CENTURY 21 ACCOUNTING

FIFTH EDITION   FIRST-YEAR COURSE

ROBERT M. SWANSON
Professor Emeritus of Business Education
and Office Administration
Ball State University
Muncie, Indiana

KENTON E. ROSS, CPA
Professor of Accounting
East Texas State University
Commerce, Texas

ROBERT D. HANSON
Associate Dean
School of Business Administration
Central Michigan University
Mount Pleasant, Michigan

BA20EA
PUBLISHED BY
SOUTH-WESTERN PUBLISHING CO.
CINCINNATI, OH   DALLAS, TX   LIVERMORE, CA

Copyright © 1992
by SOUTH-WESTERN PUBLISHING CO.
Cincinnati, Ohio

ISBN: 0-538-60600-2

Library of Congress Catalog Card Number: 90-63747

1 2 3 4 5 6 7 8 9 10 11 12 13 14 15 16 17 18 19 20 D 0 9 8 7 6 5 4 3 2 1

Printed in the United States of America

Developmental Editors: Bill Lee/Carol Volz
Production Editor: Mary H. Draper
Associate Editors/Production, Textbooks: Kimberlee Kusnerak/Leslie A. Kauffman
Associate Editors/Production, Supplements: Bradley C. Ellis/Vince Patton/Edna Stroble
Designer: Joe Devine
Production Artist: Nicola Jones
Designer, Simulations: Darren K. Wright/Jim DeSollar/J. E. Lagenaur
Production Artist, Simulations: Sophia Renieris
Photo Researcher: Fred M. Middendorf
Marketing Manager: Gregory Getter

Photo Acknowledgments

Courtesy of Coit, 3; Photo courtesy of Windsor Ind., Englewood, Colorado, 8; Larry Allan/The Image Bank, 197; Photo courtesy of Apple Computer, Inc., 219; Tandy Corporation, 246; Eric Meola/The Image Bank, 251; Location courtesy of Wooster Pike Auto Parts, 271; Tandy Corporation, 311;© Jose Carrillo, Ventura, CA, 337; Courtesy of Reynolds and Reynolds, 349; Location courtesy of Wooster Pike Auto Parts, 412; Don Carroll/The Image Bank, 436; Courtesy of International Business Machines Corporation, 463; Jay Brousseau/The Image Bank, 475; Motorola Inc., 511; Photo courtesy of Apple Computer, Inc., 548; Ford Truck Operations, 571; Photo provided by Ameritech Mobile Communications, Inc., 574; Photo of Stefan Eckert by Mark Burgess, courtesy of Cellular One, Southern Ohio, 618; Motorola Inc., 637; Photo courtesy of Recognition Equipment, Inc., 729

Preface

This preface is addressed primarily to the student. A complete examination guide for the CENTURY 21 ACCOUNTING, First-Year Course, learning package is included in the teacher's edition of this text.

This textbook is the first in a two-volume series available for use in a two-year accounting program. This fifth edition of CENTURY 21 AC-COUNTING, First-Year Course, is based on suggestions received from many sources. In addition, some changes are based on an extensive questionnaire completed by high school accounting instructors describing their accounting classroom needs. Accounting concepts and practices described in this text are in agreement with the *Statements of Financial Accounting Standards* issued by the Financial Accounting Standards Board.

This fifth edition retains the spiral approach to learning used so successfully in previous editions. Each chapter introduces new topics that build on what has been learned in previous chapters and reinforces previous learning through continued drill and practice. Learning progresses from the simple to the complex.

ORGANIZATION OF THE TEXT

Students progress through four complete accounting cycles, as shown in the table on page vi.

The textbook is organized in five parts. Each part begins with a two-page part opener that shows the general behavioral goals for each part. A different company is used in each part to illustrate accounting concepts and procedures throughout that part. The chart of accounts for each company is printed at the beginning of the part.

Chapter organization

Each chapter begins with enabling performance tasks. Enabling performance tasks are performance statements designed to guide the student through the learning experiences required in the chapter.

The content of each chapter is reinforced with numerous illustrations of key points in the chapter narrative. In addition, each chapter contains one or more summary illustrations of the content of the chapter. All chapter illustrations are numbered for ready reference.

	CYCLES			
	CYCLE 1 Chapters 1–9	CYCLE 2 Chapters 10–11	CYCLE 3 Chapters 12–19	CYCLE 4 Chapters 20–27
Type of Business	Service business	Service business	Merchandising business	Merchandising business
Business Organization	Proprietorship	Proprietorship	Partnership	Corporation
Accounting System	Manual	Automated*	Manual*	Manual*
Journal(s) Used	5-column journal	Computer input forms	11-column expanded journal	Special journals
Ledger(s) Used	General ledger	General ledger stored on computer disk	General and subsidiary ledgers	General and subsidiary ledgers

*Selected problems and activities in the second, third, and fourth accounting cycles can be automated using software available from South-Western Publishing Company.

All accounting terms are highlighted in blue. Important formulas and calculations are also highlighted in color. Distinctive background color tints are used to distinguish between journals, ledgers, and financial statements. Journals and financial statements are printed in tan. General ledger accounts, general ledger input forms, and work sheets are green. Accounts payable ledger accounts and input forms are yellow. Accounts receivable ledger accounts and input forms are blue. Also, major headings and activities are highlighted and emphasized by using color.

End-of-chapter activities

The learning activities at the end of each chapter include accounting terms, questions for individual study, cases for management decision, drills for understanding, and application problems. Each chapter also includes two enrichment problems: (1) the mastery problem provides additional practice in order to master the content of the chapter and (2) the challenge problem provides a challenge to project knowledge beyond the application problems. A recycling problem for each chapter is included at the back of the textbook for additional practice.

Reinforcement activities

Reinforcement activities are projects that include a complete accounting cycle. Reinforcement activities provide the opportunity to integrate learning from several chapters into a single activity. Three reinforcement activities are included in the textbook for Accounting Cycles 1, 3, and 4. If a reinforcement activity is desired for Accounting Cycle 2, Reinforcement Activity 1 may be automated.

Microcomputer applications

Microcomputer applications provide the opportunity to use automated accounting software to solve problems. *Automated Accounting for the Microcomputer*, 3d edition, is the accounting software used to solve the six microcomputer applications in the textbook. In addition, all three reinforcement activities may be automated if desired. The CENTURY 21 ACCOUNTING Template Disk is also needed for loading the beginning balances and charts of accounts for each microcomputer application.

Appendix A and B

Appendix A summarizes the accounting concepts that are integrated throughout the textbook. Appendix B provides instruction on using a calculator.

ACKNOWLEDGMENTS

The authors express their sincere appreciation to all persons who have contributed to this edition. The people who contributed to the fifth edition of CENTURY 21 ACCOUNTING, First-Year Course, include (1) high school instructors and students who shared their classroom experience and suggested desirable changes, (2) professional accountants who advised about accounting procedures and trends, (3) students who suggested changes based on their learning experiences, and (4) the authors of *Automated Accounting for the Microcomputer* who coordinated their software with the content of this text. The authors are also grateful to Claudia M. Gilbertson, Anoka-Ramsey Community College, and Mark W. Lehman, Mississippi State University, for assistance in revising portions of this edition.

Robert M. Swanson
Kenton E. Ross
Robert D. Hanson

Contents

PART 3
PARTNERSHIP ACCOUNTING FOR A MERCHANDISING BUSINESS

PART 4
CORPORATE ACCOUNTING FOR A MERCHANDISING BUSINESS

■ PART 5
ACCOUNTING CONTROL SYSTEMS

Welcome to Accounting

Managers and owners use accounting information as the basis for making business decisions. Accurate accounting records contribute to a business' success and help to avoid failure and bankruptcy. Failure to understand accounting information can result in poor business decisions. Training in accounting helps managers and owners make better business decisions.

This textbook is the first in a two-volume series for use in a business curriculum with two years of accounting study. The first-year text is for students who have a variety of career objectives. (1) Accounting knowledge and skill needed for beginning accounting careers. (2) Accounting knowledge and skill needed for careers in related business fields. (3) Accounting knowledge and skill to serve as a foundation on which to continue the study of accounting at the college level. The advanced text is for students with determined career objectives in accounting.

One of the most important decisions people make is how to earn a living. Individuals use accounting information to make personal financial decisions about how to earn a living and how to use their personal income. Many young people choose to prepare for a career in the exciting field of accounting.

WHAT IS ACCOUNTING?

Accounting serves people in business and in their personal lives. Accounting helps people understand business in their careers and in their personal lives.

Accounting — the language of business. Accounting is the language of business. Owners, managers, and accounting workers must understand and use this basic language. Salesclerks and general office clerks complete accounting forms and prepare accounting reports. Secretaries take dictation that includes accounting terms. These workers can do their work more efficiently if they know the language of business — accounting.

Accounting in everyday life. Nearly everyone in the United States earns money and must submit income tax reports to the federal and state governments. Everyone, personally or for a business, must plan ways to keep spending within available income. Many persons use accounting as a means of earning a living, and all persons must keep personal financial records. All persons can use accounting information and skills.

JOB OPPORTUNITIES IN ACCOUNTING

Accounting jobs fit into several classifications, including general accountants, bookkeepers, accounting clerks, and other office workers. An increasing amount of accounting work is done using computers. However, the estimated future increase in the use of computers does not appear to be decreasing the need for all kinds of accounting personnel. Computer operators are needed in addition to accounting personnel.

Accountants. Accountants plan, summarize, analyze, and interpret accounting information. Some accountants, referred to as public accountants, work as members of accounting firms that sell accounting services to other businesses. Private accountants are employed by a single business.

SENIOR ACCOUNTANT. Person with accounting degree and experience. Duties include general and cost accounting supervision.	**ACCOUNTANT.** Local business needs an accountant to supervise all accounting functions.

Bookkeepers. Bookkeepers do general accounting work plus some summarizing and analyzing of accounting information. In some businesses bookkeepers may supervise the work of accounting clerks. In small to medium-size businesses, bookkeepers may also help owners and managers interpret accounting information. Often these smaller businesses employ a public accountant to plan the accounting system.

FULL CHARGE BOOKKEEPER Work without supervision. Experience in general ledger and payroll.	**BOOKKEEPER-CLERICAL** Accounts receivable, general office, typing a must.

Accounting clerks. If a business has a large amount of accounting information to be recorded, accounting clerks may be employed to record, sort, and file accounting data. Accounting clerks are often given a title, such as payroll clerk or accounts payable clerk, to describe the specific accounting activities they perform.

PAYROLL. Opening for responsible payroll clerk. Coordination of all payroll activities. Salary depends on training and experience.	**ACCOUNTS PAYABLE CLERK** Retail store. Automated systems. Will train right person.

Other office workers. Many other office clerks and computer operators perform some accounting tasks. Regardless of who completes the accounting activities, the work must be done according to established accounting concepts and procedures. Office workers with some knowledge of accounting will better understand the importance of the accounting tasks they complete.

> **SECRETARY.** Require 4 yrs secretarial expr., word processing, type 50 wpm, 1 yr bookkeeping training or experience in similar position.

> **TYPIST.** For all phases of office work. Bookkeeping training or experience desirable.

A CAREER IN ACCOUNTING

The following career ladder represents the educational requirements and promotional possibilities in accounting careers.

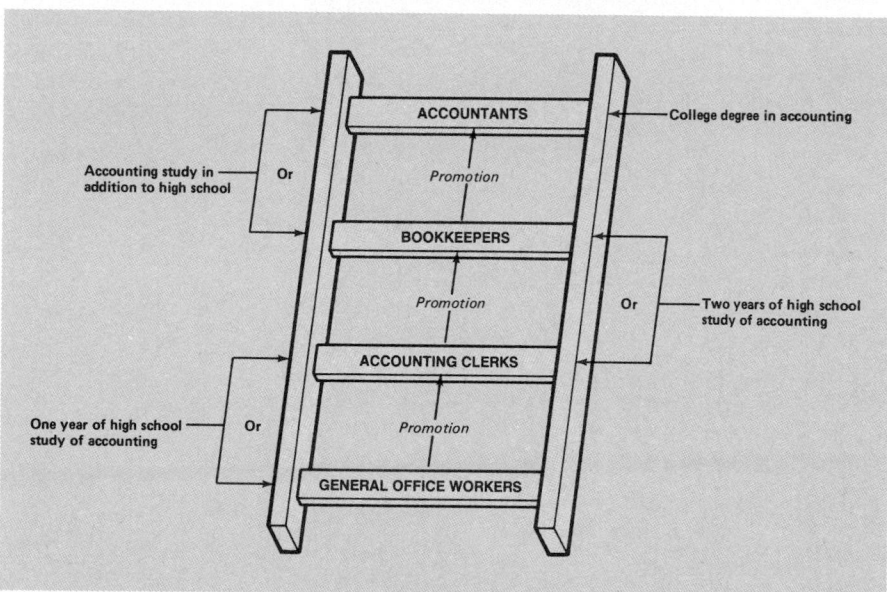

Immediately after high school graduation, individuals may start an accounting career as accounting clerks or general office workers. A few of the better students may start as bookkeepers. High school study in accounting is useful as preparation for these accounting positions. The study of high school accounting also is good preparation for the study of accounting in college.

Almost all persons seeking positions as accountants must complete some study of accounting beyond high school and must gain accounting experience. Most professional accountants also earn the Certified Public Accountant (CPA) designation. Each state sets the standards for earning a CPA certificate. Usually, the requirements include the study of college accounting, some accounting experience, and a passing score on a professional test covering all aspects of the accounting field.

With experience and additional accounting study, accounting personnel can earn promotion to higher positions on the career ladder.

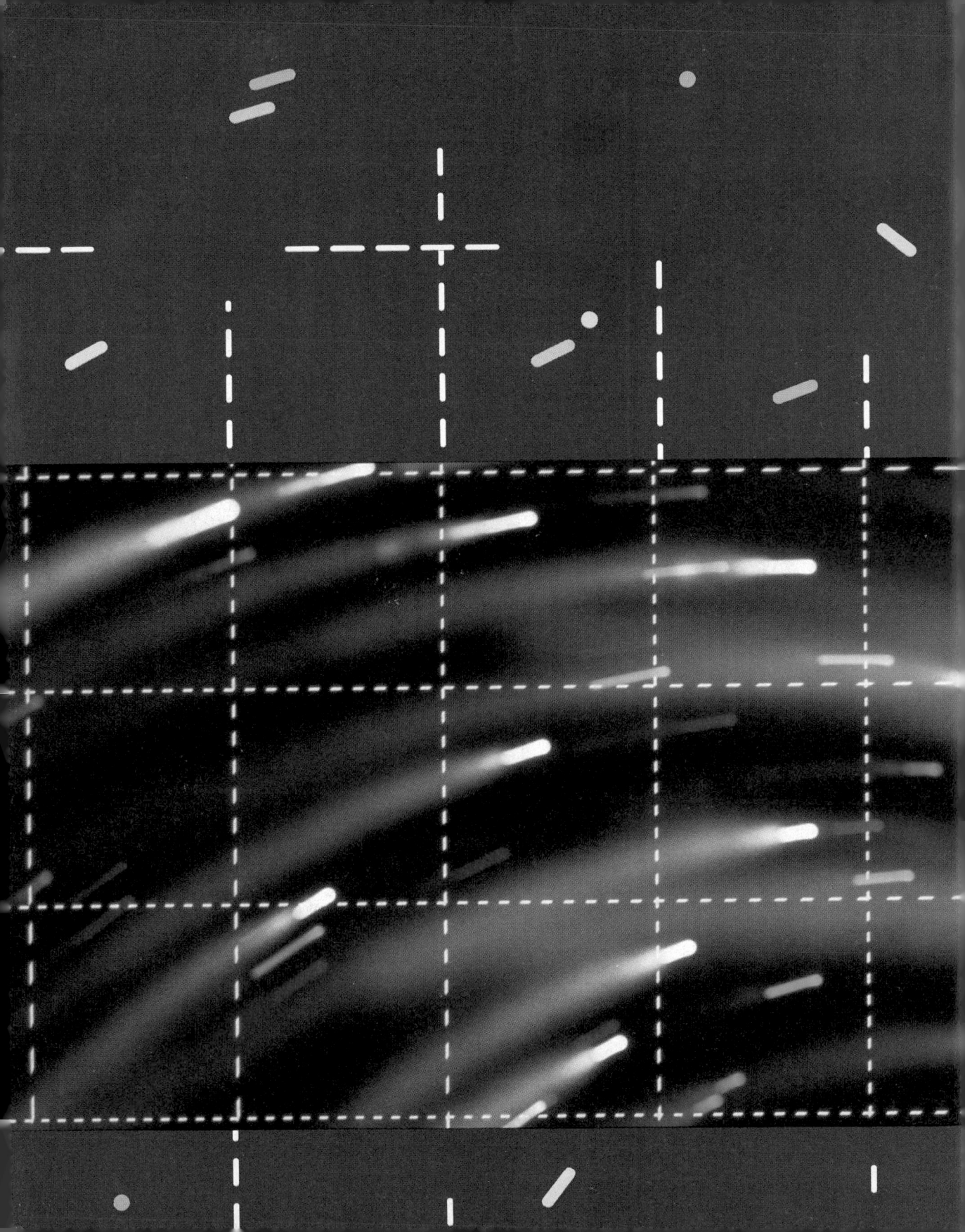

Accounting for a Service Business

1

GENERAL BEHAVIORAL GOALS

1. Know accounting terminology related to an accounting system for a service business organized as a proprietorship.
2. Understand accounting practices related to an accounting system for a service business organized as a proprietorship.
3. Demonstrate accounting procedures used in an accounting system for a service business organized as a proprietorship.

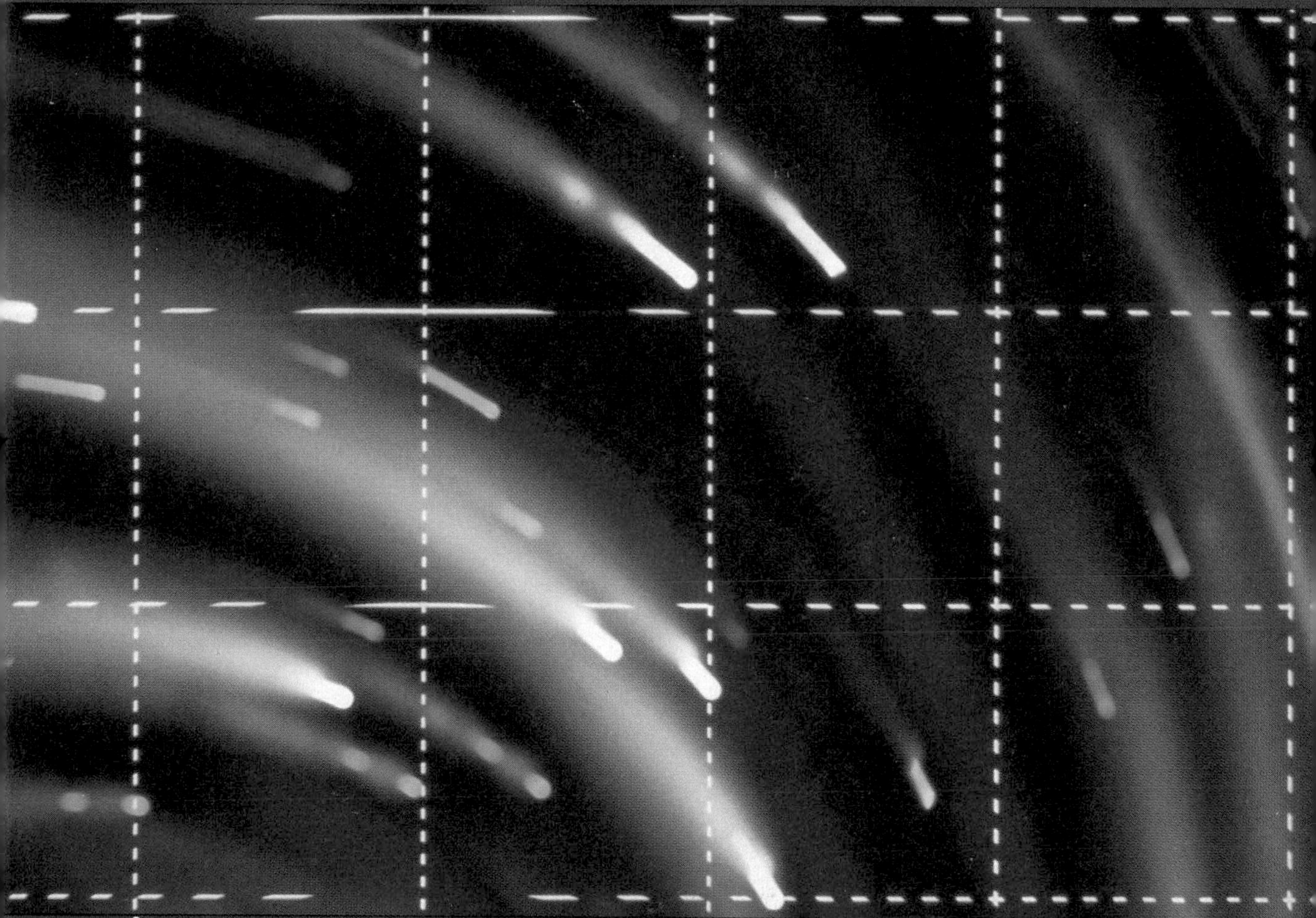

RUGCARE
Chart of Accounts

The chart of accounts for Rugcare is illustrated
above for ready reference as you study Part 1
of this textbook.

Starting a Proprietorship

ENABLING PERFORMANCE TASKS

After studying Chapter 1, you will be able to:
a. Define accounting terms related to starting a service business organized as a proprietorship.
b. Identify accounting concepts and practices related to starting a service business organized as a proprietorship.
c. Classify accounts as assets, liabilities, or owner's equity.
d. Analyze how transactions related to starting a service business organized as a proprietorship affect accounts in an accounting equation.
e. Prepare a balance sheet for a service business organized as a proprietorship from information in an accounting equation.

Many decisions are made during a person's lifetime. One important decision is how to earn a living. A person may work for others or start a new business. When a person chooses to start a business, that person must make many decisions. To make these decisions, a businessperson needs much information about the business. To provide the information, many records relating to the business must be kept.

STARTING A NEW ACCOUNTING SYSTEM

A successful business is involved in numerous financial activities. Summary reports of these financial activities are needed by several people. These reports provide the information to help the owners and managers make business decisions. *How much should be charged for the product or service? Are profits sufficient? Should new products be sold? Should new services be provided? Can costs be decreased?* The business' banker uses these reports to make loan decisions. *How much should the bank allow the business to borrow? Is the business likely to be able to repay the loan?* The government requires that the business report financial information when it pays taxes.

In order to create useful reports, financial information must be maintained in an organized way. Planning, recording, analyzing, and interpreting financial information is called accounting. A planned process for providing financial information that will be useful to management is called an accounting system. Organized summaries of a business' financial activities are called accounting records.

THE BUSINESS

A business that performs an activity for a fee is called a service business. Ben Furman worked for a service business that cleans carpets for a fee. Mr. Furman wants to be in control of his hours and his earnings. Therefore, he decided to start his own carpet-cleaning business. A business owned by one person is called a proprietorship. A proprietorship is also known as a sole proprietorship. Mr. Furman has named his new proprietorship *Rugcare*. Rugcare will rent office space and the equipment used to operate the business.

Since a new business is being started, Mr. Furman must design the accounting system that will be used to keep Rugcare's accounting records. In the accounting system, Mr. Furman must be careful to keep Rugcare's accounting records separate from his own personal financial records. For example, Mr. Furman owns a house and a personal car. Rugcare's financial records must *not* include information about Mr. Furman's house, car, or other personal belongings. For example, Mr. Furman must use one checking account for his personal expenses and another checking account for Rugcare. The financial records for Rugcare and Mr. Furman's personal belongings must be kept separate. The accounting concept, *Business Entity*, is applied when a business' financial information is recorded and reported separately from the owner's personal financial information. *(CONCEPT: Business Entity)*

> Accounting concepts are described throughout this textbook when an application of a concept first occurs. When additional applications occur, a concept reference, such as *(CONCEPT: Business Entity)*, indicates an application of a specific accounting concept. A brief description of each accounting concept used in this text is also provided in Appendix A.

THE ACCOUNTING EQUATION

A business has many items that have value. Rugcare will own items such as cash and supplies that will be used to conduct daily operations. Anything of value that is owned is called an asset. Assets have value because they can be used to acquire other assets or be used to operate a business. For example, Rugcare will use cash to buy supplies for the business.

Rugcare will then use the asset, supplies, in the operation of the rug-cleaning business.

Financial rights to the assets of a business are called equities. A business has two types of equities. (1) Equity of those to whom money is owed. For example, Rugcare may buy some supplies and agree to pay for the supplies at a later date. The business from whom supplies are bought will have a right to some of Rugcare's assets until Rugcare pays for the supplies. An amount owed by a business is called a liability. (2) Equity of the owner. Mr. Furman will own Rugcare and invest in the assets of the business. Therefore, he will have a right to decide how the assets will be used. The amount remaining after the value of all liabilities is subtracted from the value of all assets is called owner's equity.

The relationship among assets, liabilities, and owner's equity can be written as an equation. An equation showing the relationship among assets, liabilities, and owner's equity is called the accounting equation. The accounting equation is most often stated as:

$$\text{Assets} = \text{Liabilities} + \text{Owner's Equity}$$

The accounting equation must be in balance to be correct. Thus, the total of the amounts on the left side of the equation must always equal the total of the amounts on the right side. Before Mr. Furman actually starts the business, Rugcare's accounting equation would show the following amounts.

Assets	=	Liabilities + Owner's Equity
Left side amount		Right side amounts
$0	=	$0 + $0

HOW BUSINESS ACTIVITIES CHANGE THE ACCOUNTING EQUATION

Business activities change the amounts in the accounting equation. A business activity that changes assets, liabilities, or owner's equity is called a transaction. For example, a business that pays cash for supplies is engaging in a transaction. After each transaction, the accounting equation must remain in balance.

The accounting concept, *Unit of Measurement*, is applied when business transactions are stated in numbers that have common values — that is, using a common unit of measurement. (CONCEPT: *Unit of Measurement*) For example, in the United States, business transactions are recorded in dollars. In Switzerland, business transactions are recorded in Swiss francs. The unit of measurement concept is followed so that the financial reports of businesses can be clearly stated and understood in numbers that have comparable values. For example, reports would not be clear if some information was reported in United States dollars and some in Swiss francs.

Received cash from owner as an investment

Mr. Furman uses $10,000.00 of his own money to invest in Rugcare. Rugcare should only be concerned with the effect of this transaction on Rugcare's records. The business should *not* be concerned about Mr. Furman's personal records. *(CONCEPT: Business Entity)*

Transaction 1.
August 1, 19--.
Received cash from owner as an investment, $10,000.00.

A record summarizing all the information pertaining to a single item in the accounting equation is called an account. The name given to an account is called an account title. Each part of the accounting equation consists of one or more accounts. For example, one of the asset accounts is titled Cash. The cash account is used to summarize information about the amount of money the business has available.

In the accounting equation shown in Illustration 1-1, the asset account, Cash, is increased by $10,000.00, the amount of cash received by the business. This increase is on the left side of the accounting equation. The amount in an account is called the account balance. Before the owner's investment, the account balance of Cash was zero. After the owner's investment, the account balance of Cash is $10,000.00.

	Assets	=	Liabilities	+	Owner's Equity
	Cash	=			Ben Furman, Capital
Beg. Balances	$0		$0		$0
Transaction 1	+10,000				+10,000 (investment)
New Balances	$10,000		$0		$10,000

Illustration 1-1
Receiving cash from owner as an investment changes one asset and owner's equity

The account used to summarize the owner's equity in business is called capital. The capital account is an owner's equity account. Rugcare's capital account is titled Ben Furman, Capital. In the accounting equation shown in Illustration 1-1, the owner's equity account, Ben Furman, Capital, is increased by $10,000.00. This increase is on the right side of the accounting equation. Before the owner's investment, the account balance of Ben Furman, Capital was zero. After the owner's investment, the account balance of Ben Furman, Capital is $10,000.00.

The accounting equation has changed as a result of the receipt of cash as the owner's investment. However, both sides of the equation are changed by the same amount, $10,000.00. The $10,000.00 increase on the left side of the equation equals the $10,000.00 increase on the right side of the equation. Therefore, the accounting equation is still in balance.

Paid cash for supplies

Rugcare needs supplies to operate the business. Ben Furman uses some of Rugcare's cash to buy supplies.

Transaction 2.
August 3, 19--.
Paid cash for supplies, $1,577.00.

The effect of this transaction on the accounting equation is shown in Illustration 1-2. In this transaction, two asset accounts are changed. One asset, cash, has been exchanged for another asset, supplies. The asset account, Cash, is decreased by $1,577.00, the amount of cash paid out. This decrease is on the left side of the accounting equation. The asset account, Supplies, is increased by $1,577.00, the amount of supplies bought. This increase is also on the left side of the accounting equation.

For this transaction, two assets are changed. Therefore, the two changes are both on the left side of the accounting equation. When changes are made on only one side of the accounting equation, the equation must still be in balance. Therefore, if one account is increased, another account on the same side of the equation must be decreased. After this transaction, the new account balance of Cash is $8,423.00. The new account balance of Supplies is $1,577.00. The sum of the amounts on the left side is $10,000.00 (Cash, $8,423.00 + Supplies, $1,577.00). The amount on the right side is also $10,000.00. Therefore, the accounting equation is still in balance.

	Assets			= Liabilities +	Owner's Equity
	Cash	+	Supplies =		Ben Furman, Capital
Balances	$10,000		$0	$0	$10,000
Transaction 2	−1,577		+1,577		
New Balances	$ 8,423		$1,577	$0	$10,000

Total of left side:
$8,423 + $1,577 = $10,000

Total of right side:
$10,000

Illustration 1-2
Paying cash for supplies
changes two assets

Paid cash for insurance

Insurance premiums must be paid in advance. For example, Rugcare pays a $1,200.00 insurance premium for future insurance coverage.

Transaction 3.
August 4, 19--.
Paid cash for insurance, $1,200.00.

In return for this payment, Rugcare is entitled to insurance coverage for the length of the policy. The insurance coverage is something of value owned by Rugcare. Therefore, the insurance coverage is an asset. Because insurance premiums are paid in advance, or *prepaid*, the premiums are recorded in an asset account titled Prepaid Insurance.

The effect of this transaction on the accounting equation is shown in Illustration 1-3. In this transaction, two assets are changed. One asset, cash, has been exchanged for another asset, prepaid insurance. The asset account, Cash, is decreased by $1,200.00, the amount of cash paid out. This decrease is on the left side of the accounting equation. The asset account, Prepaid Insurance, is increased by $1,200.00, the amount of insurance bought. This increase is also on the left side of the accounting equation.

	Assets			= Liabilities +	Owner's Equity
	Cash	+ Supplies +	Prepaid Insurance =		Ben Furman, Capital
Balances	$8,423	$1,577	$0	$0	$10,000
Transaction 3	−1,200		+1,200		
New Balances	$7,223	$1,577	$1,200	$0	$10,000

Total of left side:
$7,223 + $1,577 + $1,200 = $10,000

Total of right side:
$10,000

Illustration 1-3
Paying cash for
insurance
changes two assets

Since two assets are changed by this transaction, both changes are on the left side of the accounting equation. Since one account is increased, the other account on the same side of the equation must be decreased. After this transaction, the new account balance of Cash is $7,223.00. The new account balance of Prepaid Insurance is $1,200.00. The sum of the amounts on the left side is $10,000.00 (Cash, $7,223.00 + Supplies, $1,577.00 + Prepaid Insurance, $1,200.00). The amount on the right side is also $10,000.00. Therefore, the accounting equation is still in balance.

Bought supplies on account

Rugcare needs to buy additional supplies. The supplies are obtained from Butler Cleaning Supplies, which is located in a different city. It is a common business practice to buy items and pay for them at a future date. Another way to state this activity is to say that these items are bought *on account*.

Transaction 4.
August 7, 19--.
Bought supplies on account from Butler Cleaning Supplies, $2,720.00.

The effect of this transaction on the accounting equation is shown in Illustration 1-4. In this transaction, one asset and one liability are changed.

	Assets			= Liabilities +	Owner's Equity
	Cash +	Supplies +	Prepaid Insurance =	Butler Cleaning Supplies +	Ben Furman, Capital
Balances	$7,223	$1,577	$1,200	$0	$10,000
Transaction 4		+2,720		+2,720	
New Balances	$7,223	$4,297	$1,200	$2,720	$10,000

Total of left side:
$7,223 + $4,297 + $1,200 = $12,720

Total of right side:
$2,720 + $10,000 = $12,720

The asset account, Supplies, is increased by $2,720.00, the amount of supplies bought. This increase is on the left side of the accounting equation. Butler Cleaning Supplies will have a claim against some of Rugcare's assets until Rugcare pays for the supplies bought. Therefore, Butler Cleaning Supplies is a liability account. The liability account, Butler Cleaning Supplies, is increased by $2,720.00, the amount owed for the supplies. This increase is on the right side of the accounting equation.

Illustration 1-4 Buying supplies on account changes one asset and one liability

This transaction changes both sides of the accounting equation. When changes are made on both sides of the equation, the change on the left side must equal the change on the right side. After this transaction, the new account balance of Supplies is $4,297.00. The new account balance of Butler Cleaning Supplies is $2,720.00. The sum of the amounts on the left side is $12,720.00 (Cash, $7,223.00 + Supplies, $4,297.00 + Prepaid Insurance, $1,200.00). The sum of the amounts on the right side is also $12,720.00 (Butler Cleaning Supplies, $2,720.00 + Ben Furman, Capital, $10,000.00). Therefore, the accounting equation is still in balance.

Paid cash on account

Since Rugcare is a new business, Butler Cleaning Supplies has not done business with Rugcare before. Butler Cleaning Supplies allows Rugcare to buy supplies on account but requires Rugcare to send a check for one-half of the amount immediately. Rugcare will pay the remaining liability at a later date.

Transaction 5.
August 11, 19--.
Paid cash on account to Butler Cleaning Supplies, $1,360.00.

The effect of this transaction on the accounting equation is shown in Illustration 1-5. In this transaction, one asset and one liability are changed. The asset account, Cash, is decreased by $1,360.00, the amount of cash paid out. This decrease is on the left side of the accounting equation. After this payment, Rugcare owes less money to Butler Cleaning Supplies. Therefore, the liability account, Butler Cleaning Supplies, is decreased by $1,360.00, the

	Assets			=	Liabilities	+	Owner's Equity
	Cash	+ Supplies	+ Prepaid Insurance	=	Butler Cleaning Supplies	+	Ben Furman, Capital
Balances	$7,223	$4,297	$1,200		$2,720		$10,000
Transaction 5	−1,360				−1,360		
New Balances	$5,863	$4,297	$1,200		$1,360		$10,000

Total of left side:
$5,863 + $4,297 + $1,200 = $11,360

Total of right side:
$1,360 + $10,000 = $11,360

Illustration 1-5
Paying cash on account
changes one asset and one
liability

amount paid on account. This decrease is on the right side of the accounting equation.

This transaction changes both sides of the accounting equation. When changes are made on both sides of the equation, the change on the left side must equal the change on the right side. After this transaction, the new account balance of Cash is $5,863.00. The new account balance of Butler Cleaning Supplies is $1,360.00. The sum of the amounts on the left side is $11,360.00 (Cash, $5,863.00 + Supplies, $4,297.00 + Prepaid Insurance, $1,200.00). The sum of the amounts on the right side is also $11,360.00 (Butler Cleaning Supplies, $1,360.00 + Ben Furman, Capital, $10,000.00). Therefore, the accounting equation is still in balance.

REPORTING FINANCIAL INFORMATION ON A BALANCE SHEET

Periodically a business reports details about its assets, liabilities, and owner's equity. The financial details about assets, liabilities, and owner's equity could be found on the last line of the accounting equation. However, most businesses prepare more formal financial statements that may be copied and sent to interested persons. A financial statement that reports assets, liabilities, and owner's equity on a specific date is called a balance sheet.

When a business is started, it is expected that the business will continue to operate indefinitely. For example, Ben Furman assumes that he will own and operate Rugcare for many years. When he retires, he expects to sell Rugcare to someone else who will continue its operation. The accounting concept, *Going Concern*, is applied when financial statements are prepared with the expectation that a business will remain in operation indefinitely. (CONCEPT: *Going Concern*)

Body of a balance sheet

A balance sheet has three major sections. (1) *Assets* are on the left side of the accounting equation. Therefore, Rugcare lists its assets on the left side of the balance sheet. (2) *Liabilities* are on the right side of the accounting equation. Therefore, Rugcare lists its liabilities on the right side of the balance sheet. (3) *Owner's equity* is also on the right side of the accounting equation. Therefore, Rugcare lists its owner's equity on the right side of the balance sheet.

Rugcare's balance sheet, prepared after the transaction on August 11, is shown in Illustration 1-6.

	Assets			= Liabilities + Owner's Equity	
	Cash	+ Supplies	+ Prepaid Insurance =	Butler Cleaning Supplies +	Ben Furman, Capital
Balances	$5,863	$4,297	$1,200	$1,360	$10,000

Rugcare				
Balance Sheet				
August 11, 19--				
Assets		**Liabilities**		
Cash	5 8 6 3 00	Butler Cleaning Supplies	1 3 6 0 00	
Supplies	4 2 9 7 00	**Owner's Equity**		
Prepaid Insurance	1 2 0 0 00	Ben Furman, Capital	10 0 0 0 00	
Total Assets	11 3 6 0 00	Total Liab. and Owner's Eq.	11 3 6 0 00	

Illustration 1-6
Balance sheet for a service business organized as a proprietorship

Preparing a balance sheet

Rugcare's balance sheet is prepared in six steps.

1 Write the *heading* on three lines at the top of the balance sheet. Center each line. The heading for Rugcare's balance sheet is:

Name of the business:	Rugcare
Name of the report:	Balance Sheet
Date of the report:	August 11, 19--

2 Prepare the *assets section* on the LEFT side. Center the word *Assets* on the first line of the wide column on the left side. Under this heading, write each asset account title and amount. The asset accounts are: Cash, $5,863.00; Supplies, $4,297.00; and Prepaid Insurance, $1,200.00.

3 Prepare the *liabilities section* on the RIGHT side. Center the word *Liabilities* on the first line of the wide column on the right side. Under this heading, write each liability account title and amount. Rugcare has only one liability account to be listed, Butler Cleaning Supplies, $1,360.00.

4 Prepare the *owner's equity section* on the RIGHT side. Center the words *Owner's Equity* on the next blank line of the wide column on the right side. Under this heading, write the owner's equity account title and amount. Rugcare's owner's equity account is Ben Furman, Capital, $10,000.00.

5 Determine if the balance sheet is *in balance*. Use a calculator, if available, or a sheet of scratch paper. Add all the asset amounts on the LEFT side. The total on the left side of Rugcare's balance sheet is $11,360.00 ($5,863.00 + $4,297.00 + $1,200.00). Add the liabilities and owner's equity amounts on the RIGHT side. The total on the right side of Rugcare's balance sheet is $11,360.00 ($1,360.00 + $10,000.00). The total of the LEFT side is the same as the total of the RIGHT side, $11,360.00. Therefore, Rugcare's balance sheet is in balance.

If the balance sheet is NOT in balance, find the errors before completing any more work.

6 *Complete* the balance sheet. Rule a single line across both amount columns. A single line means that amounts are to be added or subtracted. On the next line, write *Total Assets* in the wide column on the left side. On the same line, write the total asset amount, $11,360.00, in the left amount column. On the same line, write *Total Liabilities and Owner's Equity* in the wide column on the right side. On the same line, write the total liabilities and owner's equity amount, $11,360.00, in the right amount column. Rule double lines below the amount column totals. Double lines mean that the totals have been verified as correct.

When possible, words are spelled in full so there can be no doubt about what word was intended. However, in a few situations, where there is insufficient room to spell the words in full, words may be abbreviated. On Rugcare's balance sheet, it is necessary to abbreviate the words *Total Liab. and Owner's Eq.*

SUMMARY OF HOW TRANSACTIONS CHANGE THE ACCOUNTING EQUATION

Changes in the accounting equation caused by Transactions 1 to 5 are summarized in Illustration 1-7.

Four basic rules relate to how transactions affect the accounting equation.

1. Each transaction changes at least two accounts in the accounting equation.
2. When all the changes occur on one side of the accounting equation, increases on that side must be matched by decreases on the same side. In Illustration 1-7, Transactions 2 and 3 are examples of this rule.
3. When a transaction increases one side of the accounting equation, the other side of the equation must also be increased by the same amount. Transactions 1 and 4 are examples of this rule.

4. When a transaction decreases one side of the accounting equation, the other side of the equation must also be decreased by the same amount. Transaction 5 is an example of this rule.

Illustration 1-7
Summary of how transactions change the accounting equation

Transaction	Assets			= Liabilities +	Owner's Equity
	Cash	+ Supplies +	Prepaid Insurance =	Butler Cleaning + Supplies	Ben Furman, Capital
Beginning Balance	$0	$0	$0	$0	$0
1. Received cash from owner as an investment	+10,000				+10,000 (investment)
New Balances	$10,000	$0	$0	$0	$10,000
2. Paid cash for supplies	−1,577	+1,577			
New Balances	$8,423	$1,577	$0	$0	$10,000
3. Paid cash for insurance	−1,200		+1,200		
New Balances	$7,223	$1,577	$1,200	$0	$10,000
4. Bought supplies on account		+2,720		+2,720	
New Balances	$7,223	$4,297	$1,200	$2,720	$10,000
5. Paid cash on account	−1,360			−1,360	
New Balances	$5,863	$4,297	$1,200	$1,360	$10,000

Total of left side:
$5,863 + $4,297 + $1,200 = $11,360

Total of right side:
$1,360 + $10,000 = $11,360

ACCOUNTING TERMS

What is the meaning of each of the following?

1. accounting
2. accounting system
3. accounting records
4. service business
5. proprietorship
6. asset

7. equities
8. liability
9. owner's equity
10. accounting equation
11. transaction

12. account
13. account title
14. account balance
15. capital
16. balance sheet

QUESTIONS FOR INDIVIDUAL STUDY

1. How are financial reports used by business owners and managers?
2. How are financial reports used by a business' banker?
3. Which accounting concept is being applied when a business records and reports financial information separate from the owner's personal financial information?
4. What are the two types of equities of a business?
5. What is the accounting equation?

6. What must be true about the accounting equation after each transaction?

7. Which accounting concept is being applied when a business in the United States reports financial information in dollars?

8. What accounts are affected, and how, when the owner invests cash in a business?

9. What accounts are affected, and how, when a business pays cash for supplies?

10. Why is Prepaid Insurance an asset?

11. How are liabilities affected when a business buys supplies on account?

12. How are liabilities affected when a business pays cash for a liability?

13. Which accounting concept is being applied when financial statements are prepared with the expectation that a business will remain in operation indefinitely?

14. What are the three major sections of a balance sheet?

15. What three items are included in the heading of a balance sheet?

16. What six steps are followed in preparing a balance sheet?

17. What do double lines below a column total mean?

18. What are the four basic rules relating to how transactions affect the accounting equation?

■ CASES FOR MANAGEMENT DECISION

CASE 1 James Patton starts a new business. Mr. Patton uses his personal car in the business with the expectation that later the business can buy a car. All expenses for operating the car, including license plates, gasoline, oil, tune-ups, and new tires, are paid for out of business funds. Is this an acceptable procedure? Explain.

CASE 2 At the end of the first day of business, Quick Clean Laundry has the following assets and liabilities:

Assets	
Cash	$3,500.00
Supplies	950.00
Prepaid Insurance	1,200.00
Liabilities	
Smith Office Supplies	$ 750.00
Super Supplies Company	1,500.00

The owner, Susan Whiteford, wants to know the amount of her equity in Quick Clean Laundry. Determine this amount and explain what this amount represents.

■ DRILLS FOR UNDERSTANDING

DRILL 1-D1   Classifying assets, liabilities, and owner's equity

Use a form similar to the following.

Item	Asset	Liability	Owner's Equity
1. Cash	✓		

Instructions: Classify each item listed below as an asset, liability, or owner's equity. Place a check mark in the appropriate column. Item 1 is given as an example.

1. Cash
2. Alice Jones, Capital
3. Prepaid Insurance
4. Steward Supply Company

5. Supplies
6. Any amount owed
7. Owner's capital account
8. Anything owned

DRILL 1-D2   Determining how transactions change an accounting equation

Use a form similar to the following.

Trans. No.	Assets	=	Liabilities	+	Owner's Equity
1.	+		+		

Transactions

1. Bought supplies on account.
2. Paid cash for insurance.
3. Received cash from owner as an investment.
4. Paid cash for supplies.
5. Paid cash on account to Konroy Company.

Instructions: Decide which classification(s) are changed by each transaction. Place a plus (+) in the appropriate column if the classification is increased. Place a minus (−) in the appropriate column if the classification is decreased. Transaction 1 is given as an example.

DRILL 1-D3   Determining where items are listed on a balance sheet

Use a form similar to the following.

1	2	3
	Balance Sheet	
Items	Left Side	Right Side
1. Cash	*Asset*	

Instructions: Classify each item as an asset, liability, or owner's equity. Write the classification in Column 2 or 3 to show where each item is listed on a balance sheet. Item 1 is given as an example.

1. Cash
2. Gretchen Murphy, Capital
3. Supplies
4. Prepaid Insurance

5. Action Laundry
6. Anything owned
7. Any amount owed
8. Owner's capital account

◼ APPLICATION PROBLEMS

PROBLEM 1-1   Determining how transactions change an accounting equation

Frank March is starting March Repair Shop, a small service business. March Repair Shop uses the accounts shown in the following accounting equation. Use a form similar to the following to complete this problem.

| Trans. No. | Assets | | | = Liabilities | | + Owner's Equity |
	Cash +	Supplies +	Prepaid Insurance	= Swan's Supply Company +	York Company +	Frank March, Capital
Beg. Bal. 1.	0 +2,000	0	0	0	0	0 +2,000 (investment)
New Bal. 2.	2,000	0	0	0	0	2,000

Transactions

1. Received cash from owner as an investment, $2,000.00.
2. Paid cash for insurance, $600.00.
3. Bought supplies on account from Swan's Supply Company, $100.00.
4. Bought supplies on account from York Company, $500.00.
5. Paid cash on account to Swan's Supply Company, $100.00.
6. Paid cash on account to York Company, $300.00.
7. Paid cash for supplies, $500.00.
8. Received cash from owner as an investment, $500.00.

Instructions: For each transaction, complete the following. Transaction 1 is given as an example.

a. Analyze the transaction to determine which accounts in the accounting equation are affected.
b. Write the amount in the appropriate columns using a plus (+) if the account increases or a minus (−) if the account decreases.
c. For transactions that change owner's equity, write in parentheses a description of the transaction to the right of the amount.
d. Calculate the new balance for each account in the accounting equation.
e. Before going on to the next transaction, determine that the accounting equation is still in balance.

PROBLEM 1-2 Preparing a balance sheet from information in an accounting equation

On September 30 the Steffens Company's accounting equation indicated the following account balances.

| Trans. No. | Assets | | | = Liabilities + | Owner's Equity |
	Cash +	Supplies +	Prepaid Insurance	= Morton Company +	Steve Steffens, Capital
New Bal.	1,200	150	300	250	1,400

Instructions: Using the September 30 balance in the accounting equation, prepare a balance sheet for the Steffens Company.

PROBLEM 1-3 Determining how transactions change an accounting equation and preparing a balance sheet

Nancy Dirks is starting Dirks Company, a small service business. Dirks Company uses the accounts shown in the following accounting equation. Use a form similar to the following to complete this problem.

Trans. No.	Assets			= Liabilities +	Owner's Equity
	Cash +	Supplies +	Prepaid Insurance	= Helfrey Company +	Nancy Dirks, Capital
Beg. Bal. 1.	0 +350	0	0	0	0 +350 (investment)
New Bal. 2.	350	0	0	0	350

Transactions

1. Received cash from owner as an investment, $350.00.
2. Bought supplies on account from Helfrey Company, $100.00.
3. Paid cash for insurance, $150.00.
4. Paid cash for supplies, $50.00.
5. Received cash from owner as an investment, $300.00.
6. Paid cash on account to Helfrey Company, $75.00.

Instructions: 1. For each transaction, complete the following. Transaction 1 is given as an example.

a. Analyze the transaction to determine which accounts in the accounting equation are affected.
b. Write the amount in the appropriate columns, using a plus (+) if the account increases or a minus (−) if the account decreases.
c. For transactions that change owner's equity, write in parentheses a description of the transaction to the right of the amount.
d. Calculate the new balance for each account in the accounting equation.
e. Before going on to the next transaction, determine that the accounting equation is still in balance.

2. Using the final balances in the accounting equation, prepare a balance sheet. Use July 31 of the current year as the date of the balance sheet.

◼ ENRICHMENT PROBLEMS

MASTERY PROBLEM 1-M   Determining how transactions change an accounting equation and preparing a balance sheet

Gregory Morgan is starting a limousine service called Luxury Limo. Luxury Limo uses the accounts shown in the following accounting equation. Use a form similar to the following to complete this problem.

Trans. No.	Assets			= Liabilities +	Owner's Equity
	Cash +	Supplies +	Prepaid Insurance	= Limo Supply Company +	Gregory Morgan, Capital
Beg. Bal. 1.	0 +2,000	0	0	0	0 +2,000 (investment)
New Bal. 2.	2,000	0	0	0	2,000

Transactions
1. Received cash from owner as an investment, $2,000.00.
2. Paid cash for supplies, $250.00.
3. Bought supplies on account from Limo Supply Company, $300.00.
4. Paid cash for insurance, $600.00.
5. Paid cash on account to Limo Supply Company, $150.00.

Instructions: 1. For each transaction, complete the following. Transaction 1 is given as an example.
a. Analyze the transaction to determine which accounts in the accounting equation are affected.
b. Write the amount in the appropriate columns, using a plus (+) if the account increases or a minus (−) if the account decreases.
c. For transactions that change owner's equity, write in parentheses a description of the transaction to the right of the amount.
d. Calculate the new balance for each account in the accounting equation.
e. Before going on to the next transaction, determine that the accounting equation is still in balance.
    2. Using the final balances in the accounting equation, prepare a balance sheet. Use February 5 of the current year as the date of the balance sheet.

CHALLENGE PROBLEM 1-C   Applying accounting concepts to determine how transactions change the accounting equation

Olson Delivery Service, a new business owned by Jerome Olson, uses the accounts shown in the following accounting equation. Use a form similar to the following to complete this problem.

Trans. No.	Assets			=	Liabilities		+	Owner's Equity
	Cash +	Supplies +	Prepaid Insur.	=	Mutual Savings Bank	+ Nelson Supply Co.	+	Jerome Olson, Capital
Beg. Bal. 1.	0 +1,500	0	0		0	0		0 +1,500 (investment)
New Bal. 2.	1,500	0	0		0	0		1,500

Transactions
1. Received cash from owner as an investment, $1,500.00.
2. Paid cash for supplies, $400.00.
3. Paid cash for insurance, $240.00.
4. Bought supplies on account from Nelson Supply Company, $80.00.
5. The owner, Jerome Olson, paid $1,000.00 of his personal cash to Mutual Savings Bank for the car payment on his personal car.
6. Paid cash for supplies. The supplies were bought from a Canadian company. The supplies cost $120.00 in Canadian dollars, which is equivalent to $100.00 in United States dollars.

Instructions: For each transaction, complete the following. Transaction 1 is given as an example.
a. Analyze the transaction to determine which business accounts in the accounting equation, if any, are affected. You will need to apply the Business Entity and Unit of Measurement concepts in this problem.

b. If business accounts are affected, determine the appropriate amount of the change. Write the amount in the appropriate columns, using a plus (+) if the account increases or a minus (−) if the account decreases.

c. For transactions that change owner's equity, write in parentheses a description of the transaction to the right of the amount.

d. Calculate the new balance for each account in the accounting equation.

e. Before going on to the next transaction, determine that the accounting equation is still in balance.

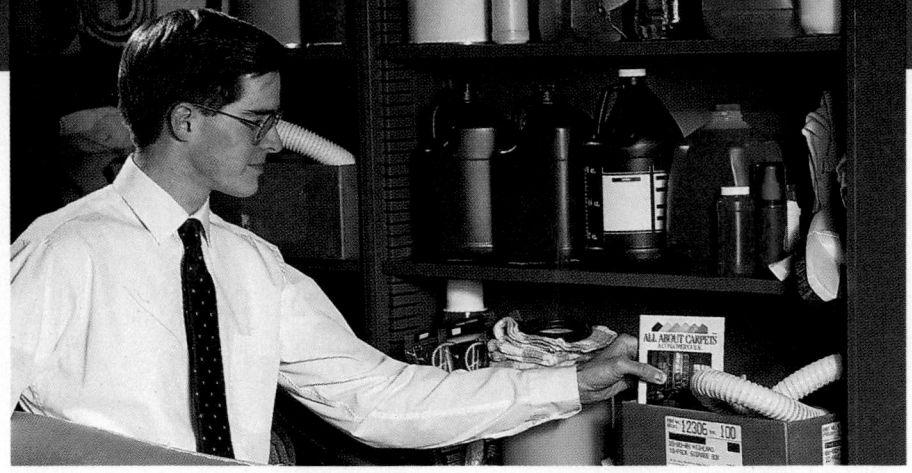

Starting a Proprietorship: Changes That Affect Owner's Equity

ENABLING PERFORMANCE TASKS

After studying Chapter 2, you will be able to:
a. Define accounting terms related to changes that affect owner's equity for a service business organized as a proprietorship.
b. Identify accounting concepts and practices related to changes that affect owner's equity for a service business organized as a proprietorship.
c. Analyze changes that affect owner's equity for a service business organized as a proprietorship in an accounting equation.
d. Prepare a balance sheet for a service business organized as a proprietorship from information in the accounting equation.

A business activity that changes assets, liabilities, or owner's equity is known as a transaction. Chapter 1 describes five transactions involved in starting Rugcare, a proprietorship. Rugcare is now ready to open for business. This chapter presents the transactions that commonly occur during the daily operations of a business. Each of these transactions changes Ben Furman's equity in Rugcare.

HOW TRANSACTIONS CHANGE OWNER'S EQUITY IN AN ACCOUNTING EQUATION

The accounting equation for Rugcare as of August 11, showing the effect of transactions for starting a business, is shown in Illustration 2-1.

The sum of the balances on the left side of the accounting equation, $11,360.00, equals the sum of the balances on the right side of the equation, $11,360.00. The equation is in balance.

Many transactions involved in the daily operations of a business increase or decrease owner's equity. Detailed information about these

	Assets			= Liabilities +	Owner's Equity
	Cash +	Supplies +	Prepaid Insurance =	Butler Cleaning Supplies +	Ben Furman, Capital
Balances	$5,863	$4,297	$1,200	$1,360	$10,000

Total of left side:	Total of right side:
$5,863 + $4,297 + $1,200 = $11,360	$1,360 + $10,000 = $11,360

changes in owner's equity is needed by owners and managers to make sound business decisions.

Illustration 2-1
Accounting equation after transactions for starting a proprietorship

Received cash from sales

A transaction for the sale of goods or services results in an increase in owner's equity. An increase in owner's equity resulting from the operation of a business is called revenue. When cash is received from a sale, the total amount of assets and owner's equity is increased.

When Rugcare receives cash for services performed, two accounts in the accounting equation are affected. The asset account, Cash, is increased by the amount of cash received. The owner's equity account, Ben Furman, Capital, is increased by the same amount.

Transaction 6.
August 12, 19--.
Received cash from sales, $525.00.

The effect of this transaction on the accounting equation is shown in Illustration 2-2. The asset account, Cash, is increased by $525.00, the amount of cash received. This increase is on the left side of the equation. The owner's equity account, Ben Furman, Capital, is also increased by $525.00. This increase is on the right side of the equation.

	Assets			= Liabilities +	Owner's Equity
	Cash +	Supplies +	Prepaid Insurance =	Butler Cleaning Supplies +	Ben Furman, Capital
Balances	$5,863	$4,297	$1,200	$1,360	$10,000
Transaction 6	+525				+525 (revenue)
New Balances	$6,388	$4,297	$1,200	$1,360	$10,525

Total of left side:	Total of right side:
$6,388 + $4,297 + $1,200 = $11,885	$1,360 + $10,525 = $11,885

After this transaction is recorded, the sum of the balances on the left side of the equation equals the sum of the balances on the right side, $11,885.00. The equation is still in balance.

Illustration 2-2
Receiving cash from sales increases assets and owner's equity

In this chapter, three different kinds of transactions that affect owner's equity are described. Therefore, a description of the transaction is shown in parentheses to the right of the amount in the accounting equation. Transaction 6 is a revenue transaction. Therefore, *(revenue)* is shown beside the $525.00 change in owner's equity in Illustration 2-2.

Paid cash for expenses

A transaction to pay for goods or services needed to operate a business results in a decrease in owner's equity. A decrease in owner's equity resulting from the operation of a business is called an expense. When cash is paid for expenses, the business has less cash. Therefore, the asset account, Cash, is decreased. The owner's equity account, Ben Furman, Capital, is also decreased by the same amount.

Transaction 7.
August 12, 19--.
Paid cash for rent, $250.00.

The effect of this transaction on the accounting equation is shown in Illustration 2-3. The asset account, Cash, is decreased by $250.00, the amount of cash paid out. This decrease is on the left side of the equation. The owner's equity account, Ben Furman, Capital, is also decreased by $250.00. This decrease is on the right side of the equation.

	Assets			= Liabilities + Owner's Equity		
	Cash	+ Supplies	+ Prepaid Insurance =	Butler Cleaning Supplies	+	Ben Furman, Capital
Balances	$6,388	$4,297	$1,200	$1,360		$10,525
Transaction 7	−250					−250 (expense)
New Balances	$6,138	$4,297	$1,200	$1,360		$10,275

Total of left side:
$6,138 + $4,297 + $1,200 = $11,635

Total of right side:
$1,360 + $10,275 = $11,635

Illustration 2-3
Paying cash for an
expense decreases assets
and owner's equity

After this transaction is recorded, the sum of the balances on the left side of the equation equals the sum of the balances on the right side, $11,635.00. The equation is still in balance.

Transaction 8.
August 12, 19--.
Paid cash for telephone bill, $45.00.

Most businesses must make payments for goods and services provided by public utilities, such as telephone companies. These goods and services are often referred to as utilities. In addition to telephone services, electricity, gas, water, and sanitation are also considered to be utilities.

The effect of this transaction on the accounting equation is shown in Illustration 2-4. The asset account, Cash, is decreased by $45.00, the amount of cash paid out. This decrease is on the left side of the equation. The owner's equity account, Ben Furman, Capital, is also decreased by $45.00. This decrease is on the right side of the equation.

Illustration 2-4
Paying cash for an expense decreases assets and owner's equity

| | Assets | | | = | Liabilities | + | Owner's Equity |
	Cash	+ Supplies	+ Prepaid Insurance	=	Butler Cleaning Supplies	+	Ben Furman, Capital
Balances	$6,138	$4,297	$1,200		$1,360		$10,275
Transaction 8	−45						−45 (expense)
New Balances	$6,093	$4,297	$1,200		$1,360		$10,230

Total of left side:
$6,093 + $4,297 + $1,200 = $11,590

Total of right side:
$1,360 + $10,230 = $11,590

After this transaction is recorded, the sum of the balances on the left side of the equation equals the sum of the balances on the right side, $11,590.00. The equation is still in balance.

Other expense transactions might be for advertising, equipment rental or repairs, charitable contributions, and other miscellaneous items. All expense transactions affect the accounting equation in the same way as Transactions 7 and 8.

Paid cash to owner for personal use

Assets taken out of a business for the owner's personal use are called withdrawals. A withdrawal decreases owner's equity. Although an owner may withdraw any kind of asset, usually an owner withdraws cash. The withdrawal decreases the account balance of the withdrawn asset, such as Cash.

Transaction 9.
August 12, 19--.
Paid cash to owner for personal use, $100.00.

The effect of this transaction on the accounting equation is shown in Illustration 2-5. The asset account, Cash, is decreased by $100.00, the amount of cash paid out. This decrease is on the left side of the accounting equation. The owner's equity account, Ben Furman, Capital, is also decreased by $100.00. This decrease is on the right side of the equation.

After this transaction is recorded, the sum of the balances on the left side of the equation equals the sum of the balances on the right side, $11,490.00. The equation is still in balance.

A decrease in owner's equity because of a withdrawal is not a result of the normal operations of a business. Therefore, a withdrawal is not an expense.

| | Assets | | = Liabilities + | Owner's Equity |
	Cash + Supplies +	Prepaid Insurance =	Butler Cleaning Supplies +	Ben Furman, Capital
Balances	$6,093 $4,297	$1,200	$1,360	$10,230
Transaction 9	−100			−100 (withdrawal)
New Balances	$5,993 $4,297	$1,200	$1,360	$10,130

Total of left side:
$5,993 + $4,297 + $1,200 = $11,490

Total of right side:
$1,360 + $10,130 = $11,490

Illustration 2-5
Paying cash to owner for
personal use decreases
assets and owner's equity

Summary of changes in owner's equity

After recording the transactions for starting Rugcare as a proprietor-ship, the total owner's equity was $10,000.00. Five transactions have af-fected owner's equity. In Chapter 1, Ben Furman made a $10,000.00 investment. In this chapter, four transactions that changed owner's equity were recorded in the accounting equation.

Transaction Number	Kind of Transaction	Change in Owner's Equity
6	Revenue	+525.00
7	Expense (rent)	−250.00
8	Expense (telephone)	−45.00
9	Withdrawal	−100.00
	Net change in owner's equity	+130.00

A revenue transaction increased owner's equity. Expense and with-drawal transactions decreased owner's equity. These transactions together increased total owner's equity by $130.00, from $10,000.00 to $10,130.00.

> For a business to succeed, revenues must be greater than expenses dur-ing most periods of time. An established business should rarely experience a decrease in its owner's equity.

REPORTING A CHANGED ACCOUNTING EQUATION ON A BALANCE SHEET

A balance sheet may be prepared on any date to report information about the assets, liabilities, and owner's equity of a business. The balance sheet prepared in Chapter 1, Illustration 1-6, reports Rugcare's financial condition at the end of business on August 11. The transactions recorded in Chapter 2 have changed the account balances of Cash and Ben Furman, Cap-ital in the accounting equation. A revised balance sheet is prepared to re-port Rugcare's financial condition after recording these transactions.

The last transaction on August 12 is recorded in the accounting equa-tion as shown in Illustration 2-5. The new account balances in the accounting equation after Transaction 9 are used to prepare the balance sheet. Rugcare's balance sheet as of August 12 is shown in Illustration 2-6.

The August 12 balance sheet is prepared using the same steps as described in Chapter 1.

	Assets			= Liabilities	+ Owner's Equity
	Cash +	Supplies +	Prepaid Insurance =	Butler Cleaning Supplies	Ben Furman, Capital
New Balances	$5,993	$4,297	$1,200	$1,360	$10,130

Rugcare				
Balance Sheet				
August 12, 19--				
Assets		**Liabilities**		
Cash	5 9 9 3 00	Butler Cleaning Supplies	1 3 6 0 00	
Supplies	4 2 9 7 00	**Owner's Equity**		
Prepaid Insurance	1 2 0 0 00	Ben Furman, Capital	10 1 3 0 00	
Total Assets	11 4 9 0 00	Total Liab. and Owner's Eq.	11 4 9 0 00	

Illustration 2-6
Balance sheet

The accounts on the left side of the accounting equation are reported on the left side of Rugcare's balance sheet. The accounts on the right side of the accounting equation are shown on the right side of the balance sheet. The total of the left side of the balance sheet, $11,490.00, is equal to the total of the right side of the balance sheet. The balance sheet is in balance.

A comparison of the August 11 and August 12 balance sheet totals is shown in Illustration 2-7.

	Assets			= Liabilities	+	Owner's Equity
	Cash +	Supplies +	Prepaid Insurance =	Butler Cleaning Supplies	+	Ben Furman, Capital
August 11	$5,863	$4,297	$1,200	$1,360		$10,000
August 12	$5,993	$4,297	$1,200	$1,360		$10,130
	+$130	$0	$0	$0		+$130

The balance sheet has an increase of $130.00 on the left side (Assets) and an increase of $130.00 on the right side (Liabilities + Owner's Equity).

Illustration 2-7
Comparison of balance sheet totals

Few businesses need to prepare a balance sheet every day. Many businesses prepare a balance sheet only on the last day of each month. Monthly balance sheets provide business owners and managers with frequent and regular information for making business decisions.

Transaction	Assets			= Liabilities +	Owner's Equity
	Cash +	Supplies +	Prepaid Insurance =	Butler Cleaning + Supplies	Ben Furman, Capital
Beginning Balance	$0	$0	$0	$0	$0
1. Received cash from owner as an investment	+10,000				+10,000 (investment)
New Balances	$10,000	$0	$0	$0	$10,000
2. Paid cash for supplies	−1,577	+1,577			
New Balances	$ 8,423	$1,577	$0	$0	$10,000
3. Paid cash for insurance	−1,200		+1,200		
New Balances	$ 7,223	$1,577	$1,200	$0	$10,000
4. Bought supplies on account		+2,720		+2,720	
New Balances	$ 7,223	$4,297	$1,200	$2,720	$10,000
5. Paid cash on account	−1,360			−1,360	
New Balances	$ 5,863	$4,297	$1,200	$1,360	$10,000
6. Received cash from sales	+525				+525 (revenue)
New Balances	$ 6,388	$4,297	$1,200	$1,360	$10,525
7. Paid cash for rent	−250				−250 (expense)
New Balances	$ 6,138	$4,297	$1,200	$1,360	$10,275
8. Paid cash for telephone bill	−45				−45 (expense)
New Balances	$ 6,093	$4,297	$1,200	$1,360	$10,230
9. Paid cash to owner for personal use	−100				−100 (withdrawal)
New Balances	$ 5,993	$4,297	$1,200	$1,360	$10,130

Illustration 2-8
Summary of how transactions affect the accounting equation

Total of left side:
$5,993 + $4,297 + $1,200 = $11,490

Total of right side:
$1,360 + $10,130 = $11,490

SUMMARY OF TRANSACTIONS THAT AFFECT OWNER'S EQUITY

Revenue, expense, and withdrawal transactions affect owner's equity. A revenue transaction increases owner's equity. Expense and withdrawal transactions decrease owner's equity.

The accounting equation has two sides. The left side of the equation shows assets. The right side of the equation shows liabilities and owner's equity. A transaction changes the account balances of two or more accounts. After each transaction, the total of accounts on the left side must equal the total of accounts on the right side. The effects of the transactions analyzed in Chapters 1 and 2 on the accounting equation are shown in Illustration 2-8. After these transactions are recorded, the total of the balances on the left side equals the total of the balances on the right side, $11,490.00. Therefore, the accounting equation is in balance.

The new balances of the accounting equation are used to prepare a balance sheet. The left side of the balance sheet contains asset accounts. The right side contains liability and owner's equity accounts.

ACCOUNTING TERMS

What is the meaning of each of the following?

1. revenue   **2.** expense   **3.** withdrawals

QUESTIONS FOR INDIVIDUAL STUDY

1. Why do owners and managers need information about changes in owner's equity?
2. What accounts are affected, and how, when cash is received from sales?
3. How does a cash payment for goods or services needed to operate a business affect owner's equity?
4. What accounts are affected, and how, by a cash payment for an expense?
5. What must be true of the accounting equation after each transaction is recorded?
6. What are four expense transactions other than rent and utilities?
7. Which asset is normally withdrawn by an owner for personal use?
8. What accounts are affected, and how, when an owner withdraws $200.00 for personal use?
9. What transactions decrease owner's equity?
10. What must be true of changes in owner's equity if a business is to be successful?
11. What are three accounts that might be found on the left side of a balance sheet?
12. How often might a business be expected to prepare a balance sheet?

CASES FOR MANAGEMENT DECISION

CASE 1 Garcia Books receives an investment from its owner, Mrs. Juanita Garcia. This transaction is recorded in the following accounting equation. Is the analysis correct? Explain.

	Assets			=	Liabilities	+	Owner's Equity
Cash	+	Supplies	+	Prepaid Insurance	=	Panther Supply Company	+	Juanita Garcia, Capital

Cash	Supplies	Prepaid Insurance	Panther Supply Company	Juanita Garcia, Capital
$1,000	$3,000	$2,000	$2,500	$3,500
+750				
$1,750	$3,000	$2,000	$2,500	$3,500

CASE 2 The manager of Phillip's Department Store prepares a balance sheet at the end of each business day. Is this a satisfactory procedure? Explain.

■ DRILLS FOR UNDERSTANDING

DRILL 2-D1   Determining how revenue, expense, and withdrawal transactions change an accounting equation

Use a form similar to the following.

Trans. No.	Assets			=	Liabilities	+	Owner's Equity
	Cash	+ Supplies +	Prepaid Insurance	=	Maxwell Company	+	Susan Sanders, Capital
1.	+						+

Transactions
1. Received cash from owner as an investment.
2. Received cash from sales.
3. Paid cash for telephone bill.
4. Paid cash for advertising.
5. Paid cash to owner for personal use.
6. Paid cash for rent.
7. Received cash from sales.
8. Paid cash for equipment repairs.

Instructions: Decide which accounts in the accounting equation are changed by each transaction. Place a plus (+) in the appropriate column if the account is increased. Place a minus (−) in the appropriate column if the account is decreased. Transaction 1 is given as an example.

DRILL 2-D2   Determining how transactions change an accounting equation

Use a form similar to the following.

Trans. No.	Assets			=	Liabilities	+	Owner's Equity
	Cash	+ Supplies +	Prepaid Insurance	=	Barrett Company	+	Sue Marist, Capital
1.		+			+		

Transactions
  1. Bought supplies on account from Barrett Company.
  2. Paid cash for electric bill.
  3. Received cash from owner as an investment.
  4. Paid cash for insurance.
  5. Received cash from sales.
  6. Paid cash for rent.
  7. Paid cash for supplies.
  8. Paid cash for advertising.
  9. Paid cash on account to Barrett Company.
 10. Paid cash to owner for personal use.

Instructions: Decide which accounts in the accounting equation are changed by each transaction. Place a plus (+) in the appropriate column if the account is increased. Place a minus (−) in the appropriate column if the account is decreased. Transaction 1 is given as an example.

 APPLICATION PROBLEMS

PROBLEM 2-1   Determining how revenue, expense, and withdrawal transactions change an accounting equation

Peter Smith operates a service business called Peter's Service Company. Peter's Service Company uses the accounts shown in the following accounting equation. Use a form similar to the following to complete this problem.

Trans. No.	Assets			= Liabilities	+ Owner's Equity
	Cash +	Supplies +	Prepaid Insurance =	Kline Company +	Peter Smith, Capital
Beg. Bal. 1.	625 −300	375	300	200	1,100 −300 (expense)
New Bal. 2.	325	375	300	200	800

Transactions
1. Paid cash for rent, $300.00.
2. Paid cash to owner for personal use, $150.00.
3. Received cash from sales, $800.00.
4. Paid cash for equipment repairs, $100.00
5. Paid cash for telephone bill, $60.00.
6. Received cash from sales, $650.00.
7. Paid cash for charitable contributions, $35.00.
8. Paid cash for miscellaneous expenses, $25.00.

Instructions: For each transaction, complete the following. Transaction 1 is given as an example.
a. Analyze the transaction to determine which accounts in the accounting equation are affected.
b. Write the amount in the appropriate columns, using a plus (+) if the account increases or a minus (−) if the account decreases.
c. For transactions that change owner's equity, write in parentheses a description of the transaction to the right of the amount.

d. Calculate the new balance for each account in the accounting equation.

e. Before going on to the next transaction, determine that the accounting equation is still in balance.

PROBLEM 2-2   Determining how transactions change an accounting equation and preparing a balance sheet

Doris Becker operates a typing business called QuickType. QuickType uses the accounts shown in the following accounting equation. Use a form similar to the following to complete this problem.

Trans. No.	Assets			=	Liabilities	+	Owner's Equity
	Cash +	Supplies +	Prepaid Insurance	=	Teale Company	+	Doris Becker, Capital
Beg. Bal. 1.	500 −50	260	300		100		960 −50 (expense)
New Bal. 2.	450	260	300		100		910

Transactions

1. Paid cash for equipment repair, $50.00.
2. Received cash from sales, $325.00.
3. Paid cash for supplies, $200.00.
4. Bought supplies on account from Teale Company, $1,200.00.
5. Paid cash for advertising, $200.00.
6. Received cash from sales, $280.00.
7. Paid cash for water bill, $60.00.
8. Paid cash for insurance, $400.00.
9. Paid cash to owner for personal use, $125.00.
10. Received cash from sales, $260.00.
11. Paid cash for equipment rental, $45.00.
12. Paid cash for charitable contributions, $25.00.
13. Received cash from sales, $300.00.
14. Paid cash on account to Teale Company, $100.00.
15. Received cash from owner as an investment, $1,000.00.
16. Paid cash for rent, $600.00.
17. Received cash from sales, $430.00.
18. Paid cash on account to Teale Company, $750.00.

Instructions: 1. For each transaction, complete the following. Transaction 1 is given as an example.

a. Analyze the transaction to determine which accounts in the accounting equation are affected.

b. Write the amount in the appropriate columns, using a plus (+) if the account increases or a minus (−) if the account decreases.

c. For transactions that change owner's equity, write in parentheses a description of the transaction to the right of the amount.

d. Calculate the new balance for each account in the accounting equation.

e. Before going on to the next transaction, determine that the accounting equation is still in balance.

2. Using the final balances in the accounting equation, prepare a balance sheet. Use the date July 17 of the current year.

■ ENRICHMENT PROBLEMS

MASTERY PROBLEM 2-M **Determining how transactions change an accounting equation and preparing a balance sheet**

Fred Nance operates a service business called Nance Company. Nance Company uses the accounts shown in the following accounting equation. Use a form similar to the following to complete this problem.

Trans. No.	Assets			=	Liabilities	+	Owner's Equity
	Cash	+	Supplies	+	Prepaid Insurance	=	Sickle Company	+	Fred Nance, Capital
Beg. Bal.	1,400	300	400	1,500	600
1.	−100				−100 (expense)
New Bal.	1,300	300	400	1,500	500
2.					

Transactions

1. Paid cash for telephone bill, $100.00.
2. Received cash from owner as an investment, $200.00.
3. Paid cash for rent, $500.00.
4. Paid cash for equipment rental, $100.00.
5. Received cash from sales, $895.00.
6. Bought supplies on account from Sickle Company, $600.00.
7. Paid cash for equipment repair, $15.00.
8. Paid cash for miscellaneous expense, $30.00.
9. Received cash from sales, $920.00.
10. Paid cash for advertising, $50.00.
11. Paid cash for charitable contribution, $10.00. *expense*
12. Paid cash for supplies, $400.00.
13. Paid cash for advertising, $250.00.
14. Received cash from sales, $795.00.
15. Paid cash on account to Sickle Company, $1,500.00.
16. Paid cash for insurance, $250.00.
17. Received cash from sales, $960.00.
18. Paid cash to owner for personal use, $1,000.00.

Instructions: 1. For each transaction, complete the following. Transaction 1 is given as an example.

a. Analyze the transaction to determine which accounts in the accounting equation are affected.

b. Write the amount in the appropriate columns, using a plus (+) if the account increases or a minus (−) if the account decreases.

c. For transactions that change owner's equity, write in parentheses a description of the transaction to the right of the amount.

d. Calculate the new balance for each account in the accounting equation.

e. Before going on to the next transaction, determine that the accounting equation is still in balance.

2. Using the final balances in the accounting equation, prepare a balance sheet. Use the date April 30 of the current year.

CHALLENGE PROBLEM 2-C   Calculating the missing amounts in an accounting equation

Each of the following statements includes four of the five amounts needed to complete an accounting equation.

Statements

1. Cash, $400.00; Supplies, $300.00; Prepaid Insurance, $800.00; Dexter Company, $500.00.
2. Cash, $200.00; Prepaid Insurance, $400.00; Dexter Company, $250.00; Pat Bouwman, Capital, $900.00.
3. Cash, $300.00; Supplies, $1,000.00; Prepaid Insurance, $750.00; Pat Bouwman, Capital, $1,200.00.
4. Supplies, $2,000.00; Prepaid Insurance, $1,200.00; Dexter Company, $2,400.00; Pat Bouwman, Capital, $3,500.00.
5. Cash, $100.00; Supplies, $2,700.00; Dexter Company, $1,100.00; Pat Bouwman, Capital, $2,500.00.
6. Cash, $250.00; Supplies, $400.00; Prepaid Insurance, $300.00; Pat Bouwman, Capital, $500.00.
7. Cash, $600.00; Supplies, $2,200.00; Prepaid Insurance, $900.00; Dexter Company, $500.00.
8. Supplies, $100.00; Prepaid Insurance, $400.00; Dexter Company, $150.00; Pat Bouwman, Capital, $500.00.

Instructions: 1. Use a form similar to the following. Record the information from each of the statements. Statement 1 is given as an example.

State-ment	Cash +	Supplies +	Prepaid Insurance	= Dexter Company +	Pat Bouwman, Capital
1.	400	300	800	500	___
	Total: ___			Total: ___	

2. Figure the sum of the balances on the side of the accounting equation that is complete. The totals of the balances on the left and right sides must be equal for the accounting equation to be in balance.

3. For each line of the form, figure the amount of the missing item in the accounting equation. Statement 1 is given as an example.

State-ment	Cash +	Supplies +	Prepaid Insurance	= Dexter Company +	Pat Bouwman, Capital
1.	400	300	800	500	1,000
	Total: 1,500			Total: 1,500	

Analyzing Transactions into Debit and Credit Parts

ENABLING PERFORMANCE TASKS

After studying Chapter 3, you will be able to:

a. Define accounting terms related to analyzing transactions into debit and credit parts.

b. Identify accounting concepts and practices related to analyzing transactions into debit and credit parts.

c. Use T accounts to analyze transactions showing which accounts are debited or credited for each transaction.

d. Verify the equality of debits and credits for each transaction.

How business transactions affect accounts in an accounting equation is described in Chapters 1 and 2. Even though the effects of transactions *can* be recorded in an accounting equation, the procedure is not practical in an actual accounting system. Accountants need more detail about the changes affecting each account than will appear in an accounting equation. Also, the number of accounts used by most businesses would make the accounting equation cumbersome to use as a major financial record. Therefore, a separate record is commonly used for each account.

ACCOUNTS

The accounting equation can be represented as a *T*, as shown in Illustration 3-1.

Assets =	Liabilities +	Owner's Equity
Left side		Right side

Illustration 3-1
Sides of an accounting equation

The values of all things owned (assets) are on the left side of the accounting equation. The values of all equities or claims against the assets (liabilities and owner's equity) are on the right side of the accounting equation.

The total of amounts on the left side of the accounting equation must always equal the total of amounts on the right side. Therefore, the total of all assets on the left side of the accounting equation must always equal the total of all liabilities and owner's equity on the right side.

A record summarizing all the information pertaining to a single item in the accounting equation is known as an account. Transactions change the balances of accounts in the accounting equation. Accounting transactions must be analyzed to determine how account balances are changed. An accounting device used to analyze transactions is called a T account. The relationship of a T account to the accounts in the accounting equation is shown in Illustration 3-2.

Assets =	Liabilities + Owner's Equity
Left side	Right side

T Account

Left side	Right side
DEBIT SIDE	CREDIT SIDE

Illustration 3-2
Relationship of a T account
to the accounting equation

Accountants have special names for amounts recorded on the left and right sides of a T account. An amount recorded on the left side of a T account is called a debit. An amount recorded on the right side of a T account is called a credit. The T account is the basic device used to analyze the effect of transactions on accounts.

The normal balance side of an asset, liability, or capital account is based on the location of the account in the accounting equation, as shown in Illustration 3-3.

Assets	=	Liabilities + Owner's Equity
Left side		Right side

ASSETS

Left side Debit side NORMAL BALANCE	Right side Credit side

LIABILITIES

Left side Debit side	Right side Credit side NORMAL BALANCE

OWNER'S CAPITAL ACCOUNT

Left side Debit side	Right side Credit side NORMAL BALANCE

Illustration 3-3
Relationship of asset,
liability, and capital
accounts to the accounting
equation

Asset accounts have normal debit balances (left side) because assets are on the left side of the accounting equation. Liability accounts have normal credit balances (right side) because liabilities appear on the right side of the accounting equation. The owner's capital account has a normal credit balance (right side) because the capital account appears on the right side of the accounting equation.

The sides of a T account are also used to show increases and decreases in account balances, as shown in Illustration 3-4.

Assets	=	Liabilities	+	Owner's Equity
Left side			Right side	

ASSETS		LIABILITIES	
Left side	Right side	Left side	Right side
Debit side	Credit side	Debit side	Credit side
Normal balance			Normal balance
INCREASE	DECREASE	DECREASE	INCREASE

OWNER'S CAPITAL	
Left side	Right side
Debit side	Credit side
	Normal balance
DECREASE	INCREASE

Illustration 3-4.
Increase and decrease
sides of asset, liability, and
capital accounts

Two basic accounting rules regulate increases and decreases of account balances. (1) Account balances increase on the normal balance side of an account. (2) Account balances decrease on the side opposite the normal balance side of an account.

Asset accounts have normal debit balances; therefore, asset accounts increase on the debit side and decrease on the credit side. Liability accounts have normal credit balances; therefore, liability accounts increase on the credit side and decrease on the debit side. The owner's capital account has a normal credit balance; therefore, the capital account increases on the credit side and decreases on the debit side.

ANALYZING HOW TRANSACTIONS AFFECT ACCOUNTS

Before a transaction is recorded in the records of a business, the information is analyzed to determine which accounts are changed and how. Each transaction changes the balances of at least two accounts. In addition, debits equal credits for each transaction, as shown in Illustration 3-5.

Supplies		Cash	
Left side	Right side	Left side	Right side
Debit side	Credit side	Debit side	Credit side
Normal balance		Normal balance	
Increase 1,577.00	Decrease	Increase	1,577.00 Decrease

DEBITS ---------------------------------- equal ----------------------------------- CREDITS

Illustration 3-5
Debits equal credits for
each transaction

The total debits, $1,577.00, equal the total credits, $1,577.00, for this transaction.

Four questions are used in analyzing a transaction into its debit and credit parts.

1 *What accounts are affected?* A list of accounts used by a business is called a chart of accounts. The account titles used by Rugcare are found on the chart of accounts on page 2.

2 *How is each account classified?* Rugcare's accounts are classified as assets, liabilities, owner's equity, revenue, and expenses.

3 *How is each account balance changed?* Is each account increased or decreased?

4 *How is each amount entered in the accounts?* The amount is either debited or credited to the account.

Received cash from owner as an investment

August 1, 19--.
Received cash from owner as an investment, $10,000.00.

The effect of this transaction in the accounting equation is shown in Illustration 3-6.

Assets	=	Liabilities	+	Owner's Equity
Left side Cash +10,000.00				Right side Ben Furman, Capital +10,000.00 (investment)

Any Asset		Owner's Capital	
Left side Debit side Normal balance Increase	Right side Credit side Decrease	Left side Debit side Decrease	Right side Credit side Normal balance Increase

Cash		Ben Furman, Capital	
Left side Debit side Normal balance Increase 10,000.00	Right side Credit side Decrease	Left side Debit side Decrease	Right side Credit side Normal balance Increase 10,000.00

DEBITS ----------------------------- equal --- CREDITS

Illustration 3-6
How debits and credits affect accounts when receiving cash from owner as an investment

Four questions are used to analyze this transaction.

1 *What accounts are affected?* Cash and Ben Furman, Capital.

2 *How is each account classified?* Cash is an asset account with a normal debit balance. Ben Furman, Capital is an owner's equity account with a normal credit balance.

3 *How is each account balance changed?* Cash is increased. Ben Furman, Capital is increased.

4 *How is each amount entered in the accounts?* The asset account, Cash, has a normal debit balance and is increased by a debit, $10,000.00. The owner's equity account, Ben Furman, Capital, has a normal credit balance and is increased by a credit, $10,000.00.

For this transaction, the total debits, $10,000.00, equal the total credits, $10,000.00.

Paid cash for supplies

August 3, 19--.
Paid cash for supplies, $1,577.00.

The effect of this transaction is shown in Illustration 3-7.

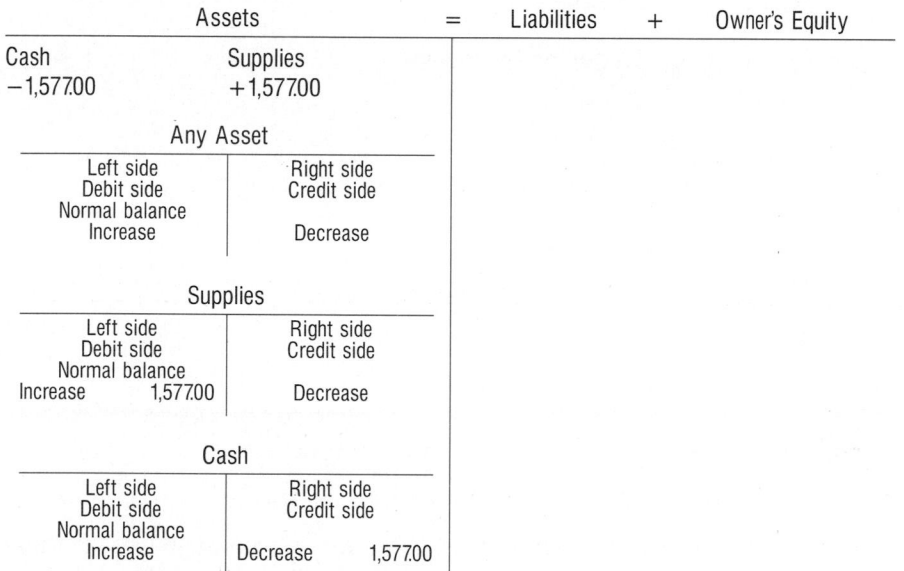

Illustration 3-7
How debits and credits affect accounts when paying cash for supplies

Four questions are used to analyze this transaction.

1 *What accounts are affected?* Cash and Supplies.

2 *How is each account classified?* Cash is an asset account with a normal debit balance. Supplies is an asset account with a normal debit balance.

3 *How is each account balance changed?* Cash is decreased. Supplies is increased.

4 *How is each amount entered in the accounts?* The asset account, Supplies, has a normal debit balance and is increased by a debit, $1,577.00. The asset account, Cash, has a normal debit balance and is decreased by a credit, $1,577.00.

For this transaction, the total debits, $1,577.00, equal the total credits, $1,577.00.

Paid cash for insurance

August 4, 19--.
Paid cash for insurance, $1,200.00.

The effect of this transaction is shown in Illustration 3-8.

Assets		=	Liabilities	+	Owner's Equity
Cash	Prepaid Insurance				
−1,200.00	+1,200.00				

Any Asset

Left side	Right side
Debit side	Credit side
Normal balance	
Increase	Decrease

Prepaid Insurance

Left side	Right side
Debit side	Credit side
Normal balance	
Increase 1,200.00	Decrease

Cash

Left side	Right side
Debit side	Credit side
Normal balance	
Increase	Decrease 1,200.00

DEBITS -------------- equal ------------ CREDITS

Illustration 3-8
How debits and credits affect accounts when paying cash for insurance

Four questions are used to analyze this transaction.

1 *What accounts are affected?* Cash and Prepaid Insurance.

2 *How is each account classified?* Cash is an asset account with a normal debit balance. Prepaid Insurance is an asset account with a normal debit balance.

3 *How is each account balance changed?* Cash is decreased. Prepaid Insurance is increased.

4 *How is each amount entered in the accounts?* The asset account, Prepaid Insurance, has a normal debit balance and is increased by a debit, $1,200.00. The asset account, Cash, has a normal debit balance and is decreased by a credit, $1,200.00.

For this transaction, the total debits, $1,200.00, equal the total credits, $1,200.00.

Bought supplies on account

August 7, 19--.
Bought supplies on account from Butler Cleaning Supplies, $2,720.00.

The effect of this transaction is shown in Illustration 3-9.

Assets	=	Liabilities	+	Owner's Equity
Supplies +2,720.00		Butler Cleaning Supplies +2,720.00		

Any Asset		Any Liability	
Left side Debit side Normal balance Increase	Right side Credit side Decrease	Left side Debit side Decrease	Right side Credit side Normal Balance Increase

Supplies		Butler Cleaning Supplies	
Left side Debit side Normal balance Increase 2,720.00	Right side Credit side Decrease	Left side Debit side Decrease	Right side Credit side Normal balance Increase 2,720.00

DEBITS ---------------------------- equal ---------------------------- CREDITS

Illustration 3-9
How debits and credits affect accounts when buying supplies on account

Four questions are used to analyze this transaction.

1 *What accounts are affected?* Supplies and Butler Cleaning Supplies.

2 *How is each account classified?* Supplies is an asset account with a normal debit balance. Butler Cleaning Supplies is a liability account with a normal credit balance.

3 *How is each account balance changed?* Supplies is increased. Butler Cleaning Supplies is increased.

4 *How is each amount entered in the accounts?* The asset account, Supplies, has a normal debit balance and is increased by a debit, $2,720.00. The liability account, Butler Cleaning Supplies, has a normal credit balance and is increased by a credit, $2,720.00.

For this transaction, the total debits, $2,720.00, equal the total credits, $2,720.00.

Paid cash on account

August 11, 19--.
Paid cash on account to Butler Cleaning Supplies, $1,360.00.

The effect of this transaction is shown in Illustration 3-10.
Four questions are used to analyze this transaction.

1 *What accounts are affected?* Cash and Butler Cleaning Supplies.

2 *How is each account classified?* Cash is an asset account with a normal debit balance. Butler Cleaning Supplies is a liability account with a normal credit balance.

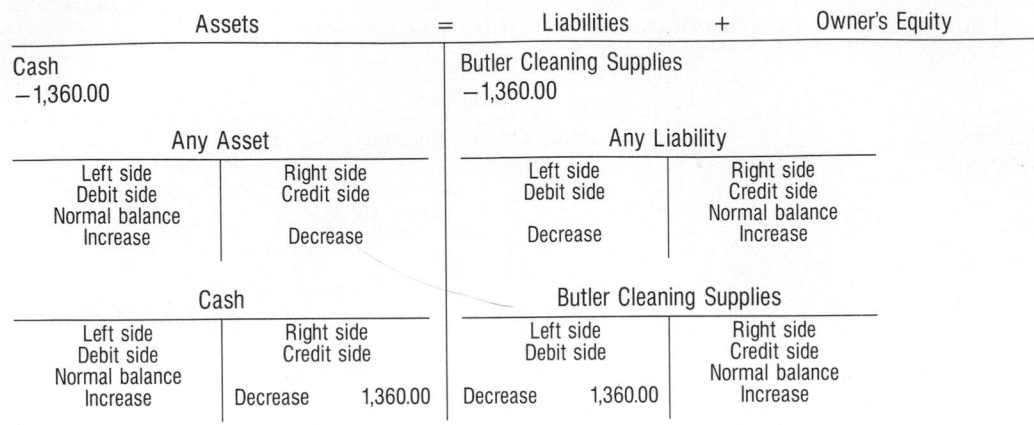

| Assets | | = | Liabilities | + | Owner's Equity |

CREDITS ------ equal ------- DEBITS

3 *How is each account balance changed?* Cash is decreased. Butler Cleaning Supplies is decreased.

4 *How is each amount entered in the accounts?* The liability account, Butler Cleaning Supplies, has a normal credit balance and is decreased by a debit, $1,360.00. The asset account, Cash, has a normal debit balance and is decreased by a credit, $1,360.00.

For this transaction, the total debits, $1,360.00, equal the total credits, $1,360.00.

Received cash from sales

Revenue increases the owner's capital. The increases from revenue could be recorded directly in the owner's capital account. However, to avoid a capital account with a large number of entries and to summarize revenue information separately from the other records, Rugcare uses a separate revenue account.

August 12, 19--.
Received cash from sales, $525.00.

The effect of this transaction is shown in Illustration 3-11.

The owner's capital account has a normal credit balance. A revenue account shows increases in capital. Therefore, a revenue account also has a normal credit balance. Revenue accounts increase on the credit side and decrease on the debit side. Rugcare's revenue account is titled Sales.

Four questions are used to analyze this revenue transaction.

1 *What accounts are affected?* Cash and Sales.

2 *How is each account classified?* Cash is an asset account with a normal debit balance. Sales is a revenue account with a normal credit balance.

Assets	=	Liabilities	+	Owner's Equity

Cash
+525.00

                                                                              Owner's Capital
                                                                              +525.00 (revenue)

Owner's Capital		Any Revenue Account	
Left side	Right side	Left side	Right side
Debit side	Credit side	Debit side	Credit side
	Normal balance		Normal balance
Decrease	Increase	Decrease	Increase

Cash		Sales	
Left side	Right side	Left side	Right side
Debit side	Credit side	Debit side	Credit side
Normal balance			Normal balance
Increase 525.00	Decrease	Decrease	Increase 525.00

DEBITS ------------------------- equal --- CREDITS

3 *How is each account balance changed?* Cash is increased. Sales is increased.

4 *How is each amount entered in the accounts?* The asset account, Cash, has a normal debit balance and is increased by a debit, $525.00. The revenue account, Sales, has a normal credit balance and is increased by a credit, $525.00.

For this transaction, the total debits, $525.00, equal the total credits, $525.00.

Illustration 3-11
How debits and credits affect accounts when receiving cash from sales

Paid cash for an expense

Expenses decrease the owner's capital. Expenses could be recorded directly in the owner's capital account. However, to avoid a capital account with a large number of entries and to summarize expense information separately from the other records, Rugcare uses separate expense accounts.

The titles of Rugcare's expense accounts are shown on the chart of accounts, page 2. The expense account, Utilities Expense, is used to record all payments of utility bills. These include payments made for electricity, telephone, gas, water, and sanitation.

August 12, 19--.
Paid cash for rent, $250.00.

The effect of this transaction is shown in Illustration 3-12.

The owner's capital account has a normal credit balance. Decreases in the owner's capital account are shown as debits. An expense account shows decreases in owner's equity. Therefore, an expense account has a normal debit balance. An expense account increases on the debit side and decreases on the credit side.

Assets	=	Liabilities	+	Owner's Equity
Cash −250.00				Owner's Capital −250.00 (expense)

Any Expense Account		Owner's Capital Account	
Left side Debit side Normal balance Increase	Right side Credit side Decrease	Left side Debit side Decrease	Right side Credit side Normal balance Increase

Cash		Rent Expense	
Left side Debit side Normal balance Increase	Right side Credit side Decrease 250.00	Left side Debit side Normal balance Increase 250.00	Right side Credit side Decrease

Illustration 3-12
How debits and credits
affect accounts when
paying cash for an
expense

CREDITS ----- equal ------ DEBITS

Four questions are used to analyze this expense transaction.

1 *What accounts are affected?* Cash and Rent Expense.

2 *How is each account classified?* Cash is an asset account with a normal debit balance. Rent Expense is an expense account with a normal debit balance.

3 *How is each account balance changed?* Cash is decreased. Rent Expense is increased.

4 *How is each amount entered in the accounts?* The expense account, Rent Expense, has a normal debit balance and is increased by a debit, $250.00. The asset account, Cash, has a normal debit balance and is decreased by a credit, $250.00.

For this transaction, the total debits, $250.00, equal the total credits, $250.00.

Paid cash to owner for personal use

Assets taken out of a business for the personal use of the owner are known as withdrawals. Withdrawals are considered to be part of the owner's equity taken out of a business. Therefore, withdrawals decrease the owner's equity. Withdrawals could be recorded as decreases directly in the owner's capital account. However, common accounting practice is to record withdrawals in a separate account to provide a separate record of the withdrawals for each fiscal period. In this way, the owner knows how much has been withdrawn from the business each fiscal period.

An account that reduces a related account on a financial statement is called a contra account. The drawing account is a contra capital account because the account shows decreases in capital.

August 12, 19--.
Paid cash to owner for personal use, $100.00.

The effect of this transaction is shown in Illustration 3-13.

Assets	=	Liabilities	+	Owner's Equity
Cash −100.00				Owner's Capital −100.00 (withdrawal)

A Contra Capital Account		Owner's Capital Account	
Left side Debit side Normal balance Increase	Right side Credit side Decrease	Left side Debit side Decrease	Right side Credit side Normal balance Increase

Cash		Ben Furman, Drawing	
Left side Debit side Normal balance Increase	Right side Credit side Decrease 100.00	Left side Debit side Normal balance Increase 100.00	Right side Credit side Decrease

CREDITS----- equal ----- DEBITS

Illustration 3-13
How debits and credits affect accounts when paying cash to owner for personal use

The owner's capital account has a normal credit balance. Decreases in the owner's capital account are shown as debits. Because a drawing account shows decreases in capital, a drawing account has a normal debit balance. A drawing account increases on the debit side and decreases on the credit side.

Four questions are used to analyze this transaction.

1 *What accounts are affected?* Cash and Ben Furman, Drawing.

2 *How is each account classified?* Cash is an asset account with a normal debit balance. Ben Furman, Drawing is a contra capital account with a normal debit balance.

3 *How is each account balance changed?* Cash is decreased. Ben Furman, Drawing is increased.

4 *How is each amount entered in the accounts?* The contra capital account, Ben Furman, Drawing, has a normal debit balance and is increased by a debit, $100.00. The asset account, Cash, has a normal debit balance and is decreased by a credit, $100.00.

For this transaction, the total debits, $100.00, equal the total credits, $100.00.

SUMMARY OF ANALYZING
TRANSACTIONS INTO DEBIT AND CREDIT PARTS

The total debits and total credits for a transaction must be equal, as shown in Illustration 3-14.

Supplies		Cash	
Debits 1,577.00	Credits	Debits	Credits 1,577.00

DEBITS-------------------- equal --------------------CREDITS

Illustration 3-14
Equality of debits and credits for a transaction

A summary of how debits and credits affect account balances is shown in Illustration 3-15.

| Assets | = | Liabilities | + | Owner's Equity |

| Equation's left side | | | | Equation's right side |

Asset Accounts		Liability Accounts		Owner's Capital Account	
Left side	Right side	Left side	Right side	Left side	Right side
Debit side	Credit side	Debit side	Credit side	Debit side	Credit side
Normal balance			Normal balance		Normal balance
Increases	Decreases	Decreases	Increases	Decreases	Increases

Owner's Drawing Account	
Left side	Right side
Debit side	Credit side
Normal balance	
Increases	Decreases

Expense Accounts		Sales	
Left side	Right side	Left side	Right side
Debit side	Credit side	Debit side	Credit side
Normal balance			Normal balance
Increases	Decreases	Decreases	Increases

Illustration 3-15
Summary of how debits
and credits affect
accounts

A summary analysis of transactions is shown in Illustration 3-16.

Illustration 3-16
Summary analysis of
transactions into debit and
credit parts

Transaction	Accounts Affected	Account Classification	How Is Account Affected?		Entered in Account as a	
			Increase	Decrease	Debit	Credit
Received cash from owner as an investment	Cash	Asset	X		X	
	Ben Furman, Capital	Owner's Equity	X			X
Paid cash for supplies	Supplies	Asset	X		X	
	Cash	Asset		X		X
Paid cash for insurance	Prepaid Insurance	Asset	X		X	
	Cash	Asset		X		X
Bought supplies on account	Supplies	Asset	X		X	
	Butler Cleaning Supplies	Liability	X			X
Paid cash on account	Butler Cleaning Supplies	Liability		X	X	
	Cash	Asset		X		X
Received cash from sales	Cash	Asset	X		X	
	Sales	Revenue	X			X
Paid cash for rent	Rent Expense	Expense	X		X	
	Cash	Asset		X		X
Paid cash to owner for personal use	Ben Furman, Drawing	Contra Capital	X		X	
	Cash	Asset		X		X

◼ ACCOUNTING TERMS

What is the meaning of each of the following?

1. T account
2. debit
3. credit
4. chart of accounts
5. contra account

◼ QUESTIONS FOR INDIVIDUAL STUDY

1. What basic accounting device is used to help analyze transactions?

2. What determines which side of a T account will be the normal balance side?

3. What is the normal balance side of an asset account? Of a liability account? Of a capital account?

4. What two basic accounting rules regulate the increases and decreases of an account?

5. On which sides of a T account are increases and decreases recorded for asset accounts? For liability accounts? For the capital account?

6. What is the relationship between total debits and total credits in accounting records?

7. What are the four questions used in analyzing a transaction into debit and credit parts?

8. What accounts are affected, and how, when cash is received from an owner as an investment?

9. What accounts are affected, and how, when cash is paid for supplies?

10. What accounts are affected, and how, when cash is paid for insurance?

11. What accounts are affected, and how, when supplies are bought on account?

12. What accounts are affected, and how, when cash is paid on account?

13. What is the normal balance side of a revenue account?

14. What accounts are affected, and how, when cash is received from sales?

15. What is the normal balance side of an expense account?

16. What accounts are affected, and how, when cash is paid for rent?

17. What is the normal balance side of a drawing account?

18. What accounts are affected, and how, when cash is paid to an owner for personal use?

◼ CASES FOR MANAGEMENT DECISION

CASE 1 When Carol Zueker invested in a business, she analyzed the transaction for her $5,000.00 investment as shown in the following T accounts.

Cash	
5,000.00	

Carol Zueker, Drawing	
5,000.00	

Did Miss Zueker analyze the transaction correctly? Explain your answer.

CASE 2 Sharon Morris records *all* cash receipts as revenue and *all* cash payments as expenses. Is Miss Morris recording her cash receipts and cash payments correctly? Explain your answer.

CASE 3 Thomas Bueler records all investments, revenue, expenses, and withdrawals in his capital account. At the end of each month, Mr. Bueler sorts the information to prepare a summary of what has caused the changes in his capital account balance. To help Mr. Bueler prepare this summary in the future, what changes would you suggest he make in his records?

■ DRILLS FOR UNDERSTANDING

DRILL 3-D1   Determining the normal balance, increase, and decrease sides for accounts

Jeff Dixon owns a service business called HouseClean. HouseClean uses the following accounts.

Cash	Sales
Supplies	Advertising Expense
Prepaid Insurance	Miscellaneous Expense
Miller Supplies	Rent Expense
Wayne Office Supplies	Repair Expense
Jeff Dixon, Capital	Utilities Expense
Jeff Dixon, Drawing	

Instructions: 1. Prepare a T account for each account. Label the debit and credit sides of each account. The T account for Cash is given as an example.

2. For each account, label the side of the T account that is used for each of the following. The T account for Cash is given as an example.
a. Normal balance
b. Increase side
c. Decrease side

```
                    Cash
     _____
        Debit side    |    Credit side
```

```
                    Cash
     _____
        Debit side    |    Credit side
      Normal balance  |
        Increase      |      Decrease
```

DRILL 3-D2   Analyzing how transactions affect accounts

Use a form similar to the following. Transaction 1 is given as an example.

1	2	3	4	5	6	7	8	9
			Account's Normal Balance		How is Account Affected?		Entered in Account as a	
Trans. No.	Accounts Affected	Account Classification	Debit	Credit	(+)	(−)	Debit	Credit
1.	Cash	Asset	✓		✓		✓	
	Jeff Dixon, Capital	Owner's Equity		✓	✓			✓

Transactions
1. Received cash from owner as an investment.
2. Paid cash for supplies.
3. Paid cash for insurance.
4. Bought supplies on account from Miller Supplies.
5. Received cash from sales.
6. Paid cash on account to Miller Supplies.
7. Paid cash for rent.
8. Paid cash for repairs.
9. Paid cash for miscellaneous expense.
10. Paid cash for telephone bill (utilities expense).
11. Paid cash to owner for personal use.

Instructions: 1. Use the account titles given in Drill 3-D1. In Column 2, write the accounts changed by each transaction.

2. For each account title, write the account classification in Column 3.

3. For each account title, place a check mark in either Column 4 or 5 to indicate the normal balance.

4. For each account title, place a check mark in either Column 6 or 7 to indicate if the account is increased (+) or decreased (−) by this transaction.

5. For each account title, place a check mark in either Column 8 or 9 to indicate if the account is changed by a debit or a credit.

■ APPLICATION PROBLEMS

PROBLEM 3-1 Analyzing transactions into debit and credit parts

Dixie Conastar owns a business called Conastar Company. Conastar Company uses the following accounts.

Cash	Sales
Supplies	Advertising Expense
Prepaid Insurance	Miscellaneous Expense
Bales Office Supplies	Rent Expense
Dixie Conastar, Capital	Utilities Expense
Dixie Conastar, Drawing	

Transactions

Apr. 1. Received cash from owner as an investment, $5,000.00.
    2. Paid cash for supplies, $50.00.
    3. Paid cash for insurance, $75.00.
    6. Bought supplies on account from Bales Office Supplies, $100.00.
    7. Received cash from sales, $400.00.
    8. Paid cash for water bill (utilities expense), $25.00.
    9. Paid cash for advertising, $40.00.
    13. Paid cash on account to Bales Office Supplies, $50.00.
    14. Received cash from sales, $400.00.
    15. Paid cash for miscellaneous expense, $5.00.
    16. Paid cash to owner for personal use, $50.00.
    18. Paid cash for rent, $250.00.

Instructions: 1. Prepare two T accounts for each transaction. On each T account, write the account title of one of the accounts affected by the transaction.

2. Write the debit or credit amount in each T account to show how the transaction affected that account. T accounts for the first transaction are given as an example.

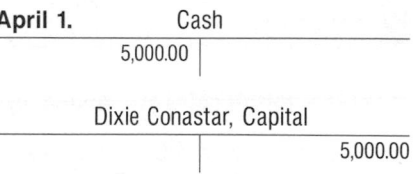

PROBLEM 3-2 Analyzing transactions into debit and credit parts

Buelah VanBorne owns a business called VanBorne Services. VanBorne Services uses the following accounts.

Cash	Sales
Supplies	Advertising Expense

Prepaid Insurance   Miscellaneous Expense
Fortune Supplies   Rent Expense
Herdle Office Supplies   Repair Expense
Buelah VanBorne, Capital   Utilities Expense
Buelah VanBorne, Drawing

Transactions

May 1. Received cash from owner as an investment, $2,000.00.
     4. Bought supplies on account from Herdle Office Supplies, $500.00.
     6. Paid cash for rent, $500.00.
     7. Received cash from sales, $400.00.
     11. Paid cash on account to Herdle Office Supplies, $250.00.
     13. Paid cash for repairs, $80.00.
     14. Received cash from sales, $500.00.
     15. Paid cash for supplies, $600.00.
     19. Paid cash for insurance, $240.00.
     20. Bought supplies on account from Fortune Supplies, $50.00.
     21. Paid cash for supplies, $500.00.
     21. Received cash from sales, $750.00.
     25. Paid cash for telephone bill (utilities expense), $90.00.
     26. Paid cash for advertising, $130.00.
     28. Paid cash for miscellaneous expense, $15.00.
     28. Received cash from sales, $520.00.
     29. Paid cash to owner for personal use, $600.00.
     31. Received cash from sales, $400.00.

Instructions: 1. Prepare a T account for each account.

2. Analyze each transaction into its debit and credit parts. Write the debit and credit amounts in the proper T accounts to show how each transaction changes account balances. Write the date of the transaction in parentheses before each amount. The amounts for Transaction 1 are given in T accounts as an example.

	Cash	
(1)	2,000.00	

	Buelah VanBorne, Capital	
		(1) 2,000.00

 ENRICHMENT PROBLEMS

MASTERY PROBLEM 3-M   Analyzing transactions into debit and credit parts

James Lands owns a business called LandScape. LandScape uses the following accounts.

Cash   Sales
Supplies   Advertising Expense
Prepaid Insurance   Miscellaneous Expense
Janitor Supplies   Rent Expense
Derner Office Supplies   Repair Expense
James Lands, Capital   Utilities Expense
James Lands, Drawing

Transactions

June 1. Received cash from owner as an investment, $3,000.00.
2. Paid cash for supplies, $60.00.
4. Paid cash for rent, $200.00.
4. Received cash from sales, $350.00.
5. Paid cash for repairs, $10.00.
9. Bought supplies on account from Janitor Supplies, $500.00.
10. Paid cash for insurance, $100.00.
11. Received cash from owner as an investment, $900.00.
11. Received cash from sales, $300.00.
12. Bought supplies on account from Derner Office Supplies, $50.00.
15. Paid cash for miscellaneous expense, $5.00.
16. Paid cash on account to Janitor Supplies, $50.00.
18. Received cash from sales, $400.00.
22. Paid cash for electric bill (utilities expense), $35.00.
23. Paid cash for advertising, $30.00.
25. Received cash from sales, $220.00.
26. Paid cash to owner for personal use, $600.00.
30. Received cash from sales, $100.00.

Instructions: 1. Prepare a T account for each account.

2. Analyze each transaction into its debit and credit parts. Write the debit and credit amounts in the proper T accounts to show how each transaction changes account balances. Write the date of the transaction in parentheses before each amount.

CHALLENGE PROBLEM 3-C   Analyzing transactions recorded in T accounts

Edward Burns owns a business for which the following T accounts show the current financial situation.

Cash

(1)	5,000.00	(2)	80.00
(6)	475.00	(4)	15.00
(8)	350.00	(5)	16.00
(9)	400.00	(7)	900.00
		(10)	150.00
		(11)	95.00
		(12)	50.00

Sales

		(6)	475.00
		(8)	350.00
		(9)	400.00

Supplies

(3)	300.00		
(11)	95.00		

Advertising Expense

(5)	16.00		

Midwest Supplies

(10)	150.00	(3)	300.00

Miscellaneous Expense

(4)	15.00		

Edward Burns, Capital

		(1)	5,000.00

Rent Expense

(7)	900.00		

Edward Burns, Drawing

(2)	80.00		

Utilities Expense

(12)	50.00		

Instructions: 1. Use a form similar to the following.

1	2	3	4	5	6
Trans. No.	Accounts Affected	Account Classification	Entered in Account as a		Description of Transaction
			Debit	Credit	
1.	Cash Edward Burns, Capital	Asset Owner's Equity	✓	✓	Received cash from owner as an investment

2. Analyze each numbered transaction in the T accounts. Write the titles of accounts affected in Column 2. For each account, write the classification of the account in Column 3.

3. For each account, place a check mark in either Column 4 or 5 to indicate if the account is affected by a debit or a credit.

4. For each transaction, write a brief statement in Column 6 describing the transaction. Information for Transaction 1 is given as an example.

Journalizing Transactions

ENABLING PERFORMANCE TASKS

After studying Chapter 4, you will be able to:
a. Define accounting terms related to recording transactions in a journal.
b. Identify accounting concepts and practices related to recording transactions in a journal.
c. Record selected transactions in a five-column journal.
d. Prove equality of debits and credits in a five-column journal.
e. Prove cash.
f. Forward totals from one journal page to another.
g. Rule a five-column journal.

As described in Chapter 3, transactions are analyzed into debit and credit parts before information is recorded. A form for recording transactions in chronological order is called a journal. Recording transactions in a journal is called journalizing.

Transactions could be recorded in the accounting equation. However, generally accepted accounting practice is to make a more permanent record by recording transactions in a journal.

A JOURNAL

Each business uses the kind of journal that best fits the needs of that business. The nature of a business and the number of transactions to be recorded determines the kind of journal to be used.

Journal form

Rugcare uses a journal that has five amount columns, as shown in Illustration 4-1.

	JOURNAL								PAGE	
					1	2	3	4	5	
DATE	ACCOUNT TITLE	DOC. NO.	POST. REF.	GENERAL		SALES CREDIT	CASH			
				DEBIT	CREDIT		DEBIT	CREDIT		
1										1
2										2
3										3
4										4
5										5

Illustration 4-1
Five-column journal

The five amount columns in Rugcare's journal are General Debit, General Credit, Sales Credit, Cash Debit, and Cash Credit. A journal amount column headed with an account title is called a special amount column. Special amount columns are used for frequently occurring transactions. For example, most of Rugcare's transactions involve receipt or payment of cash. A large number of the transactions involve receipt of cash from sales. Therefore, Rugcare uses three special amount columns in its journal: Sales Credit, Cash Debit, and Cash Credit.

Using special amount columns eliminates writing an account title in the Account Title column. Therefore, recording transactions in a journal with special amount columns saves time.

A journal amount column that is not headed with an account title is called a general amount column. In Rugcare's journal, the General Debit and General Credit columns are general amount columns.

Accuracy

Information recorded in a journal includes the debit and credit parts of each transaction recorded in one place. The information can be verified by comparing the data in the journal with the source document data to assure that all information is correct.

Chronological record

Transactions are recorded in a journal by date in the order in which the transactions occur. All the information about each transaction is recorded in one place making the information for a specific transaction easier to locate.

Double-entry accounting

Information for each transaction recorded in a journal is called an entry. The recording of debit and credit parts of a transaction is called double-entry accounting. In double-entry accounting, each transaction affects at least two accounts. Both the debit part and the credit part are recorded for each transaction. This procedure reflects the dual effect of each transaction on the business' records. For example, cash paid for advertising causes (1) a decrease in cash and (2) an increase in expenses. Double-entry accounting assures that debits equal credits.

SOURCE DOCUMENTS

A business paper from which information is obtained for a journal entry is called a source document. Each transaction is described by a source document that proves that the transaction did occur. For example, Rugcare prepares a check stub for each cash payment made. The check stub describes information about the cash payment transaction for which the check is prepared. The accounting concept, *Objective Evidence,* is applied when a source document is prepared for each transaction. *(CONCEPT: Objective Evidence)*

A transaction should be recorded only if it actually occurs. The amounts recorded must be accurate and true. Nearly all transactions result in the preparation of a source document. One way to verify the accuracy of a specific journal entry is to compare the entry with the source document. Rugcare uses four source documents: checks, calculator tapes, receipts, and memorandums.

Checks

A business form ordering a bank to pay cash from a bank account is called a check. The source document for cash payments is a check. Rugcare makes all cash payments by check. The checks are prenumbered to help Rugcare account for all checks. Rugcare's record of information on a check is the check stub prepared at the same time as the check. A check and check stub prepared by Rugcare are shown in Illustration 4-2.

Procedures for preparing checks and check stubs are described in Chapter 6.

Illustration 4-2
Check and check stub

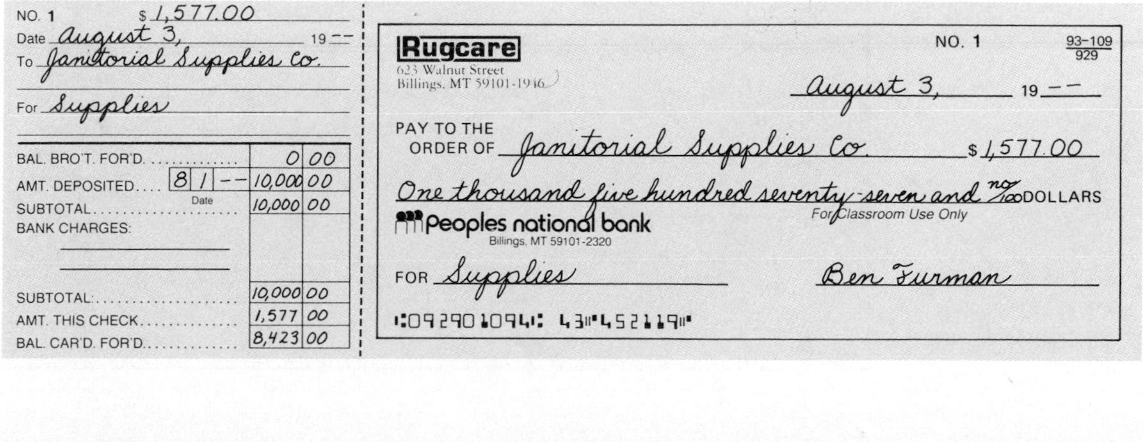
NO. 1 $ 1,577.00
Date August 3, 19 --
To Janitorial Supplies Co.
For Supplies

BAL. BRO'T. FOR'D.	0	00
AMT. DEPOSITED 8/1/-- (Date)	10,000	00
SUBTOTAL	10,000	00
BANK CHARGES:		
SUBTOTAL	10,000	00
AMT. THIS CHECK	1,577	00
BAL. CAR'D. FOR'D.	8,423	00

Rugcare
623 Walnut Street
Billings, MT 59101-1946
NO. 1
93-109/929
August 3, 19 --
PAY TO THE ORDER OF Janitorial Supplies Co. $ 1,577.00
One thousand five hundred seventy-seven and no/100 DOLLARS
For Classroom Use Only
Peoples national bank
Billings, MT 59101-2320
FOR Supplies
Ben Furman
⑆0929010941⑆ 43⑈4521191⑈

Calculator tapes

Rugcare collects cash at the time services are rendered to customers. At the end of each day, Rugcare uses a printing electronic calculator to total the amount of cash received from sales for that day. By totaling all the individual sales, a single source document is produced for the total sales of the day. Thus, time and space are saved by recording only one entry for all of a day's sales. The calculator tape is the source document for daily sales. *(CONCEPT: Objective Evidence)* A calculator tape used as a source document is shown in Illustration 4-3.

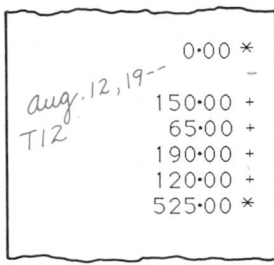

Illustration 4-3
Calculator tape used as a
source document

Rugcare dates and numbers each calculator tape. For example, in Illustration 4-3, the number, *T12*, indicates that the tape is for the twelfth day of the month.

Receipts

A business form giving written acknowledgement for cash received is called a receipt. When cash is received from sources other than sales, Rugcare prepares a receipt. The receipts are prenumbered to help account for all the receipts. A receipt is the source document for cash received from transactions other than sales. *(CONCEPT: Objective Evidence)* Rugcare's receipt is shown in Illustration 4-4.

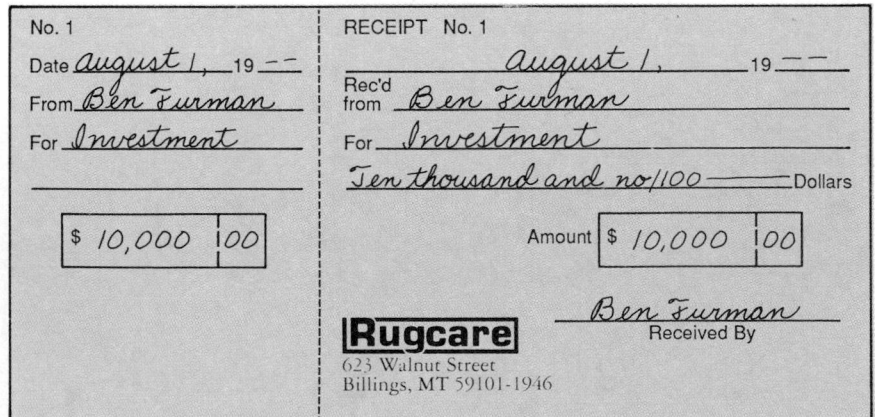

Illustration 4-4
Receipt used as a source
document

Memorandums

A form on which a brief message is written describing a transaction is called a memorandum. When no other source document is prepared for a transaction, or when additional explanation is needed about a transaction, Rugcare prepares a memorandum. *(CONCEPT: Objective Evidence)* Rugcare's memorandums are prenumbered to help account for all the memorandums. The memorandum used by Rugcare is shown in Illustration 4-5. A brief note is written on the memorandum to describe the transaction.

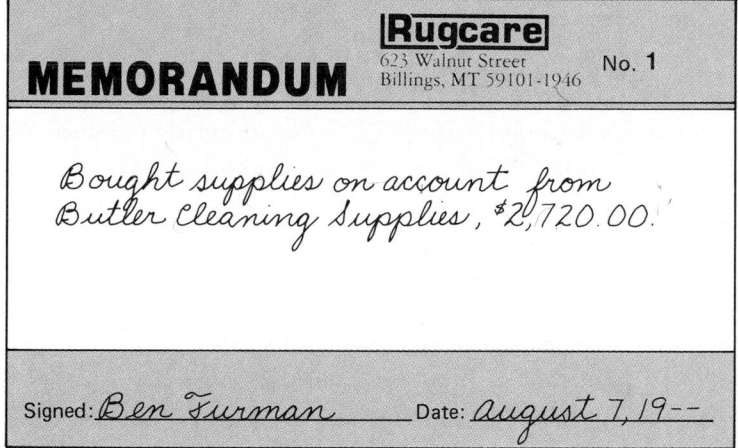

Illustration 4-5
Memorandum used as a
source document

RECORDING TRANSACTIONS IN A FIVE-COLUMN JOURNAL

Information for each transaction recorded in a journal is known as an entry. An entry consists of four parts: (1) date, (2) debit, (3) credit, and (4) source document. Before a transaction is recorded in a journal, the transaction is analyzed into its debit and credit parts.

Received cash from owner as an investment

August 1, 19--.
Received cash from owner as an investment, $10,000.00. Receipt No. 1.

The source document for this transaction is Receipt No. 1. *(CONCEPT: Objective Evidence)* The analysis of this transaction is shown in the T accounts.

All T account analysis in Chapter 4 is described in detail in Chapter 3.

The asset acount, Cash, is increased by a debit, $10,000.00. The owner's capital account, Ben Furman, Capital, is increased by a credit, $10,000.00. The journal entry for this transaction is shown in Illustration 4-6.

Cash	
10,000.00	

Ben Furman, Capital	
	10,000.00

					GENERAL		SALES CREDIT	CASH	
JOURNAL								PAGE *1*	
					1	2	3	4	5
DATE	ACCOUNT TITLE	DOC. NO.	POST. REF.	DEBIT	CREDIT	SALES CREDIT	DEBIT	CREDIT	
19-- Aug. 1	Ben Furman, Capital	R1			10 0 0 0 00		10 0 0 0 00		1

Illustration 4-6
Journal entry to record
receiving cash from owner
as an investment

1 Date. Write the date, *19--, Aug. 1,* in the Date column.
This entry is the first one on this journal page. Therefore, the year and month are both written for this entry. Neither the year nor the month are written again on the same page.

2 Debit. The journal has a special amount column for debits to Cash. The title of the account is in the column heading. Therefore, the account title does not need to be written in the Account Title column. Write the debit amount, *$10,000.00,* in the Cash Debit column.

3 Credit. Write the title of the account credited, *Ben Furman, Capital,* in the Account Title column. There is no special amount column with the title of the account credited, Ben Furman, Capital, in its heading. Therefore, the credit amount is recorded in the General Credit column. Write the credit amount, *$10,000.00,* in the General Credit column.

All amounts recorded in the General Debit or General Credit amount columns must have an account title written in the Account Title column.

4 Source document. Write the source document number, *R1,* in the Doc. No. column. The source document number, *R1,* indicates that this is Receipt No. 1.

The source document number is a cross reference from the journal to the source document. If more details are needed about this transaction, a person can refer to Receipt No. 1.

Paid cash for supplies

August 3, 19--.
Paid cash for supplies, $1,577.00. Check No. 1.

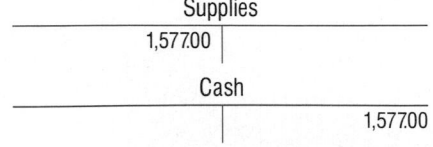

The source document for this transaction is Check No. 1. (*CONCEPT: Objective Evidence*) The analysis of this transaction is shown in the T accounts.

The asset account, Supplies, is increased by a debit, $1,577.00. The asset account, Cash, is decreased by a credit, $1,577.00. The journal entry for this transaction is shown in Illustration 4-7.

1 Date. Write the date, *3,* in the Date column. This is not the first entry on the journal page. Therefore, the year and month are not written for this entry.

		JOURNAL									PAGE *1*	
					1		2		3	4		5
	DATE	ACCOUNT TITLE	DOC. NO.	POST. REF.	GENERAL DEBIT		CREDIT		SALES CREDIT	CASH DEBIT		CREDIT
2	3	Supplies	C1		1 5 7 7 00							1 5 7 7 00	2

2 *Debit.* Write the title of the account debited, *Supplies*, in the Account Title column. There is no special amount column with the title of the account debited, Supplies, in its heading. Therefore, the debit amount is recorded in the General Debit column. Write the debit amount, *$1,577.00,* in the General Debit column.

Illustration 4-7
Journal entry to record paying cash for supplies

3 *Credit.* The journal has a special amount column for credits to Cash. The title of the account is in the column heading. Therefore, the account title does not need to be written in the Account Title column. Write the credit amount, *$1,577.00,* in the Cash Credit column.

4 *Source document.* Write the source document number, C1, in the Doc. No. column. The source document number, *C1,* indicates that this is Check No. 1.

Paid cash for insurance

August 4, 19--.
Paid cash for insurance, $1,200.00. Check No. 2.

The source document for this transaction is Check No. 2. (CONCEPT: *Objective Evidence*) The analysis of this transaction is shown in the T accounts.

The asset account, Prepaid Insurance, is increased by a debit, $1,200.00. The asset account, Cash, is decreased by a credit, $1,200.00. The journal entry for this transaction is shown in Illustration 4-8.

```
       Prepaid Insurance
       1,200.00 |

            Cash
                | 1,200.00
```

		JOURNAL									PAGE *1*	
					1		2		3	4		5
	DATE	ACCOUNT TITLE	DOC. NO.	POST. REF.	GENERAL DEBIT		CREDIT		SALES CREDIT	CASH DEBIT		CREDIT
3	4	Prepaid Insurance	C2		1 2 0 0 00							1 2 0 0 00	3

Illustration 4-8
Journal entry to record paying cash for insurance

1 *Date.* Write the date, *4,* in the Date column.

2 *Debit.* Write the title of the account debited, *Prepaid Insurance*, in the Account Title column. There is no special amount column with the title of the account debited, *Prepaid Insurance*, in its heading. Therefore, the debit amount is recorded in the General Debit column. Write the debit amount, *$1,200.00*, in the General Debit column.

3 *Credit.* The journal has a special amount column for credits to Cash. The title of the account is in the column heading. Therefore, the account title does not need to be written in the Account Title column. Write the credit amount, *$1,200.00*, in the Cash Credit column.

4 *Source document.* Write the source document number, *C2*, in the Doc. No. column.

Bought supplies on account

August 7, 19--.
Bought supplies on account from Butler Cleaning Supplies, $2,720.00. Memorandum No. 1.

Rugcare ordered these supplies by telephone. The supplies are received on August 7. Butler Cleaning Supplies has not yet sent Rugcare notice of the goods shipped. Rugcare wishes to record this transaction immediately. Therefore, Rugcare prepares a memorandum to describe the transaction.

Supplies	
2,720.00	

Butler Cleaning Supplies	
	2,720.00

The source document for this transaction is Memorandum No. 1. *(CONCEPT: Objective Evidence)* The analysis of this transaction is shown in the T accounts.

The asset account, Supplies, is increased by a debit, $2,720.00. The liability account, Butler Cleaning Supplies, is increased by a credit, $2,720.00. The journal entry for this transaction is shown in Illustration 4-9.

						GENERAL		SALES CREDIT	CASH	
	DATE	ACCOUNT TITLE	DOC. NO.	POST. REF.		DEBIT	CREDIT		DEBIT	CREDIT
4	7	Supplies	M1			2 7 2 0 00					4
5		Butler Cleaning Supp.					2 7 2 0 00				5

JOURNAL   PAGE *1*

Illustration 4-9
Journal entry to record buying supplies on account

1 *Date.* Write the date, *7*, in the Date column.

2 *Debit.* The journal does not have a special amount column for either debits to Supplies or credits to Butler Cleaning Supplies. Therefore, both account titles need to be written in the Account Title column. The debit and credit amounts are recorded in the General Debit and General Credit columns. Write the title of the account debited, *Supplies*, in the Account

Title column. Write the debit amount, *$2,720.00*, in the General Debit column.

3 *Credit.* On the next line, write the title of the account credited, *Butler Cleaning Supplies*, in the Account Title column. Write the credit amount, $2,720.00, in the General Credit column on the same line as the account title.

> This entry requires two lines in the journal because account titles for both the debit and credit amounts must be written in the Account Title column.

4 *Source document.* Write the source document number, *M1*, in the Doc. No. column on the first line of the entry.

Paid cash on account

August 11, 19--.
Paid cash on account to Butler Cleaning Supplies, $1,360.00. Check No. 3.

The source document for this transaction is Check No. 3. (*CONCEPT: Objective Evidence*) The analysis of this transaction is shown in the T accounts.

The liability account, Butler Cleaning Supplies, is decreased by a debit, $1,360.00. The asset account, Cash, is decreased by a credit, $1,360.00. The journal entry for this transaction is shown in Illustration 4-10.

Butler Cleaning Supplies
| 1,360.00 |

Cash
| | 1,360.00 |

	DATE	ACCOUNT TITLE	DOC. NO.	POST. REF.	GENERAL DEBIT	GENERAL CREDIT	SALES CREDIT	CASH DEBIT	CASH CREDIT	
JOURNAL									PAGE *1*	
6	11	Butler Cleaning Supp.	C3		1 3 6 0 00				1 3 6 0 00	6

1 *Date.* Write the date, *11*, in the Date column.

2 *Debit.* Write the title of the account debited, *Butler Cleaning Supplies*, in the Account Title column. There is no special amount column with the title of the account debited, Butler Cleaning Supplies, in its heading. Therefore, the debit amount is recorded in the General Debit column. Write the debit amount, *$1,360.00*, in the General Debit column.

3 *Credit.* The journal has a special amount column for credits to Cash. The title of the account is in the column heading. Therefore, the account title does not need to be written in the Account Title column. Write the credit amount, *$1,360.00*, in the Cash Credit column.

4 *Source document.* Write the source document number, *C3*, in the Doc. No. column.

Illustration 4-10
Journal entry to record paying cash on account

Received cash from sales

August 12, 19--.
Received cash from sales, $525.00. Tape No. 12.

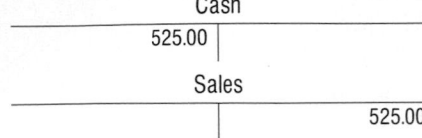

The source document for this transaction is Calculator Tape No. 12. *(CONCEPT: Objective Evidence)* The analysis of this transaction is shown in the T accounts.

The asset account, Cash, is increased by a debit, $525.00. The revenue account, Sales, is increased by a credit, $525.00. The journal entry for this transaction is shown in Illustration 4-11.

					JOURNAL						PAGE *1*	
					1	2	3		4	5		
					GENERAL		**SALES**		**CASH**			
DATE	ACCOUNT TITLE	DOC. NO.	POST. REF.		DEBIT	CREDIT	**CREDIT**		DEBIT		CREDIT	
7	*12* √	*T12* √					5 2 5 00		5 2 5 00			7

Illustration 4-11
Journal entry to record
receiving cash from sales

1   *Date.* Write the date, *12,* in the Date column.

2   *Debit.* The journal has a special amount column for debits to Cash. The title of the account is in the column heading. Therefore, the account title does not need to be written in the Account Title column. Write the debit amount, *$525.00,* in the Cash Debit column.

3   *Credit.* The journal also has a special amount column for credits to Sales. The title of the account is in the column heading. Therefore, the account title does not need to be written in the Account Title column. Write the credit amount, *$525.00,* in the Sales Credit column.

Because both amounts for this entry are recorded in special amount columns, no account titles are written in the Account Title column. Therefore, put a check mark in the Account Title column to show that no account titles need to be written for this transaction. A check mark is also placed in the Post. Ref. column to show that no separate amounts on this line are to be posted individually.

Posting procedures are described in Chapter 5.

4   *Source document.* Write the source document number, *T12,* in the Doc. No. column.

Paid cash for an expense

August 12, 19--.
Paid cash for rent, $250.00. Check No. 4.

The source document for this transaction is Check No. 4. *(CONCEPT: Objective Evidence)* The analysis of this transaction is shown in the T accounts.

The expense account, Rent Expense, is increased by a debit, $250.00. The asset account, Cash, is decreased by a credit, $250.00. The journal entry for this transaction is shown on line 8 in Illustration 4-12.

	Rent Expense	
250.00		

	Cash	
		250.00

JOURNAL   PAGE *1*

	DATE	ACCOUNT TITLE	DOC. NO.	POST. REF.	GENERAL DEBIT	GENERAL CREDIT	SALES CREDIT	CASH DEBIT	CASH CREDIT	
8	12	*Rent Expense*	*C4*		2 5 0 00				2 5 0 00	8
9	12	*Utilities Expense*	*C5*		4 5 00				4 5 00	9

Illustration 4-12
Journal entry to record paying cash for an expense

1 *Date.* Write the date, *12*, in the Date column.

2 *Debit.* Write the title of the account debited, Rent Expense, in the Account Title column. There is no special amount column with the title of the account debited, Rent Expense, in its heading. Therefore, the debit amount is recorded in the General Debit column. Write the debit amount, *$250.00*, in the General Debit column.

3 *Credit.* The journal has a special amount column for credits to Cash. The title of the account is in the column heading. Therefore, the account title does not need to be written in the Account Title column. Write the credit amount, *$250.00*, in the Cash Credit column.

4 *Source document.* Write the source document number, *C4*, in the Doc. No. column.

> The journal entry shown in Illustration 4-12 includes a cash payment for another expense, Utilities Expense. This transaction is journalized in the same way as the cash payment for rent.

Paid cash to owner for personal use

August 12, 19--.
Paid cash to owner for personal use, $100.00. Check No. 6.

The source document for this transaction is Check No. 6. *(CONCEPT: Objective Evidence)* The analysis of this transaction is shown in the T accounts.

The contra capital account, Ben Furman, Drawing, is increased by a debit, $100.00. The asset account, Cash, is decreased by a

	Ben Furman, Drawing	
100.00		

	Cash	
		100.00

credit, $100.00. The journal entry for this transaction is shown in Illustration 4-13.

					1		2		3		4		5	
					GENERAL				SALES		CASH			
	DATE	ACCOUNT TITLE	DOC. NO.	POST. REF.	DEBIT		CREDIT		CREDIT		DEBIT		CREDIT	
10	12	Ben Furman, Drawing	C6		1 0 0 00								1 0 0 00	10

JOURNAL   PAGE 1

Illustration 4-13
Journal entry to record
paying cash to owner for
personal use

1 *Date.* Write the date, *12*, in the Date column.

2 *Debit.* Write the title of the account debited, *Ben Furman, Drawing*, in the Account Title column. There is no special amount column with the title of the account debited, Ben Furman, Drawing, in its heading. Therefore, the debit amount is recorded in the General Debit column. Write the debit amount, *$100.00*, in the General Debit column.

3 *Credit.* The journal has a special amount column for credits to Cash. The title of the account is in the column heading. Therefore, the account title does not need to be written in the Account Title column. Write the credit amount, *$100.00*, in the Cash Credit column.

4 *Source document.* Write the source document number, *C6*, in the Doc. No. column.

PROVING AND RULING A JOURNAL

After Rugcare uses all but the last line on a journal page, columns are proved and ruled before totals are carried forward to the next page. At the end of each month, Rugcare also proves and rules the journal.

After all entries on August 20 are recorded, page 1 of Rugcare's journal is filled, as shown in Illustration 4-14.

Page 1 is proved and ruled before totals are carried forward to page 2.

Proving a journal page

To prove a journal page, Rugcare verifies that the total debits on the page equal the total credits. Three steps are followed in proving a journal page.

1 *Add each of the amount columns.* Use a calculator if one is available. If a calculator is not available, total the columns on a sheet of paper.

2 *Add the debit column totals, and then add the credit column totals.* The figures from page 1 of Rugcare's journal are on the next page.

Column	Debit Column Totals	Credit Column Totals
General	$ 7,920.00	$12,920.00
Sales		2,319.00
Cash	12,319.00	5,000.00
Totals	$20,239.00	$20,239.00

3 *Verify that the total debits and total credits are equal.* The total debits and the total credits on page 1 of Rugcare's journal are $20,239.00. Because the total debits equal the total credits, page 1 of Rugcare's journal is proved.

If the total debits do not equal the total credits, the errors must be found and corrected before any more work is completed.

Illustration 4-14
Completed page 1 of a journal

	DATE	ACCOUNT TITLE	DOC. NO.	POST. REF.	GENERAL DEBIT	GENERAL CREDIT	SALES CREDIT	CASH DEBIT	CASH CREDIT	
1	Aug. 1	Ben Furman, Capital	R1			10 0 0 0 00		10 0 0 0 00		1
2	3	Supplies	C1		1 5 7 7 00				1 5 7 7 00	2
3	4	Prepaid Insurance	C2		1 2 0 0 00				1 2 0 0 00	3
4	7	Supplies	M1		2 7 2 0 00					4
5		Butler Cleaning Supp.				2 7 2 0 00				5
6	11	Butler Cleaning Supp.	C3		1 3 6 0 00				1 3 6 0 00	6
7	12 ✓		T12	✓			5 2 5 00	5 2 5 00		7
8	12	Rent Expense	C4		2 5 0 00				2 5 0 00	8
9	12	Utilities Expense	C5		4 5 00				4 5 00	9
10	12	Ben Furman, Drawing	C6		1 0 0 00				1 0 0 00	10
11	13	Repair Expense	C7		2 0 00				2 0 00	11
12	13	Miscellaneous Expense	C8		2 5 00				2 5 00	12
13	13 ✓		T13	✓			2 2 9 00	2 2 9 00		13
14	14	Advertising Expense	C9		6 8 00				6 8 00	14
15	14 ✓		T14	✓			3 6 0 00	3 6 0 00		15
16	17	Petty Cash	C10		2 0 0 00				2 0 0 00	16
17	17 ✓		T17	✓			3 5 0 00	3 5 0 00		17
18	18	Miscellaneous Expense	C11		7 0 00				7 0 00	18
19	18 ✓		T18	✓			3 2 0 00	3 2 0 00		19
20	19 ✓		T19	✓			2 9 0 00	2 9 0 00		20
21	20	Repair Expense	C12		8 5 00				8 5 00	21
22	20 ✓		T20	✓			2 4 5 00	2 4 5 00		22
23	20	Supplies	M2		2 0 0 00					23
24		Dale Office Supplies				2 0 0 00				24
25	20	Carried Forward		✓	7 9 2 0 00	12 9 2 0 00	2 3 1 9 00	12 3 1 9 00	5 0 0 0 00	25

JOURNAL PAGE 1

Ruling a journal page

After a journal page is proved, the page is ruled as shown in Illustration 4-14, page 63.

1 Rule a single line across all amount columns directly below the last entry to indicate that the columns are to be added.

2 On the next line, write the date, *20,* in the Date column.

3 Write the words, *Carried Forward,* in the Account Title column. A check mark is also placed in the Post. Ref. column to show that nothing on this line needs to be posted.

4 Write each column total below the single line.

5 Rule double lines below the column totals across all amount columns. The double lines mean that the totals have been verified as correct.

Starting a new journal page

The column totals from the previous page are carried forward to a new page. The totals are recorded on the first line of the new page as shown in Illustration 4-15.

						JOURNAL			**PAGE** 2
					1	2	3	4	5
	DATE	ACCOUNT TITLE	DOC. NO.	POST. REF.	GENERAL		SALES CREDIT	CASH	
					DEBIT	CREDIT		DEBIT	CREDIT
1	Aug. 20	Brought Forward		√	7 9 2 0 00	12 9 2 0 00	2 3 1 9 00	12 3 1 9 00	5 0 0 0 00	1
2										2

Illustration 4-15
Starting a new journal
page

1 Write the page number, *2,* at the top of the journal.

2 Write the date, *19--, Aug. 20,* in the Date column. Because this is the first time that a date is written on page 2, the year, month, and day are all written in the Date column.

3 Write the words, *Brought Forward,* in the Account Title column. A check mark is also placed in the Post. Ref. column to show that nothing on this line needs to be posted.

4 Record the column totals brought forward from the previous page.

Completing a journal at the end of a month

Rugcare always proves and rules a journal at the end of each month even if the last page for the month is not full. Page 2 of Rugcare's journal on August 31 is shown in Illustration 4-16.

The entries on lines 10, 11, and 12, Illustration 4-16, are described in Chapter 6.

JOURNAL   PAGE 2

	DATE	ACCOUNT TITLE	DOC. NO.	POST. REF.	GENERAL DEBIT	GENERAL CREDIT	SALES CREDIT	CASH DEBIT	CASH CREDIT	
1	Aug. 20	Brought Forward		√	7920 00	12920 00	2319 00	12319 00	5000 00	1
2	21	√	T21	√			270 00	270 00		2
3	24	√	T24	√			300 00	300 00		3
4	25	√	T25	√			310 00	310 00		4
5	26	√	T26	√			245 00	245 00		5
6	27	Utilities Expense	C13		70 00				70 00	6
7	27	√	T27	√			290 00	290 00		7
8	28	Supplies	C14		434 00				434 00	8
9	28	√	T28	√			267 00	267 00		9
10	28	Miscellaneous Expense	M3			3 00			3 00	10
11	31	Miscellaneous Expense	C15			7 00			12 00	11
12		Repair Expense				5 00				12
13	31	Ben Furman, Drawing	C16		500 00				500 00	13
14	31	√	T31	√			290 00	290 00		14
15	31	Totals			8939 00	12920 00	4291 00	14291 00	6019 00	15

Proving page 2 of a journal. The last page of a journal for a month is proved using the same steps previously described. Then, cash is proved and the journal is ruled. The proof of page 2 of Rugcare's journal is shown below.

Illustration 4-16
Ruling a journal at the end of a month

Column	Debit Column Totals	Credit Column Totals
General	$ 8,939.00	$12,920.00
Sales		4,291.00
Cash	14,291.00	6,019.00
Totals	$23,230.00	$23,230.00

Page 2 of Rugcare's journal is proved because the total debits are equal to the total credits, $23,230.00.

Proving cash. Determining that the amount of cash agrees with the accounting records is called proving cash. Cash can be proved at any time Rugcare wishes to verify the accuracy of the cash records. However, Rugcare *always* proves cash at the end of the month when the journal is proved. Rugcare uses two steps to prove cash.

1 *Figure the cash balance.*

Cash on hand at the beginning of the month	$ 0.00

Rugcare began the month with no cash balance. Mr. Furman invested the initial cash on August 1.

Plus total cash received during the month	+14,291.00

This amount is the total of the journal's Cash Debit column.

Equals total	$14,291.00
Less total cash paid during the month	− 6,019.00

This amount is the total of the journal's Cash Credit column.

Equals cash balance at the end of the month	$ 8,272.00
Checkbook balance on the next unused check stub	8,272.00

2 *Verify that the cash balance equals the checkbook balance on the next unused check stub in the checkbook.* Because the cash balance figured from the journal and the checkbook balance are the same, *$8,272.00,* cash is proved.

Ruling a journal at the end of a month. A journal is ruled at the end of each month even if the last journal page is not full. Rugcare's journal is ruled as shown in Illustration 4-16, page 65.

The procedures for ruling a journal at the end of a month are similar to those for ruling a journal page to carry the totals forward.

Rugcare uses five steps in ruling a journal at the end of each month.

1 Rule a single line across all amount columns directly below the last entry to indicate that the columns are to be added.

2 On the next line, write the date, *31,* in the Date column.

3 Write the word, *Totals,* in the Account Title column.

Some of the column totals will be posted as described in Chapter 5. Therefore, a check mark is not placed in the Post. Ref. column for this line.

4 Write each column total below the single line.

5 Rule double lines below the column totals across all amount columns. The double lines mean that the totals have been verified as correct.

GENERALLY ACCEPTED ACCOUNTING PRACTICES

In completing accounting work, Rugcare is guided by generally accepted accounting practices, including those shown in Illustration 4-17.

1. Errors are corrected in a way that does not cause doubts about what the correct information is. If an error is recorded, cancel the error by neatly

drawing a line through the incorrect item. Write the correct item immediately above the canceled item, as shown on line 17 of Illustration 4-17.

2. Sometimes an entire entry is incorrect and is discovered before the next entry is journalized. Draw neat lines through all parts of the incorrect entry. Journalize the entry correctly on the next blank line, as shown on lines 18 and 19, Illustration 4-17.

3. Sometimes several correct entries are recorded after an incorrect entry is made. The next blank lines are several entries later. Draw neat lines through all incorrect parts of the entry. Record the correct items on the same lines as the incorrect items, directly above the canceled parts. This procedure is shown on line 20 of Illustration 4-17.

4. Words in accounting records are written in full when space permits. Words may be abbreviated only when space is limited. All items are written legibly.

5. Dollars and cents signs and decimal points are not used when writing amounts on ruled accounting paper. Sometimes a color tint or a heavy vertical rule is used on printed accounting paper to separate the dollars and cents columns.

6. Two zeros are written in the cents column when an amount is in even dollars, such as $500.00. If the cents column is left blank, doubts may arise later about the correct amount.

7. A single line is ruled across amount columns to indicate addition or subtraction as shown on line 21, Illustration 4-17.

8. A double line is ruled across amount columns to indicate that the totals have been verified as correct.

9. Neatness is very important in accounting records so that there is never any doubt about what information has been recorded. A ruler is used to make single and double lines.

Illustration 4-17
Some generally accepted accounting practices

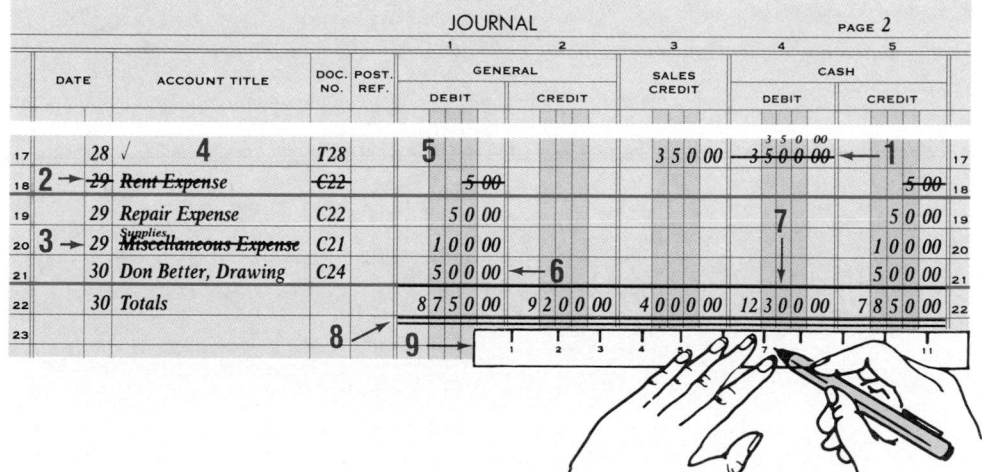

1 Analyze transactions

    a. From source document information

| Receipts | Calculator tapes |
| Checks | Memorandums |

    b. Using T accounts

Rent Expense		Cash	
50.00			50.00

    c. Verify for each entry that:

Debits ⟶ equal ⟶ Credits

2 Record entries in a journal

Transactions	Written in Account Title Column	Journal Amount Columns Used				
		General		Sales	Cash	
		Debit	Credit	Credit	Debit	Credit
Received cash from owner as an investment	Capital Account Title		√		√	
Paid cash for supplies	Supplies	√				√
Paid cash for insurance	Prepaid Insurance	√				√
Bought supplies on account	Supplies Liability Account Title	√	√			
Paid cash on account	Liability Account Title	√				√
Received cash from sales	√			√	√	
Paid cash for an expense	Expense Account Title	√				√
Paid cash to owner for personal use	Drawing Account Title	√				√

3 Prove the journal

    a. Rule a single line across amount columns.
    b. Add amount columns.
    c. Add all debit totals and add all credit totals.
    d. Verify that total debits equal total credits.

4 Prove cash

    a. Cash at beginning + Total cash received = Total
       Total − Total cash paid = Ending cash balance
    b. Verify that the cash balance is the same as the amount shown on the next unused check stub.

5 Complete the journal by ruling double lines across all amount columns.

Illustration 4-18   Summary of journalizing transactions

SUMMARY OF JOURNALIZING TRANSACTIONS

Rugcare's procedure for journalizing transactions is summarized in Illustration 4-18 on page 68.

▮ ACCOUNTING TERMS

What is the meaning of each of the following?

1. journal	**5.** entry	**9.** receipt
2. journalizing	**6.** double-entry accounting	**10.** memorandum
3. special amount column	**7.** source document	**11.** proving cash
4. general amount column	**8.** check	

▮ QUESTIONS FOR INDIVIDUAL STUDY

1. What are the five amount columns in the journal used by Rugcare?
2. Which of the columns in Rugcare's journal are special amount columns?
3. What is the source document for a cash payment transaction?
4. What is the source document for a sales transaction?
5. What is the source document for cash received from transactions other than sales?
6. What is the source document for a transaction when no other source document is prepared or when additional explanation is needed?
7. What are the four parts of a journal entry?
8. What two journal amount columns are used to record cash received from the owner as an investment?
9. What two journal amount columns are used to record cash paid for supplies?
10. What two journal amount columns are used to record cash paid for insurance?
11. What two journal amount columns are used to record supplies bought on account?
12. What two journal amount columns are used to record cash paid on account?
13. What two journal amount columns are used to record cash received from sales?
14. What two journal amount columns are used to record cash paid for an expense?
15. What two journal amount columns are used to record cash paid to the owner for personal use?
16. What is the procedure for proving a journal page?
17. What are the two steps that Rugcare uses in proving cash?

▮ CASES FOR MANAGEMENT DECISION

CASE 1 During the summer, Willard Kelly does odd jobs to earn money. Mr. Kelly keeps all his money in a single checking account. He writes checks to pay for personal items and for business expenses. These payments include personal clothing, school supplies, gasoline for his car, and recreation. Mr. Kelly uses his check stubs as his accounting records. Are Mr. Kelly's accounting procedures and records correct? Explain your answer.

CASE 2 In his business, Michael Rock uses a journal with the following columns: Date, Account Title, Check No., Cash Debit, and Cash Credit. Mr. Rock's wife, Jennifer, suggests that he needs three additional amount columns: General Debit, General Credit, and Sales Credit. Mr. Rock states that all his business transactions are for cash, and he never buys on account. Therefore, he does not see the need for more than the Cash Debit and Cash Credit special amount columns. Who is correct, Mr. or Mrs. Rock? Explain your answer.

■ DRILLS FOR UNDERSTANDING

DRILL 4-D1 Analyzing transactions

This drill provides continuing practice in analyzing transactions into debit and credit parts. Use Rugcare's chart of accounts, page 2.

Transactions
1. Paid cash for supplies, $100.00.
2. Bought supplies on account from Butler Cleaning Supplies, $500.00.
3. Paid cash to owner for personal use, $50.00.
4. Received cash from sales, $300.00.
5. Paid cash for rent, $200.00.
6. Paid cash for insurance, $250.00.
7. Received cash from owner as an investment, $1,000.00.
8. Paid cash for repairs, $25.00.
9. Paid cash for telephone bill, $30.00.
10. Paid cash for advertising, $40.00.
11. Paid cash on account to Butler Cleaning Supplies, $300.00.
12. Paid cash for miscellaneous expense, $3.00.

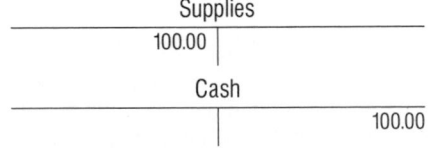

Instructions: 1. For each transaction, prepare two T accounts. On the T accounts, write the account titles affected by the transaction.
2. Write the debit or credit amount in each T account to show how the transaction affected that account. T accounts for Transaction 1 are given as an example.

DRILL 4-D2 Analyzing transactions

This drill continues the practice in analyzing transactions. Mark Jacobs owns a service business called Jacobs Secretarial Services. Jacobs Secretarial Services uses the following accounts.

Cash	Sales
Supplies	Advertising Expense
Prepaid Insurance	Miscellaneous Expense
Gable Supplies	Rent Expense
Mark Jacobs, Capital	Repair Expense
Mark Jacobs, Drawing	Utilities Expense

Use a form similar to the following. Transaction 1 is given as an example.

1	2	3	4	5	6	7
Trans. No.	Accounts Affected	Account Classification	How Is Account Affected?		Entered in Account as a	
			(+)	(−)	Debit	Credit
1.	Advertising Expense Cash	Expense Asset	√	√	√	√

Transactions

1. Paid cash for advertising.
2. Paid cash for repairs.
3. Received cash from owner as an investment.
4. Paid cash for miscellaneous expense.
5. Bought supplies on account from Gable Supplies.
6. Paid cash on account to Gable Supplies.
7. Paid cash for water bill.
8. Paid cash for supplies.
9. Paid cash for rent.
10. Paid cash to owner for personal use.
11. Received cash from sales.
12. Paid cash for insurance.

Instructions: 1. In Column 2, write the titles of the accounts changed by each transaction.

2. For each account title, write the account classification in Column 3.

3. For each account title, place a check mark in either Column 4 or 5 to indicate if each account is increased (+) or decreased (−) by this transaction.

4. For each account title, place a check mark in either Column 6 or 7 to indicate if the amount is entered in the account as a debit or a credit.

■ APPLICATION PROBLEMS

PROBLEM 4-1 **Journalizing transactions**

Dorothy Gilbert owns a service business called Lane Company. Lane Company uses the following accounts.

Cash	Sales
Supplies	Advertising Expense
Prepaid Insurance	Miscellaneous Expense
Mertz Supplies	Rent Expense
Dorothy Gilbert, Capital	Repair Expense
Dorothy Gilbert, Drawing	Utilities Expense

Instructions: 1. Journalize the following transactions completed during February of the current year. Use page 1 of a journal similar to the one described in this chapter for Rugcare. Source documents are abbreviated as follows: check, C; memorandum, M; receipt, R; calculator tape, T.

Feb. 1. Received cash from owner as an investment, $12,000.00. R1.
      3. Paid cash for rent, $600.00. C1.
      4. Paid cash for insurance, $1,200.00. C2.
      5. Bought supplies on account from Mertz Supplies, $1,500.00. M1.
      6. Paid cash for supplies, $1,000.00. C3.
      7. Paid cash on account to Mertz Supplies, $750.00. C4.
     10. Paid cash for miscellaneous expense, $5.00. C5.
     12. Received cash from sales, $500.00. T12.
     14. Received cash from sales, $450.00. T14.
     17. Paid cash for repairs, $75.00. C6.
     17. Received cash from sales, $300.00. T17.
     20. Received cash from sales, $370.00. T20.
     21. Received cash from sales, $470.00. T21.
     24. Received cash from sales, $400.00. T24.
     25. Paid cash for electric bill, $50.00. C7.
     25. Received cash from sales, $450.00. T25.
     26. Paid cash for advertising, $90.00. C8.
     26. Received cash from sales, $300.00. T26.
     27. Received cash from sales, $350.00. T27.
     28. Paid cash to owner for personal use, $250.00. C9.
     28. Received cash from sales, $500.00. T28.

2. Prove the journal. Rule a single line across all amount columns. Write the amount column totals below the single line.

3. Prove cash. The beginning cash balance on February 1 is zero. The ending cash balance on the next unused check stub is $12,070.00.

4. Rule the journal.

PROBLEM 4-2   Journalizing transactions

Rona Dowling owns a service business called LawnCare. LawnCare uses the following accounts.

Cash	Sales
Supplies	Advertising Expense
Prepaid Insurance	Miscellaneous Expense
Main Office Supplies	Rent Expense
Westley Supplies	Repair Expense
Rona Dowling, Capital	Utilities Expense
Rona Dowling, Drawing	

Instructions: 1. Journalize the following transactions completed during April of the current year. Use page 1 of a journal similar to the one described in this chapter for Rugcare. Source documents are abbreviated as follows: check, C; memorandum, M; receipt, R; calculator tape, T.

Apr. 1. Received cash from owner as an investment, $10,000.00. R1.
      2. Paid cash for rent, $800.00. C1.
      3. Paid cash for insurance, $3,000.00. C2.
      6. Bought supplies on account from Westley Supplies, $2,000.00. M1.
      7. Paid cash for supplies, $700.00. C3.
      8. Paid cash on account to Westley Supplies, $1,000.00. C4.
      8. Received cash from sales, $500.00. T8.
      9. Paid cash for telephone bill, $60.00. C5.

9. Received cash from sales, $650.00. T9.
10. Paid cash for repairs, $85.00. C6.
10. Received cash from sales, $600.00. T10.
13. Paid cash for miscellaneous expense, $15.00. C7.
13. Received cash from sales, $700.00. T13.
14. Received cash from sales, $650.00. T14.
15. Paid cash to owner for personal use, $350.00. C8.
15. Received cash from sales, $500.00. T15.
16. Paid cash for supplies, $1,000.00. C9.
16. Received cash from sales, $600.00. T16.
17. Received cash from sales, $650.00. T17.
20. Bought supplies on account from Main Office Supplies, $500.00. M2.
20. Received cash from sales, $570.00. T20.
21. Received cash from sales, $670.00. T21.

2. Prove and rule page 1 of the journal. Carry the column totals forward to page 2 of the journal.

3. Use page 2 of the journal. Journalize the following transactions completed during April of the current year.

Apr. 22. Paid cash for electric bill, $55.00. C10.
22. Received cash from sales, $600.00. T22.
23. Bought supplies on account from Main Office Supplies, $50.00. M3.
23. Received cash from sales, $650.00. T23.
24. Paid cash for advertising, $100.00. C11.
24. Received cash from sales, $500.00. T24.
27. Received cash from sales, $550.00. T27.
28. Received cash from sales, $500.00. T28.
29. Paid cash for supplies, $150.00. C12.
29. Received cash from sales, $650.00. T29.
30. Paid cash to owner for personal use, $350.00. C13.
30. Received cash from sales, $500.00. T30.

4. Prove page 2 of the journal.

5. Prove cash. The beginning cash balance on April 1 is zero. The balance on the next unused check stub is $12,375.00.

6. Rule page 2 of the journal.

◼ ENRICHMENT PROBLEMS

MASTERY PROBLEM 4-M   Journalizing transactions

Rachel Frank owns a service business called Frank's Car Wash. Frank's Car Wash uses the following accounts.

Cash	Sales
Supplies	Advertising Expense
Prepaid Insurance	Miscellaneous Expense
Delancy Supplies	Rent Expense
Long Supplies	Repair Expense
Rachel Frank, Capital	Utilities Expense
Rachel Frank, Drawing	

Instructions: 1. Journalize the following transactions completed during June of the current year. Use page 1 of a journal similar to the one described in this chapter for Rugcare. Source documents are abbreviated as follows: check, C; memorandum, M; receipt, R; calculator tape, T.

June 1. Received cash from owner as an investment, $18,000.00. R1.
      2. Paid cash for rent, $900.00. C1.
      3. Paid cash for supplies, $1,500.00. C2.
      4. Bought supplies on account from Delancy Supplies, $3,000.00. M1.
      5. Paid cash for insurance, $4,500.00. C3.
      8. Paid cash on account to Delancy Supplies, $1,500.00. C4.
      8. Received cash from sales, $750.00. T8.
      9. Paid cash for electric bill, $75.00. C5.
      9. Received cash from sales, $700.00. T9.
     10. Paid cash for miscellaneous expense, $7.00. C6.
     10. Received cash from sales, $750.00. T10.
     11. Paid cash for repairs, $100.00. C7.
     11. Received cash from sales, $850.00. T11.
     12. Received cash from sales, $700.00. T12.
     15. Paid cash to owner for personal use, $350.00. C8.
     15. Received cash from sales, $750.00. T15.
     16. Paid cash for supplies, $1,500.00. C9.
     16. Received cash from sales, $650.00. T16.
     17. Bought supplies on account from Long Supplies, $750.00. M2.
     17. Received cash from sales, $600.00. T17.
     18. Received cash from sales, $800.00. T18.
     19. Received cash from sales, $750.00. T19.

    2. Prove and rule page 1 of the journal. Carry the column totals forward to page 2 of the journal.
    3. Use page 2 of the journal. Journalize the following transactions completed during June of the current year.

June 22. Bought supplies on account from Long Supplies, $80.00. M3.
     22. Received cash from sales, $700.00. T22.
     23. Paid cash for advertising, $130.00. C10.
     23. Received cash from sales, $650.00. T23.
     24. Paid cash for telephone bill, $60.00. C11.
     24. Received cash from sales, $600.00. T24.
     25. Received cash from sales, $550.00. T25.
     26. Paid cash for supplies, $70.00. C12.
     26. Received cash from sales, $600.00. T26.
     29. Received cash from sales, $750.00. T29.
     30. Paid cash to owner for personal use, $375.00. C13.
     30. Received cash from sales, $800.00. T30.

    4. Prove page 2 of the journal.
    5. Prove cash. The beginning cash balance on June 1 is zero. The balance on the next unused check stub is $18,883.00.
    6. Rule page 2 of the journal.

CHALLENGE PROBLEM 4-C   Journalizing transactions

Wilbur Moore owns a service business called Moore's Tailors. Moore's Tailors uses the following accounts.

Cash	Sales
Supplies	Advertising Expense
Prepaid Insurance	Miscellaneous Expense
Marker Supplies	Rent Expense
O'Brien Supplies	Repair Expense
Wilbur Moore, Capital	Utilities Expense
Wilbur Moore, Drawing	

Instructions: 1. Use page 1 of a journal similar to the following.

Cash		Date	Account Title	Doc. No.	Post. Ref.	General		Sales Credit
Debit	Credit					Debit	Credit	

Journal — *Page 1*

Journalize the following transactions completed during June of the current year. Source documents are abbreviated as follows: check, C; memorandum, M; receipt, R; calculator tape, T.

June 1. Received cash from owner as an investment, $17,000.00. R1.
    2. Paid cash for supplies, $1,400.00. C1.
    3. Paid cash for rent, $800.00. C2.
    4. Paid cash for insurance, $3,000.00. C3.
    5. Bought supplies on account from Marker Supplies, $2,500.00. M1.
    7. Received cash from sales, $550.00. T7.
    9. Paid cash for telephone bill, $70.00. C4.
    9. Paid cash on account to Marker Supplies, $1,300.00. C5.
   10. Received cash from sales, $550.00. T10.
   11. Paid cash for miscellaneous expense, $6.00. C6.
   11. Received cash from sales, $550.00. T11.
   12. Paid cash for repairs, $90.00. C7.
   12. Received cash from sales, $600.00. T12.
   15. Paid cash for supplies, $1,300.00. C8.
   15. Received cash from sales, $540.00. T15.
   16. Paid cash to owner for personal use, $300.00. C9.
   16. Received cash from sales, $400.00. T16.
   17. Received cash from sales, $780.00. T17.
   18. Bought supplies on account from O'Brien Supplies, $900.00. M2.
   18. Received cash from sales, $600.00. T18.
   19. Paid cash for supplies, $85.00. C10.
   19. Received cash from sales, $850.00. T19.

2. Prove and rule page 1 of the journal. Carry the column totals forward to page 2 of the journal.
3. Use page 2 of the journal. Journalize the following transactions completed during June of the current year.

June 22. Received cash from sales, $700.00. T22.
      23. Bought supplies on account from Marker Supplies, $95.00. M3.
      23. Received cash from sales, $720.00. T23.
      24. Paid cash for advertising, $100.00. C11.
      24. Received cash from sales, $550.00. T24.
      25. Paid cash for water bill, $75.00. C12.
      25. Received cash from sales, $600.00. T25.
      26. Received cash from sales, $450.00. T26.
      29. Paid cash on account to O'Brien Supplies, $900.00. C13.
      29. Received cash from sales, $630.00. T29.
      30. Paid cash to owner for personal use, $450.00. C14.
      30. Received cash from sales, $360.00. T30.

4. Prove page 2 of the journal.
5. Prove cash. The cash balance on June 1 is zero. The balance on the next unused check stub is $16,554.00.
6. Rule page 2 of the journal.

Posting to a General Ledger

ENABLING PERFORMANCE TASKS

After studying Chapter 5, you will be able to:
a. Define accounting terms related to posting from a journal to a general ledger.
b. Identify accounting concepts and practices related to posting from a journal to a general ledger.
c. Prepare a chart of accounts for a service business organized as a proprietorship.
d. Post amounts from a journal to a general ledger.

Rugcare records transactions in a journal as described in Chapter 4. A journal is a permanent record of the debit and credit parts of each transaction with transactions recorded in chronological order. A journal does not show in one place all the changes in a single account. If only a journal is used, a business must search through all journal pages to find items affecting a single account balance. For this reason, a form is used to summarize in one place all the changes to a single account. A separate form is used for each account.

An account form is based on and includes the debit and credit sides of a T account as shown in Illustration 5-1.

Illustration 5-1
Relationship of a T account to an account form

Information needed to trace entry back to journal page			T Account	
			Left side Debit side	Right side Credit side
ACCOUNT				
DATE	ITEM	POST. REF.	DEBIT	CREDIT

In addition to debit and credit columns, space is provided in the account form for recording the transaction date and journal page number. This information can be used to trace a specific entry back to where a transaction is recorded in a journal.

The major disadvantage of the account form shown in Illustration 5-1 is that no current, up-to-date account balance is shown. If the form in Illustration 5-1 is used, an up-to-date balance must be figured each time the account is examined. Also, the balance is difficult and time consuming to figure when an account has a large number of entries. Therefore, a more commonly used account form has Debit and Credit Balance columns as shown in Illustration 5-2. Because the form has columns for the debit and credit balance, it is often referred to as the balance-ruled account form.

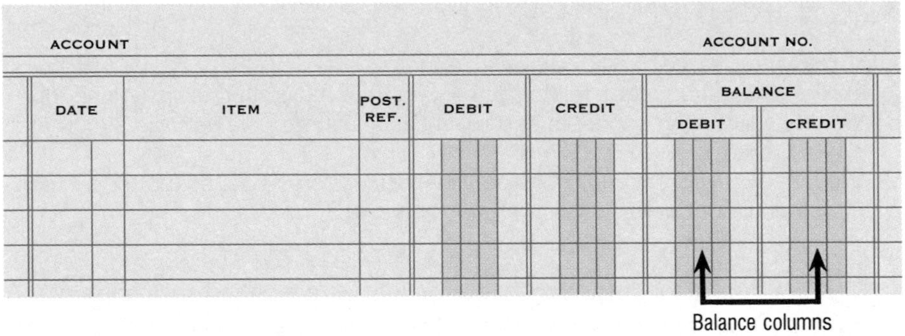

Illustration 5-2
Account form

The account balance is figured and recorded as each entry is recorded in the account. Recording information in an account is described later in this chapter. The T account is a useful device for analyzing transactions into debit and credit parts. However, the balance-ruled account form is more useful as a permanent record of changes to account balances than is the T account. Rugcare uses the balance-ruled account form.

ARRANGING ACCOUNTS IN A GENERAL LEDGER

A group of accounts is called a ledger. A ledger that contains all accounts needed to prepare financial statements is called a general ledger. The name given to an account is known as an account title. The number assigned to an account is called an account number.

Preparing a chart of accounts

A list of account titles and numbers showing the location of each account in a ledger is known as a chart of accounts. Rugcare's chart of accounts is shown in Illustration 5-3.

For ease of use while studying Part 1, Rugcare's chart of accounts is also shown on page 2.

RUGCARE
Chart of Accounts

Balance Sheet Accounts	Income Statement Accounts
(100) ASSETS	**(400) REVENUE**
110 Cash	410 Sales
120 Petty Cash	
130 Supplies	**(500) EXPENSES**
140 Prepaid Insurance	510 Advertising Expense
	520 Insurance Expense
(200) LIABILITIES	530 Miscellaneous Expense
210 Butler Cleaning Supplies	540 Rent Expense
220 Dale Office Supplies	550 Repair Expense
	560 Supplies Expense
(300) OWNER'S EQUITY	570 Utilities Expense
310 Ben Furman, Capital	
320 Ben Furman, Drawing	
330 Income Summary	

Illustration 5-3
Chart of accounts

Accounts in a general ledger are arranged in the same order as they appear on financial statements. Rugcare's chart of accounts, Illustration 5-3, shows five general ledger divisions. (1) Assets, (2) Liabilities, (3) Owner's Equity, (4) Revenue, and (5) Expenses.

Numbering general ledger accounts

Rugcare assigns a three-digit account number to each account. For example, Supplies is assigned the number *130* as shown in Illustration 5-4.

1   3   0   **Supplies**

General ledger division   Location within general ledger division

Illustration 5-4
Account numbers

The first digit of each account number shows the general ledger division in which the account is located. For example, the asset division accounts are numbered in the 100s. Therefore, the number for the asset account, Supplies, begins with a *1.*

The second two digits indicate the location of each account within a general ledger division. The *1* in the account number 130, Supplies, indicates that the account is located in the asset division. The *30* in the account number for Supplies indicates that the account is located between account number 120 and account number 140.

Rugcare initially assigns account numbers by 10s so that new accounts can be added easily. Nine numbers are unused between each account on Rugcare's chart of accounts, Illustration 5-3. For example, numbers 111 to 119 are unused between accounts numbered 110 and 120. New numbers can be assigned between existing account numbers without renumbering all existing accounts. The procedure for arranging accounts in a general ledger, assigning account numbers, and keeping records current is called file maintenance.

Unused account numbers are assigned to new accounts. Rugcare records payments for gasoline in Miscellaneous Expense. If Mr. Furman found that the amount paid each month for gasoline had become a major expense, he might decide to use a separate account. The account might be titled Gasoline Expense. Rugcare arranges expense accounts in alphabetical order in its general ledger. Therefore, the new account would be inserted between Advertising Expense and Insurance Expense.

510	Advertising Expense	(Existing account)
	GASOLINE EXPENSE	(NEW ACCOUNT)
520	Insurance Expense	(Existing account)

The number selected for the new account should leave some unused numbers on either side of it for other accounts that might need to be added. The middle, unused account number between existing numbers 510 and 520 is 515. Therefore, 515 is assigned as the account number for the new account.

510	Advertising Expense	(Existing account)
515	GASOLINE EXPENSE	(NEW ACCOUNT)
520	Insurance Expense	(Existing account)

When an account is no longer needed, it is removed from the general ledger and the chart of accounts. For example, if Rugcare were to buy its own equipment and building, there would be no need for the rent expense account. The account numbered 540 would be removed, and that number would become unused and available to assign to another account if the need should arise.

When a new account is added at the end of a ledger division, the next number in a sequence of 10s is used. For example, suppose Rugcare needs to add another expense account, Water Expense, to show more detail about one of the utility expenses. The expense accounts are arranged in alphabetical order. Therefore, the new account would be added at the end of the expense section of the chart of accounts. The last used expense account number is 570, as shown on the chart of accounts, Illustration 5-3. The next number in the sequence of 10s is 580, which is assigned as the number of the new account.

560	Supplies Expense	(Existing account)
570	Utilities Expense	(Existing account)
580	WATER EXPENSE	(NEW ACCOUNT)

Rugcare has relatively few general ledger accounts and does not anticipate adding many new accounts in the future. Therefore, a three-digit account number adequately provides for the few account numbers that might be added. However, as the number of general ledger accounts increases, a business may change to four or more digits.

Charts of accounts with more than three digits are described in later chapters.

Opening general ledger accounts

Writing an account title and number on the heading of an account is called opening an account. A general ledger account is opened for each account listed on a chart of accounts. Accounts are opened and arranged in a general ledger in the same order as on the chart of accounts.

Cash, account number 110, is the first account on Rugcare's chart of accounts. The cash account is opened as shown in Illustration 5-5.

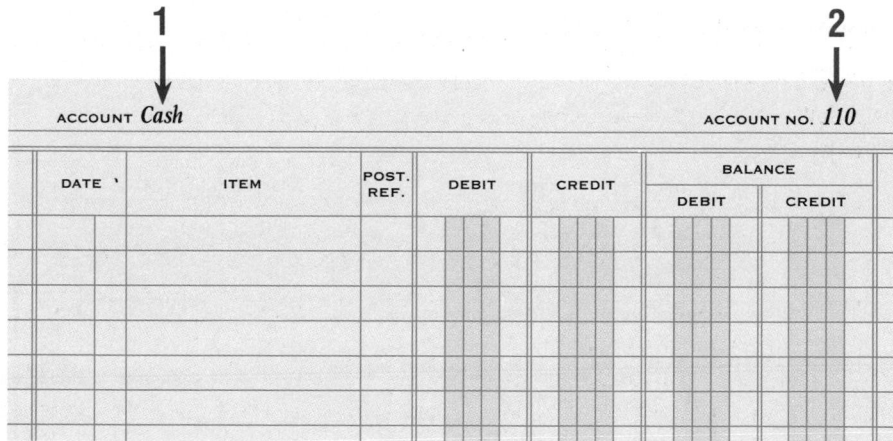

Illustration 5-5
Opening an account in a general ledger

1 Write the account title, *Cash*, after the word *Account* in the heading.

2 Write the account number, *110*, after the words *Account No.* in the heading.

The same procedure is used to open all accounts listed on Rugcare's chart of accounts.

POSTING FROM A JOURNAL TO A GENERAL LEDGER

Transferring information from a journal entry to a ledger account is called posting. Posting sorts journal entries so that all debits and credits affecting each account are brought together in one place. For example, all changes to Cash are brought together in the cash account.

Amounts in journal entries are recorded in either general amount columns or special amount columns. There are two rules for posting amounts from a journal. (1) Separate amounts in a journal's general amount columns are posted individually to the account written in the Account Title column. (2) Separate amounts in a journal's special amount columns are not posted individually. Instead, the special amount column totals are posted to the account named in the heading of the special amount column.

Posting separate amounts

For most, but not all journal entries, at least one separate amount is posted individually to a general ledger account. When an entry in a journal includes an amount in a general amount column and an account title in the Account Title column, the amount is posted individually.

Posting a separate amount from a General Debit column. Each separate amount in the General Debit and General Credit columns of a journal is posted to the account written in the Account Title column. Posting an amount from the General Debit column is shown in Illustration 5-6.

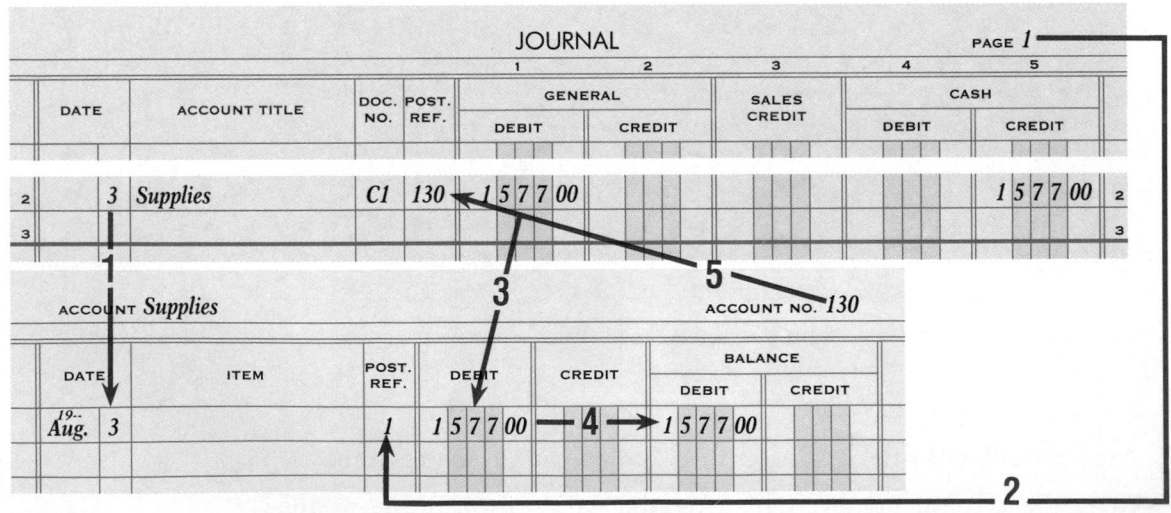

Illustration 5-6
Posting an amount from a
General Debit column

1 Write the date, *19--, Aug. 3,* in the Date column of the account, Supplies.

2 Write the journal page number, *1,* in the Post. Ref. column of the account. Post. Ref. is an abbreviation for Posting Reference.

3 Write the debit amount, *$1,577.00*, in the Debit amount column.

4 Write the new account balance, *$1,577.00*, in the Balance Debit column. Because this entry is the first in the supplies account, the previous balance is zero. The new account balance is calculated as shown below.

Previous Balance	+	Debit Column Amount	=	New Debit Balance
$0.00	+	$1,577.00	=	$1,577.00

5 Return to the journal and write the account number, *130*, in the Post. Ref. column of the journal.

The numbers in the Post. Ref. columns of the general ledger account and the journal serve three purposes. (1) An entry in an account can be traced to its source in a journal. (2) An entry in a journal can be traced to where it was posted in an account. (3) If posting is interrupted, the accounting personnel can easily see which entries in the journal still need to be posted. A blank in the Post. Ref. column of the journal indicates that posting for that line still needs to be completed. *Therefore, the posting reference is always recorded in the journal as the last step in the posting procedure.*

A second amount is posted to the supplies account from Rugcare's journal, line 4, as shown in Illustration 5-7.

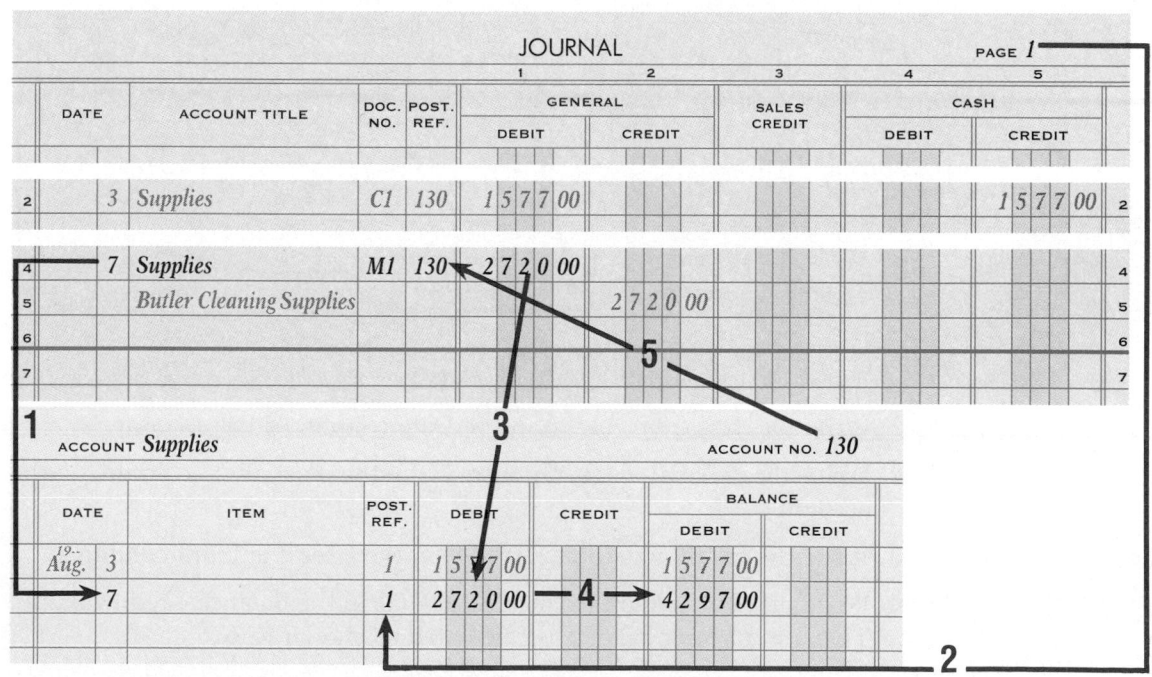

Illustration 5-7
Posting a second amount to an account

1 Write the date, *7*, in the Date column of the account.

The month and year are written only once on a page of a ledger account unless the month or year changes.

2 Write the journal page number, *1*, in the Post. Ref. column of the account.

3 Write the debit amount, *$2,720.00*, in the Debit amount column.

4 Write the new account balance, *$4,297.00*, in the Balance Debit column. The new account balance is calculated as shown below.

Previous Debit Balance	+	Debit Column Amount	=	New Debit Balance
$1,577.00	+	$2,720.00	=	$4,297.00

5 Return to the journal and write the account number, *130*, in the Post. Ref. column of the journal.

Posting a separate amount from a General Credit column. An amount in the General Credit column of a journal is posted as shown in Illustration 5-8.

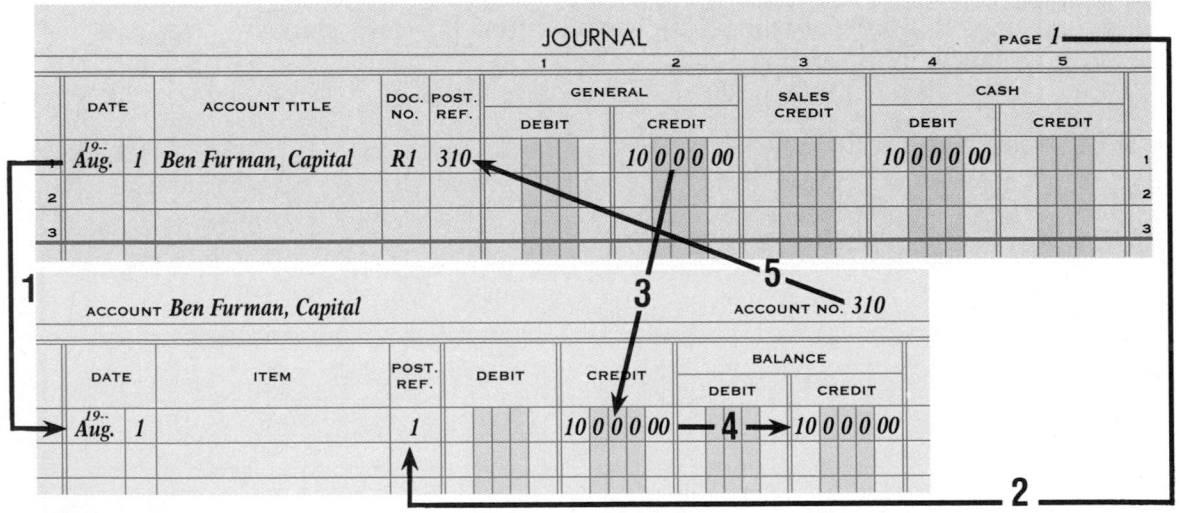

Illustration 5-8
Posting an amount from a
General Credit column

1 Write the date, *19--, Aug. 1*, in the Date column of the account.

2 Write the journal page number, *1*, in the Post. Ref. column of the account.

3 Write the credit amount, *$10,000.00*, in the Credit amount column.

4 Write the new account balance, *$10,000.00*, in the Balance Credit column. The new account balance is calculated as shown below.

Previous Balance	+	Credit Column Amount	=	New Credit Balance
$0.00	+	$10,000.00	=	$10,000.00

5 Return to the journal and write the account number, *310*, in the Post. Ref. column of the journal.

Journal entries that are not posted individually. Several lines in Rugcare's journal contain separate amounts that are not to be posted individually. These include forwarding totals and amounts recorded in special amount columns.

The totals brought forward from page 1 are shown on line 1 of the journal in Illustration 5-9. None of these separate total amounts on line 1 are posted individually to general ledger accounts. To assure that no postings are overlooked, no blank posting reference spaces should be left in the Post. Ref. column of the journal. Therefore, when the totals were forwarded to page 2 of the journal, a check mark was placed in the Post. Ref. column of line 1 to show that no separate amounts are posted individually.

	DATE	ACCOUNT TITLE	DOC. NO.	POST. REF.	GENERAL DEBIT	GENERAL CREDIT	SALES CREDIT	CASH DEBIT	CASH CREDIT	
					1	2	3	4	5	
1	Aug. 20	Brought Forward		√	7 9 2 0 00	12 9 2 0 00	2 3 1 9 00	12 3 1 9 00	5 0 0 0 00	1
11	31	Miscellaneous Expense	C15	530	7 00				1 2 00	11
12		Repair Expense		550	5 00					12
13	31	Ben Furman, Drawing	C16	320	5 0 0 00				5 0 0 00	13
14	31	√	T31	√			2 9 0 00	2 9 0 00		14
15	31	Totals			8 9 3 9 00	12 9 2 0 00	4 2 9 1 00	14 2 9 1 00	6 0 1 9 00	15
16					(√)	(√)				16
17										17

JOURNAL — PAGE 2

Check mark indicates that amounts ARE NOT posted individually

Check marks indicate that general amount column totals ARE NOT posted

Separate amounts in the special amount columns, Sales Credit, Cash Debit, and Cash Credit, are not posted individually. For example, on line 14 of the journal, Illustration 5-9, two separate $290.00 amounts are recorded in two special amount columns, Sales Credit and Cash Debit.

A check mark was placed in the Post. Ref. column on line 14 when the entry was journalized. The check mark indicates that no separate amounts are posted individually from this line. Instead, the totals of the special amount columns are posted.

Illustration 5-9
Check marks show that amounts are not posted

Posting the totals of amount columns

Separate amounts in special amount columns *are not* posted individually. The separate amounts are part of the special amount column totals. Only the totals of special amount columns *are* posted.

Totals of General Debit and General Credit amount columns. The General Debit and General Credit columns are not special amount columns because the column headings do not contain the name of an account. All of the separate amounts in the General Debit and General Credit amount columns are posted individually. Therefore, the column totals *are not* posted. A check mark in parentheses is placed below each general amount column total as shown in Illustration 5-9. The check mark indicates that the totals of the General Debit and General Credit columns are not posted.

A check mark in the Post. Ref. column indicates that amounts are not to be posted individually. On the totals line, the amounts in the special amount columns are posted. Therefore, a check mark is not placed in the Post. Ref. column for the totals line.

Posting the totals of special amount columns. Rugcare's journal has three special amount columns for which only totals are posted: Sales Credit, Cash Debit, and Cash Credit.

Posting the total of the Sales Credit column. The Sales Credit column of a journal is a special amount column with the account title Sales in the heading. Each separate amount in a special amount column could be posted individually. However, all of the separate amounts are debits or credits to the same account. Therefore, an advantage of a special amount column is that only the column total needs to be posted. For example, 14 separate sales transactions are recorded in the Sales Credit column of Rugcare's August journal. Instead of making 14 separate credit postings to Sales, only the column total is posted. As a result, only one posting is needed, which saves 13 postings. The smaller number of postings means 13 fewer opportunities to make a posting error. Posting special amount column totals saves time and results in greater accuracy.

The total of Rugcare's Sales Credit column is posted as shown in Illustration 5-10.

1 Write the date, *19--, Aug. 31*, in the Date column of the account, Sales.

2 Write the journal page number, *2*, in the Post. Ref. column of the account.

3 Write the column total, *$4,291.00*, in the Credit amount column.

4 Write the new account balance, *$4,291.00*, in the Balance Credit column. The new account balance is calculated as shown below.

Previous Balance	+	Credit Column Amount	=	New Credit Balance
$0.00	+	$4,291.00	=	$4,291.00

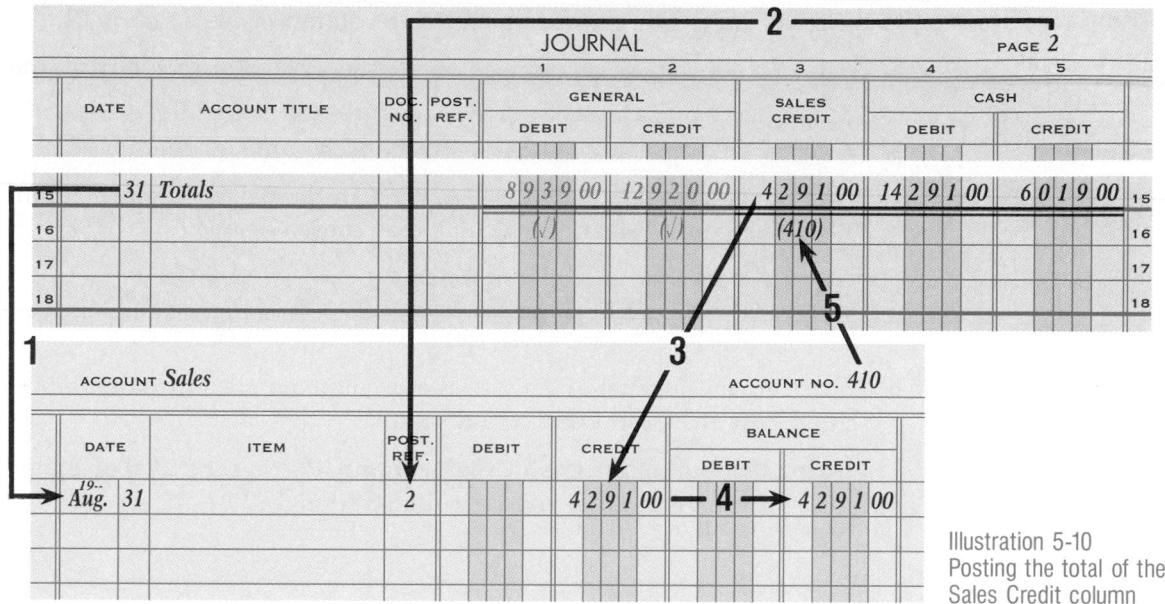

Illustration 5-10
Posting the total of the
Sales Credit column

5 Return to the journal and write the account number in parentheses, *(410)*, below the Sales Credit column total.

Posting the total of the Cash Debit column. The Cash Debit column of a journal is posted as shown in Illustration 5-11.

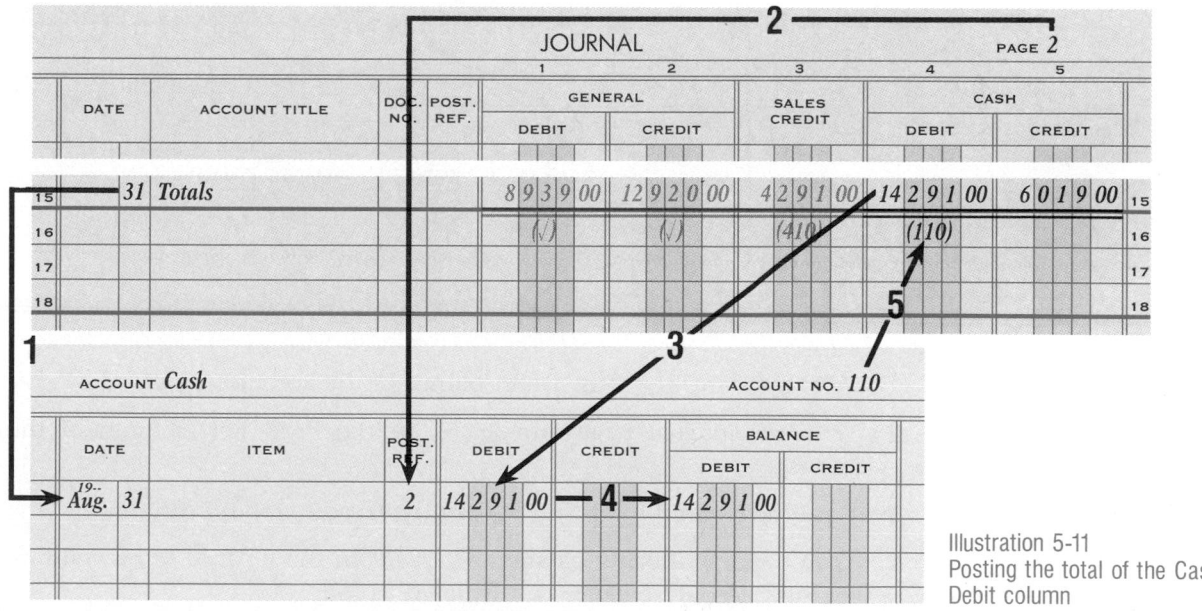

Illustration 5-11
Posting the total of the Cash
Debit column

1 Write the date, *19--, Aug. 31*, in the Date column of the account, Cash.

2 Write the journal page number, *2*, in the Post. Ref. column of the account.

3 Write the column total, *$14,291.00*, in the Debit amount column.

4 Write the new account balance, *$14,291.00*, in the Balance Debit column. The new account balance is calculated as shown below.

Previous Balance	+	Debit Column Amount	=	New Debit Balance
$0.00	+	$14,291.00	=	$14,291.00

5 Return to the journal and write the account number in parentheses, *(110)*, below the Cash Debit column total.

Posting the total of the Cash Credit column. Posting the total of a journal's Cash Credit column is shown in Illustration 5-12.

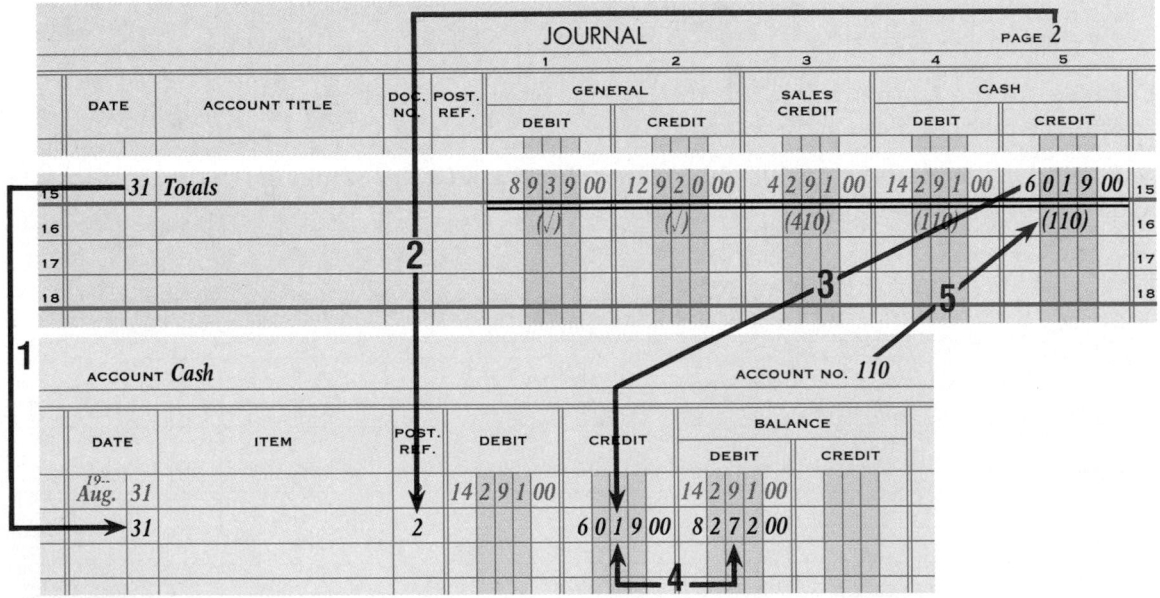

Illustration 5-12
Posting the total of the
Cash Credit column

1 Write the date, *31*, in the Date column of the account, Cash.

2 Write the journal page number, *2*, in the Post. Ref. column of the account.

3 Write the column total, *$6,019.00*, in the Credit amount column.

4 Write the new account balance, *$8,272.00*, in the Balance Debit column. The new account balance is calculated as follows.

Previous Debit Balance	–	Credit Column Amount	=	New Debit Balance
$14,291.00	–	$6,019.00	=	$8,272.00

Whenever the debits in an account exceed the credits, the account balance is a debit. Whenever the credits in an account exceed the debits, the account balance is a credit.

5 Return to the journal and write the account number in parentheses, *(110)*, below the Cash Credit column total.

Journal page with posting completed

Page 2 of Rugcare's August journal, after all posting has been completed, is shown in Illustration 5-13.

JOURNAL   PAGE 2

	DATE		ACCOUNT TITLE	DOC. NO.	POST. REF.	GENERAL DEBIT	GENERAL CREDIT	SALES CREDIT	CASH DEBIT	CASH CREDIT	
						1	2	3	4	5	
1	Aug. 19--	20	Brought Forward		√	7 9 2 0 00	12 9 2 0 00	2 3 1 9 00	12 3 1 9 00	5 0 0 0 00	1
2		21	√	T21	√			2 7 0 00	2 7 0 00		2
3		24	√	T24	√			3 0 0 00	3 0 0 00		3
4		25	√	T25	√			3 1 0 00	3 1 0 00		4
5		26	√	T26	√			2 4 5 00	2 4 5 00		5
6		27	Utilities Expense	C13	570	7 0 00				7 0 00	6
7		27	√	T27	√			2 9 0 00	2 9 0 00		7
8		28	Supplies	C14	130	4 3 4 00				4 3 4 00	8
9		28	√	T28	√			2 6 7 00	2 6 7 00		9
10		28	Miscellaneous Expense	M3	530	3 00				3 00	10
11		31	Miscellaneous Expense	C15	530	7 00				1 2 00	11
12			Repair Expense		550	5 00					12
13		31	Ben Furman, Drawing	C16	320	5 0 0 00				5 0 0 00	13
14		31	√	T31	√			2 9 0 00	2 9 0 00		14
15		31	Totals			8 9 3 9 00	12 9 2 0 00	4 2 9 1 00	14 2 9 1 00	6 0 1 9 00	15
16						(√)	(√)	(410)	(110)	(110)	16
17											17

Illustration 5-13
A journal page after posting has been completed

General ledger with posting completed

Rugcare's general ledger, after all posting from the August journal is completed, is shown in Illustration 5-14.

The use of the accounts, Income Summary, Insurance Expense, and Supplies Expense, is described in Chapter 7.

ACCOUNT *Cash*						ACCOUNT NO. *110*	

DATE	ITEM	POST. REF.	DEBIT	CREDIT	BALANCE	
					DEBIT	CREDIT
19-- Aug. 31		2	14 2 9 1 00		14 2 9 1 00	
31		2		6 0 1 9 00	8 2 7 2 00	

ACCOUNT *Petty Cash*						ACCOUNT NO. *120*	

DATE	ITEM	POST. REF.	DEBIT	CREDIT	BALANCE	
					DEBIT	CREDIT
19-- Aug. 17		1	2 0 0 00		2 0 0 00	

ACCOUNT *Supplies*						ACCOUNT NO. *130*	

DATE	ITEM	POST. REF.	DEBIT	CREDIT	BALANCE	
					DEBIT	CREDIT
19-- Aug. 3		1	1 5 7 7 00		1 5 7 7 00	
7		1	2 7 2 0 00		4 2 9 7 00	
20		1	2 0 0 00		4 4 9 7 00	
28		2	4 3 4 00		4 9 3 1 00	

ACCOUNT *Prepaid Insurance*						ACCOUNT NO. *140*	

DATE	ITEM	POST. REF.	DEBIT	CREDIT	BALANCE	
					DEBIT	CREDIT
19-- Aug. 4		1	1 2 0 0 00		1 2 0 0 00	

ACCOUNT *Butler Cleaning Supplies*						ACCOUNT NO. *210*	

DATE	ITEM	POST. REF.	DEBIT	CREDIT	BALANCE	
					DEBIT	CREDIT
19-- Aug. 7		1		2 7 2 0 00		2 7 2 0 00
11		1	1 3 6 0 00			1 3 6 0 00

ACCOUNT *Dale Office Supplies*						ACCOUNT NO. *220*	

DATE	ITEM	POST. REF.	DEBIT	CREDIT	BALANCE	
					DEBIT	CREDIT
19-- Aug. 20		1		2 0 0 00		2 0 0 00

Illustration 5-14
A general ledger after
posting has been
completed

ACCOUNT *Ben Furman, Capital*   ACCOUNT NO. *310*

DATE	ITEM	POST. REF.	DEBIT	CREDIT	BALANCE	
					DEBIT	CREDIT
19-- Aug. 1		1		10 0 0 0 00		10 0 0 0 00

ACCOUNT *Ben Furman, Drawing*   ACCOUNT NO. *320*

DATE	ITEM	POST. REF.	DEBIT	CREDIT	BALANCE	
					DEBIT	CREDIT
19-- Aug. 12		1	1 0 0 00		1 0 0 00	
31		2	5 0 0 00		6 0 0 00	

ACCOUNT *Income Summary*   ACCOUNT NO. *330*

DATE	ITEM	POST. REF.	DEBIT	CREDIT	BALANCE	
					DEBIT	CREDIT

ACCOUNT *Sales*   ACCOUNT NO. *410*

DATE	ITEM	POST. REF.	DEBIT	CREDIT	BALANCE	
					DEBIT	CREDIT
19-- Aug. 31		2		4 2 9 1 00		4 2 9 1 00

ACCOUNT *Advertising Expense*   ACCOUNT NO. *510*

DATE	ITEM	POST. REF.	DEBIT	CREDIT	BALANCE	
					DEBIT	CREDIT
19-- Aug. 14		1	6 8 00		6 8 00	

ACCOUNT *Insurance Expense*   ACCOUNT NO. *520*

DATE	ITEM	POST. REF.	DEBIT	CREDIT	BALANCE	
					DEBIT	CREDIT

Illustration 5-14
A general ledger after posting has been completed
(continued)

ACCOUNT Miscellaneous Expense — ACCOUNT NO. 530

DATE	ITEM	POST. REF.	DEBIT	CREDIT	BALANCE DEBIT	BALANCE CREDIT
Aug. 13		1	25 00		25 00	
18		1	70 00		95 00	
28		2	3 00		98 00	
31		2	7 00		105 00	

ACCOUNT Rent Expense — ACCOUNT NO. 540

DATE	ITEM	POST. REF.	DEBIT	CREDIT	BALANCE DEBIT	BALANCE CREDIT
Aug. 12		1	250 00		250 00	

ACCOUNT Repair Expense — ACCOUNT NO. 550

DATE	ITEM	POST. REF.	DEBIT	CREDIT	BALANCE DEBIT	BALANCE CREDIT
Aug. 13		1	20 00		20 00	
20		1	85 00		105 00	
31		2	5 00		110 00	

ACCOUNT Supplies Expense — ACCOUNT NO. 560

DATE	ITEM	POST. REF.	DEBIT	CREDIT	BALANCE DEBIT	BALANCE CREDIT

ACCOUNT Utilities Expense — ACCOUNT NO. 570

DATE	ITEM	POST. REF.	DEBIT	CREDIT	BALANCE DEBIT	BALANCE CREDIT
Aug. 12		1	45 00		45 00	
27		2	70 00		115 00	

Illustration 5-14
A general ledger after posting has been completed (concluded)

SUMMARY OF POSTING TO A GENERAL LEDGER

The procedures for posting from Rugcare's journal are summarized in Illustration 5-15.

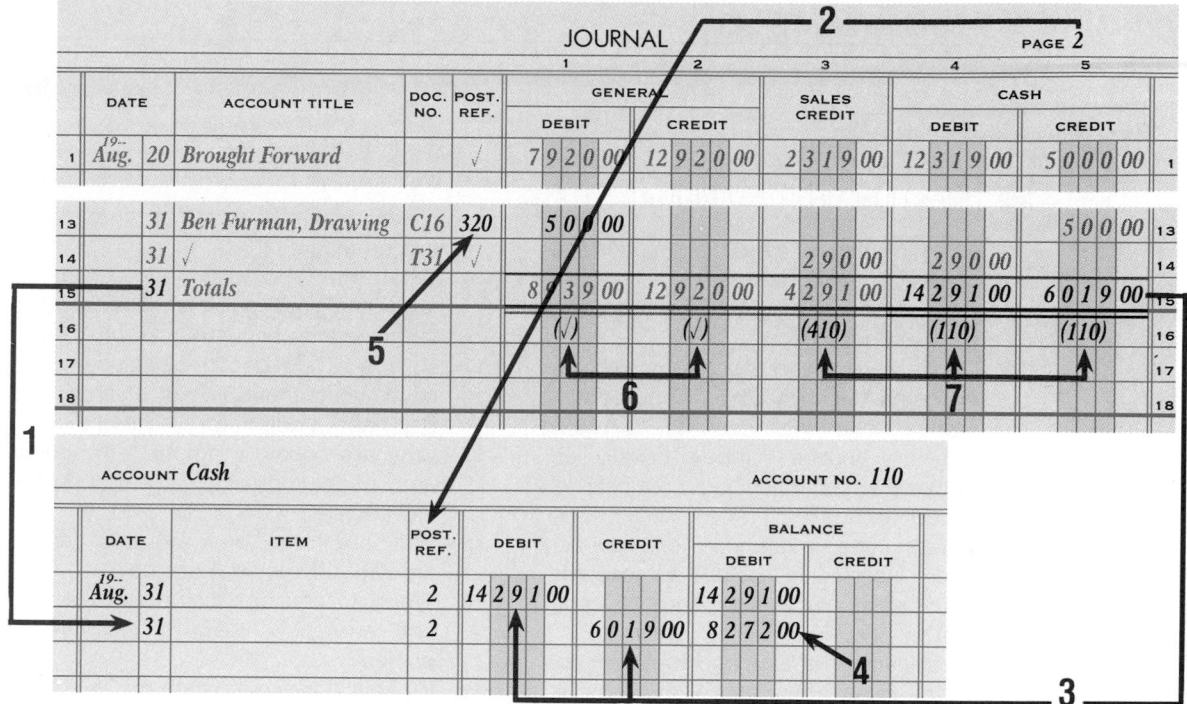

Illustration 5-15
Summary of posting to a general ledger

Seven steps are followed in posting an amount from a journal to a general ledger.

1 The date is written in the Date column of the account.

2 The journal page number is written in the Post. Ref. column of the account.

3 The amount is written in the Debit or Credit amount column of the account.

4 A new account balance is calculated and recorded in the Balance Debit or Balance Credit column of the account.

5 An account number is placed in the Post. Ref. column of the journal to show to which account a separate amount on that line has been posted. The account number is written in the journal *as the last step* in the posting procedure.

6 Check marks are placed in parentheses below general amount columns of a journal to show that the totals of these columns *are not* posted.

7 Account numbers are placed in parentheses below special amount column totals of a journal to show that these column totals have been posted.

■ ACCOUNTING TERMS

What is the meaning of each of the following?

1. ledger   **3.** account number   **5.** opening an account
2. general ledger   **4.** file maintenance   **6.** posting

■ QUESTIONS FOR INDIVIDUAL STUDY

1. Why are general ledger accounts used in an accounting system?

2. In what order are accounts arranged in a general ledger?

3. On Rugcare's chart of accounts, what is indicated by each digit in an account number?

4. Why are unused numbers usually left between account numbers on a chart of accounts?

5. What number is assigned to a new account inserted in a chart of accounts between accounts numbered 530 and 540?

6. What number is assigned to a new account added at the end of a division in which the last account is numbered 550?

7. What are the two steps in opening a new account?

8. Why are amounts posted from a journal to general ledger accounts?

9. What are the five steps in posting an amount from a journal to a general ledger account?

10. What three purposes are served by recording posting reference numbers in journals and accounts?

11. How is a new account balance calculated when the previous balance is a debit and a debit entry is posted?

12. Why are separate amounts in special amount columns of a journal not posted individually?

13. Why are totals of a journal's general amount columns not posted?

14. What is done to indicate that the general amount column totals are not posted?

15. What is done to indicate that a special amount column total in a journal has been posted?

16. How is a new account balance calculated when the previous balance is a debit, a credit entry is posted, and the previous debit balance is larger than the credit entry?

■ CASES FOR MANAGEMENT DECISION

CASE 1 Angela Desellio does not use a journal in her business records. She records the debits and credits for each transaction directly in the general ledger accounts. Is Ms. Desellio using the correct procedure? Explain your answer.

CASE 2 Philip Westing does the accounting work for his business. When posting, he first transfers all of the information to the general ledger accounts. Then he returns to the journal and, all at one time, writes the account numbers in the Post. Ref. column of the journal. Diana Young also does the accounting work for her business. When posting, she writes all the account numbers in the Post. Ref. column of the journal before she transfers any information to the accounts. Is Mr. Westing or Miss Young following the correct procedure? Explain your answer.

■ DRILLS FOR UNDERSTANDING

DRILL 5-D1   Preparing a chart of accounts

The following account descriptions refer to the location of accounts in a chart of accounts similar to the one for Rugcare, page 2.

1. The first asset account
2. The first liability account
3. The first owner's equity account
4. The first revenue account
5. The first expense account

7. The fourth expense account
8. The owner's drawing account
9. The cash account
10. The sales account
11. The owner's capital account

6. The third asset account   Use a form similar to the following. Account description 1 is given as an example.

1	2
Account Description	**Account Number**
1. The first asset account	110

Instructions: 1. In Column 1, write the account description.

2. In Column 2, write the account number. Account numbers are assigned by 10s.

3. Check your answers with Rugcare's chart of accounts, page 2. Determine if your answers are the same for each account as shown on the chart of accounts.

4. Cover your answers in Column 2. Practice rapidly recalling the account numbers for each account.

DRILL 5-D2 Analyzing posting from a journal

Instructions: 1. Use completed page 2 of the journal shown in Illustration 5-13. For each of the following lines in that illustration, write the separate amount, if any, that is posted individually. Also, write the account title to which the amount is posted.

a. Line 6
b. Line 9

c. Line 10
d. Line 11

e. Line 12
f. Line 13

2. Use the general ledger accounts shown in Illustration 5-14. Answer the following questions.

g. What item or transaction is represented by the amount in the cash account's Credit column?
h. What item or transaction is represented by the amount in the prepaid insurance account's Debit Balance column?
i. What item or transaction is represented by the amount in the sales account's Credit column?
j. Where in the journal is the information found about the item or transaction recorded in the advertising expense account's Debit column?

■ APPLICATION PROBLEMS

PROBLEM 5-1 Preparing a chart of accounts

Marie Wilson owns a service business called Wilson's Services. Wilson's Services uses the following accounts.

Automobile Expense
Bartel Supplies
Cash
Insurance Expense
Marie Wilson, Capital
Marie Wilson, Drawing

Miscellaneous Expense
Novack Office Supplies
Prepaid Insurance
Sales
Supplies
Supplies Expense

Instructions: 1. Prepare a chart of accounts similar to the one described in this chapter. Arrange expense accounts in alphabetical order. Use 3-digit account numbers and number accounts within a division by 10s.

2. Two new accounts, Gasoline Expense and Utilities Expense, are to be added to the chart of accounts prepared in Instruction 1. Assign account numbers to the two new accounts.

PROBLEM 5-2   Posting to a general ledger

Don Ley owns a service business called AquaCare. AquaCare's journal, which is needed to complete this problem, is in the working papers that accompany this textbook.

Instructions: 1. Open a general ledger account for each of the following accounts.

	Assets		Revenue
110	Cash	410	Sales
120	Supplies		Expenses
130	Prepaid Insurance	510	Advertising Expense
	Liabilities	520	Miscellaneous Expense
210	Donard Supplies	530	Rent Expense
220	Fell Office Supplies	540	Utilities Expense
	Owner's Equity		
310	Don Ley, Capital		
320	Don Ley, Drawing		

2. Post the separate amounts on each line of the journal that need to be posted individually.

3. Post the journal special amount column totals.

■ ENRICHMENT PROBLEMS

MASTERY PROBLEM 5-M   Journalizing and posting to a general ledger

Al Hiatt owns a service business called Hiatt Cleaning. Hiatt Cleaning's general ledger accounts are given in the working papers that accompany this textbook.

Instructions: 1. Journalize the following transactions completed during November of the current year. Use page 1 of the journal. Source documents are abbreviated as follows: check, C; memorandum, M; receipt, R; calculator tape, T.

Nov. 1. Received cash from owner as an investment, $7,000.00. R1.
     3. Paid cash for rent, $300.00. C1.
     5. Paid cash for insurance, $200.00. C2.
     6. Received cash from sales, $750.00. T6.
     9. Paid cash for miscellaneous expense, $5.00. C3.
   11. Paid cash for supplies, $500.00. C4.
   13. Bought supplies on account from Major Supplies, $600.00. M1.
   13. Received cash from sales, $700.00. T13.
   16. Paid cash for electric bill, $40.00. C5.
   18. Paid cash on account to Major Supplies, $300.00. C6.
   20. Paid cash for advertising, $30.00. C7.
   20. Received cash from sales, $770.00. T20.
   25. Paid cash for supplies, $150.00. C8.
   27. Paid cash for supplies, $100.00. C9.
   27. Received cash from sales, $1,150.00. T27.

Nov. 30. Paid cash to owner for personal use, $300.00. C10.
30. Received cash from sales, $410.00. T30.

2. Prove the journal.
3. Prove cash. The beginning cash balance on November 1 is zero. The balance on the next unused check stub is $8,855.00.
4. Rule the journal.
5. Post from the journal to the general ledger.

CHALLENGE PROBLEM 5-C Journalizing and posting to a general ledger

Dee Worthy owns a service business called HouseCare. HouseCare's general ledger accounts are given in the working papers that accompany this textbook.

HouseCare uses the following journal.

Journal **Page**

	Debit		Date	Account Title	Doc. No.	Post. Ref.	Credit		
	Cash	General					General	Sales	Cash
1									

Instructions: 1. Journalize the following transactions completed during March of the current year. Use page 5 of a journal. Source documents are abbreviated as follows: check, C; memorandum, M; receipt, R; calculator tape, T.

Mar. 1. Received cash from owner as an investment, $8,000.00. R1.
3. Paid cash for rent, $350.00. C1.
5. Paid cash for miscellaneous expense, $5.00. C2.
9. Paid cash for insurance, $250.00. C3.
11. Paid cash for supplies, $400.00. C4.
13. Received cash from sales, $450.00. T13.
16. Bought supplies on account from Hartwood Supplies, $700.00. M1.
18. Paid cash on account to Hartwood Supplies, $350.00. C5.
19. Paid cash for telephone bill, $60.00. C6.
20. Received cash from sales, $1,100.00. T20.
23. Paid cash for supplies, $150.00. C7.
23. Paid cash for advertising, $50.00. C8.
27. Paid cash for supplies, $150.00. C9.
27. Received cash from sales, $1,830.00. T27.
30. Paid cash to owner for personal use, $400.00. C10.
31. Received cash from sales, $410.00. T31.

2. Prove the journal.
3. Prove cash. The beginning cash balance on March 1 is zero. The balance on the next unused check stub is $9,625.00.
4. Rule the journal.
5. Post from the journal to the general ledger.

CHAPTER
6

Cash Control Systems

ENABLING PERFORMANCE TASKS

After studying Chapter 6, you will be able to:
a. Define accounting terms related to using a checking account and a petty cash fund.
b. Identify accounting concepts and practices related to using a checking account.
c. Prepare business papers related to using a checking account.
d. Reconcile a bank statement.
e. Establish and replenish a petty cash fund.
f. Record selected transactions related to using a checking account and a petty cash fund.

In accounting, money is usually referred to as cash. Most businesses make major cash payments by check. However, small cash payments for items such as postage and some supplies may be made from a cash fund kept at the place of business.

Because cash transactions occur more frequently than other types of transactions, more chances occur to make recording errors affecting cash. Cash can be transferred from one person to another without any question about ownership. Also, cash may be lost as it is moved from one place to another.

As a safety measure, Rugcare keeps most of its cash in a bank. Because all cash receipts are placed in a bank, Rugcare has written evidence to support its accounting records. Rugcare can compare its record of checks written with the bank's record of checks paid. Greater control of Rugcare's cash and greater accuracy of its cash records result from these procedures.

CHECKING ACCOUNTS

A business form ordering a bank to pay cash from a bank account is known as a check. A bank account from which payments can be ordered by a depositor is called a checking account.

98

Authorizing signatures

When a checking account is opened, the bank customer must provide a signature on a signature card for the bank records. If several persons are authorized to sign checks, each person's signature must be on the signature card. Checks should always be signed with the same signature as on the signature card. Only Ben Furman is authorized to sign checks for Rugcare.

Depositing cash

A bank customer prepares a deposit slip each time cash or checks are placed in a bank account. Deposit slips may differ slightly from one bank to another. Each bank designs its own deposit slips to fit the bank's recording machines. However, all deposit slips contain the same basic information as the slip shown in Illustration 6-1.

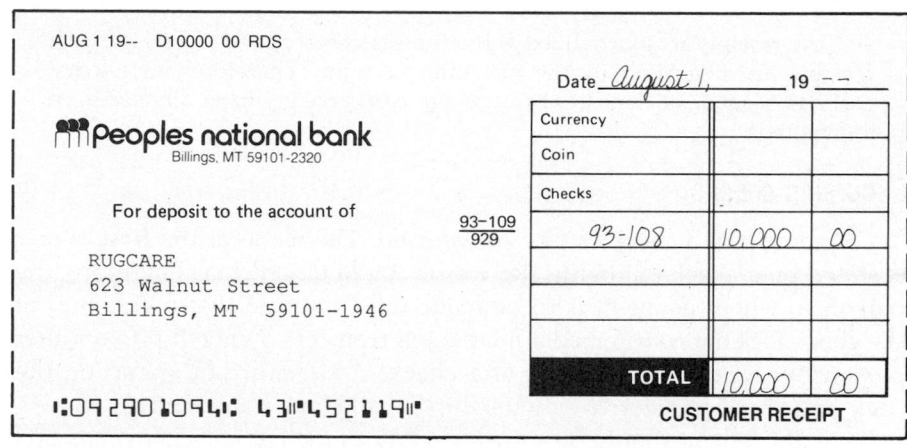

Illustration 6-1
Deposit slip

Checks are listed on a deposit slip according to the bank number on each check. For example, in Illustration 6-1, the number *93-108* identifies the bank on which the $10,000.00 check is written.

When a deposit is made, a bank gives the depositor a receipt. Many banks use a copy of the deposit slip with a printed or stamped verification as the receipt. The printed verification, *Aug 1 19-- D10000.00 RDS*, is shown along the top right edge of the deposit slip in Illustration 6-1. This printed verification means that a total of $10,000.00 was deposited on August 1. The initials *RDS* next to the amount are those of the bank employee who accepted the deposit.

Rugcare records the August 1 deposit on the next unused check stub, as shown in Illustration 6-2.

HIGHLINE SCHOOL DISTRICT
Evergreen High School
15675 Ambaum Blvd. S.W.
Seattle, Washington 98166

NO. 1	$		
Date		19	
To			
For			
BAL. BRO'T. FOR'D.		0	00
AMT. DEPOSITED. . . . . 8 / 1 --	Date	10,000	00
SUBTOTAL.		10,000	00
BANK CHARGES:			
SUBTOTAL.			
AMT. THIS CHECK.			
BAL. CAR'D. FOR'D.			

Illustration 6-2
Deposit recorded on a
check stub

After the deposit is recorded on the check stub, a checkbook subtotal is figured. The balance brought forward on Check Stub No. 1 is zero. The previous balance, $0.00, *plus* the deposit, $10,000.00, *equals* the subtotal, $10,000.00.

Cash receipts are journalized at the time cash is received. Later, the cash receipts are deposited in the checking account. Therefore, no journal entry is needed for deposits because the cash receipts have already been journalized.

Endorsing checks

Ownership of a check can be transferred. The name of the first owner is stated on a check following the words *Pay to the order of*. Therefore, the person to whom payment is to be made must indicate that ownership of the check is being transferred. One person transfers ownership to another person by signing on the back of a check. A signature or stamp on the back of a check transferring ownership is called an endorsement.

An endorsement should be signed exactly as the person's name appears on the front of the check. For example, a check made payable to B.E. Furman is endorsed on the back as *B.E. Furman*. Immediately below that endorsement, Mr. Furman writes his official signature, *Ben Furman*.

Ownership of a check might be transferred several times, resulting in several endorsements. Each endorser guarantees payment of the check. If a bank does not receive payment from the person who signed the check, each endorser is individually liable for payment.

Three types of endorsements are commonly used, each having a specific use in transferring ownership.

Blank endorsement. An endorsement consisting only of the endorser's signature is called a blank endorsement. A blank endorsement indicates that the subsequent owner is whoever has the check. A blank endorsement is shown in Illustration 6-3.

Federal regulations require that an endorsement be confined to a limited amount of space that is indicated on the back of a check.

If a check with a blank endorsement is lost or stolen, the check can be cashed by anyone who has it. Ownership may be transferred without further endorsement. A blank endorsement should be used *only* when a person is at the bank ready to cash or deposit a check.

Illustration 6-3
Blank endorsement

Special endorsement. An endorsement indicating a new owner of a check is called a special endorsement. Special endorsements are sometimes known as endorsements in full. A special endorsement is shown in Illustration 6-4.

Special endorsements include the words *Pay to the order of* and the name of the new check owner. Only the person or business named in a special endorsement can cash, deposit, or further transfer ownership of the check.

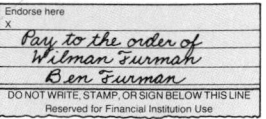

Illustration 6-4
Special endorsement

Restrictive endorsement. An endorsement restricting further transfer of a check's ownership is called a restrictive endorsement. A restrictive endorsement limits use of the check to whatever purpose is stated in the endorsement. A restrictive endorsement is shown in Illustration 6-5.

On all checks received, Rugcare stamps a restrictive endorsement which states that the check is for deposit only. This restrictive endorsement prevents unauthorized persons from cashing a check if it is lost or stolen.

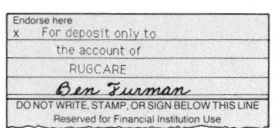

Illustration 6-5
Restrictive endorsement

Writing checks

Rugcare uses printed checks with check stubs attached. Consecutive numbers are preprinted on Rugcare's checks. Consecutive numbers on checks provide an easy way of identifying each check. Also, the numbers help keep track of all checks to assure that none are lost or misplaced.

Preparing check stubs. A check stub is a business' record of each check written for a cash payment transaction. *(CONCEPT: Objective Evidence)* To avoid forgetting to prepare a check stub, the check stub is prepared before the check is written. Rugcare's check stub and check are shown in Illustration 6-6.

Illustration 6-6
Completed check stub and check

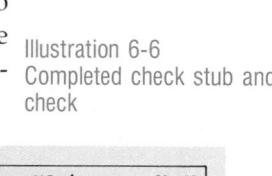

Six steps are used to complete Rugcare's Check Stub No. 1.

1 Write the amount of the check, *$1,577.00*, in the space after the dollar sign at the top of the stub.

2 Write the date of the check, *August 3, 19--*, on the Date line at the top of the stub.

3 Write to whom the check is to be paid, *Janitorial Supplies Co.*, on the To line at the top of the stub.

4 Record the purpose of the check, *Supplies*, on the For line.

5 Write the amount of the check, *$1,577.00*, in the amount column at the bottom of the stub on the line with the words "Amt. this Check."

6 Figure the new checking account balance, *$8,423.00*, and record the new balance in the amount column on the last line of the stub. The new balance is calculated as shown below.

Subtotal	−	Amount of This Check	=	New Balance
$10,000.00	−	$1,577.00	=	$8,423.00

Preparing checks. After the check stub is completed, the check is written. The check shown in Illustration 6-6 is prepared as follows.

1 Write the date, *August 3, 19--*, in the space provided.

The date should be the month, day, and year on which the check is issued. A check with a future date on it is called a postdated check. Most banks will not accept postdated checks because money cannot be withdrawn from a depositor's account until the date on the check.

2 Write to whom the check is to be paid, *Janitorial Supplies Co.*, following the words "Pay to the order of."

If the person to whom a check is to be paid is a business, use the business' name rather than the owner's name. *(CONCEPT: Business Entity)* If the person to whom the check is to be paid is an individual, use that person's name.

3 Write the amount in figures, *$1,577.00*, following the dollar sign.

Write the figures close to the printed dollar sign. This practice prevents anyone from writing another digit in front of the amount to change the amount of the check.

4 Write the amount in words, *One thousand five hundred seventy-seven and no/100*, on the line with the word "Dollars."

This written amount verifies the amount written in figures after the dollar sign. Begin the words at the extreme left. Draw a line through the unused space up to the word "Dollars." This line prevents anyone from writing in additional words to change the amount.

If the amounts in words and in figures are not the same, a bank may pay only the amount in words. Often, when the amounts do not agree, a bank will refuse to pay the check.

5 Write the purpose of the check, *Supplies*, on the line labeled "For."

On some checks this space is labeled "Memo." Some checks do not have a line for writing the purpose of the check.

6 Sign the check.

A check should not be signed until each item on the check and its stub has been verified for accuracy.

Voiding checks. Banks usually refuse to accept altered checks. If any kind of error is made in preparing a check, a new check should be prepared. Because checks are prenumbered, all checks not used should be retained for the records. This practice helps account for all checks and assures that no checks have been lost or stolen.

A check that contains errors must be marked so that others will know that it is not to be used. The word *VOID* is written in large letters across both the check and its stub.

When Rugcare records a check in its journal, the check number is placed in the journal's Doc. No. column. If a check number is missing from the Doc. No. column, there is a question whether all checks have been journalized. To assure that all check numbers are listed in the journal, Rugcare records voided checks in the journal. The date is recorded in the journal's Date column. The word *VOID* is written in the Account Title column. The check number is recorded in the Doc. No. column. A dash is placed in the Cash Credit column.

BANK STATEMENT

Banks keep separate records for each depositor. Information from deposit slips and checks are recorded daily in depositors' accounts. A report of deposits, withdrawals, and bank balance sent to a depositor by a bank is called a bank statement. Rugcare's bank statement for August 27 is shown in Illustration 6-7.

The balance for Rugcare's checking account on August 27, according to the bank's records, is $8,731.00.

When a bank receives checks, the amount of each check is deducted from the depositor's account. Then, the bank stamps the checks to indicate that the check is canceled and is not to be transferred further. Canceled checks are returned to a depositor with a bank statement. Outstanding checks are those checks issued by a depositor but not yet reported on a bank statement. Outstanding deposits are those deposits made at a bank but not yet shown on a bank statement. A bank may assess a charge for maintaining a checking account. Account service charges are also listed on a bank statement.

Banks may have different kinds of checking accounts to fit special needs of depositors. Each bank has its own regulations for its services, and fees are not charged for some checking accounts.

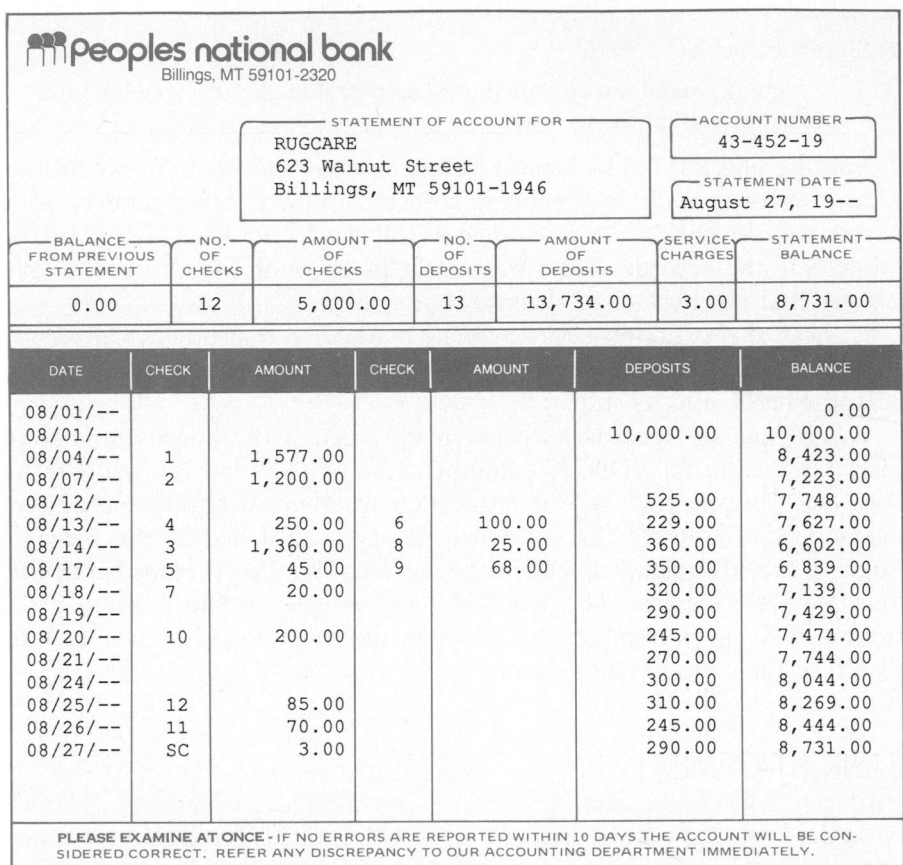

DATE	CHECK	AMOUNT	CHECK	AMOUNT	DEPOSITS	BALANCE
08/01/--						0.00
08/01/--					10,000.00	10,000.00
08/04/--	1	1,577.00				8,423.00
08/07/--	2	1,200.00				7,223.00
08/12/--					525.00	7,748.00
08/13/--	4	250.00	6	100.00	229.00	7,627.00
08/14/--	3	1,360.00	8	25.00	360.00	6,602.00
08/17/--	5	45.00	9	68.00	350.00	6,839.00
08/18/--	7	20.00			320.00	7,139.00
08/19/--					290.00	7,429.00
08/20/--	10	200.00			245.00	7,474.00
08/21/--					270.00	7,744.00
08/24/--					300.00	8,044.00
08/25/--	12	85.00			310.00	8,269.00
08/26/--	11	70.00			245.00	8,444.00
08/27/--	SC	3.00			290.00	8,731.00

Illustration 6-7
Bank statement

PLEASE EXAMINE AT ONCE - IF NO ERRORS ARE REPORTED WITHIN 10 DAYS THE ACCOUNT WILL BE CONSIDERED CORRECT. REFER ANY DISCREPANCY TO OUR ACCOUNTING DEPARTMENT IMMEDIATELY.

Verifying a bank statement

Although banks seldom make mistakes, occasionally a check or deposit might be recorded in a wrong account. When a bank statement is received, a depositor should verify its accuracy. If errors are discovered, the bank should be notified at once. However, a bank's records and a depositor's records may differ and still be correct. The difference may exist for several reasons.

1. A service charge may not have been recorded in the depositor's business records.
2. Outstanding deposits may be recorded in the depositor's records but not yet reported on a bank statement.

3. Outstanding checks may be recorded in the depositor's records but not yet reported on a bank statement.
4. A depositor may have made errors in doing arithmetic or in recording information in the business records. The most common mistakes made by depositors are arithmetic errors.
5. The bank may have made an error.

Reconciling a bank statement

A bank statement is reconciled by verifying that information on a bank statement and a checkbook are in agreement. Rugcare reconciles a bank statement on the same day that the statement is received.

Rugcare's canceled checks are received with the bank statement. The returned checks are arranged in numerical order. For each canceled check, a check mark is placed on the corresponding check stub. A check stub with no check mark indicates an outstanding check.

On August 28 Rugcare receives a bank statement dated August 27. Rugcare uses a reconciliation form printed on the back of the bank statement. Rugcare's bank statement reconciliation is shown in Illustration 6-8.

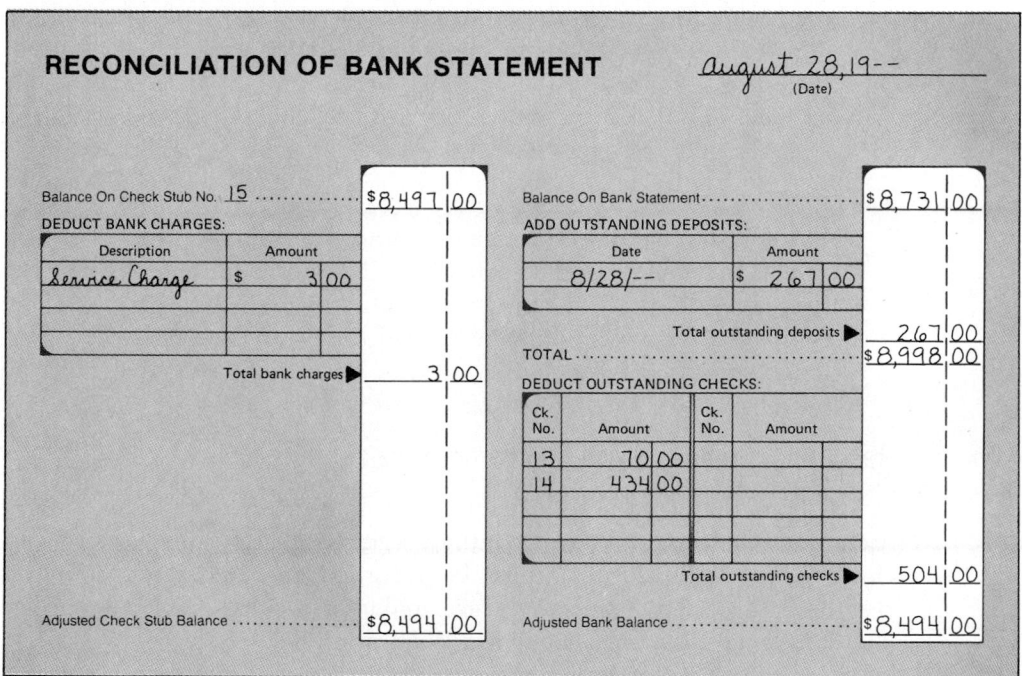

Rugcare uses three steps to reconcile a bank statement.

1 Figure the adjusted check stub balance.

- Write the date on which the reconciliation is prepared, *August 28, 19--*.
- In the left amount column, list the balance brought forward on

Illustration 6-8
Bank statement
reconciliation

Check Stub No. 15, the next unused check stub, *$8,497.00*.

- In the space for bank charges, list any charges. The only such charge for Rugcare is the bank service charge, *$3.00*. The bank service charge is labeled *SC* on the bank statement.
- Write the adjusted checkbook balance, *$8,494.00*, in the space provided at the bottom of the left amount column. The balance on the check stub, $8,497.00, *minus* the bank's service charge, $3.00, *equals* the adjusted check stub balance, $8,494.00.

2 Figure the adjusted bank balance.

- Write the ending balance shown on the bank statement, *$8,731.00*, in the right amount column.
- Write the date, *8/28/--* and the amount, *$267.00*, of any outstanding deposits in the space provided. Add the outstanding deposits. Write the total outstanding deposits, *$267.00*, in the right amount column.
- Add the ending bank statement balance to the total outstanding deposits. Write the total, *$8,998.00*, in the space for the Total.
- List the outstanding checks, *Nos. 13 and 14*, and their amounts, *$70.00 and $434.00*, in the space provided. Add the amounts of the outstanding checks, and write the total, *$504.00*, in the right amount column.
- Figure the adjusted bank balance, and write the amount, *$8,494.00*, in the space provided at the bottom of the right amount column. The total, $8,998.00, *minus* the total outstanding checks, $504.00, *equals* the adjusted bank balance, $8,494.00.

3 Compare adjusted balances.

- The adjusted balances must be the same. The adjusted check stub balance is the same as the adjusted bank balance, *$8,494.00*. Because the two amounts are the same, the bank statement is reconciled. The completed reconciliation form is filed for future reference.
- If the two adjusted balances are not the same, the errors must be found and corrected before any more work is done.

Recording a bank service charge on a check stub

The bank deducts the service charge from Rugcare's checking account each month. Although Rugcare did not write a check for the bank service charge, this cash payment must be recorded in Rugcare's accounting records as a cash payment. Rugcare makes a record of a bank service charge on a check stub as shown in Illustration 6-9.

Three steps are used to record a bank service charge on a check stub.

1 Write the words, *Service charge*, on the check stub under the heading Bank Charges.

2 Write the amount, *$3.00*, in the check stub's amount column.

3 Figure and record the new balance, *$8,494.00*, on the Subtotal line.

NO. **15**	$	
Date		19 __
To		
For		
BAL. BRO'T. FOR'D.	8,230	00
AMT. DEPOSITED.... 8 28 --	267	00
SUBTOTAL.................... Date	8,497	00
BANK CHARGES: _Service Charge_	3	00
SUBTOTAL....................	8,494	00
AMT. THIS CHECK............		
BAL. CAR'D. FOR'D.............		

Illustration 6-9
Bank service charge
recorded on a check stub

Journalizing a bank service charge

Because the bank service charge is a cash payment for which no check is written, Rugcare prepares a memorandum as the source document. Rugcare's bank service charges are relatively small and occur only once a month. Therefore, a separate ledger account for the expense is not used. Instead, Rugcare records the bank service charge as a miscellaneous expense.

> August 28, 19--.
> Received bank statement showing August bank service charge, $3.00. Memorandum No. 3.

A memorandum is the source document for a bank service charge transaction. (CONCEPT: Objective Evidence) The analysis of this transaction is shown in the T accounts.

Miscellaneous Expense is debited for $3.00 to show the increase in this expense account balance. Cash is credited for $3.00 to show the decrease in this asset account balance. The journal entry to record Rugcare's bank service charge is shown in Illustration 6-10.

Miscellaneous Expense	
3.00	

Cash	
	3.00

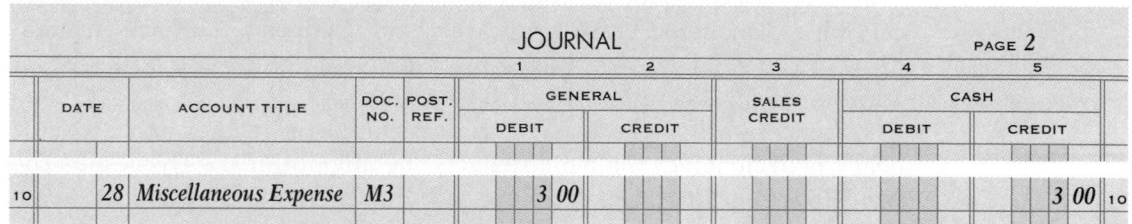

	JOURNAL						PAGE 2		
					1	2	3	4	5
DATE	ACCOUNT TITLE	DOC. NO.	POST. REF.		GENERAL		SALES CREDIT	CASH	
					DEBIT	CREDIT		DEBIT	CREDIT
10	28 _Miscellaneous Expense_	M3			3 00				3 00	10

Illustration 6-10
Journal entry to record a
bank service charge

This entry is journalized using four steps.

1 *Date.* Write the date, *28*, in the Date column.

2 *Debit.* Write the title of the account to be debited, *Miscellaneous Expense*, in the Account Title column. Record the amount debited to Miscellaneous Expense, *$3.00*, in the General Debit column.

3 *Credit.* Record the amount credited to Cash, *$3.00*, in the Cash Credit column.

4 *Source document.* Write the source document number, *M3*, in the Doc. No. column.

> Rugcare reconciled its bank statement on August 28. The entry for the bank service charge is journalized on the same date. Rugcare continues to record entries in the journal until the end of the month as shown in Illustration 5-13, Chapter 5.

DISHONORED CHECKS

A check that a bank refuses to pay is called a dishonored check. Banks may dishonor a check for a number of reasons. (1) The check appears to be altered. (2) The signature of the person who signed the check does not match the one on the signature card at the bank. (3) The amounts written in figures and in words do not agree. (4) The check is postdated. (5) The person who wrote the check has stopped payment on the check. (6) The account of the person who wrote the check has insufficient funds to pay the check.

Issuing a check on an account with insufficient funds is illegal in most states. Altering or forging a check is illegal in all states. A dishonored check may affect the credit rating of the person or business who issued the check. Checking accounts and records should be maintained in such a way that all checks will be honored when presented to the bank.

Sometimes money for a dishonored check can be collected directly from the person or business who wrote the check. Often, however, the value of a dishonored check cannot be recovered and becomes an expense to the business.

Most banks charge a fee for handling dishonored checks that have been previously accepted for deposit. This fee is an expense of the business receiving a dishonored check. Rugcare's bank charges a $5.00 fee for handling dishonored checks. Rugcare attempts to collect the $5.00 fee in addition to the amount of the dishonored check.

Rugcare records a check as a cash debit and deposits the check. When a check is dishonored, the bank deducts the amount of the check plus the fee, $5.00, from Rugcare's checking account. Therefore, Rugcare records a dishonored check in its journal as a cash payment transaction.

Recording a dishonored check on a check stub

A dishonored check recorded on a check stub is shown in Illustration 6-11.

The words, *Dishonored check*, are written on the line below the words "Bank Charges." The total amount of the dishonored check plus the fee,

```
NO. 41          $_____
Date _____ 19 ___
To _____

For _____
_____
BAL. BRO'T. FOR'D. .............    6,128 00
AMT. DEPOSITED.... [    ]
SUBTOTAL.............. Date ....    6,128 00
BANK CHARGES:
     Service Charge  3.00
     Dis. Check.    15.00
                                       18 00
SUBTOTAL.................        6,110 00
AMT. THIS CHECK.............
BAL. CAR'D. FOR'D..............
```

Illustration 6-11
Dishonored check recorded
on a check stub

$15.00, is written in the amount column on the same line. A new subtotal is figured by subtracting total bank charges, $18.00 ($3.00 service charge *plus* $15.00 dishonored check), from the balance brought forward, $6,128.00. The new subtotal, *$6,110.00*, is written on the Subtotal line. A new Balance Carried Forward is not figured until after Check No. 41 is written.

Journalizing a dishonored check

During August, Rugcare received no checks that were subsequently dishonored. However, in November Rugcare did receive a check that was dishonored.

> *November 29, 19--.*
> *Received notice from the bank of a dishonored check, $10.00, plus $5.00 fee; total, $15.00. Memorandum No. 6.*

Because Rugcare did not write a check for this cash payment, a memorandum is prepared as the source document. *(CONCEPT: Objective Evidence)*

All checks received are deposited in Rugcare's checking account. The entry for each cash receipts transaction includes a debit to Cash. If a check is subsequently returned as dishonored, the previous cash debit for the amount of the check must be offset by a cash credit. The analysis of this transaction is shown in the T accounts.

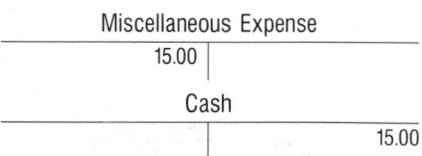

Miscellaneous Expense is debited for $15.00 to show the increase in this expense account balance. Cash is credited for $15.00 to show the decrease in this asset account balance. The journal entry to record this transaction is shown in Illustration 6-12.

This entry is journalized using four steps.

1 *Date.* Write the date, *29*, in the Date column.

2 *Debit.* Write the title of the account to be debited, *Miscellaneous Expense*, in the Account Title column. Record the amount debited to Miscellaneous Expense, *$15.00*, in the General Debit column.

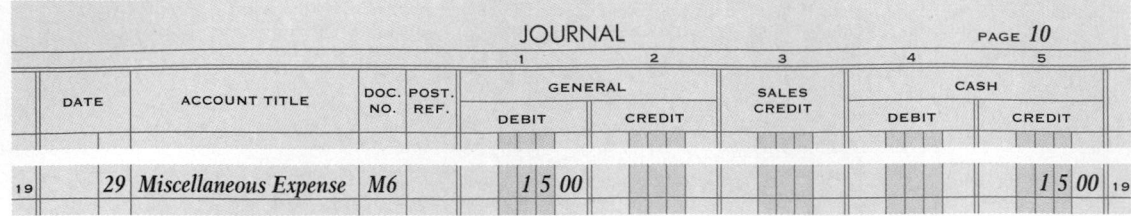

	DATE	ACCOUNT TITLE	DOC. NO.	POST. REF.	GENERAL DEBIT	GENERAL CREDIT	SALES CREDIT	CASH DEBIT	CASH CREDIT	
19	29	*Miscellaneous Expense*	M6		1 5 00				1 5 00	19

Illustration 6-12
Journal entry to record a
dishonored check

3 *Credit.* Record the amount credited to Cash, *$15.00*, in the Cash Credit column.

4 *Source document.* Write the source document number, *M6*, in the Doc. No. column.

PETTY CASH

An amount of cash kept on hand and used for making small payments is called petty cash. Cash control is effective if all cash payments are made by check and cash receipts are deposited in the bank. However, a business usually has some small payments for which writing a check is not time or cost effective. Therefore, a business may maintain a separate cash fund for making small cash payments. The actual dollar amount considered to be a small payment differs from one business to another. Mr. Furman has set $5.00 as the maximum amount to be paid at any one time from the petty cash fund.

Petty Cash	
Debit side NORMAL BALANCE Increases	Credit side Decreases

The petty cash account is an asset with a normal debit balance. The balance of the petty cash account increases on the debit side and decreases on the credit side.

Establishing a petty cash fund

On August 17 Mr. Furman decides that Rugcare needs a petty cash fund of $200.00. This amount should provide for the small cash payments anticipated during a month.

August 17, 19--.
Paid cash to establish a petty cash fund, $200.00. Check No. 10.

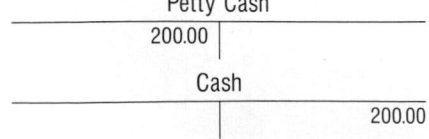

The source document for this transaction is Check No. 10. *(CONCEPT: Objective Evidence)* The analysis of this transaction is shown in the T accounts.

Petty Cash is debited for $200.00 to show the increase in this asset account balance. Cash is credited for $200.00 to show the decrease in this asset account balance. The journal entry to record this transaction is shown in Illustration 6-13. This entry is journalized using four steps.

	DATE	ACCOUNT TITLE	DOC. NO.	POST. REF.	GENERAL DEBIT	GENERAL CREDIT	SALES CREDIT	CASH DEBIT	CASH CREDIT	
					1	2	3	4	5	
16	17	Petty Cash	C10		2 0 0 00				2 0 0 00	16

JOURNAL   PAGE *1*

Illustration 6-13
Journal entry to record establishing a petty cash fund

1 *Date.* Write the date, *17*, in the Date column.

2 *Debit.* Write the title of the account to be debited, *Petty Cash*, in the Account Title column. Record the amount debited to Petty Cash, *$200.00*, in the General Debit column.

3 *Credit.* Record the amount credited to Cash, *$200.00*, in the Cash Credit column.

4 *Source document.* Write the source document number, *C10*, in the Doc. No. column.

Mr. Furman cashes the check and places the $200.00 in a locked petty cash box kept at Rugcare's place of business. Only Mr. Furman is authorized to make payments from the petty cash fund.

Making payments from a petty cash fund

Each time a small payment is made from the petty cash fund, Mr. Furman prepares a form showing the purpose and amount of the payment. A form showing proof of a petty cash payment is called a petty cash slip.

A petty cash slip used by Rugcare is shown in Illustration 6-14.

PETTY CASH SLIP   **No. 1**

Date: *August 18, 19--*

Paid to: *Bernie's Repair Shop*

For: *Hose Repair* $*5.00*

Account: *Repair Expense*

Approved: *Ben Furman*

Illustration 6-14
Petty cash slip

A petty cash slip shows the following information. (1) Petty cash slip number. (2) Date of petty cash payment. (3) To whom paid. (4) Reason for the payment. (5) Amount paid. (6) Account in which amount is to be recorded. (7) Signature of person approving the petty cash payment.

The petty cash slips are kept in the petty cash box until the fund must be replenished. No entries are made in the journal for the individual petty cash payments.

Replenishing a petty cash fund

As petty cash is paid out, the amount in the petty cash box decreases. Eventually, the petty cash fund must be replenished and the petty cash payments recorded. Rugcare replenishes its petty cash fund whenever the amount on hand is reduced to $75.00. Also, the petty cash fund is always replenished at the end of each month so that all of the expenses are recorded in the month they are incurred.

Rugcare completes four steps in replenishing the petty cash fund.

1 *Prove the petty cash fund.* On August 31 Mr. Furman proves petty cash as shown below.

Petty cash on hand $188.00
Count the cash remaining in the petty cash fund
Plus total of petty cash slips . . . .   + 12.00
Add the amounts on the petty cash slips
Equals petty cash fund $200.00

The last line of the proof must show the same total as the original balance of the petty cash fund, $200.00. If petty cash does not prove, the errors must be found and corrected before any more work is done.

2 *Prepare a petty cash report.* At the end of August, Mr. Furman totals the petty cash slips and prepares a report. Rugcare's August petty cash report is shown in Illustration 6-15.

PETTY CASH REPORT	Date: August 31, 19--		
Explanation	Amounts		
Fund total			200 00
Payments:			
Miscellaneous Expense	7	00	
Repair Expense	5	00	
Less total payments			12 00
Equals recorded amount on hand			188 00
Actual amount on hand			188 00

Illustration 6-15
Petty cash report

The report shows that a total of $12.00 has been paid out of petty cash for repairs and miscellaneous expenses. Thus, $12.00 needs to be added to the remaining $188.00 to bring the petty cash fund back to its normal size, $200.00.

3 *Write a check to replenish the petty cash fund.*

4 *Journalize the entry to replenish petty cash.*

August 31, 19--.
Paid cash to replenish the petty cash fund, $12.00: miscellaneous expense, $7.00; repairs, $5.00. Check No. 15.

The source document for this transaction is Check No. 15. (*CONCEPT: Objective Evidence*) The analysis of this transaction is shown in the T accounts.

Miscellaneous Expense is debited for $7.00 and Repair Expense is debited for $5.00 to show the increases in these expense account balances. Cash is credited for $12.00 to show a decrease in this asset account balance.

Miscellaneous Expense	
7.00	

Repair Expense	
5.00	

Cash	
	12.00

Unless the petty cash fund is permanently increased or decreased, the balance of the account is always the original amount of the fund. The check issued to replenish petty cash is a credit to Cash and does not affect Petty Cash. When the check is cashed, the money is placed in the petty cash box. The amount in the petty cash box changes as shown below.

Amount in petty cash box before fund is replenished.	$188.00
Amount from check issued to replenish petty cash	+ 12.00
Amount in petty cash box after fund is replenished	$200.00

The total amount in the petty cash box, $200.00, is again the same as the balance of the petty cash account. The journal entry to record the transaction to replenish petty cash is shown in Illustration 6-16.

Illustration 6-16
Journal entry to record
replenishing of petty cash

					GENERAL		SALES	CASH	
	DATE	ACCOUNT TITLE	DOC. NO.	POST. REF.	DEBIT	CREDIT	CREDIT	DEBIT	CREDIT
11	31	Miscellaneous Expense	C15		7 00				1 2 00
12		Repair Expense			5 00				

JOURNAL PAGE 2

This entry is journalized using four steps.

1 *Date.* Write the date, *31*, in the Date column.

2 *Debit.* Write the title of the first account to be debited, *Miscellaneous Expense*, in the Account Title column. Write the amount to be debited to Miscellaneous Expense, *$7.00*, in the General Debit column on the same line as the account title. Write the title of the second account to be debited, *Repair Expense*, on the next line in the Account Title column. Record the amount to be debited to Repair Expense, *$5.00*, in the General Debit column on the same line as the account title.

3 *Credit.* Record the amount to be credited to Cash, *$12.00*, in the Cash Credit column on the first line of this entry.

4 *Source document.* Write the source document number, *C15*, in the Doc. No. column.

The check is cashed, and the money is placed in the petty cash box. The amount in the petty cash box is now the original amount of the petty cash fund, $200.00. Petty cash on hand, $188.00, *plus* the cash to replenish, $12.00, *equals* the original amount of the petty cash fund, $200.00. The amount in the petty cash fund is now the same as the balance of the petty cash account, $200.00.

SUMMARY OF CASH CONTROL SYSTEMS PROCEDURE

Illustration 6-17
Summary of checking
account procedures

A summary of procedures for using checking accounts is shown in Illustration 6-17.

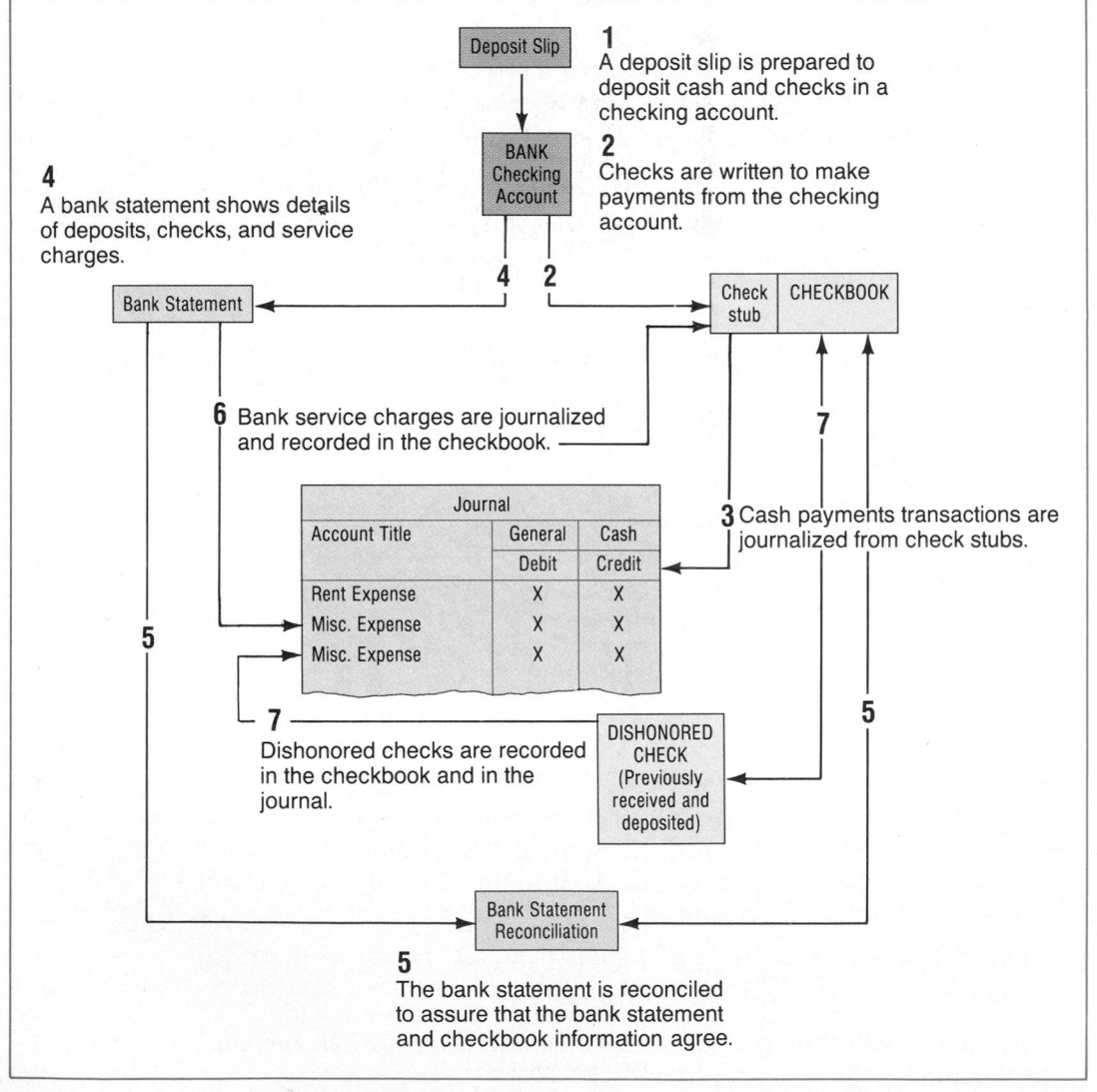

A summary of procedures for using a petty cash fund is shown in Illus- Illustration 6-18
tration 6-18.   Summary of petty cash
fund procedures

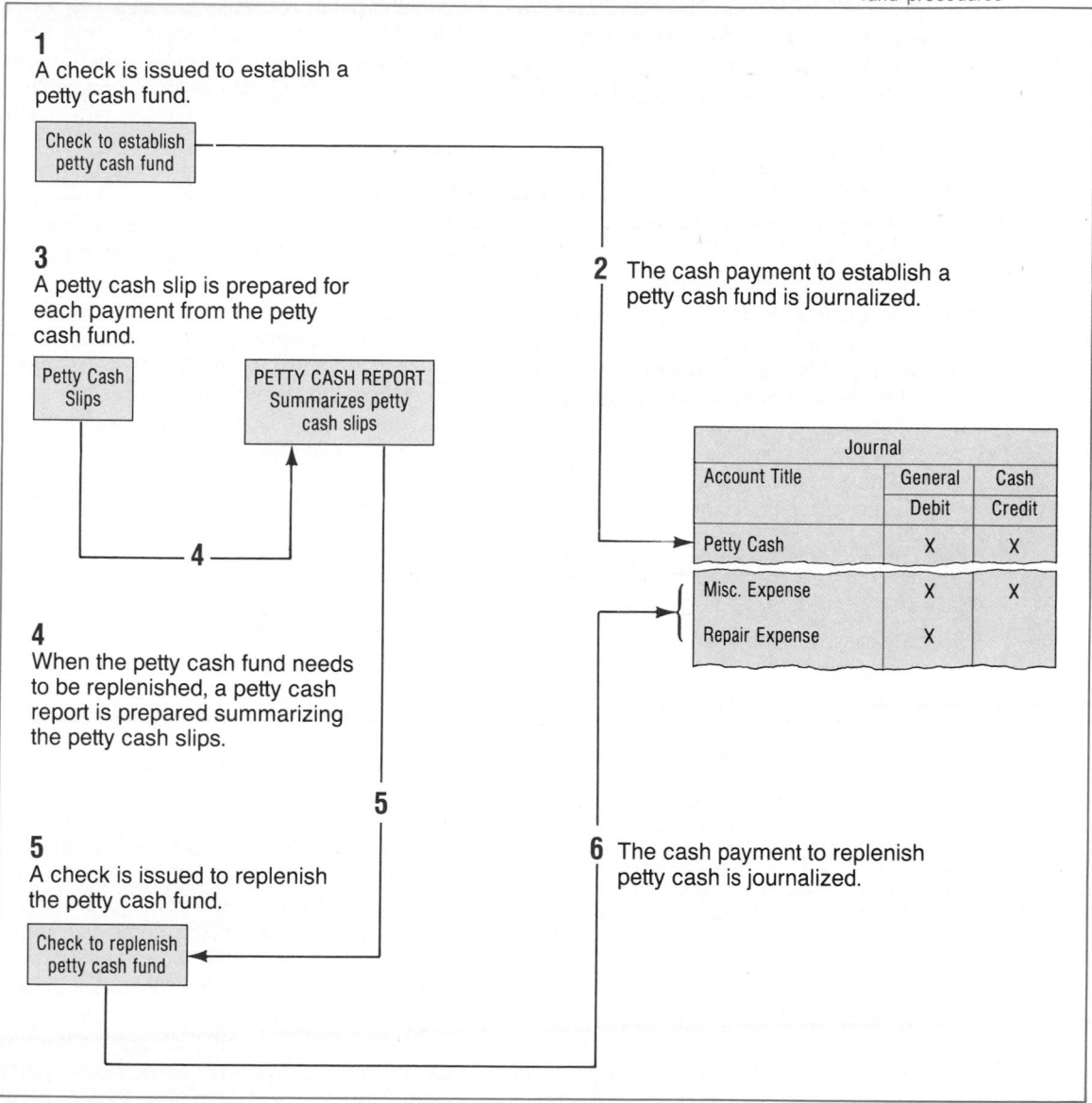

1
A check is issued to establish a
petty cash fund.

Check to establish
petty cash fund

3
A petty cash slip is prepared for
each payment from the petty
cash fund.

Petty Cash
Slips

PETTY CASH REPORT
Summarizes petty
cash slips

4

2 The cash payment to establish a
petty cash fund is journalized.

Journal		
Account Title	General	Cash
	Debit	Credit
Petty Cash	X	X
Misc. Expense	X	X
Repair Expense	X	

4
When the petty cash fund needs
to be replenished, a petty cash
report is prepared summarizing
the petty cash slips.

5

5
A check is issued to replenish
the petty cash fund.

6 The cash payment to replenish
petty cash is journalized.

Check to replenish
petty cash fund

■ ACCOUNTING TERMS

What is the meaning of each of the following?

1. checking account   **5.** restrictive endorsement   **8.** dishonored check
2. endorsement   **6.** postdated check   **9.** petty cash
3. blank endorsement   **7.** bank statement   **10.** petty cash slip
4. special endorsement

■ QUESTIONS FOR INDIVIDUAL STUDY

1. What evidence does a depositor have that money has been deposited in a checking account?
2. Why is no journal entry made by a business for a deposit in a checking account?
3. Why is the amount written in both numbers and words on a check?
4. What is the most common way of voiding a check?
5. Under what circumstances can a depositor assume that a bank statement reconciliation is correct?
6. Which accounting concept is being applied when a memorandum is prepared for the service charges deducted from a checking account?
7. What accounts are affected, and how, by an entry to record a bank service charge for a checking account?
8. What accounts are affected, and how, when Rugcare is notified that a deposited check has been dishonored?
9. What is the purpose of a petty cash fund?
10. What accounts are affected, and how, when a petty cash fund is established?
11. What is Rugcare's initial record of amounts that have been paid from the petty cash fund?
12. How is the petty cash fund proved?
13. What accounts are affected, and how, by an entry to replenish petty cash when the petty cash slips show payments for miscellaneous expense and repair expense?
14. When is a journal entry made to record payments from the petty cash fund?

■ CASES FOR MANAGEMENT DECISION

CASE 1 Iris Velez has a personal checking account in which she maintains a small balance. She receives a bank statement every three months. She files the statement and does not prepare a reconciliation. Sueanne Merker also has a personal checking account in which she maintains a balance of several hundred dollars. She receives bank statements once a month. She prepares a bank statement reconciliation for each bank statement received. Is Mrs. Velez or Ms. Merker following the better procedure? Explain your answer.

CASE 2 Dorset Company decides to establish a petty cash fund. The owner, Edna Dorset, wants to establish a $100.00 petty cash fund and limit payments to $5.00 or less. The manager, Roy Evans, suggests a petty cash fund of $3,000.00 limited to payments of $50.00 or less. Mr. Evans claims this limit will help him avoid writing so many checks. Do you agree with Ms. Dorset or Mr. Evans? Explain your answer.

CASE 3 Dot Lawn Care uses a petty cash fund. Denise Wong, the office manager, is authorized to make petty cash payments. When payments are made, she records them in a notebook on a form with the following column headings: Date, Purpose, To Whom, and Amount. She does not prepare a petty cash slip. When the petty cash fund needs replenishing, Mrs. Wong draws a single line under the last entry and summarizes the payments since petty cash was last replenished. This summary is used as the basis for writing a check to replenish petty cash. Do you agree with Mrs. Wong's petty cash procedures? Explain your answer.

■ DRILLS FOR UNDERSTANDING

DRILL 6-D1   Reconciling a bank statement

On July 29 of the current year, DeepClean received a bank statement dated July 28. The following information is obtained from the bank statement and from the records of the business.

Bank statement balance..	$1,528.00
Bank service charge	2.00
Outstanding deposit, July 28.......................................	150.00
Outstanding checks:	
No. 103	70.00
No. 105	35.00
Checkbook balance on Check Stub No. 106	1,575.00

Instructions: Prepare a bank statement reconciliation. Use July 29 of the current year as the date.

DRILL 6-D2 Reconciling a bank statement

On September 30 of the current year, Ajax Service Co. received a bank statement dated September 29. The following information is obtained from the bank statement and from the records of the business.

Bank statement balance..	$3,208.00
Bank service charge	5.00
Outstanding deposits:	
September 29	310.00
September 30	330.00
Outstanding checks:	
No. 214	90.00
No. 215	135.00
No. 217	50.00
Checkbook balance on Check Stub No. 218	3,578.00

Instructions: Prepare a bank statement reconciliation. Use September 30 of the current year as the date.

DRILL 6-D3 Replenishing a petty cash fund

KeepClean replenished petty cash on the dates shown in Column 2 of the following table. The information in Columns 3 to 5 is obtained from the petty cash reports.

1	2	3	4	5
		Summary of Petty Cash Slips		
Trans.	**Replenished on**	**Supplies**	**Advertising**	**Miscellaneous**
A	July 31	32.00	25.00	
B	August 31	21.00	20.00	5.00
C	September 30	40.00	20.00	15.00
D	October 31	10.00		20.00

Instructions: Prepare T accounts for Cash, Supplies, Advertising Expense, and Miscellaneous Expense. Use the T accounts to analyze each transaction given in the table. Label each amount in the T accounts with the corresponding transaction letter.

◼ APPLICATION PROBLEMS

PROBLEM 6-1 Endorsing checks

For each of the following situations, prepare the appropriate endorsement.

Instructions: 1. Write a blank endorsement. Use your own signature.

2. Write a special endorsement to transfer a check to Delbert Richardson. Use your own signature.

3. Write a restrictive endorsement to deposit a check in the account of OddJobs. Use your own signature.

PROBLEM 6-2   Writing checks

You are authorized to sign checks for OddJobs.

Instructions: 1. Record the balance brought forward on Check Stub No. 50, $1,396.35.

2. Record a deposit of $390.00 made on October 30 of the current year on Check Stub No. 50.

3. Prepare check stubs and write the following checks. Use October 30 of the current year as the date.

Check No. 50. To Corner Garage for repairs, $138.00.
Check No. 51. To OfficeWorld for supplies, $50.00.
Check No. 52. To Dixon Papers for supplies, $15.00.

PROBLEM 6-3   Reconciling a bank statement and recording a bank service charge

Use the bank statement, canceled checks, and check stubs given in the working papers accompanying this textbook.

Instructions: 1. Compare the canceled checks with the check stubs. For each canceled check, place a check mark next to the appropriate check stub number.

2. For each deposit shown on the bank statement, place a check mark next to the deposit amount on the appropriate check stub.

3. Prepare a bank statement reconciliation. Use August 29 of the current year as the date.

4. Record the following transactions on page 8 of a journal. The abbreviation for memorandum is M.

Sept. 1. Received bank statement showing August bank service charge, $5.00. M25.
      1. Received notice from the bank of a dishonored check, $170.00, plus $5.00 fee; total, $175.00. M26.

5. Record the bank service charge and dishonored check on Check Stub No. 165.

PROBLEM 6-4   Establishing and replenishing a petty cash fund

SweepUp established a petty cash fund on August 3 of the current year. At the end of August, the business replenished the petty cash fund.

Instructions: Journalize the following transactions completed during August of the current year. Use page 10 of a journal. The abbreviation for check is C.

Aug.   3. Paid cash to establish a petty cash fund, $100.00. C57.
      31. Paid cash to replenish the petty cash fund, $78.00: supplies, $25.00; miscellaneous expense, $8.00; repairs, $45.00. C97.

ENRICHMENT PROBLEMS

MASTERY PROBLEM 6-M   **Reconciling a bank statement; journalizing a bank service charge, a dishonored check, and petty cash transactions**

Joseph Cruz owns a business called LawnMow. LawnMow completed the following transactions during August of the current year.

Instructions: 1. Journalize the following transactions completed during August of the current year. Use page 20 of a journal. Source documents are abbreviated as follows: check, C; memorandum, M.

Aug. 21. Paid cash to establish a petty cash fund, $100.00. C61.
 24. Paid cash for repairs, $135.00. C62.
 26. Paid cash for supplies, $40.00. C63.
 27. Received notice from the bank of a dishonored check, $35.00, plus $5.00 fee; total, $40.00. M22.
 28. Paid cash for miscellaneous expense, $12.00. C64.
 31. Paid cash to owner for personal use, $300.00. C65.
 31. Paid cash to replenish the petty cash fund, $55.00: supplies, $35.00; miscellaneous expense, $20.00. C66.

2. On August 31 of the current year, LawnMow received a bank statement dated August 30. Prepare a bank statement reconciliation. Use August 31 of the current year as the date. The following information is obtained from the August 30 bank statement and from the records of the business.

Bank statement balance...	$1,521.00
Bank service charge	5.00
Outstanding deposit, August 31	430.00
Outstanding checks, Nos. 65 and 66.	
Checkbook balance on Check Stub No. 67................................	1,601.00

3. Continue using the journal and journalize the following transaction.

Aug. 31. Received bank statement showing August bank service charge, $5.00. M23.

CHALLENGE PROBLEM 6-C   **Reconciling a bank statement**

On November 30 of the current year, Johnson Company received a bank statement dated November 29. Miss Johnson placed a check mark beside the amount on each check stub for which a canceled check was received. She also placed a check mark on the check stub beside the amount of each deposit shown on the bank statement. She then prepared a bank statement reconciliation.

The last eight check stubs for the month of November and the bank statement reconciliation are given in the working papers accompanying this textbook. Both the check stubs and reconciliation contain errors.

Instructions: 1. Verify the amounts on the check stubs. Assume that the check amounts in the upper right corner of each stub are correct. Also assume that all deposits have been entered correctly on the check stubs.

2. Draw a line through all incorrect amounts on the check stubs. Write the correct amounts either above or below the incorrect amounts, depending on where space is available.

3. Prepare a correct bank statement reconciliation. Assume that the check marks written beside check and deposit amounts on the check stubs are correct. Therefore, the outstanding deposits and checks are those that are not checked.

Reinforcement Activity 1, Part A

An Accounting Cycle for a Proprietorship: Journalizing and Posting Transactions

Reinforcement activities strengthen the learning of accounting concepts and procedures. Reinforcement Activity 1 is a single problem divided into two parts. Part A includes learnings from Chapters 1 through 6. Part B includes learnings from Chapters 7 through 9. An accounting cycle is completed in Parts A and B for a single business—The Fitness Center.

THE FITNESS CENTER

In May of the current year, Gail Davis starts a service business called The Fitness Center. The business provides exercise facilities for its clients. In addition, Miss Davis, a professional dietician, offers diet and exercise counseling for clients who request her assistance. The business rents the facilities with which it operates, pays the utilities, and is responsible for maintenance. The Fitness Center charges clients for each visit.

CHART OF ACCOUNTS

The Fitness Center uses the following chart of accounts.

THE FITNESS CENTER Chart of Accounts	
Balance Sheet Accounts	**Income Statement Accounts**
(100) ASSETS	(400) REVENUE
110 Cash	410 Sales
120 Petty Cash	
130 Supplies	(500) EXPENSES
140 Prepaid Insurance	510 Advertising Expense
	520 Insurance Expense
(200) LIABILITIES	530 Miscellaneous Expense
210 Dunnel Supplies	540 Rent Expense
220 Morgan Office Supplies	550 Repair Expense
	560 Supplies Expense
(300) OWNER'S EQUITY	570 Utilities Expense
310 Gail Davis, Capital	
320 Gail Davis, Drawing	
330 Income Summary	

RECORDING TRANSACTIONS

Instructions: 1. Journalize the following transactions completed during May of the current year. Use page 1 of the journal. Source documents are abbreviated as follows: check stub, C; memorandum, M; receipt, R; calculator tape, T.

May 1. Received cash from owner as an investment, $15,000.00. R1.
     1. Paid cash for rent, $1,000.00. C1.
     2. Paid cash for electric bill, $45.00. C2.
     4. Paid cash for supplies, $500.00. C3.
     4. Paid cash for insurance, $960.00. C4.
     7. Bought supplies on account from Dunnel Supplies, $800.00. M1.
   11. Paid cash to establish a petty cash fund, $200.00. C5.
   12. Received cash from sales, $550.00. T12.
   13. Paid cash for repairs, $25.00. C6.
   13. Paid cash for miscellaneous expense, $35.00. C7.
   13. Received cash from sales, $185.00. T13.
   14. Paid cash for advertising, $100.00. C8.
   14. Received cash from sales, $335.00. T14.
   15. Paid cash to owner for personal use, $250.00. C9.
   15. Paid cash on account to Dunnel Supplies, $300.00. C10.
   15. Received cash from sales, $325.00. T15.
   18. Paid cash for miscellaneous expense, $100.00. C11.
   18. Received cash from sales, $295.00. T18.
   19. Received cash from sales, $155.00. T19.
   20. Paid cash for repairs, $125.00. C12.
   20. Bought supplies on account from Morgan Office Supplies, $150.00. M2.
   20. Received cash from sales, $195.00. T20.

    2. Prove and rule page 1 of the journal. Carry the column totals forward to page 2 of the journal.

    3. Post the separate amounts on each line of page 1 of the journal that need to be posted individually.

    4. Use page 2 of the journal. Journalize the following transactions.

May 21. Paid cash for water bill, $110.00. C13.
   21. Received cash from sales, $235.00. T21.
   25. Paid cash for supplies, $50.00. C14.
   25. Received cash from sales, $295.00. T25.
   26. Paid cash for miscellaneous expense, $25.00. C15.
   26. Received cash from sales, $300.00. T26.
   27. Received cash from sales, $195.00. T27.
   28. Paid cash for telephone bill, $210.00. C16.
   28. Received cash from sales, $275.00. T28.

    5. The Fitness Center received a bank statement dated May 27. The following information is obtained from the bank statement and from the records of the business. Prepare a bank statement reconciliation. Use May 29 as the date.

Bank statement balance...	$14,312.00
Bank service charge	3.00
Outstanding deposit, May 28	275.00

Outstanding checks:

No. 14	50.00
No. 15	25.00
No. 16	210.00
Checkbook balance on Check Stub No. 17	14,305.00

6. Continue using page 2 of the journal, and journalize the following transactions.

May 29. Received bank statement showing May bank service charge, $3.00. M3.
   29. Paid cash for supplies, $60.00. C17.
   29. Received cash from sales, $240.00. T29.
   31. Paid cash to replenish the petty cash fund, $17.00: miscellaneous expense, $10.00; repairs, $7.00. C18.
   31. Paid cash to owner for personal use, $250.00. C19.
   31. Received cash from sales, $280.00. T31.

7. Prove page 2 of the journal.

8. Prove cash. The beginning cash balance on May 1 is zero. The balance on the next unused check stub is $14,495.00.

9. Rule page 2 of the journal.

10. Post the separate amounts on each line of page 2 of the journal that need to be posted individually.

11. Post the column totals on page 2 of the journal.

The general ledger prepared in Reinforcement Activity 1, Part A, is needed to complete Reinforcement Activity 1, Part B.

Work Sheet for a Service Business

ENABLING PERFORMANCE TASKS

After studying Chapter 7, you will be able to:
a. Define accounting terms related to a work sheet for a service business organized as a proprietorship.
b. Identify accounting concepts and practices related to a work sheet for a service business organized as a proprietorship.
c. Plan adjustments for supplies and prepaid insurance.
d. Complete a work sheet for a service business organized as a proprietorship.
e. Identify selected procedures for finding and correcting errors in accounting records.

General ledger accounts contain information needed by managers and owners. Before the information can be used, however, it must be analyzed, summarized, and reported in a meaningful way. The accounting concept, *Consistent Reporting*, is applied when the same accounting procedures are followed in the same way in each accounting period. *(CONCEPT: Consistent Reporting)* For example, in one year a delivery business might report the number of deliveries made. The next year the same business reports the amount of revenue received for the deliveries made. The information for the two years cannot be compared because the business has not been consistent in reporting information about deliveries.

FISCAL PERIODS

The length of time for which a business summarizes and reports financial information is called a fiscal period. A fiscal period is also known as an accounting period. Businesses usually select a period of time, such as a month, six months, or a year, for which to summarize and report financial information. The accounting concept, *Accounting Period Cycle*, is applied when changes in financial information are reported for a specific period of time in the form of financial statements. *(CONCEPT: Accounting Period Cycle)* Each business chooses a fiscal period length that meets its needs. Because federal and state tax reports are based on one year, most businesses use a one-year fiscal period. However, because Rugcare is a new business, Mr. Furman wishes to have financial information reported frequently to help him make decisions. For this reason, Rugcare uses a one-month fiscal period.

A fiscal period can begin on any date. However, most businesses begin their fiscal periods on the first day of a month. Rugcare started business on August 1. Therefore, Rugcare's monthly fiscal period is for the period from August 1 through August 31, inclusive. Another business might use a one-year fiscal period from August 1 of one year through July 31 of the next year. Many businesses use a calendar year starting on January 1 and ending on December 31. Businesses often choose a one-year fiscal period that ends during a period of low business activity. In this way, the end-of-year accounting work comes at a time when other business activities are the lightest. For example, a store with a large volume of Christmas holiday sales might prefer to begin its fiscal period on February 1 or March 1.

> Most individuals use a one-year fiscal period that begins on January 1 and ends on December 31. This fiscal period corresponds to the period for which they must file income tax returns for the federal and state governments. However, individuals may use a different fiscal period if approved by the Internal Revenue Service.

Financial information may be analyzed, summarized, and reported on any date a business needs the information. However, financial information is always summarized and reported at the end of a fiscal period.

WORK SHEET

A columnar accounting form used to summarize the general ledger information needed to prepare financial statements is called a work sheet.

Accountants use a work sheet for four reasons. (1) To summarize general ledger account balances to prove that debits equal credits. (2) To plan needed changes to general ledger accounts to bring account balances up to date. (3) To separate general ledger account balances according to the financial statements to be prepared. (4) To figure the amount of net income or net loss for a fiscal period.

Journals and ledgers are permanent records of a business and are usually prepared in ink. However, a work sheet is a planning tool and is not considered a permanent accounting record. Therefore, a work sheet is prepared in pencil.

Preparing the heading of a work sheet

The heading on a work sheet consists of three lines. (1) Name of the business. (2) Name of the report. (3) Date of the report. The heading for Rugcare's work sheet is shown in Illustration 7-1.

Rugcare
Work Sheet
For Month Ended August 31, 19--

Illustration 7-1
Heading on a work sheet

The date on Rugcare's work sheet indicates that the work sheet covers the 31 days from August 1 through and including August 31. If the work sheet were for a calendar year fiscal period, it might have a date stated as *For Year Ended December 31, 19--*. (CONCEPT: *Accounting Period Cycle*)

Preparing a trial balance on a work sheet

The equality of debits and credits in the general ledger must be proved. The total of all debit account balances must equal the total of all credit account balances. A proof of the equality of debits and credits in a general ledger is called a trial balance. Rugcare prepares a trial balance on a work sheet. Rugcare's August 31 trial balance on a work sheet is shown in Illustration 7-2.

Information for the trial balance is taken from the general ledger. General ledger account titles are listed on a trial balance in the same order as listed on the chart of accounts. All the account titles are listed, even if some accounts do not have balances. The accounts that do not have balances in the Trial Balance columns will be needed in other parts of the work sheet.

Seven steps are used in preparing a trial balance on a work sheet.

1 Write the general ledger account titles in the work sheet's Account Title column.

2 Write the general ledger account debit balances in the Trial Balance Debit column. Write the general ledger account credit balances in the Trial Balance Credit column. If an account does not have a balance, the space in the Trial Balance columns is left blank.

Illustration 7-2
Trial balance on a work
sheet

	ACCOUNT TITLE	TRIAL BALANCE	
		DEBIT	CREDIT

Rugcare

Work Sheet

For Month Ended August 31, 19--

	ACCOUNT TITLE	TRIAL BALANCE DEBIT	TRIAL BALANCE CREDIT
1	Cash	8 2 7 2 00	
2	Petty Cash	2 0 0 00	
3	Supplies	4 9 3 1 00	
4	Prepaid Insurance	1 2 0 0 00	
5	Butler Cleaning Supplies		1 3 6 0 00
6	Dale Office Supplies		2 0 0 00
7	Ben Furman, Capital		10 0 0 0 00
8	Ben Furman, Drawing	6 0 0 00	
9	Income Summary		
10	Sales		4 2 9 1 00
11	Advertising Expense	6 8 00	
12	Insurance Expense		
13	Miscellaneous Expense	1 0 5 00	
14	Rent Expense	2 5 0 00	
15	Repair Expense	1 1 0 00	
16	Supplies Expense		
17	Utilities Expense	1 1 5 00	
18		15 8 5 1 00	15 8 5 1 00
19			
20			
21			
22			
23			
24			
25			
26			

3 Rule a single line across the two Trial Balance columns below the last line on which an account title is written. This single line shows that the two columns are to be added.

4 Add both the Trial Balance Debit and Credit columns. Use a calculator if one is available. For Rugcare's work sheet, the totals are Debit, $15,851.00 and Credit, $15,851.00.

5 Check the equality of the two amount column totals. If the two column totals are the same, then debits equal credits in the general ledger accounts. Because the totals, $15,851.00, are the same, the Trial Balance columns on Rugcare's work sheet are in balance.

If the two column totals are not the same and the trial balance is not in balance, recheck the Trial Balance columns to find the error. Other parts of a work sheet are not completed until the Trial Balance columns are proved. Suggestions for locating errors are described later in this chapter.

6 Write each column's total, *$15,851.00*, below the single line.

7 Rule double lines across both Trial Balance columns. The double lines mean that the Trial Balance column totals have been verified as correct.

Planning adjustments on a work sheet

Sometimes a business will pay cash for an expense in one fiscal period, but the expense is not used until a later period. The expense should be reported in the same fiscal period that it is used to produce revenue. The accounting concept, *Matching Expenses with Revenue*, is applied when revenue from business activities and expenses associated with earning that revenue are recorded in the same accounting period. For example, Rugcare buys supplies in quantity in August, but some of the supplies are not used until September. Only the value of the supplies used in August should be reported as expenses in August. In this way, August revenue and the supplies expense associated with earning the August revenue are recorded in the same accounting period. *(CONCEPT: Matching Expenses with Revenue)*

In order to give accurate information on financial statements, some general ledger accounts must be brought up to date at the end of a fiscal period. For example, Rugcare debits an asset account, Supplies, each time supplies are bought. Supplies on hand are items of value owned by a business until the supplies are used. The value of supplies that are used becomes an expense to the business. However, recording an expense each time an individual supply, such as a pencil, is used would be impractical. Therefore, on August 31 the balance of the asset account, Supplies, is the value of all supplies bought rather than the value of only the supplies that have not been used. The amount of supplies that have been used must be deducted from the asset account, Supplies, and recorded in the expense account, Supplies Expense.

Likewise, the amount of insurance that has been used during the fiscal period is also an expense of the business. When the insurance premium for a year of insurance coverage is paid, the entire amount is debited to an asset account, Prepaid Insurance. Each day during August a portion of the insurance coverage is used. The value of the insurance used is an expense of the business. However, recording each day's amount of insurance used is impractical. Therefore, at the end of a fiscal period, the balance of Prepaid

Insurance is the value of all insurance coverage bought, rather than the value of only the insurance coverage that still remains. The amount of the insurance coverage used must be deducted from the asset account, Prepaid Insurance, and recorded in the expense account, Insurance Expense.

Changes recorded on a work sheet to update general ledger accounts at the end of a fiscal period are called adjustments. The assets of a business, such as supplies and prepaid insurance, are used to earn revenue. The portion of the assets consumed in order to earn revenue become expenses of the business. The portions consumed are no longer assets but are now expenses. Therefore, adjustments must be made to both the asset and expense accounts for supplies and insurance. After the adjustments are made, the expenses incurred to earn revenue are reported in the same fiscal period as the revenue is earned and reported. *(CONCEPT: Matching Expenses with Revenue)*

A work sheet is used to plan adjustments. Changes are not made in general ledger accounts until adjustments are journalized and posted. The accuracy of the planning for adjustments is checked on a work sheet before adjustments are actually journalized.

Procedures for journalizing Rugcare's adjustments are described in Chapter 9.

Supplies adjustment. On August 31, before adjustments, the balance of Supplies is $4,931.00, and the balance of Supplies Expense is zero, as shown in the T accounts.

On August 31 Mr. Furman counted the supplies on hand and found that the value of supplies still unused on that date was $2,284.00. The value of the supplies used is calculated as shown below.

BEFORE ADJUSTMENT

Supplies

Aug. 31 Bal.   4,931.00

Supplies Expense

Supplies Account Balance, August 31	−	Supplies On Hand, August 31	=	Supplies Used During August
$4,931.00	−	$2,284.00	=	$2,647.00

Four questions are asked in analyzing the adjustment for the asset account, Supplies.

1. What is the balance of Supplies?.......................... $4,931.00
2. What should the balance be for this account? $2,284.00
3. What must be done to correct the account balance? Decrease $2,647.00
4. What adjustment is made?
   Debit Supplies Expense $2,647.00
   Credit Supplies $2,647.00

AFTER ADJUSTMENT

Supplies Expense

Adj. (a)   2,647.00

Supplies

| Aug. 31 Bal. | 4,931.00 | Adj. (a) | 2,647.00 |
| *(New Bal.* | *2,284.00)* | | |

The effect of this adjustment is shown in the T accounts. The expense account, Supplies Expense, is increased by a debit, $2,647.00, the value of supplies used. The balance of Supplies Expense, $2,647.00, is the value of supplies used during the fiscal period from August 1 to August 31. *(CONCEPT: Matching Expenses with Revenue)*

The asset account, Supplies, is decreased by a credit, $2,647.00, the value of supplies used. The debit balance, $4,931.00, *less* the credit adjustment, $2,647.00, *equals* the new balance, $2,284.00. The new balance of Supplies is the same as the value of supplies on hand on August 31.

Rugcare's supplies adjustment is shown on lines 3 and 16 of the work sheet in Illustration 7-3.

Illustration 7-3
Supplies adjustment on a work sheet

	ACCOUNT TITLE	TRIAL BALANCE		ADJUSTMENTS	
		DEBIT	CREDIT	DEBIT	CREDIT
3	Supplies	4 9 3 1 00			(a)2 6 4 7 00
16	Supplies Expense			(a)2 6 4 7 00	
17					

Three steps are used to record the supplies adjustment on the work sheet.

1 Write the debit amount, $2,647.00, in the work sheet's Adjustments Debit column on the line with the account title Supplies Expense (line 16).

2 Write the credit amount, $2,647.00, in the Adjustments Credit column on the line with the account title Supplies (line 3).

3 Label the two parts of this adjustment with a small letter *a* in parentheses *(a)*. The letter *a* identifies the debit and credit amounts as part of the same adjustment.

Prepaid insurance adjustment. When Rugcare pays for insurance, the amount is debited to the asset account, Prepaid Insurance. However, to debit Insurance Expense daily for the amount of that day's insurance premium used is impractical. Therefore, at the end of a fiscal period, Rugcare's prepaid insurance account does not show the actual value of the remaining prepaid insurance.

On August 31, before adjustments, the balance of Prepaid Insurance is $1,200.00, and the balance of Insurance Expense is zero, as shown in the T accounts.

On August 31 Mr. Furman checked the insurance records and found that the value of insurance coverage remaining was $1,100.00. The value of insurance coverage used during the fiscal period is calculated as shown below.

BEFORE ADJUSTMENT
Insurance Expense

Prepaid Insurance
Aug. 31 Bal.   1,200.00

Prepaid Insurance Balance, August 31	−	Insurance Coverage Remaining Unused, August 31	=	Insurance Coverage Used During August
$1,200.00	−	$1,100.00	=	$100.00

Four questions are asked in analyzing the adjustment for the asset account, Prepaid Insurance.

1. What is the balance of Prepaid Insurance $1,200.00
2. What should the balance be for this account $1,100.00
3. What must be done to correct the account balance? Decrease $ 100.00
4. What adjustment is made?
   Debit Insurance Expense .... $ 100.00
   Credit Prepaid Insurance .... $ 100.00

AFTER ADJUSTMENT

Insurance Expense

Adj. (b) 100.00	

Prepaid Insurance

Aug. 31 1,200.00	Adj. (b) 100.00
(New Bal. 1,100.00)	

The effect of this adjustment is shown in the T accounts.

The expense account, Insurance Expense, is increased by a debit, $100.00, the value of insurance used. The balance of Insurance Expense, $100.00, is the value of insurance coverage used from August 1 to August 31. *(CONCEPT: Matching Expenses with Revenue)*

The asset account, Prepaid Insurance, is decreased by a credit, $100.00, the value of insurance used. The debit balance, $1,200.00, *less* the credit adjustment, $100.00, *equals* the new balance, $1,100.00. The new balance of Prepaid Insurance is the same as the amount of insurance coverage unused on August 31.

Rugcare's prepaid insurance adjustment is shown on lines 4 and 12 of the work sheet in Illustration 7-4.

	ACCOUNT TITLE	TRIAL BALANCE		ADJUSTMENTS	
		DEBIT	CREDIT	DEBIT	CREDIT
1	Cash	8 2 7 2 00			
2	Petty Cash	2 0 0 00			
3	Supplies	4 9 3 1 00			(a) 2 6 4 7 00
4	Prepaid Insurance	1 2 0 0 00			(b) 1 0 0 00
12	Insurance Expense			(b) 1 0 0 00	
13	Miscellaneous Expense	1 0 5 00			
14	Rent Expense	2 5 0 00			
15	Repair Expense	1 1 0 00			
16	Supplies Expense			(a) 2 6 4 7 00	
17	Utilities Expense	1 1 5 00			
18		15 8 5 1 00	15 8 5 1 00	2 7 4 7 00	2 7 4 7 00
19					

Illustration 7-4
Prepaid insurance
adjustment on a work
sheet

Three steps are used to record the prepaid insurance adjustment on a work sheet.

1 Write the debit amount, *$100.00*, in the work sheet's Adjustments Debit column on the line with the account title Insurance Expense (line 12).

2 Write the credit amount, *$100.00*, in the Adjustments Credit column on the line with the account title Prepaid Insurance (line 4).

3 Label the two parts of this adjustment with a small letter *b* in parentheses *(b)*. The letter *b* identifies the debit and credit amounts as part of the same adjustment.

Proving the adjustments columns of a work sheet. After all adjustments are recorded in a work sheet's Adjustments columns, the equality of debits and credits for the two columns is proved. Rugcare's completed Adjustments columns are shown in Illustration 7-4.

Three steps are used in proving a work sheet's Adjustments columns.

1 Rule a single line across the two Adjustments columns on the same line as the single line for the Trial Balance columns.

2 Add both the Adjustments Debit and Credit columns. If the two column totals are the same, then debits equal credits for these two columns, and the work sheet's Adjustments columns are in balance. On Rugcare's work sheet, the Adjustments Debit and Credit column totals are $2,747.00. Therefore, the Adjustments columns on Rugcare's work sheet are in balance. Write each column's total below the single line.

 If the two Adjustments column totals are not the same, the Adjustments columns are rechecked and errors corrected before completing the work sheet.

3 Rule double lines across both Adjustments columns. The double lines mean that the totals have been verified as correct.

Extending financial statement information on a work sheet

At the end of each fiscal period, Rugcare prepares two financial statements from information on a work sheet. *(CONCEPT: Accounting Period Cycle)* A financial statement that reports assets, liabilities, and owner's equity on a specific date is known as a balance sheet. A financial statement showing the revenue and expenses for a fiscal period is called an income statement. The up-to-date account balances on a work sheet are extended to columns for the two financial statements.

Extending balance sheet account balances on a work sheet. The balance sheet accounts are the asset, liability, and owner's equity accounts. Up-to-date balance sheet account balances are extended to the Balance Sheet Debit and Credit columns of the work sheet. The extension of Rugcare's balance sheet account balances is shown on lines 1 through 9 of the work sheet in Illustration 7-5.

Three steps are used in extending balance sheet items on a work sheet.

1 Extend the up-to-date balance of each asset account.

Rugcare

Work Sheet

For Month Ended August 31, 19--

		TRIAL BALANCE		ADJUSTMENTS		INCOME STATEMENT		BALANCE SHEET		
	ACCOUNT TITLE	DEBIT	CREDIT	DEBIT	CREDIT	DEBIT	CREDIT	DEBIT	CREDIT	
1	Cash	8 2 7 2 00						8 2 7 2 00		1
2	Petty Cash	2 0 0 00						2 0 0 00		2
3	Supplies	4 9 3 1 00			(a) 2 6 4 7 00			2 2 8 4 00		3
4	Prepaid Insurance	1 2 0 0 00			(b) 1 0 0 00			1 1 0 0 00		4
5	Butler Cleaning Supplies		1 3 6 0 00						1 3 6 0 00	5
6	Dale Office Supplies		2 0 0 00						2 0 0 00	6
7	Ben Furman, Capital		10 0 0 0 00						10 0 0 0 00	7
8	Ben Furman, Drawing	6 0 0 00						6 0 0 00		8
9	Income Summary									9
10										10

Illustration 7-5
Balance sheet account balances extended on a work sheet

- The balance of Cash in the Trial Balance Debit column is up to date because no adjustment affects this account. Extend the balance of Cash, *$8,272.00*, to the Balance Sheet Debit column. Balances of all asset accounts not affected by adjustments are extended in the same way.
- The balance of Supplies in the Trial Balance Debit column is not up to date because it is affected by an adjustment. Figure the up-to-date adjusted balance. The debit balance, $4,931.00, *minus* the credit adjustment, $2,647.00, *equals* the up-to-date adjusted balance, $2,284.00. Extend the up-to-date balance, *$2,284.00*, to the Balance Sheet Debit column. The same procedure is used to figure and extend the up-to-date adjusted balance of the other asset account affected by an adjustment, Prepaid Insurance.

2   Extend the up-to-date balance of each liability account.

- The balance of Butler Cleaning Supplies is the up-to-date balance because no adjustment affects this account. Extend the up-to-date balance, *$1,360.00*, to the Balance Sheet Credit column. The balance of the other liability account is extended in the same way.

3   Extend the up-to-date balances of the owner's equity accounts.

- The balance of Ben Furman, Capital in the Trial Balance Credit column is the up-to-date balance because no adjustment affects this account. Extend the balance, *$10,000.00*, to the Balance Sheet Credit column.
- The balance of Ben Furman, Drawing in the Trial Balance Debit column is the up-to-date balance because no adjustment affects this account. Extend the balance, *$600.00*, to the Balance Sheet Debit column.

• Income Summary has no balance in the Trial Balance columns. There-fore, no amount needs to be extended for this account.

Extending income statement account balances on a work sheet. Rug-care's income statement accounts are the revenue and expense accounts. The extension of income statement account balances is shown on lines 10 through 17 of the work sheet in Illustration 7-6.

			Rugcare						
			Work Sheet						
			For Month Ended August 31, 19--						
		1	2	3	4	5	6	7	8
	ACCOUNT TITLE	TRIAL BALANCE		ADJUSTMENTS		INCOME STATEMENT		BALANCE SHEET	
		DEBIT	CREDIT	DEBIT	CREDIT	DEBIT	CREDIT	DEBIT	CREDIT
10	Sales		4 2 9 1 00				4 2 9 1 00		
11	Advertising Expense	6 8 00				6 8 00			
12	Insurance Expense			(b) 1 0 0 00		1 0 0 00			
13	Miscellaneous Expense	1 0 5 00				1 0 5 00			
14	Rent Expense	2 5 0 00				2 5 0 00			
15	Repair Expense	1 1 0 00				1 1 0 00			
16	Supplies Expense			(a) 2 6 4 7 00		2 6 4 7 00			
17	Utilities Expense	1 1 5 00				1 1 5 00			
18		1 5 8 5 1 00	1 5 8 5 1 00	2 7 4 7 00	2 7 4 7 00				
19									

Two steps are used in extending income statement accounts on a work sheet.

Illustration 7-6
Income statement account balances extended on a work sheet

1 Extend the up-to-date balance of the revenue account.

• The balance of Sales in the Trial Balance Credit column is the up-to-date balance because no adjustment affects this account. Extend the balance, $4,291.00, to the Income Statement Credit column.

2 Extend the up-to-date balance of each expense account.

• The balance of Advertising Expense in the Trial Balance Debit column is the up-to-date balance because no adjustment affects this account. Extend the balance, $68.00, to the Income Statement Debit column. Balances of all expense accounts not affected by adjustments are ex-tended in the same way.

• The balance of Insurance Expense in the Trial Balance columns is zero. This zero balance is not the up-to-date balance because this account is affected by an adjustment. Figure the up-to-date adjusted balance.

- The debit balance, $0.00, *plus* the debit adjustment, $100.00, *equals* the adjusted balance, $100.00. Extend the up-to-date adjusted debit balance, *$100.00*, to the Income Statement Debit column. The same procedure is used to figure and extend the up-to-date adjusted balance of each expense account affected by an adjustment.

Figuring and recording net income on a work sheet. The difference between total revenue and total expenses when total revenue is greater is called net income. Rugcare's August net income is shown on line 19 of the work sheet in Illustration 7-7.

Illustration 7-7
Completed work sheet

	ACCOUNT TITLE	1 TRIAL BALANCE DEBIT	2 TRIAL BALANCE CREDIT	3 ADJUSTMENTS DEBIT	4 ADJUSTMENTS CREDIT	5 INCOME STATEMENT DEBIT	6 INCOME STATEMENT CREDIT	7 BALANCE SHEET DEBIT	8 BALANCE SHEET CREDIT	
1	Cash	8 2 7 2 00						8 2 7 2 00		1
2	Petty Cash	2 0 0 00						2 0 0 00		2
3	Supplies	4 9 3 1 00			(a) 2 6 4 7 00			2 2 8 4 00		3
4	Prepaid Insurance	1 2 0 0 00			(b) 1 0 0 00			1 1 0 0 00		4
5	Butler Cleaning Supplies		1 3 6 0 00						1 3 6 0 00	5
6	Dale Office Supplies		2 0 0 00						2 0 0 00	6
7	Ben Furman, Capital		10 0 0 0 00						10 0 0 0 00	7
8	Ben Furman, Drawing	6 0 0 00						6 0 0 00		8
9	Income Summary									9
10	Sales		4 2 9 1 00				4 2 9 1 00			10
11	Advertising Expense	6 8 00				6 8 00				11
12	Insurance Expense			(b) 1 0 0 00		1 0 0 00				12
13	Miscellaneous Expense	1 0 5 00				1 0 5 00				13
14	Rent Expense	2 5 0 00				2 5 0 00				14
15	Repair Expense	1 1 0 00				1 1 0 00				15
16	Supplies Expense			(a) 2 6 4 7 00		2 6 4 7 00				16
17	Utilities Expense	1 1 5 00				1 1 5 00				17
18		15 8 5 1 00	15 8 5 1 00	2 7 4 7 00	2 7 4 7 00	3 3 9 5 00	4 2 9 1 00	12 4 5 6 00	11 5 6 0 00	18
19	Net Income					8 9 6 00			8 9 6 00	19
20						4 2 9 1 00	4 2 9 1 00	12 4 5 6 00	12 4 5 6 00	20
21										21

Rugcare
Work Sheet
For Month Ended August 31, 19--

Five steps are used in figuring net income on a work sheet.

1 Rule a single line across the four Income Statement and Balance Sheet columns.

2 Add both the Income Statement and Balance Sheet columns. Write the totals below the single line.

3 Figure the net income. Rugcare's net income is calculated as shown below.

Income Statement Credit Column Total	−	Income Statement Debit Column Total	=	Net Income
$4,291.00	−	$3,395.00	=	$896.00

Rugcare's August work sheet shows a net income because the Income Statement Credit column (revenue) exceeds the Income Statement Debit column (expenses).

4 Write the amount of net income, *$896.00*, below the Income Statement Debit column total. Write the words, *Net Income*, on the same line in the Account Title column.

5 Extend the amount of net income, *$896.00*, to the Balance Sheet Credit column on the same line as the words *Net Income*. The owner's equity account, Ben Furman, Capital, is increased by a credit. Therefore, the net income amount is extended to the Balance Sheet Credit column.

Totaling and ruling a work sheet. Four steps are used in totaling and ruling a work sheet.

1 Rule a single line across the four Income Statement and Balance Sheet columns just below the net income amounts.

2 Add the subtotal and net income amount for each column to get proving totals for the Income Statement and Balance Sheet columns. Write the proving totals below the single line. Proving totals are used to determine that the debits equal credits for each pair of column totals.

3 Check the equality of the proving totals for each pair of columns.
- As shown on line 20 of the work sheet in Illustration 7-7, the proving totals for the Income Statement columns, $4,291.00, are the same.
- As shown on line 20 of the work sheet in Illustration 7-7, the proving totals for the Balance Sheet columns, $12,456.00, are the same.

4 Rule double lines across the Income Statement and Balance Sheet columns. The double lines mean that the totals have been verified as correct.

A summary of preparing a work sheet is shown on the Work Sheet Overlay on pages 146A through 146C.

Figuring and recording a net loss on a work sheet. Rugcare's completed work sheet shows a net income. However, a business might have a net loss to report. The difference between total revenue and total expenses when total expenses is greater is called a net loss. A net loss on a work sheet is shown in Illustration 7-8.

			5	6	7	8	
	ACCOUNT TITLE		**INCOME STATEMENT**		**BALANCE SHEET**		
			DEBIT	CREDIT	DEBIT	CREDIT	
19			2 0 0 0 00	1 9 0 0 00	5 4 0 0 00	5 5 0 0 00	19
20	*Net Loss*			1 0 0 00	1 0 0 00		20
21			2 0 0 0 00	2 0 0 0 00	5 5 0 0 00		21
22							22
23							23

Illustration 7-8
Net loss shown on a work
sheet

Six steps are used in completing a work sheet with a net loss.

1 Rule a single line across the four Income Statement and Balance Sheet columns.

2 Add both the Income Statement and Balance Sheet columns. Write the totals below the single line.

3 The net loss is calculated as shown below.

Income Statement Debit Column Total	–	Income Statement Credit Column Total	=	Net Loss
$2,000.00	–	$1,900.00	=	$100.00

The Income Statement Debit column total (expenses) is greater than the Income Statement Credit column total (revenue). Therefore, because expenses exceed revenue, there is a net loss.

4 Write the amount of net loss, *$100.00*, below the Income Statement Credit column total. Write the words, *Net Loss*, on the same line in the Account Title column.

5 Extend the amount of net loss, *$100.00*, to the Balance Sheet Debit column on the same line as the words *Net Loss*. The owner's capital account is decreased by a debit. Therefore, a net loss is extended to the Balance Sheet Debit column.

6 Total and rule the work sheet using the same steps as when there is net income.

FINDING AND CORRECTING ERRORS

Some errors in accounting records are not discovered until a work sheet is prepared. For example, a debit to the supplies account may not have been posted from a journal to the general ledger supplies account. The omission may not be discovered until the work sheet's trial balance does not balance. Also, information may be transferred incorrectly from general ledger accounts to the work sheet's trial balance. Additional errors may be made on a work sheet, such as recording adjustment information incorrectly or adding columns incorrectly.   In addition, errors may be made in extending amounts to the Income Statement and Balance Sheet columns.

Any errors found on a work sheet must be corrected before any further work is completed. If an incorrect amount is found on a work sheet, erase the error and replace it with the correct amount. If an amount is written in an incorrect column, erase the amount and record it in the correct column. If column totals do not balance, add the columns again.

Checking for typical arithmetic errors

When two column totals are not in balance, subtract the smaller total from the larger total to find the difference. Check the difference between the two amounts against the following guides.

1 *The difference is 1, such as $.01, $.10, $1.00, or $10.00.* For example, if the totals of the two columns are Debit, $12,542.00 and Credit, $12,543.00, the difference between the two columns is $1.00. The error is most likely in addition. Add the columns again.

2 *The difference can be divided evenly by 2.* For example, the difference between two column totals is $48.00. The difference, $48.00, *divided* by 2 *equals* $24.00 with no remainder. Look for a $24.00 amount in the Trial Balance columns of the work sheet. If the amount is found, check to make sure it has been recorded in the correct Trial Balance Debit or Credit column. A $24.00 debit amount recorded in a credit column results in a difference between column totals of $48.00. If the error is not found on the work sheet, check the general ledger accounts and journal entries. An entry for $24.00 may have been recorded in an incorrect column in the journal or in an account.

3 *The difference can be divided evenly by 9.* For example, the difference between two columns is $45.00. The difference, $45.00, *divided* by 9 *equals* $5.00 with no remainder. When the difference can be divided equally by 9, look for transposed numbers such as 54 written as 45 or 19 written as 91. Also, check for a "slide." A "slide" occurs when numbers are moved to the right or left in an amount column. For example, $12.00 is recorded as $120.00 or $350.00 is recorded as $35.00.

4 *The difference is an omitted amount.* Look for an amount equal to the difference. If the difference is $50.00, look for an account balance of $50.00 that has not been extended. Look for any $50.00 amount on the work sheet and determine if it has been handled correctly. Look in the accounts and journals for a $50.00 amount, and check if that amount has been handled correctly. Failure to record a $50.00 account balance will make a work sheet's Trial Balance column totals differ by $50.00.

Checking for errors in the trial balance columns

1 Have all general ledger account balances been copied in the Trial Balance columns correctly?

2 Have all general ledger account balances been recorded in the correct Trial Balance column?

Correct any errors found and add the columns again.

Checking for errors in the adjustments columns

1 Do the debits equal the credits for each adjustment? Use the small letters that label each part of an adjustment to help check accuracy and equality of debits and credits.

2 Is the amount for each adjustment correct?

Correct any errors found and add the columns again.

Checking for errors in the income statement and balance sheet columns

1 Has each amount been copied correctly when extended to the Income Statement or Balance Sheet column?

2 Has each account balance been extended to the correct Income Statement or Balance Sheet column?

3 Has the net income or net loss been figured correctly?

4 Has the net income or net loss been recorded in the correct Income Statement or Balance Sheet column?

Correct any errors found and add the columns again.

Checking for errors in posting to general ledger accounts

Sometimes a pair of work sheet columns do not balance, and an error cannot be found on the work sheet. If this is the situation, check the posting from the journal to the general ledger accounts. As each item in an account or a journal entry is verified, a check mark should be placed next to it. The check mark indicates that the item has been checked for accuracy.

1 Have all amounts that need to be posted actually been posted from the journal?

• For an amount that has not been posted, complete the posting to the correct account.

• In all cases where posting is corrected, refigure the account balance and correct it on the work sheet.

When an omitted posting is recorded as described above, the dates in the general ledger accounts may be out of order.

2 Have all amounts been posted to the correct accounts?

- For an amount posted to the wrong account, draw a line through the entire incorrect entry. Refigure the account balance.
- Record the posting in the correct account. Refigure the account balance, and correct the work sheet. Make the correction in the general ledger accounts, as shown in Illustration 7-9.

Illustration 7-9
Correcting an error in posting to the wrong account

ACCOUNT *Supplies*					ACCOUNT NO. *130*		
DATE	ITEM	POST. REF.	DEBIT	CREDIT	BALANCE		
					DEBIT	CREDIT	
Feb. 1		1	4 0 0 00		4 0 0 00		
25		2	9 0 00		4 9 0 00		
12		1	5 0 00		5 4 0 00		

ACCOUNT *Prepaid Insurance*					ACCOUNT NO. *140*		
DATE	ITEM	POST. REF.	DEBIT	CREDIT	BALANCE		
					DEBIT	CREDIT	
Feb. 9		1	6 0 0 00		6 0 0 00		
~~12~~		~~1~~	~~5 0 00~~		~~6 5 0 00~~		

Errors in permanent records should *never* be erased. Erasures in permanent records raise questions about whether important financial information has been altered.

3 Have all amounts been written correctly? Have all amounts been posted to the correct Debit or Credit columns of an account?

- If an amount has been written incorrectly, draw a line through the incorrect amount. Write the correct amount just above the correction in the same space. Refigure the account balance, and correct the account balance on the work sheet. Correcting an error in writing an amount incorrectly is shown on the first line of the utilities expense account in Illustration 7-10.

• For an amount posted to the wrong amount column, draw a line through the incorrect item in the account. Record the posting in the correct amount column. Refigure the account balance, and correct the work sheet. Correcting an error in posting to a wrong amount column is shown on the second line of the utilities expense account in Illustration 7-10.

ACCOUNT *Utilities Expense*							ACCOUNT NO. *570*	
DATE	ITEM	POST. REF.	DEBIT	CREDIT	BALANCE			
					DEBIT		CREDIT	
Sept. 8		1	7 0 00		~~7 0 0 00~~ *7 0 0 00*			
17		1	2 7 00	~~2 7 00~~	~~6 7 3 00~~ *6 7 3 00*			

Illustration 7-10
Correcting an amount written incorrectly and an error in posting to the wrong column of an account

Checking for errors in journal entries

1 Do debits equal credits in each journal entry?

2 Is each journal entry amount recorded in the correct journal column?

3 Is information in the Account Title column correct for each journal entry?

4 Are all of the journal amount column totals correct?

5 Does the sum of debit column totals equal the sum of credit column totals in the journal?

6 Have all transactions been recorded?

Some suggestions for correcting errors in journal entries are described in Chapter 4.

Preventing errors

The best way to prevent errors is to work carefully at all times. Check the work at each step in an accounting procedure. Most errors occur in doing the required arithmetic, especially in adding columns. When possible, use a calculator to add columns. When an error is discovered, do no more work until the cause of the error is found and corrections are made.

■ ACCOUNTING TERMS

What is the meaning of each of the following?

1. fiscal period
2. work sheet
3. trial balance
4. adjustments
5. income statement
6. net income
7. net loss

■ QUESTIONS FOR INDIVIDUAL STUDY

1. What are typical lengths of fiscal periods?
2. Which accounting concept is being applied when a business summarizes and reports financial information for a fiscal period?
3. What are four reasons for preparing a work sheet?
4. Why is a work sheet prepared in pencil?
5. What are the three lines of a work sheet heading?
6. How is the equality of debits and credits proved in a general ledger?
7. Why is an adjustment for supplies planned at the end of a fiscal period?
8. What four questions are asked in analyzing the supplies adjustment?
9. What accounts are affected, and how, by the adjustment for supplies?
10. After a supplies adjustment, what does the supplies account balance represent?
11. What accounts are affected, and how, by the adjustment for prepaid insurance?
12. Why are the Adjustments columns on a work sheet totaled?
13. What two financial statements are prepared from information on a work sheet?
14. What account balances are extended to the Balance Sheet columns on Rugcare's work sheet?
15. What account balances are extended to the Income Statement columns on Rugcare's work sheet?
16. If a work sheet shows a net income, in which two columns will the net income be recorded?
17. How are the amounts in the Income Statement and Balance Sheet columns of a work sheet proved?
18. If two work sheet column totals are not equal and the difference between the totals is one, what is the most likely error?
19. If two work sheet column totals are not equal and the difference between the totals is evenly divisible by nine, what is the most likely error?

■ CASES FOR MANAGEMENT DECISION

CASE 1 Peter Dowther owns a small business. At the end of a fiscal period, he does not make an adjustment for supplies. Are Mr. Dowther's accounting procedures correct? What effect will Mr. Dowther's procedures have on the business' financial reporting? Explain your answer.

CASE 2 When posting amounts from a journal to general ledger accounts, a $10.00 debit to Miscellaneous Expense is mistakenly posted as a debit to Repair Expense. Will this error be discovered when the work sheet is prepared? Explain.

CASE 3 When posting amounts from a journal to general ledger accounts, a $10.00 debit to Supplies is mistakenly posted as a credit to Utilities Expense. Will this error be discovered when the work sheet is prepared? Explain.

CASE 4 When extending amounts on a work sheet, the debit balance for Advertising Expense is extended to the Balance Sheet Debit column. Will this error be discovered when the work sheet is prepared? Explain.

■ DRILLS FOR UNDERSTANDING

DRILL 7-D1   Extending account balances on a work sheet

Use a form similar to the following.

	1	2		5	6	7	8
Account Title	Trial Balance			Income Statement		Balance Sheet	
	Debit	Credit		Debit	Credit	Debit	Credit
1. *Advertising Expense*	✓	✓		✓	✓	✓	✓

Instructions: 1. Write each of the following account titles in the Account Title column of the form.

1. Advertising Expense
2. Bell Supply
3. Cash
4. Miscellaneous Expense
5. Maria Dorn, Capital
6. Maria Dorn, Drawing

7. Prepaid Insurance
8. Rent Expense
9. Repair Expense
10. Sales
11. Supplies
12. Utilities Expense

    2. Place a check mark in either Column 1 or 2 to indicate the Trial Balance column on a work sheet in which each account's balance will appear.
    3. Place a check mark in Columns 5, 6, 7, or 8 to indicate the column to which each up-to-date account balance will be extended.

DRILL 7-D2   Figuring net income or net loss on a work sheet

The following column totals are from the work sheets of five different businesses.

Company	Income Statement		Balance Sheet	
	Debit	Credit	Debit	Credit
A	$9,000	$9,500	$35,500	$35,000
B	1,500	2,000	7,500	7,000
C	5,200	4,800	26,500	26,900
D	5,300	8,150	34,950	32,100
E	5,300	4,130	33,400	34,570

Use a form similar to the one on page 143. The amounts for Company A are given as an example.

Instructions: Complete the following for each company.
    1. Write the Income Statement and Balance Sheet column totals on line 1.
    2. Figure the amount of net income or net loss. Write the amount on line 2 in the correct columns. Label the amount as *Net Income* or *Net Loss*.

3. Add the amounts in each column. Write the totals on line 3.
4. Verify the accuracy of your proving totals.

	Income Statement		Balance Sheet	
	Debit	Credit	Debit	Credit
Company A				
1. Column Totals	$9,000	$9,500	$35,500	$35,000
2. *Net Income*	500			500
3. Proving Totals	9,500	9,500	35,500	35,500

APPLICATION PROBLEMS

PROBLEM 7-1 Completing a work sheet

On September 30 of the current year, CleanLawn has the following general ledger accounts and balances. The business uses a monthly fiscal period.

	Account Balances	
Account Titles	**Debit**	**Credit**
Cash.	$3,000.00	
Petty Cash	100.00	
Supplies	2,000.00	
Prepaid Insurance	900.00	
Bix Supplies		$ 600.00
OfficeWorld.		100.00
Dorothy Daily, Capital		4,100.00
Dorothy Daily, Drawing	200.00	
Income Summary	—	—
Sales		2,505.00
Advertising Expense.	75.00	
Insurance Expense	—	
Miscellaneous Expense	110.00	
Rent Expense.	600.00	
Repair Expense	180.00	
Supplies Expense	—	
Utilities Expense	140.00	

Instructions: 1. Prepare the heading and trial balance on a work sheet. Total and rule the Trial Balance columns.

2. Analyze the following adjustment information into debit and credit parts. Record the adjustments on the work sheet.

Adjustment Information, September 30

Supplies on hand	$1,100.00
Value of prepaid insurance	600.00

3. Total and rule the Adjustments columns.
4. Extend the up-to-date balances to the Balance Sheet or Income Statement columns.

5. Rule a single line across the Income Statement and Balance Sheet columns. Total each column. Figure and record the net income or net loss. Label the amount in the Account Title column.

6. Total and rule the Income Statement and Balance Sheet columns.

PROBLEM 7-2   Completing a work sheet

On October 31 of the current year, Village Service Co. has the following general ledger accounts and balances. The business uses a monthly fiscal period.

Account Titles	Account Balances	
	Debit	Credit
Cash...	$4,900.00	
Petty Cash	300.00	
Supplies	2,500.00	
Prepaid Insurance.............................	2,100.00	
National Supplies		$ 1,400.00
Office Distributors............................		1,200.00
Wensk Movies		800.00
Susan Haile, Capital..........................		6,000.00
Susan Haile, Drawing..........................	1,200.00	
Income Summary	—	
Sales		20,100.00
Advertising Expense...........................	4,200.00	
Insurance Expense.............................	—	
Miscellaneous Expense	600.00	
Rent Expense.................................	8,000.00	
Repair Expense...............................	2,400.00	
Supplies Expense	—	
Utilities Expense	3,300.00	

Instructions: 1. Prepare the heading and trial balance on a work sheet. Total and rule the Trial Balance columns.

2. Analyze the following adjustment information into debit and credit parts. Record the adjustments on the work sheet.

Adjustment Information, October 31

Supplies on hand	$1,500.00
Value of prepaid insurance	900.00

3. Total and rule the Adjustments columns.

4. Extend the up-to-date balances to the Balance Sheet or Income Statement columns.

5. Rule a single line across the Income Statement and Balance Sheet columns. Total each column. Figure and record the net income or net loss. Label the amount in the Account Title column.

6. Total and rule the Income Statement and Balance Sheet columns.

PROBLEM 7-3   Finding and correcting errors in accounting records

Paul Coty has completed the September monthly work sheet for his business, LeafyLift. The work sheet and general ledger accounts are given in the working papers accompanying this textbook.

Mr. Coty believes that he has made one or more errors in preparing the work sheet. He asks you to help him verify the work sheet.

Instructions: 1. Examine the work sheet and the general ledger accounts. Make a list of the errors you find.

  2. Correct any errors you find in the general ledger accounts.

  3. Prepare a corrected work sheet.

■ ENRICHMENT PROBLEMS

MASTERY PROBLEM 7-M   **Completing a work sheet**

On April 30 of the current year, FastGrow has the following general ledger accounts and balances. The business uses a monthly fiscal period.

Account Titles	Account Balances	
	Debit	Credit
Cash...	$5,800.00	
Petty Cash	200.00	
Supplies	4,000.00	
Prepaid Insurance............................	1,000.00	
Wheaton Supplies.............................		$ 200.00
Norton Company..............................		115.00
Roger Bently, Capital		7,200.00
Roger Bently, Drawing	400.00	
Income Summary	—	—
Sales		5,300.00
Advertising Expense..........................	325.00	
Insurance Expense............................	—	
Miscellaneous Expense	140.00	
Rent Expense.................................	500.00	
Supplies Expense	—	
Utilities Expense	450.00	

Instructions: 1. Prepare the heading and trial balance on a work sheet. Total and rule the Trial Balance columns.

  2. Analyze the following adjustment information into debit and credit parts. Record the adjustments on the work sheet.

Adjustment Information, April 30

Supplies on hand	$2,050.00
Value of prepaid insurance	450.00

  3. Extend the up-to-date account balances to the Balance Sheet or Income Statement columns.

  4. Complete the work sheet.

CHALLENGE PROBLEM 7-C   **Completing a work sheet**

Clean and Mow had a small fire in its office. The fire destroyed some of the accounting records. On November 30 of the current year, the end of a monthly fiscal period, the following information was constructed from the remaining records and other sources.

Remains of the general ledger:

Account Titles	Account Balances
Supplies	$1,800.00
Donna Edwards, Drawing.	150.00
Sales	4,000.00
Advertising Expense	420.00
Rent Expense	700.00
Utilities Expense.	490.00

Information from the business' checkbook:

Cash balance on last unused check stub, $3,400.00
Total payments for miscellaneous expense, $60.00
Total payments for insurance, $325.00

Information obtained through inquiries to other businesses:

Owed to Outdoor Supplies, $2,000.00
Value of prepaid insurance, November 30, $250.00

Information obtained by counting supplies on hand after the fire:

Supplies on hand, $1,100.00

Instructions: 1. From the information given, prepare a heading and reconstruct a trial balance on a work sheet. The owner's capital account balance is the difference between the total of all debit account balances minus the total of all credit account balances.

2. Complete the work sheet.

SUMMARY OF PREPARATION OF A WORK SHEET FOR A SERVICE BUSINESS

The following overlay summarizes the preparation of a work sheet. Follow the directions below in using the overlay.

1. Before using the overlay, be sure the pages and transparent overlays are arranged correctly. The correct arrangement is shown below.

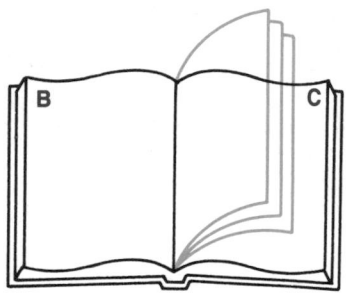

2. Place your book in a horizontal position. Study the steps on page C in preparing the work sheet. You will be able to read the text through the transparent overlays. When directed, carefully lift the transparent overlays and lay them over the work sheet as shown below.

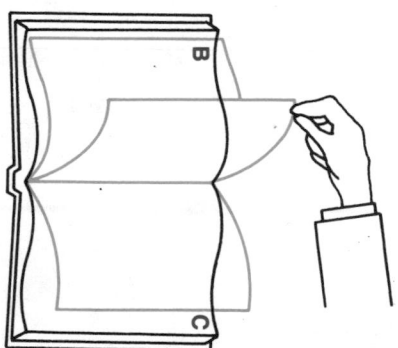

PREPARING A WORK SHEET

To correctly use the insert, read the steps below. Apply the transparent overlays when directed to do so in the steps.

Rugcare

Work Sheet

For Month Ended August 31, 19--

	ACCOUNT TITLE	TRIAL BALANCE		ADJUSTMENTS		INCOME STATEMENT		BALANCE SHEET	
		DEBIT	CREDIT	DEBIT	CREDIT	DEBIT	CREDIT	DEBIT	CREDIT
1	Cash	8272 00							
2	Petty Cash	20 00							
3	Supplies	4931 00							
4	Prepaid Insurance	1200 00							
5	Butler Cleaning Supplies		1360 00						
6	Dale Office Supplies		200 00						
7	Ben Furman, Capital		10000 00						
8	Ben Furman, Drawing	600 00							
9	Income Summary								
10	Sales		4291 00						
11	Advertising Expense	68 00							
12	Insurance Expense								
13	Miscellaneous Expense	105 00							
14	Rent Expense	250 00							
15	Repair Expense	110 00							
16	Supplies Expense								
17	Utilities Expense	115 00							
18		15851 00	15851 00						
19									
20									
21									
22									
23									
24									
25									

Write the name of this section, *Revenue:*, at the extreme left of the wide column on the first line. Write the title of the revenue account, *Sales*, on the next line indented about one centimeter. Record the balance of the account, *$4,291.00*, on the same line in the second amount column.

Expenses section of an income statement

Information from the work sheet's Account Title column and Income Statement Debit column is used to prepare the expenses section. The expenses section of Rugcare's income statement is shown in Illustration 8-5.

Expenses:			
Advertising Expense	6 8 00		
Insurance Expense	1 0 0 00		
Miscellaneous Expense	1 0 5 00		
Rent Expense	2 5 0 00		
Repair Expense	1 1 0 00		
Supplies Expense	2 6 4 7 00		
Utilities Expense	1 1 5 00		
Total Expenses		3 3 9 5 00	

Illustration 8-5
Expenses section of an
income statement

Write the name of this section, *Expenses:*, at the extreme left of the wide column on the next blank line. Write the title of each expense account in the wide column indented about one centimeter. Record the balance of each expense account in the first amount column on the same line as the account title.

To indicate addition, rule a single line across the first amount column under the last expense account balance. Write the words, *Total Expenses*, on the next blank line in the wide column. Record the amount of total expenses, *$3,395.00*, on the same line in the second amount column.

Net income section of an income statement

The amount of net income is calculated and verified using two steps.

1 The net income is calculated from information on the income statement as shown below.

Total Revenue	**− Total Expenses**	**= Net Income**
$4,291.00	− $3,395.00	= $896.00

2 The amount of net income, *$896.00*, is compared with the net income shown on the work sheet, Illustration 8-2. The net income calculated for the income statement and the net income shown on the work sheet must be the same. The net income calculated for Rugcare's income statement, $896.00, is the same as that on the work sheet.

If the net income calculated for the income statement is not the same as that shown on the work sheet, an error has been made. No more work on the income statement should be completed until the error is found and corrected.

A single line is drawn across the second amount column just below the amount of total expenses, as shown in Illustration 8-6.

				% OF SALES
Rugcare				
Income Statement				
For Month Ended August 31, 19--				
Revenue:				
Sales			4 2 9 1 00	100.0
Expenses:				
Advertising Expense		6 8 00		
Insurance Expense		1 0 0 00		
Miscellaneous Expense		1 0 5 00		
Rent Expense		2 5 0 00		
Repair Expense		1 1 0 00		
Supplies Expense		2 6 4 7 00		
Utilities Expense		1 1 5 00		
Total Expenses			3 3 9 5 00	79.1
Net Income			8 9 6 00	20.9

Illustration 8-6
An income statement

Write the words, *Net Income*, on the next line at the extreme left of the wide column. On the same line, record the amount of net income, *$896.00*, in the second amount column. Rule double lines across both amount columns below the amount of net income to show that the amount has been verified as correct. Rugcare's completed income statement is shown in Illustration 8-6.

If total expenses exceed total revenue, a net loss is reported on an income statement. When a net loss is reported, write the words, *Net Loss*, in the wide column. Subtract the total expenses from the revenue to calculate the net loss. Record the amount of net loss in the second amount column in parentheses. An amount written in parentheses on a financial statement indicates a negative amount.

Component percentage analysis of an income statement

For a service business, the revenue reported on an income statement includes two components: (1) total expenses and (2) net income. To make decisions about future operations, Mr. Furman analyzes relationships between these two income statement components and the total sales. The percentage relationship between one financial statement item and the total that includes that item is called a component percentage. On an income statement, component percentages are calculated by dividing the amount of each component by the total amount of sales. Rugcare figures a component percentage for total expenses and net income. The relationship between each component and total sales is shown in a separate column on the income statement at the right of the amount columns.

Acceptable component percentages. For a component percentage to be useful, Mr. Furman needs to know what component percentages are acceptable for businesses similar to Rugcare. Various industry organizations publish average percentages for similar businesses. In the future Mr. Furman could also compare Rugcare's component percentages from one fiscal period with the percentages of previous fiscal periods.

Total expenses component percentage. The total expenses component percentage, based on information from the August income statement shown in Illustration 8-6, is calculated as shown below.

Total Expenses	÷	Total Sales	=	Total Expenses Component Percentage
$3,395.00	÷	$4,291.00	=	79.1%

For businesses similar to Rugcare, an acceptable total expenses component percentage is not more than 80.0%. Therefore, Rugcare's percentage, 79.1%, is less than 80.0% and is acceptable.

Net income component percentage. The net income component percentage, based on information from the August income statement, is calculated as shown below.

Net Income	÷	Total Sales	=	Net Income Component Percentage
$896.00	÷	$4,291.00	=	20.9%

For businesses similar to Rugcare, an acceptable net income component percentage is not less than 20.0%. Therefore, Rugcare's percentage, 20.9%, is greater than 20.0% and is acceptable. The net income component percentage will improve if Rugcare can reduce total expenses in future months. Also, the net income component percentage will improve if Rugcare can increase the amount of revenue in future months.

When there is a net loss, the component percentage for net loss is written in parentheses. A net loss is considered unacceptable.

Income statement with two sources of revenue

Rugcare receives revenue from only one source, the sale of services for rug and carpet cleaning. Milton Lawn Service receives revenue from two sources, the sale of services to fertilize lawns and the sale of services to trim and care for trees. The business' owners want to know how much revenue is earned from each source. Therefore, the business uses two revenue accounts: Sales—Lawns and Sales—Tree Care.

When an income statement is prepared for Milton Lawn Service, both revenue accounts are listed, as shown in Illustration 8-7.

Milton Lawn Service			
Income Statement			
For Month Ended August 31, 19--			
			% OF SALES
Revenue:			
Sales—Lawns	3 3 6 0 00		
Sales—Tree Care	2 2 5 0 00		
Total Sales		5 6 1 0 00	100.0
Expenses:			

Illustration 8-7
Revenue section of an
income statement showing
two sources of revenue

Only the revenue section of Milton Lawn Service's income statement differs from the income statement prepared by Rugcare. Write the section heading, *Revenue:*, at the left of the wide column. Write the titles of both revenue accounts in the wide column indented about one centimeter. Record the balance of each account in the first amount column on the same line as the account title. Total the two revenue account balances. Write the total amount on the next line in the second amount column. Write the words, *Total Sales*, in the wide column indented about one centimeter on the same line as the total revenue amount.

BALANCE SHEET

Information about assets, liabilities, and owner's equity might be obtained from the general ledger accounts or from a work sheet. However, the information is easier to use if reported in an organized manner such as on a balance sheet. Rugcare's balance sheet information on a work sheet is shown in Illustration 8-8.

		7	8	
	ACCOUNT TITLE	BALANCE SHEET		
		DEBIT	CREDIT	
1	*Cash*	8 2 7 2 00		1
2	*Petty Cash*	2 0 0 00		2
3	*Supplies*	2 2 8 4 00		3
4	*Prepaid Insurance*	1 1 0 0 00		4
5	*Butler Cleaning Supplies*		1 3 6 0 00	5
6	*Dale Office Supplies*		2 0 0 00	6
7	*Ben Furman, Capital*		10 0 0 0 00	7
8	*Ben Furman, Drawing*	6 0 0 00		8
17				17
18		12 4 5 6 00	11 5 6 0 00	18
19	*Net Income*		8 9 6 00	19
20		12 4 5 6 00	12 4 5 6 00	20

Illustration 8-8
Balance sheet information
on a work sheet

Information needed to prepare Rugcare's balance sheet is obtained from two places on the work sheet. Account titles are obtained from the work sheet's Account Title column. Account balances are obtained from the work sheet's Balance Sheet columns.

A balance sheet has four sections: (1) heading, (2) assets, (3) liabilities, and (4) owner's equity.

Heading of a balance sheet

The heading of a balance sheet consists of three lines. (1) The name of the business. (2) The name of the statement. (3) The date of the statement. Rugcare's balance sheet heading is shown in Illustration 8-9.

Illustration 8-9
Heading of a balance sheet

Rugcare
Balance Sheet
August 31, 19--

Assets, liabilities, and owner's equity are reported on Rugcare's balance sheet as of a specific date, August 31.

Assets section of a balance sheet

A balance sheet reports information about the elements of the accounting equation.

$$\text{Assets} = \text{Liabilities} + \text{Owner's Equity}$$

The assets are on the LEFT side of the accounting equation and on the LEFT side of Rugcare's balance sheet.

The information needed to prepare the assets section is obtained from the work sheet's Account Title column and the Balance Sheet Debit column. The assets section of Rugcare's balance sheet is shown in Illustration 8-10.

Assets		
Cash	8 2 7 2 00	
Petty Cash	2 0 0 00	
Supplies	2 2 8 4 00	
Prepaid Insurance	1 1 0 0 00	
Total Assets	11 8 5 6 00	

Illustration 8-10
Assets section of a
balance sheet

Write the title of the section, *Assets*, in the middle of the left wide column. Under the heading write the titles of all asset accounts. Record the balance of each asset account in the left amount column on the same line as the account title.

Equities section of a balance sheet

Two kinds of equities are reported on a balance sheet: (1) liabilities and (2) owner's equity. Liabilities and owner's equity are on the RIGHT side of the accounting equation and on the RIGHT side of Rugcare's balance sheet.

Liabilities section of a balance sheet. The information needed to prepare the liabilities section is obtained from the work sheet's Account Title column and the Balance Sheet Credit column. The liabilities are reported on a balance sheet as shown in Illustration 8-11.

		Liabilities	
		Butler Cleaning Supplies	1 3 6 0 00
		Dale Office Supplies	2 0 0 00
		Total Liabilities	1 5 6 0 00

Illustration 8-11
Liabilities section of a
balance sheet

Write the title of the section, *Liabilities,* in the middle of the right wide column. Under this heading write the titles of all liability accounts. Record the balance of each liability account in the right amount column on the same line as the account title. To indicate addition, rule a single line across the right amount column under the last amount. Write the words, *Total Liabilities,* in the right wide column on the next blank line. Record the total of all liabilities, *$1,560.00,* in the right amount column.

Owner's equity section of a balance sheet. Only the amount of current capital is reported on Rugcare's balance sheet. The amounts needed to calculate the current capital are found in the work sheet's Balance Sheet Debit and Credit columns. The amount of current capital is calculated as shown below.

Capital Account Balance	+ Net Income	–	Drawing Account Balance	=	Current Capital
$10,000.00	+ $896.00	–	$600.00	=	$10,296.00

The title of the owner's capital account is obtained from the work sheet's Account Title column. Owner's equity is reported on a balance sheet as shown in Illustration 8-12.

	Rugcare			
	Balance Sheet			
	August 31, 19--			
Assets		*Liabilities*		
Cash	8 2 7 2 00	*Butler Cleaning Supplies*	1 3 6 0 00	
Petty Cash	2 0 0 00	*Dale Office Supplies*	2 0 0 00	
Supplies	2 2 8 4 00	*Total Liabilities*	1 5 6 0 00	
Prepaid Insurance	1 1 0 0 00	*Owner's Equity*		
		Ben Furman, Capital	10 2 9 6 00	
Total Assets	11 8 5 6 00	*Total Liab. and Owner's Eq.*	11 8 5 6 00	

Illustration 8-12
A balance sheet

Write the title of the section, *Owner's Equity,* in the middle of the right wide column on the next line. On the next line, write the title of the owner's capital account, *Ben Furman, Capital*. Record the current amount of owner's equity, *$10,296.00*, in the right amount column.

Rugcare's balance sheet prepared on August 31 is shown in Illustration 8-12. Rule a single line across both amount columns under the last amount in the amount column that is the longest. For Rugcare's balance sheet, the longest column is the right amount column. The line is ruled under the amount of Ben Furman's capital, $10,296.00. On the next line, in the right wide column, write the words, *Total Liab. and Owner's Eq.* Record the amount of total liabilities and owner's equity, *$11,856.00*, in the right amount column.

The total assets amount is not recorded at the time the rest of the assets section is prepared. The placement of the total assets line is determined after the equities section is prepared so that the two final totals are on the same line.

Write the words, *Total Assets*, in the left wide column on the same line as the words *Total Liab. and Owner's Eq.* Record the amount of total assets, *$11,856.00*, in the left amount column.

Compare the totals of the two amount columns. Because the totals are the same on both sides of Rugcare's balance sheet, $11,856.00, the balance sheet is in balance. The accounting equation being reported is also in balance.

Assets = Liabilities + Owner's Equity
$11,856.00 = $1,560.00 + $10,296.00

If the total assets do not equal the total liabilities and owner's equity, the error or errors must be found and corrected before the balance sheet is completed.

Rule double lines across both the left and right amount columns just below the column totals to show that the totals have been verified as correct.

When a business has a net loss, current capital is calculated as shown below.

Capital Account Balance	− Net Loss −	Drawing Account Balance	= Current Capital
$15,000.00	− $200.00 −	$500.00	= $14,300.00

The current capital, $14,300.00, is reported on the balance sheet in the same way as shown in Illustration 8-12.

Owner's equity reported in detail on a balance sheet

Rugcare's balance sheet reports the current capital on August 31 but does not show how this amount was calculated. Rugcare is a small business with relatively few changes in owner's equity to report. Therefore, Ben Furman decided that the business does not need to report all the details in the owner's equity section. However, some businesses prefer to report the details about how owner's equity is calculated.

If Rugcare were to report details about owner's equity, the balance sheet would be prepared as shown in Illustration 8-13.

Total Liabilities			1 5 6 0 00		
Owner's Equity					
Ben Furman, Capital, August 1		10,000.00			
Net Income	896.00				
Less Ben Furman, Drawing	600.00	296.00			
Ben Furman, Capital, August 31			10 2 9 6 00		
Total Liabilities and Owner's Equity			11 8 5 6 00		

Illustration 8-13
Owner's equity reported in detail on a balance sheet

First, the owner's capital account balance, $10,000.00, is reported. Second, the balance of the drawing account, $600.00, is subtracted from the net income for the fiscal period, $896.00. The difference, $296.00, is added to the previous capital account balance. The current capital, $10,296.00, is recorded as the amount of Ben Furman, Capital on August 31.

SUMMARY OF FINANCIAL STATEMENTS FOR A PROPRIETORSHIP

A summary of financial statements for a service business organized as a proprietorship is shown in Illustration 8-14, page 158.

1 An income statement is prepared using information from the Account Title column and Income Statement columns of a work sheet.

2 Component percentages for total expenses and net income are calculated as shown below.

Total Expenses ÷ Total Sales = Total Expenses Component Percentage
Net Income   ÷ Total Sales = Net Income Component Percentage

3 A balance sheet is prepared using information obtained from the work sheet's Account Title column and Balance Sheet columns. Current capital to be reported on the balance sheet is calculated as shown below.

$$\text{Capital Account Balance} + \text{Net Income} - \text{Drawing Account Balance} = \text{Current Capital}$$

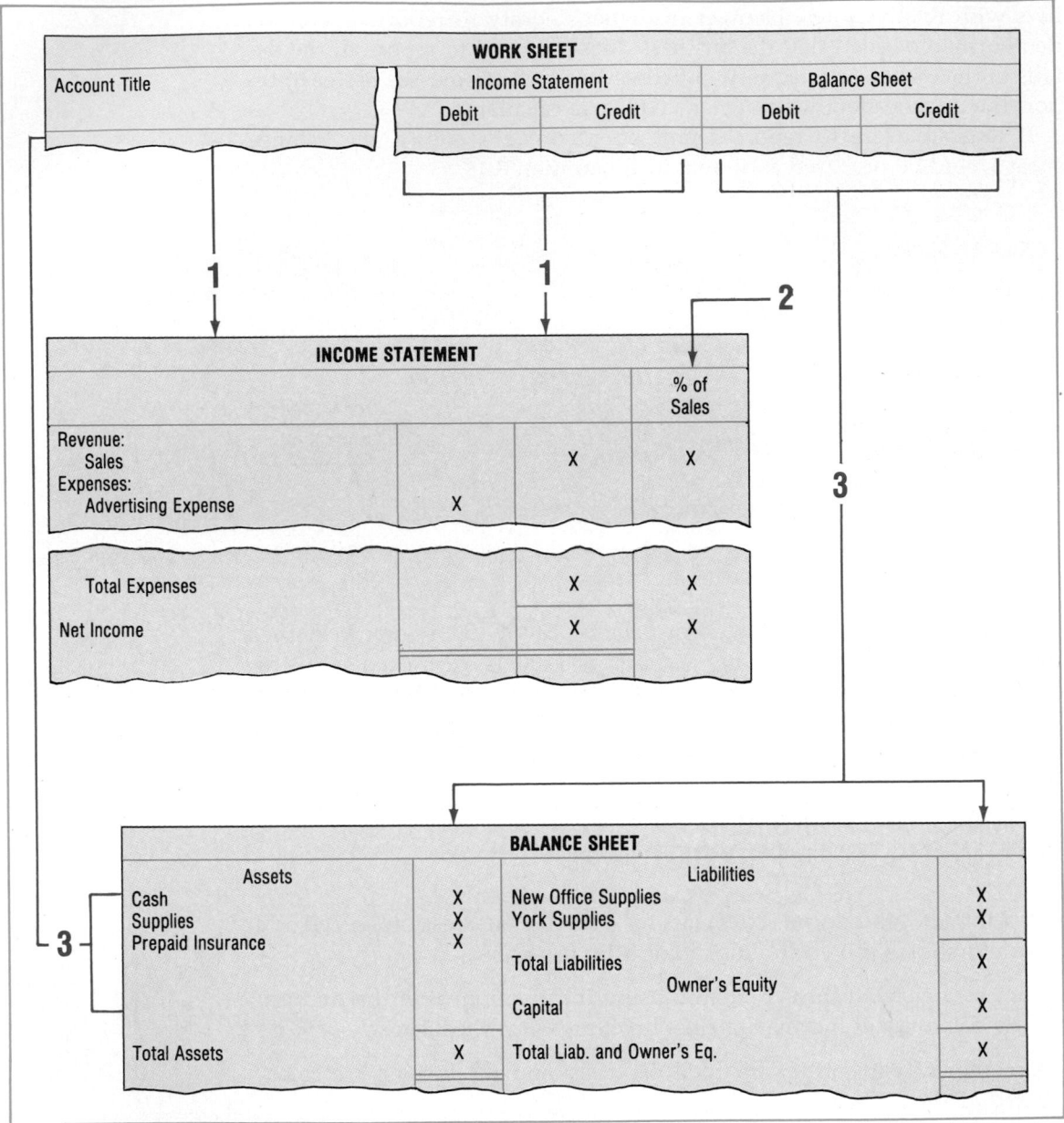

Illustration 8-14   Summary of financial statements for a proprietorship

■ ACCOUNTING TERM

What is the meaning of the following?

1. component percentage

QUESTIONS FOR INDIVIDUAL STUDY

1. Which accounting concept is being applied when all the information about a business' financial condition is reported on financial statements?
2. Which accounting concept is being applied when financial statements are prepared at least once each year?
3. For what period of time does an income statement report financial progress of a business?
4. For what period of time does a balance sheet report financial condition of a business?
5. Which accounting concept is being applied when revenue earned and the expenses incurred to earn that revenue are recorded in the same fiscal period?
6. What does Rugcare do to assist in planning the preparation of financial statements?
7. Where does Rugcare obtain the information for preparing an income statement?
8. What are the four sections of an income statement?

9. What information is found in an income statement heading?
10. What are the two steps in figuring and verifying the net income on Rugcare's income statement?
11. How does Rugcare analyze its income statement?
12. What is the formula for calculating the total expenses component percentage?
13. What is the formula for calculating the net income component percentage?
14. How is revenue shown on an income statement when a business has two sources of revenue?
15. Where does Rugcare obtain the information for preparing a balance sheet?
16. What are the four sections of a balance sheet?
17. What information is found in a balance sheet heading?
18. What is the formula for calculating the amount of capital to report on a balance sheet?

CASES FOR MANAGEMENT DECISION

CASE 1 James Worth and Mary Derner each own small businesses. Mr. Worth prepares an income statement and balance sheet at the end of each day for his business. He claims that he needs the information to make business decisions. Mrs. Derner prepares an income statement and balance sheet for her business only at the end of each one-year fiscal period. She claims that she needs the information only at the end of the year when preparing tax reports. Which

owner is using the better procedure? Explain your answer.

CASE 2 Ralph Macy owns and manages a business that has produced an average annual net income of $21,600.00 for five years. George Wayne has offered to buy Mr. Macy's business and retain him as manager at a monthly salary of $2,000.00. What should Mr. Macy consider before selling his business and accepting the position as manager?

DRILLS FOR UNDERSTANDING

DRILL 8-D1 **Classifying accounts**

Use a form similar to the following.

1	2	3	4	5	6	7	8
Account Title	Account Classification					Financial Statement	
	Asset	Liab.	Owner's Equity	Revenue	Expense	Income Statement	Balance Sheet
1. Cash	✓						✓

Instructions: 1. Write each of the following account titles in Column 1 of the form. The first account, Cash, is given as an example.

1. Cash
2. Alice Wayne, Capital
3. Alice Wayne, Drawing
4. Advertising Expense
5. Coen Office Supplies
6. Insurance Expense
7. Miscellaneous Expense
8. Mercer Supplies
9. Prepaid Insurance
10. Rent Expense
11. Sales
12. Supplies
13. Supplies Expense

2. Place a check mark in either Column 2, 3, 4, 5, or 6 to indicate the classification of each account.

3. Place a check mark in either Column 7 or 8 to indicate on which financial statement each account will be reported.

DRILL 8-D2 Figuring net income or net loss and owner's current capital

The following information is given for several companies.

	1	2	3	4	5	6
Company	Total Assets	Total Liabilities	Balance of Capital	Balance of Drawing	Total Revenue	Total Expenses
A	$ 5,600	$2,000	$ 2,320	$120	$ 2,300	$ 900
B	7,300	2,600	2,945	145	3,100	1,200
C	7,000	3,200	4,840	200	3,600	4,440
D	9,560	2,835	4,995	160	3,150	1,260
E	10,680	3,850	4,035	220	4,725	1,710
F	14,500	5,770	10,475	325	7,380	8,800
G	13,620	4,900	4,940	270	6,250	2,200
H	14,325	7,880	14,465	420	10,000	17,600

Instructions: Complete the following for each company.

1. Use the information in Columns 5 and 6. Figure the amount of net income or net loss for each company. For example, Company A: Revenue, $2,300, − expenses, $900, = net income, $1,400.

2. Figure the amount of current capital for each company using the net income or net loss from Instruction 1 and the information in Columns 3 and 4. For example, Company A: Capital account balance, $2,320, + net income, $1,400, − drawing, $120, = current capital, $3,600.

3. Use the accounting equation to check the accuracy of your answers in Instructions 1 and 2. For example, Company A: Assets, $5,600, = liabilities, $2,000, + owner's equity, $3,600. If the equation is not in balance, refigure and correct your answers to Instructions 1 and 2.

■ APPLICATION PROBLEMS

PROBLEM 8-1 **Preparing an income statement**

The following information is obtained from the work sheet of LawnMow for the month ended June 30 of the current year.

	ACCOUNT TITLE	5 INCOME STATEMENT DEBIT	6 INCOME STATEMENT CREDIT	7 BALANCE SHEET DEBIT	8 BALANCE SHEET CREDIT	
10	Sales		3 1 0 0 00			10
11	Advertising Expense	3 0 00				11
12	Insurance Expense	1 4 0 00				12
13	Miscellaneous Expense	6 5 00				13
14	Rent Expense	8 0 0 00				14
15	Supplies Expense	4 0 0 00				15
16	Utilities Expense	7 5 00				16
17		1 5 1 0 00	3 1 0 0 00			17
18	Net Income	1 5 9 0 00				18
19		3 1 0 0 00	3 1 0 0 00			19
20						20
21						21
22						22
23						23
24						24
25						25
26						26
27						27
28						28
29						29
30						30
31						31
32						32

Instructions: Prepare an income statement for the month ended June 30 of the current year. Figure and record the component percentages for total expenses and net income. Round percentage calculations to the nearest 0.1%.

PROBLEM 8-2 Preparing a balance sheet

The following information is obtained from the work sheet of LawnMow for the month ended June 30 of the current year.

Instructions: Prepare a balance sheet for June 30 of the current year.

	ACCOUNT TITLE		BALANCE SHEET		
			DEBIT	**CREDIT**	
1	Cash		7 5 3 0 00		1
2	Petty Cash		2 0 0 00		2
3	Supplies		6 8 6 0 00		3
4	Prepaid Insurance		2 5 0 0 00		4
5	Barker Supplies			4 4 0 0 00	5
6	Richmond Office Supplies			1 3 0 0 00	6
7	Clem Sutter, Capital			11 0 0 0 00	7
8	Clem Sutter, Drawing		1 2 0 0 00		8
9	Income Summary				9
16					16
17			18 2 9 0 00	16 7 0 0 00	17
18	Net Income			1 5 9 0 00	18
19			18 2 9 0 00	18 2 9 0 00	19
20					20
21					21
22					22
23					23
24					24
25					25
26					26
27					27
28					28
29					29
30					30
31					31
32					32
33					33
34					34
35					35
36					36
37					37
38					38

ENRICHMENT PROBLEMS

MASTERY PROBLEM 8-M   Preparing financial statements

The following information is obtained from the work sheet of Ace Delivery Service for the month ended July 31 of the current year.

Instructions: 1. Prepare an income statement for the month ended July 31 of the current year. Figure and record the component percentages for total expenses and net income. Round percentage calculations to the nearest 0.1%.

    2. Prepare a balance sheet for July 31 of the current year.

	ACCOUNT TITLE	INCOME STATEMENT DEBIT	INCOME STATEMENT CREDIT	BALANCE SHEET DEBIT	BALANCE SHEET CREDIT	
1	Cash			7 5 0 0 00		1
2	Petty Cash			2 0 0 00		2
3	Supplies			7 8 0 0 00		3
4	Prepaid Insurance			2 6 0 0 00		4
5	Down Supplies				4 7 0 0 00	5
6	Melton Office Supplies				1 2 0 0 00	6
7	Clark Smith, Capital				12 0 0 0 00	7
8	Clark Smith, Drawing			1 4 0 0 00		8
9	Income Summary					9
10	Sales		5 6 7 0 00			10
11	Advertising Expense	3 9 0 00				11
12	Insurance Expense	1 9 0 00				12
13	Miscellaneous Expense	1 5 0 00				13
14	Rent Expense	3 0 0 00				14
15	Supplies Expense	2 0 0 00				15
16	Utilities Expense	1 4 0 00				16
17		4 0 7 0 00	5 6 7 0 00	19 5 0 0 00	17 9 0 0 00	17
18	Net Income	1 6 0 0 00			1 6 0 0 00	18
19		5 6 7 0 00	5 6 7 0 00	19 5 0 0 00	19 5 0 0 00	19

CHALLENGE PROBLEM 8-C   **Preparing financial statements with two sources of revenue and a net loss**

The following information is obtained from the work sheet of Mercer Lawn Service for the month ended August 31 of the current year.

Instructions: 1. Prepare an income statement for the month ended August 31 of the current year. Figure and record the component percentages for total expenses and net loss. Place the percentage for net loss in parentheses to show that it is for a net loss. Round percentage calculations to the nearest 0.1%.
    2. Prepare a balance sheet for August 31 of the current year.

		5	6	7	8	
	ACCOUNT TITLE	INCOME STATEMENT		BALANCE SHEET		
		DEBIT	CREDIT	DEBIT	CREDIT	
1	Cash			6 0 2 0 00		1
2	Petty Cash			2 0 00		2
3	Supplies			6 0 0 00		3
4	Prepaid Insurance			2 5 0 00		4
5	Choice Supplies				3 0 0 00	5
6	Poll Office Supplies				2 0 00	6
7	Lydia Roland, Capital				13 0 0 00	7
8	Lydia Roland, Drawing			1 3 0 00		8
9	Income Summary					9
10	Sales—Lawn Care		4 7 0 0 00			10
11	Sales—Shrub Care		2 6 0 0 00			11
12	Advertising Expense	3 9 0 00				12
13	Insurance Expense	3 0 0 00				13
14	Miscellaneous Expense	4 5 0 00				14
15	Rent Expense	3 0 0 0 00				15
16	Supplies Expense	3 1 0 0 00				16
17	Utilities Expense	2 4 0 00				17
18		7 4 8 0 00	7 3 0 0 00	16 0 2 0 00	16 2 0 0 00	18
19	Net Loss		1 8 0 00	1 8 0 00		19
20		7 4 8 0 00	7 4 8 0 00	16 2 0 0 00	16 2 0 0 00	20

Recording Adjusting and Closing Entries for a Service Business

ENABLING PERFORMANCE TASKS

After studying Chapter 9, you will be able to:

a. Define accounting terms related to adjusting and closing entries for a service business organized as a proprietorship.

b. Identify accounting concepts and practices related to adjusting and closing entries for a service business organized as a proprietorship.

c. Record adjusting entries for a service business organized as a proprietorship.

d. Record closing entries for a service business organized as a proprietorship.

e. Prepare a post-closing trial balance for a service business organized as a proprietorship.

Rugcare prepares a work sheet at the end of each fiscal period to summarize the general ledger information needed to prepare financial statements. (CONCEPT: Accounting Period Cycle) Financial statements are prepared from information on the work sheet. (CONCEPT: Adequate Disclosure)

RECORDING ADJUSTING ENTRIES

Rugcare's adjustments are analyzed and planned on a work sheet. However, these adjustments must be journalized so that they can be posted to the general ledger accounts. Journal entries recorded to update general ledger accounts at the end of a fiscal period are called adjusting entries.

Adjusting entries are recorded on the next journal page following the page on which the last daily transactions for the month are recorded. The adjusting entries are entered in the General Debit and General Credit columns of a journal.

Rugcare records two adjusting entries. (1) An adjusting entry to bring the supplies account up to date. (2) An adjusting entry to bring the prepaid insurance account up to date.

Adjusting entry for supplies

The information needed to journalize the adjusting entry for supplies is obtained from lines 3 and 16 of Rugcare's work sheet. A partial work sheet and the adjusting entry for supplies are shown in Illustration 9-1.

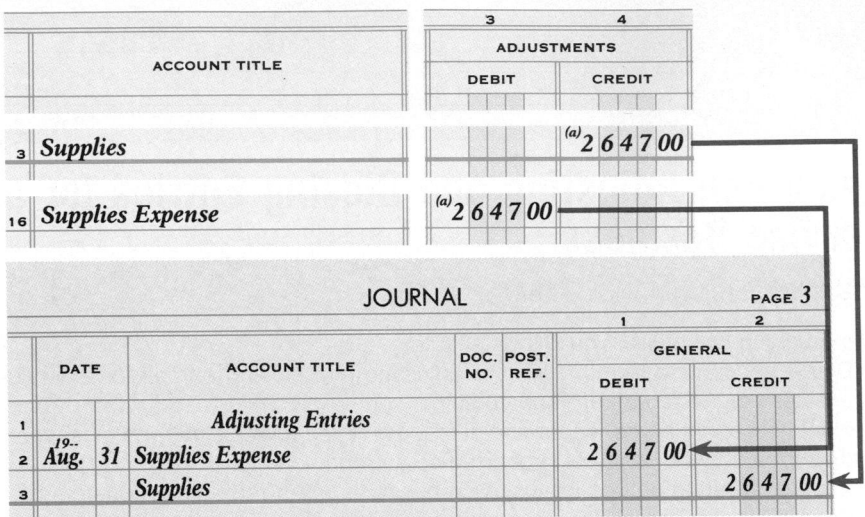

Illustration 9-1
Adjusting entry for supplies
recorded in a journal

The heading, *Adjusting Entries*, is written in the middle of the Account Title column of the journal. Because no source document is prepared for adjusting entries, the entries are identified with a heading in the journal. This heading explains all of the adjusting entries that follow. Therefore, the heading is written only once for all adjusting entries.

The date, *19--, Aug. 31*, is written in the Date column. The title of the account debited, *Supplies Expense*, is written in the Account Title column. The debit amount, *$2,647.00*, is recorded in the General Debit column on the same line as the account title. The title of the account credited, *Supplies*, is written on the next line. The credit amount, *$2,647.00*, is recorded in the General Credit column on the same line as the account title.

Supplies Expense		
Adj. (a)	2,647.00	

Supplies			
Bal.	4,931.00	Adj. (a)	2,647.00
(New Bal.	2,284.00)		

The effect of posting the adjusting entry for supplies to the general ledger accounts is shown in the T accounts.

Supplies Expense has an up-to-date balance of $2,647.00, which is the value of the supplies used during the fiscal period. Supplies has a new balance of $2,284.00, which is the value of the supplies on hand at the end of the fiscal period.

Adjusting entry for prepaid insurance

The information needed to journalize the adjusting entry for prepaid insurance is obtained from lines 4 and 12 of Rugcare's work sheet. A partial work sheet and the adjusting entry for prepaid insurance are shown in Illustration 9-2.

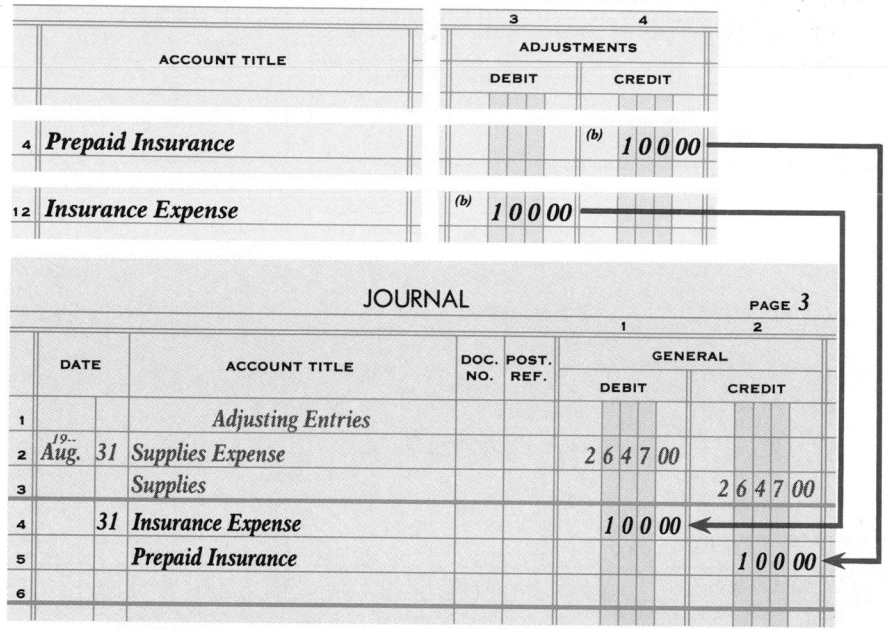

ACCOUNT TITLE			ADJUSTMENTS	
			3 DEBIT	**4** CREDIT
4 *Prepaid Insurance*				(b) 1 0 0 00
12 *Insurance Expense*			(b) 1 0 0 00	

			JOURNAL					PAGE 3	
	DATE		ACCOUNT TITLE	DOC. NO.	POST. REF.	**1** GENERAL DEBIT		**2** CREDIT	
1			*Adjusting Entries*						
2	¹⁹⁻⁻ Aug.	31	Supplies Expense			2 6 4 7 00			
3			Supplies					2 6 4 7 00	
4		31	Insurance Expense			1 0 0 00			
5			Prepaid Insurance					1 0 0 00	
6									

Illustration 9-2
Adjusting entry for prepaid insurance recorded in a journal

The date, *31*, is written in the Date column. The title of the account debited, *Insurance Expense*, is written in the Account Title column. The debit amount, *$100.00*, is recorded in the General Debit column on the same line as the account title. The title of the account credited, *Prepaid Insurance*, is written on the next line in the Account Title column. The credit amount, *$100.00*, is recorded in the General Credit column on the same line as the account title.

The effect of posting the adjusting entry for insurance to the general ledger accounts is shown in the T accounts.

Insurance Expense has an up-to-date balance of $100.00, which is the value of insurance premiums used during the fiscal period. Prepaid Insurance has a new balance of $1,100.00, which is the value of insurance premiums that remain unused at the end of the fiscal period. (CONCEPT: *Matching Expenses with Revenue*)

Insurance Expense	
Adj. (b) 100.00	

Prepaid Insurance	
Bal. 1,200.00	Adj. (b) 100.00
(New Bal. 1,100.00)	

SUMMARY OF ADJUSTING ENTRIES FOR A SERVICE BUSINESS ORGANIZED AS A PROPRIETORSHIP

The two adjusting entries for a service business organized as a proprietorship are summarized in Illustration 9-3.

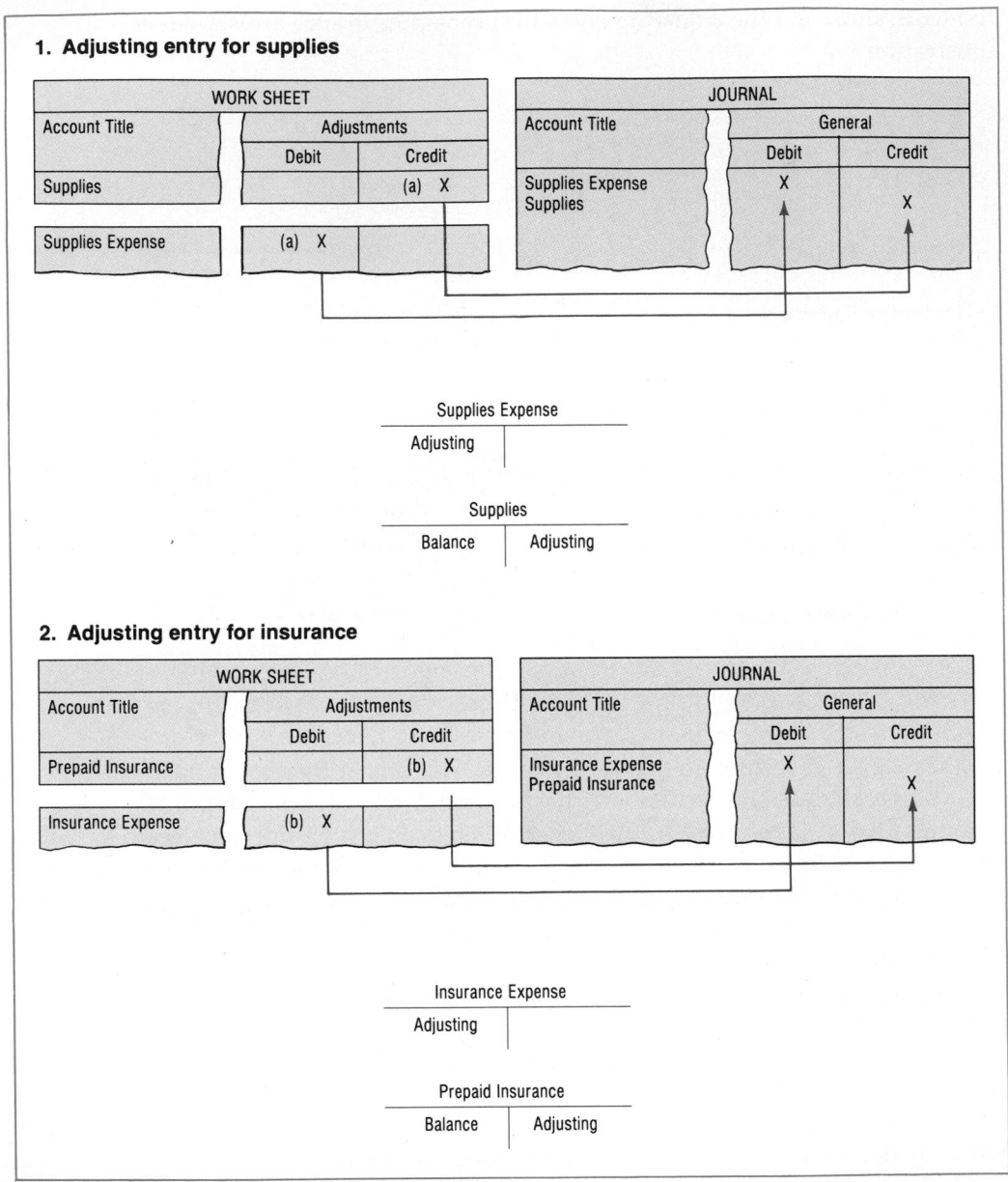

Illustration 9-3
Summary of adjusting
entries for a service
business organized as a
proprietorship

RECORDING CLOSING ENTRIES

Accounts used to accumulate information from one fiscal period to the next are called permanent accounts. Permanent accounts are also referred to as real accounts. Permanent accounts include the asset and liability accounts and the owner's capital account. The ending account balances of permanent accounts for one fiscal period are the beginning account balances for the next fiscal period.

Accounts used to accumulate information until it is transferred to the owner's capital account are called temporary accounts. Temporary accounts are also referred to as nominal accounts. Temporary accounts include the revenue, expense, and owner's drawing accounts plus the income summary account. Temporary accounts show changes in the owner's capital for a single fiscal period. Therefore, at the end of a fiscal period, the balances of temporary accounts are summarized and transferred to the owner's capital account. The temporary accounts begin a new fiscal period with zero balances.

Need for closing temporary accounts

Journal entries used to prepare temporary accounts for a new fiscal period are called closing entries. The temporary account balances must be reduced to zero at the end of each fiscal period. This procedure prepares the temporary accounts for recording information about the next fiscal period. Otherwise, the amounts for the next fiscal period would be added to amounts for previous fiscal periods. *(CONCEPT: Matching Expenses with Revenue)* The net income for the next fiscal period would be difficult to calculate because amounts from several fiscal periods remain in the accounts. Therefore, the temporary accounts must start each new fiscal period with zero balances.

To close a temporary account, an amount equal to its balance is recorded in the account on the side opposite to its balance. For example, if an account has a credit balance of $4,291.00, a debit of $4,291.00 is recorded to close the account.

Need for the income summary account

Whenever a temporary account is closed, the closing entry must have equal debits and credits. If an account is debited for $3,000.00 to close the account, some other account must be credited for the same amount. A temporary account titled *Income Summary* is used to summarize the closing entries for the revenue and expense accounts.

The income summary account is unique because it does not have a normal balance side. The balance of this account is determined by the amounts posted to the account at the end of a fiscal period. When revenue is greater than total expenses, resulting in a net income, the income summary account has a credit balance, as shown in the T account.

Income Summary	
Debit side Total expenses	Credit side Revenue (greater than expenses) (Credit balance is the net income.)

When total expenses are greater than revenue, resulting in a net loss, the income summary account has a debit balance, as shown in the T account.

Income Summary

Debit side	Credit side
Total expenses (greater than revenue)	Revenue
(Debit balance is the net loss.)	

Thus, whether the balance of the income summary account is a debit or a credit depends upon whether the business earns a net income or incurs a net loss. Because Income Summary is a temporary account, the account is also closed at the end of a fiscal period when the net income or net loss is recorded.

Rugcare records four closing entries. (1) An entry to close income statement accounts with credit balances. (2) An entry to close income statement accounts with debit balances. (3) An entry to record net income or net loss and close Income Summary. (4) An entry to close the owner's drawing account.

Information needed to record the four closing entries is found in the Income Statement and Balance Sheet columns of the work sheet.

Closing entry for an income statement account with a credit balance

Rugcare has one income statement account with a credit balance, Sales, as shown on the partial work sheet in Illustration 9-4. This credit balance

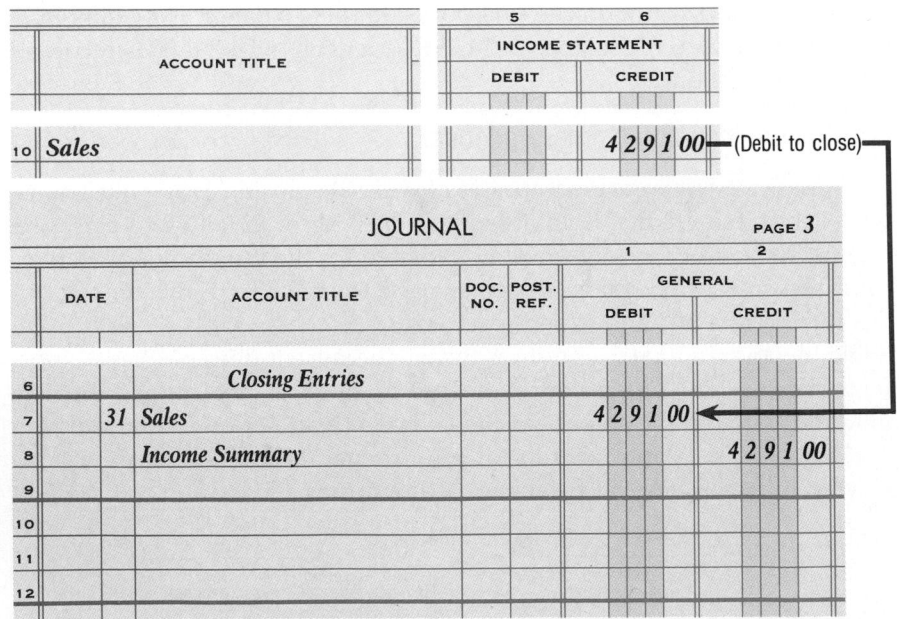

Illustration 9-4
Closing entry for an
income statement account
with a credit balance

must be reduced to zero to prepare the account for the next fiscal period. To reduce the balance to zero, Sales is debited for the amount of the balance. Because debits must equal credits for each journal entry, some other account must be credited. The account used for the credit part of this closing entry is Income Summary. The closing entry for Sales is journalized as shown in Illustration 9-4.

No source document is used for closing entries. Therefore, the heading, *Closing Entries,* is written in the Account Title column of the journal. For Rugcare, this heading is placed in the journal on the first blank line after the last adjusting entry.

The date, *31,* is written on the next line in the Date column. The title of the account debited, *Sales,* is written in the Account Title column. The debit amount, *$4,291.00,* is recorded in the General Debit column on the same line as the account title. The title of the account credited, *Income Summary,* is written in the Account Title column on the next journal line. The credit amount, *$4,291.00,* is recorded in the General Credit amount column on the same line as the account title.

The effect of this closing entry on the general ledger accounts is shown in the T accounts.

The balance of Sales is now zero, and the account is ready for the next fiscal period. The credit balance of Sales is transferred to Income Summary.

	Sales	
Closing	4,291.00	Bal. 4,291.00
		(New Bal. zero)

Income Summary	
	Closing (revenue)
	4,291.00

Closing entry for income statement accounts with debit balances

Rugcare has several income statement accounts with debit balances. The seven expense accounts have normal debit balances at the end of a fiscal period, as shown on the partial work sheet in Illustration 9-5 on page 172. The balances of the expense accounts must be reduced to zero to prepare the accounts for the next fiscal period. Each expense account is credited for an amount equal to its balance, and Income Summary is debited for the total of all the expense account balances. The closing entry for the expense accounts is journalized as shown in Illustration 9-5.

The heading for closing entries is written only once. Therefore, the closing entry for expenses starts on the next blank line in the journal.

The date, *31,* is written in the Date column. The title of the account debited, Income Summary, is written in the Account Title column. The amount debited to Income Summary is not entered in the amount column until all expenses have been journalized and the total amount calculated. The account title and balance of each expense account is recorded in the Account Title and General Credit columns. After all expense accounts and their balances have been written in the journal, the credit amounts for this entry are added. The total of all expenses, *$3,395.00,* is recorded in the General Debit column on the same line as the account title, Income Summary.

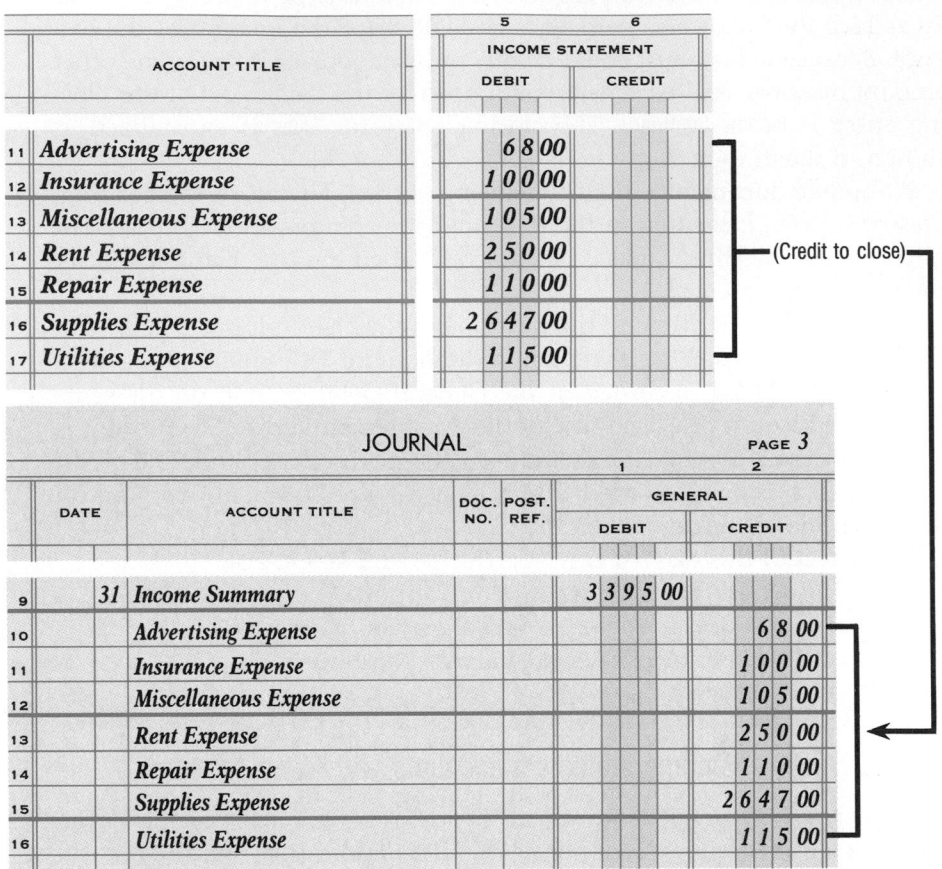

ACCOUNT TITLE	5 INCOME STATEMENT DEBIT	6 CREDIT
11 *Advertising Expense*	6 8 00	
12 *Insurance Expense*	1 0 0 00	
13 *Miscellaneous Expense*	1 0 5 00	
14 *Rent Expense*	2 5 0 00	
15 *Repair Expense*	1 1 0 00	
16 *Supplies Expense*	2 6 4 7 00	
17 *Utilities Expense*	1 1 5 00	

(Credit to close)

JOURNAL   PAGE 3

	DATE	ACCOUNT TITLE	DOC. NO.	POST. REF.	1 GENERAL DEBIT	2 CREDIT
9	31	*Income Summary*			3 3 9 5 00	
10		*Advertising Expense*				6 8 00
11		*Insurance Expense*				1 0 0 00
12		*Miscellaneous Expense*				1 0 5 00
13		*Rent Expense*				2 5 0 00
14		*Repair Expense*				1 1 0 00
15		*Supplies Expense*				2 6 4 7 00
16		*Utilities Expense*				1 1 5 00

Illustration 9-5
Closing entry for income
statement accounts with
debit balances

The effect of the closing entry for Rugcare's expense accounts is shown in the T accounts.

Income Summary

Closing (expenses)	3,395.00	Closing (revenue) *(New Bal.*	4,291.00 *896.00)*

Advertising Expense

Bal. *(New Bal. zero)*	68.00	Closing	68.00

Repair Expense

Bal. *(New Bal. zero)*	110.00	Closing	110.00

Insurance Expense

Bal. *(New Bal. zero)*	100.00	Closing	100.00

Supplies Expense

Bal. *(New Bal. zero)*	2,647.00	Closing	2,647.00

Miscellaneous Expense

Bal. *(New Bal. zero)*	105.00	Closing	105.00

Utilities Expense

Bal. *(New Bal. zero)*	115.00	Closing	115.00

Rent Expense

Bal. *(New Bal. zero)*	250.00	Closing	250.00

The balance of each expense account is returned to zero, and the accounts are ready for the next fiscal period. The debit balances of the expense accounts are recorded in Income Summary as one debit amount. The balance of Income Summary is the net income for the fiscal period, $896.00.

Closing entry to record net income or loss and close the income summary account

Rugcare's net income is on the partial work sheet shown in Illustration 9-6. The amount of net income increases the owner's capital and, therefore, must be credited to the owner's capital account. The balance of the temporary account, Income Summary, must be reduced to zero to prepare the account for the next fiscal period. The closing entry to record net income and close the income summary account is journalized as shown in Illustration 9-6.

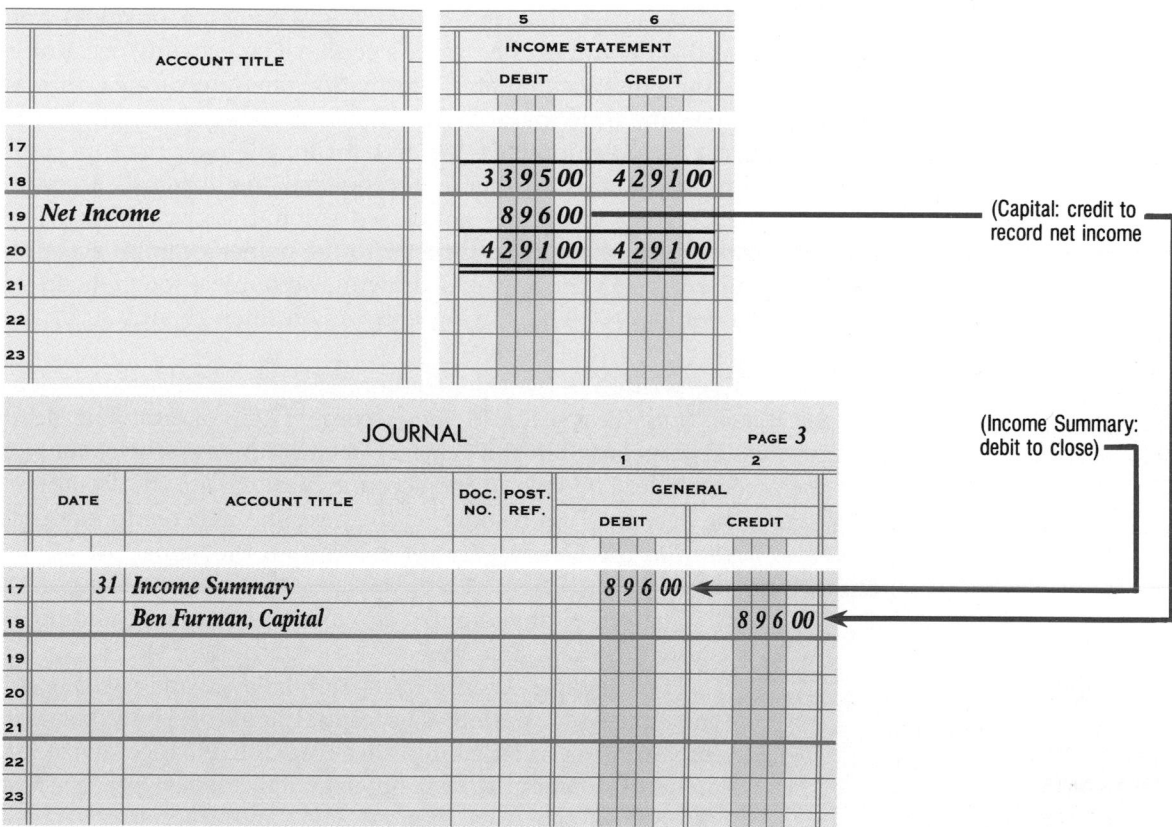

Illustration 9-6
Closing entry to record net income and close the income summary account

The date, *31*, is written in the Date column. The title of the account debited, *Income Summary*, is written in the Account Title column. The debit amount, *$896.00*, is recorded in the General Debit column on the same line as the account title. The title of the account credited, *Ben Furman, Capital*, is written in the Account Title column on the next line. The credit amount, *$896.00*, is recorded in the General Credit column on the same line as the account title.

Income Summary

Closing (expenses) 3,395.00	Closing (revenue) 4,291.00
Closing 896.00	(New Bal. zero)

Ben Furman, Capital

	Bal. 10,000.00
	Closing (net income) 896.00
	(New Bal. 10,896.00)

The effect of this closing entry on the general ledger accounts is shown in the T accounts.

The debit to the income summary account, $896.00, reduces the account balance to zero and prepares the account for the next fiscal period. The credit, $896.00, increases the balance of the owner's capital account, Ben Furman, Capital.

If the business incurs a net loss, the closing entry is a debit to the owner's capital account and a credit to the income summary account.

Closing entry for the owner's drawing account

Withdrawals are assets that the owner takes out of a business and which decrease the amount of the owner's equity. The drawing account is a temporary account that accumulates information separately for each fiscal period. Therefore, the drawing account balance is reduced to zero at the end of one fiscal period to prepare the account for the next fiscal period.

The drawing account is neither a revenue nor an expense account. Therefore, the drawing account is not closed through Income Summary. The drawing account balance is closed directly to the owner's capital account.

The closing entry for the owner's drawing account is journalized as shown in Illustration 9-7. The closing entry is on lines 19 and 20 of the journal.

The date, *31*, is written in the Date column. The title of the account debited, *Ben Furman, Capital*, is written in the Account Title column. The debit amount, *$600.00*, is recorded in the General Debit column on the same line with the account title. The title of the account credited, *Ben Furman, Drawing*, is written in the Account Title column on the next line. The credit amount, *$600.00*, is written in the General Credit column on the same line as the account title.

Ben Furman, Capital

Closing 600.00	Bal. 10,000.00
	Net Income 896.00
	(New Bal. 10,296.00)

Ben Furman, Drawing

Bal. 600.00	Closing 600.00
(New Bal. zero)	

The effect of the entry to close the drawing account is shown in the T accounts.

The drawing account has a zero balance and is ready for the next fiscal period. The capital account's new balance, $10,296.00, is verified by checking the balance with the amount of capital shown on the balance sheet prepared at the end of the fiscal period. The capital account balance shown on Rugcare's balance sheet in Chapter 8, Illustration 8-12, is $10,296.00. The two amounts are the same, and the capital account balance is verified.

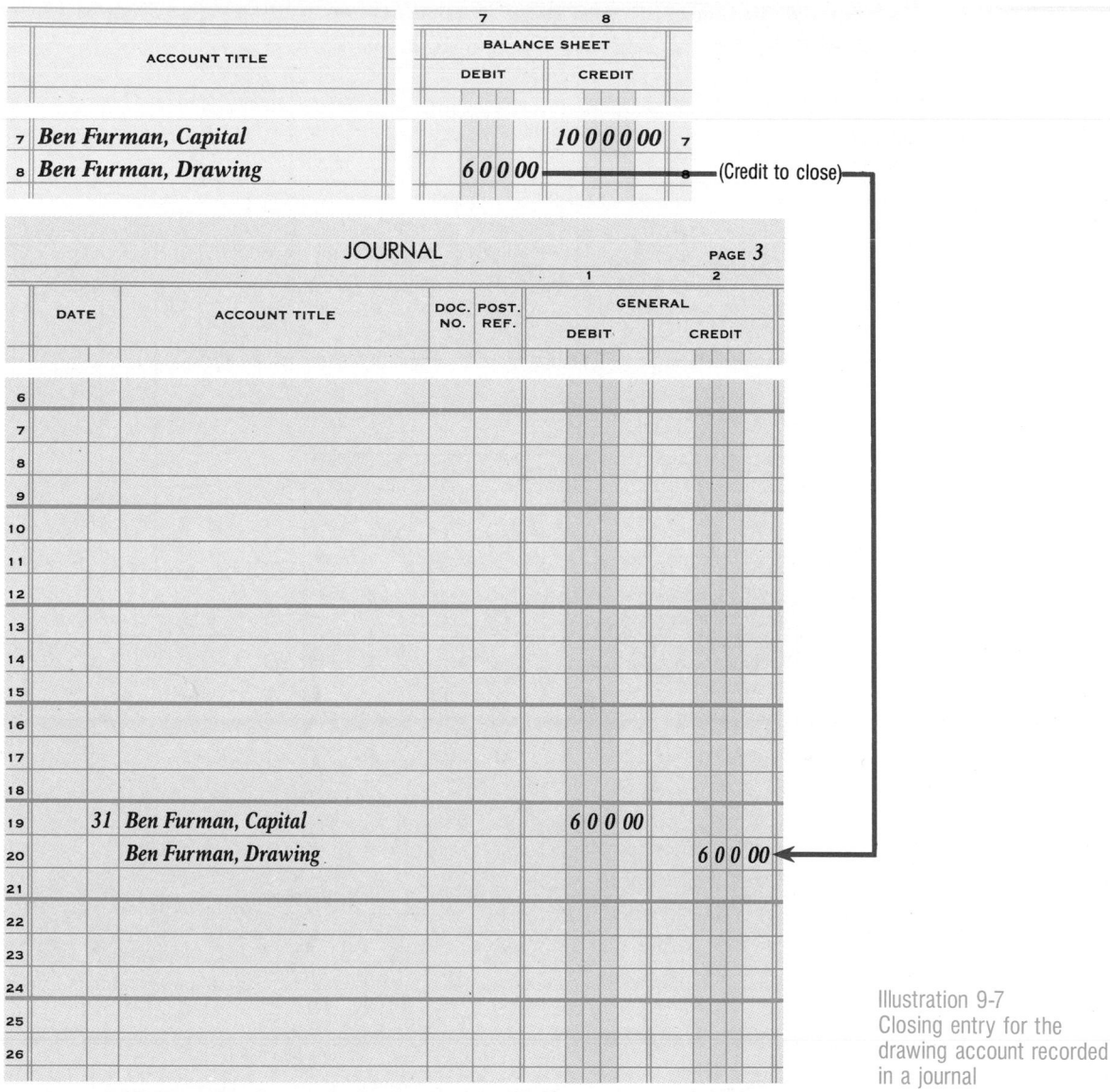

		7	8
	ACCOUNT TITLE	BALANCE SHEET	
		DEBIT	CREDIT
7	*Ben Furman, Capital*		10 0 0 0 00
8	*Ben Furman, Drawing*	6 0 0 00	—(Credit to close)—

JOURNAL   PAGE *3*

	DATE	ACCOUNT TITLE	DOC. NO.	POST. REF.	GENERAL DEBIT	GENERAL CREDIT
6						
7						
8						
9						
10						
11						
12						
13						
14						
15						
16						
17						
18						
19	31	*Ben Furman, Capital*			6 0 0 00	
20		*Ben Furman, Drawing*				6 0 0 00
21						
22						
23						
24						
25						
26						

Illustration 9-7
Closing entry for the drawing account recorded in a journal

SUMMARY OF CLOSING ENTRIES FOR A SERVICE BUSINESS ORGANIZED AS A PROPRIETORSHIP

Closing entries are journalized and posted to prepare temporary accounts for the next fiscal period. The income summary account is used to summarize all revenue and expense accounts before recording net income or net loss in the owner's capital account. A summary of closing entries is shown in Illustration 9-8.

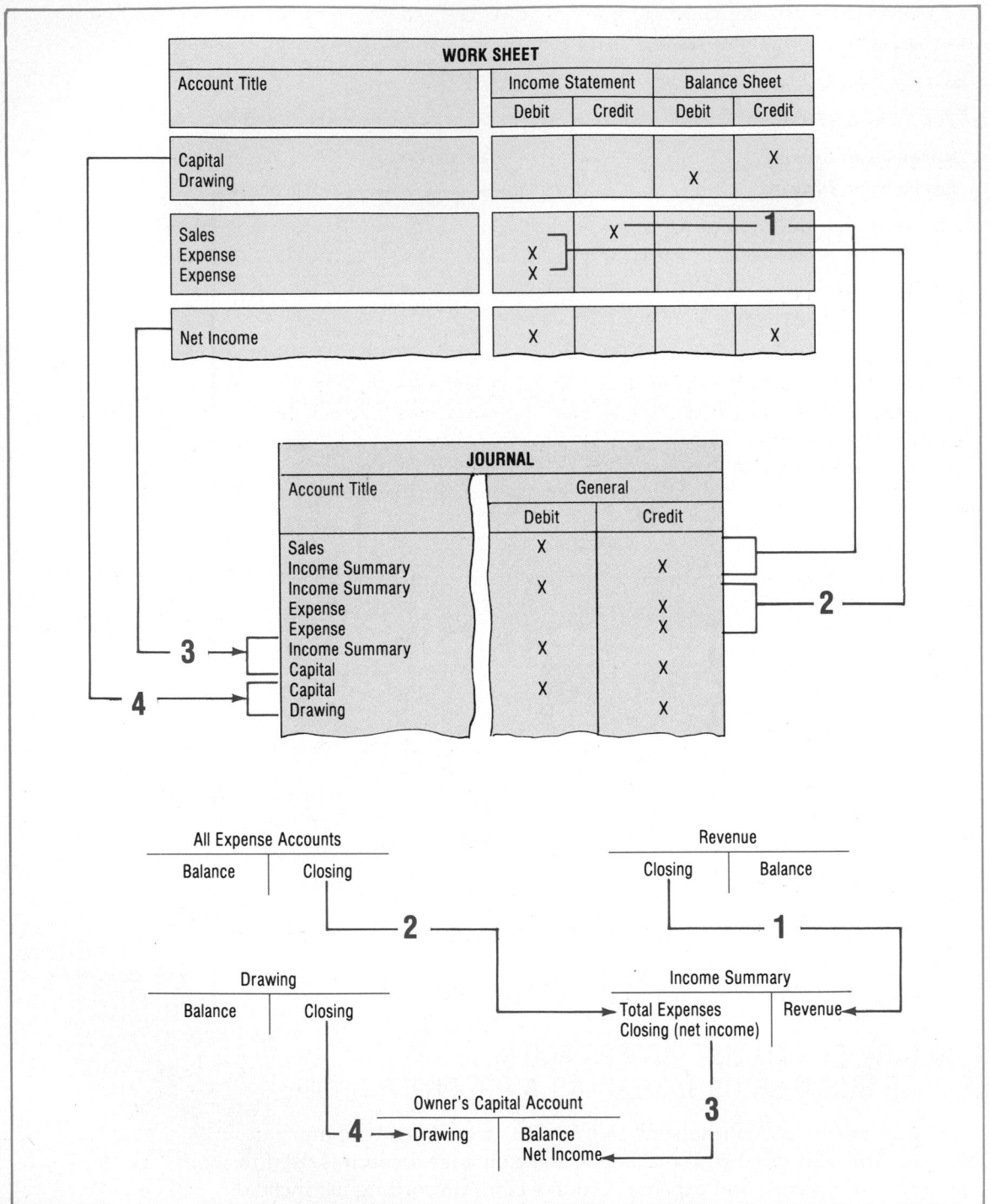

To complete a fiscal period, Rugcare records four journal entries to close temporary accounts.

1 Close income statement accounts with credit balances.

2 Close income statement accounts with debit balances.

3 Record the net income or net loss in the owner's capital account and close Income Summary.

4 Close the owner's drawing account.

GENERAL LEDGER AFTER ADJUSTING AND CLOSING ENTRIES ARE POSTED

Rugcare's general ledger after the adjusting and closing entries are posted is shown in Illustration 9-9. When an account has a zero balance, lines are drawn in both the Balance Debit and Balance Credit columns. The lines assure a reader that a balance has not been omitted.

Illustration 9-9
General ledger accounts after adjusting and closing entries are posted

ACCOUNT *Cash*   ACCOUNT NO. *110*

DATE	ITEM	POST. REF.	DEBIT	CREDIT	BALANCE DEBIT	BALANCE CREDIT
19.. Aug. 31		2	14 2 9 1 00		14 2 9 1 00	
31		2		6 0 1 9 00	8 2 7 2 00	

ACCOUNT *Petty Cash*   ACCOUNT NO. *120*

DATE	ITEM	POST. REF.	DEBIT	CREDIT	BALANCE DEBIT	BALANCE CREDIT
19.. Aug. 17		1	2 0 0 00		2 0 0 00	

ACCOUNT *Supplies*   ACCOUNT NO. *130*

DATE	ITEM	POST. REF.	DEBIT	CREDIT	BALANCE DEBIT	BALANCE CREDIT
19.. Aug. 3		1	1 5 7 7 00		1 5 7 7 00	
7		1	2 7 2 0 00		4 2 9 7 00	
20		1	2 0 0 00		4 4 9 7 00	
28		2	4 3 4 00		4 9 3 1 00	
31		3		2 6 4 7 00	2 2 8 4 00	

ACCOUNT *Prepaid Insurance*   ACCOUNT NO. *140*

DATE		ITEM	POST. REF.	DEBIT	CREDIT	BALANCE	
						DEBIT	CREDIT
Aug.^19--	4		1	1 2 0 0 00		1 2 0 0 00	
	31		3		1 0 0 00	1 1 0 0 00	

ACCOUNT *Butler Cleaning Supplies*   ACCOUNT NO. *210*

DATE		ITEM	POST. REF.	DEBIT	CREDIT	BALANCE	
						DEBIT	CREDIT
Aug.^19--	7		1		2 7 2 0 00		2 7 2 0 00
	11		1	1 3 6 0 00			1 3 6 0 00

ACCOUNT *Dale Office Supplies*   ACCOUNT NO. *220*

DATE		ITEM	POST. REF.	DEBIT	CREDIT	BALANCE	
						DEBIT	CREDIT
Aug.^19--	20		1		2 0 0 00		2 0 0 00

ACCOUNT *Ben Furman, Capital*   ACCOUNT NO. *310*

DATE		ITEM	POST. REF.	DEBIT	CREDIT	BALANCE	
						DEBIT	CREDIT
Aug.^19--	1		1		1 0 0 0 0 00		1 0 0 0 0 00
	31		3		8 9 6 00		1 0 8 9 6 00
	31		3	6 0 0 00			1 0 2 9 6 00

ACCOUNT *Ben Furman, Drawing*   ACCOUNT NO. *320*

DATE		ITEM	POST. REF.	DEBIT	CREDIT	BALANCE	
						DEBIT	CREDIT
Aug.^19--	12		1	1 0 0 00		1 0 0 00	
	31		2	5 0 0 00		6 0 0 00	
	31		3		6 0 0 00	——	——

Illustration 9-9
General ledger accounts
after adjusting and closing
entries are posted
(continued)

Illustration 9-9
General ledger accounts
after adjusting and closing
entries are posted
(continued)

ACCOUNT **Income Summary**   ACCOUNT NO. *330*

DATE	ITEM	POST. REF.	DEBIT	CREDIT	BALANCE DEBIT	BALANCE CREDIT
Aug. 19-- 31		3		4 2 9 1 00		4 2 9 1 00
31		3	3 3 9 5 00			8 9 6 00
31		3	8 9 6 00		———	———

ACCOUNT **Sales**   ACCOUNT NO. *410*

DATE	ITEM	POST. REF.	DEBIT	CREDIT	BALANCE DEBIT	BALANCE CREDIT
Aug. 19-- 31		2		4 2 9 1 00		4 2 9 1 00
31		3	4 2 9 1 00		———	———

ACCOUNT **Advertising Expense**   ACCOUNT NO. *510*

DATE	ITEM	POST. REF.	DEBIT	CREDIT	BALANCE DEBIT	BALANCE CREDIT
Aug. 19-- 14		1	6 8 00		6 8 00	
31		3		6 8 00	———	———

ACCOUNT **Insurance Expense**   ACCOUNT NO. *520*

DATE	ITEM	POST. REF.	DEBIT	CREDIT	BALANCE DEBIT	BALANCE CREDIT
Aug. 19-- 31		3	1 0 0 00		1 0 0 00	
31		3		1 0 0 00	———	———

ACCOUNT **Miscellaneous Expense**   ACCOUNT NO. *530*

DATE	ITEM	POST. REF.	DEBIT	CREDIT	BALANCE DEBIT	BALANCE CREDIT
Aug. 19-- 13		1	2 5 00		2 5 00	
18		1	7 0 00		9 5 00	
28		2	3 00		9 8 00	
31		2	7 00		1 0 5 00	
31		3		1 0 5 00	———	———

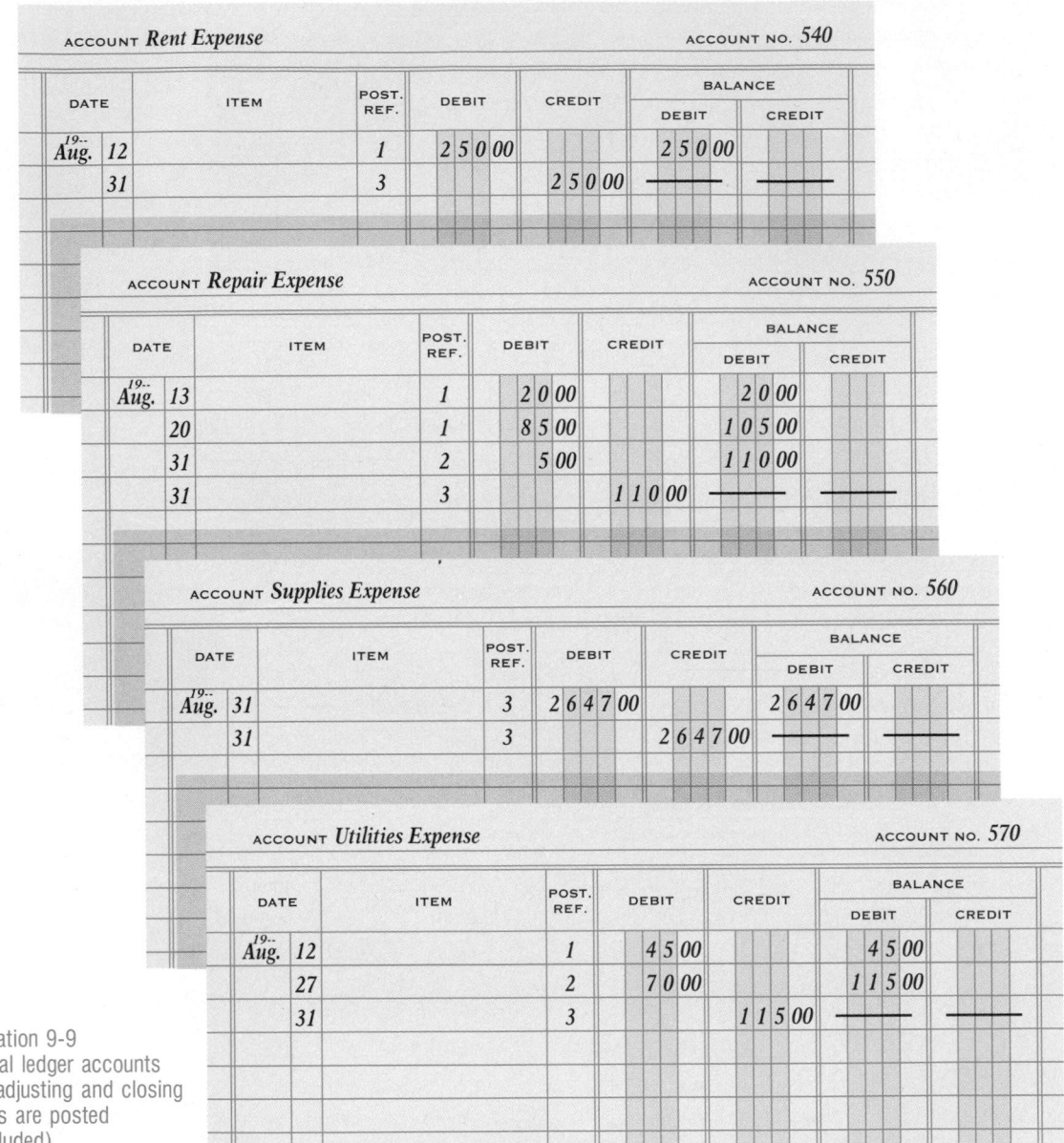

ACCOUNT *Rent Expense*					ACCOUNT NO. *540*	
DATE	ITEM	POST. REF.	DEBIT	CREDIT	BALANCE DEBIT	BALANCE CREDIT
Aug.¹⁹⁻⁻ 12		1	2 5 0 00		2 5 0 00	
31		3		2 5 0 00	——	——

ACCOUNT *Repair Expense*					ACCOUNT NO. *550*	
DATE	ITEM	POST. REF.	DEBIT	CREDIT	BALANCE DEBIT	BALANCE CREDIT
Aug.¹⁹⁻⁻ 13		1	2 0 00		2 0 00	
20		1	8 5 00		1 0 5 00	
31		2	5 00		1 1 0 00	
31		3		1 1 0 00	——	——

ACCOUNT *Supplies Expense*					ACCOUNT NO. *560*	
DATE	ITEM	POST. REF.	DEBIT	CREDIT	BALANCE DEBIT	BALANCE CREDIT
Aug.¹⁹⁻⁻ 31		3	2 6 4 7 00		2 6 4 7 00	
31		3		2 6 4 7 00	——	——

ACCOUNT *Utilities Expense*					ACCOUNT NO. *570*	
DATE	ITEM	POST. REF.	DEBIT	CREDIT	BALANCE DEBIT	BALANCE CREDIT
Aug.¹⁹⁻⁻ 12		1	4 5 00		4 5 00	
27		2	7 0 00		1 1 5 00	
31		3		1 1 5 00	——	——

Illustration 9-9
General ledger accounts
after adjusting and closing
entries are posted
(concluded)

POST-CLOSING TRIAL BALANCE

After the closing entries are posted, Rugcare verifies that debits equal credits in the general ledger accounts by preparing a trial balance. A trial balance prepared after the closing entries are posted is called a post-closing trial balance.

Only general ledger accounts with balances are included on a post-closing trial balance. The permanent accounts (assets, liabilities, and owner's capital) have balances and do appear on a post-closing trial balance. Because the temporary accounts (income summary, revenue, expense, and drawing) are closed and have zero balances, they do not appear on a post-closing trial balance. Rugcare's post-closing trial balance is shown in Illustration 9-10.

ACCOUNT TITLE	DEBIT	CREDIT
Rugcare		
Post-Closing Trial Balance		
August 31, 19--		
Cash	8 2 7 2 00	
Petty Cash	2 0 0 00	
Supplies	2 2 8 4 00	
Prepaid Insurance	1 1 0 0 00	
Butler Cleaning Supplies		1 3 6 0 00
Dale Office Supplies		2 0 0 00
Ben Furman, Capital		10 2 9 6 00
Totals	11 8 5 6 00	11 8 5 6 00

Illustration 9-10
Post-closing trial balance

Rugcare uses eight steps to prepare a post-closing trial balance.

1 Write the heading on three lines.

2 Write the titles of all general ledger accounts with balances in the Account Title column.

3 On the same line with each account title, write each account's balance in either the Debit or Credit column.

4 Rule a single line across both amount columns below the last amount, and add each amount column.

5 Compare the two column totals. The two column totals must be the same. The total of all debits must equal the total of all credits in a general ledger. The totals of both columns on Rugcare's post-closing trial balance are the same, $11,856.00. Rugcare's post-closing trial balance shows that the general ledger account balances are in balance and ready for the new fiscal period. If the two column totals are not the same, the errors must be found and corrected before any more work is completed.

6 Write the word, *Totals*, on the line below the last account title.

7 Write the column totals, *$11,856.00*, below the single line.

8 Rule double lines across both amount columns to show that the totals have been verified as correct.

SUMMARY OF AN ACCOUNTING CYCLE FOR A SERVICE BUSINESS

Chapters 1 through 9 describe Rugcare's accounting activities for a one-month fiscal period. The series of accounting activities included in recording financial information for a fiscal period is called an accounting cycle. (CONCEPT: *Accounting Period Cycle*) Rugcare's accounting cycle is summarized in Illustration 9-11.

For the next fiscal period, the cycle begins again at Step 1.

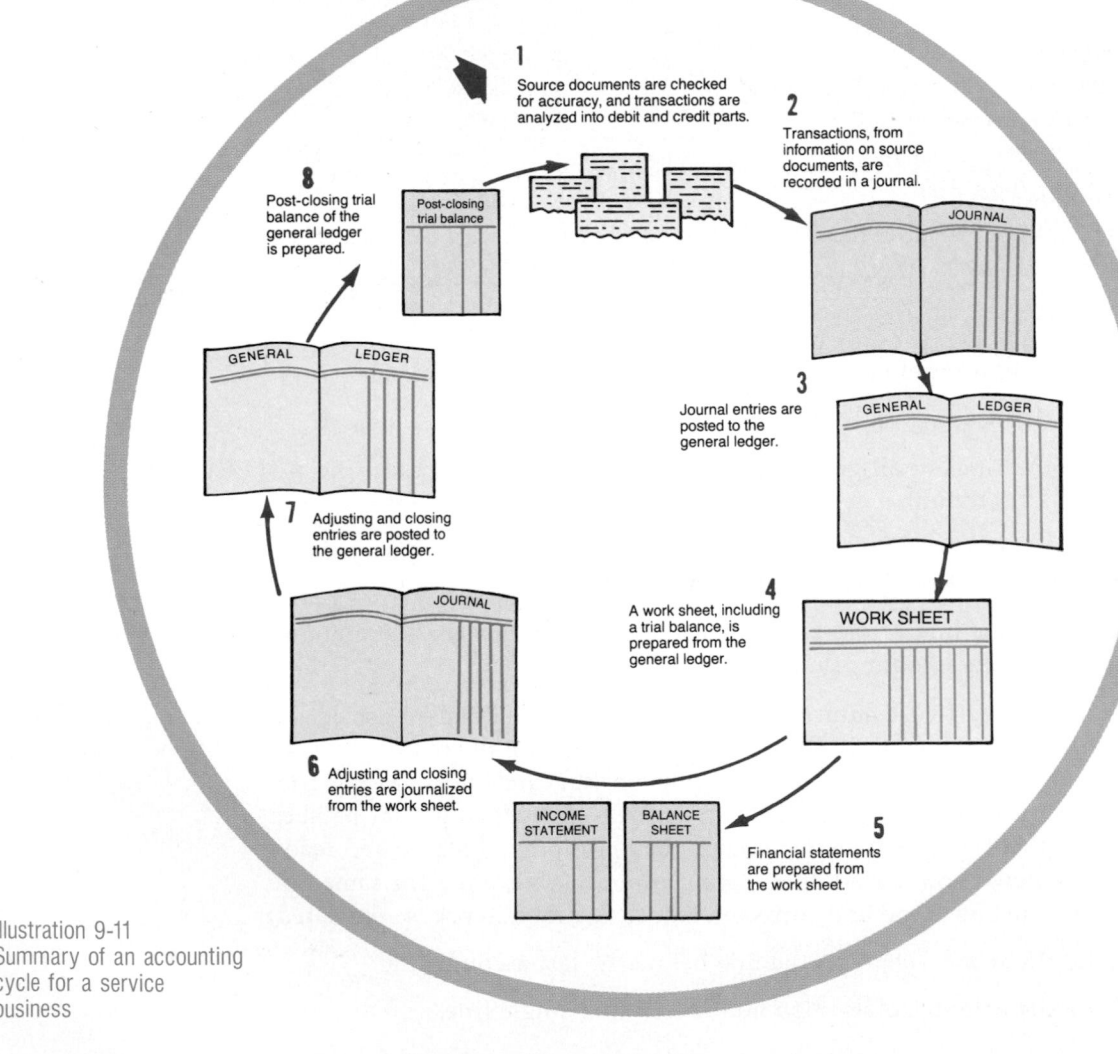

1 Source documents are checked for accuracy, and transactions are analyzed into debit and credit parts.

2 Transactions, from information on source documents, are recorded in a journal.

3 Journal entries are posted to the general ledger.

4 A work sheet, including a trial balance, is prepared from the general ledger.

5 Financial statements are prepared from the work sheet.

6 Adjusting and closing entries are journalized from the work sheet.

7 Adjusting and closing entries are posted to the general ledger.

8 Post-closing trial balance of the general ledger is prepared.

Illustration 9-11
Summary of an accounting
cycle for a service
business

ACCOUNTING TERMS

What is the meaning of each of the following?

1. adjusting entries
2. permanent accounts
3. temporary accounts
4. closing entries
5. post-closing trial balance
6. accounting cycle

QUESTIONS FOR INDIVIDUAL STUDY

1. Which accounting concept is being applied when information in a general ledger is summarized on a work sheet at the end of each fiscal period?
2. Why are adjusting entries journalized and posted at the end of a fiscal period?
3. How are adjusting entries identified in a journal?
4. What accounts are affected, and how, by the adjusting entry for supplies?
5. What accounts are affected, and how, by the adjusting entry for prepaid insurance?
6. Why are closing entries journalized and posted at the end of a fiscal period?
7. How is the income summary account used?
8. Why is the income summary account considered unique?
9. What kind of balance will the income summary account have if a business has a net income?
10. What kind of balance will the income summary account have if a business has a net loss?
11. What four closing entries are recorded by Rugcare?
12. What effect do withdrawals have on the owner's equity?
13. After the closing entries are posted, how is the balance of the capital account verified?
14. Why is a post-closing trial balance prepared after the closing entries have been posted?
15. What accounts appear on a post-closing trial balance?
16. What are the eight steps of an accounting cycle?

CASES FOR MANAGEMENT DECISION

CASE 1 Thomas Westcott forgot to journalize and post the adjusting entry for prepaid insurance at the end of the June fiscal period. What effect will this omission have on the records of Mr. Westcott's business as of June 30? Explain your answer.

CASE 2 Jason Fields states that his business is so small that he just records supplies and insurance as expenses when he pays for them. Thus, at the end of a fiscal period, Mr. Fields does not record adjusting and closing entries for his business. Do you agree with his accounting procedures? Explain your answer.

CASE 3 On July 31 Iris Medina's work sheet shows a capital account balance of $9,000.00. Miss Medina's post-closing trial balance shows a capital account balance of $8,955.00. What could have caused the change in the capital account's balance?

CASE 4 Sueanne Worth owns a business that uses only twelve general ledger accounts. She carefully checks each journal entry to assure that debits equal credits for the entry. Before preparing financial statements, she checks carefully to assure that debits equal credits in each pair of columns on the work sheet. She checks to assure that debits equal credits in each of the adjusting and closing entries. Because of these careful checks during a fiscal period, she believes that her records are accurate, and she does not need to prepare a post-closing trial balance. Do you agree with Ms. Worth? Explain your answer.

■ DRILL FOR UNDERSTANDING

DRILL 9-D1   Determining accounts affected by adjusting and closing entries

Rapid Service Company uses the following general ledger accounts.

1. Advertising Expense
2. Baer Supplies
3. Cash
4. Gates Office Supplies
5. Irma Downs, Capital
6. Irma Downs, Drawing
7. Income Summary
8. Insurance Expense

9. Miscellaneous Expense
10. Prepaid Insurance
11. Rent Expense
12. Sales
13. Supplies
14. Supplies Expense
15. Utilities Expense

Use a form similar to the following.

1	2	3	4	5	6	7
Account Title	**Account Is Affected by an Adjusting Entry**		**Account Is Affected by a Closing Entry**		**After Closing Entries Are Posted, Account Has a Balance**	
	Yes	**No**	**Yes**	**No**	**Yes**	**No**
1. *Advertising Expense*		✓	✓			✓

Instructions: 1. List the account titles in Column 1. The first account, Advertising Expense, is given as an example.

2. For each account title, place a check mark in either Column 2 or 3 to indicate whether the account is affected by an adjusting entry.

3. For each account title, place a check mark in either Column 4 or 5 to indicate whether the account is affected by a closing entry.

4. For each account title, place a check mark in either Column 6 or 7 to indicate whether the account has a balance after the closing entries are posted.

■ APPLICATION PROBLEM

PROBLEM 9-1   Journalizing and posting adjusting and closing entries; preparing a post-closing trial balance

Eiler Company's partial work sheet for the month ended October 31 of the current year is given on the next page. The general ledger accounts are given in the working papers that accompany this textbook. (The general ledger accounts do not show all details for the fiscal period. The "Balance" shown in each account is the account's balance before adjusting and closing entries are posted.)

Instructions: 1. Use page 3 of a journal. Journalize and post the adjusting entries.

2. Continue to use page 3 of the journal. Journalize and post the closing entries.

3. Prepare a post-closing trial balance.

	ACCOUNT TITLE	3 ADJUSTMENTS DEBIT	4 ADJUSTMENTS CREDIT	5 INCOME STATEMENT DEBIT	6 INCOME STATEMENT CREDIT	7 BALANCE SHEET DEBIT	8 BALANCE SHEET CREDIT	
1	Cash					2 6 0 0 00		1
2	Supplies		(a) 1 4 5 00			5 6 0 00		2
3	Prepaid Insurance		(b) 1 9 0 00			2 1 0 00		3
4	Kurtz Supplies						3 0 0 00	4
5	Wiley Supplies						9 0 00	5
6	Norma Delk, Capital						2 8 5 0 00	6
7	Norma Delk, Drawing					2 5 0 00		7
8	Income Summary							8
9	Sales				1 1 0 0 00			9
10	Insurance Expense	(b) 1 9 0 00		1 9 0 00				10
11	Miscellaneous Expense			6 5 00				11
12	Rent Expense			3 2 0 00				12
13	Supplies Expense	(a) 1 4 5 00		1 4 5 00				13
14		3 3 5 00	3 3 5 00	7 2 0 00	1 1 0 0 00	3 6 2 0 00	3 2 4 0 00	14
15	Net Income			3 8 0 00			3 8 0 00	15
16				1 1 0 0 00	1 1 0 0 00	3 6 2 0 00	3 6 2 0 00	16
17								17
18								18
19								19
20								20
21								21
22								22
23								23
24								24
25								25

ENRICHMENT PROBLEMS

MASTERY PROBLEM 9-M   **Journalizing and posting adjusting and closing entries; preparing a post-closing trial balance**

Kellerman Services' partial work sheet for the month ended November 30 of the current year is given on the next page. The general ledger accounts are given in the working papers that accompany this textbook. (The general ledger accounts do not show all details for the fiscal period. The "Balance" shown in each account is the account's balance before adjusting and closing entries are posted.)

Instructions: 1. Use page 3 of a journal. Journalize and post the adjusting entries.
   2. Continue to use page 3 of the journal. Journalize and post the closing entries.
   3. Prepare a post-closing trial balance.

ACCOUNT TITLE	3 ADJUSTMENTS DEBIT	4 ADJUSTMENTS CREDIT	5 INCOME STATEMENT DEBIT	6 INCOME STATEMENT CREDIT	7 BALANCE SHEET DEBIT	8 BALANCE SHEET CREDIT	
1 Cash					3 5 0 0 00		1
2 Supplies		(a) 1 9 5 00			7 5 0 00		2
3 Prepaid Insurance		(b) 2 6 0 00			2 8 0 00		3
4 Kern Supplies						5 0 0 00	4
5 Waite Supplies						1 2 0 00	5
6 A. Kellerman, Capital						3 7 2 5 00	6
7 A. Kellerman, Drawing					3 5 0 00		7
8 Income Summary							8
9 Sales				1 5 0 0 00			9
10 Insurance Expense	(b) 2 6 0 00		2 6 0 00				10
11 Miscellaneous Expense			8 5 00				11
12 Rent Expense			4 2 5 00				12
13 Supplies Expense	(a) 1 9 5 00		1 9 5 00				13
14	4 5 5 00	4 5 5 00	9 6 5 00	1 5 0 0 00	4 8 8 0 00	4 3 4 5 00	14
15 Net Income			5 3 5 00			5 3 5 00	15
16			1 5 0 0 00	1 5 0 0 00	4 8 8 0 00	4 8 8 0 00	16

CHALLENGE PROBLEM 9-C Preparing a work sheet; journalizing adjusting and closing entries

A trial balance on a work sheet for Reed Company is given in the working papers that accompany this textbook.

Instructions: 1. Complete the work sheet. Use December 31 of the current year as the date.

Adjustment Information, December 31

Supplies on hand $980.00
Value of prepaid insurance 700.00

2. Use page 3 of a journal. Journalize the adjusting entries.
3. Continue to use page 3 of the journal. Journalize the closing entries.

Reinforcement Activity 1, Part B

An Accounting Cycle for a Proprietorship: End-of-Fiscal-Period Work

The general ledger prepared in Reinforcement Activity 1, Part A, is needed to complete Reinforcement Activity 1, Part B.

Reinforcement Activity 1, Part B, includes end-of-fiscal-period activities studied in Chapters 7 through 9.

WORK SHEET

Instructions: 12. Prepare a trial balance on a work sheet. Use a one-month fiscal period ended May 31 of the current year.

13. Analyze the following adjustment information into debit and credit parts. Record the adjustments on the work sheet.

Adjustment Information, May 31

Supplies on hand	$515.00
Value of prepaid insurance	800.00

14. Total and rule the Adjustments columns.

15. Extend the up-to-date account balances to the Balance Sheet and Income Statement columns.

16. Complete the work sheet.

FINANCIAL STATEMENTS

17. Prepare an income statement. Figure and record the component percentages for sales, total expenses, and net income. Round percentage calculations to the nearest 0.1%.

18. Prepare a balance sheet.

ADJUSTING ENTRIES

19. Use page 3 of the journal. Journalize and post the adjusting entries.

CLOSING ENTRIES

20. Continue using page 3 of the journal. Journalize and post the closing entries.

POST-CLOSING TRIAL BALANCE

21. Prepare a post-closing trial balance.

VIDEO
TRANSFER

A BUSINESS SIMULATION   BA20EE1

This simulation covers the transactions completed by Video Transfer, a service business organized as a proprietorship. Video Transfer begins business on September 1 of the current year. The business produces personal videos for such events as weddings and family reunions. In addition, the business also transfers home movies and slides to video tape.

The activities included in the accounting cycle for Video Transfer are listed below. The company uses a journal and a general ledger similar to those described for Rugcare in Part 1. The books of account needed to complete this simulation are available from the publisher.

The following activities are included in this simulation.

1. Journalizing transactions in a journal.
2. Forwarding column totals to a new journal page.
3. Preparing a bank statement reconciliation and recording a bank service charge.
4. Proving cash.
5. Proving and ruling a journal.
6. Posting from a journal to a general ledger.
7. Preparing a trial balance on a work sheet.
8. Recording adjustments on a work sheet.
9. Completing a work sheet.
10. Preparing financial statements (income statement and balance sheet).
11. Journalizing and posting adjusting entries.
12. Journalizing and posting closing entries.
13. Preparing a post-closing trial balance.

Video Transfer
A Business Simulation

This simulation covers the transactions completed by Video Transfer, a service business organized as a proprietorship. Video Transfer begins business on September 1 of the current year. The business produces personal videos for such events as weddings and family reunions. In addition, the business also transfers home movies and slides to video tape.

ACCOUNTING CYCLE

Video Transfer uses a one-month fiscal period. The fiscal period for this simulation begins on September 1 and ends on September 30 of the current year.

ACCOUNTING RECORDS

Video Transfer uses accounting records similar to the following.

Accounting Forms and Records	Chapter	Illustration Number
Journal	4	4-14
General ledger	5	5-14
Bank statement reconciliation	6	6-8
Trial balance and work sheet	7	7-7
Income statement	8	8-6
Balance sheet	8	8-12
Adjusting entries	9	9-2
Closing entries	9	9-7

SOURCE DOCUMENTS

Video Transfer uses the following source documents. *(CONCEPT: Objective Evidence)*

Source Documents	Abbreviations	For Transactions
Calculator tapes	T	Cash received from sales
Receipts	R	Cash received from other than sales
Check stubs	C	Cash payments
Memorandums	M	Transactions not covered by the first three source documents

189

CHART OF ACCOUNTS

Video Transfer uses the following chart of accounts.

VIDEO TRANSFER Chart of Accounts		
Balance Sheet Accounts	**Income Statement Accounts**	
(100) ASSETS	**(400) REVENUE**	
110 Cash	410 Sales	
120 Petty Cash		
130 Supplies	**(500) EXPENSES**	
140 Prepaid Insurance	510 Advertising Expense	
	520 Insurance Expense	
(200) LIABILITIES	530 Miscellaneous Expense	
210 Dorn Supplies	540 Rent Expense	
220 Setter Office Supplies	550 Repair Expense	
230 Video Distributors	560 Supplies Expense	
	570 Utilities Expense	
(300) OWNER'S EQUITY		
310 Martha Day, Capital		
320 Martha Day, Drawing		
330 Income Summary		

RECORDING TRANSACTIONS

Instructions: 1. Use page 1 of the journal. Journalize the following transactions completed during September of the current year.

Trans.
No.

1	Sept. 1.	Received cash from owner as an investment, $16,000.00. R1.
2	2.	Paid cash for supplies, $800.00. C1.
3	3.	Paid cash for insurance, $400.00. C2.
4	3.	Paid cash to establish a petty cash fund, $200.00. C3.
5	3.	Bought supplies on account from Video Distributors, $450.00. M1.
6	4.	Paid cash for rent, $1,400.00. C4.
7	6.	Paid cash for electric bill, $50.00. C5.
8	7.	Received cash from sales, $475.00. T7.
9	8.	Paid cash for advertising, $100.00. C6.
10	8.	Received cash from sales, $110.00. T8.
11	9.	Paid cash on account to Video Distributors, $200.00. C7.
12	9.	Paid cash to owner for personal use, $200.00. C8.
13	9.	Received cash from sales, $280.00. T9.
14	10.	Paid cash for miscellaneous expense, $35.00. C9.
15	10.	Received cash from sales, $225.00. T10.
16	11.	Paid cash for miscellaneous expense, $50.00. C10.
17	11.	Received cash from sales, $300.00. T11.
18	12.	Paid cash for repairs, $60.00. C11.

Trans.
No.

19	Sept. 12.	Received cash from sales, $200.00. T12.
20	13.	Paid cash for supplies, $300.00. C12.
21	13.	Bought supplies on account from Setter Office Supplies, $150.00. M2.
22	13.	Received cash from sales, $175.00. T13.

2. Prove and rule page 1 of the journal. Carry the column totals forward to page 2 of the journal.

3. Prepare a report using information from page 1 of the journal. Use a form similar to the following. Give the report to your instructor.

Name _____
Today's date _____
Column totals from page ____ of the journal:

Column	Debit	Credit
General	$_____	$_____
Sales		_____
Cash	_____	_____
Totals...............	$_____	$_____

4. Post the separate amounts on each line of the journal that need to be posted individually.

5. Use page 2 of the journal. Journalize the following transactions.

Trans.
No.

23	Sept. 14.	Paid cash for miscellaneous expense, $30.00. C13.
24	14.	Bought supplies on account from Video Distributors, $140.00. M3.
25	14.	Received cash from sales, $380.00. T14.
26	15.	Paid cash for repairs, $30.00. C14.
27	15.	Paid cash for miscellaneous expense, $40.00. C15.
28	15.	Received cash from sales, $100.00. T15.
29	16.	Paid cash for miscellaneous expense, $35.00. C16.
30	16.	Paid cash for advertising, $110.00. C17.
31	16.	Paid cash to owner for personal use, $200.00. C18.
32	16.	Received cash from sales, $285.00. T16.
33	17.	Paid cash for water bill, $65.00. C19.
34	17.	Paid cash for supplies, $110.00. C20.
35	17.	Received cash from sales, $265.00. T17.
36	18.	Paid cash for miscellaneous expense, $10.00. C21.
37	18.	Received cash from sales, $310.00. T18.
38	19.	Paid cash for miscellaneous expense, $10.00. C22.
39	19.	Received cash from sales, $250.00. T19.
40	20.	Paid cash for supplies, $125.00. C23.
41	20.	Bought supplies on account from Setter Office Supplies, $160.00. M4.
42	20.	Received cash from sales, $180.00. T20.
43	21.	Received cash from sales, $120.00. T21.

6. Prove and rule page 2 of the journal. Carry the column totals forward to page 3 of the journal.

7. Prepare a report using information from page 2 of the journal. Use a form similar to the one shown in Instruction 3. Give the report to your instructor.

8. Post the separate amounts on each line of the journal that need to be posted individually.

9. Use page 3 of the journal. Journalize the following transactions.

Trans.
No.

44	Sept. 22. Bought supplies on account from Dorn Supplies, $600.00. M5.
45	22. Received cash from sales, $225.00. T22.
46	23. Paid cash for repairs, $8.00. C24.
47	23. Paid cash to owner for personal use, $200.00. C25.
48	23. Received cash from sales, $230.00. T23.
49	24. Paid cash for miscellaneous expense, $60.00. C26.
50	24. Received cash from sales, $170.00. T24.
51	25. Paid cash for telephone bill, $105.00. C27.
52	25. Received cash from sales, $185.00. T25.
53	26. Received cash from sales, $165.00. T26.
54	27. Paid cash for supplies, $100.00. C28.
55	27. Paid cash on account to Dorn Supplies, $400.00. C29.
56	27. Received cash from sales, $190.00. T27.

10. On September 27 Video Transfer received a bank statement dated September 26. The following information is obtained from the bank statement and from the records of the business. Prepare a bank statement reconciliation.

Bank statement balance	$15,700.00
Outstanding deposits:	
September 26	165.00
September 27	190.00
Outstanding checks:	
Nos. 24, 26, 27, 28, and 29	
Bank service charge	5.00
Checkbook balance on the next unused check stub	15,387.00

11. Continue using page 3 of the journal, and journalize the following transactions.

Trans.
No.

57	Sept. 27. Received bank statement showing September bank service charge, $5.00. M6.
58	28. Received cash from sales, $265.00. T28.
59	29. Received cash from sales, $250.00. T29.
60	30. Paid cash to replenish the petty cash fund, $55.00: miscellaneous expense, $30.00; repairs, $25.00. C30.
61	30. Paid cash to owner for personal use, $200.00. C31.
62	30. Received cash from sales, $265.00. T30.

12. Prove page 3 of the journal.

13. Prove cash. The beginning cash balance on September 1 is zero. The balance on the next unused check stub is $15,907.00.

14. Rule page 3 of the journal.

15. Prepare a report using information from page 3 of the journal. Use a form similar to the one shown in Instruction 3. Give the report to your instructor.

16. Post the separate amounts on each line of the journal that need to be posted individually.

17. Post the column totals of the journal.

END-OF-FISCAL-PERIOD WORK

Instructions: 18. Prepare a trial balance on a work sheet. Use a one-month fiscal period ended September 30 of the current year.

19. Analyze the following adjustment information into debit and credit parts. Record the adjustments on the work sheet. Total and rule the Adjustments columns.

Adjustment Information, September 30

Supplies on hand	$890.00
Value of prepaid insurance	300.00

20. Extend the up-to-date account balances to the Balance Sheet and Income Statement columns.

21. Complete the work sheet.

22. Prepare an income statement. Figure and record the component percentages for sales, total expenses, and net income. Round percentage calculations to the nearest 0.1%.

23. Prepare a balance sheet.

24. Use page 4 of the journal. Journalize and post the adjusting entries.

25. Continue to use page 4 of the journal. Journalize and post the closing entries.

26. Prepare a post-closing trial balance.

27. Assemble all forms and records in the following order. Be sure your name is on *each* sheet. Present your completed simulation to your instructor.

> Journal pages
> General ledger
> Bank reconciliation
> Work sheet
> Income statement
> Balance sheet
> Post-closing trial balance

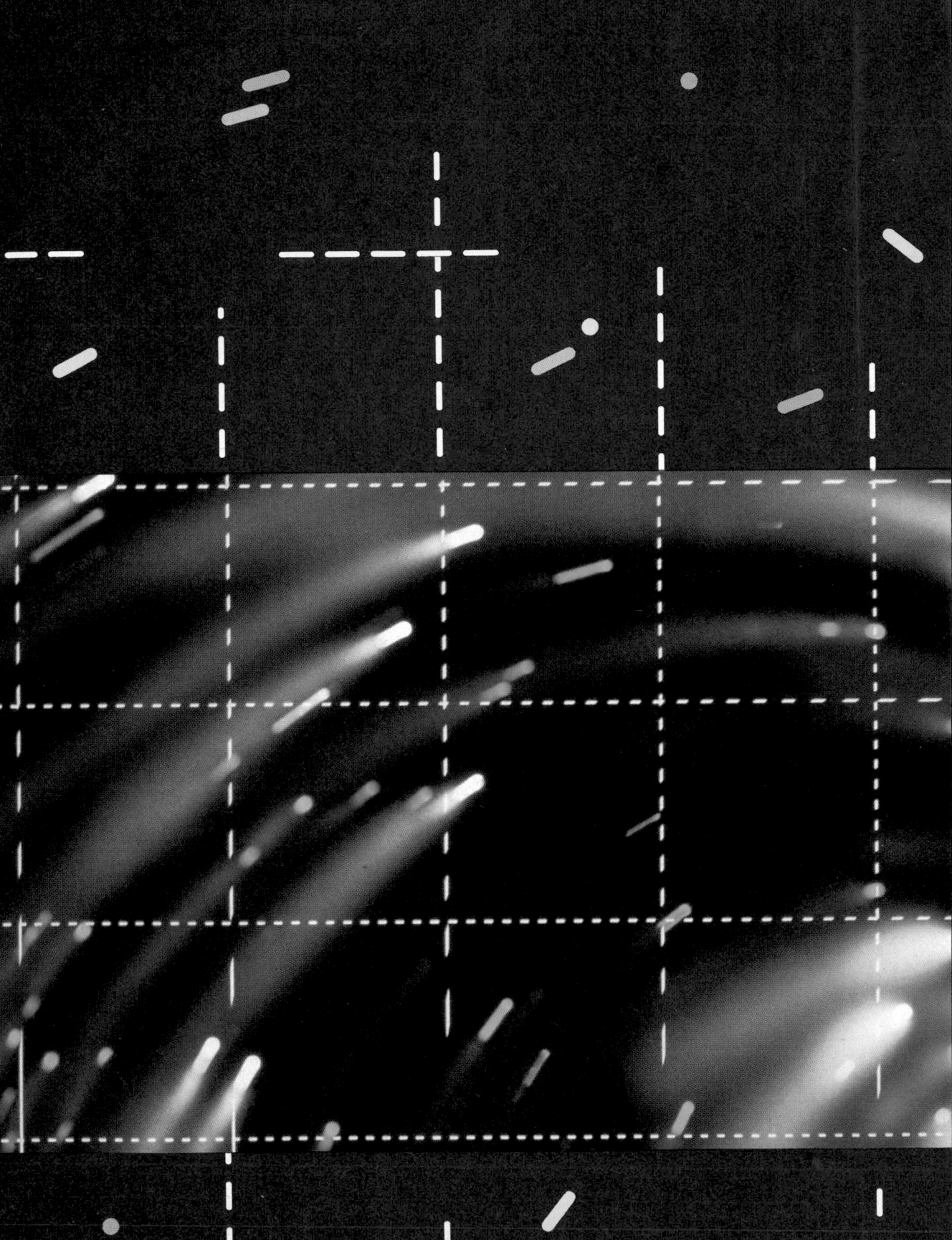

Automated Accounting for a Service Business

2

GENERAL BEHAVIORAL GOALS

1. Know accounting terminology related to an automated accounting system for a service business organized as a proprietorship.
2. Understand accounting concepts and practices related to an automated accounting system for a service business organized as a proprietorship.
3. Demonstrate accounting procedures used in an automated accounting system for a service business organized as a proprietorship.

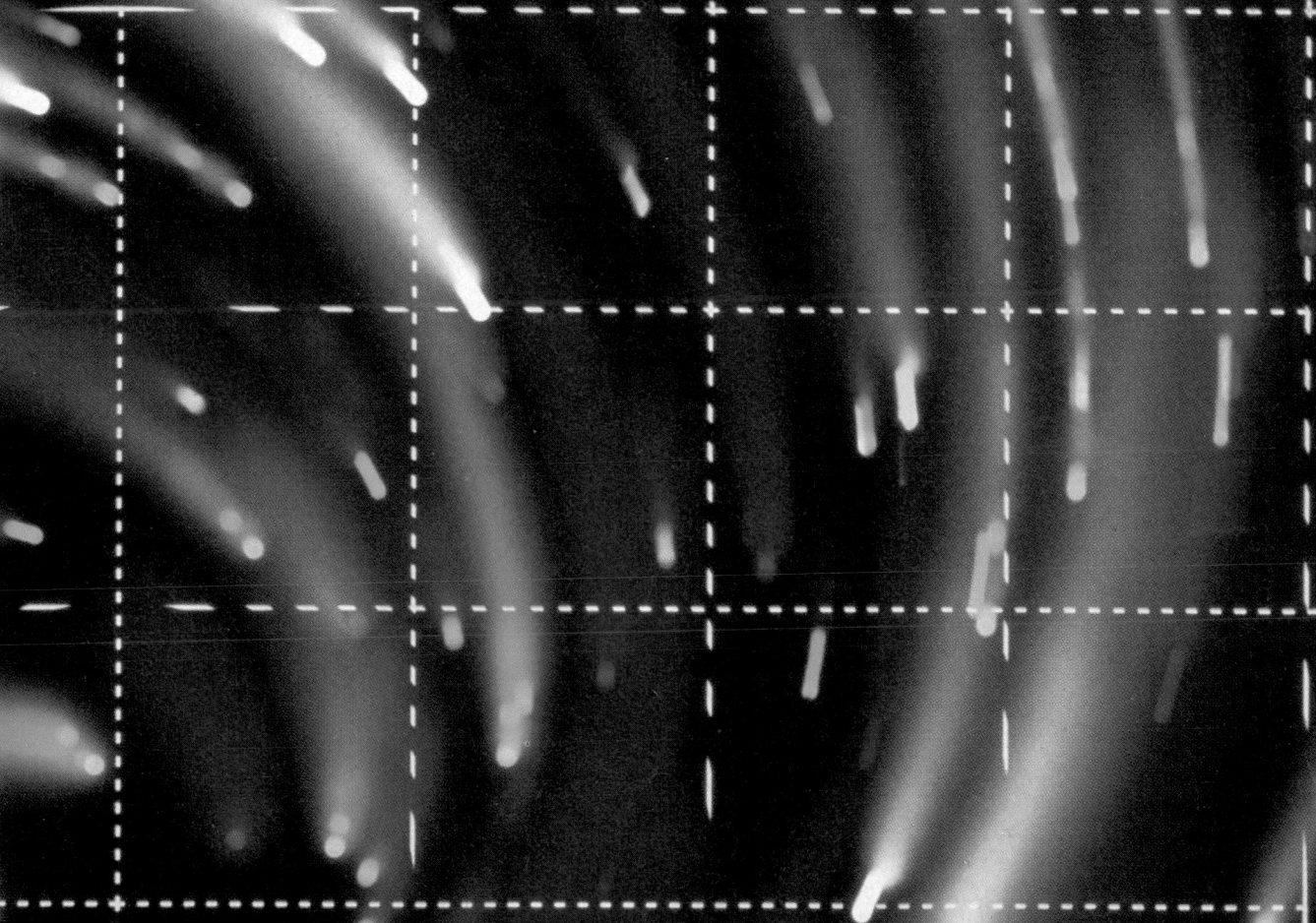

PETLODGE
Chart of Accounts

Balance Sheet Accounts	Income Statement Accounts

(100) ASSETS

110	Cash
120	Petty Cash
130	Supplies—Office
140	Supplies—Pet
150	Prepaid Insurance

(200) LIABILITIES

210	Marino Kennel Supply
220	Vega Office Supply

(300) OWNER'S EQUITY

310	Victoria Peak, Capital
320	Victoria Peak, Drawing
330	Income Summary

(400) REVENUE

410	Boarding Fees

(500) EXPENSES

510	Advertising Expense
520	Insurance Expense
530	Miscellaneous Expense
540	Rent Expense
550	Supplies Expense—Office
560	Supplies Expense—Pet
570	Utilities Expense

The chart of accounts for Petlodge is
illustrated above for ready reference as you
study Part 2 of this textbook.

Starting an Automated Accounting System

ENABLING PERFORMANCE TASKS

After studying Chapter 10, you will be able to:
a. Define accounting terms related to starting an automated accounting system.
b. Identify accounting concepts and practices related to starting an automated accounting system.
c. Prepare a general ledger file maintenance input form for a chart of accounts.
d. Prepare a general ledger input form for opening balances.

Business owners and managers depend on accounting records and reports to provide the information needed for effective decision making. These records and reports must contain current, accurate, and complete information that can be reported in useful and timely financial statements. Complete information must include the recording and reporting of all details or facts about the financial condition and progress of the business. Details or facts are called data. Although procedures used to record and report financial data may vary among businesses, the accounting concepts are the same.

Financial data may be recorded and reported by hand or by machine. An accounting system in which data are recorded and reported mostly by hand is called manual accounting. Some businesses use automated machines to speed the recording and reporting process. An accounting system in which data are recorded and reported mostly by using automated machines is called automated accounting. Even in automated accounting, some procedures are done by hand.

AUTOMATED ACCOUNTING

Victoria Peak operates a small service business known as Petlodge. *(CONCEPT: Business Entity)* Petlodge provides hourly, daily, and weekly boarding services for pets. Petlodge rents the building in which it is located as well as the furnishings needed to operate the business. Ms. Peak expects the business to make money and to continue indefinitely. *(CON-CEPT: Going Concern)*

Petlodge has been using a manual accounting system. The business wants to improve the accounting system by doing the work faster and less expensively. Petlodge is considering using an automated accounting system.

Using computers in automated accounting

Automated accounting uses a variety of machines. A machine that accepts data, applies procedures, and produces results according to stored instructions is called a computer. Both large and small businesses make use of computers to record and report accounting data. Using a computer does not change accounting concepts. Only the methods change. Regardless of the accounting system used, financial data are reported for a specified period of time. *(CONCEPT: Accounting Period Cycle)* A computer performs the routine and repetitive operations. Different types of computers are used to record and process accounting data.

Types of computers

Automated accounting systems were initially used only by larger businesses. The high cost of computers made it impractical for smaller businesses to go beyond manual systems. Today, however, computers are available for use by all businesses regardless of size. The computer cost is based on the amount of data that can be processed and the processing speed. Currently, three types of computers are used for recording and reporting accounting data: (1) mainframe computers, (2) minicomputers, and (3) microcomputers.

Mainframe computers. A large-sized computer with the greatest computing speed, largest storage capacity, and the most powerful processing capability is called a mainframe computer. A mainframe computer was the first type of computer developed to process business data. A mainframe computer is the most expensive of all types of computers. A mainframe computer is used primarily by businesses that need to process large amounts of data at very fast processing speeds.

Minicomputers. A medium-sized computer with intermediate computing speed, storage capacity, and processing capability is called a minicomputer. A minicomputer was the second type of computer developed to process business data. A minicomputer is less expensive than a mainframe computer. Minicomputers are used primarily by businesses with less data to be processed and less need for processing speed than businesses using mainframe computers.

Microcomputers. A small-sized computer with the slowest computing speed, smallest storage capacity, and the least processing capability is called a microcomputer. A microcomputer is often referred to as a personal or desktop computer. The most recent development in the computer field, the microcomputer is also the least expensive of all computers. Technological advancements have made the microcomputer very popular for business use because of increases in storage capacity and processing capability and attractive prices. A microcomputer is used primarily when data to be processed requires a processing speed greater than can be achieved with manual methods.

After gathering facts about the various types of computers, Petlodge decided to rent a microcomputer and begin using an automated accounting system. Petlodge found that an automated accounting system would reduce processing time and be less expensive than the current manual accounting system.

PLANNING FOR AUTOMATED ACCOUNTING

Planning for automated accounting is similar to planning for manual accounting. Planning any accounting system consists of two steps. (1) Setting goals—deciding what is to be recorded and reported. (2) Establishing procedures—deciding what steps to follow in carrying out the goals.

Accuracy is equally important in both manual and automated accounting. Results in any accounting system can only be as accurate as the data put into the system. For example, if $175.30 is recorded as $715.80, data on financial statements for any accounting system will be incorrect.

Phases of automated accounting

The four phases of automated accounting are (1) input, (2) processing, (3) storage, and (4) output.

Data put into a computer are called input. Input may be data on receipts, checks, and other business forms. Working with data according to precise instructions is called processing. Posting transaction data to general ledger accounts is an example of the processing phase. Filing or holding data until it is needed is called storage. Keeping data in general ledger accounts until it is needed is an example of the storage phase. Information produced by a computer is called output. Examples of output are facts about assets, liabilities, owner's equity, revenue, and expenses reported on financial statements. Output can also be printed on forms such as checks.

Computer instructions

Step-by-step instructions for completing each job must be prepared before any data can be processed by a computer. A set of instructions followed by a computer to process data is called a computer program. The term "program" may also describe a set of step-by-step instructions for processing data by manual means. Several computer programs are needed for automated accounting. Programs used to direct the operations of a computer are called software.

A person who prepares a computer program is called a computer programmer. A person needs special training to be a computer programmer. Understanding accounting concepts and procedures is helpful to a computer programmer. Just as important, an accountant needs to know basic computer concepts and procedures in order to assist a computer programmer and to use a computer.

COMPUTER UNITS

A computer is divided into four separate units. (1) Central processing unit. (2) Input unit. (3) Output unit. (4) Secondary storage unit. Each unit serves a special function. Computer units are called hardware. Illustration 10-1 shows a block diagram of the four computer units as well as the people action required before and after processing data.

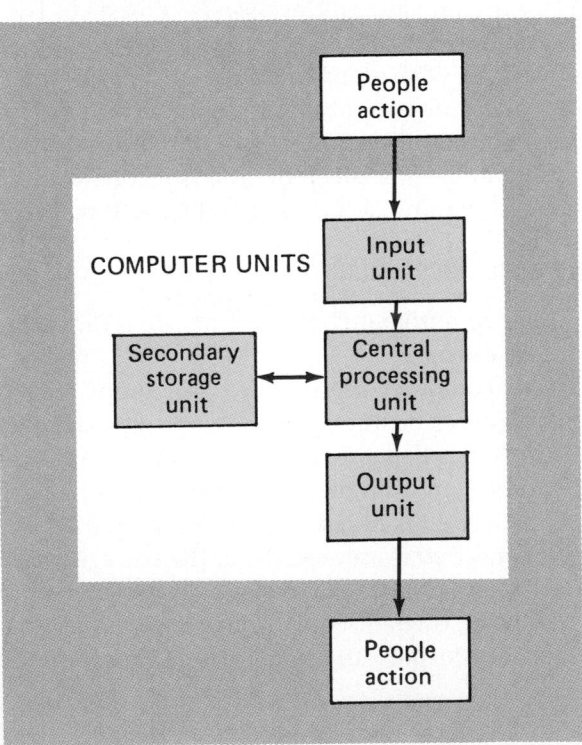

Illustration 10-1
Computer units

Four types of people action are necessary before data can be processed by a computer. (1) Describe output type and form. (2) Write instructions for the computer. (3) Arrange data to be processed (input) according to specific procedures. (4) Key-enter input into the computer.

Three types of people action are necessary after data have been processed by a computer. (1) Check output for accuracy. (2) Interpret output for decision making. (3) File output for future reference.

Central processing unit

A central processing unit (CPU) performs three distinct functions. (1) Controls all computer units. (2) Stores computer instructions and data currently being processed. (3) Processes stored data.

Illustration 10-2 shows a microcomputer with the four computer units.

Illustration 10-2
Microcomputer

Input unit

Before data can be processed by a computer, data must be converted to machine-readable form. A computer unit that converts data from human-readable to machine-readable form is referred to as an input unit. An input unit is linked to and controlled by a CPU.

A common input unit is a computer keyboard. A computer keyboard looks much like a typewriter keyboard. Operation of a computer keyboard is also similar to operation of a typewriter keyboard. After each character has been key-entered, the character is displayed on a television-like screen often referred to as a computer monitor.

The terms "key-enter," "key-entered," and "key-entering" are used in this textbook to indicate keying information using the keyboard and then pressing the Enter key. The Enter key is called "Return" on some keyboards.

Output unit

The end result of processing data by a computer is the output. A computer unit that converts data from machine-readable to human-readable form is referred to as an output unit. An output unit is linked to and controlled by a CPU. Different kinds of output units, such as monitors and printers, may be used by computers.

Computer monitor. A computer monitor is used to display data entered from a keyboard as well as data that has been processed.

Computer printer. An output unit that produces a printed, human-readable copy of processed data is known as a printer. Computer output in printed, human-readable form is called a printout. Petlodge's microcomputer uses a printer to produce printed output.

Secondary storage unit

A CPU has limited space for internal data storage. A computer's storage capacity can be expanded by using secondary storage units. Secondary storage units are sometimes known as auxiliary or external storage. Data are transferred from secondary storage to a CPU as needed during processing.

Magnetic disks are the most widely used secondary storage for microcomputers. Petlodge's microcomputer uses a disk for secondary storage. Illustration 10-3 shows a microcomputer with a disk being inserted.

Illustration 10-3
Microcomputer with a disk
being inserted

AUTOMATED GENERAL LEDGER ACCOUNTING

Petlodge's automated accounting system is based on the same accounting concepts as a manual accounting system. Only equipment and procedures differ. Software to process accounting data is included with the microcomputer that Petlodge rents.

Building a chart of accounts

Chart of accounts numbering systems are similar for both automated and manual accounting. Petlodge uses the same three-digit numbering system described for Rugcare in Chapter 5. Petlodge also uses the same procedures for making changes to its chart of accounts as described for Rugcare. The procedures for arranging accounts in a general ledger, assigning account numbers, and keeping records current is known as file maintenance.

The chart of accounts, page 196, shows all balance sheet and income statement divisions. The chart also lists all accounts within a division. The accounts are listed in the order that they appear on financial statements.

Before data from a chart of accounts are key-entered into a computer, a general ledger file maintenance input form (FORM GL-1) is prepared. Petlodge's general ledger file maintenance input form is shown in Illustration 10-4.

	GENERAL LEDGER FILE MAINTENANCE Input Form	
RUN DATE _09 / 01 / --_ MM DD YY		FORM GL-1

	ACCOUNT NUMBER	ACCOUNT TITLE	
1	110	Cash	1
2	120	Petty Cash	2
3	130	Supplies - Office	3
4	140	Supplies - Pet	4
5	150	Prepaid Insurance	5
6	210	Marino Kennel Supply	6
7	220	Vega Office Supply	7
8	310	Victoria Peak, Capital	8
9	320	Victoria Peak, Drawing	9
10	330	Income Summary	10
11	410	Boarding Fees	11
12	510	Advertising Expense	12
13	520	Insurance Expense	13
14	530	Miscellaneous Expense	14
15	540	Rent Expense	15
16	550	Supplies Expense - Office	16
17	560	Supplies Expense - Pet	17
18	570	Utilities Expense	18

Illustration 10-4
General ledger file maintenance input form

The input form shows the account numbers and account titles. The computer software requires that chart of accounts data be key-entered into the computer sequentially—account number first followed by account title. Therefore, the file maintenance input form used by Petlodge arranges the chart of accounts data in the same order as data are entered on the computer keyboard. The computer software also specifies the maximum number of spaces that can be used for account numbers and account titles. Any account titles that contain more characters than the software will accept must be abbreviated when recorded on the file maintenance input form (FORM GL-1).

The general ledger file maintenance input form has marks in the Account Title column to indicate how many characters the software will accept for an account title. All of Petlodge's account titles fit the 25-character space allowed, so none have to be abbreviated.

Three steps are followed in preparing each line of Petlodge's general ledger file maintenance input form for the chart of accounts.

1 Write the run date, *09/01/--*, in the space provided at the top of the form. After all accounts have been recorded on the input form, the chart of accounts data are key-entered into the computer. The date to be printed on reports prepared by a computer is called the run date. Petlodge changed from manual to automated accounting on September 1. Therefore, the run date, 09/01/--, indicates that the chart of accounts data entered on the file maintenance input form are effective as of 09/01/--.

2 Write each account number in the Account Number column.

3 Write each account title in the Account Title column just as it will appear on the output.

The account numbers and account titles are obtained from the chart of accounts, page 196. Petlodge's revenue account is titled *Boarding Fees* to describe the type of revenue received for boarding services.

Processing a chart of accounts

In manual accounting data for each account are kept on separate ledger forms. A ledger represents the storage phase of manual accounting. In Petlodge's automated accounting system, data about each account are stored on a disk. The disk serves the same purpose in automated accounting as the ledger in manual accounting. The disk represents the automated accounting storage phase.

In an automated accounting system, the activities are arranged so that each activity may be selected using a keyboard or some other input device. A list of options from which an activity may be selected is called a menu. Petlodge's software has a General Ledger Main Menu. An entry selected using the keyboard displays the General Ledger Main Menu shown in Illustration 10-5.

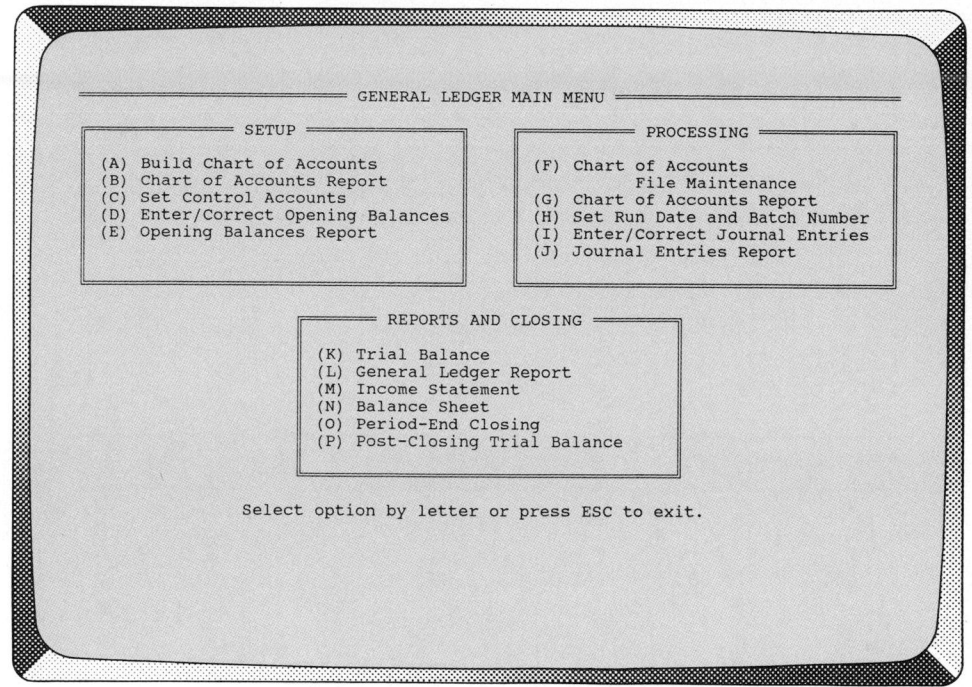

Illustration 10-5
General ledger main menu
displayed on a computer
monitor

The activities listed in the *Setup* section of the menu are described in this chapter. The activities listed in the *Processing* and *Reports and Closing* sections are described in Chapter 11.

Option A is selected to build a chart of accounts. Spaces for entering general ledger chart of accounts data are displayed on the computer monitor. Chart of accounts data are then key-entered, as shown for the cash account in Illustration 10-6, page 206.

After all accounts have been key-entered, Option B is selected from the General Ledger Main Menu, Illustration 10-5. This option directs the computer to prepare a chart of accounts report. Petlodge's chart of accounts report is shown in Illustration 10-7, page 206.

The report is checked for accuracy by comparing it with the data recorded on the file maintenance input form. After the accuracy check, the report is filed for future reference.

Setting control accounts

Computer software is generally written for use by many different types of businesses. Therefore, general ledger account numbers may not be the same from one business to the next. For this reason, most computer software requires that selected general ledger accounts be identified for special handling by the software. General ledger accounts that must be

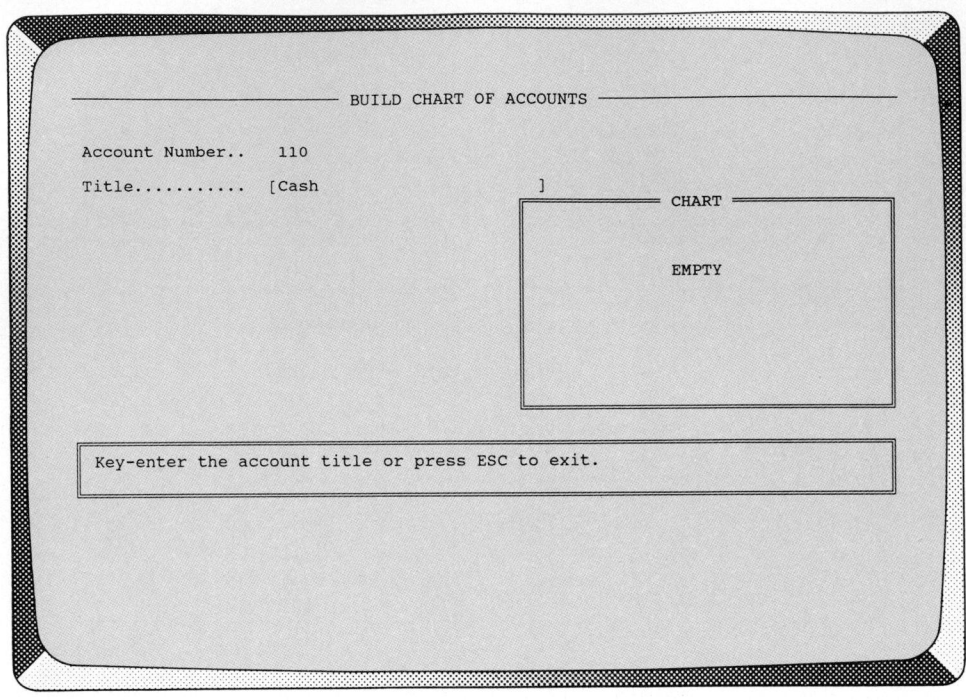

Illustration 10-6   Computer monitor display for chart of accounts data

```
  RUN DATE: 09/01/--                  PETLODGE
                                 CHART OF ACCOUNTS

     -------------------
     ACCOUNT    ACCOUNT
     NUMBER     TITLE
     -------------------
     110        Cash
     120        Petty Cash
     130        Supplies--Office
     140        Supplies--Pet
     150        Prepaid Insurance
     210        Marino Kennel Supply
     220        Vega Office Supply
     310        Victoria Peak, Capital
     320        Victoria Peak, Drawing
     330        Income Summary
     410        Boarding Fees
     510        Advertising Expense
     520        Insurance Expense
     530        Miscellaneous Expense
     540        Rent Expense
     550        Supplies Expense--Office
     560        Supplies Expense--Pet
     570        Utilities Expense
```

Illustration 10-7   Chart of accounts report

identified for special handling by computer software are called control accounts. The software used by Petlodge requires that control accounts be identified from the chart of accounts report. Option C is selected from the General Ledger Main Menu to set the control accounts. The computer monitor displays the control accounts needed and spaces for recording the account numbers from the chart of accounts report. The computer monitor display with the control accounts set is shown in Illustration 10-8.

```
───────────────────────── SET CONTROL ACCOUNTS ─────────────────────────

     Cash Account Number............   [110   ]
     Capital Account Number.........   [310   ]
     Drawing Account Number.........   [320   ]
     Income Summary Account Number..   [330   ]










    ┌────────────────────────────────────────────────────────────────┐
    │ Key-enter the data.  Move cursor with arrow keys to correct data.  Press │
    │ ENTER from last field to record.  Press ESC to ignore this entry and exit. │
    └────────────────────────────────────────────────────────────────┘

                          F1=CHART
```

The cash account number is needed to allow the computer to keep track of all entries to the cash account. This feature makes it easy to do a cash proof at any time during a fiscal period.

Illustration 10-8
Computer monitor display
with control accounts set

The capital, drawing, and income summary account numbers are needed for end-of-fiscal-period work.

Journalizing opening balances

The books for Petlodge's manual accounting system are closed on August 31. Petlodge changes to an automated accounting system on September 1. Data from the August 31 manually prepared post-closing trial balance are used to journalize the account balances for the new automated accounting system. A memorandum is used as the source document for the account balances. *(CONCEPT: Objective Evidence)* A copy of the post-closing trial balance is stapled to the memorandum to avoid having to copy the data to the memorandum. Petlodge's August 31 post-closing trial balance is shown in Illustration 10-9.

ACCOUNT TITLE	DEBIT	CREDIT
Cash	12 5 0 0 00	
Petty Cash	3 0 0 00	
Supplies—Office	1 2 6 0 00	
Supplies—Pet	1 5 1 5 00	
Prepaid Insurance	7 6 5 00	
Marino Kennel Supply		9 4 3 00
Vega Office Supply		3 8 7 00
Victoria Peak, Capital		15 0 1 0 00
Totals	16 3 4 0 00	16 3 4 0 00

Petlodge
Post-Closing Trial Balance
August 31, 19--

Illustration 10-9
Post-closing trial balance

Before general ledger account balances are key-entered into a computer, an input form is prepared. The form shows all data needed for recording account balances. The computer software requires that entries to the general ledger be key-entered into the computer in a certain sequence. Therefore, the input form used by Petlodge arranges the data in the same order as data are entered on the computer keyboard. By having data arranged in the correct sequence, key-entering the data is faster. Petlodge uses a general ledger input form (FORM GL-2) to journalize general ledger account balances. The input form resembles a journal used in manual accounting. However, there is one major difference between the type of data journalized on an input form and on a journal used in manual accounting. In manual accounting account titles are used to identify the accounts affected by each journal entry. In automated accounting account numbers are used because computers work more efficiently with numbers than with alphabetic characters. Account titles are stored on secondary storage during the processing of the chart of accounts. The computer obtains the account titles from secondary storage when the account titles are needed for financial reports. Petlodge's completed general ledger input form for the account balances from the post-closing trial balance is shown in Illustration 10-10.

	DAY	DOC. NO.	ACCOUNT NUMBER	DEBIT AMOUNT	CREDIT AMOUNT	
	1	2	3	4	5	
1	01	M1	110	12500 00		1
2			120	300 00		2
3			130	1260 00		3
4			140	1515 00		4
5			150	765 00		5
6			210		943 00	6
7			220		387 00	7
8			310		15010 00	8
25						25
BATCH TOTALS				16340 00	16340 00	

RUN DATE _09 / 01 / --_ MM DD YY

BATCH NO. _1_

GENERAL LEDGER
Input Form

FORM GL-2

Illustration 10-10
General ledger input form
for account balances

Eight steps are followed in journalizing account balances on Petlodge's general ledger input form.

1 Write the run date, _09/01/--,_ in the space provided at the top of the form. The run date is the date Petlodge starts its automated accounting system.

2 Write the batch number, _1,_ in the space provided at the top of the form. Each group of journal entries to be processed by a computer, regardless of the number of entries, is identified by a number. The number assigned to a group of journal entries is called a batch number. As the opening balances entry is the first group of journal entries, batch number 1 is automatically assigned by the computer.

3 Write the day, _01,_ on line 1 in the Day column. Enter the day only on line 1 because the day is the same for all lines.

4 Write the document number, _M1,_ on the same line in the Doc. No. column. Enter the document number only on line l because the document number is the same for all lines.

5 Write the account number in the Account Number column for each general ledger account with a balance. These accounts are listed on the post-closing trial balance, Illustration 10-9. The account numbers are listed on the chart of accounts report, Illustration 10-7.

6 Write the account balance in either the Debit Amount or Credit Amount column. The account balances are given on the post-closing trial balance, Illustration 10-9.

7 After all account balances have been journalized, total the Debit Amount and Credit Amount columns. Enter the totals on the Batch Totals line provided at the bottom of the form.

8 Compare the two totals to be sure that debits equal credits. Also compare the batch totals with the totals on the trial balance to be sure that amounts were recorded correctly.

Processing account balances

In manual accounting account balances are journalized in a journal and posted to accounts stored in a ledger. In Petlodge's automated accounting system, account balances are journalized and posted to accounts stored on a disk.

Option D is selected from the General Ledger Main Menu to enter the opening account balances. Spaces for key-entering each account balance are displayed on the computer monitor. Data for entering the account balance for the first line of the general ledger input form are shown in Illustration 10-11.

Illustration 10-11
Computer monitor display
with an account balance
entered

```
———————————— ENTER/CORRECT OPENING BALANCES BATCH 1 ————————————

Journal Entry Number     1
Day of Month........  [01]
Document Number.....  [M1       ]
Acct.#  Debit Amt. Credit Amt.
[110   ][12500    ][            ]
[      ][          ][            ]
[      ][          ][            ]
[      ][          ][            ]
[      ][          ][            ]
[      ][          ][            ]
[      ][          ][            ]
[      ][          ][            ]

Proof Total:
         .00

Note:  Press END key to move cursor to the last data field.

 Key-enter the data.  Move cursor with arrow keys to correct data.  Press
 ENTER from last field to record.  Press ESC to ignore this entry and exit.

        F1=CHART    F2=JOURNAL ENTRIES    F3=CORRECTIONS
```

The computer automatically assigns a sequential number to each journal entry, beginning with the number *1*. This procedure allows an entry needing correction at a later date to be easily retrieved from computer storage by referencing the journal entry number.

After all account balances have been key-entered and posted, Option E is selected from the General Ledger Main Menu. This option directs the computer to prepare an opening balances report. Petlodge's opening balances report is shown in Illustration 10-12.

```
RUN DATE: 09/01/--                      PETLODGE
                             OPENING BALANCES BATCH 1

 -----------------------------------------------------------------------
 JE#    DATE      ACCOUNT NUMBER & TITLE          DEBIT AMOUNT   CREDIT AMOUNT
 -----------------------------------------------------------------------
 0001   09/01/--  110     Cash                      12500.00
                  120     Petty Cash                  300.00
                  130     Supplies--Office           1260.00
                  140     Supplies--Pet              1515.00
                  150     Prepaid Insurance           765.00
                  210       Marino Kennel Supply                    943.00
                  220       Vega Office Supply                      387.00
                  310       Victoria Peak, Capital               15010.00
                          DOCUMENT: M1

                                            ---------------  ---------------
                  TOTALS                        16340.00         16340.00
                                            ===============  ===============
                  IN BALANCE
```

The opening balances report is checked for accuracy by comparing the totals on the report with the batch totals on the input form. If the totals are the same, the opening balances report is assumed to be correct. The opening balances report is filed for future reference.

Illustration 10-12
Opening balances report

SUMMARY OF STARTING AN AUTOMATED ACCOUNTING SYSTEM

The steps followed by Petlodge to start an automated general ledger accounting system are summarized in Illustration 10-13.

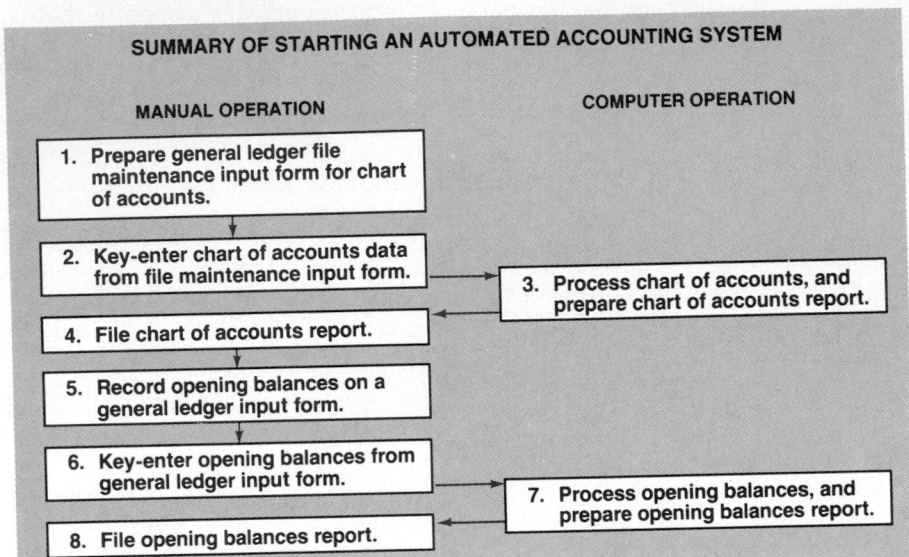

SUMMARY OF STARTING AN AUTOMATED ACCOUNTING SYSTEM

MANUAL OPERATION

1. Prepare general ledger file maintenance input form for chart of accounts.
2. Key-enter chart of accounts data from file maintenance input form.
4. File chart of accounts report.
5. Record opening balances on a general ledger input form.
6. Key-enter opening balances from general ledger input form.
8. File opening balances report.

COMPUTER OPERATION

3. Process chart of accounts, and prepare chart of accounts report.
7. Process opening balances, and prepare opening balances report.

Illustration 10-13
Summary of steps for starting an automated general ledger accounting system

ACCOUNTING TERMS

What is the meaning of each of the following?

1. data
2. manual accounting
3. automated accounting
4. computer
5. mainframe computer
6. minicomputer
7. microcomputer
8. input
9. processing
10. storage
11. output
12. computer program
13. software
14. computer programmer
15. hardware
16. printout
17. run date
18. menu
19. control accounts
20. batch number

QUESTIONS FOR INDIVIDUAL STUDY

1. What type of information do owners and managers depend on for effective decision making?
2. Which accounting concept is being applied when a business expects to make money and continue indefinitely?
3. Does using a computer change accounting concepts? Why?
4. Which accounting concept is being applied when financial data are reported for a specified period of time?
5. What are the three types of computers used for recording and reporting accounting data?
6. What are the two steps necessary for planning an accounting system?

7. What are the four phases of automated accounting?
8. What does an accountant need to know in order to assist a computer programmer and to use a computer?
9. What three types of people action are necessary after data have been processed by a computer?
10. What is the most widely used secondary storage for microcomputers?
11. Why does Petlodge use a special form

to enter the general ledger chart of accounts?
12. How is a chart of accounts report checked for accuracy?
13. Which accounting concept is being applied when a memorandum is used as the source document for opening balances?
14. Why does Petlodge use a special form to journalize opening balances?

▇ CASES FOR MANAGEMENT DECISION

CASE 1 Floyd Ulicki owns and operates a service business. The business uses a manual accounting system. Mr. Ulicki does the accounting himself; however, operating the business has been taking more and more of his time. Consequently, he has been having difficulty finding time to run an efficient accounting system. Mr. Ulicki is considering hiring an accountant or renting a computer to improve his accounting system. What factors should he consider in making the decision to either hire an accountant or rent a computer and automate his accounting system?

CASE 2 Susan Lane owns and operates a physical fitness center. She has been using a manual accounting system. She wants to improve her accounting system by having work done faster and less expensively. After gathering facts about the various types of accounting systems, she decides to rent a microcomputer and begin using automated accounting. Mrs. Lane is concerned, however, about not knowing how to program a computer. She is considering either learning how to write computer programs or hiring a computer programmer. What would you recommend?

▇ DRILLS FOR UNDERSTANDING

DRILL 10-D1 Preparing a chart of accounts for automated accounting

The following account descriptions refer to the location of accounts in a chart of accounts similar to the one for Petlodge.

1. The first asset account.
2. The first liability account.
3. The first owner's equity account.
4. The first revenue account.
5. The first expense account.
6. The second asset account.
7. The second liability account.
8. The second owner's equity account.
9. The second expense account.
10. The third expense account.

Use a form similar to the following.

1	2
Account Descriptions	**Account Number**
1. *The first asset account.*	*110*

Instructions: 1. In Column 1 write the account description. Account description 1 is given as an example.

2. In Column 2 write the account number. Account numbers are assigned by 10s.

3. Check your answers with Petlodge's chart of accounts, page 196.

DRILL 10-D2   Analyzing steps for starting an automated accounting system

Instructions: Refer to Illustration 10-13, page 212, and answer the following questions.

1. What form is prepared to build the chart of accounts?
2. Is key-entering the chart of accounts into the computer a manual or computer operation?
3. In which step is the chart of accounts processed by the computer?
4. Is the preparation of a chart of accounts report a manual or computer operation?
5. What form is prepared for the opening balances?
6. In which step are the opening balances key-entered into the computer?
7. In which step is an opening balances report prepared?
8. Is the preparation of an opening balances report a manual or computer operation?

■ APPLICATION PROBLEMS

PROBLEM 10-1   Preparing a general ledger file maintenance input form

E-Z Rest Motel has the following general ledger chart of accounts.

Balance Sheet Accounts		Income Statement Accounts	
(100) ASSETS		**(400) REVENUE**	
110	Cash	410	Room Rentals
120	Petty Cash		
130	Supplies—Cleaning	**(500) EXPENSES**	
140	Supplies—Office		
150	Prepaid Insurance	510	Advertising Expense
		520	Insurance Expense
(200) LIABILITIES		530	Miscellaneous Expense
		540	Rent Expense
210	Gentec Enterprises	550	Supplies Expense—Cleaning
220	Superior Office Supply	560	Supplies Expense—Office
		570	Utilities Expense
(300) OWNER'S EQUITY			
310	Darrell King, Capital		
320	Darrell King, Drawing		
330	Income Summary		

Instructions: Prepare a general ledger file maintenance input form (FORM GL-1) for the general ledger chart of accounts. Use December 1 of the current year as the run date.

PROBLEM 10-2   Journalizing opening balances in an automated accounting system

E-Z Rest Motel has the following post-closing trial balance on November 30 of the current year.

ACCOUNT TITLE	DEBIT	CREDIT
E-Z Rest Motel **Post-Closing Trial Balance** **November 30, 19--**		
Cash	14 6 4 0 00	
Petty Cash	3 0 0 00	
Supplies—Cleaning	1 4 8 0 00	
Supplies—Office	1 1 6 0 00	
Prepaid Insurance	1 8 4 0 00	
Gentec Enterprises		1 2 2 5 00
Superior Office Supply		7 4 3 00
Darrell King, Capital		17 4 5 2 00
Totals	19 4 2 0 00	19 4 2 0 00

Instructions: 1. Journalize the opening balances for E-Z Rest Motel on a general ledger input form (FORM GL-2). Use December 1 of the current year as the run date and the date of the opening balances. Use account numbers from the chart of accounts given in Problem 10-1. Batch No. 1; Memorandum No. 1.

2. Total and prove the Debit Amount and Credit Amount columns. Record the batch totals.

■ ENRICHMENT PROBLEMS

MASTERY PROBLEM 10-M   Preparing a general ledger file maintenance input form and journalizing opening balances

AAA Secretarial Service has the following general ledger chart of accounts and post-closing trial balance on June 30 of the current year.

Balance Sheet Accounts		Income Statement Accounts	
(100) ASSETS		**(400) REVENUE**	
110	Cash	410	Secretarial Fees
120	Petty Cash		
130	Supplies		**(500) EXPENSES**
140	Prepaid Insurance	510	Advertising Expense
		520	Insurance Expense
(200) LIABILITIES		530	Miscellaneous Expense
		540	Rent Expense
210	Armeda Office Products	550	Supplies Expense
220	Perez Office Supply	560	Utilities Expense
(300) OWNER'S EQUITY			
310	Kay Dewitt, Capital		
320	Kay Dewitt, Drawing		
330	Income Summary		

AAA Secretarial Service Post-Closing Trial Balance June 30, 19--		
ACCOUNT TITLE	DEBIT	CREDIT
Cash	13 9 2 0 00	
Petty Cash	3 0 0 00	
Supplies	3 9 1 0 00	
Prepaid Insurance	2 0 7 0 00	
Armeda Office Products		1 4 6 5 00
Perez Office Supply		6 3 5 00
Kay Dewitt, Capital		18 1 0 0 00
Totals	20 2 0 0 00	20 2 0 0 00

Instructions: 1. Prepare a general ledger file maintenance input form (FORM GL-1) for the general ledger chart of accounts. Use July 1 of the current year as the run date.

2. Journalize the opening balances for AAA Secretarial Service on a general ledger input form (FORM GL-2). Use July 1 of the current year as the run date and the date of the opening balances. Batch No. 1; Memorandum No. 1.

3. Total and prove the Debit Amount and Credit Amount columns. Record the batch totals.

CHALLENGE PROBLEM 10-C **Preparing a general ledger file maintenance input form and journalizing opening balances**

Sutton Auto Towing has the following general ledger chart of accounts and post-closing trial balance on May 31 of the current year.

Balance Sheet Accounts		Income Statement Accounts	
(100) ASSETS		**(400) REVENUE**	
110	Cash	410	Towing Fees
120	Petty Cash		
130	Supplies		**(500) EXPENSES**
140	Prepaid Insurance	510	Advertising Expense
		520	Gasoline Expense
	(200) LIABILITIES	530	Insurance Expense
		540	Miscellaneous Expense
210	Beck Office Supplies	550	Rent Expense—Building
220	Sandel Service Station	560	Rent Expense—Truck
		570	Supplies Expense
	(300) OWNER'S EQUITY	580	Utilities Expense
310	Dale Irvin, Capital		
320	Dale Irvin, Drawing		
330	Income Summary		

ACCOUNT TITLE	DEBIT	CREDIT
Sutton Auto Towing		
Post-Closing Trial Balance		
May 31, 19--		
Cash	10 2 5 0 00	
Petty Cash	3 0 0 00	
Supplies	1 1 4 5 00	
Prepaid Insurance	5 2 5 00	
Beck Office Supply		2 8 5 00
Sandel Service Station		8 4 0 00
Dale Irvin, Capital		11 0 9 5 00
Totals	12 2 2 0 00	12 2 2 0 00

Instructions: 1. Prepare a general ledger file maintenance input form (FORM GL-1) for the general ledger chart of accounts. Use June 1 of the current year as the run date.

2. Journalize the opening balances for Sutton Auto Towing on a general ledger input form (FORM GL-2). Use June 1 of the current year as the run date and the date of the opening balances. Batch No. 1; Memorandum No. 1.

3. Total and prove the Debit Amount and Credit Amount columns. Record the batch totals.

The solution to Challenge Problem 10-C is needed to complete Computer Application 1.

ELECTRICAL EQUIPMENT

The following rules protect the operator of the equipment, other persons in the environment, and the equipment itself.

1. Do not unplug equipment by pulling on the electrical cord. Instead, grasp the plug at the outlet and remove it.
2. Do not stretch electrical cords across an aisle where someone might trip over them.
3. Avoid food and beverages near equipment where a spill might result in an electrical short.
4. Do not attempt to remove the cover of equipment for any reason while the power is turned on.
5. Do not attempt to repair equipment while it is plugged in. To avoid damage most repairs should be done by an authorized service technician.
6. Always turn the power off when finished using equipment.
7. Do not overload extension cords.
8. Follow manufacturer recommendations for safe use.
9. Replace frayed electrical cords immediately.

MICROCOMPUTERS

1. To avoid damage to the drives, do not insert pencils or other implements in floppy disk drives.
2. To prevent overheating, avoid blocking air vents.
3. Position keyboards to prevent bumping or dropping them off the work surface.

MONITORS

1. Most manufacturers advise repair by authorized service technicians only.

2. Adjust brightness and focus for comfortable viewing.
3. Avoid glare on the monitor screen.
4. Do not leave fingerprints on the screen. Keep the screen clear of dust. Only use a soft cloth for cleaning the screen.

PRINTERS

1. Do not let jewelry, ties, scarves, loose sleeves, or other clothing get caught in the machinery. This could result in damage to the machinery and could cause personal injury.
2. Exercise caution when using toxic chemicals such as toner in order to avoid spills.

DISKETTES

1. Put write/protect tabs on all program software to avoid accidental erasure.
2. Do not bend or fold diskettes.
3. Do not write on a diskette with a hard or sharp-pointed pen or pencil; use a felt-tip marker.
4. Do not touch exposed surfaces of diskettes.
5. Be sure the disk drive is not running when you insert or remove a diskette.
6. Keep diskettes away from extreme hot or cold temperatures. Do not leave diskettes in a car during very hot or cold weather.
7. Keep diskettes away from magnetic fields such as transformers and magnets.
8. Store diskettes in the storage envelopes.
9. Keep diskettes away from smoke, ashes, and dust, including chalk dust.
10. Do not leave diskettes in the disk drive for prolonged periods, such as overnight.

Computer Application 1
Starting an Automated Accounting System

The general ledger file maintenance input form and the general ledger input form completed in Challenge Problem 10-C, Chapter 10, are needed to complete Computer Application 1.

Sutton Auto Towing completed the required input forms for starting an automated accounting system. Chapter 10 describes the required manual and computer operations. Computer Application 1 provides an opportunity to process the data from the completed forms using a microcomputer.

Computer Application 1 is designed to be used with the *Automated Accounting for the Microcomputer*, 3d edition, software. The software provides the option of either displaying or printing reports. If a printer is available, select the *Print* option when given the choice of displaying or printing reports. If a printer is not available, select the *Display* option. Selecting the *Display* option causes the report to be displayed on the computer monitor.

■ COMPUTER APPLICATION PROBLEM

COMPUTER APPLICATION PROBLEM 1 Starting an automated accounting system

Instructions: 1. Load the *Automated Accounting for the Microcomputer* software. Select Computer Application 1 (CA-1) from the CENTURY 21 ACCOUNTING Template Disk. The accounting system setup data and company name have been entered and are stored on the Template Disk.

2. Key-enter the chart of accounts data from the completed general ledger input form prepared in Challenge Problem 10-C.

3. Display/Print the chart of accounts report. Check the report for accuracy.

4. Key-enter the control account numbers.

5. Key-enter the opening balances from the completed general ledger input form prepared in Challenge Problem 10-C.

6. Display/Print the opening balances report. Check the report for accuracy by comparing the report totals with the batch totals on the general ledger input form.

Using an Automated Accounting System

ENABLING PERFORMANCE TASKS

After studying Chapter 11, you will be able to:
a. Define accounting terms related to using an automated accounting system.
b. Identify accounting concepts and practices related to using an automated accounting system.
c. Perform file maintenance activities.
d. Journalize transactions on a general ledger input form.
e. Journalize adjusting entries on a general ledger input form.

A business should study immediate and future accounting needs before deciding to change from a manual to an automated accounting system. The cost of changing accounting systems must also be considered. Petlodge determined that an automated accounting system would reduce processing time and be less expensive than the manual accounting system. Chapter 10 describes accounting procedures used by Petlodge to start an automated accounting system. Chapter 11 describes procedures followed by Petlodge to use an automated accounting system for daily accounting activities and end-of-fiscal-period work.

FILE MAINTENANCE

In manual accounting file maintenance activities for a general ledger chart of accounts require working with individual ledger accounts. (1) An account is deleted by removing the account from the file. (2) An account title or number is changed by preparing a new ledger account. (3) An account is added by preparing a new ledger form and inserting the account in the proper order within the file. In automated accounting a general ledger chart of accounts is stored on secondary computer storage. File maintenance activities include recording deletions and additions on a general ledger file maintenance input form. The deletions and additions are key-entered into the computer to change the file on secondary storage.

Deleting an account

Petlodge has limited advertising expense. Therefore, a decision is made to delete this account from the general ledger and record advertising as a miscellaneous expense. The entry on a general ledger file maintenance input form to delete Advertising Expense is shown on line 1 of Illustration 11-1.

RUN   DATE __09 01 , --__
　　　　　　　MM DD YY

GENERAL LEDGER
FILE MAINTENANCE
Input Form

FORM GL-1

	1 ACCOUNT NUMBER	2 ACCOUNT TITLE	
1	510	(D e l e t e)	1
2	540	R e n t E x p e n s e — B u i l d i n g	2
3	545	R e n t E x p e n s e — C o m p u t e r	3

Illustration 11-1
Entries for file maintenance

Three steps are followed to complete a general ledger file maintenance input form to delete an account.

1 Write the run date, *09/01/--*, in the space provided at the top of the form. This run date indicates the effective date of the file maintenance data.

2 Write the account number of the account to be deleted, *510*, in the Account Number column. Obtain the account number from the chart of accounts report, Illustration 10-7, page 206.

3 Write the word, *(Delete)*, on the same line in the Account Title column. A word that is not to be key-entered into the computer is placed in parentheses. Placing the word *Delete* in parentheses indicates that the word is not an account title and is not to be key-entered into the computer.

Adding an account

Petlodge decides to keep a separate record of the rent paid for the microcomputer and software. Petlodge records the payment of the monthly rent on the building in the rent expense account. Petlodge decides to use a second rent expense account for the computer rental. Because renting the computer represents a major expense, Petlodge wants to be able to record and report the exact amount of this expense. *(CONCEPT: Adequate Disclosure)*

Changing an account title. Because a second rent expense account is being added, Petlodge wishes to clearly identify each type of rent expense. Therefore, the current account titled *Rent Expense* is changed to *Rent Expense—Building*. The entry to change an account title is shown on line 2 of Illustration 11-1.

Two steps are followed to complete a general ledger file maintenance input form to change an account title.

1 Write the account number of the account to be changed, *540*, on the next blank line in the Account Number column. Obtain the account number from the chart of accounts report.

2 Write the new account title, *Rent Expense—Building*, on the same line in the Account Title column.

Adding a new account. A new account number is determined using procedures described in Chapter 5. The account number assigned must place the account in the proper order within the expenses division in the chart of accounts. Expense accounts are listed in alphabetical order. Petlodge assigns accounts by 10s within each general ledger division. Using the unused middle number, the new account number for Rent Expense—Computer is assigned as follows.

540	Rent Expense—Building	(New account title of existing account)
545	RENT EXPENSE—COMPUTER	(NEW ACCOUNT)
550	Supplies Expense—Office	(Existing account)

If no exact middle number is available, the nearest *even whole number* is used. For example, the middle number between 545 and 550 is 547.5. The number 547.5 contains four digits and cannot be assigned in a three-digit numbering system. Therefore, 548, the nearest *even whole number* would be used.

New accounts that are added after the last account in a division are assigned the next number in the sequence of 10s. For example, an account added as the last account in a division ending with the number 550 would be assigned the number 560.

Two steps are followed to complete a general ledger file maintenance input form to add an account, as shown on line 3 of Illustration 11-1.

1 Write the account number of the new account to be added, *545*, on the next blank line in the Account Number column.

2 Write the new account title, *Rent Expense—Computer*, on the same line in the Account Title column.

Processing file maintenance data

The General Ledger Main Menu is shown in Illustration 11-2.

Option F is selected to perform file maintenance. Spaces for entering file maintenance data are displayed on the computer monitor.

Data on each line of the input form are then key-entered. After all changes have been key-entered and processed, Option G is selected from the General Ledger Main Menu. This option directs the computer to prepare a revised chart of accounts report. The report reflects all changes

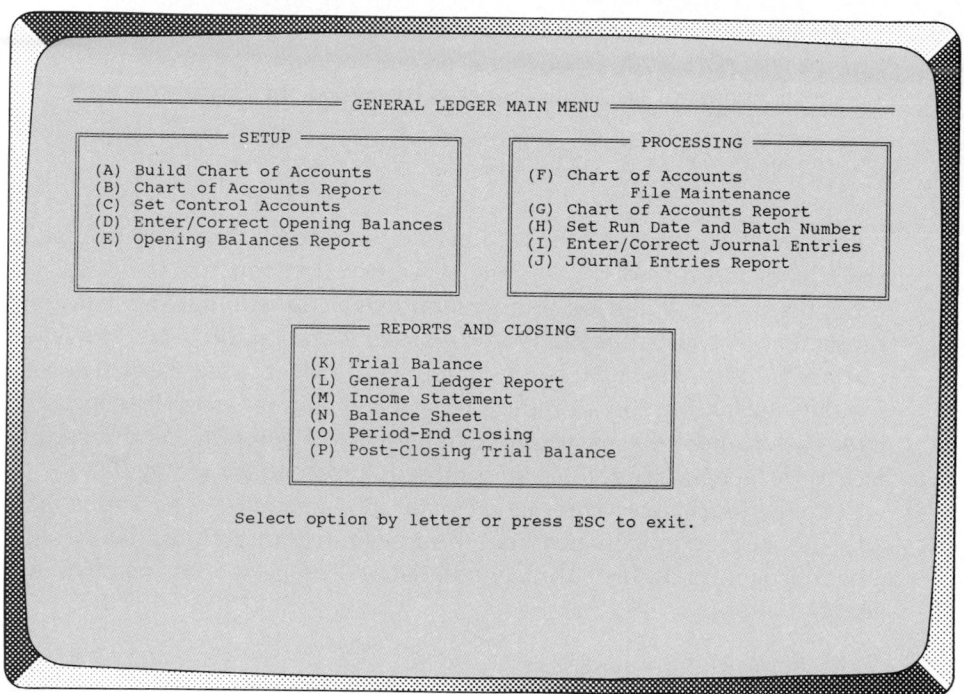

made to the chart of accounts. The revised chart of accounts report is shown in Illustration 11-3.

Illustration 11-2
General ledger main menu

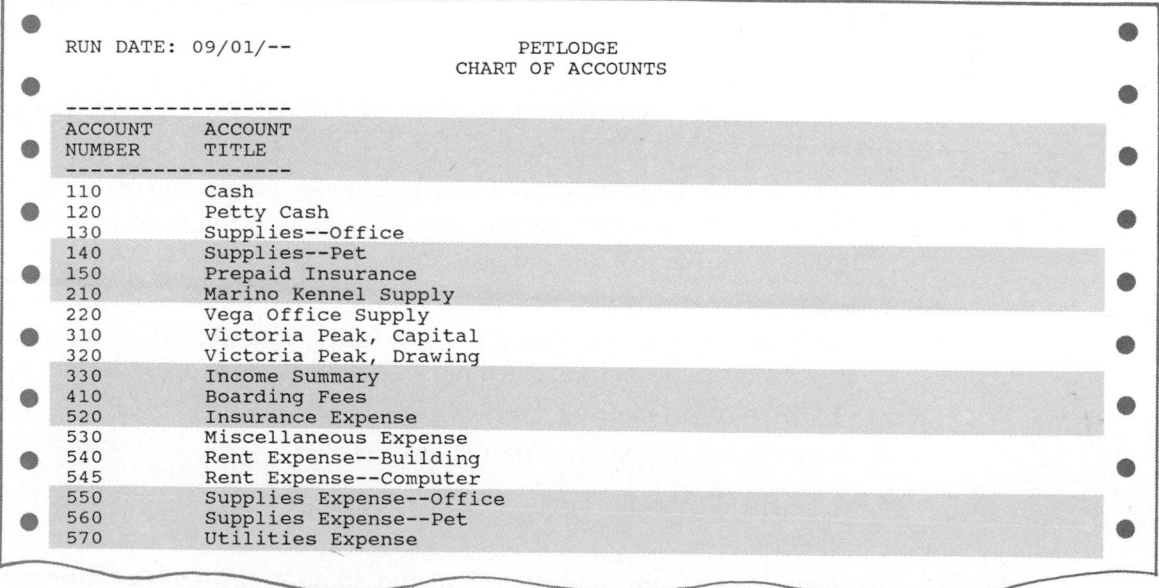

RUN DATE: 09/01/--	PETLODGE CHART OF ACCOUNTS

ACCOUNT NUMBER	ACCOUNT TITLE
110	Cash
120	Petty Cash
130	Supplies--Office
140	Supplies--Pet
150	Prepaid Insurance
210	Marino Kennel Supply
220	Vega Office Supply
310	Victoria Peak, Capital
320	Victoria Peak, Drawing
330	Income Summary
410	Boarding Fees
520	Insurance Expense
530	Miscellaneous Expense
540	Rent Expense--Building
545	Rent Expense--Computer
550	Supplies Expense--Office
560	Supplies Expense--Pet
570	Utilities Expense

Illustration 11-3   Revised chart of accounts report

Petlodge checks the accuracy of the revised chart of accounts by comparing the report with the general ledger file maintenance input form. The revised chart of accounts report is then filed for future reference.

RECORDING TRANSACTIONS

In manual accounting transactions are analyzed into their debit and credit parts and recorded in a journal. Transaction data are then periodically posted from a journal to a general ledger. In automated accounting transactions are also analyzed into their debit and credit parts. However, transaction data are journalized on a general ledger input form. Transaction data journalized on an input form are key-entered into the computer. After each transaction has been key-entered, the computer is directed to post to the general ledger accounts stored on secondary storage.

Petlodge journalizes transaction data on a general ledger input form daily. Because Petlodge has a limited number of transactions, data from a general ledger input form are key-entered and processed on the computer weekly.

Cash payment of an expense

September 1, 19--.
Paid cash for building rental, $1,200.00. Check No. 245.

The source document for this transaction is Check No. 245. *(CONCEPT: Objective Evidence)* The analysis of this kind of transaction is described in Chapter 3. Rent Expense—Building is debited and Cash is credited for $1,200.00. The general ledger input form entry to record this transaction is shown on lines 1 and 2 of Illustration 11-4.

Eight steps are followed to journalize transactions on a general ledger input form.

1 Write the run date, *09/05/--*, in the space provided at the top of the form. The run date indicates that the transaction data entered on the input form are for the week ended September 5.

2 Write the batch number, *2*, in the space provided at the top of the form. Batch number 1 was assigned to the opening balances, Illustration 10-10, Chapter 10. Therefore, batch number 2 is assigned to the first group of transactions.

3 Write the day, *01*, on line 1 in the Day column.

4 Write the document number, *C245*, on the same line in the Doc. No. column.

5 Write the account number, *540*, of the account debited, Rent Expense— Building, on the same line in the Account Number column.

RUN DATE 09 05 / --		GENERAL LEDGER		
MM DD YY		Input Form		FORM GL-2
BATCH NO. 2				

	DAY	DOC. NO.	ACCOUNT NUMBER	DEBIT AMOUNT	CREDIT AMOUNT	
	1	2	3	4	5	
1	01	C245	540	1200 00		1
2			110		1200 00	2
3	01	C246	545	875 00		3
4			110		875 00	4
5	02	C247	530	85 00		5
6			110		85 00	6
7	02	C248	320	600 00		7
8			110		600 00	8
9	03	C249	210	250 00		9
10			110		250 00	10
11	03	C250	130	63 00		11
12			110		63 00	12
13	04	C251	130	87 00		13
14			140	46 00		14
15			530	69 00		15
16			110		202 00	16
17	04	R12	110	1000 00		17
18			310		1000 00	18
19	05	T5	110	935 00		19
20			410		935 00	20

BATCH TOTALS	5210 00	5210 00

Illustration 11-4
General ledger input form
with transactions recorded

6 Write the debit amount, *$1,200.00*, on the same line in the Debit Amount column.

7 On the second line, write the account number, *110*, of the account credited, Cash, in the Account Number column. The Day and Doc. No. columns are left blank on the second line of an entry. The date and document number are recorded only once for each transaction.

8 Write the credit amount, *$1,200.00*, on the same line in the Credit Amount column.

These same procedures are used to record all cash payment transactions.

Cash payment to owner as a withdrawal

Assets taken out of a business for an owner's personal use are known as withdrawals. Petlodge's general ledger has an account titled *Victoria Peak, Drawing* for recording withdrawals. A drawing account balance decreases an owner's capital account balance. Therefore, a drawing account has a normal debit balance.

September 2, 19--.
Paid cash to owner for personal use, $600.00. Check No. 248.

The source document for this transaction is Check No. 248. *(CONCEPT: Objective Evidence)* The analysis of this kind of transaction is described in Chapter 3. Victoria Peak, Drawing is debited and Cash is credited for $600.00. The general ledger input form entry to record this transaction is shown on lines 7 and 8 of Illustration 11-4. Petlodge follows the same procedures to complete lines 7 and 8 as described for lines 1 and 2.

Cash payment of a liability

September 3, 19--.
Paid cash on account to Marino Kennel Supply, $250.00. Check No. 249.

The source document for this transaction is Check No. 249. *(CONCEPT: Objective Evidence)* The analysis of this kind of transaction is described in Chapter 3. Marino Kennel Supply is debited and Cash is credited for $250.00. The general ledger input form entry to record this transaction is shown on lines 9 and 10 of Illustration 11-4.

Cash payment for supplies

September 3, 19--.
Paid cash for office supplies, $63.00. Check No. 250.

The source document for this transaction is Check No. 250. *(CONCEPT: Objective Evidence)* The analysis of this kind of transaction is described in Chapter 3. Supplies—Office is debited and Cash is credited for $63.00. The general ledger input form entry to record this transaction is shown on lines 11 and 12 of Illustration 11-4.

Cash payment to replenish petty cash

Petlodge deposits all cash in a bank. However, some cash is kept in a petty cash fund for making change at the cash register and for making small cash payments. Petlodge has a petty cash fund of $300.00 that is replenished whenever the fund drops below $100.00.

September 4, 19--.
Paid cash to replenish the petty cash fund, $202.00: office supplies, $87.00; pet supplies, $46.00; miscellaneous, $69.00. Check No. 251.

The source document for this transaction is Check No. 251. *(CONCEPT: Objective Evidence)* The analysis of this kind of transaction is described in Chapter 6. Supplies—Office is debited for $87.00, and Supplies—Pet is debited for $46.00. Miscellaneous Expense is debited for $69.00. Cash is credited for $202.00, the total amount needed to replenish the petty cash fund. The general ledger input form entry to record this transaction is shown on lines 13 through 16 of Illustration 11-4.

Cash receipt from owner as an investment

From time to time, Victoria Peak invests cash in Petlodge. When cash is invested, both the cash account balance and the capital account balance are increased.

> September 4, 19--.
> Received cash from owner as an investment, $1,000.00. Receipt No. 12.

The source document for this transaction is Receipt No. 12. *(CONCEPT: Objective Evidence)* The analysis of this kind of transaction is described in Chapter 3. Cash is debited and Victoria Peak, Capital is credited for $1,000.00. The general ledger input form entry to record this transaction is shown on lines 17 and 18 of Illustration 11-4.

Cash receipt from boarding fees

Petlodge receives a fee for boarding pets. Cash is collected and recorded when the boarding is finished.

> September 5, 19--.
> Received cash from boarding fees, $935.00. Cash Register Tape No. 5.

The source document for this transaction is Cash Register Tape No. 5. *(CONCEPT: Objective Evidence)* Petlodge uses a cash register to record all boarding fees collected. The cash register prints each transaction on a paper tape inside the machine. A printed receipt is also provided for each customer. Amounts on the cash register tape may be totaled daily or weekly. Petlodge records the total boarding fees collected weekly. The tape is marked with the letter *T* and the day of the month it is removed from the cash register.

The analysis of this kind of transaction is described in Chapter 3. Cash is debited and Boarding Fees is credited for $935.00. The general ledger input form entry to record this transaction is shown on lines 19 and 20 of Illustration 11-4.

Completing a general ledger input form

After all transactions have been recorded, Petlodge totals the Debit Amount and Credit Amount columns. The totals are recorded on the Batch Totals line provided at the bottom of the input form. If more than one general ledger input form is required to record transactions, the amount columns for all pages are totaled. A journal entry should not be split on two different general ledger input forms. Therefore, if a complete journal entry cannot be entered on an input form, a new input form is started. The totals for all pages are then entered *only* on the last page on the Batch Totals line. The two totals are compared to assure that debits equal credits. Because the two totals are the same, *$5,210.00*, the entries on this input form are assumed to be correct.

Processing journal entries

Option H is selected from the General Ledger Main Menu, to set the run date, 09/05/--, and the batch number, 2, as shown in Illustration 11-5.

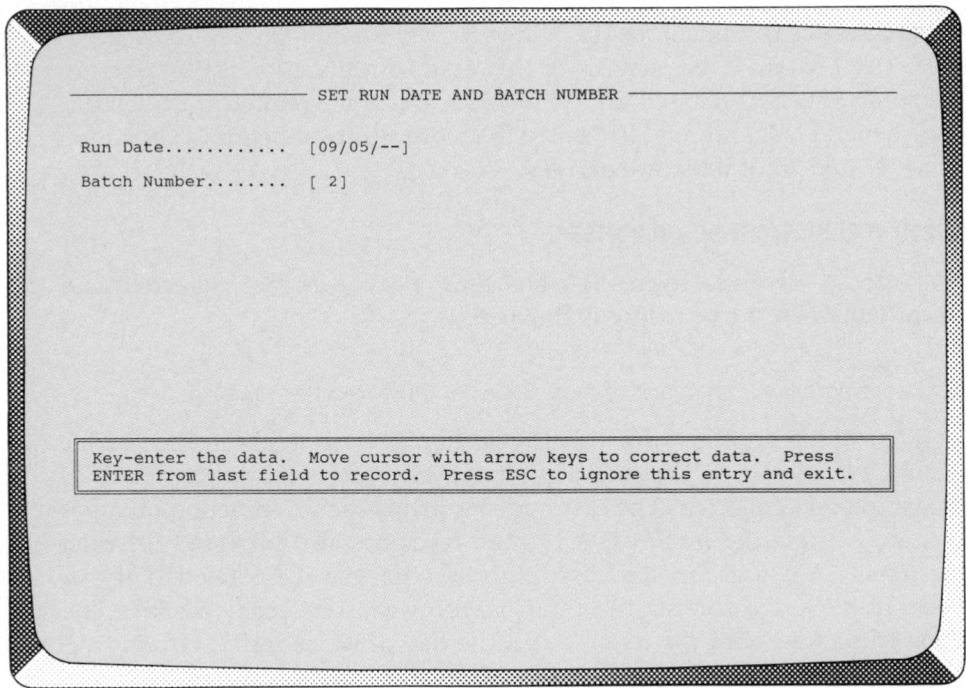

```
─────────────────────── SET RUN DATE AND BATCH NUMBER ───────────────────────


   Run Date...........   [09/05/--]

   Batch Number........  [ 2]














  ┌────────────────────────────────────────────────────────────────────────┐
  │ Key-enter the data.  Move cursor with arrow keys to correct data.  Press │
  │ ENTER from last field to record.  Press ESC to ignore this entry and exit.│
  └────────────────────────────────────────────────────────────────────────┘
```

Illustration 11-5
Computer monitor display
with run date and batch
number recorded

Option I is selected from the General Ledger Main Menu to key-enter journal entries. Spaces for entering the data are displayed on the computer monitor. Petlodge key-enters the transaction data from the general ledger input form one line at a time. Lines 1 and 2 are shown entered in Illustration 11-6.

After all lines on the input form have been entered and posted, Option J is selected from the General Ledger Main Menu. This option directs the

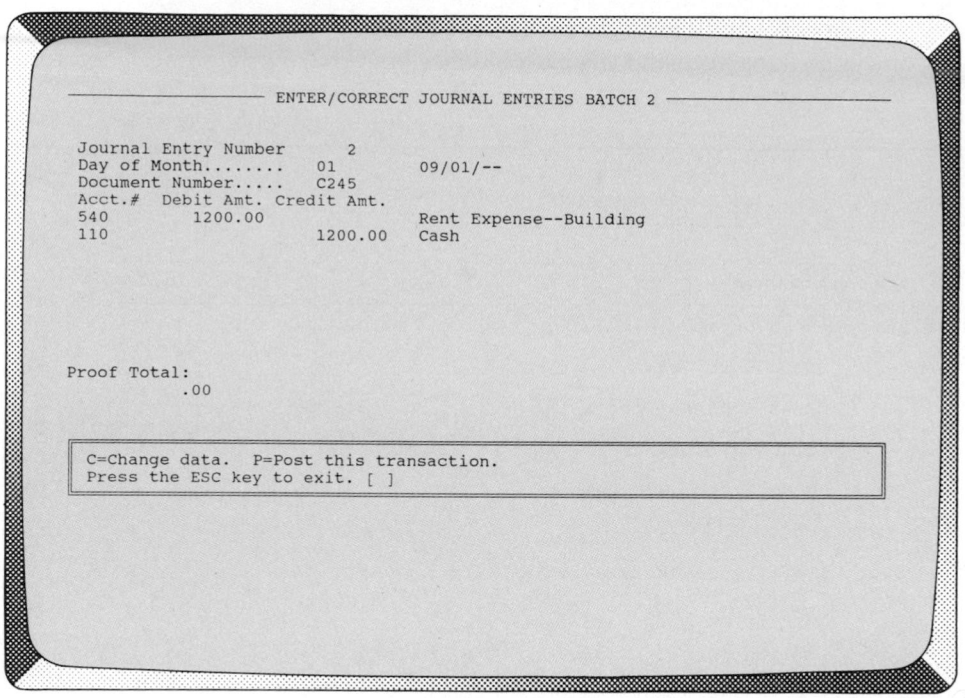

```
──────────────── ENTER/CORRECT JOURNAL ENTRIES BATCH 2 ────────────────

    Journal Entry Number       2
    Day of Month........     01        09/01/--
    Document Number.....    C245
    Acct.#   Debit Amt. Credit Amt.
    540        1200.00                Rent Expense--Building
    110                    1200.00    Cash




    Proof Total:
             .00


    ┌─────────────────────────────────────────────────────────────────┐
    │ C=Change data.   P=Post this transaction.                        │
    │ Press the ESC key to exit. [ ]                                    │
    └─────────────────────────────────────────────────────────────────┘
```

computer to prepare a journal entries report. The journal entries report for batch number 2 is shown in Illustration 11-7, page 230.

Petlodge checks the journal entries report for accuracy by comparing the report totals, *$5,210.00*, with the batch totals on the general ledger input form, *$5,210.00*. Because the totals are the same, the journal entries report is assumed to be correct. The journal entries report is then filed for future reference.

Illustration 11-6
Computer monitor display
of a journal entry

Proving cash

Petlodge also proves cash after each journal entries report involving cash transactions is prepared. The computer keeps track of cash receipts and cash payments. The total cash receipts and cash payments are listed on the journal entries report, Illustration 11-7, to aid in proving cash. Petlodge proves cash on September 5 as shown below.

Cash on hand at the beginning of the month	$12,500.00
(Opening balances report, Illustration 10-12)	
Plus total cash receipts	+ 1,935.00
(Journal entries report, Illustration 11-7)	
Equals total	$14,435.00
Less total cash payments	− 3,275.00
(Journal entries report, Illustration 11-7)	
Equals cash on hand, September 5	$11,160.00

The checkbook balance on the next unused check stub is $11,160.00. The checkbook balance and the cash balance on hand are the same. Therefore, cash is proved.

```
RUN DATE: 09/05/--                      PETLODGE
                               JOURNAL ENTRIES BATCH# 2
---------------------------------------------------------------------------
JE#   DATE      ACCOUNT NUMBER & TITLE          DEBIT AMOUNT  CREDIT AMOUNT
---------------------------------------------------------------------------
0002  09/01/--  540   Rent Expense--Building       1200.00
                110     Cash                                     1200.00
                      DOCUMENT: C245

0003  09/01/--  545   Rent Expense--Computer        875.00
                110     Cash                                      875.00
                      DOCUMENT: C246

0004  09/02/--  530   Miscellaneous Expense          85.00
                110     Cash                                       85.00
                      DOCUMENT: C247

0005  09/02/--  320   Victoria Peak, Drawing        600.00
                110     Cash                                      600.00
                      DOCUMENT: C248

0006  09/03/--  210   Marino Kennel Supply          250.00
                110     Cash                                      250.00
                      DOCUMENT: C249

0007  09/03/--  130   Supplies--Office               63.00
                110     Cash                                       63.00
                      DOCUMENT: C250

0008  09/04/--  130   Supplies--Office               87.00
                140   Supplies--Pet                  46.00
                530   Miscellaneous Expense          69.00
                110     Cash                                      202.00
                      DOCUMENT: C251

0009  09/04/--  110   Cash                         1000.00
                310     Victoria Peak, Capital                  1000.00
                      DOCUMENT: R12

0010  09/05/--  110   Cash                          935.00
                410     Boarding Fees                             935.00
                      DOCUMENT: T5

                                                  -------------- --------------
                TOTALS                              5210.00       5210.00
                                                  ============== ==============
                IN BALANCE

Cash Receipts          1935.00
Cash Payments          3275.00
```

Illustration 11-7
Journal entries report

COMPLETING END-OF-FISCAL-PERIOD WORK

In manual accounting a trial balance is prepared on a work sheet to prove the equality of debits and credits in a general ledger. Adjustments are then planned and the work sheet is completed as described in Part 1 for Rugcare. Financial statements are then manually prepared from data on a completed work sheet. Adjusting and closing entries are entered in a journal and manually posted to general ledger accounts. A post-closing trial balance is prepared manually from general ledger accounts to prove equality of debits and credits after posting adjusting and closing entries.

In automated accounting end-of-fiscal-period reports are printed by a computer according to instructions in the computer software. The run date used for all end-of-fiscal-period reports is the ending date of the accounting period. Petlodge prepares financial statements at the end of each monthly fiscal period. *(CONCEPT: Accounting Period Cycle)* Two financial statements are prepared. (1) Income statement. (2) Balance sheet. Before printing financial statements, Option K is selected from the General Ledger Main Menu to direct the computer to prepare a trial balance. The trial balance is prepared to prove equality of general ledger debits and credits. The trial balance is also used to plan adjustments to general ledger accounts. Petlodge's trial balance is shown in Illustration 11-8.

```
RUN DATE: 09/30/--                      PETLODGE
                                     TRIAL BALANCE
-----------------------------------------------------------------------
ACCOUNT     ACCOUNT
NUMBER      TITLE                         DEBIT AMOUNT       CREDIT AMOUNT
-----------------------------------------------------------------------
110         Cash                            14393.00
120         Petty Cash                        300.00
130         Supplies--Office                 1410.00
140         Supplies--Pet                    2136.00
150         Prepaid Insurance                 765.00
210         Marino Kennel Supply                                1323.00
220         Vega Office Supply                                   195.00
310         Victoria Peak, Capital                             16010.00
320         Victoria Peak, Drawing           1200.00
410         Boarding Fees                                       5455.00
530         Miscellaneous Expense             439.00
540         Rent Expense--Building           1200.00
545         Rent Expense--Computer            875.00
570         Utilities Expense                 265.00
                                        --------------     --------------
            TOTALS                          22983.00           22983.00
                                        ==============     ==============
```

Illustration 11-8
Trial balance

Planning adjusting entries

At the end of an accounting period, certain general ledger accounts need to be brought up to date. *(CONCEPT: Matching Expenses with Revenue)*

Supplies adjustments. Petlodge has two accounts for supplies, Supplies—Office and Supplies—Pet. Two accounts are used in adjusting each supplies account—an asset account and an expense account. Petlodge's two adjustments for the supplies accounts are similar to those described for Rugcare in Part 1.

The value of office supplies used, *$295.00*, is debited to Supplies Expense—Office. Supplies—Office is credited for the same amount. The value of pet supplies used, *$530.00*, is debited to Supplies Expense—Pet. Supplies—Pet is credited for the same amount.

Prepaid insurance adjustment. Insurance premiums, when paid, are debited to the asset account Prepaid Insurance. Insurance expense, however, must be recorded for the month in which the insurance coverage is actually used. *(CONCEPT: Matching Expenses with Revenue)* Prepaid Insurance and Insurance Expense are, therefore, adjusted at the end of each fiscal period. Petlodge's prepaid insurance adjustment is the same as the one described in Part 1. The value of insurance used, *$85.00*, is debited to Insurance Expense. The same amount is credited to Prepaid Insurance.

Petlodge's adjusting entries are recorded on a general ledger input form, as shown in Illustration 11-9.

RUN DATE *09 30 --* MM DD YY

BATCH NO. **7**

GENERAL LEDGER Input Form

FORM GL-2

	DAY	DOC. NO.	ACCOUNT NUMBER	DEBIT AMOUNT	CREDIT AMOUNT	
1	30	Adj. Ent.	550	295 00		1
2			130		295 00	2
3	30	Adj. Ent.	560	530 00		3
4			140		530 00	4
5	30	Adj. Ent.	520	85 00		5
6			150		85 00	6

BATCH TOTALS   910 00   910 00

Illustration 11-9 General ledger input form with adjusting entries recorded

The run date, *09/30/--*, is used to indicate that the adjusting entries are for the month ended 09/30/--. The batch number, *7*, is used as the next sequential number for all batches recorded during the month of September. Batch numbers 3 through 6 were used for the four remaining weekly transaction batches journalized during the month. The day, *30*, is written in the Day Column for each entry. The abbreviation for adjusting entries, *Adj.Ent.*, is written in the Doc. No. column for each entry.

Processing adjusting entries

Option H is selected from the General Ledger Main Menu to record a new run date and batch number. Option I is selected from the General

Ledger Main Menu to enter the adjusting entries. Spaces are displayed on the computer monitor for entering the adjusting entries. Petlodge key-enters the adjusting entries from the input form one line at a time. After all lines on the input form have been key-entered and posted, Option J is selected from the General Ledger Main Menu. This option directs the computer to prepare a journal entries report for the adjusting entries. The journal entries report for the adjusting entries is shown in Illustration 11-10.

```
RUN DATE: 09/30/--                       PETLODGE
                                  JOURNAL ENTRIES BATCH# 7

----------------------------------------------------------------------------
JE#    DATE      ACCOUNT NUMBER & TITLE           DEBIT AMOUNT   CREDIT AMOUNT
----------------------------------------------------------------------------
0038  09/30/-- 550    Supplies Expense--Office        295.00
               130       Supplies--Office                             295.00
                      DOCUMENT: Adj.Ent.

0039  09/30/-- 560    Supplies Expense--Pet           530.00
               140       Supplies--Pet                                530.00
                      DOCUMENT: Adj.Ent.

0040  09/30/-- 520    Insurance Expense                85.00
               150       Prepaid Insurance                             85.00
                      DOCUMENT: Adj.Ent.

                                                  ---------------  ---------------
              TOTALS                                   910.00          910.00
                                                  ===============  ===============
              IN BALANCE
```

Petlodge checks the journal entries report for accuracy by comparing the report with the input form. The journal entries report is then filed for future reference.

Illustration 11-10
Journal entries report for adjusting entries

General ledger report

If individual accounts from the general ledger need to be examined, a general ledger report may be prepared. This report shows all entries to general ledger accounts during the fiscal period. Option L is selected from the General Ledger Main Menu to direct the computer to prepare a general ledger report. A partial general ledger report showing all entries posted to Supplies—Office is shown in Illustration 11-11.

Illustration 11-11
Partial general ledger report

```
RUN DATE: 09/30/--                       PETLODGE
                                     GENERAL LEDGER

-------------------------------------------------------------------------------
ACCOUNT              J.E.   BATCH          DOCUMENT
NUMBER   TITLE       NO.    NUMBER  DATE   NUMBER     DEBIT AMOUNT  CREDIT AMOUNT
-------------------------------------------------------------------------------
130      Supplies--Office
                     0001    01    09/01/-- M1           1260.00
                     0007    02    09/03/-- C250           63.00
                     0008    02    09/04/-- C251           87.00
                     0038    07    09/30/-- Adj.Ent.                    295.00
                                           End.Bal.       1115.00
```

Processing an income statement

After the general ledger report has been prepared, Option M is selected from the General Ledger Main Menu. This option directs the computer to prepare an income statement. Petlodge's income statement is shown in Illustration 11-12.

```
                                    PETLODGE
                                INCOME STATEMENT
                         FOR PERIOD ENDED 09/30/--
                                                                  % OF NET
    R E V E N U E                                                 REVENUE
    -------------                                                 --------
    Boarding Fees                       5455.00                    100.00
                                    ---------------
    NET REVENUE                                        5455.00     100.00


    E X P E N S E S
    ---------------
    Insurance Expense                     85.00                      1.56
    Miscellaneous Expense                439.00                      8.05
    Rent Expense--Building              1200.00                     22.00
    Rent Expense--Computer               875.00                     16.04
    Supplies Expense--Office             295.00                      5.41
    Supplies Expense--Pet                530.00                      9.72
    Utilities Expense                    265.00                      4.86
                                    ---------------
    TOTAL EXPENSES                                     3689.00      67.63
                                                   ----------------
    NET INCOME                                         1766.00      32.37
                                                   ================
```

Illustration 11-12
Income statement

Income statement analysis

The percentage relationship between one financial statement item and the total that includes that item is known as a component percentage. Petlodge's software computes a component percentage for each expense, total expenses, and net income. The relationship between each component and sales is shown in a separate column of the income statement.

Ms. Peak first analyzes the total expenses and net income components to determine if the percentages are acceptable. Acceptable component percentages are determined by comparing the component percentages with percentages published by industry organizations or similar businesses. Ms. Peak also compares the component percentages with the percentages reported on prior income statements. If the total expenses percentage is not acceptable, each individual expense is analyzed to determine causes for an unacceptable component percentage for total expenses.

Total expenses component percentage. For businesses similar to Petlodge, an acceptable total expenses percentage is not more than 70.00%. Therefore, Petlodge's component percentage, 67.63%, is acceptable.

Net income component percentage. For businesses similar to Petlodge, an acceptable net income component percentage is not less than 30.00%.

Therefore, Petlodge's net income component percentage, 32.37%, is acceptable. Reducing the total expenses component percentage in future fiscal periods will result in an improvement in the net income component percentage.

Processing a balance sheet

Option N is selected from the General Ledger Main Menu to direct the computer to prepare a balance sheet. Petlodge's balance sheet is shown in Illustration 11-13.

```
                              PETLODGE
                           BALANCE SHEET
                             09/30/--

        A S S E T S
        -----------
        Cash                           14393.00
        Petty Cash                       300.00
        Supplies--Office                1115.00
        Supplies--Pet                   1606.00
        Prepaid Insurance                680.00
                                    ---------------
        TOTAL ASSETS                                  18094.00
                                                  ================
        L I A B I L I T I E S
        --------------------
        Marino Kennel Supply            1323.00
        Vega Office Supply               195.00
                                    ---------------
        TOTAL LIABILITIES                              1518.00

        O W N E R ' S   E Q U I T Y
        --------------------------
        Victoria Peak, Capital          16010.00
        Victoria Peak, Drawing          -1200.00
        NET INCOME                       1766.00
                                    ---------------
        TOTAL CAPITAL                                 16576.00
                                                  ---------------
        TOTAL LIABILITIES & CAPITAL                   18094.00
                                                  ================
```

Illustration 11-13
Balance sheet

A balance sheet may be prepared in one of two forms: (1) account form or (2) report form. A balance sheet listing assets on the left and equities on the right is called an account form of balance sheet. The account form of balance sheet, used by Rugcare, is described in Part 1. A balance sheet listing the assets, liabilities, and owner's equity vertically is called a report form of balance sheet. Petlodge's computer prints the report form of balance sheet, as shown in Illustration 11-13.

After the income statement and balance sheet have been reviewed and analyzed, the statements are filed for future reference.

Closing temporary accounts

In manual accounting closing entries for all temporary accounts are manually entered in a journal and posted to general ledger accounts. *(CONCEPT: Matching Expenses with Revenue)* In Petlodge's automated accounting system, the computer software contains instructions for closing temporary accounts. When Petlodge wants to close temporary accounts, Option O is selected from the General Ledger Main Menu. This option directs the computer to post closing entries to general ledger accounts. Because no journal entries need to be entered on the keyboard, no general ledger input form or journal entries report is prepared.

Processing a post-closing trial balance

After the financial statements have been prepared and closing entries have been posted, Option P is selected from the General Ledger Main Menu. This option directs the computer to prepare a post-closing trial balance. Petlodge's post-closing trial balance is shown in Illustration 11-14.

```
RUN DATE: 09/30/--                        PETLODGE
                               POST-CLOSING TRIAL BALANCE
------------------------------------------------------------------------------

ACCOUNT        ACCOUNT
NUMBER         TITLE                   DEBIT AMOUNT        CREDIT AMOUNT
------------------------------------------------------------------------------
110            Cash                       14393.00
120            Petty Cash                   300.00
130            Supplies--Office            1115.00
140            Supplies--Pet               1606.00
150            Prepaid Insurance            680.00
210            Marino Kennel Supply                          1323.00
220            Vega Office Supply                             195.00
310            Victoria Peak, Capital                       16576.00
                                        --------------      --------------
               TOTALS                     18094.00           18094.00
                                        ==============      ==============
```

Illustration 11-14
Post-closing trial balance

After the post-closing trial balance has been checked for equality of debits and credits, the trial balance is filed for future reference.

ELECTRONIC SPREADSHEETS

Accountants regularly use paper with columns and rows to analyze financial data. This paper is frequently referred to as analysis paper. Work sheets are prepared manually on analysis paper. Sometimes a work sheet completed on analysis paper is referred to as a spreadsheet. Analysis paper is often used to answer "what if" questions about business operations. An example of "What if?" analysis is figuring the result on net income if revenue is increased by various percentages. When changes are made manually, amounts must be erased and new amounts must be entered. Also, totals must be recalculated, which increases the possibility of errors. If a number of "What if?" questions are needed, a new version must be manually prepared for each set of data. Therefore, preparing a number of versions manually is time consuming.

Computers have made analyzing financial data much easier by increasing the speed and accuracy of calculations. Computers can automatically perform calculations and display and print the results in rows and columns similar to an accountant's analysis paper. A form generated by computer software and consisting of multiple rows and columns in which data can be entered and analyzed is called an electronic spreadsheet. Electronic spreadsheets eliminate the need to manually erase data and recalculate totals when a change is made. Electronic spreadsheets are regularly used by accountants to perform "What if?" financial analysis.

SUMMARY OF USING AN AUTOMATED GENERAL LEDGER ACCOUNTING SYSTEM

Petlodge's automated general ledger accounting system is summarized in Illustration 11-15 below and on page 238. Steps 1 through 8 were described in Chapter 10. Steps 9 through 23 are presented in this chapter.

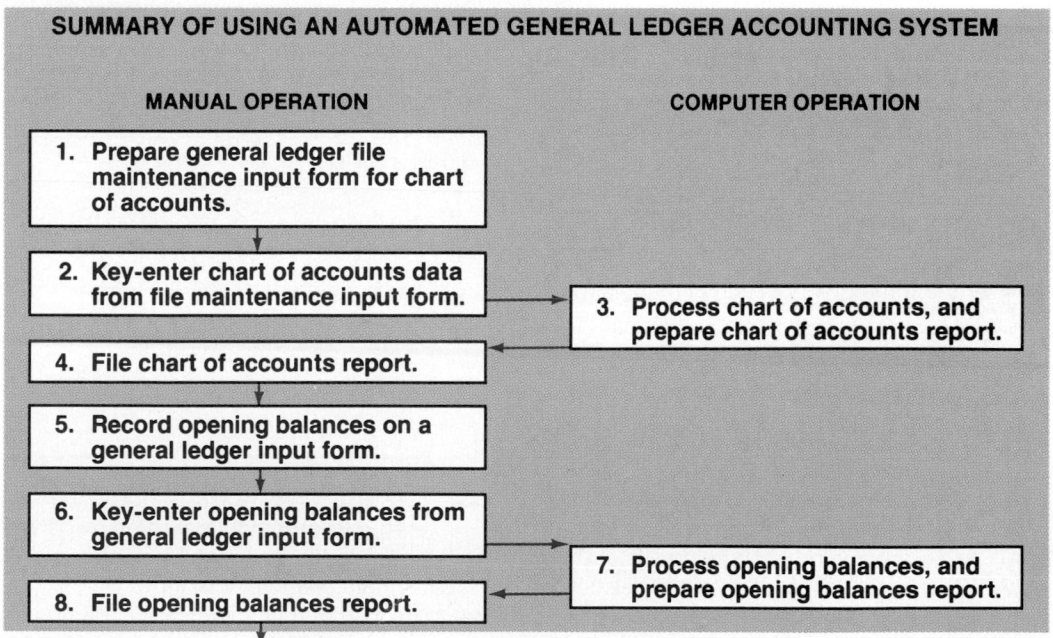

Illustration 11-15   Summary of using an automated general ledger accounting system

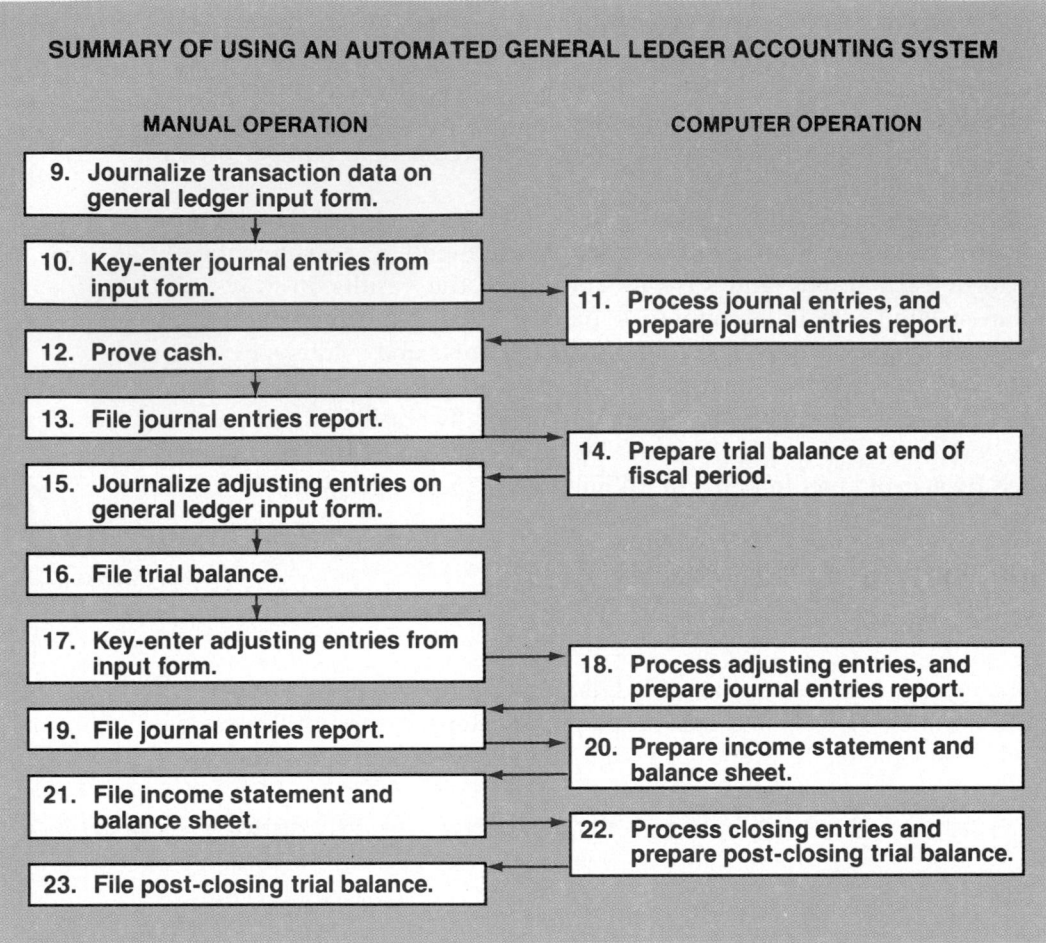

Illustration 11-15   Summary of using an automated general ledger accounting system (concluded)

ACCOUNTING TERMS

What is the meaning of each of the following?

1. account form of balance sheet
2. report form of balance sheet
3. electronic spreadsheet

QUESTIONS FOR INDIVIDUAL STUDY

1. What items should be considered before deciding to change from a manual to an automated accounting system?
2. What form is used to enter deletions from and additions to a general ledger chart of accounts?

3. Why is a word which is not to be entered into a computer written in parentheses in the Account Title column of a file maintenance input form?
4. Which accounting concept is being applied when Petlodge decides to add a

second rent expense account?

5. How does Petlodge assign account numbers within each general ledger division?

6. Where is transaction data recorded before being entered into a computer?

7. In automated accounting, how are transaction data posted to general ledger accounts?

8. Why does Petlodge enter transaction data into the computer weekly instead of daily?

9. Why does Petlodge keep some money in a petty cash fund?

10. After a journal entries report is prepared, how does Petlodge check the report for accuracy?

11. How often does Petlodge prove cash?

12. Why is a computer generated trial balance prepared at the end of a fiscal period?

13. How does Petlodge determine acceptable component percentages?

14. Why does Petlodge's automated accounting system not require manual recording of closing entries?

15. Why do accountants use electronic spreadsheets?

CASES FOR MANAGEMENT DECISION

CASE 1 Irma Angulo is starting a new business called Quality Tailor Services. She has rented a microcomputer and software for an automated general ledger accounting system. In building her general ledger chart of accounts, she plans to use a two-digit general ledger account number. What problems, if any, will a two-digit general ledger account number create?

CASE 2 Bruce Miller owns and operates a chain of five health clubs. One club is located in the downtown business area. Four clubs are located in suburban areas. A computer system is installed in the downtown club. All five clubs use a general ledger input form to record daily transactions for computer processing. Each morning a general ledger input form is prepared for the previous day's business. The completed forms are delivered to the downtown club to be processed by the computer. The automated accounting procedures do not provide a way to distinguish in which club transactions occurred. Data are processed as if only one club were involved. A need exists to be able to analyze business activity by club. What changes might be made so that transactions could be identified by club?

DRILLS FOR UNDERSTANDING

DRILL 11-D1 Adding new general ledger account numbers

This drill provides practice in assigning account numbers to new accounts being added to a general ledger chart of accounts. Use the following partial chart of accounts and list of new accounts to be added to the chart of accounts.

Account No.	Account Title	New Accounts to Be added
110	Cash	Petty Cash
120	Supplies—Office	Supplies—Store
130	Prepaid Insurance	Draper Enterprises
210	Adkins Supply Company	Equipment Repair Expense
510	Advertising Expense	Insurance Expense
520	Miscellaneous Expense	Rent Expense—Computer
530	Rent Expense—Store	Supplies Expense—Store
540	Supplies Expense—Office	Utilities Expense

Use a form similar to the following.

1	2
New General Ledger Account Title	**Account Number Assigned**
Petty Cash	*115*

Instructions: 1. In Column 1 write the account titles of the new accounts to be added to the general ledger chart of accounts.

2. In Column 2 write the account number assigned to each new account title. Use the unused middle number method of assigning new account numbers. The account number assigned to Petty Cash is given as an example.

DRILL 11-D2   Analyzing steps completed in an automated accounting system

Instructions: Refer to Illustration 11-15, pages 237–238, and answer the following questions.

1. What form is used to journalize transactions?
2. Is proving cash a manual or computer operation?
3. What form is used to journalize adjusting entries?
4. Does the printing of a trial balance at the end of a fiscal period precede or follow the planning of adjusting entries?
5. Is the processing of adjusting entries a manual or computer operation?
6. Is the preparation of an income statement and a balance sheet a manual or computer operation?
7. Is the processing of closing entries a manual or computer operation?
8. Is the preparation of a post-closing trial balance a manual or computer operation?

■ APPLICATION PROBLEMS

PROBLEM 11-1   Performing file maintenance activities

Kortage Small Engine Repair performed the following file maintenance activities.

	Accounts Deleted		**Accounts Added**
220	Lapham Services Co.	135	Supplies—Parts
560	Utilities Expense	550	Supplies Expense—Parts

Instructions: Prepare a general ledger file maintenance input form (FORM GL-1). Use November 1 of the current year as the run date.

PROBLEM 11-2   Journalizing transactions on a general ledger input form

Sowle Travel Agency has the following general ledger chart of accounts.

Account No.	Account Title	Account No.	Account Title
110	Cash	410	Fees
120	Petty Cash	510	Advertising Expense
130	Supplies—Computer	530	Miscellaneous Expense
140	Supplies—Office	540	Rent Expense—Computer
210	Grant Computer Products	550	Rent Expense—Office
220	Poyer Office Supply	580	Utilities Expense
310	Hazel Sowle, Capital		
320	Hazel Sowle, Drawing		

Instructions: 1. Journalize the following transactions on a general ledger input form (FORM GL-2). Use June 6 of the current year as the run date. Batch No. 2. Source documents are abbreviated as follows: check, C; receipt, R; cash register tape, T.

Transactions

June 1. Paid cash for office rent, $950.00. C145.
1. Paid cash for computer rent, $825.00. C146.
1. Paid cash to owner for personal use, $600.00. C147.
2. Paid cash for office supplies, $263.00. C148.
2. Paid cash on account to Grant Computer Products, $360.00. C149.
3. Paid cash for advertising, $85.00. C150.
3. Paid cash for computer supplies, $135.00. C151.
4. Paid cash for miscellaneous expense, $45.00. C152.
4. Received cash from owner as an investment, $3,500.00. R23.
5. Paid cash on account to Poyer Office Supply, $265.00. C153.
5. Paid cash for electric bill, $145.00. C154.
6. Paid cash to replenish the petty cash fund, $201.00: computer supplies, $76.00; office supplies, $72.00; miscellaneous, $53.00. C155.
6. Received cash from fees, $1,986.00. T6.

2. Total and prove the Debit Amount and Credit Amount columns. Record the batch totals.

PROBLEM 11-3   Journalizing adjusting entries on a general ledger input form

Velo Accounting Service has the following general ledger accounts that need adjustment at the end of the fiscal period.

Account No.	Account Title	Account Balance
130	Supplies—Computer....................	$1,220.00
140	Supplies—Office	1,740.00
150	Prepaid Insurance	1,280.00
530	Insurance Expense	—
560	Supplies Expense—Computer	—
570	Supplies Expense—Office..............	—

Adjustment Information, August 31

Value of computer supplies on hand....................	$ 865.00
Value of office supplies on hand	1,380.00
Value of prepaid insurance	1,120.00

Instructions: 1. Journalize the adjusting entries on a general ledger input form (FORM GL-2). Use August 31 of the current year as the run date. Batch No. 7.
    2. Total and prove the Debit Amount and Credit Amount columns. Record the batch totals.

■ ENRICHMENT PROBLEMS

MASTERY PROBLEM 11-M   **Preparing input forms for an automated accounting system**

Arthur's Bowling Lanes has the following general ledger chart of accounts.

Balance Sheet Accounts		Income Statement Accounts	
(100) ASSETS		**(400) REVENUE**	
110	Cash	410	Sales
120	Supplies—Bowling		
130	Supplies—Office		
140	Prepaid Insurance	**(500) EXPENSES**	
(200) LIABILITIES		510	Advertising Expense
		520	Insurance Expense
		530	Miscellaneous Expense
210	Costello Bowling Supplies	540	Rent Expense
220	Hayes Office Supply	550	Supplies Expense—Bowling
230	Top-Line Bowling Supplies	560	Supplies Expense—Office
(300) OWNER'S EQUITY			
310	Clyde Arthur, Capital		
320	Clyde Arthur, Drawing		
330	Income Summary		

Arthur's Bowling Lanes performed the following file maintenance activities.

Account Deleted	**Account Title Change**	**Accounts Added**
Advertising Expense	Rent Expense	Petty Cash
	TO	Rent Expense—Computer
	Rent Expense—Building	Utilities Expense

Instructions: 1. Assign account numbers to the new accounts using the unused middle number method.

2. Prepare a general ledger file maintenance input form (FORM GL-1). Use December 1 of the current year as the run date.

3. Journalize the following transactions on a general ledger input form (FORM GL-2). Use December 31 of the current year as the run date. Batch No. 6. Source documents are abbreviated as follows: check, C; receipt, R; cash register tape, T.

Transactions

Dec. 27. Paid cash for miscellaneous expense, $125.00. C235.
27. Paid cash for bowling supplies, $185.00. C236.
28. Paid cash for office supplies, $143.00. C237.
29. Paid cash on account to Costello Bowling Supplies, $438.00. C238.
29. Received cash from owner as an investment, $4,000.00. R12.
30. Paid cash for miscellaneous expense, $95.00. C239.
30. Paid cash to replenish the petty cash fund, $103.00: bowling supplies, $42.00; office supplies, $36.00; miscellaneous, $25.00. C240.
30. Paid cash for telephone bill, $116.00. C241.
31. Paid cash for computer rent, $835.00. C242.
31. Paid cash to owner for personal use, $850.00. C243.
31. Received cash from sales, $1,980.00. T31.

4. Total and prove the Debit Amount and Credit Amount columns. Record the batch totals.

5. The following accounts need adjustment at the end of the fiscal period. Journalize the adjusting entries on a general ledger input form (FORM GL-2). Use December 31 of the current year as the run date. Batch No. 7.

Account Title	**Account Balance**
Supplies—Bowling	$2,110.00
Supplies—Office	1,427.00
Prepaid Insurance	1,890.00

Adjustment Information, December 31

Value of bowling supplies on hand	$1,480.00
Value of office supplies on hand	940.00
Value of prepaid insurance	1,680.00

6. Total and prove the Debit Amount and Credit Amount columns. Record the batch totals.

CHALLENGE PROBLEM 11-C   Preparing input forms for an automated accounting system

ShurFit Tailors has the following general ledger chart of accounts.

Balance Sheet Accounts		Income Statement Accounts	
(100) ASSETS		**(400) REVENUE**	
110	Cash	410	Tailoring Fees
120	Petty Cash		
130	Supplies—Fabric	**(500) EXPENSES**	
140	Supplies—Office		
150	Prepaid Insurance	510	Advertising Expense
		520	Insurance Expense
(200) LIABILITIES		530	Miscellaneous Expense
		540	Rent Expense
210	Empire Fabrics	550	Supplies Expense—Fabric
220	Ganto Office Supply	560	Supplies Expense—Office
230	Palm Fabrics		
(300) OWNER'S EQUITY			
310	Linda Kline, Capital		
320	Linda Kline, Drawing		
330	Income Summary		

ShurFit Tailors performed the following file maintenance activities.

Account Deleted	**Account Title Change**	**Accounts Added**
Empire Fabrics	Rent Expense	Regarus Textiles
	TO	Rent Expense—Computer
	Rent Expense—Building	Utilities Expense

Instructions: 1. Assign account numbers to the new accounts using the unused middle number method.

2. Prepare a general ledger file maintenance input form (FORM GL-1). Use July 1 of the current year as the run date.

3. Journalize the following transactions on a general ledger input form (FORM GL-2). Use July 31 of the current year as the run date. Batch No. 6. Source documents are abbreviated as follows: check, C; receipt, R; cash register tape, T.

Transactions

July 27. Paid cash for fabric supplies, $255.00. C335.
   27. Paid cash for advertising, $130.00. C336.
   28. Paid cash for office supplies, $93.00. C337.
   29. Paid cash on account to Palm Fabrics, $387.00. C338.
   29. Received cash from owner as an investment, $3,000.00. R15.
   30. Paid cash for miscellaneous expense, $45.00. C339.
   30. Paid cash to replenish the petty cash fund, $205.00: fabric supplies, $102.00; office supplies, $57.00; miscellaneous, $46.00. C340.

July 30. Paid cash for electric bill, $146.00. C341.
    31. Paid cash for computer rent, $780.00. C342.
    31. Paid cash to owner for personal use, $750.00. C343.
    31. Received cash from tailoring fees, $1,740.00. T31.

4. Total and prove the Debit Amount and Credit Amount columns. Record the batch totals.

5. The following accounts need adjustment at the end of the fiscal period. Journalize the adjusting entries on a general ledger input form (FORM GL-2). Use July 31 of the current year as the run date. Batch No. 7.

Account Title	Account Balance
Supplies—Fabric......................................	$1,930.00
Supplies—Office......................................	1,480.00
Prepaid Insurance....................................	1,520.00

Adjustment Information, July 31

Value of fabric supplies on hand	$1,360.00
Value of office supplies on hand	1,233.00
Value of prepaid insurance	1,330.00

6. Total and prove the Debit Amount and Credit Amount columns. Record the batch totals.

The solution to Challenge Problem 11-C is needed to complete Computer Application 2.

Computer Application 2
Using an Automated Accounting System

The general ledger file maintenance input form and the general ledger input forms completed in Challenge Problem 11-C, Chapter 11, are needed to complete Computer Application 2.

ShurFit Tailors completed the input forms for using an automated accounting system. The manual and computer operations required are described in Chapter 11. Computer Application 2 provides an opportunity to process the data from the completed forms using a microcomputer.

Computer Application 2 is designed to be used with the *Automated Accounting for the Microcomputer*, 3d edition, software. The software provides the option of either displaying or printing reports. If a printer is available, select the *Print* option when given the choice of displaying or printing reports. If a printer is not available, select the *Display* option. Selecting the *Display* option causes the report to be displayed on the computer monitor.

■ COMPUTER APPLICATION PROBLEM

COMPUTER APPLICATION PROBLEM 2   **Using an automated accounting system**

Instructions: 1. Load the *Automated Accounting for the Microcomputer* software. Select Computer Application 2 (CA-2) from the CENTURY 21 ACCOUNTING Template Disk. The accounting system data, chart of accounts, opening balances, and company name have been entered and are stored on the Template Disk.

2. Key-enter the file maintenance data from the completed general ledger file maintenance input form prepared in Challenge Problem 11-C.

3. Display/Print the revised chart of accounts report. Check the report for accuracy.

4. Key-enter the transactions from the completed general ledger input form prepared in Challenge Problem 11-C.

5. Display/Print the journal entries report. Check the report for accuracy by comparing the report totals with the batch totals on the general ledger input form.

6. Prove cash. The beginning cash balance was $10,850.00. The balance on the next unused check stub is $12,799.00.

7. Display/Print the trial balance.

8. Key-enter the adjusting entries from the completed general ledger input form prepared in Challenge Problem 11-C.

9. Display/Print the journal entries report. Check the report for accuracy by comparing the report totals with the totals on the general ledger input form.

10. Display/Print the income statement.

11. Display/Print the balance sheet.

12. Close the ledger.

13. Display/Print the post-closing trial balance.

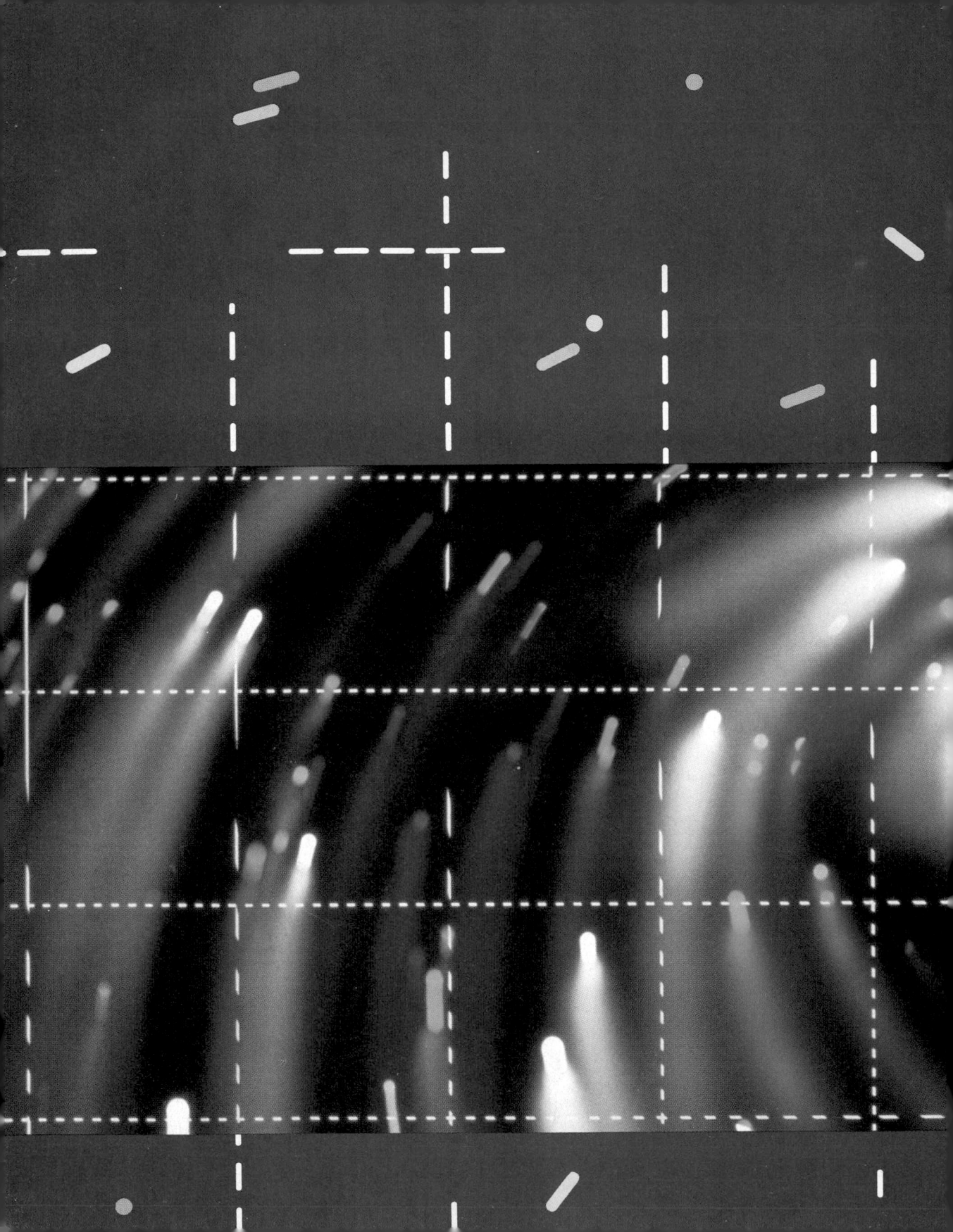

Partnership Accounting for a Merchandising Business

3

GENERAL BEHAVIORAL GOALS

1. Know accounting terminology related to an accounting system for a merchandising business organized as a partnership.
2. Understand accounting concepts and practices related to an accounting system for a merchandising business organized as a partnership.
3. Demonstrate accounting procedures used in an accounting system for a merchandising business organized as a partnership.

CARLAND
Chart of Accounts
General Ledger

Balance Sheet Accounts

(1000) ASSETS

1110   Cash
1120   Petty Cash
1130   Accounts Receivable
1140   Merchandise Inventory
1145   Supplies—Office
1150   Supplies—Store
1160   Prepaid Insurance

(2000) LIABILITIES

2110   Accounts Payable
2120   Employee Income Tax Payable
2130   FICA Tax Payable
2140   Sales Tax Payable
2150   Unemployment Tax Payable—
      Federal
2160   Unemployment Tax Payable—
      State
2170   Health Insurance Premiums
      Payable
2180   U.S. Savings Bonds Payable
2190   United Way Donations Payable

(3000) OWNERS' EQUITY

3110   Amy Kramer, Capital
3120   Amy Kramer, Drawing
3130   Dario Mesa, Capital
3140   Dario Mesa, Drawing
3150   Income Summary

Income Statement Accounts

(4000) OPERATING REVENUE

4110   Sales

(5000) COST OF MERCHANDISE

5110   Purchases

(6000) OPERATING EXPENSES

6110   Advertising Expense
6120   Credit Card Fee Expense
6130   Insurance Expense
6140   Miscellaneous Expense
6150   Payroll Taxes Expense
6160   Rent Expense
6170   Salary Expense
6175   Supplies Expense—Office
6180   Supplies Expense—Store
6190   Utilities Expense

Subsidiary Ledgers

Accounts Receivable Ledger

110   Ashley Delivery
120   Autohaus Service
130   Friendly Auto Service
140   Keystone Delivery
150   Powell Rent-A-Car
160   Wood Sales & Service

Accounts Payable Ledger

210   Antelo Supply
220   Bell Office Products
230   Filtrex Tires
240   Nilon Motor Parts
250   Q-Ban Distributors
260   Veloz Automotive

The charts of accounts for CarLand are illustrated above for
ready reference as you study Part 3 of this textbook.

12

Journalizing Purchases and Cash Payments

ENABLING PERFORMANCE TASKS

After studying Chapter 12, you will be able to:

a. Define accounting terms related to purchases and cash payments for a merchandising business.

b. Identify accounting concepts and practices related to purchases and cash payments for a merchandising business.

c. Analyze purchases and cash payments transactions for a merchandising business.

d. Journalize purchases and cash payments transactions for a merchandising business.

Rugcare, the business described in Part 1, is owned by one person. Petlodge, described in Part 2, is also owned by one person. A business owned by one person is known as a proprietorship.

Many businesses require the skills of more than one person. Many businesses also need more capital than one owner can provide. Therefore, many businesses are owned by two or more persons. A business in which two or more persons combine their assets and skills is called a partnership. Each member of a partnership is called a partner. Partners must agree on how each partner will share the business' profit or loss. As in proprietorships, reports and financial records of the business are kept separate from the personal records of the partners. (CONCEPT: Business Entity)

Both Rugcare and Petlodge, the businesses described in Parts 1 and 2, sell services for a fee. A business that sells a service for a fee is known as a service business. However, many other businesses purchase goods to sell. A business that purchases and sells goods is called a merchandising business. Goods that a merchandising business purchases to sell are called merchandise. The selling of merchandise rather than a service is what makes the activities of a merchandising business different from those of a service business.

251

CarLand, the business described in this part, is a merchandising business organized as a partnership. The business is owned by Amy Kramer and Dario Mesa. The business purchases and sells automotive supplies. CarLand rents the building in which the business is located as well as the equipment used for operation. CarLand expects to make money and continue in business indefinitely. *(CONCEPT: Going Concern)*

USING AN EXPANDED JOURNAL

A service business generally has a large number of cash transactions and a limited number of noncash transactions. Noncash transactions are those that do not involve either the receipt or payment of cash. Rugcare uses a 5-column journal, described in Part 1, to record all cash and noncash transactions.

Need for expanded journal

CarLand, a merchandising business, has many noncash and other frequently occurring transactions that affect single accounts. CarLand could use the same journal as the one used by Rugcare. However, without adding more special amount columns to the journal, the large number of transactions would require many entries in the General Debit and Credit columns.

Form of expanded journal

To save time and space in journalizing transactions, CarLand uses an 11-column journal. The journal includes additional special amount columns for recording frequently occurring transactions that affect single accounts. A journal expanded to provide for the recording of frequently occurring transactions that affect single accounts is shown in Illustration 12-1.

Illustration 12-1
Amount columns of an
expanded journal

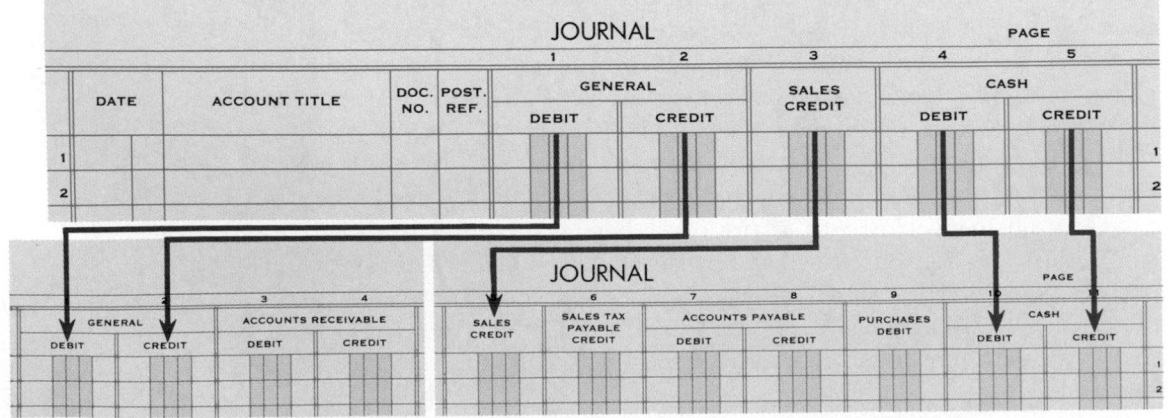

An expanded journal is commonly used by small merchandising businesses in which only one person records transactions. Amy Kramer records all transactions for CarLand.

CarLand's journal, Illustration 12-1, has special amount columns for the recording of frequently occurring transactions related to the purchasing and selling of merchandise. The columns are arranged to make accurate journalizing and posting easier. Debit and credit columns for *Cash*, *Accounts Receivable*, and *Accounts Payable* are arranged in pairs. This arrangement helps avoid errors in recording amounts in the wrong columns. All columns are placed to the right of the Account Title column. The General Debit and Credit amount columns are placed first so that amounts in these columns will be close to the titles in the Account Title column.

> The number and arrangement of columns in a journal is determined by the type and frequency of transactions. CarLand determined that the journal described above would best meet the needs of the business.

JOURNALIZING PURCHASES OF MERCHANDISE

The price a business pays for goods it purchases to sell is called cost of merchandise. The selling price of merchandise must be greater than the cost of merchandise for a business to make a profit. The amount added to the cost of merchandise to establish the selling price is called markup. Revenue earned from the sale of merchandise includes both the cost of merchandise and markup. Only the markup increases capital. Accounts for the cost of merchandise are kept in a separate division of the general ledger. The cost of merchandise division is shown in CarLand's chart of accounts, page 250.

In addition to purchasing merchandise to sell, a merchandising business also buys supplies and other assets for use in the business. A business from which merchandise is purchased or supplies or other assets are bought is called a vendor.

The account used for recording the cost of merchandise purchased to sell is titled *Purchases*. Purchases is classified as a cost account because it is in the cost of merchandise division in the chart of accounts. The cost account *Purchases* is a temporary account. Because the cost of merchandise pur-

Purchases	
Debit side	Credit side
Normal balance	
Increase	Decrease

chased for resale reduces capital when the merchandise is sold, the cost account *Purchases* has a normal debit balance. Therefore, the purchases account is increased by a debit and decreased by a credit, as shown in the T account.

The cost account, *Purchases*, is used only to record the value of merchandise purchased. Therefore, only purchases of merchandise are recorded in the Purchases Debit column of the journal. All other items bought, such as supplies, are recorded in the General Debit column of the journal. Merchandise and other items bought are recorded and reported at the price agreed upon at the time the transactions occur. The price agreed upon at the time the transaction occurs may be lower than the given price. The accounting concept, *Historical Cost*, is applied when the actual amount paid for merchandise or other items bought is recorded. *(CONCEPT: Historical Cost)*

Purchase of merchandise for cash

CarLand pays cash for some purchases. All cash payments are made by check.

November 2, 19--.
Purchased merchandise for cash, $483.00. Check No. 259.

The source document for a cash purchase is the check issued. *(CONCEPT: Objective Evidence)*

A cash purchase transaction increases the purchases account balance and decreases the cash account balance. The analysis of the cash purchase transaction is shown in the T accounts.

Because the purchases account has a normal debit balance, Purchases is debited for $483.00 to show the increase in this cost account. The cash account also has a normal debit balance. Therefore, Cash is credited for $483.00 to show the decrease in this asset account.

The journal entry to record this transaction is shown in Illustration 12-2.

```
          Purchases
    483.00 |
    _____
            Cash
           |  483.00
```

Illustration 12-2
Journal entry to record a
purchase of merchandise
for cash

							9	10	11	
PAGE 21				JOURNAL				PAGE 21		
							PURCHASES DEBIT	CASH		
	DATE	ACCOUNT TITLE	DOC. NO.	POST. REF.				DEBIT	CREDIT	
1	Nov. 2	√	C259	√			483 00		483 00	1

The date, *19--, Nov. 2,* is recorded in the Date column. Both the debit and credit amounts will be recorded in special amount columns. Therefore, a check mark is placed in the Account Title column to show that no account title needs to be written. The check number, *C259,* is recorded in the Doc. No. column. Both the debit and credit amounts will be posted as part of special amount column totals. Therefore, a check mark is placed in the Post. Ref. column to show that amounts on this line are not to be posted individually. The debit to Purchases, *$483.00,* is entered in the Purchases Debit column. The credit to Cash, *$483.00,* is entered in the Cash Credit column.

Purchase of merchandise on account

A transaction in which the merchandise purchased is to be paid for later is called a purchase on account. Some businesses that purchase on account from only a few vendors keep a separate general ledger account for each vendor to whom money is owed. Businesses that purchase on account from many vendors will have many accounts for vendors. To avoid a bulky general ledger, the total amount owed to all vendors can be summarized in a single general ledger account. A liability account that summarizes the amounts owed to all vendors is titled Accounts Payable. CarLand uses an accounts payable account.

The liability account, Accounts Payable, has a normal credit balance. Therefore, the accounts payable account is increased by a credit and decreased by a debit, as shown in the T account.

Accounts Payable	
Debit side	Credit side
	Normal balance
Decrease	Increase

When a vendor sells merchandise to a buyer, the vendor prepares a form showing what has been sold. A form describing the goods sold, the quantity, and the price is called an invoice. An invoice used as a source document for recording a purchase on account transaction is called a purchase invoice. (CONCEPT: Objective Evidence) A purchase invoice received by CarLand is shown in Illustration 12-3.

veloz automotive
2611 Industrial
Fremont, NH 03044-2672

REC'D 11/02/-- P74

TO: CarLand
1374 Parklane
Rockville, RI 02873-4121

DATE: 10/26/--
INV. NO.: 2768
TERMS: 30 days
ACCT. NO.: 260

QUANTITY	CAT. NO.	DESCRIPTION	UNIT PRICE	TOTAL
8	4422	All-season tires	73.00	584.00✓
6	4424	All-season tires	73.00	438.00✓
12	6620	Floor mats	16.00	192.00✓
12	7715	Seat covers	45.00	540.00✓
		Total		1,754.00

Illustration 12-3
Purchase invoice

A purchase invoice lists the quantity, the description, the price of each item, and the total amount of the invoice. A purchase invoice provides the information needed for recording a purchase on account.

When CarLand receives a purchase invoice, a date and a number are stamped in the upper right-hand corner. The date stamped is the date the invoice is received. CarLand received the invoice in Illustration 12-3 on 11/02/--. This date should not be confused with the vendor's date on the invoice, 10/26/--. CarLand assigns numbers in sequence to easily identify all purchase invoices. The number stamped on the invoice, *P74*, is the number assigned by CarLand to this purchase invoice. This number should not be confused with the invoice number, 2768, assigned by the vendor. Each vendor uses a different numbering system. Therefore, vendor invoice numbers could not be recorded in sequence, which would make it impossible to detect a missing invoice.

A buyer needs to know that all items ordered have been received and that the prices are correct. The check marks on the invoice show that the items have been received and that amounts have been checked and are correct. The initials near the total are those of the person at CarLand who checked the invoice.

An agreement between a buyer and a seller about payment for merchandise is called the terms of sale. The terms of sale on the invoice, Illustration 12-3, are 30 days. These terms mean that payment is due within 30 days from the date of the invoice. The invoice is dated October 26. Therefore, payment must be made by November 25.

November 2, 19--.
Purchased merchandise on account from Veloz Automotive, $1,754.00. Purchase Invoice No. 74.

The source document for a purchase on account is the purchase invoice received with the merchandise. *(CONCEPT: Objective Evidence)*

A purchase on account transaction increases the amount owed to a vendor. This transaction increases the purchases account balance and increases the accounts payable account balance. The analysis of this purchase on account transaction is shown in the T accounts.

Because the purchases account has a normal debit balance, Purchases is debited for $1,754.00 to show the increase in this cost account. The accounts payable account has a normal credit balance. Therefore, Accounts Payable is credited for $1,754.00 to show the increase in this liability account.

The journal entry to record this purchase on account transaction is shown in Illustration 12-4.

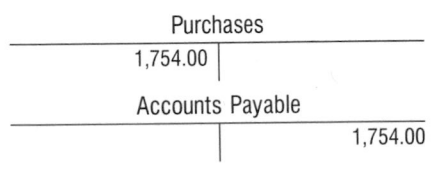

Purchases	
1,754.00	

Accounts Payable	
	1,754.00

Illustration 12-4
Journal entry to record a
purchase of merchandise
on account

PAGE 21			JOURNAL						7		8		9	
									ACCOUNTS PAYABLE				PURCHASES DEBIT	
	DATE	ACCOUNT TITLE		DOC. NO.	POST. REF.				DEBIT		CREDIT			
2	2	*Veloz Automotive*		P74							1 7 5 4 00		1 7 5 4 00	

The date, 2, is written in the Date column. No special amount column is provided for Veloz Automotive. Therefore, the vendor's name, *Veloz Automotive*, is recorded in the Account Title column. CarLand's purchase invoice number, *P74*, is entered in the Doc. No. column. The credit to Accounts Payable, *$1,754.00*, is recorded in the Accounts Payable Credit column. The debit to Purchases, *$1,754.00*, is recorded in the Purchases Debit column.

The debit to Purchases and the credit to Accounts Payable are recorded in special amount columns. Therefore, writing the titles of either general ledger account in the Account Title column is not necessary. However, the name of the vendor is written in the Account Title column to show to whom the amount is owed. The way CarLand keeps records of the amount owed to each vendor is described in Chapter 14.

JOURNALIZING BUYING SUPPLIES

CarLand buys supplies for use in the business. Supplies are not recorded in the purchases account because supplies are not intended for sale. Cash register tapes and price tags are examples of supplies used in a merchandising business.

Buying supplies for cash

CarLand buys most of its supplies for cash.

November 5, 19--.
Paid cash for office supplies, $87.00. Check No. 261.

The source document for buying supplies for cash is the check issued in payment. *(CONCEPT: Objective Evidence)*

This transaction increases the office supplies account balance and decreases the cash account balance. The analysis of the buying supplies for cash transaction is shown in the T accounts.

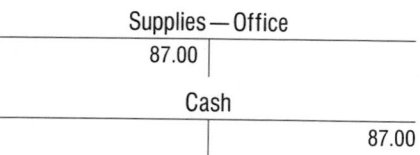

Because the office supplies account has a normal debit balance, Supplies—Office is debited for $87.00 to show the increase in this asset account. The cash account also has a normal debit balance. Therefore, Cash is credited for $87.00 to show the decrease in this asset account.

The journal entry to record this buying supplies for cash transaction is shown in Illustration 12-5, page 258.

The date, *5*, is recorded in the Date column. No special amount column is provided for Supplies—Office. Therefore, the account title, *Supplies—Office*, is written in the Account Title column. The check number, *C261*, is entered in the Doc. No. column. The debit to Supplies—Office, *$87.00*, is recorded in the General Debit column. The credit to Cash, *$87.00*, is recorded in the Cash Credit column.

PAGE *21*	JOURNAL				1	2		PAGE *21*		
					GENERAL				10	11
DATE	ACCOUNT TITLE	DOC. NO.	POST. REF.	DEBIT	CREDIT			CASH	DEBIT	CREDIT
6	5	Supplies—Office	C261	8 7 00						8 7 00	6
7											7
8											8

Illustration 12-5
Journal entry to record
buying supplies for cash

Buying supplies on account

CarLand usually buys supplies for cash. Occasionally, however, Car-Land buys some supplies on account.

*November 6, 19--.
Bought store supplies on account from Antelo Supply, $160.00. Memorandum No. 43.*

When CarLand buys supplies on account, an invoice is received from the vendor. This invoice is similar to the purchase invoice received when merchandise is purchased. To assure that no mistake is made, a memorandum is attached to the invoice noting that the invoice is for supplies and not for purchases. Memorandum 43 is shown in Illustration 12-6.

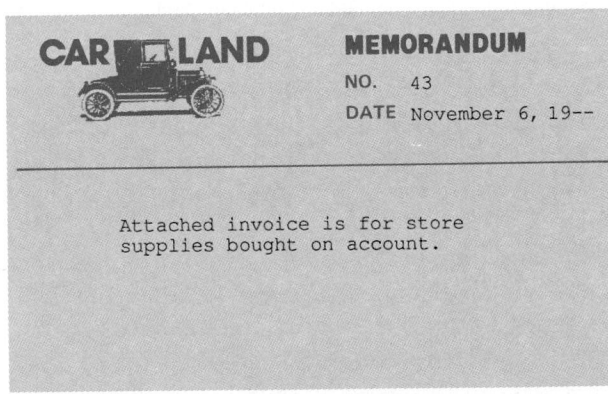

Illustration 12-6
Memorandum for buying
supplies on account

The source document for buying supplies on account is the memorandum with its attached invoice. (CONCEPT: *Objective Evidence*)

This transaction increases the store supplies account balance and increases the accounts payable account balance. The analysis of the buying supplies on account transaction is shown in the T accounts.

Because the store supplies account has a normal debit balance, Supplies—Store is debited for $160.00 to show the in-

Supplies—Store

160.00 |

Accounts Payable

| 160.00

crease in this asset account. The accounts payable account has a normal credit balance. Therefore, Accounts Payable is credited for $160.00 to show the increase in this liability account.

The journal entry to record this buying supplies on account transaction is shown in Illustration 12-7.

Illustration 12-7
Journal entry to record
buying supplies on account

	DATE	ACCOUNT TITLE	DOC. NO.	POST. REF.	GENERAL DEBIT	GENERAL CREDIT	ACCOUNTS PAYABLE DEBIT	ACCOUNTS PAYABLE CREDIT
9	6	Supplies—Store	M43		1 6 0 00			
10		Antelo Supply						1 6 0 00

PAGE 21 — JOURNAL

The date, *6*, is written in the Date column. No special amount column is provided for Supplies—Store. Therefore, the account title, *Supplies—Store*, is recorded in the Account Title column. The memorandum number, *M43*, is entered in the Doc. No. column. The debit to Supplies—Store, *$160.00*, is written in the General Debit column on the same line. An account title is also required for the credit part of the entry. Therefore, the vendor name, *Antelo Supply*, is recorded in the Account Title column on the next line. The credit to Accounts Payable, *$160.00*, is entered in the Accounts Payable Credit column on the same line.

JOURNALIZING CASH PAYMENTS

Most of CarLand's cash payments are to vendors or for expenses. Payment to vendors is made according to the terms of sale on the purchase invoices. Payment for an expense is usually made at the time the expense occurs.

Cash payment on account

CarLand pays by check for all cash purchases and for payments on account.

November 7, 19--.
Paid cash on account to Filtrex Tires, $970.00, covering Purchase Invoice No. 72. Check No. 263.

The source document for a cash payment on account is the check issued in payment. (CONCEPT: *Objective Evidence*)

This cash payment on account transaction decreases the amount owed to vendors. This transaction decreases the accounts payable account balance and decreases the cash account balance. The analysis of the cash payment on account transaction is shown in the T accounts.

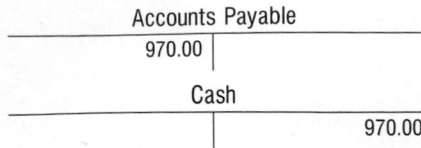

Because the accounts payable account has a normal credit balance, Accounts Payable is debited for $970.00 to show the decrease in this liability account. The cash account has a normal debit balance. Therefore, Cash is credited for $970.00 to show the decrease in this asset account.

The journal entry to record this cash payment on account transaction is shown in Illustration 12-8.

PAGE *21*		JOURNAL			7	8	10	11 PAGE *21*
					ACCOUNTS PAYABLE		**CASH**	
DATE	ACCOUNT TITLE		DOC. NO.	POST. REF.	DEBIT	CREDIT	DEBIT	CREDIT
13	7	*Filtrex Tires*		C263	9 7 0 00			9 7 0 00	13
14									14
15									15
16									16

Illustration 12-8
Journal entry to record a
cash payment on account

The date, 7, is written in the Date column. No special amount column is provided for Filtrex Tires. Therefore, the vendor name, *Filtrex Tires*, is recorded in the Account Title column. The check number, *C263*, is entered in the Doc. No. column. The debit to Accounts Payable, *$970.00*, is written in the Accounts Payable Debit column. The credit to Cash, *$970.00*, is written in the Cash Credit column.

Cash payment of an expense

CarLand usually pays for an expense at the time the transaction occurs.

November 9, 19--.
Paid cash for advertising, $125.00. Check No. 265.

The source document for a cash payment of an expense is the check issued in payment. *(CONCEPT: Objective Evidence)*

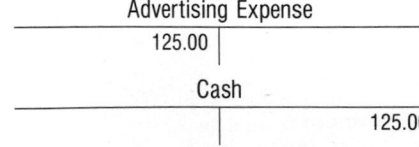

This cash payment increases the advertising expense account balance and decreases the cash account balance. The analysis of the cash payment of an expense transaction is shown in the T accounts.

Because the advertising expense account has a normal debit balance, Advertising Expense is debited for $125.00 to show the increase in this expense account. The cash account also has a normal debit balance. Therefore, Cash is credited for $125.00 to show the decrease in this asset account.

The journal entry to record this cash payment of an expense transaction is shown in Illustration 12-9.

	DATE	ACCOUNT TITLE	DOC. NO.	POST. REF.	GENERAL DEBIT	GENERAL CREDIT	CASH DEBIT	CASH CREDIT	
PAGE *21*		JOURNAL			1	2	PAGE *21* 10	11	
17	*9*	*Advertising Expense*	*C265*		1 2 5 00			1 2 5 00	17
18									18
19									19

The date, *9*, is written in the Date column. No special amount column is provided for Advertising Expense. Therefore, the account title, *Advertising Expense*, is recorded in the Account Title column. The check number, *C265*, is entered in the Doc. No. column. The debit to Advertising Expense, *$125.00*, is written in the General Debit column. The credit to Cash, *$125.00*, is written in the Cash Credit column.

Illustration 12-9
Journal entry to record a cash payment of an expense

Cash payment to replenish petty cash

CarLand deposits all cash in a bank. Some cash, however, is kept in a petty cash fund for making change at the cash register and for making small cash payments. CarLand has a petty cash fund of $500.00, which is replenished whenever the petty cash on hand drops below $200.00.

> November 9, 19--.
> Paid cash to replenish the petty cash fund, $301.00: office supplies, $58.00; store supplies, $65.00; advertising, $92.00; miscellaneous, $86.00. Check No. 266.

The source document for a cash payment to replenish petty cash is the check issued. *(CONCEPT: Objective Evidence)*

This cash payment increases the balances of the supplies accounts and several expense accounts and decreases the cash account balance. The analysis of the cash payment transaction to replenish petty cash is shown in the T accounts.

The supplies accounts have normal debit balances. Therefore, Supplies—Office is debited for $58.00 and Supplies—Store is debited for $65.00 to show the increases in these two asset accounts. The expense accounts also have normal debit balances. Therefore, Advertising Expense is debited for $92.00 and Miscellaneous Expense is debited for $86.00 to show the increases in these expense accounts. The cash account has a normal debit balance. Therefore, Cash is credited for $301.00, the total amount needed to replenish the petty cash fund, to show the decrease in this asset account.

Supplies—Office	
58.00	

Supplies—Store	
65.00	

Advertising Expense	
92.00	

Miscellaneous Expense	
86.00	

Cash	
	301.00

The journal entry to record this cash payment to replenish petty cash transaction is shown in Illustration 12-10, page 262.

	DATE		ACCOUNT TITLE	DOC. NO.	POST. REF.	GENERAL			CASH	
						DEBIT	CREDIT		DEBIT	CREDIT
18		9	*Supplies—Office*	C266		5 8 00		18		3 0 1 00
19			*Supplies—Store*			6 5 00		19		
20			*Advertising Expense*			9 2 00		20		
21			*Miscellaneous Expense*			8 6 00		21		

PAGE *21*   JOURNAL   PAGE *21*

Illustration 12-10
Journal entry to record a cash payment to replenish petty cash

The date, *9*, is written once in the Date column, line 18. No special amount columns are provided for any of the accounts for which the petty cash fund was used. Therefore, the account titles are recorded in the Account Title column. The check number, *C266*, is entered once in the Doc. No. column, line 18. The debit amounts are written in the General Debit column. The credit amount is recorded in the Cash Credit column.

JOURNALIZING OTHER TRANSACTIONS

Most transactions of merchandising businesses are related to purchasing and selling merchandise. A merchandising business, however, has other transactions that must be recorded. CarLand records these other transactions in its journal.

Withdrawals by partners

Amy Kramer, Drawing	
Debit side	Credit side
Normal balance Increase	Decrease

Dario Mesa, Drawing	
Debit side	Credit side
Normal balance Increase	Decrease

Assets taken out of a business for the personal use of an owner are known as withdrawals. The two assets generally taken out of a merchandising business are cash and merchandise. Withdrawals reduce the amount of a business' capital. The account titles of the partners' drawing accounts are Amy Kramer, Drawing and Dario Mesa, Drawing. The drawing accounts are classified as contra capital accounts. Since capital accounts have credit balances, partners' drawing accounts have normal debit balances. Therefore, the drawing accounts are increased by a debit and decreased by a credit, as shown in the T accounts.

Withdrawals could be recorded as debits directly to the partners' capital accounts. However, withdrawals are normally recorded in separate accounts so that the total amounts are easily determined for each accounting period.

Cash withdrawal. When either Amy Kramer or Dario Mesa withdraws cash from CarLand, a check is written for the payment.

November 10, 19--.
Dario Mesa, partner, withdrew cash for personal use, $1,500.00. Check No. 267.

The source document for a cash withdrawal is the check issued. *(CONCEPT: Objective Evidence)*

This cash withdrawal increases Dario Mesa's drawing account balance and decreases the cash account balance. The analysis of the cash withdrawal transaction is shown in the T accounts.

Dario Mesa, Drawing	
1,500.00	

Cash	
	1,500.00

Because the drawing account has a normal debit balance, Dario Mesa, Drawing is debited for $1,500.00 to show the increase in this contra capital account. The cash account also has a normal debit balance. Therefore, Cash is credited for $1,500.00 to show the decrease in this asset account.

The journal entry to record this cash withdrawal is shown in Illustration 12-11.

					1	2		10	11	
PAGE *21*		JOURNAL						PAGE *21*		
	DATE	ACCOUNT TITLE	DOC. NO.	POST. REF.	GENERAL DEBIT	GENERAL CREDIT		CASH DEBIT	CASH CREDIT	
22	10	*Dario Mesa, Drawing*	C267		1 5 0 0 00				1 5 0 0 00	22

Illustration 12-11
Journal entry to record a cash withdrawal by a partner

The date, *10*, is written in the Date column. No special amount column is provided for Dario Mesa, Drawing. Therefore, the contra capital account title, *Dario Mesa, Drawing*, is recorded in the Account Title column. The check number, *C267*, is entered in the Doc. No. column. The debit to Dario Mesa, Drawing, *$1,500.00*, is written in the General Debit column. The credit to Cash, *$1,500.00*, is written in the Cash Credit column.

Merchandise withdrawal. A partner may also withdraw merchandise for personal use.

November 12, 19--.
Dario Mesa, partner, withdrew merchandise for personal use, $200.00. Memorandum No. 44.

The source document for a withdrawal of merchandise is the memorandum prepared by the partner withdrawing the merchandise. *(CONCEPT: Objective Evidence)*

This merchandise withdrawal increases Dario Mesa's drawing account balance and decreases the purchases account balance. The analysis of the merchandise withdrawal transaction is shown in the T accounts.

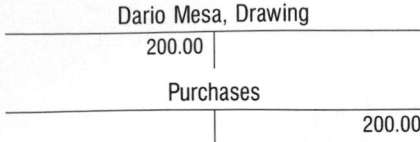

Dario Mesa, Drawing

| 200.00 | |

Purchases

| | 200.00 |

Because the drawing account has a normal debit balance, Dario Mesa, Drawing is debited for $200.00 to show the increase in this contra capital account. The purchases account also has a normal debit balance. Therefore, Purchases is credited for $200.00 to show the decrease in this cost account.

The journal entry to record this merchandise withdrawal is shown in Illustration 12-12.

					1	2
PAGE *21*		JOURNAL				
					GENERAL	
	DATE	ACCOUNT TITLE	DOC. NO.	POST. REF.	DEBIT	CREDIT
26	*12*	*Dario Mesa, Drawing*	*M44*		2 0 0 00	
27		*Purchases*				2 0 0 00

Illustration 12-12
Journal entry to record a merchandise withdrawal by a partner

The date, *12*, is written in the Date column. Neither a Drawing Debit nor a Purchases Credit column is provided in the journal because merchandise withdrawals do not occur frequently. Therefore, the account title, *Dario Mesa, Drawing*, is recorded in the Account Title column. The memorandum number, *M44*, is entered in the Doc. No. column. The debit to Dario Mesa, Drawing, *$200.00*, is written in the General Debit column. The account title, *Purchases*, is recorded in the Account Title column on the next line. The credit to Purchases, *$200.00*, is entered in the General Credit column.

Correcting entry

Errors may be made even though care is taken in recording transactions. Simple errors may be corrected by ruling through the incorrect item, as described in Chapter 4. However, a transaction may have been improperly journalized and posted to the ledger. When an error in a journal entry has already been posted, the incorrect journal entry should be corrected with an additional journal entry. A journal entry made to correct an error in the ledger is called a correcting entry.

November 13, 19--.
Discovered that a payment of cash for advertising in October was journalized and posted in error as a debit to Miscellaneous Expense *instead of* Advertising Expense, *$120.00. Memorandum No. 45.*

If an accounting error is discovered, a memorandum is prepared describing the correction to be made. The source document for a correcting entry is the memorandum prepared. *(CONCEPT: Objective Evidence)* A memorandum for this correcting entry is shown in Illustration 12-13.

To correct the error, an entry is made to add $120.00 to the advertising expense account. The entry must also deduct $120.00 from the miscellaneous expense account. The correcting entry increases the advertising expense account balance and decreases the miscellaneous expense account balance. The analysis of the correcting entry is shown in the T accounts.

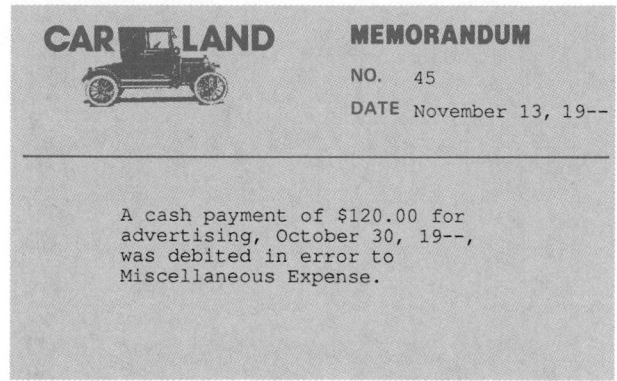

Illustration 12-13
Memorandum for a
correcting entry

Because the advertising expense account has a normal debit balance, Advertising Expense is debited for $120.00 to show the increase in this expense account. The miscellaneous expense account also has a normal debit balance. Therefore, Miscellaneous Expense is credited for $120.00 to show the decrease in this expense account.

Advertising Expense	
120.00	

Miscellaneous Expense	
	120.00

The journal entry to record this correcting entry is shown in Illustration 12-14.

			JOURNAL				
PAGE 21							
						1	2
	DATE	ACCOUNT TITLE	DOC. NO.	POST. REF.		GENERAL	
						DEBIT	CREDIT
28	13	*Advertising Expense*	M45			1 2 0 00	
29		*Miscellaneous Expense*					1 2 0 00

Illustration 12-14
Journal entry to record a
correcting entry

The date, *13,* is written in the Date column. The account title, *Advertising Expense,* is recorded in the Account Title column. The memorandum number, *M45,* is entered in the Doc. No. column. The debit to Advertising Expense, *$120.00,* is entered in the General Debit column. The account title, *Miscellaneous Expense,* is written in the Account Title column on the next line. The credit to Miscellaneous Expense, *$120.00,* is recorded in the General Credit column.

SUMMARY OF JOURNALIZING PURCHASES, CASH PAYMENTS, AND OTHER TRANSACTIONS

The chart shown in Illustration 12-15 summarizes the entries for purchases, cash payments, and other transactions in an expanded journal.

TRANSACTION	JOURNAL										
	1	2	3	4	5	6	7	8	9	10	11
	GENERAL		ACCOUNTS RECEIVABLE		SALES CREDIT	SALES TAX PAYABLE CREDIT	ACCOUNTS PAYABLE		PURCHASES DEBIT	CASH	
	DEBIT	CREDIT	DEBIT	CREDIT			DEBIT	CREDIT		DEBIT	CREDIT
Purchase merchandise for cash									X		X
Purchase merchandise on account								X	X		
Buying supplies for cash	X										X
Buying supplies on account	X							X			
Cash payment on account							X				X
Cash payment of an expense	X										X
Cash payment to replenish petty cash	X										X
Cash withdrawal	X										X
Merchandise withdrawal	X	X									

Illustration 12-15   Summary of entries for purchases, cash payments, and other transactions in an expanded journal

◼ ACCOUNTING TERMS

What is the meaning of each of the following?

1. partnership
2. partner
3. merchandising business
4. merchandise
5. cost of merchandise
6. markup
7. vendor
8. purchase on account
9. invoice
10. purchase invoice
11. terms of sale
12. correcting entry

◼ QUESTIONS FOR INDIVIDUAL STUDY

1. Why would two or more persons want to own a single business?
2. What makes the activities of a merchandising business different from those of a service business?
3. What are noncash transactions?
4. Why does CarLand use an 11-column journal rather than a 5-column journal like the one used by Rugcare?
5. What is the title of the account that shows the cost of merchandise purchased for sale?
6. What is the account classification of Purchases?
7. Which accounting concept is being applied when merchandise and other items bought are recorded and reported at the price agreed upon at the time the transactions occur?
8. What accounts are affected, and how, when merchandise is purchased for cash?
9. Why is a check mark placed in the Account Title column of an expanded journal for a cash purchase transaction?
10. Why would a business use a single general ledger account to summarize the amount owed to all vendors?
11. What is the name of the liability account that summarizes the amounts owed to all vendors?
12. Why does CarLand use its own set of sequential purchase invoice numbers rather than using the numbers assigned by vendors?

13. What accounts are affected, and how, when merchandise is purchased on account?

14. Why are the account titles (Purchases and Accounts Payable) for a purchase on account entry not written in the Account Title column?

15. Why are supplies bought recorded in a separate supplies account rather than in the purchases account?

16. What accounts are affected, and how, when store supplies are bought on account?

17. What accounts are affected, and how, when a cash payment on account is made?

18. How does CarLand use a petty cash fund?

19. What accounts are affected, and how, when a withdrawal of merchandise is made?

20. When should a journal entry be made to correct errors in recording transactions?

◼ CASES FOR MANAGEMENT DECISION

CASE 1 Deborah Butler owns and operates a gift shop in a downtown shopping area. Because of a shopping mall that has opened in one of the suburbs, the gift shop's business has been declining. Ms. Butler has an opportunity to move the business to the shopping mall. Additional capital, however, is required to move and operate the business in a new location. The local bank has agreed to lend the money needed. The business hours would be extended at the new location. The business would also be open seven days a week. The extended hours plus the expected increase in business would require the hiring of one additional employee. Ms. Butler has been contacted by Fred Chaney, a person with similar merchandising experience, who would like to become a partner. As an alternative to borrowing cash, Mr. Chaney would provide the capital necessary to move the business to the new location. For the capital provided, Mr. Chaney would share equally in the net income or loss of the business. Mr. Chaney would also share equally in the operation of the business. Should Ms. Butler (1) borrow the money from the bank, or (2) bring in a partner? Explain your answer.

CASE 2 Daryl Hodges is a high school student who works part-time in a local clothing store. As part of his duties, he records daily transactions in a journal. One day he asks the owner: "You use the purchase invoice as your source document for recording purchases of merchandise on account. You use a memorandum as your source document for recording the entry when supplies are bought on account. Why don't you use the invoice for both entries?" How would you respond to this question?

◼ DRILLS FOR UNDERSTANDING

DRILL 12-D1   **Analyzing transactions into debit and credit parts**

Instructions: Prepare two T accounts for each of the following transactions. Use the T accounts to analyze each transaction. Use account titles similar to CarLand's, as shown in the chart of accounts, page 250. The partners' names are Irma Gilbert and Alex Jensen. The first transaction is given as an example.

Purchases		Cash	
200.00			200.00

Transactions

1. Purchased merchandise for cash, $200.00.
2. Purchased merchandise on account from Klein Co., $900.00.
3. Paid cash for office supplies, $75.00.
4. Bought store supplies on account from Central Supply, $240.00.
5. Bought office supplies on account from Cratin Supply, $125.00.
6. Purchased merchandise for cash, $175.00.
7. Paid cash for office supplies, $70.00.
8. Paid cash on account to Matson Company, $750.00.
9. Purchased merchandise on account from Garber Company, $1,200.00.
10. Paid cash for advertising, $85.00.
11. Irma Gilbert, partner, withdrew cash for personal use, $1,000.00.
12. Alex Jensen, partner, withdrew cash for personal use, $1,000.00.
13. Irma Gilbert, partner, withdrew merchandise for personal use, $130.00.
14. Paid cash on account to Butler Enterprises, $360.00.
15. Discovered that a transaction for office supplies bought last month was journalized and posted in error as a debit to Prepaid Insurance instead of Supplies—Office, $60.00.
16. Alex Jensen, partner, withdrew merchandise for personal use, $95.00.

The solution to Drill 12-D1 is needed to complete Drill 12-D2.

DRILL 12-D2   Analyzing journal entries

The solution to Drill 12-D1 is needed to complete Drill 12-D2.

Instructions: Use a form similar to the following. Based on the answers in Drill 12-D1, write the amounts in the amount columns to be used to journalize each transaction. Transaction 1 is given as an example.

Transaction	General		Accounts Payable		Purchases Debit	Cash	
	Debit	Credit	Debit	Credit		Debit	Credit
1. Debit amount					$200.00		
Credit amount							$200.00

▮ APPLICATION PROBLEM

PROBLEM 12-1   Journalizing purchases, cash payments, and other transactions

Mary Demski and Eileen Ivan, partners, own a gift shop.

Instructions: Journalize the following transactions completed during September of the current year. Use page 21 of a journal similar to the one described in this chapter for CarLand. Source documents are abbreviated as follows: check, C; memorandum, M; purchase invoice, P.

Sept. 1. Purchased merchandise for cash, $150.00. C220.
       1. Purchased merchandise on account from Kemp Fashions, $1,350.00. P60.
       2. Paid cash for office supplies, $75.00. C221.
       2. Purchased merchandise on account from Bonner & Co., $740.00. P61.
       3. Purchased merchandise on account from Burton Fabrics, $585.00. P62.

Sept. 4. Paid cash for office supplies, $55.00. C222.
7. Bought store supplies on account from Pulver Supply, $135.00. M42.
7. Purchased merchandise for cash, $120.00. C223.
8. Paid cash for telephone bill, $120.00. C224.
9. Bought office supplies on account from Lorand Supply, $85.00. M43.
11. Purchased merchandise for cash, $110.00. C225.
12. Paid cash for store supplies, $60.00. C226.
14. Mary Demski, partner, withdrew cash for personal use, $1,200.00. C227.
14. Eileen Ivan, partner, withdrew cash for personal use, $1,200.00. C228.
18. Paid cash on account to Kemp Fashions, $1,350.00, covering P60. C229.
21. Paid cash for advertising, $87.00. C230.
22. Paid cash on account to Bonner & Co., $740.00, covering P61. C231.
24. Mary Demski, partner, withdrew merchandise for personal use, $160.00. M44.
25. Discovered that a transaction for office supplies bought in August was journalized and posted in error as a debit to Purchases instead of Supplies—Office, $88.00. M45.
26. Paid cash on account to Burton Fabrics, $585.00, covering P62. C232.
29. Eileen Ivan, partner, withdrew merchandise for personal use, $120.00. M46.
30. Paid cash to replenish the petty cash fund, $305.00: office supplies, $63.00; store supplies, $51.00; advertising, $88.00; miscellaneous, $103.00. C233.
30. Paid cash on account to Pulver Supply, $135.00, covering M42. C234.

ENRICHMENT PROBLEMS

MASTERY PROBLEM 12-M   **Journalizing purchases, cash payments, and other transactions**

Sylvia Prior and Julia Steger, partners, own a bookstore.

Instructions: Journalize the following transactions completed during November of the current year. Use page 23 of a journal similar to the one described in this chapter for CarLand. Source documents are abbreviated as follows: check, C; memorandum, M; purchase invoice, P.

Nov. 2. Paid cash for rent, $1,250.00. C261.
2. Sylvia Prior, partner, withdrew cash for personal use, $1,500.00. C262.
2. Julia Steger, partner, withdrew cash for personal use, $1,500.00. C263.
3. Purchased merchandise for cash, $130.00. C264.
4. Paid cash on account to BFL Publishing, $920.00, covering P71. C265.
4. Purchased merchandise on account from Quality Books, $1,450.00. P74.
5. Paid cash for office supplies, $48.00. C266.
7. Julia Steger, partner, withdrew merchandise for personal use, $42.00. M32.
9. Paid cash for electric bill, $154.00. C267.
9. Paid cash on account to Quality Books, $1,235.00, covering P72. C268.
10. Bought store supplies on account from Carson Supply Co., $106.00. M33.
11. Paid cash on account to Matson Book Service, $975.00, covering P73. C269.
14. Purchased merchandise on account from Falk Book Co., $1,525.00. P75.
16. Paid cash for store supplies, $62.00. C270.
16. Sylvia Prior, partner, withdrew merchandise for personal use, $64.00. M34.
17. Bought store supplies on account from Gray Supplies, $214.00. M35.
18. Purchased merchandise for cash, $145.00. C271.
18. Paid cash to replenish the petty cash fund, $302.00: office supplies, $73.00; store supplies, $47.00; advertising, $92.00; miscellaneous, $90.00. C272.
19. Paid cash on account to Quality Books, $1,450.00, covering P74. C273.

Nov. 21. Purchased merchandise on account from Voss Publishing, $925.00. P76.

    24. Paid cash on account to Falk Book Co., $1,525.00, covering P75. C274.

    26. Discovered that a transaction for office supplies bought in October was journalized and posted in error as a debit to Purchases instead of Supplies—Office, $94.00. M36.

    28. Bought store supplies on account from Carson Supply, $118.00. M37.

    30. Purchased merchandise for cash, $68.00. C275.

CHALLENGE PROBLEM 12-C   Journalizing correcting entries

A review of Meir Decorating's accounting records for last month revealed the following errors.

Instructions: Journalize the needed correcting entries on page 8 of a journal similar to the one described in this chapter for CarLand. Use December 2 of the current year.

Dec. 2. Discovered that a withdrawal of merchandise by Alice Reyes, partner, was journalized and posted in error as a credit to Cash instead of Purchases, $116.00. M35.

    2. Discovered that a transaction for office supplies bought for cash was journalized and posted in error as a debit to Purchases instead of Supplies—Office, $95.00. M36.

    2. Discovered that a payment for advertising was journalized and posted in error as a debit to Miscellaneous Expense instead of Advertising Expense, $125.00. M37.

    2. Discovered that a transaction for store supplies bought on account was journalized and posted in error as a debit to Utilities Expense instead of Supplies—Store, $52.00. M38.

    2. Discovered that a purchase of merchandise on account was journalized and posted in error as a debit to Supplies—Office instead of Purchases, $850.00. M39.

    2. Discovered that a payment for rent was journalized and posted in error as a debit to Salary Expense instead of Rent Expense, $1,200.00. M40.

    2. Discovered that a withdrawal of cash by Harold Atkins, partner, was journalized and posted in error as a credit to Purchases instead of Cash, $200.00. M41.

    2. Discovered that a payment for a miscellaneous expense was journalized and posted in error as a debit to Supplies Expense—Store instead of Miscellaneous Expense, $89.00. M42.

    2. Discovered that a transaction for office supplies bought for cash was journalized and posted in error as a debit to Prepaid Insurance instead of Supplies—Office, $160.00. M43.

    2. Discovered that a payment for store supplies was journalized and posted in error as a debit to Supplies—Office instead of Supplies—Store, $151.00. M44.

Journalizing Sales and Cash Receipts

ENABLING PERFORMANCE TASKS

After studying Chapter 13, you will be able to:
a. Define accounting terms related to sales and cash receipts for a merchandising business.
b. Identify accounting concepts and practices related to sales and cash receipts for a merchandising business.
c. Analyze sales and cash receipts transactions for a merchandising business.
d. Journalize sales and cash receipts transactions for a merchandising business.
e. Prove and rule a journal.

Purchases and sales of merchandise are the two major activities of a merchandising business. A person or business to whom merchandise or services are sold is called a customer. Rugcare, described in Part 1, sells services. CarLand, described in this part, sells merchandise. Other businesses may sell both services and merchandise.

SALES TAX

Laws of most states and some cities require that a tax be collected from customers for each sale made. A tax on a sale of merchandise or services is called a sales tax. Sales tax rates are usually stated as a percentage of sales. Regardless of the tax rates used, accounting procedures are the same.

Every business collecting a sales tax needs accurate records of the amount of tax collected. Businesses must file reports with the proper government unit and pay the amount of sales tax collected. Records need to show (1) total sales and (2) total sales tax. The amount of sales tax collected by CarLand is a business liability until paid to the state government. Therefore, the sales tax amount is recorded in a separate liability account titled *Sales Tax Payable*. The liability account, Sales Tax Payable, has a normal

Sales Tax Payable	
Debit side	Credit side
	Normal balance
Decrease	Increase

credit balance. This account is increased by a credit and decreased by a debit, as shown in the T account.

CarLand operates in a state with a 6% sales tax rate. A customer must pay for the price of the goods plus the sales tax. The total amount of a sale of merchandise priced at $200.00 is calculated as shown below.

Price of Goods	×	Sales Tax Rate	=	Sales Tax
$200.00	×	6%	=	$12.00
Price of Goods	+	Sales Tax	=	Total Amount Received
$200.00	+	$12.00	=	$212.00

A customer must pay $212.00 for the merchandise ($200.00 for the goods plus $12.00 for the sales tax). CarLand records the price of goods sold, the sales tax, and the total amount received.

JOURNALIZING SALES AND CASH RECEIPTS FOR SALES

A sale of merchandise may be (1) for cash or (2) on account. A sale of merchandise increases the revenue of a business. Regardless of when payment is made, the revenue should be recorded at the time of a sale, not on the date cash is received. For example, on June 15 CarLand sells merchandise on account to a customer. The customer pays CarLand for the merchandise on July 12. CarLand records the revenue on June 15, the date of the sale. The accounting concept, *Realization of Revenue*, is applied when revenue is recorded at the time goods or services are sold. *(CONCEPT: Realization of Revenue)*

Cash and credit card sales

CarLand sells most of its merchandise for cash. A sale in which cash is received for the total amount of the sale at the time of the transaction is called a cash sale. CarLand also sells merchandise to customers who have a bank approved credit card. A sale in which a credit card is used for the total amount of the sale at the time of the transaction is called a credit card sale. Major bank approved credit cards include VISA, MasterCard, Discover Card, and Carte Blanche. CarLand accepts all major bank approved credit cards from customers. A customer who uses a credit card promises to pay the amount due on the credit card transaction to the bank issuing the credit card.

CarLand prepares a credit card slip for each credit card sale. At the end of each week, these credit card slips are included with CarLand's bank deposit. CarLand's bank accepts the credit card slips the same way it accepts checks and cash for deposit. The bank increases CarLand's bank account by the total amount of the credit card sales deposited. If a credit card was issued by another bank, CarLand's bank sends the credit card slips to the issuing bank. The bank that issues the credit card then bills the customer and collects the amount owed. The bank that accepts and processes the credit card slips for a business charges a fee for this service. This fee is included on CarLand's monthly bank statement.

Cash and credit card sales are both revenue items that increase the revenue account, Sales. Because the bank accepts credit card slips the same way it accepts cash, CarLand's bank account increases after each deposit as though cash had been deposited. Therefore, CarLand combines all sales for cash and credit cards and records the two revenue items as a single cash sales transaction.

November 7, 19--.
Recorded cash and credit card sales, $6,450.00, plus sales tax, $387.00; total, $6,837.00. Cash Register Tape No. 7.

CarLand uses a cash register to list all cash and credit card sales. When a transaction is entered on the cash register, a paper tape is printed as a receipt for the customer. The cash register also internally accumulates data about total cash and credit card sales.

At the end of each week, a cash register tape is printed showing total cash and credit card sales. The tape is removed from the cash register and marked with a *T* and the date (T7). The cash register tape is used by CarLand as the source document for weekly cash and credit card sales transactions. *(CONCEPT: Objective Evidence)*

A cash and credit card sales transaction increases the balances of the cash account, the sales account, and the sales tax payable account. The analysis of this transaction is shown in the T accounts.

Because the asset account, Cash, has a normal debit balance, Cash is debited for the total sales and sales tax, $6,837.00, to show the increase in this asset account. The sales account has a normal credit balance. Therefore, Sales is credited for the total price of all goods sold, $6,450.00, to show the increase in this revenue account. The sales tax payable account also has a normal credit balance. Therefore, Sales Tax Payable is credited for the total sales tax, $387.00, to show the increase in this liability account.

The journal entry to record this cash and credit card sales transaction is shown in Illustration 13-1.

Cash	
6,837.00	

Sales	
	6,450.00

Sales Tax Payable	
	387.00

Illustration 13-1
Journal entry to record
cash and credit card sales

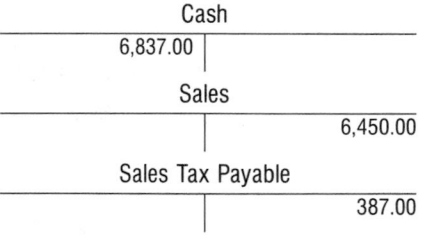

PAGE *21*		JOURNAL			5 SALES CREDIT	6 SALES TAX PAYABLE CREDIT	PAGE *21*	
DATE	ACCOUNT TITLE		DOC. NO.	POST. REF.			10 CASH DEBIT	11 CASH CREDIT
14 7	√		T7	√	6 4 5 0 00	3 8 7 00	6 8 3 7 00	14

The date, 7, is written in the Date column. Special amount columns are provided for all accounts in this transaction. Therefore, a check mark is placed in the Account Title column to show that no account title needs to be written. The cash register tape number, *T7*, is recorded in the Doc. No. column. A check mark is also placed in the Post. Ref. column to show that amounts on this line do not need to be posted individually. The credit to Sales, *$6,450.00*, is written in the Sales Credit column. The credit to Sales Tax Payable, *$387.00*, is recorded in the Sales Tax Payable Credit column. The debit to Cash, *$6,837.00*, is entered in the Cash Debit column.

Sales on account

A sale for which cash will be received at a later date is called a sale on account. A sale on account is also known as a charge sale. CarLand sells on account only to businesses. Other customers must either pay cash or use a credit card.

Accounts Receivable	
Debit side	Credit side
Normal balance	
Increase	Decrease

CarLand summarizes the total due from all charge customers in a general ledger account titled *Accounts Receivable*. Accounts Receivable is an asset account with a normal debit balance. Therefore, the accounts receivable account is increased by a debit and decreased by a credit, as shown in the T account.

When merchandise is sold on account, the seller prepares a form showing what has been sold. A form describing the goods sold, the quantity, and the price is known as an invoice. An invoice used as a source document for recording a sale on account is called a sales invoice. *(CONCEPT: Objective Evidence)* A sales invoice is also known as a sales ticket or a sales slip. The sales invoice used by CarLand is shown in Illustration 13-2.

CAR LAND

1374 Parklane
Rockville, RI 02873-4121

Sold to: Friendly Auto Service
430 Main Street
Alton, RI 02803-1163

Cust. No. 130

No. 72
Date 11/3/--
Terms 30 days

Stock No.	Description	Quantity	Unit Price	Amount
4422	All-season tires	2	110.00	220.00
7710	Seat covers	8	57.50	460.00
			Subtotal	680.00
Customer's Signature		Salesclerk	Sales Tax	40.80
Jean Friendly		*a. j.*	Total	720.80

Illustration 13-2
Sales invoice

The seller considers an invoice for a sale on account to be a sales invoice. The same invoice is considered by the customer to be a purchase invoice.

A sales invoice is prepared in duplicate. The original copy is given to the customer. The carbon copy is used as the source document for the sale on account transaction. *(CONCEPT: Objective Evidence)* Sales invoices are numbered in sequence. The number *72* is the number of the sales invoice issued to Friendly Auto Service.

November 3, 19--.
Sold merchandise on account to Friendly Auto Service, $680.00, plus sales tax, $40.80; total, $720.80. Sales Invoice No. 72.

A sale on account transaction increases the amount to be collected later from a customer. Payment for this sale will be received at a later date. However, the sale is recorded at the time the sale is made because the sale has taken place and payment is due to CarLand. *(CONCEPT: Realization of Revenue)* The analysis of the sale on account transaction is shown in the T accounts.

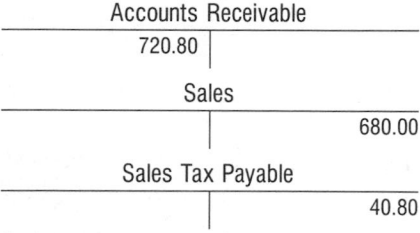

Because the accounts receivable account has a normal debit balance, Accounts Receivable is debited for the total sales and sales tax, $720.80, to show the increase in this asset account. The sales account has a normal credit balance. Therefore, Sales is credited for the price of the goods, $680.00, to show the increase in this revenue account. The sales tax payable account also has a normal credit balance. Therefore, Sales Tax Payable is credited for the total sales tax, $40.80, to show the increase in this liability account.

The journal entry to record this sale on account transaction is shown in Illustration 13-3.

PAGE *21*			JOURNAL			**3**		**4**			**5**	**6**
	DATE	ACCOUNT TITLE	DOC. NO.	POST. REF.		ACCOUNTS RECEIVABLE					SALES CREDIT	SALES TAX PAYABLE CREDIT
						DEBIT		CREDIT				
4	*3*	*Friendly Auto Service*	*S72*			7 2 0 80					6 8 0 00	4 0 80
5												

Illustration 13-3
Journal entry to record a sale on account

The date, *3*, is written in the Date column. The customer name, *Friendly Auto Service*, is recorded in the Account Title column. The sales invoice number, *S72*, is entered in the Doc. No. column. The debit to Accounts Receivable, *$720.80*, is written in the Accounts Receivable Debit column. The credit to Sales, *$680.00*, is recorded in the Sales Credit column. The credit to Sales Tax Payable, *$40.80*, is entered in the Sales Tax Payable Credit column.

The debit and credit amounts are recorded in special amount columns. Therefore, writing the titles of the ledger accounts in the Account Title column is not necessary. However, the name of the customer is written in the Account Title column to show from whom the amount is due. Car-Land's procedures for keeping records of the amounts to be collected from each customer are described in Chapter 14.

Cash receipts on account

When cash is received on account from a customer, CarLand prepares a receipt. The receipts are prenumbered so that all receipts can be accounted for. Receipts are prepared in duplicate. The original copy of the receipt is given to the customer. The carbon copy of the receipt is used as the source document for the cash receipt on account transaction. (CONCEPT: *Objective Evidence*)

November 6, 19--.
Received cash on account from Autohaus Service, $1,802.00, covering S65.
Receipt No. 86.

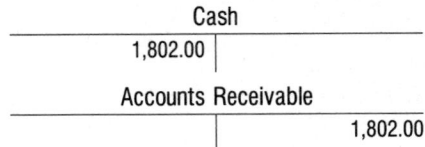

A cash receipt on account transaction decreases the amount to be collected from a customer. This transaction increases the cash account balance and decreases the accounts receivable account balance. The analysis of the cash receipt on account transaction is shown in the T accounts.

Because the cash account has a normal debit balance, Cash is debited for the amount of cash received, $1,802.00, to show the increase in this asset account. The accounts receivable account also has a normal debit balance. Therefore, Accounts Receivable is credited for $1,802.00 to show the decrease in this asset account.

Illustration 13-4
Journal entry to record a cash receipt on account

The journal entry to record this cash receipt on account transaction is shown in Illustration 13-4.

					ACCOUNTS RECEIVABLE		CASH		
PAGE *21*		JOURNAL			3	4	10	11	PAGE *21*
	DATE	ACCOUNT TITLE	DOC. NO.	POST. REF.	DEBIT	CREDIT	DEBIT	CREDIT	
11	6	*Autohans Service*	R86			1 8 0 2 00	1 8 0 2 00		11
12									12

The date, 6, is written in the Date column. The customer name, *Autohaus Service*, is recorded in the Account Title column. The receipt number, *R86*, is entered in the Doc. No. column. The credit to Accounts Receivable, *$1,802.00*, is written in the Accounts Receivable Credit column. The debit to Cash, *$1,802.00*, is recorded in the Cash Debit column.

PROVING AND RULING AN EXPANDED JOURNAL

A journal is proved and ruled whenever a journal page is filled and always at the end of a month.

Totaling and proving an expanded journal page

After all November 14 entries are recorded, page 21 of CarLand's journal is filled. Page 21 is totaled and proved before column totals are forwarded to page 22. To prove a journal page, CarLand uses a calculator to verify that the total debit amounts equal the total credit amounts. CarLand's debit totals equal the credit totals on page 21 of the journal. Therefore, the equality of debits and credits has been proved.

Ruling an expanded journal page to carry totals forward

After a journal page has been proved, the journal must be prepared for forwarding. CarLand's journal column totals prepared for forwarding are shown on line 34, Illustration 13-5 on pages 278 and 279.

Five steps are followed to rule CarLand's journal.

1 Rule a single line across all amount columns directly below the last entry to indicate that the columns are to be added.

2 On the next line write the date, *14*, in the Date column.

3 Write the words, *Carried Forward*, in the Account Title column. A check mark is also placed in the Post. Ref. column to show that nothing on this line needs to be posted.

4 Write each column total below the single line.

5 Rule double lines below the column totals across all amount columns to show that the totals have been verified as correct.

Starting a new expanded journal page

The totals from the previous journal page are carried forward to the next journal page. The totals are recorded on the first line of the new page. Column totals brought forward to a new page are shown on line 1, Illustration 13-6 on pages 278 and 279.

Four steps are followed for forwarding totals.

1 Write the page number, *22*, at the top of the journal.

2 Write the date, *19--, Nov. 14*, in the Date column.

3 Write the words, *Brought Forward*, in the Account Title column. A check mark is also placed in the Post. Ref. column to show that nothing on this line needs to be posted.

4 Record the column totals brought forward from page 21 of the journal.

PAGE 21	JOURNAL								
					1	2	3	4	
DATE	ACCOUNT TITLE	DOC. NO.	POST. REF.		GENERAL		ACCOUNTS RECEIVABLE		
					DEBIT	CREDIT	DEBIT	CREDIT	
1	Nov. 2	√	C259	√					1
2	2	Veloz Automotive	P74						2
32	14	Powell Rent-A-Car	R89					3 1 8 00	32
33	14	√	T14	√					33
34	14	Carried Forward		√	4 2 9 3 00	3 2 0 00	3 3 9 2 00	3 9 7 5 00	34

Illustration 13-5   Journal prepared for forwarding (left page)

PAGE 22	JOURNAL								
					1	2	3	4	
DATE	ACCOUNT TITLE	DOC. NO.	POST. REF.		GENERAL		ACCOUNTS RECEIVABLE		
					DEBIT	CREDIT	DEBIT	CREDIT	
1	Nov. 14	Brought Forward		√	4 2 9 3 00	3 2 0 00	3 3 9 2 00	3 9 7 5 00	1

Illustration 13-6   Journal totals brought forward to a new page (left page)

Proving an expanded journal at the end of a month

Equality of debits and credits in a journal is proved at the end of each month. All columns are totaled using a calculator. A journal is proved when the debit totals equal the credit totals. The proof for CarLand's journal, Illustration 13-7, pages 280 and 281, is calculated as shown below.

Col. No.	Column Title	Debit Totals	Credit Totals
1	General Debit	$15,686.22	
2	General Credit		$ 2,029.02
3	Accounts Receivable Debit..............	9,222.00	
4	Accounts Receivable Credit.............		7,950.00
5	Sales Credit		31,600.00
6	Sales Tax Payable Credit...............		1,896.00
7	Accounts Payable Debit.................	10,820.00	
8	Accounts Payable Credit................		15,870.00
9	Purchases Debit	14,773.00	
10	Cash Debit	32,224.00	
11	Cash Credit		23,380.20
	Totals...............................	$82,725.22	$82,725.22

The two totals, *$82,725.22*, are equal. Equality of debits and credits in CarLand's journal for November is proved.

PAGE 21

	5 SALES CREDIT	6 SALES TAX PAYABLE CREDIT	7 ACCOUNTS PAYABLE DEBIT	8 ACCOUNTS PAYABLE CREDIT	9 PURCHASES DEBIT	10 CASH DEBIT	11 CASH CREDIT	
1					483 00		483 00	1
2				1754 00	1754 00			2
32						318 00		32
33	5100 00	306 00				5406 00		33
34	14750 00	885 00	5360 00	11690 00	12013 00	16218 00	9656 00	34

Illustration 13-5   Journal prepared for forwarding (right page)

PAGE 22

	5 SALES CREDIT	6 SALES TAX PAYABLE CREDIT	7 ACCOUNTS PAYABLE DEBIT	8 ACCOUNTS PAYABLE CREDIT	9 PURCHASES DEBIT	10 CASH DEBIT	11 CASH CREDIT	
1	14750 00	885 00	5360 00	11690 00	12013 00	16218 00	9656 00	1

Illustration 13-6   Journal totals brought forward to a new page (right page)

Proving cash at the end of a month

CarLand's cash proof at the end of November is calculated as shown below.

Cash on hand at the beginning of the month $14,706.20
   (November 1 balance of cash account in general ledger)
Plus total cash received during the month 32,224.00
   (Cash Debit column total, line 16, Illustration 13-7)
Equals total. $46,930.20
Less total cash paid during the month. 23,380.20
   (Cash Credit column total, line 16, Illustration 13-7)
Equals cash balance on hand at end of the month. $23,550.00

The last check written in November is Check No. 276. The balance on the next unused check stub is $23,550.00. Since the balance on the next unused check stub is the same as the cash proof, cash is proved.

Ruling an expanded journal at the end of a month

CarLand's journal is ruled at the end of each month. CarLand's expanded journal totaled and ruled at the end of November is shown on line 16, Illustration 13-7. Five steps are followed to rule a journal.

					GENERAL		ACCOUNTS RECEIVABLE	
					1	2	3	4
	DATE	ACCOUNT TITLE	DOC. NO.	POST. REF.	DEBIT	CREDIT	DEBIT	CREDIT
15	30 √		T30	√					15
16	30	Totals			15 686 22	2 029 02	9 222 00	7 950 00	16

PAGE 23 — JOURNAL

Illustration 13-7   Journal page totaled and ruled at the end of a month (left page)

1 Rule a single line across all amount columns directly below the last entry to indicate that the columns are to be added.

2 On the next line write the date, *30*, in the Date column.

3 Write the word, *Totals*, in the Account Title column.

4 Write each column total below the single line.

5 Rule double lines across all amount columns to show that the totals have been verified as correct.

Some of the column totals will be posted as described in Chapter 14. Therefore, a check mark is not placed in the Post. Ref. column for this line.

Illustration 13-8
Summary of entries for
sales and cash receipts
transactions in an
expanded journal

SUMMARY OF JOURNALIZING SALES AND CASH RECEIPTS

The chart shown in Illustration 13-8 summarizes the entries for sales and cash receipts transactions in an expanded journal.

	JOURNAL										
	1	2	3	4	5	6	7	8	9	10	11
TRANSACTION	GENERAL		ACCOUNTS RECEIVABLE		SALES CREDIT	SALES TAX PAYABLE CREDIT	ACCOUNTS PAYABLE		PURCHASES DEBIT	CASH	
	DEBIT	CREDIT	DEBIT	CREDIT			DEBIT	CREDIT		DEBIT	CREDIT
Cash and credit card sale					X	X				X	
Sale on account			X		X	X					
Cash receipt on account				X						X	

▮ ACCOUNTING TERMS

What is the meaning of each of the following?

1. customer
2. sales tax
3. cash sale
4. credit card sale
5. sale on account
6. sales invoice

PAGE *23*

	5		6		7		8		9		10		11	
	SALES CREDIT		SALES TAX PAYABLE CREDIT		ACCOUNTS PAYABLE				PURCHASES DEBIT		CASH			
					DEBIT		CREDIT				DEBIT		CREDIT	
15	1 1 5 0 00		6 9 00								1 2 1 9 00				15
16	31 6 0 0 00		1 8 9 6 00		10 8 2 0 00		15 8 7 0 00		14 7 7 3 00		32 2 2 4 00		23 3 8 0 20		16

Illustration 13-7   Journal page totaled and ruled at the end of a month (right page)

■ QUESTIONS FOR INDIVIDUAL STUDY

1. What are the two major activities of a merchandising business?
2. How are sales tax rates usually stated?
3. Why must every business that collects a sales tax keep accurate records of the amount of tax collected?
4. What two amounts must sales tax records show?
5. Why is sales tax collected considered a liability?
6. What is the normal balance of the sales tax payable account, and how is the account increased and decreased?
7. Which accounting concept is being applied when revenue is recorded at the time a sale is made, regardless of when payment is made?
8. Which accounting concept is being applied when a cash register tape is used as the source document for cash and credit card sales?
9. How often does CarLand journalize cash sales?
10. What accounts are affected, and how, for a cash and credit card sales transaction?
11. Why is a check mark placed in the Account Title column of an expanded journal when journalizing cash and credit card sales?
12. What is another name used for a sale on account?
13. What is the title of the general ledger account used to summarize the total amount due from all charge customers?
14. What is the source document for a sale on account transaction?
15. What are other names used for a sales invoice?
16. What accounts are affected, and how, for a sale on account transaction?
17. Which amount columns in a journal are used to record a sale on account transaction?
18. What accounts are affected, and how, for a cash receipt on account transaction?
19. How often is the equality of debits and credits in a journal proved?
20. How often is a journal page ruled?

■ CASES FOR MANAGEMENT DECISION

CASE 1 Carrie and Karl Lott, partners, operate a shoe store. A 5-column journal similar to the one described in Chapter 4 is used to record all transactions. The business sells merchandise for cash and on account. The business also purchases most of its merchandise on account. Mrs. Lott asked an accountant to check the accounting system and recommend changes. The accountant suggests that an expanded journal similar to the one described in Chapters 12 and 13 be used. Which journal would be better? Why?

CASE 2 Amy Pryor, an accountant for a sporting goods store, has noted a major increase in overdue amounts from charge customers. All invoice amounts from sales on account are due within 30 days. The amounts due have reduced the amount of cash available for the day-to-day operation of the business. Miss Pryor recommends that the business (1) stop all sales on account and (2) begin accepting bank credit cards. The owner is reluctant to accept the recom- mendations because the business might lose some reliable customers who do not have credit cards. Also, the business will have increased expenses because of the credit card fee. How would you respond to Miss Pryor's recommendations? What alter- natives might the owner consider?

■ DRILLS FOR UNDERSTANDING

DRILL 13-D1   Analyzing transactions into debit and credit parts

Instructions: Prepare T accounts for each of the following transactions. Use the T accounts to analyze each transaction. A 5% sales tax has been added to each sale. The first transaction is given as an example.

Cash	Sales	Sales Tax Payable
1,575.00	1,500.00	75.00

Transactions

1. Recorded cash and credit card sales, $1,500.00, plus sales tax, $75.00; total, $1,575.00.
2. Sold merchandise on account to Steven Kramer, $300.00, plus sales tax, $15.00; total, $315.00.
3. Sold merchandise on account to Mark Fields, $360.00, plus sales tax, $18.00; total, $378.00.
4. Received cash on account from Jackson White, $157.50.
5. Received cash on account from Gloria Burton, $68.25.
6. Recorded cash and credit card sales, $1,750.00, plus sales tax, $87.50; total, $1,837.50.

The solution to Drill 13-D1 is needed to complete Drill 13-D3.

DRILL 13-D2   Analyzing the effect of sales transactions on accounts

Instructions: 1. Prepare a T account for each of the following accounts: Cash, Accounts Re- ceivable, Sales, and Sales Tax Payable.

2. Using the T accounts, show which accounts are debited and credited for the following transactions. Add a 6% sales tax to each sale. Write the transaction number in parentheses to the left of each amount. The first transaction is given as an example.

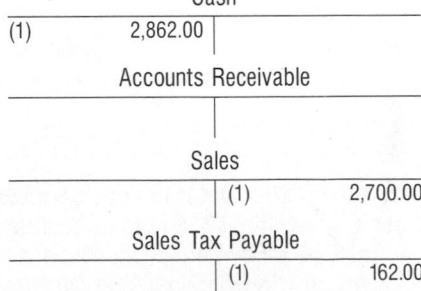

Transactions

1. Recorded cash and credit card sales, $2,700.00.
2. Sold merchandise on account to Melissa Bedo, $180.00.
3. Sold merchandise on account to Kim Lea, $170.00.
4. Received cash on account from Maria Jones, $148.40.
5. Received cash on account from Jack Mumford, $79.50.
6. Recorded cash and credit card sales, $2,375.00.

DRILL 13-D3 Analyzing journal entries

The solution to Drill 13-D1 is needed to complete Drill 13-D3.

Instructions: Use a form similar to the following. Based on the answers in Drill 13-D1, write the amounts in the amount columns to be used to journalize each transaction. Transaction 1 is given as an example.

Transaction	Accounts Rec.		Sales Credit	Sales Tax Payable Credit	Cash	
	Debit	Credit			Debit	Credit
1. Debit amount					$1,575.00	
Credit amount			$1,500.00			
Credit amount				$75.00		

■ APPLICATION PROBLEM

PROBLEM 13-1 Journalizing sales and cash receipts

Mark Butler and Betty Rivers, partners, own a tennis equipment and clothing store.

Instructions: 1. Journalize the following transactions completed during September of the current year. Use page 16 of a journal similar to the one described in this chapter. A 4% sales tax has been added to each sale. Source documents are abbreviated as follows: receipt, R; sales invoice, S; cash register tape, T.

Sept.   1. Sold merchandise on account to Valerie Seeley, $50.00, plus sales tax, $2.00; total, $52.00. S66.
   2. Sold merchandise on account to Jill Folker, $125.00, plus sales tax, $5.00; total, $130.00. S67.
   4. Sold merchandise on account to Jerome Hodges, $85.00, plus sales tax, $3.40; total, $88.40. S68.
   5. Received cash on account from Rita Picken, $140.40, covering S62. R93.
   5. Recorded cash and credit card sales, $2,360.00, plus sales tax, $94.40; total, $2,454.40. T5.
   7. Received cash on account from Karla Doyle, $182.00, covering S63. R94.
   9. Sold merchandise on account to Anthony Zolte, $115.00, plus sales tax, $4.60; total, $119.60. S69.
   12. Recorded cash and credit card sales, $2,890.00, plus sales tax, $115.60; total, $3,005.60. T12.
   12. Received cash on account from Jonathan Ames, $50.40, covering S64. R95.
   14. Received cash on account from Robert Hall, $67.60, covering S65. R96.
   15. Sold merchandise on account to Beth Klein, $115.00, plus sales tax, $4.60; total, $119.60. S70.
   17. Received cash on account from Valerie Seeley, $52.00, covering S66. R97.
   19. Recorded cash and credit card sales, $2,810.00, plus sales tax, $112.40; total, $2,922.40. T19.
   25. Received cash on account from Jill Folker, $130.00, covering S67. R98.
   26. Sold merchandise on account to Jill Folker, $75.00, plus sales tax, $3.00; total, $78.00. S71.

Sept. 26. Recorded cash and credit card sales, $2,650.00, plus sales tax, $106.00; total, $2,756.00. T26.

28. Received cash on account from Jerome Hodges, $88.40, covering S68. R99.

29. Sold merchandise on account to Karla Doyle, $95.00, plus sales tax, $3.80; total, $98.80. S72.

30. Recorded cash and credit card sales, $1,540.00, plus sales tax, $61.60; total, $1,601.60. T30.

2. Total the journal. Prove the equality of debits and credits.

3. Rule the journal.

◼ ENRICHMENT PROBLEMS

MASTERY PROBLEM 13-M   Journalizing transactions

Kevin Sykes and David Webb, partners, own a bicycle and motorcycle store.

Instructions: 1. Journalize the following transactions completed during November of the current year. Use page 18 of a journal similar to the one described in this chapter. A 6% sales tax has been added to each sale. Source documents are abbreviated as follows: check, C; memorandum, M; purchase invoice, P; receipt, R; sales invoice, S; cash register tape, T.

Nov. 2. Paid cash for rent, $1,250.00. C244.

2. Kevin Sykes, partner, withdrew cash for personal use, $600.00. C245.

2. David Webb, partner, withdrew cash for personal use, $600.00. C246.

3. Paid cash for electric bill, $130.00. C247.

3. Purchased merchandise on account from Vista Cycle Co., $2,275.00. P58.

4. Paid cash on account to Daley Motorcycles, $1,360.00, covering P56. C248.

5. Sold merchandise on account to Loree Adams, $1,130.00, plus sales tax, $67.80; total, $1,197.80. S61.

5. Paid cash for office supplies, $62.00. C249.

6. Purchased merchandise for cash, $165.00. C250.

7. Recorded cash and credit card sales, $5,850.00, plus sales tax, $351.00; total, $6,201.00. T7.

9. Sold merchandise on account to Victor Droste, $358.00, plus sales tax, $21.48; total, $379.48. S62.

9. Received cash on account from Wayne Ivory, $1,775.50, covering S57. R112.

11. Bought office supplies on account from Walden Supply, $68.00. M43.

12. Purchased merchandise for cash, $180.00. C251.

12. Received cash on account from Robert Melvin, $996.40, covering S58. R113.

13. Paid cash on account to Action Cycles, $1,365.00, covering P57. C252.

14. David Webb, partner, withdrew merchandise for personal use, $385.00. M44.

14. Recorded cash and credit card sales, $2,680.00, plus sales tax, $160.80; total, $2,840.80. T14.

16. Kevin Sykes, partner, withdrew cash for personal use, $600.00. C253.

16. David Webb, partner, withdrew cash for personal use, $600.00. C254.

17. Purchased merchandise on account from United Bicycle Co., $825.00. P59.

18. Purchased merchandise for cash, $196.00. C255.

18. Bought store supplies on account from Baker Supply, $92.00. M45.

19. Paid cash on account to Walden Supply, $68.00, covering M43. C256.

21. Recorded cash and credit card sales, $2,430.00, plus sales tax, $145.80; total, $2,575.80. T21.

Nov. 23. Discovered that a payment of cash for advertising in October was journalized and posted in error as a debit to Miscellaneous Expense instead of Advertising Expense, $125.00. M46.

23. Paid cash for office supplies, $44.00. C257.

2. Prepare page 18 of the journal for forwarding. Total the amount columns. Prove the equality of debits and credits, and record the totals to be carried forward on line 32.

3. Record the totals brought forward on line 1 of page 19 of the journal. Prove the equality of debits and credits again.

4. Journalize the following transactions on page 19 of the journal.

Nov. 23. Received cash on account from Esther Lorand, $630.70, covering S59. R114.

24. Sold merchandise on account to Celia Sotelo, $325.00, plus sales tax, $19.50; total, $344.50. S63.

27. Purchased merchandise on account from Cycle World, $1,240.00. P60.

27. Paid cash for advertising, $85.00. C258.

28. Recorded cash and credit card sales, $2,680.00, plus sales tax, $160.80; total, $2,840.80. T28.

28. Received cash on account from Leonard Kane, $1,147.00, covering S60. R115.

30. Sold merchandise on account to Jonathan Hunt, $45.00, plus sales tax, $2.70; total, $47.70. S64.

30. Paid cash to replenish the petty cash fund, $301.00: office supplies, $62.00; store supplies, $71.00; advertising, $88.00; miscellaneous, $80.00. C259.

30. Recorded cash and credit card sales, $640.00, plus sales tax, $38.40; total, $678.40. T30.

5. Total page 19 of the journal. Prove the equality of debits and credits.

6. Prove cash. The November 1 cash account balance in the general ledger was $9,431.00. On November 30 the balance on the next unused check stub was $21,511.40.

7. Rule page 19 of the journal.

CHALLENGE PROBLEM 13-C   Journalizing transactions

The columns of a journal may be arranged in different ways. For example, the journal used in this chapter is referred to as an expanded journal. All of the amount columns are to the right of the Account Title column. However, another arrangement is to have the amount columns divided by the Account Title column. Some of the amount columns are to the left and some are to the right of the Account Title column.

Instructions: 1. Use a journal with the columns arranged as follows.

Cash		Date	Account Title	Doc. No.	Post. Ref.	General		Accts. Rec.		Sales Cr.	Sales Tax Pay. Cr.	Accts. Payable		Purchases Dr.
Dr.	Cr.					Dr.	Cr.	Dr.	Cr.			Dr.	Cr.	

2. Use the transactions and instructions for Mastery Problem 13-M. Complete all of the instructions using the journal above.

CHAPTER

14

Posting to General and Subsidiary Ledgers

ENABLING PERFORMANCE TASKS

After studying Chapter 14, you will be able to:
a. Define accounting terms related to posting to ledgers.
b. Identify accounting practices related to posting to ledgers.
c. Post to a general ledger from a journal.
d. Open accounts in ledgers.
e. Post to subsidiary ledgers from a journal.
f. Prepare subsidiary schedules.

A journal provides a permanent record of transactions listed in chronological order. Journal entries are sorted and summarized by transferring information to ledger accounts. Transferring information from journal entries to ledger accounts is known as posting. Posting information from a journal to ledger accounts summarizes in one place transactions affecting each account.

LEDGERS AND CONTROLLING ACCOUNTS

A business' size, number of transactions, and type of transactions determine the number of ledgers used in an accounting system.

General ledger

A ledger that contains all accounts needed to prepare financial statements is known as a general ledger. A general ledger sorts and summarizes all information affecting income statement and balance sheet accounts. A business with transactions involving mostly the receipt and payment of cash may use only a general ledger. Rugcare, described in Part 1, uses only a general ledger. CarLand also uses a general ledger. CarLand's general ledger chart of accounts is on page 250. However, because of the business' size and the number and type of transactions, CarLand also uses additional ledgers in its accounting system.

Subsidiary ledgers

A business needs to know the amount owed each vendor as well as the amount to be collected from each charge customer. Therefore, a separate account is needed for each vendor and each customer. A general ledger could contain an account for each vendor and for each customer. However, a business with many vendors and customers would have a bulky general ledger and a long trial balance. CarLand eliminates these problems by keeping a separate ledger for vendors and a separate ledger for customers. Each separate ledger is summarized in a single general ledger account. A ledger that is summarized in a single general ledger account is called a subsidiary ledger. A subsidiary ledger containing only accounts for vendors from whom items are purchased or bought on account is called an counts payable ledger. A subsidiary ledger containing only accounts for charge customers is called an accounts receivable ledger.

Controlling accounts

The total amount owed to all vendors is summarized in a single general ledger account, Accounts Payable. The total amount to be collected from all charge customers is summarized in a single general ledger account, Accounts Receivable.

An account in a general ledger that summarizes all accounts in a subsidiary ledger is called a controlling account. The balance of a controlling account equals the total of all account balances in its related subsidiary ledger. Thus, the balance of the controlling account, Accounts Payable, equals the total of all vendor account balances in the accounts payable subsidiary ledger. The balance of the controlling account, Accounts Receivable, equals the total of all charge customer account balances in the accounts receivable subsidiary ledger.

POSTING TO A GENERAL LEDGER

Daily general ledger account balances are usually not necessary. Balances of general ledger accounts are needed only when financial statements are prepared. Posting from a journal to a general ledger can be done periodically throughout a month. The number of transactions determines how often to post to a general ledger. A business with many transactions would normally post more often than a business with few transactions. Posting often helps keep the work load evenly distributed throughout a month. However, posting must always be done at the end of a month. CarLand uses the same 4-column general ledger account form and posting procedures as described for Rugcare in Chapter 5.

Posting a journal's general amount columns

Amounts recorded in a journal's general amount columns are amounts for which no special amount columns are provided. Therefore, separate amounts in a journal's General Debit and General Credit columns *ARE* posted individually to the accounts written in the journal's Account Title column. The posting of the General Debit entry on line 6 of CarLand's journal is shown in Illustration 14-1.

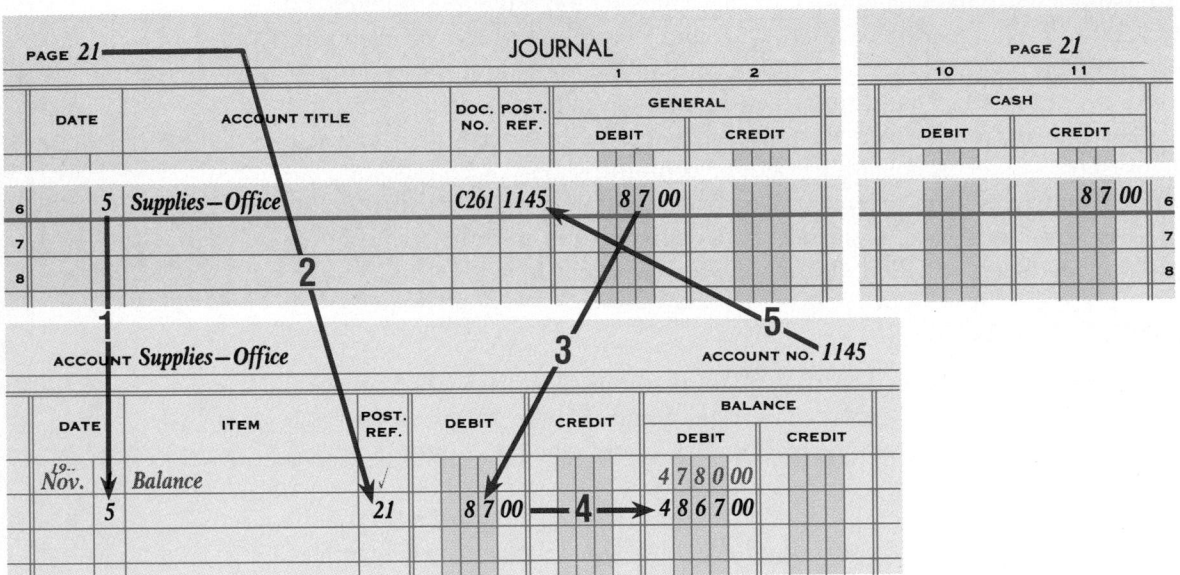

Illustration 14-1
Posting from a journal's
General Debit column

Five steps are followed to post the debit entry to the general ledger.

1 Write the date, *5*, in the Date column of the account.

2 Write the journal page number, *21*, in the Post. Ref. column of the account.

3 Write the debit amount, *$87.00*, in the account's Debit amount column.

4 Add the amount in the Debit amount column to the previous balance in the Balance Debit column ($4,780.00 + $87.00 = $4,867.00). Write the new account balance, *$4,867.00*, in the Balance Debit column.

5 Write the general ledger account number, *1145*, in the Post. Ref. column of the journal.

Posting a journal's special amount columns

CarLand's journal has nine special amount columns. Separate amounts written in these special amount columns *ARE NOT* posted individually to the general ledger. Separate amounts in a special amount column all affect the same general ledger account. Therefore, only the totals of special amount columns *ARE* posted to the general ledger. Each special amount column total is posted to the general ledger account listed in the column heading. Posting of the Cash Credit amount column total is shown in Illustration 14-2.

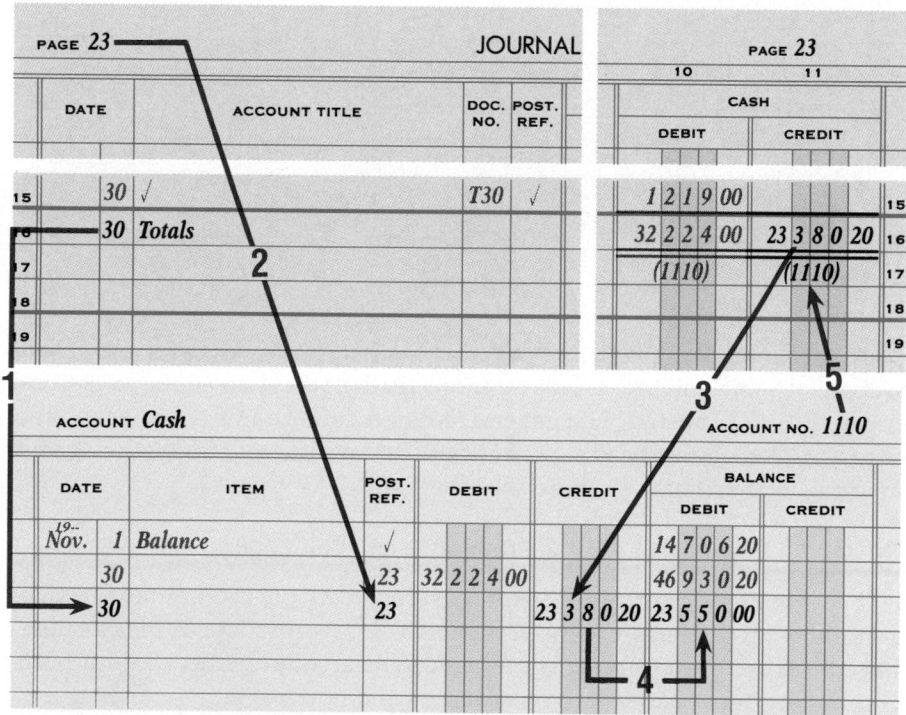

Illustration 14-2
Posting the Cash Credit
column total

Five steps are followed to post the Cash Credit column total.

1 Write the date, *30*, in the Date column of the account.

2 Write the journal page number, *23*, in the Post. Ref. column of the account.

3 Write the Cash Credit column total, *$23,380.20*, in the account's Credit amount column.

4 Subtract the amount in the Credit amount column from the previous balance in the Balance Debit column ($46,930.20 − $23,380.20 = $23,550.00). Write the new account balance, *$23,550.00*, in the Balance Debit column.

5 Return to the journal and write the general ledger account number, *1110*, in parentheses below the Cash Credit column total.

Rules for posting a journal's column totals

Rules for posting a journal's column totals are shown in Illustration 14-3.

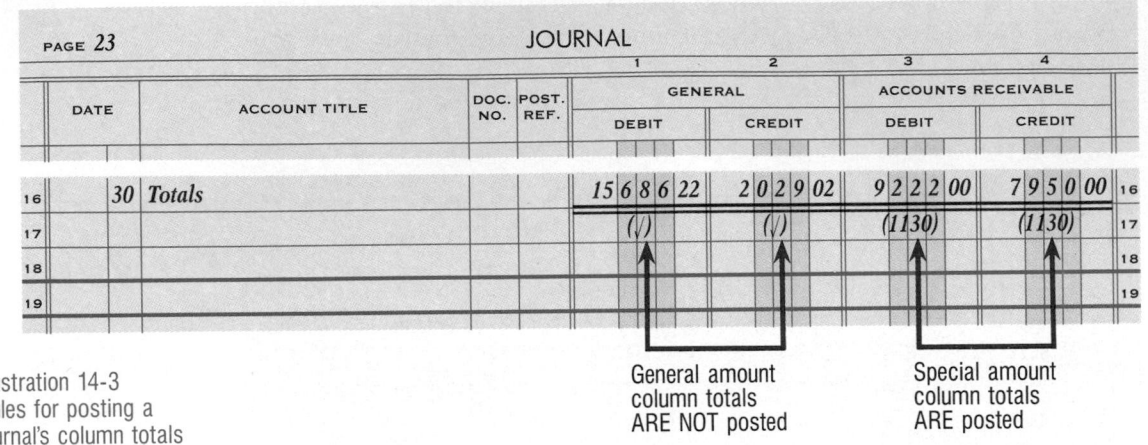

Illustration 14-3
Rules for posting a
journal's column totals

General amount column totals ARE NOT posted

Special amount column totals ARE posted

A check mark is placed in parentheses below the General Debit and General Credit column totals to indicate that the two amount column totals *ARE NOT* posted. The general ledger account number of the account listed in the column heading is written in parentheses below the special amount column totals to show that the totals *ARE* posted.

Opening a new page for an account in a general ledger

The number of entries that may be recorded on each general ledger account form depends on the number of lines provided. When all lines have been used, a new page is prepared. The account name, account number, and account balance are recorded on the new page.

On November 1 CarLand prepared a new page for Cash in the general ledger because the existing page was full. On that day, the account balance was $14,706.20. The new page for Cash in the general ledger is shown in Illustration 14-4.

ACCOUNT Cash						ACCOUNT NO. 1110	
			POST.			BALANCE	
DATE		ITEM	REF.	DEBIT	CREDIT	DEBIT	CREDIT
19-- Nov.	1	Balance	√			14 7 0 6 20	

Illustration 14-4
Opening a new page for an
account in a general ledger

The account title and account number are written on the heading at the top of the new page. The date, *19--, Nov. 1,* is recorded in the Date column. The word *Balance* is written in the Item column. A check mark is placed in the Post. Ref. column to show that the entry has been carried forward from a previous page rather than posted from a journal. The account balance, *$14,706.20,* is written in the Balance Debit column.

ASSIGNING ACCOUNT NUMBERS TO SUBSIDIARY LEDGER ACCOUNTS

CarLand assigns a vendor number to each account in the accounts payable ledger. A customer number is also assigned to each account in the accounts receivable ledger. A three-digit number is used. The first digit identifies the division in which the controlling account appears in the general ledger. The second two digits show each account's location within a subsidiary ledger. Accounts are assigned by 10s beginning with the second digit. Accounts in the subsidiary ledgers can be located by either number or name.

The vendor number for Antelo Supply is 210. The first digit, *2,* shows that the controlling account is a liability, Accounts Payable. The second and third digits, *10,* show the vendor number assigned to Antelo Supply.

The customer number for Ashley Delivery is 110. The first digit, *1,* shows that the controlling account is an asset, Accounts Receivable. The second and third digits, *10,* show the customer number assigned to Ashley Delivery.

The procedure for adding new accounts to subsidiary ledgers is the same as described for Rugcare's general ledger in Chapter 5. Accounts are arranged in alphabetic order within the subsidiary ledgers. New accounts are assigned the unused middle number. If the proper alphabetic order places a new account as the last account, the next number in the sequence of 10s is assigned. CarLand's chart of accounts for the subsidiary ledgers is on page 250.

POSTING TO AN ACCOUNTS PAYABLE LEDGER

When the balance of a vendor account in an accounts payable ledger is changed, the balance of the controlling account, Accounts Payable, is also changed. The total of all vendor account balances in the accounts payable ledger equals the balance of the controlling account, Accounts Payable. The relationship between the accounts payable ledger and the general ledger controlling account, Accounts Payable, is shown in Illustration 14-5.

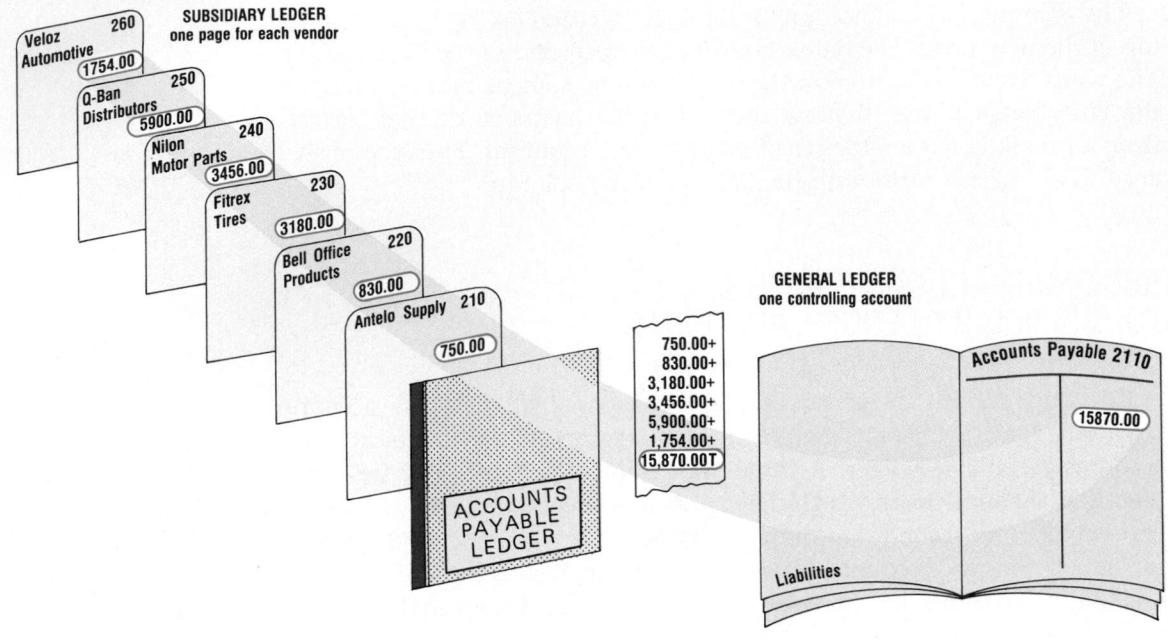

Illustration 14-5
Relationship of accounts
payable ledger and general
ledger controlling account

Accounts payable ledger form

CarLand uses the 3-column accounts payable subsidiary account form shown in Illustration 14-6.

Illustration 14-6
Three-column account
form used in an accounts
payable ledger

VENDOR *Veloz Automotive*						VENDOR NO. *260*
DATE	ITEM	POST. REF.	DEBIT	CREDIT	CREDIT BALANCE	

Information to be recorded in the accounts payable ledger is essentially the same as that recorded in the 4-column general ledger account. The information includes the date, posting reference, debit or credit amount, and new account balance. Accounts payable are liabilities, and liabilities have normal credit balances. Therefore, the Debit Balance column is usually not needed for the accounts payable ledger accounts. The accounts payable account form is the same as the general ledger account form except that there is no Debit Balance column.

Accounts in CarLand's accounts payable ledger are arranged in alphabetic order and kept in a loose-leaf binder. Periodically, accounts for new vendors are added and accounts no longer used are removed from the accounts payable ledger.

If the number of accounts becomes large enough to make a loose-leaf binder inappropriate, ledger pages may be kept in a file cabinet.

Opening vendor accounts

Each new account is opened by writing the vendor name and vendor number on the heading of the ledger account. The account opened for Veloz Automotive is shown in Illustration 14-6.

The vendor name is obtained from the first purchase invoice received. The vendor number is assigned using the three-digit numbering system described on page 291. The correct alphabetic order for Veloz Automotive places the account as the sixth account in the accounts payable subsidiary ledger. Vendor number 260 is assigned to Veloz Automotive.

> Some businesses record both the vendor name and vendor address on the ledger form. However, the address information is usually kept in a separate name and address file. This practice eliminates having to record the vendor address on the ledger form each time a new ledger page is opened or the address changes.

Posting from a journal to an accounts payable ledger

Each entry in the Accounts Payable columns of a journal affects the vendor named in the Account Title column. CarLand posts each amount in these two columns often. Posting often keeps each vendor account balance up to date. Totals of Accounts Payable special amount columns are posted to the general ledger at the end of each month.

Posting a credit to an accounts payable ledger. Posting a credit for a purchase on account from the journal to the accounts payable ledger is shown in Illustration 14-7.

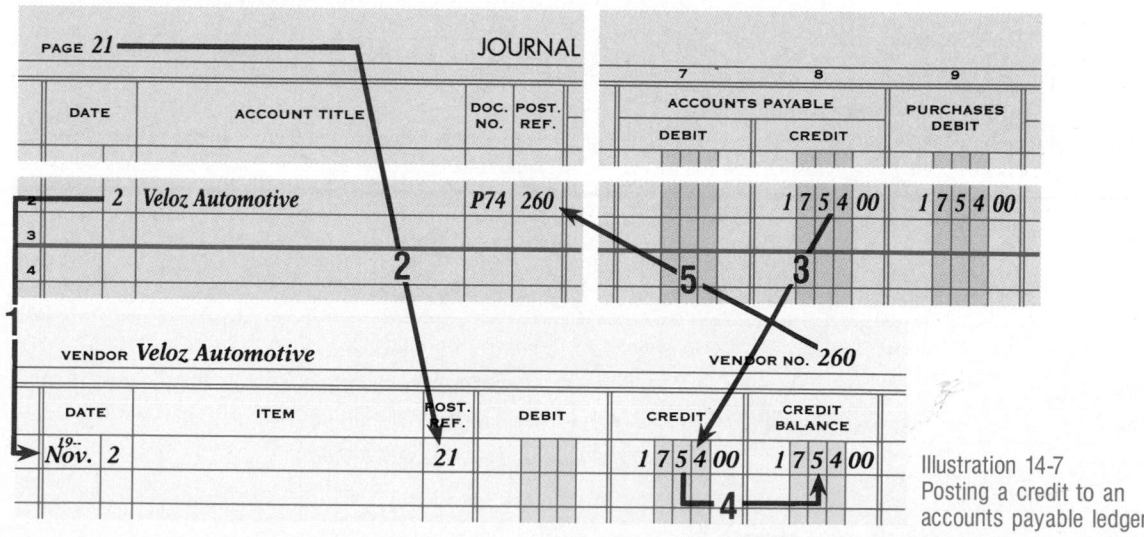

Illustration 14-7
Posting a credit to an
accounts payable ledger

Five steps are followed to post the entry on line 2 of the journal to the accounts payable ledger.

1 Write the date, *19--, Nov. 2*, in the Date column of the account.

2 Write the journal page number, *21*, in the Post. Ref. column of the account.

3 Write the credit amount, *$1,754.00*, in the Credit amount column of the account for Veloz Automotive.

4 Add the amount in the Credit amount column to the previous balance in the Credit Balance column. (Veloz Automotive has no previous balance; therefore, $0 + $1,754.00 = $1,754.00.) Write the new account balance, *$1,754.00*, in the Credit Balance column.

5 Write the vendor number, *260*, in the Post. Ref. column of the journal. The vendor number shows that the posting for this entry is completed.

The controlling account in the general ledger, Accounts Payable, is also increased by this entry. At the end of the month, the journal's Accounts Payable Credit column total is posted to the controlling account, Accounts Payable.

Posting a debit to an accounts payable ledger. The same steps are followed to post a debit to a vendor account as are used to post a credit. However, the debit amount is entered in the Debit amount column of the vendor account. The debit amount is subtracted from the previous credit balance. Posting a cash payment on account from the journal to the accounts payable ledger is shown in Illustration 14-8.

Illustration 14-8
Posting a debit to an
accounts payable ledger

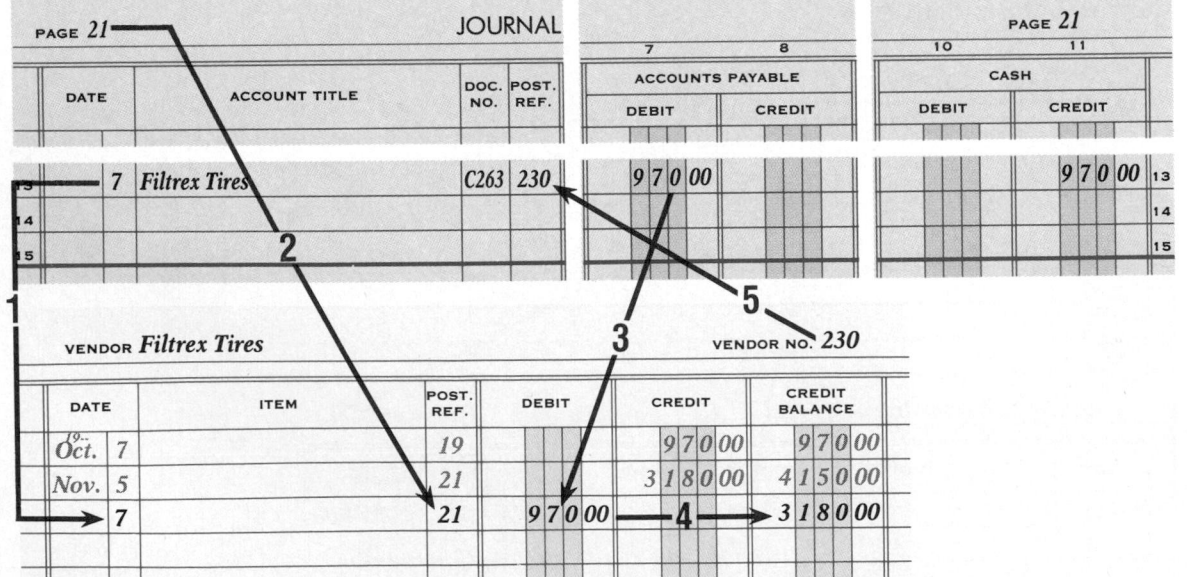

The controlling account in the general ledger, Accounts Payable, is decreased by this entry. At the end of the month, the journal's Accounts Payable Debit column total is posted to the controlling account, Accounts Payable.

Opening a new page for a vendor in an accounts payable ledger

The number of entries that may be recorded on each account form depends on the number of lines provided. When all lines have been used, a new page is prepared. The vendor name, vendor number, and account balance are recorded on the new page.

On November 1 CarLand prepared a new page for Nilon Motor Parts in the accounts payable ledger because the existing page was full. On that day, the account balance was $4,840.00. The new page for Nilon Motor Parts in the accounts payable ledger is shown in Illustration 14-9.

VENDOR *Nilon Motor Parts*   VENDOR NO. *240*

DATE	ITEM	POST. REF.	DEBIT	CREDIT	CREDIT BALANCE
19-- Nov. 1	Balance	✓			4 8 4 0 00

Illustration 14-9
Opening a new page for a vendor in the accounts payable ledger

The vendor name and vendor number are written at the top of the account page. The date, *19--, Nov. 1*, is recorded in the Date column. The word *Balance* is written in the Item column. A check mark is placed in the Post. Ref. column to show that the amount has been carried forward from a previous page rather than posted from a journal. The account balance, *$4,840.00*, is written in the Credit Balance column.

Completed accounts payable ledger

CarLand's accounts payable ledger after all posting has been completed is shown in Illustration 14-10.

VENDOR *Antelo Supply*   VENDOR NO. *210*

DATE	ITEM	POST. REF.	DEBIT	CREDIT	CREDIT BALANCE
19-- Oct. 12		19		4 3 0 00	4 3 0 00
Nov. 6		21		1 6 0 00	5 9 0 00
12		21	4 3 0 00		1 6 0 00
23		22		5 9 0 00	7 5 0 00

Illustration 14-10
Accounts payable ledger after posting has been completed

VENDOR *Bell Office Products*   VENDOR NO. *220*

DATE		ITEM	POST. REF.	DEBIT	CREDIT	CREDIT BALANCE
19-- Oct.	23		20		6 2 0 00	6 2 0 00
Nov.	23		22	6 2 0 00		
	24		22		8 3 0 00	8 3 0 00

VENDOR *Filtrex Tires*   VENDOR NO. *230*

DATE		ITEM	POST. REF.	DEBIT	CREDIT	CREDIT BALANCE
19-- Oct.	7		19		9 7 0 00	9 7 0 00
Nov.	5		21		3 1 8 0 00	4 1 5 0 00
	7		21	9 7 0 00		3 1 8 0 00

VENDOR *Nilon Motor Parts*   VENDOR NO. *240*

DATE		ITEM	POST. REF.	DEBIT	CREDIT	CREDIT BALANCE
19-- Nov.	1	Balance	√			4 8 4 0 00
	4		21		3 4 5 6 00	8 2 9 6 00
	20		22	4 8 4 0 00		3 4 5 6 00

VENDOR *Q-Ban Distributors*   VENDOR NO. *250*

DATE		ITEM	POST. REF.	DEBIT	CREDIT	CREDIT BALANCE
19-- Nov.	1	Balance	√			3 9 6 0 00
	6		21	3 9 6 0 00		
	13		21		3 1 4 0 00	3 1 4 0 00
	20		22		2 7 6 0 00	5 9 0 0 00

VENDOR *Veloz Automotive*   VENDOR NO. *260*

DATE		ITEM	POST. REF.	DEBIT	CREDIT	CREDIT BALANCE
19-- Nov.	2		21		1 7 5 4 00	1 7 5 4 00

Illustration 14-10
Accounts payable ledger
after posting has been
completed
(concluded)

POSTING TO AN ACCOUNTS RECEIVABLE LEDGER

When the balance of a customer account in an accounts receivable ledger is changed, the balance of the controlling account, Accounts Receivable, is also changed. The total of all customer account balances in the accounts receivable ledger equals the balance of the controlling account, Accounts Receivable. The relationship between the accounts receivable ledger and the general ledger controlling account, Accounts Receivable, is shown in Illustration 14-11.

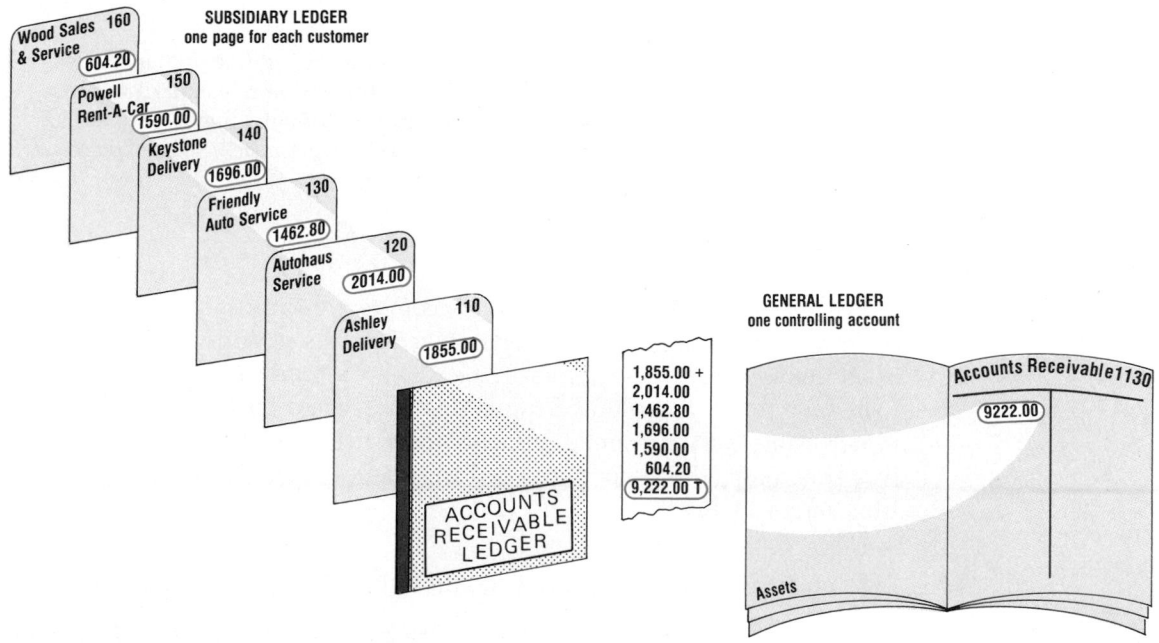

Illustration 14-11
Relationship of accounts
receivable ledger and
general ledger controlling
account

Accounts receivable ledger form

CarLand uses the 3-column accounts receivable subsidiary account form shown in Illustration 14-12.

CUSTOMER *Friendly Auto Service*					CUSTOMER NO. *130*
DATE	ITEM	POST. REF.	DEBIT	CREDIT	DEBIT BALANCE

Illustration 14-12
Three-column account
form used in an accounts
receivable ledger

The accounts receivable account form is similar to the one used for the accounts payable ledger. Accounts receivable are assets, and assets have normal debit balances. Therefore, the form used in the accounts receivable ledger has a Debit Balance column instead of a Credit Balance column.

Accounts in CarLand's accounts receivable ledger are arranged in alphabetic order and kept in a loose-leaf binder. Periodically, accounts for new customers are added and accounts no longer used are removed from the accounts receivable ledger. The customer number 130 had been assigned to a former customer. That account, however, had been removed from the ledger. Therefore, customer number 130 is available for assignment to Friendly Auto Service.

> Some businesses record both the customer name and customer address on the ledger form. However, the address information is usually kept in a separate name and address file. This practice eliminates having to record the customer address on the ledger form each time a new ledger page is opened or the address changes.

Opening customer accounts

Procedures for opening customer accounts are similar to those used for opening vendor accounts. The customer name is obtained from the first sales invoice prepared for a customer. The customer number is assigned using the three-digit numbering system described on page 291. The customer name and customer number are written on the heading of the ledger account. The account opened for Friendly Auto Service is shown in Illustration 14-12.

Posting from a journal to an accounts receivable ledger

Each entry in the Accounts Receivable columns of a journal affects the customer named in the Account Title column. Each amount listed in these two columns is posted to a customer account in the accounts receivable ledger often. Posting often keeps each customer account balance up to date. Totals of Accounts Receivable special amount columns are posted to the general ledger at the end of each month.

Posting a debit to an accounts receivable ledger. Posting a debit for a sale on account from the journal to the accounts receivable ledger is shown in Illustration 14-13.

Five steps are followed to post the entry on line 4 of the journal to the accounts receivable ledger.

1 Write the date, *3*, in the Date column of the account.

2 Write the journal page number, *21*, in the Post. Ref. column of the account.

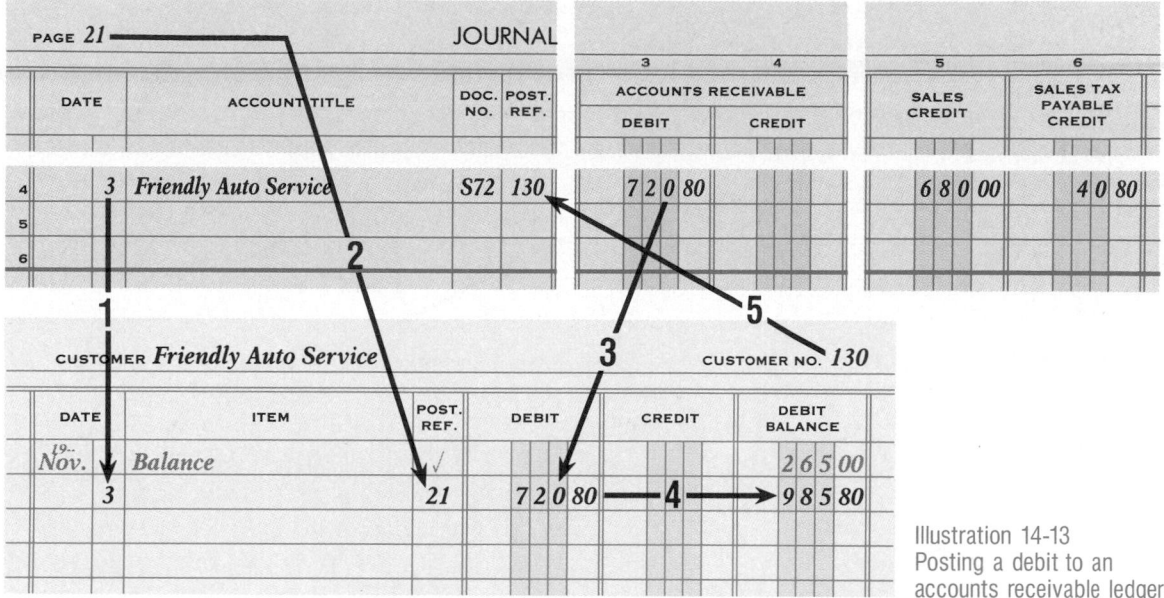

Illustration 14-13
Posting a debit to an
accounts receivable ledger

3 Write the debit amount, *$720.80*, in the Debit amount column of the account for Friendly Auto Service.

4 Add the amount in the Debit amount column to the previous balance in the Debit Balance column ($265.00 + $720.80 = $985.80). Write the new account balance, *$985.80*, in the Debit Balance column.

5 Write the customer number, *130*, in the Post. Ref. column of the journal. The customer number shows that the posting for this entry is completed.

The controlling account in the general ledger, Accounts Receivable, is also increased by this entry. At the end of the month, the journal's Accounts Receivable Debit column total is posted to the controlling account, Accounts Receivable.

Posting a credit to an accounts receivable ledger. The same steps are followed to post a credit to a customer account as are used to post a debit. However, the credit amount is written in the Credit amount column of the customer account. The credit amount is subtracted from the previous debit balance. Posting a cash receipt on account from the journal to the accounts receivable ledger is shown in Illustration 14-14 on page 300.

The controlling account in the general ledger, Accounts Receivable, is decreased by this entry. However, the amount is not posted individually to the accounts receivable account. At the end of the month, the amount, *$318.00*, is posted as part of the special amount column total to Accounts Receivable.

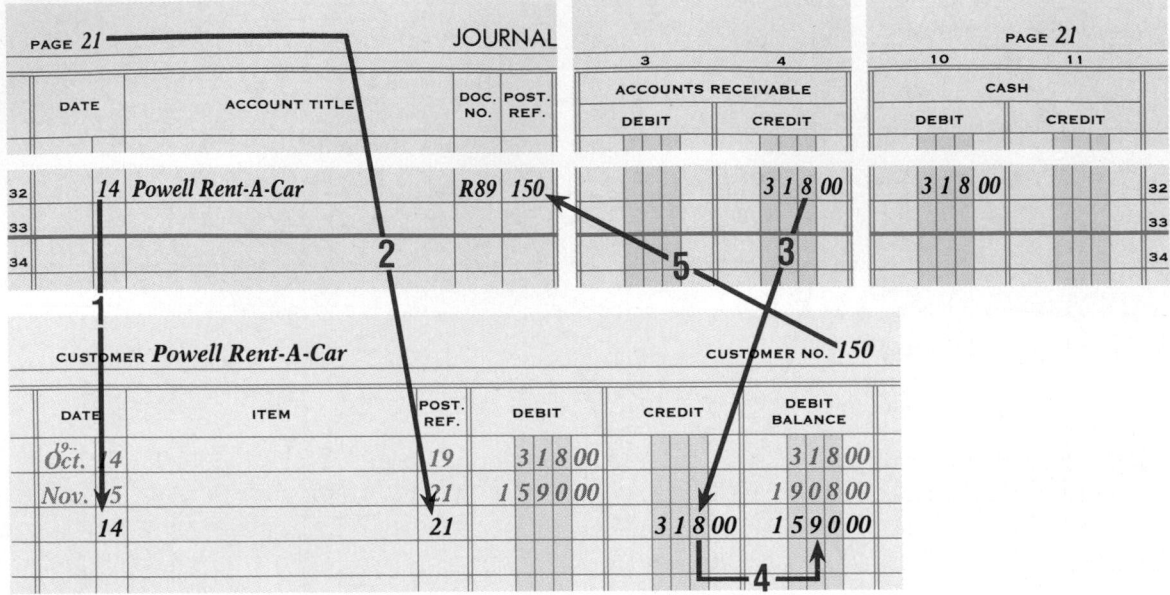

Illustration 14-14
Posting a credit to an
accounts receivable ledger

Opening a new page for a customer in an accounts receivable ledger

Procedures for opening a new page in an accounts receivable ledger are similar to those for an accounts payable ledger. The customer name and customer number are written at the top of the new account page. The date is recorded in the Date column. The word *Balance* is written in the Item column. A check mark is placed in the Post. Ref. column to show that the amount has been carried forward from a previous page rather than posted from a journal. The account balance is recorded in the Debit Balance column.

Completed accounts receivable ledger

CarLand's accounts receivable ledger after all posting has been completed is shown in Illustration 14-15.

Illustration 14-15
Accounts receivable ledger
after posting has been
completed

CUSTOMER *Ashley Delivery*   CUSTOMER NO. *110*

DATE		ITEM	POST. REF.	DEBIT	CREDIT	DEBIT BALANCE
Nov.	1	Balance	√			2 49 1 00
	9		21	4 77 00		2 96 8 00
	16		22	1 3 78 00		4 34 6 00
	17		22		2 49 1 00	1 85 5 00

Illustration 14-15
Accounts receivable ledger
after posting has been
completed
(concluded)

CUSTOMER *Autohaus Service*   CUSTOMER NO. *120*

DATE		ITEM	POST. REF.	DEBIT	CREDIT	DEBIT BALANCE
Nov. 19--	1	Balance	√			1 8 0 2 00
	6		21		1 8 0 2 00	
	18		22	2 0 1 4 00		2 0 1 4 00

CUSTOMER *Friendly Auto Service*   CUSTOMER NO. *130*

DATE		ITEM	POST. REF.	DEBIT	CREDIT	DEBIT BALANCE
Nov. 19--	1	Balance	√			2 6 5 00
	3		21	7 2 0 80		9 8 5 80
	24		22	7 4 2 00		1 7 2 7 80
	25		22		2 6 5 00	1 4 6 2 80

CUSTOMER *Keystone Delivery*   CUSTOMER NO. *140*

DATE		ITEM	POST. REF.	DEBIT	CREDIT	DEBIT BALANCE
Oct. 19--	10		19	9 5 4 00		9 5 4 00
Nov.	10		21		9 5 4 00	
	24		22	3 1 8 00		3 1 8 00
	29		22	1 3 7 8 00		1 6 9 6 00

CUSTOMER *Powell Rent-A-Car*   CUSTOMER NO. *150*

DATE		ITEM	POST. REF.	DEBIT	CREDIT	DEBIT BALANCE
Oct. 19--	14		19	3 1 8 00		3 1 8 00
Nov.	5		21	1 5 9 0 00		1 9 0 8 00
	14		21		3 1 8 00	1 5 9 0 00

CUSTOMER *Wood Sales & Service*   CUSTOMER NO. *160*

DATE		ITEM	POST. REF.	DEBIT	CREDIT	DEBIT BALANCE
Nov. 19--	1	Balance	√			2 1 2 0 00
	11		21	6 0 4 20		2 7 2 4 20
	13		21		9 0 1 00	1 8 2 3 20
	20		22		1 2 1 9 00	6 0 4 20

PROVING THE ACCURACY OF POSTING

A single error in posting to a ledger account may cause the trial balance to be out of balance. An error in posting may cause the cash account balance to disagree with the actual cash on hand. An error in posting may also cause the income to be understated or overstated on an income statement. An error in posting may also cause a business to overpay or underpay its vendors. Posting must be accurate to assure correct account balances. Therefore, to prove the accuracy of posting, three things are done. (1) Cash is proved. (2) Subsidiary schedules are prepared to prove that the total of the balances in the subsidiary ledgers equals the balance of the controlling account in the general ledger. (3) A trial balance is prepared to prove that debits equal credits in the general ledger.

Preparation of a trial balance is described in Chapter 17.

Proving cash

The method used to prove cash is described in Chapter 13. The cash proof total is compared with the balance on the next unused check stub in the checkbook.

Proving the subsidiary ledgers

A controlling account balance in a general ledger must equal the sum of all account balances in a subsidiary ledger. CarLand proves the accounts payable and accounts receivable subsidiary ledgers at the end of each month.

Proving accounts payable. A listing of vendor accounts, account balances, and total amount due all vendors is called a schedule of accounts payable. A schedule of accounts payable is prepared after all entries in a journal are posted. CarLand's schedule of accounts payable, prepared on November 30, is shown in Illustration 14-16.

CarLand	
Schedule of Accounts Payable	
November 30, 19--	
Antelo Supply	7 5 0 00
Bell Office Products	8 3 0 00
Filtrex Tires	3 1 8 0 00
Nilon Motor Parts	3 4 5 6 00
Q-Ban Distributors	5 9 0 0 00
Veloz Automotive	1 7 5 4 00
Total Accounts Payable	15 8 7 0 00

Illustration 14-16
Schedule of accounts
payable

The balance of Accounts Payable in the general ledger is $15,870.00. The total of the schedule of accounts payable is $15,870.00. Because the two amounts are the same, the accounts payable ledger is proved.

Proving accounts receivable. A listing of customer accounts, account balances, and total amount due from all customers is called a schedule of accounts receivable. A schedule of accounts receivable is prepared after all entries in a journal are posted. CarLand's schedule of accounts receivable, prepared on November 30, is shown in Illustration 14-17.

CarLand	
Schedule of Accounts Receivable	
November 30, 19--	
Ashley Delivery	1 8 5 5 00
Autohaus Service	2 0 1 4 00
Friendly Auto Service	1 4 6 2 80
Keystone Delivery	1 6 9 6 00
Powell Rent-A-Car	1 5 9 0 00
Wood Sales & Service	6 0 4 20
Total Accounts Receivable	9 2 2 2 00

Illustration 14-17
Schedule of accounts receivable

The balance of Accounts Receivable in the general ledger is $9,222.00. The total of the schedule of accounts receivable is $9,222.00. Because the two amounts are the same, the accounts receivable ledger is proved.

SUMMARY OF POSTING TO GENERAL AND SUBSIDIARY LEDGERS

A summary of the posting steps from Rugcare's journal is in Chapter 5. The steps described for Rugcare also apply to posting from an expanded journal. However, special amount columns and controlling accounts require an additional set of posting steps.

Posting from a journal's general columns

As shown in Illustration 14-18 on page 304, separate amounts in General columns *ARE* posted individually. Totals of General Debit and Credit columns *ARE NOT* posted.

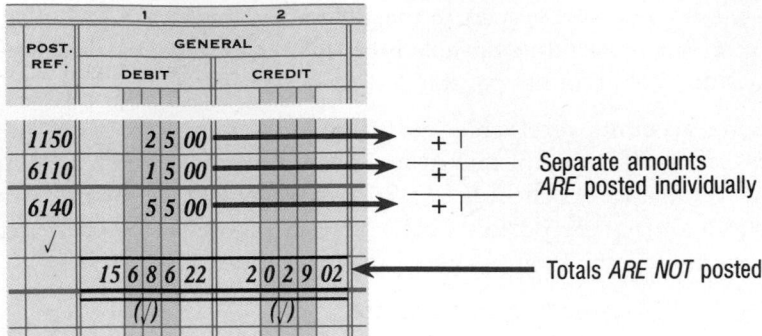

Illustration 14-18
Summary of posting from
a journal's general columns

Posting from a journal's special columns

As shown in Illustration 14-19, totals of special amount columns *ARE* posted to the account named in the column heading. The column total shown *IS* posted as a credit to the named account. Separate amounts in special columns *ARE NOT* posted individually unless the columns affect a controlling account.

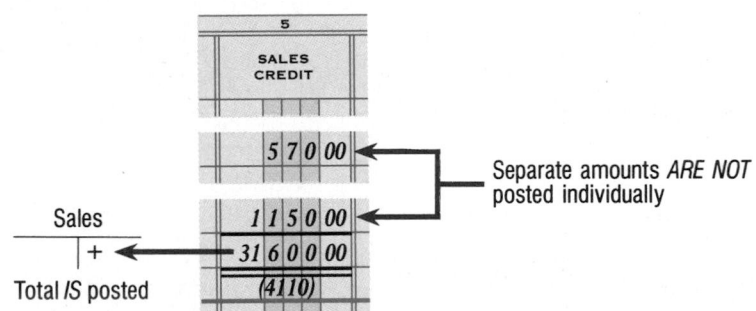

Illustration 14-19
Summary of posting from
a journal's special columns

Posting from a journal's special columns for controlling accounts

As shown in Illustration 14-20, separate amounts and total amounts are posted from special columns for controlling accounts. Separate amounts in the Accounts Receivable Debit and Credit columns *ARE* posted individually to customer accounts. These accounts are found in the accounts receivable ledger. As the last posting step, a customer number is written in the Post. Ref. column of the journal. The customer number shows that posting of a separate amount to a customer account has been completed.

Totals of special columns *ARE* posted to the controlling accounts named in the column headings. The total of an Accounts Receivable Debit column is posted as a debit to Accounts Receivable in the general ledger. The total of an Accounts Receivable Credit column is posted as a credit to Accounts Receivable in the general ledger. As a last posting step, an account number is placed in parentheses under the total of a special amount column. The number shows the general ledger account to which the total was posted.

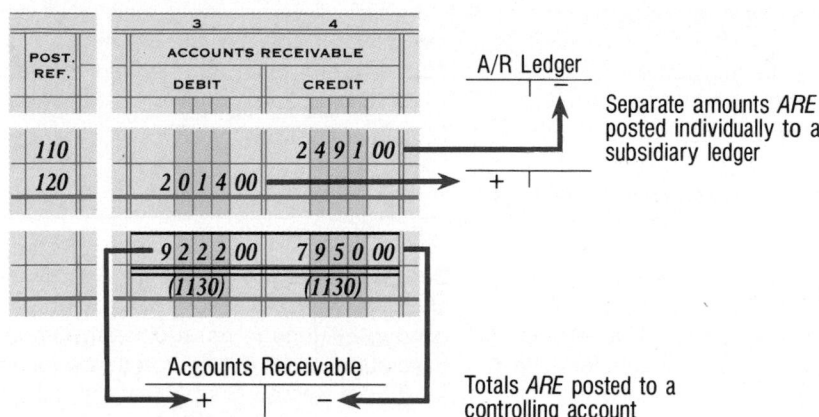

Illustration 14-20
Summary of posting from special columns for controlling accounts

The same principles used for Accounts Receivable amount columns also apply to Accounts Payable amount columns in a journal.

ACCOUNTING TERMS

What is the meaning of each of the following?

1. subsidiary ledger
2. accounts payable ledger
3. accounts receivable ledger
4. controlling account
5. schedule of accounts payable
6. schedule of accounts receivable

QUESTIONS FOR INDIVIDUAL STUDY

1. How is journal entry information sorted and summarized?
2. What determines the number of ledgers used in an accounting system?
3. What ledger contains all accounts needed to prepare an income statement and a balance sheet?
4. What type of business would generally use a single ledger?
5. Why would a business keep a separate account for each vendor and each customer?
6. Why would a business keep a separate ledger for vendors and a separate ledger for customers?
7. What is the title of the general ledger controlling account for vendors?
8. What is the title of the general ledger controlling account for customers?
9. Why is posting to a general ledger done only periodically throughout the month?
10. What determines the frequency of posting to a general ledger?
11. Why are amounts recorded in a journal's general amount columns posted individually?
12. Why are separate amounts in special amount columns not posted individually to the general ledger?
13. Why is a check mark placed in parentheses below the General Debit and General Credit column totals?
14. What does the first digit in a vendor or customer number identify?

15. Why does the 3-column account form used in an accounts payable ledger have a Credit Balance column?
16. Why is posting of separate amounts in the Accounts Payable columns done often?
17. How often are the totals of the Accounts Payable columns of a journal posted?

18. Why is a check mark entered in the Post. Ref. column when a new page is opened for a vendor?
19. Why does the 3-column account form used in an accounts receivable ledger have a Debit Balance column?
20. How are subsidiary ledgers proved at the end of a month?

◼ CASES FOR MANAGEMENT DECISION

CASE 1 Edna Doyle, an accountant, is asked to evaluate the accounting system of Dotson's Department Store. The general ledger includes individual accounts for each vendor and customer. When checking the records and accounting procedures, Ms. Doyle notes the bulky general ledger and long trial balance. Dotson's Department Store uses a 5-column journal to record all transactions. A general ledger is used to maintain all income statement, balance sheet, vendor, and customer accounts. Transactions affecting vendor or customer accounts are recorded in the General Debit or General Credit columns of the journal. Separate vendor and customer entries are then posted individually to accounts in the general ledger. What recommendations should Ms. Doyle make concerning the handling of vendor and customer accounts?

CASE 2 Automart purchased merchandise on account six weeks ago for $400.00 from

Belview Supply. A check for $400.00 was sent three weeks ago in payment of the account. Although no additional purchases have been made, Automart recently received a bill from Belview Supply that listed the balance due as $800.00. What probably caused this error? When would the error probably be discovered?

CASE 3 Leon Reyes observes his accountant at work and says, "You post each individual accounts receivable entry in the journal. Then you post the totals of the Accounts Receivable columns. You are posting these entries twice, which will make the records wrong." The accountant does not agree that the posting procedure is incorrect. Is Mr. Reyes or his accountant correct? Why?

◼ DRILLS FOR UNDERSTANDING

DRILL 14-D1   Analyzing transactions of a merchandising business

Instructions: Prepare T accounts for each of the following transactions. Use the T accounts to analyze each transaction. A 6% sales tax has been added to each sale. The first transaction is given as an example.

Accounts Receivable		Sales		Sales Tax Payable	
127.20			120.00		7.20

Transactions

1. Sold merchandise on account to Sarah Burke, $120.00, plus sales tax, $7.20; total, $127.20.
2. Paid cash on account to Casa Enterprises, $950.00.
3. Paid cash for rent, $1,250.00.
4. Discovered that a payment for advertising was journalized and posted in error as a debit to Miscellaneous Expense instead of Advertising Expense, $125.00.
5. Paid cash for office supplies, $80.00.
6. Recorded cash and credit card sales, $1,850.00, plus sales tax, $111.00; total, $1,961.00.
7. Joyce Berling, partner, withdrew merchandise for personal use, $90.00.
8. Purchased merchandise on account from Irvine Products, $1,640.00.
9. Received cash on account from Carl Downing, $227.90.
10. Purchased merchandise for cash, $130.00.
11. Michael Zolty, partner, withdrew cash for personal use, $700.00.
12. Bought store supplies on account from Carter Supply, $315.00.

The solution to Drill 14-D1 is needed to complete Drill 14-D2.

DRILL 14-D2   Analyzing, journalizing, and posting transactions of a merchandising business

The solution to Drill 14-D1 is needed to complete Drill 14-D2.

Instructions: 1. Use a form similar to the following. Based on the answers in Drill 14-D1, place a check mark in the amount columns to be used to journalize each transaction. Transaction 1 is given as an example.

Transaction	Amount columns in the journal										
	General		Accts. Rec.		Sales Credit	Sales Tax Pay. Credit	Accts. Payable		Purch. Debit	Cash	
	Debit	Credit	Debit	Credit			Debit	Credit		Debit	Credit
1. Debit amount			√								
Credit amount					√						
Credit amount						√					

2. Use a form similar to the following. Based on the answers to Instruction 1, place a check mark in the proper column to indicate whether the amount will or will not be posted individually to the ledgers. Transaction 1 is given as an example.

Transaction	Posted individually to			Not posted individually to any ledger
	General Ledger	Accts. Receivable Ledger	Accts. Payable Ledger	
1. Debit amount		√		
Credit amount				√
Credit amount				√

▮ APPLICATION PROBLEM

PROBLEM 14-1   Opening accounts and posting to ledgers from a journal

The journal for Carpet Magic is given in the working papers accompanying this textbook.

Instructions: 1. Open new pages for the following accounts in the general ledger. Record the balances as of September 1 of the current year.

Account No.	Account Title	Account Balance
1110	Cash	$ 18,300.00
1130	Accounts Receivable	8,470.00
1150	Supplies—Office......................................	3,680.00
1160	Supplies—Store	4,260.00
1170	Prepaid Insurance....................................	1,560.00
2110	Accounts Payable....................................	10,555.00
2120	Sales Tax Payable....................................	1,235.00
3120	Diane Engler, Drawing	8,000.00
3140	Paul Sisco, Drawing	8,340.00
4110	Sales	172,420.00
5110	Purchases..	96,500.00
6110	Advertising Expense..................................	1,860.00
6140	Miscellaneous Expense	1,310.00
6160	Rent Expense.......................................	8,000.00

2. Open new pages for the following vendor accounts in the accounts payable ledger. Record the balances as of September 1 of the current year.

Vendor No.	Vendor Name	Purchase No.	Account Balance
210	Crown Carpet Co.	52	$2,575.00
220	Marlow Industries..............................	53	4,220.00
230	Superior Carpeting	—	—
240	V & P Carpet Co...............................	51	3,760.00

3. Open new pages for the following customer accounts in the accounts receivable ledger. Record the balances as of September 1 of the current year.

Customer No.	Customer Name	Sales No.	Account Balance
110	Cameo Shoe Store............................	44	$3,680.00
120	Paula Hughs	42	1,850.00
130	Elsa Leyba....................................	43	2,940.00
140	Scott Ward....................................	—	—

4. Post the separate items recorded in the following columns of the journal. (a) General Debit and Credit. (b) Accounts Receivable Debit and Credit. (c) Accounts Payable Debit and Credit.

5. Post the totals of the special columns of the journal.

6. Prepare a schedule of accounts payable. Compare the total of the schedule with the balance of the controlling account, Accounts Payable, in the general ledger. If the totals are not the same, find and correct the errors.

7. Prepare a schedule of accounts receivable. Compare the total of the schedule with the balance of the controlling account, Accounts Receivable, in the general ledger. If the totals are not the same, find and correct the errors.

■ ENRICHMENT PROBLEMS

MASTERY PROBLEM 14-M   Posting to ledgers from a journal

The journal and ledgers for Anton Leather Goods are given in the working papers accompanying this textbook.

Instructions: 1. Post the separate items recorded in the following columns of the journal. (a) General Debit and Credit. (b) Accounts Receivable Debit and Credit. (c) Accounts Payable Debit and Credit.

2. Post the totals of the special columns of the journal.

3. Prepare a schedule of accounts payable and a schedule of accounts receivable. Prove the accuracy of the subsidiary ledgers by comparing the schedule totals with the balances of the controlling accounts in the general ledger. If the totals are not the same, find and correct the errors.

CHALLENGE PROBLEM 14-C   Journalizing and posting business transactions

The general ledger, accounts payable, and accounts receivable accounts for Par Golf Products are given in the working papers accompanying this textbook. The balances are recorded as of November 1 of the current year.

PARTIAL GENERAL LEDGER

Account No.	Account Title	Account Balance
1110	Cash	$ 16,850.00
1130	Accounts Receivable	2,867.30
1150	Supplies—Office	2,635.00
1160	Supplies—Store	2,160.00
2110	Accounts Payable	8,023.00
2120	Sales Tax Payable	1,312.00
3120	Maria Adolfo, Drawing	12,800.00
3140	Lawrence Phipps, Drawing	12,540.00
4110	Sales	218,749.00
5110	Purchases	112,500.00
6110	Advertising Expense	2,940.00
6140	Miscellaneous Expense	1,410.00
6160	Rent Expense	9,500.00
6190	Utilities Expense	1,785.00

ACCOUNTS PAYABLE LEDGER

Vendor No.	Vendor Name	Purchase No.	Account Balance
210	Artex Golf Products	P74	$2,430.00
220	Ecola Golf Equipment	P72	1,965.00
230	Garcia Supply	—	—
240	Patton Golf Co.	P75	948.00
250	Valiant Golf Co.	P73	2,680.00

ACCOUNTS RECEIVABLE LEDGER

Customer No.	Customer Name	Sales No.	Account Balance
110	William Backus	S52	$ 795.00
120	Linda Boge	S50	678.40
130	Jonathan Dunbar	—	—
140	James Patco	S53	1,160.70
150	Bertha Welsh	S51	233.20

Instructions: 1. Journalize the following transactions completed during November of the current year. Use page 18 of a journal similar to the one described in this chapter. Add a 6% sales tax to all sales transactions. Source documents are abbreviated as follows: check, C; memorandum, M; purchase invoice, P; receipt, R; sales invoice, S; cash register tape, T.

Nov. 2. Paid cash for rent, $950.00. C275.
       3. Purchased merchandise on account from Valiant Golf Co., $1,625.00. P76.
       4. Purchased merchandise for cash, $119.00. C276.
       5. Received cash on account from Linda Boge, $678.40, covering S50. R45.
       7. Paid cash on account to Ecola Golf Equipment, $1,965.00, covering P72. C277.
       7. Recorded cash and credit card sales, $4,730.00. T7.
          Posting. Post the items that are to be posted individually.
       9. Maria Adolfo, partner, withdrew merchandise for personal use, $165.00. M35.
      11. Sold merchandise on account to James Patco, $255.00. S54.
      12. Discovered that store supplies bought for cash was journalized and posted in error as a debit to Advertising Expense instead of Supplies—Store, $93.00. M36.
      14. Bought store supplies on account from Garcia Supply, $215.00. M37.
      14. Recorded cash and credit card sales, $4,840.00. T14.
          Posting. Post the items that are to be posted individually.
      16. Maria Adolfo, partner, withdrew cash for personal use, $1,200.00. C278.
      16. Lawrence Phipps, partner, withdrew cash for personal use, $1,200.00. C279.
      17. Paid cash for electric bill, $183.50. C280.
      20. Paid cash on account to Valiant Golf Co., $2,680.00, covering P73. C281.
      21. Recorded cash and credit card sales, $4,480.00. T21.
          Posting. Post the items that are to be posted individually.
      23. Paid cash on account to Artex Golf Products, $2,430.00, covering P74. C282.
      24. Sold merchandise on account to Jonathan Dunbar, $1,095.00. S55.
      26. Received cash on account from Bertha Welsh, $233.20, covering S51. R46.
      26. Purchased merchandise on account from Patton Golf Co., $1,285.00. P77.
      27. Received cash on account from William Backus, $795.00, covering S52. R47.
      28. Purchased merchandise on account from Artex Golf Products, $2,325.00. P78.
      28. Sold merchandise on account to Bertha Welsh, $1,095.00. S56.
      28. Recorded cash and credit card sales, $4,630.00. T28.
          Posting. Post the items that are to be posted individually.
      30. Paid cash to replenish the petty cash fund, $302.00: office supplies, $48.00; store supplies, $62.00; advertising, $74.00; miscellaneous, $118.00. C283.
      30. Recorded cash and credit card sales, $840.00. T30.
          Posting. Post the items that are to be posted individually.

   2. Total the journal. Prove the equality of debits and credits.
   3. Prove cash. The balance on the next unused check stub is $28,218.30.
   4. Rule the journal.
   5. Post the totals of the special columns of the journal.
   6. Prepare a schedule of accounts payable and a schedule of accounts receivable. Prove the accuracy of the subsidiary ledgers by comparing the schedule totals with the balances of the controlling accounts in the general ledger. If the totals are not the same, find and correct the errors.

Computer Application 3
Automated Accounting Cycle for a
Partnership: Journalizing and
Posting Transactions

A business' financial information may be recorded, summarized, and reported using either a manual or an automated accounting system. Pet-lodge, the service business described in Part 2, uses an automated accounting system. CarLand, the merchandising business described in Part 3, uses a manual accounting system. CarLand's manual journalizing procedures for purchases, cash payments, sales, and cash receipts are described in Chapters 12 and 13. Manual posting procedures are described in Chapter 14. Computer Application 3 describes procedures for using a microcomputer to journalize and post CarLand's business transactions. Computer Application Problem 3 contains instructions for using a micro-computer to solve Challenge Problem 14-C, Chapter 14.

AUTOMATED ACCOUNTING PROCEDURES FOR CARLAND

CarLand uses six forms to arrange its data for automated accounting.

1. General ledger file maintenance input form (FORM GL-1)—for building or changing a general ledger chart of accounts.
2. Accounts payable file maintenance input form (FORM AP-1)—for building or changing an accounts payable chart of accounts.
3. Accounts receivable file maintenance input form (FORM AR-1)—for building or changing an accounts receivable chart of accounts.
4. General ledger input form (FORM GL-2)—for recording general ledger opening account balances and for recording journal entries not affecting either accounts payable or accounts receivable.
5. Accounts payable input form (FORM AP-2)—for recording vendor

opening account balances and for recording purchases on account, buying supplies on account, and cash payments on account.
6. Accounts receivable input form (FORM AR-2)—for recording customer opening account balances and for recording sales on account and cash receipts on account.

BUILDING A CHART OF ACCOUNTS

CarLand's chart of accounts for the general and subsidiary ledgers is on page 250.

Building a general ledger chart of accounts

The same procedures described for Petlodge in Part 2 are used to build CarLand's general ledger chart of accounts. A general ledger file maintenance input form (FORM GL-1) is used to describe the general ledger chart of accounts for computer processing. The cash account is entered as shown in Illustration C3-1. All general ledger account numbers and titles are entered on the input form in the same way.

Illustration C3-1
General ledger file maintenance input form for chart of accounts

The General Ledger Main Menu is shown in Illustration C3-2.

Option A is selected from the General Ledger Main Menu to display spaces for key-entering the general ledger chart of accounts data into the computer. After all chart of accounts data are entered, Option B is selected from the General Ledger Main Menu. This option directs the computer to prepare a chart of accounts report.

Building an accounts payable chart of accounts

An accounts payable file maintenance input form (FORM AP-1) is used to describe CarLand's accounts payable chart of accounts for computer processing. The vendor account of Antelo Supply is shown recorded on

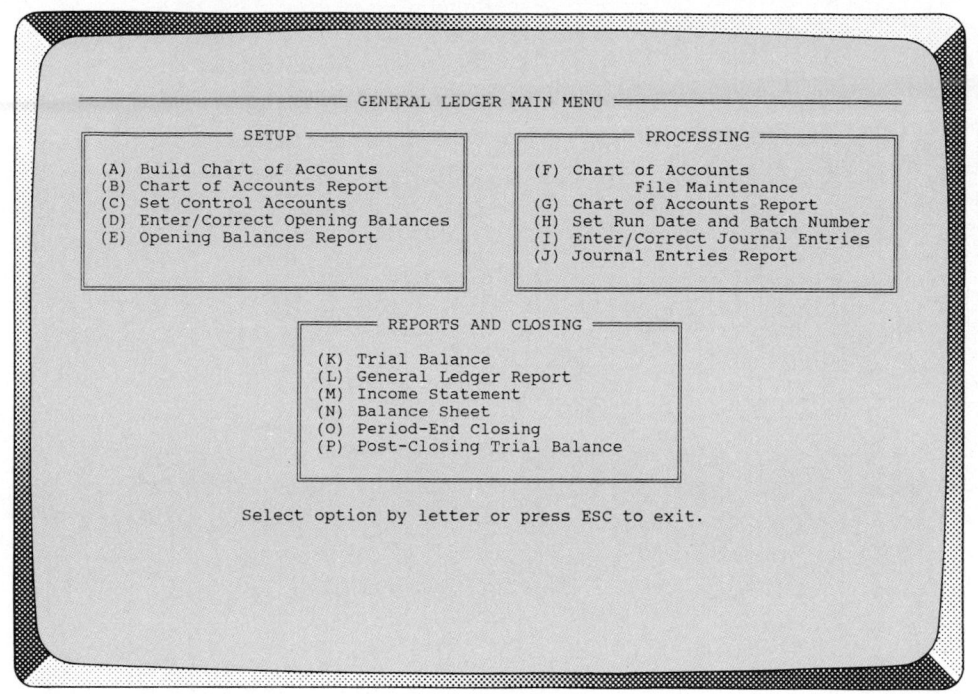

```
═══════════════════ GENERAL LEDGER MAIN MENU ═══════════════════

  ┌═ SETUP ══════════════════╗        ┌═ PROCESSING ════════════════╗
  ║                          ║        ║                             ║
  ║ (A) Build Chart of Accounts      ║ (F) Chart of Accounts         ║
  ║ (B) Chart of Accounts Report     ║         File Maintenance      ║
  ║ (C) Set Control Accounts         ║ (G) Chart of Accounts Report  ║
  ║ (D) Enter/Correct Opening Balances ║ (H) Set Run Date and Batch Number ║
  ║ (E) Opening Balances Report      ║ (I) Enter/Correct Journal Entries ║
  ║                          ║        ║ (J) Journal Entries Report    ║
  ╚══════════════════════════╝        ╚═════════════════════════════╝

            ┌═ REPORTS AND CLOSING ══════════════╗
            ║                                    ║
            ║ (K) Trial Balance                  ║
            ║ (L) General Ledger Report          ║
            ║ (M) Income Statement               ║
            ║ (N) Balance Sheet                  ║
            ║ (O) Period-End Closing             ║
            ║ (P) Post-Closing Trial Balance     ║
            ╚════════════════════════════════════╝

        Select option by letter or press ESC to exit.
```

line 1 in Illustration C3-3. All vendor numbers and names are entered on the input form in the same way.

Illustration C3-2
General ledger main menu

RUN	DATE 11/01/-- MM DD YY	ACCOUNTS PAYABLE FILE MAINTENANCE Input Form	FORM AP-1

	1	2	
	VENDOR NUMBER	VENDOR NAME	
1	210	A n t e l o S u p p l y	1
2	220	B e l l O f f i c e P r o d u c t s	2
3	230	F i l t r e x T i r e s	3
4	240	N i l o n M o t o r P a r t s	4
5	250	Q - B a n D i s t r i b u t o r s	5
6	260	V e l o z A u t o m o t i v e	6

Illustration C3-3
Accounts payable file maintenance input form for chart of accounts

The Accounts Payable Main Menu is shown in Illustration C3-4.

Option A is selected from the Accounts Payable Main Menu to display spaces for key-entering the accounts payable chart of accounts data. After all vendor accounts have been key-entered, Option B is selected from the Accounts Payable Main Menu. This option directs the computer to prepare a vendor list.

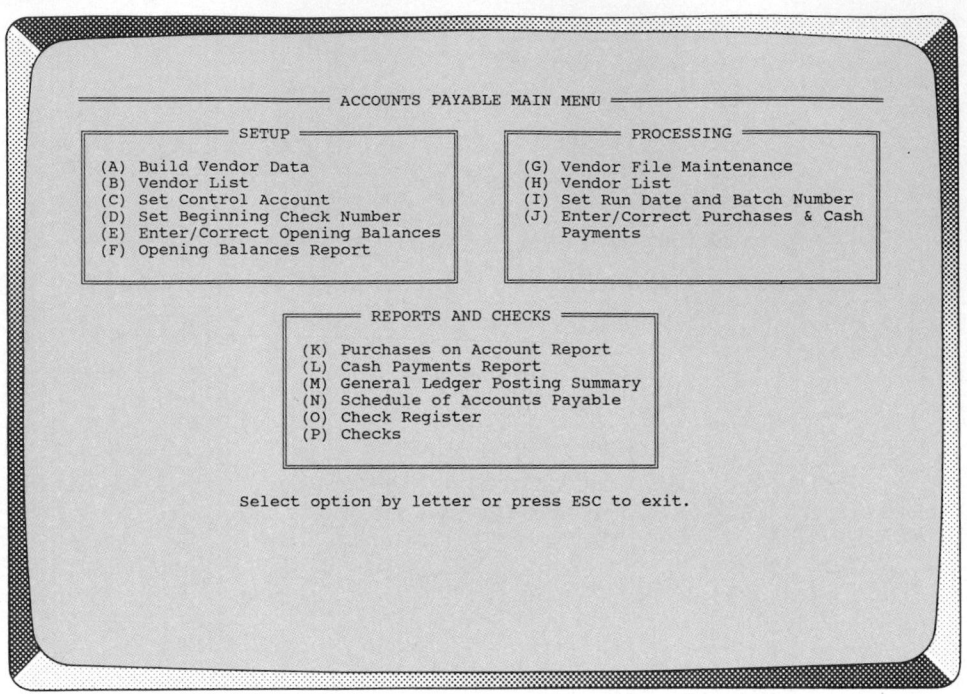

ACCOUNTS PAYABLE MAIN MENU

SETUP
(A) Build Vendor Data
(B) Vendor List
(C) Set Control Account
(D) Set Beginning Check Number
(E) Enter/Correct Opening Balances
(F) Opening Balances Report

PROCESSING
(G) Vendor File Maintenance
(H) Vendor List
(I) Set Run Date and Batch Number
(J) Enter/Correct Purchases & Cash
    Payments

REPORTS AND CHECKS
(K) Purchases on Account Report
(L) Cash Payments Report
(M) General Ledger Posting Summary
(N) Schedule of Accounts Payable
(O) Check Register
(P) Checks

Select option by letter or press ESC to exit.

Illustration C3-4
Accounts payable main
menu

Building an accounts receivable chart of accounts

An accounts receivable file maintenance input form (FORM AR-1) is used to describe CarLand's accounts receivable chart of accounts for computer processing. The customer account of Ashley Delivery is shown recorded on line 1 in Illustration C3-5. All customer numbers and names are entered on the input form in the same way.

ACCOUNTS RECEIVABLE
FILE MAINTENANCE
Input Form

FORM AR-1

RUN   DATE 11/01/--
            MM DD YY

	CUSTOMER NUMBER	CUSTOMER NAME	
1	110	Ashley Delivery	1
2	120	Autohaus Service	2
3	130	Friendly Auto Service	3
4	140	Keystone Delivery	4
5	150	Powell Rent-A-Car	5
6	160	Wood Sales & Service	6
7			7

Illustration C3-5
Accounts receivable file
maintenance input form for
chart of accounts

The Accounts Receivable Main Menu is shown in Illustration C3-6.

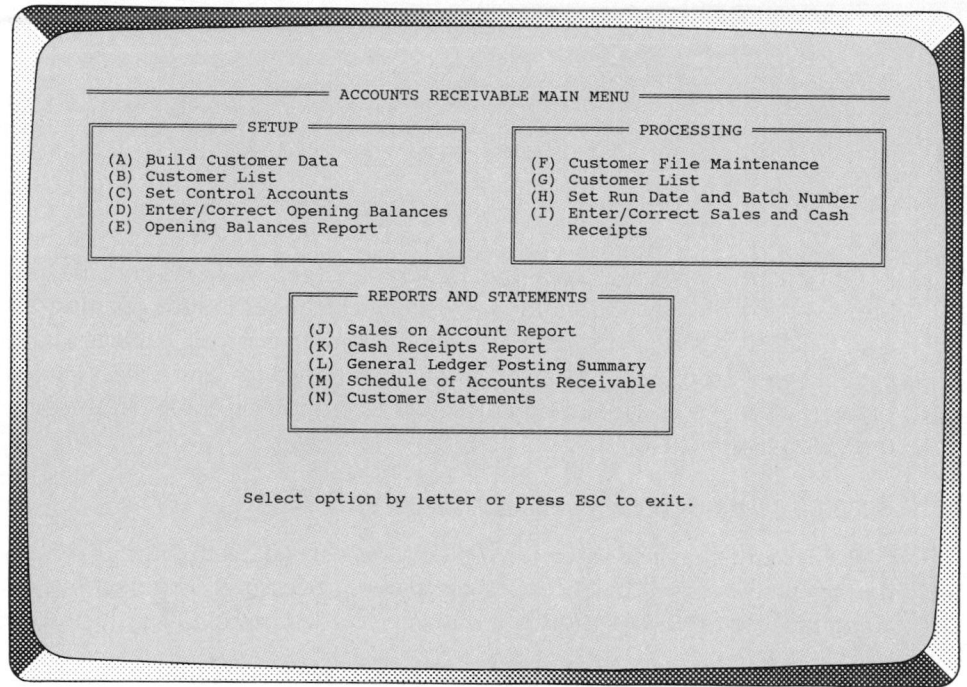

```
══════════════════ ACCOUNTS RECEIVABLE MAIN MENU ══════════════════

   ═══════ SETUP ═══════                  ═══════ PROCESSING ═══════
   (A) Build Customer Data                (F) Customer File Maintenance
   (B) Customer List                      (G) Customer List
   (C) Set Control Accounts               (H) Set Run Date and Batch Number
   (D) Enter/Correct Opening Balances     (I) Enter/Correct Sales and Cash
   (E) Opening Balances Report                Receipts


           ═══════ REPORTS AND STATEMENTS ═══════
           (J) Sales on Account Report
           (K) Cash Receipts Report
           (L) General Ledger Posting Summary
           (M) Schedule of Accounts Receivable
           (N) Customer Statements



        Select option by letter or press ESC to exit.
```

Option A is selected from the Accounts Receivable Main Menu to display spaces for key-entering the accounts receivable chart of accounts data. After all customer accounts have been key-entered, Option B is selected from the Accounts Receivable Main Menu. This option directs the computer to prepare a customer list.

Illustration C3-6
Accounts receivable main menu

RECORDING OPENING ACCOUNT BALANCES

In an automated accounting system, opening account balances for the general and subsidiary ledgers are recorded on input forms.

Recording general ledger opening account balances

A general ledger input form (FORM GL-2) is used to journalize general ledger opening account balances. The same procedures described for Petlodge, Chapter 10, are followed by CarLand to journalize general ledger opening account balances. The opening account balance for CarLand's cash account is shown in Illustration C3-7. All general ledger opening account balances are journalized in the same way.

Illustration C3-7
General ledger input form
for opening account
balances

		RUN DATE **11/01/--** MM DD YY	GENERAL LEDGER Input Form			FORM GL-2

		RUN DATE				
BATCH NO.	**1**					
	1	2	3	4	5	
	DAY	DOC. NO.	ACCOUNT NUMBER	DEBIT AMOUNT	CREDIT AMOUNT	
1	*01*	*M1*	*1110*	*14706 20*		1
2						2

Option D is selected from the General Ledger Main Menu, Illustration C3-2, to display spaces for key-entering general ledger opening account balances. After all general ledger opening account balances have been key-entered and posted, Option E is selected from the General Ledger Main Menu. This option directs the computer to prepare an opening balances report.

Recording vendor opening account balances

An accounts payable input form (FORM AP-2) is used to journalize vendor opening account balances for computer processing. The opening account balance for Q-Ban Distributors is shown recorded on line 1 in Illustration C3-8.

RUN DATE **11/01/--** MM DD YY

BATCH NO. **1**

ACCOUNTS PAYABLE
Input Form

FORM AP-2

	1	2	3			4	5	6			7	8	
			PURCHASES					CASH PAYMENTS					
	PURCH. INVOICE NO.	VEND. NO.	DATE			GEN. LEDGER ACCT. NO.	INVOICE AMOUNT	DATE			DISP. CODE	MANUAL CHECK NO.	
			MO.	DAY	YR.			MO.	DAY	YR.			
1	*P71*	*250*	*10*	*06*	*--*	*5110*	*3960 00*				*A*		1
2	*P72*	*230*	*10*	*07*	*--*	*5110*	*970 00*				*A*		2
3	*M35*	*210*	*10*	*12*	*--*	*1150*	*430 00*				*A*		3
4	*P73*	*240*	*10*	*20*	*--*	*5110*	*4840 00*				*A*		4
5	*M39*	*220*	*10*	*23*	*--*	*1145*	*620 00*				*A*		5
6													6
24													24
25													25

BATCH TOTAL   *10820 00*

DISPOSITION CODE:
A = ON ACCOUNT
M = MANUAL CHECK

Illustration C3-8
Accounts payable input
form for vendor opening
account balances

Nine steps are followed to journalize the opening account balance for Q-Ban Distributors on an accounts payable input form.

1 Enter the run date, *11/01/--*, in the space provided at the top of the form. The run date is the date CarLand starts its automated accounting system.

2 Enter the batch number, *1*, in the space provided at the top of the form. The number assigned to a group of journal entries is known as a batch number. Since the vendor opening account balances represent the first entries to the accounts payable ledger, batch number 1 is assigned.

3 Enter the purchase invoice number, *P71*, in the Purch. Invoice No. column. The purchase invoice number is the source document number for merchandise purchased on account still owed by CarLand. (CON-CEPT: *Objective Evidence*)

4 Enter the vendor number, *250*, in the Vend. No. column. The vendor number is obtained from the vendor list.

5 Enter the date, *10/06/--*, in the Purchases Date column. This date is the date of Purchase Invoice No. 71.

6 Enter the general ledger account number for Purchases, *5110*, in the Gen. Ledger Acct. No. column.

7 Enter the amount, *$3,960.00*, in the Invoice Amount column.

8 Enter the disposition code, *A*, in the Disp. Code column. A disposition code indicates the action to be performed on the entry. Entering an *A* in this column indicates that the entry is a purchase of merchandise on account or a supplies bought on account transaction. This action is similar to recording a debit to Purchases and a credit to Accounts Payable in a journal. Entering an *M* in this column indicates that a previously recorded entry to Accounts Payable is to be paid with a check prepared manually. This action is similar to recording a debit to Accounts Payable and a credit to Cash in a journal.

9 After all vendor opening account balances have been journalized, the Invoice Amount column is totaled. The total is entered on the Batch Total line provided at the bottom of the form. If more than one accounts payable input form is required to journalize vendor opening account balances, the Invoice Amount column for all pages is totaled. The total for all pages is then entered *only* on the last page on the Batch Total line.

All vendor opening account balances are journalized in the same way. Some vendor account opening balances, however, are for supplies bought on account rather than purchases of merchandise on account. The entry for Antelo Supply on line 3 of the accounts payable input form in Illustration C3-8 is for supplies bought on account. The source document number recorded in the Purch. Invoice No. column is *M35*, the memorandum prepared when the supplies were bought on account. The general ledger account number recorded in the Gen. Ledger Acct. No. column is *1150*, the account number for Supplies—Store. This has the effect of recording a debit to Supplies—Store and a credit to Accounts Payable.

Option E is selected from the Accounts Payable Main Menu, Illustration C3-4, to display spaces for key-entering each vendor account balance. After all vendor opening account balances have been key-entered and posted, Option F is selected from the Accounts Payable Main Menu. This option directs the computer to prepare an opening balances report. The vendor opening balances report is checked for accuracy by comparing the report total with the batch total on the accounts payable input form. If the totals are not the same, the errors must be found and corrected. If the totals are the same, the vendor opening balances report is assumed to be correct.

Recording customer opening account balances

An accounts receivable input form (FORM AR-2) is used to journalize customer opening account balances for computer processing. The opening account balance for Autohaus Service is shown recorded on line 1 in Illustration C3-9. All customer opening account balances are journalized in the same way.

	SALES INVOICE NO.	CUST. NO.	DATE MO.	DATE DAY	DATE YR.	GEN. LEDGER ACCT. NO.	INVOICE AMOUNT	SALES TAX %	DATE MO.	DATE DAY	DATE YR.	DOC. NO.	CASH RECEIVED	
1	S65	120	10	06	--	4110	1700 00	6						1
2	S66	140	10	10	--	4110	900 00	6						2
3	S67	160	10	13	--	4110	850 00	6						3
4	S68	150	10	14	--	4110	300 00	6						4
5	S69	110	10	17	--	4110	2350 00	6						5
6	S70	160	10	20	--	4110	1150 00	6						6
7	S71	130	10	25	--	4110	250 00	6						7
8														8
24														24
25														25

RUN DATE 11 01 / -- (MM DD YY)   BATCH NO. 1

ACCOUNTS RECEIVABLE Input Form   FORM AR-2

BATCH TOTALS   7500 00

Illustration C3-9
Accounts receivable input form for customer opening account balances

Nine steps are followed to journalize the opening account balance for Autohaus Service on an accounts receivable input form.

1 Enter the run date, *11/01/--*, in the space provided at the top of the form. The run date is the date CarLand starts its automated accounting system.

2 Enter the batch number, *1*, in the space provided at the top of the form. Since the customer opening account balances represent the first entries to the accounts receivable ledger, batch number 1 is assigned.

3 Enter the sales invoice number, *S65*, in the Sales Invoice No. column. This sales invoice number is the source document number for a sale of merchandise on account still due CarLand. *(CONCEPT: Objective Evidence)*

4 Enter the customer number, *120*, in the Cust. No. column. The customer number is obtained from the customer list.

5 Enter the date, *10/06/--*, in the Sales Date column. This date is the date CarLand issued Sales Invoice No. 65.

6 Enter the general ledger account number for Sales, *4110*, in the Gen. Ledger Acct. No. column.

7 Enter the amount, *$1,700.00*, in the Invoice Amount column.

8 Enter the sales tax percent, *6*, in the Sales Tax % column. The computer figures the sales tax amount based on the sales tax rate entered in the Sales Tax % column. CarLand operates in a state with a 6% sales tax rate.

9 After all customer opening account balances have been journalized, the Invoice Amount column is totaled. The total is recorded on the Batch Totals line provided at the bottom of the form. If more than one accounts receivable input form is required to record opening account balances, the Invoice Amount column for all pages is totaled. The total for all pages is then recorded *only* on the last page on the Batch Totals line.

Option D is selected from the Accounts Receivable Main Menu, Illustration C3-6, to display spaces for key-entering each customer account balance. After all customer opening account balances have been key-entered and posted, Option E is selected from the Accounts Receivable Main Menu. This option directs the computer to prepare an opening balances report. The customer opening balances report is checked for accuracy by comparing the report total with the batch total on the accounts receivable input form. If the totals are not the same, the errors must be found and corrected. If the totals are the same, the customer opening balances report is assumed to be correct.

RECORDING TRANSACTIONS
NOT AFFECTING SUBSIDIARY LEDGERS

CarLand records all transactions that affect vendor and customer accounts on accounts payable and accounts receivable input forms. All other transactions are recorded on a general ledger input form.

Purchase of merchandise for cash

November 2, 19--.
Purchased merchandise for cash, $483.00. Check No. 259.

The entry to journalize this transaction is on lines 1 and 2 of the general ledger input form shown in Illustration C3-10. Purchases is debited and Cash is credited for $483.00.

The run date, *11/30/--*, is written in the space provided at the top of the form. The run date indicates that the transaction data entered on the input form are for November 1 through 30. The batch number, 2, is written in the space provided at the top of the form. Since batch number 1 was assigned to the general ledger opening account balances, batch number 2 is used for the group of journal entries for November 1 through 30.

On line 1, the day, *02*, is written in the Day column. The document number, *C259*, is entered in the Doc. No. column. The purchases account number, *5110*, is written in the Account Number column. The amount debited to Purchases, *$483.00*, is entered in the Debit Amount column.

On line 2, the cash account number, *1110*, is written in the Account Number column. The Day and Doc. No. columns are left blank starting with the second line of an entry. The date and document number are entered only once for each complete transaction. The amount credited to Cash, *$483.00*, is written in the Credit Amount column.

The same procedures are used to journalize any transactions that do not affect either the accounts payable or accounts receivable subsidiary ledgers.

Buying supplies for cash

November 5, 19--.
Paid cash for office supplies, $87.00. Check No. 261.

The entry to journalize this transaction is on lines 5 and 6 of Illustration C3-10. Supplies—Office is debited and Cash is credited for $87.00.

Cash and credit card sales

November 7, 19--.
Recorded cash and credit card sales, $6,450.00, plus sales tax, $387.00; total, $6,837.00. Cash Register Tape No. 7.

The entry to journalize this transaction is on lines 7 through 9 of Illustration C3-10. Cash is debited for $6,837.00. Sales Tax Payable is credited for $387.00. Sales is credited for $6,450.00.

RUN DATE _11 / 30 / --_
MM DD YY

BATCH NO. 2

GENERAL LEDGER
Input Form

FORM GL-2

	DAY	DOC. NO.	ACCOUNT NUMBER	DEBIT AMOUNT	CREDIT AMOUNT	
1	02	C259	5110	483 00		1
2			1110		483 00	2
3	02	C260	6160	1500 00		3
4			1110		1500 00	4
5	05	C261	1145	87 00		5
6			1110		87 00	6
7	07	T7	1110	6837 00		7
8			2140		387 00	8
9			4110		6450 00	9
10	09	C264	6190	300 00		10
11			1110		300 00	11
12	09	C265	6110	125 00		12
13			1110		125 00	13
14	09	C266	1145	58 00		14
15			1150	65 00		15
16			6110	92 00		16
17			6140	86 00		17
18			1110		301 00	18
19	10	C267	3140	1500 00		19
20			1110		1500 00	20
21	12	M44	3140	200 00		21
22			5110		200 00	22
23	13	M45	6110	120 00		23
24			6140		120 00	24
25						25
22	30	T30	1110	1219 00		22
23			2140		69 00	23
24			4110		1150 00	24
25						25
			BATCH TOTALS	38863 22	38863 22	

Illustration C3-10
General ledger input form
with transactions entered

Cash payment of an expense

November 9, 19--.
Paid cash for advertising, $125.00. Check No. 265.

The entry to journalize this transaction is on lines 12 and 13 of Illustration C3-10. Advertising Expense is debited and Cash is credited for $125.00.

Cash payment to replenish petty cash

November 9, 19--.
Paid cash to replenish the petty cash fund, $301.00: office supplies, $58.00; store supplies, $65.00; advertising, $92.00; miscellaneous, $86.00. Check No. 266.

The entry to journalize this transaction is on lines 14 through 18 of Illustration C3-10. Supplies—Office is debited for $58.00, and Supplies—Store is debited for $65.00. Advertising Expense is debited for $92.00, and Miscellaneous Expense is debited for $86.00. Cash is credited for $301.00, the total amount needed to replenish the petty cash fund.

Changes in capital

November 10, 19--.
Dario Mesa, partner, withdrew cash for personal use, $1,500.00. Check No. 267.

The entry to journalize this transaction is on lines 19 and 20 of Illustration C3-10. Dario Mesa, Drawing is debited and Cash is credited for $1,500.00.

November 12, 19--.
Dario Mesa, partner, withdrew merchandise for personal use, $200.00. Memorandum No. 44.

The entry to journalize this transaction is on lines 21 and 22 of Illustration C3-10. Dario Mesa, Drawing is debited and Purchases is credited for $200.00.

Correcting entry

November 13, 19--.
Discovered that a payment of cash for advertising in October was journalized and posted in error as a debit to Miscellaneous Expense instead of Advertising Expense, $120.00. Memorandum No. 45.

The entry to journalize this transaction is on lines 23 and 24 of Illustration C3-10. Advertising Expense is debited and Miscellaneous Expense is credited for $120.00.

Carland's general ledger input form has 25 lines. After the correcting entry is recorded on lines 23 and 24, only one line remains on the form. The debit and credit parts of a transaction should always be recorded on the same page of an input form. Therefore, the next transaction is recorded on the second page of a general ledger input form.

CarLand's general ledger entries required three pages of general ledger input forms. The last four lines of the third page are shown at the bottom of Illustration C3-10.

After all transactions have been journalized, the Debit Amount and Credit Amount columns are totaled. The totals are entered on the Batch

Totals line provided at the bottom of the last page of general ledger input forms. The amount columns for all pages are totaled. The totals for all pages are then entered *only* on the last page on the Batch Totals line. The two totals are compared to assure that debits equal credits. As the two totals are the same, $38,863.22, the entries on the general ledger input form are assumed to be correct.

Processing transactions not affecting subsidiary ledgers

Option H is selected from the General Ledger Main Menu, Illustration C3-2, to set the run date, *11/30/--*, and the batch number, 2. Option I is selected from the General Ledger Main Menu to display spaces for entering the journal entries. After all lines on the input forms for batch number 2 have been entered and posted, Option J is selected from the General Ledger Main Menu. This option directs the computer to prepare a journal entries report. CarLand's journal entries report is shown in Illustration C3-11 on page 324.

Each journal entries report is checked for accuracy by comparing the report totals with the totals on the general ledger input form. As the totals are the same, $38,863.22, the journal entries report is assumed to be correct and is filed for future reference. If the totals are not the same, the errors must be found and corrected.

RECORDING ACCOUNTS PAYABLE TRANSACTIONS

Three types of transactions affect CarLand's accounts payable. (1) Purchases of merchandise on account. (2) Buying supplies on account. (3) Cash payments on account. An accounts payable input form (FORM AP-2) is used to journalize all transactions affecting accounts payable.

Purchase of merchandise on account

November 2, 19--.
Purchased merchandise on account from Veloz Automotive, $1,754.00. Purchase Invoice No. 74.

The entry to journalize this transaction is on line 1 of Illustration C3-12 on page 325.

The run date, *11/30/--*, is written in the space provided at the top of the form. The run date indicates that the transaction data journalized on the input form are for the month ended November 30. The batch number, 2, is written in the space provided at the top of the form. Batch number 1 was assigned to the accounts payable opening balances. The purchase invoice number, *P74*, is entered in the Purch. Invoice No. column. The vendor number, *260*, is recorded in the Vend. No. column. The day, *11/02/--*, is written in the Purchases Date columns. The purchases account number, *5110*, is entered in the Gen. Ledger Acct. No. column. The invoice amount,

```
RUN DATE: 11/30/--                          CARLAND
                                    JOURNAL ENTRIES BATCH# 2

------------------------------------------------------------------------
JE#   DATE       ACCOUNT NUMBER & TITLE           DEBIT AMOUNT  CREDIT AMOUNT
------------------------------------------------------------------------
0005  11/02/-- 5110     Purchases                    483.00
               1110        Cash                                    483.00
                        DOCUMENT: C259

0006  11/02/-- 6160     Rent Expense                1500.00
               1110        Cash                                   1500.00
                        DOCUMENT: C260

0007  11/05/-- 1145     Supplies--Office              87.00
               1110        Cash                                     87.00
                        DOCUMENT: C261

0008  11/07/-- 1110     Cash                        6837.00
               2140        Sales Tax Payable                      387.00
               4110        Sales                                 6450.00
                        DOCUMENT: T7

0009  11/09/-- 6190     Utilities Expense            300.00
               1110        Cash                                    300.00
                        DOCUMENT: C264

0010  11/09/-- 6110     Advertising Expense          125.00
               1110        Cash                                    125.00
                        DOCUMENT: C265

0011  11/09/-- 1145     Supplies--Office              58.00
               1150     Supplies--Store               65.00
               6110     Advertising Expense           92.00
               6140     Miscellaneous Expense         86.00
               1110        Cash                                    301.00
                        DOCUMENT: C266

0012  11/10/-- 3140     Dario Mesa, Drawing         1500.00
               1110        Cash                                   1500.00
                        DOCUMENT: C267

0013  11/12/-- 3140     Dario Mesa, Drawing          200.00
               5110        Purchases                              200.00
                        DOCUMENT: M44

0014  11/13/-- 6110     Advertising Expense          120.00
               6140        Miscellaneous Expense                  120.00
                        DOCUMENT: M45

0026  11/30/-- 1110     Cash                        1219.00
               2140        Sales Tax Payable                       69.00
               4110        Sales                                  1150.00
                        DOCUMENT: T30

                                                 --------------- ---------------
               TOTALS                               38863.22      38863.22
                                                 =============== ===============
               IN BALANCE

Cash Receipts        24274.00
Cash Payments        12560.20
```

Illustration C3-11   Journal entries report

$1,754.00, is written in the Invoice Amount column. The disposition code, *A*, is entered in the Disp. Code column. Entering an *A* in this column indicates that the entry is on account.

Buying supplies on account

November 6, 19--.
Bought store supplies on account from Antelo Supply, $160.00. Memorandum No. 43.

The entry to journalize this transaction is on line 4 of Illustration C3-12. The procedures for journalizing this entry are the same as for a purchase of merchandise on account except for the entries in the Purch. Invoice No. and Gen. Ledger Acct. No. columns. The memorandum number, *M43*, is written in the Purch. Invoice No. column. The store supplies account number, *1150*, is entered in the Gen. Ledger Acct. No. column.

RUN DATE 11 / 30 / --
MM DD YY

BATCH NO. 2

ACCOUNTS PAYABLE
Input Form

FORM AP-2

	1	2	3			4	5	6			7	8	
			PURCHASES					CASH PAYMENTS					
	PURCH. INVOICE NO.	VEND. NO.	DATE			GEN. LEDGER ACCT. NO.	INVOICE AMOUNT	DATE			DISP. CODE	MANUAL CHECK NO.	
			MO.	DAY	YR.			MO.	DAY	YR.			
1	P74	260	11	02	--	5110	1754 00				A		1
2	P75	240	11	04	--	5110	3456 00				A		2
3	P76	230	11	05	--	5110	3180 00				A		3
4	M43	210	11	06	--	1150	160 00				A		4
5	P71							11	06	--	M	262	5
6	P72							11	07	--	M	263	6
7	M35							11	12	--	M	268	7
8	P77	250	11	13	--	5110	3140 00				A		8
9	P78	250	11	20	--	5110	2760 00				A		9
10	P73							11	20	--	M	273	10
11	M47	210	11	23	--	1150	590 00				A		11
12	M39							11	23	--	M	274	12
13	M48	220	11	24	--	1145	830 00				A		13
14													14
24													24
25													25

BATCH TOTAL   15870 00

DISPOSITION CODE:
A = ON ACCOUNT
M = MANUAL CHECK

Illustration C3-12
Accounts payable input form with transactions entered

Cash payment on account

November 7, 19--.
Paid cash on account to Filtrex Tires, $970.00, covering Purchase Invoice
No. 72. Check No. 263.

The entry to journalize this transaction is on line 6 of Illustration C3-12.

The purchase invoice number to be paid, *P72*, is entered in the Purch. Invoice No. column. The Purchases columns are left blank for a cash payment on account transaction. These data were stored on secondary storage when the initial purchase of merchandise on account was journalized and posted. The date, *11/07/--*, is entered in the Cash Payments Date columns. The disposition code, *M*, is written in the Disp. Code column. Writing an *M* in the Disp. Code column indicates that a check is to be manually prepared. The manual check number, *263*, is entered in the Manual Check No. column.

After all accounts payable transactions have been journalized, the Invoice Amount column is totaled. The total is entered on the Batch Total line provided at the bottom of the accounts payable input form, as shown in Illustration C3-12. If more than one accounts payable input form is required to journalize accounts payable transactions, the Invoice Amount column for all pages is totaled. The total for all pages is then entered *only* on the last page on the Batch Total line.

Processing accounts payable transactions

Option I is selected from the Accounts Payable Main Menu, Illustration C3-4, to set the run date, *11/30/--*, and the batch number, 2. Option J is selected from the Accounts Payable Main Menu to display spaces for entering purchases and cash payments. After all lines on the input form have been entered and posted, Option K is selected from the Accounts Payable Main Menu. This option directs the computer to prepare a purchases on account report. CarLand's purchases on account report is shown in Illustration C3-13.

Illustration C3-13
Purchases on account
report

```
RUN DATE: 11/30/--                    CARLAND
                         PURCHASES ON ACCOUNT BATCH# 2

     -----------------------------------------------------------
     VENDOR                     PURCH.       G.L.
     NO. NAME                   INV.  DATE   ACCOUNT    AMOUNT
     -----------------------------------------------------------
     260 Veloz Automotive       P74   11/02/-- 5110     1754.00
     240 Nilon Motor Parts      P75   11/04/-- 5110     3456.00
     230 Filtrex Tires          P76   11/05/-- 5110     3180.00
     210 Antelo Supply          M43   11/06/-- 1150      160.00
     250 Q-Ban Distributors     P77   11/13/-- 5110     3140.00
     250 Q-Ban Distributors     P78   11/20/-- 5110     2760.00
     210 Antelo Supply          M47   11/23/-- 1150      590.00
     220 Bell Office Products   M48   11/24/-- 1145      830.00
                                                      ----------
        TOTALS                                        15870.00
                                                      ==========
```

The purchases on account report is checked for accuracy by comparing the report total with the batch total of the accounts payable input form. As the total is the same, $15,870.00, the purchases on account report is assumed to be correct. The accounts payable input form and purchases on account report are filed for future reference.

Option L is selected from the Accounts Payable Main Menu to direct the computer to prepare a cash payments report. CarLand's cash payments report is shown in Illustration C3-14.

```
RUN DATE: 11/30/--                   CARLAND
                              CASH PAYMENTS BATCH# 2

         -----------------------------------------------------------------
         VENDOR                         INVOICE                      MAN.
         NO. NAME                       NO.   DATE    AMOUNT  TYPE    CHK.
         -----------------------------------------------------------------
         250 Q-Ban Distributors         P71 11/06/--  3960.00 Payment 262
         230 Filtrex Tires              P72 11/07/--   970.00 Payment 263
         210 Antelo Supply              M35 11/12/--   430.00 Payment 268
         240 Nilon Motor Parts          P73 11/20/--  4840.00 Payment 273
         220 Bell Office Products       M39 11/23/--   620.00 Payment 274

            TOTAL CASH PAYMENTS   10820.00
```

Illustration C3-14
Cash payments report

Option M is selected from the Accounts Payable Main Menu to direct the computer to prepare a general ledger posting summary. This summary lists all entries posted by the computer to the general ledger resulting from processing the accounts payable transactions. The general ledger posting summary for accounts payable transactions is shown in Illustration C3-15.

```
RUN DATE: 11/30/--                   CARLAND
                       GENERAL LEDGER POSTING SUMMARY BATCH# 2

         -----------------------------------------------------------------
         ACCOUNT ACCOUNT
         NUMBER  TITLE                     DEBIT        CREDIT
         -----------------------------------------------------------------
         1110    Cash                                  10820.00
         1145    Supplies--Office          830.00
         1150    Supplies--Store           750.00
         2110    Accounts Payable        10820.00
         2110    Accounts Payable                      15870.00
         5110    Purchases               14290.00
                                         -----------  -----------
                 TOTALS                    26690.00     26690.00
                                         ===========  ===========
```

Illustration C3-15
General ledger posting summary for accounts payable transactions

Option N is selected from the Accounts Payable Main Menu to prepare a schedule of accounts payable. CarLand's schedule of accounts payable on November 30 is shown in Illustration C3-16.

```
RUN DATE: 11/30/--                      CARLAND
                               SCHEDULE OF ACCOUNTS PAYABLE

  -----------------------------------------
  VENDOR NUMBER AND NAME
          INVOICE    DATE        AMOUNT
  -----------------------------------------
  210   Antelo Supply
              M43    11/06/--     160.00
              M47    11/23/--     590.00
          VENDOR TOTAL            750.00

  220   Bell Office Products
              M48    11/24/--     830.00
          VENDOR TOTAL            830.00

  230   Filtrex Tires
              P76    11/05/--    3180.00
          VENDOR TOTAL           3180.00

  240   Nilon Motor Parts
              P75    11/04/--    3456.00
          VENDOR TOTAL           3456.00

  250   Q-Ban Distributors
              P77    11/13/--    3140.00
              P78    11/20/--    2760.00
          VENDOR TOTAL           5900.00

  260   Veloz Automotive
              P74    11/02/--    1754.00
          VENDOR TOTAL           1754.00

                                -----------
  FINAL TOTAL                    15870.00
                                ===========
```

Illustration C3-16
Schedule of accounts
payable

RECORDING ACCOUNTS RECEIVABLE TRANSACTIONS

Two types of transactions affect CarLand's accounts receivable. (1) Sales on account. (2) Cash receipts on account. An accounts receivable input form (FORM AR-2) is used to journalize all transactions affecting accounts receivable.

Sale on account

November 3, 19--.
Sold merchandise on account to Friendly Auto Service, $680.00, plus sales tax, $40.80; total, $720.80. Sales Invoice No. 72.

The entry to journalize this transaction is shown recorded on line 1 of Illustration C3-17.

The run date, *11/30/--*, is written in the space provided at the top of the form. The run date indicates that the transaction data entered on the input form are for the month ended November 30. The batch number, 2, is written in the space provided at the top of the form. Batch number 1 was assigned to the opening accounts receivable balances. The sales invoice number, *S72*, is entered in the Sales Invoice No. column. The customer number is entered in the Cust. No. column. The date, *11/03/--*, is entered in the Sales Date columns. The sales account number, *4110*, is written in the Gen. Ledger Acct. No. column. The invoice amount, *$680.00*, is entered in the Invoice Amount column. The sales tax rate, *6*, is written in the Sales Tax % column. The Cash Receipts columns are left blank for a sale on account entry. These columns are used only to enter a cash receipt on account entry.

RUN DATE 11/30/-- MM DD YY

BATCH NO. 2

ACCOUNTS RECEIVABLE
Input Form

FORM AR-2

	SALES INVOICE NO.	CUST. NO.	MO.	DAY	YR.	GEN. LEDGER ACCT. NO.	INVOICE AMOUNT	SALES TAX %	MO.	DAY	YR.	DOC. NO.	CASH RECEIVED	
1	S72	130	11	03	--	4110	680 00	6						1
2	S73	150	11	05	--	4110	1500 00	6						2
3	S65								11	06	--	R86	1802 00	3
4	S74	110	11	09	--	4110	450 00	6						4
5	S66								11	10	--	R87	954 00	5
6	S75	160	11	11	--	4110	570 00	6						6
7	S67								11	13	--	R88	901 00	7
8	S68								11	14	--	R89	318 00	8
9	S76	110	11	16	--	4110	1300 00	6						9
10	S69								11	17	--	R90	2491 00	10
11	S77	120	11	18	--	4110	1900 00	6						11
12	S70								11	20	--	R91	1219 00	12
13	S78	130	11	24	--	4110	700 00	6						13
14	S79	140	11	24	--	4110	300 00	6						14
15	S71								11	25	--	R92	265 00	15
16	S80	140	11	29	--	4110	1300 00	6						16

BATCH TOTALS 8700 00   7950 00

Illustration C3-17
Accounts receivable input form with transactions entered

Cash receipt on account

November 6, 19--.
Received cash on account from Autohaus Service, $1,802.00, covering S65. Receipt No. 86.

The entry to journalize this transaction is on line 3 of Illustration C3-17.

The sales invoice number for the cash received, *S65*, is written in the Sales Invoice No. column. The Sales columns are left blank for a cash receipt on account transaction. These data were stored on secondary storage when the initial sale on account transaction was journalized and posted. The date, *11/06/--*, is written in the Cash Receipts Date columns. The source document number, *R86*, is entered in the Doc. No. column. The amount of cash received, *$1,802.00*, is written in the Cash Received column.

After all accounts receivable transactions have been journalized, the Invoice Amount and Cash Received columns are totaled. The totals are entered on the Batch Totals line provided at the bottom of the form. If more than one accounts receivable input form is required to journalize accounts receivable transactions, the amount columns for all pages are totaled. The totals for all pages are then entered *only* on the last page on the Batch Totals line.

Processing accounts receivable transactions

Option H is selected from the Accounts Receivable Main Menu, Illustration C3-6, to set the run date, *11/30/--*, and the batch number, *2*. Option I is selected from the Accounts Receivable Main Menu to display spaces for entering sales and cash receipts. After all lines on the input form have been entered and posted, Option J is selected from the Accounts Receivable Main Menu. This option directs the computer to prepare a sales on account report. CarLand's sales on account report is shown in Illustration C3-18.

Illustration C3-18
Sales on account report

```
RUN DATE: 11/30/--                    CARLAND
                           SALES ON ACCOUNT BATCH# 2

      -------------------------------------------------------------------
      CUSTOMER                    INVOICE           G.L.    INVOICE    SALES
      NO. NAME                    NO.     DATE    ACCOUNT   AMOUNT     TAX
      -------------------------------------------------------------------
      130 Friendly Auto Service   S72   11/03/--   4110      680.00    40.80
      150 Powell Rent-A-Car       S73   11/05/--   4110     1500.00    90.00
      110 Ashley Delivery         S74   11/09/--   4110      450.00    27.00
      160 Wood Sales & Service    S75   11/11/--   4110      570.00    34.20
      110 Ashley Delivery         S76   11/16/--   4110     1300.00    78.00
      120 Autohaus Service        S77   11/18/--   4110     1900.00   114.00
      130 Friendly Auto Service   S78   11/24/--   4110      700.00    42.00
      140 Keystone Delivery       S79   11/24/--   4110      300.00    18.00
      140 Keystone Delivery       S80   11/29/--   4110     1300.00    78.00
                                                         ---------  ---------
      TOTALS                                             8700.00    522.00
                                                         =========  =========
```

The sales on account report is checked for accuracy by comparing the report total with the input form batch total of the Invoice Amount column. As the total is the same, $8,700.00, the sales on account total is assumed to be correct.

Option K is selected from the Accounts Receivable Main Menu to direct the computer to prepare a cash receipts report. CarLand's cash receipts report is shown in Illustration C3-19.

```
RUN DATE: 11/30/--                    CARLAND
                            CASH RECEIPTS BATCH# 2
     --------------------------------------------------------------
     CUSTOMER                    INVOICE          DOC.
     NO. NAME                    NO.    DATE      NO.      AMOUNT TYPE
     --------------------------------------------------------------
     120 Autohaus Service        S65   11/06/--   R86     1802.00 Receipt
     140 Keystone Delivery       S66   11/10/--   R87      954.00 Receipt
     160 Wood Sales & Service    S67   11/13/--   R88      901.00 Receipt
     150 Powell Rent-A-Car       S68   11/14/--   R89      318.00 Receipt
     110 Ashley Delivery         S69   11/17/--   R90     2491.00 Receipt
     160 Wood Sales & Service    S70   11/20/--   R91     1219.00 Receipt
     130 Friendly Auto Service   S71   11/25/--   R92      265.00 Receipt
                                                        ----------
         TOTALS                                          7950.00
                                                        ==========
```

The cash receipts report is checked for accuracy by comparing the report total with the input form batch total of the Cash Received column. As the totals are the same, $7,950.00, the cash received amount is assumed to be correct. The accounts receivable input form and the sales on account and cash receipts reports are then filed for future reference.

Illustration C3-19
Cash receipts report

Option L is selected from the Accounts Receivable Main Menu to direct the computer to prepare a general ledger posting summary. This summary lists all entries posted by the computer to the general ledger resulting from processing the accounts receivable transactions. CarLand's general ledger posting summary for accounts receivable transactions is shown in Illustration C3-20.

Illustration C3-20
General ledger posting
summary for accounts
receivable transactions

```
RUN DATE: 11/30/--                    CARLAND
                  GENERAL LEDGER POSTING SUMMARY BATCH# 2
     --------------------------------------------------------------
     ACCOUNT ACCOUNT
     NUMBER  TITLE                      DEBIT        CREDIT
     --------------------------------------------------------------
     1110    Cash                       7950.00
     1130    Accounts Receivable        9222.00
     1130    Accounts Receivable                     7950.00
     2140    Sales Tax Payable                        522.00
     4110    Sales                                   8700.00
                                      -----------  -----------
             TOTALS                     17172.00     17172.00
                                      ===========  ===========
```

Option M is selected from the Accounts Receivable Main Menu to direct the computer to prepare a schedule of accounts receivable. CarLand's schedule of accounts receivable on November 30 is shown in Illustration C3-21.

Illustration C3-21
Schedule of accounts
receivable

```
RUN DATE: 11/30/--                      CARLAND
                          SCHEDULE OF ACCOUNTS RECEIVABLE

-----------------------------------------------------------
CUSTOMER                        INVOICE
NO. NAME                        NO.   DATE       AMOUNT
-----------------------------------------------------------
110 Ashley Delivery             S74   11/09/--    477.00
110 Ashley Delivery             S76   11/16/--   1378.00
    CUSTOMER TOTAL                               1855.00

120 Autohaus Service            S77   11/18/--   2014.00
    CUSTOMER TOTAL                               2014.00

130 Friendly Auto Service       S72   11/03/--    720.80
130 Friendly Auto Service       S78   11/24/--    742.00
    CUSTOMER TOTAL                               1462.80

140 Keystone Delivery           S79   11/24/--    318.00
140 Keystone Delivery           S80   11/29/--   1378.00
    CUSTOMER TOTAL                               1696.00

150 Powell Rent-A-Car           S73   11/05/--   1590.00
    CUSTOMER TOTAL                               1590.00

160 Wood Sales & Service        S75   11/11/--    604.20
    CUSTOMER TOTAL                                604.20

                                             -----------
    FINAL TOTAL                                  9222.00
                                             ===========
```

■ COMPUTER APPLICATION PROBLEM

COMPUTER APPLICATION PROBLEM 3   Journalizing and posting transactions

Instructions: 1. Journalize transactions from Challenge Problem 14-C, Chapter 14, on appropriate computer input forms.

a. Journalize entries *NOT* affecting either accounts payable or accounts receivable on a general ledger input form (FORM GL-2). Use November 30 of the current year as the run date. Batch No. 2.

b. Journalize purchases on account, supplies bought on account, and cash payments on account on an accounts payable input form (FORM AP-2). Use November 30 of the current year as the run date. Batch No. 2.

c. Journalize sales on account and cash received on account on an accounts receivable input form (FORM AR-2). Use November 30 of the current year as the run date. Batch No. 2.

2. Load the *Automated Accounting for the Microcomputer* software. Select Computer Application 3 (CA-3) from the CENTURY 21 ACCOUNTING Template Disk. The accounting system data, chart of accounts, opening balances, and company name have been entered and are stored on the Template Disk.

3. Key-enter data from the completed general ledger input form.
4. Display/Print the journal entries report.
5. Key-enter data from the completed accounts payable input form.
6. Display/Print the purchases on account report.
7. Display/Print the cash payments report.
8. Display/Print the general ledger posting summary.
9. Display/Print the schedule of accounts payable.
10. Key-enter data from the completed accounts receivable input form.
11. Display/Print the sales on account report.
12. Display/Print the cash receipts report.
13. Display/Print the general ledger posting summary.
14. Display/Print the schedule of accounts receivable.

Preparing Payroll Records

ENABLING PERFORMANCE TASKS

After studying Chapter 15, you will be able to:
a. Define accounting terms related to payroll records.
b. Identify accounting practices related to payroll records.
c. Figure employee earnings and deductions.
d. Complete payroll records.
e. Prepare payroll checks.

CarLand employs several people to work in the business. These employees record the time they work for CarLand each day. Periodically CarLand pays its employees for the number of hours each employee has worked. The money paid for employee services is called a salary. The period covered by a salary payment is called a pay period. A business may decide to pay employee salaries every week, every two weeks, twice a month, or once a month. CarLand uses a semimonthly pay period. Employees are paid twice a month, on the 15th and last day of each month.

The total amount earned by all employees for a pay period is called a payroll. The payroll is reduced by state and federal taxes and other deductions, such as health insurance, to determine the amount paid to all employees. Special payroll records support the recording of payroll transactions in a journal. The business also uses these records to inform employees of their annual earnings and to prepare payroll reports for the government.

PAYROLL TIME CARDS

A payroll system must include an accurate record of the time each employee has worked. Several methods are used for keeping time records. Employee time records are frequently kept on time cards. Time cards are used as the basic source of information to prepare a payroll.

Some time cards only require employees to record the total hours worked each day. Employees who record the total hours worked each day usually complete time cards by hand.

A business may use a time card that requires employees to record their arrival and departure times. CarLand uses a time clock to record the daily arrival and departure times of its employees. The time card for Patrick S. Turner for the pay period December 1-15 is shown in Illustration 15-1.

Illustration 15-1
Payroll time card

Analyzing a payroll time card

Mr. Turner's employee number is at the top of the card. Below the employee number are the employee name and the ending date of the pay period.

CarLand's time cards have three sections, Morning, Afternoon, and Overtime, with In and Out columns under each section. When Mr. Turner reported for work on December 1, he inserted the card in the time clock. The clock recorded his time of arrival, 7:58, on the first line of the time card. The other entries on this line indicate that he left for lunch at 12:02. He returned at 12:59 and left for the day at 5:06. On December 3 he worked overtime, starting at 7:01 and leaving at 9:33.

CarLand figures overtime pay for each employee who works more than 8 hours in one day. No employee works more than 5 days in any one week.

Figuring hours worked

The first task in preparing a payroll is to figure the number of hours worked by each employee. Four steps are followed to figure employee hours worked.

1 Figure the number of regular hours for each day and enter the amounts in the Hours Reg column.

Mr. Turner works 8 hours during a normal day. The hours worked on December 3, the third line of the time card, are figured using the arrival and departure times imprinted on the time card. Times are rounded to the nearest quarter hour to figure the hours worked.

	Departure Time	−	Arrival Time	=	Hours Worked
Morning:					
Time card	12:01		7:55		
Nearest quarter hour	12:00	−	8:00	=	4:00
Afternoon:					
Time card	5:02		12:56		
Nearest quarter hour	5:00	−	1:00	=	4:00
Total regular hours worked on December 3					8:00

The hours worked in the morning and afternoon are figured separately. The morning departure time of 12:01 is rounded to the nearest quarter hour, 12:00. The rounded arrival time, 8:00, *subtracted* from the departure time, 12:00, *equals* the morning hours worked. Hours worked of 4:00 means that Mr. Turner worked 4 hours and no (00) minutes. The total regular hours worked, *8*, is recorded in the Hours Reg column on line 3 of the time card.

2 Figure the number of overtime hours for each day and enter the amounts in the Hours OT column.

Overtime hours for December 3 are figured using the same procedure as for regular hours.

	Departure Time	−	Arrival Time	=	Hours Worked
Time card	9:33		7:01		
Nearest quarter hour	9:30	−	7:00	=	2:30

The hours worked of 2:30 means that Mr. Turner worked 2 hours and 30 minutes (1/2 hour) of overtime. Therefore, 2 1/2 is recorded in the Hours OT column.

3 Add the hours worked in the Hours Reg and OT columns. Enter the totals in the spaces provided at the bottom of the time card.

Mr. Turner worked 88 regular hours (8 hours × 11 days) and 4 1/2 overtime hours during the semimonthly pay period. Therefore, *88* is recorded in the Regular Hours space at the bottom of the card and *4 1/2* is recorded in the Overtime Hours space.

4 Add the Hours column to figure the total hours. Enter the total in the Hours column at the bottom of the time card.

Mr. Turner worked 88 regular hours and 4 1/2 overtime hours for a total of 92 1/2 hours. Total hours, *92 1/2*, are entered in the Total Hours space.

Figuring employee total earnings

Once the total regular and overtime hours are determined, employee earnings can be calculated. The total pay due for a pay period before deductions is called total earnings. Total earnings are sometimes referred to as gross pay or gross earnings. Four steps are followed to figure employee total earnings.

1 Enter the rate for regular time in the Rate column. Figure the regular earnings by multiplying regular hours times the regular rate.

Mr. Turner's regular hourly rate, *$8.00*, is entered in the Regular Rate space. The regular earnings are calculated as shown below.

Regular Hours	×	Regular Rate	=	Regular Earnings
88	×	$8.00		$704.00

The amount of regular earnings, *$704.00*, is entered in the Regular Amount space.

2 Enter the rate for overtime in the Rate column.

Mr. Turner is paid 1 1/2 times his regular rate for overtime work. The overtime rate for Mr. Turner is calculated as shown below.

Regular Rate	×	1 1/2	=	Overtime Rate
$8.00	×	1 1/2	=	$12.00

The overtime rate, *$12.00*, is entered in the Overtime Rate space.

3 Figure the overtime earnings by multiplying overtime hours times the overtime rate.

The overtime earnings for Mr. Turner are calculated as shown below.

Overtime Hours	×	Overtime Rate	=	Overtime Earnings
4 1/2	×	$12.00	=	$54.00

The amount of overtime earnings, *$54.00*, is entered in the Overtime Amount space.

4 Add the Amount column to figure the total earnings.

The total earnings for Mr. Turner are calculated as shown below.

Regular Earnings	+	Overtime Earnings	=	Total Earnings
$704.00	+	$54.00	=	$758.00

The amount of total earnings, *$758.00*, is entered in the Total Earnings space.

CarLand owes Mr. Turner $758.00 for his work during the pay period ending December 15. However, taxes and other deductions must be subtracted from total earnings to determine the actual amount CarLand will pay Mr. Turner. Therefore, CarLand will not pay Mr. Turner the entire $758.00.

PAYROLL TAXES

Taxes based on the payroll of a business are called payroll taxes. A business is required by law to withhold certain payroll taxes from employee salaries. A business is also required to pay additional payroll taxes. All payroll taxes are based on employee total earnings. Therefore, accurate and detailed payroll records must be maintained. Errors in payroll records could cause incorrect payroll tax payments. Federal and state governments may charge a business a penalty for failure to pay correct payroll taxes on time.

Payroll taxes withheld represent a liability for the employer until payment is made. Federal payroll taxes may be paid to a Federal Reserve Bank. The taxes may also be paid to a bank authorized to receive such funds for the government. Local and state governments that assess payroll taxes also designate how, when, and where a business will pay the liability for employee taxes withheld.

Employee income tax

A business must withhold federal income taxes from employee total earnings. Federal income taxes withheld must be forwarded periodically to the federal government. Federal income tax is withheld from employee earnings in all 50 states. Employers in many states also are required to withhold state, city, or county income taxes from employee earnings.

The information used to determine the amount of income tax withheld is identified on Form W-4, Employee's Withholding Allowance Certificate. The completed Form W-4 for Mr. Turner is shown in Illustration 15-2.

Information from the completed Form W-4 is used when a business figures the amount of federal income taxes to be withheld. Employers are required to have on file a current Form W-4 for all employees. The amount of income tax withheld is based on employee marital status and withholding allowances.

Marital status. Employees identify on Form W-4 whether they are married or single. A married employee will have less income tax withheld than a single employee with the same total earnings.

Mr. Turner checked the married box for item 3 of the Form W-4 shown in Illustration 15-2.

Form **W-4**	**Employee's Withholding Allowance Certificate**	OMB No. 1545-0010
Department of the Treasury Internal Revenue Service	► **For Privacy Act and Paperwork Reduction Act Notice, see reverse.**	

1 Type or print your first name and middle initial	Last name	2 Your social security number
Patrick S. Turner		450-70-6432

Home address (number and street or rural route) 1625 Northland Drive	3 Marital Status	☐ Single ☒ Married
City or town, state, and ZIP code Rockville, RI 02873		☐ Married, but withhold at higher Single rate. **Note:** *If married, but legally separated, or spouse is a nonresident alien, check the Single box.*

4	Total number of allowances you are claiming (from line G above or from the Worksheets on back if they apply)	**4**	4
5	Additional amount, if any, you want deducted from each pay	**5**	$ –0–

6 I claim exemption from withholding and I certify that I meet **ALL** of the following conditions for exemption:
- Last year I had a right to a refund of **ALL** Federal income tax withheld because I had **NO** tax liability; **AND**
- This year I expect a refund of **ALL** Federal income tax withheld because I expect to have **NO** tax liability; **AND**
- This year if my income exceeds $500 and includes nonwage income, another person cannot claim me as a dependent.

If you meet all of the above conditions, enter the year effective and "EXEMPT" here . . . . . . ►	**6**	19

7 Are you a full-time student? (**Note:** *Full-time students are not automatically exempt.*)	**7**	☐ Yes ☐ No

Under penalties of perjury, I certify that I am entitled to the number of withholding allowances claimed on this certificate or entitled to claim exempt status.

Employee's signature ► *Patrick S. Turner*   Date ► *June 27*   19– –

8 Employer's name and address (**Employer:** Complete 8 and 10 **only if sending to IRS**)	9 Office code (optional)	10 Employer identification number

Withholding allowance. A deduction from total earnings for each person legally supported by a taxpayer is called a withholding allowance. The larger the number of the withholding allowances claimed, the smaller the income tax withheld from employee salaries.

Mr. Turner claimed four withholding allowances, one each for himself, his wife, and his two children. The number of withholding allowances was recorded in item 4 of the Form W-4.

Most employees are required to have federal income taxes withheld from their salaries. An exemption from withholding is available for certain low-income and part-time employees. The employee must meet the requirements listed in the instructions which accompany Form W-4. The requirements are very restrictive. Most students with part-time jobs who live with their parents do *not* qualify for the exemption. Students who earn over $500 in salary or any interest from a savings or checking account are not eligible to claim the exemption.

The federal government occasionally changes the way income taxes are withheld from employee total earnings. The Form W-4 shown in Illustration 15-2 was the form in use when the materials for this textbook were prepared. Employers must be aware of changes in tax laws and forms. If Form W-4 is changed, an employer must obtain a new W-4 from each employee.

Employee and employer social security tax

The federal social security law includes three programs.

1. Old-age, survivors, and disability insurance benefits for qualified employees and their spouses, widows or widowers, dependent children, and parents.

2. Payments to senior citizens for the cost of certain hospital and related services. The federal health insurance program for people who have reached retirement age is called Medicare.
3. Grants to states that provide benefits for persons temporarily unemployed and for certain relief and welfare purposes.

Each employee must have a social security number. Most employees will have received their social security number as a child. Employees without social security numbers can apply for a number at the nearest Social Security office.

FICA tax. A federal tax paid by employees and employers for old-age, survivors, disability, and hospitalization insurance is called FICA tax. FICA is the abbreviation for the Federal Insurance Contributions Act. FICA tax is based on the total earnings of the employees. Employers are required to withhold FICA tax from a specified amount of employee salary paid in a calendar year. In addition, employers must pay the same amount of FICA tax as withheld from employee salaries.

Federal unemployment tax. A federal tax used for state and federal administrative expenses of the unemployment program is called federal unemployment tax. This tax is paid entirely by employers.

State unemployment tax. A state tax used to pay benefits to unemployed workers is called state unemployment tax. This tax is usually paid by employers. The Social Security Act specifies certain standards for unemployment compensation laws. Therefore, a high degree of uniformity exists in state unemployment laws. However, details of state unemployment laws do differ. Because of these differences, employers must know the requirements of the states in which they operate.

Retention of records. Employers are required to retain all payroll records showing payments and deductions. Some records must be retained longer than others. Records pertaining to social security tax payments and deductions must be retained for four years. The length of time state unemployment tax payment records must be retained varies from state to state.

PAYROLL REGISTER

A business form used to record payroll information is called a payroll register. A payroll register summarizes the total earnings and payroll withholdings of all employees. CarLand's payroll register for the semimonthly period ended December 15 is shown in Illustration 15-3.

Regular, overtime, and total earnings are recorded in a payroll register from information on time cards. Amounts deducted for payroll taxes, health insurance, and charitable contributions are calculated and recorded in a payroll register. Also, the total amount to be paid to each employee and the check number of each payroll check are recorded in a payroll register.

	EMPL. NO	EMPLOYEE NAME	MARITAL STATUS	NO. OF ALLOWANCES	EARNINGS REGULAR	OVERTIME	TOTAL	DEDUCTIONS FEDERAL INCOME TAX	FICA TAX	HEALTH INSUR- ANCE	OTHER	TOTAL	NET PAY	CHECK. NO.	
1	2	Bauch, Mary R.	M	2	660 00		660 00	57 00	52 80	38 00	B 5 00	152 80	507 20	419	1
2	5	Clay, Richard P.	S	1	80 00		80 00	00	6 40			6 40	73 60	420	2
3	1	Javorski, Adam B.	M	2	384 00	18 00	402 00	17 00	32 16	38 00		87 16	314 84	421	3
4	6	Maggio, Brenda A.	S	1	40 00		40 00	00	3 20			3 20	36 80	422	4
5	4	Turner, Patrick S.	M	4	704 00	54 00	758 00	45 00	60 64	50 00	B 10 00 UW 10 00	175 64	582 36	423	5
6	3	Wilkes, Samuel R.	S	1	616 00		616 00	73 00	49 28	32 00		154 28	461 72	424	6
7					2484 00	72 00	2556 00	192 00	204 48	158 00	B 15 00 UW 10 00	579 48	1976 52		7
8															8

Table header: SEMIMONTHLY PERIOD ENDED *December 15, 19--* · PAYROLL REGISTER · DATE OF PAYMENT *December 15, 19--*

Illustration 15-3
Payroll register

The two partners of CarLand, Amy Kramer and Dario Mesa, are not listed on the payroll register. Owners of partnerships are not employees of the company. Cash payments to partners are recorded as withdrawals rather than as salaries.

Recording earnings in a payroll register

The employee number, name, marital status, and withholding allowances are listed in a payroll register. Employee earnings for a pay period are written in the appropriate columns of a payroll register.

Recorded on line 5 of the payroll register are Mr. Turner's employee number, 4, and name, *Turner, Patrick S.* Also recorded are Mr. Turner's marital status, M for married; the number of withholding allowances, 4; regular earnings, $704.00; overtime earnings, $54.00; and total earnings, $758.00. This information is obtained from Mr. Turner's Form W-4 and time card.

Recording deductions in a payroll register

The deductions section of a payroll register is used to record the payroll taxes and other deductions withheld from employee earnings. Also, some companies deduct amounts for retirement plans. These deductions will vary from one company to another depending on policies established between management and employees.

Five steps are followed to figure and record deductions.

1 The Federal Income Tax column is used to record the amount of federal income tax withheld from employee earnings. This amount is determined from tables furnished by the federal government. Portions of the tables showing the tax to be withheld are shown in Illustration 15-4 on pages 342 and 343.

SEMIMONTHLY PAYROLL PERIOD — MARRIED PERSONS

| And the wages are— | | And the number of withholding allowances claimed is— | | | | | | | | | | |
At least	But less than	0	1	2	3	4	5	6	7	8	9	10
		The amount of income tax to be withheld shall be—										
$0	$130											
130	135	1										
135	140	2										
140	145	2										
145	150	3										
400	410	42	30	17	5							
410	420	43	31	19	7							
420	430	45	33	20	8							
430	440	46	34	22	10							
440	450	48	36	23	11							
450	460	49	37	25	13							
460	470	51	39	26	14	2						
470	480	52	40	28	16	3						
480	490	54	42	29	17	5						
490	500	55	43	31	19	6						
500	520	57	45	33	21	9						
520	540	60	48	36	24	12						
540	560	63	51	39	27	15	3					
560	580	66	54	42	30	18	6					
580	600	69	57	45	33	21	9					
600	620	72	60	48	36	24	12					
620	640	75	63	51	39	27	15	2				
640	660	78	66	54	42	30	18	5				
660	680	81	69	57	45	33	21	8				
680	700	84	72	60	48	36	24	11				
700	720	87	75	63	51	39	27	14	2			
720	740	90	78	66	54	42	30	17	5			
740	760	93	81	69	57	45	33	20	8			
760	780	96	84	72	60	48	36	23	11			
780	800	99	87	75	63	51	39	26	14	2		
800	820	102	90	78	66	54	42	29	17	5		
820	840	105	93	81	69	57	45	32	20	8		
840	860	108	96	84	72	60	48	35	23	11		
860	880	111	99	87	75	63	51	38	26	14	2	
880	900	114	102	90	78	66	54	41	29	17	5	
900	920	117	105	93	81	69	57	44	32	20	8	
920	940	120	108	96	84	72	60	47	35	23	11	
940	960	123	111	99	87	75	63	50	38	26	14	2
960	980	126	114	102	90	78	66	53	41	29	17	5
980	1,000	129	117	105	93	81	69	56	44	32	20	8
1,000	1,020	132	120	108	96	84	72	59	47	35	23	11
1,020	1,040	135	123	111	99	87	75	62	50	38	26	14
1,040	1,060	138	126	114	102	90	78	65	53	41	29	17
1,060	1,080	141	129	117	105	93	81	68	56	44	32	20
1,080	1,100	144	132	120	108	96	84	71	59	47	35	23
1,100	1,120	147	135	123	111	99	87	74	62	50	38	26
1,120	1,140	150	138	126	114	102	90	77	65	53	41	29
1,140	1,160	153	141	129	117	105	93	80	68	56	44	32
1,160	1,180	156	144	132	120	108	96	83	71	59	47	35
1,180	1,200	159	147	135	123	111	99	86	74	62	50	38
1,200	1,220	162	150	138	126	114	102	89	77	65	53	41
1,220	1,240	165	153	141	129	117	105	92	80	68	56	44
1,240	1,260	168	156	144	132	120	108	95	83	71	59	47
1,260	1,280	171	159	147	135	123	111	98	86	74	62	50
1,280	1,300	174	162	150	138	126	114	101	89	77	65	53
1,300	1,320	177	165	153	141	129	117	104	92	80	68	56
1,320	1,340	180	168	156	144	132	120	107	95	83	71	59
1,340	1,360	183	171	159	147	135	123	110	98	86	74	62
1,360	1,380	187	174	162	150	138	126	113	101	89	77	65
1,380	1,400	192	177	165	153	141	129	116	104	92	80	68

SEMIMONTHLY MARRIED PERSONS

Illustration 15-4
Section of income tax withholding tables for semimonthly pay period

Mr. Turner's federal income tax on total earnings of $758.00 is found in the table for married persons. Since CarLand pays its payroll twice a month, the table for a semimonthly pay period is used. The proper wage bracket is from $740.00 to $760.00. The income tax to be withheld is the amount shown on this line under the column for four allowances, $45.00.

No federal income tax was withheld from the earnings of Richard Clay and Brenda Maggio. Although they are students who work part-time, they are not exempt from federal income tax withholding. They did not, however, have enough total earnings *in this pay period* to require any income tax to be withheld. Federal income tax withholding tables are also available for daily, weekly, biweekly, and monthly pay periods. The tables in Illustration 15-4 are those available when materials for this textbook were prepared.

SEMIMONTHLY PAYROLL PERIOD — SINGLE PERSONS

And the wages are—		And the number of withholding allowances claimed is—										
At least	But less than	0	1	2	3	4	5	6	7	8	9	10
		The amount of income tax to be withheld shall be—										
$0	$45											
45	50	1										
50	55	1										
55	60	2										
60	65	3										
65	70	4										
70	75	4										
75	80	5										
80	85	6										
85	90	7										
380	390	51	39	27	15	2						
390	400	53	41	28	16	4						
400	410	54	42	30	18	5						
410	420	56	44	31	19	7						
420	430	57	45	33	21	8						
430	440	59	47	34	22	10						
440	450	60	48	36	24	11						
450	460	62	50	37	25	13	1					
460	470	63	51	39	27	14	2					
470	480	65	53	40	28	16	4					
480	490	66	54	42	30	17	5					
490	500	68	56	43	31	19	7					
500	520	70	58	46	33	21	9					
520	540	73	61	49	36	24	12					
540	560	76	64	52	39	27	15	3				
560	580	79	67	55	42	30	18	6				
580	600	82	70	58	45	33	21	9				
600	620	85	73	61	48	36	24	12				
620	640	88	76	64	51	39	27	15	3			
640	660	91	79	67	54	42	30	18	6			
660	680	94	82	70	57	45	33	21	9			
680	700	97	85	73	60	48	36	24	12			
700	720	100	88	76	63	51	39	27	15	2		
720	740	103	91	79	66	54	42	30	18	5		
740	760	106	94	82	69	57	45	33	21	8		
760	780	109	97	85	72	60	48	36	24	11		
780	800	112	100	88	75	63	51	39	27	14	2	
800	820	118	103	91	78	66	54	42	30	17	5	
820	840	123	106	94	81	69	57	45	33	20	8	
840	860	129	109	97	84	72	60	48	36	23	11	
860	880	135	112	100	87	75	63	51	39	26	14	2
880	900	140	118	103	90	78	66	54	42	29	17	5
900	920	146	123	106	93	81	69	57	45	32	20	8
920	940	151	129	109	96	84	72	60	48	35	23	11
940	960	157	134	112	99	87	75	63	51	38	26	14
960	980	163	140	117	102	90	78	66	54	41	29	17
980	1,000	168	146	123	105	93	81	69	57	44	32	20
1,000	1,020	174	151	128	108	96	84	72	60	47	35	23
1,020	1,040	179	157	134	111	99	87	75	63	50	38	26
1,040	1,060	185	162	140	117	102	90	78	66	53	41	29
1,060	1,080	191	168	145	122	105	93	81	69	56	44	32
1,080	1,100	196	174	151	128	108	96	84	72	59	47	35
1,100	1,120	202	179	156	134	111	99	87	75	62	50	38
1,120	1,140	207	185	162	139	116	102	90	78	65	53	41
1,140	1,160	213	190	168	145	122	105	93	81	68	56	44
1,160	1,180	219	196	173	150	128	108	96	84	71	59	47
1,180	1,200	224	202	179	156	133	111	99	87	74	62	50
1,200	1,220	230	207	184	162	139	116	102	90	77	65	53
1,220	1,240	235	213	190	167	144	122	105	93	80	68	56
1,240	1,260	241	218	196	173	150	127	108	96	83	71	59

Illustration 15-4
Section of income tax withholding tables for semimonthly pay period

2 The FICA Tax column is used to record the amount deducted for social security tax. FICA tax is calculated by multiplying total earnings by the tax rate. From time to time, Congress changes the tax rate used to figure FICA taxes. A FICA tax rate of 8% is used to illustrate the FICA tax calculations in this textbook. The FICA tax for Mr. Turner is calculated as shown below.

Total Earnings	×	FICA Tax Rate	=	FICA Tax Deduction
$758.00	×	8%	=	$60.64

Congress has limited the amount of FICA tax that each individual must pay. The FICA tax is not calculated on total earnings over a specified amount. The maximum amount of earnings on which a tax is calculated is called a tax base. A tax base of $50,000.00 is used for the FICA tax calculations in this textbook.

Before recording Mr. Turner's $60.64 FICA tax in the payroll register, his accumulated earnings are compared to the tax base. Between January 1 and December 1, Mr. Turner has earned $16,794.00. Since his earnings are less than the tax base, the FICA tax is recorded in the payroll register. If Mr. Turner had accumulated earnings over $50,000.00, no FICA tax would be owed and no amount would have been recorded in the payroll register.

3   The Health Insurance column is used to record health insurance premiums. Full-time employees of CarLand participate in a group health insurance plan to take advantage of lower group rates.

Mr. Turner's semimonthly health insurance premium is $50.00. Premiums are set by the insurance company and are usually based on the employee marital status and whether coverage is for an individual or a family. Some health insurance premiums may be based on the number of individuals covered.

4   The Other column is used to record voluntary deductions requested by an employee. Entries are identified by code letters. CarLand uses the letter *B* to identify amounts withheld for buying U.S. Savings Bonds. *UW* is used to identify amounts withheld for employee contributions to United Way.

Mr. Turner has authorized CarLand to withhold $10.00 each pay period to buy U.S. Savings Bonds for him. Mr. Turner has also authorized that $10.00 be withheld as a contribution to the United Way.

5   The Total column is used to record total deductions. All deductions on a line for each employee are added. The total deductions for Mr. Turner are calculated as shown below.

Federal Income Tax	+	FICA Tax	+	Health Insurance	+	Other	=	Total Deductions
$45.00	+	$60.64	+	$50.00	+	$20.00	=	$175.64

Figuring net pay in a payroll register

The total earnings paid to an employee after payroll taxes and other deductions is called net pay. Net pay is figured by subtracting total deductions from total earnings. The Net Pay column is used to record the amount. The net pay for Mr. Turner is calculated as shown below.

Total Earnings	–	Total Deductions	=	Net Pay
$758.00	–	$175.64	=	$582.36

Completing a payroll register

After the net pay has been recorded for each employee, each amount column is totaled. A separate total is shown for each different type of deduction in the Other column. Accuracy of these totals is verified by subtracting the Total Deductions column total from the Total Earnings column total as shown below.

Total Earnings	–	Total Deductions	=	Net Pay
$2,556.00	–	$579.48	=	$1,976.52

The net pay calculated above, $1,976.52, is compared to the total of the Net Pay column. The payroll register is proved because these amounts are equal. If the amounts are not equal, the errors must be found and corrected. After the payroll register is proved, a double rule is drawn below the totals across all amount columns. When the payroll register is completed and proved, the register is given to a partner of the company for approval.

Before checks are written for employee net pay, the payroll calculations are checked for accuracy. A partner approves the payroll after the accuracy is verified. After each check is written, the check number is recorded in the Ck. No. column.

PAYROLL CHECKS

CarLand pays its employees with checks written on a special payroll checking account. A check for the total net pay is written on CarLand's general checking account. The check is deposited in the payroll checking account. Illustration 15-5 shows the check written for the December 1-15 pay period. The check amount, $1,976.52, is the total of the Net Pay column of the payroll register in Illustration 15-3.

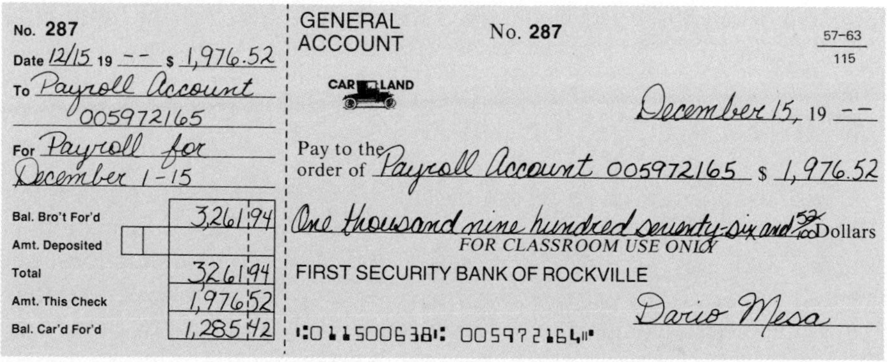
No. 287
Date 12/15 19 -- $ 1,976.52
To Payroll Account 005972165
For Payroll for December 1-15

Bal. Bro't For'd	3,261.94
Amt. Deposited	
Total	3,261.94
Amt. This Check	1,976.52
Bal. Car'd For'd	1,285.42

GENERAL ACCOUNT
No. 287
57-63/115
CARLAND
December 15, 19 --
Pay to the order of Payroll Account 005972165 $ 1,976.52
One thousand nine hundred seventy-six and 52/100 Dollars
FOR CLASSROOM USE ONLY
FIRST SECURITY BANK OF ROCKVILLE
Dario Mesa
⑆0115006381⑆ 005972164⑈

Illustration 15-5
Check for total net pay

The information used to prepare payroll checks is taken from a payroll register. The payroll check for Mr. Turner is shown in Illustration 15-6. A special payroll check form is used that has a detachable stub for recording earnings and amounts deducted. Employees keep the stubs for a record of deductions and cash received.

Check No. **423**		PAYROLL						57–63

Check No. **423**

PERIOD ENDING	12 / 15 --
EARNINGS	$ 758 00
REG.	$ 704.00
O.T.	$ 54.00
DEDUCTIONS	$ 175 64
INC. TAX	$ 45.00
FICA TAX	$ 60.64
HEALTH INS.	$ 50.00
OTHER	$ 10.00
NET PAY	$ 582 36

PAYROLL ACCOUNT

57–63 / 115

December 15, 19 --   No. **423**

Pay to the order of ___Patrick S. Turner___ $ 582.36

Five hundred eighty-two and ³⁶/₁₀₀ _____ Dollars

FOR CLASSROOM USE ONLY

FIRST SECURITY BANK OF ROCKVILLE   CAR LAND

Dario Mesa

⑆011500638⑆ 0059721650⑈

Illustration 15-6
Payroll check with
detachable stub

A separate checking account for payroll checks helps to protect and control payroll payments. The exact amount needed to pay the payroll is deposited in the special payroll account. If amounts on checks are altered or unauthorized payroll checks are prepared, the amount in the special payroll account would be insufficient to cover all the checks. Thus, the bank and CarLand would be alerted quickly to an unauthorized payroll check. Also, since payroll checks are drawn on the separate account, any balance in this account will correspond to the sum of outstanding payroll checks.

Some businesses deposit employee net pay directly to each employee bank account by using electronic funds transfer (EFT). When EFT is used, the bank's computer deducts the amount of net pay from the business' bank account and adds the amount to each employee bank account. The payroll must still be figured, but individual checks are not written and do not have to be distributed. Under this system, each employee receives a statement of earnings and deductions similar to the detachable stub on a payroll check.

EMPLOYEE EARNINGS RECORDS

A business form used to record details affecting payments made to an employee is called an employee earnings record. This information is recorded each pay period. The record includes earnings, deductions, net pay, and accumulated earnings for the calendar year. Employee earnings records enable the company to complete required tax forms at the end of the year.

Recording information in an employee earnings record

CarLand keeps all employee earnings records on cards. One card for each employee is used for each quarter in the calendar year. After a payroll register has been prepared, the payroll data for each employee are recorded in each employee earnings record. The December 15 payroll register data for Patrick S. Turner are recorded in his fourth quarter employee earnings record shown in Illustration 15-7.

EARNINGS RECORD FOR QUARTER ENDED September 30, 19--

EMPLOYEE NO. _4_ Turner (LAST NAME) Patrick (FIRST) S. (MIDDLE INITIAL) MARITAL STATUS _M_ WITHHOLDING ALLOWANCES _4_

10 ACCUMULATED EARNINGS
9376 00
10190 00
10874 00
11692 00
12456 00
13918 00
13814 00
13918 00

EARNINGS RECORD FOR QUARTER ENDED December 31, 19--

EMPLOYEE NO. _4_ Turner (LAST NAME) Patrick (FIRST) S. (MIDDLE INITIAL) MARITAL STATUS _M_ WITHHOLDING ALLOWANCES _4_

RATE OF PAY _$8.00_ PER HR. SOCIAL SECURITY NO. _450-70-6432_ POSITION _Sales Clerk_

PAY PERIOD		EARNINGS			DEDUCTIONS					NET PAY	ACCUMULATED EARNINGS
NO.	ENDED	REGULAR (1)	OVERTIME (2)	TOTAL (3)	FEDERAL INCOME TAX (4)	FICA TAX (5)	HEALTH INSURANCE (6)	OTHER (7)	TOTAL (8)	(9)	(10)
1	10/15	640 00	60 00	700 00	39 00	56 00	50 00	B 10 00 / UW 10 00	165 00	535 00	14618 00
2	10/31	768 00		768 00	48 00	61 44	50 00	B 10 00 / UW 10 00	179 44	588 56	15386 00
3	11/15	704 00		704 00	39 00	56 32	50 00	B 10 00 / UW 10 00	165 32	538 68	16090 00
4	11/30	704 00		704 00	39 00	56 32	50 00	B 10 00 / UW 10 00	165 32	538 68	16794 00
5	12/15	704 00	54 00	758 00	45 00	60 64	50 00	B 10 00 / UW 10 00	175 64	582 36	17552 00
6	12/31	640 00		640 00	30 00	51 20	50 00	B 10 00 / UW 10 00	151 20	488 80	18192 00
7											
QUARTERLY TOTALS		4160 00	114 00	4274 00	240 00	341 92	300 00	B 60 00 / UW 60 00	1001 92	3272 08	

OTHER DEDUCTIONS: B—U.S. SAVINGS BONDS; UW—UNITED WAY

Illustration 15-7
Employee earnings record

Quarterly totals are used in the preparation of payroll reports required by the government. The accumulated earnings are also used to determine if the employee has earned more than the FICA tax base.

Analyzing an employee earnings record

Mr. Turner's name, employee number, social security number, and other payroll data are entered at the top of his fourth quarter employee earnings record.

Amount columns of an employee earnings record are the same as amount columns of a payroll register. Amounts opposite an employee name in a payroll register are recorded in the corresponding columns of the employee earnings record. The pay period ending December 15 is the fifth pay period in the fourth quarter. Therefore, Mr. Turner's earnings and deductions for that pay period are entered on line 5 of his employee earnings record.

The earnings record also has an Accumulated Earnings column. The first entry in this column is the accumulated earnings at the end of the previous quarter. Accumulated earnings of $13,918.00 were carried forward from the third quarter earnings record to the fourth quarter earnings record, as shown in Illustration 15-7.

Total earnings for a pay period are added to the accumulated earnings in the previous line to figure the new total accumulated earnings. Accumulated earnings are sometimes referred to as year-to-date earnings. Mr. Turner's accumulated earnings as of December 15 are calculated as shown below.

Accumulated Earnings as of December 1	+	Total Earnings for Pay Period Ended December 15	=	Accumulated Earnings as of December 15
$16,794.00	+	$758.00	=	$17,552.00

The Accumulated Earnings column shows the total earnings for Mr. Turner since the first of the year. The amounts in the Accumulated Earnings column supply an up-to-date reference for an employee's year-to-date earnings. When employee earnings reach the tax base, certain payroll taxes do not apply. For example, employers pay state and federal unemployment taxes only on a specified amount of each employee earnings. Also, the FICA taxes are paid only on the first $50,000 of total earnings.

Quarterly totals will be calculated on Mr. Turner's employee earnings record after the payroll for the pay period ended December 31 is recorded. The Quarterly Totals line provides space for the totals for the quarter. The accuracy of the quarterly totals is verified with the same steps used to verify payroll register totals. The Total Deductions column total is subtracted from the Total Earnings column total as shown below.

Total Earnings	–	Total Deductions	=	Net Pay
$4,274.00	–	$1,001.92	=	$3,272.08

The net pay calculated above, $3,272.08, is compared to the total of the Net Pay column. The earnings record is proved because these amounts are equal. These totals are needed to prepare required government reports.

PROCESSING A PAYROLL USING A PEGBOARD

Preparing a payroll requires figuring, recording, and reporting payroll information. Each business selects a system for processing the payroll that results in adequate control for the least amount of cost.

A special device used to write the same information at one time on several forms is called a pegboard. One type of pegboard is shown in Illustration 15-8.

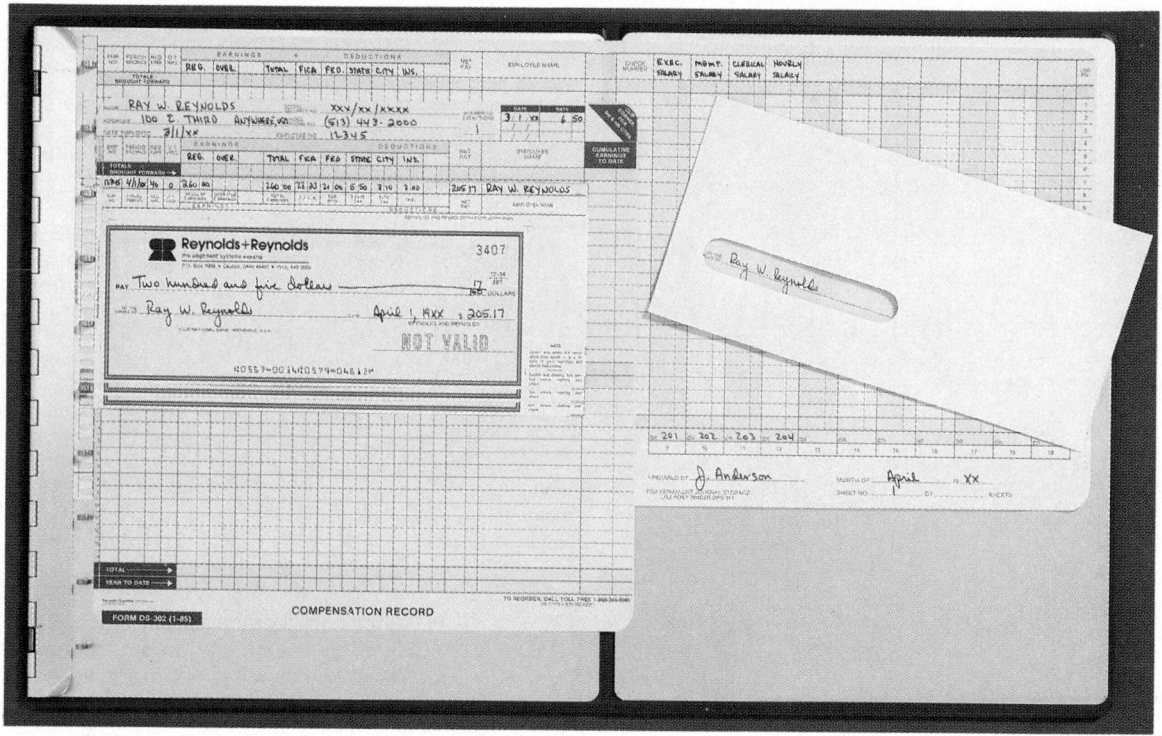

Illustration 15-8
A pegboard

The name pegboard comes from the pegs along one side of the board. The forms used with this device have holes punched along one side. Each of the forms is placed on the pegs. Thus, the line on each form on which information is to be written is aligned one below the other.

When a payroll is recorded, a page of the payroll register is attached to the pegboard. Next, the employee earnings record is properly positioned on top of the payroll register page. Then the check is positioned on top of both of these sheets. As the check stub is written, the carbonless paper imprints the same information on the employee earnings record and the payroll register. The information is written only once. However, the information is recorded on three different records at the same time. Recording information on several forms with one writing is referred to as the write-it-once principle.

The pegboard has two major purposes. First, the pegboard provides a solid writing base for writing on the forms by hand. Second, information is recorded on several forms with one writing, thus saving time and reducing the chance of error.

SUMMARY OF PREPARING PAYROLL RECORDS

The steps required to prepare payroll records are summarized in Illustration 15-9.

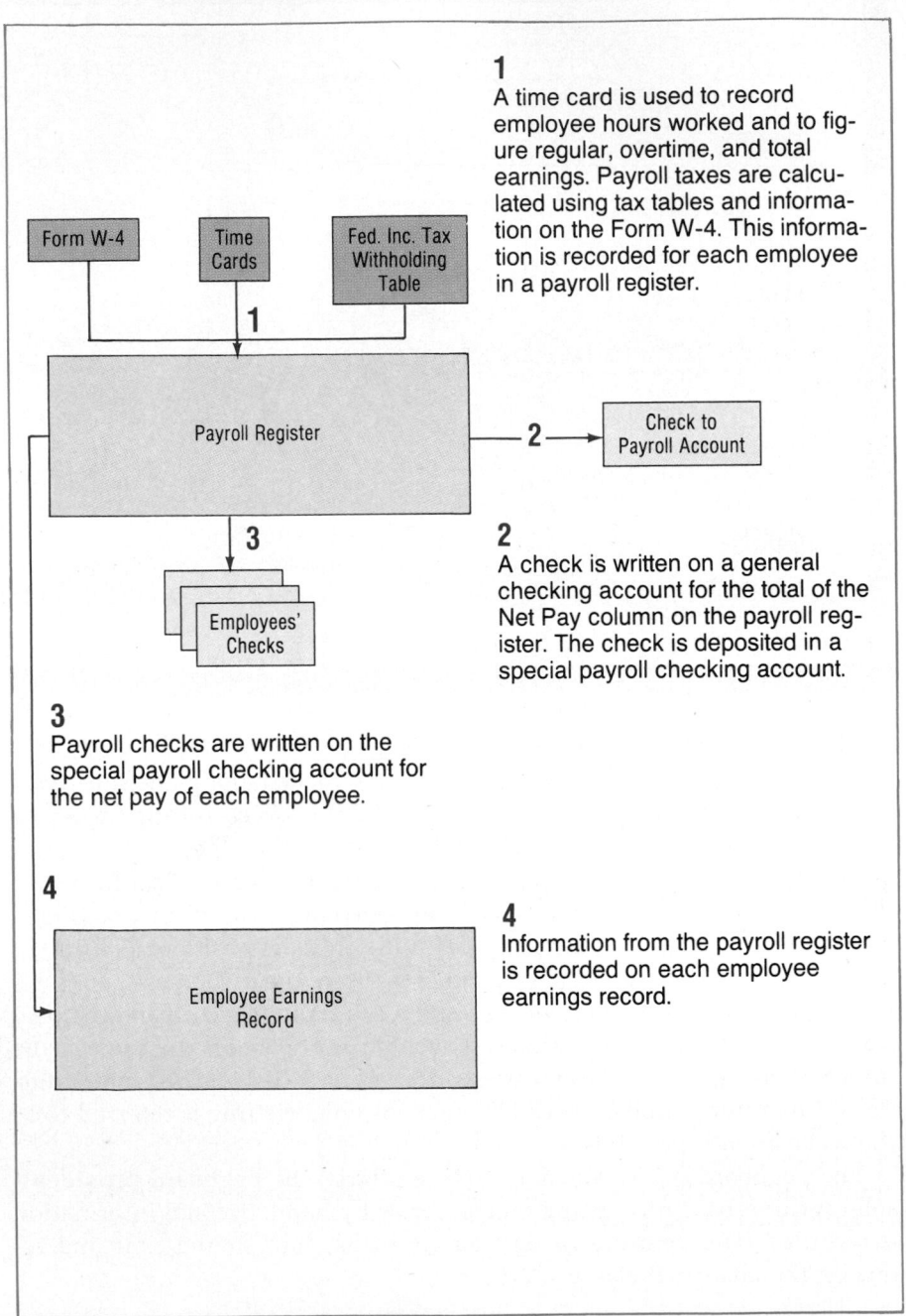

1
A time card is used to record employee hours worked and to figure regular, overtime, and total earnings. Payroll taxes are calculated using tax tables and information on the Form W-4. This information is recorded for each employee in a payroll register.

2
A check is written on a general checking account for the total of the Net Pay column on the payroll register. The check is deposited in a special payroll checking account.

3
Payroll checks are written on the special payroll checking account for the net pay of each employee.

4
Information from the payroll register is recorded on each employee earnings record.

Illustration 15-9
Summary of preparing
payroll records

ACCOUNTING TERMS

What is the meaning of each of the following?

1. salary
2. pay period
3. payroll
4. total earnings
5. payroll taxes
6. withholding allowance
7. Medicare
8. FICA tax
9. federal unemployment tax
10. state unemployment tax
11. payroll register
12. tax base
13. net pay
14. employee earnings record
15. pegboard

QUESTIONS FOR INDIVIDUAL STUDY

1. How often may a business decide to pay its employees?
2. What information is presented at the top of a time card?
3. To compute hours worked to the nearest quarter hour, how would an arrival time of 7:54 be rounded?
4. On what amount are employee payroll taxes based?
5. What factors determine the amount of federal income tax withheld from an employee?
6. How does the number of withholding allowances affect the amount of federal income tax withheld?
7. Who pays FICA tax?
8. How long must records pertaining to social security tax payments and deductions be retained?
9. What is the source of the earnings amounts reported in a payroll register?
10. Why are partners of a company not listed in the company's payroll register?
11. How is the amount of federal income tax withheld from employee salaries determined?
12. Under what circumstances can an employee who is not exempt from federal income tax withholding have no tax withheld on a payroll register?
13. What must an employer know to be able to figure the amount of FICA tax to be withheld from the salary of an employee?
14. How is a payroll register proved?
15. What amount is deposited into a payroll checking account?
16. Where is the information obtained to prepare a payroll check?
17. What is the major purpose of the Accumulated Earnings column of an employee earnings record?
18. What are two major purposes for using a pegboard for processing a payroll?

CASES FOR MANAGEMENT DECISION

CASE 1 Kilton Hardware currently requires each employee to inform the accounting clerk of the total hours worked each day during the pay period. The total number of hours worked by all employees has been steadily increasing during the prior pay periods. The new store manager has suggested that a time clock be installed to record arrival and departure times. The accounting clerk believes the current system is satisfactory. Do you agree with the new manager or the accounting clerk? Explain your response.

CASE 2 A banker has recommended that Tillman Construction Company open a second checking account. The company would write payroll checks against the new checking account. The company's 50 employees are currently paid with checks written against its general checking account. Do you agree with the banker's recommendation? Explain the reason for your decision.

DRILLS FOR UNDERSTANDING

DRILL 15-D1   Figuring employee earnings

The following information is taken from the time card of each employee.

Employee Number	Hours Worked		Regular Rate
	Regular	Overtime	
1	40	1	$6.00
2	40	5	9.00
3	30	0	6.50
4	25	0	7.75
5	40	4	8.50
6	35	0	7.00

Instructions: For each employee, figure the amount of regular, overtime, and total earnings. Overtime hours are paid at one and one-half times the regular rate.

DRILL 15-D2   Determining payroll tax withholdings

The following information is taken from the semimonthly payroll register.

Employee		Marital Status	No. of Allowances	Total Earnings
No.	Name			
2	Adams, Winston	M	2	$870.00
6	Forte, Peter	M	3	780.00
3	Gable, Joanne	S	1	670.00
1	Jenkins, Mary	M	5	760.00
8	Little, Edward	S	1	650.00
7	Nelson, Janice	S	2	710.00
4	Pate, Kim	S	1	640.00
5	Sanders, Michael	M	3	890.00

Instructions: 1. Determine the federal income tax that must be withheld for each of the eight employees. Use the tax withholding tables shown in Illustration 15-4.

2. Calculate the amount of FICA tax that must be withheld for each employee using an 8% tax rate. None of the eight employees has accumulated earnings greater than the tax base.

 APPLICATION PROBLEMS

PROBLEM 15-1   Completing payroll time cards

Employee time cards are given in the working papers accompanying this textbook.

Instructions: 1. Figure the regular, overtime, and total hours worked by each employee. Any hours over the regular 8-hour day are considered overtime. Record the hours on the time cards.

2. Determine the regular, overtime, and total earnings for each employee. The overtime rate is 1 1/2 times the regular rate. Complete the time cards.

PROBLEM 15-2   Preparing a semimonthly payroll

The following information is for the semimonthly pay period April 1-15 of the current year.

Employee		Marital Status	No. of Allowances	Earnings		Deductions	
No.	Name			Regular	Overtime	Health Insurance	Savings Bonds
2	Agne, Roberta	S	1	$704.00	36.00	$28.00	$10.00
10	Beville, Michael	M	3	424.00		45.00	
9	Day, Mellisa	M	2	739.20	63.00	36.00	5.00
3	Finley, Lisa	M	2	560.00		36.00	5.00
6	Gunter, Jill	S	1	484.00	33.00		
11	Locke, Alan	S	1	589.60			
1	O'Neal, Barton	S	2	756.80	64.50	28.00	
5	Soehn, Lucille	M	4	809.60		45.00	25.00
4	Webb, Ronald	M	3	686.40	23.40	45.00	
7	Wyatt, Pamela	S	1	809.40	41.40		10.00
8	Yang, Kim	M	2	598.40		28.00	
12	Zucconi, Robert	S	1	572.00	19.50		5.00

Instructions: 1. Prepare a payroll register. The date of payment is April 15. Use the federal income tax withholding tables in Illustration 15-4 to find the income tax withholding for each employee. Calculate FICA tax withholding using an 8% tax rate. None of the employee accumulated earnings has exceeded the FICA tax base.

2. Prepare a check for the total amount of the net pay. Make the check payable to Payroll Account, and sign your name as partner of City Hardware Company. The beginning check stub balance is $8,365.79.

3. Prepare payroll checks for Jill Gunter, Check No. 765, and Ronald Webb, Check No. 769. Sign your name as a partner of City Hardware Company. Record the two payroll check numbers in the payroll register.

PROBLEM 15-3   Preparing an employee earnings record

Derrick Hammond had the following earnings for the six semimonthly pay periods in April, May, and June of the current year.

Pay Period Ended	Earnings		
	Regular	Overtime	Total
4/15	$1,232.00	$105.00	$1,337.00
4/30	1,120.00	63.00	1,183.00
5/15	1,232.00	—	1,232.00
5/31	952.00	—	952.00
6/15	1,232.00	147.00	1,379.00
6/30	1,120.00	—	1,120.00

The following additional data about Derrick Hammond are needed to complete the employee earnings record.

1. Employee number: 32
2. Marital status: married
3. Withholding Allowances: 2
4. Rate of pay: regular, $14.00
5. Social security number: 218-78-2164
6. Position: service manager
7. Accumulated earnings for the first quarter: $7,928.00
8. Deductions from total earnings:
   a. Health insurance: $40.00 each semimonthly pay period
   b. U. S. Savings Bonds: $10.00 each semimonthly pay period
   c. Federal income tax: determined each pay period by using the withholding tables in Illustration 15-4
   d. FICA taxes: 8% of total earnings each pay period

Instructions: 1. Prepare an employee earnings record for Derrick Hammond for the second quarter of the year.
2. Verify the accuracy of the completed employee earnings record. The Quarter Total for Regular and Overtime Earnings should equal the Quarter Total for Net Pay plus Total Deductions. The Quarter Total for Total Earnings should equal the end-of-quarter Accumulated Earnings minus the beginning-of-quarter Accumulated Earnings.

ENRICHMENT PROBLEMS

MASTERY PROBLEM 15-M   Preparing a semimonthly payroll

The following information is for the semimonthly pay period May 16-31 of the current year.

Employee		Marital Status	No. of Allowances	Earnings		Deductions	
No.	Name			Regular	Overtime	Health Insurance	Savings Bonds
3	Abney, Patricia	M	2	$512.00	$12.80	$30.00	$10.00
6	Blanks, Wilma	S	1	576.00	21.60		
8	Fitts, Deborah	M	3	624.00	11.70	38.00	5.00
1	Greer, Daniel	M	2	399.00	34.20	30.00	5.00
5	Habig, Vincent	S	1	672.00			
9	Jones, Phyllis	M	2	608.00	79.80	30.00	10.00
10	Malloy, Timothy	S	2	544.00	10.20	30.00	10.00
2	Paxton, Alice	M	4	496.00		44.00	
4	Tait, Michelle	S	1	640.00	36.00		
7	Walzak, Thomas	S	1	472.00			15.00

Instructions: 1. Prepare a payroll register. The date of payment is May 31. Use the income tax withholding tables in Illustration 15-4 to find the income tax withholding for each employee. Calculate FICA tax withholding using an 8% tax rate. None of the employee accumulated earnings has exceeded the FICA tax base.
2. Prepare a check for the total amount of the net pay. Make the check payable to Payroll Account, and sign your name as a partner of Mercer Company. The beginning check stub balance is $10,287.20.

3. Prepare payroll checks for Daniel Greer, Check No. 426, and Michelle Tait, Check No. 431. Sign your name as a partner of Mercer Company. Record the two payroll check numbers in the payroll register.

CHALLENGE PROBLEM 15-C   Figuring piecework wages

Production workers in factories are frequently paid on the basis of the number of units they produce. This payroll method is referred to as the piecework incentive wage plan. Most piecework incentive wage plans include a guaranteed hourly rate to employees regardless of the number of units they produce. This guaranteed hourly rate is referred to as the base rate.

Time and motion study engineers usually determine the standard time required for producing a single unit. Assume, for example, that time studies determine that one-third of an hour is the standard time required to produce a unit. Then the standard rate for an 8-hour day would be 24 units (8 hours divided by 1/3 hour = 24 units per day). If a worker's daily base pay is $66.00, the incentive rate per unit is $2.75 ($66.00 divided by 24 units = $2.75 per unit). Therefore, the worker who produces 24 or fewer units per day is paid the base pay, $66.00. However, each worker is paid an additional $2.75 for each unit over 24 produced each day.

Southern Woodworks Company has eight employees in production departments that are paid on a piecework incentive wage plan. The following standard and incentive wage rates are listed by department.

Department	Standard Production per Employee	Incentive Rate per Unit
Cutting	30 units per day	$2.30
Assembly	20 units per day	$4.10
Finishing	40 units per day	$1.80

Each employee worked eight hours a day during the semimonthly pay period, August 1-15. Payroll records for August 1-15 are summarized in the following table.

Employee		Marital Status	No. of Allow-ances	Guaranteed Daily Rate	Units Produced per Day									
					Pay Period August 1–15									
No.	Name				2	3	4	5	6	9	10	11	12	13
Cutting Department														
C2	Simpson, Alan	S	1	$69.00	29	32	31	34	28	27	30	32	36	26
C4	Creek, Janice	M	1	$69.00	32	31	28	29	27	29	31	32	27	28
C8	Pate, Marie	M	2	$69.00	31	28	27	24	31	33	32	29	30	29
Assembly Department														
A1	Meese, Frank	S	1	$82.00	20	21	19	19	18	18	19	21	20	21
A6	Harris, Kevin	M	3	$82.00	25	21	17	18	19	21	20	20	21	18
A7	Martin, Angela	S	1	$82.00	22	24	25	21	20	19	23	21	18	17
Finishing Department														
F5	Quinn, Karen	M	2	$72.00	41	40	38	39	42	43	41	40	38	37
F3	Raines, Jon	M	2	$72.00	37	37	38	38	39	38	40	41	41	42

Instructions: Prepare a payroll register. The earnings column headed Incentive is used instead of Overtime. The date of payment is August 16. Use the income tax withholding tables in Illustration 15-4. Calculate the employee FICA tax withholding using an 8% tax rate. None of the employees has health insurance or other deductions.

Payroll Accounting, Taxes, and Reports

ENABLING PERFORMANCE TASKS

After studying Chapter 16, you will be able to:
a. Identify accounting concepts and practices related to payroll accounts, taxes, and reports.
b. Analyze payroll transactions.
c. Journalize and post payroll transactions.
d. Prepare selected payroll tax reports.

Payroll information for each pay period is recorded in a payroll register. Each pay period the payroll information for each employee is also recorded on each employee earnings record. Separate payroll accounts for each employee are not kept in the general ledger. Instead, accounts are kept in the general ledger to summarize total earnings and deductions for all employees.

The payroll register and employee earnings records provide all the payroll information needed to prepare a payroll and payroll tax reports. Journal entries are made to record the payment of the payroll and the employer payroll taxes. In addition, various quarterly and annual payroll tax reports are required to report the payment of payroll taxes.

RECORDING A PAYROLL

The payroll register for CarLand's semimonthly pay period ended December 15 is shown in Illustration 16-1.

Analyzing payment of a payroll

The column totals of a payroll register provide the debit and credit amounts needed to journalize a payroll. CarLand's December 15 payroll is summarized in the following T accounts.

```
                                          Employee Income Tax Payable
                                                    │  Dec. 15      192.00
                                               FICA Tax Payable
                                                    │  Dec. 15      204.48
                                          Health Insurance Premiums Payable
                                                    │  Dec. 15      158.00
              Salary Expense
  Dec. 15      2,556.00    │        =       U.S. Savings Bonds Payable
                                                    │  Dec. 15       15.00
                                          United Way Donations Payable
                                                    │  Dec. 15       10.00
                                                   Cash
                                                    │  Dec. 15    1,976.52
```

SEMIMONTHLY PERIOD ENDED *December 15, 19--*   **PAYROLL REGISTER**   **DATE OF PAYMENT** *December 15, 19--*

	EMPL. NO.	EMPLOYEE NAME	MARITAL STATUS	NO. OF ALLOWANCES	EARNINGS REGULAR	OVERTIME	TOTAL	DEDUCTIONS FEDERAL INCOME TAX	FICA TAX	HEALTH INSUR-ANCE	OTHER		TOTAL	NET PAY	CHECK NO.	
1	2	Bauch, Mary R.	M	2	660 00		660 00	57 00	52 80	38 00	B	5 00	152 80	507 20	419	1
2	5	Clay, Richard P.	S	1	80 00		80 00	00	6 40				6 40	73 60	420	2
3	1	Javorski, Adam B.	M	2	384 00	18 00	402 00	17 00	32 16	38 00			87 16	314 84	421	3
4	6	Maggio, Brenda A.	S	1	40 00		40 00	00	3 20				3 20	36 80	422	4
5	4	Turner, Patrick S.	M	4	704 00	54 00	758 00	45 00	60 64	50 00	B 10 00 / UW 10 00		175 64	582 36	423	5
6	3	Wilkes, Samuel R.	S	1	616 00		616 00	73 00	49 28	32 00			154 28	461 72	424	6
7					2484 00	72 00	2556 00	192 00	204 48	158 00	B 15 00 / UW 10 00		579 48	1976 52		7

The Total Earnings column total, $2,556.00, is the salary expense for the period. Salary Expense is debited for this amount.

Illustration 16-1 Payroll register

The Federal Income Tax column total, $192.00, is the amount withheld from employee salaries for federal income tax. The amount withheld is a liability of the business until the taxes are sent to the federal government. Employee Income Tax Payable is credited for $192.00 to record this liability.

The FICA Tax column total, $204.48, is the amount withheld from salaries of all employees for FICA tax. The amount withheld is a liability of the business until the tax is paid to the government. FICA Tax Payable is credited for $204.48.

The Health Insurance column total, $158.00, is the amount withheld from salaries for health insurance premiums. The amount withheld is a liability of the business until the premiums are paid to the insurance company. Health Insurance Premiums Payable is credited for $158.00 to record this liability.

The Other column of the deductions section may contain more than one total. Two types of *Other* deductions are recorded in CarLand's payroll register. The $15.00 Other column total identified with the letter *B* is withheld to buy savings bonds for employees. The $10.00 total identified with the letters *UW* is withheld for employee United Way pledges. Until these amounts have been paid by the employer, they are liabilities of the business. U.S. Savings Bonds Payable is credited for $15.00. United Way Donations Payable is credited for $10.00.

The Net Pay column total, $1,976.52, is the net amount paid to employees. Cash is credited for $1,976.52. A check for the total net pay amount, $1,976.52, is written on CarLand's general checking account. This amount is deposited in a special payroll checking account used only for employee payroll checks. Individual payroll checks are then written on the special payroll checking account.

Journalizing payment of a payroll

December 15, 19--.
Paid cash for semimonthly payroll, $1,976.52 (total payroll, $2,556.00, less deductions: employee income tax, $192.00; FICA tax, $204.48; health insurance premiums, $158.00; U.S. Savings Bonds, $15.00; United Way donations, $10.00). Check No. 287.

The source document for payment of a payroll is the check written for the total net pay. *(CONCEPT: Objective Evidence)* The journal entry to record payment of CarLand's December 15 payroll is shown in Illustration 16-2.

					GENERAL			CASH	
PAGE *24*		JOURNAL			1	2		PAGE *24*	
								10	11
	DATE	ACCOUNT TITLE	DOC. NO.	POST. REF.	DEBIT	CREDIT		DEBIT	CREDIT
21	15	*Salary Expense*	C287		2 5 5 6 00				1 9 7 6 52
22		*Employee Income Tax Pay.*				1 9 2 00			
23		*FICA Tax Payable*				2 0 4 48			
24		*Health Insurance Premiums Pay.*				1 5 8 00			
25		*U.S. Savings Bonds Payable*				1 5 00			
26		*United Way Donations Payable*				1 0 00			

Illustration 16-2
Journal entry to record
a payroll

The date, *15*, is written in the Date column. The title of the account debited, *Salary Expense*, is recorded in the Account Title column. The check number, *C287*, is entered in the Doc. No. column. The amount debited to Salary Expense, *$2,556.00*, is written in the General Debit column. On the same line, the net amount paid to employees, *$1,976.52*, is written in the Cash Credit column. Five liability accounts are credited for the amounts deducted from employee salaries. The five account titles are written in the Account Title column. The five credit amounts are written in the General Credit column.

Posting the journal entry for payment of a payroll

Amounts recorded in the General columns of a journal are posted individually to general ledger accounts. After the December 15 payroll entry is posted, the liability and salary expense accounts appear as shown in Illustration 16-3.

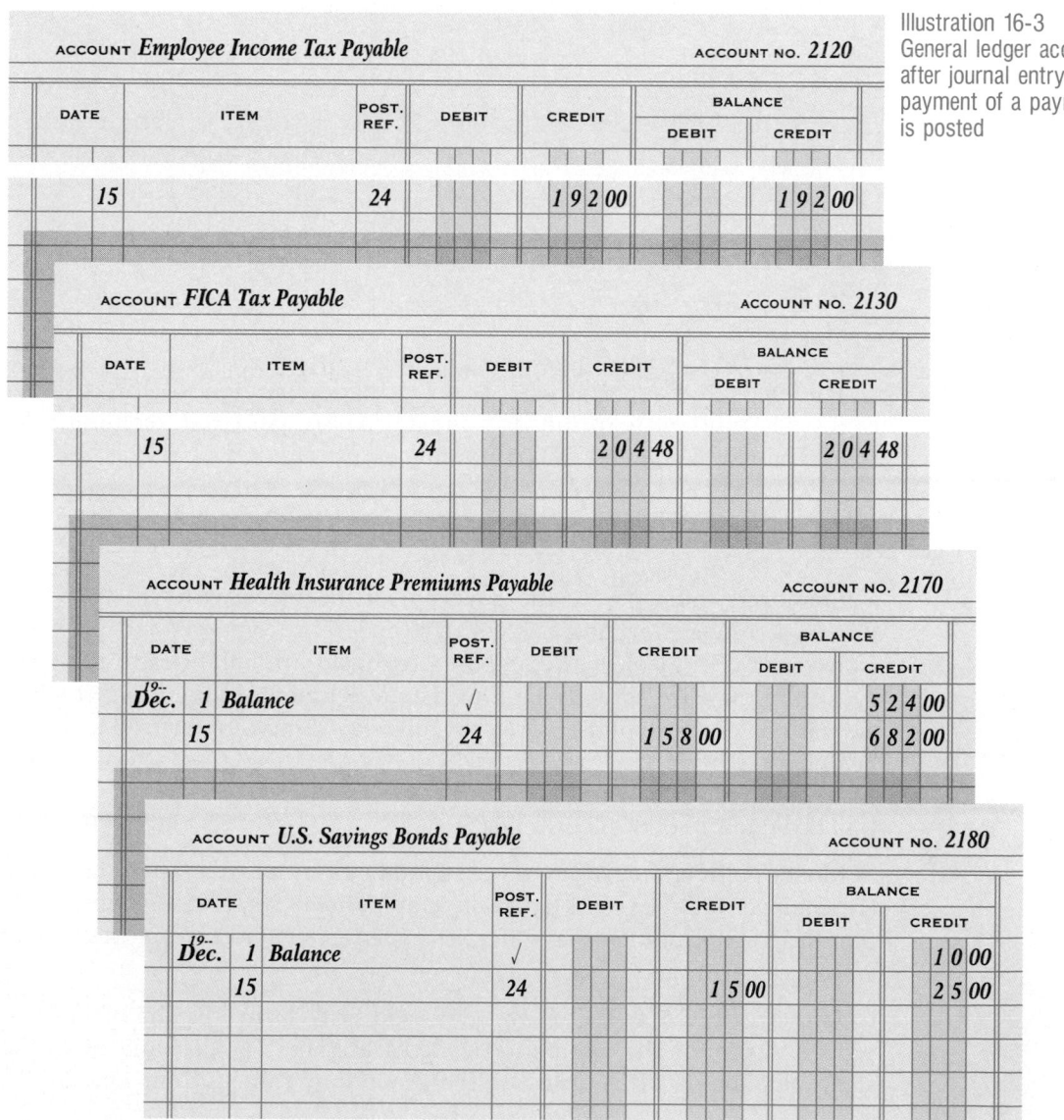

Illustration 16-3
General ledger accounts after journal entry for payment of a payroll is posted

ACCOUNT *Employee Income Tax Payable*   ACCOUNT NO. *2120*

DATE	ITEM	POST. REF.	DEBIT	CREDIT	BALANCE DEBIT	BALANCE CREDIT
15		24		1 9 2 00		1 9 2 00

ACCOUNT *FICA Tax Payable*   ACCOUNT NO. *2130*

DATE	ITEM	POST. REF.	DEBIT	CREDIT	BALANCE DEBIT	BALANCE CREDIT
15		24		2 0 4 48		2 0 4 48

ACCOUNT *Health Insurance Premiums Payable*   ACCOUNT NO. *2170*

DATE	ITEM	POST. REF.	DEBIT	CREDIT	BALANCE DEBIT	BALANCE CREDIT
Dec. 1	Balance	✓				5 2 4 00
15		24		1 5 8 00		6 8 2 00

ACCOUNT *U.S. Savings Bonds Payable*   ACCOUNT NO. *2180*

DATE	ITEM	POST. REF.	DEBIT	CREDIT	BALANCE DEBIT	BALANCE CREDIT
Dec. 1	Balance	✓				1 0 00
15		24		1 5 00		2 5 00

ACCOUNT *United Way Donations Payable*					ACCOUNT NO. *2190*	
DATE	ITEM	POST. REF.	DEBIT	CREDIT	BALANCE DEBIT	BALANCE CREDIT
Dec. 1	Balance	√				4 0 00
15		24		1 0 00		5 0 00

ACCOUNT *Salary Expense*					ACCOUNT NO. *6170*	
DATE	ITEM	POST. REF.	DEBIT	CREDIT	BALANCE DEBIT	BALANCE CREDIT
Dec. 1	Balance	√			54 9 5 2 00	
15		24	2 5 5 6 00		57 5 0 8 00	

Illustration 16-3
General ledger accounts after journal entry for payment of a payroll is posted (concluded)

The credit to Cash, $1,976.52, is not posted separately to the cash account. The amount is included in the journal's Cash Credit column total that is posted at the end of the month.

RECORDING EMPLOYER PAYROLL TAXES

Employers must pay to the government the taxes withheld from employee earnings. CarLand has withheld federal income tax and FICA tax from employee salaries. The amounts withheld are liabilities to the business until they are actually paid to the government. In addition, employers must pay several of their own payroll taxes. Employer payroll taxes are business expenses.

Calculating employer payroll taxes

Most employers must pay three separate payroll taxes. These taxes are (1) employer FICA tax, (2) federal unemployment tax, and (3) state unemployment tax. Employer payroll taxes expense is based on a percentage of employee earnings.

Employer FICA tax. CarLand withheld $204.48 in FICA tax from employee wages for the pay period ended December 15. CarLand owes the same amount of FICA taxes as the amount withheld from employees.

Therefore, CarLand's FICA tax for the pay period ended December 15 is also $204.48.

Congress sets the FICA tax rate for employees and employers. Periodically, Congress may change the tax rate and tax base. The employer FICA tax rate is the same as the employee FICA tax rate. A tax rate of 8% and a tax base of $50,000.00 are used in this textbook.

The FICA tax is the only payroll tax paid by *both* the employees and the employer. Employees pay 8% of their total earnings up to the $50,000.00 tax base as a FICA tax. Employers also pay 8% of each employee's total earnings up to the $50,000.00 tax base as a FICA tax.

Federal unemployment tax. Federal unemployment insurance laws require that employers pay taxes for unemployment compensation. These tax funds are used to pay workers benefits for limited periods of unemployment and to administer the unemployment compensation program. All of the federal unemployment tax is paid by the employer.

The federal unemployment tax for most businesses is 0.8% of total earnings of each employee up to a tax base of $7,000.00 during a calendar year. The total earnings of CarLand's December 1-15 pay period subject to the federal unemployment tax is referred to as unemployment taxable earnings. The amount of unemployment taxable earnings is figured as shown in Illustration 16-4.

CarLand Taxable Earnings for December 15, 19-- Pay Period			
	Accumulated Earnings as of Nov. 30, 19--	Total Earnings for Dec. 15, 19-- Pay Period	Unemployment Taxable Earnings
Bauch, Mary R........	$14,520.00	$660.00	$ —
Clay, Richard P.	2,160.00	80.00	80.00
Javorski, Adam B......	5,792.50	402.00	402.00
Maggio, Brenda A.....	1,680.00	40.00	40.00
Turner, Patrick S......	16,794.00	758.00	—
Wilkes, Samuel R.	4,976.50	616.00	616.00
			$1,138.00

Illustration 16-4
Total earnings subject to federal unemployment tax

Accumulated earnings are figured on each employee earnings record. Patrick S. Turner's accumulated earnings as of November 30, *$16,794.00*, are recorded in the first column. Total earnings for Mr. Turner for the December 15 pay period, *$758.00*, are recorded in the second column. Since the accumulated earnings for Mr. Turner are greater than $7,000.00, none of his current earnings are subject to federal unemployment tax. Thus, the amount of unemployment taxable earnings recorded in the third column is zero.

The accumulated earnings for Samuel R. Wilkes, $4,976.50, are less than $7,000.00. Therefore, his total earnings for the December 15 pay period are subject to federal unemployment tax. Total earnings for Mr. Wilkes for the December 15 pay period, *$616.00*, are recorded in the Unemployment Taxable Earnings column.

The total earnings for the pay period are entered in the Unemployment Taxable Earnings column for employees whose accumulated earnings are less than $7,000.00. The sum of the Unemployment Taxable Earnings Column, $1,138.00, is the amount used to calculate federal unemployment tax.

CarLand's federal unemployment tax is calculated as shown below.

Unemployment Taxable Earnings	×	Federal Unemployment Tax Rate	=	Federal Unemployment Tax
$1,138.00	×	.8%	=	$9.10

State unemployment tax. Most states require that employers pay unemployment tax of 5.4% on the first $7,000.00 earned by each employee. The unemployment taxable earnings used to calculate the federal unemployment tax are also used to calculate the state unemployment tax. The unemployment taxable earnings subject to the state unemployment tax are figured in Illustration 16-4. Thus, the state employment tax to be paid by CarLand is calculated as shown below.

Unemployment Taxable Earnings	×	State Unemployment Tax Rate	=	State Unemployment Tax
$1,138.00	×	5.4%	=	$61.45

Journalizing employer payroll taxes

Employer payroll taxes are paid to the government at a later date. However, the transaction to record employer payroll taxes expense is journalized on the same date the payroll is journalized. The salary expense and the employer payroll taxes expense are, therefore, both recorded in the same accounting period.

December 15, 19--.
Recorded employer payroll taxes expense, $275.03, for the semimonthly pay period ended December 15. Taxes owed are: FICA tax, $204.48; federal unemployment tax, $9.10; state unemployment tax, $61.45. Memorandum No. 54.

The source document for journalizing employer payroll taxes is a memorandum. *(CONCEPT: Objective Evidence)* The entry to record employer payroll taxes is analyzed in the T accounts.

Payroll Taxes Expense is debited for $275.03 to show the increase in the balance of this expense account. Three liability accounts are credited to show the increase in payroll tax liabilities. FICA Tax Payable is credited for $204.48. Unemployment Tax Payable—Federal is credited for $9.10. Unemployment Tax Payable—State is credited for $61.45.

CarLand's journal entry to record the employer payroll taxes expense is shown in Illustration 16-5.

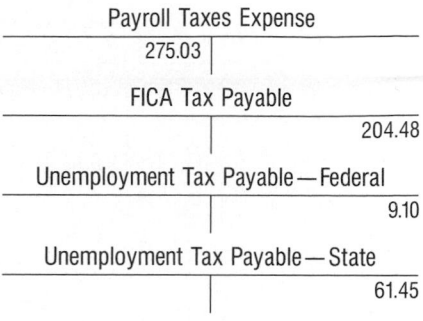

Payroll Taxes Expense	
275.03	

FICA Tax Payable	
	204.48

Unemployment Tax Payable—Federal	
	9.10

Unemployment Tax Payable—State	
	61.45

PAGE *24* — JOURNAL — PAGE *24*

		DATE	ACCOUNT TITLE	DOC. NO.	POST. REF.	GENERAL DEBIT	GENERAL CREDIT	CASH DEBIT	CASH CREDIT	
27		15	*Payroll Taxes Expense*	M54		2 7 5 03				27
28			*FICA Tax Payable*				2 0 4 48			28
29			*Unemployment Tax Pay.—Federal*				9 10			29
30			*Unemployment Tax Pay.—State*				6 1 45			30
31										31

The date, *15,* is written in the Date column. The title of the account debited, *Payroll Taxes Expense,* is written in the Account Title column. The memorandum number, *M54,* is entered in the Doc. No. column. The debit amount, *$275.03,* is entered in the General Debit column. The titles of the liability accounts are entered in the Account Title column. The amounts credited to the liability accounts are entered in the General Credit column.

Illustration 16-5
Journal entry to record employer payroll taxes

Posting an employer payroll taxes entry

After the entry for the employer payroll taxes is posted, the accounts involved appear as shown in Illustration 16-6.

ACCOUNT *FICA Tax Payable*   ACCOUNT NO. *2130*

	DATE	ITEM	POST. REF.	DEBIT	CREDIT	BALANCE DEBIT	BALANCE CREDIT
	15		24		2 0 4 48		2 0 4 48
	15		24		2 0 4 48		4 0 8 96

Illustration 16-6
General ledger accounts after journal entry for employer payroll taxes expense is posted

ACCOUNT Unemployment Tax Payable—Federal						ACCOUNT NO. 2150

DATE		ITEM	POST. REF.	DEBIT	CREDIT	BALANCE DEBIT	BALANCE CREDIT
Dec. 19--	1	Balance	✓				40 48
	15		24		9 10		49 58

ACCOUNT Unemployment Tax Payable—State						ACCOUNT NO. 2160

DATE		ITEM	POST. REF.	DEBIT	CREDIT	BALANCE DEBIT	BALANCE CREDIT
Dec. 19--	1	Balance	✓				273 22
	15		24		61 45		334 67

ACCOUNT Payroll Taxes Expense						ACCOUNT NO. 6150

DATE		ITEM	POST. REF.	DEBIT	CREDIT	BALANCE DEBIT	BALANCE CREDIT
Dec. 19--	1	Balance	✓			6738 96	
	15		24	275 03		7013 99	

Illustration 16-6
General ledger accounts
after journal entry for
employer payroll taxes
expense is posted
(concluded)

The FICA Tax Payable account has two credits. The first credit, $204.48, is the FICA tax withheld from *employee* wages for the semimonthly period ended December 15. This amount was posted from the journal entry that recorded payment of the payroll, Illustration 16-2. The second credit, $204.48, is the *employer* liability for FICA tax. This amount was posted from the journal entry that recorded the employer payroll taxes, Illustration 16-5.

Summary of amounts posted to the general ledger

Both the employees and employer owe payroll taxes. Federal income tax and FICA tax are withheld from employee salaries. An equal amount of FICA tax is owed by the employer. The employer must also record federal and state unemployment taxes. The payroll taxes resulting from Car-Land's December 1-15 pay period are summarized below.

	Employees	Employer
Federal Income Tax	$192.00	—
FICA Tax	204.48	$204.48
Federal Unemployment Tax	—	9.10
State Unemployment Tax	—	61.45
Total	$396.48	$275.03

Only the employer payroll taxes, $275.03, are recorded as payroll taxes expense in CarLand's general ledger accounts. The payroll taxes of both the employees and the employer create liabilities to the business which must be paid at times specified by the government.

REPORTING WITHHOLDING AND PAYROLL TAXES

Each employer is required by law to periodically report the payroll taxes withheld from employee salaries and the employer payroll taxes due the government. Some reports are submitted quarterly and others are submitted annually.

Employer quarterly federal tax return

Each employer must file a quarterly federal tax return showing the federal income tax and FICA taxes due the government. This information is submitted every three months on Form 941, Employer's Quarterly Federal Tax Return. Form 941 is filed before the last day of the month following the end of a calendar quarter. CarLand's Form 941 for the calendar quarter ended December 31 is shown in Illustration 16-7, page 366. The information needed to prepare Form 941 is obtained from employee earnings records.

Total earnings, $15,192.90, are recorded on line 2 of Form 941. This amount is the sum of the fourth quarter total earnings of all CarLand employees. The amount of total earnings, $15,192.90, is also recorded on the line to the left of line 6. The income tax withheld, $1,168.00, is recorded on line 3 of Form 941. The amount is the total of the fourth quarter federal income tax withheld from CarLand's employees.

The social security (FICA) taxes due are calculated as shown below.

Total Earnings	×	FICA Tax Rate	=	Social Security (FICA) Tax
$15,192.90	×	16%	=	$2,430.86

The 16% tax rate is the sum of the *employee* 8% FICA tax rate and the *employer* 8% FICA tax rate. The FICA tax amount, $2,430.86, is recorded on line 6 of Form 941.

CarLand is required to pay the federal government the sum of the FICA tax and federal income tax withheld. The amount of the payment is figured as shown below.

Federal Income Tax Withheld	+	FICA Tax	=	Total Payment
$1,168.00	+	$2,430.86	=	$3,598.86

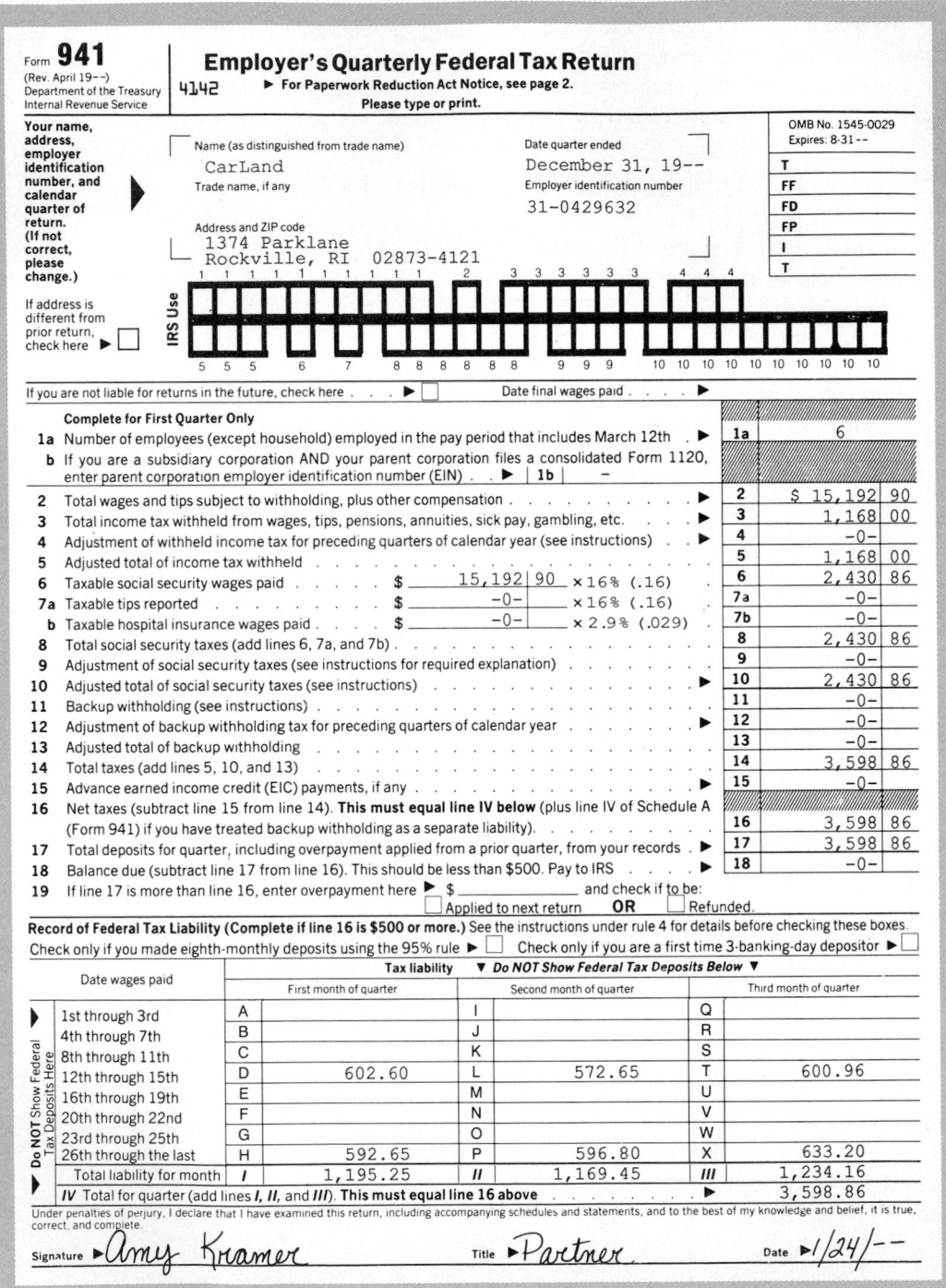

Form **941**
(Rev. April 19--)
Department of the Treasury
Internal Revenue Service
4142

Employer's Quarterly Federal Tax Return
▶ For Paperwork Reduction Act Notice, see page 2.
Please type or print.

Your name, address, employer identification number, and calendar quarter of return. (If not correct, please change.)

Name (as distinguished from trade name)
CarLand
Trade name, if any

Address and ZIP code
1374 Parklane
Rockville, RI 02873-4121

Date quarter ended
December 31, 19--
Employer identification number
31-0429632

OMB No. 1545-0029
Expires: 8-31 --

T
FF
FD
FP
I
T

If address is different from prior return, check here ▶ ☐

If you are not liable for returns in the future, check here . . . ▶ ☐   Date final wages paid . . . . ▶

Complete for First Quarter Only

1a	Number of employees (except household) employed in the pay period that includes March 12th . . ▶	**1a**	6	
b	If you are a subsidiary corporation AND your parent corporation files a consolidated Form 1120, enter parent corporation employer identification number (EIN) . . ▶ **1b** –			
2	Total wages and tips subject to withholding, plus other compensation . . . . ▶	**2**	$ 15,192	90
3	Total income tax withheld from wages, tips, pensions, annuities, sick pay, gambling, etc. . . . ▶	**3**	1,168	00
4	Adjustment of withheld income tax for preceding quarters of calendar year (see instructions) . . ▶	**4**	-0-	
5	Adjusted total of income tax withheld	**5**	1,168	00
6	Taxable social security wages paid . . . . $ _15,192|90_ × 16% (.16)	**6**	2,430	86
7a	Taxable tips reported . . . . . . $ _-0-_ × 16% (.16)	**7a**	-0-	
b	Taxable hospital insurance wages paid . . . $ _-0-_ × 2.9% (.029) . .	**7b**	-0-	
8	Total social security taxes (add lines 6, 7a, and 7b)	**8**	2,430	86
9	Adjustment of social security taxes (see instructions for required explanation)	**9**	-0-	
10	Adjusted total of social security taxes (see instructions) . . . . ▶	**10**	2,430	86
11	Backup withholding (see instructions)	**11**	-0-	
12	Adjustment of backup withholding tax for preceding quarters of calendar year . . . . . ▶	**12**	-0-	
13	Adjusted total of backup withholding	**13**	-0-	
14	Total taxes (add lines 5, 10, and 13)	**14**	3,598	86
15	Advance earned income credit (EIC) payments, if any . . . . ▶	**15**	-0-	
16	Net taxes (subtract line 15 from line 14). **This must equal line IV below** (plus line IV of Schedule A (Form 941) if you have treated backup withholding as a separate liability).	**16**	3,598	86
17	Total deposits for quarter, including overpayment applied from a prior quarter, from your records . ▶	**17**	3,598	86
18	Balance due (subtract line 17 from line 16). This should be less than $500. Pay to IRS . . . ▶	**18**	-0-	
19	If line 17 is more than line 16, enter overpayment here ▶ $ _____ and check if to be: ☐ Applied to next return **OR** ☐ Refunded.			

Record of Federal Tax Liability (Complete if line 16 is $500 or more.) See the instructions under rule 4 for details before checking these boxes.

Check only if you made eighth-monthly deposits using the 95% rule ▶ ☐   Check only if you are a first time 3-banking-day depositor ▶ ☐

Do NOT Show Federal Tax Deposits Here

Date wages paid	Tax liability	▼ Do NOT Show Federal Tax Deposits Below ▼					
		First month of quarter		Second month of quarter		Third month of quarter	
1st through 3rd	A		I		Q		
4th through 7th	B		J		R		
8th through 11th	C		K		S		
12th through 15th	D	602.60	L	572.65	T	600.96	
16th through 19th	E		M		U		
20th through 22nd	F		N		V		
23rd through 25th	G		O		W		
26th through the last	H	592.65	P	596.80	X	633.20	
Total liability for month	I	1,195.25	II	1,169.45	III	1,234.16	

IV Total for quarter (add lines *I*, *II*, and *III*). **This must equal line 16 above** . . . . ▶   3,598.86

Under penalties of perjury, I declare that I have examined this return, including accompanying schedules and statements, and to the best of my knowledge and belief, it is true, correct, and complete.

Signature ▶ *Amy Kramer*   Title ▶ *Partner*   Date ▶ 1/24/--

Illustration 16-7   Form 941, Employer's Quarterly Federal Tax Return

The total payment owed to the federal government, *$3,598.86*, is recorded on line 14 of Form 941.

The lower section of Form 941 lists the amounts and dates when payroll taxes were withheld from employees and are due from the employer. For the pay period ended December 15, the amount of taxes owed is figured as shown below.

Federal Income Tax Withheld		Employee FICA Tax		Employer FICA Tax		Federal Tax Liability
$192.00	+	$204.48	+	$204.48	=	$600.96

The federal tax liability for the December 15 pay period, *$600.96*, is recorded on line T of Form 941. The December 15 pay period ended in the third month of the quarter between the 12th and 15th of the month. The December 15 pay period is, therefore, recorded on line T.

Employer annual report to employees of taxes withheld

Each employer who withholds income tax and FICA tax from employee earnings must furnish each employee with an annual report of these withholdings. The report shows total year's earnings and the amounts withheld for taxes for an employee. These amounts are obtained from the employee earnings records. The report is prepared on the Internal Revenue Service Form W-2, Wage and Tax Statement.

Employers are required to furnish Form W-2 to each employee by January 31 of the next year. If an employee ends employment before December 31, Form W-2 must be furnished within 30 days of the last date of employment.

The Form W-2 prepared by CarLand for Patrick S. Turner is shown in Illustration 16-8, on page 368.

Four copies (A to D) of Form W-2 are prepared for each employee. Copies B and C are given to the employee. The employee attaches Copy B to a personal federal income tax return and keeps Copy C for a personal record. The employer sends Copy A to the Social Security Administration and keeps Copy D for the business' records.

> Businesses in states with state income tax must prepare additional copies of Form W-2. The employee attaches the additional copy to the personal state income tax return.

Employer annual reporting of payroll taxes

Form W-3, Transmittal of Income and Tax Statements, is sent to the Social Security Administration by February 28 each year. Form W-3 reports the previous year's earnings and payroll taxes withheld for all employees. Attached to Form W-3 is Copy A of each employee Form W-2. A Form W-3 prepared by CarLand is shown in Illustration 16-9.

1 Control number	22222	OMB No. 1545-0008					

Form W-2 Wage and Tax Statement 19 --

Form W-2 Wage and Tax Statement (Copy A For Social Security Administration — Dept. of the Treasury—Internal Revenue Service):

- 1 Control number: 22222 OMB No. 1545-0008
- 2 Employer's name, address, and ZIP code:
  CarLand
  1374 Parklane
  Rockville, RI 02873-4121
- 6 Statutory employee / Deceased / Pension plan / Legal rep / 942 emp. / Subtotal / Deferred compensation / Void
- 7 Allocated tips
- 8 Advance EIC payment
- 9 Federal income tax withheld: 1,032.00
- 10 Wages, tips, other compensation: 18,192.00
- 3 Employer's identification number: 31-0429632
- 4 Employer's state I.D. number
- 11 Social security tax withheld: 1,455.36
- 12 Social security wages: 18,192.00
- 5 Employee's social security number: 450-70-6432
- 13 Social security tips
- 14 Nonqualified plans
- 19 Employee's name, address and ZIP code:
  Patrick S. Turner
  1625 Northland Drive
  Rockville, RI 02873-5073
- 15 Dependent care benefits
- 16 Fringe benefits incl. in Box 10
- 17
- 18 Other
- 20 / 21 / 22 / 23
- 24 State income tax
- 25 State wages, tips, etc.
- 26 Name of state
- 27 Local income tax
- 28 Local wages, tips, etc.
- 29 Name of locality

Copy A For Social Security Administration   Dept. of the Treasury—Internal Revenue Service

Illustration 16-8
Form W-2, Wage and Tax Statement

Form W-3 Transmittal of Income and Tax Statements 19 --   Department of the Treasury Internal Revenue Service

- 1 Control number: 33333   OMB No. 1545-0008
- Kind of Payer:
  - 2 941/941E [X] Military [ ] 943 [ ]
  - CT-1 [ ] 942 [ ] Medicare gov't. emp. [ ]
- 3 Employer's state I.D. number
- 5 Total number of statements: 6
- 4
- 6 Establishment number
- 7 Allocated tips
- 8 Advance EIC payments
- 9 Federal income tax withheld: 4,612.00
- 10 Wages, tips, and other compensation: 60,153.00
- 11 Social security tax withheld: 4,812.24
- 12 Social security wages: 60,153.00
- 13 Social security tips
- 14 Nonqualified plans
- 15 Dependent care benefits
- 16 Adjusted total social security wages and tips
- 17 Deferred compensation
- 18 Employer's identification number: 31 — 0429632
- 19 Other EIN used this year
- 20 Employer's name: CarLand
- 21 Gross annuity, pension, etc. (Form W-2P)
- 23 Taxable amount (Form W-2P)
- 24 Income tax withheld by third-party payer
- 22 Employer's address and ZIP code:
  1374 Parklane
  Rockville, RI 02873-4121

Under penalties of perjury, I declare that I have examined this return and accompanying documents, and to the best of my knowledge and belief, they are true, correct, and complete.

Signature ▶ *Amy Kramer*   Title ▶ *Partner*   Date ▶ 2/27/--

Telephone number (optional)

Illustration 16-9
Form W-3, Transmittal of Income and Tax Statements

At the end of a calendar year, employers must also report to the federal and state governments a summary of all earnings paid to employees during the twelve months.

Employers with more than 250 employees have different procedures for reporting withholding tax information. The information is sent to the Internal Revenue Service in computer files rather than the actual Forms W-2 and W-3.

PAYING WITHHOLDING AND PAYROLL TAXES

At least quarterly, employers must pay to the federal government the federal income taxes and FICA taxes withheld from employee salaries. The payment also includes the amount of employer FICA taxes.

Paying the liability for employee income tax and FICA tax

Employee withheld income tax, employee FICA tax, and employer FICA tax are paid periodically in a combined payment. Tax payments are made to banks authorized by the Internal Revenue Service to accept these payments or to a Federal Reserve bank. The timing of these tax payments is based on the amount of taxes owed. A payment is accompanied by a Form 8109, Federal Tax Deposit Coupon, which shows the amount and purpose of the payment.

In December, CarLand withheld $402.00 from employee salaries for federal income taxes. The liability for FICA tax for December is $832.16. This amount includes both the employer share and the amounts withheld from employees. CarLand's federal tax payment is sent January 15 to an authorized bank with Form 8109 as shown in Illustration 16-10.

Illustration 16-10
Form 8109, Federal Tax Deposit Coupon for withheld income tax and FICA taxes

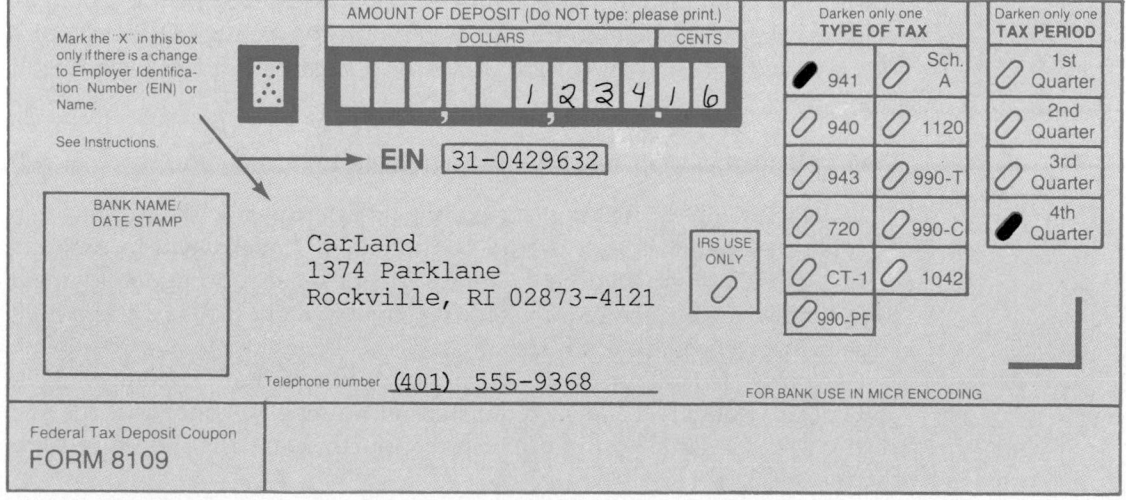

The type of tax, federal income and FICA taxes, is identified by marking the 941 circle. These taxes are reported to the government using Form 941. The calendar quarter is identified on the right side of the form.

January 15, 19--.
Paid cash for liability for employee income tax, $402.00, and for FICA tax, $832.16; total, $1,234.16. Check No. 305.

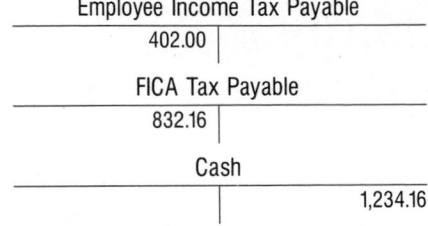

Employee Income Tax Payable	
402.00	

FICA Tax Payable	
832.16	

Cash	
	1,234.16

The source document for this transaction is the check written to pay the payroll taxes liability. *(CONCEPT: Objective Evidence)* This transaction is analyzed in the T accounts.

The balances of the liability accounts are reduced by this transaction. Therefore, Employee Income Tax Payable is debited for $402.00. FICA Tax Payable is debited for $832.16. The balance of the Cash account is decreased by a credit for the total payment, $1,234.16.

The journal entry to record payment of these liabilities is shown in Illustration 16-11.

						GENERAL				CASH	
PAGE 27		JOURNAL				1	2		PAGE 27	10	11
	DATE	ACCOUNT TITLE	DOC. NO.	POST. REF.		DEBIT	CREDIT			DEBIT	CREDIT
25	15	*Employee Income Tax Payable*	C305			4 0 2 00					1 2 3 4 16	25
26		*FICA Tax Payable*				8 3 2 16						26
27												27

Illustration 16-11
Journal entry to record payment of liability for employee income tax and FICA tax

The date, *15*, is written in the Date column. The titles of the two accounts debited, *Employee Income Tax Payable* and *FICA Tax Payable*, are written in the Account Title column. The check number, *C305*, is entered in the Doc. No. column. The two debit amounts are entered in the General Debit column. The amount of the credit to Cash, *$1,234.16*, is recorded in the Cash Credit column.

Paying the liability for federal unemployment tax

Federal unemployment tax is usually paid after the end of each quarter. Federal unemployment tax is paid to the federal government by sending the check to a designated bank. The payment for federal unemployment tax is similar to the one required for income tax and FICA tax. Form 8109, Federal Tax Deposit Coupon, accompanies the unemployment tax payment.

CarLand's federal unemployment tax at the end of December 31 is $59.15. A payment is made each quarter but no report is due until the end of the year. CarLand's Form 8109 for the fourth quarter is shown in Illustration 16-12.

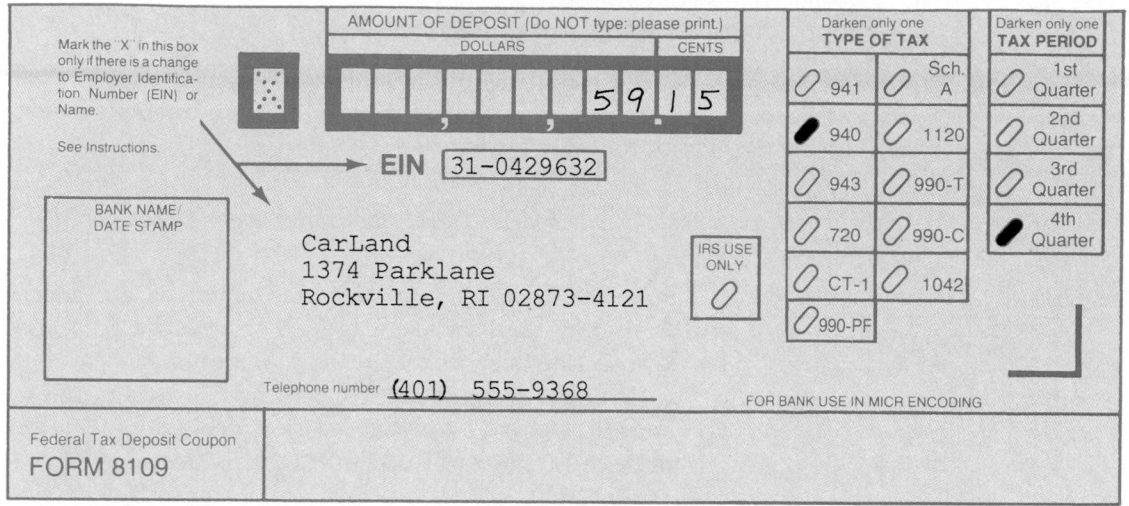

The type of tax, federal unemployment tax, is identified by marking the 940 circle since this tax is reported to the government using Form 940. The calendar quarter is identified on the right side of the form.

Illustration 16-12
Form 8109, Federal Tax Deposit Coupon for federal unemployment tax

January 31, 19--.
Paid cash for federal unemployment tax liability for quarter ended December 31, $59.15. Check No. 318.

The source document for this transaction is the check written to pay the payroll tax liability. *(CONCEPT: Objective Evidence)* This transaction is analyzed in the T accounts.

The balance of the liability account is reduced by this transaction. Therefore, Unemployment Tax Payable—Federal is debited for $59.15. The balance of the asset account, Cash, is decreased by a credit for the payment, $59.15.

The journal entry to record payment of the liability for federal unemployment taxes is shown in Illustration 16-13.

Unemployment Tax Payable—Federal	
59.15	

Cash	
	59.15

PAGE 28						JOURNAL					PAGE 28	
						1	2			10	11	
	DATE	ACCOUNT TITLE	DOC. NO.	POST. REF.		GENERAL				CASH		
						DEBIT	CREDIT			DEBIT	CREDIT	
27	31	*Unemployment Tax Pay.—Federal*	C318			5 9 15					5 9 15	27
28												28

The date, *31*, is written in the Date column. The title of the account debited, *Unemployment Tax Payable—Federal*, is written in the Account Title column. The check number, *C318*, is entered in the Doc. No. column. The check amount, *$59.15*, is entered in the General Debit and Cash Credit columns.

Illustration 16-13
Journal entry to record payment of liability for federal unemployment tax

Paying the liability for state unemployment tax

State requirements for reporting and paying state unemployment taxes vary. In general, employers are required to pay the state unemployment tax during the month following each calendar quarter.

January 31, 19--.
Paid cash for state unemployment tax liability for quarter ended December 31, $399.26. Check No. 319.

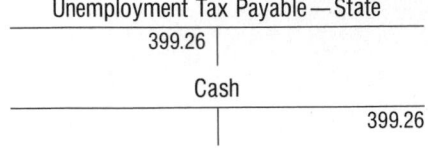

The source document for this transaction is the check written to pay the liability. *(CONCEPT: Objective Evidence)* This transaction is analyzed in the T accounts.

The liability account is reduced by this transaction. Therefore, Unemployment Tax Payable—State is debited for $399.26. The balance of the asset account, Cash, is decreased by a credit, $399.26.

The journal entry to record payment of the liability for state unemployment tax is shown in Illustration 16-14.

PAGE 28	JOURNAL								
					GENERAL			CASH	
DATE	ACCOUNT TITLE	DOC. NO.	POST. REF.		DEBIT	CREDIT		DEBIT	CREDIT
31	Unemployment Tax Pay.—State	C319			399 26				399 26

Illustration 16-14
Journal entry to record payment of liability for state unemployment tax

The date, *31*, is written in the Date column. The title of the account debited, *Unemployment Tax Payable—State*, is written in the Account Title column. The check number, *C319*, is entered in the Doc. No. column. The check amount, *$399.26*, is entered in the General Debit and Cash Credit columns.

SUMMARY OF PAYROLL ACCOUNTING, TAXES, AND REPORTS

The payroll register provides the amounts required to journalize the payroll. Employer payroll taxes are calculated and recorded in the journal. Later, the employee and employer payroll taxes are paid to the federal and state governments. The entries to journalize a payroll and payroll taxes are summarized in Illustration 16-15.

ACCOUNT TITLE	1	2	10	11
	GENERAL		CASH	
	DEBIT	CREDIT	DEBIT	CREDIT
Pay the Payroll:				
Salary Expense	X			X
Employee Income Tax Payable		X		
FICA Tax Payable		X		
Health Insurance Premiums Payable		X		
U.S. Savings Bonds Payable		X		
United Way Donations Payable		X		
Record Employer Payroll Taxes:				
Payroll Taxes Expense	X			
FICA Tax Payable		X		
Unemployment Tax Payable—Federal		X		
Unemployment Tax Payable—State		X		
Pay Employee and Employer Taxes:				
Employee Income Tax Payable	X			X
FICA Tax Payable	X			
Unemployment Tax Payable—Federal	X			X
Unemployment Tax Payable—State	X			X

Illustration 16-15
Summary of payroll journal entries

The chart in Illustration 16-16 summarizes the types of payroll taxes and who pays each tax.

Tax	Who Pays the Tax	
	Employee	Employer
Federal Income Tax	X	
FICA Tax	X	X
Federal Unemployment Tax		X
State Unemployment Tax		X

Illustration 16-16
Summary of payroll taxes

■ QUESTIONS FOR INDIVIDUAL STUDY

1. Why does a business need to keep payroll information about individual employees?
2. What two business forms provide the payroll information needed about individual employees?
3. What accounts are affected, and how, by an entry to record a payroll?
4. Where is the amount obtained which is used to write a payroll check?
5. What is the source document for journalizing payment of a payroll?
6. What are the three payroll taxes paid by most employers?
7. What is the only payroll tax paid by both the employee and the employer?
8. What amount is used to calculate federal unemployment tax?
9. When is the transaction to record employer payroll taxes expense journalized?
10. Which accounting concept is being applied when a memorandum is used as the source document for journalizing employer payroll taxes?
11. What accounts are affected, and how, by an entry to record employer payroll taxes?
12. Where is the information obtained that is needed to prepare a quarterly federal tax return, Form 941?
13. How is the 16% FICA tax rate used on Form 941 figured?
14. What amounts are used to figure the tax liability for a pay period as reported on the quarterly federal tax return, Form 941?
15. What information is reported on a Form W-2, Wage and Tax Statement?
16. Who receives a completed Form W-2, Wage and Tax Statement?
17. What should an employee do with Copies B and C of Form W-2, Wage and Tax Statement, received from an employer?
18. What is the purpose of Form W-3, Transmittal of Income and Tax Statements?
19. What payroll taxes are deposited using Form 8109, Federal Tax Deposit Coupon?
20. What accounts are affected, and how, by an entry to record payment of an employer liability for federal unemployment tax?

■ CASES FOR MANAGEMENT DECISION

CASE 1 The partners of Smith and Tyson have decided to hire a sales manager. They agree that the business can only afford to pay the manager a salary of $30,000.00. The accounting clerk informs the partners that hiring the manager will cost the business more than the $30,000.00 salary. Do you agree with the accounting clerk? Explain your response.

CASE 2 Miller Manufacturing had total salary expense for the month of November of $40,000.00. Sandra Peterson, accounting clerk, figured the November employer FICA tax as $3,200.00 ($40,000.00 × 8%). Samuel Grissom, accountant, stated that the FICA taxes withheld from employee earnings were $2,850.00. What is the most likely reason for the difference between Ms. Peterson's and Mr. Grissom's figures for FICA taxes? Explain.

■ DRILLS FOR UNDERSTANDING

DRILL 16-D1   Analyzing payroll transactions

Instructions: 1. Prepare the following T accounts for four different businesses: Cash, Employee Income Tax Payable, FICA Tax Payable, Unemployment Tax Payable — Federal, Unemployment Tax Payable — State, Payroll Taxes Expense, and Salary Expense.

Busi-ness	Total Earnings	Federal Income Tax Withheld	Employee FICA Tax	Employer FICA Tax	Federal Unemploy-ment Tax	State Unemploy-ment Tax
A	$ 9,000.00	$1,350.00	$ 720.00	$ 720.00	$ 72.00	$486.00
B	4,200.00	590.00	336.00	336.00	33.60	226.80
C	12,600.00	2,016.00	1,008.00	1,008.00	100.80	680.40
D	7,800.00	1,140.00	624.00	624.00	62.40	421.20

2. Use T accounts to analyze the following payroll entries for each business. (a) Entry to record payment of a payroll. (b) Entry to record employer payroll taxes.

DRILL 16-D2   Calculating employer payroll taxes

The following payroll information is taken from a payroll register and employee earnings records.

Employee Name	Accumulated Earnings, April 30	Total Earnings for May 1–15 Pay Period
Blette, Kathryn	$ 4,689.00	$ 586.00
Easton, Phillip	3,882.50	427.00
Goodpaster, Sandra	8,450.00	1,045.00
Lake, Margaret	5,725.90	827.75
Raymond, Peter	7,329.00	945.60
Saenz, Raul	10,426.00	1,236.00
Williams, Patricia	4,107.25	518.50

Instructions: 1. Calculate the amount of earnings subject to unemployment taxes. Unemployment taxes are owed on the first $7,000.00 of earnings for each employee.

2. Calculate the amount of employer payroll taxes owed for the May 1-15 pay period. Employer payroll tax rates are as follows: FICA, 8%; federal unemployment, 0.8%; state unemployment, 5.4%.

■ APPLICATION PROBLEMS

PROBLEM 16-1   Journalizing and posting payment of semimonthly payrolls

Lambert's payroll register has the following totals for two semimonthly pay periods, August 1-15 and August 16-31 of the current year.

Period	Total Earnings	Deductions				Net Pay
		Federal Income Tax	FICA Tax	Other	Total	
Aug. 1–15	$3,670.00	$514.00	$293.60	B $90.00	$897.60	$2,772.40
Aug. 16–31	$3,180.00	$437.00	$254.40	B $75.00	$766.40	$2,413.60
Other Deductions: B—U.S. Savings Bonds						

Instructions: 1. Journalize payment of the two payrolls on page 17 of a journal. The first payroll was paid by Check No. 756 on August 15 of the current year. The second payroll was paid by Check No. 768 on August 31 of the current year.

2. Post the items that are to be posted individually. The balances in the general ledger are recorded as of August 1 of the current year.

Account No.	Account Title	August 1 Balance
2120	Employee Income Tax Payable	$ —
2130	FICA Tax Payable	—
2150	Unemployment Tax Payable—Federal	—
2160	Unemployment Tax Payable—State	—
2180	U.S. Savings Bonds Payable	—
6150	Payroll Taxes Expense	4,939.23
6170	Salary Expense	38,609.00

The general ledger accounts used in Problem 16-1 are needed to complete Problem 16-2.

PROBLEM 16-2   Calculating, journalizing, and posting employer payroll taxes

The general ledger accounts used in Problem 16-1 are needed to complete Problem 16-2.

Lambert's semimonthly payroll register totals are shown in Problem 16-1. Employer payroll tax rates are as follows: FICA, 8%; federal unemployment, 0.8%; state unemployment, 5.4%. Unemployment taxes are owed on the first $7,000.00 of earnings for each employee.

Use the following information about accumulated earnings and total earnings for the August 1-15 pay period.

Employee Name	Accumulated Earnings, July 31	Total Earnings for August 1–15 Pay Period	Total Earnings for August 16–31 Pay Period
Carson, Michael	$ 4,634.00	$767.50	$634.50
Franks, Janice	5,623.50	430.00	324.50
Hester, Mary	12,230.00	924.00	874.00
Marchese, Thomas	2,346.50	213.00	138.00
Pait, Kim	3,243.00	624.50	573.00
Toler, Troy	10,532.00	711.00	636.00

Instructions: 1. Figure the amount of earnings subject to unemployment taxes for the August 1-15 pay period.

2. Calculate the employer payroll tax amounts for the August 1-15 pay period.

3. Journalize the employer payroll taxes on page 18 of a journal. Use the date of August 15 of the current year. The source document is Memorandum No. 75.

4. Post the items that are to be posted individually.

5. Total earnings for the August 16-31 pay period are as follows.

Carson, Michael	$634.50
Franks, Janice	324.50
Hester, Mary	874.00
Marchese, Thomas	138.00
Pait, Kim	573.00
Toler, Troy	636.00

Calculate the employer payroll taxes for the August 16-31 pay period. Figure August 15 accumulated earnings by adding total earnings for the August 1-15 pay period to the July 31 accumulated earnings.

6. Journalize the employer payroll taxes on page 18 of a journal. Use the date of August 31 of the current year. The source document is Memorandum No. 82.

7. Post the items that are to be posted individually.

PROBLEM 16-3 Reporting employer quarterly withholding and payroll taxes

The following payroll data is for Jenson Clothing Company for the second quarter of the current year.

Date Paid	Total Earnings	Federal Income Tax Withheld	Employee FICA Tax Withheld
April 15	$2,825.00	$416.00	$226.00
April 30	2,987.00	438.00	238.96
May 15	3,142.00	468.00	251.36
May 31	2,936.00	428.00	234.88
June 15	3,212.00	489.00	256.96
June 30	2,849.00	422.00	227.92

Additional data.
1. Company address: 669 Eagle Street, Warrenville, IL 62325-4600
2. Employer identification number: 60-8909267
3. Number of employees: 5
4. Federal tax payments have been made on May 15, June 15, and July 15.

Instructions: Prepare a Form 941, Employer's Quarterly Federal Tax Return, for Jenson Clothing Company. The return is for the second quarter of the current year. Use the date July 21. Sign your name as a partner of the company.

PROBLEM 16-4 Calculating and journalizing withholding and payroll taxes

The following payroll data is for Hawbecker Company for the first quarter of the current year.

Period	Total Earnings	Federal Income Tax Withheld
March	$12,537.00	$2,138.00
First Quarter	37,293.00	—

In addition, total earnings are subject to 8% employee and 8% employer FICA tax. The federal unemployment tax rate is 0.8% and the state unemployment tax rate is 5.4% of total earnings. No total earnings have exceeded the tax base for calculating unemployment taxes.

Instructions: 1. Calculate the appropriate liability amount of FICA tax for March. Journalize the payment of the federal income tax and FICA tax liabilities on page 7 of a journal. The taxes were paid by Check No. 785 on April 3 of the current year.

2. Calculate the appropriate federal unemployment tax liability for the first quarter. Journalize payment of this liability in the journal. The tax was paid by Check No. 802 on April 30 of the current year.

3. Calculate the appropriate state unemployment tax liability for the first quarter. Journalize payment of this liability in the journal. The tax was paid by Check No. 803 on April 30 of the current year.

■ ENRICHMENT PROBLEMS

MASTERY PROBLEM 16-M   Journalizing and posting payroll transactions

Star Equipment completed payroll transactions during the period April 1 to May 15 of the current year. Payroll tax rates are as follows: FICA, 8%; federal unemployment, 0.8%; state unemployment, 5.4%. The company buys savings bonds for employees as accumulated withholdings reach the necessary amount to purchase a bond. No total earnings have exceeded the tax base for calculating unemployment taxes.

The balances in the general ledger are recorded as of April 1 of the current year.

Account No.	Account Title	April 1 Balance
2120	Employee Income Tax Payable	$ 945.00
2130	FICA Tax Payable	984.99
2150	Unemployment Tax Payable—Federal	147.75
2160	Unemployment Tax Payable—State	997.30
2180	U.S. Savings Bonds Payable	200.00
6150	Payroll Taxes Expense	2,622.53
6170	Salary Expense	18,468.50

Instructions: 1. Journalize the following transactions on page 14 of a journal. Source documents are abbreviated as follows: check, C, and memorandum, M.

Apr. 15. Paid cash for liability for employee income tax, $945.00, and for FICA tax, $984.99; total, $1,929.99. C356.

   15. Paid cash for semimonthly payroll, $2,463.52 (total payroll, $3,256.00, less deductions: employee income tax, $482.00; FICA tax, $260.48; U.S. Savings Bonds, $50.00). C357.

   15. Recorded employer payroll taxes expense. M25.

   15. Paid cash for U.S. Savings Bonds for employees, $250.00. C358.

   30. Paid cash for semimonthly payroll, $2,527.36, (total payroll, $3,358.00, less deductions: employee income tax, $512.00; FICA tax, $268.64; U.S. Savings Bonds, $50.00). C376.

   30. Recorded employer payroll taxes expense. M29.

   30. Paid cash for federal unemployment tax liability for quarter ended March 31, $147.75. C377.

   30. Paid cash for state unemployment tax liability for quarter ended March 31, $997.30. C378.

      Posting. Post the items that are to be posted individually.

May 15. Paid cash for liability for employee income tax, $994.00, and for FICA tax, $1,058.24; total, $2,052.24. C405.

   15. Paid cash for semimonthly payroll, $2,373.40 (total payroll, $3,145.00, less deductions: employee income tax, $470.00; FICA tax, $251.60; U.S. Savings Bonds, $50.00). C406.

   15. Recorded employer payroll taxes expense. M36.

      Posting. Post the items that are to be posted individually.

2. Prove and rule the journal.

CHALLENGE PROBLEM 16-C   Journalizing and posting payroll transactions

Danner Hardware completed payroll transactions during the period January 1 to April 30 of the current year. Payroll tax rates are as follows: FICA, 8%; federal unemployment, 0.8%; and state unemployment, 5.4%. The company buys savings bonds for employees as the accumulated withholdings reach the necessary amount to purchase a bond. No total earnings have exceeded the tax base for calculating unemployment taxes.

The balances in the general ledger are recorded as of January 1 of the current year.

Account No.	Account Title	January 1 Balance
2120	Employee Income Tax Payable	$1,215.00
2130	FICA Tax Payable	1,342.68
2150	Unemployment Tax Payable—Federal	83.62
2160	Unemployment Tax Payable—State	564.45
2180	U.S. Savings Bonds Payable	300.00
6150	Payroll Taxes Expense	—
6170	Salary Expense	—

Instructions: 1. Journalize the following transactions on page 1 of a journal. Source documents are abbreviated as follows: check, C, and memorandum, M.

Jan. 2. Paid cash for 12 U.S. Savings Bonds at $25.00 each for employees. C143.
   15. Paid cash for December liability for employee income tax and for FICA tax. C152.
   31. Paid cash for federal unemployment tax liability for quarter ended December 31. C158.
   31. Paid cash for state unemployment tax liability for quarter ended December 31. C159.
   31. Paid cash for monthly payroll, $6,283.04 (total payroll, $8,487.00, less deductions: employee income tax, $1,425.00; FICA tax, $678.96; U.S. Savings Bonds, $100.00). C164.
   31. Recorded employer payroll taxes expense. M95.
        Posting. Post the items that are to be posted individually.
Feb. 15. Paid cash for January liability for employee income tax and for FICA tax. C170.
   28. Paid cash for monthly payroll, $6,348.16 (total payroll, $8,598.00, less deductions: employee income tax, $1,462.00; FICA tax, $687.84; U.S. Savings Bonds, $100.00). C180.
   28. Recorded employer payroll taxes expense. M104.
        Posting. Post the items that are to be posted individually.
Mar. 15. Paid cash for February liability for employee income tax and for FICA tax. C195.
   31. Paid cash for monthly payroll, $6,660.76 (total payroll, $9,028.00, less deductions: employee income tax, $1,545.00; FICA tax, $722.24; U.S. Savings Bonds, $100.00). C206.
   31. Recorded employer payroll taxes expense. M113.
        Posting. Post the items that are to be posted individually.
Apr. 1. Paid cash for 12 U.S. Savings Bonds at $25.00 each for employees. C207.
   15. Paid cash for March liability for employee income tax and for FICA tax. C218.
   30. Paid cash for federal unemployment tax liability for quarter ended March 31. C224.
   30. Paid cash for state unemployment tax liability for quarter ended March 31. C225.
        Posting. Post the items that are to be posted individually.

2. Prove and rule the journal.

Reinforcement Activity 2, Part A

An Accounting Cycle for a Partnership: Journalizing and Posting Transactions

Reinforcement Activity 2 reinforces learnings from Part 3, Chapters 12 through 19. Activities cover a complete accounting cycle for a merchandising business organized as a partnership. Reinforcement Activity 2 is a single problem divided into two parts. Part A includes learnings from Chapters 12 through 16. Part B includes learnings from Chapters 17 through 19.

The accounting work of a single merchandising business for the last month of a yearly fiscal period is used in this reinforcement activity. The records kept and reports prepared, however, illustrate the application of accounting concepts for all merchandising businesses.

CLEARVIEW OPTICAL

Tara Bruski and James Myler, partners, own and operate ClearView Optical, a merchandising business. The business sells a complete line of fashion, sun, and sport eyewear. ClearView is located in a downtown shopping area and is open for business Monday through Saturday. A monthly rent is paid for the building and fixtures. ClearView accepts credit cards from customers.

CHART OF ACCOUNTS

ClearView Optical uses the chart of accounts shown on the next page.

JOURNAL AND LEDGERS

The journal and ledgers used by ClearView Optical are listed in the following chart. Models of the journal and ledgers are shown in the textbook illustrations given in the chart.

Journal and Ledgers	Chapter	Illustration Number
Expanded journal..	13	13–5
Accounts payable ledger	14	14–10
Accounts receivable ledger	14	14–15
General ledger...	17	17–1

RECORDING TRANSACTIONS

The December 1 account balances for the general and subsidiary ledgers are given in the working papers accompanying this textbook.

Instructions: 1. Journalize the transactions beginning on the bottom of page 382 on page 23 of a journal. A 6% sales tax has been added to each sale. Source documents are abbreviated as follows: check, C; memorandum, M; purchase invoice, P; receipt, R; sales invoice, S; cash register tape, T.

CLEARVIEW OPTICAL
Chart of Accounts

Balance Sheet Accounts

(1000) ASSETS
1110 Cash
1120 Petty Cash
1130 Accounts Receivable
1140 Merchandise Inventory
1145 Supplies—Office
1150 Supplies—Store
1160 Prepaid Insurance

(2000) LIABILITIES
2110 Accounts Payable
2120 Employee Income Tax Payable
2130 FICA Tax Payable
2140 Sales Tax Payable
2150 Unemployment Tax Payable—Federal
2160 Unemployment Tax Payable—State
2170 Health Insurance Premiums Payable
2180 U.S. Savings Bonds Payable
2190 United Way Donations Payable

(3000) OWNERS' EQUITY
3110 Tara Bruski, Capital
3120 Tara Bruski, Drawing
3130 James Myler, Capital
3140 James Myler, Drawing
3150 Income Summary

Income Statement Accounts

(4000) OPERATING REVENUE
4110 Sales

(5000) COST OF MERCHANDISE
5110 Purchases

(6000) OPERATING EXPENSES
6110 Advertising Expense
6120 Credit Card Fee Expense
6130 Insurance Expense
6140 Miscellaneous Expense
6150 Payroll Taxes Expense
6160 Rent Expense
6170 Salary Expense
6175 Supplies Expense—Office
6180 Supplies Expense—Store
6190 Utilities Expense

Subsidiary Ledgers

Accounts Receivable Ledger

110 Theresa Abbey
120 Nancy Bonner
130 Jonathan Doran
140 Irma Iznaga
150 Brian Patco
160 Norman Witte

Accounts Payable Ledger

210 A & B Optical Co.
220 Central Office Supply
230 Kosh Optical Lab
240 Optical Imports
250 Trend Optics Co.
260 Weaver Supply

Dec. 1. Paid cash for rent, $1,000.00. C272.
  1. Tara Bruski, partner, withdrew cash for personal use, $1,200.00. C273.
  1. James Myler, partner, withdrew cash for personal use, $1,200.00. C274.
  2. Paid cash for electric bill, $288.50. C275.
  2. Received cash on account from Nancy Bonner, $344.50, covering S64. R82.
  3. Paid cash for miscellaneous expense, $60.00. C276.

Dec. 3. Paid cash on account to Trend Optics Co., $483.80, covering P73. C277.
      4. Sold merchandise on account to Theresa Abbey, $375.00, plus sales tax, $22.50; total, $397.50. S67.
      5. Recorded cash and credit card sales, $4,830.00, plus sales tax, $289.80; total, $5,119.80. T5.
         Posting. Post the items that are to be posted individually.
      7. Sold merchandise on account to Jonathan Doran, $385.00, plus sales tax, $23.10; total, $408.10. S68.
      7. Received cash on account from Norman Witte, $360.40, covering S65. R83.
      8. Bought office supplies on account from Central Office Supply, $293.00. M43.
      9. Purchased merchandise on account from Optical Imports, $1,125.00. P77.
      9. Bought store supplies on account from Weaver Supply, $275.00. M44.
     10. Tara Bruski, partner, withdrew merchandise for personal use, $250.00. M45.
     10. Paid cash for office supplies, $145.00. C278.
     10. Discovered that a payment of cash for advertising in November was journalized and posted in error as a debit to Miscellaneous Expense instead of Advertising Expense, $125.00. M46.
     11. Paid cash on account to Kosh Optical Lab, $975.80, covering P74. C279.
     11. Purchased merchandise on account from Trend Optics Co., $860.00. P78.
     12. Paid cash for store supplies, $220.00. C280.
     12. Recorded cash and credit card sales, $5,940.00, plus sales tax, 356.40; total, $6,296.40. T12.
         Posting. Post the items that are to be posted individually.
     14. James Myler, partner, withdrew merchandise for personal use, $325.00. M47.
     14. Purchased merchandise on account from Kosh Optical Lab, $2,730.00. P79.
     14. Sold merchandise on account to Brian Patco, $140.00, plus sales tax, $8.40; total, $148.40. S69.
     14. Paid cash for advertising, $345.00. C281.
     15. Paid cash on account to A & B Optical Co., $1,060.40, covering P75. C282.
     15. Received cash on account from Irma Iznaga, $683.70, covering S66. R84.
     15. Sold merchandise on account to Nancy Bonner, $410.00, plus sales tax, $24.60; total, $434.60. S70.
         Posting. Post the items that are to be posted individually.

   2. Prove and rule page 23 of the journal.
   3. Carry the column totals forward to page 24 of the journal.
   4. Journalize the following transactions on page 24 of the journal.

Dec. 15. Paid cash for semimonthly payroll, $1,751.80 (total payroll, $2,315.00, less deductions: employee income tax, $181.00; FICA tax, $185.20; health insurance, $142.00; U.S. Savings Bonds, $25.00; United Way donations, $30.00). C283.
     15. Recorded employer payroll taxes, $250.30, for the semimonthly pay period ended December 15. Taxes owed are: FICA tax, $185.20; federal unemployment tax, $8.40; and state unemployment tax, $56.70. M48.
     19. Recorded cash and credit card sales, $5,760.00, plus sales tax, $345.60; total, $6,105.60. T19.
     23. Paid cash on account to Optical Imports, $1,840.00, covering P76. C284.
     26. Recorded cash and credit card sales, $5,820.00, plus sales tax, $349.20; total, $6,169.20. T26.
         Posting. Post the items that are to be posted individually.

ClearView Optical's bank charges a fee for handling the collection of credit card sales deposited during the month. The credit card fee is deducted from ClearView Optical's bank account. The amount is then shown on the bank statement. The credit card fee is recorded in the journal as a reduction in cash.

Dec. 28. Recorded credit card fee expense, $285.20. M49. (Debit Credit Card Fee Expense; credit Cash.)

  30. Purchased merchandise on account from A & B Optical Co., $1,620.00. P80.

  31. Paid cash to replenish the petty cash fund, $304.00: office supplies, $62.00; store supplies, $59.00; advertising, $87.00; miscellaneous, $96.00. C285.

  31. Paid cash for semimonthly payroll, $1,882.00 (total payroll, $2,460.00, less deductions: employee income tax, $184.20; FICA tax, $196.80; health insurance, $142.00; U.S. Savings Bonds, $25.00; United Way donations, $30.00). C286.

  31. Recorded employer payroll taxes, $263.92, for the semimonthly pay period ended December 31. Taxes owed are: FICA tax, $196.80; federal unemployment tax, $8.66; and state unemployment tax, $58.46. M50.

  31. Received bank statement showing December bank service charge, $4.50. M51.

  31. Recorded cash and credit card sales, $3,240.00, plus sales tax, $194.40; total, $3,434.40. T31.

   Posting. Post the items that are to be posted individually.

5. Total page 24 of the journal. Prove the equality of debits and credits.

6. Prove cash. The balance on the next unused check stub was $34,918.00.

7. Rule the journal.

8. Post the totals of the special columns of the journal.

9. Prepare a schedule of accounts payable and a schedule of accounts receivable. Prove the accuracy of the subsidiary ledgers by comparing the schedule totals with the balances of the controlling accounts in the general ledger. If the totals are not the same, find and correct the errors.

The ledgers used in Reinforcement Activity 2, Part A, are needed to complete Reinforcement Activity 2, Part B.

Stellar Attractions Pegboard Payroll System provides experience in preparing records using a pegboard and no-carbon-required forms. When data are entered on the statement of earnings and deductions stub on the check, the employee earnings record and the payroll register are simultaneously prepared. Posting is eliminated. The following activities are included in the accounting cycle for Stellar Attractions. This business simulation is available from the publisher.

Activities in Stellar Attractions

1. Preparing necessary forms for new employees.
2. Completing time cards by entering summary data.
3. Assembling forms on a pegboard: checks with earnings and deductions stubs, employee earnings records, and payroll register. All records are completed with one writing.
4. Recording time card summary data on the statement of earnings and deductions stubs of checks on the pegboard.
5. Determining appropriate deductions using tax tables and figuring net pay.
6. Recording deductions and net pay on the statement of earnings and deductions stubs.
7. Totaling, proving, ruling, and filing the payroll register. Filing employee earnings records.
8. Separating, writing, and signing payroll checks.
9. Totaling and proving employee earnings records for the end of the quarter and year to date.
10. Preparing quarterly and annual reports.

Work Sheet for a Merchandising Business

ENABLING PERFORMANCE TASKS

After studying Chapter 17, you will be able to:
a. Define accounting terms related to a work sheet for a merchandising business.
b. Identify accounting concepts and practices related to a work sheet for a merchandising business.
c. Plan adjustments on a work sheet for a merchandising business.
d. Complete a work sheet for a merchandising business.

Management decisions about future business operations are often based on financial information. Financial information shows whether a profit is being made or a loss is being incurred. Profit or loss information helps an owner or manager determine future changes. Financial information is also needed to prepare required tax reports. A business summarizes financial information at least once each fiscal period. CarLand uses a one-year fiscal period that begins on January 1 and ends on December 31. Therefore, CarLand summarizes its financial information on December 31 of each year.

GENERAL LEDGER WITH POSTING COMPLETED

CarLand's completed general ledger on December 31, after all transactions have been posted, is shown in Illustration 17-1. No entries have been posted in the following accounts: Income Summary, Insurance Expense, Supplies Expense—Office, and Supplies Expense—Store. Transactions during the year did not affect these accounts.

ACCOUNT *Cash*   ACCOUNT NO. *1110*

DATE		ITEM	POST. REF.	DEBIT	CREDIT	BALANCE	
						DEBIT	CREDIT
Dec. 19..	1	Balance	√			23 55 00 00	
	31		25	30 9 8 4 00		54 5 3 4 00	
	31		25		30 3 00 43	24 2 33 57	

ACCOUNT *Petty Cash*   ACCOUNT NO. *1120*

DATE		ITEM	POST. REF.	DEBIT	CREDIT	BALANCE	
						DEBIT	CREDIT
Jan. 19..	1	Balance	√			5 0 0 00	

ACCOUNT *Accounts Receivable*   ACCOUNT NO. *1130*

DATE		ITEM	POST. REF.	DEBIT	CREDIT	BALANCE	
						DEBIT	CREDIT
Dec. 19..	1	Balance	√			9 2 2 2 00	
	31		25	8 6 9 2 00		17 9 1 4 00	
	31		25		8 5 8 2 00	9 3 3 2 00	

ACCOUNT *Merchandise Inventory*   ACCOUNT NO. *1140*

DATE		ITEM	POST. REF.	DEBIT	CREDIT	BALANCE	
						DEBIT	CREDIT
Jan. 19..	1	Balance	√			225 4 0 0 00	

ACCOUNT *Supplies—Office*   ACCOUNT NO. *1145*

DATE		ITEM	POST. REF.	DEBIT	CREDIT	BALANCE	
						DEBIT	CREDIT
Dec. 19..	1	Balance	√			4 9 8 0 00	
	3		24	1 6 0 00		5 1 4 0 00	
	9		24	8 6 00		5 2 2 6 00	
	18		25	1 2 4 00		5 3 5 0 00	
	31		25	5 0 00		5 4 0 0 00	

Illustration 17-1
General ledger with posting
completed

Illustration 17-1
General ledger with posting
completed (continued)

ACCOUNT *Supplies—Store*   **ACCOUNT NO.** *1150*

DATE		ITEM	POST. REF.	DEBIT	CREDIT	BALANCE DEBIT	BALANCE CREDIT
Dec.	1	Balance	√			5 1 3 0 00	
	7		24	2 3 0 00		5 3 6 0 00	
	31		25	7 3 00		5 4 3 3 00	
	31		25	3 4 7 00		5 7 8 0 00	

ACCOUNT *Prepaid Insurance*   **ACCOUNT NO.** *1160*

DATE		ITEM	POST. REF.	DEBIT	CREDIT	BALANCE DEBIT	BALANCE CREDIT
Dec.	1	Balance	√			4 8 4 0 00	

ACCOUNT *Accounts Payable*   **ACCOUNT NO.** *2110*

DATE		ITEM	POST. REF.	DEBIT	CREDIT	BALANCE DEBIT	BALANCE CREDIT
Dec.	1	Balance	√				15 8 7 0 00
	31		25	15 5 4 5 59			3 2 4 41
	31		25		10 1 2 7 49		10 4 5 1 90

ACCOUNT *Employee Income Tax Payable*   **ACCOUNT NO.** *2120*

DATE		ITEM	POST. REF.	DEBIT	CREDIT	BALANCE DEBIT	BALANCE CREDIT
Dec.	1	Balance	√				3 8 4 00
	15		24	3 8 4 00		—	
	15		24		1 9 2 00		1 9 2 00
	31		25		2 1 0 00		4 0 2 00

ACCOUNT **FICA Tax Payable**   ACCOUNT NO. *2130*

DATE		ITEM	POST. REF.	DEBIT	CREDIT	BALANCE DEBIT	BALANCE CREDIT
Dec.¹⁹⁻⁻	1	Balance	√				8 1 7 92
	15		24	8 1 7 92		———	———
	15		24		2 0 4 48		2 0 4 48
	15		24		2 0 4 48		4 0 8 96
	31		25		2 1 1 60		6 2 0 56
	31		25		2 1 1 60		8 3 2 16

ACCOUNT **Sales Tax Payable**   ACCOUNT NO. *2140*

DATE		ITEM	POST. REF.	DEBIT	CREDIT	BALANCE DEBIT	BALANCE CREDIT
Dec.¹⁹⁻⁻	1	Balance	√				1 8 9 6 00
	15		24	1 8 9 6 00		———	———
	31		25		1 7 6 0 00		1 7 6 0 00

ACCOUNT **Unemployment Tax Payable—Federal**   ACCOUNT NO. *2150*

DATE		ITEM	POST. REF.	DEBIT	CREDIT	BALANCE DEBIT	BALANCE CREDIT
Dec.¹⁹⁻⁻	1	Balance	√				4 0 48
	15		24		9 10		4 9 58
	31		25		9 57		5 9 15

ACCOUNT **Unemployment Tax Payable—State**   ACCOUNT NO. *2160*

DATE		ITEM	POST. REF.	DEBIT	CREDIT	BALANCE DEBIT	BALANCE CREDIT
Dec.¹⁹⁻⁻	1	Balance	√				2 7 3 22
	15		24		6 1 45		3 3 4 67
	31		25		6 4 59		3 9 9 26

Illustration 17-1
General ledger with posting
completed (continued)

Illustration 17-1
General ledger with posting
completed (continued)

ACCOUNT **Health Insurance Premiums Payable**   ACCOUNT NO. *2170*

DATE		ITEM	POST. REF.	DEBIT	CREDIT	BALANCE	
						DEBIT	CREDIT
Dec.	1	Balance	✓				5 2 4 00
	15		24		1 5 8 00		6 8 2 00
	31		25		1 5 8 00		8 4 0 00

ACCOUNT **U.S. Savings Bonds Payable**   ACCOUNT NO. *2180*

DATE		ITEM	POST. REF.	DEBIT	CREDIT	BALANCE	
						DEBIT	CREDIT
Dec.	1	Balance	✓				1 0 00
	15		24		1 5 00		2 5 00
	31		25		1 5 00		4 0 00

ACCOUNT **United Way Donations Payable**   ACCOUNT NO. *2190*

DATE		ITEM	POST. REF.	DEBIT	CREDIT	BALANCE	
						DEBIT	CREDIT
Dec.	1	Balance	✓				4 0 00
	15		24		1 0 00		5 0 00
	31		25		1 0 00		6 0 00

ACCOUNT **Amy Kramer, Capital**   ACCOUNT NO. *3110*

DATE		ITEM	POST. REF.	DEBIT	CREDIT	BALANCE	
						DEBIT	CREDIT
Jan.	1	Balance	✓				101 1 1 8 00

ACCOUNT **Amy Kramer, Drawing**   ACCOUNT NO. *3120*

DATE		ITEM	POST. REF.	DEBIT	CREDIT	BALANCE	
						DEBIT	CREDIT
Dec.	1	Balance	✓			16 7 0 0 00	
	15		24	1 5 0 0 00		18 2 0 0 00	

ACCOUNT *Dario Mesa, Capital*   ACCOUNT NO. *3130*

DATE		ITEM	POST. REF.	DEBIT	CREDIT	BALANCE	
						DEBIT	CREDIT
Jan.	1	Balance	√				101 2 2 8 00

ACCOUNT *Dario Mesa, Drawing*   ACCOUNT NO. *3140*

DATE		ITEM	POST. REF.	DEBIT	CREDIT	BALANCE	
						DEBIT	CREDIT
Dec.	1	Balance	√			17 1 0 0 00	
	15		24	1 5 0 0 00		18 6 0 0 00	

ACCOUNT *Income Summary*   ACCOUNT NO. *3150*

DATE	ITEM	POST. REF.	DEBIT	CREDIT	BALANCE	
					DEBIT	CREDIT

ACCOUNT *Sales*   ACCOUNT NO. *4110*

DATE		ITEM	POST. REF.	DEBIT	CREDIT	BALANCE	
						DEBIT	CREDIT
Dec.	1	Balance	√				323 2 6 6 00
	31		25		29 3 3 4 00		352 6 0 0 00

ACCOUNT *Purchases*   ACCOUNT NO. *5110*

DATE		ITEM	POST. REF.	DEBIT	CREDIT	BALANCE	
						DEBIT	CREDIT
Dec.	1	Balance	√			148 1 7 2 51	
	31		25	10 1 2 7 49		158 3 0 0 00	

ACCOUNT *Advertising Expense*   ACCOUNT NO. *6110*

DATE		ITEM	POST. REF.	DEBIT	CREDIT	BALANCE	
						DEBIT	CREDIT
Dec.	1	Balance	√			4 8 6 0 00	
	4		24	1 6 5 00		5 0 2 5 00	
	16		25	8 3 00		5 1 0 8 00	
	22		25	3 9 2 00		5 5 0 0 00	

Illustration 17-1
General ledger with posting
completed (continued)

Illustration 17-1
General ledger with posting
completed (continued)

ACCOUNT *Credit Card Fee Expense*   ACCOUNT NO. *6120*

DATE		ITEM	POST. REF.	DEBIT	CREDIT	BALANCE DEBIT	BALANCE CREDIT
Dec.	1	Balance	√			2 1 7 5 00	
	28		25	7 1 5 00		2 8 9 0 00	

ACCOUNT *Insurance Expense*   ACCOUNT NO. *6130*

DATE	ITEM	POST. REF.	DEBIT	CREDIT	BALANCE DEBIT	BALANCE CREDIT

ACCOUNT *Miscellaneous Expense*   ACCOUNT NO. *6140*

DATE		ITEM	POST. REF.	DEBIT	CREDIT	BALANCE DEBIT	BALANCE CREDIT
Dec.	1	Balance	√			1 7 3 2 15	
	9		24	3 9 00		1 7 7 1 15	
	17		25	1 6 3 00		1 9 3 4 15	
	22		25	1 0 6 00		2 0 4 0 15	
	31		25	1 4 2 00		2 1 8 2 15	

ACCOUNT *Payroll Taxes Expense*   ACCOUNT NO. *6150*

DATE		ITEM	POST. REF.	DEBIT	CREDIT	BALANCE DEBIT	BALANCE CREDIT
Dec.	1	Balance	√			6 7 3 8 96	
	15		24	2 7 5 03		7 0 1 3 99	
	31		25	2 8 5 76		7 2 9 9 75	

ACCOUNT *Rent Expense*   ACCOUNT NO. *6160*

DATE		ITEM	POST. REF.	DEBIT	CREDIT	BALANCE DEBIT	BALANCE CREDIT
Dec.	1	Balance	√			16 5 0 0 00	
	1		24	1 5 0 0 00		18 0 0 0 00	

ACCOUNT *Salary Expense*					ACCOUNT NO. *6170*	

DATE	ITEM	POST. REF.	DEBIT	CREDIT	BALANCE DEBIT	BALANCE CREDIT
19-- Dec. 1	Balance	√			54 9 5 2 00	
15		24	2 5 5 6 00		57 5 0 8 00	
31		25	2 6 4 5 00		60 1 5 3 00	

ACCOUNT *Supplies Expense—Office*					ACCOUNT NO. *6175*	

DATE	ITEM	POST. REF.	DEBIT	CREDIT	BALANCE DEBIT	BALANCE CREDIT

ACCOUNT *Supplies Expense—Store*					ACCOUNT NO. *6180*	

DATE	ITEM	POST. REF.	DEBIT	CREDIT	BALANCE DEBIT	BALANCE CREDIT

ACCOUNT *Utilities Expense*					ACCOUNT NO. *6190*	

DATE	ITEM	POST. REF.	DEBIT	CREDIT	BALANCE DEBIT	BALANCE CREDIT
19-- Dec. 1	Balance	√			2 9 1 5 00	
3		24	1 8 0 00		3 0 9 5 00	
9		24	8 5 00		3 1 8 0 00	

Illustration 17-1
General ledger with posting
completed (concluded)

AN 8-COLUMN WORK SHEET
FOR A MERCHANDISING BUSINESS

A columnar accounting form on which the financial information needed to prepare financial statements is summarized is known as a work sheet. A work sheet is used to plan adjustments and sort financial statement information. A work sheet may be prepared whenever a business wishes to summarize and report financial information. A work sheet is always prepared at the end of each fiscal period because financial statements are prepared at the end of each fiscal period. *(CONCEPT: Accounting Period Cycle)* CarLand prepares a work sheet and financial statements annually.

Work sheets for service and merchandising businesses are similar.

CarLand's work sheet is similar to the one used by Rugcare described in Chapter 7. CarLand's work sheet, however, also includes accounts for accounts receivable, merchandise inventory, accounts payable, sales tax, and purchases.

RECORDING A TRIAL BALANCE ON A WORK SHEET

To prove the equality of debits and credits in the general ledger, a trial balance is prepared. CarLand prepares a trial balance in the Trial Balance columns of a work sheet. CarLand's trial balance on December 31 is shown in Illustration 17-2, page 394.

General ledger accounts are listed in the work sheet's Account Title column in the same order in which they appear in the general ledger. All accounts are listed regardless of whether there is a balance or not. Listing all accounts reduces the possibility of overlooking an account that needs to be brought up to date.

PLANNING ADJUSTMENTS ON A WORK SHEET

After posting is completed at the end of a fiscal period, some general ledger accounts, such as the two supplies accounts and the prepaid insurance account, are not up to date. Adjustments for supplies and prepaid insurance are described in Chapter 7. In addition to supplies and prepaid insurance, CarLand needs to adjust the merchandise inventory account. Changes recorded on a work sheet to update general ledger accounts at the end of a fiscal period are known as adjustments.

Adjustments are planned in the Adjustments columns of a work sheet. Adjustments recorded on a work sheet are for planning purposes only. The general ledger account balances are not changed until journal entries are recorded and posted. Journal entries made to bring general ledger accounts up to date are known as adjusting entries.

Merchandise inventory adjustment

The amount of goods on hand is called an inventory. The amount of goods on hand for sale to customers is called merchandise inventory. The general ledger account in which merchandise inventory is recorded is titled *Merchandise Inventory*. Merchandise Inventory is an asset account with a normal debit balance, as shown in the T account.

Merchandise Inventory	
Debit side Normal balance Increase	Credit side Decrease

Analyzing a merchandise inventory adjustment. CarLand's merchandise inventory account on January 1, the beginning of the fiscal year, has a debit balance of $225,400.00, as shown in the T account.

CarLand
Work Sheet
For Year Ended December 31, 19--

	ACCOUNT TITLE	TRIAL BALANCE	
		DEBIT	CREDIT
1	Cash	24 2 3 3 57	
2	Petty Cash	5 0 0 00	
3	Accounts Receivable	9 3 3 2 00	
4	Merchandise Inventory	225 4 0 0 00	
5	Supplies—Office	5 4 0 0 00	
6	Supplies—Store	5 7 8 0 00	
7	Prepaid Insurance	4 8 4 0 00	
8	Accounts Payable		10 4 5 1 90
9	Employee Income Tax Payable		4 0 2 00
10	FICA Tax Payable		8 3 2 16
11	Sales Tax Payable		1 7 6 0 00
12	Unemploy. Tax Payable—Fed.		5 9 15
13	Unemploy. Tax Payable—State		3 9 9 26
14	Health Ins. Premiums Pay.		8 4 0 00
15	U.S. Savings Bonds Payable		4 0 00
16	United Way Donations Payable		6 0 00
17	Amy Kramer, Capital		101 1 1 8 00
18	Amy Kramer, Drawing	18 2 0 0 00	
19	Dario Mesa, Capital		101 2 2 8 00
20	Dario Mesa, Drawing	18 6 0 0 00	
21	Income Summary		
22	Sales		352 6 0 0 00
23	Purchases	158 3 0 0 00	
24	Advertising Expense	5 5 0 0 00	
25	Credit Card Fee Expense	2 8 9 0 00	
26	Insurance Expense		
27	Miscellaneous Expense	2 1 8 2 15	
28	Payroll Taxes Expense	7 2 9 9 75	
29	Rent Expense	18 0 0 0 00	
30	Salary Expense	60 1 5 3 00	
31	Supplies Expense—Office		
32	Supplies Expense—Store		
33	Utilities Expense	3 1 8 0 00	
34		569 7 9 0 47	569 7 9 0 47
35			

Illustration 17-2   Trial balance on a work sheet

The balance of the merchandise inventory account on December 31, the end of the fiscal year, is the same amount, $225,400.00. The January 1 and December 31 balances are the same because no entries have been made in the account during the fiscal year. The changes in inventory resulting from purchases and sales transactions have not been recorded in the merchandise inventory account.

Merchandise Inventory
Jan. 1 Bal. 225,400.00	

Each purchase transaction increases the amount of merchandise on hand. However, all purchases are recorded in the purchases account. Each sales transaction decreases the amount of merchandise on hand. However, all sales are recorded in the sales account. This procedure makes it easier to determine quickly the total purchases and sales during a fiscal period. During a fiscal period, the amount of merchandise on hand increases each time merchandise is purchased. The amount of merchandise on hand also decreases each time merchandise is sold. The merchandise inventory account balance, therefore, must be adjusted to reflect the changes resulting from purchases and sales during a fiscal period.

The two accounts used to adjust the merchandise inventory are Merchandise Inventory and Income Summary. The T accounts show the merchandise inventory and income summary accounts before the merchandise inventory adjustment is made.

BEFORE ADJUSTMENT
Income Summary

Merchandise Inventory
Jan. 1 Bal. 225,400.00	

Before the adjustment, the merchandise inventory account has a January 1 debit balance of $225,400.00. The merchandise inventory account balance, however, is not up to date. The actual count of merchandise on December 31 shows that the inventory is valued at $212,200.00. Therefore, the merchandise inventory account balance must be adjusted to show the current value of merchandise on hand.

Most accounts needing adjustment at the end of a fiscal period have a related temporary account. For example, when the account Supplies is adjusted, Supplies Expense is the related expense account, a temporary account. Merchandise Inventory, however, does not have a related expense account. Therefore, Income Summary, a temporary account, is used to adjust the merchandise inventory account at the end of a fiscal period.

Four questions are asked in analyzing the adjustment for merchandise inventory.

1. What is the balance of Merchandise Inventory? . . $225,400.00
2. What should the balance be for this account? $212,200.00
3. What must be done to correct the account
   balance? Decrease. . . . . $ 13,200.00
4. What adjustment is made?
   Debit Income Summary . . . . $ 13,200.00
   Credit Merchandise Inventory. . . . . $ 13,200.00

The merchandise inventory adjustment is shown in the T accounts.

AFTER ADJUSTMENT

Income Summary

Adj. (a) 13,200.00	

Merchandise Inventory

Jan. 1 Bal. 225,400.00	Adj. (a) 13,200.00
(New Bal. 212,200.00)	

Income Summary is debited and Merchandise Inventory is credited for $13,200.00. The beginning debit balance of Merchandise Inventory, $225,400.00, *minus* the adjustment credit amount, $13,200.00, *equals* the ending debit balance of Merchandise Inventory, $212,200.00.

Recording a merchandise inventory adjustment on a work sheet. The merchandise inventory adjustment is shown on lines 4 and 21 in the work sheet's Adjustments columns in Illustration 17-3.

Illustration 17-3
Merchandise inventory
adjustment on a
work sheet

Three steps are used to record CarLand's adjustment for merchandise inventory on a work sheet.

1 Write the debit amount, *$13,200.00*, in the Adjustments Debit column on the line with the account title Income Summary (line 21).

2 Write the credit amount, *$13,200.00*, in the Adjustments Credit column on the line with the account title Merchandise Inventory (line 4).

3 Label the two parts of this adjustment with the small letter *a* in parentheses, *(a)*.

AFTER ADJUSTMENT

Merchandise Inventory

Jan. 1 Bal. 245,600.00	
Adj. (a) 5,200.00	
(New Bal. 250,800.00)	

Income Summary

	Adj. (a) 5,200.00

If the amount of merchandise inventory on hand is greater than the balance of Merchandise Inventory, opposite entries would be made—debit Merchandise Inventory and credit Income Summary. For example, Kobrin Company's merchandise inventory account on January 1 has a debit balance of $245,600.00. The count of merchandise on December 31 shows that the inventory is valued at $250,800.00. The merchandise on hand is $5,200.00 *greater* than the balance of Merchandise Inventory. This merchandise inventory adjustment is shown in the T accounts.

Merchandise Inventory is debited and Income Summary is credited for $5,200.00.

Supplies adjustments

CarLand uses office and store supplies in the daily operation of the business. The amount of supplies *not used* during a fiscal period represents an asset. The amount of supplies *used* during a fiscal period represents an expense. Accurate financial reporting includes recording expenses in the fiscal period in which the expenses contribute to earning revenue. *(CONCEPT: Matching Expenses with Revenue)*

Analyzing an office supplies inventory adjustment. CarLand's office supplies account on December 31, the end of the fiscal period, has a debit balance of $5,400.00, as shown in the T account.

Supplies — Office

Dec. 31 Bal. 5,400.00	

The account balance for Supplies — Office, $5,400.00, includes two items. (1) The account balance on January 1. (2) The cost of office supplies bought during the year. The account balance does not reflect the value of any office supplies *used* during the year (an expense). Therefore, the office supplies account balance must be adjusted to show the value of office supplies on hand on December 31. The amount of supplies on hand on December 31 is determined by counting the supplies on hand and calculating their value.

The two accounts used to adjust office supplies are Supplies — Office and Supplies Expense — Office. The T accounts show the two accounts before the adjustment is made.

BEFORE ADJUSTMENT

Supplies Expense — Office

Supplies — Office

Dec. 31 Bal. 5,400.00	

Before the adjustment, the office supplies account has a December 31 debit balance of $5,400.00. However, office supplies have been used throughout the fiscal period. These changes in office supplies were not recorded in the office supplies account. Therefore, the office supplies account balance is not up to date. The actual count of office supplies on December 31 shows that the value of the office supplies inventory is $1,460.00. The office supplies account balance must be adjusted to show the current value of the office supplies inventory.

Four questions are asked in analyzing the adjustment for office supplies inventory.

1. What is the balance of Supplies — Office $5,400.00
2. What should the balance be for this account? . $1,460.00
3. What must be done to correct the account balance? Decrease. $3,940.00
4. What adjustment is made?
    Debit Supplies Expense — Office. $3,940.00
    Credit Supplies — Office. $3,940.00

The office supplies inventory adjustment is shown in the T accounts.

Supplies Expense — Office is debited and Supplies — Office is credited for $3,940.00. The beginning debit balance of Supplies — Office, $5,400.00, *minus* the adjustment credit amount, $3,940.00, *equals* the ending debit balance of Supplies — Office, $1,460.00.

AFTER ADJUSTMENT

Supplies Expense — Office

Adj. (b) 3,940.00	

Supplies — Office

Dec. 31 Bal. 5,400.00	Adj. (b) 3,940.00
(New Bal. 1,460.00)	

Recording supplies inventory adjustments on a work sheet. CarLand makes a similar adjustment for store supplies. The steps in recording the *two* supplies inventory adjustments are the same as those described for Rugcare in Chapter 7. The *two* supplies inventory adjustments are shown in the Adjustments columns of the work sheet in Illustration 17-4. The adjustment for Supplies—Office is labeled *(b)* and is shown on lines 5 and 31. The adjustment for Supplies—Store is labeled *(c)* and is shown on lines 6 and 32.

| | | TRIAL BALANCE | | ADJUSTMENTS | |
	ACCOUNT TITLE	DEBIT	CREDIT	DEBIT	CREDIT
5	*Supplies—Office*	5 4 0 0 00			(b) 3 9 4 0 00
6	*Supplies—Store*	5 7 8 0 00			(c) 3 2 6 0 00
31	*Supplies Expense—Office*			(b) 3 9 4 0 00	
32	*Supplies Expense—Store*			(c) 3 2 6 0 00	
33					

Illustration 17-4
Supplies inventory
adjustments on a
work sheet

Prepaid insurance adjustment

Payment for insurance protection is paid in advance. The value of prepaid insurance *not expired* during a fiscal period is an asset. The value of prepaid insurance *expired* during a fiscal period is an expense.

Analyzing a prepaid insurance adjustment. CarLand's prepaid insurance account on December 31, the end of the fiscal period, has a debit balance of $4,840.00, as shown in the T account.

Prepaid Insurance	
Dec. 31 Bal. 4,840.00	

The account balance for Prepaid Insurance, $4,840.00, includes two items. (1) The account balance on January 1. (2) The cost of insurance premiums paid during the year. The account balance does not reflect the value of the insurance *expired* during the year (an expense). Therefore, the prepaid insurance account balance must be adjusted to bring the balance up to date. (CONCEPT: *Matching Expenses with Revenue*)

The two accounts used to adjust the prepaid insurance account are Prepaid Insurance and Insurance Expense. The T accounts show the two accounts before the adjustment is made.

BEFORE ADJUSTMENT

Insurance Expense	

Prepaid Insurance	
Dec. 31 Bal. 4,840.00	

Before the adjustment, the prepaid insurance account has a December 31 debit balance of $4,840.00. The account balance, however, is not up to date. The value of the prepaid insurance *not expired* is determined to be $2,200.00. The prepaid insurance account balance must be adjusted to show its current value.

Four questions are asked in analyzing the adjustment for prepaid insurance.

1. What is the balance of Prepaid Insurance?........ $4,840.00
2. What should the balance be for this account? . $2,200.00
3. What must be done to correct the account
    balance? Decrease.......................... $2,640.00
4. What adjustment is made?
    Debit Insurance Expense.................... $2,640.00
    Credit Prepaid Insurance $2,640.00

The prepaid insurance adjustment is shown in the T accounts.

Insurance Expense is debited and Prepaid Insurance is credited for $2,640.00. The beginning debit balance of Prepaid Insurance, $4,840.00, *minus* the adjustment credit amount, $2,640.00, *equals* the ending debit balance of Prepaid Insurance, $2,200.00.

AFTER ADJUSTMENT

Insurance Expense

Adj. (d) 2,640.00	

Prepaid Insurance

Dec. 31 Bal. 4,840.00	Adj. (d) 2,640.00
(New Bal. *2,200.00)*	

Recording a prepaid insurance adjustment on a work sheet. The steps in recording the prepaid insurance adjustment on a work sheet are the same as those followed by Rugcare in Chapter 7. The adjustment for Prepaid Insurance is labeled *(d)* and is shown in the Adjustments columns on lines 7 and 26 of the work sheet in Illustration 17-5.

		1	2	3	4
	ACCOUNT TITLE	TRIAL BALANCE		ADJUSTMENTS	
		DEBIT	CREDIT	DEBIT	CREDIT
7	*Prepaid Insurance*	4 8 4 0 00			*(d)*2 6 4 0 00
26	*Insurance Expense*			*(d)*2 6 4 0 00	

Illustration 17-5
Prepaid insurance
adjustment on a
work sheet

COMPLETING A WORK SHEET

CarLand follows the same procedures for completing a work sheet as described for Rugcare in Chapter 7 with the exception of the income summary account. Rugcare sells a service, not merchandise. Therefore, Rugcare has no amount recorded in the income summary account, a related account used to adjust Merchandise Inventory. CarLand sells merchandise. Therefore, the income summary account is used as the related account to adjust Merchandise Inventory. The merchandise inventory adjustment reflects the increases and decreases in the amount of goods on hand resulting from sales and purchases. Therefore, the amount recorded in Income Summary is extended to the work sheet's Income Statement Debit or Credit column. An Income Summary debit amount is extended to the Income Statement Debit column. An Income Summary credit amount is extended to the Income Statement Credit column. CarLand's completed work sheet is shown in Illustration 17-6 on pages 400 and 401.

CarLand

Work Sheet

For Year Ended December 31, 19--

	TRIAL BALANCE		ADJUSTMENTS		INCOME STATEMENT		BALANCE SHEET	
ACCOUNT TITLE	DEBIT (1)	CREDIT (2)	DEBIT (3)	CREDIT (4)	DEBIT (5)	CREDIT (6)	DEBIT (7)	CREDIT (8)
1 Cash	24 2 33 57						24 2 33 57	
2 Petty Cash	5 0 0 00						5 0 0 00	
3 Accounts Receivable	9 3 3 2 00						9 3 3 2 00	
4 Merchandise Inventory	225 4 0 0 00			(a) 13 2 0 0 00			212 2 0 0 00	
5 Supplies—Office	5 4 0 0 00			(b) 3 9 4 0 00			1 4 6 0 00	
6 Supplies—Store	5 7 8 0 00			(c) 3 2 6 0 00			2 5 2 0 00	
7 Prepaid Insurance	4 8 4 0 00			(d) 2 6 4 0 00			2 2 0 0 00	
8 Accounts Payable		10 4 5 1 90						10 4 5 1 90
9 Employee Income Tax Pay.		4 0 2 00						4 0 2 00
10 FICA Tax Payable		8 3 2 16						8 3 2 16
11 Sales Tax Payable		1 7 6 0 00						1 7 6 0 00
12 Unemploy. Tax Pay.—Federal		5 9 15						5 9 15
13 Unemploy. Tax Pay.—State		3 9 9 26						3 9 9 26
14 Health Ins. Premiums Pay.		8 4 0 00						8 4 0 00
15 U.S. Savings Bonds Payable		4 0 00						4 0 00
16 United Way Donations Payable		6 0 00						6 0 00
17 Amy Kramer, Capital		101 1 1 8 00						101 1 1 8 00
18 Amy Kramer, Drawing	18 2 0 0 00						18 2 0 0 00	
19 Dario Mesa, Capital		101 2 2 8 00						101 2 2 8 00
20 Dario Mesa, Drawing	18 6 0 0 00						18 6 0 0 00	

	Account Title	Trial Balance Dr	Trial Balance Cr	Adjustments Dr	Adjustments Cr	Income Statement Dr	Income Statement Cr	Balance Sheet Dr	Balance Sheet Cr
21	*Income Summary*				(a) 13 2 0 0 00		13 2 0 0 00		
22	*Sales*		352 6 0 0 00				352 6 0 0 00		
23	*Purchases*	158 3 0 0 00				158 3 0 0 00			
24	*Advertising Expense*	5 5 0 00				5 5 0 00			
25	*Credit Card Fee Expense*	2 8 9 0 00				2 8 9 0 00			
26	*Insurance Expense*			(a) 2 6 4 0 00		2 6 4 0 00			
27	*Miscellaneous Expense*	2 1 8 2 15				2 1 8 2 15			
28	*Payroll Taxes Expense*	7 2 9 9 75				7 2 9 9 75			
29	*Rent Expense*	18 0 0 0 00				18 0 0 0 00			
30	*Salary Expense*	60 1 5 3 00				60 1 5 3 00			
31	*Supplies Expense—Office*			(b) 3 9 4 0 00		3 9 4 0 00			
32	*Supplies Expense—Store*			(c) 3 2 6 0 00		3 2 6 0 00			
33	*Utilities Expense*	3 1 8 0 00				3 1 8 0 00			
34		569 7 9 0 47	569 7 9 0 47	23 0 4 0 00	23 0 4 0 00	280 5 4 4 90	352 6 0 0 00	289 2 4 5 57	217 1 9 0 47
35	*Net Income*					72 0 5 5 10			72 0 5 5 10
36						352 6 0 0 00	352 6 0 0 00	289 2 4 5 57	289 2 4 5 57
37									
38									

Illustration 17-6
Completed work sheet for
a merchandising business

SUMMARY OF COMPLETING AN 8-COLUMN WORK SHEET FOR A MERCHANDISING BUSINESS

Illustration 17-7
Summary of an 8-column
work sheet for a
merchandising business

Illustration 17-7 summarizes the steps followed in completing an 8-column work sheet for a merchandising business.

	ACCOUNT TITLE	TRIAL BALANCE		ADJUSTMENTS		INCOME STATEMENT		BALANCE SHEET		
		DEBIT	CREDIT	DEBIT	CREDIT	DEBIT	CREDIT	DEBIT	CREDIT	
1	Cash	24 2 3 3 57						24 2 3 3 57		1
2	Petty Cash	5 0 0 00						5 0 0 00		2
4	Merchandise Inventory	225 4 0 0 00			(a) 13 2 0 0 00			212 2 0 0 00		4
5	Supplies—Office	5 4 0 0 00			(b) 3 9 4 0 00			1 4 6 0 00		5
8	Accounts Payable		10 4 5 1 90						10 4 5 1 90	8
19	Dario Mesa, Capital		101 2 2 8 00						101 2 2 8 00	19
20	Dario Mesa, Drawing	18 6 0 0 00						18 6 0 0 00		20
21	Income Summary			(a) 13 2 0 0 00		13 2 0 0 00				21
22	Sales		352 6 0 0 00				352 6 0 0 00			22
23	Purchases	158 3 0 0 00				158 3 0 0 00				23
32	Supplies Expense—Store			(c) 3 2 6 0 00		3 2 6 0 00				32
33	Utilities Expense	2 1 8 0 00				3 1 8 0 00				33
34		569 7 9 0 47	569 7 9 0 47	23 0 4 0 00	23 0 4 0 00	280 5 4 4 90	352 6 0 0 00	289 2 4 5 57	217 1 9 0 47	34
35	Net Income					72 0 5 5 10			72 0 5 5 10	35
36						352 6 0 0 00	352 6 0 0 00	289 2 4 5 57	289 2 4 5 57	36
37										37

1 Prepare a trial balance in the Trial Balance columns.

2 Analyze and record adjustments in the Adjustments columns.

3 Extend balance sheet items to the work sheet's Balance Sheet columns.

4 Extend income statement items, including Income Summary, to the work sheet's Income Statement columns.

5 Total the Income Statement and Balance Sheet columns.

6 Figure the net income or net loss. If the Income Statement Credit column total (revenue) is larger than the Debit column total (costs and

expenses), a net income has occurred. If the Income Statement Debit column total (costs and expenses) is larger than the Credit column total (revenue), a net loss has occurred. CarLand's net income is calculated as shown below.

Income Statement Credit Column Total	−	Income Statement Debit Column Total	=	Net Income
$352,600.00	−	$280,544.90	=	$72,055.10

7 Extend the amount of net income or net loss to the Balance Sheet Debit or Credit column. When a net income occurs, the net income amount is extended to the Balance Sheet Credit amount column, as shown for CarLand on line 35. When a net loss occurs, the net loss amount is extended to the Balance Sheet Debit amount column.

8 Total the four Income Statement and Balance Sheet amount columns.

9 Check that the totals for each pair of columns are in balance. As shown on CarLand's work sheet on line 36, the totals for the Income Statement columns, $352,600.00, are the same. The totals for the Balance Sheet columns, $289,245.57, are also the same. CarLand's work sheet is in balance.

A 10-COLUMN WORK SHEET FOR A MERCHANDISING BUSINESS

Some large merchandising businesses *with many accounts to be adjusted* at the end of a fiscal period may use a 10-column work sheet. A 10-column work sheet includes an additional pair of amount columns titled *Adjusted Trial Balance*, as shown in the 10-column work sheet in Illustration 17-8.

After adjustments have been recorded, the balance for each account listed in the Trial Balance columns is extended to the Adjusted Trial Balance columns. The Adjusted Trial Balance columns are then totaled to prove equality of debits and credits after adjustments. Following proof of debits and credits, amounts in the Adjusted Trial Balance columns are extended to the Balance Sheet and Income Statement columns. The Income Statement and Balance Sheet columns are totaled and ruled the same way as on an 8-column work sheet.

Any business with adjustments to make at the end of a fiscal period could use either an 8-column or a 10-column work sheet. However, completing two extra amount columns when most of the account balances *are not* adjusted requires extra time and work. Account balances not adjusted must be extended from the Trial Balance columns to the Adjusted Trial Balance columns. Whereas, with an 8-column work sheet, account balances *not* adjusted are extended directly to the Balance Sheet or Income Statement columns. CarLand prefers to use an 8-column work sheet because only four adjustments are needed at the end of each fiscal period.

CarLand

Work Sheet

For Year Ended December 31, 19--

	ACCOUNT TITLE	TRIAL BALANCE		ADJUSTMENTS		
		DEBIT	CREDIT	DEBIT	CREDIT	
1	Cash	24 2 3 3 57				1
2	Petty Cash	5 0 0 00				2
3	Accounts Receivable	9 3 3 2 00				3
4	Merchandise Inventory	225 4 0 0 00			(a)13 2 0 0 00	4
5	Supplies—Office	5 4 0 0 00			(b) 3 9 4 0 00	5
6	Supplies—Store	5 7 8 0 00			(c) 3 2 6 0 00	6
7	Prepaid Insurance	4 8 4 0 00			(d) 2 6 4 0 00	7
8	Accounts Payable		10 4 5 1 90			8
9	Employee Income Tax Payable		4 0 2 00			9
10	FICA Tax Payable		8 3 2 16			10
11	Sales Tax Payable		1 7 6 0 00			11
29	Rent Expense	18 0 0 0 00				29
30	Salary Expense	60 1 5 3 00				30
31	Supplies Expense—Office			(b) 3 9 4 0 00		31
32	Supplies Expense—Store			(c) 3 2 6 0 00		32
33	Utilities Expense	3 1 8 0 00				33
34		569 7 9 0 47	569 7 9 0 47	23 0 4 0 00	23 0 4 0 00	34
35	Net Income					35
36						36

Illustration 17-8   Ten-column work sheet (left page)

ACCOUNTING TERMS

What is the meaning of each of the following?

1. inventory   **2.** merchandise inventory

QUESTIONS FOR INDIVIDUAL STUDY

1. Why do some general ledger accounts not have any entries posted and, therefore, zero balances at the end of a fiscal period?

2. Why is a work sheet used at the end of a fiscal period?

3. Which accounting concept is being applied when a work sheet is prepared at the end of each fiscal period?

4. Why are all general ledger accounts listed on the Trial Balance columns of a work sheet?

5. Which of CarLand's general ledger accounts need to be brought up to date at the end of a fiscal period?

6. What type of account is Merchandise Inventory, and what is its normal balance?

	5 ADJUSTED TRIAL BALANCE DEBIT	6 CREDIT	7 INCOME STATEMENT DEBIT	8 CREDIT	9 BALANCE SHEET DEBIT	10 CREDIT	
1	24 2 3 3 57				24 2 3 3 57		1
2	5 0 0 00				5 0 0 00		2
3	9 3 3 2 00				9 3 3 2 00		3
4	212 2 0 0 00				212 2 0 0 00		4
5	1 4 6 0 00				1 4 6 0 00		5
6	2 5 2 0 00				2 5 2 0 00		6
7	2 2 0 0 00				2 2 0 0 00		7
8		10 4 5 1 90				10 4 5 1 90	8
9		4 0 2 00				4 0 2 00	9
10		8 3 2 16				8 3 2 16	10
11		1 7 6 0 00				1 7 6 0 00	11
29	18 0 0 0 00		18 0 0 0 00				29
30	60 1 5 3 00		60 1 5 3 00				30
31	3 9 4 0 00		3 9 4 0 00				31
32	3 2 6 0 00		3 2 6 0 00				32
33	3 1 8 0 00		3 1 8 0 00				33
34	592 8 3 0 47	592 8 3 0 47	280 5 4 4 90	352 6 0 0 00	289 2 4 5 57	217 1 9 0 47	34
35			72 0 5 5 10			72 0 5 5 10	35
36			352 6 0 0 00	352 6 0 0 00	289 2 4 5 57	289 2 4 5 57	36

Illustration 17-8   Ten-column work sheet (right page)

7. Why are the beginning and ending balances of the merchandise inventory account before adjustments the same?

8. What accounts are affected, and how, by the adjustment for merchandise inventory?

9. What does the amount of supplies not used during a fiscal period represent to a business?

10. Which accounting concept is being applied when expenses are recorded in the same accounting period in which the expenses contribute to earning revenue?

11. What two items are included in Car-Land's office supplies account balance before adjustment?

12. What accounts are affected, and how, by the adjustment for office supplies inventory?

13. What two items are included in Car-Land's prepaid insurance account balance before adjustment?

14. What accounts are affected, and how, by a prepaid insurance adjustment?

15. What type of merchandising business might use a 10-column work sheet?

16. What two additional amount columns are found on a 10-column work sheet?

CASES FOR MANAGEMENT DECISION

CASE 1 After completing a work sheet, Kramer Merchandising Outlet finds that through an oversight, paper bags still in boxes were overlooked in figuring the supplies inventory. The value of the paper bags overlooked is $50.00. Joseph Kramer suggests that the accountant not worry about such a small amount because the oversight does not have any effect on balancing the Income Statement and Balance Sheet columns of the work sheet. Mr. Kramer further indicates that the oversight will be corrected anyway when the store supplies are counted at the end of the next fiscal period.

The accountant recommends that the work sheet be redone to reflect the refigured supplies inventory. Do you agree with Mr. Kramer or the accountant? Explain your answer.

CASE 2 Quality Shoes paid $1,440.00 for a one-year fire insurance policy. The company prepares an income statement and balance sheet every three months. However, the accountant prepares a prepaid insurance adjustment only at the end of the year. Rachel Delfield, one of the partners in the business, thinks the prepaid insurance should be adjusted every three months. Who is correct? Why?

◼ DRILLS FOR UNDERSTANDING

DRILL 17-D1   Analyzing adjusting entries

The following chart contains adjustment information related to the preparation of work sheets for three businesses.

Business	Account Title and Balance		End-of-Fiscal-Period Information	
A	Merchandise Inventory...	$148,000.00	Merchandise inventory ..	$134,000.00
	Supplies—Office	5,750.00	Office supp. inventory ...	4,200.00
	Supplies—Store	4,920.00	Store supp. inventory....	3,840.00
	Prepaid Insurance	1,860.00	Value of prepaid insurance	1,240.00
B	Merchandise Inventory...	$182,000.00	Merchandise inventory ..	$166,000.00
	Supplies—Office	4,680.00	Office supp. inventory ...	3,460.00
	Supplies—Store	5,930.00	Store supp. inventory....	4,320.00
	Prepaid Insurance	2,520.00	Value of prepaid insurance	1,260.00
C	Merchandise Inventory...	$166,500.00	Merchandise inventory ..	$178,000.00
	Supplies—Office	5,460.00	Office supp. inventory ...	4,520.00
	Supplies—Store	6,480.00	Store supp. inventory....	4,960.00
	Prepaid Insurance	2,160.00	Value of prepaid insurance	1,080.00

Use a form similar to the following.

1	2	3	4	5
Business	Adjustment Number	Accounts Affected	Adjustment Column	
			Debit	Credit
A	1.	Income Summary	$14,000.00	
		Merchandise Inventory		$14,000.00

Instructions: For each business list the accounts affected and the amounts for each of the following adjustments. List the account titles in Column 3 and the amounts in either Column 4 or 5. Adjustment 1 for Business A is given as an example.

Adjustments
1. Merchandise inventory adjustment.
2. Office supplies inventory adjustment.
3. Store supplies inventory adjustment.
4. Prepaid insurance adjustment.

DRILL 17-D2 Extending balance sheet and income statement items

Madison Enterprise's work sheet has the following Trial Balance and Adjustments columns.

	Madison Enterprises				
	Work Sheet				
	For Year Ended December 31, 19--				
ACCOUNT TITLE	TRIAL BALANCE		ADJUSTMENTS		
	DEBIT	CREDIT	DEBIT	CREDIT	
1 Cash	21 770 00				1
2 Petty Cash	500 00				2
3 Accounts Receivable	8 911 00				3
4 Merchandise Inventory	211 870 00			(a) 12 408 00	4
5 Supplies—Office	5 076 00			(b) 3 704 00	5
6 Supplies—Store	5 430 00			(c) 3 065 00	6
7 Prepaid Insurance	4 620 00			(d) 2 520 00	7
8 Accounts Payable		8 950 00			8
9 Sales Tax Payable		1 654 00			9
10 Diane Casey, Capital		98 230 00			10
11 Diane Casey, Drawing	17 108 00				11
12 Julia Gibbs, Capital		98 764 00			12
13 Julia Gibbs, Drawing	17 482 00				13
14 Income Summary			(a) 12 408 00		14
15 Sales		263 700 00			15
16 Purchases	148 800 00				16
17 Advertising Expense	5 170 00				17
18 Credit Card Fee Expense	2 720 00				18
19 Insurance Expense			(d) 2 520 00		19
20 Miscellaneous Expense	2 051 00				20
21 Rent Expense	16 800 00				21
22 Supplies Expense—Office			(b) 3 704 00		22
23 Supplies Expense—Store			(c) 3 065 00		23
24 Utilities Expense	2 990 00				24
25	471 298 00	471 298 00	21 697 00	21 697 00	25

Instructions: 1. Extend the balance sheet items to the Balance Sheet columns of the work sheet.

2. Extend the income statement items to the Income Statement columns of the work sheet.

3. Complete the work sheet.

a. Total the Income Statement and Balance Sheet columns.

b. Figure and record the net income or net loss.

c. Total and rule the Income Statement and Balance Sheet columns.

◼ APPLICATION PROBLEMS

PROBLEM 17-1 Completing a work sheet

On December 31 of the current year, Eastside Supply has the following general ledger accounts and balances. The trial balance is recorded on the work sheet in the working papers accompanying this textbook.

Account Title	Balance
Cash	$ 22,460.00
Petty Cash	500.00
Accounts Receivable	9,195.00
Merchandise Inventory	218,600.00
Supplies—Office	5,230.00
Supplies—Store	5,610.00
Prepaid Insurance	4,515.00
Accounts Payable	9,235.00
Sales Tax Payable	1,145.00
Pablo Sanchez, Capital	81,236.00
Pablo Sanchez, Drawing	14,640.00
Carmen Zapata, Capital	81,778.00
Carman Zapata, Drawing	14,820.00
Income Summary	—
Sales	274,900.00
Purchases	123,705.00
Advertising Expense	5,335.00
Credit Card Fee Expense	2,810.00
Insurance Expense	—
Miscellaneous Expense	2,134.00
Rent Expense	15,600.00
Supplies Expense—Office	—
Supplies Expense—Store	—
Utilities Expense	3,140.00

Instructions: 1. Analyze the following adjustment information, and record the adjustments on the work sheet.

Adjustment Information, December 31	
Merchandise inventory	$196,610.00
Office supplies inventory	1,410.00
Store supplies inventory	2,450.00
Value of prepaid insurance	1,935.00

2. Figure and record the net income or net loss.

3. Complete the work sheet.

PROBLEM 17-2   **Completing a work sheet**

On December 31 of the current year, Jomar has the following general ledger accounts and balances. The trial balance is recorded on the work sheet in the working papers accompanying this textbook.

Account Title	Balance
Cash	$ 22,100.00
Petty Cash	300.00
Accounts Receivable	9,620.00
Merchandise Inventory	243,600.00
Supplies—Office	5,730.00
Supplies—Store	5,380.00
Prepaid Insurance	5,060.00
Accounts Payable	9,864.00
Sales Tax Payable	916.00
Lidia Jomar, Capital	151,850.00
Lidia Jomar, Drawing	12,860.00
Philip Jomar, Capital	150,894.00
Philip Jomar, Drawing	12,674.00
Income Summary	—
Sales	183,110.00
Purchases	147,150.00
Advertising Expense	5,820.00
Credit Card Fee Expense	1,615.00
Insurance Expense	—
Miscellaneous Expense	2,285.00
Rent Expense	19,200.00
Supplies Expense—Office	—
Supplies Expense—Store	—
Utilities Expense	3,240.00

Instructions: 1. Analyze the following adjustment information, and record the adjustments on the work sheet.

Adjustment Information, December 31	
Merchandise inventory	$246,600.00
Office supplies inventory	1,790.00
Store supplies inventory	1,510.00
Value of prepaid insurance	2,300.00

2. Figure and record the net income or net loss.
3. Complete the work sheet.

ENRICHMENT PROBLEMS

MASTERY PROBLEM 17-M   **Completing a work sheet**

On December 31 of the current year, Marine Supply has the following general ledger accounts and balances. The trial balance is recorded on the work sheet in the working papers accompanying this textbook.

Account Title	Balance
Cash	$ 23,740.00
Petty Cash	500.00

Accounts Receivable	10,200.00
Merchandise Inventory	185,300.00
Supplies—Office	5,585.00
Supplies—Store	5,735.00
Prepaid Insurance	4,275.00
Accounts Payable	9,680.00
Sales Tax Payable	1,376.00
Mark Edwards, Capital	88,740.00
Mark Edwards, Drawing	18,380.00
David Parker, Capital	89,459.00
David Parker, Drawing	18,610.00
Income Summary	—
Sales	275,300.00
Purchases	161,290.00
Advertising Expense	5,920.00
Credit Card Fee Expense	2,735.00
Insurance Expense	—
Miscellaneous Expense	2,365.00
Rent Expense	16,800.00
Supplies Expense—Office	—
Supplies Expense—Store	—
Utilities Expense	3,120.00

Instructions: Use the following adjustment information. Complete the work sheet.

Adjustment Information, December 31

Merchandise inventory	$208,600.00
Office supplies inventory	1,855.00
Store supplies inventory	2,355.00
Value of prepaid insurance	1,575.00

CHALLENGE PROBLEM 17-C   Completing a 10-column work sheet

On December 31 of the current year, Ultimate Fashion has the following general ledger accounts and balances. The trial balance is recorded on the work sheet in the working papers accompanying this textbook.

Account Title	Balance
Cash	$ 25,340.00
Petty Cash	500.00
Accounts Receivable	9,485.00
Merchandise Inventory	215,870.00
Supplies—Office	5,130.00
Supplies—Store	5,335.00
Prepaid Insurance	3,960.00
Accounts Payable	10,320.00
Sales Tax Payable	810.00
Debra Brown, Capital	109,635.00
Debra Brown, Drawing	18,340.00
Richard Leyba, Capital	108,845.00
Richard Leyba, Drawing	18,560.00
Income Summary	—
Sales	192,380.00
Purchases	86,570.00
Advertising Expense	6,140.00

Credit Card Fee Expense 2,385.00
Insurance Expense. . . . .   —
Miscellaneous Expense. 2,530.00
Rent Expense 18,600.00
Supplies Expense—Office . . . .   —
Supplies Expense—Store. . . . .   —
Utilities Expense. 3,245.00

Instructions: Use the following adjustment information. Complete the 10-column work sheet.

Adjustment Information, December 31

Merchandise inventory $205,370.00
Office supplies inventory. 2,160.00
Store supplies inventory 2,195.00
Value of prepaid insurance 1,320.00

Financial Statements for a Partnership

ENABLING PERFORMANCE TASKS

After studying Chapter 18, you will be able to:
a. Define accounting terms related to financial statements for a merchandising business organized as a partnership.
b. Identify accounting concepts and practices related to financial statements for a merchandising business organized as a partnership.
c. Prepare an income statement for a merchandising business organized as a partnership.
d. Analyze an income statement using component percentages for a merchandising business organized as a partnership.
e. Prepare a distribution of net income statement for a merchandising business organized as a partnership.
f. Prepare an owners' equity statement for a merchandising business organized as a partnership.
g. Prepare a balance sheet for a merchandising business organized as a partnership.

The financial activities of a business are recorded in journals and ledgers during a fiscal period. At the end of a fiscal period, a work sheet is prepared to organize and summarize this financial information. The completed work sheet is used to prepare financial statements. Financial statements provide the primary source of information needed by owners and managers to make decisions on the future activity of a business.

All financial information must be reported in order to make sound business decisions. The financial statements should provide information about a business' financial condition, changes in this financial condition, and the progress of operations. (CONCEPT: Adequate Disclosure)

Comparing financial condition and progress for more than one fiscal period also helps owners and managers make sound business decisions. Therefore, financial information must be reported the same way from one fiscal period to the next. (CONCEPT: Consistent Reporting)

FINANCIAL STATEMENTS FOR A PARTNERSHIP

A business organized as a partnership prepares four financial statements to report financial progress and condition. A partnership prepares an income statement and a balance sheet similar to those used by a proprietorship. A partnership also prepares two additional financial statements. One statement reports the distribution of net income or net loss for each partner. The other statement reports the changes in owners' equity for the fiscal period.

INCOME STATEMENT

An income statement is used to report a business' financial progress. Merchandising businesses report revenue, cost of merchandise sold, gross profit on sales, expenses, and net income or loss. Current and previous income statements can be compared to determine the reasons for increases or decreases in net income. This comparison is helpful in making management decisions about future operations.

Preparing an income statement

Information from a completed work sheet is used to prepare an income statement. CarLand's income statement information on a work sheet for the year ended December 31 is shown in Illustration 18-1.

Illustration 18-1
Income statement
information on a work
sheet

	ACCOUNT TITLE	TRIAL BALANCE		ADJUSTMENTS		INCOME STATEMENT		BALANCE SHEET		
		DEBIT	CREDIT	DEBIT	CREDIT	DEBIT	CREDIT	DEBIT	CREDIT	
4	Merchandise Inventory	225 4 0 0 00			(b) 13 2 0 0 00			212 2 0 0 00		4
22	Sales		352 6 0 0 00				352 6 0 0 00			22
23	Purchases	158 3 0 0 00				158 3 0 0 00				23
24	Advertising Expense	5 5 0 0 00				5 5 0 0 00				24
25	Credit Card Fee Expense	2 8 9 0 00				2 8 9 0 00				25
26	Insurance Expense			(a) 2 6 4 0 00		2 6 4 0 00				26
27	Miscellaneous Expense	2 1 8 2 15				2 1 8 2 15				27
28	Payroll Taxes Expense	7 2 9 9 75				7 2 9 9 75				28
29	Rent Expense	18 0 0 0 00				18 0 0 0 00				29
30	Salary Expense	60 1 5 3 00				60 1 5 3 00				30
31	Supplies Expense—Office			(c) 3 9 4 0 00		3 9 4 0 00				31
32	Supplies Expense—Store			(d) 3 2 6 0 00		3 2 6 0 00				32
33	Utilities Expense	3 1 8 0 00				3 1 8 0 00				33
34		569 7 9 0 47	569 7 9 0 47	23 0 4 0 00	23 0 4 0 00	280 5 4 4 90	352 6 0 0 00	289 2 4 5 57	217 1 9 0 47	34
35	Net Income					72 0 5 5 10			72 0 5 5 10	35
36						352 6 0 0 00	352 6 0 0 00	289 2 4 5 57	289 2 4 5 57	36

The income statement of a merchandising business has three main sections. (1) Revenue section. (2) Cost of merchandise sold section. (3) Expenses section. The total original price of all merchandise sold during a fiscal period is called the cost of merchandise sold. *(CONCEPT: Historical Cost)* Cost of merchandise sold is sometimes known as cost of goods sold or cost of sales. CarLand's completed income statement is shown in Illustration 18-2.

				% OF SALES
CarLand				
Income Statement				
For Year Ended December 31, 19--				
Revenue:				
Sales			352 6 0 0 00	100.0
Cost of Merchandise Sold:				
Merchandise Inventory, January 1, 19--	225 4 0 0 00			
Purchases	158 3 0 0 00			
Total Cost of Mdse. Available for Sale	383 7 0 0 00			
Less Mdse. Inventory, December 31, 19--	212 2 0 0 00			
Cost of Merchandise Sold			171 5 0 0 00	48.6
Gross Profit on Sales			181 1 0 0 00	51.4
Expenses:				
Advertising Expense	5 5 0 0 00			
Credit Card Fee Expense	2 8 9 0 00			
Insurance Expense	2 6 4 0 00			
Miscellaneous Expense	2 1 8 2 15			
Payroll Taxes Expense	7 2 9 9 75			
Rent Expense	18 0 0 0 00			
Salary Expense	60 1 5 3 00			
Supplies Expense—Office	3 9 4 0 00			
Supplies Expense—Store	3 2 6 0 00			
Utilities Expense	3 1 8 0 00			
Total Expenses			109 0 4 4 90	30.9
Net Income			72 0 5 5 10	20.4

Illustration 18-2
Income statement for a
merchandising business

CarLand uses seven steps in preparing an income statement.

1 Write the income statement heading on three lines.

2 Prepare the revenue section. Use the information from the Income Statement Credit column of the work sheet.

- Write the name of this section, *Revenue:*, at the extreme left of the wide column on the first line.

- Write the title of the revenue account, Sales, on the next line, indented about one centimeter.

- Write the balance of the sales account, *$352,600.00*, in the second amount column. For CarLand, this amount is also the total of the revenue section.

> For businesses with more than one source of revenue, each revenue account title is listed in the wide column. Each account balance is written in the first amount column. The words *Total Revenue* are written in the wide column on the next line below the last revenue account title. The total amount of revenue is written in the second amount column.

3 Prepare the cost of merchandise sold section.

- Write the name of this section, *Cost of Merchandise Sold:*, at the extreme left of the wide column.

- Indent about one centimeter on the next line, and write the items needed to figure cost of merchandise sold. Write the amount of each item in the first amount column.

Beginning merchandise inventory, January 1.......... (This amount is the debit balance of Merchandise Inventory in the Trial Balance Debit Column of the work sheet.)	$ 225,400.00
Plus purchases made during the fiscal period .... (This amount is the debit balance of Purchases in the Income Statement Debit column of the work sheet.)	+158,300.00
Equals total cost of merchandise available for sale during the fiscal period	$ 383,700.00
Less ending merchandise inventory, December 31...... (This amount is the debit balance of Merchandise Inventory in the Balance Sheet Debit column of the work sheet.)	−212,200.00
Equals cost of merchandise sold during the fiscal period	$ 171,500.00

- Indent about one centimeter on the next line, and write the words *Cost of Merchandise Sold*. Write the cost of merchandise sold amount, *$171,500.00*, in the second amount column.

4 Figure the gross profit on sales. The revenue remaining after cost of merchandise sold has been deducted is called gross profit on sales.

- Write the words *Gross Profit on Sales* on the next line at the extreme left of the wide column.

- Write the gross profit on sales amount, *$181,100.00*, in the second amount column. (Total revenue, $352,600.00, *less* cost of merchandise sold, $171,500.00, *equals* gross profit on sales, $181,100.00.)

5 Prepare the expenses section. Use the information from the Income Statement Debit column of the work sheet.

- Write the name of this section, *Expenses:*, at the extreme left of the wide column.
- Indent about one centimeter on the next line, and list the expense account titles in the order in which they appear on the work sheet. Write the amount of each expense account balance in the first amount column.
- Indent about one centimeter, and write the words *Total Expenses* on the next line in the wide column below the last expense account title. Total the individual expense amounts and write the total, *$109,044.90*, in the second amount column on the total line.

6 Figure the net income.

- Write the words *Net Income* on the next line at the extreme left of the wide column.
- Write the net income amount, *$72,055.10*, in the second amount column on the net income line. (Gross profit on sales, $181,100.00, *less* total expenses, $109,044.90, *equals* net income, $72,055.10.)

   Verify accuracy by comparing the amount of net income figured on the income statement, $72,055.10, with the amount on the work sheet, $72,055.10. The two amounts must be the same.

7 Rule double lines across both amount columns to show that the income statement has been verified as correct.

Analyzing an income statement showing a net income

For a merchandising business, every sales dollar reported on the income statement includes four components. (1) Cost of merchandise sold. (2) Gross profit on sales. (3) Total expenses. (4) Net income. To help make decisions about future operations, CarLand analyzes relationships between these four income statement components and sales. The percentage relationship between one financial statement item and the total that includes that item is known as a component percentage. On an income statement, component percentages are figured by dividing the amount of each component by the amount of sales. CarLand figures a component percentage for cost of merchandise sold, gross profit on sales, total expenses, and net income. The relationship between each component and sales is shown in a separate column on the income statement.

Acceptable component percentages

For a component percentage to be useful, a business must know acceptable percentages. This information is determined by making comparisons with prior fiscal periods as well as with industry standards that are published by industry organizations. Based on these sources, CarLand determines the acceptable component percentages shown in the following table.

Income Statement Items	Acceptable Component Percentages	Actual Component Percentages
Sales	100.0%	100.0%
Cost of merchandise sold	not more than 50.0%	48.6%
Gross profit on sales	not less than 50.0%	51.4%
Total expenses	not more than 32.0%	30.9%
Net income	not less than 18.0%	20.4%

Each percentage represents the amount of each sales dollar that is considered acceptable. For example, CarLand determines that no more than 50 cents, or 50.0%, of each sales dollar should be devoted to cost of merchandise sold.

Cost of merchandise sold component percentage. The cost of merchandise sold is a major cost. Therefore, this cost must be kept as low as possible. Analysis of CarLand's income statement, Illustration 18-2, shows that the cost of merchandise sold is 48.6% of sales. This component percentage is calculated as shown below.

Cost of Merchandise Sold	÷	Sales	=	Cost of Merchandise Sold Component Percentage
$171,500.00	÷	$352,600.00	=	48.6%

The component percentage for cost of merchandise sold, 48.6%, is *less than* the maximum acceptable percentage, 50.0%. Therefore, CarLand's component percentage for cost of merchandise sold is considered acceptable.

Gross profit on sales component percentage. Gross profit must be large enough to cover total expenses and the desired amount of net income. CarLand determines that at least 50 cents, or 50.0%, of each sales dollar should result in gross profit. Analysis of CarLand's income statement shows that the component percentage for gross profit on sales is 51.4%. This component percentage is calculated as shown below.

Gross Profit on Sales	÷	Sales	=	Gross Profit on Sales Component Percentage
$181,100.00	÷	$352,600.00	=	51.4%

The component percentage for gross profit on sales, 51.4%, is *not less than* the minimum acceptable percentage, 50.0%. Therefore, CarLand's component percentage for gross profit on sales is considered acceptable.

Total expenses component percentage. Total expenses must be less than gross profit on sales to provide a desirable net income. CarLand determines that no more than 32 cents, or 32.0%, of each sales dollar should be devoted to total expenses. Analysis of CarLand's income statement shows that the component percentage for total expenses is 30.9%. This component percentage is calculated as shown below.

Total Expenses	÷	Sales	=	Total Expenses Component Percentage
$109,044.90	÷	$352,600.00	=	30.9%

The component percentage for total expenses, 30.9%, is *not more than* the maximum acceptable percentage, 32.0%. Therefore, CarLand's component percentage for total expenses is considered acceptable.

Net income component percentage. The component percentage for net income shows the progress being made by a business. CarLand determines that at least 18 cents, or 18.0%, of each sales dollar should result in net income. Analysis of CarLand's income statement shows that the component percentage for net income is 20.4%. This component percentage is calculated as shown below.

Net Income	÷	Sales	=	Net Income Component Percentage
$72,055.10	÷	$352,600.00	=	20.4%

The component percentage for net income, 20.4%, is *not less than* the minimum acceptable percentage, 18.0%. Therefore, CarLand's component percentage for net income is considered acceptable.

Analyzing an income statement showing a net loss

When a business' total expenses are greater than the gross profit on sales, the difference is known as a net loss. For example, the income statement shown in Illustration 18-3 shows a net loss of $3,770.00 for the fiscal period.

Total expenses, $109,120.00, *less* gross profit on sales, $105,350.00, *equals* net loss, $3,770.00. The net loss amount, *$3,770.00*, is written in parentheses in the second amount column on the line with the words *Net Loss*. An amount written in parentheses on a financial statement indicates a negative amount.

Autoworks uses the same acceptable component percentages as CarLand. Analysis of the income statement, Illustration 18-3, indicates unacceptable component percentages. (1) The component percentage for cost of merchandise sold, 53.3%, is *more than* the maximum acceptable component percentage, 50.0%. (2) The component percentage for gross profit on sales, 46.7%, is *less than* the minimum acceptable component percentage, 50.0%. (3) The component percentage for total expenses, 48.4%, is *more than* the

Autoworks Income Statement For Year Ended December 31, 19--			% OF SALES
Revenue:			
Sales		225 4 0 0 00	100.0
Cost of Merchandise Sold:			
Merchandise Inventory, Janaury 1, 19--	243 2 0 0 00		
Purchases	138 9 0 0 00		
Total Cost of Mdse. Available for Sale	382 1 0 0 00		
Less Mdse. Inventory, December 31, 19--	262 0 5 0 00		
Cost of Merchandise Sold		120 0 5 0 00	53.3
Gross Profit on Sales		105 3 5 0 00	46.7
Expenses:			
Advertising Expense	5 2 0 0 00		
Credit Card Fee Expense	3 1 2 0 00		
Insurance Expense	1 0 5 0 00		
Miscellaneous Expense	2 3 9 0 00		
Payroll Taxes Expense	8 3 4 0 00		
Rent Expense	14 4 0 0 00		
Salary Expense	62 3 1 0 00		
Supplies Expense—Office	4 6 2 0 00		
Supplies Expense—Store	4 2 8 0 00		
Utilities Expense	3 4 1 0 00		
Total Expenses		109 1 2 0 00	48.4
Net Loss		(3 7 7 0 00)	(1.67)

Illustration 18-3
Income statement showing a net loss

maximum acceptable component percentage, 32.0%. (4) Because a net loss occurred, the component percentage for net income, (1.67%), means that Autoworks lost 1.67 cents on each sales dollar. The net loss amount, $3,770.00, is considered unacceptable.

Actions to correct unacceptable component percentages

The goal of any business is to earn an acceptable net income. When component percentages are not acceptable, regardless of whether a net income or net loss occurred, management action is necessary.

Unacceptable component percentage for gross profit on sales. The component percentage for gross profit on sales is directly related to sales revenue and cost of merchandise sold. An unacceptable component percentage for gross profit on sales requires one of three actions. (1) Increase sales revenue. (2) Decrease cost of merchandise sold. (3) Increase sales revenue and also decrease cost of merchandise sold.

Increasing sales revenue while keeping the cost of merchandise sold the same will increase gross profit on sales. To increase sales revenue, management may consider increasing the markup on merchandise purchased for sale. However, a business must be cautious on the amount of the markup increase. If the increase in markup is too large, a decrease in sales revenue could occur for two reasons. (1) The sales price is beyond what customers are willing to pay. (2) The sales price is higher than what competing businesses charge for the same merchandise.

Decreasing the cost of merchandise sold while keeping the sales revenue the same will also increase gross profit on sales. To decrease cost of merchandise sold, management should review purchasing practices. For example, would purchasing merchandise in larger quantities or from other vendors result in a lower cost?

Combining a small increase in sales revenue and a small decrease in the cost of merchandise sold may also result in an acceptable component percentage for gross profit on sales.

Unacceptable component percentage for total expenses. Each expense account balance must be reviewed to determine if major increases have occurred. This review should include comparisons with prior fiscal periods as well as with industry standards. Actions must then be taken to reduce any expenses for which major increases have occurred or that are beyond industry standards.

Unacceptable component percentage for net income. If the component percentages for cost of merchandise sold, gross profit on sales, and total expenses are brought within acceptable ranges, net income will also be acceptable.

DISTRIBUTION OF NET INCOME STATEMENT

A partnership's net income or net loss may be divided in any way agreed upon by the partners. Amy Kramer and Dario Mesa, partners in CarLand, agreed to share net income or net loss equally.

A partnership distribution of net income or net loss is usually shown on a separate financial statement. A partnership financial statement showing net income or loss distribution to partners is called a distribution of net income statement.

Preparing a distribution of net income statement

The net income, $72,055.10, from the income statement shown in Illustration 18-2 is used to prepare the distribution of net income statement. CarLand's distribution of net income statement is shown in Illustration 18-4.

CarLand							
Distribution of Net Income Statement							
For Year Ended December 31, 19--							
Amy Kramer							
50.0% of Net Income			36	0	2	7	55
Dario Mesa							
50.0% of Net Income			36	0	2	7	55
Net Income			72	0	5	5	10

Illustration 18-4
Distribution of net income
statement for a partnership

CarLand uses seven steps in preparing a distribution of net income statement.

1 Write the heading of the distribution of net income statement on three lines.

2 Write one partner's name, *Amy Kramer*, on the first line at the extreme left of the wide column.

3 Indent about one centimeter on the next line, and write Amy Kramer's share of net income as a percentage, *50.0% of Net Income*. Write Miss Kramer's share of net income, $36,027.55 (50.0% × $72,055.10), in the amount column on the same line.

4 Write the other partner's name, *Dario Mesa*, on the next line at the extreme left of the wide column.

5 Indent about one centimeter on the next line, and write Dario Mesa's share of net income as a percentage, *50.0% of Net Income*. Write Mr. Mesa's share of net income, $36,027.55 (50.0% × $72,055.10), in the amount column on the same line.

6 Write the words *Net Income* on the next line at the extreme left of the wide column. Add the distribution of net income for Amy Kramer, $36,027.55, and for Dario Mesa, $36,027.55. Write the total amount, $72,055.10, in the amount column. Verify accuracy by comparing the total amount, $72,055.10, with the net income reported on the income statement, $72,055.10. The two amounts must be the same.

7 Rule double lines across the amount column to show that the distribution of net income statement has been verified as correct.

Distribution of net income statement with unequal distribution of earnings

Regardless of how earnings are shared, the steps in preparing a distribution of net income statement are the same. The only difference is the description of how the earnings are to be shared by the partners. A distribution of net income statement with unequal shares of earnings is shown in Illustration 18-5.

Illustration 18-5
Distribution of net income
statement with unequal
distribution of earnings

Central Sporting Goods	
Distribution of Net Income Statement	
For Year Ended December 31, 19--	
Dolores Demski	
60.0% of Net Income	40 8 0 0 00
Linda Kemp	
40.0% of Net Income	27 2 0 0 00
Net Income	68 0 0 0 00

Dolores Demski and Linda Kemp are partners in a business. Because Mrs. Demski spends more time in the business than Ms. Kemp, the partners agree to share net income or loss unequally. Mrs. Demski gets 60.0% of net income or loss. Ms. Kemp gets 40.0% of net income or loss. With a net income of $68,000.00, Mrs. Demski receives 60.0%, or $40,800.00. Ms. Kemp receives 40.0%, or $27,200.00.

OWNERS' EQUITY STATEMENT

The amount of net income earned is important to business owners. Owners are also interested in changes that occur in owners' equity during a fiscal period. A financial statement that summarizes the changes in owners' equity during a fiscal period is called an owners' equity statement. Business owners can review an owners' equity statement to determine if owners' equity is increasing or decreasing and what is causing the change. Three factors can change owners' equity. (1) Additional investments. (2) Withdrawals. (3) Net income or net loss.

Preparing an owners' equity statement

An owners' equity statement shows information about changes during a fiscal period in each partner's capital. Information needed to prepare an owners' equity statement is obtained from the distribution of net income statement and the general ledger capital and drawing accounts. The distribution of net income statement shows each partner's share of net income or net loss. Three kinds of information are obtained from each partner's capital and drawing account. (1) Beginning capital amount. (2) Any additional investments made during the fiscal period. (3) Each partner's withdrawal of assets during the fiscal period.

The general ledger capital and drawing accounts of Amy Kramer and Dario Mesa, partners, are shown in Illustration 18-6.

Illustration 18-6
Partners' capital and
drawing accounts

ACCOUNT **Amy Kramer, Capital**   ACCOUNT NO. *3110*

DATE		ITEM	POST. REF.	DEBIT	CREDIT	BALANCE	
						DEBIT	CREDIT
Jan.	1	Balance	√				101 1 1 8 00

ACCOUNT **Amy Kramer, Drawing**   ACCOUNT NO. *3120*

DATE		ITEM	POST. REF.	DEBIT	CREDIT	BALANCE	
						DEBIT	CREDIT
Dec.	1	Balance	√			16 7 0 0 00	
	15		24	1 5 0 0 00		18 2 0 0 00	

ACCOUNT **Dario Mesa, Capital**   ACCOUNT NO. *3130*

DATE		ITEM	POST. REF.	DEBIT	CREDIT	BALANCE	
						DEBIT	CREDIT
Jan.	1	Balance	√				101 2 2 8 00

ACCOUNT **Dario Mesa, Drawing**   ACCOUNT NO. *3140*

DATE		ITEM	POST. REF.	DEBIT	CREDIT	BALANCE	
						DEBIT	CREDIT
Dec.	1	Balance	√			17 1 0 0 00	
	15		24	1 5 0 0 00		18 6 0 0 00	

Neither Amy Kramer nor Dario Mesa invested any additional capital during the year ended December 31. The beginning and ending capital balances, therefore, are the same as recorded in the accounts on January 1. Both partners withdrew cash and merchandise during the year ended December 31.

CarLand's owners' equity statement, prepared for the year ended December 31, is shown in Illustration 18-7.

CarLand Owners' Equity Statement For Year Ended December 31, 19--				
Amy Kramer				
Capital, January 1, 19--			101 1 1 8 00	
Share of Net Income	36 0 2 7 55			
Less Withdrawals	18 2 0 0 00			
Net Increase in Capital			17 8 2 7 55	
Capital, December 31, 19--				118 9 4 5 55
Dario Mesa				
Capital, January 1, 19--			101 2 2 8 00	
Share of Net Income	36 0 2 7 55			
Less Withdrawals	18 6 0 0 00			
Net Increase in Capital			17 4 2 7 55	
Capital, December 31, 19--				118 6 5 5 55
Total Owners' Equity, December 31, 19--				237 6 0 1 10

Illustration 18-7
Owners' equity statement

CarLand uses seven steps in preparing an owners' equity statement.

1 Write the heading of the owners' equity statement on three lines.

2 Write the name, *Amy Kramer*, on the first line at the extreme left of the wide column.

3 Figure the net increase in capital for Amy Kramer.

- Indent about one centimeter on the next line, and write the words *Capital, January 1, 19--*. Write the beginning capital amount, $101,118.00, in the second amount column on the same line. (This amount is obtained from Miss Kramer's capital account in the general ledger.)

- Indent about one centimeter on the next line, and write the words *Share of Net Income*. On the same line, write Miss Kramer's share of net income amount, $36,027.55, in the first amount column. (This amount is obtained from the distribution of net income statement.)

- Indent about one centimeter on the next line, and write the words *Less Withdrawals*. On the same line, write the withdrawals amount, $18,200.00, in the first amount column. (This amount is obtained from Miss Kramer's drawing account in the general ledger.)

- Indent about one centimeter on the next line, and write the words *Net Increase in Capital*. Write the net increase in capital amount,

$17,827.55, on the same line in the second amount column. (The share of net income, $36,027.55, *less* withdrawals, $18,200.00, *equals* the net increase in capital, $17,827.55.)

- Indent about one centimeter on the next line, and write the words *Capital, December 31, 19--*. Write the December 31 capital amount, *$118,945.55*, on the same line in the third amount column. (The January 1 capital, $101,118.00, *plus* the net increase in capital, $17,827.55, *equals* the December 31 capital, $118,945.55.)

4 Write the name, *Dario Mesa*, on the next line at the extreme left of the wide column.

5 Figure the net increase in capital for Dario Mesa.

- Indent about one centimeter on the next line, and write the words *Capital, January 1, 19--*. On the same line, write the beginning capital amount, *$101,228.00*, in the second amount column.

- Indent about one centimeter on the next line, and write the words *Share of Net Income*. On the same line, write Mr. Dario's share of net income amount, *$36,027.55*, in the first amount column.

- Indent about one centimeter on the next line, and write the words *Less Withdrawals*. On the same line, write the withdrawals amount, *$18,600.00*, in the first amount column.

- Indent about one centimeter on the next line, and write the words *Net Increase in Capital*. On the same line, write the difference, *$17,427.55*, in the second amount column.

- Indent about one centimeter on the next line, and write the words *Capital, December 31, 19--*. On the same line, write the December 31 capital amount, *$118,655.55*, in the third amount column.

6 Write the words *Total Owners' Equity, December 31, 19--* on the next line at the extreme left of the wide column. On the same line, write the total amount, *$237,601.10*, in the third amount column.

7 Rule double lines across the three amount columns to show that the totals have been verified as correct.

Some businesses include the owners' equity statement information as part of the balance sheet. An example of this method of reporting changes in owner's equity is shown in Illustration 8-13, Chapter 8.

Owners' equity statement with an additional investment and a net loss

On December 31 the capital accounts of Kevin Blaine and David Lamont showed additional investments of $10,000.00 each. Also, the income statement, Illustration 18-3, showed a net loss of $3,770.00. The partners agreed to share net income or net loss equally. The owners' equity statement for Autoworks is shown in Illustration 18-8.

Autoworks				
Owners' Equity Statement				
For Year Ended December 31, 19--				
Kevin Blaine				
Capital, January 1, 19--	104 3 0 0 00			
Plus Additional Investment	10 0 0 0 00			
Total		114 3 0 0 00		
Share of Net Loss	1 8 8 5 00			
Plus Withdrawals	14 8 0 0 00			
Net Decrease in Capital		16 6 8 5 00		
Capital, December 31, 19--			97 6 1 5 00	
David Lamont				
Capital, January 1, 19--	102 8 0 0 00			
Plus Additional Investment	10 0 0 0 00			
Total		112 8 0 0 00		
Share of Net Loss	1 8 8 5 00			
Plus Withdrawals	15 1 0 0 00			
Net Decrease in Capital		16 9 8 5 00		
Capital, December 31, 19--			95 8 1 5 00	
Total Owners' Equity, December 31, 19--			193 4 3 0 00	

Illustration 18-8
Owners' equity statement
showing an additional
investment and a net loss

BALANCE SHEET

Some management decisions can best be made after owners have determined the amount of assets, liabilities, and owners' equity. Owners could obtain some of the information needed by inspecting general ledger accounts. The information needed might also be found on a work sheet. However, the information is easier to use when organized and reported on a balance sheet. A balance sheet reports a business' financial condition on a specific date. A balance sheet may be prepared in account form or report form. Rugcare, described in Chapter 8, uses the account form. Petlodge, described in Chapter 11, uses the report form. CarLand also uses the report form.

Preparing a balance sheet

The information used to prepare a balance sheet is obtained from two sources. (1) The Balance Sheet columns of a work sheet, as shown in Illustration 18-9. (2) The owners' equity statement, as shown in Illustration 18-7.

	ACCOUNT TITLE	TRIAL BALANCE		ADJUSTMENTS		INCOME STATEMENT		BALANCE SHEET		
		DEBIT	CREDIT	DEBIT	CREDIT	DEBIT	CREDIT	DEBIT	CREDIT	
1	Cash	24233 57						24233 57		1
2	Petty Cash	500 00						500 00		2
3	Accounts Receivable	9332 00						9332 00		3
4	Merchandise Inventory	225400 00			(a)13200 00			212200 00		4
5	Supplies—Office	5400 00			(b)3940 00			1460 00		5
6	Supplies—Store	5780 00			(c)3260 00			2520 00		6
7	Prepaid Insurance	4840 00			(d)2640 00			2200 00		7
8	Accounts Payable		10451 90						10451 90	8
9	Employee Income Tax Payable		402 00						402 00	9
10	FICA Tax Payable		832 16						832 16	10
11	Sales Tax Payable		1760 00						1760 00	11
12	Unemployment Tax Payable—Fed.		59 15						59 15	12
13	Unemployment Tax Payable—State		399 26						399 26	13
14	Health Insurance Premiums Pay.		840 00						840 00	14
15	U.S. Savings Bonds Payable		40 00						40 00	15
16	United Way Donations Payable		60 00						60 00	16
17										17

CarLand's completed balance sheet on December 31, the last day of the fiscal year, is shown in Illustration 18-10 on page 428.

CarLand uses six steps in preparing a balance sheet.

Illustration 18-9
Balance sheet information on a work sheet

1 Write the balance sheet heading on three lines.

2 Prepare the assets section of the balance sheet. Use information from the work sheet given in Illustration 18-9.

* Write the section title, *Assets*, on the first line in the middle of the wide column.

* Beginning on the next line, at the extreme left of the wide column, write the asset account titles in the order in which they appear on the work sheet. Write the balance of each asset account in the first amount column.

* Write the words *Total Assets* on the next line below the last asset account title. Total the individual asset amounts, and write the total assets, $252,445.57, on the same line in the second amount column.

3 Prepare the liabilities section of the balance sheet. Use information from the work sheet given in Illustration 18-9.

* Write the section title, *Liabilities*, on the next line in the middle of the wide column.

CarLand						
Balance Sheet						
December 31, 19--						
Assets						
Cash	24 2 3 3 57					
Petty Cash	5 0 0 00					
Accounts Receivable	9 3 3 2 00					
Merchandise Inventory	212 2 0 0 00					
Supplies—Office	1 4 6 0 00					
Supplies—Store	2 5 2 0 00					
Prepaid Insurance	2 2 0 0 00					
Total Assets		252 4 4 5 57				
Liabilities						
Accounts Payable	10 4 5 1 90					
Employee Income Tax Payable	4 0 2 00					
FICA Tax Payable	8 3 2 16					
Sales Tax Payable	1 7 6 0 00					
Unemployment Tax Payable—Federal	5 9 15					
Unemployment Tax Payable—State	3 9 9 26					
Health Insurance Premiums Payable	8 4 0 00					
U.S. Savings Bonds Payable	4 0 00					
United Way Donations Payable	6 0 00					
Total Liabilities		14 8 4 4 47				
Owners' Equity						
Amy Kramer, Capital	118 9 4 5 55					
Dario Mesa, Capital	118 6 5 5 55					
Total Owners' Equity		237 6 0 1 10				
Total Liabilities and Owners' Equity		252 4 4 5 57				

Illustration 18-10
Balance sheet for a
partnership

- Beginning on the next line, at the extreme left of the wide column, write the liability account titles in the order in which they appear on the work sheet. Write the balance of each liability account in the first amount column.

- Write the words *Total Liabilities* on the next line below the last liability account title. Total the individual liability amounts, and write the total liabilities, $14,844.47, on the same line in the second amount column.

4 Prepare the owners' equity section of the balance sheet. Use information from the owners' equity statement given in Illustration 18-7.

- Write the section title, *Owners' Equity*, on the next line in the middle of the wide column.

- Write the account title, Amy Kramer, Capital, on the next line at the extreme left of the wide column. On the same line, write the amount of Amy Kramer's current capital, *$118,945.55*, in the first amount column.

- Write the account title, Dario Mesa, Capital, on the next line at the extreme left of the wide column. On the same line, write the amount of Dario Mesa's current capital, *$118,655.55*, in the first amount column.

- Write the words *Total Owners' Equity* on the next line at the extreme left of the wide column. Add the two capital amounts, and write the total, *$237,601.10*, on the same line in the second amount column.

5 Total the liabilities and owners' equity sections of the balance sheet.

- Write the words *Total Liabilities and Owners' Equity* on the next line at the extreme left of the wide column. Total the liabilities and owners' equity, and write the total, *$252,445.57*, on the same line in the second amount column.

    Verify accuracy by comparing the total amount of assets and the total amount of liabilities and owners' equity. These two amounts must be the same. The two amounts, $252,445.57, are the same. The balance sheet is assumed to be correct.

6 Rule double lines across both amount columns below Total Assets and below Total Liabilities and Owners' Equity. These two sets of double lines show that the amounts have been verified as correct.

Supporting schedules for a balance sheet

A report prepared to give details about an item on a principal financial statement is called a supporting schedule. A supporting schedule is sometimes known as a supplementary report or an exhibit.

CarLand prepares two supporting schedules to accompany the balance sheet. The supporting schedules are a schedule of accounts payable and a schedule of accounts receivable. A balance sheet shows only the accounts payable total amount. The account balance for each vendor is not shown. When detailed information is needed, a supporting schedule of accounts payable is prepared showing the balance for each vendor. A balance sheet also shows only the accounts receivable total amount. When information about the account balance for each customer is needed, a supporting schedule of accounts receivable is prepared. CarLand's supporting schedules on December 31 are similar to the supporting schedules for November 30 shown in Chapter 14.

SUMMARY OF FINANCIAL STATEMENTS FOR A PARTNERSHIP

The chart shown in Illustration 18-11 summarizes the financial statements for a partnership.

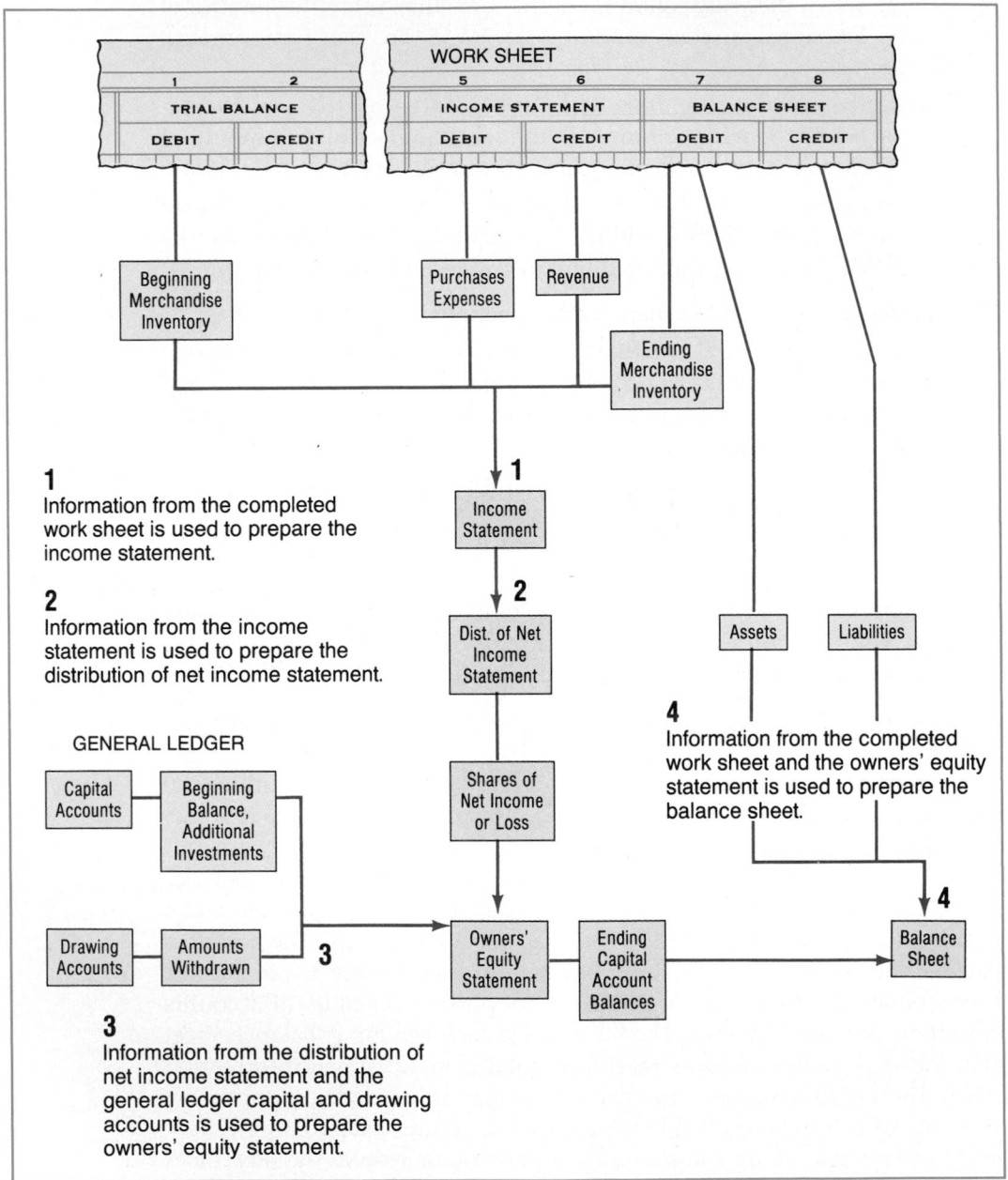

Illustration 18-11   Summary of financial statements for a partnership

◼ ACCOUNTING TERMS

What is the meaning of each of the following?

1. cost of merchandise sold
2. gross profit on sales
3. distribution of net income statement
4. owners' equity statement
5. supporting schedule

◼ QUESTIONS FOR INDIVIDUAL STUDY

1. Why is a work sheet prepared at the end of a fiscal period?
2. What is the primary source of information needed by owners and managers to make decisions on future activities of a business?
3. Which accounting concept is being applied when financial statements contain all information necessary for a reader to understand a business' financial condition and progress?
4. Which accounting concept is being applied when accounting principles are applied the same way in preparing financial statements from one fiscal period to the next?
5. Which financial statement reports the financial progress of a business?
6. How may income statements be used to determine reasons for increases or decreases in net income?
7. Where does a business find the information needed to prepare an income statement?
8. What are the three main sections of an income statement for a merchandising business?
9. How is the cost of merchandise sold calculated?
10. How is the gross profit on sales calculated?
11. How is net income calculated?
12. What four component percentages does CarLand calculate to analyze its income statement?
13. How does a business determine acceptable component percentages?
14. How is net loss calculated?
15. What are two reasons why an increase in markup could result in a decrease in sales revenue?
16. Why does a partnership prepare a distribution of net income statement?
17. Why do businesses prepare an owners' equity statement?
18. What three factors can cause changes in owners' equity to occur?
19. Where does a business find the information needed to prepare an owners' equity statement?
20. Which financial statement reports the financial condition of a business?

◼ CASES FOR MANAGEMENT DECISION

CASE 1 Jun Mori and Victoria Leben, partners, compared their current income statement with their income statement of a year ago. They noted that sales were 15.0% higher than a year ago. They also noted that the total expenses were 20.0% higher than a year ago. What type of analysis should be done to determine whether the increase in expenses is justified?

CASE 2 Rhoda Chalupa and Jonathan Fulton are partners in a paint and decorating store. The store operates on a yearly fiscal period. At the end of each year, an accountant is hired to prepare financial statements. At the end of each month during the year, Mrs. Chalupa prepares a work sheet. The work sheet is prepared to determine if the business made or lost money that month. The accountant suggests that monthly financial statements also be prepared. Mrs. Chalupa believes, however, that the monthly work sheet is sufficient to determine how the business is doing. Do you agree with Mrs. Chalupa or the accountant? Why?

■ DRILLS FOR UNDERSTANDING

DRILL 18-D1   Figuring the cost of merchandise sold

The work sheets of three businesses show the following information.

Business	Account Title	Trial Balance Debit	Income Statement Debit	Balance Sheet Debit
A	Merchandise inventory . . . Purchases	$118,000.00	 $23,800.00	$124,000.00
B	Merchandise inventory . . . Purchases	$174,000.00	 $38,200.00	$192,000.00
C	Merchandise inventory . . . Purchases	$152,000.00	 $29,400.00	$144,000.00

Instructions: Figure the cost of merchandise sold for each business.

DRILL 18-D2   Figuring net income or loss

The work sheets of three businesses show the following information.

Business	Account Title	Trial Balance Debit	Income Statement Debit	Income Statement Credit	Balance Sheet Debit
A	Merchandise Inventory . . Sales. . . . . Purchases . . . . Total Expenses.	$225,000.00	 $64,600.00 42,300.00	 $162,400.00	$214,000.00
B	Merchandise Inventory . . Sales. . . . . Purchases . . . . Total Expenses.	$186,400.00	 $82,000.00 53,800.00	 $122,000.00	$198,000.00
C	Merchandise Inventory . . Sales. . . . . Purchases . . . . Total Expenses.	$210,000.00	 $58,800.00 29,600.00	 $135,400.00	$202,600.00

Instructions: Figure the net income or loss for each business.

DRILL 18-D3   Figuring component percentages

The income statements of three businesses show the following information.

Business	Component	Amount
A	Sales Cost of Merchandise Sold Gross Profit on Sales Total Expenses Net Income	$186,000.00 91,000.00 95,000.00 41,000.00 54,000.00
B	Sales Cost of Merchandise Sold Gross Profit on Sales Total Expenses Net Income	$164,000.00 78,000.00 86,000.00 48,000.00 38,000.00
C	Sales Cost of Merchandise Sold Gross Profit on Sales Total Expenses Net Income	$226,000.00 121,000.00 105,000.00 68,000.00 37,000.00

Instructions: Figure component percentages for cost of merchandise sold, gross profit on sales, total expenses, and net income for each business. Round percentage calculations to the nearest 0.1%.

DRILL 18-D4 **Figuring the distribution of net income or loss**

The following information concerns net income or loss distribution for three businesses.

Business	Partner	Agreement on Sharing Income or Loss
A	1 2	50.0% of income or loss 50.0% of income or loss
B	1 2	40.0% of income or loss 60.0% of income or loss
C	1 2 3	25.0% of income or loss 30.0% of income or loss 45.0% of income or loss

Instructions: 1. Assume that each business earned a net income of $64,000.00. What is the amount of income to be distributed to each partner in each business?

2. Assume that each business had a net loss of $8,000.00. What is the amount of loss to be distributed to each partner in each business?

 APPLICATION PROBLEMS

PROBLEM 18-1 **Preparing financial statements**

The work sheet for Midwest Supply for the year ended December 31 of the current year is provided in the working papers accompanying this textbook.

Instructions: 1. Prepare an income statement. Figure and record the following component percentages: (a) cost of merchandise sold, (b) gross profit on sales, (c) total expenses, and (d) net income or loss. Round percentage calculations to the nearest 0.1%.

2. Prepare a distribution of net income statement. Net income or loss is to be shared equally.

3. Prepare an owners' equity statement. No additional investments were made.

4. Prepare a balance sheet in report form.

PROBLEM 18-2 **Preparing a distribution of net income statement and an owners' equity statement (net income)**

Louise Cova and Diane Landon are partners in a merchandising business. The following information was taken from the records on December 31 of the current year.

Partner	Balance of Capital Account January 1	Balance of Drawing Account	Distribution of Net Income
Cova	$138,000.00	$15,260.00	60.0%
Landon	$124,000.00	$16,340.00	40.0%

Instructions: 1. On December 31 the partnership had a net income of $72,400.00. Prepare a distribution of net income statement for the partnership of C.L. Sales.

2. Prepare an owners' equity statement. No additional investments were made.

PROBLEM 18-3 **Preparing an owners' equity statement (net loss)**

Paul Chapman and Lawrence Jaffa are partners in a merchandising business. The following information was taken from the records on December 31 of the current year.

Partner	Balance of Capital Account January 1	Balance of Drawing Account	Distribution of Net Loss
Chapman	$113,000.00	$12,680.00	$3,400.00
Jaffa	$107,000.00	$13,540.00	$3,400.00

Instructions: Prepare an owners' equity statement for Riverside Supply. Additional investments made during the year: Paul Chapman, $11,000.00; Lawrence Jaffa, $9,000.00.

ENRICHMENT PROBLEMS

MASTERY PROBLEM 18-M **Preparing financial statements**

Gallery Furniture prepared the following work sheet for the year ended December 31 of the current year.

Instructions: 1. Prepare an income statement. Figure and record the following component percentages: (a) cost of merchandise sold, (b) gross profit on sales, (c) total expenses, and (d) net income or loss. Round percentage calculations to the nearest 0.1%.

2. Prepare a distribution of net income statement. Net income or loss is to be shared equally.

3. Prepare an owners' equity statement. No additional investments were made.

4. Prepare a balance sheet in report form.

Gallery Furniture

Work Sheet

For Year Ended December 31, 19--

		1	2	3	4	5	6	7	8	
	ACCOUNT TITLE	TRIAL BALANCE		ADJUSTMENTS		INCOME STATEMENT		BALANCE SHEET		
		DEBIT	CREDIT	DEBIT	CREDIT	DEBIT	CREDIT	DEBIT	CREDIT	
1	Cash	28 7 9 2 00						28 7 9 2 00		1
2	Petty Cash	5 0 0 00						5 0 0 00		2
3	Accounts Receivable	12 8 3 5 00						12 8 3 5 00		3
4	Merchandise Inventory	290 6 0 0 00			(a) 14 5 1 0 00			276 0 9 0 00		4
5	Supplies—Office	5 3 7 5 00			(b) 3 3 6 0 00			2 0 1 5 00		5
6	Supplies—Store	5 8 4 0 00			(c) 3 7 2 0 00			2 1 2 0 00		6
7	Prepaid Insurance	5 1 4 5 00			(d) 2 9 4 0 00			2 2 0 5 00		7
8	Accounts Payable		9 1 3 0 00						9 1 3 0 00	8
9	Sales Tax Payable		1 0 7 2 00						1 0 7 2 00	9
10	Jennifer Faust, Capital		142 9 6 0 00						142 9 6 0 00	10
11	Jennifer Faust, Drawing	18 9 1 0 00						18 9 1 0 00		11
12	David Mason, Capital		137 4 5 0 00						137 4 5 0 00	12
13	David Mason, Drawing	18 3 6 0 00						18 3 6 0 00		13
14	Income Summary			(a) 14 5 1 0 00		14 5 1 0 00				14
15	Sales		257 3 0 0 00				257 3 0 0 00			15
16	Purchases	129 2 8 0 00				129 2 8 0 00				16
17	Advertising Expense	5 5 8 5 00				5 5 8 5 00				17
18	Credit Card Fee Expense	2 3 6 0 00				2 3 6 0 00				18
19	Insurance Expense			(d) 2 9 4 0 00		2 9 4 0 00				19
20	Miscellaneous Expense	2 6 4 0 00				2 6 4 0 00				20
21	Rent Expense	19 2 0 0 00				19 2 0 0 00				21
22	Supplies Expense—Office			(b) 3 3 6 0 00		3 3 6 0 00				22
23	Supplies Expense—Store			(c) 3 7 2 0 00		3 7 2 0 00				23
24	Utilities Expense	2 4 9 0 00				2 4 9 0 00				24
25		547 9 1 2 00	547 9 1 2 00	24 5 3 0 00	24 5 3 0 00	186 0 8 5 00	257 3 0 0 00	361 8 2 7 00	290 6 1 2 00	25
26	Net Income					71 2 1 5 00			71 2 1 5 00	26
27						257 3 0 0 00	257 3 0 0 00	361 8 2 7 00	361 8 2 7 00	27
28										28

CHALLENGE PROBLEM 18-C **Preparing financial statements (unequal distribution of net income; additional investment)**

Gallery Furniture's work sheet is shown in Mastery Problem 18-M.

Instructions: 1. Prepare a distribution of net income statement. The net income is to be shared as follows: Jennifer Faust, 75.0%; David Mason, 25.0%.

2. Prepare an owners' equity statement. Mr. Mason made an additional investment of $15,000.00 during the year. He had a beginning capital of $122,450.00.

Recording Adjusting and Closing Entries for a Partnership

ENABLING PERFORMANCE TASKS

After studying Chapter 19, you will be able to:
a. Identify accounting concepts and practices related to adjusting and closing entries for a merchandising business organized as a partnership.
b. Record adjusting entries for a merchandising business organized as a partnership.
c. Record closing entries for a merchandising business organized as a partnership.
d. Prepare a post-closing trial balance for a merchandising business organized as a partnership.

General ledger account balances are changed only by posting journal entries. Two types of journal entries change general ledger account balances at the end of a fiscal period. (1) Adjusting entries bring general ledger account balances up to date. (2) Closing entries prepare temporary accounts for the next fiscal period. *(CONCEPT: Matching Expenses with Revenue)* Information needed for journalizing adjusting entries is taken from the Adjustments columns of a work sheet. Information needed for journalizing closing entries is taken from the Income Statement and Balance Sheet columns of a work sheet and a distribution of net income statement.

RECORDING ADJUSTING ENTRIES

Four adjustments in the partial work sheet's Adjustments columns are shown in Illustration 19-1.

	ACCOUNT TITLE	TRIAL BALANCE		ADJUSTMENTS	
		DEBIT	CREDIT	DEBIT	CREDIT
4	*Merchandise Inventory*	225 4 0 0 00			(a)13 2 0 0 00
5	*Supplies—Office*	5 4 0 0 00			(b) 3 9 4 0 00
6	*Supplies—Store*	5 7 8 0 00			(c) 3 2 6 0 00
7	*Prepaid Insurance*	4 8 4 0 00			(d) 2 6 4 0 00
21	*Income Summary*			(a)13 2 0 0 00	
26	*Insurance Expense*			(d) 2 6 4 0 00	
31	*Supplies Expense—Office*			(b) 3 9 4 0 00	
32	*Supplies Expense—Store*			(c) 3 2 6 0 00	
33					

Illustration 19-1
Partial work sheet showing
adjustments

Adjusting entries are recorded on the next journal page following the page on which the last daily transaction for the month is recorded. The adjusting entries are entered in the General Debit and Credit columns of a journal. CarLand's four adjusting entries are recorded in a journal as shown in Illustration 19-2.

PAGE 26 · JOURNAL

	DATE	ACCOUNT TITLE	DOC. NO.	POST. REF.	GENERAL		ACCOUNTS RECEIVABLE	
					DEBIT	CREDIT	DEBIT	CREDIT
1		*Adjusting Entries*						
2	*Dec.* 19.. 31	*Income Summary*			13 2 0 0 00			
3		*Merchandise Inventory*				13 2 0 0 00		
4	31	*Supplies Expense—Office*			3 9 4 0 00			
5		*Supplies—Office*				3 9 4 0 00		
6	31	*Supplies Expense—Store*			3 2 6 0 00			
7		*Supplies—Store*				3 2 6 0 00		
8	31	*Insurance Expense*			2 6 4 0 00			
9		*Prepaid Insurance*				2 6 4 0 00		

Illustration 19-2
Adjusting entries recorded
in a journal

The heading, *Adjusting Entries*, is written in the middle of the journal's Account Title column. This heading explains all of the adjusting entries that follow. Therefore, indicating a source document is unnecessary. The first adjusting entry is recorded on the first two lines below the heading.

Adjusting entry for merchandise inventory

Income Summary

Adj. (a)	13,200.00	

Merchandise Inventory

Bal.	225,400.00	Adj. (a)	13,200.00	
(New Bal.	212,200.00)			

The debit and credit parts of the merchandise inventory adjustment are identified on the work sheet by the letter (a), Illustration 19-1. The merchandise inventory adjustment includes a debit to Income Summary and a credit to Merchandise Inventory of $13,200.00.

CarLand's adjusting entry for merchandise inventory is shown on lines 2 and 3 of the journal, Illustration 19-2.

The effect of posting the adjusting entry for merchandise inventory is shown in the T accounts.

Adjusting entry for office supplies inventory

Supplies Expense — Office

Adj. (b)	3,940.00	

Supplies — Office

Bal.	5,400.00	Adj. (b)	3,940.00	
(New Bal.	1,460.00)			

The debit and credit parts of the office supplies adjustment are identified on the work sheet by the letter (b), Illustration 19-1. The office supplies inventory adjustment includes a debit to Supplies Expense — Office and a credit to Supplies — Office of $3,940.00.

CarLand's adjusting entry for office supplies inventory is shown on lines 4 and 5 of the journal, Illustration 19-2.

The effect of posting the adjusting entry for office supplies inventory is shown in the T accounts.

Adjusting entry for store supplies inventory

Supplies Expense — Store

Adj. (c)	3,260.00	

Supplies — Store

Bal.	5,780.00	Adj. (c)	3,260.00	
(New Bal.	2,520.00)			

The debit and credit parts of the store supplies adjustment are identified on the work sheet by the letter (c), Illustration 19-1. The store supplies inventory adjustment includes a debit to Supplies Expense — Store and a credit to Supplies — Store of $3,260.00.

CarLand's adjusting entry for store supplies inventory is shown on lines 6 and 7 of the journal, Illustration 19-2.

The effect of posting the adjusting entry for store supplies inventory is shown in the T accounts.

Adjusting entry for prepaid insurance

Insurance Expense

Adj. (d)	2,640.00	

Prepaid Insurance

Bal.	4,840.00	Adj. (d)	2,640.00	
(New Bal.	2,200.00)			

The debit and credit parts of the prepaid insurance adjustment are identified on the work sheet by the letter (d), Illustration 19-1. The prepaid insurance adjustment includes a debit to Insurance Expense and a credit to Prepaid Insurance of $2,640.00.

CarLand's adjusting entry for prepaid insurance is shown on lines 8 and 9 of the journal, Illustration 19-2.

The effect of posting the adjusting entry for prepaid insurance is shown in the T accounts.

SUMMARY OF ADJUSTING ENTRIES FOR A MERCHANDISING BUSINESS ORGANIZED AS A PARTNERSHIP

The four adjusting entries for a merchandising business organized as a partnership are summarized in Illustration 19-3.

ADJUSTING ENTRY	JOURNAL		
	ACCOUNT TITLE	GENERAL	
		DEBIT	CREDIT
1. Adjust merchandise inventory (increase in inventory)	Merchandise Inventory Income Summary	X	X
(decrease in inventory)	Income Summary Merchandise Inventory	X	X
2. Adjust office supplies inventory	Supplies Expense—Office Supplies—Office	X	X
3. Adjust store supplies inventory	Supplies Expense—Store Supplies—Store	X	X
4. Adjust prepaid insurance	Insurance Expense Prepaid Insurance	X	X

Illustration 19-3
Summary of adjusting entries for a merchandising business organized as a partnership

RECORDING CLOSING ENTRIES

At the end of a fiscal period, the temporary accounts are closed to prepare the general ledger for the next fiscal period. *(CONCEPT: Matching Expenses with Revenue)* To close a temporary account, an amount equal to its balance is recorded on the side opposite the balance. CarLand records four kinds of closing entries.

1 An entry to close income statement accounts with credit balances.
2 An entry to close income statement accounts with debit balances.
3 An entry to record net income or loss and close the income summary account.
4 Entries to close the partners' drawing accounts.

The income summary account

A temporary account is used to summarize the closing entries for revenue, cost, and expenses. The account is titled *Income Summary* because it is used to summarize information about net income. Income Summary is used only at the end of a fiscal period to help prepare other accounts for a new fiscal period. The income summary account is a unique account because it does not have a normal balance side.

Amounts needed for the closing entries are obtained from the Income Statement and Balance Sheet columns of the work sheet and from the distribution of net income statement.

Closing entries are entered in the General Debit and Credit columns of a journal. The heading, *Closing Entries,* is written in the middle of the journal's Account Title column on the next line following the last adjusting entry. This heading explains all of the closing entries that follow. Therefore, indicating a source document is unnecessary. The first closing entry is recorded on the first two lines below the heading.

Closing entry for an income statement account with a credit balance

Rugcare's work sheet has one income statement account with a credit balance, Sales, as shown in Illustration 19-4. This revenue account has a normal credit balance at the end of a fiscal period. This credit balance must be reduced to zero to prepare the account for the next fiscal period. *(CONCEPT: Matching Expenses with Revenue)* The closing entry for Sales is journalized as shown in Illustration 19-4.

Illustration 19-4
Closing entry for an income statement account with a credit balance

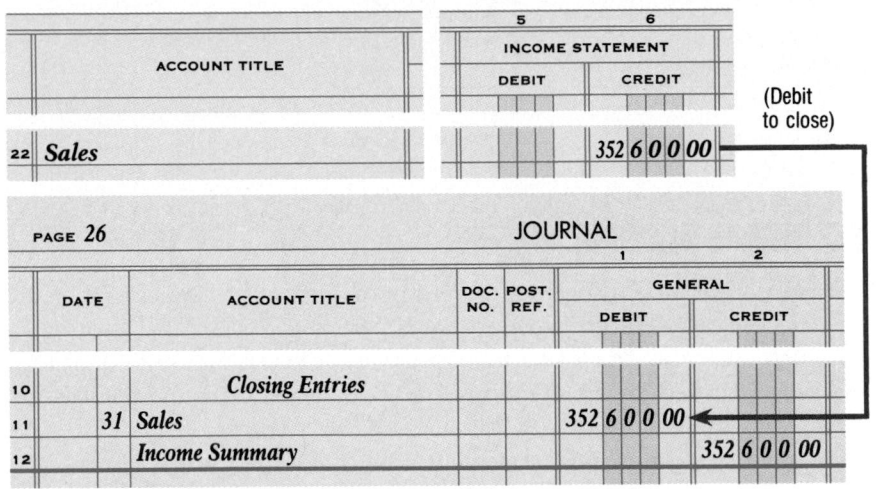

To reduce the balance to zero, Sales is debited for the amount of the balance, $352,600.00. Income Summary is credited for $352,600.00 so that debits equal credits in this entry.

The effect of this closing entry on the general ledger accounts is shown in the T accounts.

Sales			
Closing	352,600.00	Bal.	352,600.00
		(New Bal. zero)	

Income Summary			
Adj. (mdse. inv.)	13,200.00	Closing (revenue)	352,600.00

The balance of Sales is now zero, and the account is ready for the next fiscal period.

Closing entry for income statement accounts with debit balances

Rugcare's work sheet has eleven income statement accounts with debit balances, as shown in Illustration 19-5. These eleven accounts are the cost account, Purchases, and the ten expense accounts. The cost and expense accounts have normal debit balances at the end of a fiscal period. These debit balances must be reduced to zero to prepare the accounts for the next

		5	6
	ACCOUNT TITLE	**INCOME STATEMENT**	
		DEBIT	**CREDIT**
21	*Income Summary*	13 2 0 0 00	
22	*Sales*		352 6 0 0 00
23	*Purchases*	158 3 0 0 00	
24	*Advertising Expense*	5 5 0 0 00	
25	*Credit Card Fee Expense*	2 8 9 0 00	
26	*Insurance Expense*	2 6 4 0 00	
27	*Miscellaneous Expense*	2 1 8 2 15	
28	*Payroll Taxes Expense*	7 2 9 9 75	
29	*Rent Expense*	18 0 0 0 00	
30	*Salary Expense*	60 1 5 3 00	
31	*Supplies Expense—Office*	3 9 4 0 00	
32	*Supplies Expense—Store*	3 2 6 0 00	
33	*Utilities Expense*	3 1 8 0 00	

(Credit to close)

PAGE 26		JOURNAL				
					1	2
	DATE	ACCOUNT TITLE	DOC. NO.	POST. REF.	**GENERAL**	
					DEBIT	**CREDIT**
13	31	*Income Summary*			267 3 4 4 90	
14		*Purchases*				158 3 0 0 00
15		*Advertising Expense*				5 5 0 0 00
16		*Credit Card Fee Expense*				2 8 9 0 00
17		*Insurance Expense*				2 6 4 0 00
18		*Miscellaneous Expense*				2 1 8 2 15
19		*Payroll Taxes Expense*				7 2 9 9 75
20		*Rent Expense*				18 0 0 0 00
21		*Salary Expense*				60 1 5 3 00
22		*Supplies Expense—Office*				3 9 4 0 00
23		*Supplies Expense—Store*				3 2 6 0 00
24		*Utilities Expense*				3 1 8 0 00

Illustration 19-5
Closing entry for income statement accounts with debit balances

fiscal period. *(CONCEPT: Matching Expenses with Revenue)* To reduce the balances to zero, the cost and expense accounts are credited for the amount of their balances. The account used for the debit of this closing entry is Income Summary. The closing entry for the cost and expense accounts is journalized as shown in Illustration 19-5.

The income summary amount shown on the work sheet, $13,200.00, is the amount of the adjustment for merchandise inventory. Income Summary is used to summarize the amounts that contribute to net income. The adjustment for merchandise inventory contributes to net income. However, Income Summary is not closed as part of this closing entry. Instead, the account is closed with the third closing entry when net income is recorded.

The debit to Income Summary is not entered in the amount column until all cost and expense balances have been journalized and the total amount calculated. The account title and balance of each cost and expense account is written in the Account Title and General Credit columns. After all cost and expense accounts and their balances have been written in the journal, add the credit amounts for this entry. Write the total of the cost and expense accounts, *$267,344.90,* in the General Debit column on the same line as the account title Income Summary.

The effect of this closing entry on the general ledger accounts is shown in the T accounts.

Income Summary

Adj. (mdse. inv.)	13,200.00	Closing (revenue)	352,600.00
Closing (cost and expenses)	267,344.90	*(New Bal.*	*72,055.10)*

Purchases

Bal.	158,300.00	Closing	158,300.00
(New Bal. zero)			

Rent Expense

Bal.	18,000.00	Closing	18,000.00
(New Bal. zero)			

Advertising Expense

Bal.	5,500.00	Closing	5,500.00
(New Bal. zero)			

Salary Expense

Bal.	60,153.00	Closing	60,153.00
(New Bal. zero)			

Credit Card Fee Expense

Bal.	2,890.00	Closing	2,890.00
(New Bal. zero)			

Supplies Expense — Office

Bal.	3,940.00	Closing	3,940.00
(New Bal. zero)			

Insurance Expense

Bal.	2,640.00	Closing	2,640.00
(New Bal. zero)			

Supplies Expense — Store

Bal.	3,260.00	Closing	3,260.00
(New Bal. zero)			

Miscellaneous Expense

Bal.	2,182.15	Closing	2,182.15
(New Bal. zero)			

Utilities Expense

Bal.	3,180.00	Closing	3,180.00
(New Bal. zero)			

Payroll Taxes Expense

Bal.	7,299.75	Closing	7,299.75
(New Bal. zero)			

The cost account, Purchases, and the expense accounts are now closed and have zero balances. Income Summary has three amounts. (1) A debit of $13,200.00, the amount of the merchandise inventory adjustment. (2) A credit of $352,600.00, the amount of the entry to close the revenue account. (3) A debit of $267,344.90, the total amount of the entry to close the cost and expense accounts. The balance of Income Summary is the net income for the fiscal period, $72,055.10.

Closing entry to record net income or loss and close the income summary account

Net income increases the partners' equity and, therefore, must be credited to the partners' capital accounts. The share of the net income to be recorded for each partner is shown on the distribution of net income statement. The balance of the temporary account Income Summary must be reduced to zero to prepare the account for the next fiscal period. The distribution of net income statement and the closing entry to record net income and close Income Summary are shown in Illustration 19-6.

Illustration 19-6
Closing entry to record net income and close the income summary account

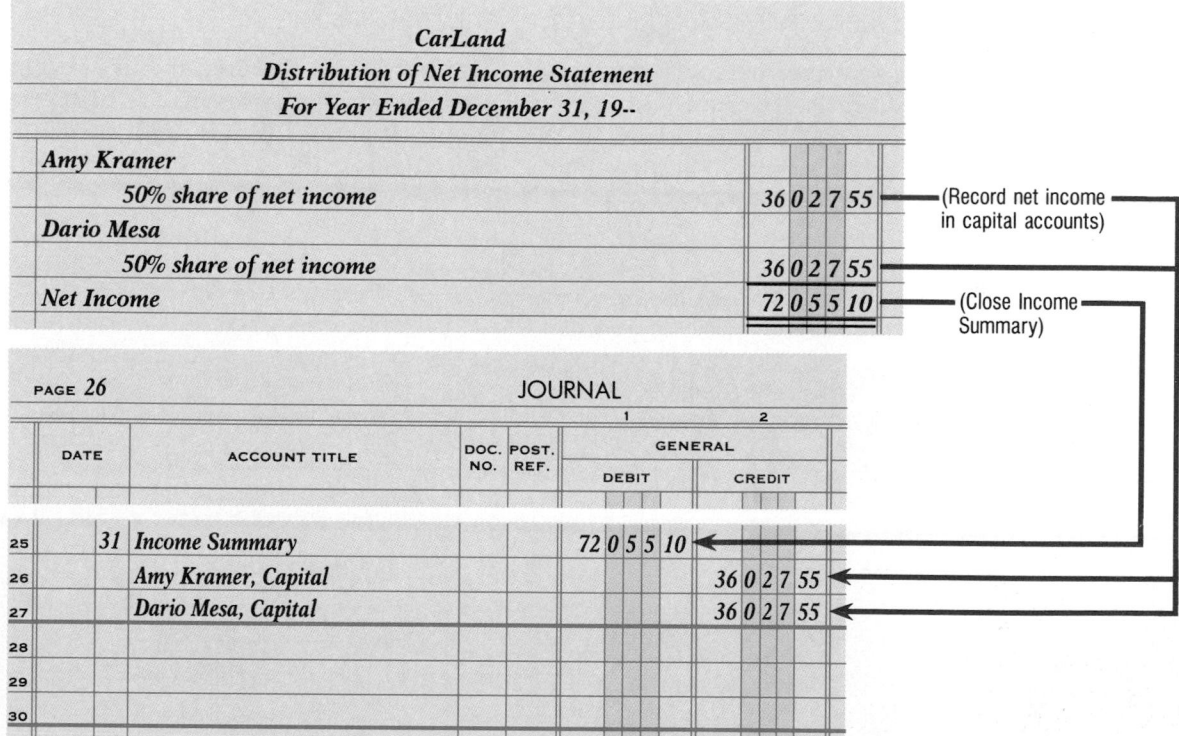

The effect of this closing entry on the general ledger accounts is shown in the T accounts.

Income Summary

Adj. (mdse. inv.)	13,200.00	Closing (revenue)	352,600.00
Closing (cost and expenses	267,344.90		
Closing (net income)	72,055.10	*(New Bal. zero)*	

Amy Kramer, Capital

		Bal.	101,118.00
		Closing (net income)	36,027.55

Dario Mesa, Capital

		Bal.	101,228.00
		Closing (net income)	36,027.55

The credits to the two partners' capital accounts, $36,027.55, record the partners' share of the net income. The debit to the income summary account, $72,055.10, reduces the account balance to zero and prepares the account for the next fiscal period.

If the business has a net loss, the partners' capital accounts are debited for their share of the net loss. Income Summary is credited for the total net loss.

Closing entries for the partners' drawing accounts

The partners' drawing accounts are temporary accounts and must begin each fiscal period with zero balances. Because withdrawals are neither a revenue, cost, nor expense, the drawing accounts are not closed through Income Summary. The drawing account balances are closed directly to the partners' capital accounts.

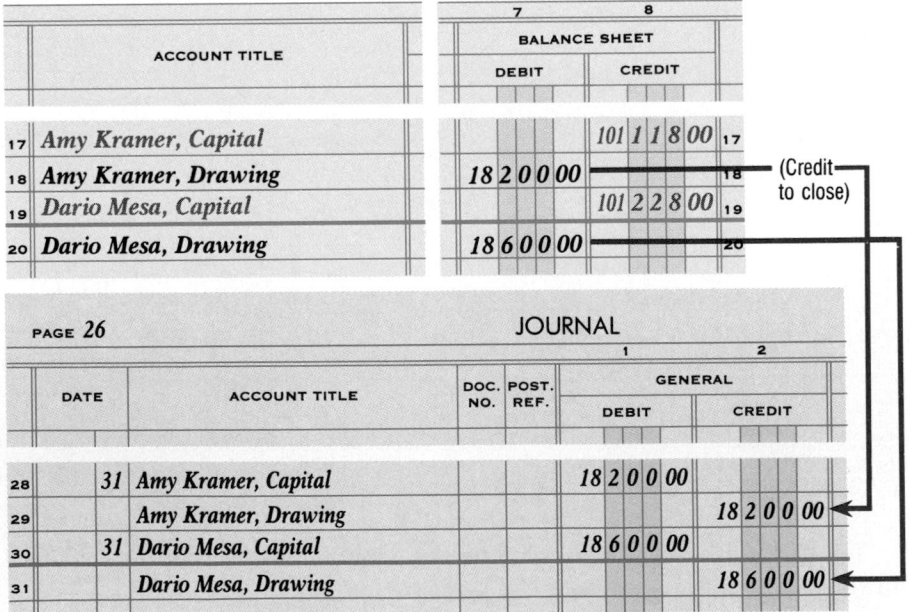

Illustration 19-7
Closing entries for the
partners' drawing accounts

A partial work sheet and the closing entries for the partners' drawing accounts are shown in Illustration 19-7. The closing entry is on lines 28-31 of the journal.

The credits to Amy Kramer, Drawing and Dario Mesa, Drawing reduce the account balances to zero. The accounts are prepared for the next fiscal period. The debits to Amy Kramer, Capital and Dario Mesa, Capital reduce the balances of these accounts by the amount of the partners' withdrawals during the fiscal period.

The effect of these closing entries on the general ledger accounts is shown in the T accounts.

Amy Kramer, Capital

Closing (drawing)	18,200.00	Bal.	101,118.00
		Closing (net income)	36,027.55
		(New Bal.	*118,945.55)*

Amy Kramer, Drawing

Bal.	18,200.00	Closing	18,200.00
(New Bal. zero)			

Dario Mesa, Capital

Closing (drawing)	18,600.00	Bal.	101,228.00
		Closing (net income)	36,027.55
		(New Bal.	*118,655.55)*

Dario Mesa, Drawing

Bal.	18,600.00	Closing	18,600.00
(New Bal. zero)			

After the closing entry for the partners' drawing accounts, the balances of the partners' capital accounts are the same as reported in the owners' equity section of the balance sheet, Illustration 19-8.

CarLand		
Balance Sheet		
December 31, 19--		
Owners' Equity		
Amy Kramer, Capital	118 9 4 5 55	
Dario Mesa, Capital	118 6 5 5 55	
Total Owners' Equity		237 6 0 1 10
Total Liabilities and Owners' Equity		252 4 4 5 57

Illustration 19-8
Owners' equity section of a balance sheet

CarLand's closing entries recorded in a journal are shown in Illustration 19-9.

	DATE	ACCOUNT TITLE	DOC. NO.	POST. REF.	GENERAL		ACCOUNTS RECEIVABLE	
					DEBIT	CREDIT	DEBIT	CREDIT
10		*Closing Entries*						
11	31	Sales			352 6 0 0 00			
12		Income Summary				352 6 0 0 00		
13	31	Income Summary			267 3 4 4 90			
14		Purchases				158 3 0 0 00		
15		Advertising Expense				5 5 0 0 00		
16		Credit Card Fee Expense				2 8 9 0 00		
17		Insurance Expense				2 6 4 0 00		
18		Miscellaneous Expense				2 1 8 2 15		
19		Payroll Taxes Expense				7 2 9 9 75		
20		Rent Expense				18 0 0 0 00		
21		Salary Expense				60 1 5 3 00		
22		Supplies Expense—Office				3 9 4 0 00		
23		Supplies Expense—Store				3 2 6 0 00		
24		Utilities Expense				3 1 8 0 00		
25	31	Income Summary			72 0 5 5 10			
26		Amy Kramer, Capital				36 0 2 7 55		
27		Dario Mesa, Capital				36 0 2 7 55		
28	31	Amy Kramer, Capital			18 2 0 0 00			
29		Amy Kramer, Drawing				18 2 0 0 00		
30	31	Dario Mesa, Capital			18 6 0 0 00			
31		Dario Mesa, Drawing				18 6 0 0 00		

PAGE 26 — JOURNAL

Illustration 19-9
Closing entries for a partnership recorded in a journal

SUMMARY OF CLOSING ENTRIES FOR A MERCHANDISING BUSINESS ORGANIZED AS A PARTNERSHIP

The closing entries for a merchandising business organized as a partnership are summarized in Illustration 19-10.

CLOSING ENTRY	JOURNAL		
	ACCOUNT TITLE	GENERAL	
		DEBIT	CREDIT
1. Transfers income statement accounts with credit balances to Income Summary	Revenue account Income Summary	X	 X
2. Transfers income statement accounts with debit balances to Income Summary	Income Summary Cost and expense accounts	X	 X
3. Transfers net income or loss to partners' capital accounts and closes Income Summary	Income Summary Partners' capital accounts (net income)	X	 X
	Partners' capital accounts Income Summary (net loss)	X	 X
4. Transfers partners' drawing account balances to partners' capital accounts	Partners' capital accounts Partners' drawing accounts	X	 X

Illustration 19-10
Summary of closing entries

CHECKING A GENERAL LEDGER'S ACCURACY AFTER POSTING ADJUSTING AND CLOSING ENTRIES

CarLand's 4-column general ledger account form has separate Balance Debit and Balance Credit columns. Each time an entry is posted to a general ledger account, the account balance is figured. The balance is then recorded in the appropriate balance column. Each general ledger account shows its current balance at all times. When an account is closed, a short line is drawn in both the Balance Debit and Credit columns. The ending balance for one fiscal period is the beginning balance for the next fiscal period.

Completed general ledger

CarLand's completed general ledger after adjusting and closing entries are posted is shown in Illustration 19-11.

ACCOUNT *Cash*   ACCOUNT NO. *1110*

DATE	ITEM	POST. REF.	DEBIT	CREDIT	BALANCE	
					DEBIT	CREDIT
Dec. 31 19--	Balance	√			24 2 3 3 57	

Illustration 19-11
General ledger after adjusting and closing entries are posted

ACCOUNT *Petty Cash*   ACCOUNT NO. *1120*

DATE		ITEM	POST. REF.	DEBIT	CREDIT	BALANCE	
						DEBIT	CREDIT
19-- Dec.	31	Balance	√			5 0 0 00	

ACCOUNT *Accounts Receivable*   ACCOUNT NO. *1130*

DATE		ITEM	POST. REF.	DEBIT	CREDIT	BALANCE	
						DEBIT	CREDIT
19-- Dec.	31	Balance	√			9 3 3 2 00	

ACCOUNT *Merchandise Inventory*   ACCOUNT NO. *1140*

DATE		ITEM	POST. REF.	DEBIT	CREDIT	BALANCE	
						DEBIT	CREDIT
19-- Jan.	1	Balance	√			225 4 0 0 00	
Dec.	31		26		13 2 0 0 00	212 2 0 0 00	

ACCOUNT *Supplies—Office*   ACCOUNT NO. *1145*

DATE		ITEM	POST. REF.	DEBIT	CREDIT	BALANCE	
						DEBIT	CREDIT
19-- Dec.	31	Balance	√			5 4 0 0 00	
	31		26		3 9 4 0 00	1 4 6 0 00	

ACCOUNT *Supplies—Store*   ACCOUNT NO. *1150*

DATE		ITEM	POST. REF.	DEBIT	CREDIT	BALANCE	
						DEBIT	CREDIT
19-- Dec.	31	Balance	√			5 7 8 0 00	
	31		26		3 2 6 0 00	2 5 2 0 00	

ACCOUNT *Prepaid Insurance*   ACCOUNT NO. *1160*

DATE		ITEM	POST. REF.	DEBIT	CREDIT	BALANCE	
						DEBIT	CREDIT
19-- Dec.	31	Balance	√			4 8 4 0 00	
	31		26		2 6 4 0 00	2 2 0 0 00	

Illustration 19-11
General ledger after
adjusting and closing
entries are posted
(continued)

ACCOUNT	Accounts Payable					ACCOUNT NO.	2110
DATE	ITEM	POST. REF.	DEBIT	CREDIT	BALANCE		
					DEBIT	CREDIT	
19-- Dec. 31	Balance	√				10 4 5 1 90	

Illustration 19-11
General ledger after
adjusting and closing
entries are posted
(continued)

ACCOUNT	Employee Income Tax Payable					ACCOUNT NO.	2120
DATE	ITEM	POST. REF.	DEBIT	CREDIT	BALANCE		
					DEBIT	CREDIT	
19-- Dec. 31	Balance	√				4 0 2 00	

ACCOUNT	FICA Tax Payable					ACCOUNT NO.	2130
DATE	ITEM	POST. REF.	DEBIT	CREDIT	BALANCE		
					DEBIT	CREDIT	
19-- Dec. 31	Balance	√				8 3 2 16	

ACCOUNT	Sales Tax Payable					ACCOUNT NO.	2140
DATE	ITEM	POST. REF.	DEBIT	CREDIT	BALANCE		
					DEBIT	CREDIT	
19-- Dec. 31	Balance	√				1 7 6 0 00	

ACCOUNT	Unemployment Tax Payable—Federal					ACCOUNT NO.	2150
DATE	ITEM	POST. REF.	DEBIT	CREDIT	BALANCE		
					DEBIT	CREDIT	
19-- Dec. 31	Balance	√				5 9 15	

ACCOUNT	Unemployment Tax Payable—State					ACCOUNT NO.	2160
DATE	ITEM	POST. REF.	DEBIT	CREDIT	BALANCE		
					DEBIT	CREDIT	
19-- Dec. 31	Balance	√				3 9 9 26	

ACCOUNT *Health Insurance Premiums Payable*   ACCOUNT NO. 2170

DATE		ITEM	POST. REF.	DEBIT	CREDIT	BALANCE	
						DEBIT	CREDIT
Dec.	31	Balance	✓				8 4 0 00

ACCOUNT *U.S. Savings Bonds Payable*   ACCOUNT NO. 2180

DATE		ITEM	POST. REF.	DEBIT	CREDIT	BALANCE	
						DEBIT	CREDIT
Dec.	31	Balance	✓				4 0 00

ACCOUNT *United Way Donations Payable*   ACCOUNT NO. 2190

DATE		ITEM	POST. REF.	DEBIT	CREDIT	BALANCE	
						DEBIT	CREDIT
Dec.	31	Balance	✓				6 0 00

ACCOUNT *Amy Kramer, Capital*   ACCOUNT NO. 3110

DATE		ITEM	POST. REF.	DEBIT	CREDIT	BALANCE	
						DEBIT	CREDIT
Dec.	31	Balance	✓				101 1 1 8 00
	31		26		36 0 2 7 55		137 1 4 5 55
	31		26	18 2 0 0 00			118 9 4 5 55

ACCOUNT *Amy Kramer, Drawing*   ACCOUNT NO. 3120

DATE		ITEM	POST. REF.	DEBIT	CREDIT	BALANCE	
						DEBIT	CREDIT
Dec.	31	Balance	✓			18 2 0 0 00	
	31		26		18 2 0 0 00	——	——

Illustration 19-11
General ledger after
adjusting and closing
entries are posted
(continued)

Illustration 19-11
General ledger after adjusting and closing entries are posted (continued)

ACCOUNT *Dario Mesa, Capital*   ACCOUNT NO. *3130*

DATE		ITEM	POST. REF.	DEBIT	CREDIT	BALANCE DEBIT	BALANCE CREDIT
Dec.¹⁹⁻⁻	31	Balance	√				101 2 2 8 00
	31		26		36 0 2 7 55		137 2 5 5 55
	31		26	18 6 0 0 00			118 6 5 5 55

ACCOUNT *Dario Mesa, Drawing*   ACCOUNT NO. *3140*

DATE		ITEM	POST. REF.	DEBIT	CREDIT	BALANCE DEBIT	BALANCE CREDIT
Dec.¹⁹⁻⁻	31	Balance	√			18 6 0 0 00	
	31		26		18 6 0 0 00	—	—

ACCOUNT *Income Summary*   ACCOUNT NO. *3150*

DATE		ITEM	POST. REF.	DEBIT	CREDIT	BALANCE DEBIT	BALANCE CREDIT
Dec.¹⁹⁻⁻	31		26	13 2 0 0 00		13 2 0 0 00	
	31		26		352 6 0 0 00		339 4 0 0 00
	31		26	267 3 4 4 90			72 0 5 5 10
	31		26	72 0 5 5 10		—	—

ACCOUNT *Sales*   ACCOUNT NO. *4110*

DATE		ITEM	POST. REF.	DEBIT	CREDIT	BALANCE DEBIT	BALANCE CREDIT
Dec.¹⁹⁻⁻	31	Balance	√				352 6 0 0 00
	31		26	352 6 0 0 00		—	—

ACCOUNT *Purchases*   ACCOUNT NO. *5110*

DATE		ITEM	POST. REF.	DEBIT	CREDIT	BALANCE DEBIT	BALANCE CREDIT
Dec.¹⁹⁻⁻	31	Balance	√			158 3 0 0 00	
	31		26		158 3 0 0 00	—	—

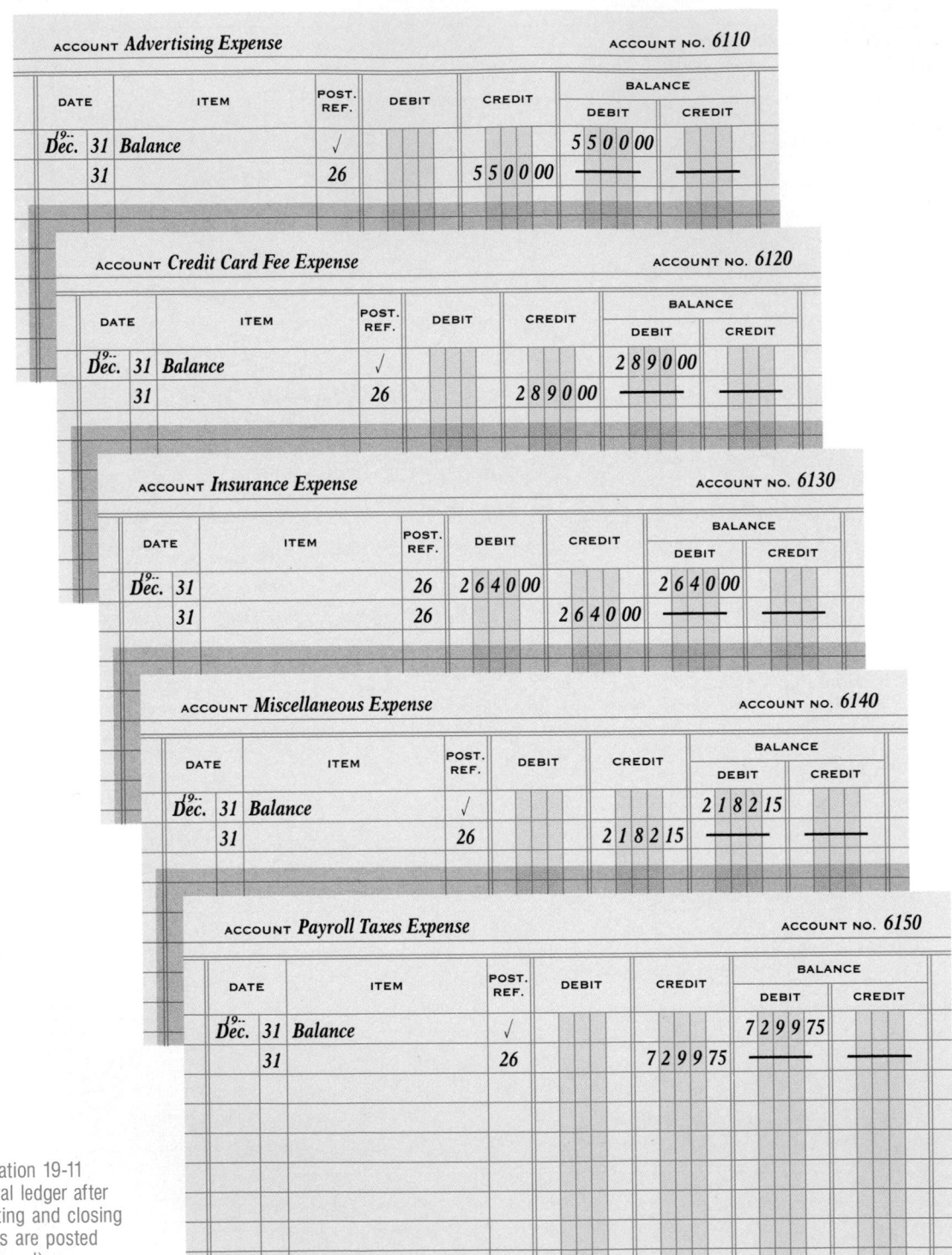

ACCOUNT Advertising Expense					ACCOUNT NO. 6110	
DATE	ITEM	POST. REF.	DEBIT	CREDIT	BALANCE DEBIT	BALANCE CREDIT
Dec. 31	Balance	√			5 5 0 0 00	
31		26		5 5 0 0 00	——	——

ACCOUNT Credit Card Fee Expense					ACCOUNT NO. 6120	
DATE	ITEM	POST. REF.	DEBIT	CREDIT	BALANCE DEBIT	BALANCE CREDIT
Dec. 31	Balance	√			2 8 9 0 00	
31		26		2 8 9 0 00	——	——

ACCOUNT Insurance Expense					ACCOUNT NO. 6130	
DATE	ITEM	POST. REF.	DEBIT	CREDIT	BALANCE DEBIT	BALANCE CREDIT
Dec. 31		26	2 6 4 0 00		2 6 4 0 00	
31		26		2 6 4 0 00	——	——

ACCOUNT Miscellaneous Expense					ACCOUNT NO. 6140	
DATE	ITEM	POST. REF.	DEBIT	CREDIT	BALANCE DEBIT	BALANCE CREDIT
Dec. 31	Balance	√			2 1 8 2 15	
31		26		2 1 8 2 15	——	——

ACCOUNT Payroll Taxes Expense					ACCOUNT NO. 6150	
DATE	ITEM	POST. REF.	DEBIT	CREDIT	BALANCE DEBIT	BALANCE CREDIT
Dec. 31	Balance	√			7 2 9 9 75	
31		26		7 2 9 9 75	——	——

Illustration 19-11
General ledger after
adjusting and closing
entries are posted
(continued)

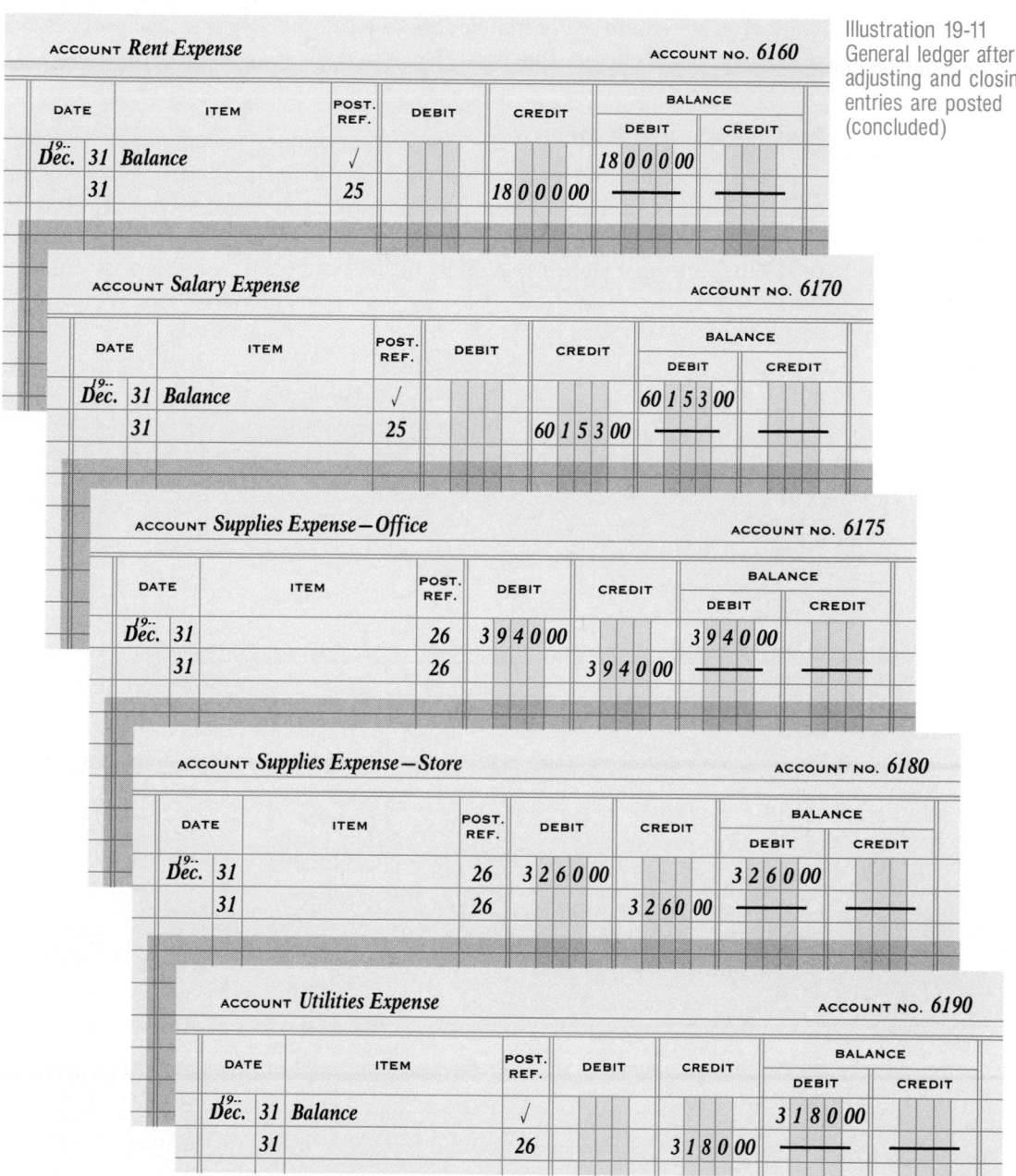

Illustration 19-11
General ledger after
adjusting and closing
entries are posted
(concluded)

ACCOUNT *Rent Expense*   ACCOUNT NO. *6160*

DATE		ITEM	POST. REF.	DEBIT	CREDIT	BALANCE DEBIT	BALANCE CREDIT
Dec. 19--	31	Balance	✓			18 0 0 0 00	
	31		25		18 0 0 0 00	———	———

ACCOUNT *Salary Expense*   ACCOUNT NO. *6170*

DATE		ITEM	POST. REF.	DEBIT	CREDIT	BALANCE DEBIT	BALANCE CREDIT
Dec. 19--	31	Balance	✓			60 1 5 3 00	
	31		25		60 1 5 3 00	———	———

ACCOUNT *Supplies Expense—Office*   ACCOUNT NO. *6175*

DATE		ITEM	POST. REF.	DEBIT	CREDIT	BALANCE DEBIT	BALANCE CREDIT
Dec. 19--	31		26	3 9 4 0 00		3 9 4 0 00	
	31		26		3 9 4 0 00	———	———

ACCOUNT *Supplies Expense—Store*   ACCOUNT NO. *6180*

DATE		ITEM	POST. REF.	DEBIT	CREDIT	BALANCE DEBIT	BALANCE CREDIT
Dec. 19--	31		26	3 2 6 0 00		3 2 6 0 00	
	31		26		3 2 6 0 00	———	———

ACCOUNT *Utilities Expense*   ACCOUNT NO. *6190*

DATE		ITEM	POST. REF.	DEBIT	CREDIT	BALANCE DEBIT	BALANCE CREDIT
Dec. 19--	31	Balance	✓			3 1 8 0 00	
	31		26		3 1 8 0 00	———	———

Balance sheet accounts (asset, liability, and capital accounts) have up-to-date balances to begin the new fiscal period. Balances in the balance sheet accounts agree with the amounts on the balance sheet, Illustration 18-10, Chapter 18. General ledger account balances on December 31 of one year are the beginning balances for January 1 of the next year.

Income statement accounts (revenue, cost, and expense accounts) have zero balances to begin the new fiscal period. *(CONCEPT: Matching Expenses with Revenue)*

Post-closing trial balance

After adjusting and closing entries have been posted, a post-closing trial balance is prepared. The post-closing trial balance is prepared to prove the equality of debits and credits in the general ledger. CarLand's post-closing trial balance prepared on December 31 is shown in Illustration 19-12.

ACCOUNT TITLE	DEBIT	CREDIT
CarLand		
Post-Closing Trial Balance		
December 31, 19--		
Cash	24 2 3 3 57	
Petty Cash	5 0 0 00	
Accounts Receivable	9 3 3 2 00	
Merchandise Inventory	212 2 0 0 00	
Supplies—Office	1 4 6 0 00	
Supplies—Store	2 5 2 0 00	
Prepaid Insurance	2 2 0 0 00	
Accounts Payable		10 4 5 1 90
Employee Income Tax Payable		4 0 2 00
FICA Tax Payable		8 3 2 16
Sales Tax Payable		1 7 6 0 00
Unemployment Tax Payable—Federal		5 9 15
Unemployment Tax Payable—State		3 9 9 26
Health Insurance Premiums Payable		8 4 0 00
U.S. Savings Bonds Payable		4 0 00
United Way Donations Payable		6 0 00
Amy Kramer, Capital		118 9 4 5 55
Dario Mesa, Capital		118 6 5 5 55
Totals	252 4 4 5 57	252 4 4 5 57

Illustration 19-12
Post-closing trial balance

All general ledger accounts that have balances are listed on a post-closing trial balance. Accounts are listed in the same order as they appear in the general ledger. Accounts with zero balances are not listed on a post-closing trial balance.

Account balances on the post-closing trial balance, Illustration 19-12, agree with the balances on the balance sheet, Illustration 18-10, Chapter 18. Also, because the post-closing trial balance debit and credit balance totals are the same, $252,445.57, the equality of debits and credits in the general ledger is proved. The general ledger is ready for the next fiscal period. (CONCEPT: *Accounting Period Cycle*)

SUMMARY OF AN ACCOUNTING CYCLE FOR A MERCHANDISING BUSINESS

Service and merchandising businesses use a similar accounting cycle. The accounting cycles are also similar for a proprietorship and a partnership. Variations occur when subsidiary ledgers are used. Variations also occur in preparing financial statements. CarLand's accounting cycle for a merchandising business is summarized in Illustration 19-13.

Illustration 19-13
Summary of an accounting cycle for a merchandising business

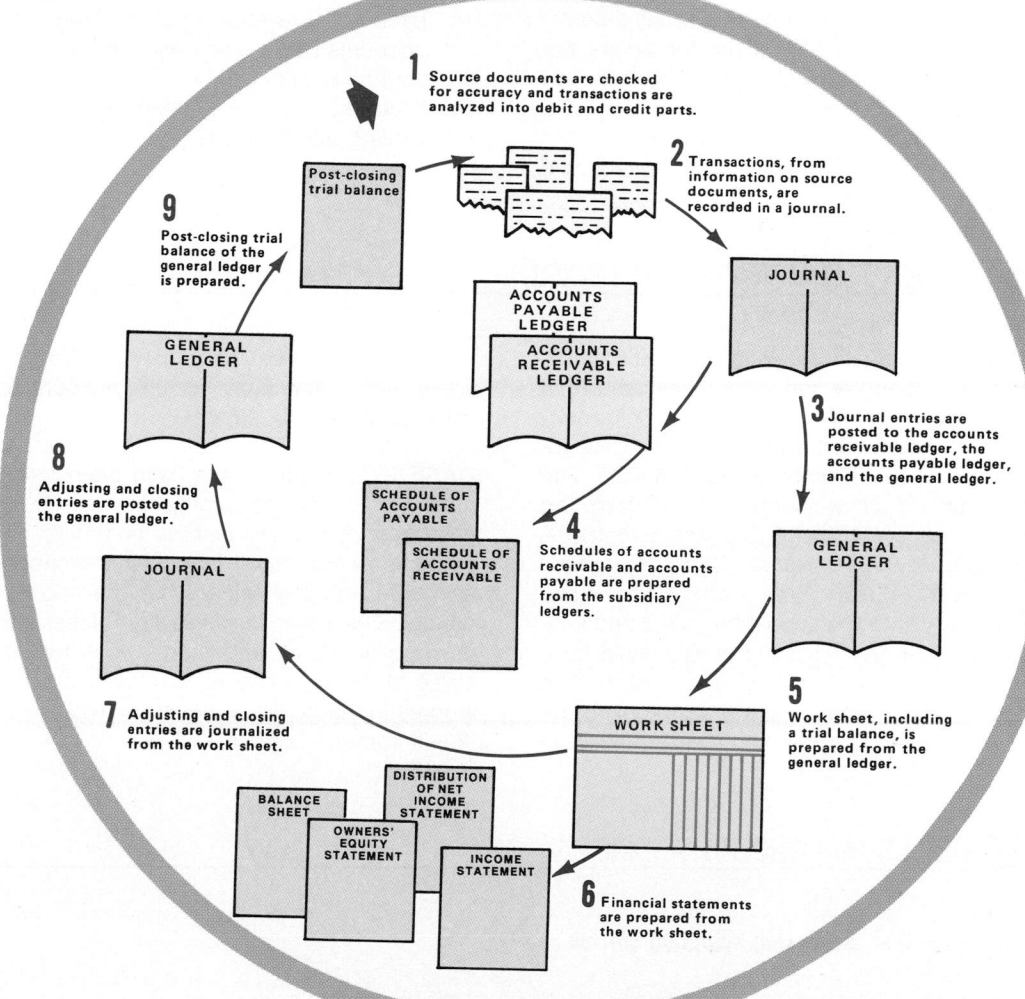

■ QUESTIONS FOR INDIVIDUAL STUDY

1. What two types of journal entries change general ledger account balances at the end of a fiscal period?
2. Where is the information obtained for journalizing adjusting entries?
3. Where is the information obtained for journalizing closing entries?
4. Where is the explanation for adjusting entries written in a journal?
5. Which accounting concept is being applied when temporary accounts are closed at the end of a fiscal period?
6. What four kinds of closing entries are recorded at the end of a fiscal period?
7. What is the title of the temporary account used to summarize information about net income at the end of a fiscal period?
8. Why is the income summary account considered a unique account?
9. Where is the explanation for closing entries written in a journal?
10. What are the three amounts recorded in the income summary account after closing the revenue, cost, and expense accounts?
11. Why are partners' withdrawals not closed to the income summary account?
12. What is recorded in the Balance Debit and Credit columns of a general ledger account when an account is closed?
13. Which accounting concept is being applied when revenue, cost, and expense accounts begin a new fiscal period with zero balances?
14. What accounts are listed on a post-closing trial balance?

■ CASES FOR MANAGEMENT DECISION

CASE 1 Household Furniture's Trial Balance Debit column of the work sheet shows a debit balance of $2,400.00 for the office supplies account. The ending office supplies inventory is determined to be $1,800.00. The accounting clerk journalized the following adjusting entry: debit Supplies Expense—Office, $1,800.00; credit Supplies—Office, $1,800.00. Susan Gray, partner, discussed the entry with the accounting clerk and suggested that the adjusting entry should have been for $600.00 instead of $1,800.00. The clerk indicates that there is no problem because the amounts will be adjusted again at the end of the next fiscal period. Do you agree with Miss Gray or the accounting clerk? Explain your answer.

CASE 2 Two businesses have been using different accounting practices. One business first closes the income summary account to record the net income in the capital accounts and then closes the drawing accounts. The other business first closes the drawing accounts and then closes the income summary account to record the net income in the capital accounts. Which practice is correct? Explain.

■ DRILLS FOR UNDERSTANDING

DRILL 19-D1   Analyzing adjusting entries

The following information is from the work sheet of Chaney's Giftware.

		1	2	3	4
	ACCOUNT TITLE	TRIAL BALANCE		ADJUSTMENTS	
		DEBIT	CREDIT	DEBIT	CREDIT
4	*Merchandise Inventory*	248 0 0 0 00			(a) 16 0 0 0 00
5	*Supplies—Office*	3 9 4 0 00			(b) 2 3 4 0 00
6	*Supplies—Store*	4 3 1 0 00			(c) 2 6 8 0 00
7	*Prepaid Insurance*	4 3 7 0 00			(d) 2 8 4 0 00
21	*Income Summary*			(a) 16 0 0 0 00	
26	*Insurance Expense*			(d) 2 8 4 0 00	
31	*Supplies Expense—Office*			(b) 2 3 4 0 00	
32	*Supplies Expense—Store*			(c) 2 6 8 0 00	

Instructions: 1. Prepare a T account for each account. For those accounts that have a balance, enter the balance on the proper side of the T account.

2. Enter the adjusting entries in the appropriate T accounts.

DRILL 19-D2 Analyzing adjusting entries

The following information is related to adjustments needed at the end of a fiscal period for three businesses.

Business	Account Title	Account Balance in General Ledger	Adjustment Information	
			Ending Inventories	Ending Value
1	Merchandise Inventory	$388,000.00	$365,000.00	
	Supplies—Office	4,730.00	2,910.00	
	Supplies—Store	5,230.00	3,470.00	
	Prepaid Insurance	3,360.00		$840.00
2	Merchandise Inventory	$274,000.00	$286,000.00	
	Supplies—Office	3,620.00	1,840.00	
	Supplies—Store	3,950.00	2,110.00	
	Prepaid Insurance	2,850.00		$570.00
3	Merchandise Inventory	$292,000.00	$278,000.00	
	Supplies—Office	4,480.00	2,250.00	
	Supplies—Store	4,130.00	2,320.00	
	Prepaid Insurance	3,200.00		$800.00

Instructions: 1. Prepare eight T accounts for each of the three businesses. (1) Merchandise Inventory. (2) Supplies—Office. (3) Supplies—Store. (4) Prepaid Insurance. (5) Income Summary. (6) Insurance Expense. (7) Supplies Expense—Office. (8) Supplies Expense—Store. For those accounts that have a balance, enter the balance on the proper side of the T account.

2. Enter the adjusting entries in the appropriate T accounts for each business.

DRILL 19-D3   **Analyzing closing entries**

The following information is from the work sheet of Novak's Sport Center.

	ACCOUNT TITLE	INCOME STATEMENT DEBIT	INCOME STATEMENT CREDIT
21	*Income Summary*	12 0 0 0 00	
22	*Sales*		236 0 0 0 00
23	*Purchases*	94 4 0 0 00	
24	*Advertising Expense*	3 2 5 0 00	
25	*Credit Card Fee Expense*	2 1 3 0 00	
26	*Insurance Expense*	2 5 2 0 00	
27	*Miscellaneous Expense*	1 3 8 0 00	
28	*Rent Expense*	14 4 0 0 00	
29	*Supplies Expense—Office*	2 9 8 0 00	
30	*Supplies Expense—Store*	3 1 2 0 00	

Instructions: 1. Prepare a T account for each account. In each T account, enter the amount that is shown in the Income Statement columns.
    2. Enter the debit and credit amounts to close the income statement credit balance account. Enter the debit and credit amounts to close the income statement debit balance accounts.

▮ APPLICATION PROBLEM

PROBLEM 19-1   Journalizing and posting adjusting and closing entries; preparing a post-closing trial balance

Use the following partial work sheet of Jewel Box Company for the year ended December 31 of the current year. The general ledger accounts and their balances are in the working papers accompanying this textbook.

		3	4	5	6
	ACCOUNT TITLE	ADJUSTMENTS		INCOME STATEMENT	
		DEBIT	CREDIT	DEBIT	CREDIT
4	*Merchandise Inventory*		(a)13 0 0 0 00		
5	*Supplies—Office*		(b) 2 1 4 0 00		
6	*Supplies—Store*		(c) 2 4 5 0 00		
7	*Prepaid Insurance*		(d) 2 6 4 0 00		
21	*Income Summary*	(a)13 0 0 0 00		13 0 0 0 00	
22	*Sales*				316 0 0 0 00
23	*Purchases*			126 4 5 0 00	
24	*Advertising Expense*			4 7 2 0 00	
25	*Credit Card Fee Expense*			3 2 6 0 00	
26	*Insurance Expense*	(d) 2 6 4 0 00		2 6 4 0 00	
27	*Miscellaneous Expense*			1 9 3 0 00	
28	*Payroll Taxes Expense*			6 7 7 3 00	
29	*Rent Expense*			15 6 0 0 00	
30	*Salary Expense*			56 7 8 7 00	
31	*Supplies Expense—Office*	(b) 2 1 4 0 00		2 1 4 0 00	
32	*Supplies Expense—Store*	(c) 2 4 5 0 00		2 4 5 0 00	
33	*Utilities Expense*			2 9 4 0 00	
34		20 2 3 0 00	20 2 3 0 00	238 6 9 0 00	316 0 0 0 00
35	*Net Income*			77 3 1 0 00	
36				316 0 0 0 00	316 0 0 0 00

Instructions: 1. Use page 25 of a journal. Journalize the adjusting entries using information from the partial work sheet.

2. Post the adjusting entries.

3. Continue using page 25 of the journal. Journalize the closing entries using information from the work sheet. The distribution of net income statement shows equal distribution of earnings. The partners' drawing accounts show the following debit balances in the work sheet's Balance Sheet Debit column: Paula Chaney, Drawing, $14,580.00; Scott Chaney, Drawing, $14,720.00.

4. Post the closing entries.

5. Prepare a post-closing trial balance.

ENRICHMENT PROBLEMS

MASTERY PROBLEM 19-M   **Journalizing and posting adjusting and closing entries; preparing a post-closing trial balance**

Use the following partial work sheet of Robco Toys for the year ended December 31 of the current year. The general ledger accounts and their balances are in the working papers accompanying this textbook.

	ADJUSTMENTS		INCOME STATEMENT	
ACCOUNT TITLE	DEBIT	CREDIT	DEBIT	CREDIT
4 Merchandise Inventory		(a) 12 50 0 00		
5 Supplies—Office		(b) 2 43 0 00		
6 Supplies—Store		(c) 2 27 0 00		
7 Prepaid Insurance		(d) 2 28 0 00		
21 Income Summary	(a) 12 50 0 00		12 50 0 00	
22 Sales				325 63 0 00
23 Purchases			130 45 0 00	
24 Advertising Expense			5 18 0 00	
25 Credit Card Fee Expense			3 42 0 00	
26 Insurance Expense	(d) 2 28 0 00		2 28 0 00	
27 Miscellaneous Expense			2 06 0 00	
28 Payroll Taxes Expense			7 12 4 00	
29 Rent Expense			15 60 0 00	
30 Salary Expense			59 36 0 00	
31 Supplies Expense—Office	(b) 2 43 0 00		2 43 0 00	
32 Supplies Expense—Store	(c) 2 27 0 00		2 27 0 00	
33 Utilities Expense			2 88 0 00	
34	19 48 0 00	19 48 0 00	245 55 4 00	325 63 0 00
35 Net Income			80 07 6 00	
36			325 63 0 00	325 63 0 00
37				

Instructions: 1. Use page 25 of a journal. Journalize the adjusting entries using information from the partial work sheet.

2. Post the adjusting entries.

3. Continue using page 25 of the journal. Journalize the closing entries using information from the work sheet. The distribution of net income statement shows equal distribution of earnings. The partners' drawing accounts show the following debit balances in the work sheet's Balance Sheet Debit column: Marcus Florie, Drawing, $18,230.00; Karen Rader, Drawing, $18,710.00.

4. Post the closing entries.

5. Prepare a post-closing trial balance.

CHALLENGE PROBLEM 19-C   Completing end-of-fiscal-period work

Plaza Book Center's trial balance is recorded on a 10-column work sheet in the working papers accompanying this textbook. The general ledger accounts and their balances are also given.

Instructions: 1. Use the following adjustment information. Complete the 10-column work sheet.

Adjustment Information, December 31

Merchandise inventory.................................	$204,680.00
Office supplies inventory..............................	2,635.00
Store supplies inventory..............................	2,310.00
Value of prepaid insurance	2,200.00

    2. Prepare an income statement from the information on the work sheet. Calculate and record the following component percentages: (a) cost of merchandise sold, (b) gross profit on sales, (c) total expenses, and (d) net income or loss. Round percentage calculations to the nearest 0.1%.

    3. Prepare a distribution of net income statement. Net income or loss is to be shared equally.

    4. Prepare an owners' equity statement. No additional investments were made.

    5. Prepare a balance sheet in report form.

    6. Use page 25 of a journal. Journalize the adjusting entries.

    7. Post the adjusting entries.

    8. Continue using page 25 of the journal. Journalize the closing entries.

    9. Post the closing entries.

    10. Prepare a post-closing trial balance.

Reinforcement Activity 2, Part B

An Accounting Cycle for a Partnership: End-of-Fiscal-Period Work

The ledgers used in Reinforcement Activity 2, Part A, are needed to complete Reinforcement Activity 2, Part B.

Reinforcement Activity 2, Part B, includes those accounting activities needed to complete the accounting cycle of ClearView Optical.

END-OF-FISCAL-PERIOD WORK

Instructions: 10. Prepare a trial balance on a work sheet. Use December 31 of the current year as the date.

11. Complete the work sheet using the following adjustment information.

Adjustment Information, December 31

Merchandise inventory	$203,200.00
Office supplies inventory	2,370.00
Store supplies inventory	3,240.00
Value of prepaid insurance	260.00

12. Prepare an income statement. Figure and record the following component percentages: (a) cost of merchandise sold, (b) gross profit on sales, (c) total expenses, and (d) net income or loss. Round percentage calculations to the nearest 0.1%.

13. Prepare a distribution of net income statement. Net income or loss is to be shared equally.

14. Prepare an owners' equity statement. No additional investments were made.

15. Prepare a balance sheet in report form.

16. Use page 25 of a journal. Journalize and post the adjusting entries.

17. Continue using page 25 of the journal. Journalize and post the closing entries.

18. Prepare a post-closing trial balance.

Computer Application 4
Automated Accounting Cycle for a
Partnership: End-of-Fiscal-Period Work

Chapters 17 through 19 describe CarLand's manual accounting procedures for completing end-of-fiscal-period work. Computer Application 4 describes procedures for using a microcomputer to complete CarLand's end-of-fiscal-period work. Computer Application Problem 4 contains instructions for using a microcomputer to solve Challenge Problem 19-C, Chapter 19.

PLANNING ADJUSTMENTS

Procedures for bringing CarLand's general ledger account balances up to date are similar to those described for Petlodge in Chapter 11.

Option K is selected from the General Ledger Main Menu, Illustration C4-1, page 464, to direct the computer to prepare a trial balance.

A trial balance is prepared to check the equality of debits and credits in the general ledger and to plan adjusting entries. CarLand's trial balance is shown in Illustration C4-2, page 464.

Recording adjusting entries

Adjusting entries are journalized on a general ledger input form (FORM GL-2). CarLand's completed general ledger input form for the adjusting entries is shown in Illustration C4-3, page 465.

Illustration C4-1
General ledger
main menu

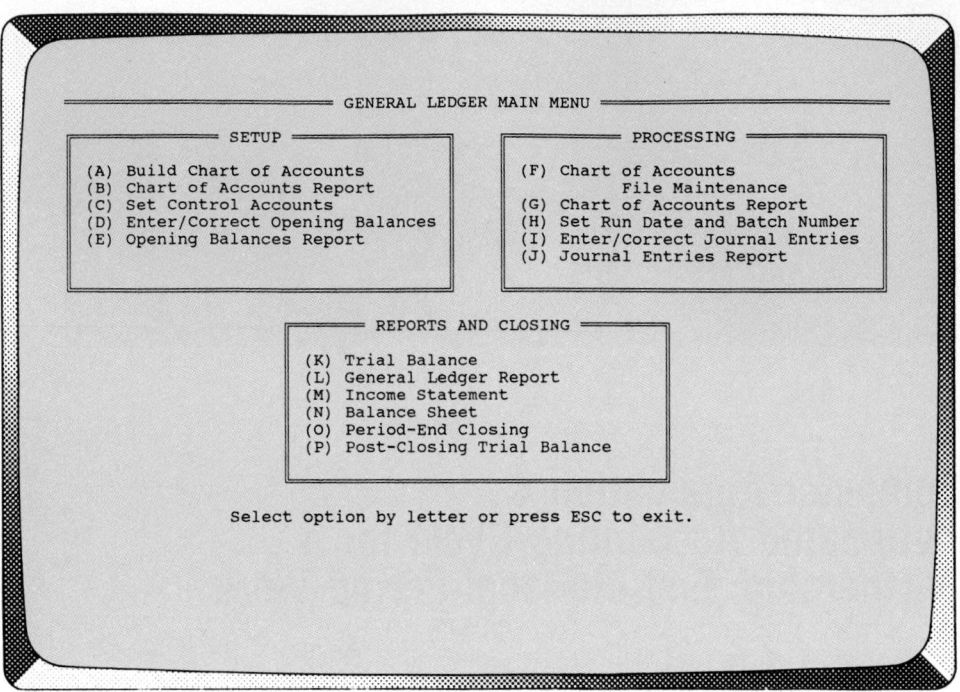

```
═══════════════════════ GENERAL LEDGER MAIN MENU ═══════════════════════

   ┌──────── SETUP ────────┐           ┌───────── PROCESSING ─────────┐
   │ (A) Build Chart of Accounts       │ (F) Chart of Accounts
   │ (B) Chart of Accounts Report      │          File Maintenance
   │ (C) Set Control Accounts          │ (G) Chart of Accounts Report
   │ (D) Enter/Correct Opening Balances│ (H) Set Run Date and Batch Number
   │ (E) Opening Balances Report       │ (I) Enter/Correct Journal Entries
   └───────────────────────┘           │ (J) Journal Entries Report
                                        └───────────────────────────┘

              ┌──────── REPORTS AND CLOSING ────────┐
              │ (K) Trial Balance
              │ (L) General Ledger Report
              │ (M) Income Statement
              │ (N) Balance Sheet
              │ (O) Period-End Closing
              │ (P) Post-Closing Trial Balance
              └─────────────────────────────────────┘


              Select option by letter or press ESC to exit.
```

Illustration C4-2
Trial balance

RUN DATE: 12/31/--   CARLAND
                                   TRIAL BALANCE

ACCOUNT NUMBER	ACCOUNT TITLE	DEBIT AMOUNT	CREDIT AMOUNT
1110	Cash	24233.57	
1120	Petty Cash	500.00	
1130	Accounts Receivable	9332.00	
1140	Merchandise Inventory	225400.00	
1145	Supplies--Office	5400.00	
1150	Supplies--Store	5780.00	
1160	Prepaid Insurance	4840.00	
2110	Accounts Payable		10451.90
2120	Empl. Income Tax Payable		402.00
2130	FICA Tax Payable		832.16
2140	Sales Tax Payable		1760.00
2150	Unempl. Tax Pay.--Federal		59.15
2160	Unempl. Tax Pay.--State		399.26
2170	Health Ins. Prem. Payable		840.00
2180	U.S. Savings Bonds Pay.		40.00
2190	United Way Don. Payable		60.00
3110	Amy Kramer, Capital		101118.00
3120	Amy Kramer, Drawing	18200.00	
3130	Dario Mesa, Capital		101228.00
3140	Dario Mesa, Drawing	18600.00	
4110	Sales		352600.00
5110	Purchases	158300.00	
6110	Advertising Expense	5500.00	
6120	Credit Card Fee Expense	2890.00	
6140	Miscellaneous Expense	2182.15	
6150	Payroll Taxes Expense	7299.75	
6160	Rent Expense	18000.00	
6170	Salary Expense	60153.00	
6190	Utilities Expense	3180.00	
	TOTALS	569790.47	569790.47

RUN DATE 12/31/--			GENERAL LEDGER			
MM DD YY			Input Form			
BATCH NO. 4					FORM GL-2	

	1	2	3	4	5	
	DAY	DOC. NO.	ACCOUNT NUMBER	DEBIT AMOUNT	CREDIT AMOUNT	
1	31	Adj.Ent.	3150	13200 00		1
2			1140		13200 00	2
3	31	Adj.Ent.	6175	3940 00		3
4			1145		3940 00	4
5	31	Adj.Ent.	6180	3260 00		5
6			1150		3260 00	6
7	31	Adj.Ent.	6130	2640 00		7
8			1160		2640 00	8
20						20
21						21
22						22
23						23
24						24
25						25
			BATCH TOTALS	23040 00	23040 00	

Illustration C4-3
General ledger input form with adjusting entries entered

CarLand has the following adjustment data on December 31.

Adjustment Information, December 31

Merchandise inventory	$212,200.00
Office supplies inventory	1,460.00
Store supplies inventory	2,520.00
Value of prepaid insurance	2,200.00

After all adjusting entries have been journalized, the Debit Amount and Credit Amount columns are totaled. The totals are entered on the Batch Totals line provided at the bottom of the input form. The two totals are compared to assure that debits equal credits. As the two totals are the same, $23,040.00, the adjusting entries journalized on the general ledger input form are assumed to be correct.

Processing adjusting entries

Option H is selected from the General Ledger Main Menu, Illustration C4-1, to set the run date, 12/31/--, and the batch number, 4. Option I is selected from the General Ledger Main Menu to display spaces for entering the adjusting entries. After all lines on the input form have been entered

Illustration C4-4
Journal entries report for
adjusting entries

and posted, Option J is selected from the General Ledger Main Menu. This option directs the computer to prepare a journal entries report for the adjusting entries. CarLand's journal entries report for adjusting entries is shown in Illustration C4-4.

```
RUN DATE: 12/31/--                      CARLAND
                             JOURNAL ENTRIES BATCH# 4

    ------------------------------------------------------------------
    JE#   DATE       ACCOUNT NUMBER & TITLE         DEBIT AMOUNT   CREDIT AMOUNT
    ------------------------------------------------------------------
    0050  12/31/-- 3150   Income Summary              13200.00
                   1140     Merchandise Inventory                    13200.00
                   DOCUMENT: Adj.Ent.

    0051  12/31/-- 6175   Supplies Expense--Office     3940.00
                   1145     Supplies--Office                          3940.00
                   DOCUMENT: Adj.Ent.

    0052  12/31/-- 6180   Supplies Expense--Store      3260.00
                   1150     Supplies--Store                           3260.00
                   DOCUMENT: Adj.Ent.

    0053  12/31/-- 6130   Insurance Expense            2640.00
                   1160     Prepaid Insurance                         2640.00
                   DOCUMENT: Adj.Ent.

                                                     ---------------  ---------------
                   TOTALS                               23040.00        23040.00
                                                     ===============  ===============
                   IN BALANCE
```

The journal entries report for adjusting entries is checked against the general ledger input form for adjusting entries. The totals shown on the report, $23,040.00, are the same as on the general ledger input form. Therefore, the journal entries report is assumed to be correct.

PREPARING END-OF-FISCAL-PERIOD REPORTS

In automated accounting end-of-fiscal-period reports are prepared by a computer based on instructions in computer software.

Processing financial statements

After the journal entries report for adjusting entries has been prepared and checked for accuracy, Option M is selected from the General Ledger

Main Menu. This option directs the computer to print an income statement. CarLand's income statement is shown in Illustration C4-5.

Illustration C4-5
Income statement prepared by computer

```
                            CARLAND
                        INCOME STATEMENT
                    FOR PERIOD ENDED 12/31/--
                                                              % OF NET
    R E V E N U E                                             REVENUE
    -------------                                             --------
    Sales                          352600.00                  100.00
                                ----------------
    NET REVENUE                                    352600.00   100.00

    C O S T   O F   M D S E .   S O L D
    -----------------------------------
    BEGINNING INVENTORY            225400.00                    63.93
    Purchases                      158300.00                    44.90
                                ----------------
    MDSE. AVAILABLE FOR SALE       383700.00                   108.82
    LESS ENDING INVENTORY          212200.00                    60.18
                                ----------------
    COST OF MDSE. SOLD                             171500.00    48.64
                                                ----------------
    GROSS PROFIT ON OPERATIONS                     181100.00    51.36

    E X P E N S E S
    ---------------
    Advertising Expense              5500.00                     1.56
    Credit Card Fee Expense          2890.00                      .82
    Insurance Expense                2640.00                      .75
    Miscellaneous Expense            2182.15                      .62
    Payroll Taxes Expense            7299.75                     2.07
    Rent Expense                    18000.00                     5.10
    Salary Expense                  60153.00                    17.06
    Supplies Expense--Office         3940.00                     1.12
    Supplies Expense--Store          3260.00                      .92
    Utilities Expense                3180.00                      .90
                                ----------------
    TOTAL EXPENSES                                 109044.90    30.93
                                                ----------------
    NET INCOME                                      72055.10    20.44
                                                ================
```

CarLand's net income or net loss is distributed equally to each partner based on the partnership agreement. In CarLand's manual accounting system, a distribution of net income statement is prepared to show how the net income or net loss is divided. Then, an owners' equity statement is prepared to show changes in each partner's capital during a fiscal period. In CarLand's automated accounting system, distribution of income and changes in capital are both shown on the balance sheet.

Illustration C4-6
Balance sheet prepared by
computer

Option N is selected from the General Ledger Main Menu to direct the computer to print a balance sheet. CarLand's balance sheet is shown in Illustration C4-6.

```
                             CARLAND
                           BALANCE SHEET
                             12/31/--

   A S S E T S
   -----------
   Cash                          24233.57
   Petty Cash                      500.00
   Accounts Receivable            9332.00
   Merchandise Inventory        212200.00
   Supplies--Office               1460.00
   Supplies--Store                2520.00
   Prepaid Insurance              2200.00
                                ----------
   TOTAL ASSETS                                252445.57
                                              ==========

   L I A B I L I T I E S
   ---------------------
   Accounts Payable              10451.90
   Empl. Income Tax Payable        402.00
   FICA Tax Payable                832.16
   Sales Tax Payable              1760.00
   Unempl. Tax Pay.--Federal        59.15
   Unempl. Tax Pay.--State         399.26
   Health Ins. Prem. Payable       840.00
   U.S. Savings Bonds Pay.          40.00
   United Way Don. Payable          60.00
                                ----------
   TOTAL LIABILITIES                            14844.47

   O W N E R ' S   E Q U I T Y
   ---------------------------
   Amy Kramer, Capital          101118.00
   Amy Kramer, Drawing          -18200.00
   SHARE OF NET INCOME @ 50%     36027.55
   Dario Mesa, Capital          101228.00
   Dario Mesa, Drawing          -18600.00
   SHARE OF NET INCOME @ 50%     36027.55
                                ----------
   TOTAL CAPITAL                               237601.10
                                              ----------
   TOTAL LIABILITIES & CAPITAL                 252445.57
                                              ==========
```

In manual accounting closing entries for all temporary accounts are manually entered in a journal and posted to general ledger accounts. In automated accounting the computer software contains instructions for closing temporary accounts. After the balance sheet has been prepared, Option O is selected from the General Ledger Main Menu to perform period-end closing.

After completing period-end closing, Option P is selected from the General Ledger Main Menu. This option directs the computer to print a post-closing trial balance. CarLand's post-closing trial balance is shown in Illustration C4-7.

Illustration C4-7
Post-closing trial balance prepared by computer

```
RUN DATE: 12/31/--                    CARLAND
                              POST-CLOSING TRIAL BALANCE

  --------------------------------------------------------------------------
  ACCOUNT      ACCOUNT
  NUMBER       TITLE                        DEBIT AMOUNT      CREDIT AMOUNT
  --------------------------------------------------------------------------
  1110         Cash                            24233.57
  1120         Petty Cash                        500.00
  1130         Accounts Receivable              9332.00
  1140         Merchandise Inventory          212200.00
  1145         Supplies--Office                 1460.00
  1150         Supplies--Store                  2520.00
  1160         Prepaid Insurance                2200.00
  2110         Accounts Payable                                  10451.90
  2120         Empl. Income Tax Payable                            402.00
  2130         FICA Tax Payable                                    832.16
  2140         Sales Tax Payable                                  1760.00
  2150         Unempl. Tax Pay.--Federal                            59.15
  2160         Unempl. Tax Pay.--State                             399.26
  2170         Health Ins. Prem. Payable                           840.00
  2180         U.S. Savings Bonds Pay.                              40.00
  2190         United Way Don. Payable                              60.00
  3110         Amy Kramer, Capital                              118945.55
  3130         Dario Mesa, Capital                              118655.55

                                           --------------    --------------
               TOTALS                         252445.57          252445.57
                                           ==============    ==============
```

COMPUTER APPLICATION PROBLEM

COMPUTER APPLICATION PROBLEM 4   End-of-fiscal-period work

Instructions: 1. Load the *Automated Accounting for the Microcomputer* software. Select Computer Application 4 (CA-4) from the CENTURY 21 ACCOUNTING Template Disk. The general ledger chart of accounts and current balances have been entered and stored on the Template Disk.

2. Display/Print a trial balance.

3. Refer to the adjustment information given in Challenge Problem 19-C, Chapter 19. Journalize the adjusting entries on a general ledger input form. Use December 31 of the current year as the run date. Batch No. 3. Use the following account numbers and titles.

Acct. No.	Account Title	Balance before Adjustments
1130	Merchandise Inventory	$218,320.00
1140	Supplies—Office	5,180.00
1150	Supplies—Store	4,275.00
1160	Prepaid Insurance	3,960.00
3150	Income Summary.............................	—
6120	Insurance Expense	—
6150	Supplies Expense—Office.....................	—
6160	Supplies Expense—Store.....................	—

4. Key-enter the adjusting entries from the completed general ledger input form.

5. Display/Print the journal entries report.

6. Display/Print the income statement.

7. Display/Print the balance sheet.

8. Close the general ledger.

9. Display/Print the post-closing trial balance.

VIKING MARINE

A BUSINESS SIMULATION

BA20EE2

Viking Marine is a merchandising business organized as a partnership. This business simulation covers the realistic transactions completed by Viking Marine, which sells personal watercraft and water sports items. Transactions are recorded in a journal similar to the one used by CarLand in Part 3. The following activities are included in the accounting cycle for Viking Marine. This business simulation is available from the publisher in either manual or automated versions.

Activities in Viking Marine

1. Recording transactions in a journal from source documents.
2. Posting items to be posted individually to a general ledger and subsidiary ledger.
3. Recording a payroll in a payroll register. Updating the employee earnings record. Recording payroll journal entries.
4. Posting column totals to a general ledger.
5. Preparing schedules of accounts receivable and accounts payable from subsidiary ledgers.
6. Preparing a trial balance on a work sheet.
7. Planning adjustments and completing a work sheet.
8. Preparing financial statements.
9. Journalizing and posting adjusting entries.
10. Journalizing and posting closing entries.
11. Preparing a post-closing trial balance.

471

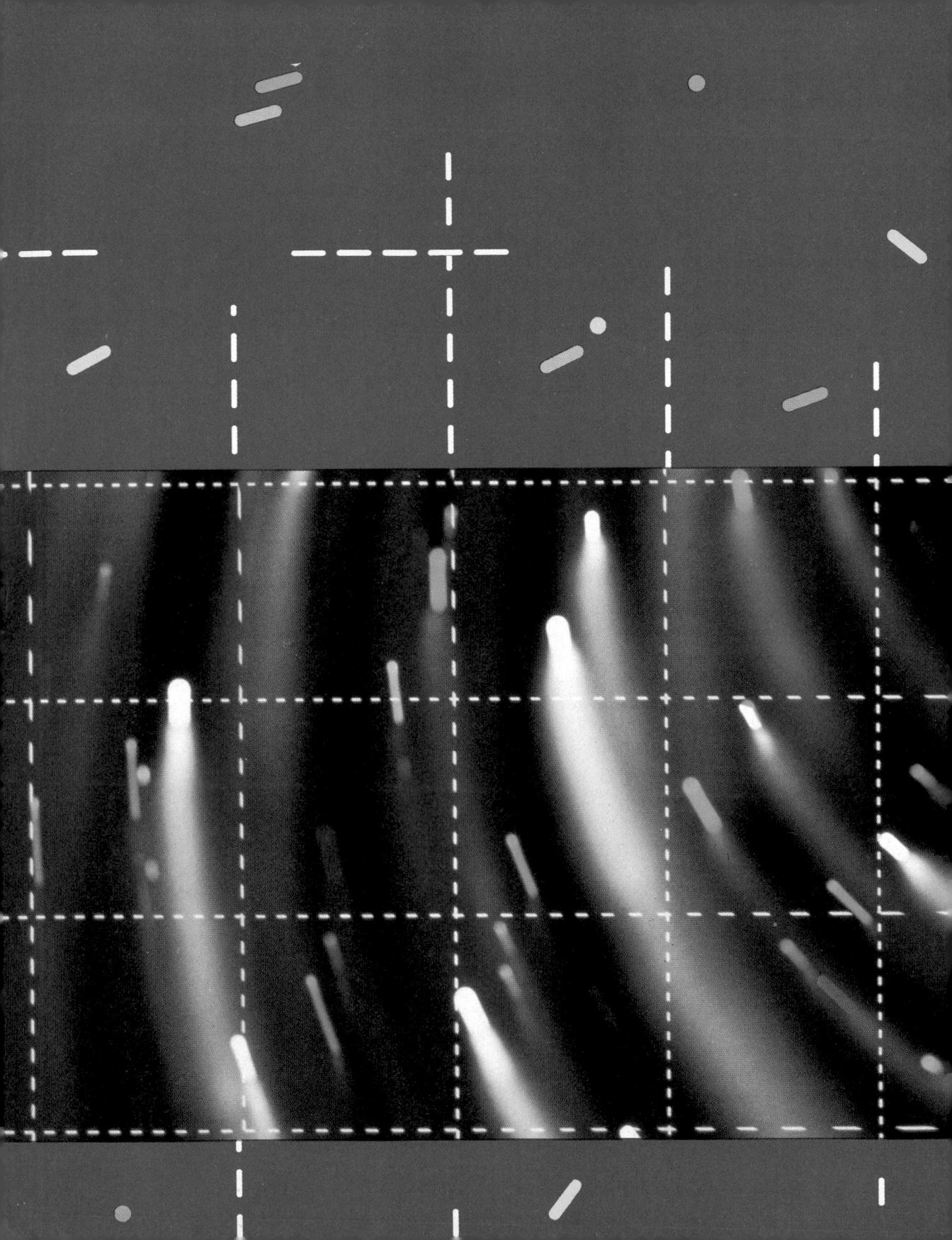

Corporate Accounting for a Merchandising Business

4

GENERAL BEHAVIORAL GOALS

1. Know accounting terminology related to an accounting system for a merchandising business organized as a corporation.
2. Understand accounting concepts and practices related to an accounting system for a merchandising business organized as a corporation.
3. Demonstrate accounting procedures used in an accounting system for a merchandising business organized as a corporation.

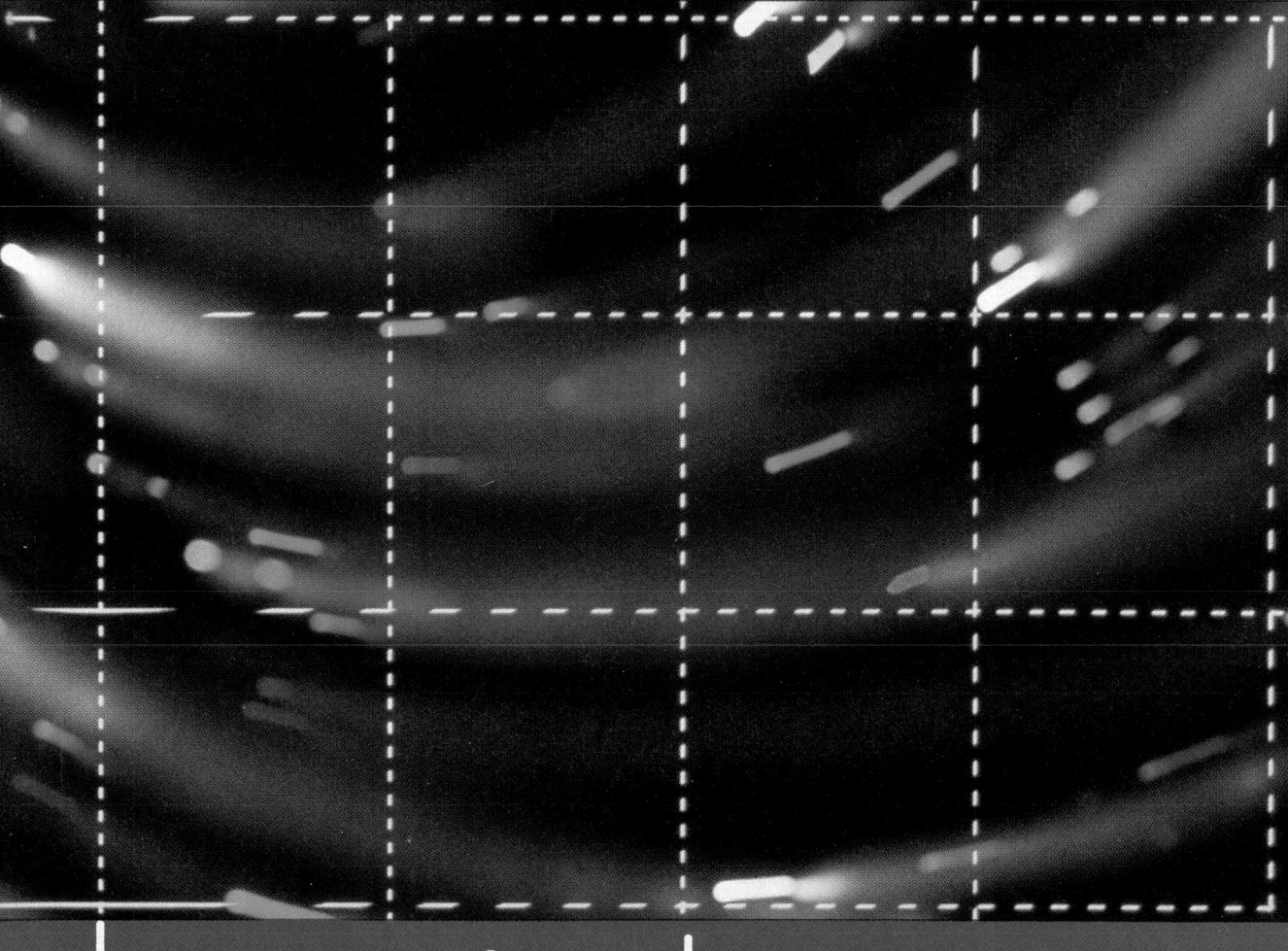

CELLUPHONE, INC.
Chart of Accounts

Balance Sheet Accounts

(1000) ASSETS

1100   Current Assets

1105   Cash
1110   Petty Cash
1115   Notes Receivable
1120   Interest Receivable
1125   Accounts Receivable
1130   Allowance for Uncollectible
       Accounts
1135   Merchandise Inventory
1140   Supplies
1145   Prepaid Insurance

1200   Plant Assets

1205   Office Equipment
1210   Accumulated Depreciation—
       Office Equipment
1215   Store Equipment
1220   Accumulated Depreciation—
       Store Equipment

(2000) LIABILITIES

2100   Current Liabilities

2105   Notes Payable
2110   Interest Payable
2115   Accounts Payable
2120   Employee Income Tax Payable
2125   Federal Income Tax Payable
2130   FICA Tax Payable
2135   Sales Tax Payable
2140   Unemployment Tax Payable—
       Federal
2145   Unemployment Tax Pay.—State
2150   Health Insurance Premiums
       Payable
2155   Dividends Payable

(3000) STOCKHOLDERS' EQUITY
3105   Capital Stock
3110   Retained Earnings
3115   Dividends
3120   Income Summary

Income Statement Accounts

(4000) OPERATING REVENUE
4105   Sales
4110   Sales Discount
4115   Sales Returns and Allowances

(5000) COST OF MERCHANDISE
5105   Purchases
5110   Purchases Discount
5115   Purchases Returns and
       Allowances

(6000) OPERATING EXPENSES
6105   Advertising Expense
6110   Credit Card Fee Expense
6115   Depreciation Expense—Office
       Equipment
6120   Depreciation Expense—Store
       Equipment
6125   Insurance Expense
6130   Miscellaneous Expense
6135   Payroll Taxes Expense
6140   Rent Expense
6145   Salary Expense
6150   Supplies Expense
6155   Uncollectible Accounts Expense
6160   Utilities Expense

(7000) OTHER REVENUE
7105   Gain on Plant Assets
7110   Interest Income

(8000) OTHER EXPENSES
8105   Cash Short and Over
8110   Interest Expense
8115   Loss on Plant Assets

(9000) INCOME TAX EXPENSE
9105   Federal Income Tax Expense

The chart of accounts for Celluphone, Inc., is illustrated above for
ready reference as you study Part 4 of this textbook.

CHAPTER 20

Recording Purchases and Cash Payments Using Special Journals

ENABLING PERFORMANCE TASKS

After studying Chapter 20, you will be able to:
a. Define accounting terms related to purchases and cash payments.
b. Identify accounting concepts and practices related to purchases and cash payments.
c. Analyze transactions affecting purchases and cash payments.
d. Journalize and post transactions related to purchases and cash payments.

Reliable financial information is important for the successful operation of a business. However, the amount of information a business needs and can afford varies with the business' size and complexity. Several types of accounting systems may be used to record, summarize, and report a business' financial information. An accounting system may vary from a small manual system operated by one accounting clerk to a large computerized system that requires hundreds of accountants and clerks. A business should use an accounting system that provides the desired financial information with the least amount of effort and cost. Regardless of the accounting system used, financial information is reported for a specified period of time. (CONCEPT: Accounting Period Cycle)

CORPORATIONS

Many businesses need amounts of capital that cannot be easily provided by a proprietorship or a partnership. An organization with the legal rights of a person and which may be owned by many persons is called a corporation. Many businesses are organized as corporations. A corporation is formed by receiving approval from a state or federal agency. A corporation can own property, incur liabilities, and enter into contracts in its

475

own name. A corporation may also sell ownership in itself. Each unit of ownership in a corporation is called a share of stock. Total shares of ownership in a corporation are called capital stock.

Celluphone, Inc., is organized as a corporation. Celluphone, Inc., is a business that sells cellular phones to corporate customers for use in their company cars and trucks. Celluphone was formed as a corporation because several owners can provide larger amounts of capital than one owner. The principal difference among the accounting records of proprietorships, partnerships, and corporations is in the capital accounts. Proprietorships and partnerships have a single capital and drawing account for each owner. A corporation has separate capital accounts for the stock issued and for the earnings kept in the business. The use of the different capital accounts is explained in more detail in Chapter 26. As in proprietorships and partnerships, information in a corporation's accounting system is kept separate from the personal records of the owners. *(CONCEPT: Business Entity)*

SPECIAL JOURNALS

A business with few transactions may need only one bookkeeper or accounting clerk to record transactions. When one person records transactions, a business may record all entries in one journal. In Part 1, Rugcare uses a 5-column journal to record all transactions. In Part 3, CarLand uses an 11-column expanded journal to record all transactions. However, a business with many daily transactions may use several different journals. A journal used to record only one kind of transaction is called a special journal. Using special journals allows the work of journalizing to be divided among several accounting clerks. The accounting clerks then specialize in the kind of transactions recorded. This specialization helps improve the efficiency of recording transactions.

Whether a single journal or several special journals are used, all business transactions are recorded in a common unit of measurement—the dollar. Recording all transactions in dollar values permits more meaningful comparisons with previous accounting periods and with other businesses. *(CONCEPT: Unit of Measurement)*

Celluphone uses four special journals along with a general journal to record its transactions.

1. Purchases journal — for all purchases on account
2. Cash payments journal — for all cash payments
3. Sales journal — for all sales on account
4. Cash receipts journal — for all cash receipts

A general journal is used for all other transactions.

RECORDING PURCHASES ON
ACCOUNT USING A PURCHASES JOURNAL

A special journal used to record *only* purchase on account transactions is called a purchases journal. The relationship between Celluphone's purchases journal and the expanded journal described in Chapter 12 is shown in Illustration 20-1.

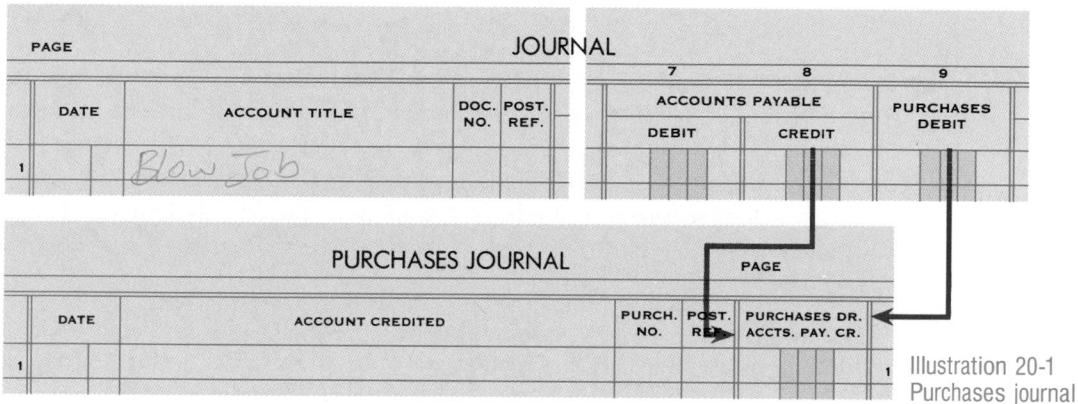

Illustration 20-1
Purchases journal

A purchase on account transaction can be recorded on one line of Celluphone's purchases journal. Each entry in the single amount column is both a debit to Purchases and a credit to Accounts Payable. The titles of both general ledger accounts are listed in the single amount column heading. Since the debit and credit entries always affect the same two accounts, recording time is reduced by using only one amount column.

Journalizing purchases on account

The source document for recording a purchase on account is a purchase invoice received from a vendor. *(CONCEPT: Objective Evidence)* Celluphone dates, numbers, and verifies each purchase invoice.

> *March 1, 19--.*
> *Purchased merchandise on account from Cell Systems, $6,672.00. Purchase Invoice No. 39.*

The analysis of this transaction is shown in the T accounts. The balance of the purchases account is increased by this transaction. Thus, Purchases is debited for $6,672.00. The amount owed to a vendor is increased by this transaction. Therefore, Accounts Payable is credited for $6,672.00. The same amount is also credited to the account of Cell Systems in the accounts payable ledger.

Purchases are recorded at their cost. *(CONCEPT: Historical Cost)* The purchases journal entry to record this purchase on account transaction is shown in Illustration 20-2.

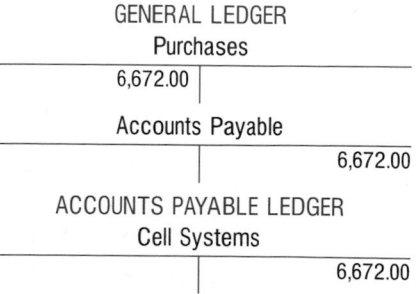

	PURCHASES JOURNAL			PAGE 3	

	DATE		ACCOUNT CREDITED	PURCH. NO.	POST. REF.	PURCHASES DR. ACCTS. PAY. CR.	
1	Mar. 1		Cell Systems	39		6 6 7 2 00	1
2							2
3							3
4							4

Illustration 20-2
Purchases journal entry to record a purchase on account

The date, *19--, Mar.1*, is written in the Date column. The vendor name, *Cell Systems*, is written in the Account Credited column. The number stamped on the invoice, *39*, is entered in the Purch. No. column. The amount of the invoice, *$6,672.00*, is recorded in the amount column.

Each purchase on account is recorded in a purchases journal in the same way.

In Part 3, CarLand uses an abbreviation to indicate the type of source document in the Post. Ref. column of the expanded journal because all kinds of transactions are recorded in one journal. However, only purchase invoices are recorded in the purchases journal so the abbreviation *P* is not needed in the Purch. No. column.

Posting from a purchases journal to an accounts payable ledger

The amount on each line of a purchases journal is posted as a credit to the named vendor account in the accounts payable ledger.

Celluphone posts frequently to the accounts payable ledger. By posting frequently, each vendor account always shows an up-to-date balance. Posting from line 1 of a purchases journal to a vendor account in the accounts payable ledger is shown in Illustration 20-3.

	PURCHASES JOURNAL				PAGE 3	

	DATE		ACCOUNT CREDITED	PURCH. NO.	POST. REF.	PURCHASES DR. ACCTS. PAY. CR.	
1	Mar. 1		Cell Systems	39	220	6 6 7 2 00	1
2							2

VENDOR *Cell Systems*   VENDOR NO. *220*

	DATE		ITEM	POST. REF.	DEBIT	CREDIT	CREDIT BALANCE
	Mar. 1		Balance	√			2 0 7 9 00
		1		P3		6 6 7 2 00	8 7 5 1 00

Illustration 20-3
Posting from a purchases journal to an accounts payable ledger

The date, *1*, is recorded in the Date column of the vendor account. The abbreviation for the purchases journal and the page number of the journal, *P3*, is written in the Post. Ref. column of the account. The amount, *$6,672.00*, is entered in the Credit column of the vendor account. The amount in the Credit column is added to the previous balance in the Credit Balance column ($2,079.00 + $6,672.00 = $8,751.00). The new balance, *$8,751.00*, is recorded in the Credit Balance column. The vendor number for Cell Systems, *220*, is written in the Post. Ref. column of the purchases journal to show that posting has been completed for this line.

> When several journals are used, an abbreviation is used to show the journal from which the posting is made. The abbreviation *P* is used for the purchases journal. The abbreviation *P3* means page 3 of the purchases journal.

Posting from a purchases journal to an accounts payable ledger is the same as posting from an expanded journal's Accounts Payable Credit column, as described in Chapter 14.

Posting from a purchases journal to a general ledger

At the end of each month, a purchases journal is totaled and ruled, as shown in Illustration 20-4, page 480.

A single line is ruled across the amount column of the purchases journal under the last amount recorded. The date of the last day of the month, *31*, is entered in the Date column. The word *Total* is written in the Account Credited column. The amount column is added, and the total is written directly below the single line. Double lines are ruled across the amount column under the total amount.

Illustration 20-4 also shows the posting of a purchases journal to a general ledger. The total amount of the purchases journal is posted to two general ledger accounts. The total amount, $108,046.00, is posted to Purchases as a debit and to Accounts Payable as a credit. This maintains the equality of debits and credits in the general ledger.

After the total is posted to Purchases, the account number, *5105*, is written under the total in the purchases journal. After this total is posted to Accounts Payable, the account number, *2115*, is written under the purchases journal total. Both account numbers are written in parentheses. This procedure is the same as posting totals of special amount columns in any journal.

Illustration 20-5, page 480, shows a summary of the procedure for journalizing and posting using a purchases journal.

1 Celluphone records a purchase on account transaction on a single line of a one-column purchases journal.

2 Items in the purchases journal's amount column are posted separately to vendor accounts in the accounts payable ledger.

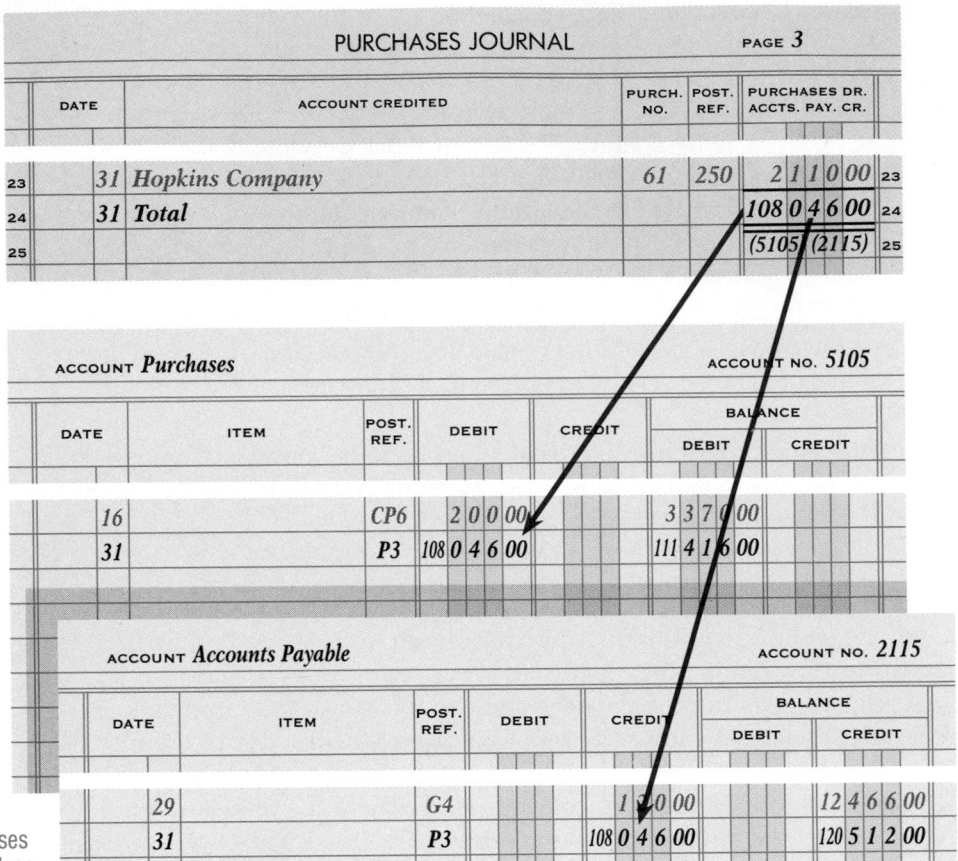

Illustration 20-4
Posting from a purchases
journal to a general ledger

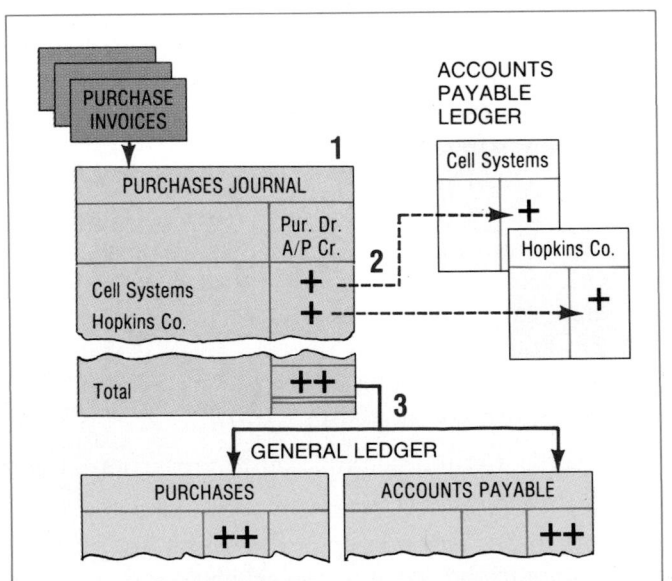

Illustration 20-5
Summary of journalizing
and posting using a
purchases journal

3 At the end of the month, the purchases journal amount column total is posted to two general ledger accounts. Purchases is debited; Accounts Payable is credited.

RECORDING CASH PAYMENTS
USING A CASH PAYMENTS JOURNAL

Celluphone uses another special journal for recording *only* cash payments. A special journal used to record only cash payment transactions is called a cash payments journal. The relationship between Celluphone's cash payments journal and the expanded journal described in Chapter 12 is shown in Illustration 20-6.

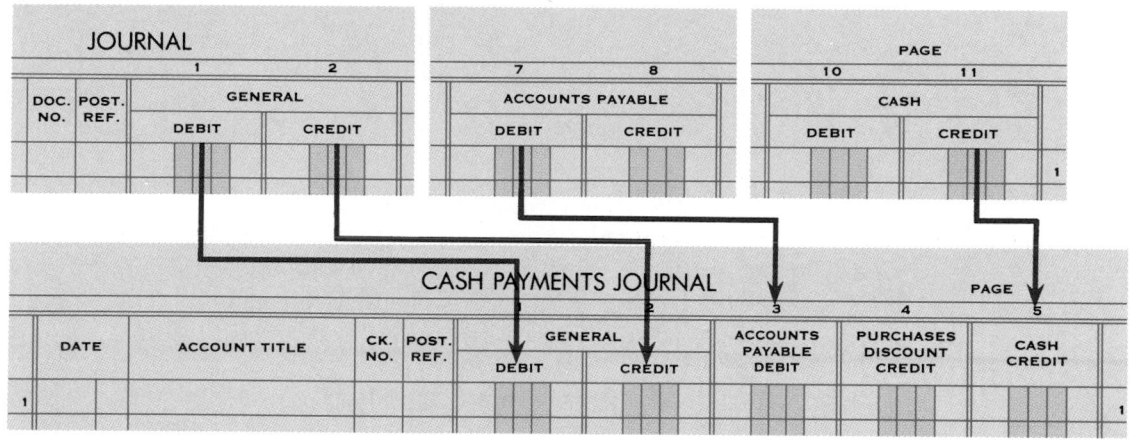

Illustration 20-6
Cash payments journal

Those columns of an expanded journal needed to record only cash payments are included in Celluphone's cash payments journal. In addition, Celluphone has many cash payment transactions that include a discount on the purchases. Therefore, a special amount column is provided in the cash payments journal to record this discount. Transactions that do not occur often, such as monthly rent, are recorded in the General columns.

Journalizing cash payments for expenses

All of Celluphone's cash payments are recorded in a cash payments journal. The source document for most cash payments is a check. *(CONCEPT: Objective Evidence)* A few payments, such as bank service charges, are made as direct withdrawals from the company's bank account. For these payments not using a check, the source document is a memorandum. Most cash payments are for (1) expenses, (2) cash purchases, and (3) payments to vendors.

March 1, 19--.
Paid cash for rent, $3,000.00. Check No. 148.

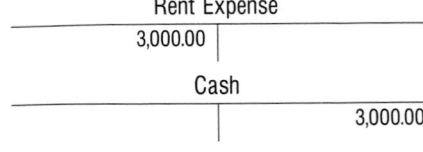

The source document for this cash payment transaction is a check. *(CONCEPT: Objective Evidence)* The analysis of this transaction is shown in the T accounts. The amount of rent expense is increased by this transaction. Therefore, Rent Expense is debited for $3,000.00. The amount of cash is decreased by this transaction. Therefore, Cash is credited for $3,000.00.

The cash payments journal entry to record this cash payment for an expense is shown on line 1, Illustration 20-7.

					CASH PAYMENTS JOURNAL			PAGE 6
					1	2	3	4	5
	DATE	ACCOUNT TITLE	CK. NO.	POST. REF.	GENERAL DEBIT	GENERAL CREDIT	ACCOUNTS PAYABLE DEBIT	PURCHASES DISCOUNT CREDIT	CASH CREDIT
1	*Mar.* 1	*Rent Expense*	*148*		3 0 0 0 00				3 0 0 0 00	1
2	1	*Purchases*	*149*		4 8 0 00				4 8 0 00	2

Illustration 20-7
Cash payment recorded in a cash payments journal

The date, *19--, Mar. 1*, is written in the Date column. The account debited, Rent Expense, is entered in the Account Title column. The number of the check, *148*, is written in the Ck. No. column. The amount debited to Rent Expense, *$3,000.00*, is recorded in the General Debit column. The amount credited to Cash, *$3,000.00*, is recorded in the Cash Credit column.

Journalizing cash payments for cash purchases

Businesses purchase much of their merchandise on account. However, some vendors may require that merchandise be paid for at the time of purchase. In other situations, paying cash at the time of purchase may be more convenient for the business.

Trade discount. Many manufacturers and wholesalers print price lists and catalogs to describe their products. Generally, prices listed in catalogs are the manufacturers' suggested retail prices. A business' printed or catalog price is called a list price. When a merchandising business purchases a number of products from a manufacturer, the price frequently is quoted as "list price less trade discount." A reduction in the list price granted to customers is called a trade discount. Trade discounts are used to quote different prices for different quantities purchased without changing catalog or list prices.

When a trade discount is granted, the seller's invoice shows the actual amount charged. This amount after the trade discount has been deducted from the list price is known as the invoice amount. Only the invoice amount is used in a journal entry. *(CONCEPT: Historical Cost)* The invoice is recorded by both the seller and buyer at the same amount. No journal entry is made to show the amount of a trade discount.

Cash purchases. Celluphone wishes to buy 80 cellular phone carrying cases for cash. The price quoted to Celluphone was $10.00 list price per case less 40% trade discount. The total invoice amount is calculated in three steps.

Step 1: **List Price × Trade Discount Rate = Trade Discount**
    $10.00 ×   40%   = $4.00
Step 2: **List Price − Trade Discount = Invoice Amount per Case**
    $10.00 − $4.00 = $6.00
Step 3: **Invoice Amount per Case × Number of Cases = Total Invoice Amount**
     $6.00   ×   80 = $480.00

Celluphone's purchase price for the 80 carrying cases will be $480.00, the list price less the trade discount.

March 1, 19--.
Purchased merchandise for cash, $480.00. Check No. 149.

The source document for recording this purchase of merchandise for cash is a check. *(CONCEPT: Objective Evidence)* The analysis of this transaction is shown in the T accounts.

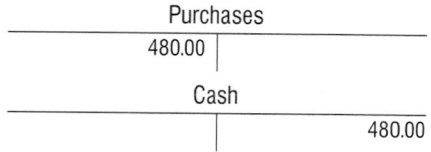

The amount of purchases is increased by this transaction. Thus, Purchases is debited for $480.00. The amount of cash is decreased by this transaction. Therefore, Cash is credited for $480.00.

The entry to record this cash purchase of merchandise is shown on line 2 of the cash payments journal, Illustration 20-7, page 482.

The date, *1*, is written in the Date column. The account debited, Purchases, is entered in the Account Title column. The number of the check, *149*, is written in the Ck. No. column. The amount debited to Purchases, *$480.00*, is recorded in the General Debit column. The amount credited to Cash, $480.00, is recorded in the Cash Credit column.

Journalizing cash payments for purchases on account

Normally, the total amount shown on a purchase invoice is the amount that a customer is expected to pay by an agreed due date. However, some vendors offer their customers an incentive to pay before the due date.

Cash discount. A customer is expected to pay the vendor for a sale within the credit period agreed upon. To encourage early payment, a vendor may allow a deduction from the invoice amount. A deduction that a vendor allows on the invoice amount to encourage prompt payment is called a cash discount. A cash discount is usually stated as a percentage that can be deducted from the invoice amount.

The terms of sale on an invoice may be written as *2/10, n/30*. These terms are commonly read *two ten, net thirty*. *Two ten* means 2% of the invoice amount may be deducted if the invoice is paid within 10 days of the invoice date. *Net thirty* means that the total invoice amount must be paid within 30 days. A business may also indicate the date for full payment of an invoice as *EOM*. Payment specified as *EOM* means that full payment is expected not later than the end of the month.

Purchases discount. A cash discount on purchases taken by a customer is called a purchases discount. When a purchases discount is taken, the customer pays less cash than the invoice amount previously recorded in the purchases account. Therefore, purchases discounts are deducted from purchases. Purchases discounts are recorded in a general ledger account titled *Purchases Discount*.

In Celluphone's general ledger, the account Purchases Discount is numbered 5110. The purchases discount account is in the cost of merchandise division of Celluphone's general ledger. An account that offsets a related account is known as a contra account. Thus, on an income statement, the contra account, Purchases Discount, is deducted from the balance of its related account, Purchases.

Purchases	
Debit side	Credit side
Normal balance	
Increase	Decrease

Purchases Discount	
Debit side	Credit side
	Normal balance
Decrease	Increase

Since contra accounts are deductions from their related accounts, contra account normal balances are opposite the normal balances of their related accounts. The normal balance for a purchases account is a debit. Therefore, the normal balance for Purchases Discount, a contra account to Purchases, is a credit as shown in the T accounts.

Cash payments on account with purchases discounts. Celluphone tries to pay all vendors on or before the date for taking the purchases discount. This policy reduces the cost of merchandise purchased by Celluphone.

March 8, 19--.
Paid cash on account to Cell Systems, $6,538.56, covering Purchase Invoice No. 39 for $6,672.00, less 2% discount, $133.44. Check No. 168.

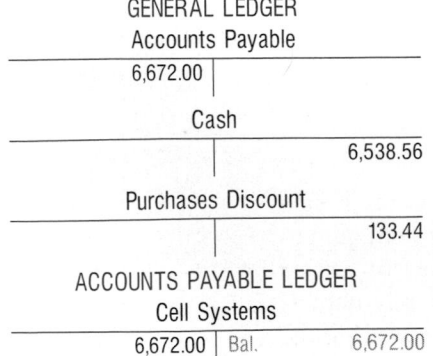

GENERAL LEDGER
Accounts Payable

6,672.00	

Cash

	6,538.56

Purchases Discount

	133.44

ACCOUNTS PAYABLE LEDGER
Cell Systems

6,672.00	Bal.	6,672.00

The source document for this payment on account transaction is a check. (*CONCEPT: Objective Evidence*) The analysis of this transaction is shown in the T accounts. Accounts Payable is debited for the amount of the purchase invoice, $6,672.00. This debit decreases the amount owed to vendors. This same amount, $6,672.00, is also debited to the account of Cell Systems in the accounts payable ledger.

Cash is credited for the amount of the check, $6,538.56. Purchases Discount is credited for the amount of the purchases discount, $133.44. The discount is figured by multiplying the amount of the purchase invoice, $6,672.00, by the discount rate, 2% ($6,672.00 × 2% = $133.44).

The cash payments journal entry to record this payment on account with a purchases discount is shown in Illustration 20-8.

	DATE	ACCOUNT TITLE	CK. NO.	POST. REF.	GENERAL DEBIT	GENERAL CREDIT	ACCOUNTS PAYABLE DEBIT	PURCHASES DISCOUNT CREDIT	CASH CREDIT	
21	8	Cell Systems	168				6 6 7 2 00	1 3 3 44	6 5 3 8 56	21
22										22

CASH PAYMENTS JOURNAL   PAGE 6

Illustration 20-8
Cash payments journal entry to record a cash payment on account with a purchases discount

The date, *8*, is written in the Date column. The vendor name, *Cell Systems*, is recorded in the Account Title column. The check number, *168*, is written in the Ck. No. column. The purchase invoice amount, *$6,672.00*, is entered in the Accounts Payable Debit column. The purchases discount amount, *$133.44*, is recorded in the Purchases Discount Credit column. The invoice amount less the purchases discount, *$6,538.56*, is entered in the Cash Credit column. The total of the two credits ($133.44 + $6,538.56) is $6,672.00, which is equal to the one debit of $6,672.00.

Purchases discounts are recorded frequently by Celluphone. Therefore, a special amount column for Purchases Discount Credit is provided in the cash payments journal.

Cash payments on account without purchases discounts. Some vendors do not provide purchases discounts. In this case the full invoice amount is paid. Celluphone purchased merchandise on account from Electro Sound on February 2. Electro Sound's credit terms are n/30. Therefore, Celluphone will pay the full amount of the purchase invoice, $1,740.00, within 30 days of the invoice date, February 2.

> March 2, 19--.
> Paid cash on account to Electro Sound, $1,740.00, covering Purchase Invoice No. 21. Check No. 150.

The source document for this payment on account transaction is a check. (CONCEPT: *Objective Evidence*) The analysis of this transaction is shown in the T accounts. Accounts Payable is debited for the amount of the purchase invoice, $1,740.00. This debit decreases the amount owed to vendors. This same amount, $1,740.00, is also debited to the account of Electro Sound in the accounts payable ledger. Cash is decreased by this transaction. Therefore, Cash is credited for the amount of the check, $1,740.00, which is also the full amount of the purchase invoice.

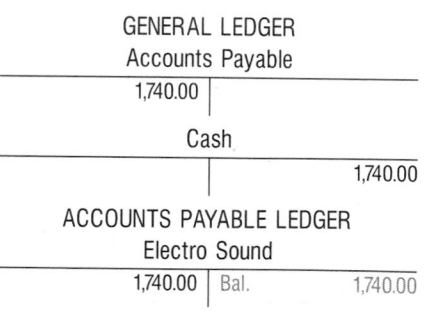

GENERAL LEDGER
Accounts Payable

1,740.00	

Cash

	1,740.00

ACCOUNTS PAYABLE LEDGER
Electro Sound

1,740.00	Bal.	1,740.00

The cash payments journal entry to record this payment on account without a purchases discount is shown in Illustration 20-9.

	DATE	ACCOUNT TITLE	CK. NO.	POST. REF.	GENERAL DEBIT	GENERAL CREDIT	ACCOUNTS PAYABLE DEBIT	PURCHASES DISCOUNT CREDIT	CASH CREDIT	
3	2	Electro Sound	150				1 7 4 0 00		1 7 4 0 00	3
4										4

CASH PAYMENTS JOURNAL   PAGE 6

Illustration 20-9
Cash payments journal
entry to record a cash
payment on account
without a purchases
discount

The date, 2, is written in the Date column. The vendor name, *Electro Sound*, is recorded in the Account Title column. The check number, *150*, is written in the Ck. No. column. The purchase invoice amount, *$1,740.00*, is entered in the Accounts Payable Debit column. The same amount, *$1,740.00*, is entered in the Cash Credit column.

Journalizing cash payments to replenish a petty cash fund

Establishing and replenishing a petty cash fund is described for Rugcare in Chapter 6. Celluphone follows procedures similar to those used by Rugcare to account for and safeguard its petty cash fund.

Regardless of how careful a petty cash custodian may be, errors may be made when making payments from a petty cash fund. These errors cause a difference between actual cash on hand and the custodian's record of the amount of cash that should be on hand. The amount of petty cash that should be on hand is the established amount of the petty cash fund less the amount of petty cash payments for the period. To keep the petty cash fund at a constant amount, differences are recorded at the end of a fiscal period as well as at other times when the petty cash fund is replenished. Differences are determined by comparing the amount that should be on hand with the amount of cash in the petty cash box.

Cash short and over account. Cash in the petty cash box may be less than what the cash balance should be according to the custodian's records. A petty cash on hand amount that is less than a recorded amount is called cash short. Cash in the petty cash box may also be more than the cash balance should be according to the custodian's records. A petty cash on hand amount that is more than a recorded amount is called cash over. Amounts of petty cash short and petty cash over are recorded in an account titled *Cash Short and Over*.

A cash short and over account is a temporary account. The account is used to record shortages and overages, if any, each time the petty cash fund is replenished throughout the year. At the end of the fiscal year, the cash short and over account is closed to Income Summary. The cash short and over account is unique because it may have the characteristics of an expense account or the characteristics of a revenue account. If the balance of the account is a debit, similar to expense accounts, the account balance is an expense. If the balance of the account is a credit, similar to revenue accounts, the account balance is revenue. Therefore, the balance side of a cash short and over account determines whether it is an expense or revenue.

Cash short is an expense and, therefore, is debited to the account Cash Short and Over. Cash over is revenue and, therefore, is credited to Cash Short and Over. The increase sides for both cash short and cash over are shown in the T account.

Cash Short and Over	
Debit side Increase cash short	Credit side Increase cash over

Petty cash short. A petty cash on hand amount that is less than a recorded amount is known as cash short. Celluphone has an established petty cash fund of $300.00. Prior to replenishment of the petty cash fund on March 31, the custodian had receipts for the following total payments: supplies, $87.80; advertising, $43.75; and miscellaneous, $97.90. A cash count shows $66.55 in the petty cash box. A comparison is made between the cash that should be on hand and the amount actually on hand in the petty cash box. From the information above, Celluphone's petty cash custodian prepares a petty cash report, as shown in Illustration 20-10.

PETTY CASH REPORT Date: March 31, 19--		
Explanation	Amounts	
Fund total		300 00
Payments:		
Supplies	87 80	
Advertising	43 75	
Miscellaneous	97 90	
Less total payments		229 45
Equals recorded amount on hand		70 55
Less actual amount on hand		66 55
Equals cash short		4 00
Total payments		229 45
Plus cash short		4 00
Equals amount to replenish		233 45

Illustration 20-10
Petty cash report for replenishment of a petty cash fund with cash short

The petty cash report in Illustration 20-10 shows that the actual cash on hand ($66.55) is $4.00 less than the amount the records show should be on hand ($70.55). Therefore, the petty cash fund is short.

The petty cash fund is replenished for the amount paid out, $229.45, plus cash short, $4.00. This total amount, $233.45, restores the fund's cash balance to its original amount, $300.00 ($229.45 + $4.00 + $66.55 cash on hand).

March 31, 19--.
Paid cash to replenish the petty cash fund, $233.45: supplies, $87.80; advertis-
ing, $43.75; miscellaneous, $97.90; cash short, $4.00. Check No. 209.

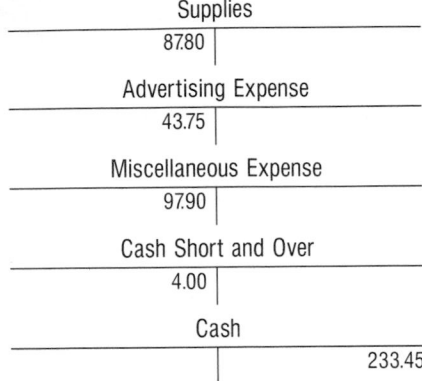

The source document for this replenishment of a petty cash fund transaction is a check. *(CONCEPT: Objective Evidence)* The analysis of this transaction to replenish petty cash is shown in the T accounts.

Debit entries include the accounts for which cash payments have been made plus Cash Short and Over. Cash is decreased by this transaction. Therefore, Cash is credited for the amount of the check to replenish the petty cash fund, $233.45, which is also the sum of the debit entries.

The cash payments journal entry to record this replenishment of the petty cash fund with cash short is shown in Illustration 20-11.

						GENERAL		ACCOUNTS PAYABLE DEBIT	PURCHASES DISCOUNT CREDIT	CASH CREDIT	
	DATE	ACCOUNT TITLE	CK. NO.	POST. REF.		DEBIT	CREDIT				
19	31	*Supplies*	209			87 80				233 45	19
20		*Advertising Expense*				43 75					20
21		*Miscellaneous Exp.*				97 90					21
22		*Cash Short and Over*				4 00					22
23											23

CASH PAYMENTS JOURNAL   PAGE 8

Illustration 20-11
Cash payments journal entry to record replenishment of a petty cash fund with cash short

Petty cash over. A petty cash on hand amount that is more than a recorded amount is known as cash over.

Prior to Celluphone's replenishment of the petty cash fund on April 30, the custodian had receipts for the following total payments: supplies, $107.45; advertising, $57.00; and miscellaneous, $121.90. A cash count shows $16.20 in the petty cash box. A comparison is made between the cash that should be on hand and the amount actually on hand in the petty cash box. From the information above, Celluphone's petty cash custodian prepares a petty cash report, as shown in Illustration 20-12.

The petty cash report in Illustration 20-12 shows that cash on hand ($16.20) is $2.55 more than what the records show should be on hand ($13.65). Therefore, the petty cash fund is over.

The petty cash fund will be replenished for the amount paid out, $286.35, less cash over, $2.55. This net amount, $283.80, will restore the

PETTY CASH REPORT	Date: April 30, 19--		
Explanation	Amounts		
Fund total			300 00
Payments:			
Supplies	107 45		
Advertising	57 00		
Miscellaneous	121 90		
Less total payments			286 35
Equals recorded amount on hand			13 65
Less actual amount on hand			16 20
Equals cash over			2 55
Total payments			286 35
Less cash over			2 55
Equals amount to replenish			283 80

Illustration 20-12
Petty cash report for
replenishment of a petty
cash fund with cash over

fund's cash balance to its original amount, $300.00 ($286.35 − $2.55 +
$16.20 cash on hand).

April 30, 19--.
Paid cash to replenish the petty cash fund, $283.80: supplies, $107.45; advertising, $57.00; miscellaneous, $121.90; cash over, $2.55. Check No. 267.

The source document for this transaction is a check. (CONCEPT: *Objective Evidence*) The analysis of this transaction to replenish petty cash is shown in the T accounts.

Debit entries include the accounts for which cash payments have been made. Credit entries are Cash, $283.80, and Cash Short and Over, $2.55, since cash on hand was over this period. The sum of the debit entries equals the sum of the credit entries to Cash and Cash Short and Over.

The cash payments journal entry to record this replenishment of the petty cash fund with cash over is shown in Illustration 20-13.

Supplies	
107.45	

Advertising Expense	
57.00	

Miscellaneous Expense	
121.90	

Cash Short and Over	
	2.55

Cash	
	283.80

CASH PAYMENTS JOURNAL   PAGE *11*

	DATE	ACCOUNT TITLE	CK. NO.	POST. REF.	GENERAL DEBIT	GENERAL CREDIT	ACCOUNTS PAYABLE DEBIT	PURCHASES DISCOUNT CREDIT	CASH CREDIT	
18	30	Supplies	267		107 45				283 80	18
19		Advertising Expense			57 00					19
20		Miscellaneous Exp.			121 90					20
21		Cash Short and Over				2 55				21
22										22

Illustration 20-13   Cash payments journal entry to record replenishment of a petty cash fund with cash over

In Celluphone's general ledger, the account Cash Short and Over is numbered 8105. The cash short and over account may be an expense or a revenue, depending on whether it has a debit or credit balance. Celluphone lists the account in the other expense division of its general ledger, however, because the balance at year end normally is a debit, making the balance of the account an expense.

Posting from a cash payments journal to an accounts payable ledger

Illustration 20-14 shows the posting of a cash payments journal entry to a vendor account. Each entry in the Accounts Payable Debit column of a cash payments journal affects the vendor named in the Account Title column. Each amount listed in this column is posted separately to the proper vendor account in the accounts payable ledger. In this way, each vendor account shows an up-to-date balance.

CASH PAYMENTS JOURNAL PAGE *6*

	DATE	ACCOUNT TITLE	CK. NO.	POST. REF.	1 GENERAL DEBIT	2 GENERAL CREDIT	3 ACCOUNTS PAYABLE DEBIT	4 PURCHASES DISCOUNT CREDIT	5 CASH CREDIT	
3	*2*	*Electro Sound*	*150*	*240*			*1 740 00*		*1 740 00*	3
4										4

VENDOR *Electro Sound* VENDOR NO. *240*

DATE		ITEM	POST. REF.	DEBIT	CREDIT	CREDIT BALANCE
19-- Mar.	*1*	*Balance*	✓			*2 460 00*
	2		*CP6*	*1 740 00*		*720 00*

Illustration 20-14
Posting from a cash payments journal to an accounts payable ledger

The date, 2, is written in the Date column of the vendor account. *CP6* is entered in the Post. Ref. column. The abbreviation *CP6* means page 6 of the cash payments journal. The amount in the Accounts Payable Debit column, *$1,740.00,* is posted to the Debit column of the vendor account. The amount in the Debit column of the vendor account is subtracted from the previous balance in the Credit Balance column ($2,460.00 − $1,740.00 = $720.00). The new balance, *$720.00,* is recorded in the Credit Balance column. The vendor number for Electro Sound, *240,* is written in the Post. Ref. column of the cash payments journal. This last step shows completion of posting of this line.

Posting from a cash payments journal to a general ledger

Each amount in the General columns of a cash payments journal is posted separately to a general ledger account. Therefore, the totals of the general amount columns are not posted. However, the monthly total of each special amount column is posted to a general ledger account.

Posting from the general columns of a cash payments journal. Separate amounts in the General columns are posted individually to the general ledger account named in the Account Title column. Illustration 20-15 shows the posting from a General column of a cash payments journal to a general ledger account.

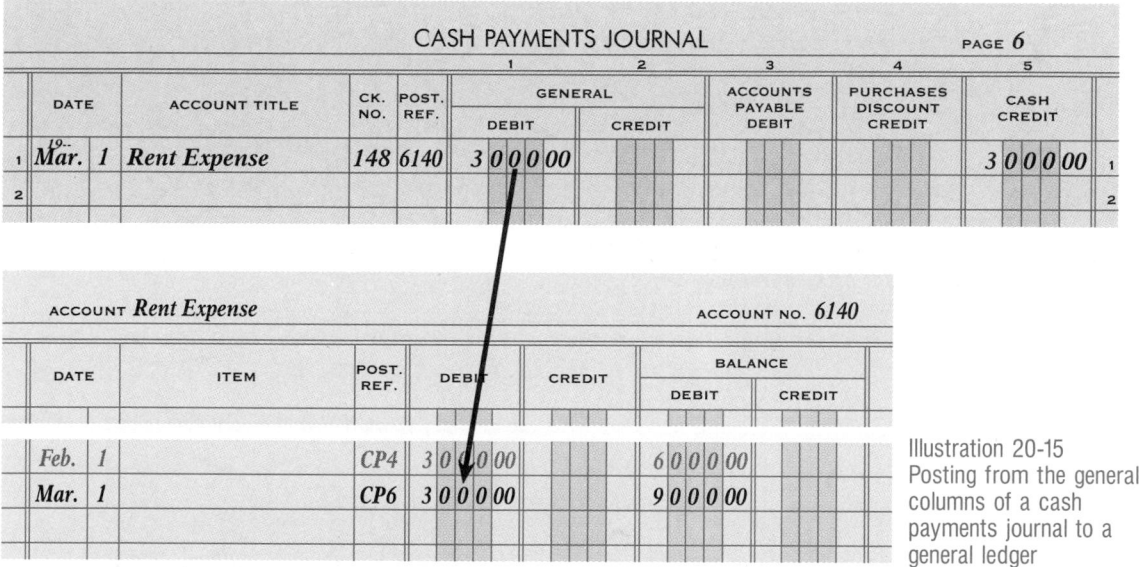

Illustration 20-15
Posting from the general columns of a cash payments journal to a general ledger

The date, *Mar. 1*, is written in the Date column of the account Rent Expense. *CP6* is recorded in the Post. Ref. column to show that the amount is from page 6 of the cash payments journal. The amount in the General Debit column, *$3,000.00*, is posted to the Debit column of the general ledger account Rent Expense. The existing amount in the Balance Debit column, *$6,000.00*, is added to the March 1 debit entry, *$3,000.00*. The new balance, *$9,000.00*, is written in the Balance Debit column. The number of the rent expense account, *6140*, is entered in the Post. Ref. column of the cash payments journal. This account number shows that posting of the general amount on this line in the journal is complete.

Posting totals from the special columns of a cash payments journal. At the end of each month, equality of debits and credits is proved for a cash payments journal. The cash payments journal is ruled as shown in Illustration 20-16. The total of each special column is then posted to the account named in the journal's column headings. The date and CP8 are recorded in the Date and Post. Ref. columns of the account. The total is entered in the appropriate amount column, and the new account balance is recorded. As a last step, the account number is written in parentheses below the journal column total. This procedure is followed until all special amount column totals are posted.

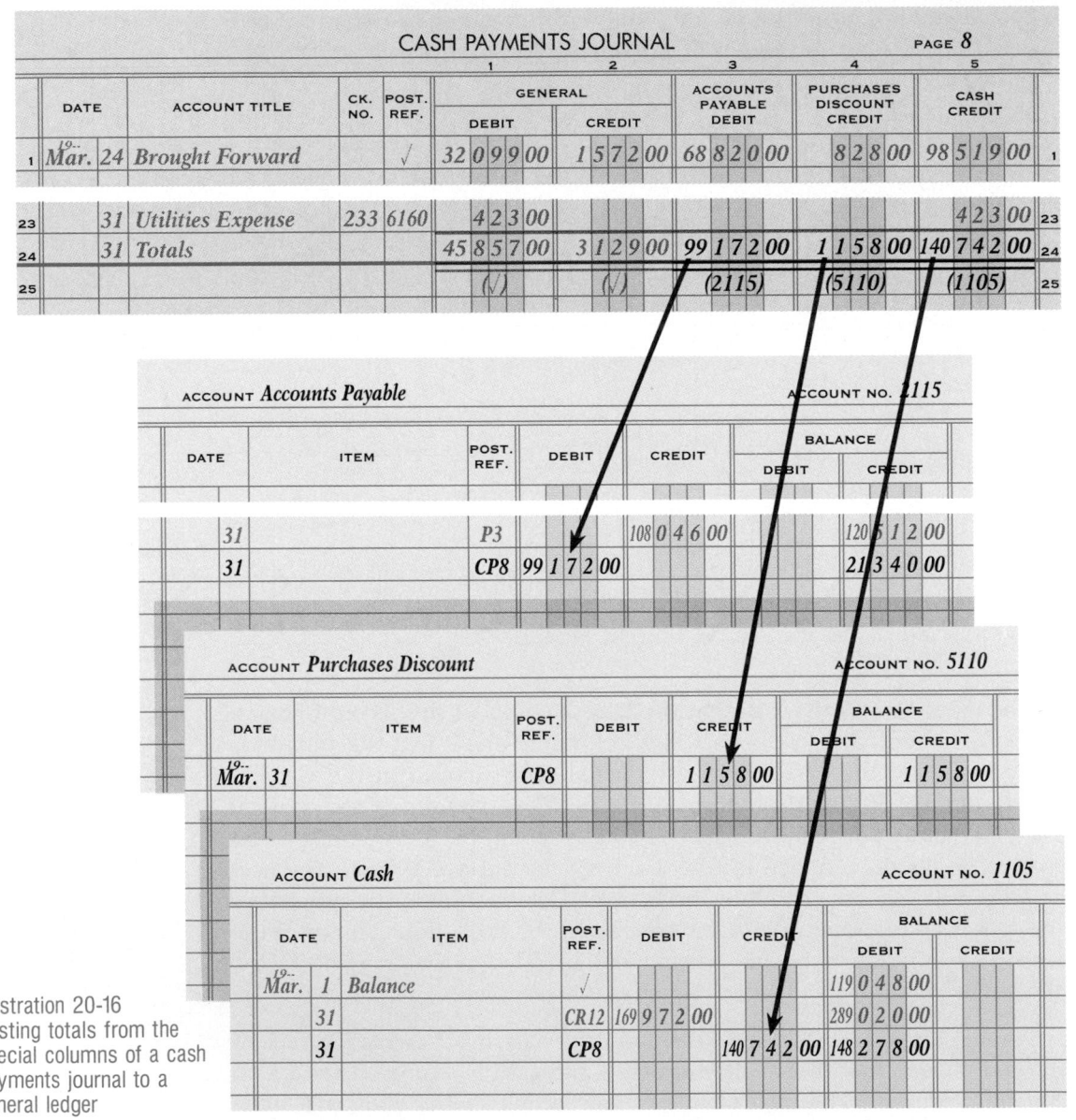

Illustration 20-16
Posting totals from the special columns of a cash payments journal to a general ledger

Posting from a cash receipts journal to the cash account, shown on line 2 of the cash account, Illustration 20-16, is described in Chapter 21.

The totals of the General columns are not posted. Each amount in these columns was posted separately to a general ledger account. To indicate that these totals are not to be posted, a check mark is placed in parentheses below each column total.

Illustration 20-17 shows a summary of the procedure for journalizing and posting cash payments using a cash payments journal.

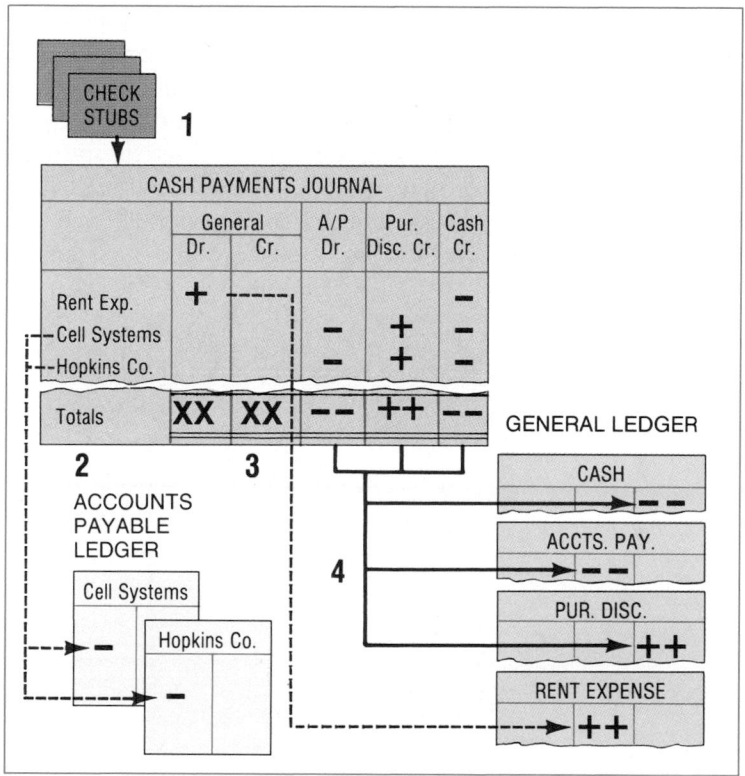

Illustration 20-17
Summary of journalizing and posting using a cash payments journal

1 Celluphone records all cash payments in a 5-column cash payments journal.

2 Amounts in the Accounts Payable Debit column are posted frequently to the named vendor account in the accounts payable ledger.

3 Individual items in the General Debit and Credit columns are posted frequently during the month to the general ledger.

4 At the end of the month, the totals of the special columns are posted to the general ledger.

RECORDING TRANSACTIONS USING A GENERAL JOURNAL

Not all transactions are recorded in Celluphone's special journals. For example, when Celluphone buys supplies on account, the transaction is not recorded in any of the special journals. The transaction is not a cash payment transaction, so it is not recorded in the cash payments journal. The transaction is not a purchase of merchandise on account, so it is not recorded in the purchases journal.

A journal with two amount columns in which all kinds of entries can be recorded is called a general journal. A general journal has only two amount columns: a Debit amount column and a Credit amount column. Any journal entry can be recorded in a general journal by writing the account title and amount for each account affected. Celluphone uses a general journal for recording journal entries that cannot be recorded in any of the special journals. Celluphone records transactions for purchases returns and allowances and for buying supplies on account in its general journal. The relationship between Celluphone's general journal and the expanded journal described in Chapter 12 is shown in Illustration 20-18.

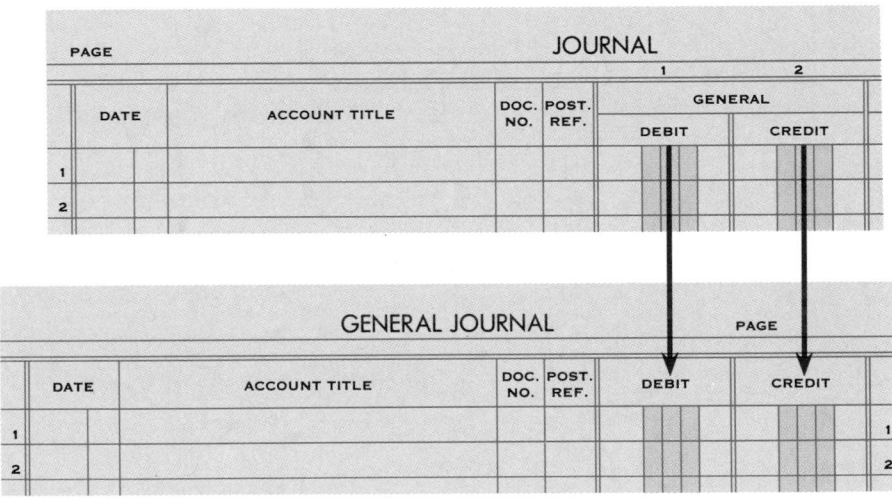

Illustration 20-18
General journal

Purchases returns and allowances

A customer may not want to keep merchandise that is inferior in quality or is damaged when received. A customer may be allowed to return part or all of the merchandise purchased. Credit allowed for the purchase price of returned merchandise, resulting in a decrease in the customer's accounts payable, is called a purchases return. When merchandise is damaged but still usable or is of a different quality than that ordered, the vendor may let the customer keep the merchandise at a reduced price. Credit allowed for part of the purchase price of merchandise that is not returned, resulting in a decrease in the customer's accounts payable, is called a pur-chases allowance.

A purchases return or allowance should be confirmed in writing. The details may be stated in a letter or on a form. A form prepared by the customer showing the price deduction taken by the customer for returns and allowances is called a debit memorandum. The form is called a debit memorandum because the customer records the amount as a debit (deduction) to the vendor account to show the decrease in the amount owed.

The customer may use a copy of the debit memorandum as the source document for journalizing purchases returns and allowances. However, the customer may wait for written confirmation from the vendor and use that confirmation as the source document. Celluphone issues a debit memorandum for each purchases return or allowance. This debit memorandum is used as the source document for purchases returns and allowances transactions. *(CONCEPT: Objective Evidence)* The transaction can be recorded immediately without waiting for written confirmation from the vendor. The original of the debit memorandum is sent to the vendor. The carbon copy is kept by Celluphone. The debit memorandum form used by Celluphone is shown in Illustration 20-19.

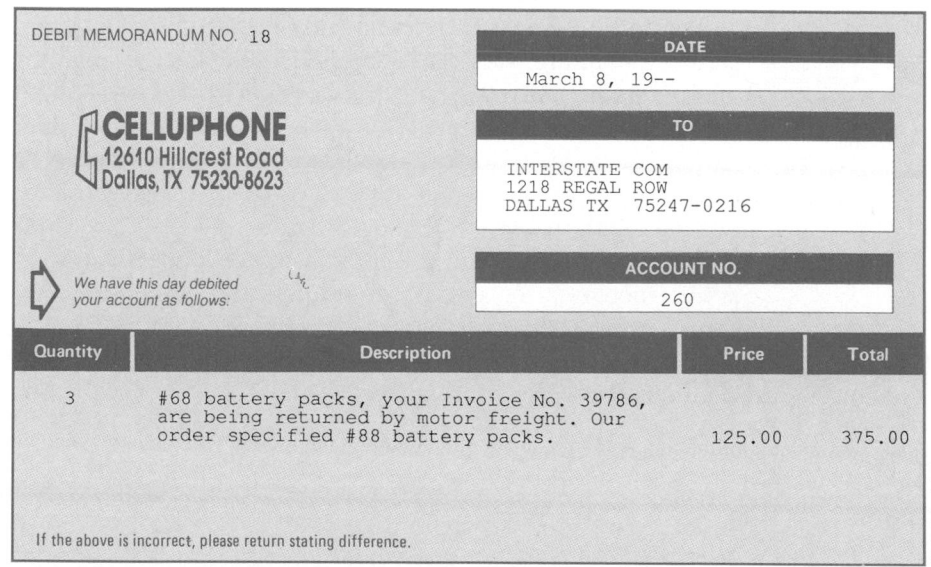

Illustration 20-19
Debit memorandum for purchases returns and allowances

Some businesses credit the purchases account for the amount of the purchases return or allowance. However, better information is provided if these amounts are credited to a separate account titled *Purchases Returns and Allowances.* A business can see how large its purchases returns and allowances are. Also, a business can see if purchases returns and allowances are increasing or decreasing from year to year. If the amounts are large, one account may be kept for purchases returns and another account for purchases allowances. Usually a single purchases returns and allowances account is satisfactory.

Purchases	
Debit side	Credit side
Normal balance	
Increase	Decrease

Purchases Returns and Allowances	
Debit side	Credit side
	Normal balance
Decrease	Increase

Purchases returns and allowances decrease the amount of purchases. Therefore, the account Purchases Returns and Allowances is a contra account to Purchases. Thus, the normal account balance of Purchases Returns and Allowances is a credit, the opposite of the normal account balance of Purchases, a debit, as shown in the T accounts.

Journalizing purchases returns and allowances

Celluphone uses a single account, Purchases Returns and Allowances. The account is in the cost of merchandise division of Celluphone's chart of accounts.

March 8, 19--.
Returned merchandise to Interstate Com, $375.00, covering Purchase Invoice No. 30. Debit Memorandum No. 18.

The source document for recording a purchases return or allowance is a debit memorandum. *(CONCEPT: Objective Evidence)* The analysis of this transaction is shown in the T accounts.

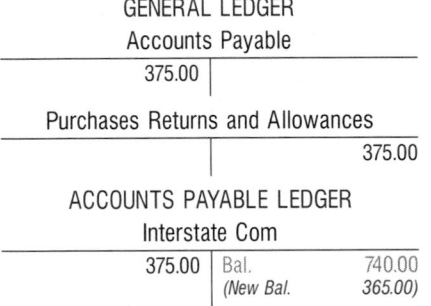

GENERAL LEDGER
Accounts Payable

| 375.00 | |

Purchases Returns and Allowances

| | 375.00 |

ACCOUNTS PAYABLE LEDGER
Interstate Com

| 375.00 | Bal.   740.00 |
| | (New Bal.   365.00) |

The amount owed to a vendor is decreased by this transaction. Therefore, Accounts Payable is debited for the amount of the return, $375.00. The same amount is also debited to the account of Interstate Com in the accounts payable ledger. Because Purchases has a normal debit balance, the contra purchases account, Purchases Returns and Allowances, has a normal credit balance. Therefore, the purchases returns and allowances account is increased by a credit. Since this transaction increases the purchases returns and allowances account, Purchases Returns and Allowances is credited for $375.00.

The general journal entry to record this purchases returns and allowances transaction is shown in Illustration 20-20.

Illustration 20-20
General journal entry to record purchases returns and allowances

		DATE		ACCOUNT TITLE	DOC. NO.	POST. REF.	DEBIT	CREDIT	
			GENERAL JOURNAL					PAGE 3	
1		*Mar.* 8		*Accounts Payable/Interstate Com*	DM18	/	3 7 5 00		1
2				*Purchases Ret. and Allow.*				3 7 5 00	2
3									3

The date, *19--, Mar. 8*, is written in the Date column. The single debit amount is posted both to the general ledger account and the accounts payable ledger account. Therefore, the accounts to be debited, *Accounts Payable/Interstate Com*, are entered in the Account Title column. A diagonal line is placed between the two account titles to separate them clearly. A diagonal line is also placed in the Post. Ref. column to show that the debit amount is to be posted to two accounts. The source document for the entry, *DM18*, is entered in the Doc. No. column. The amount of the debit, *$375.00*, is recorded in the Debit column. The account to be credited, *Purchases Returns and Allowances*, is written on the next line in the Account Title column. This account title is indented about one centimeter. The amount of the credit, *$375.00*, is recorded in the Credit column.

Journalizing buying supplies on account

Celluphone generally buys supplies on account. Supplies are not merchandise. Only merchandise purchased on account is recorded in the purchases journal. Therefore, when any item that is not merchandise is bought on account, the transaction is recorded in the general journal.

March 9, 19--.
Bought supplies on account from Kryger Supplies, $228.00. Memorandum No. 38.

The source document for this buying supplies on account transaction is a memorandum. *(CONCEPT: Objective Evidence)* A memorandum is used as the source document so that the supplies will not be recorded unintentionally as merchandise. The invoice received from Kryger Supplies is attached to the memorandum to confirm the price paid.

The analysis of this transaction is shown in the T accounts. This transaction increases the balance of the supplies account. Therefore, Supplies is debited for $228.00. The amount owed to a vendor is also increased by this transaction. Therefore, Accounts Payable is credited for $228.00. The same amount is also credited to the account of Kryger Supplies in the accounts payable ledger.

The general journal entry to record this buying supplies on account transaction is shown in Illustration 20-21.

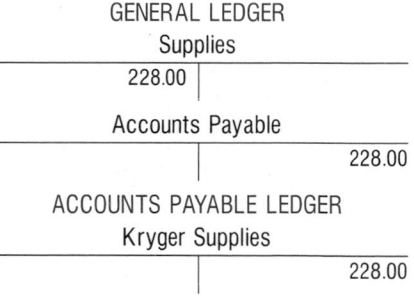

```
            GENERAL LEDGER
                Supplies
        228.00    |
        _____
            Accounts Payable
                  |      228.00
        _____
       ACCOUNTS PAYABLE LEDGER
            Kryger Supplies
                  |      228.00
```

GENERAL JOURNAL   PAGE *3*

	DATE	ACCOUNT TITLE	DOC. NO.	POST. REF.	DEBIT	CREDIT	
3	9	*Supplies*	M38		2 2 8 00		3
4		*Accounts Pay./Kryger Supp.*		/		2 2 8 00	4
5							5

Illustration 20-21
General journal entry to record buying supplies on account

The date, *9*, is written in the Date column. The account to be debited, *Supplies*, is recorded in the Account Title column. The source document, *M38*, is entered in the Doc. No. column. The amount of the debit, *$228.00*, is entered in the Debit column. The accounts to be credited, *Accounts Payable/ Kryger Supplies*, are written on the next line in the Account Title column. These accounts are indented about one centimeter. A diagonal line is placed between the two account titles. A diagonal line is also placed in the Post. Ref. column to show that the credit is to be posted to two accounts. The amount of the credit, *$228.00*, is entered in the Credit column.

Posting from a general journal

Each amount in the general journal Debit and Credit columns is posted separately to a general ledger account. The posting of an entry for supplies bought on account from a general journal is shown in Illustration 20-22.

The debit amount is posted first. The date, *9*, is written in the Date column of the general ledger account Supplies. The abbreviation for the general journal, *G3*, is entered in the Post. Ref. column of the supplies account. The amount from the general journal Debit column, *$228.00*, is recorded in the Debit column of the supplies account. The amount in the Debit column is added to the previous balance in the Balance Debit column ($870.00 + $228.00 = $1,098.00). The new balance, *$1,098.00*, is recorded in the Balance Debit column. The supplies account number, *1140*, is written in the Post. Ref. column of the general journal to show the completion of posting for this line.

Next the credit amount is posted. The date, *9*, is written in the Date column of the general ledger account Accounts Payable. The abbreviation for the general journal, *G3*, is entered in the Post. Ref. column of the accounts payable account. The amount from the general journal Credit column, *$228.00*, is recorded in the Credit column of the accounts payable account. The amount in the Credit column is added to the previous balance in the Balance Credit column ($14,900.00 + $228.00 = $15,128.00). The new balance, *$15,128.00*, is recorded in the Balance Credit column. The accounts payable account number, *2115*, is written at the left of the diagonal line in the Post. Ref. column of the general journal. The account number shows the completion of posting for this line to the general ledger.

After posting to the general ledger accounts is complete, the credit amount is also posted to the accounts payable subsidiary ledger. The date, *19--, Mar. 9*, is written in the Date column of the Kryger Supplies account. The abbreviation for the general journal, *G3*, is entered in the Post. Ref. column. The amount from the general journal Credit column, *$228.00*, is recorded in the Credit column of the Kryger Supplies account. Since there is no previous balance in the subsidiary account, the amount in the Credit column is also the balance of the account. Therefore, *$228.00*, is also entered in the Credit Balance column. The Kryger Supplies account number,

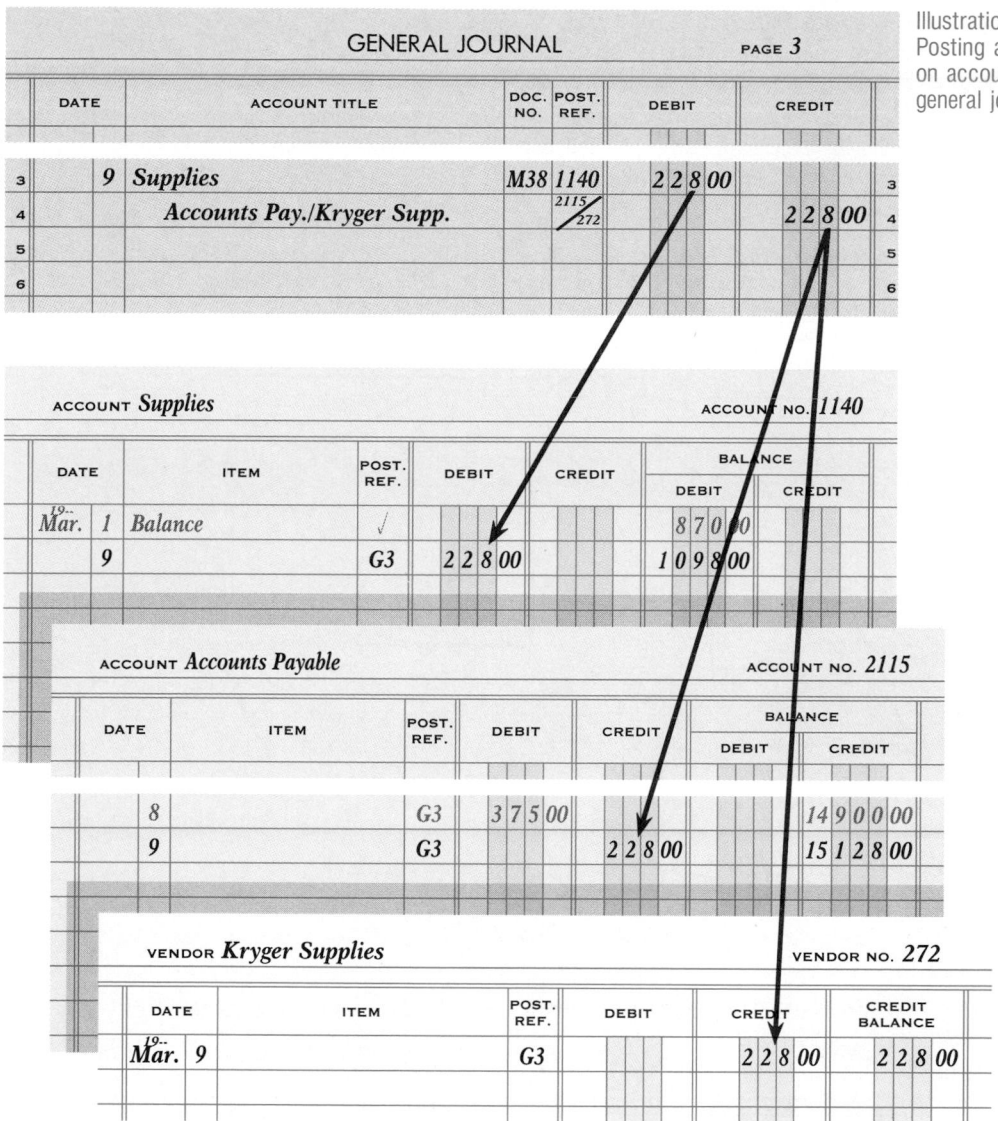

Illustration 20-22
Posting a buying supplies
on account entry from a
general journal

272, is written at the right of the diagonal line in the Post. Ref. column of the general journal. The vendor account number shows the completion of posting for this line to the subsidiary ledger.

Illustration 20-23 shows a summary of the procedure for journalizing and posting transactions using a general journal.

1 Celluphone records in a general journal all transactions that cannot be recorded in any of the special journals.

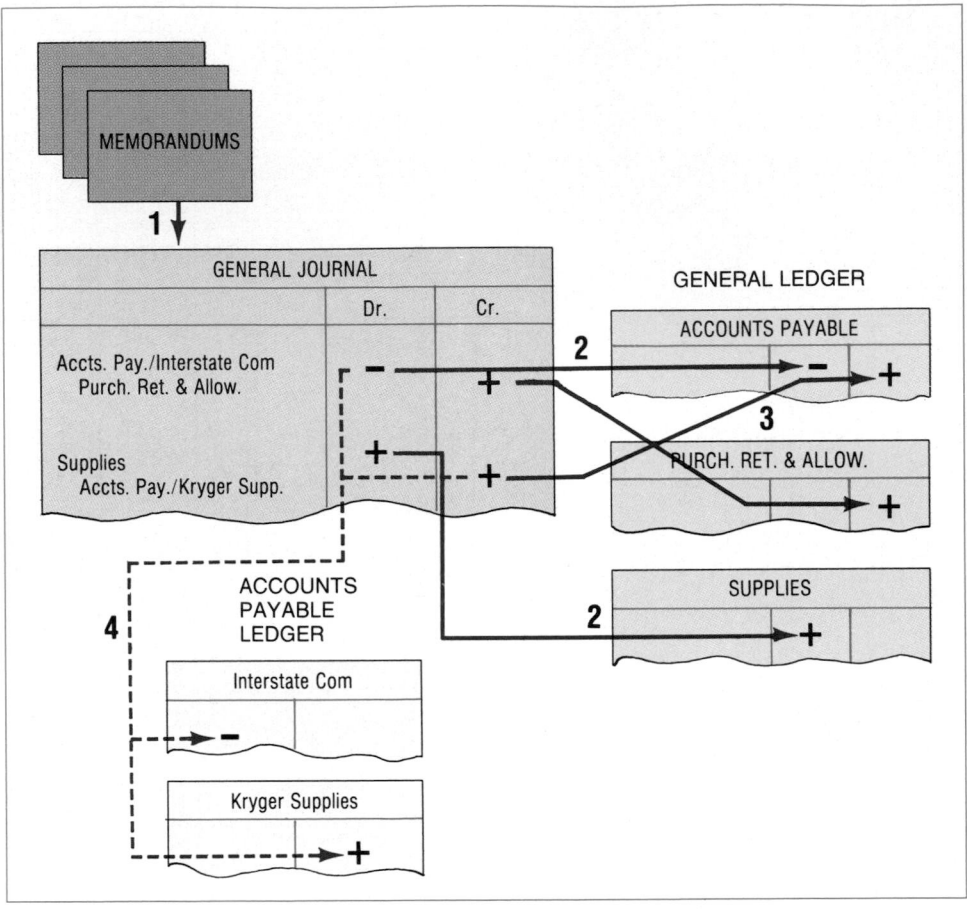

Illustration 20-23
Summary of journalizing
and posting using a
general journal

2 Amounts in the Debit column are posted to the general ledger.

3 Amounts in the Credit column are posted to the general ledger.

4 Amounts debited or credited to Accounts Payable are posted to the named vendor account in the accounts payable subsidiary ledger.

PREPARING A SCHEDULE OF ACCOUNTS PAYABLE

A listing of vendor accounts, account balances, and total amount due all vendors is known as a schedule of accounts payable. A schedule of accounts payable is prepared before financial statements are prepared to prove the accounts payable ledger. If the total amount due on the schedule of accounts payable equals the accounts payable controlling account balance in the general ledger, the accounts payable ledger is proved. Preparation of a schedule of accounts payable is described in Chapter 14.

SUMMARY OF RECORDING PURCHASES AND CASH PAYMENTS USING SPECIAL JOURNALS

The charts shown in Illustration 20-24 summarize the entries for purchases, cash payments, and other transactions in special journals and a general journal.

TRANSACTION	PURCHASES JOURNAL
	PURCHASES DEBIT ACCTS. PAY. CR.
Purchases on account	X

TRANSACTIONS	CASH PAYMENTS JOURNAL				
	1	2	3	4	5
	GENERAL		ACCOUNTS PAYABLE DEBIT	PURCHASES DISCOUNT CREDIT	CASH CREDIT
	DEBIT	CREDIT			
Cash payment for expenses	X				X
Cash purchases	X				X
Cash payment for purchases on account with purchases discount			X	X	X
Cash payment for purchases on account without purchases discount			X		X
Cash payment to replenish petty cash with cash short	X				X
Cash payment to replenish petty cash with cash over	X	X			X

TRANSACTIONS	GENERAL JOURNAL	
	DEBIT	CREDIT
Purchases returns and allowances	X	X
Buying supplies on account	X	X

Illustration 20-24
Summary of recording purchases and cash payments using special journals

■ ACCOUNTING TERMS

What is the meaning of each of the following?

1. corporation
2. share of stock
3. capital stock
4. special journal
5. purchases journal
6. cash payments journal

7. list price
8. trade discount
9. cash discount
10. purchases discount
11. cash short

12. cash over
13. general journal
14. purchases return
15. purchases allowance
16. debit memorandum

■ QUESTIONS FOR INDIVIDUAL STUDY

1. What kind of accounting system should a business use?

2. Which accounting concept is being applied when a business reports financial information for a specified period of time?

3. What are some business transactions a corporation can conduct in its own name?

4. What is the principal difference between the accounting records of a corporation and those of a proprietorship or partnership?

5. Which accounting concept is being applied when a corporation keeps only information in its accounting system that relates to the corporation?

6. What is the major purpose for applying the Unit of Measurement concept by recording all business transactions in a common unit of measurement — the dollar?

7. What is a common source document for recording a purchase on account?

8. Which accounting concept is being applied when a business requires a source document as the basis for recording a transaction?

9. Which accounting concept is being applied when a business records purchases at the actual amount paid for the merchandise?

10. What accounts are affected, and how, when the total amount of the purchases journal is posted?

11. What is the last step in posting a purchases journal to a general ledger to show that posting is complete?

12. Which cash payments made by Celluphone are recorded in a cash payments journal?

13. When a trade discount is received on purchases, what journal entry is made to show the amount of the trade discount?

14. Why would a vendor grant a cash discount to a customer?

15. What is meant by terms of sale 2/10, n/30?

16. What kind of account offsets a related account?

17. What accounts are affected, and how, when a check is issued as payment on account for a purchase with a purchases discount?

18. How is a balance in the cash short and over account treated at the end of a fiscal period?

19. If cash is short when a petty cash fund is replenished, what entry is made to Cash Short and Over to record the shortage?

20. If cash is over when a petty cash fund is replenished, what entry is made to Cash Short and Over to record the overage?

21. Why are the totals for the General Debit and Credit columns of a cash payments journal not posted?

22. If purchases returns and allowances are a decrease in purchases, why are returns and allowances credited to a separate account?

23. When supplies are bought on account, why is the entry made in a general journal instead of a purchases journal?

CASES FOR MANAGEMENT DECISION

CASE 1 McLain Florists, Inc., has employed an accounting firm to install a new accounting system using special journals. You and two other accountants are designing the special journals. Alisa Matthews, one of the accountants, recommends a cash payments journal with one special column — Cash Credit. Jose Ramundo, the other accountant, recommends a cash payments journal with three special columns — Accounts Payable Debit, Purchases Discount Credit, and Cash Credit. You have been asked to decide which cash payments journal should be used. Give your decision and the reason for that decision.

CASE 2 Gemini Company has established a $300.00 petty cash fund. During a routine review of the petty cash records, you discover that small shortages totaling $20.00 have occurred over the past four months. The fund custodian, Elaine Hilton, has not listed cash short or over on any of the reports prepared for replenishment. When asked about this practice, Miss Hilton said that she always waits until the amount of the shortage is significant — approximately $50.00. Then she requests replenishment for the amount of the shortage. What is your opinion of this practice? What action do you recommend?

CASE 3 Thomas Hill has just been hired as an accountant by the Fit-Right Clothing Company. Soon after starting to work, Mr. Hill suggested that the purchases journal be used to record all items acquired by the company on account, including merchandise and office supplies. He contends that besides eliminating the confusion of deciding which journal to use for each item acquired, net income will also be easier to figure because all items bought would be summarized together. Is Mr. Hill's suggestion an acceptable alternative? Explain your response.

DRILLS FOR UNDERSTANDING

DRILL 20-D1   Figuring petty cash short and petty cash over

Four different companies have the following information related to petty cash transactions.

Company	Petty Cash Record				Amount of Cash in Cash Box
	Beginning Balance	Distribution of Payments			
		Supplies	Advertising Expense	Miscellaneous Expense	
A	$300.00	$46.25	$76.32	$91.87	$ 85.56
B	250.00	24.76	82.35	18.21	120.68
C	150.00	12.43	51.45	14.15	78.97
D	200.00	53.98	25.34	34.25	84.43

Instructions: For each company, determine the amount, if any, of petty cash short or petty cash over.

DRILL 20-D2   Analyzing replenishing a petty cash fund

Petty cash is replenished for the amounts and on the dates shown in the following table.

Date on Which Replenished	Monthly Totals of Petty Cash Payment Records				
	Supplies	Advertising Expense	Miscellaneous Expense	Cash Short	Cash Over
May 31	$54.50	$15.30	$31.30	$4.01	
June 30	25.60	45.90	16.70	2.54	
July 31	14.20	64.00	42.20		$6.39
August 31	66.00	45.50	22.30	1.51	

Instructions: For each date, prepare T accounts for the accounts affected by the cash payments journal entry to replenish petty cash. Record the amounts on the debit or credit side of each T account to show how the accounts are affected.

DRILL 20-D3 Analyzing the journalizing of purchases and cash payments transactions

Use a form similar to the following.

Trans. No.	(A) Account(s) Debited	(B) Account(s) Credited	(C) Journal in Which Recorded	(D) Name of Amount Column(s) Used in Journal	(E)
				For Amount Debited	For Amount Credited
1.	Accounts Payable Hubburd Co.	Cash	Cash Payments	Accounts Payable Debit	Cash Credit

Instructions: Complete the form for each of the following transactions. Write in Column A the title of the account(s) debited. Write in Column B the title of the account(s) credited. Write in Column C the name of the journal in which the transaction is recorded. Write in Columns D and E the names of the journal amount column(s) in which debit and credit amounts are recorded. Transaction 1 is given as an example.

Transactions
1. Paid cash on account to Hubburd Co.; no discount.
2. Purchased merchandise on account from Westward Company.
3. Bought supplies for cash.
4. Paid cash for rent.
5. Paid cash on account to Westward Company; no discount.
6. Purchased merchandise on account from Sadler, Inc.
7. Paid cash for advertising.
8. Returned merchandise to Westward Company.
9. Purchased merchandise for cash.
10. Returned merchandise to Sadler, Inc.
11. Paid cash on account to Olympus Gauge Company for a purchase invoice less discount.

The solution to Drill 20-D3 is needed to complete Drill 20-D4.

DRILL 20-D4 Analyzing the posting of purchases and cash payments transactions

The solution to Drill 20-D3 is needed to complete Drill 20-D4.

Use a form similar to the following.

Trans. No.	(A) Accounts Affected	(B) Amounts Posted Individually to		(D) Amounts Not Posted Individually to Any Ledger
		General Ledger	(C) Accounts Payable Ledger	
1.	Accounts Payable			✓
	Hubburd Co.		✓	
	Cash			✓

Instructions: 1. Write in Column A the titles of the accounts affected by each transaction in Drill 20-D3. These account titles are taken from Columns A and B of completed Drill 20-D3.

2. Place a check mark in Column B if the amount is posted individually to the general ledger. Place a check mark in Column C if the amount is posted individually to the accounts payable ledger. Place a check mark in Column D if the amount is not posted individually to any ledger. Transaction 1 is given as an example.

 APPLICATION PROBLEMS

PROBLEM 20-1 Journalizing and posting purchase on account transactions

The general ledger and accounts payable ledger accounts for Wholesale Office Supply Company are given in the working papers accompanying this textbook. The balances are recorded as of May 1 of the current year.

PARTIAL GENERAL LEDGER

Account Number	Account Title	Account Balance
2115	Accounts Payable...	$3,153.00
5105	Purchases..	—

ACCOUNTS PAYABLE LEDGER

Vendor Number	Vendor Name	Terms	Purchase Number	Account Balance
210	Bird Enterprises.................	2/10, n/30	P22	$1,245.00
220	Johnston Company...............	1/10, n/30	P21	257.00
230	Preston Office Supply............	n/30	—	—
240	PXR, Inc.......................	2/10, n/30	P23	1,535.00
250	Reznik Paper Company	1/10, n/30	P24	116.00

Instructions: 1. Journalize the following purchases on account completed during May of the current year. Use page 5 of a purchases journal. The abbreviation for purchase invoice is P.

May 2. Purchased merchandise on account from PXR, Inc., $1,500.00. P25.
    5. Purchased merchandise on account from Preston Office Supply, $154.00. P26.
    8. Purchased merchandise on account from Reznik Paper Company, $642.00. P27.
  11. Purchased merchandise on account from PXR, Inc., $414.00. P28.
  14. Purchased merchandise on account from Bird Enterprises, $2,268.00. P29.
  18. Purchased merchandise on account from Johnston Company, $1,849.00. P30.
  20. Purchased merchandise on account from PXR, Inc., $602.00. P31.
  24. Purchased merchandise on account from Preston Office Supply, $314.00. P32.
  26. Purchased merchandise on account from Reznik Paper Company, $1,988.00. P33.
  29. Purchased merchandise on account from Bird Enterprises, $735.00. P34.

2. Post each amount in the purchases journal to the accounts payable ledger.
3. Total and rule the purchases journal. Post the total.

PROBLEM 20-2 Journalizing and posting cash payment transactions

The general ledger and accounts payable ledger accounts for Jenson Company are given in the working papers accompanying this textbook. The balances are recorded as of July 1 of the current year.

PARTIAL GENERAL LEDGER

Account Number	Account Title	Account Balance
1105	Cash	$22,046.00
1110	Petty Cash	250.00
1140	Supplies	735.00
2115	Accounts Payable	5,573.00
5105	Purchases	—
5110	Purchases Discount	—
6105	Advertising Expense	—
6130	Miscellaneous Expense	—
6140	Rent Expense	—
8105	Cash Short and Over	—

ACCOUNTS PAYABLE LEDGER

Vendor Number	Vendor Name	Terms	Purchase Number	Account Balance
210	Briggs Steel Company	n/30	P126	$ 804.00
220	Gray's Decorum	1/10, n/30	P127	1,216.00
230	Lipson Company	1/10, n/30	P128	2,114.00
240	Varsity Co.	2/10, n/30	P124	1,439.00

Instructions: 1. Journalize the following cash payments completed during July of the current year. Use page 7 of a cash payments journal. The abbreviation for check is C.

July 1. Paid cash for rent, $600.00. C216.
    5. Paid cash on account to Gray's Decorum, $1,203.84, covering P127 for $1,216.00, less 1% discount, $12.16. C217.
    7. Paid cash for supplies, $128.00. C218.
    8. Paid cash on account to Lipson Company, $2,092.86, covering P128 for $2,114.00, less 1% discount, $21.14. C219.
    9. Paid cash for miscellaneous expense, $140.00. C220.
  12. Purchased merchandise for cash, $263.00. C221.

July 14. Paid cash on account to Varsity Co., $1,410.22, covering P124 for $1,439.00, less 2% discount, $28.78. C222.
   19. Paid cash for supplies, $93.00. C223.
   23. Paid cash on account to Briggs Steel Company, $804.00, covering P126; no discount. C224.
   28. Paid cash for miscellaneous expense, $124.00. C225.
   30. Paid cash to replenish the petty cash fund, $105.00: advertising, $61.50; miscellaneous, $38.45; cash short, $5.05. C226.

2. Post accounts payable amounts to the appropriate accounts in the accounts payable ledger.

3. Post the amounts in the general columns to the appropriate general ledger accounts.

4. Prove and rule the cash payments journal. Post the totals of the special columns to the appropriate general ledger accounts.

PROBLEM 20-3   Journalizing and posting purchases and cash payment transactions

The general ledger and accounts payable ledger accounts for Sandy's Sewing Company are given in the working papers accompanying this textbook. The balances are recorded as of April 1 of the current year.

PARTIAL GENERAL LEDGER

Account Number	Account Title	Account Balance
1105	Cash	$41,418.00
1110	Petty Cash	200.00
1140	Supplies	1,509.00
2115	Accounts Payable.	7,532.00
5105	Purchases.	—
5110	Purchases Discount	—
5115	Purchases Returns and Allowances	—
6105	Advertising Expense	—
6130	Miscellaneous Expense.	—
6140	Rent Expense	—
8105	Cash Short and Over.	—

ACCOUNTS PAYABLE LEDGER

Vendor Number	Vendor Name	Terms	Purchase Number	Account Balance
210	Kelmans Supply.	2/10, n/30	P63	$1,678.00
220	Office Emporium	1/10, n/30	—	—
230	Potters Equipment.	1/10, n/30	P64	5,250.00
240	Threads, Inc.	1/15, n/30	P62	604.00
250	York Company	n/30	—	—

Instructions: 1. Journalize the following transactions affecting purchases and cash payments completed during April of the current year. Use page 4 of a purchases journal, a general journal, and a cash payments journal. Source documents are abbreviated as follows: check, C; debit memorandum, DM; memorandum, M; purchase invoice, P.

April 1. Paid cash for rent, $1,450.00. C57.
   2. Purchased merchandise on account from Threads, Inc., $2,565.00. P65.
   2. Bought supplies on account from Office Emporium, $536.00. M15.

Posting. Post the items that are to be posted individually. Post from the journals in this order: purchases journal, general journal, and cash payments journal.

April 5. Purchased merchandise on account from York Company, $2,995.00. P66.

7. Paid cash on account to Potters Equipment, $5,197.50, covering P64 for $5,250.00, less 1% discount, $52.50. C58.

8. Returned merchandise to York Company, $188.00, from P66. DM7.

10. Paid cash on account to Kelmans Supply, $1,644.44 covering P63 for $1,678.00, less 2% discount, $33.56. C59.

Posting. Post the items that are to be posted individually.

12. Purchased merchandise on account from Kelmans Supply, $4,683.00. P67.

12. Paid cash on account to Threads, Inc., $597.96, covering P62 for $604.00, less 1% discount, $6.04. C60.

15. Paid cash to replenish the petty cash fund, $96.20: supplies, $21.40; advertising, $43.20; miscellaneous, $35.00; cash over, $3.40. C61.

16. Purchased merchandise for cash, $706.00. C62.

16. Purchased merchandise on account from Threads, Inc., $4,243.00. P68.

Posting. Post the items that are to be posted individually.

19. Paid cash for miscellaneous expense, $114.00. C63.

22. Paid cash on account to Kelmans Supply, $4,589.34, covering P67 for $4,683.00, less 2% discount, $93.66. C64.

22. Purchased merchandise on account from Kelmans Supply, $1,976.00. P69.

23. Purchased merchandise on account from Potters Equipment, $3,204.00. P70.

23. Purchased merchandise on account from Threads, Inc., $1,020.00. P71.

Posting. Post the items that are to be posted individually.

26. Returned merchandise to Threads, Inc., $340.00, from P71. DM8.

26. Paid cash on account to Office Emporium, $536.00, covering M15; no discount. C65.

28. Paid cash for miscellaneous expense, $214.00. C66.

28. Purchased merchandise on account from York Company, $1,768.00. P72.

30. Paid cash on account to York Company, $2,807.00, covering P66 for $2,995.00, less DM7, $188.00; no discount. C67.

30. Paid cash on account to Threads, Inc., $4,200.57, covering P68 for $4,243.00, less 1% discount, $42.43. C68.

30. Paid cash to replenish the petty cash fund, $75.00: supplies, $32.50; advertising, $16.40; miscellaneous, $23.25; cash short, $2.85. C69.

Posting. Post the items that are to be posted individually.

2. Total and rule the purchases journal. Post the total.

3. Prove and rule the cash payments journal. Post the totals of the special columns.

4. Prepare a schedule of accounts payable similar to the one described in Chapter 14. Compare the schedule total with the balance of the accounts payable account in the general ledger. The total and balance should be the same.

■ ENRICHMENT PROBLEMS

MASTERY PROBLEM 20-M **Journalizing and posting purchases and cash payment transactions**

The general ledger and accounts payable ledger accounts of City Plumbing Supply Company are given in the working papers accompanying this textbook. The balances are recorded as of August 1 of the current year.

PARTIAL GENERAL LEDGER

Account Number	Account Title	Account Balance
1105	Cash	$14,789.00
1110	Petty Cash	250.00
1140	Supplies	315.00
2115	Accounts Payable..	2,015.00
5105	Purchases...	—
5110	Purchases Discount	—
5115	Purchases Returns and Allowances	—
6105	Advertising Expense	—
6130	Miscellaneous Expense.....................................	—
6140	Rent Expense	—
8105	Cash Short and Over.......................................	—

ACCOUNTS PAYABLE LEDGER

Vendor Number	Vendor Name	Terms	Purchase Number	Account Balance
210	Barker Pipe Co.	1/10, n/30	P74	$365.00
220	Edson Tools, Inc..................	1/10, n/30	—	—
230	Fullers Tape Company	n/30	P72	708.00
240	Renson Supplies..................	n/15	M14	942.00
250	TenCorp Tubing	2/10, n/30	—	—

Instructions: 1. Journalize the following transactions affecting purchases and cash payments completed during August of the current year. Use page 8 of a purchases journal, a cash payments journal, and a general journal. Source documents are abbreviated as follows: check, C; debit memorandum, DM; memorandum, M; purchase invoice, P.

Aug. 2. Returned merchandise to Fullers Tape Company, $152.00, from P72. DM17.

2. Paid cash for rent, $690.00. C504.

4. Paid cash on account to Barker Pipe Co., $361.35, covering P74 for $365.00, less 1% discount, $3.65. C505.

6. Purchased merchandise on account from TenCorp Tubing, $602.00. P75.

6. Paid cash on account to Renson Supplies, $942.00, covering M14; no discount. C506.
   Posting. Post the items that are to be posted individually. Post from the journals in this order: purchases journal, general journal, and cash payments journal.

9. Purchased merchandise on account from Edson Tools, Inc., $446.00. P76.

10. Paid cash on account to Fullers Tape Company, $556.00, covering P72 for $708.00, less DM17, $152.00; no discount. C507.

13. Paid cash for miscellaneous expense, $147.00. C508.

13. Bought supplies on account from Renson Supplies, $206.00. M15.

16. Paid cash to replenish the petty cash fund, $165.35: supplies, $22.50; advertising, $34.00; miscellaneous, $114.00; cash over, $5.15. C509.

16. Purchased merchandise on account from Fullers Tape Company, $687.00. P77.

16. Paid cash on account to TenCorp Tubing, $589.96, covering P75 for $602.00, less 2% discount, $12.04. C510.

18. Paid cash on account to Edson Tools, Inc., $441.54, covering P76 for $446.00, less 1% discount, $4.46. C511.
    Posting. Post the items that are to be posted individually.

19. Returned merchandise to Fullers Tape Company, $88.00, from P77. DM18.

20. Purchased merchandise on account from TenCorp Tubing, $315.00. P78.

Aug. 23. Purchased merchandise on account from Barker Pipe Co., $1,463.00. P79.
 25. Paid cash on account to Renson Supplies, $206.00, covering M15; no discount. C512.
 26. Bought supplies on account from Renson Supplies, $341.00. M16.
 27. Paid cash for miscellaneous expense, $76.00. C513.
 30. Purchased merchandise on account from Edson Tools, Inc., $1,161.00. P80.
 30. Paid cash on account to TenCorp Tubing, $308.70, covering P78 for $315.00, less 2% discount, $6.30. C514.
 31. Paid cash on account to Barker Pipe Co., $1,448.37, covering P79 for $1,463.00, less 1% discount, $14.63. C515.
 31. Paid cash to replenish the petty cash fund, $201.75: supplies, $45.45; advertising, $80.40; miscellaneous, $72.40; cash short, $3.50. C516.
  Posting. Post the items that are to be posted individually.

2. Total and rule the purchases journal. Post the total.

3. Prove and rule the cash payments journal. Post the totals of the special columns.

4. Prepare a schedule of accounts payable. Compare the schedule total with the balance of the accounts payable account in the general ledger. The total and balance should be the same.

CHALLENGE PROBLEM 20-C   Journalizing transactions in a combined purchases-cash payments journal

The accountant for City Plumbing Supply Company has suggested that time could be saved if the purchases journal and the cash payments journal were combined into one journal. The accountant suggests using a journal such as the following.

Purchases—Cash Payments Journal									
				1	2	3	4	5	6	7
Date	Account Title	Doc. No.	Post. Ref.	General		Purchases Debit	Accounts Payable		Purchases Discount Credit	Cash Credit
				Debit	Credit		Debit	Credit		

Christopher Howard, manager, has asked the accountant to show him how the journal would appear after transactions have been recorded.

Instructions: 1. Use page 8 of a purchases—cash payments journal and a general journal. Journalize the transactions given in Mastery Problem 20-M.

2. Prove and rule the combined purchases-cash payments journal.

3. Do you agree with the accountant that the combined purchases-cash payments journal used in this problem saves time in journalizing and posting? Why?

Recording Sales and Cash Receipts Using Special Journals

ENABLING PERFORMANCE TASKS

After studying Chapter 21, you will be able to:
a. Define accounting terms related to sales and cash receipts.
b. Identify accounting concepts and practices related to sales and cash receipts.
c. Analyze transactions affecting sales and cash receipts.
d. Journalize and post transactions related to sales and cash receipts.

As the volume of business and the number of transactions increase for a business, efficiency of operation becomes more important in completing work accurately and on time. Celluphone has sales of about $2,000,000.00 annually and has numerous transactions to record each day. Because of the size and the numerous transactions of the business, Celluphone uses a system of special journals. Using special journals improves the efficiency of recording transactions and permits more than one accounting clerk to record transactions at the same time. Celluphone uses four special journals and a general journal. A sales journal, a cash receipts journal, and selected uses of a general journal are described in this chapter. A purchases journal, a cash payments journal, and selected uses of a general journal are described in Chapter 20.

RECORDING SALES ON ACCOUNT USING A SALES JOURNAL

Celluphone sells much of its merchandise for cash. However, to encourage additional sales, Celluphone sells on account to customers with approved credit. Regardless of when cash is received, revenue should be recorded when merchandise is sold. *(CONCEPT: Realization of Revenue)* Since many sales are made on account, Celluphone uses a special journal to record *only* sales on account transactions. A special journal used to record only sales on account transactions is called a sales journal. The relationship between Celluphone's sales journal and the expanded journal described in Chapter 12 is shown in Illustration 21-1.

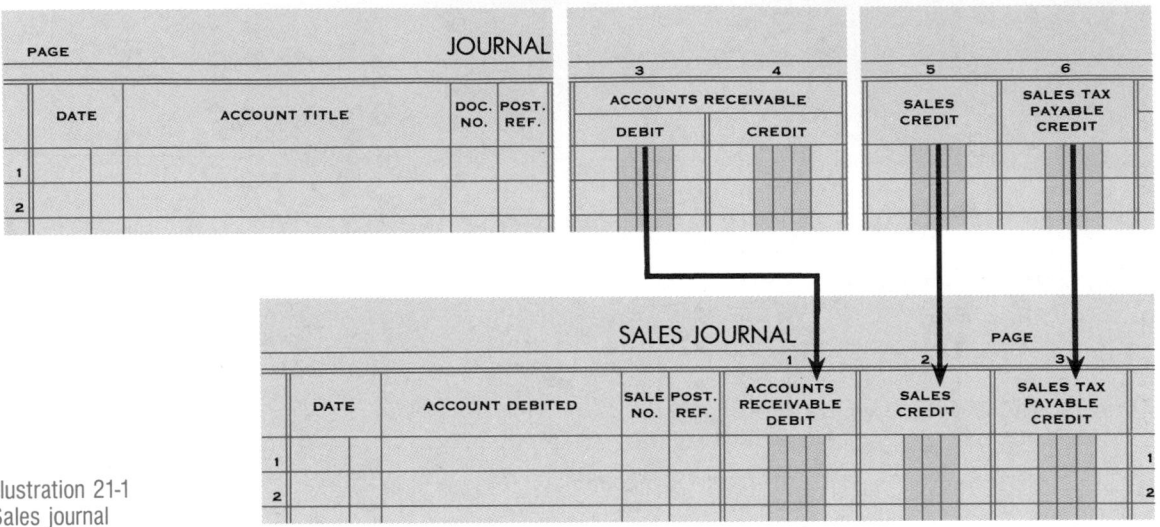

Illustration 21-1
Sales journal

Those columns used in an expanded journal and needed to record *only* sales on account are included in Celluphone's sales journal. These amount columns are Accounts Receivable Debit, Sales Credit, and Sales Tax Payable Credit. With these special amount columns, each sale on account transaction can be recorded on one line in Celluphone's sales journal.

Sales tax rates vary from state to state and may even vary within a state. An 8% sales tax is collected on items sold at retail in the city in which Celluphone is located. A retail business must collect the sales tax from customers and periodically send the sales tax collected to the state. Therefore, Celluphone uses a sales journal with a Sales Tax Payable Credit column to keep a separate record of sales tax.

Journalizing sales on account

Celluphone prepares a sales invoice in duplicate for each sale on account. The original copy is given to the customer. The carbon copy of the sales invoice is the source document for recording a sales on account transaction. *(CONCEPT: Objective Evidence)* Celluphone's sales invoice is similar to the one described in Chapter 13.

> *March 1, 19--.*
> *Sold merchandise on account to DTex Imports, $1,600.00, plus sales tax, $128.00; total, $1,728.00. Sales Invoice No. 148.*

The source document for this transaction is a sales invoice. *(CONCEPT: Objective Evidence)*

The analysis of this transaction is shown in the T accounts. Accounts Receivable is debited for $1,728.00, the amount of the sale plus the sales tax. Sales is credited for $1,600.00, the amount of the sale. Sales Tax Payable is credited for $128.00, the amount of sales tax on this sale. Celluphone owes the tax to the state government. Therefore, the amount of sales tax charged each customer is a liability. DTex Imports' account in the accounts receivable ledger is also debited for $1,728.00.

The sales journal entry to record this sales on account transaction is shown in Illustration 21-2.

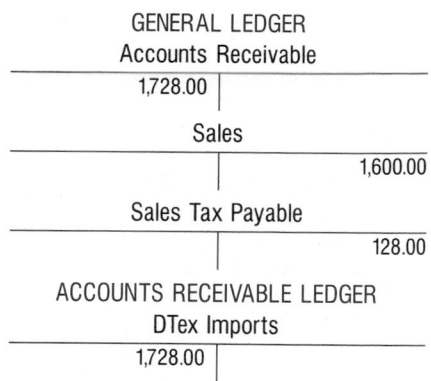

GENERAL LEDGER
Accounts Receivable

| 1,728.00 | |

Sales

| | 1,600.00 |

Sales Tax Payable

| | 128.00 |

ACCOUNTS RECEIVABLE LEDGER
DTex Imports

| 1,728.00 | |

		SALES JOURNAL						PAGE 8	
					1		2		3
	DATE	ACCOUNT DEBITED	SALE NO.	POST. REF.	ACCOUNTS RECEIVABLE DEBIT		SALES CREDIT		SALES TAX PAYABLE CREDIT
1	19-- Mar. 1	*DTex Imports*	148		1 7 2 8 00		1 6 0 0 00		1 2 8 00
2									

Illustration 21-2
Sales journal entry to record a sale on account

The date, *19--, Mar. 1*, is written in the Date column. The customer name, *DTex Imports*, is recorded in the Account Debited column. The sales invoice number, *148*, is entered in the Sale No. column. The sale amount plus the sales tax, *$1,728.00*, is written in the Accounts Receivable Debit column. The sale amount, *$1,600.00*, is entered in the Sales Credit column. The sales tax amount, *$128.00*, is written in the Sales Tax Payable Credit column. Each sale on account is recorded in the sales journal in this same way.

> Since the source document for all entries in the sales journal is a sales invoice, it is not necessary to use an *S* with the document number.

Posting from a sales journal to an accounts receivable ledger

Each amount in a sales journal's Accounts Receivable Debit column is posted individually to the customer account in the accounts receivable ledger. Each amount is posted as a debit to the customer account listed in the Account Debited column. Celluphone posts frequently to the accounts receivable ledger so that each customer account will show an up-to-date balance. Illustration 21-3 shows the posting of this entry on line 1 of the sales journal.

The date, *1*, is written in the Date column of the account. The abbreviation for the sales journal and the page number, *S8*, are recorded in the

		SALES JOURNAL				PAGE 8	
					1	2	3
	DATE	ACCOUNT DEBITED	SALE NO.	POST. REF.	ACCOUNTS RECEIVABLE DEBIT	SALES CREDIT	SALES TAX PAYABLE CREDIT
1	Mar. 1	DTex Imports	148	120	1 7 2 8 00	1 6 0 0 00	1 2 8 00	1
2								2

CUSTOMER DTex Imports						CUSTOMER NO. 120
DATE	ITEM	POST. REF.	DEBIT	CREDIT	DEBIT BALANCE
Mar. 1	Balance	✓			4 8 6 00
1		S8	1 7 2 8 00		2 2 1 4 00

Illustration 21-3
Posting from a sales
journal to an accounts
receivable ledger

Post. Ref. column. The amount, *$1,728.00*, is entered in the Debit column of the customer account. The amount in the Debit column is added to the previous balance in the Debit Balance column ($486.00 + $1,728.00 = $2,214.00). The new balance, *$2,214.00*, is written in the Debit Balance column. The customer number for DTex Imports, *120*, is recorded in the Post. Ref. column of the sales journal to show that posting has been completed for this line.

Posting from a sales journal to a general ledger

Equality of debits and credits is proved for a sales journal at the end of each month. The sales journal is then ruled, and the totals of special columns are posted, as shown in Illustration 21-4.

A single line is ruled across the amount columns of the sales journal under the last amounts recorded. The date of the last day of the month, *31*, is written in the Date column. The word *Totals* is written in the Account Debited column. The column totals are written below the single line. Double lines are ruled across the amount columns under the totals. Next, each amount column total is posted to the general ledger account named in the sales journal column headings.

When each sales journal amount column total is posted, *S11* is written in the Post. Ref. column of the account. The account number is written in parentheses under the amount column total in the sales journal. The accounts receivable account number, *1125*, is written under the Accounts Receivable Debit column total in the sales journal. The sales account number, *4105*, is written under the Sales Credit column total. The sales tax payable account number, *2135*, is written under the Sales Tax Payable Credit column total.

Illustration 21-4
Posting from a sales journal to a general ledger

SALES JOURNAL PAGE 11

	DATE		ACCOUNT DEBITED	SALE NO.	POST. REF.	1 ACCOUNTS RECEIVABLE DEBIT	2 SALES CREDIT	3 SALES TAX PAYABLE CREDIT	
23		31	Kirby's	221	130	1 404 00	1 300 00	104 00	23
24		31	Totals			88 614 00	82 050 00	6 564 00	24
25						(1125)	(4105)	(2135)	25
26									26

ACCOUNT *Accounts Receivable* ACCOUNT NO. *1125*

DATE		ITEM	POST. REF.	DEBIT	CREDIT	BALANCE DEBIT	BALANCE CREDIT
	30		G5		2 555 00	33 182 00	
	31		S11	88 614 00		121 796 00	

ACCOUNT *Sales* ACCOUNT NO. *4105*

DATE		ITEM	POST. REF.	DEBIT	CREDIT	BALANCE DEBIT	BALANCE CREDIT
19-- Mar.	31		S11		82 050 00		82 050 00

ACCOUNT *Sales Tax Payable* ACCOUNT NO. *2135*

DATE		ITEM	POST. REF.	DEBIT	CREDIT	BALANCE DEBIT	BALANCE CREDIT
	31		CP8	10 656 00		—	—
	31		S11		6 564 00		6 564 00

A summary of the procedure for journalizing and posting using a sales journal is shown in Illustration 21-5.

1 Celluphone records all sales on account in a 3-column sales journal.

2 Individual items in the sales journal are posted frequently to the customer accounts in the accounts receivable ledger.

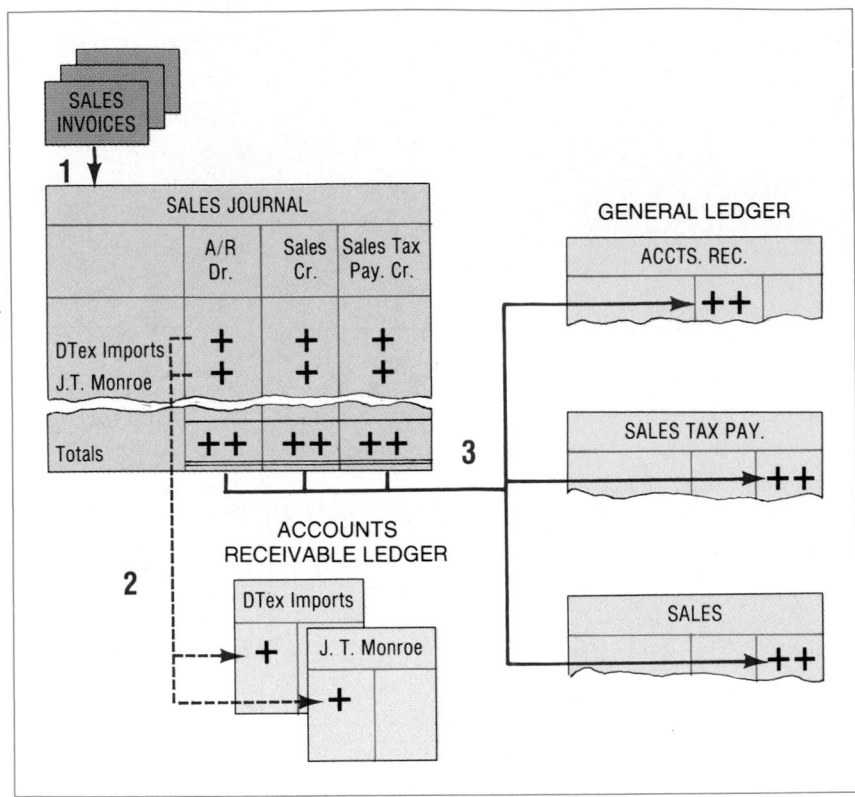

Illustration 21-5
Summary of journalizing
and posting using a sales
journal

3 At the end of each month, each amount column total is posted. The Accounts Receivable Debit column total is posted to Accounts Receivable as a debit. The Sales Credit column total is posted to Sales as a credit. The Sales Tax Payable Credit column total is posted to Sales Tax Payable as a credit.

RECORDING CASH RECEIPTS
USING A CASH RECEIPTS JOURNAL

Celluphone has many transactions involving the receipt of cash. Because of the numerous transactions involving sizable amounts of cash, Celluphone has two objectives. (1) To avoid the loss of any cash. (2) To efficiently account for the cash. To help meet these objectives, Celluphone uses a special journal to record *only* cash receipt transactions. A special journal used to record only cash receipt transactions is called a cash receipts journal.

Using a cash receipts journal permits Celluphone to record all cash receipts in one location—the cash receipts journal. Thus the amount of cash received can be determined much more quickly and easily.

The relationship between Celluphone's cash receipts journal and the expanded journal described in Chapter 12 is shown in Illustration 21-6.

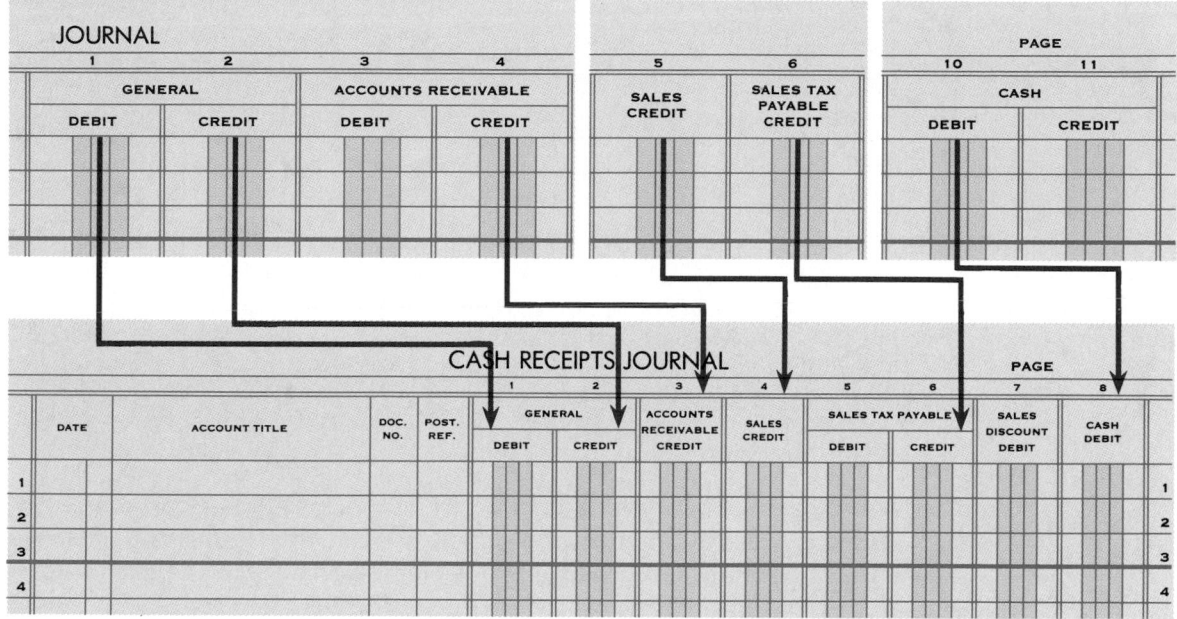

Illustration 21-6
Cash receipts journal

Those columns used in an expanded journal and needed to record *only* cash receipts are included in Celluphone's cash receipts journal. In addition, Celluphone has many transactions with cash discounts. Two additional special amount columns are provided in the cash receipts journal for recording cash received on account with a cash discount. These special amount columns are Sales Tax Payable Debit and Sales Discount Debit. With these additional special amount columns, each cash receipt transaction can be recorded on one line in Celluphone's cash receipts journal.

All cash receipts are recorded in a cash receipts journal. Most cash receipts are for (1) cash and credit card sales and (2) cash received from customers on account.

Journalizing cash and credit card sales

March 1, 19--.
Recorded cash and credit card sales, $2,870.00, plus sales tax, $229.60; total, $3,099.60. Cash Register Tape No. 1.

The source document for this transaction is a cash register tape. (CONCEPT: *Objective Evidence*)

The analysis of this transaction is shown in the T accounts. Cash is debited for $3,099.60. Sales is credited for $2,870.00, and Sales Tax Payable is credited for $229.60.

The cash receipts journal entry to record this cash receipt transaction is shown in Illustration 21-7.

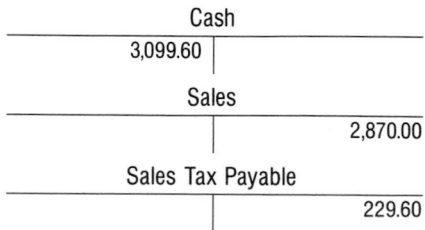

CASH RECEIPTS JOURNAL   PAGE 9

					1	2	3	4	5	6	7	8
					GENERAL		ACCOUNTS RECEIVABLE	SALES	SALES TAX PAYABLE		SALES DISCOUNT	CASH
	DATE	ACCOUNT TITLE	DOC. NO.	POST. REF.	DEBIT	CREDIT	CREDIT	CREDIT	DEBIT	CREDIT	DEBIT	DEBIT
1	19-- Mar. 1	√	T1	√				2 870 00		229 60		3 099 60	1

Illustration 21-7
Cash receipts journal entry to record cash and credit card sales

The date, *19--, Mar. 1*, is written in the Date column. A check mark is recorded in the Account Title column to show that no account title needs to be written. The cash register tape number, *T1*, is entered in the Doc. No. column. A check mark is also recorded in the Post. Ref. column to show that separate amounts on this line are not posted individually. The amount credited to Sales, *$2,870.00*, is written in the Sales Credit column. The amount credited to Sales Tax Payable, *$229.60*, is recorded in the Sales Tax Payable Credit column. The amount of cash received, *$3,099.60*, is written in the Cash Debit column.

Sales discounts

Selling merchandise on account usually helps a business increase the volume of its sales by providing more convenience to the customer. The sales transaction can be made by telephone or mail. The merchandise can be shipped to a customer when a sales agreement is reached. A customer can then pay for the merchandise after it is received. Because of this convenience, many sales are made on account. A customer is expected to pay the amount due within the credit period agreed upon.

To encourage early payment for a sale on account, a deduction on the invoice amount may be allowed. A deduction on the invoice amount to encourage prompt payment is known as a cash discount. A cash discount on sales is called a sales discount. When a sales discount is taken, a customer pays less cash than the invoice amount previously recorded in the sales account. Therefore, the amount of a sales discount is deducted from sales. Sales discounts are recorded in a general ledger account titled *Sales Discount*. The contra account Sales Discount follows the account to which it is related, Sales, in Celluphone's general ledger operating revenue division. The account is numbered 4110. Since sales discounts decrease sales, the account Sales Discount is a contra account to Sales. Thus, as shown in the T accounts, the normal account balance of Sales Discount is a debit, the opposite of the normal account balance of Sales, a credit.

Sales	
Debit side	Credit side
	Normal balance
Decrease	Increase

Sales Discount	
Debit side	Credit side
Normal balance	
Increase	Decrease

Some businesses debit the sales account for the amount of the sales discount. However, better information is provided if these amounts are debited to a separate account, Sales Discount. A separate account shows the amount being given as a sales discount. The amount of sales, sales discounts, and time of collections can be analyzed to determine whether sales discounts are effective and worth the cost.

Calculating and journalizing cash receipts on account with sales discounts

To encourage prompt payment, Celluphone gives credit terms of 1/10, n/30. When a customer pays the amount owed within 10 days, the sales invoice amount is reduced 1%.

On March 1, as shown in Illustration 21-2, Celluphone sold merchandise on account to DTex Imports for $1,600.00 plus 8% sales tax, $128.00, for a total invoice amount of $1,728.00. On March 11 Celluphone received payment for this sale on account within the discount period.

In the state where Celluphone is located, state regulations require that sales taxes be paid only on actual sales realized. When Celluphone prepares an invoice for a sale on account, the company does not know whether the customer will pay within the sales discount period. Therefore, the customer is invoiced for the full sales amount plus sales tax on that amount. Thus, on March 1, DTex Imports was invoiced for the full amount of the sale, $1,600.00, plus sales tax on that amount, $128.00, for a total invoice amount of $1,728.00. If payment for a sale on account is received within the discount period, the sales amount is reduced by the amount of the sales discount. The amount of sales tax is also reduced because the amount of the sale is reduced.

> In some states sales taxes must be paid on the original invoice amount of sale. In these states a sales discount would not result in a reduction in the sales tax liability.

Three amounts must be calculated to prepare the journal entry and verify that the customer paid the correct amount. (1) The amount of the sales discount, which is a percentage of the amount originally credited to Sales. (2) The amount the sales tax liability is reduced, which is the amount of sales tax on the sales discount. (3) The amount of cash received, which is the original total invoice amount (the Accounts Receivable Debit amount at the time of the sale) less the sales discount and the reduction in sales tax liability. These three amounts are calculated as shown below for cash received on account within the discount period for Sales Invoice No. 148 to DTex Imports.

(1) *Sales Discount:*

Sales Invoice Amount	×	**Sales Discount Rate**	=	**Sales Discount**
$1,600.00	×	1%	=	$16.00

(2) *Sales Tax Liability Reduction:*

Sales Discount	×	**Sales Tax Rate**	=	**Reduction in Sales Tax Payable**
$16.00	×	8%	=	$1.28

(3) *Cash Received:*

Total Invoiced Amount	−	**Sales Discount**	−	**Sales Tax Reduction**	=	**Cash Received**
$1,728.00	−	$16.00	−	$1.28	=	$1,710.72

March 11, 19--.
Received cash on account from DTex Imports, $1,710.72, covering Sales Invoice No. 148 for $1,728.00 ($1,600.00 plus sales tax, $128.00), less 1% discount, $16.00, and less sales tax, $1.28. Receipt No. 232.

GENERAL LEDGER

Cash

Mar. 11	1,710.72	

Sales Discount

Mar. 11	16.00	

Sales Tax Payable

Mar. 11	1.28	Mar. 1	128.00

Accounts Receivable

Mar. 1	1,728.00	Mar. 11	1,728.00

ACCOUNTS RECEIVABLE LEDGER

DTex Imports

Mar. 1	1,728.00	Mar. 11	1,728.00

The source document for this transaction is a receipt. *(CONCEPT: Objective Evidence)*

The analysis of this transaction for cash received on account with a sales discount is shown in the T accounts. Cash is debited for the total amount received, $1,710.72. Sales Discount is debited for the sales discount amount, $16.00. Sales Tax Payable is debited for $1.28, the amount of the reduction in sales tax liability. The sales tax payable on this discounted sale is now $126.72 ($128.00 less $1.28). Accounts Receivable is credited for $1,728.00, the amount debited to Accounts Receivable at the time of the sale on account. DTex Imports' account is also credited for the same amount as Accounts Receivable, $1,728.00.

The amounts for this transaction can be proved by making the calculations shown below.

Sales invoice amount....................	$1,600.00
Less sales discount......................	− 16.00
($1,600.00 × 1%)	
Equals reduced invoice amount...........	$1,584.00
Plus sales tax on reduced invoice amount .	+ 126.72
($1,584.00 × 8%)	
Equals cash received....................	$1,710.72

The cash receipts journal entry to record this cash receipt on account with a sales discount is shown in Illustration 21-8.

CASH RECEIPTS JOURNAL   PAGE 9

DATE	ACCOUNT TITLE	DOC. NO.	POST. REF.	GENERAL DEBIT	GENERAL CREDIT	ACCOUNTS RECEIVABLE CREDIT	SALES CREDIT	SALES TAX PAYABLE DEBIT	SALES TAX PAYABLE CREDIT	SALES DISCOUNT DEBIT	CASH DEBIT	
20	11 DTex Imports	R232				1 728 00		1 28		16 00	1 710 72	20
21												21

Illustration 21-8
Cash receipts journal entry to record a cash receipt on account with sales discount

The date, *11*, is written in the Date column. The customer name, *DTex Imports*, is entered in the Account Title column. The receipt number, *R232*, is written in the Doc. No. column. The amount credited to Accounts Receivable, *$1,728.00*, is recorded in the Accounts Receivable Credit column. The reduction in Sales Tax Payable, *$1.28*, is written in the Sales Tax Payable Debit column.

The debit to Sales Discount, *$16.00*, is entered in the Sales Discount Debit column. The debit to Cash, *$1,710.72*, is written in the Cash Debit column. The total of the three debits ($1.28 + $16.00 + $1,710.72) is $1,728.00 and is equal to the one credit of $1,728.00.

If a customer does not pay the amount owed within the sales discount period, the full invoice amount is due. If DTex Imports had not taken the sales discount, the journal entry would be a debit to Cash, $1,728.00, and a credit to Accounts Receivable, $1,728.00. The same amount, $1,728.00, would also be credited to the account of DTex Imports in the accounts receivable ledger.

Posting from a cash receipts journal to an accounts receivable ledger

Each entry in the Accounts Receivable Credit column affects the account of the customer named in the Account Title column. Each amount listed in the Accounts Receivable Credit column is posted individually to the proper customer account in the accounts receivable ledger. Illustration 21-9 shows the posting of a cash receipts journal entry to a customer account.

CASH RECEIPTS JOURNAL — PAGE 9

	Date	Account Title	Doc. No.	Post. Ref.	1 General Debit	2 General Credit	3 Accounts Receivable Credit	4 Sales Credit	5 Sales Tax Payable Debit	6 Sales Tax Payable Credit	7 Sales Discount Debit	8 Cash Debit	
20	11	DTex Imports	R232	120			1,728 00		1 28		16 00	1,710 72	20
21													21

CUSTOMER *DTex Imports* — CUSTOMER NO. *120*

Date	Item	Post. Ref.	Debit	Credit	Debit Balance
1		S8	1,728 00		2,214 00
4		CR9		486 00	1,728 00
11		CR9		1,728 00	—

Illustration 21-9
Posting from a cash receipts journal to an accounts receivable ledger

The date, *11*, is written in the Date column of the customer account. The abbreviation and page number of the cash receipts journal, *CR9*, is recorded in the Post. Ref. column. The amount in the Accounts Receivable Credit column, *$1,728.00*, is written in the Credit column of the customer account. The amount in the Credit column of the customer account is sub-

tracted from the previous balance in the Debit Balance column ($1,728.00 − $1,728.00 = 0). A horizontal line is drawn in the Debit Balance column to indicate a new balance of zero. The customer number for DTex Imports, *120*, is recorded in the Post. Ref. column of the cash receipts journal to show that posting has been completed for this line.

Posting from a cash receipts journal to a general ledger

Each amount in the General amount columns of a cash receipts journal is posted to a general ledger account. However, only the total of each special amount column is posted to the general ledger account given in the column heading. Posting the special amount column totals of Celluphone's cash receipts journal is shown in Illustration 21-10.

Posting from the general columns of a cash receipts journal. Each amount in the General columns is posted separately to the general ledger account named in the Account Title column. Entries that are recorded in the General columns are described in Chapter 24.

Posting totals from the special columns of a cash receipts journal. At the end of each month, equality of debits and credits is proved for a cash receipts journal. Cash is then proved. Celluphone's beginning cash account balance, March 1, 19--, was $119,048.00. The cash proof for Celluphone at the end of March is calculated as shown below.

Cash on hand at the beginning of the month . . . . (March 1, 19--, balance of cash account in general ledger)	$119,048.00
Plus total cash received during the month . . . . (Cash Debit column total, cash receipts journal, Illustration 21-10)	+169,972.00
Total	$289,020.00
Less total cash paid during the month. . . . . (Cash Credit column total, cash payments journal, Illustration 20-16, Chapter 20)	−140,742.00
Equals cash on hand at the end of the month.	$148,278.00

The balance on the next unused check stub is $148,278.00. The balance on the check stub agrees with the balance figured above. Therefore, cash is proved.

After cash is proved, the cash receipts journal is ruled as shown in Illustration 21-10. Each special amount column total is posted to the account named in the cash receipts journal column heading.

Posting from a cash payments journal to the cash account is described in Chapter 20.

When each special amount column total is posted, *CR12* is written in the Post. Ref. column of the account. The general ledger account number is

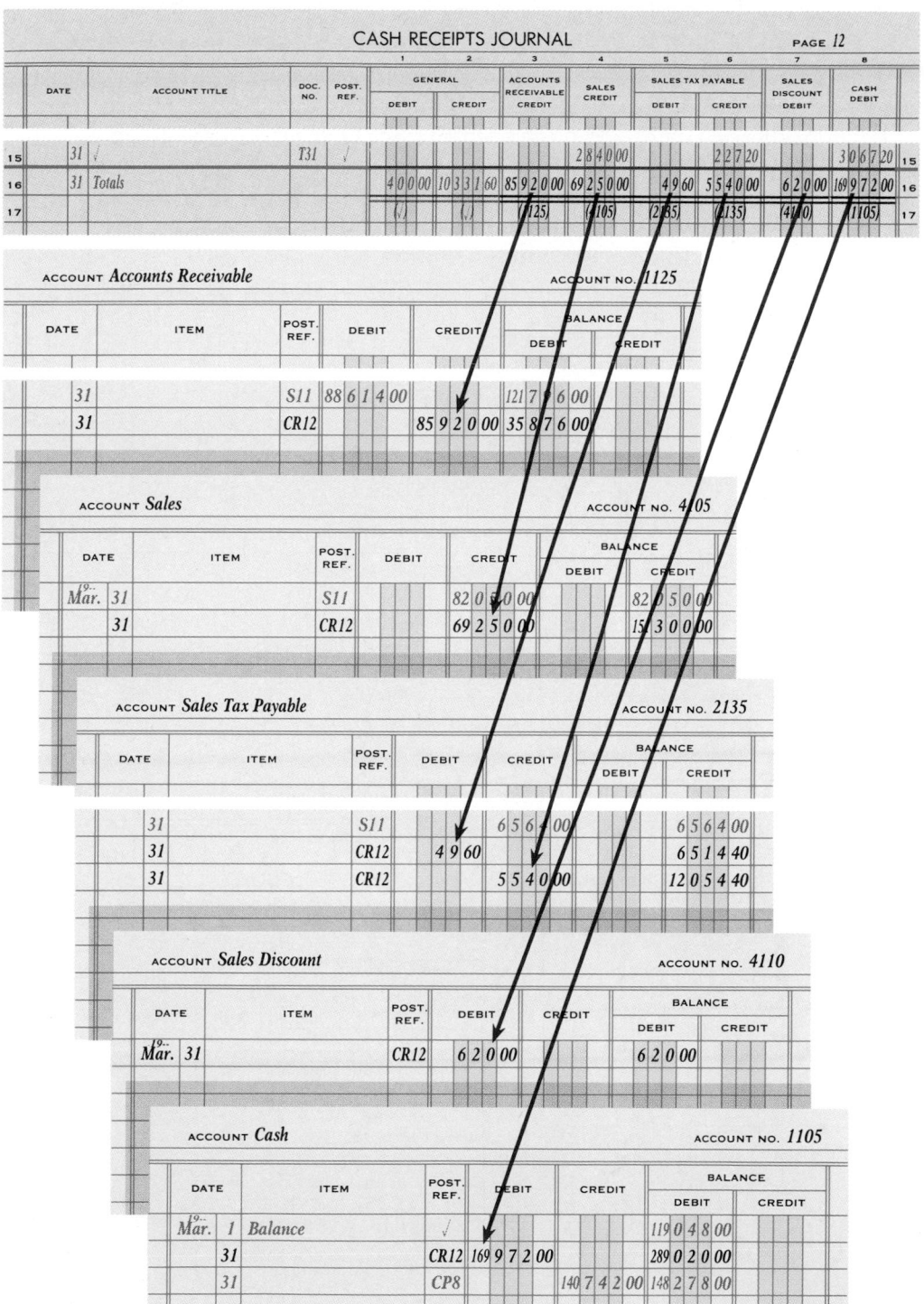

Illustration 21-10   Posting totals of the special amount columns in a cash receipts journal to a general ledger

written below the related cash receipts journal column total. The account number, written in parentheses, shows that posting of a column total is complete.

The totals of the General amount columns are not posted. Each amount in these columns was posted separately to a general ledger account. To indicate that these totals are not posted, a check mark is placed in parentheses below each column total.

A summary of the procedure for journalizing and posting using a cash receipts journal is shown in Illustration 21-11.

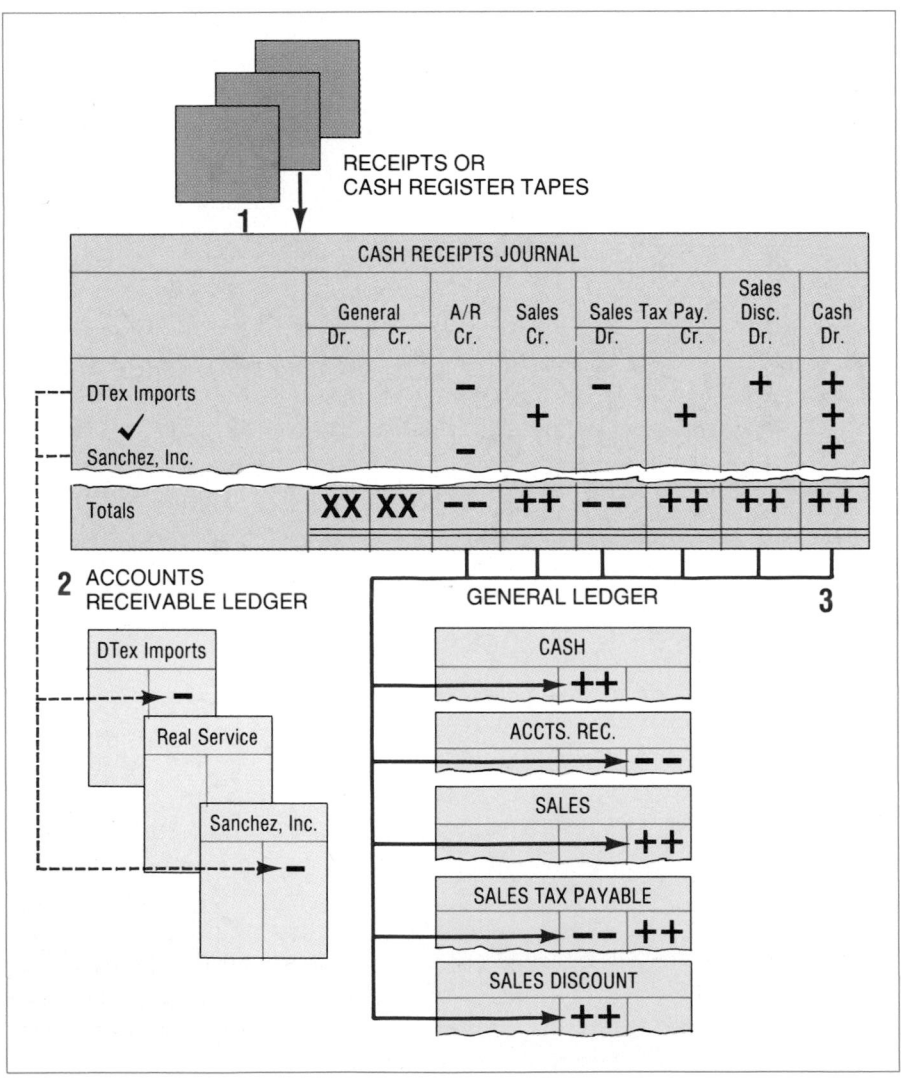

Illustration 21-11
Summary of journalizing and posting using a cash receipts journal

1 Celluphone records all cash receipts in an 8-column cash receipts journal.

2 Amounts in the Accounts Receivable Credit column are posted frequently to the customer accounts in the accounts receivable ledger.

3 At the end of the month, the totals of the special columns are posted to the general ledger.

RECORDING TRANSACTIONS USING A GENERAL JOURNAL

Purchases related transactions recorded in a general journal are described in Chapter 20. Celluphone also records two sales related transactions in a general journal. These two transactions are not sales on account or cash receipts. Thus, they are not appropriate for either the sales journal or the cash receipts journal. These two transactions are (1) sales returns and allowances and (2) correcting entries that affect customer accounts but not the controlling account.

Sales returns and allowances

Most merchandising businesses expect to have some merchandise returned because a customer decides not to keep the merchandise. A customer may have received the wrong style, the wrong size, or damaged goods. A customer may return merchandise and ask for a credit on account or a cash refund. Credit allowed a customer for the sales price of returned merchandise, resulting in a decrease in the vendor's accounts receivable, is called a sales return.

Credit may be granted to a customer without asking for the return of damaged or imperfect merchandise. An allowance also may be given because of a shortage in a shipment. Credit allowed a customer for part of the sales price of merchandise that is not returned, resulting in a decrease in the vendor's accounts receivable, is called a sales allowance.

A vendor usually informs a customer in writing when a sales return or a sales allowance is granted. A form prepared by the vendor showing the amount deducted for returns and allowances is called a credit memorandum. The form is called a credit memorandum because the vendor records the amount as a credit to the customer account to show the decrease in Accounts Receivable.

Celluphone issues a credit memorandum in duplicate for each sales return or sales allowance. The original copy is given to the customer. The second copy is used as the source document for sales returns and allowances. (CONCEPT: Objective Evidence) The credit memorandum form used by Celluphone is shown in Illustration 21-12.

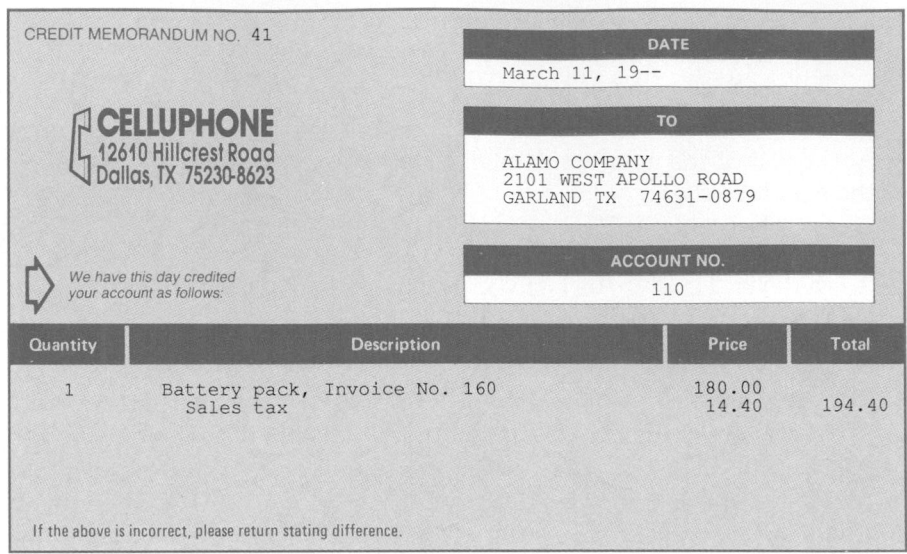

Illustration 21-12
Credit memorandum

Sales	
Debit side	Credit side
	Normal balance
Decrease	Increase

Sales Returns and Allowances	
Debit side	Credit side
Normal balance	
Increase	Decrease

Sales returns and sales allowances decrease the amount of sales. Therefore, the account Sales Returns and Allowances is a contra account to the revenue account Sales. Thus, the normal account balance of Sales Returns and Allowances is a debit, the opposite of the normal balance of Sales, a credit, as shown in the T accounts.

Some businesses debit the sales account for the amount of a return or allowance. However, better information is provided if these amounts are debited to a separate account, Sales Returns and Allowances. A separate account shows how large the sales returns and allowances are. Also, a business can see if returns and allowances are increasing or decreasing from year to year. If the amounts are large, separate accounts may be kept for sales returns and for sales allowances. Usually a single, combined account is sufficient.

Celluphone uses a single contra revenue account, Sales Returns and Allowances. The account is in the general ledger's revenue division.

Journalizing sales returns and allowances

On March 8 Celluphone sold merchandise on account to Alamo Company for $360.00. Alamo's account was debited for $388.80 ($360.00 sales and $28.80 sales tax). Later, Alamo returned part of the merchandise. A customer is entitled to credit for the amount of a sales return or allowance. The credit must include the sales tax on the return or allowance.

March 11, 19--.
Granted credit to Alamo Company for merchandise returned, $180.00, plus sales tax, $14.40, from S160; total, $194.40. Credit Memorandum No. 41.

The source document for this sales return is a credit memorandum. *(CONCEPT: Objective Evidence)* The analysis of this transaction is shown in the T accounts.

Because Sales has a normal credit balance, the contra revenue account, Sales Returns and Allowances, has a normal debit balance. Therefore, the sales returns and allowances account is increased by a debit. This transaction increases the balance of the account. Therefore, Sales Returns and Allowances is debited for $180.00, the amount of the sale that was returned.

The sales tax payable account, a liability account, has a normal credit balance. Therefore, the sales tax payable account is increased by a credit. However, this transaction decreases the balance of this account. Therefore, Sales Tax Payable is debited for $14.40, the amount of tax on the returned merchandise.

The amount to be collected from the customer is decreased. Alamo is entitled to a $180.00 credit for the merchandise returned and a $14.40 credit for sales tax. Therefore, Accounts Receivable is credited for the total amount of the return, $194.40. The same amount is also credited to Alamo's account in the accounts receivable ledger.

The general journal entry to record this sales returns and allowances transaction is shown in Illustration 21-13.

GENERAL LEDGER

Sales Returns and Allowances

Mar. 11	180.00	

Sales Tax Payable

Mar. 11	14.40	Mar. 8	28.80

Accounts Receivable

Mar. 8	388.80	Mar. 11	194.40

ACCOUNTS RECEIVABLE LEDGER

Alamo Company

Mar. 8	388.80	Mar. 11	194.40

		GENERAL JOURNAL				PAGE *3*	
	DATE	ACCOUNT TITLE	DOC. NO.	POST. REF.	DEBIT	CREDIT	
12	*11*	*Sales Returns and Allowances*	*CM41*		1 8 0 00		12
13		*Sales Tax Payable*			1 4 40		13
14		*Accounts Receivable/Alamo Co.*	/			1 9 4 40	14
15							15
16							16
17							17

Illustration 21-13
General journal entry to record sales returns and allowances

The date, *11*, is written in the Date column. *Sales Returns and Allowances* is recorded in the Account Title column. The source document, *CM41*, is entered in the Doc. No. column. The amount of the debit, *$180.00*, is entered in the Debit column. *Sales Tax Payable* is written on the next line in the Account Title column. The amount of the debit, *$14.40*, is recorded in the Debit column. The accounts credited, *Accounts Receivable/Alamo Company*, are written on the next line in the Account Title column. These account titles are indented about one centimeter. A diagonal line is placed between the two account titles. A diagonal line also is placed in the Post. Ref. column to show that the credit is posted to two accounts. The amount of the credit, *$194.40*, is entered in the Credit column.

Journalizing correcting entries affecting customer accounts

Errors may be made in recording amounts in subsidiary ledgers that do not affect the general ledger controlling account. For example, a sale on account may be recorded to the wrong customer in the sales journal. The column total posted from the sales journal to the general ledger is correct. The accounts receivable account shows the correct balance. However, two of the customer accounts in the accounts receivable ledger show incorrect balances. To correct this error, only the subsidiary ledger accounts need to be corrected.

March 12, 19--.
Discovered that a sale on account to Ridgecrest Co. on February 26, S133, was incorrectly charged to the account of Ridgepoint Co., $297.00. Memorandum No. 40.

ACCOUNTS RECEIVABLE LEDGER

Ridgecrest Co.			
Mar. 12	297.00		

Ridgepoint Co.			
Feb. 26	297.00	Mar. 12	297.00

The source document for this correcting entry is a memorandum. *(CONCEPT: Objective Evidence)* The analysis of this correcting entry is shown in the T accounts.

On February 28 the total of the Accounts Receivable Debit column in the sales journal was posted correctly. No correction is needed for this amount.

The account of Ridgepoint Co. was debited for $297.00 when the account of Ridgecrest Co. should have been debited. The correcting entry involves only subsidiary ledger accounts. Ridgecrest Co.'s account is debited for $297.00 to record the charge sale in the correct account. Ridgepoint Co.'s account is credited for $297.00 to cancel the incorrect entry. The general journal entry to record this correcting entry is shown in Illustration 21-14.

Illustration 21-14
General journal entry to record a correcting entry affecting customer accounts

	GENERAL JOURNAL					PAGE 3	
DATE	ACCOUNT TITLE	DOC. NO.	POST. REF.	DEBIT		CREDIT	
15	**12** **Ridgecrest Co.**	*M40*		2 9 7 00			15
16	**Ridgepoint Co.**					2 9 7 00	16
17							17
18							18

The date, *12*, is written in the Date column. The name of the correct customer, *Ridgecrest Co.*, is entered in the Account Title column. The source document, *M40*, is entered in the Doc. No. column. The debit amount, *$297.00*, is recorded in the Debit column. On the next line, the name of the incorrectly charged customer, *Ridgepoint Co.*, is entered in the Account Title column. This account name is indented about one centimeter. The credit amount, *$297.00*, is recorded in the Credit column.

Posting from a general journal

Each amount in the Debit and Credit columns of a general journal is posted to the account or accounts named in the Account Title column. The two general journal entries discussed in this chapter are posted in the same way as described in Chapter 20.

A summary of the procedure for journalizing and posting transactions using a general journal is shown in Illustration 21-15.

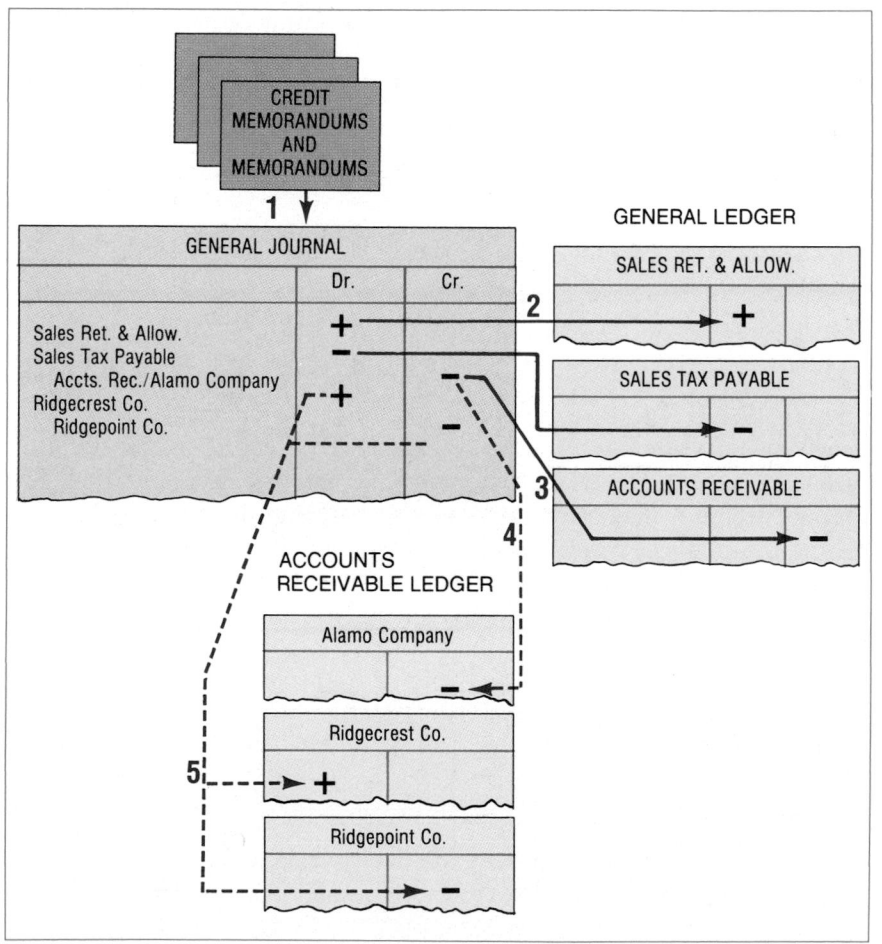

Illustration 21-15
Summary of journalizing and posting using a general journal

1 Celluphone records in a general journal all transactions that cannot be recorded in any of the special journals.

2 Amounts in the Debit column are posted frequently to the general ledger.

3 Amounts in the Credit column are posted frequently to the general ledger.

4 Amounts debited or credited to Accounts Receivable are posted to the named vendor account in the accounts receivable ledger.

5 Correcting entries involving only subsidiary ledger accounts are posted only to the appropriate subsidiary ledger.

PREPARING A SCHEDULE OF ACCOUNTS RECEIVABLE

A listing of customer accounts, account balances, and total amount due from all customers is known as a schedule of accounts receivable. A schedule of accounts receivable is prepared before financial statements are prepared to prove the accounts receivable ledger. If the total amount shown on a schedule of accounts receivable equals the accounts receivable controlling account balance in the general ledger, the accounts receivable ledger is proved. Preparation of a schedule of accounts receivable is described in Chapter 14.

ORDER OF POSTING FROM SPECIAL JOURNALS

Items affecting customer or vendor accounts are posted often during the month. Some businesses post daily so that the balances of the subsidiary ledger accounts will be up to date. Since general ledger account balances are needed only when financial statements are prepared, the general ledger accounts may be posted less often during the month. All items, including the totals of special columns, must be posted before a trial balance is prepared.

The best order in which to post the journals is listed below.

1. Sales journal.
2. Purchases journal.
3. General journal.
4. Cash receipts journal.
5. Cash payments journal.

This order of posting usually puts the debits and credits in the accounts in the order the transactions occurred.

SUMMARY OF RECORDING SALES AND CASH RECEIPTS USING SPECIAL JOURNALS

The charts shown in Illustration 21-16 summarize the entries for sales, cash receipts, and other transactions in special journals and a general journal.

TRANSACTION	SALES JOURNAL		
	1	2	3
	ACCOUNTS RECEIVABLE DEBIT	SALES CREDIT	SALES TAX PAYABLE CREDIT
Sales on account	X	X	X

TRANSACTIONS	CASH RECEIPTS JOURNAL							
	1	2	3	4	5	6	7	8
	GENERAL		ACCOUNTS RECEIVABLE CREDIT	SALES CREDIT	SALES TAX PAYABLE		SALES DISCOUNT DEBIT	CASH DEBIT
	DEBIT	CREDIT			DEBIT	CREDIT		
Cash receipts from sales				X		X		X
Cash receipts on account with sales discount			X		X		X	X

TRANSACTIONS	GENERAL JOURNAL	
	DEBIT	CREDIT
Sales returns and allowances	X	X
Correcting entry	X	X

Illustration 21-16
Summary of recording sales and cash receipts using special journals

ACCOUNTING TERMS

What is the meaning of each of the following?

1. sales journal
2. cash receipts journal

3. sales discount
4. sales return

5. sales allowance
6. credit memorandum

QUESTIONS FOR INDIVIDUAL STUDY

1. Why do some companies sell merchandise on account?
2. Which accounting concept is being applied when revenue is recorded as merchandise is sold regardless of when cash is received?
3. What are the special amount columns in Celluphone's 3-column sales journal?
4. What source document does Celluphone use for a sale on account transaction?
5. Which accounting concept is being applied when a copy of a sales invoice is used as the basis for recording a sale on account?
6. Why does Celluphone post frequently to customer accounts?
7. What objectives do companies with numerous transactions involving sizable amounts of cash frequently have?
8. What source document does Celluphone use for a cash and credit card sales transaction?
9. Why do companies offer sales discounts?
10. What is the normal account balance of the sales discount account?
11. Are businesses that offer sales discounts required to use a sales discount account?
12. When cash is received on account within the discount period and sales tax is charged on the amount less the discount, what amounts must be calculated to prepare the journal entry for receipt of cash?
13. What source document does Celluphone use for a cash receipt on account transaction?
14. What general ledger accounts are affected, and how, by a cash receipt from a customer on account when there is a sales discount and sales tax?
15. Which amounts in a cash receipts journal are posted separately to general ledger accounts?
16. What source document does Celluphone use for a sales returns and allowances transaction?
17. What general ledger accounts are affected, and how, by a sales returns and allowances transaction?
18. How can an error involving posting a debit amount to the wrong customer account be corrected?
19. In what order should special journals be posted? Why?

CASES FOR MANAGEMENT DECISION

CASE 1 Latson Company uses a 3-column sales journal with special amount columns similar to the one in this chapter. The company records sales tax payable at the time a sale on account is made. Christopher Chenault, the office manager, questions this practice. He suggests that sales tax payable not be recorded until cash is actually collected for a sale. Which procedure is preferable? Why?

CASE 2 Regents Office Supply sells office

supplies to many local firms. Most of the store's sales are made on account. In order to encourage early payment, Regents offers a sales discount for those who pay within the discount period. Regents is considering changing its payroll policy for sales personnel from a salary plan to a commission-on-sales plan in order to encourage sales personnel to increase their sales efforts. Commissions would be 5% of sales. Various sales personnel have asked you, the manager, whether commissions would be based on gross sales or on sales after sales discounts and returns and allowances. What should your response be? Explain.

 DRILLS FOR UNDERSTANDING

DRILL 21-D1 Analyzing the journalizing of sales and cash receipts transactions

Use a form similar to the following.

Trans. No.	(A) Account(s) Debited	(B) Account(s) Credited	(C) Journal in Which Recorded	(D) For Amount Debited	(E) For Amount Credited
				Name of Amount Column(s) Used in Journal	
1.	Accts. Rec. James Harding	Sales Sales Tax Pay.	Sales	Accts. Rec. Debit	Sales Credit Sales Tax Pay. Credit

Instructions: Complete the form for each of the following transactions. Write in Column A the title of the account(s) debited. Write in Column B the title of the account(s) credited. Write in Column C the name of the journal in which the transaction is recorded. Write in Columns D and E the names of the journal amount column(s) in which debit and credit amounts are recorded. Transaction 1 is given as an example.

Transactions
1. Sold merchandise on account to James Harding plus sales tax.
2. Recorded cash and credit card sales plus sales tax.
3. Received cash on account from Accent Company; no sales discount.
4. Granted credit to Richco for merchandise returned plus sales tax.
5. Sold merchandise on account to Kennel Co. plus sales tax.
6. Granted credit to Silver Star for damaged merchandise plus sales tax.
7. Discovered that a sale on account to Rebecca Hind was incorrectly charged to Rebecca Hindle.
8. Received cash on account from Forms Co. less sales discount and sales tax.

The solution to Drill 21-D1 is needed to complete Drill 21-D2.

DRILL 21-D2 Analyzing the posting of sales and cash receipts transactions

The solution to Drill 21-D1 is needed to complete Drill 21-D2.

Use a form similar to the following.

Trans. No.	(A) Accounts Affected	(B) Amounts Posted Individually to		(D) Amounts Not Posted Individually to Any Ledger
		General Ledger	Accounts Receivable Ledger	
1.	Accts. Rec.			✓
	James Harding		✓	
	Sales			✓
	Sales Tax Payable			✓

Instructions: 1. Write in Column A the titles of the accounts affected by each transaction in Drill 21-D1.

2. Place a check mark in Column B if the amount is posted individually to the general ledger. Place a check mark in Column C if the amount is posted individually to the accounts receivable ledger. Place a check mark in Column D if the amount is not posted individually to any ledger. Transaction 1 is given as an example.

◼ APPLICATION PROBLEMS

PROBLEM 21-1   Journalizing and posting sales on account transactions

The general ledger and accounts receivable ledger accounts for Capitol Sales Company are given in the working papers accompanying this textbook. The balances are recorded as of March 1 of the current year.

PARTIAL GENERAL LEDGER

Account No.	Account Title	Account Balance
1125	Accounts Receivable	$2,420.00
2135	Sales Tax Payable	—
4105	Sales..	—

ACCOUNTS RECEIVABLE LEDGER

Customer No.	Customer Name	Sale No.	Account Balance
110	Austin Equipment Co.	S54	$406.00
120	Theresa Briggs....................	S52	321.00
130	Crawford Company.................	S57	618.00
140	Daniel Noble......................	S56	257.00
150	Midori Saga	S53	355.00
160	Tensil Company...................	S55	463.00

Instructions: 1. Journalize the following sales on account completed during March of the current year. Use page 3 of a sales journal. The sales tax rate is 8%. The abbreviation for sales invoice is S.

March 1. Sold merchandise on account to Daniel Noble, $204.00, plus sales tax, $16.32; total, $220.32. S58.

3. Sold merchandise on account to Austin Equipment Co., $330.65, plus sales tax, $26.45; total, $357.10. S59.

March 5. Sold merchandise on account to Crawford Company, $145.25, plus sales tax, $11.62; total, $156.87. S60.

8. Sold merchandise on account to Theresa Briggs, $215.90, plus sales tax, $17.27; total, $233.17. S61.

10. Sold merchandise on account to Tensil Company, $154.00, plus sales tax, $12.32; total, $166.32. S62.

12. Sold merchandise on account to Crawford Company, $198.55, plus sales tax, $15.88; total, $214.43. S63.

15. Sold merchandise on account to Midori Saga, $114.00, plus sales tax, $9.12; total, $123.12. S64.

20. Sold merchandise on account to Austin Equipment Co., $234.90, plus sales tax, $18.79; total, $253.69. S65.

26. Sold merchandise on account to Midori Saga, $233.00, plus sales tax, $18.64; total, $251.64. S66.

31. Sold merchandise on account to Daniel Noble, $164.25, plus sales tax, $13.14; total, $177.39. S67.

2. Post each amount in the Accounts Receivable Debit column of the sales journal to the accounts receivable ledger.

3. Prove and rule the sales journal. Post the totals of the special columns.

PROBLEM 21-2 Journalizing and posting cash receipts transactions

The general ledger and accounts receivable ledger accounts for The General Store are given in the working papers accompanying this textbook. The balances are recorded as of May 1 of the current year.

PARTIAL GENERAL LEDGER

Account No.	Account Title	Account Balance
1105	Cash.......................................	$10,233.00
1125	Accounts Receivable	1,808.00
2135	Sales Tax Payable...........................	—
4105	Sales.......................................	—
4110	Sales Discount..............................	—

ACCOUNTS RECEIVABLE LEDGER

Customer No.	Customer Name	Sale No.	Account Balance
110	Cynthia Anson....................	S217	$324.00
120	Brandon Company	S219	648.00
130	Jason Denison.....................	S218	216.00
140	Kitchen Kettle	S223	157.00
150	Stan's Eatery	S220	463.00

Instructions: 1. Journalize the following cash receipts completed during May of the current year. Use page 5 of a cash receipts journal. The General Store offers terms of 1/10, n/30. The sales tax rate is 8%. Source documents are abbreviated as follows: receipt, R; sales invoice, S; cash register tape, T.

May 2. Received cash on account from Brandon Company, $641.52, covering S219 for $648.00 ($600.00 plus sales tax, $48.00), less 1% discount, $6.00, and less sales tax, $0.48. R65.

May   5. Received cash on account from Kitchen Kettle, $157.00, covering S223; no discount. R66.

7. Received cash on account from Jason Denison, $213.84, covering S218 for $216.00 ($200.00 plus sales tax, $16.00), less 1% discount, $2.00, and less sales tax, $0.16. R67.

8. Received cash on account from Cynthia Anson, $320.76, covering S217 for $324.00 ($300.00 plus sales tax, $24.00), less 1% discount, $3.00, and less sales tax, $0.24. R68.

14. Recorded cash and credit card sales, $7,177.00, plus sales tax, $574.16; total, $7,751.16. T14.

21. Received cash on account from Stan's Eatery, $463.00, covering S220; no discount. R69.

31. Recorded cash and credit card sales, $6,947.00, plus sales tax, $555.76; total, $7,502.76. T31.

2. Post each amount in the Accounts Receivable Credit column of the cash receipts journal to the accounts receivable ledger.

3. Prove the equality of debits and credits for the cash receipts journal.

4. Prove cash. The cash balance on hand on May 1 was $10,233.00. The total of the Cash Credit column of the cash payments journal for The General Store is $14,003.83. The balance on the next unused check stub on May 31 is $13,279.21.

5. Rule the cash receipts journal. Post the totals of the special columns.

PROBLEM 21-3   Journalizing and posting sales and cash receipts transactions

The general ledger and accounts receivable ledger accounts for Pierce Imports are given in the working papers accompanying this textbook. The balances are recorded as of June 1 of the current year.

PARTIAL GENERAL LEDGER

Account No.	Account Title	Account Balance
1105	Cash..	$9,211.00
1125	Accounts Receivable	3,361.48
2135	Sales Tax Payable............................	—
4105	Sales.......................................	—
4110	Sales Discount...............................	—
4115	Sales Returns and Allowances................	—

ACCOUNTS RECEIVABLE LEDGER

Customer No.	Customer Name	Sale No.	Account Balance
110	Beverly's Gift Shop	S136	$303.25
120	Frank Finnely.....................	S145	415.00
		S150	276.48
130	Geno's	S147	346.00
140	Susan Malta......................	S146	475.75
150	Nan and Jenkins Decorators	—	—
160	The Import Shop...................	S151	924.00
170	Hana Victor.......................	S149	621.00

Instructions: 1. Journalize the following transactions affecting sales and cash receipts completed during June of the current year. Use page 6 of a sales journal, a general journal, and a cash receipts journal. Pierce Imports offers terms of 1/10, n/30. The sales tax rate is 8%. Source documents are abbreviated as follows: credit memorandum, CM; memorandum, M; receipt, R; sales invoice, S; cash register tape, T.

June 3. Received cash on account from Beverly's Gift Shop, $300.22, covering S136 for $303.25 ($280.79 plus sales tax, $22.46), less 1% discount, $2.81, and less sales tax, $0.22. R83.

4. Sold merchandise on account to Geno's, $416.25, plus sales tax, $33.30; total, $449.55. S152.

4. Recorded cash and credit card sales, $3,556.00, plus sales tax, $284.48; total, $3,840.48. T4.

7. Received cash on account from Geno's, $342.54, covering S147 for $346.00 ($320.37 plus sales tax, $25.63), less 1% discount, $3.20, and less sales tax, $0.26. R84.

9. Received cash on account from Hana Victor, $614.79, covering S149 for $621.00 ($575.00 plus sales tax, $46.00), less 1% discount, $5.75, and less sales tax, $0.46. R85.

9. Discovered that a sale on account to Nan and Jenkins Decorators on May 26, S145, was incorrectly charged to the account of Frank Finnely, $415.00 ($384.26 plus sales tax, $30.74). M27.

10. Received cash on account from Frank Finnely, $273.72, covering S150 for $276.48 ($256.00 plus sales tax, $20.48), less 1% discount, $2.56, and less sales tax, $0.20. R86.

11. Sold merchandise on account to Hana Victor, $604.15, plus sales tax, $48.33; total, $652.48. S153.

11. Recorded cash and credit card sales, $4,122.00, plus sales tax, $329.76; total, $4,451.76. T11.

Posting. Post the items that are to be posted individually. Post from the journals in this order: sales journal, general journal, and cash receipts journal.

14. Granted credit to The Import Shop for merchandise returned, $67.00, plus sales tax, $5.36, from S151; total, $72.36. CM31.

15. Sold merchandise on account to Beverly's Gift Shop, $414.00, plus sales tax, $33.12; total, $447.12. S154.

15. Sold merchandise on account to Susan Malta, $305.80, plus sales tax, $24.46; total, $330.26. S155.

17. Received cash on account from Nan and Jenkins Decorators, $415.00, covering M27; no discount. R87.

18. Recorded cash and credit card sales, $2,997.00, plus sales tax, $239.76; total, $3,236.76. T18.

Posting. Post the items that are to be posted individually.

21. Sold merchandise on account to Frank Finnely, $348.00, plus sales tax, $27.84; total, $375.84. S156.

21. Received cash on account from The Import Shop, $851.64 (covering S151 less CM31), no discount. R88.

21. Received cash on account from Hana Victor, $645.96, covering S153 for $652.48 ($604.15 plus sales tax, $48.33), less 1% discount, $6.04, and less sales tax, $0.48. R89.

22. Received cash on account from Geno's, $449.55, covering S152; no discount. R90.

24. Sold merchandise on account to Frank Finnely, $149.80, plus sales tax, $11.98; total, $161.78. S157.

25. Sold merchandise on account to The Import Shop, $415.50, plus sales tax, $33.24; total, $448.74. S158.

June 27. Sold merchandise on account to Nan and Jenkins Decorators, $637.00, plus sales tax, $50.96; total, $687.96. S159.

30. Received cash on account from Susan Malta, $475.75, covering S146; no discount. R91.

30. Recorded cash and credit card sales, $1,582.00, plus sales tax, $126.56; total, $1,708.56. T30.

Posting. Post the items that are to be posted individually.

2. Prove and rule the sales journal. Post the totals of the special columns.

3. Prove the equality of debits and credits for the cash receipts journal.

4. Prove cash. The cash balance on hand on June 1 was $9,211.00. The total of the Cash Credit column of the cash payments journal for Pierce Imports is $15,672.58. The balance on the next unused check stub on June 30 is $11,145.15.

5. Rule the cash receipts journal. Post the totals of the special columns.

6. Prepare a schedule of accounts receivable similar to the one described in Chapter 14. Compare the schedule total with the balance of the accounts receivable account in the general ledger. The total and balance should be the same.

■ ENRICHMENT PROBLEMS

MASTERY PROBLEM 21-M   Journalizing and posting sales and cash receipts transactions

The general ledger and accounts receivable accounts for Founders Corporation are given in the working papers accompanying this textbook. The balances are recorded as of February 1 of the current year.

PARTIAL GENERAL LEDGER

Account No.	Account Title	Account Balance
1105	Cash..	$6,354.00
1125	Accounts Receivable	2,568.76
2135	Sales Tax Payable	—
4105	Sales..	—
4110	Sales Discount	—
4115	Sales Returns and Allowances	—

ACCOUNTS RECEIVABLE LEDGER

Customer No.	Customer Name	Sale No.	Account Balance
110	Andrew Anderson	S91	$229.50
120	Brady and Co.	S94	404.56
130	Jessica Howe......................	S88	367.20
140	Kindercraft	S87	150.00
150	Alford Lein	S93	216.00
160	Mandon, Inc.	S90	378.00
170	Platter Company	S92	432.00
180	Glenda Stevens	S95	391.50

Instructions: 1. Journalize the following transactions affecting sales and cash receipts completed during February of the current year. Use page 2 of a sales journal, a general journal, and a cash receipts journal. Founders Corporation offers terms of 2/10, n/30. The sales tax rate is 8%. Source documents are abbreviated as follows: credit memorandum, CM; memorandum, M; receipt, R; sales invoice, S; cash register tape, T.

Feb. 1. Sold merchandise on account to Jessica Howe, $330.00, plus sales tax, $26.40; total, $356.40. S96.

1. Granted credit to Mandon, Inc., for merchandise returned, $48.00, plus sales tax, $3.84, from S90; total, $51.84. CM27.

5. Received cash on account from Platter Company, $423.36, covering S92 for $432.00 ($400.00 plus sales tax, $32.00), less 2% discount, $8.00, and less sales tax, $0.64. R42.

8. Received cash on account from Glenda Stevens, $383.67, covering S95 for $391.50 ($362.50 plus sales tax, $29.00), less 2% discount, $7.25, and less sales tax, $0.58. R43.

8. Recorded cash and credit card sales, $1,420.00, plus sales tax, $113.60; total, $1,533.60. T8.

   Posting. Post the items that are to be posted individually. Post from the journals in this order: sales journal, general journal, and cash receipts journal.

9. Sold merchandise on account to Mandon, Inc., $214.00, plus sales tax, $17.12; total, $231.12. S97.

11. Received cash on account from Jessica Howe, $367.20, covering S88; no discount. R44.

11. Granted credit to Andrew Anderson for merchandise returned, $112.50, plus sales tax, $9.00, from S91; total $121.50. CM28.

12. Received cash on account from Kindercraft, $150.00, covering S87; no discount. R45.

12. Received cash on account from Mandon, Inc., $326.16 (covering S90 less CM27), no discount. R46.

12. Recorded cash and credit card sales, $2,215.00, plus sales tax, $177.20; total, $2,392.20. T12.

   Posting. Post the items that are to be posted individually.

15. Received cash on account from Brady and Co., $404.56, covering S94; no discount. R47.

18. Sold merchandise on account to Platter Company, $205.00, plus sales tax, $16.40; total, $221.40. S98.

18. Received cash on account from Mandon, Inc., $226.50, covering S97 for $231.12 ($214.00 plus sales tax, $17.12), less 2% discount, $4.28, and less sales tax, $0.34. R48.

19. Sold merchandise on account to Brady and Co., $420.00, plus sales tax, $33.60; total, $453.60. S99.

19. Recorded cash and credit card sales, $1,897.00, plus sales tax, $151.76; total, $2,048.76. T19.

   Posting. Post the items that are to be posted individually.

22. Received cash on account from Jessica Howe, $356.40, covering S96; no discount. R49.

22. Discovered that a sale on account to Platter Company on January 15, S93, was incorrectly charged to the account of Alford Lein, $216.00 ($200.00 plus sales tax, $16.00). M52.

23. Sold merchandise on account to Kindercraft, $296.00, plus sales tax, $23.68; total, $319.68. S100.

23. Received cash on account from Andrew Anderson, $108.00 (covering S91 less CM28), no discount. R50.

23. Received cash on account from Brady and Co., $444.53, covering S99 for $453.60 ($420.00 plus sales tax, $33.60), less 2% discount, $8.40, and less sales tax, $0.67. R51.

Feb. 25. Sold merchandise on account to Andrew Anderson, $356.00, plus sales tax, $28.48; total, $384.48. S101.

28. Received cash on account from Kindercraft, $313.29, covering S100 for $319.68 ($296.00 plus sales tax, $23.68), less 2% discount, $5.92, and less sales tax, $0.47. R52.

28. Recorded cash and credit card sales, $2,197.00, plus sales tax, $175.76; total, $2,372.76. T28.

    Posting. Post the items that are to be posted individually.

2. Prove and rule the sales journal. Post the totals of the special columns.

3. Prove the equality of debits and credits for the cash receipts journal.

4. Prove cash. The cash balance on hand on February 1 was $6,354.00. The total of the Cash Credit column of the cash payments journal for Founders Corporation is $11,234.00. The balance on the next unused check stub on February 28 is $6,970.99.

5. Rule the cash receipts journal. Post the totals of the special columns.

6. Prepare a schedule of accounts receivable similar to the one described in Chapter 14. Compare the schedule total with the balance of the accounts receivable account in the general ledger. The total and balance should be the same.

CHALLENGE PROBLEM 21-C **Journalizing and posting sales, purchases, cash receipts, and cash payments transactions**

The general ledger, accounts receivable ledger, and accounts payable ledger accounts for Princess Company are given in the working papers accompanying this textbook. The balances are recorded as of April 1 of the current year.

PARTIAL GENERAL LEDGER

Account No.	Account Title	Account Balance
1105	Cash	$7,690.00
1110	Petty Cash	300.00
1125	Accounts Receivable	1,479.60
1140	Supplies	240.00
2115	Accounts Payable...	6,734.00
2135	Sales Tax Payable	—
4105	Sales	—
4110	Sales Discount	—
4115	Sales Returns and Allowances	—
5105	Purchases..	—
5110	Purchases Discount	—
5115	Purchases Returns and Allowances	—
6105	Advertising Expense	—
6130	Miscellaneous Expense....................................	—
6140	Rent Expense	—
8105	Cash Short and Over......................................	—

ACCOUNTS RECEIVABLE LEDGER

Customer No.	Customer Name	Sale No.	Account Balance
110	Barbra Almon	S51	$330.48
120	Bland Company	—	—
130	James Hart	S50	167.40
140	Jefferson Co..	S53	556.20
150	Linda Ponder.......................................	S54	425.52

ACCOUNTS PAYABLE LEDGER

Vendor No.	Vendor Name	Terms	Purchase No.	Account Balance
210	Dunn Supplies	n/30	M14	$1,413.00
220	Gibson Electric Co.	n/30	P64	1,945.00
230	Roland and Barnes	1/10, n/30	P74	366.00
240	Webb Co.	2/15, n/30	P75	3,010.00

Instructions: 1. Journalize the following transactions affecting sales, purchases, cash receipts, and cash payments completed during April of the current year. Calculate and record sales tax on all sales and sales returns and allowances as described in this chapter. Use page 4 of a sales journal, a purchases journal, a general journal, a cash receipts journal, and a cash payments journal. Princess Company offers its customers terms of 2/10, n/30. The sales tax rate is 8%. Source documents are abbreviated as follows: check, C; credit memorandum, CM; debit memorandum, DM; memorandum, M; purchase invoice, P; receipt, R; sales invoice, S; cash register tape, T.

April 1. Paid cash for April rent, $850.00. C84.
 1. Paid cash on account to Roland and Barnes, covering P74 for $366.00, less 1% discount. C85.
 2. Received cash on account from Jefferson Co., $545.08, covering S53 for $556.20 ($515.00 plus sales tax, $41.20), less 2% discount and less sales tax on discount. R26.
 2. Recorded cash and credit card sales, $1,926.00, plus sales tax. T2.
 Posting. Post the items that are to be posted individually. Post the journals in this order: sales journal, purchases journal, general journal, cash receipts journal, and cash payments journal.
 5. Returned merchandise to Webb Co., $468.32, from P75. DM9.
 6. Sold merchandise on account to Bland Company, $247.00, plus sales tax. S55.
 6. Paid cash on account to Gibson Electric Co., $1,945.00, covering P64; no discount. C86.
 6. Received cash on account from Linda Ponder, $417.01, covering S54 for $425.52 ($394.00 plus sales tax, $31.52), less 2% discount and less sales tax on discount. R27.
 7. Bought supplies on account from Dunn Supplies, $537.00. M15.
 9. Received cash on account from Barbra Almon, $330.48, covering S51; no discount. R28.
 9. Recorded cash and credit card sales, $1,820.00, plus sales tax. T9.
 Posting. Post the items that are to be posted individually.
 12. Purchased merchandise on account from Gibson Electric Co., $1,675.00. P77.
 13. Paid cash on account to Webb Co., covering P75 for $3,010.00, less DM9, $468.32, and less 2% discount. C87.
 14. Sold merchandise on account to Jefferson Co., $746.00, plus sales tax. S56.
 14. Paid cash for advertising, $450.00. C88.
 14. Paid cash on account to Dunn Supplies, $1,413.00, covering M14; no discount. C89.
 15. Granted credit to Bland Company for merchandise returned, $126.00, plus sales tax, from S55. CM18.
 16. Sold merchandise on account to Barbra Almon, $742.00, plus sales tax. S57.
 16. Received cash on account from Bland Company, $128.07, covering S55 for $266.76 ($247.00 plus sales tax, $19.76), less CM18 ($126.00 plus sales tax), less 2% discount and less sales tax on discount. R29.
 16. Recorded cash and credit card sales, $2,246.00, plus sales tax. T16.
 Posting. Post the items that are to be posted individually.

April 19. Received cash on account from James Hart, $167.40, covering S50; no discount. R30.
 20. Purchased merchandise on account from Roland and Barnes, $216.00. P78.
 21. Sold merchandise on account to Linda Ponder, $623.00, plus sales tax. S58.
 23. Paid cash for miscellaneous expense, $205.00. C90.
 23. Received cash on account from Jefferson Co., $789.57, covering S56 for $805.68 ($746.00 plus sales tax, $59.68), less 2% discount and less sales tax on discount. R31.
 23. Recorded cash and credit card sales, $2,152.00, plus sales tax. T23.
     Posting. Post the items that are to be posted individually.
 26. Sold merchandise on account to Bland Company, $915.00, plus sales tax. S59.
 26. Purchased merchandise on account from Gibson Electric Co., $1,975.00. P79.
 29. Paid cash on account to Roland and Barnes, covering P78 for $216.00, less 1% discount. C91.
 29. Purchased merchandise on account from Webb Co., $985.00. P80.
 30. Recorded cash and credit card sales, $1,847.00, plus sales tax. T30.
 30. Paid cash to replenish the petty cash fund, $130.25: supplies, $45.15; advertising, $60.00; miscellaneous, $22.50; cash short, $2.60. C92.
     Posting. Post the items that are to be posted individually.

2. Prove and rule the sales journal. Post the totals of the special columns.

3. Total and rule the purchases journal. Post the total.

4. Prove the equality of debits and credits for the cash receipts and cash payments journals.

5. Prove cash. The cash balance on hand on April 1 was $7,690.00. The balance on the next unused check stub on April 30 is $12,797.61.

6. Rule the cash receipts journal. Post the totals of the special columns.

7. Rule the cash payments journal. Post the totals of the special columns.

8. Prepare a schedule of accounts receivable and a schedule of accounts payable similar to the ones described in Chapter 14. Compare each schedule total with the balance of the controlling account in the general ledger. The total and balance should be the same.

Reinforcement Activity 3, Part A

An Accounting Cycle for a Corporation: Journalizing and Posting Transactions

Reinforcement Activity 3 reinforces learnings from Part 4, Chapters 20 through 27, and covers a complete accounting cycle for a merchandising business organized as a corporation. Part A reinforces learnings from Chapters 20 and 21. Part B reinforces learnings from Chapters 22 through 27.

The general ledger account balances summarize transactions for the first eleven months of a fiscal year. The transactions given for December of the current year are for the last month of the fiscal year.

HARDWARE MART

Reinforcement Activity 3 includes accounting records for Hardware Mart. Hardware Mart sells home repair materials, electrical supplies, and small hand and power tools. The business, which is located in a shopping center, is open Monday through Saturday. Space for the business is rented. However, the corporation owns the office and store equipment.

CHART OF ACCOUNTS

Hardware Mart uses the chart of accounts shown on the next page.

JOURNALS AND LEDGERS

Hardware Mart uses the following journals and ledgers. Models of journals and ledgers are shown in the textbook illustrations given in the chart.

Journals and Ledgers	Chapter	Illustration Number
Sales journal	21	21-4
Purchases journal	20	20-4
General journal	20	20-22
Cash receipts journal	21	21-10
Cash payments journal	20	20-16
Accounts receivable ledger	21	21-9
Accounts payable ledger	20	20-14
General ledger	20	20-4

RECORDING TRANSACTIONS

The account balances for the general and subsidiary ledgers are given in the working papers accompanying this textbook.

HARDWARE MART
Chart of Accounts

Balance Sheet Accounts

(1000) ASSETS

1100 Current Assets

1105 Cash
1110 Petty Cash
1115 Notes Receivable
1120 Interest Receivable
1125 Accounts Receivable
1130 Allowance for Uncollectible
Accounts
1135 Merchandise Inventory
1140 Supplies
1145 Prepaid Insurance

1200 Plant Assets

1205 Office Equipment
1210 Accumulated Depreciation—
Office Equipment
1215 Store Equipment
1220 Accumulated Depreciation—
Store Equipment

(2000) LIABILITIES

2100 Current Liabilities

2105 Notes Payable
2110 Interest Payable
2115 Accounts Payable
2120 Employee Income Tax Payable
2125 Federal Income Tax Payable
2130 FICA Tax Payable
2135 Sales Tax Payable
2140 Unemployment Tax Payable—
Federal
2145 Unemployment Tax Payable—
State
2150 Health Insurance Premiums
Payable
2155 Dividends Payable

(3000) STOCKHOLDERS' EQUITY

3105 Capital Stock
3110 Retained Earnings
3115 Dividends
3120 Income Summary

Income Statement Accounts

(4000) OPERATING REVENUE

4105 Sales
4110 Sales Discount
4115 Sales Returns and Allowances

(5000) COST OF MERCHANDISE

5105 Purchases
5110 Purchases Discount
5115 Purchases Returns and
Allowances

(6000) OPERATING EXPENSES

6105 Advertising Expense
6110 Credit Card Fee Expense
6115 Depreciation Expense—Office
Equipment
6120 Depreciation Expense—Store
Equipment
6125 Insurance Expense
6130 Miscellaneous Expense
6135 Payroll Taxes Expense
6140 Rent Expense
6145 Salary Expense
6150 Supplies Expense
6155 Uncollectible Accounts Expense
6160 Utilities Expense

(7000) OTHER REVENUE

7105 Gain on Plant Assets
7110 Interest Income

(8000) OTHER EXPENSES

8105 Cash Short and Over
8110 Interest Expense
8115 Loss on Plant Assets

(9000) INCOME TAX EXPENSE

9105 Federal Income Tax Expense

Instructions: 1. Journalize the following transactions completed during December of the current year. Use page 12 of a sales journal, a purchases journal, a general journal, and a cash receipts journal. Use pages 23 and 24 of a cash payments journal. Hardware Mart offers its customers terms of 1/10, n/30. The sales tax rate is 8%. Source documents are abbreviated as follows: check, C; credit memorandum, CM; debit memorandum, DM; memorandum, M; purchase invoice, P; receipt, R; sales invoice, S; cash register tape, T.

Dec. 1. Paid cash for rent, $1,750.00. C310.

1. Received cash on account from Gerald Bell, $3,143.45, covering S180 for $3,175.20 ($2,940.00 plus sales tax, $235.20), less 1% discount, $29.40, and less sales tax, $2.35. R169.

1. Purchased merchandise on account from Granger Company, $11,728.00. P95.

2. Granted credit to Linda Franz for merchandise returned, $555.00, plus sales tax, $44.40, from S170; total, $599.40. CM23.

2. Received cash on account from Linda Franz, $2,975.40 (covering S170 less CM23), no discount. R170.

3. Sold merchandise on account to Paul Rodriguez, $2,130.00, plus sales tax, $170.40; total, $2,300.40. S188.

3. Paid cash on account to Beta Hardware Supplies, $4,176.37, covering P92 for $4,261.60, less 2% discount, $85.23. C311.

3. Recorded cash and credit card sales, $7,755.80, plus sales tax, $620.46; total, $8,376.26. T3.

> *Posting.* Post the items that are to be posted individually. Post the journals in this order: sales journal, purchases journal, general journal, cash receipts journal, and cash payments journal.

5. Returned merchandise to Granger Company, $1,620.00, from P90. DM25.

6. Paid cash on account to Sunbelt Corp., $3,132.86, covering P93 for $3,196.80, less 2% discount, $63.94. C312.

7. Received cash on account from Paul Rodriguez, $5,116.12, covering S185 for $5,167.80 ($4,785.00 plus sales tax, $382.80), less 1% discount, $47.85, and less sales tax, $3.83. R171.

7. Purchased merchandise on account from Western Tools, $5,730.00. P96.

8. Sold merchandise on account to Roy Heflin, $2,481.00, plus sales tax, $198.48; total, $2,679.48. S189.

8. Paid cash on account to Western Tools, $2,637.76, covering P94 for $2,664.40, less 1% discount, $26.64. C313.

9. Received cash on account from Roy Heflin, $4,374.00, covering S183; no discount. R172.

10. Paid cash for liability for November health insurance premiums, $625.00. C314.

10. Recorded cash and credit card sales, $14,542.20, plus sales tax, $1,163.38; total, $15,705.58. T10.

> *Posting.* Post the items that are to be posted individually.

12. Purchased merchandise on account from Sunbelt Corp., $11,652.00. P97.

13. Paid cash for miscellaneous expense, $227.50. C315.

13. Paid cash for supplies, $176.10. C316.

13. Received cash on account from Paul Rodriguez, $2,277.40, covering S188 for $2,300.40 ($2,130.00 plus sales tax, $170.40), less 1% discount, $21.30, and less sales tax, $1.70. R173.

14. Sold merchandise on account to Patricia Nielsen, $750.00, plus sales tax, $60.00; total, $810.00. S190.

Dec. 14. Paid cash for advertising, $579.50. C317.
15. Paid cash for semimonthly payroll, $3,247.50 (total payroll, $4,450.00, less deductions: employee income tax, $534.00; FICA tax, $356.00; health insurance premiums, $312.50). C318.
15. Recorded employer payroll taxes expense, $405.60 (FICA tax, $356.00; federal unemployment tax, $6.40; state unemployment tax, $43.20). M31.
15. Paid cash for liability for employee income tax, $1,075.00, and for FICA tax, $1,360.00; total, $2,435.00. C319.
15. Paid cash for quarterly estimated federal income tax, $3,500.00. C320. (Debit Federal Income Tax Expense; credit Cash.)
15. Paid cash to replenish the petty cash fund, $178.50: supplies, $26.75; advertising, $44.00; miscellaneous, $109.75; cash over, $2.00. C321.
16. Paid cash on account to Western Tools, $5,672.70, covering P96 for $5,730.00, less 1% discount, $57.30. C322.
16. Received cash on account from Patricia Nielsen, $2,381.40, covering S186; no discount. R174.
17. Received cash on account from Roy Heflin, $2,652.69, covering S189 for $2,679.48 ($2,481.00 plus sales tax, $198.48), less 1% discount, $24.81, and less sales tax, $1.98. R175.
17. Purchased merchandise for cash, $470.00. C323.
17. Recorded cash and credit card sales, $18,096.00, plus sales tax, $1,447.68; total, $19,543.68. T17.
   Posting. Post the items that are to be posted individually.
19. Paid cash for miscellaneous expense, $124.60. C324.
19. Sold merchandise on account to Linda Franz, $2,675.00, plus sales tax, $214.00; total, $2,889.00. S191.
20. Paid cash on account to Granger Company, $2,464.70, covering P90 for $4,084.70, less DM25, $1,620.00; no discount. C325.
21. Paid cash on account to Decorator Systems, $3,552.50, covering P91; no discount. C326.

2. Prove and rule page 23 of the cash payments journal.
3. Forward the totals from page 23 to page 24 of the cash payments journal.
4. Continue recording the following transactions.

Dec. 21. Paid cash for miscellaneous expense, $288.00. C327.
22. Purchased merchandise on account from Beta Hardware Supplies, $7,165.00. P98.
22. Paid cash on account to Sunbelt Corp., $11,418.96, covering P97 for $11,652.00, less 2% discount, $233.04. C328.
23. Purchased merchandise for cash, $617.50. C329.
24. Sold merchandise on account to Roy Heflin, $650.00, plus sales tax, $52.00; total, $702.00. S192.
24. Recorded cash and credit card sales, $14,003.60, plus sales tax, $1,120.29; total, $15,123.89. T24.
   Posting. Post the items that are to be posted individually.
26. Bought supplies on account from HiValue Electrical Co., $339.00. M32.
27. Sold merchandise on account to Gerald Bell, $1,854.00, plus sales tax, $148.32; total, $2,002.32. S193.
27. Paid cash for advertising, $441.30. C330.
28. Purchased merchandise on account from Western Tools, $11,474.00. P99.

Dec. 29. Received cash on account from Linda Franz, $2,860.11, covering S191 for $2,889.00 ($2,675.00 plus sales tax, $214.00), less 1% discount, $26.75, and less sales tax, $2.14. R176.

    29. Paid cash on account to Granger Company, $11,728.00, covering P95; no discount. C331.

    30. Sold merchandise on account to Paul Rodriguez, $875.00, plus sales tax, $70.00; total, $945.00. S194.

    30. Paid cash for liability for sales tax, $4,932.60. C332. (Debit Sales Tax Payable; credit Cash.)

    31. Paid cash for semimonthly payroll, $3,170.50 (total payroll, $4,300.00, less deductions: employee income tax, $473.00; FICA tax, $344.00; health insurance premiums, $312.50). C333.

    31. Recorded employer payroll taxes expense, $368.80 (FICA tax, $344.00; federal unemployment tax, $3.20; state unemployment tax, $21.60). M33.

    31. Recorded credit card fee expense for December, $776.60. M34. (Debit Credit Card Fee Expense; credit Cash.)

    31. Paid cash to replenish the petty cash fund, $171.20: supplies, $21.80; advertising, $52.00; miscellaneous, $96.40; cash short, $1.00. C334.

    31. Recorded cash and credit card sales, $4,524.00, plus sales tax, $361.92; total, $4,885.92. T31.

      Posting. Post the items that are to be posted individually.

5. Prove and rule the sales journal. Post the totals of the special columns.

6. Total and rule the purchases journal. Post the total.

7. Prove the equality of debits and credits for the cash receipts and cash payments journals.

8. Prove cash. The balance on the next unused check stub on December 31 is $54,777.45.

9. Rule the cash receipts journal. Post the totals of the special columns.

10. Rule the cash payments journal. Post the totals of the special columns.

11. Prepare a schedule of accounts receivable and a schedule of accounts payable. Compare each schedule total with the balance of the controlling account in the general ledger. The total and balance should be the same.

The general ledger used in Reinforcement Activity 3, Part A, is needed to complete Reinforcement Activity 3, Part B.

Computer Application 5
Automated Accounting Cycle for a Corporation: Journalizing and Posting Transactions

Businesses may use different accounting systems depending on the size and kind of business. Celluphone, the merchandising business described in Part 4, uses a manual accounting system. Celluphone manually records purchases, cash payments, sales, and cash receipts. Computer Application 5 describes procedures for using a microcomputer to record Celluphone's transactions. Computer Application 5 also contains instructions for using a microcomputer to solve Challenge Problem 21-C, Chapter 21.

AUTOMATED ACCOUNTING PROCEDURES FOR CELLUPHONE

Celluphone uses six forms to arrange its data for automated accounting.

1. General ledger file maintenance input form (FORM GL-1)—for building or changing a general ledger chart of accounts.
2. Accounts payable file maintenance input form (FORM AP-1)—for building or changing an accounts payable chart of accounts.
3. Accounts receivable file maintenance input form (FORM AR-1)—for building or changing an accounts receivable chart of accounts.
4. General ledger input form (FORM GL-2)—for recording general ledger opening account balances and for recording journal entries not affecting either accounts payable or accounts receivable.
5. Accounts payable input form (FORM AP-3)—for recording vendor opening account balances and for recording purchases on account, buying supplies on account, purchases returns and allowances, and cash payments on account.
6. Accounts receivable input form (FORM AR-3)—for recording customer opening account balances and for recording sales on account, sales returns and allowances, and cash receipts on account.

BUILDING A CHART OF ACCOUNTS

A general ledger file maintenance input form (FORM GL-1) is used to describe the general ledger chart of accounts. An accounts payable file maintenance input form (FORM AP-1) is used to describe the accounts payable chart of accounts. An accounts receivable file maintenance input form (FORM AR-1) is used to describe the accounts receivable chart of accounts.

After all lines on each file maintenance input form have been key-entered into the computer and posted, three reports are prepared. (1) General ledger chart of accounts. (2) Vendor list. (3) Customer list.

RECORDING OPENING ACCOUNT BALANCES

A general ledger input form (FORM GL-2) is used to journalize general ledger opening account balances. An accounts payable input form (FORM AP-3) is used to journalize vendor opening account balances. An accounts receivable input form (FORM AR-3) is used to journalize customer opening account balances.

After the opening account balances from each input form have been journalized on the input form, the amount columns are totaled. The totals are entered on the Batch Totals line provided at the bottom of the input form. If more than one input form is required to journalize opening account balances, the amount columns for all pages are totaled. The totals for all pages are then entered *only* on the last page on the Batch Totals line.

After the opening account balances on each input form have been key-entered into the computer and posted, three opening balances reports are prepared. (1) General ledger opening balances report. (2) Accounts payable opening balances report. (3) Accounts receivable opening balances report.

RECORDING TRANSACTIONS NOT AFFECTING SUBSIDIARY LEDGERS

A general ledger input form (FORM GL-2) is used to journalize transactions not affecting the accounts payable or accounts receivable subsidiary ledgers.

Each journal entry requires at least two lines on the general ledger input form. A journal entry should not be split between two different pages. Therefore, if a complete entry cannot be entered on a page, a new page is started.

After all transactions have been journalized on the input form, the Debit Amount and Credit Amount columns are totaled. The totals are entered on the Batch Totals line provided at the bottom of the general ledger

input form. If more than one general ledger input form is required to journalize transactions, the Debit Amount and Credit Amount columns for all
pages are totaled. The totals for all pages are then entered *only* on the last
page on the Batch Totals line.

After all lines on the input form have been key-entered into the computer and posted, a journal entries report is prepared.

RECORDING ACCOUNTS PAYABLE TRANSACTIONS

Four types of transactions affect Celluphone's accounts payable. (1) Purchases of merchandise on account. (2) Cash payments on account with or
without a purchase discount. (3) Purchases returns and allowances.
(4) Buying supplies on account. An accounts payable input form (FORM
AP-3) is used to journalize all transactions affecting accounts payable.

Celluphone's accounts payable input form (FORM AP-3) has more special columns than the input form used by CarLand in Computer Application 3. (1) A Debit Memos section is used for recording information about
debit memorandums. (2) A Disc. % column is included in the Cash Payments section. Use of these additional columns is described later in this
computer application.

Purchase of merchandise on account

March 1, 19--.
*Purchased merchandise on account from Cell Systems, $6,672.00. Purchase
Invoice No. 39.*

Illustration C5-1
Accounts payable input
form with transactions
entered

The entry to journalize this transaction is on line 1 of Illustration C5-1.

	PURCH. INVOICE NO.	VEND. NO.	DATE MO.	DATE DAY	DATE YR.	GEN. LEDGER ACCT. NO.	INVOICE AMOUNT	DATE MO.	DATE DAY	DATE YR.	MEMO. NO.	DEBIT MEMO. AMOUNT	DATE MO.	DATE DAY	DATE YR.	DISC. %	DISP. CODE	MANUAL CHECK NO.	
1	P39	220	03	01	--	5105	6672 00										A		1
2	P39												03	08	--	2	M	168	2
3	P30							03	08	--	DM18	375 00					A		3
4	M38	272	03	09	--	1140	228 00										A		4
20																			20

RUN DATE 03 31 / --   MM DD YY

BATCH NO. 2

ACCOUNTS PAYABLE
Input Form

FORM AP-3

BATCH TOTALS 108274 00   375 00

DISPOSITION CODE:
A = ON ACCOUNT
M = MANUAL CHECK

Cash payment on account with a purchase discount

March 8, 19--.
Paid cash on account to Cell Systems, $6,538.56, covering Purchase Invoice
No. 39 for $6,672.00, less 2% discount, $133.44. Check No. 168.

The entry to journalize this transaction is on line 2 of Illustration C5-1.

The purchase invoice number to be paid, *P39*, is written in the Purch. Invoice No. column. The Purchases and Debit Memos sections are left blank for a cash payment on account transaction. The date of the payment, *03/08/--*, is entered in the Cash Payments Date columns. The discount percent, *2*, is written in the Disc. % column. The disposition code, *M*, is written in the Disp. Code column. Writing an *M* in this column indicates that a check is to be manually prepared. The check number, *168*, is written in the Manual Check No. column.

Purchase return

March 8, 19--.
Returned merchandise to Interstate Com, $375.00, covering Purchase Invoice
No. 30. Debit Memorandum No. 18.

The entry to journalize this transaction is on line 3 of Illustration C5-1.

The purchase invoice number to which the returned merchandise applies, *P30*, is written in the Purch. Invoice No. column. The date on which the merchandise was returned, *03/08/--*, is entered in the Debit Memos Date columns. The debit memorandum number, *DM18*, is entered in the Memo. No. column. The amount of the purchase return, *$375.00*, is written in the Debit Memo. Amount column. The disposition code, *A*, is written in the Disp. Code column.

Buying supplies on account

March 9, 19--.
Bought supplies on account from Kryger Supplies, $228.00. Memorandum
No. 38.

The entry to journalize this transaction is on line 4 of Illustration C5-1.

After all accounts payable transactions have been journalized on the input form, the Invoice Amount and Debit Memo. Amount columns are totaled. The totals are entered on the Batch Totals line provided at the bottom of the accounts payable input form. If more than one accounts payable input form is required to journalize accounts payable transactions, the amount columns for all pages are totaled. The totals for all pages are then entered *only* on the last page on the Batch Totals line.

Processing accounts payable transactions

After all lines on the input form have been key-entered into the computer and posted, two reports are prepared. (1) Purchases on account report. (2) Cash payments report. The purchases on account report is checked for accuracy by comparing the report total with the Purchases Invoice Amount Batch Total on the input form. The cash payments report is checked for accuracy by comparing the report total debit memos amount with the Debit Memo Amount Batch Total on the input form.

Next, a general ledger posting summary is prepared. This summary lists all entries posted by the computer to the general ledger based on the accounts payable transactions. Lastly, a schedule of accounts payable is prepared.

RECORDING ACCOUNTS RECEIVABLE TRANSACTIONS

Three types of transactions affect Celluphone's accounts receivable. (1) Sales on account. (2) Cash receipts on account with or without a sales discount. (3) Sales returns and allowances. An accounts receivable input form (FORM AR-3) is used to journalize all transactions affecting accounts receivable.

Celluphone's accounts receivable input form (FORM AR-3) has more special columns than the input form used by CarLand in Computer Application 3. (1) A Credit Memos section is used for recording information about credit memorandums. (2) A Disc. % column in the Cash Receipts section. Use of these additional columns is described later in this computer application.

Sale on account

> March 1, 19--.
> Sold merchandise on account to DTex Imports, $1,600.00, plus sales tax, $128.00; total, $1,728.00. Sales Invoice No. 148.

The entry to journalize this transaction is on line 1 of Illustration C5-2.

Cash receipt on account with a sales discount

> March 11, 19--.
> Received cash on account from DTex Imports, $1,710.72, covering Sales Invoice No. 148 for $1,728.00 ($1,600.00 plus sales tax, $128.00), less 1% discount, $16.00, and less sales tax, $1.28. Receipt No. 232.

The entry to journalize this transaction is on line 2 of Illustration C5-2. The sales invoice number to which the sales discount applies, S148, is written in the Sales Invoice No. column. The date on which cash is received, 03/11/--, is entered in the Cash Receipts Date columns. The source document number, R232, is entered in the Doc. No. column. The sales discount percent, 1, is written in the Disc. % column. The amount of cash received, $1,710.72, is written in the Cash Received column.

When cash received on account does not include a sales discount, the Disc. % column is left blank.

	SALES INVOICE NO.	CUST. NO.	DATE MO.	DATE DAY	DATE YR.	GEN. LEDGER ACCT. NO.	INVOICE AMOUNT	SALES TAX %	DATE MO.	DATE DAY	DATE YR.	MEMO. NO.	CREDIT MEMO AMOUNT	DATE MO.	DATE DAY	DATE YR.	DOC. NO.	DISC. %	CASH RECEIVED	
1	S148	120	03	01	--	4105	1600 00	8												1
2	S148													03	11	--	R232	1	1710 72	2
15	S160								03	11	--	CM41	180 00							15
20																				20
	BATCH TOTALS						82050 00						180 00						85920 00	

RUN DATE 03 31 / --   MM DD YY

BATCH NO. 2

ACCOUNTS RECEIVABLE
Input Form

FORM AR-3

Illustration C5-2
Accounts receivable input
form with transactions
entered

Sales return

March 11, 19--.
Granted credit to Alamo Company for merchandise returned, $180.00, plus sales tax, $14.40, from Sales Invoice No. 160; total, $194.40. Credit Memorandum No. 41.

The entry to journalize this transaction is on line 15 of Illustration C5-2.

The sales invoice number for which the credit is granted, *S160*, is written in the Sales Invoice No. column. The date on which the credit is granted, *03/11/--*, is entered in the Credit Memos Date columns. The credit memorandum number, *CM41*, is written in the Memo. No. column. The amount of the credit for merchandise returned, *$180.00*, is entered in the Credit Memo Amount column. The software calculates the amount of sales tax on the sales return.

After all accounts receivable transactions have been journalized on the input form, the Invoice Amount, Credit Memo Amount, and Cash Received columns are totaled. The totals are entered on the Batch Totals line provided at the bottom of the input form. If more than one accounts receivable input form is required to journalize accounts receivable transactions, the amount columns for all pages are totaled. The totals for all pages are then entered *only* on the last page on the Batch Totals line.

Processing accounts receivable transactions

After all lines on the input form have been key-entered into the computer and posted, two reports are prepared. (1) Sales on account report. (2) Cash receipts report. The sales on account report is checked for accuracy by comparing the report's invoice amount total with the Sales Invoice Amount Batch Total on the input form. The cash receipts report is checked for accuracy by comparing the Total Credit Memos and Total Cash Receipts amounts with the Batch Totals on the input form for Credit Memo Amount and Cash Received.

Next, a general ledger posting summary is prepared. This summary lists all entries posted by the computer to the general ledger based on accounts receivable transactions. Lastly, a schedule of accounts receivable is prepared.

■ COMPUTER APPLICATION PROBLEM

COMPUTER APPLICATION PROBLEM 5   **Journalizing and posting transactions**

Instructions: 1. Journalize transactions from Challenge Problem 21-C, Chapter 21, on appropriate computer input forms.
a. Journalize entries *NOT* affecting either accounts payable or accounts receivable on a general ledger input form (FORM GL-2). Use April 30 of the current year as the run date. Batch No. 2.
b. Journalize purchases on account, purchases returns and allowances, supplies bought on account, and cash payments on account on an accounts payable input form (FORM AP-3). Use April 30 of the current year as the run date. Batch No. 2.
c. Journalize sales on account, sales returns and allowances, and cash received on account on an accounts receivable input form (FORM AR-3). Use April 30 of the current year as the run date. Batch No. 2.

2. Load the *Automated Accounting for the Microcomputer* software. Select Computer Application 5 (CA-5) from the CENTURY 21 ACCOUNTING Template Disk. The accounting system data, chart of accounts, opening balances, and company name have been entered and are stored on the Template Disk.
3. Key-enter data from the completed general ledger input form.
4. Display/Print the journal entries report.
5. Key-enter data from the completed accounts payable input form.
6. Display/Print the purchases on account report.
7. Display/Print the cash payments report.
8. Display/Print the general ledger posting summary.
9. Display/Print the schedule of accounts payable.
10. Key-enter data from the completed accounts receivable input form.
11. Display/Print the sales on account report.
12. Display/Print the cash receipts report.
13. Display/Print the general ledger posting summary.
14. Display/Print the schedule of accounts receivable.

DANGER HARD HAT AREA

22

Accounting for Uncollectible Accounts Receivable

ENABLING PERFORMANCE TASKS

After studying Chapter 22, you will be able to:
a. Define accounting terms related to uncollectible accounts.
b. Identify accounting concepts and practices related to uncollectible accounts.
c. Figure estimated uncollectible accounts expense.
d. Journalize and post entries related to uncollectible accounts.

A business generally sells on account to encourage sales. If sales on account are offered, customers may buy merchandise today even though they will not have the cash needed until later. Also, when sales on account are offered, sales can be made over the telephone or by mail more easily without requiring immediate cash payment.

Although many businesses sell on account, they do expect full payment within the terms of sale. Most businesses thoroughly investigate customers before selling to them on credit. Even with a thorough credit investigation, however, some accounts receivable will be uncollectible. Accounts receivable that cannot be collected are called uncollectible accounts. Uncollectible accounts are also known as bad debts.

If a business fails to collect from a customer, the business loses part of the asset *Accounts Receivable*. The amount of the accounts receivable not collected is recorded as an expense. Celluphone records the expense caused by uncollectible accounts in an account titled *Uncollectible Accounts Expense*. Uncollectible Accounts Expense is also referred to as bad debts expense. An uncollectible amount does not decrease revenue. Instead, the loss is considered a regular expense of doing business. Revenue was earned when the sale was made. *(CONCEPT: Realization of Revenue)* Failing to collect an account does not cancel the sale. Therefore the loss is treated as an expense.

ESTIMATING AND RECORDING UNCOLLECTIBLE ACCOUNTS EXPENSE

Risk of loss occurs when a business sells on account. This potential loss is present even though several months may pass before the actual loss becomes known. Accurate financial reporting requires that expenses be recorded in the fiscal period in which the expenses contribute to earning revenue. *(CONCEPT: Matching Expenses with Revenue)* The balance of Accounts Receivable, a controlling account, must equal the sum of the customer accounts in the subsidiary ledger. A business does not know at the time sales are made which customer accounts will become uncollectible. If a business knew exactly which accounts would become uncollectible in the future, it could credit Accounts Receivable and each customer account for the uncollectible amounts. Uncollectible Accounts Expense could then be debited for the same amount. However, businesses do not know which customers will not pay their accounts in the future. Therefore, specific customer accounts cannot be credited for uncollectible amounts. The accounts receivable general ledger account also cannot be credited for these amounts. However, at the end of each fiscal period, a business can calculate and record an *estimated* amount of uncollectible accounts expense.

Estimating and recording uncollectible accounts expense at the end of a fiscal period accomplishes two objectives. (1) An up-to-date value of uncollectible accounts prevents an overstatement of the value of accounts receivable on the balance sheet. (2) Recording the estimated uncollectible accounts expense prevents an understatement of expenses on the income statement.

To record estimated uncollectible accounts, an adjusting entry is made affecting two accounts: Uncollectible Accounts Expense and Allowance for Uncollectible Accounts. The estimated value of uncollectible accounts is debited to Uncollectible Accounts Expense. An expense account has a normal debit balance. Therefore, the uncollectible accounts expense account is increased by a debit and decreased by a credit, as shown in the T account.

The estimated value of uncollectible accounts is also credited to an account titled *Allowance for Uncollectible Accounts*. An account that reduces a related account is known as a contra account. Allowance for Uncollectible Accounts is a contra account to its related asset account, Accounts Receivable. A contra asset account has a normal credit balance because it reduces the balance of an asset account. Therefore, Allowance for Uncollectible Accounts is increased by a credit and decreased by a debit, as shown in the T account.

Uncollectible Accounts Expense	
Debit side Normal balance Increase	Credit side Decrease

Accounts Receivable	
Debit side Normal balance Increase	Credit side Decrease

Allowance for Uncollectible Accounts	
Debit side Decrease	Credit side Normal balance Increase

Allowance for Bad Debts and Allowance for Doubtful Accounts are account titles sometimes used instead of Allowance for Uncollectible Accounts.

Crediting the estimated value of uncollectible accounts to a contra account is called the allowance method of recording losses from uncollectible accounts. The difference between the balance of Accounts Receivable and its contra account, Allowance for Uncollectible Accounts, is called the book value of accounts receivable. The book value of accounts receivable is reported on a balance sheet as shown in Chapter 27.

A contra account is usually assigned the next account number following its related account. Celluphone's accounts receivable account is numbered 1125. Allowance for Uncollectible Accounts is numbered 1130.

Estimating uncollectible accounts expense

Many businesses use a percentage of total sales on account to estimate uncollectible accounts expense. Each sale on account represents a risk of loss from an uncollectible account. Therefore, if the estimated percentage of loss is accurate, the amount of uncollectible accounts expense will be accurate regardless of when the actual losses occur. Since a sale on account creates a risk of loss, estimating the percentage of uncollectible accounts expense for the same period matches sales revenue with related uncollectible accounts expense. (CONCEPT: Matching Expenses with Revenue)

Celluphone estimates uncollectible accounts expense by figuring a percentage of total sales on account. A review of Celluphone's previous experience in collecting sales on account shows that actual uncollectible accounts expense has been about 1% of total sales on account. The company's total sales on account for the year is $922,700.00. Thus, Celluphone's uncollectible accounts expense is calculated as shown below.

Total Sales on Account	× Percentage =	Estimated Uncollectible Accounts Expense
$922,700.00 ×	1% =	$9,227.00

Celluphone estimates that of the $922,700.00 sales on account during the year, $9,227.00 will eventually be uncollectible.

Analyzing an adjustment for uncollectible accounts expense

An adjustment is made to record estimated uncollectible accounts expense for a fiscal year. The effect of Celluphone's uncollectible accounts expense adjustment is shown in the T accounts.

Uncollectible Accounts Expense is debited for $9,227.00 to show the increase in the balance of this expense account. The balance of this account, $9,227.00, is the uncollectible accounts expense for the fiscal period.

Allowance for Uncollectible Accounts is credited for $9,227.00 to show the increase in the balance of this contra asset account. The previous balance,

Uncollectible Accounts Expense	
Dec. 31 Adj. 9,227.00	

Allowance for Uncollectible Accounts	
	Bal. 265.00
	Dec. 31 Adj. 9,227.00
	(New Bal. 9,492.00)

$265.00, plus the fiscal year increase, $9,227.00, equals the December 31 balance, $9,492.00. After the adjustment, Celluphone estimates that $9,492.00 of accounts receivable will be uncollectible.

Entering an adjustment for uncollectible accounts expense on a work sheet

At the end of a fiscal period, an adjustment for uncollectible accounts expense is planned on a work sheet. Celluphone's adjustment for uncollectible accounts expense is shown in the Adjustments columns of the partial work sheet in Illustration 22-1.

		1	2	3	4
---	ACCOUNT TITLE	TRIAL BALANCE		ADJUSTMENTS	
		DEBIT	CREDIT	DEBIT	CREDIT
6	*Allowance for Uncollectible Accts.*		2 6 5 00		(b)9 2 2 7 00
45	*Uncollectible Accounts Exp.*			(b)9 2 2 7 00	

Illustration 22-1
Uncollectible accounts
expense adjustment on a
work sheet

On line 45 of the work sheet, Uncollectible Accounts Expense is debited for $9,227.00 in the Adjustments Debit column. On line 6 Allowance for Uncollectible Accounts is credited for $9,227.00 in the Adjustments Credit column.

The percentage of total sales on account method of estimating uncollectible accounts expense assumes that a portion of every sale on account dollar will become uncollectible. An Allowance for Uncollectible Accounts balance in the Trial Balance Credit column means that previous fiscal period estimates have not yet been identified as uncollectible. When the allowance account has a previous credit balance, the amount of the adjustment is added to the previous balance. The new balance is then extended to the Balance Sheet Credit column. This new balance of the allowance account is the estimated amount of accounts receivable that will eventually become uncollectible.

Journalizing an adjusting entry for uncollectible accounts expense

Information used to journalize an uncollectible accounts expense adjusting entry is obtained from a work sheet's Adjustments columns. The adjusting entry for uncollectible accounts expense is shown in the general journal in Illustration 22-2.

Posting an adjusting entry for uncollectible accounts expense

After the adjusting entry is posted, Accounts Receivable, Allowance for Uncollectible Accounts, and Uncollectible Accounts Expense appear as shown in Illustration 22-3.

GENERAL JOURNAL

PAGE *15*

	DATE	ACCOUNT TITLE	DOC. NO.	POST. REF.	DEBIT	CREDIT	
1		*Adjusting Entries*					1
4	31	*Uncollectible Accounts Expense*			9 2 2 7 00		4
5		*Allow. for Uncollectible Accts.*				9 2 2 7 00	5

Illustration 22-2
Adjusting entry for
uncollectible accounts
expense

Illustration 22-3
General ledger accounts
after adjusting entry for
uncollectible accounts
expense is posted

ACCOUNT *Accounts Receivable*   ACCOUNT NO. *1125*

DATE	ITEM	POST. REF.	DEBIT	CREDIT	BALANCE DEBIT	BALANCE CREDIT
Dec. 31		S50	83 8 4 0 00		129 6 6 0 00	
31		CR49		61 4 2 0 00	68 2 4 0 00	

ACCOUNT *Allowance for Uncollectible Accounts*   ACCOUNT NO. *1130*

DATE	ITEM	POST. REF.	DEBIT	CREDIT	BALANCE DEBIT	BALANCE CREDIT
Dec. 27		G14	4 9 0 00			2 6 5 00
31		G15		9 2 2 7 00		9 4 9 2 00

ACCOUNT *Uncollectible Accounts Expense*   ACCOUNT NO. *6155*

DATE	ITEM	POST. REF.	DEBIT	CREDIT	BALANCE DEBIT	BALANCE CREDIT
Dec. 31		G15	9 2 2 7 00		9 2 2 7 00	

Accounts Receivable has a debit balance of $68,240.00, the total amount due from customers on December 31. Allowance for Uncollectible Accounts has a credit balance of $9,492.00 on December 31. The balance of this contra account is to be subtracted from the balance of its related account, Accounts Receivable, on the balance sheet. The debit balance of Uncollectible Accounts Expense is $9,227.00. This amount is the estimated uncollectible accounts expense for the current fiscal year ended December 31.

The December 27 Allowance for Uncollectible Accounts entry, $490.00, is the amount of an account that was determined to be uncollectible. Canceling uncollectible accounts is described in the next section of this chapter.

The book value of accounts receivable on December 31 is calculated as shown below.

Accounts Receivable	−	Balance of Allowance for Uncollectible Accounts	=	Book Value of Accounts Receivable
$68,240.00	−	$9,492.00	=	$58,748.00

CANCELING UNCOLLECTIBLE ACCOUNTS RECEIVABLE

Celluphone uses a planned collection procedure to collect customer accounts. Most customers pay when accounts are due. However, a few accounts, regardless of collection efforts, prove to be uncollectible. When a customer account is determined to be uncollectible, a journal entry is made to cancel the uncollectible account. This entry cancels the uncollectible amount from the general ledger account Accounts Receivable as well as the customer account in the accounts receivable subsidiary ledger. Canceling the balance of a customer account because the customer does not pay is called writing off an account.

Journalizing writing off an uncollectible account receivable

After several months of unsuccessful collection efforts, Celluphone decides that the past-due account of North Star Co. is uncollectible.

January 3, 19--.
Wrote off North Star Co.'s past-due account as uncollectible, $556.00. Memorandum No. 2.

GENERAL LEDGER

Allowance for Uncollectible Accounts

Jan. 3	556.00	Bal.	9,492.00
		(New Bal.	*8,936.00)*

Accounts Receivable

Bal.	68,240.00	Jan. 3	556.00
(New Bal.	*67,684.00)*		

ACCOUNTS RECEIVABLE LEDGER

North Star Co.

Bal.	556.00	Jan. 3	556.00

The entry to write off this uncollectible account is analyzed in the T accounts.

Allowance for Uncollectible Accounts is debited for $556.00 to reduce the balance of this contra asset account. This specific amount, $556.00, is no longer an estimate because the account of North Star Co. has been determined to be uncollectible. Therefore, the amount of the uncollectible account is deducted from the allowance account. The new balance of the allowance account is $8,936.00 ($9,492.00 less $556.00).

Accounts Receivable is credited for $556.00 to reduce the balance due from customers. The new balance of the accounts receivable account is $67,684.00 ($68,240.00 less $556.00).

North Star's account in the accounts receivable ledger is also credited for $556.00. This entry cancels the debit balance of the account. North Star's account is written off.

The book value of accounts receivable is the same both before and after writing off an uncollectible account. The book value of accounts receivable before writing off North Star's account is calculated as shown below.

	Balance of Allowance for	Book Value of
Accounts Receivable −	Uncollectible Accounts =	Accounts Receivable
$68,240.00 −	$9,492.00 =	$58,748.00

The book value of accounts receivable after writing off North Star's account is calculated as shown below.

	Balance of Allowance for	Book Value of
Accounts Receivable −	Uncollectible Accounts =	Accounts Receivable
$67,684.00 −	$8,936.00 =	$58,748.00

The book value remains the same because the same amount is deducted from both the accounts receivable account and the allowance account.

The general journal entry to write off North Star's account is shown in Illustration 22-4.

GENERAL JOURNAL   PAGE *18*

	DATE	ACCOUNT TITLE	DOC. NO.	POST. REF.	DEBIT	CREDIT	
8	3	*Allowance for Uncollectible Accts.*	M2		5 5 6 00		8
9		*Accts. Receivable/North Star Co.*		/		5 5 6 00	9
10							10
11							11
12							12
13							13
14							14

Illustration 22-4
General journal entry to write off an uncollectible account

Allowance for Uncollectible Accounts is debited for $556.00. Accounts Receivable and North Star's account are both credited for $556.00.

Posting an entry to write off an uncollectible account receivable

After the journal entry to write off an uncollectible account is posted, the two general ledger accounts, Accounts Receivable and Allowance for Uncollectible Accounts, and the customer account appear as shown in Illustration 22-5. The words *Written off* are written in the Item column of the customer account to show the full credit history for the customer.

ACCOUNT *Accounts Receivable*   **ACCOUNT NO.** *1125*

DATE		ITEM	POST. REF.	DEBIT	CREDIT	BALANCE DEBIT	BALANCE CREDIT
	31		CR49		61 420 00	68 240 00	
19X2 Jan.	3		G18		5 56 00	67 684 00	

ACCOUNT *Allowance for Uncollectible Accounts*   **ACCOUNT NO.** *1130*

DATE		ITEM	POST. REF.	DEBIT	CREDIT	BALANCE DEBIT	BALANCE CREDIT
	31		G15		9 227 00		9 492 00
19X2 Jan.	3		G18	5 56 00			8 936 00

CUSTOMER *North Star Co.*   **CUSTOMER NO.** *150*

DATE		ITEM	POST. REF.	DEBIT	CREDIT	DEBIT BALANCE
19X1 Apr.	6		S12	5 56 00		5 56 00
19X2 Jan.	3	Written off	G18		5 56 00	——

Illustration 22-5
General ledger and customer accounts after entry for writing off an uncollectible account is posted

COLLECTING WRITTEN-OFF ACCOUNTS RECEIVABLE

A business writes off a specific account receivable after determining that the account probably will not be collected. Occasionally, after an account has been written off, the customer pays the delinquent account. Several accounts must be changed to recognize payment of a written-off account receivable.

Journalizing collecting a written-off account receivable

January 7, 19--.
Received cash in full payment of North Star Co.'s account, previously written off as uncollectible, $556.00. Memorandum No. 3 and Receipt No. 4.

The accounts must be changed to show that North Star did pay its account. The accounts also should be changed to show a complete credit history of North Star's dealings with Celluphone. Two journal entries are recorded for the collection of a written-off account receivable. (1) A general journal entry to reopen the customer account. (2) A cash receipts journal entry to record the cash received on account.

GENERAL LEDGER
Accounts Receivable

Bal.	68,240.00	Jan. 3	556.00
Jan. 7	556.00		

Allowance for Uncollectible Accounts

Jan. 3	556.00	Bal.	9,492.00
		Jan. 7	556.00

ACCOUNTS RECEIVABLE LEDGER
North Star Co.

Bal.	556.00	Jan. 3	556.00
Jan. 7	556.00		
(New Bal.	556.00)		

General journal entry to reopen the customer account.
To show an accurate credit history, North Star's account is reopened. The effect of this entry to reopen North Star's account is shown in the T accounts.

Accounts Receivable is debited for $556.00. This debit entry replaces the amount previously written off in the general ledger account Accounts Receivable. Allowance for Uncollectible Accounts is credited for $556.00. This credit entry replaces the amount in the allowance account that was removed when North Star's account was previously written off. Also, North Star's account in the accounts receivable ledger is debited for $556.00. This entry to reopen the account is the exact reverse of the entry to write off North Star's account.

The general journal entry to reopen North Star's account in the accounts receivable ledger is shown in Illustration 22-6.

	DATE	ACCOUNT TITLE	DOC. NO.	POST. REF.	DEBIT	CREDIT	
16	7	*Accounts Receivable/North Star Co.*	M3	/	556 00		16
17		*Allow. for Uncollectible Accts.*				556 00	17
18							18

GENERAL JOURNAL PAGE *18*

Illustration 22-6
General journal entry to reopen customer account previously written off

Cash receipts journal entry to record cash received for an account previously written off. After the entry to reopen North Star's account is recorded, an entry is made to record the cash received on North Star's account. The effect of this entry to record a cash receipt on account is shown in the T accounts.

Cash is debited for $556.00. Accounts Receivable is credited for $556.00. North Star's account in the accounts receivable ledger is also credited for $556.00.

The cash receipts journal entry to record the receipt of cash on account from North Star Co. is shown in Illustration 22-7.

GENERAL LEDGER
Cash

Jan. 7	556.00	

Accounts Receivable

Bal.	68,240.00	Jan. 3	556.00
Jan. 7	556.00	Jan. 7	556.00

ACCOUNTS RECEIVABLE LEDGER
North Star Co.

Bal.	556.00	Jan. 3	556.00
Jan. 7	556.00	Jan. 7	556.00
		(New Bal.	zero)

CASH RECEIPTS JOURNAL   PAGE 51

	DATE	ACCOUNT TITLE	DOC. NO.	POST. REF.	GENERAL DEBIT	GENERAL CREDIT	ACCOUNTS RECEIVABLE CREDIT	SALES CREDIT	SALES TAX PAYABLE DEBIT	SALES TAX PAYABLE CREDIT	SALES DISCOUNT DEBIT	CASH DEBIT	
1	19X2 Jan. 7	North Star Co.	R4				5 5 6 00					5 5 6 00	1
2													2

Illustration 22-7
Cash receipts journal entry
to record cash received for
an account previously
written off

Posting an entry for collecting a written-off account receivable

After posting the two entries to reopen North Star's account and to
record collection of the account, the accounts affected appear as shown in
Illustration 22-8.

ACCOUNT **Accounts Receivable**   ACCOUNT NO. 1125

DATE	ITEM	POST. REF.	DEBIT	CREDIT	BALANCE DEBIT	BALANCE CREDIT
31		CR49		61 4 2 0 00	68 2 4 0 00	
19X2 Jan. 3		G18		5 5 6 00	67 6 8 4 00	
7		G18	5 5 6 00		68 2 4 0 00	

ACCOUNT **Allowance for Uncollectible Accounts**   ACCOUNT NO. 1130

DATE	ITEM	POST. REF.	DEBIT	CREDIT	BALANCE DEBIT	BALANCE CREDIT
31		G15		9 2 2 7 00		9 4 9 2 00
19X2 Jan. 3		G18	5 5 6 00			8 9 3 6 00
7		G18		5 5 6 00		9 4 9 2 00

CUSTOMER **North Star Co.**   CUSTOMER NO. 150

DATE	ITEM	POST. REF.	DEBIT	CREDIT	DEBIT BALANCE
19X1 Apr. 6		S12	5 5 6 00		5 5 6 00
19X2 Jan. 3	Written off	G18		5 5 6 00	——
7	Reopen account	G18	5 5 6 00		5 5 6 00
7		CR51		5 5 6 00	——

Illustration 22-8
General ledger and
customer accounts after
collection of a previously
written-off account

North Star's account balance is zero. The entries in North Star's account show a complete history of North Star's credit dealings with Celluphone. The account shows the April 6 balance, $556.00, and the balance written off on January 3. On January 7 the account is debited for the same amount, $556.00, to reopen North Star's account. The words *Reopen account* are written in the Item column to describe this entry. Also, on January 7 the account is credited for $556.00 to record payment of the account.

Entries resulting from cash received for a previously written-off account are recorded in a cash receipts journal's special amount columns. These amounts are posted to the general ledger accounts at the end of the month as part of the column totals.

SUMMARY OF ACCOUNTING FOR UNCOLLECTIBLE ACCOUNTS RECEIVABLE

The chart shown in Illustration 22-9 summarizes the entries for transactions related to uncollectible accounts.

Illustration 22-9
Summary of entries for uncollectible accounts receivable

TRANSACTIONS		GENERAL LEDGER								ACCTS. REC. SUBSIDIARY LEDGER	
		CASH		ACCTS. REC.		ALLOW. FOR UNCOLL. ACCTS.		UNCOLL. ACCTS. EXPENSE		CUSTOMER ACCOUNT	
		DEBIT	CREDIT	DEBIT	CREDIT	DEBIT	CREDIT	DEBIT	CREDIT	DEBIT	CREDIT
Adjusting entry for uncollectible accounts expense							X	X			
Write off uncollectible account receivable					X	X					X
Collect previously written off account receivable	Entry 1			X			X			X	
	2	X			X						X

ACCOUNTING TERMS

What is the meaning of each of the following?
1. uncollectible accounts
2. allowance method of recording losses from uncollectible accounts
3. book value of accounts receivable
4. writing off an account

QUESTIONS FOR INDIVIDUAL STUDY

1. Why might a business sell merchandise on account?
2. Why is an uncollectible account recorded as an expense rather than a reduction in revenue?
3. When does the risk of loss from a sale on account occur?
4. Which accounting concept is being ap-

plied when uncollectible accounts expense is recorded in the same fiscal period in which the expense contributes to earning revenue?

5. When do businesses normally estimate the amount of their uncollectible accounts expense?

6. What two objectives will be accomplished by recording an estimated amount of uncollectible accounts expense?

7. Why is Allowance for Uncollectible Accounts called a contra account?

8. Why would a business use a percentage of total sales on account to estimate uncollectible accounts expense?

9. What is the procedure for estimating uncollectible accounts expense based on total sales on account?

10. What accounts are affected, and how, when an adjusting entry is made to record uncollectible accounts expense?

11. What kind of situation would cause Allowance for Uncollectible Accounts to have a balance in the work sheet's Trial Balance Credit column?

12. How is the book value of accounts receivable figured?

13. What accounts are affected, and how, when an uncollectible account is written off?

14. Why is Allowance for Uncollectible Accounts debited when a customer account is written off?

15. Does the book value of accounts receivable differ before and after writing off an account? Explain.

16. Why is a customer account reopened when the account is paid after being previously written off?

17. What accounts are affected, and how, when a written-off account receivable is collected?

18. How does the journal entry for reopening an account previously written off differ from an entry for writing off an account?

◼ CASES FOR MANAGEMENT DECISION

CASE 1 CompuCraft Corporation has always assumed that an account receivable is good until the account is proven to be uncollectible. When an account proves to be uncollectible, the credit manager notifies the accounting clerk to write off the account. The accounting clerk then debits Uncollectible Accounts Expense and credits Accounts Receivable. Recently the company's new accountant, Diane Wilson, suggested that the method be changed for recording uncollectible accounts expense. Mrs. Wilson recommended that the company estimate uncollectible accounts expense based on a percentage of total sales on account. Mrs. Wilson stated that the change would provide more accurate information on the income statement and balance sheet. Do you agree with Mrs. Wilson that her recommended method would provide more accurate information? Explain.

CASE 2 Ulrick Corporation credits Accounts Receivable for the amount of estimated uncollectible accounts expense at the end of each fiscal period. Lindsey Company credits Allowance for Uncollectible Accounts for the amount of estimated uncollectible accounts expense at the end of each fiscal period. Which company is using the better method? Why?

CASE 3 Gates, Inc., debits Cash and credits Accounts Receivable when an account is paid that was previously written off. The new accounting clerk, James Thompson, recommends that when a previously written-off account is collected, the account be reopened. Cash is then debited and Accounts Receivable and the customer account are credited. Which is the better procedure? Why?

DRILLS FOR UNDERSTANDING

DRILL 22-D1 Estimating uncollectible accounts expense

The accounting records of six stores show the following summary information for the fiscal period ended December 31 of the current year.

Store	Total Sales on Account	Estimated Uncollectible Accounts as Percentage of Sales on Account	Balance of Allowance for Uncollectible Accounts Before Adjustment
1	$48,700.00	0.6%	$32.00 Credit
2	73,900.00	0.5%	63.00 Credit
3	95,200.00	1.0%	24.00 Debit
4	61,400.00	0.7%	79.00 Credit
5	54,800.00	0.4%	Zero
6	89,600.00	0.8%	57.00 Debit

Instructions: For each of the six stores, calculate the following:
a. Uncollectible accounts expense.
b. Balance of allowance for Uncollectible Accounts after adjustment.

DRILL 22-D2 Analyzing entries for uncollectible accounts

Instructions: Use a form similar to the following. Analyze each entry. For each entry indicate how each account is affected by writing one of the following: *DR* if debited, *CR* if credited, or *NE* if no entry is made.

Transaction	General Ledger				Accounts Receivable Ledger Customer Account
	Cash	Accounts Receivable	Allowance for Uncollectible Accounts	Uncollectible Accounts Expense	
A. Adjusting entry for uncollectible accounts expense at end of fiscal period					
B. Wrote off an uncollectible account					
C. Collected account previously written off 1) Entry 1:					
2) Entry 2:					

■ APPLICATION PROBLEMS

PROBLEM 22-1   Estimating and journalizing entries for uncollectible accounts expense

Use the following information from the records of Caraway Company for three successive years.

Year	Total Sales on Account	Balance of Allowance for Uncollectible Accounts Before Adjustment
19X1	$473,221.00	$171.00 Credit
19X2	495,074.00	279.00 Credit
19X3	516,978.00	392.80 Credit

Caraway Company estimates uncollectible accounts expense as 1.0% of its total sales on account.

Instructions: 1. For each year record the uncollectible accounts expense adjustment on a work sheet.

    2. For each year journalize the adjusting entry on page 13 of a general journal.

PROBLEM 22-2   Recording entries to write off uncollectible accounts receivable

During June of the current year, Alphacom Corporation determined that three accounts were uncollectible.

Instructions: 1. Journalize the entries to write off the following accounts. Use page 6 of a general journal. The abbreviation for memorandum is M.

June   4. Wrote off Davidson Corporation's past-due account as uncollectible, $347.00. M13.
      15. Wrote off Jordan Equipment Co.'s past-due account as uncollectible, $521.00. M20.
      30. Wrote off Porter, Inc.'s past-due account as uncollectible, $179.00, M27.

    2. Post each entry to the customer accounts in the accounts receivable ledger.

PROBLEM 22-3   Recording transactions for collection of written-off accounts receivable

Abbott Electronics received payment for accounts that had previously been written off.

Instructions: 1. Journalize the following transactions completed during August of the current year. Use page 8 of a general journal and page 15 of a cash receipts journal. Source documents are abbreviated as follows: memorandum, M; receipt, R.

Aug.   6. Received cash in full payment of Hargrove Inc.'s account, previously written off as uncollectible, $715.00. M4 and R34.
      20. Received cash in full payment of Andrews Corp.'s account, previously written off as uncollectible, $384.00. M27 and R92.
      27. Received cash in full payment of Tyler Co.'s account, previously written off as uncollectible, $443.00. M38 and R121.

    2. Post each entry to the customer accounts in the accounts receivable ledger.

ENRICHMENT PROBLEMS

MASTERY PROBLEM 22-M Recording entries for uncollectible accounts

Travis Industries has the following accounts in its accounts receivable ledger.

PARTIAL ACCOUNTS RECEIVABLE LEDGER

Account No. and Title	Date	Post. Ref.	Debit	Debit Balance
125 Burrell Company	Mar. 28	S3	$714.15	$714.15
135 Fiber-Tech	Mar. 15	S3	829.35	829.35
140 Gentry Corporation	Jan. 16	S1	482.50	482.50
150 Kingston Corporation	Feb. 4	S2	247.60	247.60

Instructions: 1. Journalize the following transactions completed during October, November, and December of the current year. Use pages 10, 11, and 12 of a general journal and pages 11 and 12 of a cash receipts journal. Source documents are abbreviated as follows: memorandum, M; receipt, R.

Oct. 7. Wrote off Kingston Corporation's past-due account as uncollectible, $247.60. M202.
  18. Wrote off Gentry Corporation's past-due account as uncollectible, $482.50. M206.
    Posting. Post each entry to the customer accounts in the accounts receivable ledger.
Nov. 8. Wrote off Burrell Company's past-due account as uncollectible, $714.15. M219.
  17. Received cash in full payment of Kingston Corporation's account, previously written off as uncollectible, $247.60. M223 and R461.
    Posting. Post each entry to the customer accounts in the accounts receivable ledger.
Dec. 3. Wrote off Fiber-Tech's past-due account as uncollectible, $829.35. M226.
  9. Received cash in full payment of Burrell Company's account, previously written off as uncollectible, $714.15. M229 and R514.
  28. Received cash in full payment of Gentry Corporation's account, previously written off as uncollectible, $482.50. M235 and R547.
    Posting. Post each entry to the customer accounts in the accounts receivable ledger.

2. Journalize the December 31 adjusting entry for estimated uncollectible accounts expense for the year. Use page 13 of the general journal. Uncollectible accounts expense is estimated as 1.0% of total sales on account. Total sales on account for the year were $1,051,080.00.

CHALLENGE PROBLEM 22-C Recording entries for uncollectible accounts

Sunrise Nursery has general ledger accounts for account number 1130, Allowance for Uncollectible Accounts, and account number 6165, Uncollectible Accounts Expense. At the beginning of the current year, the credit balance of Allowance for Uncollectible Accounts was $1,573.25. Uncollectible accounts expense is estimated as 0.75% of the total sales on account each quarter.

Instructions: 1. Journalize entries for the following transactions and adjusting entries completed during the current year. Use page 1 of a general journal and a cash receipts journal. (Usually a new journal page is started each month and adjusting entries are also recorded on a new journal page. To conserve space in the working papers, record all of the year's entries on the same page of the appropriate journal.) Source documents are abbreviated as follows: memorandum, M; receipt, R.

Jan. 11. Received cash in full payment of Taylor Corporation's account, previously written off as uncollectible, $317.40. M2 and R4.

Mar. 3. Wrote off Gibson Company's past-due account as uncollectible, $629.80. M7.

31. End of first quarterly fiscal period. Record the adjusting entry for estimated uncollectible accounts expense. Total sales on account for the first quarterly fiscal period were $174,920.00.

Posting. Post entries to Allowance for Uncollectible Accounts and Uncollectible Accounts Expense.

May 5. Received cash in full payment of Bowman, Inc.'s account, previously written off as uncollectible, $62.15. M13 and R39.

18. Wrote off Kirkwood Corporation's past-due account as uncollectible, $281.75. M16.

June 14. Wrote off Liberty Landscapes' past-due account as uncollectible, $753.40. M19.

30. End of second quarterly fiscal period. Record the adjusting entry for estimated uncollectible accounts expense. Total sales on account for the second quarterly fiscal period were $195,800.00.

Posting. Post entries to Allowance for Uncollectible Accounts and Uncollectible Accounts Expense.

July 6. Wrote off Plant Dimension Co.'s past-due account as uncollectible, $594.30. M20.

28. Wrote off Parker Fertilizer Company's past-due account as uncollectible, $256.10. M24.

Sept. 28. Wrote off Jacobsen Corporation's past-due account as uncollectible, $74.80. M37.

30. End of third quarterly fiscal period. Record the adjusting entry for estimated uncollectible accounts expense. Total sales on account for the third quarterly fiscal period were $201,760.00.

Posting. Post entries to Allowance for Uncollectible Accounts and Uncollectible Accounts Expense.

Nov. 1. Wrote off Superior Design's past-due account as uncollectible, $789.20. M38.

23. Received cash in full payment of Parker Fertilizer Company's account, previously written off as uncollectible, $256.10. M41 and R114.

Dec. 31. End of fourth quarterly fiscal period. Record the adjusting entry for estimated uncollectible accounts expense. Total sales on account for the fourth quarterly fiscal period were $219,860.00.

Posting. Post entries to Allowance for Uncollectible Accounts and Uncollectible Accounts Expense.

2. Assume that you are the accountant for Sunrise Nursery. You have determined that all possible procedures are now being used to reduce uncollectible accounts. Examine the year's activity in the account Allowance for Uncollectible Accounts. Are the accounting procedures for uncollectible accounts adequate and accurate? Should any changes in procedure be recommended? If so, what? Explain the reason for your response.

Accounting for Plant Assets and Depreciation

ENABLING PERFORMANCE TASKS

After studying Chapter 23, you will be able to:

a. Define accounting terms related to plant assets and depreciation.
b. Identify accounting concepts and practices related to accounting for plant assets and depreciation.
c. Calculate depreciation expense and book value of a plant asset.
d. Record plant asset information in a plant asset record.
e. Journalize entries related to accounting for plant assets and depreciation.

Most businesses use two broad categories of assets in the operations of their businesses. Cash and other assets expected to be exchanged for cash or consumed within a year are called current assets. Assets which will be used for a number of years in the operation of a business are called plant assets. Some of the more significant current assets used by Celluphone are cash, accounts receivable, merchandise inventory, supplies, and prepaid insurance. Celluphone also has a number of assets that will be used for a number of years in the operation of its business. Some of Celluphone's plant assets are typewriters, computers, cash registers, sales display cases, and furniture. These assets are used in the business and are not intended for sale to its customers. Celluphone's complete list of current and plant assets is in the chart of accounts, page 474.

The telephones Celluphone uses in operating the business are classified as plant assets. The telephones Celluphone buys and resells to its customers are merchandise inventory and classified as current assets. The difference in classification is determined by the way the asset is used. Assets purchased to be resold are merchandise inventory and classified as current assets. Assets bought to be used in operating the business are classified as plant assets.

Businesses may have three major types of plant assets—equipment, buildings, and land. Celluphone owns equipment, such as typewriters, cash registers, and sales display cases, that it uses to operate the business. However, the company rents the building and the land where the business is located. Therefore, Celluphone has accounts for equipment, which is the only type of plant asset it owns.

To provide more detailed financial information, Celluphone records its equipment in two different equipment accounts—Office Equipment and Store Equipment. (CONCEPT: Adequate Disclosure)

BUYING AND RECORDING PLANT ASSETS

Procedures for recording the buying of a plant asset are similar to procedures for recording the buying of current assets such as supplies. The amount paid for a plant asset is debited to a plant asset account with a title such as Office Equipment. (CONCEPT: Historical Cost) A plant asset account has a normal debit balance. Therefore, a plant asset account such as Office Equipment is increased by a debit and decreased by a credit, as shown in the T account.

Office Equipment

Debit side	Credit side
Normal balance Increase	Decrease

January 2, 19X1.
Paid cash for a new typewriter, $820.00. Check No. 4.

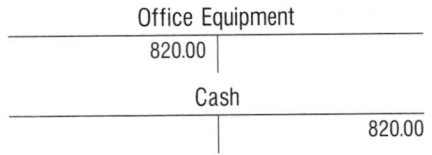

Office Equipment

820.00 |

Cash

| 820.00

The source document for this cash payment transaction is a check. (CONCEPT: Objective Evidence) The analysis of this transaction is shown in the T accounts. Celluphone has a separate plant asset account for office equipment. Therefore, Office Equipment is increased by an $820.00 debit. Cash is decreased by an $820.00 credit.

The cash payments journal entry to record this transaction is shown in Illustration 23-1.

	DATE	ACCOUNT TITLE	CK. NO.	POST. REF.	GENERAL DEBIT	GENERAL CREDIT	ACCOUNTS PAYABLE DEBIT	PURCHASES DISCOUNT CREDIT	CASH CREDIT	
					1	2	3	4	5	
4	2	*Office Equipment*	4		820 00				820 00	4
5										5

CASH PAYMENTS JOURNAL   PAGE *1*

Illustration 23-1
Cash payments journal entry to record the buying of a plant asset

After the entry for buying a typewriter is posted, the office equipment account in the general ledger appears as shown in Illustration 23-2.

The $12,830.00 balance of Office Equipment is the original cost of office equipment owned on January 1. The $13,650.00 balance of Office Equipment is

ACCOUNT *Office Equipment*					ACCOUNT NO. *1205*			
DATE	ITEM	POST. REF.	DEBIT	CREDIT	BALANCE			
					DEBIT		CREDIT	
Jan. ¹⁹ˣ¹ 1	*Balance*	√			12 8 3 0 00			
2		CP1	8 2 0 00		13 6 5 0 00			

Illustration 23-2
A plant asset account in the general ledger

the original cost of office equipment owned on January 2. The debit balance of Office Equipment always shows the original cost of all office equipment owned. *(CONCEPT: Historical Cost)*

EFFECTS OF DEPRECIATION ON PLANT ASSETS

A business buys plant assets to use in earning revenue. Celluphone bought a new typewriter to use for typing invoices and other correspondence for the business. Celluphone plans to use the typewriter for its entire useful life. However, plant assets such as Celluphone's typewriter decrease in value because of use. Plant assets also decrease in value with the passage of time as they become older and newer models become available. All plant assets, with the exception of land, have a limited useful life. However, plant assets generally have a useful life of several years.

In order to match revenue with the expenses used to earn the revenue, the cost of a plant asset should be allocated to an expense over the plant asset's useful life. Therefore, a portion of a plant asset's cost is transferred to an expense account in each fiscal period that a plant asset is used to earn revenue. *(CONCEPT: Matching Expenses with Revenue)* The portion of a plant asset's cost that is transferred to an expense account in each fiscal period during a plant asset's useful life is called depreciation expense.

Depreciation expense differs from many other business expenses in one significant way. For many business expenses, cash is paid out in the same fiscal period in which the expense is recorded. For example, cash is generally paid for salaries during the same fiscal period in which salary expense is recorded for those salaries. However, cash is generally paid out when a plant asset is bought, but depreciation expense is recorded over several years. Celluphone paid $820.00 for a new typewriter in 19X1, but a portion of the new typewriter's cost will be recorded as depreciation expense each year during the estimated useful life of the typewriter.

Two factors affect the useful life of a plant asset: (1) physical depreciation and (2) functional depreciation. Physical depreciation is caused by wear from use and deterioration from aging and weathering. Functional depreciation occurs when a plant asset becomes inadequate or obsolete.

An asset is inadequate when it can no longer satisfactorily perform needed service. An asset is obsolete when a newer machine can operate more efficiently or produce better service.

Land, because of its permanent nature, generally is not subject to depreciation. Buildings, after years of use, eventually become unusable to a business. However, the building may be torn down and a new building constructed on the same land. Since land can be used indefinitely it is considered permanent and is not depreciated.

CALCULATING DEPRECIATION EXPENSE

Depreciation expense is recorded for each fiscal period a plant asset is used. *(CONCEPT: Accounting Period Cycle)* Several factors are considered in calculating depreciation expense.

Factors affecting depreciation expense

Three factors affect the amount of depreciation expense for a plant asset.

1. The original cost of a plant asset.
2. The estimated salvage value of a plant asset.
3. The estimated useful life of a plant asset.

Original cost. The original cost of a plant asset includes all costs paid to make the asset usable to a business. These costs include the price of the asset, delivery costs, and any necessary installation costs. The original cost of the new typewriter bought by Celluphone is $820.00.

Estimated salvage value. Generally, a business removes a plant asset from use and disposes of it when the asset is no longer usable. The amount that will be received for an asset at the time of its disposal is not known when the asset is bought. Thus, the amount that may be received at disposal must be estimated. The estimated salvage value is the amount an owner expects to receive when a plant asset is removed from use. Estimated salvage value may also be referred to as residual value or scrap value.

Celluphone estimates a salvage value of $100.00 for the new typewriter at the end of its useful life.

Estimated useful life. The total amount of depreciation expense is distributed over the estimated useful life of a plant asset. When a plant asset is bought, the exact length of useful life is impossible to predict. Therefore, the number of years of useful life must be estimated.

Celluphone estimates that the useful life of a typewriter is five years. An estimate of useful life should be based on prior experience with similar assets and on available guidelines. Trade associations frequently publish guidelines for specialized plant assets. For tax purposes the Internal Revenue Service also publishes depreciation guidelines for plant assets.

Calculating depreciation expense for a fiscal year

The total cost of a plant asset that should be allocated to an expense over the asset's useful life is the amount paid for the asset (original cost) less the estimated salvage value. This difference, original cost less estimated salvage value, is the estimated total depreciation expense for the asset's entire useful life.

The total amount of estimated depreciation expense for the typewriter bought on January 2 is calculated as shown below.

Original Cost	−	Estimated Salvage Value	=	Estimated Total Depreciation Expense
$820.00	−	$100.00	=	$720.00

Depreciation expense for a fiscal year is calculated by dividing a plant asset's estimated total depreciation expense by the estimated useful life in years.

Estimated Total Depreciation Expense	÷	Years of Estimated Useful Life	=	Annual Depreciation Expense
$720.00	÷	5	=	$144.00

The depreciation expense for Celluphone's typewriter is $144.00 each year of use. Since Celluphone used the typewriter for all of the year it was bought, January 2 to December 31, one year's depreciation expense, $144.00, is charged as an expense for the year.

Charging an equal amount of depreciation expense for a plant asset in each year of useful life is called the straight-line method of depreciation. Celluphone uses the straight-line method to calculate depreciation.

> There are other methods of calculating depreciation expense. However, the straight-line method is widely used because it allocates a plant asset's original cost equally to each accounting period and is simple to calculate.

Calculating depreciation expense for part of a fiscal year

Depreciation expense is calculated for a fiscal year for those plant assets used throughout the entire fiscal year. However, if a plant asset is bought during the year the asset will be used only part of that fiscal year. Thus, depreciation expense should be calculated for only the part of the year the asset is used. To calculate depreciation expense for part of a year, the annual depreciation expense is divided by 12 to determine the depreciation expense for a month. The monthly depreciation expense is then multiplied by the number of months the plant asset is used that year.

Celluphone bought a new computer on July 1, 19X1. The original cost is $4,600.00, the estimated salvage value is $1,000.00, and the estimated useful life is four years. Celluphone calculates the computer depreciation expense for 19X1 by following four steps. The first two steps are similar to those illustrated previously for Celluphone's typewriter. The third and fourth steps are used to calculate depreciation expense for part of a year.

STEP 1:

Original Cost	−	Estimated Salvage Value	=	Estimated Total Depreciation Expense
$4,600.00	−	$1,000.00	=	$3,600.00

STEP 2:

Estimated Total Depreciation Expense	÷	Years of Estimated Useful Life	=	Annual Depreciation Expense
$3,600.00	÷	4	=	$900.00

STEP 3:

Annual Depreciation Expense	÷	Months in a Year	=	Monthly Depreciation Expense
$900.00	÷	12	=	$75.00

STEP 4:

Monthly Depreciation Expense	×	Number of Months Asset Is Used	=	Partial Year's Depreciation Expense
$75.00	×	6	=	$450.00

The depreciation expense for the part of the year Celluphone used the new computer is $450.00.

When determining the number of months to use in calculating depreciation for part of a year, most businesses round to the nearest whole month. For example, if an asset is bought on July 7, the asset is used for more than half the month. Thus, depreciation expense would be calculated for all of July. If an asset is bought on July 19, the asset is used for less than half the month. Thus, depreciation expense is not calculated for any of July.

PREPARING PLANT ASSET RECORDS

A separate record is kept for each plant asset. An accounting form on which a business records information about each plant asset is called a plant asset record.

Plant asset records may vary in arrangement for different businesses, but most records contain similar information. Celluphone's plant asset record has three sections. The first section of Celluphone's plant asset record for the typewriter bought on January 2, 19X1, is shown in Illustration 23-3. The first section contains a complete description of the plant asset, including the general ledger account title and number, purchase date, serial number, original cost, estimated useful life, estimated salvage value, and annual depreciation expense.

The second section of Celluphone's plant asset record includes information about the disposal of the asset—how disposed of, date of disposal,

PLANT ASSET RECORD

Description _____ *Typewriter* _____

Date Bought *January 2, 19X1*	Serial Number *48C79623*	Original Cost *$820.00*
Estimated Useful Life *5 years*	Estimated Salvage Value *$100.00*	Annual Depreciation *$144.00*

General Ledger Account No. _____ *1205* _____

General Ledger Account _____ *Office Equipment* _____

Disposed of: Discarded _____   Sold _____   Traded _____

Date _____   Disposal Amount _____

YEAR	ANNUAL DEPRECIATION EXPENSE	ACCUMULATED DEPRECIATION	ENDING BOOK VALUE

Illustration 23-3
Plant asset record showing description of plant asset

and amount received for the asset. This information will be filled in when the asset is disposed of.

The third section of Celluphone's plant asset record for the computer bought on July 1, 19X1, is shown in Illustration 23-4. The third section of Celluphone's plant asset record includes information about the depreciation expense and changing value of the asset for each year it is used.

At the end of each fiscal period, Celluphone brings each plant asset record up to date by calculating and recording three amounts: (1) annual

PLANT ASSET RECORD

Description _____ *Computer* _____

Date Bought *July 1, 19X1*	Serial Number *19X5-24867*	Original Cost *$4,600.00*
Estimated Useful Life *4 years*	Estimated Salvage Value *$1,000.00*	Annual Depreciation *$900.00*

General Ledger Account No. _____ *1205* _____

General Ledger Account _____ *Office Equipment* _____

Disposed of: Discarded _____   Sold _____   Traded _____

Date _____   Disposal Amount _____

YEAR	ANNUAL DEPRECIATION EXPENSE	ACCUMULATED DEPRECIATION	ENDING BOOK VALUE
19X1	450.00	450.00	4,150.00
19X2	900.00	1,350.00	3,250.00
19X3	900.00	2,250.00	2,350.00
19X4	900.00	3,150.00	1,450.00
19X5	450.00	3,600.00	1,000.00

Continue record on back of card

Illustration 23-4
Plant asset record brought up to date each fiscal year of a plant asset's life

depreciation expense, (2) accumulated depreciation, and (3) ending book value.

The amount recorded in the Annual Depreciation Expense column is always the amount recorded for the fiscal year. The annual depreciation expense for the computer bought July 1, 19X1, is $900.00. However, the amount recorded for the year 19X1 in the Annual Depreciation Expense column is $450.00, the amount of depreciation expense for the part of the year Celluphone actually used the computer.

Depreciation is the portion of a plant asset's cost that is transferred to an expense account at the end of each fiscal period during the plant asset's useful life. Therefore, as the amount of depreciation expense increases, the remaining value of the plant asset decreases. However, important information would be lost if the plant asset account is reduced each time depreciation expense is recorded. Thus, information about the original cost of a plant asset and the total amount of depreciation expense recorded over the life of a plant asset should be retained. Therefore, the cumulative total of depreciation expense is recorded. The total amount of depreciation expense that has been recorded since the purchase of a plant asset is called accumulated depreciation.

At the end of the fiscal year 19X1, Celluphone has used its computer six months or half a year. Since the computer had no previous depreciation expense in 19X1, the accumulated depreciation for 19X1 is the same amount as the depreciation expense, $450.00, as shown in Illustration 23-4.

A plant asset's accumulated depreciation each fiscal period is calculated as shown below for the first two years of life for Celluphone's computer.

Year	Previous Year's Balance of Accumulated Depreciation	+	Current Year's Depreciation Expense	=	Current Year's Balance of Accumulated Depreciation
19X1	0	+	$450.00	=	$ 450.00
19X2	$450.00	+	$900.00	=	$1,350.00

For 19X1, $450.00 is recorded and for 19X2, $1,350.00 is recorded in the plant asset record's Accumulated Depreciation column.

The original cost of a plant asset minus accumulated depreciation is called the book value of a plant asset. To complete the end-of-fiscal-period updating of a plant asset, the ending book value is calculated. The ending book value for Celluphone's computer is calculated as shown below.

Year	Original Cost	−	Accumulated Depreciation	=	Ending Book Value
19X1	$4,600.00	−	$ 450.00	=	$4,150.00
19X2	$4,600.00	−	$1,350.00	=	$3,250.00

The book value is recorded each year in the plant asset record's Ending Book Value column, as shown in Illustration 23-4.

A plant asset is never depreciated below its estimated salvage value. Therefore, when a plant asset's book value equals its estimated salvage value, no further depreciation expense is recorded. The book value of Celluphone's computer at the end of 19X4, as shown in Illustration 23-4, is $1,450.00. Only $450.00 depreciation expense is needed to reduce the book value to the estimated salvage value, $1,000.00. Therefore, on December 31, 19X5, only $450.00 depreciation expense is recorded for Celluphone's computer. Thus, at the end of 19X5, and thereafter, the book value for the computer will remain at $1,000.00.

ACCOUNTS AFFECTING THE VALUATION OF PLANT ASSETS

Three general ledger accounts are used to record information about each kind of plant asset. (1) An asset account is used to record the original cost of the asset. (2) An expense account is used to record the amount of depreciation expense. (3) A contra asset account is used to record the accumulated depreciation.

Plant asset accounts

Celluphone uses two plant asset accounts: Office Equipment and Store Equipment. The appropriate plant asset account is debited for the original cost when equipment is bought. The account is credited for the original cost when equipment is disposed of. Therefore, the balance of a plant asset account always shows the original cost of all equipment in current use.

Depreciation expense accounts

Depreciation is an expense to a business. To record depreciation expense for a fiscal period, an adjusting entry is made to two accounts. The amount of depreciation for a fiscal period is debited to an expense account titled *Depreciation Expense*.

Celluphone uses two depreciation expense accounts: Depreciation Expense— Office Equipment and Depreciation Expense—Store Equipment. The location of these expense accounts is shown in Celluphone's chart of accounts.

Accumulated depreciation accounts

The adjusting entry for the amount of depreciation for a fiscal period also has a credit to a contra asset account titled *Accumulated Depreciation*. A contra asset account has a normal credit balance. Therefore, the accumulated depreciation account is increased by a credit and decreased by a debit, as shown in the T account.

Accumulated Depreciation	
Debit side	Credit side
	Normal balance
Decrease	Increase

The account title Allowance for Depreciation is sometimes used instead of Accumulated Depreciation.

Celluphone uses two accumulated depreciation accounts: Accumulated Depreciation—Office Equipment and Accumulated Depreciation—Store Equipment. The location of these contra asset accounts is shown in Celluphone's chart of accounts.

RECORDING DEPRECIATION EXPENSE

At the end of the fiscal year, Celluphone figures the depreciation expense for each plant asset. Next, the total depreciation expense is figured for all plant assets of the same kind. For example, in 19X1 the depreciation expense for the new typewriter is $144.00. The depreciation expense for other office equipment is $1,606.00. Thus, the total office equipment depreciation expense for the year is $1,750.00. Celluphone's accumulated depreciation for each kind of plant asset on December 31, 19X1, is calculated as shown below.

Kind of Equipment	Previous Year's Balance of Accumulated Depreciation	+	Current Year's Depreciation Expense	=	Current Year's Balance of Accumulated Depreciation
Office equipment	$3,625.00	+	$1,750.00	=	$ 5,375.00
Store equipment	$9,125.00	+	$6,325.00	=	$15,450.00

Analyzing an adjustment for depreciation expense

An adjusting entry is made to record estimated depreciation expense for a fiscal period. The T accounts show the office equipment account, depreciation expense account, and accumulated depreciation account before the adjustment for depreciation expense is made.

The effect of Celluphone's adjustment for office equipment depreciation expense is shown in the T accounts.

Depreciation Expense—Office Equipment is debited for $1,750.00 to show the increase in the balance of this expense account. The balance of this account, $1,750.00, is the estimated depreciation expense for the accounting period.

Accumulated Depreciation—Office Equipment is credited for $1,750.00 to show the increase in the balance of this contra asset account. The January 1 balance, $3,625.00, plus the annual increase, $1,750.00, equals the December 31 balance, $5,375.00. The office equipment account balance, $18,250.00, *minus* the accumulated depreciation account balance, $5,375.00, *equals* the office equipment book value, $12,875.00.

A similar adjusting entry is made to record estimated depreciation expense for store equipment. The book value of each kind of plant asset after the adjustments on December 31, 19X1, is calculated as shown on the next page.

BEFORE ADJUSTMENT

Office Equipment

Jan. 1 Bal.	12,830.00	
Jan. 2	820.00	
July 1	4,600.00	
Dec. 31 Bal.	18,250.00	

Depreciation Expense—Office Equipment

Accumulated Depreciation— Office Equipment

		Jan. 1 Bal.	3,625.00

AFTER ADJUSTMENT

Office Equipment

Jan. 1 Bal.	12,830.00	
Jan. 2	820.00	
July 1	4,600.00	
Dec. 31 Bal.	18,250.00	

Depreciation Expense—Office Equipment

Dec. 31 Adj.	1,750.00	

Accumulated Depreciation— Office Equipment

		Jan. 1 Bal.	3,625.00
		Dec. 31 Adj.	1,750.00
		Dec. 31 Bal.	5,375.00

Kind of Equipment	Balance of Asset Account	–	Total Accumulated Depreciation	=	Ending Book Value 12/31/X1
Office equipment	$18,250.00	–	$ 5,375.00	=	$12,875.00
Store equipment	$77,190.00	–	$15,450.00	=	$61,740.00

Planning depreciation expense adjustments on a work sheet

Celluphone plans the adjustments for depreciation expense in the Adjustments columns of a work sheet. The adjustments for depreciation expense are on the partial work sheet shown in Illustration 23-5.

Celluphone, Inc.

Work Sheet

For Year Ended December 31, 19X1

	ACCOUNT TITLE	TRIAL BALANCE DEBIT	TRIAL BALANCE CREDIT	ADJUSTMENTS DEBIT	ADJUSTMENTS CREDIT
10	*Office Equipment*	18 2 5 0 00			
11	*Accum. Depr.—Office Equipment*		3 6 2 5 00		(f) 1 7 5 0 00
12	*Store Equipment*	77 1 9 0 00			
13	*Accum. Depr.—Store Equipment*		9 1 2 5 00		(g) 6 3 2 5 00
37	*Depr. Exp.—Office Equipment*			(f) 1 7 5 0 00	
38	*Depr. Exp.—Store Equipment*			(g) 6 3 2 5 00	
39					

Illustration 23-5
Adjustments for depreciation expense on a work sheet

Adjustment for depreciation of office equipment. On line 37 the increase in Depreciation Expense—Office Equipment, *$1,750.00*, is entered in the Adjustments Debit column. On line 11 the increase in Accumulated Depreciation—Office Equipment, *$1,750.00*, is entered in the Adjustments Credit column.

Adjustment for depreciation of store equipment. On line 38 the increase in Depreciation Expense—Store Equipment, *$6,325.00*, is entered in the Adjustments Debit column. On line 13 the increase in Accumulated Depreciation—Store Equipment, *$6,325.00*, is entered in the Adjustments Credit column.

Journalizing adjusting entries for depreciation expense

Information needed to journalize adjustments for depreciation expense is obtained from the work sheet's Adjustments columns. Celluphone's two adjusting entries to record depreciation expense are shown in Illustration 23-6.

GENERAL JOURNAL							PAGE 15	
	DATE	ACCOUNT TITLE	DOC. NO.	POST. REF.	DEBIT		CREDIT	
12	31	Depr. Exp.—Office Equipment			1 75 0 00			12
13		Accum. Depr.—Office Equip.					1 75 0 00	13
14	31	Depr. Exp.—Store Equipment			6 32 5 00			14
15		Accum. Depr.—Store Equip.					6 32 5 00	15
16								16
17								17

Illustration 23-6
Adjusting entries to
journalize depreciation
expense

Posting adjusting entries for depreciation expense

After adjusting entries for depreciation expense are posted, the accounts appear as shown in Illustration 23-7.

Office Equipment and Store Equipment have debit balances showing the original cost of equipment. The two contra accounts for the equipment accounts have credit balances showing the accumulated depreciation recorded to date. The two depreciation expense accounts have debit balances showing depreciation expense for the current fiscal period.

DISPOSING OF A PLANT ASSET

A business uses a plant asset for its useful life. A plant asset may no longer be useful to a business for a number of reasons. The asset may not be needed. The asset may be worn out or more productive new assets may be available. Whatever the reason, when a plant asset is no longer useful to a business, the asset may be disposed of. The old plant asset may be sold, traded for a new asset, or discarded.

When a plant asset is disposed of, a journal entry is recorded that achieves the following three effects in the accounts.

1. Removes the original cost of the plant asset and its related accumulated depreciation.
2. Recognizes any cash or other asset received for the old plant asset.
3. Recognizes the gain or loss on the disposal, if any.

Sale of a plant asset for book value

After five years of use, Celluphone sold a typewriter.

January 3, 19X6.
Received cash from sale of the typewriter bought on January 2, 19X1, $100.00: original cost, $820.00; total accumulated depreciation through December 31, 19X5, $720.00. Receipt No. 4.

ACCOUNT *Office Equipment*   ACCOUNT NO. *1205*

DATE		ITEM	POST. REF.	DEBIT	CREDIT	BALANCE	
						DEBIT	CREDIT
19X1 Jan.	1	Balance	√			12 8 3 0 00	
	2		CP1	8 2 0 00		13 6 5 0 00	
July	1		CP16	4 6 0 0 00		18 2 5 0 00	

ACCOUNT *Accumulated Depreciation—Office Equipment*   ACCOUNT NO. *1210*

DATE		ITEM	POST. REF.	DEBIT	CREDIT	BALANCE	
						DEBIT	CREDIT
19X1 Jan.	1	Balance	√				3 6 2 5 00
Dec.	31		G15		1 7 5 0 00		5 3 7 5 00

ACCOUNT *Store Equipment*   ACCOUNT NO. *1215*

DATE		ITEM	POST. REF.	DEBIT	CREDIT	BALANCE	
						DEBIT	CREDIT
19X1 Jan.	1	Balance	√			77 1 9 0 00	

ACCOUNT *Accumulated Depreciation—Store Equipment*   ACCOUNT NO. *1220*

DATE		ITEM	POST. REF.	DEBIT	CREDIT	BALANCE	
						DEBIT	CREDIT
19X1 Jan.	1	Balance	√				9 1 2 5 00
Dec.	31		G15		6 3 2 5 00		15 4 5 0 00

ACCOUNT *Depreciation Expense—Office Equipment*   ACCOUNT NO. *6115*

DATE		ITEM	POST. REF.	DEBIT	CREDIT	BALANCE	
						DEBIT	CREDIT
19X1 Dec.	31		G15	1 7 5 0 00		1 7 5 0 00	

ACCOUNT *Depreciation Expense—Store Equipment*   ACCOUNT NO. *6120*

DATE		ITEM	POST. REF.	DEBIT	CREDIT	BALANCE	
						DEBIT	CREDIT
19X1 Dec.	31		G15	6 3 2 5 00		6 3 2 5 00	

Illustration 23-7
General ledger accounts
after posting adjusting
entries for depreciation
expense

A notation is made in the second section of the plant asset record for this typewriter, as shown in Illustration 23-8.

| PLANT ASSET RECORD | | | General Ledger Account No. _____ *1205* | |
| Description _____ *Typewriter* | | | General Ledger Account _____ *Office Equipment* | |

| Date Bought *January 2, 19X1* | Serial Number _____ 48C79623 | | Original Cost *$820.00* | |
| Estimated Useful Life *5 years* | Estimated Salvage Value *$100.00* | | Annual Depreciation *$144.00* | |

| Disposed of: | Discarded _____ | Sold ✓ | Traded _____ | |
| Date _____ *January 3, 19X6* | | Disposal Amount *$100.00* | | |

YEAR	ANNUAL DEPRECIATION EXPENSE	ACCUMULATED DEPRECIATION	ENDING BOOK VALUE
19X1	*144.00*	*144.00*	*676.00*
19X2	*144.00*	*288.00*	*532.00*
19X3	*144.00*	*432.00*	*388.00*
19X4	*144.00*	*576.00*	*244.00*
19X5	*144.00*	*720.00*	*100.00*

Illustration 23-8
Plant asset record showing disposal of a plant asset

A check mark indicates whether the asset was discarded, sold, or traded. The date the typewriter is sold, *January 3, 19X6*, is written in the space for the disposition date. The amount received, *$100.00*, is written in the space for the disposal amount. Celluphone then files the typewriter's plant asset record in a file for plant assets that have been disposed of so that information about the asset is available if needed.

The typewriter is sold for $100.00. The ending book value of the typewriter when the typewriter is sold is $100.00, as shown on the last line of the plant asset record, Illustration 23-8. Before analyzing the accounts affected in this transaction, the amount of any gain or loss that is realized from the sale should be determined. The gain or loss on the sale of a plant asset is the difference between the book value of the asset sold and the value of the asset received. The gain or loss on the sale of Celluphone's typewriter is calculated as shown below.

Value of Asset Received	–	Book Value of Asset Sold		=	Gain or Loss on Disposal of Plant Asset
		Cost	$820.00		
		Accum. Dep.	720.00		
Cash $100.00	–	Book Value	$100.00	=	0

Celluphone sold its typewriter for the typewriter's book value. Therefore, no gain or loss exists. The journal entry for the sale of a plant asset for book value must achieve the following two effects in the accounts.

1. Remove the original cost of the plant asset and its related accumulated depreciation.
2. Recognize the cash received.

The source document for this cash receipt transaction is a receipt. (CONCEPT: *Objective Evidence*) The analysis of this transaction is shown in the T accounts.

Cash is debited for $100.00 to show the increase in the balance of this asset account.

The accumulated depreciation account should show only the depreciation for plant assets still in use. Therefore, Accumulated Depreciation—Office Equipment is debited for $720.00 to show the decrease in this contra asset account's balance. The amount, $720.00, is the total depreciation recorded during the typewriter's entire life.

Office Equipment is credited for $820.00 to show the decrease in the balance of this plant asset account. This entry cancels the original cost, $820.00, that was debited to the office equipment account when the typewriter was bought.

The cash receipts journal entry to record the sale of the typewriter is shown in Illustration 23-9.

Cash	
100.00	

Accumulated Depreciation— Office Equipment	
720.00	Bal. 720.00

Office Equipment	
Bal. 820.00	820.00

CASH RECEIPTS JOURNAL

PAGE 1

	DATE	ACCOUNT TITLE	DOC. NO.	POST. REF.	GENERAL DEBIT	GENERAL CREDIT	ACCOUNTS RECEIVABLE CREDIT	SALES CREDIT	SALES TAX PAYABLE DEBIT	SALES TAX PAYABLE CREDIT	SALES DISCOUNT DEBIT	CASH DEBIT	
8	3	Accum. Depr.—Office Equipment	R4		720 00							100 00	8
9		Office Equipment				820 00							9
10													10

Illustration 23-9
Cash receipts journal entry to record the sale of a plant asset for book value

Sale of a plant asset for more than book value

Revenue that results when a plant asset is sold for more than book value is called gain on plant assets. After five years of use, Celluphone sold a cash register for $150.00.

April 1, 19X7.
Received cash from sale of the cash register bought on April 1, 19X2, $150.00: original cost, $470.00; total accumulated depreciation through December 31, 19X6, $399.00; additional depreciation to be recorded through April 1, 19X7, $21.00. Memorandum No. 14 and Receipt No. 38.

The source documents for this transaction are a memorandum, detailing the need for an additional three months' depreciation, and a receipt. (CONCEPT: *Objective Evidence*)

Journalizing depreciation for part of a year. A plant asset may be disposed of at any time during the asset's useful life. When a plant asset is disposed of, its depreciation from the beginning of the current fiscal year to the date of disposal is recorded. For example, Celluphone last recorded adjusting entries for depreciation expense on December 31, 19X6. The cash register is sold on April 1, 19X7. Before entries are made for the sale of the cash register, three months' depreciation must be recorded for the period January 1 through April 1. The additional depreciation for the cash register is calculated as shown below.

Annual Depreciation Expense	÷	Months in a Year	=	Monthly Depreciation Expense
$84.00	÷	12	=	$7.00

Monthly Depreciation Expense	×	Number of Months Asset Is Used	=	Partial Year's Depreciation Expense
$7.00	×	3	=	$21.00

The analysis of this entry is shown in the T accounts.

Depreciation Expense—Store Equipment is debited for $21.00 to show the increase in the balance of this expense account. Accumulated Depreciation—Store Equipment is credited for $21.00 to show the increase in this contra asset account.

The general journal entry to record the three months' depreciation is shown in Illustration 23-10.

Depreciation Expense—Store Equipment

Add. Depr. 21.00	

Accumulated Depreciation—Store Equipment

	Bal. 399.00
	Add. Depr. 21.00
	(New Bal. 420.00)

GENERAL JOURNAL   PAGE 4

	DATE	ACCOUNT TITLE	DOC. NO.	POST. REF.	DEBIT	CREDIT	
1	19X7 Apr. 1	Depr. Exp.—Store Equipment	M14		21 00		1
2		Accum. Depr.—Store Equipment				21 00	2
3							3

Illustration 23-10
General journal entry to record depreciation for part of a year

Journalizing the sale of a plant asset. After the partial year's depreciation is recorded, a journal entry is made to record the sale of the cash register. The cash register is sold for $150.00. The ending book value when the cash register is sold is $50.00. The gain on the sale of Celluphone's cash register is calculated as shown below.

Value of Asset Received	−	Book Value of Asset Sold		=	Gain on Disposal
		Cost	$470.00		
		Accum. Dep.	−420.00		
Cash $150.00	−	Book Value	$ 50.00	=	$100.00 Gain

Celluphone sold its cash register for $100.00 more than its book value. Since the asset received has greater value than the book value of the plant asset disposed of, the difference is recognized as a gain on plant assets. The gain is caluated as $150.00 cash received, *less* $50.00 book value of plant asset, *equals* $100.00 gain on plant asset.

The amount of gain realized on the disposal of a plant asset is credited to a revenue account titled *Gain on Plant Assets*. A revenue account has a normal credit balance. Therefore, the gain on plant assets account is increased by a credit and decreased by a debit, as shown in the T account.

Gain on Plant Assets	
Debit side	Credit side
	Normal balance
Decrease	Increase

A gain from the sale of plant assets is not an operating revenue. Therefore, Gain on Plant Assets is not listed under Operating Revenue in a chart of accounts. Gain on Plant Assets is listed in a classification titled *Other Revenue* in a chart of accounts.

The journal entry for the sale of a plant asset for more than book value must achieve the following three effects in the accounts.

1. Remove the original cost of the plant asset and its related accumulated depreciation.
2. Recognize the cash received.
3. Recognize the gain on disposal of the asset.

The analysis of this transaction is shown in the T accounts.

Cash is debited for $150.00 to show the increase in the balance of this asset account. Accumulated Depreciation—Store Equipment is debited for $420.00 to show the decrease in this contra asset account. This amount, $420.00, is the sum of all depreciation expense recorded during the entire time Celluphone has used this cash register. Store Equipment is credited for $470.00 to show the decrease in the balance of this plant asset account. This entry removes the original cost, $470.00, that was debited to the store equipment account when the cash register was bought. Gain on Plant Assets is credited for $100.00 to show the increase in this other revenue account.

Cash	
150.00	

Accumulated Depreciation— Store Equipment	
420.00	Bal. 420.00

Store Equipment	
Bal. 470.00	470.00

Gain on Plant Assets	
	100.00

The cash receipts journal entry to record the sale of the cash register is shown in Illustration 23-11, page 588.

Notations are made on the plant asset record to record the partial year's depreciation and disposal information.

Sale of a plant asset for less than book value

Loss that results when a plant asset is sold for less than book value is called loss on plant assets. Celluphone sold a computer for $800.00 after four years of use.

							1	2	3	4	5	6	7	8		
CASH RECEIPTS JOURNAL															PAGE *10*	
	DATE		ACCOUNT TITLE	DOC. NO.	POST. REF.	GENERAL		ACCOUNTS RECEIVABLE CREDIT	SALES CREDIT	SALES TAX PAYABLE		SALES DISCOUNT DEBIT	CASH DEBIT			
						DEBIT	CREDIT			DEBIT	CREDIT					
1	*19X7 Apr.*	*1*	*Accum. Depr.—Store Equipment*	*R38*		*4 2 0 00*							*1 5 0 00*			1
2			*Store Equipment*				*4 7 0 00*									2
3			*Gain on Plant Assets*				*1 0 0 00*									3

Illustration 23-11
Cash receipts journal entry to record the sale of a plant asset for more than book value

September 1, 19X5.
Received cash from sale of the computer bought on September 1, 19X1, $800.00: original cost, $4,000.00; total accumulated depreciation through December 31, 19X4, $2,000.00; additional depreciation to be recorded through September 1, 19X5, $400.00. Memorandum No. 82 and Receipt No. 281.

The source documents for this transaction are a memorandum, detailing the need for an additional eight months' depreciation, and a receipt. (CONCEPT: *Objective Evidence*)

Journalizing depreciation for part of a year. Celluphone last recorded adjusting entries for depreciation expense on December 31, 19X4. Celluphone sells its computer on September 1, 19X5. Before entries are made for the sale of the computer, eight months' depreciation must be recorded. The eight months' depreciation is for the period January 1 through September 1. The additional depreciation for the computer is calculated as shown below.

Annual Depreciation Expense	÷	**Months in a Year**	=	**Monthly Depreciation Expense**
$600.00	÷	12	=	$50.00

Monthly Depreciation Expense	×	**Number of Months Asset Is Used**	=	**Partial Year's Depreciation Expense**
$50.00	×	8	=	$400.00

Depreciation Expense—Office Equipment

Add. Depr.	400.00	

Accumulated Depreciation— Office Equipment

	Bal.	2,000.00
	Add. Depr.	400.00
	(New Bal.	*2,400.00)*

The analysis of this entry is shown in the T accounts.
Depreciation Expense—Office Equipment is debited for $400.00 to show the increase in the balance of this expense account. Accumulated Depreciation—Office Equipment is credited for $400.00 to show the increase in this contra asset account.

The general journal entry to record the eight months' depreciation is shown in Illustration 23-12.

Journalizing the sale of a plant asset. After the partial year's depreciation is recorded, a journal entry is made to record the sale of the computer. The computer is sold for $800.00. The ending book value when the computer is sold is $1,600.00. The loss on the sale of Celluphone's computer is calculated as shown on the next page.

		GENERAL JOURNAL				PAGE 9	
	DATE	ACCOUNT TITLE	DOC. NO.	POST. REF.	DEBIT	CREDIT	
1	*19X5* *Sept.* *1*	*Depr. Exp.—Office Equipment*	M82		4 0 0 00		1
2		*Accum. Depr.—Office Equip.*				4 0 0 00	2
3							3

Illustration 23-12
General journal entry to record depreciation for part of a year

Book Value of Asset Sold	−	Value of Asset Received	=	Loss on Disposal
Cost $4,000.00				
Accum. Dep. −2,400.00				
Book Value $1,600.00	−	Cash $800.00	=	$800.00 Loss

Celluphone sold its computer for $800.00 less than its book value. Since the asset received has less value than the book value of the plant asset disposed of, the difference is recognized as a loss on plant assets. The loss is calculated as $1,600.00 book value of plant asset, *less* $800.00 cash received, *equals* $800.00 loss on plant asset.

The amount of loss realized on the disposal of a plant asset is debited to an expense account titled *Loss on Plant Assets*. An expense account has a normal debit balance. Therefore, Loss on Plant Assets is increased by a debit and decreased by a credit, as shown in the T account.

Loss on Plant Assets	
Debit side Normal balance Increase	Credit side Decrease

A loss from the sale of plant assets is not an operating expense. Therefore, Loss on Plant Assets is listed in a classification titled *Other Expense* in a chart of accounts.

The journal entry for the sale of a plant asset for less than book value must achieve the following three effects in the accounts.

1. Remove the original cost of the plant asset and its related accumulated depreciation.
2. Recognize the cash received.
3. Recognize the loss on disposal of the asset.

The analysis of this transaction is shown in the T accounts.
Cash is debited for $800.00 to show the increase in the balance of this asset account. Accumulated Depreciation—Office Equipment is debited for $2,400.00 to show the decrease in this contra asset account. This amount, $2,400.00, is the sum of all depreciation expense recorded during the entire period Celluphone has used this computer. Loss on Plant Assets is debited for $800.00 to show the increase in this expense account. Office Equipment is credited for $4,000.00 to show the

Cash	
800.00	

Accumulated Depreciation— Office Equipment	
2,400.00	Bal. 2,400.00

Loss on Plant Assets	
800.00	

Office Equipment	
Bal. 4,000.00	4,000.00

decrease in the balance of this plant asset account. This entry removes the original cost, $4,000.00, which was debited to the office equipment account when the computer was bought.

The cash receipts journal entry to record the sale of Celluphone's computer is shown in Illustration 23-13.

							GENERAL		ACCOUNTS RECEIVABLE CREDIT	SALES CREDIT	SALES TAX PAYABLE		SALES DISCOUNT DEBIT	CASH DEBIT	
	DATE		ACCOUNT TITLE	DOC. NO.	POST. REF.		DEBIT	CREDIT			DEBIT	CREDIT			
1	19X5 Sept.	1	Accum. Depr.—Office Equipment	R281			2 4 0 0 00							8 0 0 00	1
2			Loss on Plant Assets				8 0 0 00								2
3			Office Equipment					4 0 0 0 00							3

CASH RECEIPTS JOURNAL — PAGE 19

Illustration 23-13
Cash receipts journal entry to record the sale of a plant asset for less than book value

Notations are made on the plant asset record to record the partial year's depreciation and disposal information.

SUMMARY OF ACCOUNTING FOR PLANT ASSETS AND DEPRECIATION

Illustration 23-14
Summary of entries related to plant assets and depreciation

The chart shown in Illustration 23-14 summarizes the entries for transactions related to plant assets and depreciation.

	GENERAL LEDGER											
TRANSACTIONS	CASH		EQUIPMENT		ACCUMULATED DEPRECIATION		DEPRECIATION EXPENSE		GAIN ON PLANT ASSETS		LOSS ON PLANT ASSETS	
	DEBIT	CREDIT	DEBIT	CREDIT	DEBIT	CREDIT	DEBIT	CREDIT	DEBIT	CREDIT	DEBIT	CREDIT
Buying a plant asset		X	X									
Recording depreciation expense for a fiscal period							X	X				
Sale of plant asset for book value	X				X	X						
Sale of plant asset for more than book value	X				X	X				X		
Sale of plant asset for less than book value	X				X	X					X	

The chart shown in Illustration 23-15 summarizes the calculations for amounts related to depreciation and sale of plant assets.

AMOUNTS	CALCULATIONS				
Annual Depreciation Expense	Original Cost	− Estimated Salvage Value	= Estimated Total Depreciation Expense	÷ Years of Estimated Useful Life	= Annual Depreciation Expense
Partial Year's Depreciation Expense	Annual Depreciation Expense	÷ Months in a Year	= Monthly Depreciation Expense	× Number of Months Asset Is Used	= Partial Year's Depreciation Expense
Current Year's Balance of Accumulated Depreciation	Previous Year's Balance of Accumulated Depreciation		+ Current Year's Depreciation Expense	= Current Year's Balance of Accumulated Depreciation	
Book Value of a Plant Asset	Original Cost		− Accumulated Depreciation	= Ending Book Value	
Gain on Sale of a Plant Asset	Value of Asset Received		− Book Value of Asset Sold	= Gain on Disposal	
Loss on Sale of a Plant Asset	Book Value of Asset Sold		− Value of Asset Received	= Loss on Disposal	

Illustration 23-15   Summary of calculations for amounts related to depreciation and sale of plant assets

ACCOUNTING TERMS

What is the meaning of each of the following?

1. current assets
2. plant assets
3. depreciation expense
4. straight-line method of depreciation
5. plant asset record

6. accumulated depreciation
7. book value of a plant asset
8. gain on plant assets
9. loss on plant assets

QUESTIONS FOR INDIVIDUAL STUDY

1. What are the two broad categories of assets used by most businesses in the operations of their businesses?
2. Which accounting concept is being applied when a business debits its equipment account for $800.00 when it pays $800.00 for a new typewriter?
3. What accounts are affected, and how, when a plant asset is bought for cash?
4. What is the reason for recording depreciation expense?

5. Which accounting concept is being applied when depreciation is recorded?
6. In what significant way does depreciation expense differ from many other business expenses?
7. Why is land generally not subject to depreciation?
8. What three factors affect the amount of depreciation expense for a plant asset?
9. What is included in the original cost of a plant asset?

10. Why is the estimated salvage value used in determining depreciation expense rather than the actual salvage value?
11. If, when purchased, the useful life of an asset cannot be reasonably estimated from past experience, where might this information be obtained?
12. How is the annual depreciation expense figured for a plant asset using the straight-line method of depreciation?
13. When a plant asset record is brought up to date, what three amounts are generally recorded on the record?
14. How is the book value of a plant asset calculated?
15. When a plant asset's book value equals its estimated salvage value, how is the depreciation expense for the succeeding periods recorded?
16. What amount is always shown as the balance of a plant asset account?
17. On a work sheet, what accounts are affected, and how, in planning adjustments for depreciation of a plant asset?
18. What accounts are affected, and how, when a plant asset is sold for book value?
19. What accounts are affected, and how, when a plant asset is sold for more than book value?
20. What accounts are affected, and how, when a plant asset is sold for less than book value?

■ CASES FOR MANAGEMENT DECISION

CASE 1 Carol Ebener, owner of a small business, does not record depreciation expense for the business' plant assets. Ms. Ebener says that she does not make actual cash payments for depreciation. Therefore, she records an expense for the use of plant assets only when cash is paid for a plant asset. Do you agree with Ms. Ebener's method? Explain.

CASE 2 AutoType, a word processing service company, has more business than can be handled with the number of word processors it presently owns. The company is investigating the cost of buying an additional word processor. One dealer recommends a word processor costing $4,500.00. The useful life of this word processor is estimated to be five years with an estimated salvage value of $500.00. Another dealer recommends a larger word processor with 50% more memory capacity and 10% faster processing speed. The cost is $7,300.00, with a useful life of eight years and an estimated salvage value of $900.00. Which word processor would you recommend AutoType buy? Why?

CASE 3 Jennifer Mays has been working for a short time for Joel Enterprises. She recently asked her manager why the balance of the contra account, Accumulated Depreciation, grew larger at the end of each year while the balance for the contra account, Allowance for Uncollectible Accounts, seemed to stay about the same at the end of the year. As manager, how would you answer Ms. Mays?

CASE 4 TriState Company sold a typewriter for $100.00 after using it for five years. TriState paid $800.00 for the typewriter and at that time estimated the useful life to be five years with an estimated salvage value of $50.00. When the typewriter was sold, a total of $750.00 accumulated depreciation had been recorded in its plant asset record. Jonathan Yancey, a new accounting clerk, recorded the sale as a $100.00 debit to Cash and a $100.00 credit to Gain on Plant Assets. When asked why he made that entry, Mr. Yancey said that since the typewriter had been used for its full estimated useful life, he thought any amount realized from its sale should be recorded as a gain. Is Mr. Yancey correct? Explain.

■ DRILLS FOR UNDERSTANDING

DRILL 23-D1   Calculating depreciation expense

Instructions: Use the straight-line method of calculating depreciation described in this chapter. Calculate the amount of annual depreciation expense for each of the following plant assets.

Plant Asset	Original Cost	Estimated Salvage Value	Estimated Useful Life
1	$ 730.00	$ 50.00	4 years
2	5,200.00	1,400.00	5 years
3	2,170.00	250.00	3 years
4	1,610.00	170.00	6 years
5	8,950.00	2,350.00	8 years
6	17,480.00	950.00	10 years
7	12,600.00	3,150.00	9 years
8	57,200.00	5,500.00	25 years
9	9,220.00	480.00	4 years
10	26,500.00	5,950.00	15 years

DRILL 23-D2   Calculating book value of plant assets

Instructions: Calculate two amounts for each of the following plant assets.

a. Calculate the amount of total accumulated depreciation that should be recorded through December 31, 19X6. Calculate the time of depreciation to the nearest number of months. Round amounts to the nearest cent.
b. Calculate the ending book value as of December 31, 19X6.

Plant Asset	Date Bought	Original Cost	Estimated Salvage Value	Estimated Useful Life
1	Jan. 1, 19X1	$ 1,050.00	$ 150.00	6 years
2	July 1, 19X1	4,700.00	400.00	10 years
3	Apr. 1, 19X2	25,500.00	1,500.00	15 years
4	Sept. 1, 19X2	12,800.00	1,250.00	7 years
5	Mar. 1, 19X3	10,700.00	1,100.00	8 years
6	Aug. 1, 19X4	6,200.00	500.00	5 years
7	Dec. 31, 19X4	930.00	110.00	4 years
8	Oct. 1, 19X5	2,700.00	300.00	3 years
9	May 1, 19X6	15,600.00	3,600.00	8 years
10	Nov. 1, 19X6	7,800.00	240.00	9 years

■ APPLICATION PROBLEMS

PROBLEM 23-1   Journalizing the buying of plant assets

Holloway Company records plant assets in two accounts: Office Equipment and Store Equipment.

Instructions: Journalize the following transactions completed during the current year. Use page 12 of a cash payments journal. (Usually a new journal page is started each month. However, to conserve space in the working papers, record all of the year's entries on the same page of the cash payments journal.) The abbreviation for check is C.

Jan. 1. Paid cash for office equipment, $9,270.00. C127.
Feb. 1. Paid cash for store equipment, $12,850.00. C159.
May 1. Paid cash for office equipment, $313.00. C228.
June 1. Paid cash for office equipment, $1,740.00. C263.
Nov. 1. Paid cash for store equipment, $3,684.00. C401.
Dec. 1. Paid cash for office equipment, $920.00. C442.

PROBLEM 23-2   Calculating depreciation expense

Creative Concepts, Inc., owns the following plant assets.

Plant Asset	Date Bought	Original Cost	Estimated Salvage Value	Estimated Useful Life
1	July 1, 19X1	$ 5,600.00	$ 800.00	12 years
2	Nov. 1, 19X1	5,000.00	380.00	7 years
3	May 1, 19X2	21,600.00	2,250.00	15 years
4	Feb. 1, 19X3	10,750.00	1,750.00	9 years
5	Apr. 1, 19X3	3,820.00	220.00	6 years
6	Aug. 1, 19X3	1,440.00	200.00	2 years

Instructions: For each plant asset, calculate the depreciation expense to be recorded for the year ended December 31, 19X3. Use the straight-line method of calculating depreciation described in this chapter.

PROBLEM 23-3   Preparing a plant asset record

PhotoCraft bought a new high-speed photocopying machine on July 1 of the current year. Use the following additional information pertaining to the copier.

Account number: 1225
General ledger account: Store Equipment
Serial number of copier: KP3044987
Cost: $12,500.00
Estimated useful life: 7 years
Estimated salvage value: $2,000.00

Instructions: Prepare a plant asset record. For each year of the plant asset's life, record year-end date, annual depreciation expense, accumulated depreciation, and ending book value. Use the straight-line method of calculating depreciation.

PROBLEM 23-4   Recording work sheet adjustments and journal entries for depreciation expense

Landmark Contractors' general ledger has the following accounts and balances on December 31 of the current year.

PARTIAL GENERAL LEDGER

Account Title	Balance Debit	Credit
Office Equipment	$ 8,740.00	—
Accumulated Depreciation—Office Equipment	—	$2,130.00
Store Equipment	37,820.00	—
Accumulated Depreciation—Store Equipment	—	7,564.00
Depreciation Expense—Office Equipment	—	—
Depreciation Expense—Store Equipment	—	—

Instructions: 1. Record the account titles and balances in a work sheet's Account Title and Trial Balance columns for the current year ended December 31.

2. Record on the work sheet the adjustments for estimated depreciation for the year. Annual depreciation expenses are office equipment, $1,150.00, and store equipment, $1,890.00.

3. Journalize the adjusting entries on page 13 of a general journal.

PROBLEM 23-5   Journalizing the disposing of plant assets

Horizon Company records plant assets in two accounts: Office Equipment and Store Equipment.

Instructions: Journalize the following transactions completed during 19X2. Use page 12 of a general journal and a cash receipts journal. Source documents are abbreviated as follows: memorandum, M; receipt, R.

Feb. 1. Received cash from sale of office equipment, $1,400.00: original cost, $10,700.00; total accumulated depreciation through December 31, 19X1, $9,000.00; additional depreciation to be recorded through February 1, 19X2, $300.00. M25 and R43.

Apr. 1. Received cash from sale of store equipment, $500.00: original cost, $5,200.00; total accumulated depreciation through December 31, 19X1, $4,500.00; additional depreciation to be recorded through April 1, 19X2, $200.00. M52 and R74.

June 1. Received cash from sale of office equipment, $200.00: original cost, $3,800.00; total accumulated depreciation through December 31, 19X1, $3,500.00; additional depreciation to be recorded through June 1, 19X2, $100.00. M97 and R133.

Aug. 1. Received cash from sale of office equipment, $1,200.00: original cost, $8,100.00; total accumulated depreciation through December 31, 19X1, $6,120.00; additional depreciation to be recorded through August 1, 19X2, $400.00. M132 and R206.

Oct. 1. Received cash from sale of store equipment, $600.00: original cost, $1,450.00; total accumulated depreciation through December 31, 19X1, $1,050.00; additional depreciation to be recorded through October 1, 19X2, $50.00. M197 and R289.

■ ENRICHMENT PROBLEMS

MASTERY PROBLEM 23-M   Calculating depreciation expense and book value of plant assets; journalizing entries affecting plant assets

Taylor Lumber records plant assets in two accounts: Office Equipment and Store Equipment. Taylor Lumber owns the following plant assets.

Plant Asset	Asset Account	Date Bought	Original Cost	Estimated Salvage Value	Estimated Useful Life
1	Office Equipment	Apr. 1, 19X1	$ 7,300.00	$ 700.00	6 years
2	Store Equipment	July 1, 19X1	6,900.00	600.00	9 years
3	Store Equipment	Oct. 1, 19X1	5,700.00	900.00	3 years
4	Store Equipment	Aug. 1, 19X2	2,600.00	500.00	5 years
5	Store Equipment	Sept. 1, 19X2	3,100.00	700.00	4 years
6	Office Equipment	Nov. 1, 19X3	10,800.00	1,800.00	10 years
7	Office Equipment	May 1, 19X4	1,400.00	200.00	4 years
8	Office Equipment	July 1, 19X4	22,500.00	1,500.00	14 years

Instructions: 1. Calculate each plant asset's depreciation expense for the year ended December 31, 19X4. Use the straight-line method of calculating depreciation. Round amounts to the nearest cent.

2. Calculate each plant asset's ending book value as of December 31, 19X4.

3. Journalize the two adjusting entries for depreciation expense for the year ended December 31, 19X4. Use page 13 of a general journal.

4. Journalize the following transaction. Use page 4 of a cash receipts journal. Source documents are abbreviated as follows: memorandum, M; receipt, R.

19X5

Apr. 2. Received cash from sale of plant asset number 2, $4,200.00: original cost, $6,900.00; total accumulated depreciation through December 31, 19X4, $2,450.00; additional depreciation to be recorded through April 2, 19X5, $175.00. M125 and R193.

CHALLENGE PROBLEM 23-C   Calculating depreciation expense and book value of plant assets; journalizing entries affecting plant assets

Candlewick Company records plant assets in two accounts: Office Equipment and Store Equipment. Candlewick Company owns the following plant assets.

Plant Asset	Asset Account	Date Bought	Original Cost	Estimated Salvage Value	Estimated Useful Life
1	Office Equipment	Jan. 1, 19X1	$ 1,750.00	$ 250.00	5 years
2	Store Equipment	Jan. 1, 19X2	7,250.00	1,000.00	5 years
3	Store Equipment	Apr. 1, 19X2	12,500.00	1,500.00	10 years
4	Office Equipment	July 1, 19X2	3,500.00	300.00	4 years
5	Office Equipment	Apr. 1, 19X3	4,400.00	500.00	6 years
6	Store Equipment	July 1, 19X3	1,400.00	200.00	3 years
7	Store Equipment	July 1, 19X5	6,050.00	800.00	7 years
8	Office Equipment	Oct 1, 19X5	3,000.00	600.00	8 years

Instructions: 1. Calculate each plant asset's depreciation expense for the year ended December 31, 19X5. Use the straight-line method of calculating depreciation. Round amounts to the nearest cent.

2. Calculate each plant asset's total accumulated depreciation as of December 31, 19X5.

3. Calculate each plant asset's ending book value as of December 31, 19X5.

4. Journalize the two adjusting entries for depreciation expense for the year ended December 31, 19X5. Use page 13 of a general journal.

5. Journalize the following transactions completed during 19X6. Use page 25 of a cash receipts journal. Continue using page 13 of the general journal. Source documents are abbreviated as follows: memorandum, M; receipt, R.

19X6

Mar. 15. Received cash from sale of plant asset number 1, $250.00. R72.

Apr. 30. Received cash from sale of plant asset number 2, $2,000.00. M97 and R115.

Aug. 1. Received cash from sale of plant asset number 4, $850.00. M173 and R209.

Accounting for Notes and Interest

ENABLING PERFORMANCE TASKS

After studying Chapter 24, you will be able to:
a. Define accounting terms related to notes and interest.
b. Identify accounting concepts and practices related to notes and interest.
c. Calculate interest and maturity dates for notes.
d. Analyze and record transactions for notes payable and notes receivable.

Cash is the primary medium of exchange for business transactions. *(CONCEPT: Unit of Measurement)* Cash is used to purchase merchandise and to pay salaries and other expenses. In turn, businesses receive cash when they sell their products or services and collect payment. The cash received for products or services can be used to purchase more merchandise and continue to pay salaries and other expenses. Thus, the business cycle continues.

Sometimes a business receives more cash from sales than is needed to pay for purchases and expenses. When this occurs, a business may deposit the extra cash in a bank or other financial institution for a short period. At other times, the receipt of cash from sales does not occur at the same time and in sufficient amounts to pay for needed purchases and expenses. When this occurs, a business needs to borrow additional cash or make arrangements with its vendors to delay payment for a period of time. Generally, when a bank or other business lends money to another business, the loan agreement is made in writing.

PROMISSORY NOTES

A written and signed promise to pay a sum of money at a specified time is called a promissory note. A promissory note frequently is referred to as a note.

Promissory notes are used when money is borrowed for a period of time from a bank or other lending agency. Sometimes a business requests a note from a customer who wants credit beyond the usual time given for sales on account. Notes have an advantage over oral promises and accounts receivable or payable. A note, like a check, can be endorsed and transferred to a bank in return for cash. Thus, the business can get its money before the note is due. Notes can also be useful in a court of law as written evidence of a debt. One form of a promissory note is shown in Illustration 24-1.

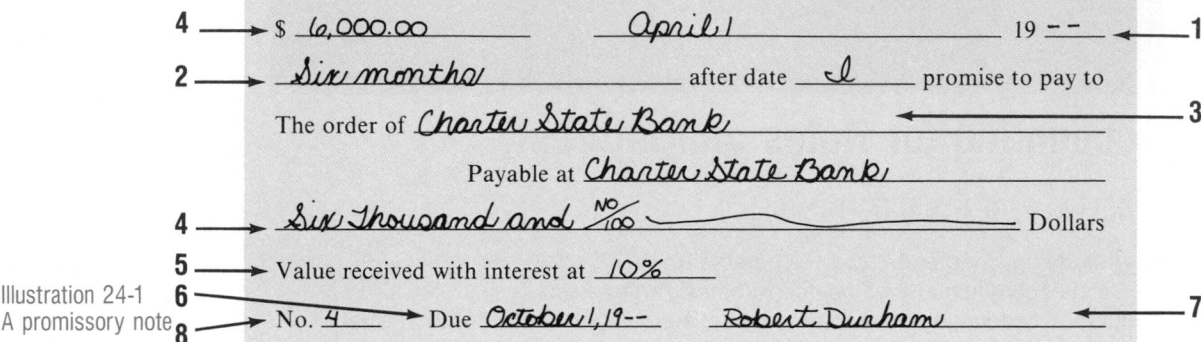

Illustration 24-1
A promissory note

The terms defined below apply to the promissory note shown in Illustration 24-1.

	Term	Definition	Illustration
1	Date of a note	The day a note is issued.	April 1, 19--
2	Time of a note	The days, months, or years from the date of issue until a note is to be paid.	Six months
3	Payee of a note	The person or business to whom the amount of a note is payable.	Charter State Bank
4	Principal of a note	The original amount of a note. Sometimes known as face amount of a note.	$6,000.00
5	Interest rate of a note	The percentage of the principal that is paid for use of the money.	10%
6	Maturity date of a note	The date a note is due.	October 1, 19--
7	Maker of a note	The person or business who signs a note and thus promises to make payment.	Robert Durham
8	Number of a note	The number assigned by the maker to identify a specific note.	4

INTEREST ON PROMISSORY NOTES

An amount paid for the use of money for a period of time is called interest. Banks and other lending institutions generally charge interest on money loaned to their customers.

When businesses borrow money from banks, other lending institutions, or other businesses, promissory notes generally are prepared to provide written evidence of the transaction. Most promissory notes require the payment of interest. A promissory note that requires the payment of principal plus interest when the note is due is called an interest-bearing note. A promissory note that requires only the payment of the principal when the note is due is called a non-interest-bearing note.

The interest rate is stated as a percentage of the principal. *Interest at 10% means that 10 cents will be paid for the use of each dollar borrowed* for a full year. The interest on $100.00 for a full year at 10% is $10.00 ($100.00 × 10% = $10.00).

The amount that is due on the maturity date of a note is called the maturity value. A one-year interest-bearing note with a principal of $100.00 and interest rate of 10% will have a maturity value of $110.00 ($100.00 principal + $10.00 interest).

> Sometimes partial payments on a note are made each month. This arrangement is particularly true when an individual buys a car and signs a note for the amount owed. The monthly payment includes part of the principal and part of the interest to be paid.

Calculating interest

To calculate interest for one year, the principal is multiplied by the interest rate. The interest on a 12% interest-bearing note for $1,000.00 for one year is calculated as shown below.

Principal	×	Interest Rate	×	Time in Years	=	Interest for One Year
$1,000.00	×	12%	×	1	=	$120.00

When the time of a note is expressed in months, the time used in calculating interest is stated as a fraction of 12 months. The interest on a 12% interest-bearing note for $1,000.00 for three months (3/12 of a year) is calculated as shown below.

Principal	×	Interest Rate	×	Time as Fraction of Year	=	Interest for Fraction of Year
$1,000.00	×	12%	×	$\frac{3}{12}$	=	$\frac{\$360.00}{12} = \$30.00$

The time of a note is often stated as a number of days, such as 30 days, 60 days, or 90 days. When the time of a note is stated in days, the time used in calculating interest is stated as a fraction of 360 days. The interest on a 12% interest-bearing note for $1,000.00 for 60 days (60/360 of a year) is calculated as shown below.

Principal	×	Interest Rate	×	Time as Fraction of Year	=	Interest for Fraction of Year
$1,000.00	×	12%	×	$\dfrac{60}{360}$	=	$\dfrac{\$7,200.00}{360} = \$20.00$

Agencies of the federal government generally use a 365-day year when calculating interest. Consumer interest is also generally calculated on a 365-day year. However, many banks use a 360-day year when calculating interest. Therefore, the interest calculations in this textbook use a 360-day year.

Calculating maturity date

The time between the date a note is issued and the date a note is due may be expressed in either years, months, or days. When the time of a note is stated in months, the maturity date is calculated by counting the number of months from the date of issuance. For example, a six-month note dated April 11 would be due on October 11.

When the time of a note is expressed in days, the maturity date is calculated by counting the exact number of days. The date the note is written is not counted, but the maturity date is counted. To figure this maturity date, find the number of days remaining in the month the note was written. Then add the days in the following months until the total equals the required number of days. For example, a 60-day note dated March 3 is due on May 2. The maturity date is calculated as shown below.

March 3 through 31	28 days (31 − 3 = 28)
April 1 through 30	30 days
May 1 through 2	2 days (Maturity date: May 2)
	60 days

NOTES PAYABLE

A person or organization to whom a liability is owed is called a creditor. Promissory notes that a business issues to creditors are called notes payable. Liabilities due within a short time, usually within a year, are called current liabilities. Since notes payable generally are paid within one year, they are classified as current liabilities.

Issuing a note payable to borrow money from a bank

When a business issues a note payable, the principal or face amount of the note is credited to a liability account titled *Notes Payable*. A liability account has a normal credit balance. Therefore, the notes payable account is increased by a credit and decreased by a debit, as shown in the T account.

Notes Payable

Debit side	Credit side
Decrease	Normal balance Increase

On April 1 Celluphone arranges to borrow money from its bank. A note payable is issued to the bank as evidence of the debt. The bank deposits the principal amount of the note in Celluphone's checking account.

April 1, 19--.
Issued a 6-month, 10% note, $6,000.00. Note Payable No. 4.

The bank retains the original of the note until Celluphone pays the maturity value. A copy of the note payable is the source document used by Celluphone to record this transaction. *(CONCEPT: Objective Evidence)* The analysis of this transaction to issue a note payable is shown in the T accounts.

Cash

Apr. 1	6,000.00	

Notes Payable

	Apr. 1	6,000.00

Cash is debited for $6,000.00 to show the increase in the balance of this asset account. Notes Payable is credited for $6,000.00 to show the increase in the balance of this liability account. No entry is made for interest until a later date when the interest is paid.

The cash receipts journal entry to record this transaction is shown in Illustration 24-2.

CASH RECEIPTS JOURNAL — PAGE 13

DATE	ACCOUNT TITLE	DOC. NO.	POST. REF.	GENERAL DEBIT	GENERAL CREDIT	ACCOUNTS RECEIVABLE CREDIT	SALES CREDIT	SALES TAX PAYABLE DEBIT	SALES TAX PAYABLE CREDIT	SALES DISCOUNT DEBIT	CASH DEBIT
6	1 Notes Payable	NP4			6000 00						6000 00
7											

Illustration 24-2
Cash receipts journal entry to record cash received for the issuance of a note payable

Paying principal and interest on a note payable at maturity

When a note payable reaches the maturity date, the maker of the note pays the maturity value to the payee. The maturity value of a note is the principal (original amount borrowed) plus the interest that has accrued during the time of the note. The interest accrued on money borrowed is called interest expense.

The interest accrued on a note payable is debited to an expense account titled *Interest Expense.* An expense account has a normal debit balance. Therefore, the interest expense account is increased by a debit and decreased by a credit, as shown in the T account.

Interest Expense

Debit side Normal balance Increase	Credit side Decrease

Interest expense is a financial expense rather than an expense of the business' normal operations. Therefore, Interest Expense is listed in a classification titled *Other Expense* in a chart of accounts.

Celluphone paid the six-month note payable it had issued on April 1.

October 1, 19--.
Paid cash for the maturity value of Note Payable No. 4: principal, $6,000.00,
plus interest, $300.00; total, $6,300.00. Check No. 573.

Notes Payable

| Oct. 1 | 6,000.00 | Apr. 1 | 6,000.00 |

Interest Expense

| Oct. 1 | 300.00 | |

Cash

| | | Oct. 1 | 6,300.00 |

A check is the source document for recording this transaction. *(CONCEPT: Objective Evidence)* The analysis of this transaction to pay the maturity value of a note payable is shown in the T accounts.

Notes Payable is debited for $6,000.00 to show the decrease in the balance of this liability account. Interest Expense is debited for $300.00 to show the increase in the balance of this other expense account. Cash is paid for the maturity value of the note. Thus, Cash is credited for $6,300.00 ($6,000.00 principal + $300.00 interest) to show the decrease in the balance of this asset account.

The cash payments journal entry to record this transaction is shown in Illustration 24-3.

CASH PAYMENTS JOURNAL															PAGE **28**	
					1		2		3		4		5			
	DATE	ACCOUNT TITLE	CK. NO.	POST. REF.	GENERAL			ACCOUNTS PAYABLE DEBIT		PURCHASES DISCOUNT CREDIT		CASH CREDIT				
					DEBIT		CREDIT									
1	Oct. 1	*Notes Payable*	573		6 0 0 0 00							6 3 0 0 00				1
2		*Interest Expense*			3 0 0 00											2
3																3
4																4

Illustration 24-3
Cash payments journal entry to record payment of maturity value of a note payable

Issuing and paying a note payable for an extension of time

A business may ask for an extension of time if it is unable to pay an account when due. When a request for more time is made, sometimes the business is asked to issue a note payable. The note payable does not pay the amount owed to the vendor. However, the form of the liability is changed from an account payable to a note payable.

April 5, 19--.
Issued a 60-day, 12% note to Action Phone Company for an extension of time on this account payable, $2,000.00. Note Payable No. 5.

GENERAL LEDGER

Accounts Payable

| 2,000.00 | |

Notes Payable

| | 2,000.00 |

ACCOUNTS PAYABLE LEDGER
Action Phone Company

| 2,000.00 | Bal. | 2,000.00 |

A copy of the note is the source document for recording this transaction. *(CONCEPT: Objective Evidence)* The analysis of this transaction to issue a note payable is shown in the T accounts.

Accounts Payable is debited for $2,000.00 to show the decrease in the balance of this liability account. Notes Payable is credited for $2,000.00 to show the increase in the balance of this liability account. The vendor account, Action Phone

Company, is debited for $2,000.00 to show the decrease in the balance of this accounts payable ledger account. Whenever Accounts Payable is decreased, the vendor account in the accounts payable ledger is also decreased by the same amount. No entry is made for interest expense until a later date when interest is paid.

The general journal entry to record this transaction is shown in Illustration 24-4.

		GENERAL JOURNAL				PAGE 5	
DATE		ACCOUNT TITLE	DOC. NO.	POST. REF.	DEBIT	CREDIT	
17	5	*Accounts Payable/Action Phone Co.*	NP5	/	2 0 0 0 00		17
18		*Notes Payable*				2 0 0 0 00	18

Illustration 24-4
General journal entry to record issuing a note payable for an extension of time on an account payable

When this entry is posted, the balance of the accounts payable account for Action Phone Company will be zero. One liability, Accounts Payable, is replaced by another liability, Notes Payable.

Note Payable No. 5 is due on June 4. The maturity date for Note Payable No. 5 is calculated as shown below.

April 5 through 30	25 days (30 − 5 = 25)
May 1 through 31	31 days
June 1 through 4	4 days (Maturity date: June 4)
	60 days

June 4, 19--.
Paid cash for the maturity value of Note Payable No. 5: principal, $2,000.00, plus interest, $40.00; total, $2,040.00. Check No. 328.

The interest expense is calculated as shown below.

Principal	×	Interest Rate	×	Time as Fraction of Year	=	Interest for Fraction of Year
$2,000.00	×	12%	×	$\dfrac{60}{360}$	=	$\dfrac{\$14,400.00}{360} = \$40.00$

The analysis of this transaction to record payment of the maturity value of a note is shown in the T accounts.

Notes Payable is debited for $2,000.00 to show the decrease in the balance of this liability account. Interest Expense is debited for $40.00 to show the increase in the balance of this other expense account. Cash is credited for the principal of the note plus the interest, $2,040.00, to show the decrease in the balance of this asset account.

Notes Payable	
June 4 2,000.00	Apr. 5 2,000.00

Interest Expense	
June 4 40.00	

Cash	
	June 4 2,040.00

The cash payments journal entry to record this transaction is shown in Illustration 24-5.

CASH PAYMENTS JOURNAL

	DATE	ACCOUNT TITLE	CK. NO.	POST. REF.	GENERAL DEBIT	GENERAL CREDIT	ACCOUNTS PAYABLE DEBIT	PURCHASES DISCOUNT CREDIT	CASH CREDIT	
1	*June* 4	*Notes Payable*	328		2 0 0 0 00				2 0 4 0 00	1
2		*Interest Expense*			4 0 00					2
3										3

PAGE *15*

Illustration 24-5
Cash payments journal entry to record payment of maturity value of a note payable issued for an extension of time

Issuing and paying a discounted note payable

Some banks require that the interest be paid at the time a note is issued. Interest collected in advance on a note is called bank discount. A note on which interest is paid in advance is called a discounted note. The amount received for a note after the bank discount has been deducted is called proceeds.

> May 3, 19--.
> Discounted at 10% a 3-month non-interest-bearing note, $3,000.00; proceeds, $2,925.00, interest, $75.00. Note Payable No. 6.

The bank deposited the proceeds, $2,925.00, in Celluphone's checking account. The amount of the discount and the proceeds are calculated as shown below.

Maturity Value	×	Discount Rate	×	Time as Fraction of Year	=	Bank Discount
$3,000.00	×	10%	×	$\frac{3}{12}$	=	$\frac{\$900.00}{12}$ = $75.00

Maturity Value	−	Bank Discount	=	Proceeds
$3,000.00	−	$75.00	=	$2,925.00

Cash

May 3	2,925.00	

Interest Expense

May 3	75.00	

Notes Payable

	May 3	3,000.00

A copy of the note is the source document for recording this transaction. *(CONCEPT: Objective Evidence)* The analysis of this transaction to record a discounted note payable is shown in the T accounts.

Cash is debited for $2,925.00 ($3,000.00 − $75.00 interest expense) to show the increase in the balance of this asset account. Interest Expense is debited for the discount, $75.00, to show the increase in the balance of this other expense account. Notes Payable is credited for $3,000.00 to show the increase in the balance of this liability account.

The cash receipts journal entry to record this transaction is shown in Illustration 24-6.

							GENERAL		ACCOUNTS RECEIVABLE CREDIT	SALES CREDIT	SALES TAX PAYABLE		SALES DISCOUNT DEBIT	CASH DEBIT	
	DATE	ACCOUNT TITLE	DOC. NO.	POST. REF.		DEBIT	CREDIT				DEBIT	CREDIT			
6	3	Interest Expense	NP6			7 5 00								2 9 2 5 00	6
7		Notes Payable					3 0 0 0 00								7

CASH RECEIPTS JOURNAL — PAGE 17

Illustration 24-6
Cash receipts journal entry to record cash received for a discounted note payable

When Note Payable No. 6 is paid on August 3, Check No. 450 is issued to the bank. This check is in payment of the principal. No payment of interest expense is necessary at this time because the bank collected the interest in advance when the note was discounted. Therefore, the maturity value of a discounted note is the principal of the note. Because no interest is paid on the maturity date, a discounted note is considered a non-interest-bearing note.

August 3, 19--.
Paid cash for the maturity value of non-interest-bearing Note Payable No. 6, $3,000.00. Check No. 450.

The analysis of this transaction to record payment of a discounted note payable is shown in the T accounts.

Notes Payable is debited for $3,000.00 to show the decrease in the balance of this liability account. Cash is credited for the amount paid, $3,000.00, to show the decrease in the balance of this asset account.

Notes Payable			
Aug. 3	3,000.00	May 3	3,000.00

Cash			
		Aug. 3	3,000.00

The cash payments journal entry to record this transaction is shown in Illustration 24-7.

						GENERAL		ACCOUNTS PAYABLE DEBIT	PURCHASES DISCOUNT CREDIT	CASH CREDIT	
	DATE	ACCOUNT TITLE	CK. NO.	POST. REF.		DEBIT	CREDIT				
3	3	Notes Payable	450			3 0 0 0 00				3 0 0 0 00	3
4											4

CASH PAYMENTS JOURNAL — PAGE 20

Illustration 24-7
Cash payments journal entry to record payment of a discounted note payable

NOTES RECEIVABLE

Promissory notes that a business accepts from customers are called notes receivable. Notes receivable generally are paid within one year. Therefore, they are classified as current assets.

Accepting a note receivable from a customer

A customer who is unable to pay an account on the due date may request additional time. When a request for more time is made, a business may agree to accept a note receivable. A note receivable does not pay the amount the customer owes. However, the form of the asset is changed from an account receivable to a note receivable.

If a customer needs extra time to pay, most businesses prefer a note receivable over an account receivable for several reasons. A note receivable usually earns interest whereas an account receivable does not. By signing the promissory note, the customer provides a written confirmation of the amount owed, which provides evidence of the debt in case legal action is required to collect.

Notes Receivable	
Debit side	Credit side
Normal balance	
Increase	Decrease

When a business accepts a note receivable, the principal or face amount of the note is debited to an asset account titled *Notes Receivable*. An asset account has a normal debit balance. Therefore, the notes receivable account is increased by a debit and decreased by a credit, as shown in the T account.

Celluphone agrees to accept a promissory note from Ann Nance. Celluphone accepts the note because Mrs. Nance is unable to pay the account receivable when due. The note Mrs. Nance issues, which will be payable to Celluphone, is an interest-bearing note. Although Celluphone has not yet collected the cash Mrs. Nance owes, the promissory note does provide a written promise to pay the amount owed plus interest.

As defined earlier, a promissory note is a written and signed promise to pay a sum of money at a specified time. A note is recorded as a note receivable by the person or business to whom the amount of a note is payable. A note is recorded as a note payable by the maker of the note, the person or business who signs a note and thus promises to make payment. Therefore, the note issued by Mrs. Nance to Celluphone is recorded by Celluphone as a note receivable. This same note is recorded by Mrs. Nance as a note payable.

April 22, 19--.
Received a 2-month, 12% note from Ann Nance for an extension of time on her account, $800.00. Note Receivable No. 10.

A copy of the note is the source document for recording this transaction. *(CONCEPT: Objective Evidence)* The analysis of this transaction to record a note receivable is shown in the T accounts.

Notes Receivable is debited for $800.00 to show the increase in the balance of this asset account. Accounts Receivable is credited for $800.00 to show the decrease in the balance of this asset account. The customer account, Ann Nance, is also credited for $800.00 to show the decrease in the balance of this accounts receivable ledger account. Whenever Accounts Receiv-

GENERAL LEDGER
Notes Receivable

Apr. 22	800.00	.	

Accounts Receivable

		Apr. 22	800.00

ACCOUNTS RECEIVABLE LEDGER
Ann Nance

Bal.	800.00	Apr. 22	800.00

able is decreased, the customer account in the accounts receivable ledger is also decreased by the same amount.

The general journal entry to record this transaction is shown in Illustration 24-8.

	DATE		ACCOUNT TITLE	DOC. NO.	POST. REF.	DEBIT	CREDIT	
			GENERAL JOURNAL				PAGE 6	
6	22		Notes Receivable	NR10		8 0 0 00		6
7			Accounts Receivable/Ann Nance		/		8 0 0 00	7
8								8
9								9
10								10

Illustration 24-8
General journal entry to record a note receivable for an extension of time on an account

When this entry is posted, the balance of the accounts receivable account for Mrs. Nance will be zero. One asset, Accounts Receivable, is replaced by another asset, Notes Receivable.

Collecting principal and interest on a note receivable at maturity

When a note receivable reaches the maturity date, the payee of the note receives the maturity value from the maker of the note. The maturity value of a note is the principal (original amount of the note) plus the interest earned during the time of the note. The interest earned on money loaned is called interest income.

The interest earned on a note receivable is credited to a revenue account titled *Interest Income.* A revenue account has a normal credit balance. Therefore, the interest income account is increased by a credit and decreased by a debit, as shown in the T account.

Interest Income	
Debit side	Credit side
	Normal balance
Decrease	Increase

Interest income is investment revenue rather than revenue from the business' normal operations. Therefore, Interest Income is listed in a classification titled *Other Revenue* in a chart of accounts.

Celluphone received cash from Ann Nance for the principal and interest of the note accepted from Mrs. Nance on April 22.

June 22, 19--.
Received cash for the maturity value of Note Receivable No. 10: principal, $800.00, plus interest, $16.00; total, $816.00. Receipt No. 497.

A receipt issued for cash received from Ann Nance is the source document for recording this transaction. *(CONCEPT: Objective Evidence)* The analysis of this transaction to record receipt of the maturity value of a note receivable is shown in the T accounts.

Cash

June 22	816.00	

Notes Receivable

Apr. 22	800.00	June 22	800.00

Interest Income

		June 22	16.00

Cash is debited for $816.00 ($800.00 principal + $16.00 interest income) to show the increase in the balance of this asset account. Notes Receivable is credited for $800.00 to show the decrease in the balance of this asset account. Interest Income is credited for $16.00 ($800.00 × 12% × 2/12 = $16.00) to show the increase in the balance of this other revenue account.

The cash receipts journal entry to record this transaction is shown in Illustration 24-9.

					GENERAL		ACCOUNTS RECEIVABLE CREDIT	SALES CREDIT	SALES TAX PAYABLE		SALES DISCOUNT DEBIT	CASH DEBIT	
	DATE	ACCOUNT TITLE	DOC. NO.	POST. REF.	DEBIT	CREDIT			DEBIT	CREDIT			
18	22	Notes Receivable	R497			800 00						816 00	18
19		Interest Income				16 00							19
20													20
21													21
22													22

CASH RECEIPTS JOURNAL — PAGE 22

Illustration 24-9
Cash receipts journal entry to record receipt of maturity value of a note receivable

After the entry is recorded, the original copy of Note Receivable No. 10 is marked *Paid* and returned to Ann Nance, the maker.

Recording a dishonored note receivable

A note that is not paid when due is called a dishonored note. The balance of the notes receivable account should show only the total amount of notes that probably will be collected. The amount of a dishonored note receivable should therefore be removed from the notes receivable account. The amount of the note plus interest income earned on the note is still owed by the customer. Therefore, the total amount owed should be debited to the accounts receivable account in the general ledger. The amount owed should also be debited to the customer account in the accounts receivable ledger. The customer account will then show the total amount owed by the customer, including the amount of the dishonored note and interest earned. This information may be important if the customer requests credit in the future or if collection is achieved later.

May 12, 19--.
Keith Leising dishonored Note Receivable No. 9, a 1-month, 12% note maturity value due today: principal, $200.00; interest, $2.00; total, $202.00. Memorandum No. 65.

A memorandum is the source document for recording this transaction. *(CONCEPT: Objective Evidence)* The analysis of this transaction for a dishonored note receivable is shown in the T accounts.

Accounts Receivable is debited for $202.00 ($200.00 principal + $2.00 interest income) to show the increase in the balance of this asset account. Notes Receivable is credited for $200.00 to show the decrease in the balance of this asset account. Interest Income is credited for $2.00 ($200.00 × 12% × 1/12 = $2.00) to show the increase in the balance of this other revenue account. The customer account, Keith Leising, is also debited for $202.00 ($200.00 principal + $2.00 interest) to show the increase in the balance of this accounts receivable ledger account.

The interest income has been earned even though it has not been paid. Keith Leising owes the principal amount of the note plus the interest earned. Therefore, the total of principal plus interest ($200.00 + $2.00 = $202.00) is debited to Accounts Receivable and to the customer account.

The general journal entry to record this transaction is shown in Illustration 24-10.

GENERAL LEDGER

Accounts Receivable

May 12	202.00		

Notes Receivable

Apr. 12	200.00	May 12	200.00

Interest Income

		May 12	2.00

ACCOUNTS RECEIVABLE LEDGER

Keith Leising

May 12	202.00		

GENERAL JOURNAL   PAGE 8

	DATE	ACCOUNT TITLE	DOC. NO.	POST. REF.	DEBIT	CREDIT	
9	12	Accounts Receivable/Keith Leising	M65	/	202 00		9
10		Notes Receivable				200 00	10
11		Interest Income				2 00	11
12							12
13							13
14							14

Illustration 24-10
General journal entry to record a dishonored note receivable

Celluphone does not write off Mr. Leising's account when the note is dishonored. Instead, the company continues to try to collect the account.

Later Celluphone may decide that the account cannot be collected from Mr. Leising. At that time the balance of the account will be written off as an uncollectible account. Allowance for Uncollectible Accounts will be debited, and Accounts Receivable and Keith Leising's account will be credited.

SUMMARY OF ACCOUNTING FOR NOTES AND INTEREST

The chart shown in Illustration 24-11 summarizes the journal entries for recording notes payable and notes receivable transactions.

The chart shown in Illustration 24-12 summarizes the calculations for interest and discounted notes.

TRANSACTIONS	GENERAL LEDGER														SUBSIDIARY LEDGERS			
	CASH		NOTES REC.		ACCTS. REC.		NOTES PAY.		ACCTS. PAY.		INTEREST INCOME		INTEREST EXPENSE		ACCTS. REC.		ACCTS. PAY.	
	DR.	CR.	DR.	CR.	DR.	CR.	DR.	CR.	DR.	CR.	DR.	CR.	DR.	CR.	DR.	CR.	DR.	CR.
Issuing a note payable to borrow money from a bank	X							X										
Paying principal and interest on a note payable at maturity		X					X						X					
Issuing a note payable for an extension of time							X	X									X	
Paying principal and interest on a note for an extension of time		X					X						X					
Issuing a discounted note payable for cash	X							X					X					
Paying a discounted note payable		X					X											
Accepting a note receivable from a customer			X			X										X		
Collecting principal and interest on a note receivable at maturity	X			X								X						
Recording a dishonored note receivable					X	X						X			X			

Illustration 24-11   Summary of journal entries for recording notes payable and notes receivable transactions

AMOUNTS	CALCULATIONS						
Interest for Years	Principal	×	Interest Rate	×	Time in Years	=	Interest for Years
Interest for Fraction of Year	Principal	×	Interest Rate	×	Time as Fraction of Year	=	Interest for Fraction of Year
Bank Discount	Maturity Value	×	Discount Rate	×	Time as Fraction of Year	=	Bank Discount
Proceeds	Maturity Value	−	Bank Discount		=	Proceeds	

Illustration 24-12   Summary of calculations for interest and discounted notes

ACCOUNTING TERMS

What is the meaning of each of the following?

1. promissory note
2. date of a note
3. time of a note
4. payee of a note
5. principal of a note
6. interest rate of a note
7. maturity date of a note
8. maker of a note

9. number of a note
10. interest
11. interest-bearing note
12. non-interest-bearing note
13. maturity value
14. creditor
15. notes payable
16. current liabilities

17. interest expense
18. bank discount
19. discounted note
20. proceeds
21. notes receivable
22. interest income
23. dishonored note

QUESTIONS FOR INDIVIDUAL STUDY

1. What conditions would cause a business to have extra cash to deposit in a bank, yet at another time of year, need to borrow extra cash from a bank?
2. Why does a business sometimes request a promissory note from a credit customer?
3. What is the advantage of a promissory note over an account receivable?
4. What is the difference between the payee and the maker of a note?
5. What does *interest at 10%* mean?
6. How is interest calculated for a fraction of a year?
7. Why are notes payable generally classified as current liabilities?
8. Which accounting concept is being applied when a copy of a note payable is used as the source document for recording the issuance of a note payable?
9. What accounts are affected, and how, when a business issues a note payable to borrow money from a bank?
10. When an interest-bearing note is paid, why is the credit to Cash greater than the debit to Notes Payable?
11. What accounts are affected, and how, when a business issues an interest-bearing note payable for an extension of time on its account payable?

12. What accounts are affected, and how, when a business pays an interest-bearing note payable that had been issued for an extension of time on its account payable?
13. How much will the maker receive from a one-year non-interest-bearing note with a face value of $1,000.00, discounted at 10%?
14. What accounts are affected, and how, when a non-interest-bearing note payable is discounted at a bank?
15. What accounts are affected, and how, when a discounted note payable is paid at maturity?
16. When a business accepts a note receivable from a credit customer for an extension of time on the customer's account receivable, how does the amount and form of the business asset change?
17. What accounts are affected, and how, when a business receives the principal and interest on a note receivable at maturity?
18. What accounts are affected, and how, when a customer dishonors an interest-bearing note receivable?
19. Why is interest income recorded at the time a note is dishonored even though cash has not been received?

■ CASES FOR MANAGEMENT DECISION

CASE 1 BelTech purchased $8,000.00 worth of merchandise on account from Major Supplies on April 1. Major Supplies' terms of sale require payment on account within 30 days. However, BelTech purchased the merchandise with the understanding that it could issue a 10% note payable with payment due no later than October 1. On April 1 BelTech's accountant was instructed to issue the note payable to Major Supplies. As payments on account are due in 30 days, the accountant suggested that the note be issued on May 1. On what date would you suggest that the note be issued? Why?

CASE 2 Because of a temporary cash shortage, Jupiter Company has had to request an extension of time on its purchases on account. Jupiter's regular vendor, Custom Suppliers, requires that a 12% interest-bearing note be issued to them for any extension of time over one month. Jupiter usually needs 3 months from time of purchase to time of payment. Because of the extra costs for interest expense, Jupiter has been exploring other vendor options. Another vendor, Page Supplies, has been located that will sell merchandise on account with credit terms of net due in 3 months. For the same quantity and brand of merchandise, Custom Suppliers' cost is $10,000.00; for Page Supplies, $10,250.00. Since Page Supplies offers 3 months credit terms without any interest charges and the merchandise is only 2.5% higher than that from Custom Suppliers, Jupiter's purchasing manager, Robert Jimerson, has decided to buy the merchandise from Page. When asked why he is buying from the company with costs 2.5% higher, he said, "A 2.5% higher price is better than the 12% interest we would have to pay Custom Suppliers." Do you agree with Mr. Jimerson? Explain.

CASE 3 Alexandra Davis requested a $1,000.00 bank loan for one year. The loan officer agreed to the loan and offered Miss Davis her choice of a 10% interest-bearing note or a note discounted at 10%. Which choice should Miss Davis accept?

CASE 4 Solar Company has a $5,000.00, 3-month, 12% note receivable that has been dishonored. Two company accounting clerks cannot agree on the best way to record the dishonored note. David Rinehart recommends crediting Notes Receivable for $5,000.00 and debiting Allowance for Uncollectible Accounts for $5,000.00. Deborah Sadovsky recommends debiting Accounts Receivable and the customer account for $5,150.00 and crediting Notes Receivable for $5,000.00 and Interest Income for $150.00. Which is the more desirable entry? Why?

■ DRILLS FOR UNDERSTANDING

DRILL 24-D1 Calculating interest on notes

Instructions: Calculate the interest for each of the following notes.

No. of Note	Principal of Note	Interest Rate	Time of Note
1	$ 700.00	8%	1 year
2	1,200.00	12%	6 months
3	500.00	15%	30 days
4	800.00	9%	4 months
5	600.00	10%	60 days

DRILL 24-D2 Calculating maturity dates of notes

Instructions: Calculate the maturity date for each of the following notes.

No. of Note	Date of Note	Time of Note
1	Jan. 11	90 days
2	Feb. 5	1 year
3	May 17	30 days
4	July 1	3 months
5	Oct. 20	6 months

DRILL 24-D3 Calculating maturity dates and interest on notes

Instructions: For each of the following notes, calculate (1) the maturity date and (2) the interest.

No. of Note	Date of Note	Principal of Note	Interest Rate	Time of Note
1	Jan. 4	$ 400	9%	30 days
2	Mar. 21	800	11%	1 year
3	May 8	1,200	13%	60 days
4	July 15	1,700	12%	6 months
5	Sept. 1	2,000	10%	90 days

DRILL 24-D4 Analyzing recording notes payable transactions

Instructions: Use a form similar to the following. For each transaction, write the title of the accounts affected in the Account Title column. For each account title, place a check mark in the Debit or Credit column to show whether the account is debited or credited. Transaction 1 is given as an example. The abbreviation for note payable is NP.

Trans. No.	Account Title	Debit	Credit
1.	Cash Interest Expense Notes Payable	✓ ✓	 ✓

Transactions
1. Discounted at 14% a 60-day non-interest-bearing note. NP135.
2. Issued a 1-year, 12% note. NP136.
3. Issued a 6-month, 10% note. NP137.
4. Discounted at 11% a 90-day non-interest-bearing note. NP138.
5. Discounted at 13% a 2-month non-interest-bearing note. NP139.
6. Issued a 30-day, 15% note for an extension of time on an account payable. NP140.
7. Paid cash for the maturity value of non-interest-bearing NP135.
8. Paid cash for the maturity value of NP136.

DRILL 24-D5 Analyzing recording notes receivable transactions

Instructions: Use a form similar to the following. For each transaction, write the title of the accounts affected in the Account Title column. For each account title, place a check mark in the

Debit or Credit column to show whether the account is debited or credited. Transaction 1 is given as an example. The abbreviation for note receivable is NR.

Trans. No.	Account Title	Debit	Credit
1.	Notes Receivable	✓	
	Accounts Receivable		✓

Transactions

1. Received a 60-day, 14% note for an extension of time on an account. NR26.
2. Received a 1-year, 10% note for an extension of time on an account. NR27.
3. Received a 3-month, 12% note for an extension of time on an account. NR28.
4. Received a 90-day, 11% note for an extension of time on an account. NR29.
5. Received a 6-month, 13% note for an extension of time on an account. NR30.
6. Received cash for the maturity value of NR26.
7. Received cash for the maturity value of NR27.
8. Maker dishonored NR28, a 3-month, 12% note, maturity value due today.

▊ APPLICATION PROBLEMS

PROBLEM 24-1   Journalizing notes payable transactions

The following transactions were completed by Coastal Construction during the current year.

Instructions: 1. Journalize the following transactions. Use page 10 of a general journal, page 20 of a cash receipts journal, and page 18 of a cash payments journal. (Usually a new journal page is started each month. However, to conserve space in the working papers, record all of the year's entries on the same page of each journal.) Source documents are abbreviated as follows: check, C; note payable, NP.

Mar.   3. Issued a 90-day, 13% note, $6,000.00. NP179.
  12. Paid cash for the maturity value of NP169: principal, $3,500.00, plus interest, $35.00; total, $3,535.00. C2117.
  31. Issued a 30-day, 12% note to Santa Fe Company for an extension of time on this account payable, $1,500.00. NP180.
Apr.   8. Paid cash for the maturity value of NP158: principal, $12,500.00, plus interest, $375.00; total, $12,875.00. C2189.
  30. Paid cash for the maturity value of NP180: principal, $1,500.00, plus interest, $15.00; total, $1,515.00. C2234.
May 13. Issued a 60-day, 12% note, $5,500.00. NP181.
June 1. Paid cash for the maturity value of NP179: principal, $6,000.00, plus interest, $195.00; total, $6,195.00. C2415.
  17. Issued a 30-day, 11% note to Universal Lumber for an extension of time on this account payable, $8,000.00. NP182.
July 12. Paid cash for the maturity value of NP181: principal, $5,500.00, plus interest, $110.00; total, $5,610.00. C2543.
  17. Paid cash for the maturity value of NP182: principal, $8,000.00, plus interest, $73.33; total, $8,073.33. C2561.

  2. Prove the cash receipts and cash payments journals.

PROBLEM 24-2   Journalizing notes payable transactions

The following transactions were completed by Manhattan Concepts, Inc., during the current year.

Instructions: 1. Journalize the following transactions. Use page 16 of a general journal, page 23 of a cash receipts journal, and page 20 of a cash payments journal. Source documents are abbreviated as follows: check, C; note payable, NP.

Jan. 17. Issued a 90-day, 12% note, $9,000.00. NP134.

    29. Paid cash for the maturity value of NP112: principal, $2,000.00, plus interest, $18.33; total, $2,018.33. C1073.

Feb. 2. Discounted at 13% a 60-day non-interest-bearing note, $7,000.00; proceeds, $6,848.33, interest, $151.67. NP135.

    9. Paid cash for the maturity value of NP120: principal, $3,000.00, plus interest, $30.00; total, $3,030.00. C1103.

   21. Issued a 30-day, 11% note to Newport Company for an extension of time on this account payable, $5,000.00. NP136.

Mar. 8. Discounted at 12% a 45-day non-interest-bearing note, $4,500.00; proceeds, $4,432.50, interest, $67.50. NP137.

   23. Paid cash for the maturity value of NP136: principal, $5,000.00, plus interest, $45.83; total, $5,045.83. C1234.

Apr. 3. Paid cash for the maturity value of non-interest-bearing NP135, $7,000.00. C1279.

   17. Paid cash for the maturity value of NP134: principal, $9,000.00, plus interest, $270.00; total, $9,270.00. C1312.

   22. Paid cash for the maturity value of non-interest-bearing NP137, $4,500.00. C1335.

2. Prove the cash receipts and cash payments journals.

PROBLEM 24-3   Journalizing notes receivable transactions

The following transactions were completed by Westport Company during the current year.

Instructions: 1. Journalize the following transactions. Use page 19 of a general journal and page 22 of a cash receipts journal. Source documents are abbreviated as follows: memorandum, M; note receivable, NR; receipt, R.

Jan. 10. Received a 90-day, 11% note from Gary Shelton for an extension of time on his account, $1,500.00. NR67.

   18. Received cash for the maturity value of NR49: principal, $500.00, plus interest, $25.00; total, $525.00. R37.

Feb. 3. Received a 30-day, 10% note from Joanne Davis for an extension of time on her account, $800.00. NR68.

   12. Received cash for the maturity value of NR53: principal, $4,000.00, plus interest, $80.00; total, $4,080.00. R83.

   27. Received a 60-day, 12% note from Andrew McCormick for an extension of time on his account, $2,400.00. NR69.

Mar. 5. Received cash for the maturity value of NR68: principal, $800.00, plus interest, $6.67; total, $806.67. R99.

Apr. 10. Gary Shelton dishonored NR67, a 90-day, 11% note, maturity value due today: principal, $1,500.00; interest, $41.25; total, $1,541.25. M251.

   28. Received cash for the maturity value of NR69: principal, $2,400.00, plus interest, $48.00; total, $2,448.00. R154.

2. Prove the cash receipts journal.

ENRICHMENT PROBLEMS

MASTERY PROBLEM 24-M   Journalizing notes payable and notes receivable transactions

The following transactions were completed by Peterson Sporting Goods during the current year.

Instructions: 1. Journalize the following transactions. Use page 14 of a general journal, page 20 of a cash receipts journal, and page 16 of a cash payments journal. Source documents are abbreviated as follows: check, C; memorandum, M; note payable, NP; note receivable, NR; receipt, R.

Apr. 2. Issued a 30-day, 12% note to Devco Supply Company for an extension of time on this account payable, $6,500.00. NP120.

 7. Received a 90-day, 13% note from Jill Bankston for an extension of time on her account, $700.00. NR154.

 14. Discounted at 11% a 90-day non-interest-bearing note, $12,000.00; proceeds, $11,670.00, interest, $330.00. NP121.

 26. Issued a 30-day, 13% note to Dayton Corporation for an extension of time on this account payable, $4,000.00. NP122.

 30. Received a 60-day, 12% note from Jeremy Hicks for an extension of time on his account, $300.00. NR155.

May 2. Paid cash for the maturity value of NP120: principal, $6,500.00, plus interest, $65.00; total, $6,565.00. C175.

 5. Received a 30-day, 11% note from Suzanne Johnson for an extension of time on her account, $550.00. NR156.

 11. Issued a 60-day, 10% note, $7,000.00. NP123.

 26. Paid cash for the maturity value of NP122: principal, $4,000.00, plus interest, $43.33; total, $4,043.33. C189.

June 4. Received cash for the maturity value of NR156: principal, $550.00, plus interest, $5.04; total, $555.04. R225.

 8. Issued a 30-day, 12% note to Winston Company for an extension of time on this account payable, $2,500.00. NP124.

 17. Received a 60-day, 10% note from Melissa Albertson for an extension of time on her account, $600.00. NR157.

 29. Jeremy Hicks dishonored NR155, a 60-day, 12% note, maturity value due today: principal, $300.00; interest, $6.00; total $306.00. M310.

July 6. Received cash for the maturity value of NR154: principal, $700.00, plus interest, $22.75; total, $722.75. R253.

 8. Paid cash for the maturity value of NP124: principal, $2,500.00, plus interest, $25.00; total, $2,525.00. C251.

 10. Paid cash for the maturity value of NP123: principal, $7,000.00, plus interest, $116.67; total, $7,116.67. C262.

 13. Paid cash for the maturity value of non-interest-bearing NP121, $12,000.00. C274.

Aug. 16. Received cash for the maturity value of NR157: principal, $600.00, plus interest, $10.00; total, $610.00. R278.

2. Prove the cash receipts and cash payments journals.

CHALLENGE PROBLEM 24-C   Journalizing notes payable and notes receivable transactions

The following transactions were completed by Briarcraft Apparel Company during the current year.

Instructions: 1. Journalize the following transactions. Use page 20 of a general journal, page 27 of a cash receipts journal, and page 31 of a cash payments journal. Source documents are abbreviated as follows: check, C; memorandum, M; note payable, NP; note receivable, NR; receipt, R.

Feb.   3. Issued a 90-day, 13% note to Rainbow Manufacturing for an extension of time on this account payable, $7,550.00. NP158.

      7. Discounted at 10% a 6-month non-interest-bearing note, $15,000.00. NP159.

      9. Received a 30-day, 12% note dated February 6 from William Andrews for an extension of time on his account, $985.00. NR84.

   24. Received a 2-month, 13% note dated February 23 from Elizabeth Townsend for an extension of time on her account, $1,275.00. NR85.

Mar.   1. Issued a 3-month, 12% note to Livingston Company for an extension of time on this account payable, $6,995.00. NP160.

      8. Received cash for the maturity value of NR84. R273.

   15. Bought store equipment from Warner Company, $2,875.00. Paid cash, $1,200.00, and issued a 4-month, 11% note for the balance, $1,675.00. C124 and NP161. Journalize the transaction in the cash payments journal in one combined entry. Record the check number in the Ck. No. column. Write *NP161* in parentheses after the account title for notes payable to complete the audit trail.

Apr. 24. Elizabeth Townsend dishonored NR85, maturity value due today. M64.

May   4. Paid cash for the maturity value of NP158. C172.

June   1. Paid cash for the maturity value of NP160. C183.

July 15. Paid cash for the maturity value of NP161. C197.

   21. Received cash from Elizabeth Townsend, $600.00, for part of the balance charged to her account on April 24. R325. Wrote off the remainder of this account receivable as uncollectible. M99. Journalize the check in the cash receipts journal. Journalize the write-off of the customer account in the general journal.

Aug.   7. Paid cash for the maturity value of non-interest-bearing NP159. C215.

  2. Prove the cash receipts and cash payments journals.

CHAPTER
25

Accounting for Accrued Revenue and Expenses

ENABLING PERFORMANCE TASKS

After studying Chapter 25, you will be able to:
a. Define accounting terms related to accrued revenue and accrued expenses.
b. Identify accounting concepts and practices related to accrued revenue and accrued expenses.
c. Record adjusting, closing, and reversing entries for accrued revenue.
d. Record adjusting, closing, and reversing entries for accrued expenses.

Accepted accounting procedures require that revenue and expenses be recorded in the accounting period in which revenue is earned and expenses are incurred. (CONCEPT: Matching Expenses with Revenue) Some revenues, however, are earned each day but are usually recorded only when cash is actually received. For example, interest is earned for each day an interest-bearing note receivable is held. However, the interest may not be received until the maturity date of the note. Likewise, some expenses may be incurred before they are actually paid. An interest-bearing note payable incurs interest expense each day the note is outstanding. Yet, the interest generally is not paid until the note's maturity date.

To record revenue that has been earned but not yet received, an adjusting entry is made at the end of the fiscal period. As a result of this adjusting entry, revenue is reported for the fiscal period in which the revenue is actually earned. (CONCEPT: Realization of Revenue) An adjusting entry is also made at the end of a fiscal period to record an expense that has been incurred but not yet paid. As a result of this adjusting entry, the expense is reported for the fiscal period in which the expense is actually incurred. (CONCEPT: Matching Expenses with Revenue)

ACCRUED REVENUE

Revenue earned in one fiscal period but not received until a later fiscal period is called accrued revenue. At the end of a fiscal period, accrued revenue is recorded by an adjusting entry. *(CONCEPT: Realization of Revenue)* The adjusting entry for accrued revenue increases the accrued revenue account, an other revenue account. The adjusting entry also increases the accrued revenue receivable account, an asset account. The income statement will then report all revenue earned for the period even though some of the revenue has not yet been received. The balance sheet will report all the assets, including the accrued revenue receivable. *(CONCEPT: Adequate Disclosure)*

Adjusting entry for accrued interest income

At the end of each fiscal period, Celluphone examines the notes receivable on hand. The amount of interest income earned but not yet collected is figured. Interest earned but not yet received is called accrued interest income. On December 31 Celluphone has one note receivable on hand, Note Receivable No. 15. Note Receivable No. 15 is a 3-month, 12% note for $550.00 from J.T. Monroe, dated October 31. The accounting records should show all the interest income for the fiscal period. *(CONCEPT: Adequate Disclosure)* Therefore, an adjusting entry must be made to record the amount of interest earned to date on this note.

The time period from October 31 to December 31 is two months. Therefore, the time stated as a fraction of a year is 2/12. Accrued interest on this note to the end of the fiscal year is calculated as shown below.

Principal	×	Interest Rate	×	Time as Fraction of Year	=	Accrued Interest Income
$550.00	×	12%	×	$\dfrac{2}{12}$	=	$11.00

The analysis of Celluphone's adjusting entry for accrued interest income is shown in the T accounts.

Interest Receivable is debited for $11.00 to show the increase in the balance of this asset account. The interest receivable account balance is the amount of interest income that has accrued at the end of the fiscal period. However, this revenue will not be collected until the next fiscal period.

Interest Income is credited for $11.00 to show the increase in the balance of this other revenue account. The new interest income account balance, $214.00, is the total amount of interest income earned during the fiscal period.

Interest Receivable

Dec. 31 Adj. 11.00	

Interest Income

	Dec. 31 Bal. 203.00
	Dec. 31 Adj. 11.00
	(New Bal. 214.00)

The adjustment for accrued interest income is planned on a work sheet. Celluphone's accrued interest income adjustment for the year ended December 31 is shown in Illustration 25-1.

	ACCOUNT TITLE	TRIAL BALANCE		ADJUSTMENTS		INCOME STATEMENT		BALANCE SHEET		
		1 DEBIT	2 CREDIT	3 DEBIT	4 CREDIT	5 DEBIT	6 CREDIT	7 DEBIT	8 CREDIT	
4	*Interest Receivable*			(a) 11 00				11 00		4
48	*Interest Income*		203 00		(a) 11 00		214 00			48

Celluphone, Inc.
Work Sheet
For Year Ended December 31, 19--

Illustration 25-1
Accrued interest income
adjustment on a work
sheet

On line 4 of the work sheet, Interest Receivable is debited for $11.00 in the Adjustments Debit column. This amount, $11.00, is extended to the Balance Sheet Debit column. On line 48 Interest Income is credited for $11.00 in the Adjustments Credit column. The interest income adjustment, $11.00, is added to the previous balance in the Trial Balance Credit column, $203.00. The new balance, $214.00 ($11.00 + $203.00), is extended to the Income Statement Credit column.

Information used to journalize an adjustment for accrued interest income is obtained from the Adjustments columns of a work sheet. The adjusting entry is shown in Illustration 25-2.

GENERAL JOURNAL   PAGE *15*

	DATE	ACCOUNT TITLE	DOC. NO.	POST. REF.	DEBIT	CREDIT	
1		*Adjusting Entries*					1
2	*Dec.* 31	*Interest Receivable*			11 00		2
3		*Interest Income*				11 00	3
4							4

Illustration 25-2
Adjusting entry for accrued
interest income

After the adjusting entry is posted, the interest receivable and interest income accounts appear as shown in Illustration 25-3.

The interest receivable account has a debit balance of $11.00 and will appear on the December 31 balance sheet as a current asset. This debit balance is the accrued interest income earned but not yet collected at the end of the year. The interest income account has a credit balance of $214.00 and will appear on the income statement for the year ended December 31 as other revenue. This amount is the total interest income for the year.

ACCOUNT *Interest Receivable*   **ACCOUNT NO.** *1120*

DATE	ITEM	POST. REF.	DEBIT	CREDIT	BALANCE DEBIT	BALANCE CREDIT
Dec. 31		*G15*	1 1 00		1 1 00	

ACCOUNT *Interest Income*   **ACCOUNT NO.** *7110*

DATE	ITEM	POST. REF.	DEBIT	CREDIT	BALANCE DEBIT	BALANCE CREDIT
Dec. 29		*CR49*		2 3 00		2 0 3 00
31		*G15*		1 1 00		2 1 4 00

Illustration 25-3
General ledger accounts after adjusting entry for accrued interest income is posted

Closing entry for interest income

Information needed to record closing entries is obtained from the Income Statement columns of a work sheet. Interest Income is closed to the income summary account. The analysis of Celluphone's entry to close the interest income account is shown in the T accounts.

Interest Income is closed as part of the regular closing entry for income statement accounts with credit balances. Interest Income is debited for $214.00 to reduce the account balance to zero. The $214.00 is also credited to Income Summary as part of the entry to close all income statement accounts with credit balances. After the closing entry is posted, the interest income account is closed. Closing entries for all revenue and expense accounts are described in Chapter 27.

Interest Income		
Dec. 31 Clos. 214.00	Dec. 31 Bal.	203.00
	Dec. 31 Adj.	11.00
	(New Bal. zero)	

Income Summary	
	Dec. 31 Clos. 214.00

Reversing entry for accrued interest income

Adjusting entries for accrued revenues have an effect on transactions to be recorded in the following fiscal period. For example, on the maturity date of Note Receivable No. 15, January 31, Celluphone will receive cash for the note's principal and interest. Total interest earned for the 3-month note is $16.50, calculated as shown below.

Principal	×	Interest Rate	×	Time as Fraction of Year	=	Interest
$550.00	×	12%	×	$\frac{3}{12}$	=	$16.50

However, an adjusting entry was made to record the amount of interest earned last year, $11.00, by debiting Interest Receivable and crediting Interest Income. Thus, $11.00 of the $16.50 total interest income has already been recorded as revenue. The remaining $5.50 of the $16.50 total interest was earned during the current year. Determining how much of the cash received is for interest income earned and accrued during the previous year and how much is earned during the current year is inconvenient. To avoid this inconvenience, a reversing entry is made at the beginning of the new fiscal period. An entry made at the beginning of one fiscal period to reverse an adjusting entry made in the previous fiscal period is called a reversing entry.

Interest Income

Dec. 31 Clos.	214.00	Dec. 31 Bal.	203.00
Jan. 1. Rev.	11.00	Dec. 31 Adj.	11.00
(New Bal.	11.00)		

Interest Receivable

| Dec. 31 Adj. | 11.00 | Jan. 1 Rev. | 11.00 |
| | | (New Bal. zero) | |

The analysis of Celluphone's reversing entry for accrued interest income is shown in the T accounts.

The reversing entry results in a debit balance of $11.00 in Interest Income. A debit balance is the opposite of the normal balance of the interest income account. When the full amount of interest is received, $16.50, this amount will be credited to Interest Income. The account will then have a credit balance of $5.50 ($16.50 credit − $11.00 debit), the amount earned in the new year.

The reversing entry to Interest Receivable reduces that account to a zero balance. Thus, when the interest is received, no credit entry will be required to recognize collection of the balance of Interest Receivable. The total amount of interest received will be credited to Interest Income. Celluphone's reversing entry for accrued interest income is shown in Illustration 25-4.

	GENERAL JOURNAL				PAGE 17	
	DATE	ACCOUNT TITLE	DOC. NO.	POST. REF.	DEBIT	CREDIT
1		*Reversing Entries*				
2	*Jan.* 1	*Interest Income*			1 1 00	
3		*Interest Receivable*				1 1 00
4						

Illustration 25-4
Reversing entry for
accrued interest income

The reversing entry is the opposite of the adjusting entry shown in Illustration 25-2.

Celluphone uses the following rule of thumb to determine whether or not reversing entries are made. If an adjusting entry creates a balance in an asset or liability account, the adjusting entry is reversed. The adjusting entry for accrued interest income creates a balance in the asset account, Interest Receivable. Therefore, Celluphone uses reversing entries for all accrued interest income adjusting entries.

A balance is "created" in an account when the account balance is changed from a zero balance to an amount.

Collecting a note receivable issued in a previous fiscal period

On January 31 Celluphone received the maturity value (principal plus interest) of the one note receivable on hand December 31, the end of the previous fiscal year. The maturity value for Note Receivable No. 15 is calculated as shown below.

Principal	×	Interest Rate	×	Time as Fraction of Year	=	Interest
$550.00	×	12%	×	$\frac{3}{12}$	=	$16.50

Principal	+	Interest	=	Maturity Value
$550.00		$16.50		$566.50

January 31, 19--.
Received cash for the maturity value of Note Receivable No. 15: principal, $550.00, plus interest, $16.50; total, $566.50. Receipt No. 38.

The total interest, $16.50, was earned during two fiscal periods, $11.00 during the previous fiscal period and $5.50 during the current fiscal period. Since Celluphone uses reversing entries, the entry to record the collection of this note receivable and interest is the same as the entry to record a note accepted and collected in a single fiscal year. The analysis of Celluphone's receipt of principal and interest is shown in the T accounts.

When Note Receivable No. 15 is collected on January 31, Cash is debited for the total amount received, $566.50, to record the increase in this current asset account. Notes Receivable is credited for the principal of the note, $550.00, to record the decrease in the balance of this current asset account. Interest Income is credited for the total amount of interest, $16.50, to record the increase in this other revenue account. The interest income account now has a credit balance of $5.50 ($16.50 credit − $11.00 debit), the amount of interest earned during the current fiscal period.

The cash receipts journal entry to record this receipt of cash for a note receivable when reversing entries are used is shown in Illustration 25-5.

Cash		
Jan. 31 Rec'd	566.50	

Notes Receivable			
Oct. 31 NR15	550.00	Jan. 31 Rec'd	550.00

Interest Income			
Dec. 31 Clos.	214.00	Dec. 31 Bal.	203.00
Jan. 1 Rev.	11.00	Dec. 31 Adj.	11.00
		Jan. 31 Rec'd	16.50
		(New Bal.	*5.50)*

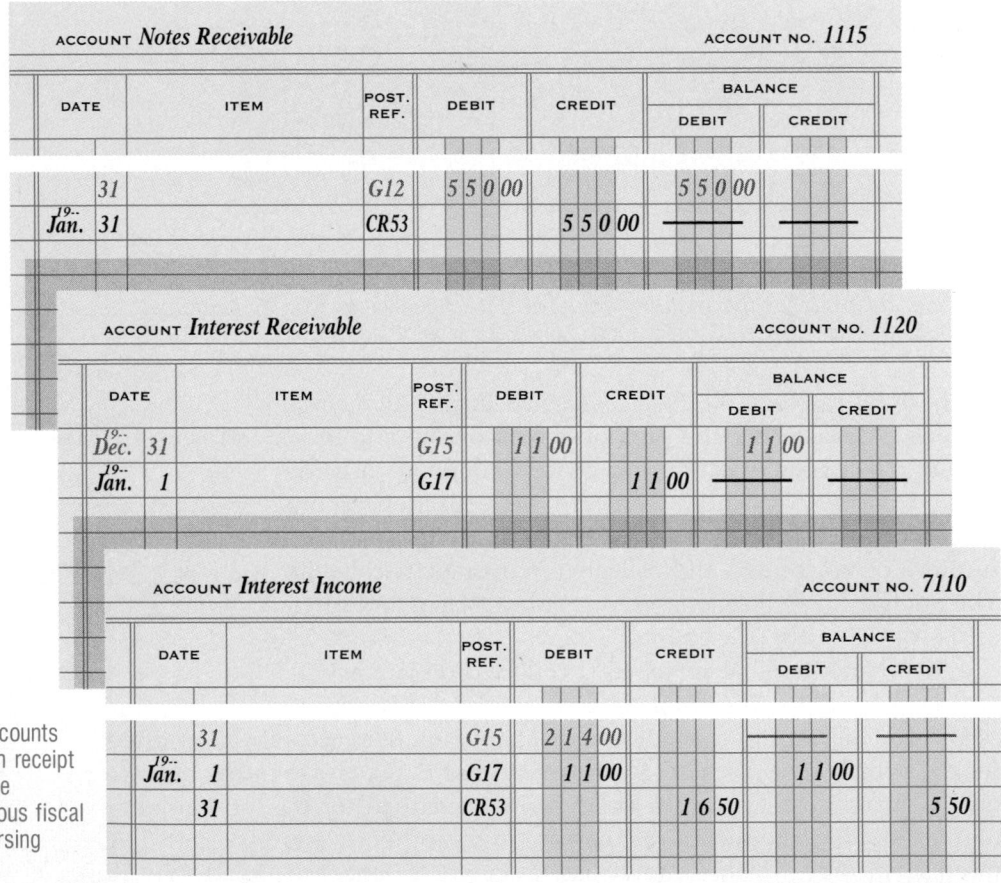

			CASH RECEIPTS JOURNAL							PAGE 53	
					1	2	3	4	5	6	7	8
DATE	ACCOUNT TITLE	DOC. NO.	POST. REF.	GENERAL		ACCOUNTS RECEIVABLE CREDIT	SALES CREDIT	SALES TAX PAYABLE		SALES DISCOUNT DEBIT	CASH DEBIT
				DEBIT	CREDIT			DEBIT	CREDIT		
12	31	Notes Receivable	R38		5 50 00						5 66 50	12
13		Interest Income			16 50							13

Illustration 25-5
Cash receipts journal entry to record note receivable accepted in previous fiscal period when reversing entries are used

After the cash receipts journal entry is posted, the notes receivable, interest receivable, and interest income accounts appear as shown in Illustration 25-6.

ACCOUNT **Notes Receivable**   ACCOUNT NO. **1115**

DATE	ITEM	POST. REF.	DEBIT	CREDIT	BALANCE DEBIT	BALANCE CREDIT
31		G12	5 50 00		5 50 00	
Jan. 31		CR53		5 50 00	——	——

ACCOUNT **Interest Receivable**   ACCOUNT NO. **1120**

DATE	ITEM	POST. REF.	DEBIT	CREDIT	BALANCE DEBIT	BALANCE CREDIT
Dec. 31		G15	1 1 00		1 1 00	
Jan. 1		G17		1 1 00	——	——

ACCOUNT **Interest Income**   ACCOUNT NO. **7110**

DATE	ITEM	POST. REF.	DEBIT	CREDIT	BALANCE DEBIT	BALANCE CREDIT
31		G15	2 14 00		——	——
Jan. 1		G17	1 1 00		1 1 00	
31		CR53		16 50		5 50

Illustration 25-6
General ledger accounts after posting cash receipt for note receivable accepted in previous fiscal period when reversing entries are used

Notes Receivable has a zero balance. This account will be used again when additional notes receivable are accepted. After the reversing entry is recorded, Interest Receivable has a zero balance. Interest Receivable will not be used again until it is needed for an adjusting entry at the end of the current fiscal year. Interest Income has a credit balance of $5.50, the amount of interest earned on Note Receivable No. 15 in the current year.

ACCRUED EXPENSES

Expenses incurred in one fiscal period but not paid until a later fiscal period are called accrued expenses. At the end of a fiscal period, accrued expense is recorded by an adjusting entry. (CONCEPT: *Matching Expenses with Revenue*) The adjusting entry for accrued expense increases the accrued expense account, an other expense account. The adjusting entry also increases the accrued expense payable account, a liability account. The income statement will then report all expenses for the period even though some of the expenses have not yet been paid. The balance sheet will report all liabilities, including the accrued expenses payable. (CONCEPT: *Adequate Disclosure*)

Adjusting entry for accrued interest expense

Interest incurred but not yet paid is called accrued interest expense. At the end of each fiscal period, Celluphone examines the notes payable outstanding and figures the accrued interest expense. On December 31, Celluphone has one note payable outstanding, Note Payable No. 10. Note Payable No. 10 is a 9-month, 10% note for $2,800.00 issued to First National Bank on September 30. The accounting records should show all the interest expense for the fiscal period. (CONCEPT: *Adequate Disclosure*) Therefore, an adjusting entry is made to record the amount of accrued interest expense to date on this note.

The time period from September 30 to December 31 is three months. Therefore, the time stated as a fraction of a year is 3/12. Accrued interest on this note at the end of the fiscal year is calculated as shown below.

Principal		Interest Rate		Time as Fraction of Year		Accrued Interest Expense
$2,800.00	×	10%	×	$\frac{3}{12}$	=	$70.00

The analysis of Celluphone's adjusting entry for accrued interest expense is shown in the T accounts.

Interest Expense is debited for $70.00 to show the increase in the balance of this other expense account. The new interest expense account balance, $1,445.00, is the amount of interest expense incurred during the fiscal period.

Interest Expense

Dec. 31 Bal.	1,375.00	
Dec. 31 Adj.	70.00	
(New Bal.	1,445.00)	

Interest Payable

| | | Dec. 31 Adj. | 70.00 |

Interest Payable is credited for $70.00 to show the increase in the balance of this liability account. The interest payable account balance, $70.00, is the amount of accrued interest at the end of the fiscal period. However, this interest will not be paid until the next fiscal period.

The adjustment for accrued interest expense is planned on a work sheet. Celluphone's accrued interest expense adjustment for the year ended December 31 is shown in Illustration 25-7.

	Celluphone, Inc.		
	Work Sheet		
	For Year Ended December 31, 19--		

	ACCOUNT TITLE	TRIAL BALANCE		ADJUSTMENTS		INCOME STATEMENT		BALANCE SHEET		
		DEBIT	CREDIT	DEBIT	CREDIT	DEBIT	CREDIT	DEBIT	CREDIT	
15	*Interest Payable*				(h) 70 00				70 00	15
50	*Interest Expense*	1 375 00		(h) 70 00		1 445 00				50

Illustration 25-7
Accrued interest expense adjustment on a work sheet

On line 50 of the work sheet, Interest Expense is debited for $70.00 in the Adjustments Debit column. The interest expense adjustment, $70.00, is added to the previous balance in the Trial Balance Debit column, $1,375.00. The new balance, $1,445.00 ($70.00 + $1,375.00), is extended to the Income Statement Debit column. On line 15 Interest Payable is credited for $70.00 in the Adjustments Credit column. This amount, $70.00, is extended to the Balance Sheet Credit column.

Information used to journalize an adjustment for accrued interest expense is obtained from the Adjustments columns of a work sheet. The adjusting entry is shown in Illustration 25-8.

				GENERAL JOURNAL				PAGE 15	
		DATE		ACCOUNT TITLE	DOC. NO.	POST. REF.	DEBIT	CREDIT	
1				*Adjusting Entries*					1
16		31		*Interest Expense*			70 00		16
17				*Interest Payable*				70 00	17
18									18

Illustration 25-8
Adjusting entry for accrued interest expense

After the adjusting entry is posted, the interest payable and interest expense accounts appear as shown in Illustration 25-9.

Illustration 25-9
General ledger accounts
after adjusting entry for
accrued interest expense is
posted

ACCOUNT **Interest Payable**   ACCOUNT NO. **2110**

DATE	ITEM	POST. REF.	DEBIT	CREDIT	BALANCE DEBIT	BALANCE CREDIT
Dec. 31		G15		70 00		70 00

ACCOUNT **Interest Expense**   ACCOUNT NO. **8110**

DATE	ITEM	POST. REF.	DEBIT	CREDIT	BALANCE DEBIT	BALANCE CREDIT
Dec. 21		CP35	200 00		1 375 00	
31		G15	70 00		1 445 00	

The interest payable account has a credit balance of $70.00 and will appear on the December 31 balance sheet as a current liability. This credit balance is the accrued interest expense incurred but not yet paid at the end of the year. The interest expense account has a debit balance of $1,445.00 and will appear on the income statement for the year ended December 31 as an other expense. This amount is the total interest expense for the year.

Closing entry for interest expense

Information needed to record closing entries is obtained from the Income Statement columns of a work sheet. Interest Expense is closed to the income summary account. The analysis of Celluphone's entry to close the interest expense account is shown in the T accounts.

Income Summary
Dec. 31 Clos. 1,445.00 |

Interest Expense
Dec. 31 Bal. 1,375.00 | Dec. 31 Clos. 1,445.00
Dec. 31 Adj. 70.00 | (New Bal. zero)

Interest Expense is closed as part of the regular closing entries. The $1,445.00 will also be a part of the debit entry to Income Summary to close all income statement accounts with debit balances. Interest Expense is credited for $1,445.00 to reduce the account balance to zero. After the closing entry is posted, the interest expense account is closed.

Reversing entry for accrued interest expense

On the maturity date of Note Payable No. 10, June 30, Celluphone will pay the note's maturity value (principal and interest). Total interest incurred for the 9-month note is $210.00, calculated as shown on page 628.

Principal	×	Interest Rate	×	Time as Fraction of Year	=	Interest
$2,800.00	×	10%	×	$\dfrac{9}{12}$	=	$210.00

However, an adjusting entry was made to record the amount of accrued interest expense last year, $70.00, by debiting Interest Expense and crediting Interest Payable. Thus, $70.00 of the $210.00 total interest expense was incurred and recorded in the previous year. The remaining $140.00 of the $210.00 total interest expense was incurred during the current year. Determining how much of the cash paid is for accrued interest expense and how much applies to the current year is an inconvenient process. To avoid this inconvenient process, a reversing entry is made at the beginning of the new fiscal period.

The adjusting entry for accrued interest expense "creates" a balance in the liability account Interest Payable. Therefore, Celluphone uses reversing entries for all accrued interest expense adjusting entries.

Interest Payable

Jan. 1 Rev.	70.00	Dec. 31 Adj.	70.00
(New Bal. zero)			

Interest Expense

Dec. 31 Bal.	1,375.00	Dec. 31 Clos.	1,445.00
Dec. 31 Adj.	70.00	Jan. 1 Rev.	70.00
		(New Bal.	*70.00)*

The analysis of Celluphone's reversing entry for accrued interest expense is shown in the T accounts.

The reversing entry results in a credit balance of $70.00 in Interest Expense. A credit balance is the opposite of the normal balance of the interest expense account. When the full amount of interest is paid, $210.00, this amount will be debited to Interest Expense. The account will then have a debit balance of $140.00 ($210.00 debit − $70.00 credit), the amount of interest expense incurred in the new year.

The reversing entry to Interest Payable reduces that account to a zero balance. Thus, when the interest is received, no debit entry will be required to recognize payment of the balance of Interest Payable. The total amount of interest paid will be debited to Interest Expense. Celluphone's reversing entry for accrued interest expense is shown in Illustration 25-10.

Illustration 25-10
Reversing entry for accrued interest expense

	DATE	ACCOUNT TITLE	DOC. NO.	POST. REF.	DEBIT	CREDIT	
1		*Reversing Entries*					1
4	1	*Interest Payable*			70 00		4
5		*Interest Expense*				70 00	5
6							6

GENERAL JOURNAL   PAGE *17*

The reversing entry is the opposite of the adjusting entry shown in Illustration 25-8.

Paying a note payable issued in a previous fiscal period

On June 30 Celluphone paid the maturity value (principal plus interest) of the one note payable on hand December 31, the end of the previous fiscal year. The maturity value for Note Payable No. 10 is calculated as shown below.

Principal	×	Interest Rate	×	Time as Fraction of Year	=	Interest
$2,800.00	×	10%	×	$\frac{9}{12}$	=	$210.00

Principal	+	Interest	=	Maturity Value
$2,800.00		$210.00		$3,010.00

June 30, 19--.
Paid cash for the maturity value of Note Payable No. 10: principal, $2,800.00, plus interest, $210.00; total, $3,010.00. Check No. 982.

The total interest, $210.00, was incurred during two fiscal periods, $70.00 during the previous fiscal period and $140.00 during the current fiscal period. Since Celluphone uses reversing entries, the entry to record the payment of this note payable and interest is the same as the entry to record a note issued and paid in a single fiscal year. The analysis of Celluphone's entry to record payment of principal and interest is shown in the T accounts.

Notes Payable is debited for the principal of the note, $2,800.00, to record the decrease in the balance of this current liability account. Interest Expense is debited for the total amount of interest, $210.00, to record the increase in this other expense account. The interest expense account now has a debit balance of $140.00, the amount of interest expense incurred during the current fiscal period. Cash is credited for the total amount paid, $3,010.00, to record the decrease in this current asset account.

Notes Payable	
June 30 Paid 2,800.00	Sept. 30 NP10 2,800.00

Interest Expense	
Dec. 31 Bal. 1,375.00	Dec. 31 Clos. 1,445.00
Dec. 31 Adj. 70.00	Jan. 1 Rev. 70.00
June 30 Paid 210.00	
(New Bal. 140.00)	

Cash	
	June 30 Paid 3,010.00

The cash payments journal entry to record this payment of a note payable when reversing entries are used is shown in Illustration 25-11, page 630.

After the cash payments journal entry is posted, the notes payable, interest payable, and interest expense accounts appear as shown in Illustration 25-12, page 630.

	DATE	ACCOUNT TITLE	CK. NO.	POST. REF.	GENERAL DEBIT	GENERAL CREDIT	ACCOUNTS PAYABLE DEBIT	PURCHASES DISCOUNT CREDIT	CASH CREDIT	
					1	2	3	4	5	
21	30	Notes Payable	982		2 80 0 00				3 01 0 00	21
22		Interest Expense			2 1 0 00					22

CASH PAYMENTS JOURNAL   PAGE 55

Illustration 25-11   Cash payments journal entry to record note payable issued in previous fiscal period when reversing entries are used

ACCOUNT Notes Payable   ACCOUNT NO. 2105

DATE	ITEM	POST. REF.	DEBIT	CREDIT	BALANCE DEBIT	BALANCE CREDIT
30		CR26		2 80 0 00		2 80 0 00
June 30		CP55	2 80 0 00		——	——

ACCOUNT Interest Payable   ACCOUNT NO. 2110

DATE	ITEM	POST. REF.	DEBIT	CREDIT	BALANCE DEBIT	BALANCE CREDIT
Dec. 31		G15		7 0 00		7 0 00
Jan. 1		G17	7 0 00		——	——

ACCOUNT Interest Expense   ACCOUNT NO. 8110

DATE	ITEM	POST. REF.	DEBIT	CREDIT	BALANCE DEBIT	BALANCE CREDIT
31		G16		1 44 5 00	——	——
Jan. 1		G17		7 0 00		7 0 00
June 30		CP55	2 1 0 00		1 4 0 00	

Illustration 25-12
General ledger accounts after posting cash payment for note payable issued in previous fiscal period when reversing entries are used

Notes Payable has a zero balance. This account will be used again when additional notes payable are issued. After the reversing entry is recorded, Interest Payable has a zero balance. Interest Payable will not be used again until it is needed for an adjusting entry at the end of the current fiscal year. Interest Expense has a debit balance of $140.00, the amount of interest incurred on Note Payable No. 10 in the current year.

SUMMARY OF ACCOUNTING FOR ACCRUED REVENUE AND EXPENSES

The chart shown in Illustration 25-13 summarizes the journal entries for recording accrued revenue and expenses.

Illustration 25-13
Summary of journal entries for recording accrued revenue and expenses

JOURNAL ENTRIES	GENERAL LEDGER															
	CASH		NOTES RECEIVABLE		INTEREST RECEIVABLE		NOTES PAYABLE		INTEREST PAYABLE		INCOME SUMMARY		INTEREST INCOME		INTEREST EXPENSE	
	DR	CR	DR	CR	DR	CR	DR	CR	DR	CR	DR	CR	DR	CR	DR	CR
Adjusting entry for accrued interest income on note receivable					X									X		
Entry to close interest income account												X	X			
Reversing entry for accrued interest income						X							X			
Received cash for note receivable accepted in previous fiscal period when reversing entries are used	X			X										X		
Adjusting entry for accrued interest expense on note payable										X					X	
Entry to close interest expense account											X					X
Reversing entry for accrued interest expense									X							X
Paid cash for note payable issued in previous fiscal period when reversing entries are used		X					X								X	

■ ACCOUNTING TERMS

What is the meaning of each of the following?

1. accrued revenue
2. accrued interest income
3. reversing entry
4. accrued expenses
5. accrued interest expense

■ QUESTIONS FOR INDIVIDUAL STUDY

1. When do accepted accounting procedures require that revenue and expenses be recorded?
2. Which accounting concept is being applied when an adjusting entry is made at the end of the fiscal period to record accrued revenue?
3. Which accounting concept is being applied when an adjusting entry is made at the end of a fiscal period to record an expense that has been incurred but not yet paid?
4. Why should accrued revenue be recorded by an adjusting entry before financial statements are prepared at the end of a fiscal period?
5. What accounts are affected, and how, by the adjusting entry for accrued interest income?
6. Where is the information obtained that is needed to journalize an adjustment for accrued interest income?
7. After closing entries are posted, what is the balance of the interest income account?
8. Why does a business use reversing entries as part of its procedures for accounting for accrued interest income?
9. What accounts are affected, and how, by the reversing entry for accrued interest income?
10. Interest of $15.00 on a note receivable is earned and accrued on December 31 and an additional $25.00 interest is earned by the note's maturity date. What entry will be made to Interest Income when the maturity value of the note is received? (The business uses reversing entries for all accrual adjusting entries.)
11. Why should accrued expenses be recorded by an adjusting entry before financial statements are prepared at the end of a fiscal period?
12. What accounts are affected, and how, by the adjusting entry for accrued interest expense?
13. What accounts are affected, and how, by the reversing entry for accrued interest expense?
14. Immediately after a reversing entry for accrued interest expense is recorded, what is the balance of the interest payable account?

■ CASES FOR MANAGEMENT DECISION

CASE 1 As a new accounting clerk at The Print Shop, you discover that $80.00 accrued interest income on notes receivable was not recorded at the end of the current fiscal period. When you consult with the manager, the manager says, "Don't worry about recording the interest income. It will be recorded when we collect the note and interest." Is the manager's approach acceptable? Explain your answer. What effect will the omission of accrued interest income have on the current fiscal year's (a) income statement and (b) balance sheet?

CASE 2 At the end of each fiscal period, Jet-Air prepares adjusting entries to record accrued interest expense. However, the company does not record reversing entries for the accrued interest expense. At the end of the current fiscal year, Jet-Air had Note Payable No. 12 outstanding, a $3,000.00, 3-month, 10% note issued October 31. Jet-Air made the following journal entries related to Note Payable No. 12.

Issued Oct. 31

Cash	$3,000.00	
Notes Payable		$3,000.00

Adj. Entry Dec. 31

Interest Expense	50.00	
Interest Payable		50.00

Clos. Entry Dec. 31

Income Summary	50.00	
Interest Expense		50.00

Paid Note Jan. 31

Notes Payable	3,000.00	
Interest Payable	50.00	
Interest Expense	25.00	
Cash		3,075.00

Winifred Harwick, a newly employed accounting supervisor, says that generally accepted accounting principles require that reversing entries be used in conjunction with adjusting entries for accrued expenses. Thus, Ms. Harwick says Jet-Air must begin using reversing entries for all accrued expenses. Is Ms. Harwick correct? Do the procedures Jet-Air has been using result in incorrect financial statements? Explain your answer.

 ## DRILLS FOR UNDERSTANDING

DRILL 25-D1 Analyzing entries for notes receivable and accrued revenue

Use a form similar to the following.

Entry No.	Cash		Notes Receivable		Accounts Receivable		Interest Receivable		Interest Income		Income Summary	
	Debit	Credit	Debit	Credit	Debit	Credit	Debit	Credit	Debit	Credit	Debit	Credit
1.												

Instructions: For each of the following entries, indicate by a check mark which account(s) should be debited and which account(s) should be credited.

Entries

1. Received a note receivable from a customer for an extension of time on account.
2. Recorded an adjusting entry at the end of the fiscal period for interest earned but not yet received.
3. Closed interest income account.
4. Recorded reversing entry for accrued interest income.
5. Received cash for maturity value of a note receivable accepted in previous fiscal period.

DRILL 25-D2 Analyzing entries for notes payable and accrued expenses

Use a form similar to the following.

Entry No.	Cash		Notes Payable		Accounts Payable		Interest Payable		Interest Expense		Income Summary	
	Debit	Credit	Debit	Credit	Debit	Credit	Debit	Credit	Debit	Credit	Debit	Credit
1.												

Instructions: For each of the following entries, indicate by a check mark which account(s) should be debited and which account(s) should be credited.

Entries

1. Issued a note payable to a vendor for an extension of time on an account payable.
2. Recorded an adjusting entry at the end of the fiscal period for interest incurred but not yet paid.
3. Closed interest expense account.
4. Recorded reversing entry for accrued interest expense.
5. Paid cash for maturity value of a note payable issued in previous fiscal period.

■ APPLICATION PROBLEMS

PROBLEM 25-1 Journalizing and posting entries for accrued revenue

The following accounts are from Citation Corporation's general ledger. The balances are recorded as of December 31 of the current year before adjusting entries.

PARTIAL GENERAL LEDGER

Account No.	Account Title	Account Balance
1115	Notes Receivable.	$800.00
1120	Interest Receivable	—
3120	Income Summary	—
7110	Interest Income	226.00

Citation Corporation completed the following transactions related to notes receivable during the current year and the following year. The first transaction has already been journalized and posted. Note Receivable No. 11 is the only note receivable on hand at the end of the fiscal period. Source documents are abbreviated as follows: note receivable, NR; receipt, R.

19X1

Nov. 1. Received a 3-month, 12% note from Peter Mendoza for an extension of time on his account, $800.00. NR11.

19X2

Feb. 1. Received cash for the maturity value of NR11: principal, $800.00, plus interest, $24.00; total, $824.00. R110.

Instructions: 1. Use page 14 of a general journal. Journalize the adjusting entry for accrued interest income on December 31. Post this entry.

2. Continue to use page 14 of a general journal. Journalize the closing entry for interest income. Post this entry.

3. Use page 15 of a general journal. Journalize the reversing entry for accrued interest income. Post this entry.

4. Use page 18 of a cash receipts journal. Journalize the receipt of cash for the maturity value of NR11. Post this entry.

PROBLEM 25-2 Journalizing and posting entries for accrued expenses

The following accounts are from Charter Corporation's general ledger. The balances are recorded as of December 31 of the current year before adjusting entries.

PARTIAL GENERAL LEDGER

Account No.	Account Title	Account Balance
2105	Notes Payable	$4,000.00
2110	Interest Payable	—
3120	Income Summary	—
8110	Interest Expense	634.00

Charter Corporation completed the following transactions related to notes payable during the current year and the following year. The first transaction has already been journalized and posted. Note Payable No. 5 is the only note payable on hand at the end of the fiscal period. Source documents are abbreviated as follows: check, C; note payable, NP.

19X1

Sept. 1. Issued a 6-month, 12% note, $4,000.00. NP5.

19X2

Mar. 1. Paid cash for the maturity value of NP5: principal, $4,000.00, plus interest, $240.00; total, $4,240.00. C189.

Instructions: 1. Use page 15 of a general journal. Journalize the adjusting entry for accrued interest expense on December 31. Post this entry.

2. Continue to use page 15 of a general journal. Journalize the closing entry for interest expense. Post this entry.

3. Use page 16 of a general journal. Journalize the reversing entry for accrued interest expense. Post this entry.

4. Use page 20 of a cash payments journal. Journalize the cash payment for the maturity value of NP5. Post this entry.

■ ENRICHMENT PROBLEMS

MASTERY PROBLEM 25-M Journalizing and posting entries for accrued revenue and expenses

The following accounts are from Hahn Company's general ledger. The balances are recorded as of December 31 of the current year before adjusting entries.

PARTIAL GENERAL LEDGER

Account No.	Account Title	Account Balance
1115	Notes Receivable..................................	$ 600.00
1120	Interest Receivable	—
2105	Notes Payable	2,400.00
2110	Interest Payable...................................	—
3120	Income Summary	—
7110	Interest Income	104.00
8110	Interest Expense	325.00

Hahn Company completed the following transactions related to notes receivable and notes payable during the current year and the following year. The first two transactions have already been journalized and posted. Note Receivable No. 8 and Note Payable No. 4 are the only notes on hand at the end of the fiscal period. Source documents are abbreviated as follows: check, C; note payable, NP; note receivable, NR; receipt, R.

19X1

Oct. 31. Received a 3-month, 12% note from Donald Ritter for an extension of time on his account, $600.00. NR8.

31. Issued a 4-month, 14% note, $2,400.00. NP4.

19X2

Jan. 31. Received cash for the maturity value of NR8: principal, $600.00, plus interest, $18.00; total, $618.00. R207.

Feb. 28. Paid cash for the maturity value of NP4: principal, $2,400.00, plus interest, $112.00; total, $2,512.00. C423.

Instructions: 1. Use page 15 of a general journal. Journalize the adjusting entries for accrued interest income and accrued interest expense on December 31. Post these entries.

2. Continue to use page 15 of a general journal. Journalize the closing entries for interest income and interest expense. Post these entries.

3. Use page 16 of a general journal. Journalize the reversing entries for accrued interest income and accrued interest expense. Post these entries.

4. Use page 19 of a cash receipts journal. Journalize the receipt of cash for the maturity value of NR8. Post this entry.

5. Use page 25 of a cash payments journal. Journalize the cash payment for the maturity value of NP4. Post this entry.

CHALLENGE PROBLEM 25-C   **Journalizing and posting entries for accrued revenue and expenses**

The following accounts are from Castoldo Corporation's general ledger. The balances are recorded as of December 31 of the current year before adjusting entries.

PARTIAL GENERAL LEDGER

Account No.	Account Title	Account Balance
1115	Notes Receivable...................................	$ 400.00
1120	Interest Receivable	—
1125	Accounts Receivable	—
2105	Notes Payable	2,500.00
2110	Interest Payable...................................	—
3120	Income Summary	—
7110	Interest Income	326.50
8110	Interest Expense	1,248.00

Castoldo Corporation completed the following transactions related to notes receivable and notes payable during the current year and the following year. The first two transactions have already been journalized and posted. Note Receivable No. 6 and Note Payable No. 11 are the only notes on hand at the end of the fiscal period. Source documents are abbreviated as follows: check, C; memorandum, M; note payable, NP; note receivable, NR; receipt, R.

19X1

Nov. 30. Received a 4-month, 12% note from Margaret Snider for an extension of time on her account, $400.00. NR6.

Dec. 15. Issued a 5-month, 12% note, $2,500.00. NP11.

19X2

Mar. 31. Margaret Snider dishonored NR6, maturity value due today. M83.

May 15. Paid cash for the maturity value of NP11. C465.

Instructions: 1. Use page 13 of a general journal. Journalize the adjusting entries for accrued interest income and accrued interest expense on December 31. Post these entries.

2. Continue to use page 13 of a general journal. Journalize the closing entries for interest income and interest expense. Post these entries.

3. Use page 14 of a general journal. Journalize the reversing entries for accrued interest income and accrued interest expense. Post these entries.

4. Use page 16 of a general journal. Journalize the dishonored note, NR6. Post this entry to the general ledger accounts.

5. Use page 33 of a cash payments journal. Journalize the cash payment for the maturity value of NP11. Post this entry.

Distributing Dividends and Preparing a Work Sheet for a Corporation

ENABLING PERFORMANCE TASKS

After studying Chapter 26, you will be able to:

a. Define accounting terms related to distributing dividends and preparing a work sheet for a merchandising business organized as a corporation.

b. Identify accounting concepts and practices related to distributing dividends and preparing a work sheet for a merchandising business organized as a corporation.

c. Journalize the declaration and payment of a dividend for a merchandising business organized as a corporation.

d. Plan end-of-fiscal-period adjustments for a merchandising business organized as a corporation.

e. Complete a work sheet for a merchandising business organized as a corporation.

Many accounting procedures used for a corporation are similar to the procedures used for a proprietorship or a partnership. Consequently, preparing a work sheet for a corporation is similar to preparing a work sheet for a proprietorship or a partnership.

There are, however, three principal differences between accounting for a proprietorship or partnership and accounting for a corporation. (1) Different accounts are used to record owners' equity. (2) Different procedures are used to distribute income to owners. (3) Corporations calculate and pay federal income tax. Corporations must pay income tax on their net income. Proprietorship and partnership net income is treated as part of each owner's personal income for income tax purposes. Thus, income tax is not figured for a proprietorship or partnership business.

STOCKHOLDERS' EQUITY
ACCOUNTS USED BY A CORPORATION

A corporation's ownership is divided into units. Each unit of ownership in a corporation is known as a share of stock. An owner of one or more shares of a corporation is called a stockholder. Each stockholder is an owner of a corporation.

Separate general ledger owners' equity accounts are maintained for each owner of a proprietorship or a partnership. However, a corporation may have many stockholders. Therefore, a separate owners' equity account is not maintained for each owner of a corporation. Instead, a single owners' equity account, titled Capital Stock, is used for the investment of all owners.

Owners' equity accounts for a corporation normally are listed under a major chart of accounts division titled *Stockholders' Equity*. The stockholders' equity section of Celluphone's chart of accounts is shown in Illustration 26-1.

Illustration 26-1
Stockholders' equity
section of a corporation
chart of accounts

(3000) STOCKHOLDERS' EQUITY
3105 Capital Stock
3110 Retained Earnings
3115 Dividends
3120 Income Summary

A second stockholders' equity account is used to record a corporation's earnings. An amount earned by a corporation and not yet distributed to stockholders is called retained earnings. Retained Earnings is the title of the account used to record a corporation's earnings.

A third stockholders' equity account is used to record the distribution of a corporation's earnings to stockholders. Earnings distributed to stockholders are called dividends. A corporation's dividend account is a temporary account similar to a proprietorship's or partnership's drawing account. Each time a dividend is declared, an account titled Dividends is debited. At the end of each fiscal period, the balance in the dividends account is closed to Retained Earnings. Dividends could be recorded as debits to a corporation's retained earnings account. However, many corporations record dividends in a separate account so that the total amounts are easily determined for each fiscal period.

DISTRIBUTING CORPORATE DIVIDENDS TO STOCKHOLDERS

Net income increases a corporation's total stockholders' equity. Some income may be retained by a corporation for business expansion. Also, some income may be given to stockholders as a return on their investments. Dividends can be distributed to stockholders *ONLY* by formal action of a corporation's board of directors. *(CONCEPT: Business Entity)* A group of persons elected by the stockholders to manage a corporation is called a board of directors.

Declaring a dividend

Action by a board of directors to distribute corporate earnings to stockholders is called declaring a dividend. Dividends normally are declared on one date and paid on a later date. A corporation's board of directors is not required to declare a dividend. In fact, dividends cannot be declared that would exceed the balance of the retained earnings account. However, when a board of directors does declare a dividend, the corporation is then obligated to pay the dividend. The dividend is a liability that must be recorded in the corporation's accounts.

Celluphone's board of directors declares a dividend every three months so that stockholders can share the corporation's earnings throughout the year. Celluphone declares dividends each March 15, June 15, September 15, and December 15. The dividends are then paid on the 15th of the month following the declaration.

December 15, 19--.
Celluphone's board of directors declared a quarterly dividend of $2.00 per share; capital stock issued is 10,000 shares; total dividend, $20,000.00. Date of payment is January 15, 19--. Memorandum No. 195.

A memorandum is the source document for journalizing this transaction. *(CONCEPT: Objective Evidence)* The analysis of the December 15 quarterly dividend declaration is shown in the T accounts.

A dividend declaration increases the balance of the dividends account. The stockholders' equity account, Dividends, has a normal debit balance and is increased by a debit. Dividends, therefore, is debited for $20,000.00 (10,000 shares × $2.00 per share). Dividends Payable is credited for $20,000.00 to show the increase in this liability account.

A transaction for a declaration of a dividend is not appropriately journalized in any of the special journals. Therefore, the entry is journalized in a general journal. The general journal entry to record Celluphone's quarterly declaration of a dividend is shown in Illustration 26-2.

Dividends

3/15 Decl.	20,000.00	
6/15 Decl.	20,000.00	
9/15 Decl.	20,000.00	
12/15 Decl.	20,000.00	

Dividends Payable

4/15 Paid	20,000.00	3/15 Decl.	20,000.00
7/15 Paid	20,000.00	6/15 Decl.	20,000.00
10/15 Paid	20,000.00	9/15 Decl.	20,000.00
		12/15 Decl.	20,000.00

GENERAL JOURNAL PAGE 14

	DATE		ACCOUNT TITLE	DOC. NO.	POST. REF.	DEBIT	CREDIT	
1	Dec.	15	Dividends	M195		20 00 0 00		1
2			Dividends Payable				20 00 0 00	2
3								3
4								4
5								5
6								6

Illustration 26-2
General journal entry to record the declaration of a dividend by a corporation

Dividends is debited for the dividend declared, $20,000.00. Dividends Payable is credited for the liability incurred by the dividend declaration, $20,000.00.

Paying a dividend

Celluphone issues one check for the amount of the total dividend to be paid. This check is deposited in a special dividend checking account. A separate check for each stockholder is drawn on this special account. The special account avoids a large number of cash payments journal entries and also reserves cash specifically for paying dividends.

A check is often made payable to an agent, such as a bank. The agent then handles the details of sending dividend checks to individual stockholders.

January 15, 19--.
Paid cash for quarterly dividend declared December 15, 19--, $20,000.00.
Check No. 794.

Dividends Payable

4/15 Paid	20,000.00	3/15 Decl.	20,000.00
7/15 Paid	20,000.00	6/15 Decl.	20,000.00
10/15 Paid	20,000.00	9/15 Decl.	20,000.00
1/15 Paid	20,000.00	12/15 Decl.	20,000.00

Cash

	1/15 Paid	20,000.00

The check is the source document for recording this payment. *(CONCEPT: Objective Evidence)* The analysis of the January 15 payment of Celluphone's quarterly dividend is shown in the T accounts.

In this transaction the balance of the liability account, Dividends Payable, is decreased. The balance of the asset account, Cash, is also decreased. Therefore, Dividends Payable is debited for $20,000.00 and Cash is credited for $20,000.00.

The cash payments journal entry to record Celluphone's quarterly dividend payment of $20,000.00 is shown in Illustration 26-3.

CASH PAYMENTS JOURNAL   PAGE 37

	DATE	ACCOUNT TITLE	CK. NO.	POST. REF.	GENERAL DEBIT	GENERAL CREDIT	ACCOUNTS PAYABLE DEBIT	PURCHASES DISCOUNT CREDIT	CASH CREDIT	
					1	2	3	4	5	
1	Jan. 15	Dividends Payable	794		20 00 0 00				20 00 0 00	1
2										2
3										3
4										4
5										5
6										6
7										7
8										8

Illustration 26-3
Cash payments journal entry to record the payment of a dividend

Dividends Payable is debited for the amount of dividends paid, $20,000.00. Cash is credited for the total amount of cash paid, $20,000.00. When this entry is posted, the dividends payable account has a zero balance.

PREPARING A WORK SHEET FOR A CORPORATION

Work sheets for proprietorships, partnerships, and corporations are similar. Businesses use work sheets to plan adjustments and provide information needed to prepare financial statements. Celluphone may prepare a work sheet at any time financial statements are needed. However, Celluphone always prepares a work sheet and financial statements at the end of a fiscal year. (CONCEPT: *Accounting Period Cycle*)

Entering a trial balance on a work sheet

To prepare a work sheet, a trial balance is first entered in the Trial Balance columns. All general ledger accounts are listed in the same order as they appear in the general ledger. Trial Balance columns are totaled to prove equality of debits and credits.

Celluphone's trial balance on December 31 is shown on the work sheet, Illustration 26-4. A corporation's accounts are similar to those of a proprietorship or partnership except for the capital stock, retained earnings, dividends, and federal income tax accounts.

Planning adjustments on a work sheet

Some general ledger accounts need to be brought up to date before financial statements are prepared. Accounts are brought up to date by planning and entering adjustments on a work sheet. Most adjustments on a corporation's work sheet are similar to those for proprietorships and partnerships.

The adjustments for merchandise inventory, supplies, and prepaid insurance are described in earlier chapters. Celluphone also makes six other adjustments. (1) Interest Income. (2) Uncollectible Accounts Expense. (3) Depreciation Expense—Office Equipment. (4) Depreciation Expense—Store Equipment. (5) Interest Expense. (6) Federal Income Tax Expense.

Adjustments for depreciation expense, uncollectible accounts expense, interest income, and interest expense could also be made by proprietorships and partnerships. However, the adjustment for federal income tax is unique to corporations. This adjustment is not made for proprietorships and partnerships because taxes are paid by the owners, not the business. Adjustments generally are made in the order that accounts are listed on a work sheet.

Interest income adjustment. Interest income earned during the current fiscal period but not yet received needs to be recorded. Two accounts are used for the adjustment for accrued interest income: Interest Receivable and Interest Income. An analysis of Celluphone's adjustment for accrued interest income is described in Chapter 25. Celluphone's accrued interest income adjustment is labeled *a* on lines 4 and 48 in the work sheet Adjustments columns, Illustration 26-4, pages 642 and 643.

Celluphone, Inc.
Work Sheet
For Year Ended December 31, 19--

	TRIAL BALANCE		ADJUSTMENTS		INCOME STATEMENT		BALANCE SHEET	
ACCOUNT TITLE	DEBIT	CREDIT	DEBIT	CREDIT	DEBIT	CREDIT	DEBIT	CREDIT
1 Cash	40968 00						40968 00	
2 Petty Cash	300 00						300 00	
3 Notes Receivable	550 00						550 00	
4 Interest Receivable			(a) 11 00				11 00	
5 Accounts Receivable	6824 00						6824 00	
6 Allow. for Uncollectible Accts.		265 00		(b) 9227 00				9492 00
7 Merchandise Inventory	205160 00		(c) 7018 00				212178 00	
8 Supplies	15455 00			(d) 11690 00			3765 00	
9 Prepaid Insurance	13550 00			(e) 8598 00			4952 00	
10 Office Equipment	18250 00						18250 00	
11 Accum. Depr.—Office Equip.		3625 00		(f) 1750 00				5375 00
12 Store Equipment	77190 00						77190 00	
13 Accum. Depr.—Store Equip.		9125 00		(g) 6325 00				15450 00
14 Notes Payable		2800 00						2800 00
15 Interest Payable				(h) 70 00				70 00
16 Accounts Payable		83965 75						83965 75
17 Employee Income Tax Payable		2340 00						2340 00
18 Federal Income Tax Payable				(i) 2219 23				2219 23
19 FICA Tax Payable		2695 00						2695 00
20 Sales Tax Payable		10982 00						10982 00
21 Unemploy. Tax Payable—Federal		47 00						47 00
22 Unemploy. Tax Payable—State		317 25						317 25
23 Health Insur. Premiums Payable		995 00						995 00
24 Dividends Payable		20000 00						20000 00
25 Capital Stock		100000 00						100000 00

	Account	Trial Balance Debit	Trial Balance Credit	Adjustments Debit	Adjustments Credit	Income Statement Debit	Income Statement Credit	Balance Sheet Debit	Balance Sheet Credit
26	Retained Earnings		149 118 00						149 118 00
27	Dividends	80 000 00						80 000 00	
28	Income Summary				(c) 7 018 00		7 018 00		
29	Sales		2050 440 00				2050 440 00		
30	Sales Discount	5 642 00				5 642 00			
31	Sales Returns and Allowances	24 318 00				24 318 00			
32	Purchases	1454 798 00				1454 798 00			
33	Purchases Discount		10 766 00				10 766 00		
34	Purchases Returns and Allowances		5 310 00				5 310 00		
35	Advertising Expense	32 600 00				32 600 00			
36	Credit Card Fee Expense	20 468 00				20 468 00			
37	Depr. Expense—Office Equipment			(f) 17 500 00		17 500 00			
38	Depr. Expense—Store Equipment			(g) 63 250 00		63 250 00			
39	Insurance Expense			(e) 8 598 00		8 598 00			
40	Miscellaneous Expense	22 350 00				22 350 00			
41	Payroll Taxes Expense	23 720 00				23 720 00			
42	Rent Expense	56 400 00				56 400 00			
43	Salary Expense	251 932 00				251 932 00			
44	Supplies Expense			(d) 11 690 00		11 690 00			
45	Uncollectible Accounts Expense			(b) 9 227 00		9 227 00			
46	Utilities Expense	48 900 00				48 900 00			
47	Gain on Plant Assets		2 250 00				2 250 00		
48	Interest Income		2 030 00		(a) 1 10 00		2 140 00		
49	Cash Short and Over	3 00				3 00			
50	Interest Expense	1 375 00		(h) 7 00		1 445 00			
51	Loss on Plant Assets	4 600 00				4 600 00			
52	Federal Income Tax Expense	34 600 00		(i) 2 219 23		36 819 23			
53		2453 219 00	2453 219 00	46 908 23	46 908 23	1973 435 23	2073 973 00	506 404 00	405 866 23
54	Net Income after Fed. Inc. Tax					100 537 77			100 537 77
55						2073 973 00	2073 973 00	506 404 00	506 404 00

Illustration 26-4
Completed work sheet for
a corporation

Interest Receivable is debited for the amount of accrued interest income, $11.00. Interest Income is credited for the same amount.

Uncollectible accounts expense adjustment. The estimated amount of uncollectible accounts expense for a fiscal period needs to be brought up to date. Two accounts are used for the adjustment for uncollectible accounts expense: Uncollectible Accounts Expense and Allowance for Uncollectible Accounts. An analysis of Celluphone's uncollectible accounts expense adjustment is described in Chapter 22. The uncollectible accounts expense adjustment is labeled *b* on lines 6 and 45 in the work sheet Adjustments columns, Illustration 26-4. Uncollectible Accounts Expense is debited for the amount of estimated uncollectible accounts expense, $9,227.00. Allowance for Uncollectible Accounts is credited for the same amount.

Merchandise inventory adjustment. The merchandise inventory account balance in a trial balance is the beginning inventory for a fiscal period. The amount of the ending inventory is determined by counting the merchandise on hand at the end of the fiscal period. An adjusting entry is made to bring merchandise inventory up to date so that the end-of-fiscal-period balance will be shown in the merchandise inventory account. The merchandise inventory adjustment is labeled *c* on lines 7 and 28 in the work sheet Adjustments columns, Illustration 26-4.

Celluphone's beginning merchandise inventory, $205,160.00, is shown on line 7 in the Trial Balance Debit column on the work sheet. Celluphone's ending merchandise inventory on December 31 is counted and determined to be $212,178.00. To bring Celluphone's merchandise inventory account up to date, the balance of Merchandise Inventory needs to be increased by $7,018.00 ($212,178.00 ending inventory − $205,160.00 beginning inventory). Merchandise Inventory is debited for the amount of the increase, $7,018.00. Income Summary is credited for the same amount.

> If the ending merchandise inventory is less than the beginning merchandise inventory, the difference (decrease) is debited to Income Summary and credited to Merchandise Inventory.

Supplies adjustment. Two accounts are used for the adjustment for supplies: Supplies and Supplies Expense. The supplies adjustment is labeled *d* on lines 8 and 44 in the work sheet Adjustments columns, Illustration 26-4. Supplies Expense is debited for the value of supplies used, $11,690.00. Supplies is credited for the same amount.

Prepaid insurance adjustment. Insurance premiums are debited to a prepaid insurance account when paid. Insurance expense, however, must be recorded for the fiscal period in which the insurance is used. *(CONCEPT: Matching Expenses with Revenue)* Therefore, Prepaid Insurance and Insurance Expense are adjusted at the end of the fiscal period. The prepaid insurance adjustment is labeled *e* on lines 9 and 39 in the work sheet

Adjustments columns, Illustration 26-4. Insurance Expense is debited for the value of insurance used, $8,598.00. Prepaid Insurance is credited for the same amount.

Depreciation expense adjustments. An analysis of Celluphone's depreciation expense adjustments is described in Chapter 23. The depreciation expense adjustments are labeled *f* and *g* on lines 11, 13, 37, and 38 in the work sheet Adjustments columns, Illustration 26-4.

Depreciation Expense—Office Equipment is debited for the amount of office equipment depreciation expense, $1,750.00. Accumulated Depreciation—Office Equipment is credited for the same amount. Depreciation Expense—Store Equipment is debited for the amount of store equipment depreciation expense, $6,325.00. Accumulated Depreciation—Store Equipment is credited for the same amount.

Interest expense adjustment. Interest expense incurred during the current fiscal period but not yet paid needs to be recorded. Two accounts are used for the adjustment for accrued interest expense: Interest Payable and Interest Expense. An analysis of Celluphone's adjustment for accrued interest expense is described in Chapter 25. The interest expense adjustment is labeled *h* on lines 15 and 50 in the work sheet Adjustments columns, Illustration 26-4.

Interest Expense is debited for the amount of accrued interest expense, $70.00. Interest Payable is credited for the same amount.

Federal income tax expense adjustment

Corporations anticipating annual federal income taxes of $500.00 or more are required to pay their estimated taxes each quarter. Estimated income tax is paid in quarterly installments in April, June, September, and December. However, the actual income tax owed is figured at the end of a fiscal year. Based on the actual tax owed for a year, a corporation must file an annual return. Any additional tax owed that was not paid in quarterly installments must be paid when the final return is sent.

Early in the current year, Celluphone estimated $34,600.00 federal income tax for the year. Celluphone paid $8,650.00 in each quarterly installment for a total of $34,600.00. Each tax payment is recorded as a debit to Federal Income Tax Expense and a credit to Cash.

Federal income tax is an expense of a corporation. However, the amount of tax depends on net income before the tax is recorded. Five steps are used to figure the total amount of federal income tax expense and the amount of the adjustment needed on a work sheet.

1 Complete all adjustments on a work sheet except the federal income tax expense adjustment.

2 Extend all amounts except the federal income tax expense account balance to the appropriate Income Statement or Balance Sheet columns.

3 On a separate sheet of paper, total the work sheet's Income Statement columns. Figure the difference between the two totals. This difference is the net income before federal income tax expense. Celluphone's net income before federal income tax is figured from the Income Statement columns of the work sheet, Illustration 26-4.

Total of Income Statement Credit column.............	$2,073,973.00
Less total of Income Statement Debit column before federal income tax	−1,936,616.00
Equals net income before federal income tax...........	$ 137,357.00

4 Figure the amount of federal income tax expense using a tax rate table furnished by the Internal Revenue Service. Celluphone's federal income tax for the current year is $36,819.23.

Tax rate tables showing income tax rates for corporations are distributed by the Internal Revenue Service. Each corporation should check a current table to find the applicable rates. Corporation tax rates in effect when this text was written were used to figure Celluphone's federal income tax expense.

5 Figure the amount of the federal income tax expense adjustment.

The difference between the total federal income tax expense and the estimated tax already paid is the amount of the adjustment, $2,219.23 ($36,819.23 − $34,600.00 = $2,219.23).

Celluphone's federal income tax expense adjustment is shown in the T accounts. Celluphone paid quarterly federal income tax installments of $8,650.00 each. Federal Income Tax Expense has a debit balance of $34,600.00 at the end of the fiscal period before the adjustment is made.

Federal Income Tax Expense

4/15	8,650.00
6/15	8,650.00
9/15	8,650.00
12/15	8,650.00
(12/15 Bal.	*34,600.00)*
12/31 Adj. (i)	2,219.23
(New Bal.	*36,819.23)*

Federal Income Tax Payable

	12/31 Adj. (i) 2,219.23

To enter the adjustment for income tax expense, Celluphone debits Federal Income Tax Expense for $2,219.23 to show the increase in the balance of this expense account. The new balance of this account, $36,819.23, is the total federal income tax expense for the fiscal period. Federal Income Tax Payable is credited for $2,219.23 to show the increase in this liability account. Celluphone's federal income tax payable account balance, $2,219.23, is the amount of income tax expense still unpaid at year end. Celluphone's federal income tax expense adjustment is labeled *i* on lines 18 and 52 in the work sheet Adjustments columns, Illustration 26-4.

Federal Income Tax Expense is debited for the amount of the increase, $2,219.23. Federal Income Tax Payable is credited for the same amount.

Federal Income Tax Expense is an expense account. The account appears under a major division titled *Income Tax Expense* as the last item in Celluphone's chart of accounts. Federal Income Tax Payable, a liability account, appears under the heading *Current Liabilities*.

After the federal income tax expense adjustment is recorded, the Adjustments columns are totaled and ruled. Next, the balances of the income tax accounts are extended to the appropriate work sheet columns. The federal income tax expense account balance is extended to the Income Statement Debit column. The federal income tax payable account balance is extended to the Balance Sheet Credit column.

Completing a work sheet

The Income Statement and Balance Sheet columns are totaled. Totals are written as shown on line 53 of Celluphone's work sheet, Illustration 26-4. The Income Statement Credit column total for Celluphone is $2,073,973.00, which is more than the Income Statement Debit column total of $1,973,435.23. (The Credit column total, $2,073,973.00, *less* the Debit column total, $1,973,435.23, *equals* the difference, $100,537.77.) This amount, *$100,537.77*, is written in the Income Statement Debit column on line 54 of the work sheet. *Net Income after Federal Income Tax* is written in the Account Title column on the same line. Income Statement columns are then totaled as shown on line 55 of the work sheet.

The net income after federal income tax amount, $100,537.77, is written in the Balance Sheet Credit column, line 54. Balance Sheet columns are totaled as shown on line 55. The totals of both the Balance Sheet Debit and Balance Sheet Credit columns are the same and assumed to be correct. Double lines are ruled across the Income Statement and Balance Sheet columns on line 55 to show that the totals have been verified as correct.

SUMMARY OF PREPARING A WORK SHEET FOR A CORPORATION

The chart shown in Illustration 26-5 summarizes the steps followed in preparing an 8-column work sheet for a corporation.

1 Prepare a trial balance in the Trial Balance columns.

2 Analyze and record all adjustments except the federal income tax expense adjustment in the Adjustments columns.

3 Extend all amounts except the federal income tax expense account balance to the appropriate Income Statement or Balance Sheet columns.

4 On a separate sheet of paper, total the work sheet's Income Statement columns. Figure the difference between the two totals. This difference is the net income before federal income tax.

Income Statement Credit column......................	$2,073,973.00
Less total of Income Statement Debit column..........	−1,936,616.00
Equals net income before federal income tax...........	$ 137,357.00

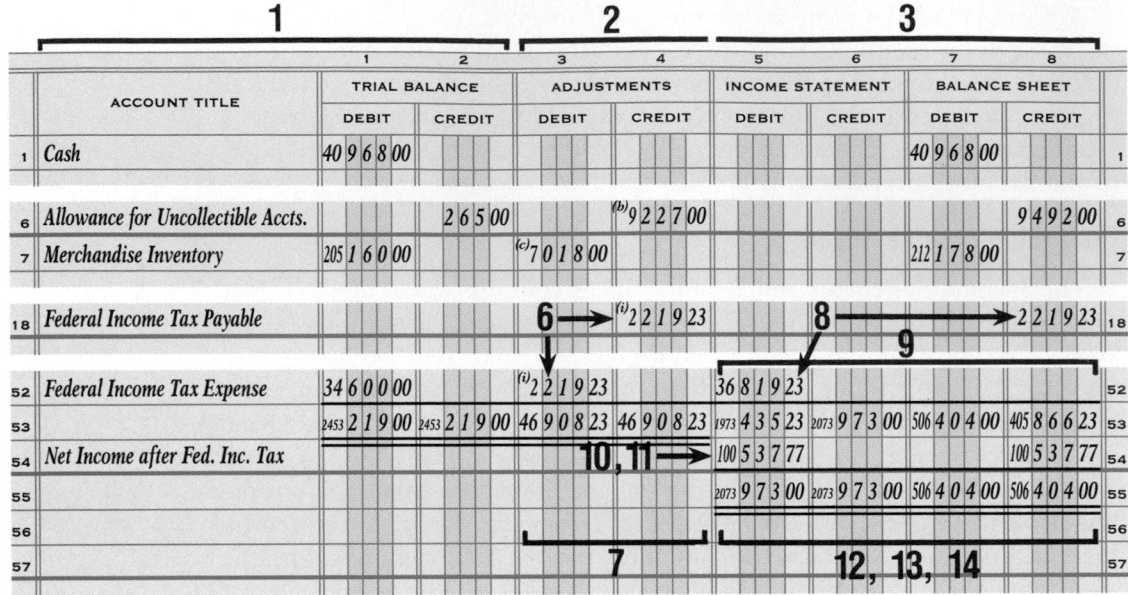

Illustration 26-5
Summary of preparing a
work sheet for a
corporation

5 Figure the amount of federal income tax expense.

6 Calculate and enter the federal income tax expense adjustment in the Adjustments columns.

Total federal income tax expense......................	$36,819.23
Less balance of Federal Income Tax Expense.................	−34,600.00
Equals federal income tax expense adjustment	$ 2,219.23

7 Total and rule the Adjustments columns.

8 Extend the federal income tax expense account balance to the Income Statement Debit column. Extend the federal income tax payable account balance to the Balance Sheet Credit column.

9 Total the Income Statement and Balance Sheet columns.

10 Figure the net income or net loss. If the Income Statement Credit column total (revenue) is larger than the Debit column total (costs and expenses), a net income has occurred. If the Income Statement Debit column total (costs and expenses) is larger than the Credit column total (revenue), a net loss has occurred.

11 Enter the amount of net income in the Income Statement Debit column and in the Balance Sheet Credit column. If there is a net loss, enter the amount of net loss in the Income Statement Credit column and in the Balance Sheet Debit column.

12 Total the four Income Statement and Balance Sheet amount columns.

13 Check that both totals of the Income Statement columns are the same and that both totals of the Balance Sheet columns are the same.

14 Rule double lines across the Income Statement and Balance Sheet column totals to show that the totals have been verified as correct.

ACCOUNTING TERMS

What is the meaning of each of the following?

1. stockholder

2. retained earnings

3. dividends

4. board of directors

5. declaring a dividend

QUESTIONS FOR INDIVIDUAL STUDY

1. How does accounting for a corporation differ from accounting for a proprietorship or partnership?
2. Why don't partnerships and proprietorships pay federal income tax?
3. How many accounts are kept for the investment of all owners of a corporation?
4. In which chart of accounts division is the capital stock account listed?
5. What account does a corporation use to record earnings not yet distributed to stockholders?
6. Why do many corporations record dividends declared in a separate dividends account?
7. What action is required before a corporation can distribute income to its stockholders?
8. When is a dividend recorded as a liability in a corporation's general ledger accounts?
9. What accounts are affected, and how, when a dividend is declared?
10. What accounts are affected, and how, when a dividend is paid?
11. In what order are general ledger accounts listed on a corporation work sheet?
12. Why is Celluphone's merchandise inventory adjustment a debit to Merchandise Inventory?
13. What circumstances would require an adjustment that credits Merchandise Inventory?
14. What accounts are affected, and how, by the adjustment for accrued interest expense?
15. Why is federal income tax expense not figured until all other adjustments have been planned on a work sheet?
16. What accounts are affected, and how, by the adjustment for federal income tax expense?

CASES FOR MANAGEMENT DECISION

CASE 1 Fahle Company's net income has been fluctuating between a small net income and a small net loss during the first four years of the corporation's existence. The company is hoping to earn $12.00 per share during its fifth year. Janet Riley, newly appointed president of Fahle Company, believes the corporation needs to take some positive action to regain the confidence of the stockholders. She suggests the corpora-tion declare a $10.00 per share dividend December 15 to be paid February 1. By February 1 financial statements for Fahle's fifth year ending December 31 will be completed so the net income earned for the year will be known. Mrs. Riley also suggests that if the net income is not as high as expected, the board of directors can cancel the declared dividend before it is paid. Do you agree with Mrs. Riley's proposal? Explain.

CASE 2 At the beginning of the current year, Bower Company changed its organization from a partnership to a corporation. The president suggested that since the same six individuals owned the corporation as had owned the partnership, the same procedures should be used for paying income tax on the earnings of the business. The net in-come of the corporation would be treated as part of each corporation owner's personal in-come for income tax purposes. "If this pro-cedure is followed," said the president, "the corporation will not need to pay any income tax." Do you agree with the president's sug-gestion? Explain.

◼ DRILLS FOR UNDERSTANDING

DRILL 26-D1   Analyzing adjustments on a work sheet

Use a form similar to the following.

Adjustment No.	Work Sheet Adjustment	
	Account Debited	**Account Credited**
1.	*Supplies Expense*	*Supplies*

Instructions: For each of the following adjustments, write the title of the account debited and the title of the account credited. Adjustment No. 1 is given as an example.

Adjustments
1. Supplies
2. Accrued interest income
3. Merchandise inventory (increased)
4. Merchandise inventory (decreased)
5. Uncollectible accounts expense
6. Prepaid insurance
7. Depreciation expense—store equipment
8. Accrued interest expense
9. Additional federal income tax owed

DRILL 26-D2   Extending account balances on a work sheet

Use a form similar to the following.

Account	Work Sheet Columns			
	Income Statement		Balance Sheet	
	Debit	**Credit**	**Debit**	**Credit**
1. *Allowance for Uncollectible Accounts*				✓

Instructions: For each of the following accounts, place a check mark in the work sheet column to which the account balance should be extended. Account No. 1 is given as an example.

Accounts
1. Allowance for Uncollectible Accounts
2. Sales Returns and Allowances
3. Notes Payable
4. Retained Earnings
5. Accounts Receivable
6. Purchases Discount
7. Merchandise Inventory
8. Dividends
9. Federal Income Tax Expense
10. Accumulated Depreciation — Store Equipment

◼ APPLICATION PROBLEMS

PROBLEM 26-1 Journalizing dividends

Century Center Corporation completed the following transactions during December of the current year and January of the next year. Source documents are abbreviated as follows: check, C; memorandum, M.

Dec. 15. The board of directors declared a dividend of $10.00 per share; capital stock issued is 1,500 shares; total dividend, $15,000.00. Date of payment is January 15. M126.
Jan. 15. Paid cash for dividend declared December 15, $15,000.00. C432.

Instructions: 1. Use page 12 of a general journal. Journalize the dividend declared on December 15.
   2. Use page 15 of a cash payments journal. Journalize payment of the dividend.

PROBLEM 26-2 Preparing a work sheet for a corporation

Eagle System Corporation's general ledger accounts and balances are recorded on a work sheet in the working papers.

Instructions: Complete the work sheet for the current year ended December 31. Record the adjustments on the work sheet using the following information.

Adjustment Information, December 31

Accrued interest income	$ 277.20
Uncollectible accounts expense estimated as 1.5% of sales on account. Sales on account for year, $499,000.00.	
Merchandise inventory	90,066.26
Supplies inventory	327.88
Value of prepaid insurance	3,023.60
Annual depreciation expense — office equipment	2,690.00
Annual depreciation expense — store equipment	1,607.60
Accrued interest expense	545.16
Federal income tax expense for the year	21,446.41

■ ENRICHMENT PROBLEMS

MASTERY PROBLEM 26-M   Journalizing dividends and preparing a work sheet for a corporation

Universal Corporation's general ledger accounts and balances are recorded on a work sheet in the working papers.

Instructions: 1. Complete the work sheet for the current year ended December 31. Record the adjustments on the work sheet using the following information.

Adjustment Information, December 31

Accrued interest income	$ 118.00
Uncollectible accounts expense estimated as 1.0% of sales on account.	
Sales on account for year, $407,800.00.	
Merchandise inventory	123,952.00
Supplies inventory	1,592.10
Value of prepaid insurance	5,906.00
Annual depreciation expense—office equipment	1,386.00
Annual depreciation expense—store equipment	9,800.00
Accrued interest expense	94.00
Federal income tax expense for the year	12,950.28

2. Use page 36 of a cash payments journal. Journalize the following transaction completed during the next year. The abbreviation for check is C.

Jan. 15. Paid cash for quarterly dividend declared December 15, $10,500.00. C604.

CHALLENGE PROBLEM 26-C   Preparing a 10-column work sheet for a corporation

Austin Sports Center's general ledger accounts and balances are recorded on a 10-column work sheet in the working papers.

Instructions: Complete the 10-column work sheet for the current year ended December 31. Record the adjustments on the work sheet using the following information.

Adjustment Information, December 31

Accrued interest income	$ 119.25
Uncollectible accounts expense estimated as 1.5% of sales on account.	
Sales on account for year, $306,933.33.	
Merchandise inventory	81,356.00
Supplies inventory	1,872.00
Value of prepaid insurance	4,440.00
Annual depreciation expense—office equipment	1,360.00
Annual depreciation expense—store equipment	15,304.00
Accrued interest expense	57.00

Federal income tax expense for the year is figured at the following rates:
  15% of net income before taxes, zero to $50,000.00.
  Plus 25% of net income before taxes, $50,000.00 to $75,000.00.
  Plus 34% of net income before taxes, $75,000.00 to $100,000.00.
  Plus 39% of net income before taxes, $100,000.00 to $335,000.00.
  Plus 34% of net income before taxes over $335,000.00.

Financial Statements and End-of-Fiscal-Period Entries for a Corporation

ENABLING PERFORMANCE TASKS

After studying Chapter 27, you will be able to:

a. Define accounting terms related to financial statements for a merchandising business organized as a corporation.

b. Identify accounting concepts and practices related to financial statements and end-of-fiscal-period entries for a merchandising business organized as a corporation.

c. Prepare and analyze an income statement for a merchandising business organized as a corporation.

d. Prepare a statement of stockholders' equity for a merchandising business organized as a corporation.

e. Prepare and analyze a balance sheet for a merchandising business organized as a corporation.

f. Record adjusting and closing entries for a merchandising business organized as a corporation.

g. Record reversing entries for a merchandising business organized as a corporation.

Corporations prepare financial statements that report financial information similar to the information reported by proprietorships and partnerships. To provide the corporation's managers and stockholders with information on how well the corporation is progressing, financial statements are prepared annually and sometimes monthly or quarterly. *(CONCEPT: Accounting Period Cycle)*

FINANCIAL STATEMENTS FOR A CORPORATION

Financial statements are used to report a business' financial progress and condition as well as changes in the owners' equity. To report this information, Celluphone prepares three financial statements. (1) Income statement. (2) Statement of stockholders' equity. (3) Balance sheet.

Celluphone, Inc.
Work Sheet
For Year Ended December 31, 19--

	TRIAL BALANCE		ADJUSTMENTS		INCOME STATEMENT		BALANCE SHEET	
ACCOUNT TITLE	DEBIT	CREDIT	DEBIT	CREDIT	DEBIT	CREDIT	DEBIT	CREDIT
1 Cash	40968 00						40968 00	
2 Petty Cash	300 00						300 00	
3 Notes Receivable	550 00						550 00	
4 Interest Receivable			(a) 11 00				11 00	
5 Accounts Receivable	68240 00						68240 00	
6 Allow. for Uncollectible Accts.		265 00		(b) 9227 00				9492 00
7 Merchandise Inventory	205160 00		(c) 7018 00				212178 00	
8 Supplies	15455 00			(d) 11690 00			3765 00	
9 Prepaid Insurance	13550 00			(e) 8598 00			4952 00	
10 Office Equipment	18250 00						18250 00	
11 Accum. Depr.—Office Equip.		3625 00		(f) 1750 00				5375 00
12 Store Equipment	77190 00						77190 00	
13 Accum. Depr.—Store Equip.		9125 00		(g) 6325 00				15450 00
14 Notes Payable		2800 00						2800 00
15 Interest Payable				(h) 70 00				70 00
16 Accounts Payable		83965 75						83965 75
17 Employee Income Tax Payable		2340 00						2340 00
18 Federal Income Tax Payable				(i) 2219 23				2219 23
19 FICA Tax Payable		2695 00						2695 00
20 Sales Tax Payable		10982 00						10982 00
21 Unemploy. Tax Payable—Federal		47 00						47 00
22 Unemploy. Tax Payable—State		317 25						317 25
23 Health Insur. Premiums Payable		995 00						995 00
24 Dividends Payable		20000 00						20000 00
25 Capital Stock		100000 00						100000 00

Account Title	Trial Balance Debit	Trial Balance Credit	Adjustments Debit	Adjustments Credit	Income Statement Debit	Income Statement Credit	Balance Sheet Debit	Balance Sheet Credit
26 Retained Earnings		149 1 1 8 00						149 1 1 8 00
27 Dividends	8 0 0 0 00						8 0 0 0 00	
28 Income Summary				(c) 7 0 1 8 00		7 0 1 8 00		
29 Sales		2050 4 4 0 00				2050 4 4 0 00		
30 Sales Discount	5 6 4 2 00				5 6 4 2 00			
31 Sales Returns and Allowances	24 3 1 8 00				24 3 1 8 00			
32 Purchases	1454 7 9 8 00				1454 7 9 8 00			
33 Purchases Discount		10 7 6 6 00				10 7 6 6 00		
34 Purchases Returns and Allowances		5 3 1 0 00				5 3 1 0 00		
35 Advertising Expense	32 6 0 0 00				32 6 0 0 00			
36 Credit Card Fee Expense	20 4 6 8 00				20 4 6 8 00			
37 Depr. Expense—Office Equipment			(f) 1 7 5 0 00		1 7 5 0 00			
38 Depr. Expense—Store Equipment			(g) 6 3 2 5 00		6 3 2 5 00			
39 Insurance Expense			(e) 8 5 9 8 00		8 5 9 8 00			
40 Miscellaneous Expense	22 3 5 0 00				22 3 5 0 00			
41 Payroll Taxes Expense	23 7 2 0 00				23 7 2 0 00			
42 Rent Expense	56 4 0 0 00				56 4 0 0 00			
43 Salary Expense	251 9 3 2 00				251 9 3 2 00			
44 Supplies Expense			(d) 11 6 9 0 00		11 6 9 0 00			
45 Uncollectible Accounts Expense			(b) 9 2 2 7 00		9 2 2 7 00			
46 Utilities Expense	48 9 0 0 00				48 9 0 0 00			
47 Gain on Plant Assets		2 2 5 00				2 2 5 00		
48 Interest Income		2 0 3 00		(a) 1 1 00		2 1 4 00		
49 Cash Short and Over	3 00				3 00			
50 Interest Expense	13 7 5 00		(h) 7 0 00		14 4 5 00			
51 Loss on Plant Assets	4 6 0 00				4 6 0 00			
52 Federal Income Tax Expense	34 6 0 0 00		(i) 2 2 1 9 23		36 8 1 9 23			
53	2453 2 1 9 00	2453 2 1 9 00	46 9 0 8 23	46 9 0 8 23	1973 4 3 5 23	2073 9 7 3 00	506 4 0 4 00	405 8 6 6 23
54 Net Income after Fed. Inc. Tax					100 5 3 7 77			100 5 3 7 77
55					2073 9 7 3 00	2073 9 7 3 00	506 4 0 4 00	506 4 0 4 00
56								

Illustration 27-1   Work sheet for a corporation

A corporation prepares an income statement and a balance sheet similar to those used by proprietorships and partnerships. However, a corporation reports changes in owners' equity differently. First, owners' equity for all owners is reported as a single amount rather than for each owner. Second, owners' equity is reported in two categories. (1) Capital contributed by the owners. (2) Capital earned by the corporation.

Income statement

An income statement reports financial progress of a business during a fiscal period. *(CONCEPT: Accounting Period Cycle)* Revenue, cost of merchandise sold, gross profit on operations, operating expenses, and net income or net loss are reported on an income statement. *(CONCEPT: Adequate Disclosure)* To help make decisions about current and future operations, Celluphone also analyzes relationships between revenue and expense items. Based on this analysis, Celluphone reports component percentages for all major income statement items.

Preparing an income statement. Celluphone's income statement is prepared from information found in the Trial Balance, Income Statement, and Balance Sheet columns of the work sheet, Illustration 27-1, shown on pages 654–655..

Procedures for preparing Celluphone's income statement are similar to those used by any merchandising business. Celluphone's income statement for the current year ended December 31 is shown in Illustration 27-3.

Celluphone's income statement differs in four ways from CarLand's income statement shown in Part 3.

1. Net sales is listed in the Operating Revenue section. Total sales less sales discount and sales returns and allowances is called net sales. Net sales is reported in the Operating Revenue section of Celluphone's income statement, as shown in Illustration 27-2.

				% of Net Sales
Operating Revenue:				
Sales............................			$2,050,440.00	
Less: Sales Discount..............	$	5,642.00		
Sales Ret. and Allow.........		24,318.00	29,960.00	
Net Sales.........................			$2,020,480.00	100.0

Illustration 27-2
Net sales reported on an income statement

2. Net purchases is reported in the Cost of Merchandise Sold section. Total purchases less purchases discount and purchases returns and allowances is called net purchases. Net purchases is reported in the Cost

Celluphone, Inc.
Income Statement
For Year Ended December 31, 19--

				% of Net Sales
Operating Revenue:				
Sales............................		$2,050,440.00		
Less: Sales Discount...............	$ 5,642.00			
Sales Ret. and Allow.........	24,318.00	29,960.00		
Net Sales........................			$2,020,480.00	100.0
Cost of Merchandise Sold:				
Merchandise Inv., Jan. 1, 19--		$ 205,160.00		
Purchases	$1,454,798.00			
Less: Purchases Discount $10,766.00				
Purch. Ret. and Allow......... 5,310.00	16,076.00			
Net Purchases		1,438,722.00		
Total Cost of Mdse. Avail. for Sale ...		$1,643,882.00		
Less Mdse. Inventory, Dec. 31, 19-- ..		212,178.00		
Cost of Merchandise Sold			1,431,704.00	70.9
Gross Profit on Operations...........			$ 588,776.00	29.1
Operating Expenses:				
Advertising Expense...............		$ 32,600.00		
Credit Card Fee Expense...........		20,468.00		
Depreciation Exp.—Office Equip.....		1,750.00		
Depreciation Exp.—Store Equip......		6,325.00		
Insurance Expense		8,598.00		
Miscellaneous Expense		22,350.00		
Payroll Taxes Expense		23,720.00		
Rent Expense.....................		56,400.00		
Salary Expense		251,932.00		
Supplies Expense		11,690.00		
Uncollectible Accounts Expense		9,227.00		
Utilities Expense		4,890.00		
Total Operating Expenses..........			449,950.00	22.3
Income from Operations			$ 138,826.00	6.9
Other Revenue:				
Gain on Plant Assets	$ 225.00			
Interest Income....................	214.00			
Total Other Revenue		$ 439.00		
Other Expenses:				
Cash Short and Over	$ 3.00			
Interest Expense	1,445.00			
Loss on Plant Assets	460.00			
Total Other Expenses..............		1,908.00		
Net Deduction.....................			1,469.00	0.1
Net Income before Fed. Inc. Tax			$ 137,357.00	6.8
Less Federal Income Tax Exp......			36,819.23	1.8
Net Income after Fed. Inc. Tax			$ 100,537.77	5.0

Illustration 27-3   Income statement for a corporation

of Merchandise Sold section of Celluphone's income statement, as shown in Illustration 27-4.

Cost of Merchandise Sold:			
Merchandise Inv., Jan. 1, 19--			$ 205,160.00
Purchases		$1,454,798.00	
Less: Purchases Discount	$10,766.00		
Purch. Ret. and Allow.	5,310.00	16,076.00	
Net Purchases			1,438,722.00

Illustration 27-4
Net purchases reported on
an income statement

3. Income from operations is reported separately from net income. Income from operations is the income earned only from normal business activities. Celluphone's normal business activities are selling cellular phones to corporate customers. Other revenue and expenses, such as interest income, interest expense, and gains or losses on plant assets, are not normal business activities. Other revenue and expenses are not included in figuring income from operations.

4. Net income before and net income after federal income tax are reported separately. Reporting net income before and after federal income tax is unique to corporation income statements. Corporations pay federal income tax on their net income. However, federal income taxes are not paid by proprietorships and partnerships because they are paid by the owners. Thus, proprietorships and partnerships do not report federal income tax on their income statements. Net income is reported in the Net Income section of Celluphone's income statement as shown in Illustration 27-5.

Net Income before Fed. Inc. Tax		$ 137,357.00	6.8
Less Federal Income Tax Exp.		36,819.23	1.8
Net Income after Fed. Inc. Tax		$ 100,537.77	5.0

Illustration 27-5
Federal income tax
reported on an income
statement

Analyzing an income statement. For a business to determine whether it is progressing satisfactorily, results of operations are compared with industry standards and/or previous fiscal periods. To provide meaningful comparisons, the same accounting concepts must be followed for preparing the income statements for each fiscal period. (CONCEPT: Consistent Reporting)

To help management improve future fiscal periods, items contributing to net income should be analyzed. By analyzing items of revenue, cost, and expense, items that should be improved can be identified.

The percentage relationship between one financial statement item and the total that includes that item is known as a component percentage. Celluphone prepares component percentages for six major items on its income statement. Celluphone uses net sales as the base for calculating component percentages. The amount of each item on the income statement is divided by the amount of net sales. Thus, each component percentage shows the percentage that item is of net sales. For example, Celluphone's cost of merchandise sold component percentage is calculated as shown below.

Cost of Merchandise Sold	÷	Net Sales	=	Cost of Merchandise Sold Component Percentage
$1,431,704.00	÷	$2,020,480.00	=	70.9%

This component percentage indicates that during the current fiscal year, Celluphone spent 70.9 cents out of each $1.00 of sales for the merchandise sold. Component percentages for each major item on Celluphone's income statement are listed in a separate column in Illustration 27-2.

When analyzing an income statement, Celluphone first reviews the component percentages for the six major items. (1) Cost of merchandise sold. (2) Gross profit on operations. (3) Total operating expenses. (4) Income from operations. (5) Net addition or deduction from other revenue and expenses. (6) Net income before federal income tax. The last two items on the income statement, federal income tax expense and net income after federal income tax, are important. Celluphone does not have much control over these two items because the tax rate, set by the Internal Revenue Service, determines these amounts. However, the company is interested in what portion of each sales dollar is paid to the federal government for income taxes. Therefore, the component percentage for federal income tax is calculated. Celluphone also calculates the component percentage for net income after federal income tax.

Acceptable component percentages. Based on comparisons with industry standards as well as previous accounting periods, Celluphone has determined acceptable component percentages for each major item of cost and expense on its income statement. For comparative purposes, Celluphone's acceptable and actual component percentages are shown in Illustration 27-6.

Income Statement Items	Acceptable Component Percentages	Actual Component Percentages
Net sales	100.0%	100.0%
Cost of merchandise sold	not more than 71.0%	70.9%
Gross profit on operations	not less than 29.0%	29.1%
Total operating expenses	not more than 22.4%	22.3%
Income from operations	not less than 6.6%	6.9%
Net deduction	not more than 0.1%	0.1%
Net income before federal income tax	not less than 6.5%	6.8%

Illustration 27-6
Income statement acceptable component percentages

If the component percentage of any cost or expense item for a fiscal period exceeds the acceptable percentage, that cost or expense is reviewed further to determine the reason. After determining the reason why a cost or expense exceeded the acceptable percentage, ways are sought to bring the expense within acceptable limits.

Achieving acceptable component percentages for the six major income statement items indicates that the business is keeping costs and expenses at an acceptable level compared with revenue. For the current year ended December 31, Celluphone has achieved acceptable percentages for all six major items. Component percentages for cost of merchandise sold, 70.9%, total operating expenses, 22.3%, and deductions for other revenue and expenses, 0.1%, are all equal to or less than the maximum acceptable level for each item, a positive result. The component percentages for gross profit on operations, 29.1%, income from operations, 6.9%, and net income before federal income tax, 6.8%, are all more than the minimum acceptable percentage for each item, a positive result.

However, if a major item shows a negative result, further analysis should be made of each item to determine and correct any negative results of individual income statement items. For example, in the previous fiscal period, the component percentage for Celluphone's total operating expenses was more than the acceptable level, a negative result. A further review of each expense item showed that component percentages for salary expense and payroll taxes expense were higher than the acceptable percentages, a negative result. Further investigation revealed that Celluphone had employed additional temporary employees during the company's busy season. However, during the year, Celluphone retained these temporary employees two months longer than needed because of a lack of coordination between managers. Since the cause of the excessive salary expense was identified, Celluphone took action to more carefully control these expenses in the future.

Statement of stockholders' equity

A financial statement that shows changes in a corporation's ownership for a fiscal period is called a statement of stockholders' equity. A statement of stockholders' equity is similar to the owners' equity statement for a partnership.

A statement of stockholders' equity contains two major sections. (1) Capital stock. (2) Earnings retained in a corporation. Celluphone's statement of stockholders' equity for the current year ended December 31 is shown in Illustration 27-7.

The first section of Celluphone's statement of stockholders' equity shows that the corporation started the current fiscal year on January 1 with $100,000.00 in capital stock. This capital stock consisted of 1,000 shares of stock issued in previous years at $100.00 per share. During the current fiscal year, no additional capital stock was issued. Thus, at the end of the current fiscal year, Celluphone still has $100,000.00 capital stock issued. This information is obtained from the previous year's statement and the capital stock account.

Celluphone, Inc.			
Statement of Stockholders' Equity			
For Year Ended December 31, 19--			
Capital Stock:			
$100.00 Per Share			
January 1, 19--, 1,000 Shares Issued		$100,000.00	
Issued during Current Year, None		0	
Balance, December 31, 19--, 1,000 Shares Issued			$100,000.00
Retained Earnings:			
Balance, January 1, 19--		$149,118.00	
Net Income after Federal Income Tax for 19--	$100,537.77		
Less Dividends Declared during 19--	80,000.00		
Net Increase during 19--		20,537.77	
Balance, December 31, 19--			169,655.77
Total Stockholders' Equity, December 31, 19--			$269,655.77

The second section of Celluphone's statement of stockholders' equity shows that Celluphone started the current fiscal year on January 1 with $149,118.00 retained earnings. This amount represents previous years' earnings that have been kept in the business and not distributed to stockholders. For the current fiscal year ended December 31, Celluphone earned net income after federal income tax of $100,537.77. This amount is obtained from line 54 of the work sheet, Illustration 27-1.

Illustration 27-7
Statement of stockholders' equity for a corporation

Net income increases a corporation's total capital. Some income may be retained by a corporation for business expansion. Some income may be distributed to stockholders as a return on their investments.

During the year, Celluphone's board of directors declared $80,000.00 in dividends. The amount of dividends declared is obtained from line 27 of the work sheet's Balance Sheet Debit column. Changes in Celluphone's retained earnings during the current fiscal year are calculated as shown below.

Retained earnings balance, January 1, 19-- . . .		$149,118.00
Net income after federal income tax for 19-- . .	$100,537.77	
Less dividends declared during 19--	− 80,000.00	
Net increase during 19--		+ 20,537.77
Retained earings balance, December 31, 19-- . .		$169,655.77

Celluphone's capital stock, $100,000.00, plus retained earnings, $169,655.77, equals total stockholders' equity on December 31, $269,655.77.

Balance sheet

A corporation balance sheet reports assets, liabilities, and stockholders' equity on a specific date. *(CONCEPT: Accounting Period Cycle)*

Celluphone's balance sheet, shown in Illustration 27-8, is prepared from information found in the Balance Sheet columns of the work sheet, Illustration 27-1, and the statement of stockholders' equity, Illustration 27-7.

Illustration 27-8
Balance sheet for a corporation

Celluphone, Inc.
Balance Sheet
December 31, 19--

ASSETS

Current Assets:			
Cash		$ 40,968.00	
Petty Cash		300.00	
Notes Receivable		550.00	
Interest Receivable		11.00	
Accounts Receivable	$68,240.00		
Less Allowance for Uncollectible Accounts	9,492.00	58,748.00	
Merchandise Inventory		212,178.00	
Supplies		3,765.00	
Prepaid Insurance		4,952.00	
Total Current Assets			$321,472.00
Plant Assets:			
Office Equipment	$18,250.00		
Less Accumulated Depreciation—Office Equipment	5,375.00	$ 12,875.00	
Store Equipment	$77,190.00		
Less Accumulated Depreciation—Store Equipment	15,450.00	61,740.00	
Total Plant Assets			74,615.00
Total Assets			$396,087.00

LIABILITIES

Current Liabilities:		
Notes Payable	$ 2,800.00	
Interest Payable	70.00	
Accounts Payable	83,965.75	
Employee Income Tax Payable	2,340.00	
Federal Income Tax Payable	2,219.23	
FICA Tax Payable	2,695.00	
Sales Tax Payable	10,982.00	
Unemployment Tax Payable—Federal	47.00	
Unemployment Tax Payable—State	317.25	
Health Insurance Premiums Payable	995.00	
Dividends Payable	20,000.00	
Total Liabilities		$126,431.23

STOCKHOLDERS' EQUITY

Capital Stock	$100,000.00	
Retained Earnings	169,655.77	
Total Stockholders' Equity		269,655.77
Total Liabilities and Stockholders' Equity		$396,087.00

Classifying assets. Celluphone classifies its assets into two categories. (1) Current assets. (2) Plant assets. These categories are based on the length of time the assets will be in use. A business owning both current assets and plant assets usually lists them under separate headings on a balance sheet.

Cash and other assets expected to be exchanged for cash or consumed within a year are known as current assets. Current assets include such items as cash, accounts receivable, merchandise inventory, supplies, and prepaid insurance. Assets that will be used for a number of years in the operation of a business are known as plant assets. Plant assets include such items as cash registers, computers, and display cases.

Reporting book value of assets. An account that reduces a related account on financial statements is known as a contra account. Celluphone reports three contra accounts on its balance sheet. (1) Allowance for Uncollectible Accounts. (2) Accumulated Depreciation—Office Equipment. (3) Accumulated Depreciation—Store Equipment. The difference between an asset's account balance and its related contra account balance is called book value. Celluphone reports the book value for Accounts Receivable and the two equipment accounts on its balance sheet. An asset's book value is reported on a balance sheet by listing three amounts. (1) The balance of the asset account. (2) The balance of the asset's contra account. (3) Book value. Book value of Celluphone's accounts receivable and plant asset accounts is reported as shown on the partial balance sheet, Illustration 27-9.

Illustration 27-9
Book value of asset accounts reported on a balance sheet

Celluphone, Inc. Balance Sheet December 31, 19--		
ASSETS		
Current Assets:		
Accounts Receivable...	$68,240.00	
Less Allowance for Uncollectible Accounts.................	9,492.00	58,748.00
Plant Assets:		
Office Equipment...	$18,250.00	
Less Accumulated Depreciation—Office Equipment..........	5,375.00	$ 12,875.00
Store Equipment..	$77,190.00	
Less Accumulated Depreciation—Store Equipment	15,450.00	61,740.00
Total Plant Assets		74,615.00

Celluphone uses the following procedure to report the book value of accounts receivable on the balance sheet. The total amount of accounts receivable, *$68,240.00*, is written in the first amount column of the balance sheet. *Less Allowance for Uncollectible Accounts* is written on the next line, indented about one centimeter. The amount, *$9,492.00*, is written below the $68,240.00. The difference between the two amounts, *$58,748.00*, is written in the second amount column on the same line. The amount of the difference, $58,748.00, is the book value of accounts receivable on December 31. Similar procedures are followed to report book values of the plant asset accounts. The total of the two individual book values, *$74,615.00*, is written in the third amount column of the balance sheet.

Classifying liabilities. Liabilities are classified according to the length of time until they are due. Liabilities due within a short time, usually within a year, are known as current liabilities. All of Celluphone's liabilities are listed on the balance sheet in Illustration 27-8 as current liabilities because they come due within a year.

Liabilities owed for more than a year are called long-term liabilities. An example of a long-term liability is Mortgage Payable. On December 31 of the current year, Celluphone does not have any long-term liabilities.

Electro Company has both current liabilities and long-term liabilities. A portion of Electro's balance sheet is shown in Illustration 27-10.

LIABILITIES	
Current Liabilities:	
Notes Payable	$ 12,560.00

Dividends Payable	25,000.00	
Total Current Liabilities		$ 48,369.00
Long-term Liabilities:		
Mortgage Payable		86,000.00
Total Liabilities		$134,369.00

Illustration 27-10
Liabilities section of a balance sheet showing current and long-term liabilities

Reporting a corporation's stockholders' equity. A major difference between corporation balance sheets and proprietorship or partnership balance sheets is the owners' equity section. The owners' equity section of Celluphone's balance sheet, Illustration 27-8, is labeled *Stockholders' Equity*. Some corporations use the same label, Owners' Equity, as proprietorships and partnerships. Either label is acceptable.

The Stockholders' Equity section contains accounts related to capital stock and earnings kept in the business. For Celluphone, these accounts are Capital Stock and Retained Earnings. Total stockholders' equity on Celluphone's balance sheet, Illustration 27-8, is $269,655.77, the same as on Celluphone's statement of stockholders' equity, Illustration 27-7.

Analyzing a balance sheet. To continue operating successfully, a business must have adequate financial resources. A business must be able to buy additional merchandise, pay employee salaries, and pay for other operating expenses. Financial strength analysis measures the ability of a business to pay its debts. The balance sheet is the primary source of data to determine the financial strength of a business.

Celluphone analyzes its financial strength to assist the company in planning for future periods and to insure that adequate resources are available to operate the business. Creditors and investors also use financial strength analysis to determine if the company is a good credit and investment risk. Before a creditor sells merchandise to a company on account, the creditor must believe that the company will later pay for the merchandise. A company that is considered to be a poor credit risk is usually a bad investment for an investor.

Celluphone uses two analyses to evaluate financial strength. (1) Working capital. (2) Current ratio.

Current assets less current liabilities is the amount of financial resources a company has available to conduct its daily operations. Current assets include cash, notes receivable, interest receivable, accounts receivable, merchandise inventory, supplies, and prepaid insurance. Current liabilities include notes payable, interest payable, accounts payable, taxes payable, health insurance premiums payable, and dividends payable. For a company to operate efficiently, an adequate supply of resources must be available after current liabilities are paid.

The amount of total current assets less total current liabilities is called working capital. Working capital is the amount of current assets available for use in the business after current liabilities are paid. The amount is stated in dollars. Celluphone's working capital for December 31 of the current year is calculated as shown below.

Total Current Assets		Total Current Liabilities		Working Capital
$321,472.00	−	$126,431.23	=	$195,040.77

Working capital should not be confused with cash. Celluphone does not have $195,040.77 of excess cash. However, Celluphone does have $195,040.77 of assets that will be converted to cash and will be available for use in daily operations during the next fiscal year.

Working capital is a measure of the amount of financial resources available for the daily operations of the business. Although working capital is a useful measure, working capital does not permit a business to compare itself to its industry or to provide a convenient relative measurement from year to year.

A more useful measure results from comparing the amount of total current assets to total current liabilities. A comparison between two numbers showing how many times one number exceeds the other is called a ratio. A ratio that shows the numeric relationship of current assets to current liabilities is called the current ratio. The current ratio is a measure of a company's ability to pay its current liabilities. Creditors use the ratio to determine if merchandise should be sold to a company on account.

Based on the balance sheet information, Celluphone's current ratio is calculated as shown below.

Total Current Assets	÷	Total Current Liabilities	=	Current Ratio
$321,472.00	÷	$126,431.23	=	2.5 to 1

Celluphone's current ratio is stated as 2.5 to 1, which means that total current assets are 2.5 times total current liabilities.

Based on previous experience and industry guidelines, Celluphone has established a minimum acceptable current ratio of 2.0 to 1. On December 31 of the current year, Celluphone's current ratio, 2.5 to 1, exceeds the minimum acceptable ratio. This year's current ratio indicates a favorable condition of financial strength.

SUMMARY OF FINANCIAL STATEMENTS FOR A CORPORATION

The chart shown in Illustration 27-11 summarizes the financial statements for a corporation.

ADJUSTING, CLOSING, AND REVERSING ENTRIES FOR A CORPORATION

The end-of-fiscal-period work of corporations is similar to the work of proprietorships and partnerships except for differences in the equity accounts. After corporate financial statements are prepared, adjusting and closing entries are journalized and posted. A post-closing trial balance is then prepared. Finally, reversing entries are journalized and posted.

Adjusting entries

A corporation's adjusting entries are made from the Adjustments columns of a work sheet. Each adjustment is journalized and posted to

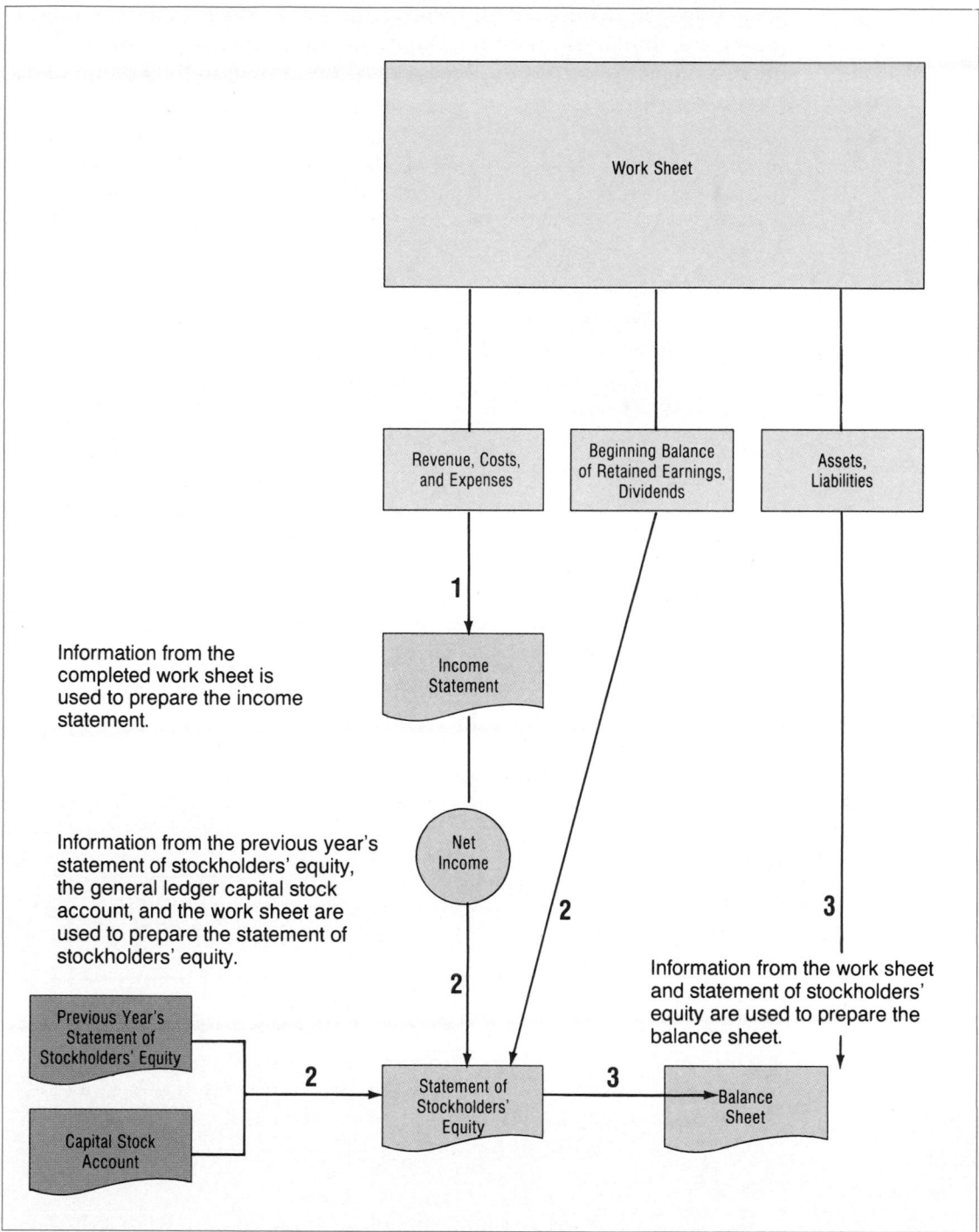

Illustration 27-11   Summary of financial statements for a corporation

general ledger accounts. With the exception of federal income tax, adjustments are similar to those for proprietorships and partnerships. Celluphone's adjusting entries for December 31 are shown in Illustration 27-12.

	DATE		ACCOUNT TITLE	DOC. NO.	POST. REF.	DEBIT	CREDIT	
1			*Adjusting Entries*					1
2	*Dec.*	*31*	*Interest Receivable*			1 1 00		2
3			*Interest Income*				1 1 00	3
4		*31*	*Uncollectible Accounts Expense*			9 2 2 7 00		4
5			*Allowance for Uncoll. Accts.*				9 2 2 7 00	5
6		*31*	*Merchandise Inventory*			7 0 1 8 00		6
7			*Income Summary*				7 0 1 8 00	7
8		*31*	*Supplies Expense*			11 6 9 0 00		8
9			*Supplies*				11 6 9 0 00	9
10		*31*	*Insurance Expense*			8 5 9 8 00		10
11			*Prepaid Insurance*				8 5 9 8 00	11
12		*31*	*Depreciation Exp.—Office Equip.*			1 7 5 0 00		12
13			*Accum. Depr.—Office Equip.*				1 7 5 0 00	13
14		*31*	*Depreciation Exp.—Store Equip.*			6 3 2 5 00		14
15			*Accum. Depr.—Store Equip.*				6 3 2 5 00	15
16		*31*	*Interest Expense*			7 0 00		16
17			*Interest Payable*				7 0 00	17
18		*31*	*Federal Income Tax Expense*			2 2 1 9 23		18
19			*Federal Income Tax Payable*				2 2 1 9 23	19
20								20
21								21
22								22
23								23
24								24
25								25
26								26
27								27
28								28
29								29
30								30

GENERAL JOURNAL   PAGE 15

Illustration 27-12
Adjusting entries for a
corporation

Procedures for journalizing Celluphone's adjusting entries are similar to those previously described for other businesses.

Closing entries

Closing entries for a corporation are made from information in a work sheet. Closing entries for revenue and expense accounts are similar to those for proprietorships or partnerships. A corporation's last two closing entries are similar to those previously studied but affect different accounts. A corporation records the following four closing entries.

1. Closing entry for income statement accounts with credit balances (revenue and contra cost accounts).
2. Closing entry for income statement accounts with debit balances (cost, contra revenue, and expense accounts).
3. Closing entry to record net income or net loss in the retained earnings account and close the income summary account.
4. Closing entry for the dividends account.

Closing entry for income statement accounts with credit balances. The closing entry for Celluphone's income statement credit balance accounts on December 31 is shown in Illustration 27-13, page 670. Income statement credit balance accounts are revenue (Sales, Gain on Plant Assets, and Interest Income) and the contra cost accounts (Purchases Discount and Purchases Returns and Allowances). Information needed for closing income statement credit balance accounts is obtained from the work sheet's Income Statement Credit column as shown in Illustration 27-13.

Celluphone begins its closing entries on a new page of the general journal. Thus, all the closing entries are together on one page.

Closing entry for income statement accounts with debit balances. The closing entry for Celluphone's income statement debit balance accounts on December 31 is shown in Illustration 27-14, page 671. Income statement debit balance accounts are the contra revenue accounts (Sales Discount and Sales Returns and Allowances) and the cost (Purchases) and expense accounts. Information needed for closing income statement debit balance accounts is obtained from the work sheet's Income Statement Debit column, as shown in Illustration 27-14.

If Cash Short and Over has a credit balance, the account balance amount is closed to Income Summary with the credit balance accounts.

After closing entries for the income statement debit balance accounts are posted, Income Summary has a credit balance of $100,537.77. This credit balance is the amount of net income. This amount is the same as on line 54 of Celluphone's work sheet.

	Celluphone, Inc.			
	Work Sheet			
	For Year Ended December 31, 19--			
			5	6
	ACCOUNT TITLE		INCOME STATEMENT	
			DEBIT	CREDIT
28	Income Summary			7 0 1 8 00
29	Sales			2050 4 4 0 00
30	Sales Discount		5 6 4 2 00	
31	Sales Returns and Allowances		24 3 1 8 00	
32	Purchases		1454 7 9 8 00	
33	Purchases Discount			10 7 6 6 00
34	Purchases Returns and Allowances			5 3 1 0 00
35	Advertising Expense		32 6 0 0 00	
36	Credit Card Fee Expense		20 4 6 8 00	
37	Depr. Expense—Office Equipment		1 7 5 0 00	
38	Depr. Expense—Store Equipment		6 3 2 5 00	
39	Insurance Expense		8 5 9 8 00	
40	Miscellaneous Expense		22 3 5 0 00	
41	Payroll Taxes Expense		23 7 2 0 00	
42	Rent Expense		56 4 0 0 00	
43	Salary Expense		251 9 3 2 00	
44	Supplies Expense		11 6 9 0 00	
45	Uncollectible Accounts Expense		9 2 2 7 00	
46	Utilities Expense		4 8 9 0 00	
47	Gain on Plant Assets			2 2 5 00
48	Interest Income			2 1 4 00
49	Cash Short and Over		3 00	
50	Interest Expense		1 4 4 5 00	
51	Loss on Plant Assets		4 6 0 00	
52	Federal Income Tax Expense		36 8 1 9 23	
53			1973 4 3 5 23	2073 9 7 3 00
54	Net Income after Fed. Inc. Tax		100 5 3 7 77	
55			2073 9 7 3 00	2073 9 7 3 00
56				
57				

			GENERAL JOURNAL		PAGE 16		
	DATE	ACCOUNT TITLE	DOC. NO.	POST. REF.	DEBIT	CREDIT	
1		Closing Entries					1
2	Dec. 31	Sales			2050 4 4 0 00		2
3		Purchases Discount			10 7 6 6 00		3
4		Purchases Returns and Allowances			5 3 1 0 00		4
5		Gain on Plant Assets			2 2 5 00		5
6		Interest Income			2 1 4 00		6
7		Income Summary				2066 9 5 5 00	7
8							8

Illustration 27-13
Closing entry for a
corporation's income
statement accounts with
credit balances

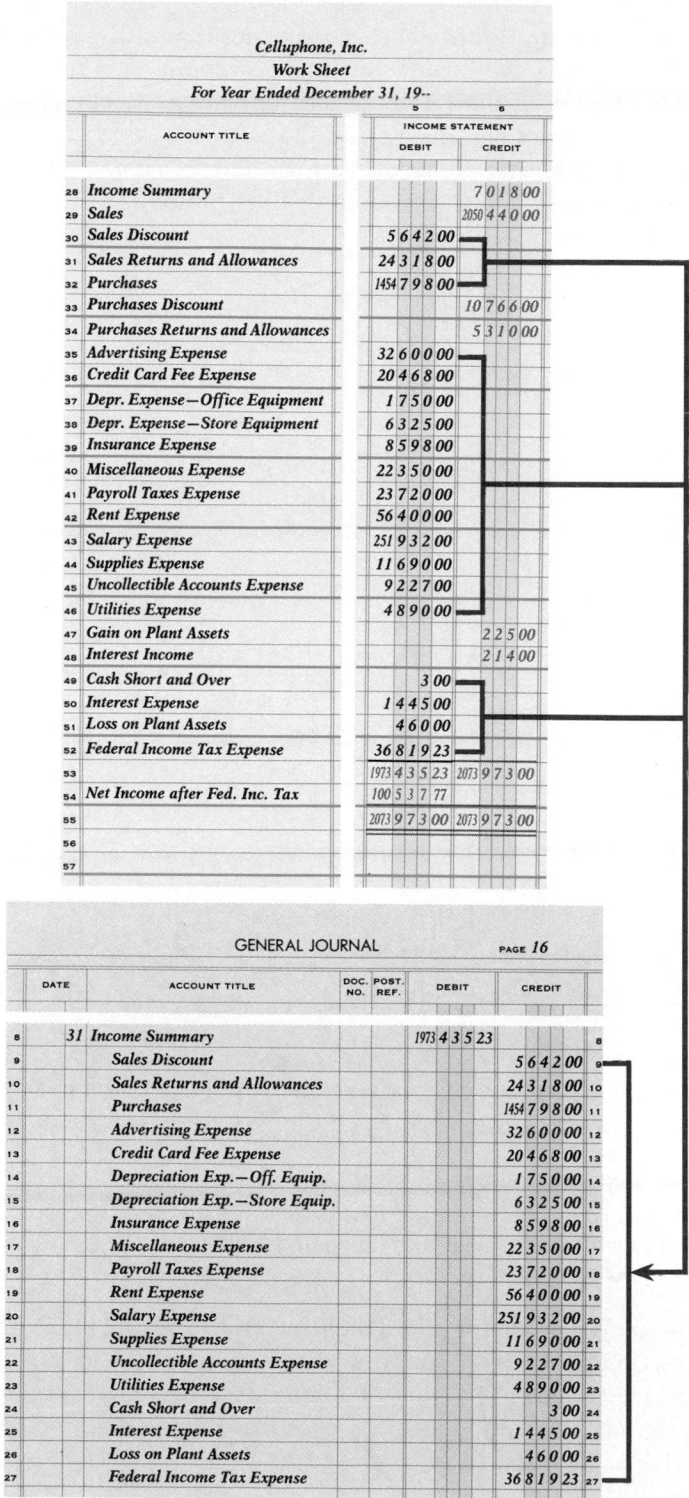

Illustration 27-14
Closing entry for a corporation's income statement accounts with debit balances

Closing entry to record net income or net loss in the retained earnings account and close the income summary account. A corporation's net income is recorded in the retained earnings account. The closing entry to record Celluphone's net income and close Income Summary is shown in Illustration 27-15. Information needed for this entry is obtained from line 54 of Celluphone's work sheet, as shown in Illustration 27-15.

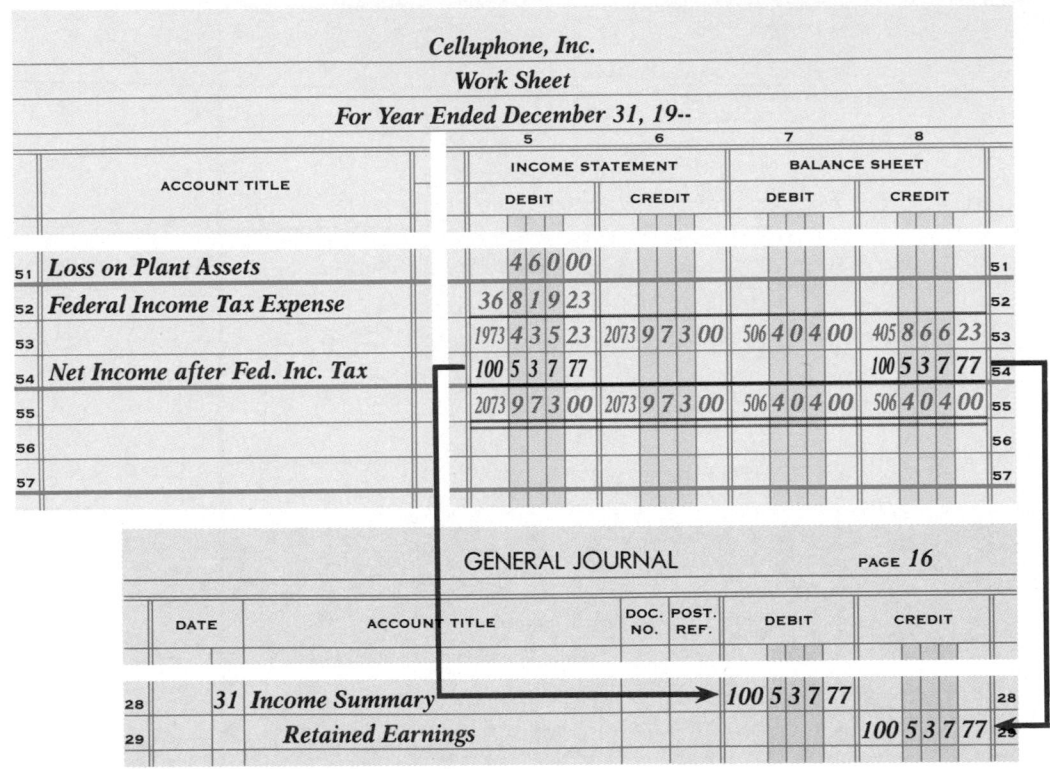

Illustration 27-15
Closing entry to record a corporation's net income in the retained earnings account and close the income summary account

After the entry to record net income is posted, Income Summary has a zero balance. The net income, $100,537.77, has been recorded as a credit to Retained Earnings.

If a corporation has a net loss, Income Summary has a debit balance. Retained Earnings would then be debited and Income Summary credited for the net loss amount.

Closing entry for the dividends account. The closing entry for Celluphone's dividends account is shown in Illustration 27-16. The debit balance of a dividends account is the total amount of dividends declared during a fiscal period. Since dividends decrease the earnings retained by a corporation, the dividends account is closed to Retained Earnings.

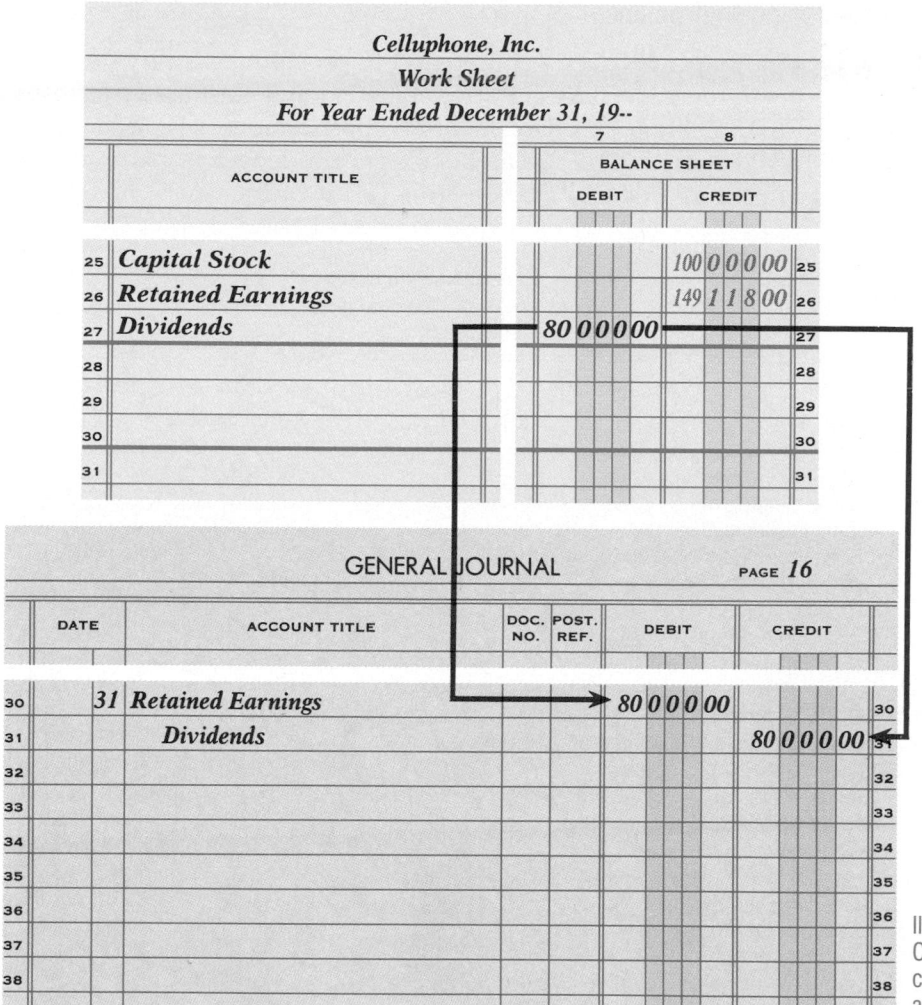

Illustration 27-16
Closing entry for a corporation's dividends account

Information needed for closing Celluphone's dividends account is obtained from line 27 of the work sheet's Balance Sheet Debit column, as shown in Illustration 27-16.

After the closing entry for the dividends account is posted, Dividends has a zero balance. The amount of the dividends, $80,000.00, has been recorded as a debit to Retained Earnings.

After adjusting and closing entries are journalized and posted, balance sheet accounts all have up-to-date balances. Asset, liability, and stockholders' equity account balances agree with amounts on the balance sheet, Illustration 27-8. Revenue, cost, expense, and dividends accounts all begin the new fiscal period with zero balances.

Post-closing trial balance

A post-closing trial balance is prepared to prove the equality of debits and credits in the general ledger after adjusting and closing entries have been posted. Celluphone's December 31 post-closing trial balance is shown in Illustration 27-17. Celluphone's general ledger is ready for the next fiscal period. *(CONCEPT: Accounting Period Cycle)*

Celluphone, Inc.
Post-Closing Trial Balance
December 31, 19--

Account Title	Debit	Credit
Cash	$ 40,968.00	
Petty Cash	300.00	
Notes Receivable	550.00	
Interest Receivable	11.00	
Accounts Receivable	68,240.00	
Allowance for Uncollectible Accounts		$ 9,492.00
Merchandise Inventory	212,178.00	
Supplies	3,765.00	
Prepaid Insurance	4,952.00	
Office Equipment	18,250.00	
Accumulated Depreciation—Office Equipment		5,375.00
Store Equipment	77,190.00	
Accumulated Depreciation—Store Equipment		15,450.00
Notes Payable		2,800.00
Interest Payable		70.00
Accounts Payable		83,965.75
Employee Income Tax Payable		2,340.00
Federal Income Tax Payable		2,219.23
FICA Tax Payable		2,695.00
Sales Tax Payable		10,982.00
Unemployment Tax Payable—Federal		47.00
Unemployment Tax Payable—State		317.25
Health Insurance Premiums Payable		995.00
Dividends Payable		20,000.00
Capital Stock		100,000.00
Retained Earnings		169,655.77
Totals	$426,404.00	$426,404.00

Illustration 27-17
Post-closing trial balance
for a corporation

Reversing entries

If an adjusting entry creates a balance in an asset or liability account, Celluphone reverses the adjusting entry. A review of Celluphone's adjusting entries shows that the adjusting entry for accrued interest income created a balance in the interest receivable account. The adjusting entry for accrued interest expense created a balance in the interest payable account. Therefore, reversing entries are recorded for these two adjusting entries, as shown in Illustration 27-18.

GENERAL JOURNAL

PAGE *17*

	DATE		ACCOUNT TITLE	DOC. NO.	POST. REF.	DEBIT	CREDIT	
1			*Reversing Entries*					1
2	*19..* *Jan.*	*1*	*Interest Income*			*1 1 00*		2
3			*Interest Receivable*				*1 1 00*	3
4		*1*	*Interest Payable*			*7 0 00*		4
5			*Interest Expense*				*7 0 00*	5
6								6
7								7
8								8
9								9
10								10
11								11
12								12
13								13
14								14

Illustration 27-18
Reversing entries for
accrual adjusting entries

Celluphone's adjusting entry for income tax expense does create a balance in the federal income tax payable account. During the new year, cash will be paid for accrued income tax expense for the previous year plus periodic payments for the current year's income tax expense. To avoid confusing the amount of tax expense recorded for each of these years and to provide year-to-date income tax expense information for each year, Celluphone does not reverse this adjusting entry. For similar reasons many corporations do not reverse accrued income tax adjusting entries.

SUMMARY OF END-OF-FISCAL-PERIOD ENTRIES FOR A CORPORATION

The chart shown in Illustration 27-19, page 676, summarizes the end-of-fiscal-period entries for a corporation.

◼ ACCOUNTING TERMS

What is the meaning of each of the following?

1. net sales
2. net purchases
3. statement of stockholders' equity
4. book value
5. long-term liabilities
6. working capital
7. ratio
8. current ratio

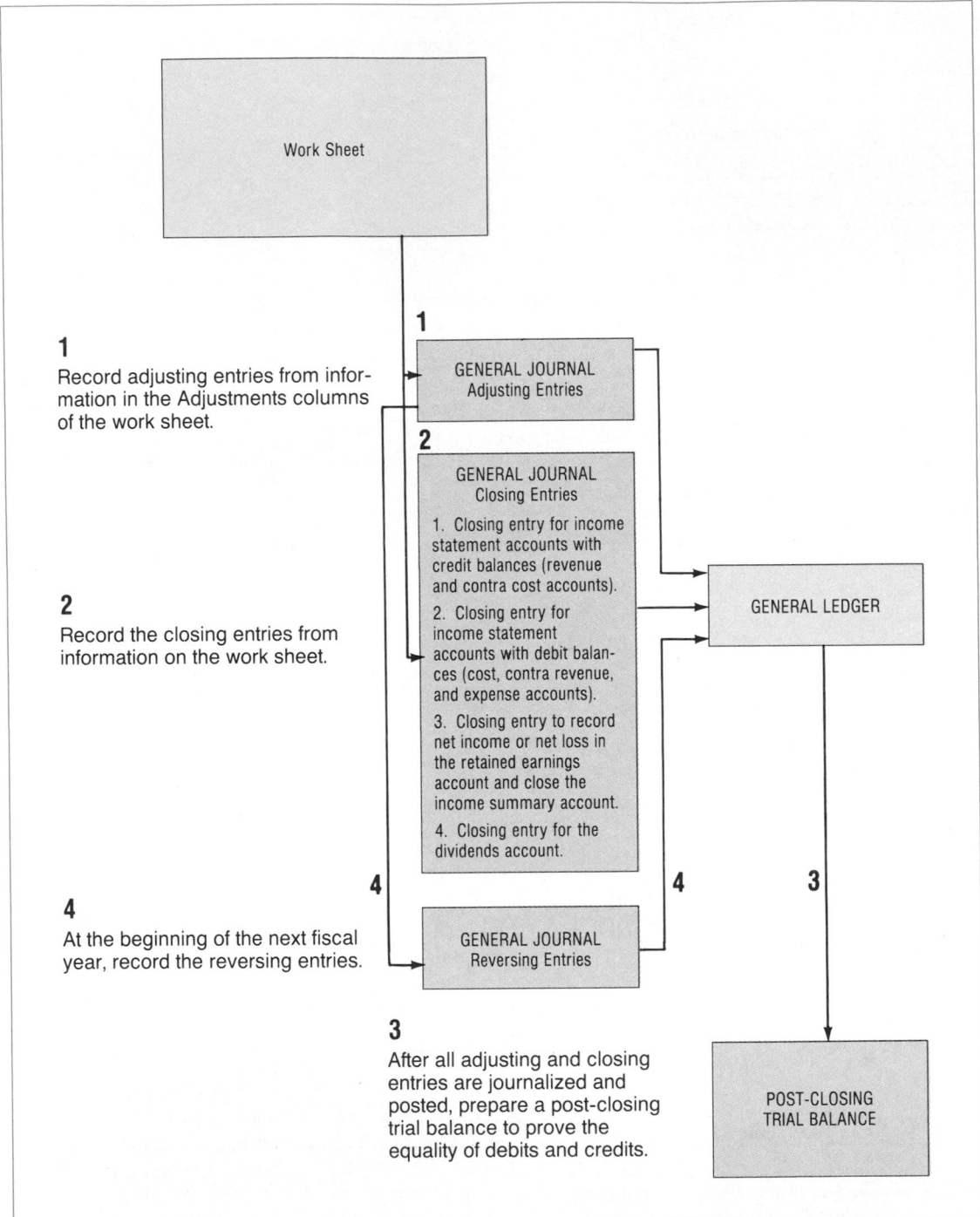

1

Record adjusting entries from information in the Adjustments columns of the work sheet.

2

Record the closing entries from information on the work sheet.

4

At the beginning of the next fiscal year, record the reversing entries.

3

After all adjusting and closing entries are journalized and posted, prepare a post-closing trial balance to prove the equality of debits and credits.

Illustration 27-19   Summary of end-of-fiscal-period entries for a corporation

■ QUESTIONS FOR INDIVIDUAL STUDY

1. Which accounting concept is being applied when a corporation prepares financial statements annually and sometimes monthly or quarterly?
2. In what two ways does a corporation report changes in owners' equity differently from a proprietorship or partnership?
3. What financial information does an income statement report?
4. Where is the information found to prepare a corporation income statement?
5. What is the difference between sales and net sales reported on an income statement?
6. Why are other revenue and other expenses reported separately on the income statement from sales, cost of merchandise sold, and operating expenses?
7. How may the information on an income statement be used to determine whether the business is progressing satisfactorily?
8. Which accounting concept is being applied when the same accounting concepts are used for preparing income statements for each fiscal period?
9. What information is shown by component percentages on an income statement?
10. What financial information does a statement of stockholders' equity report?
11. Where is the information found to prepare a statement of stockholders' equity?
12. What financial information does a corporation balance sheet report?
13. Where is the information found to prepare a balance sheet?
14. What three amounts are reported on a balance sheet to show book value of a plant asset?
15. What determines whether a liability on a balance sheet is classified as current or long term?
16. For what purposes is the financial strength of a business analyzed?
17. What is working capital?
18. What kind of balances do income statement accounts have immediately after adjusting and closing entries are journalized and posted?
19. Why is a post-closing trial balance prepared?

■ CASES FOR MANAGEMENT DECISION

CASE 1 The president of Kalikow Company asked the accounting department to provide as much information as possible to help management improve the company's net income. Paul Jayroe, a senior accountant, suggests that an income statement showing all the revenue and expense amounts should provide all the information management needs to analyze the company's results of operations. Do you agree with the accountant's suggestion? If not, what additional information do you recommend? Explain your answer.

CASE 2 Riverside Company recently organized as a corporation with five stockholders. Tamara Connell, the bookkeeper, is developing the accounting system. She suggested that although there are five stockholders, only one equity account be used. The account would be titled Corporation Capital. The president of Riverside questions the bookkeeper's recommendation. Is the bookkeeper's recommendation acceptable? If not, how should capital be recorded and reported? Explain your answer.

■ DRILLS FOR UNDERSTANDING

DRILL 27-D1 Classifying a corporation's revenue, cost, and expense accounts

Use a form similar to the following.

Account No.	Operating Revenue	Contra Account of Operating Revenue	Cost of Merchandise	Contra Account of Cost of Merchandise	Operating Expense	Other Revenue	Other Expenses
1.					✓		

Instructions: For each of the following accounts, place a check mark in the column that correctly classifies the account. Account No. 1 is given as an example.

Accounts
1. Advertising Expense
2. Sales
3. Interest Income
4. Salary Expense
5. Sales Returns and Allowances
6. Purchases
7. Depreciation Expense
8. Purchases Discount
9. Interest Expense
10. Sales Discount
11. Uncollectible Accounts Expense
12. Purchases Returns and Allowances
13. Gain on Plant Assets
14. Utilities Expense
15. Cash Short and Over (cash short)

DRILL 27-D2 Classifying a corporation's assets, liabilities, and stockholders' equity accounts

Use a form similar to the following.

Account No.	Current Asset	Contra Acct. of a Current Asset	Plant Asset	Contra Acct. of a Plant Asset	Current Liability	Long-Term Liability	Stockholders' Equity
1.	✓						

Instructions: For each of the following accounts, place a check mark in the column that correctly classifies the account. Account No. 1 is given as an example.

Accounts
1. Cash
2. Accumulated Depreciation—Office Equipment
3. Federal Income Tax Payable

4. Prepaid Insurance
5. Notes Payable
6. Interest Receivable
7. Accounts Payable
8. Notes Receivable
9. Office Equipment
10. Interest Payable
11. Capital Stock
12. Mortgage Payable
13. Employee Income Tax Payable
14. Dividends Payable
15. Retained Earnings
16. Petty Cash
17. Accumulated Depreciation—Store Equipment
18. FICA Tax Payable
19. Merchandise Inventory
20. Allowance for Uncollectible Accounts

 APPLICATION PROBLEMS

PROBLEM 27-1   **Preparing financial statements for a corporation**

AmTech Company completed the work sheet shown on pages 680–681 for the current year ended December 31.

Instructions: 1. Prepare an income statement. Calculate and record the following component percentages. (a) Cost of merchandise sold. (b) Gross profit on operations. (c) Total operating expenses. (d) Income from operations. (e) Net addition or deduction resulting from other revenue and expenses. (f) Net income before federal income tax. Round percentage calculations to the nearest 0.1%.

2. Analyze AmTech's income statement by determining if component percentages are within acceptable levels. If any component percentage is not within an acceptable level, suggest steps that the company should take. AmTech considers the following component percentages acceptable.

Cost of merchandise sold...............................	Not more than 73.0%
Gross profit on operations	Not less than 27.0%
Total operating expenses	Not more than 24.9%
Income from operations	Not less than 2.1%
Net deduction from other revenue and expenses	Not more than 0.1%
Net income before federal income tax...................	Not less than 2.0%

3. Prepare a statement of stockholders' equity. Use the following additional information.

January 1 balance of capital stock account.........................	$100,000.00
(1,000 shares issued for $100.00 per share)	
January 1 balance of retained earnings account.....................	68,085.20

4. Prepare a balance sheet.
5. Calculate AmTech's (a) working capital and (b) current ratio. Determine if these items are within acceptable levels. AmTech considers the following levels acceptable.

Working capital................................	Not less than $100,000.00
Current ratio...................................	Between 2.2 to 1 and 2.8 to 1

AmTech Company

Work Sheet

For Year Ended December 31, 19--

| | TRIAL BALANCE | | ADJUSTMENTS | | INCOME STATEMENT | | BALANCE SHEET | |
ACCOUNT TITLE	DEBIT	CREDIT	DEBIT	CREDIT	DEBIT	CREDIT	DEBIT	CREDIT
1 Cash	85 399 00						85 399 00	
2 Petty Cash	250 00						250 00	
3 Notes Receivable	3 500 00						3 500 00	
4 Interest Receivable			(a) 1 31 00				1 31 00	
5 Accounts Receivable	55 618 00						55 618 00	
6 Allow. for Uncollectible Accts.		3 78 00		(b) 5 064 00				5 442 00
7 Merchandise Inventory	40 537 00		(c) 2 954 60				43 491 60	
8 Supplies	7 726 40			(d) 5 667 20			2 059 20	
9 Prepaid Insurance	14 652 00			(e) 9 768 00			4 884 00	
10 Office Equipment	12 821 60						12 821 60	
11 Accum. Depr.—Office Equipment		2 574 00		(f) 1 496 00				4 070 00
12 Store Equipment	77 880 00						77 880 00	
13 Accum. Depr.—Store Equipment		14 949 00		(g) 16 834 40				31 783 40
14 Notes Payable		1 650 00						1 650 00
15 Interest Payable				(h) 62 70				62 70
16 Accounts Payable		56 953 50						56 953 50
17 Employee Income Tax Payable		1 535 00						1 535 00
18 Federal Income Tax Payable				(i) 4 15 51				4 15 51
19 FICA Tax Payable		8 06 00						8 06 00
20 Sales Tax Payable		6 256 00						6 256 00
21 Unemploy. Tax Payable—Federal		38 00						38 00
22 Unemploy. Tax Payable—State		2 56 50						2 56 50
23 Health Insur. Premiums Payable		5 26 00						5 26 00
24 Dividends Payable		6 000 00						6 000 00
25 Capital Stock		100 000 00						100 000 00

#	Account Title	Trial Balance Debit	Trial Balance Credit	Adjustments Debit	Adjustments Credit	Income Statement Debit	Income Statement Credit	Balance Sheet Debit	Balance Sheet Credit
26	Retained Earnings		68 0 8 5 20						68 0 8 5 20
27	Dividends	24 0 0 0 00						24 0 0 0 00	
28	Income Summary				(c) 2 9 5 4 60		2 9 5 4 60		
29	Sales		1443 9 6 1 20				1443 9 6 1 20		
30	Sales Discount	4 4 3 1 90				4 4 3 1 90			
31	Sales Returns and Allowances	17 5 1 7 00				17 5 1 7 00			
32	Purchases	1056 2 9 0 00				1056 2 9 0 00			
33	Purchases Discount		7 8 2 4 30				7 8 2 4 30		
34	Purchases Returns and Allowances		3 8 5 0 00				3 8 5 0 00		
35	Advertising Expense	23 3 5 5 20				23 3 5 5 20			
36	Credit Card Fee Expense	13 0 3 5 00				13 0 3 5 00			
37	Depr. Expense—Office Equipment			(f) 1 4 9 6 00		1 4 9 6 00			
38	Depr. Expense—Store Equipment			(g) 16 8 3 4 40		16 8 3 4 40			
39	Insurance Expense			(e) 9 7 6 8 00		9 7 6 8 00			
40	Miscellaneous Expense	27 7 3 5 40				27 7 3 5 40			
41	Payroll Taxes Expense	16 2 9 2 10				16 2 9 2 10			
42	Rent Expense	46 2 0 0 00				46 2 0 0 00			
43	Salary Expense	181 0 3 1 00				181 0 3 1 00			
44	Supplies Expense			(d) 5 6 6 7 20		5 6 6 7 20			
45	Uncollectible Accounts Expense			(b) 5 0 6 4 00		5 0 6 4 00			
46	Utilities Expense	3 4 6 5 00				3 4 6 5 00			
47	Gain on Plant Assets		2 6 4 00				2 6 4 00		
48	Interest Income		3 9 4 00		(a) 1 3 1 00		5 2 5 00		
49	Cash Short and Over	8 80				8 80			
50	Interest Expense	1 8 4 80		(h) 6 2 70		2 4 7 50			
51	Loss on Plant Assets	1 7 0 50				1 7 0 50			
52	Federal Income Tax Expense	4 2 0 0 00		(i) 4 1 5 51		4 6 1 5 51			
53		1716 3 0 0 70	1716 3 0 0 70	42 3 9 3 41	42 3 9 3 41	1433 2 2 4 51	1459 3 7 9 10	283 8 7 9 81	310 0 3 4 40
54	Net Income after Fed. Inc. Tax					26 1 5 4 59			26 1 5 4 59
55						1459 3 7 9 10	1459 3 7 9 10	310 0 3 4 40	310 0 3 4 40
56									
57									

PROBLEM 27-2   Journalizing adjusting, closing, and reversing entries for a corporation

Use the completed work sheet shown in Problem 27-1 to complete Problem 27-2.

Instructions: 1. Use page 18 of a general journal. Journalize the adjusting entries.

2. Use page 19 of a general journal. Journalize the closing entries.

3. Use page 20 of a general journal. Journalize the reversing entries for the accrued interest income and accrued interest expense.

■ ENRICHMENT PROBLEMS

MASTERY PROBLEM 27-M   Preparing financial statements and end-of-fiscal-period entries for a corporation

Accent, Inc., completed the work sheet shown on pages 684–685 for the current year ended December 31.

Instructions: 1. Prepare an income statement. Calculate and record the following component percentages. (a) Cost of merchandise sold. (b) Gross profit on operations. (c) Total operating expenses. (d) Income from operations. (e) Net addition or deduction resulting from other revenue and expenses. (f) Net income before federal income tax. Round percentage calculations to the nearest 0.1%.

2. Analyze Accent's income statement by determining if component percentages are within acceptable levels. If any component percentage is not within an acceptable level, suggest steps that the company should take. Accent considers the following component percentages acceptable.

Cost of merchandise sold.............................	Not more than 72.0%
Gross profit on operations	Not less than 28.0%
Total operating expenses	Not more than 22.0%
Income from operations	Not less than 6.0%
Net deduction from other revenue and expenses	Not more than 0.1%
Net income before federal income tax...................	Not less than 5.9%

3. Prepare a statement of stockholders' equity. Use the following additional information.

January 1 balance of capital stock account.........................	$150,000.00
(15,000 shares issued for $10.00 per share)	
January 1 balance of retained earnings account.....................	42,387.20

4. Prepare a balance sheet.

5. Calculate Accent's (a) working capital and (b) current ratio. Determine if these items are within acceptable levels. Accent considers the following levels acceptable.

Working capital................................	Not less than $125,000.00
Current ratio.................................	Between 2.0 to 1 and 2.6 to 1

6. Use page 20 of a general journal. Journalize the adjusting entries.

7. Use page 21 of a general journal. Journalize the closing entries.

8. Use page 22 of a general journal. Journalize the reversing entries for the accrued interest income and accrued interest expense.

CHALLENGE PROBLEM 27-C   Preparing financial statements and end-of-fiscal-period entries for a corporation

Glass Design Corporation's general ledger accounts and balances are recorded on a 10-column work sheet in the working papers.

Instructions: 1. Complete a 10-column work sheet for the current year ended December 31. Record the adjustments on the work sheet using the following information.

Adjustment Information, December 31

Accrued interest income	$ 250.00
Uncollectible accounts expense estimated as 1.2% of sales on account.	
Sales on account for year, $561,375.00.	
Merchandise inventory	85,059.56
Supplies inventory	295.12
Value of prepaid insurance	2,720.80
Annual depreciation expense—office equipment	2,421.00
Annual depreciation expense—store equipment	1,446.84
Accrued interest expense	490.64

Federal income tax for the year is figured at the following rates:
  15% of net income before taxes, zero to $50,000.00.
  Plus 25% of net income before taxes, $50,000.00 to $75,000.00.
  Plus 34% of net income before taxes, $75,000.00 to $100,000.00.
  Plus 39% of net income before taxes, $100,000.00 to $335,000.00.
  Plus 34% of net income before taxes over $335,000.00.

2. Prepare an income statement. Calculate and record the following component percentages. (a) Cost of merchandise sold. (b) Gross profit on operations. (c) Total operating expenses. (d) Income from operations. (e) Net addition or deduction resulting from other revenue and expenses. (f) Net income before federal income tax. Round percentage calculations to the nearest 0.1%.

3. Analyze Glass Design's income statement by determining if component percentages are within acceptable levels. If any component percentage is not within an acceptable level, suggest steps that the company should take. Glass Design considers the following component percentages acceptable.

Cost of merchandise sold	Not more than 70.0%
Gross profit on operations	Not less than 30.0%
Total operating expenses	Not more than 24.0%
Income from operations	Not less than 6.0%
Net deduction from other revenue and expenses	Not more than 0.1%
Net income before federal income tax	Not less than 5.9%

4. Prepare a statement of stockholders' equity. Use the following additional information.

January 1 balance of capital stock account	$100,000.00
(10,000 shares issued for $10.00 per share)	
January 1 balance of retained earnings account	33,028.87

5. Prepare a balance sheet.
6. Calculate Glass Design's (a) working capital and (b) current ratio. Determine if these items are within acceptable levels. Glass Design considers the following levels acceptable.

Working capital	Not less than $125,000.00
Current ratio	Between 2.0 to 1 and 2.5 to 1

 7. Use page 13 of a general journal. Journalize the adjusting entries.
8. Use page 14 of a general journal. Journalize the closing entries.
9. Use page 15 of a general journal. Journalize the reversing entries for the accrued interest income and accrued interest expense.

Accent, Inc.

Work Sheet

For Year Ended December 31, 19--

	TRIAL BALANCE		ADJUSTMENTS		INCOME STATEMENT		BALANCE SHEET	
ACCOUNT TITLE	DEBIT	CREDIT	DEBIT	CREDIT	DEBIT	CREDIT	DEBIT	CREDIT
	1	2	3	4	5	6	7	8
1 Cash	52 283 00						52 283 00	
2 Petty Cash	3 00 00						3 00 00	
3 Notes Receivable	4 4 00 00						4 4 00 00	
4 Interest Receivable			(a) 1 29 80				1 29 80	
5 Accounts Receivable	59 0 96 40						59 0 96 40	
6 Allow. for Uncollectible Accts.		3 86 10		(b) 4 4 85 80				4 8 71 90
7 Merchandise Inventory	105 5 64 10		(c) 12 7 83 10				118 3 47 20	
8 Supplies	8 2 32 40			(d) 6 4 81 09			1 7 51 31	
9 Prepaid Insurance	15 5 92 50			(e) 9 0 95 90			6 4 96 60	
10 Office Equipment	13 6 21 30						13 6 21 30	
11 Accum. Depr.—Office Equipment		2 7 34 60		(f) 1 5 24 60				4 2 59 20
12 Store Equipment	82 7 46 40						82 7 46 40	
13 Accum. Depr.—Store Equipment		15 8 82 90		(g) 10 7 78 00				26 6 62 90
14 Notes Payable		2 7 43 40						2 7 43 40
15 Interest Payable				(h) 1 03 40				1 03 40
16 Accounts Payable		68 2 65 00						68 2 65 00
17 Employee Income Tax Payable		1 6 29 10						1 6 29 10
18 Federal Income Tax Payable				(i) 1 5 05 60				1 5 05 60
19 FICA Tax Payable		1 9 77 80						1 9 77 80
20 Sales Tax Payable		6 6 47 30						6 6 47 30
21 Unemploy. Tax Payable—Federal		3 4 00						3 4 00
22 Unemploy. Tax Payable—State		2 29 50						2 29 50
23 Health Insur. Premiums Payable		5 56 60						5 56 60
24 Dividends Payable		12 0 00 00						12 0 00 00
25 Capital Stock		150 0 00 00						150 0 00 00

Account Title	Trial Balance Debit	Trial Balance Credit	Adjustments Debit	Adjustments Credit	Income Statement Debit	Income Statement Credit	Balance Sheet Debit	Balance Sheet Credit
Retained Earnings		42,387.20						42,387.20
Dividends	48,000.00						48,000.00	
Income Summary				(c)12,783.10		12,783.10		
Sales		1,506,985.70				1,506,985.70		
Sales Discount	7,593.30				7,593.30			
Sales Returns and Allowances	17,867.30				17,867.30			
Purchases	1,077,414.80				1,077,414.80			
Purchases Discount		5,890.50				5,890.50		
Purchases Returns and Allowances		3,927.00				3,927.00		
Advertising Expense	20,742.70				20,742.70			
Credit Card Fee Expense	13,555.30				13,555.30			
Depr. Expense—Office Equipment			(f)1,524.60		1,524.60			
Depr. Expense—Store Equipment			(g)10,780.00		10,780.00			
Insurance Expense			(e)9,095.90		9,095.90			
Miscellaneous Expense	28,289.80				28,289.80			
Payroll Taxes Expense	17,355.80				17,355.80			
Rent Expense	48,000.00				48,000.00			
Salary Expense	184,650.40				184,650.40			
Supplies Expense			(a)6,481.09		6,481.09			
Uncollectible Accounts Expense			(b)4,485.80		4,485.80			
Utilities Expense	3,619.00				3,619.00			
Gain on Plant Assets		225.00				225.00		
Interest Income		390.50		(d)129.80		520.30		
Cash Short and Over	12.10				12.10			
Interest Expense	309.10		(h)103.40		412.50			
Loss on Plant Assets	346.50				346.50			
Federal Income Tax Expense	13,300.00		(c)1,505.60		14,805.60			
	1,822,892.20	1,822,892.20	46,889.29	46,889.29	1,467,032.49	1,530,331.60	387,172.01	323,872.90
Net Income after Fed. Inc. Tax					63,299.11			63,299.11
					1,530,331.60	1,530,331.60	387,172.01	387,172.01

Reinforcement Activity 3, Part B

An Accounting Cycle for a Corporation: End-of-Fiscal-Period Work

The general ledger used in Reinforcement Activity 3, Part A, is needed to complete Reinforcement Activity 3, Part B.

Reinforcement Activity 3, Part B, includes those accounting activities needed to complete an accounting cycle for a corporation. In Part A Hardware Mart's transactions were recorded for the last month of a fiscal year. In Part B end-of-fiscal-period work is completed.

END-OF-FISCAL-PERIOD WORK

Instructions: 12. Prepare a work sheet for the fiscal year ended December 31 of the current year. Use the following adjustment information.

Adjustment Information, December 31

Accrued interest income	$ 84.00
Uncollectible accounts expense is estimated as 1.5% of sales on account. Sales on account for the year, $120,800.00.	
Merchandise inventory	65,661.20
Supplies inventory	242.50
Value of prepaid insurance	2,160.00
Annual depreciation expense—office equipment	2,130.00
Annual depreciation expense—store equipment	3,410.00
Accrued interest expense	500.00
Federal income tax for the year	14,579.41

13. Prepare an income statement. Calculate and record the following component percentages as a percent of net sales: (a) cost of merchandise sold, (b) gross profit on operations, (c) total operating expenses, (d) income from operations, and (e) net additions/deductions from other revenue and expenses, and (f) net income before federal income tax. Round percentage calculations to the nearest 0.1%.

14. Analyze Hardware Mart's income statement by determining if component percentages are within acceptable levels. If any component percentage is not within an acceptable level, suggest steps that the company should take. Hardware Mart considers the following percentages acceptable.

Cost of merchandise sold	Not more than 66.0%
Gross profit on operations	Not less than 34.0%
Total operating expenses	Not more than 25.0%
Income from operations	Not less than 9.0%
Net deductions from other revenue and expenses	Not more than 0.5%
Net income before federal income tax	Not less than 8.5%

15. Prepare a statement of stockholders' equity. Use the following additional information.

January 1 balance of capital stock account........................... $40,000.00
    (4,000 shares issued for $10.00 per share)
January 1 balance of retained earnings account...................... 34,894.40

16. Prepare a balance sheet.

17. Calculate Hardware Mart's (a) working capital and (b) current ratio. Determine if these items are within acceptable levels. Hardware Mart considers the following amounts acceptable.

Working capital	Not less than $50,000.00
Current ratio	Between 2.0 to 1 and 2.5 to 1

18. Journalize the adjusting entries on page 13 of a general journal. Post the adjusting entries.

19. Journalize the closing entries on page 14 of a general journal. Post the closing entries.

20. Prepare a post-closing trial balance.

21. Journalize the reversing entries on page 15 of a general journal for the accrued interest income and accrued interest expense adjusting entries. Post the reversing entries.

Computer Application 6
Automated Accounting Cycle for a
Corporation: End-of-Fiscal-Period Work

Celluphone's manual accounting procedures for completing a corporation's end-of-fiscal-period work are described in Chapter 27. Computer Application 6 describes procedures for using a microcomputer to complete Celluphone's end-of-fiscal-period work. Computer Application Problem 6 contains instructions for using a microcomputer to solve Challenge Problem 27-C, Chapter 27.

PLANNING ADJUSTMENTS

A trial balance is prepared by the computer to check the equality of debits and credits in the general ledger. Celluphone's trial balance is shown in Illustration C6-1.

The trial balance also serves as the basis for planning adjusting entries. Adjusting entries are journalized on a general ledger input form (FORM GL-2). Celluphone has the following adjustment data on December 31.

Accrued interest income	$ 11.00
Uncollectible accounts expense	9,227.00
Merchandise inventory	212,178.00
Supplies inventory	3,765.00
Value of prepaid insurance	4,952.00
Annual depreciation expense—office equipment	1,750.00
Annual depreciation expense—store equipment	6,325.00
Accrued interest expense	70.00
Federal income tax expense for the year	36,819.23

After all adjusting entries have been journalized on the input form, the Debit Amount and Credit Amount columns are totaled. The totals are en-

```
RUN DATE: 12/31/--                    CELLUPHONE, INC.
                                       TRIAL BALANCE


------------------------------------------------------------------------
ACCOUNT    ACCOUNT
NUMBER     TITLE                        DEBIT AMOUNT        CREDIT AMOUNT
------------------------------------------------------------------------
1105       Cash                           40968.00
1110       Petty Cash                       300.00
1115       Notes Receivable                 550.00
1125       Accounts Receivable            68240.00
1130       Allow. For Uncoll. Accts.                            265.00
1135       Merchandise Inventory         205160.00
1140       Supplies                       15455.00
1145       Prepaid Insurance              13550.00
1205       Office Equipment               18250.00
1210       Acc. Depr.--Office Equip.                           3625.00
1215       Store Equipment                77190.00
1220       Acc. Depr.--Store Equip.                            9125.00
2105       Notes Payable                                       2800.00
2115       Accounts Payable                                   83965.75
2120       Empl. Inc. Tax Payable                              2340.00
2130       FICA Tax Payable                                    2695.00
2135       Sales Tax Payable                                  10982.00
2140       Unempl. Tax Pay.--Federal                             47.00
2145       Unempl. Tax Pay.--State                              317.25
2150       Health Ins. Prem. Payable                            995.00
2155       Dividends Payable                                  20000.00
3105       Capital Stock                                     100000.00
3110       Retained Earnings                                 149118.00
3115       Dividends                      80000.00
4105       Sales                                            2050440.00
4110       Sales Discount                  5642.00
4115       Sales Ret. and Allowances      24318.00
5105       Purchases                    1454798.00
5110       Purchases Discount                                 10766.00
5115       Pur. Ret. and Allowances                            5310.00
6105       Advertising Expense            32600.00
6110       Credit Card Fee Expense        20468.00
6130       Miscellaneous Expense          22350.00
6135       Payroll Taxes Expense          23720.00
6140       Rent Expense                   56400.00
6145       Salary Expense                251932.00
6160       Utilities Expense               4890.00
7105       Gain on Plant Assets                                 225.00
7110       Interest Income                                      203.00
8105       Cash Short and Over                3.00
8110       Interest Expense                1375.00
8115       Loss on Plant Assets             460.00
9105       Federal Inc. Tax Expense       34600.00
                                        --------------      --------------
           TOTALS                        2453219.00          2453219.00
                                        ==============      ==============
```

Illustration C6-1
Trial balance prepared by computer

tered on the Batch Totals line provided at the bottom of the input form. The two totals are compared to assure that debits and credits are equal. As the two totals are the same, $46,908.23, the adjusting entries journalized on the general ledger input form are assumed to be correct. Celluphone's completed general ledger input form for the adjusting entries is shown in Illustration C6-2.

	DAY	DOC. NO.	ACCOUNT NUMBER	DEBIT AMOUNT	CREDIT AMOUNT	
	1	2	3	4	5	
1	31	Adj.Ent.	1120	11 00		1
2			7110		11 00	2
3	31	Adj.Ent.	6155	9227 00		3
4			1130		9227 00	4
5	31	Adj.Ent.	1135	7018 00		5
6			3120		7018 00	6
7	31	Adj.Ent.	6150	11690 00		7
8			1140		11690 00	8
9	31	Adj.Ent.	6125	8598 00		9
10			1145		8598 00	10
11	31	Adj.Ent.	6115	1750 00		11
12			1210		1750 00	12
13	31	Adj.Ent.	6120	6325 00		13
14			1220		6325 00	14
15	31	Adj.Ent.	8110	70 00		15
16			2110		70 00	16
17	31	Adj.Ent.	9105	2219 23		17
18			2125		2219 23	18
25						25

RUN DATE 12/31/--   MM DD YY

BATCH NO. 4

GENERAL LEDGER
Input Form

FORM GL-2

BATCH TOTALS   46908 23   46908 23

Illustration C6-2
General ledger input form with adjusting entries entered

Processing adjusting entries

After all lines on the input form have been key-entered into the computer and posted, a journal entries report is prepared. Celluphone's journal entries report is shown in Illustration C6-3.

PREPARING END-OF-FISCAL-PERIOD REPORTS

After the journal entries report for adjusting entries has been prepared, an income statement is prepared. Celluphone's income statement is shown in Illustration C6-4, page 692.

```
RUN DATE: 12/31/--                    CELLUPHONE, INC.
                                 JOURNAL ENTRIES BATCH# 4

-----------------------------------------------------------------------------
JE#   DATE      ACCOUNT NUMBER & TITLE            DEBIT AMOUNT   CREDIT AMOUNT
-----------------------------------------------------------------------------
0031  12/31/--  1120   Interest Receivable            11.00
                7110      Interest Income                             11.00
                       DOCUMENT: Adj.Ent.

0032  12/31/--  6155   Uncoll. Accounts Expense     9227.00
                1130      Allow. For Uncoll. Accts.                 9227.00
                       DOCUMENT: Adj.Ent.

0033  12/31/--  1135   Merchandise Inventory        7018.00
                3120      Income Summary                            7018.00
                       DOCUMENT: Adj.Ent.

0034  12/31/--  6150   Supplies Expense            11690.00
                1140      Supplies                                 11690.00
                       DOCUMENT: Adj.Ent.

0035  12/31/--  6125   Insurance Expense            8598.00
                1145      Prepaid Insurance                         8598.00
                       DOCUMENT: Adj.Ent.

0036  12/31/--  6115   Depr. Exp.--Office Equip.    1750.00
                1210      Acc. Depr.--Office Equip.                 1750.00
                       DOCUMENT: Adj.Ent.

0037  12/31/--  6120   Depr. Exp.--Store Equip.     6325.00
                1220      Acc. Depr.--Store Equip.                  6325.00
                       DOCUMENT: Adj.Ent.

0038  12/31/--  8110   Interest Expense               70.00
                2110      Interest Payable                            70.00
                       DOCUMENT: Adj.Ent.

0039  12/31/--  9105   Federal Inc. Tax Expense     2219.23
                2125      Fed. Income Tax Payable                   2219.23
                       DOCUMENT: Adj.Ent.


                                                  ---------------  ---------------
                TOTALS                                46908.23        46908.23
                                                  ===============  ===============
                IN BALANCE
```

Illustration C6-3
Journal entries report for adjusting entries

In Celluphone's manual accounting system, a statement of stockholders' equity is prepared to show changes in stockholders' equity during the fiscal period. In Celluphone's automated accounting system, changes in stockholders' equity are shown on the balance sheet. Celluphone's balance sheet is shown in Illustration C6-5, page 693.

After the balance sheet has been prepared, the computer is directed to post closing entries to general ledger accounts.

After the closing entries have been posted, a post-closing trial balance is prepared. Celluphone's post-closing trial balance is shown in Illustration C6-6, page 694.

```
                          CELLUPHONE, INC.
                          INCOME STATEMENT
                       FOR PERIOD ENDED 12/31/--
                                                              % OF NET
 O P E R A T I N G    R E V E N U E                            REVENUE
 ---------------------------------                            --------
 Sales                             2050440.00                   101.48
 Sales Discount                      -5642.00                     -.28
 Sales Ret. and Allowances          -24318.00                    -1.20
                                  ------------
 NET OPERATING REVENUE                            2020480.00     100.00

 C O S T    O F    M D S E .    S O L D
 --------------------------------------
 BEGINNING INVENTORY                205160.00                     10.15
 Purchases                         1454798.00                     72.00
 Purchases Discount                 -10766.00                      -.53
 Pur. Ret. and Allowances            -5310.00                      -.26
                                  ------------
 MDSE. AVAILABLE FOR SALE          1643882.00                     81.36
 LESS ENDING INVENTORY              212178.00                     10.50
                                  ------------
 COST OF MDSE. SOLD                               1431704.00      70.86
                                                 ------------
 GROSS PROFIT ON OPERATIONS                        588776.00      29.14

 O P E R A T I N G    E X P E N S E S
 -----------------------------------
 Advertising Expense                 32600.00                      1.61
 Credit Card Fee Expense             20468.00                      1.01
 Depr. Exp.--Office Equip.            1750.00                       .09
 Depr. Exp.--Store Equip.             6325.00                       .31
 Insurance Expense                    8598.00                       .43
 Miscellaneous Expense               22350.00                      1.11
 Payroll Taxes Expense               23720.00                      1.17
 Rent Expense                        56400.00                      2.79
 Salary Expense                     251932.00                     12.47
 Supplies Expense                    11690.00                       .58
 Uncoll. Accounts Expense             9227.00                       .46
 Utilities Expense                    4890.00                       .24
                                  ------------
 TOTAL OPERATING EXPENSES                          449950.00      22.27
                                                 ------------
 NET INCOME FROM OPERATIONS                        138826.00       6.87

 O T H E R    R E V E N U E
 --------------------------
 Gain on Plant Assets                  225.00                       .01
 Interest Income                       214.00                       .01

 O T H E R    E X P E N S E S
 ----------------------------
 Cash Short and Over                     3.00                       .00
 Interest Expense                     1445.00                       .07
 Loss on Plant Assets                  460.00                       .02
                                  ------------
 NET DEDUCTION                                       1469.00        .07
                                                 ------------
 NET INCOME BEFORE INCOME TAX                      137357.00       6.80

 I N C O M E    T A X
 --------------------
 Federal Inc. Tax Expense            36819.23                      1.82
                                  ------------
 NET INCOME AFTER INCOME TAX                       100537.77       4.98
                                                 ==============
```

Illustration C6-4   Income statement prepared by computer

```
                        CELLUPHONE, INC.
                         BALANCE SHEET
                           12/31/--

       A S S E T S
       -----------
       Cash                           40968.00
       Petty Cash                       300.00
       Notes Receivable                 550.00
       Interest Receivable               11.00
       Accounts Receivable            68240.00
       Allow. For Uncoll. Accts.      -9492.00
       Merchandise Inventory         212178.00
       Supplies                        3765.00
       Prepaid Insurance               4952.00
       Office Equipment               18250.00
       Acc. Depr.--Office Equip.      -5375.00
       Store Equipment                77190.00
       Acc. Depr.--Store Equip.      -15450.00
                                    ----------------
       TOTAL ASSETS                               396087.00
                                                ================

       L I A B I L I T I E S
       ---------------------
       Notes Payable                   2800.00
       Interest Payable                  70.00
       Accounts Payable               83965.75
       Empl. Inc. Tax Payable          2340.00
       Fed. Income Tax Payable         2219.23
       FICA Tax Payable                2695.00
       Sales Tax Payable              10982.00
       Unempl. Tax Pay.--Federal         47.00
       Unempl. Tax Pay.--State          317.25
       Health Ins. Prem. Payable        995.00
       Dividends Payable              20000.00
                                    ----------------
       TOTAL LIABILITIES                          126431.23

       S T O C K H O L D E R S '   E Q U I T Y
       ----------------------------------------------
       Capital Stock                 100000.00
       Retained Earnings             149118.00
       Dividends                     -80000.00
       NET INCOME                    100537.77
                                    ----------------
       TOTAL STOCKHOLDERS' EQUITY                 269655.77
                                                ----------------
       TOTAL LIABILITIES & EQUITY                 396087.00
                                                ================


       NET WORKING CAPITAL:      195040.77
       CURRENT RATIO:            2.54 TO 1
```

Illustration C6-5
Balance sheet prepared by computer

RECORDING REVERSING ENTRIES

Celluphone records two reversing entries after the post-closing trial balance is prepared. (1) An entry to reverse the adjusting entry for accrued interest income. (2) An entry to reverse the adjusting entry for accrued interest expense. The reversing entries are recorded on a general ledger in-

```
RUN DATE: 12/31/--                          CELLUPHONE, INC.
                                      POST-CLOSING TRIAL BALANCE

-----------------------------------------------------------------------------
ACCOUNT        ACCOUNT
NUMBER         TITLE                         DEBIT AMOUNT        CREDIT AMOUNT
-----------------------------------------------------------------------------
1105           Cash                            40968.00
1110           Petty Cash                        300.00
1115           Notes Receivable                  550.00
1120           Interest Receivable                11.00
1125           Accounts Receivable             68240.00
1130           Allow. For Uncoll. Accts.                             9492.00
1135           Merchandise Inventory          212178.00
1140           Supplies                          3765.00
1145           Prepaid Insurance                 4952.00
1205           Office Equipment                18250.00
1210           Acc. Depr.--Office Equip.                             5375.00
1215           Store Equipment                 77190.00
1220           Acc. Depr.--Store Equip.                             15450.00
2105           Notes Payable                                         2800.00
2110           Interest Payable                                        70.00
2115           Accounts Payable                                     83965.75
2120           Empl. Inc. Tax Payable                                2340.00
2125           Fed. Income Tax Payable                               2219.23
2130           FICA Tax Payable                                      2695.00
2135           Sales Tax Payable                                    10982.00
2140           Unempl. Tax Pay.--Federal                               47.00
2145           Unempl. Tax Pay.--State                                317.25
2150           Health Ins. Prem. Payable                              995.00
2155           Dividends Payable                                    20000.00
3105           Capital Stock                                       100000.00
3110           Retained Earnings                                   169655.77
                                             ---------------     ---------------
               TOTALS                           426404.00           426404.00
                                             ===============     ===============
```

Illustration C6-6
Post-closing trial balance
prepared by computer

put form (FORM GL-2). Celluphone's reversing entries are shown on the general ledger input form in Illustration C6-7.

RUN DATE 01 01 -- MM DD YY BATCH NO. 5	GENERAL LEDGER Input Form			FORM GL-2
	1	2	3	4	5

	DAY	DOC. NO.	ACCOUNT NUMBER	DEBIT AMOUNT	CREDIT AMOUNT	
1	01	Rev.Ent.	7110	11 00		1
2			1120		11 00	2
3	01	Rev.Ent.	2110	70 00		3
4			8110		70 00	4
25						25
			BATCH TOTALS	81 00	81 00	

Illustration C6-7
General ledger input form
with reversing entries
entered

After all lines on the input form have been key-entered into the computer and posted, a journal entries report is prepared. Celluphone's journal entries report is shown in Illustration C6-8.

Illustration C6-8
Journal entries report for reversing entries

```
  RUN DATE: 01/01/--                    CELLUPHONE, INC.
                                     JOURNAL ENTRIES BATCH# 5
  --------------------------------------------------------------------------------
  JE#   DATE       ACCOUNT NUMBER & TITLE           DEBIT AMOUNT   CREDIT AMOUNT
  --------------------------------------------------------------------------------
  0001  01/01/-- 7110    Interest Income                 11.00
                  1120       Interest Receivable                        11.00
                  DOCUMENT: Rev.Ent.

  0002  01/01/-- 2110    Interest Payable                70.00
                  8110       Interest Expense                           70.00
                  DOCUMENT: Rev.Ent.

                                                    --------------  --------------
                  TOTALS                                  81.00          81.00
                                                    ==============  ==============
                  IN BALANCE
```

▓ COMPUTER APPLICATION PROBLEM

COMPUTER APPLICATION PROBLEM 6   End-of-fiscal-period work

Instructions: 1. Load the *Automated Accounting for the Microcomputer* software. Select Computer Application 6 (CA-6) from the CENTURY 21 ACCOUNTING Template Disk. The general ledger chart of accounts and current balances have been entered and stored on the Template Disk.

2. Display/Print a trial balance.

3. Refer to the adjustment information given in Challenge Problem 27-C, Chapter 27. Journalize the adjusting entries on a general ledger input form. Net income before federal income tax for the year is $87,030.57. Use December 31 of the current year as the run date. Batch No. 4. Use the following account numbers and titles.

Acct. No.	Account Title
1120	Interest Receivable
1130	Allowance for Uncollectible Accounts
1135	Merchandise Inventory
1140	Supplies
1145	Prepaid Insurance
1210	Accumulated Depreciation—Office Equipment
1220	Accumulated Depreciation—Store Equipment
2110	Interest Payable
2125	Federal Income Tax Payable
3120	Income Summary
6115	Depreciation Expense—Office Equipment
6120	Depreciation Expense—Store Equipment
6125	Insurance Expense

6150	Supplies Expense
6155	Uncollectible Accounts Expense
7110	Interest Income
8110	Interest Expense
9105	Federal Income Tax Expense

4. Key-enter the adjusting entries from the completed general ledger input form.

5. Display/Print the journal entries report.

6. Display/Print the income statement.

7. Display/Print the balance sheet.

8. Close the general ledger.

9. Display/Print the post-closing trial balance.

10. Journalize the reversing entries on a general ledger input form. Use January 1 of the year following the current year as the run date. Batch No. 5.

11. Key-enter the reversing entries from the completed general ledger input form.

12. Display/Print the journal entries report.

WESTERN RIDER, INC.
A BUSINESS SIMULATION

Western Rider, Inc., is a merchandising business organized as a corporation. This business simulation covers the realistic transactions completed by Western Rider, Inc., which sells clothing, tack, and other items to those who own and show horses or who simply ride horses for pleasure. Transactions are recorded in special journals and a general journal similar to the ones used by Celluphone, Inc., in Part 4. The following activities are included in the accounting cycle for Western Rider, Inc. This business simulation is available from the publisher in either manual or automated versions.

Activities in Western Rider, Inc.

1. Recording transactions in special journals from source documents.
2. Posting items to be posted individually to a general ledger and subsidiary ledger.
3. Posting column totals to a general ledger.
4. Preparing schedules of accounts receivable and accounts payable from subsidiary ledgers.
5. Preparing a trial balance on a work sheet.
6. Planning adjustments and completing a work sheet.
7. Preparing financial statements.
8. Journalizing and posting adjusting entries.
9. Journalizing and posting closing entries.
10. Preparing a post-closing trial balance.
11. Journalizing and posting reversing entries.

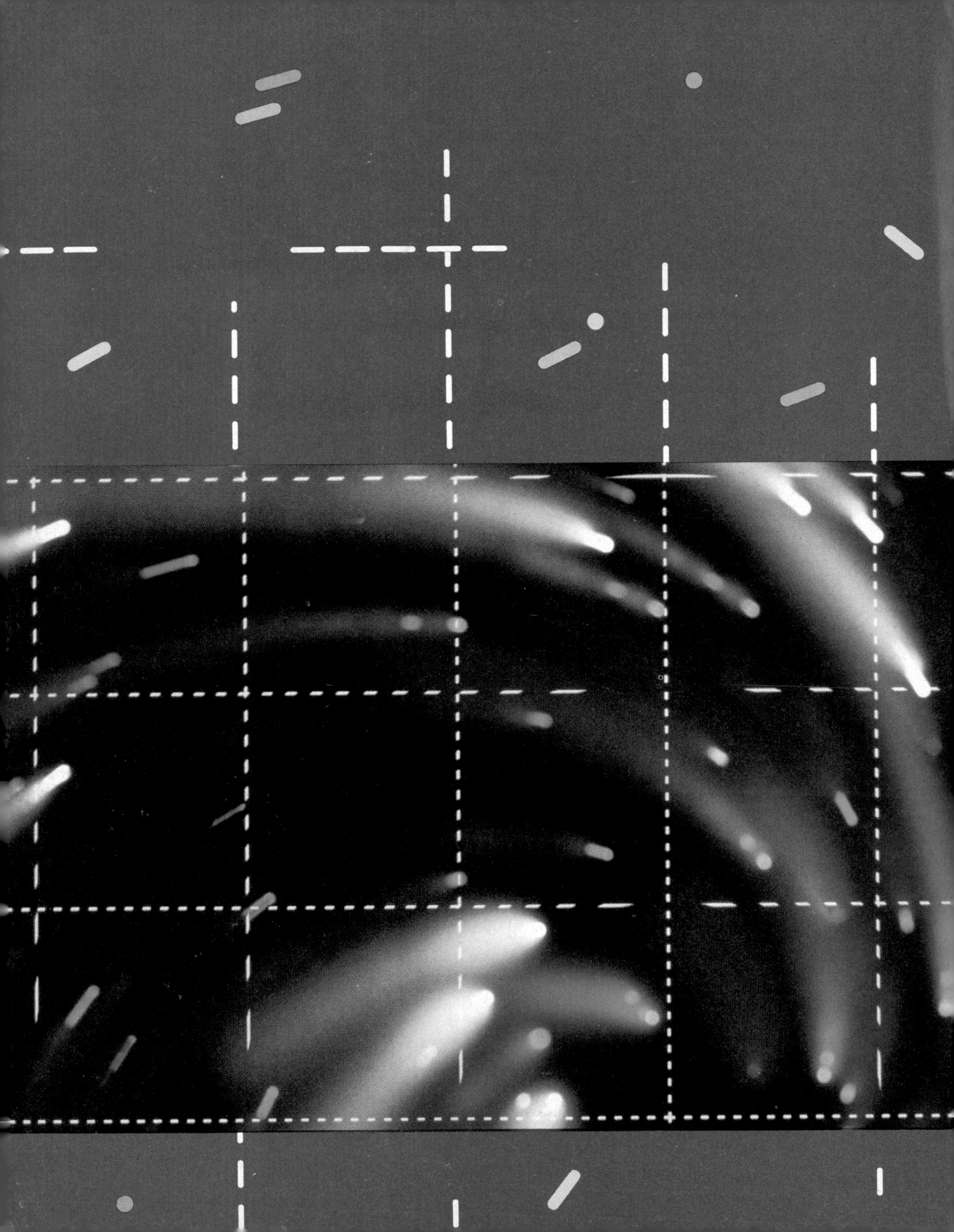

Accounting Control Systems

5

GENERAL BEHAVIORAL GOALS

1. Know accounting terminology related to selected accounting control systems.
2. Understand accounting concepts and practices related to selected accounting control systems.
3. Demonstrate accounting procedures for selected accounting control systems.

MUSICO, INC.
Chart of Accounts

Balance Sheet Accounts

(1000) ASSETS

1100 Current Assets

1105 Cash
1110 Petty Cash
1115 Notes Receivable
1120 Interest Receivable
1125 Accounts Receivable
1130 Allowance for Uncollectible Accounts
1135 Merchandise Inventory
1140 Supplies
1145 Prepaid Insurance

1200 Plant Assets

1205 Delivery Equipment
1210 Accumulated Depreciation—Delivery Equipment
1215 Office Equipment
1220 Accumulated Depreciation—Office Equipment
1225 Store Equipment
1230 Accumulated Depreciation—Store Equipment

(2000) LIABILITIES

2100 Current Liabilities

2105 Notes Payable
2110 Interest Payable
2115 Vouchers Payable
2120 Employee Income Tax Pay.—Federal
2125 Employee Income Tax Pay.—State
2130 FICA Tax Payable
2135 Income Tax Payable—Federal
2140 Income Tax Payable—State
2145 Sales Tax Payable
2150 Unemployment Tax Payable—Federal
2155 Unemployment Tax Payable—State
2160 Dividends Payable

(3000) STOCKHOLDERS' EQUITY

3105 Capital Stock
3110 Retained Earnings
3115 Dividends
3120 Income Summary

Income Statement Accounts

(4000) OPERATING REVENUE

4105 Sales
4110 Sales Discount
4115 Sales Returns and Allowances

(5000) COST OF MERCHANDISE

5105 Purchases
5110 Purchases Discount
5115 Purchases Returns and Allowances

(6000) OPERATING EXPENSES

6105 Advertising Expense
6110 Credit Card Fee Expense
6115 Delivery Expense
6120 Depreciation Expense—Delivery Equipment
6125 Depreciation Expense—Office Equipment
6130 Depreciation Expense—Store Equipment
6135 Insurance Expense
6140 Miscellaneous Expense
6145 Payroll Taxes Expense
6150 Rent Expense
6155 Salary Expense
6160 Supplies Expense
6165 Uncollectible Accounts Expense
6170 Utilities Expense

(7000) OTHER REVENUE

7105 Gain on Plant Assets
7110 Interest Income

(8000) OTHER EXPENSES

8105 Cash Short and Over
8110 Interest Expense
8115 Loss on Plant Assets

(9000) INCOME TAX EXPENSE

9105 Income Tax Expense—Federal
9110 Income Tax Expense—State

The chart of accounts for MusiCo, Inc., is illustrated above for ready reference as you study Part 5 of this textbook.

A Voucher System

ENABLING PERFORMANCE TASKS

After studying Chapter 28, you will be able to:
a. Define accounting terms related to a voucher system.
b. Identify accounting concepts and practices related to a voucher system.
c. Prepare a voucher.
d. Journalize data from vouchers in a voucher register.
e. Journalize voucher payment transactions in a check register.
f. Journalize purchases returns and allowances and payroll transactions in a voucher system.

An accounting system includes procedures for the recording and reporting of accurate and up-to-date financial information useful to management. In addition, an accounting system should include procedures to assist management in controlling daily operations. Of particular concern to management are procedures and records to control and protect assets. One asset that should be controlled and protected is cash. Cash is the asset most likely to be misused because ownership is easily transferred. Also, transactions generally affect the cash account more often than other general ledger accounts. Many businesses, therefore, use specific cash control procedures.

Cash control procedures include storing cash in a safe place, making bank deposits regularly, and approving all cash payments. Cash payments are approved before being paid to ensure that the goods or services were ordered, have been received, and the amounts due are correct. In small businesses the owner or manager usually approves cash payments. In large businesses several persons may have authority to approve cash payments. A business form used to show an authorized person's approval for a cash payment is called a voucher. A set of procedures for controlling cash payments by preparing and approving vouchers before payments are made is called a voucher system. In a voucher system *NO* check can be issued without a properly authorized voucher.

Any business paper used to authorize an accounting entry may be referred to as a voucher. However, when a voucher system is used, *voucher* refers only to the cash payments approval form.

A VOUCHER

A voucher is prepared for each invoice received from a vendor. An invoice is checked for accuracy before a voucher is prepared.

August 1, 19--.
Purchased merchandise on account from Kemp Instrument Company, $3,500.00. Voucher No. 647.

```
            Purchases
      ──────────────────────────
          3,500.00  │

          Vouchers Payable
      ──────────────────────────
                    │   3,500.00
```

The source document for this transaction is Voucher No. 647. *(CONCEPT: Objective Evidence)* The analysis of this transaction is shown in the T accounts.

In a voucher system, the general ledger liability account, Vouchers Payable, is used instead of Accounts Payable. Accounts Payable has been used to record only amounts of items bought on account. In a voucher system, Vouchers Payable is used to record *ALL* amounts to be paid by check. Since Vouchers Payable is a liability account, the normal balance of Vouchers Payable is on the credit side of the account. Also, an accounts payable ledger is not kept. Instead, vouchers needing to be paid are kept in an unpaid vouchers file. The unpaid vouchers file shows all amounts owed and to whom amounts are owed.

Verifying an invoice

MusiCo, a merchandising business, sells musical instruments. When MusiCo receives an invoice, a verification form is stamped on the invoice, as shown in Illustration 28-1.

MusiCo's receiving clerk verifies that the items were received in the correct quantities. A clerk in MusiCo's purchasing department verifies that the terms and prices are correct. The calculations on the invoice are also verified. Each person doing a part of the work places a check mark next to the items verified and initials the verification form to show responsibility for that part.

Preparing a voucher from an invoice

A form is printed on the outside of a voucher to summarize the contents and provide space for approving payments. The outside of MusiCo's voucher for the invoice from Kemp Instrument Company is shown in Illustration 28-2. After the invoice is summarized on the voucher, the voucher is folded so that related documents can be placed inside the fold. For this reason a voucher is sometimes known as a voucher jacket.

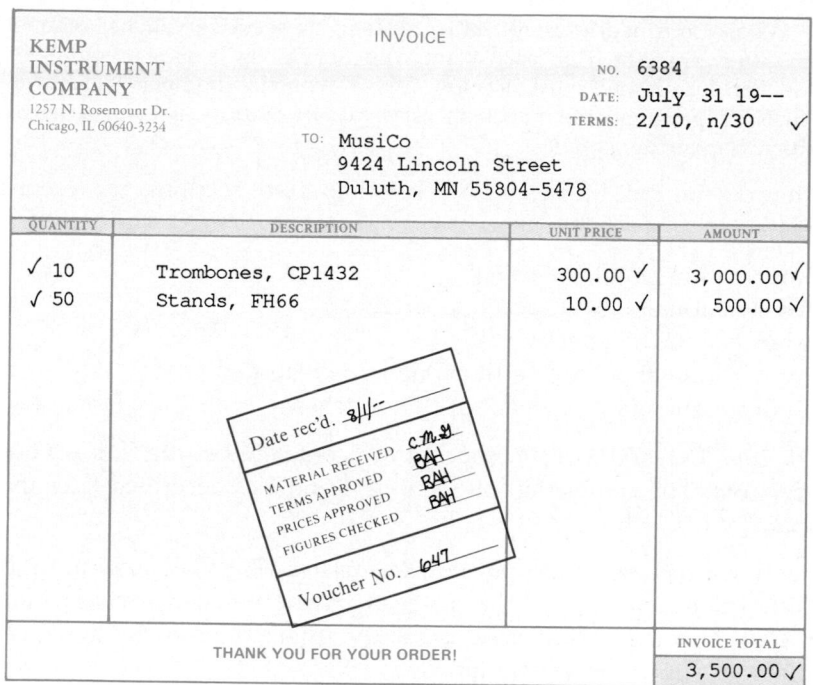

Illustration 28-1
Verification of an invoice

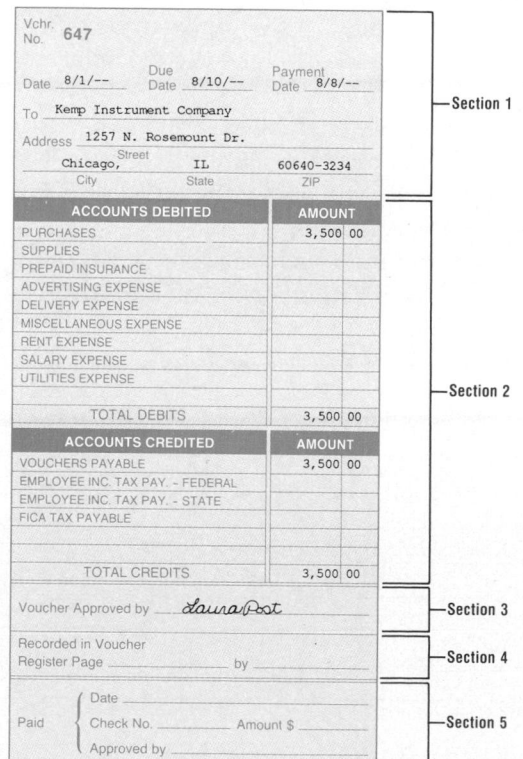

Illustration 28-2
Outside of a voucher for an invoice

When a business uses a voucher system, consecutive voucher numbers are often preprinted on each blank voucher. MusiCo uses prenumbered voucher forms and must account for all voucher numbers. Therefore, MusiCo's prenumbered vouchers serve as an additional control within MusiCo's voucher system.

The outside of MusiCo's voucher has five sections for recording information.

1. Information about the payee.
2. Information about the accounts affected.
3. Approval of the voucher.
4. Information about where the voucher is recorded.
5. Information about payment of the voucher.

Sections 1, 2, and 3 of the voucher are completed at the time a voucher is prepared. The completion of Sections 4 and 5 is described later in this chapter.

Section 1 of a voucher—payee information. MusiCo's accounting clerk obtains information about the payee from the verified invoice, Illustration 28-1. The accounting clerk enters the information in Section 1 of the voucher, as shown in Illustration 28-2.

The due date of Voucher No. 647 is calculated using information on the invoice, Illustration 28-1. The invoice is dated July 31. The invoice terms, 2/10, n/30, indicate that a 2% discount can be taken by paying the invoice within ten days. Therefore, to take the discount, the invoice must be paid no later than August 10.

Most cash payments are mailed. From experience, MusiCo has learned that most checks are received within two days. Therefore, MusiCo writes and mails checks two days before the due date. Thus, the payment date for Voucher No. 647 is August 8.

After Section 1 of the voucher is completed, the voucher number, *647*, is recorded on the verification stamp on the invoice, as shown in Illustration 28-1.

	DATE		PAYEE	VCHR. NO.	PAID		VOUCHERS PAYABLE CREDIT	
					DATE	CK. NO.		
1	Aug.	1	*Kemp Instrument Company*	647			3 5 0 0 00	1
2								2
3								3
4								4
5								5

VOUCHER

Illustration 28-3
Voucher recorded in a
voucher register (left page)

Section 2 of a voucher—accounts affected. As previously described, two accounts are affected by this transaction: the cost account, Purchases, is debited; the liability account, Vouchers Payable, is credited. Section 2 of the voucher lists several preprinted account titles. Purchases is preprinted under the heading Accounts Debited. Vouchers Payable is preprinted under the heading Accounts Credited. Therefore, only the amount of the invoice, $3,500.00, must be entered in Section 2, as shown in Illustration 28-2. Total Debits and Total Credits are also calculated and entered.

Titles of the accounts that are most often affected by cash payments are printed on the voucher form. If additional account titles are needed, they are entered on the blank lines in Section 2.

Section 3 of a voucher—voucher approval. As a double check, someone is usually authorized to approve vouchers before they are journalized. Laura Post, accountant, is authorized to approve vouchers for MusiCo. When Miss Post verifies that the voucher is correct, she approves it by signing her name in Section 3, as shown in Illustration 28-2.

A VOUCHER REGISTER

A voucher is recorded after it has been approved. A journal used to record vouchers is called a voucher register. A voucher register is similar to and replaces a purchases journal. The source document for an entry in a voucher register is a voucher. *(CONCEPT: Objective Evidence)* Vouchers are recorded in the voucher register as they are approved. Since MusiCo's vouchers are prenumbered, all vouchers can be accounted for. A missing voucher number shows that a voucher has not been recorded.

MusiCo's voucher register is shown in Illustration 28-3 below and on page 704. Special columns are provided for Vouchers Payable Credit, Purchases Debit, Delivery Expense Debit, and Supplies Debit. For accounts with no special amount columns, information is recorded in the General columns.

Illustration 28-3
Voucher recorded in a voucher register (right page)

	PURCHASES DEBIT	DELIVERY EXPENSE DEBIT	SUPPLIES DEBIT	ACCOUNT TITLE	POST. REF.	DEBIT	CREDIT	
1	3 5 0 0 00							1
2								2
3								3
4								4
5								5

Journalizing a voucher in a voucher register's special columns

The entry for Voucher No. 647 is shown in Illustration 28-3.

The date of the voucher, *19--, Aug. 1,* is written in the Date column. The name of the payee, *Kemp Instrument Company,* is written in the Payee column. The voucher number, *647,* is recorded in the Vchr. No. column. This information is obtained from Section 1 of the voucher.

The credit amount, *$3,500.00,* is written in the Vouchers Payable Credit column. The debit amount, *$3,500.00,* is written in the Purchases Debit column. This information is obtained from Section 2 of the voucher.

Section 4 of a voucher—where voucher is recorded

The person who records the voucher in the voucher register also completes Section 4 of the voucher. A notation is made in Section 4 of the voucher indicating the page on which the information is recorded in the voucher register. The person's initials are also recorded in the space provided on the voucher. Placing the voucher register page number on the voucher provides easy reference to where the entry is located in the voucher register. Section 4 of Voucher No. 647 is shown in Illustration 28-4.

Illustration 28-4
Notation on voucher
showing where voucher is
recorded

> Recorded in Voucher
> Register Page _____ 21 _____ by _ *G.R.S.* _

After Voucher No. 647 is journalized and the notation is made in Section 4, the voucher is filed in an unpaid vouchers file. The vouchers are placed in this file according to the payment date. Filing the vouchers by payment date makes it easier to determine which vouchers need to be paid each day. This method helps assure payment of invoices within the discount period. Thus, Voucher No. 647 is filed under the date on which it is to be paid, August 8.

Payment of a voucher is described later in this chapter.

Journalizing a voucher in a voucher register's general columns

MusiCo's voucher register has special debit amount columns for Purchases Debit, Delivery Expense Debit, and Supplies Debit. When an account other than these three is affected, the information is recorded in the General columns.

August 2, 19--.
Received invoice for miscellaneous expense from Glenhill Glass Repair Company, $40.00. Voucher No. 648.

The source document for this transaction is Voucher No. 648. *(CONCEPT: Objective Evidence)* This voucher is prepared in the same way as described for Voucher No. 647, Illustration 28-2. The analysis of this transaction is shown in the T accounts.

Miscellaneous Expense	
40.00	

Vouchers Payable	
	40.00

The entry for Voucher No. 648 is shown on line 2 of the voucher register, Illustration 28-5, pages 708 and 709.

The date, 2, is written in the Date column. The name of the payee, *Glenhill Glass Repair Company*, is written in the Payee column. The voucher number, *648*, is recorded in the Vchr. No. column. The credit amount, *$40.00*, is recorded in the Vouchers Payable Credit column. Since MusiCo's voucher register does not have a special debit amount column for Miscellaneous Expense, the debit amount, *$40.00*, is recorded in the General Debit column. When an amount is recorded in a general amount column, an account title must also be written in the Account Title column. The account to be debited, *Miscellaneous Expense*, is written in the Account Title column.

A notation is made on Voucher No. 648 in Section 4 to show where the voucher was recorded and by whom.

Proving, ruling, and posting a voucher register

Separate amounts recorded in a voucher register's General Debit and General Credit columns are posted individually during the month. As each amount is posted, the account number is written in the voucher register's Post. Ref. column. MusiCo's voucher register after posting is completed is shown in Illustration 28-5, pages 708 and 709.

At the end of each month, MusiCo's voucher register is proved and ruled. The procedures for proving and ruling a voucher register are the same as those previously described for special journals.

Totals of special amount columns are posted to the general ledger accounts listed in the column headings. Totals of General Debit and General Credit amount columns are not posted. Posting procedures for a voucher register's column totals are the same as previously described for special journals.

A CHECK REGISTER

MusiCo pays each voucher by check. A check is prepared for the amount of each voucher less any purchases discount. The check and voucher are presented to a person authorized to approve payment. A check with space for writing details about a cash payment is called a voucher check. MusiCo prepares voucher checks in duplicate. The original copy is given to the payee and MusiCo keeps the duplicate copy.

	DATE	PAYEE	VCHR. NO.	PAID		VOUCHERS PAYABLE CREDIT	
				DATE	CK. NO.		
1	Aug. 1	Kemp Instrument Company	647	Aug. 8	783	3 5 0 0 00	1
2	2	Glenhill Glass Repair Company	648			4 0 00	2
3	4	Jacobs Music	649	Aug. 11	784	9 7 3 91	3
4	5	Salem Wholesale Instruments	650			4 5 1 00	4
5	7	Bob's Delivery Service	651	Aug. 17	786	6 3 00	5
6	7	Ramsey, Inc.	652	See Vchr. 655		1 8 0 00	6
7	10	Superior Office Supplies	653			8 7 00	7
8	12	Kuker Company	654	Aug. 19	788	2 7 6 00	8
9	12	Ramsey, Inc.	655			9 5 00	9
10							10
11	14	Petty Cash Custodian, MusiCo	656	Aug. 14	785	2 1 2 50	11
12							12
27	31	Payroll	694	Aug. 31	800	4 3 3 1 96	27
28							28
29							29
30							30
31	31	Totals				105 0 7 7 41	31
32						(2115)	32
33							33
34							34
35							35
36							36

Illustration 28-5
Voucher register (left page)

MusiCo does not prepare check stubs when checks are written. Instead, the duplicate check is used as the source document for a cash payment transaction. (CONCEPT: *Objective Evidence*)

MusiCo's procedures for keeping a record of the checking account balance are explained later in this chapter.

Preparing a voucher check

On August 8, vouchers to be paid on that day are removed from the unpaid vouchers file. Included in this group is Voucher No. 647. To pay Voucher No. 647, MusiCo's cash payments clerk prepares Check No. 783, as shown in Illustration 28-6.

Each voucher check provides space in which details about the cash payment are shown. MusiCo's voucher checks have space at the right in

REGISTER PAGE *21*

	PURCHASES DEBIT	DELIVERY EXPENSE DEBIT	SUPPLIES DEBIT	GENERAL ACCOUNT TITLE	POST. REF.	DEBIT	CREDIT	
1	3 5 0 0 00							1
2				Miscellaneous Expense	6140	4 0 00		2
3	9 7 3 91							3
4	4 5 1 00							4
5		6 3 00						5
6	1 8 0 00							6
7			8 7 00					7
8	2 7 6 00							8
9				Vouchers Payable	2115	1 8 0 00		9
10				Purchases Returns and Allow.	5115		8 5 00	10
11		4 0 00	5 5 25	Advertising Expense	6105	4 7 00		11
12				Miscellaneous Expense	6140	7 0 25		12
27				Salary Expense	6155	5 8 5 4 00		27
28				Employee Inc. Tax Pay.—Fed.	2120		8 7 8 10	28
29				Employee Inc. Tax Pay.—State	2125		1 7 5 62	29
30				FICA Tax Payable	2130		4 6 8 32	30
31	5 3 8 0 6 91	1 2 2 4 00	1 4 5 2 25			5 6 1 7 5 25	7 5 8 1 0 00	31
32	(5105)	(6115)	(1140)			(✓)	(✓)	32
33								33
34								34
35								35
36								36

which the details are recorded. On Check No. 783 the information includes the items listed on page 710.

Illustration 28-5
Voucher register (right page)

Illustration 28-6
Voucher check

MusiCo
9424 Lincoln Street
Duluth, MN 55804-5478

No. 783   75-3 / 919

August 8 19 --

PAY TO THE ORDER OF Kemp Instrument Company $ 3,430.00

Three thousand four hundred thirty and no/100------------------ Dollars

For Classroom Use Only

FIRST NATIONAL BANK
DULUTH, MN 55813-1073

Shane Meyer

⑆091900038⑆ 372 1238⑈

MusiCo
Voucher No. 647
In Payment Of:
Invoice No. 6384
$3,500.00
Less 2% discount   70.00
Amount $3,430.00
Check No. 783

Detach This Stub Before Cashing

1. MusiCo's voucher number, *647*.
2. Payee's invoice number, *6384*.
3. Amount of invoice, *$3,500.00*.
4. Amount of discount, *$70.00*.
5. Net amount for which check is written, *$3,430.00*.

Before a payee deposits or cashes a voucher check, the stub showing details of the transaction is removed. The stub is kept by the payee as a record of the check.

Section 5 of a voucher—payment of a voucher

The person who prepares the check also completes part of Section 5 of the voucher. A notation is made in Section 5 of the voucher indicating the date paid, the check number, and the amount. Payment notation for Voucher No. 647 is shown in Illustration 28-7.

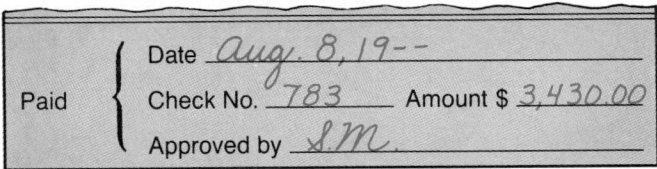

The manager, Shane Meyer, verifies that the information on the check and voucher agrees and is accurate. When he is satisfied that the payment is in order, he signs the check and initials Section 5 of the voucher, as shown in Illustration 28-7.

Information about this payment must also be recorded in the voucher register. The person who prepares the check usually makes this notation. The date on which this voucher is paid, *Aug. 8*, and the check number, *783*, are written in the voucher register. This information is written on the same line as the original entry for Voucher No. 647. This notation is shown on line 1 of Illustration 28-5.

The check is given or sent to the payee, and the voucher is filed in the paid vouchers file according to the name of the vendor.

Journalizing cash payments in a check register

A journal used in a voucher system to record cash payments is called a check register. MusiCo's check register, a form of a cash payments journal, is shown in Illustration 28-8. This check register is similar to and replaces a cash payments journal.

Maintaining bank columns in a check register. MusiCo does not use a checkbook with check stubs. MusiCo needs some way to know the checking account balance. Therefore, in addition to recording cash payments in

	DATE		PAYEE	CK. NO.	VCHR. NO.	VOUCHERS PAYABLE DEBIT	PURCHASES DISCOUNT CREDIT	CASH CREDIT	BANK DEPOSITS	BANK BALANCE	
1	*Aug.*	*8*	*Brought Forward*		√	23 1 0 9 90	2 6 8 30	22 8 4 1 60		97 7 6 8 13	1
2		*8*	*Kemp Instrument Co.*	*783*	*647*	3 5 0 0 00	7 0 00	3 4 3 0 00		94 3 3 8 13	2
3											3

CHECK REGISTER   PAGE *19*

Illustration 28-8
Check recorded in a check register

the voucher register, MusiCo uses a check register to maintain the checking account balance.

MusiCo's check register, Illustration 28-8, has two Bank columns, *Deposits* and *Balance*. These two Bank columns are used to keep an up-to-date record of cash in MusiCo's checking account. The Bank Deposits column is used to record the amounts deposited in the checking account. The Bank Balance column shows the checking account balance after each check and deposit is recorded in the check register.

Journalizing checks in a check register. MusiCo prepares a voucher for each payment. Therefore, each check is issued in payment of a voucher. Checks are recorded in the check register in the order they are written.

In MusiCo's voucher system, only three general ledger accounts are affected by a cash payment: Vouchers Payable, Purchases Discount, and Cash. Therefore, MusiCo's check register has only three special amount columns: Vouchers Payable Debit, Purchases Discount Credit, and Cash Credit. Each check is recorded in a check register as a debit to the liability account, Vouchers Payable, and a credit to the asset account, Cash. If a discount is taken for prompt payment, the discount amount is recorded as a credit to the contra cost account, Purchases Discount.

August 8, 19--.
Paid cash to Kemp Instrument Company, $3,430.00, covering Voucher No. 647 for $3,500.00, less 2% discount, $70.00. Check No. 783.

The source document for this transaction is the copy of Check No. 783. *(CONCEPT: Objective Evidence)* The analysis of this transaction is shown in the T accounts.

The liability account, Vouchers Payable, is debited for $3,500.00. The contra cost account, Purchases Discount, is credited for $70.00. Cash is credited for the net amount paid, $3,430.00.

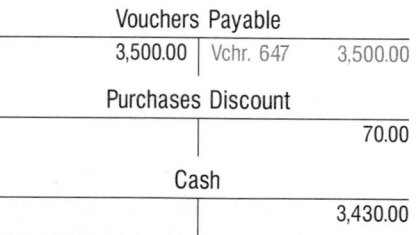

Vouchers Payable	
3,500.00	Vchr. 647 3,500.00

Purchases Discount	
	70.00

Cash	
	3,430.00

The check register entry to record Check No. 783 is shown on line 2 of Illustration 28-8.

The date, *8*, is recorded in the Date column. The name of the payee, *Kemp Instrument Company*, is written in the Payee column. The check number, *783*, is entered in the Ck. No. column. The number of the voucher being paid, *647*, is entered in the Vchr. No. column. The debit to Vouchers Payable, *$3,500.00*, is recorded in the Vouchers Payable Debit column. The credit to Purchases Discount, *$70.00*, is recorded in the Purchases Discount Credit column. The credit to Cash, *$3,430.00*, is recorded in the Cash Credit column. A new checking account balance is calculated. The previous balance, *$97,768.13*, *minus* this payment, *$3,430.00*, *equals* the new balance, *$94,338.13*. The new balance, *$94,338.13*, is recorded in the Bank Balance column.

Proving, ruling, and posting a check register

At the end of each month, the check register's special amount columns are proved, ruled, and posted. MusiCo's check register after it has been posted is shown in Illustration 28-9.

CHECK REGISTER   PAGE *19*

	DATE	PAYEE	CK. NO.	VCHR. NO.	VOUCHERS PAYABLE DEBIT (1)	PURCHASES DISCOUNT CREDIT (2)	CASH CREDIT (3)	BANK DEPOSITS (4)	BANK BALANCE (5)	
1	*Aug.* ¹⁹⁻⁻ 8	*Brought Forward*		√	23 1 0 9 90	2 6 8 30	22 8 4 1 60		97 7 6 8 13	1
2	8	*Kemp Instrument Co.*	783	647	3 5 0 0 00	7 0 00	3 4 3 0 00		94 3 3 8 13	2
3	11	*Jacobs Music*	784	649	9 7 3 91	1 9 48	9 5 4 43		93 3 8 3 70	3
4	14	*Petty Cash Cust., MusiCo*	785	656	2 1 2 50		2 1 2 50		93 1 7 1 20	4
5	14	*Deposit*		√				18 7 6 7 15	111 9 3 8 35	5
22	31	*Payroll*	800	694	4 3 3 1 96		4 3 3 1 96		95 3 7 3 21	22
23	31	*Deposit*		√				19 2 9 4 78	114 6 6 7 99	23
24	31	*Totals*			103 4 5 2 22	5 6 6 88	102 8 8 5 34			24
25					*(2115)*	*(5110)*	*(1105)*			25
26										26

Illustration 28-9
Ruling and posting a check register

Procedures for posting from MusiCo's check register are the same as those previously described for special journals. However, no separate amounts are posted individually because the check register does not have a General Debit or General Credit column. The three special amount column totals are posted to the general ledger accounts listed in the column headings. After each total is posted, the account number is written in parentheses below the column total.

MusiCo's check register also has two Bank columns: Deposits and Balance. The Bank columns are used to summarize the status of the checking account balance. The Bank Deposits column is used to record all deposits in the checking account. A deposit is shown on line 5 of Illustration 28-9. The Bank Balance column shows the current checking account balance after each entry in the check register. These two columns are neither ruled nor posted.

The Deposits column does not need to be totaled and posted because each cash receipt is recorded in the cash receipts journal and posted from that journal. At the end of each month, cash is proved by comparing the last amount in the check register's Balance column with the balance in the general ledger cash account. Cash is proved if the two amounts are the same.

Starting a new page of a check register

A new page of a check register may be needed either during a month or at the start of a new month. When a new page is started during a month, the totals of the Vouchers Payable Debit, Purchases Discount Credit, and Cash Credit columns are brought forward from the previous page. The balance of the Bank Balance column is also brought forward. No amount is brought forward for the Bank Deposits column. This procedure is shown on line 1 of the check register in Illustration 28-8, page 711.

MusiCo begins a new page of the check register at the beginning of each month. Only the balance of the Bank Balance column is brought forward. The totals of the special amount columns are not brought forward because they were posted at the end of the previous month. A new page of a check register started at the beginning of a month is shown in Illustration 28-10.

	DATE	PAYEE	CK. NO.	VCHR. NO.	VOUCHERS PAYABLE DEBIT	PURCHASES DISCOUNT CREDIT	CASH CREDIT	BANK	
					1	2	3	4 DEPOSITS	5 BALANCE
1	Sept. 1	Brought Forward		√					114 66 7 99
2									

CHECK REGISTER   PAGE *20*

Illustration 28-10
Starting a new page of a check register at the beginning of a month

USING A VOUCHER SYSTEM FOR SELECTED TRANSACTIONS

A voucher was prepared for each transaction described previously in this chapter. Each voucher was paid in full when due. Some transactions, however, require different procedures. Two examples are purchases returns and allowances and payroll transactions.

Purchases returns and allowances

A purchases returns and allowances transaction reduces the total amount owed for an invoice. Therefore, the voucher record for that invoice must be changed to show the reduction in the amount owed.

August 12, 19--.
Issued Debit Memorandum No. 98 to Ramsey, Inc., for return of merchandise purchased, $85.00. Cancel Voucher No. 652. Voucher No. 655.

Vouchers Payable		
Vchr. 655 180.00	Vchr. 652	180.00
	Vchr. 655	95.00

Purchases Returns and Allowances	
	Vchr. 655 85.00

Voucher No. 655 is prepared for this transaction and is the source document for the entry. *(CONCEPT: Objective Evidence)* The analysis of this transaction is shown in the T accounts.

The liability account, Vouchers Payable, is debited for $180.00 to cancel Voucher No. 652. Vouchers Payable is credited for $95.00, the difference between Voucher No. 652 ($180.00) and Debit Memorandum No. 98 ($85.00). The contra cost account, Purchases Returns and Allowances, is credited for $85.00, the amount of merchandise returned.

MusiCo follows five steps in changing the original amount owed for Voucher No. 652 because of the purchases return.

1 Remove Voucher No. 652 from the unpaid vouchers file. Write *Canceled* across Section 5 to show cancellation of the voucher.

2 Prepare Voucher No. 655 as shown in Illustration 28-11. Place the canceled Voucher No. 652 and Debit Memorandum No. 98 inside of Voucher No. 655.

Illustration 28-11
Outside of a voucher for the return of merchandise purchased

3 Write the words, *See Vchr. 655,* in the voucher register's Paid columns on the same line as Voucher No. 652. This notation is shown on line 6 of Illustration 28-5.

4 Record Voucher No. 655 in the voucher register as shown on lines 9 and 10 of Illustration 28-5. The date, *12,* is recorded in the Date column. The name of the payee, *Ramsey, Inc.,* is written in the Payee column. The voucher number, *655,* is entered in the Vchr. No. column. The new credit amount, *$95.00,* is entered in the Vouchers Payable Credit column. The title of the account debited, Vouchers Payable, is written in the General Account Title column. The amount of the canceled Voucher No. 652, *$180.00,* is recorded in the General Debit column. On the next line, the title of the account credited, Purchases Returns and Allowances, is written in the General Account Title column. The amount of the return, *$85.00,* is recorded in the General Credit column. A notation is made in Section 4 on Voucher No. 655 showing the voucher register page number on which this voucher is recorded.

5 File Voucher No. 655 by its due date in the unpaid vouchers file. The due date is based on the terms of the original invoice. Therefore, Voucher No. 655 has the same due date as canceled Voucher No. 652.

Payroll

MusiCo pays its employees semimonthly. A payroll register is prepared showing details for each payroll. The payroll register is prepared in the same way as described in Part 3. Information from a payroll register is used in preparing a voucher for payroll.

August 31, 19--.
Recorded voucher for semimonthly payroll for period ended August 31, $4,331.96 (total payroll, $5,854.00, less deductions: employee income tax payable—federal, $878.10; employee income tax payable—state, $175.62; FICA tax payable, $468.32). Voucher No. 694.

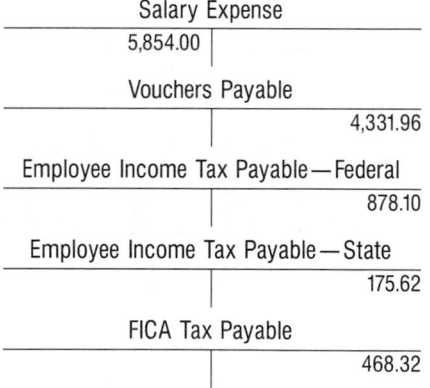

The analysis of this payroll transaction is shown in the T accounts.

A payroll register is needed for several purposes, as described in Part 3. Therefore, the payroll register cannot be placed inside a voucher for payroll. For this reason information from the payroll register is summarized on the inside of Voucher No. 694, as shown in Illustration 28-12.

The outside of Voucher No. 694 is shown in Illustration 28-13.

The voucher register entry to record Voucher No. 694 is shown on lines 27 to 30 in Illustration 28-5, pages 708 and 709.

VOUCHER		Vchr. No. **694**
	Payment Date August 31	19 --
Date August 31 19 -- Terms _____	Due August 31	19 --
To Payroll		

Address _____

City _____   State _____   Zip _____

For the following: Enclose all invoices or other papers.

DATE	VOUCHER DETAILS		AMOUNT
Aug. 31	Payroll for period ended 8/31/--		
	Salary Expense		$5,854.00
	Deductions:		
	Employee Inc. Tax Pay.--Federal	$878.10	
	Employee Inc. Tax Pay.--State	175.62	
	FICA Tax Payable	468.32	1,522.04
	Net cash payment		$4,331.96

MusiCo

Illustration 28-12
Inside of a voucher for
payroll

Vchr. No. **694**		
Date 8/31/--	Due Date 8/31/--	Payment Date 8/31/--
To Payroll		

Address _____
          Street

City _____   State _____   ZIP _____

ACCOUNTS DEBITED	AMOUNT
PURCHASES	
SUPPLIES	
PREPAID INSURANCE	
ADVERTISING EXPENSE	
DELIVERY EXPENSE	
MISCELLANEOUS EXPENSE	
RENT EXPENSE	
SALARY EXPENSE	5,854 00
UTILITIES EXPENSE	
TOTAL DEBITS	5,854 00

ACCOUNTS CREDITED	AMOUNT
VOUCHERS PAYABLE	4,331 96
EMPLOYEE INC. TAX PAY. - FEDERAL	878 10
EMPLOYEE INC. TAX PAY. - STATE	175 62
FICA TAX PAYABLE	468 32
TOTAL CREDITS	5,854 00

Voucher Approved by _Laura Bot_

Recorded in Voucher
Register Page _21_   by _J.R.S._

Paid { Date _Aug. 31, 19--_
       Check No. _800_   Amount $ _4,331.96_
       Approved by _L M._ }

Illustration 28-13
Outside of a voucher for
payroll

August 31, 19--.
Paid cash for semimonthly payroll, $4,331.96, covering Voucher No. 694.
Check No. 800.

Vouchers Payable		
4,331.96	Vchr. 694	4,331.96

Cash	
	4,331.96

A copy of Check No. 800 is the source document for this transaction. *(CONCEPT: Objective Evidence)* Section 5 of Voucher No. 694 is completed to show that the voucher has been paid. Voucher No. 694 is then placed in the paid vouchers file.

The analysis of this transaction to pay a voucher for payroll is shown in the T accounts.

The check register entry to record Check No. 800 is shown on line 22 in Illustration 28-9, page 712.

A notation of the payment of Voucher No. 694 is made in the voucher register, as shown on line 27 in Illustration 28-5, pages 708 and 709.

An entry is made in MusiCo's general journal for the employer's payroll taxes. This entry is the same as described in Part 3. Later, when payroll taxes are due, vouchers are prepared, approved, and paid. One voucher is prepared for total payroll taxes owed to the federal government. Another voucher is prepared for total payroll taxes owed to the state government.

ADVANTAGES OF A VOUCHER SYSTEM

A voucher system has the following advantages for businesses that make many cash payments.

1. Authorizing and approving all cash payments is limited to a few persons. This procedure helps protect and control cash.
2. Providing a voucher jacket is a convenient method of filing invoices and related business papers for future reference. This is especially true when invoices received from vendors are of different sizes.
3. Filing unpaid vouchers according to their payment dates helps assure payment of invoices within the discount periods.
4. Using an unpaid vouchers file and a paid vouchers file eliminates posting to an accounts payable ledger.
5. Using a paid vouchers file provides three different and easy ways to find information about a paid voucher.
   a. *If only the voucher number is known,* look in the voucher register for that number and find the payee's name on the same line. The voucher will be in the paid vouchers file under the name of the payee.
   b. *If only the check number used to pay the voucher is known,* look in the check register for the check number. The payee's name is on the same line. The voucher will be in the paid vouchers file under the name of the payee.
   c. *If only the name of the payee is known,* look in the paid vouchers file where vouchers are filed under the name of the payee.

SUMMARY OF A VOUCHER SYSTEM

The chart shown in Illustration 28-14, page 718, summarizes the steps followed when using a voucher system.

◼ ACCOUNTING TERMS

What is the meaning of each of the following?

1. voucher
2. voucher system
3. voucher register
4. voucher check
5. check register

◼ QUESTIONS FOR INDIVIDUAL STUDY

1. What three procedures are used to control and protect cash?
2. What account title is used in place of Accounts Payable when a voucher system is used?
3. What items are verified on an invoice before a voucher is prepared?
4. What information is shown in Sections 1, 2, and 3 of a voucher?
5. Which accounting concept is being applied when a business uses a voucher as the source document for an entry in a voucher register?
6. In what order are unpaid vouchers filed in the unpaid vouchers file?
7. Where are account titles and amounts

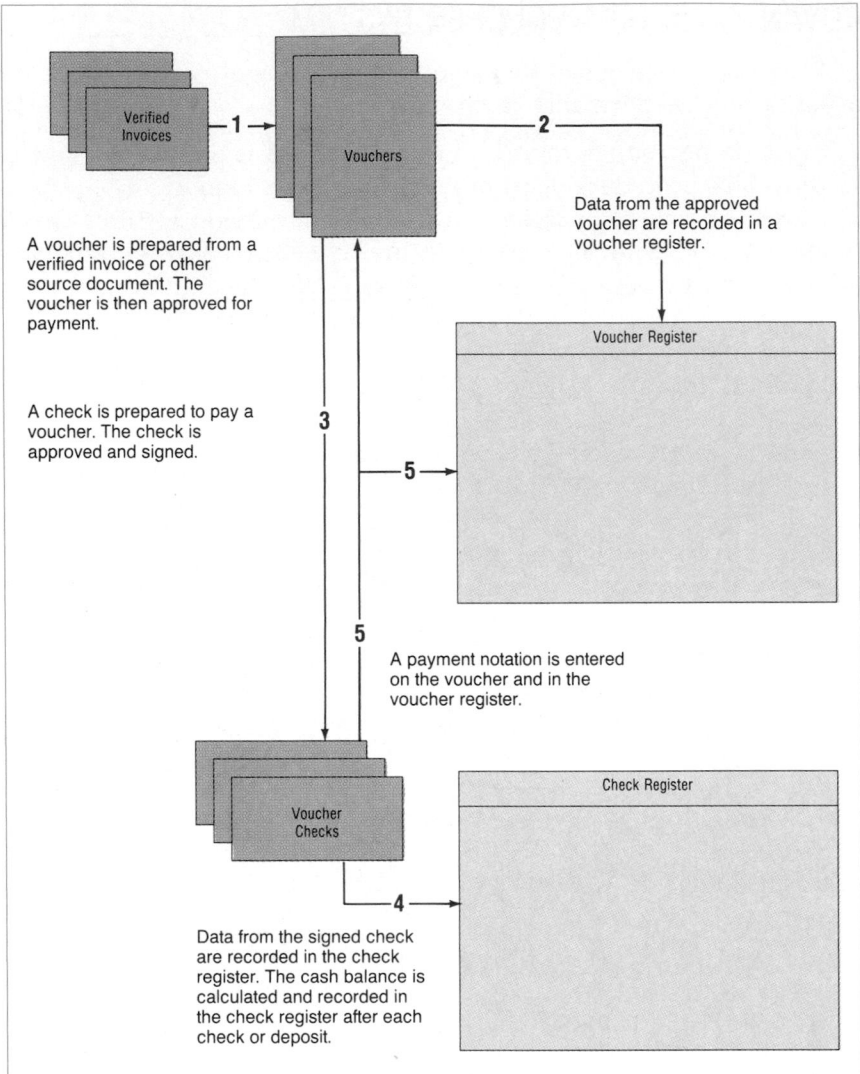

A voucher is prepared from a verified invoice or other source document. The voucher is then approved for payment.

A check is prepared to pay a voucher. The check is approved and signed.

Data from the approved voucher are recorded in a voucher register.

A payment notation is entered on the voucher and in the voucher register.

Data from the signed check are recorded in the check register. The cash balance is calculated and recorded in the check register after each check or deposit.

Illustration 28-14
Summary of a voucher
system

recorded that cannot be recorded in one of the special amount columns of a voucher register?

8. Which amounts in a voucher register are posted as totals?

9. What is the source document for an entry in a check register?

10. When a voucher is paid, what information is recorded in the voucher register?

11. Why does MusiCo use the Bank Deposits and Bank Balance columns in its check register?

12. Which three special amount columns are used in MusiCo's check register?

13. What amounts are posted from MusiCo's check register?

14. When a purchases return is made, how is the new voucher amount calculated?

15. What is the source of information used in preparing a voucher for payroll?

16. What are five advantages of using a voucher system?

CASES FOR MANAGEMENT DECISION

CASE 1 Kelly White, the bookkeeper for Greenfield, Inc., is setting up a voucher system for Greenfield. In her planning, she is trying to decide how many columns to use in the voucher register. She is also trying to decide what headings to use for the special columns in the voucher register. What should Ms. White consider in making her decision about these special columns?

CASE 2 The Harper Company uses a voucher system for cash payments.

Jonathan Bartell, the bookkeeper, receives and verifies the invoices. He then prepares the voucher and enters the voucher in the voucher register. When the voucher is due, Mr. Bartell prepares and signs the check and enters the payment in the check register. What is your opinion of the procedure Harper Company follows for its voucher system? Explain.

DRILLS FOR UNDERSTANDING

DRILL 28-D1 Preparing vouchers

Otto Company uses a voucher form similar to the one described in this chapter.

Instructions: For each of the following transactions, complete Sections 1 and 2 on the outside of a voucher. Assume that payment dates are two days before the due date of each invoice. Use April of the current year. The abbreviation for voucher is V.

April 10. Purchased merchandise on account from Lockett Company, 985 Jordan Street, Santa Clara, CA 95050-2675, $3,156.80. (Terms 2/10, n/30.) V42.
   12. Received invoice for advertising from Mountain View News, 6752 Malarin Street, Mountain View, CA 94042-2176, $150.00. (Payment due May 10.) V43.
   13. Bought supplies on account from Bay Area Supplies, 586 West Edith Avenue, Los Altos, CA 94022-7223, $312.87. (Terms n/30.) V44.

DRILL 28-D2 Analyzing journalizing transactions in a voucher register

Use a form similar to the following.

Item No.	Amount Columns in a Voucher Register					
	Vouchers Payable Credit	Purchases Debit	Delivery Expense Debit	Supplies Debit	General Debit	General Credit
1.	✓	✓				

Instructions: Place a check mark in each voucher register column that will be used in journalizing each of the following items. Item No. 1 is given as an example.

Items
1. Purchased merchandise on account.
2. Received invoice for delivery expense for the month.
3. Received invoice for advertising expense for the month.

4. Issued a debit memorandum for a purchases return. Cancel original voucher and issue a new voucher.
5. Bought supplies on account.
6. Record data from the payroll register affecting the following accounts: Employee Income Tax Payable—Federal and Salary Expense.
7. Received invoice for current month's rent.

DRILL 28-D3   Analyzing journalizing transactions in a check register

Use a form similar to the following.

Item No.	Amount Columns in a Check Register				
	Vouchers Payable Debit	Purchases Discount Credit	Cash Credit	Bank	
				Deposits	Balance
1.	✓		✓		✓

Instructions: Place a check mark in each check register column that will be used in journalizing each of the following items. Item No. 1 is given as an example.

Items
1. Paid a voucher with no discount.
2. Paid a voucher less a discount.
3. Made a deposit in the bank account.

▊ APPLICATION PROBLEMS

PROBLEM 28-1   Journalizing vouchers in a voucher register

TeleTronics uses a voucher register similar to the one described in this chapter.

Instructions: 1. Journalize the following transactions completed during September of the current year. Use page 9 of a voucher register. The abbreviation for voucher is V.

Sept.   1. Purchased merchandise on account from Eastern Company, $3,100.00. V87.
    2. Received invoice for September rent from Post Real Estate Developers, $1,150.00. V88.
    5. Bought supplies on account from Supra Supply Company, $258.00. V89.
    8. Received invoice for advertising from Newport News, $87.50. V90.
   11. Purchased merchandise on account from Hoyer Company, $3,347.75. V91.
   18. Received invoice for delivery service from Rapid Rabbit, $235.15. V92.
   19. Purchased merchandise on account from Beggen Company, $1,973.00. V93.
   23. Bought office furniture on account from Syracuse Furniture Company, $1,315.00. V94.
   25. Received invoice for utilities from Northside Electric Cooperative, $185.00. V95.
   29. Bought supplies on account from Northern Supply, $317.00. V96.
   30. Received invoice for miscellaneous expense from Manley Maintenance Company, $25.00. V97.

2. Prove and rule the voucher register.

The voucher register prepared in Problem 28-1 is needed to complete Problem 28-2.

PROBLEM 28-2   Journalizing cash payments and deposits in a check register

The voucher register prepared in Problem 28-1 is needed to complete Problem 28-2.

TeleTronics uses a check register similar to the one described in this chapter.

Instructions: 1. Use page 9 of a check register. Record the bank balance brought forward on September 1 of the current year, $19,443.13.

2. Continue using page 9 of the check register. Journalize the following cash payments and deposits completed during September of the current year. As each cash payment is journalized, make the appropriate notation in the voucher register. Source documents are abbreviated as follows: check, C; voucher, V.

Sept. 2. Paid cash to Post Real Estate Developers, $1,150.00, covering V88. C83.
     8. Paid cash to Newport News, $87.50, covering V90. C84.
     9. Paid cash to Eastern Company, $3,038.00, covering V87 for $3,100.00, less 2% discount, $62.00. C85.
   13. Paid cash to Supra Supply Company, $258.00, covering V89. C86.
   18. Paid cash to Rapid Rabbit, $235.15, covering V92. C87.
   19. Paid cash to Hoyer Company, $3,280.79, covering V91 for $3,347.75, less 2% discount, $66.96. C88.
   24. Made a deposit in the checking account, $5,684.54.
   25. Paid cash to Northside Electric Cooperative, $185.00, covering V95. C89.
   30. Paid cash to Manley Maintenance Company, $25.00, covering V97. C90.

3. Prove and rule the check register.

PROBLEM 28-3   Journalizing purchases returns and allowances in a voucher register

Nygren Supply Company uses a voucher register similar to the one described in this chapter.

Instructions: Journalize the following transactions completed during February of the current year. Use page 2 of a voucher register. When a voucher is canceled, make appropriate notations in the voucher register. Source documents are abbreviated as follows: debit memorandum, DM; voucher, V.

Feb. 1. Purchased merchandise on account from Hamline Corporation, $2,700.00. V10.
    4. Issued DM2 to Hamline Corporation for return of merchandise purchased, $200.00. Cancel V10. V11.
   15. Purchased merchandise on account from Moorhead, Inc., $1,778.00. V12.
   17. Issued DM3 to Moorhead, Inc., for return of merchandise purchased, $350.00. Cancel V12. V13.

PROBLEM 28-4   Preparing and journalizing a voucher for payroll

Bowman Service Center uses a voucher form and a voucher register similar to the ones described in this chapter. Bowman Service Center's payroll register for May 15 of the current year shows the following information. The abbreviation for voucher is V.

May 15. Recorded voucher for semimonthly payroll for period ended May 15, $3,120.97 (total payroll, $4,217.53, less deductions: employee income tax payable—federal, $632.63; employee income tax payable—state, $126.53; FICA tax payable, $337.40). V51.

Instructions: 1. Prepare a voucher for the payroll on May 15 of the current year.

2. Use page 5 of a voucher register. Journalize the voucher for the payroll. Assume the voucher has been approved. After the voucher is journalized, complete Section 4 of the voucher.

■ ENRICHMENT PROBLEMS

MASTERY PROBLEM 28-M   Journalizing transactions in a voucher system

Jameson Company uses a voucher register and a check register similar to the ones described in this chapter.

Instructions: 1. Use page 20 of a check register. Record the bank balance brought forward on November 1 of the current year, $11,676.77.

2. Journalize the following transactions completed during November of the current year. Use page 22 of a voucher register and page 20 of a check register. When a voucher is paid or canceled, make appropriate notations in the voucher register. Source documents are abbreviated as follows: check, C; debit memorandum, DM; voucher, V.

Nov. 1. Purchased merchandise on account from Georgia Company, $975.00. V68.
      2. Bought supplies on account from Supply World, $216.80. V69.
      4. Bought store equipment on account from Equipment Plus, $1,998.00. V70.
      8. Purchased merchandise on account from North Heights Corporation, $1,695.15. V71.
      8. Paid cash to Georgia Company, $955.50, covering V68 for $975.00, less 2% discount, $19.50. C57.
     10. Made a deposit in the checking account, $3,579.00.
     14. Received invoice for delivery service from Quick Delivery, $24.10. V72.
     14. Paid cash to Quick Delivery, $24.10, covering V72. C58.
     14. Issued DM10 to North Heights Corporation for return of merchandise purchased, $225.00. Cancel V71. V73.
     15. Paid cash to North Heights Corporation, $1,440.75, covering V73 for $1,470.15, less 2% discount, $29.40. C59.
     16. Recorded voucher for semimonthly payroll for period ended November 15, $1,459.64 (total payroll, $1,972.50, less deductions: employee income tax payable—federal, $295.88; employee income tax payable—state, $59.18; FICA tax payable, $157.80). V74.
     16. Paid cash for semimonthly payroll, $1,459.64, covering V74. C60.
     22. Paid cash to Supply World, $216.80, covering V69. C61.
     25. Bought office furniture on account from Fischer Furniture, $2,350.00. V75.
     29. Made a deposit in the checking account, $1,170.15.
     30. Purchased merchandise on account from Georgia Company, $2,258.50. V76.

3. Prove and rule both the voucher register and the check register.

**CHALLENGE PROBLEM 28-C   Journalizing purchase invoices at the net amount in a
                          voucher system**

Cayman Company uses a voucher system. All of the vendors with whom Cayman Company does business offer terms of 2/10, n/30. Cayman has a policy of paying all invoices within the discount period. The business records invoice vouchers at the net amount (invoice total less a 2% discount). Thus, a $1,000.00 invoice, allowing a 2% discount of $20.00, is recorded at the net amount, $980.00. Purchases is debited and Vouchers Payable is credited for $980.00. A purchases discount account is not used.

If an invoice *is not* paid within the discount period, the discount is lost by Cayman Company. This loss is recorded in an account titled Discounts Lost. Thus, if the $1,000.00 invoice described above *is not* paid within the discount period, the business must pay the full $1,000.00. However, one of the controls in a voucher system is that no check can be written for more than the voucher amount. Therefore, in order for a check to be written for the full $1,000.00, the original voucher must be canceled. A new voucher for $1,000.00 must be prepared, approved, and recorded.

This new voucher would include a debit to Discounts Lost of $20.00, a debit to Vouchers Payable of $980.00 (the amount of the original voucher), and a credit to Vouchers Payable of $1,000.00. Once this voucher is approved, a check can be written for $1,000.00 to pay the full amount due.

If an invoice is recorded at its net amount, then all purchases returns and allowances are recorded at net amounts. An invoice, $1,000.00, recorded at net with a 2% discount, has a $100.00 purchase return and allowance. Thus, the $100.00 return is discounted by 2% and recorded as $98.00. For the return, Vouchers Payable is debited $980.00 (the amount of original voucher), Purchases Returns and Allowances is credited for $98.00, and Vouchers Payable is credited for $882.00 (the amount of the new voucher).

Cayman's voucher register is similar to the one described for MusicCo in this chapter, except for Column 3. Instead of Delivery Expense Debit, Cayman's voucher register third column is titled *Discounts Lost Debit.* Cayman's check register has two special amount columns: Vouchers Payable Debit and Cash Credit.

Instructions: 1. Use page 20 of a check register. Record the amounts brought forward on December 11 of the current year.

Vouchers Payable Debit	$1,395.00
Cash Credit	1,395.00
Bank Balance	8,500.00

2. Journalize the following transactions completed during December of the current year. Use page 25 of a voucher register and page 20 of a check register similar to those described for Cayman Company. Assume that for all purchases of merchandise, equipment, or supplies the invoice terms are 2/10, n/30. When a voucher is paid or canceled, make appropriate notations in the voucher register. Number vouchers consecutively starting with Voucher No. 109. Source documents are abbreviated as follows: check, C; debit memorandum, DM; voucher, V.

Dec. 11. Purchased merchandise on account from Knotts Company, $2,000.00.
 15. Made a deposit in the checking account, $1,000.00.
 15. Bought supplies on account from Fairgate Supply Company, $200.00.
 18. Bought store equipment on account from Hightop Company, $1,000.00.
 18. Paid cash to Knotts Company covering V109. C80.
 19. Purchased merchandise on account from Neal Company, $500.00.
 22. Made a deposit in the checking account, $2,000.00.
 25. Paid cash to Hightop Company covering V111. C81.
 26. Paid cash to Fairgate Supply Company covering V110. C82.
 28. Bought supplies on account from Peerless Supply Company, $300.00.
 28. Issued DM30 to Neal Company for return of merchandise purchased, $50.00. Cancel V112.
 29. Made a deposit in the checking account, $1,000.00.
 31. Paid cash to Neal Company covering V115. C83.

3. Prove and rule both the voucher register and the check register.

CHAPTER
29

An Inventory System

ENABLING PERFORMANCE TASKS

After studying Chapter 29, you will be able to:
a. Define accounting terms related to an inventory system.
b. Identify accounting concepts and practices related to an inventory system.
c. Determine the cost of merchandise inventory using the fifo, lifo, and weighted-average inventory costing methods.
d. Estimate the cost of merchandise inventory using the gross profit method of estimating inventory.

Merchandise inventory on hand is typically the largest asset of a merchandising business. Successful businesses must have merchandise available for sale that customers want. A business, therefore, needs controls that assist managers in maintaining a merchandise inventory of sufficient quantity, variety, and price.

The cost of merchandise inventory is reported on both the balance sheet and the income statement. An accurate cost of merchandise inventory is required to correctly report current assets and retained earnings on the balance sheet. The accuracy of the inventory cost will also assure that gross profit and net income are reported correctly on the income statement. *(CONCEPT: Adequate Disclosure)*

CONTROLLING THE QUANTITY OF MERCHANDISE INVENTORY

To determine the most efficient size of inventory, a business makes frequent analysis of purchases, sales, and inventory records. Many businesses fail because too much or too little merchandise inventory is kept on hand. A business that stocks merchandise that does not satisfy the demand of its customers is also likely to fail.

A merchandise inventory that is larger than needed may decrease the net income of a business for several reasons.

1. Excess inventory requires that a business spend money for expensive store and warehouse space.
2. Excess inventory uses capital that could be invested in other assets to earn a profit for the business.
3. Excess inventory requires that a business spend money for expenses, such as taxes and insurance premiums, that increase with the cost of the merchandise inventory.
4. Excess inventory may become obsolete and unsaleable.

Merchandise inventory that is smaller than needed may also decrease the net income of a business for several reasons.

1. Sales may be lost to competitors if items wanted by customers are not on hand.
2. Sales may be lost to competitors if there is an insufficient variety of merchandise to satisfy customers.
3. When a business frequently orders small quantities of an item, the price paid is often more per unit than when merchandise is ordered in large quantities.

DETERMINING THE QUANTITY OF MERCHANDISE INVENTORY

The quantity of items in inventory at the end of a fiscal period must be determined in order to figure the cost of merchandise sold. Two principal methods are used to determine the quantity of each item of merchandise on hand.

1. A merchandise inventory determined by counting, weighing, or measuring items of merchandise on hand is called a periodic inventory. A periodic inventory is also referred to as a physical inventory.
2. A merchandise inventory determined by keeping a continuous record of increases, decreases, and balance on hand is called a perpetual inventory. A perpetual inventory is also referred to as a book inventory.

Periodic inventory

Counting, weighing, or measuring merchandise on hand for a periodic inventory is commonly referred to as "taking an inventory." Employees count each item of inventory and record the quantities on special forms. To assure an accurate and complete count, a business will typically be closed during the periodic inventory. Taking an inventory is often a large and expensive task. Therefore, a periodic inventory usually is taken only at the end of a fiscal period.

Businesses frequently establish their fiscal period to end when inventory is at a minimum because it takes less time to count a smaller inventory. For example, a department store may take an inventory at the end of

January. The amount of merchandise on hand is smaller because of Christmas sales and January clearance sales. Few purchases of additional merchandise are made in January. All of these activities make the merchandise inventory smaller at the end of January.

MusiCo has found from past experience that relatively few sales are made after the holiday season. Thus, the quantity of merchandise on hand is relatively small at the end of January. Therefore, MusiCo ends its annual fiscal period on January 31. MusiCo takes its periodic inventory during the last week of January.

A form used during a periodic inventory to record information about each item of merchandise on hand is called an inventory record. The inventory record has space to record the stock number, unit description, number of units on hand, unit price, and total cost of each item. The inventory record used by MusiCo is shown in Illustration 29-1.

MusiCo	MERCHANDISE INVENTORY		Form No. __3__	
Date January 31, 19--		Item Guitar strings		
Stock No.	Unit Description	No. of Units on Hand	Unit Price	Total Cost
3410	extra light gauge, steel	25	$ 6.80	$ 170.00
3420	light gauge, steel	13	6.50	84.50
3430	medium gauge, steel	34	10 @ 6.30 } 24 @ 6.40	216.60
3440	heavy gauge, steel	8	5.95	47.60
3510	extra light gauge, nylon	16	7.20	115.20
3540	heavy gauge, nylon	28	6.75	189.00 $ 862.50

Illustration 29-1
Inventory record

Information is typed in the Stock No. column and Unit Description column before the periodic inventory begins. Employees taking the inventory write the actual count in the No. of Units on Hand column. Inventory records are then sent to the accounting department where the Unit Price and Total Cost columns are completed.

Perpetual inventory

Some businesses keep inventory records that show continuously the quantity on hand for each kind of merchandise. A form used to show the kind of merchandise, quantity received, quantity sold, and balance on hand is called a stock record. A separate stock record is prepared for each kind of merchandise on hand. A file of stock records for all merchandise on hand is called a stock ledger. A stock record for MusiCo is shown in Illustration 29-2.

Description *marching band hats*				Stock No. *4516B*		
Maximum *40*		Minimum *10*		Location *aisle F*		

INCREASES			DECREASES			BALANCE
DATE	PURCHASE NO.	QUANTITY	DATE	SALES INVOICE NO.	QUANTITY	QUANTITY
19-- *Jan. 1*						*23*
			19-- *Jan. 12*	*3269*	*15*	*8*
Feb. 1	*9281*	*32*				*40*
			Mar. 4	*3461*	*12*	*28*

Illustration 29-2
Stock record

A perpetual inventory system provides day-to-day information about the quantity of merchandise on hand. The minimum balance allowed before a reorder must be placed is also shown on each stock record. When the quantity falls below the minimum, additional merchandise is ordered to increase the balance up to the maximum. The minimum balance is the quantity of merchandise that will typically last until the ordered merchandise can be received from the vendors. A stock record shows the quantity but usually not the cost of the merchandise.

When a perpetual inventory of merchandise is kept, entries are made on the stock records to show the following information.

1. Increases in the quantity on hand when additional merchandise is received.
2. Decreases in the quantity on hand when merchandise is sold.
3. The balance on hand after each increase or decrease is recorded.

Each time merchandise is purchased, an entry is recorded in the Increases columns. The balance on hand is then updated in the Balance column. Each time merchandise is sold, an entry is recorded in the Decreases columns and the balance is updated. The quantity of merchandise on hand is the last amount in the Balance column of a stock record.

When a perpetual inventory is kept manually, errors may be made in recording or figuring amounts. Also, some stock records may be incorrect because merchandise is taken from stock and not recorded on stock records. A customary practice is to take a periodic inventory at least once a fiscal period. The periodic inventory is then compared with the perpetual inventory records. The perpetual records are corrected to reflect the actual quantity on hand as determined by the periodic inventory.

Perpetual inventory using a computer

Many merchandising businesses use a computer to keep perpetual inventory records. Special cash registers and checkout counters are used.

The checkout counters have devices to read the Universal Product Codes (UPC codes) marked on products. An example of a UPC code is shown in Illustration 29-3.

A stock ledger for all merchandise on hand is stored on the computer. Each time a UPC code is read at the checkout counter, the computer checks the stock ledger to obtain the product description and the sales price. The product description and price are then displayed on the cash register. At the same time, the computer reduces the units on hand to reflect the item sold. The computer periodically checks the quantities in the stock ledger and prints a list of the items that need to be reordered.

DETERMINING THE COST OF MERCHANDISE INVENTORY

Costs are not recorded on inventory records at the time a periodic inventory is taken. After the quantities of merchandise on hand are counted, purchase invoices are used to find merchandise unit prices. The total costs are then calculated using the quantities and unit prices recorded on the inventory records. Most businesses use one of three inventory costing methods to calculate the cost of merchandise inventory: (1) first-in, first-out, (2) last-in, first-out, or (3) weighted-average.

First-in, first-out inventory costing method

MusiCo takes a periodic inventory at the end of each fiscal period. The quantity of each item on hand is recorded on an inventory record. The inventory records are sent to the accounting department to determine the unit price and total cost of each item on hand. MusiCo uses the most recent invoices for purchases to determine the unit price of an item. The earliest invoices for purchases, therefore, are used to determine the cost of merchandise sold.

Using the price of merchandise purchased first to calculate the cost of merchandise sold first is called the first-in, first-out inventory costing method. The cost of the ending inventory, therefore, consists of the most recent price of merchandise purchased. The first-in, first-out method is frequently abbreviated as *fifo* (the first letter of each of the four words). On January 31 a periodic inventory of music stands, Stock No. MS130, showed 16 music stands on hand. Purchase information for this item during the fiscal period is shown below.

	Units	Unit Price	Total Cost
February 1, beginning inventory...........	4	$40.00	$ 160.00
April 14, purchases.......................	10	42.00	420.00
June 22, purchases	8	44.00	352.00
September 6, purchases	16	45.00	720.00
November 28, purchases	12	48.00	576.00
Totals................................	50		$2,228.00

During the fiscal period, 34 music stands were sold. Using the fifo method, the 16 inventory units on hand on January 31 are priced using the most recent unit prices. The most recent unit prices are $48.00 and $45.00. The inventory cost using the fifo method is calculated as shown below.

Most recent purchase, November 28, 12 units @ $48.00	$576.00
Next most recent purchase, September 6, 4 units @ $45.00	180.00
Total cost of 16 units	$756.00

The most recent purchase, November 28, is used to price 12 of the 16 units in ending inventory. The remaining 4 units in ending inventory are priced using the next most recent purchase, September 6.

On the inventory record, the 16 music stands are shown as having a total cost of $756.00. The cost of the 34 music stands sold is calculated as shown below.

Total Purchases	−	Cost of Ending Inventory	=	Cost of Merchandise Sold
$2,228.00	−	$756.00	=	$1,472.00

Last-in, first-out inventory costing method

Using the price of merchandise purchased last to calculate the cost of merchandise sold first is called the last-in, first-out inventory costing method. The last-in, first-out method is frequently abbreviated as *lifo*. This method is based on the idea that the most recent prices of merchandise should be charged against current revenue. (*CONCEPT: Matching Expenses with Revenue*)

Using the lifo method, each item on the inventory records is recorded at the earliest prices paid for the merchandise. The lifo inventory cost for the 16 music stands described previously is calculated as shown below.

Beginning inventory, February 1, 4 units @ $40.00	$160.00
Next earliest purchase, April 14, 10 units @ $42.00	420.00
Next earliest purchase, June 22, 2 units @ $44.00...............	88.00
Total cost of 16 units	$668.00

The earliest prices consist of the 4 units in the February 1 beginning inventory. The earliest purchase, April 14, of 10 units is then used to price 10 units in ending inventory. The remaining 2 units in ending inventory are priced using the next earliest purchase, June 22.

On the inventory record, the 16 music stands would show a total cost of $668.00. The cost of merchandise sold for the 34 music stands sold would be recorded as $1,560.00, the difference between total purchases, $2,228.00, and the cost of ending inventory, $668.00.

Weighted-average inventory costing method

Using the average cost of beginning inventory plus merchandise purchased during a fiscal period to calculate the cost of merchandise sold is called the weighted-average inventory costing method. The ending inventory and cost of merchandise sold are calculated using the same unit price, the average amount paid for the merchandise during the fiscal period. The average cost of merchandise is charged against current revenue. (CONCEPT: Matching Expenses with Revenue)

Using the weighted-average method, the inventory is priced at the average price per unit of the beginning inventory plus the cost of all purchases during the fiscal year. The weighted-average inventory cost for the 16 music stands described previously is calculated as shown below.

Total of Beginning Inventory and Purchases	÷	Total Units	=	Weighted-Average Price per Unit
$2,228.00	÷	50	=	$44.56

Units in Ending Inventory	×	Weighted-Average Price per Unit	=	Cost of Ending Inventory
16	×	$44.56	=	$712.96

On the inventory record, the 16 music stands would show a total cost of $712.96. The cost of merchandise sold for the 34 units sold would be recorded as $1,515.04, the difference between total purchases, $2,228.00, and the cost of ending inventory, $712.96. Since the weighted-average method uses an average unit price, the same unit price may be used to calculate the cost of both ending inventory and cost of merchandise sold. Thus, the cost of merchandise sold could also be calculated as shown below.

Units Sold	×	Weighted-Average Price per Unit	=	Cost of Merchandise Sold
34	×	$44.56	=	$1,515.04

A business usually determines the order in which products are sold based on the type of inventory. A grocery store, for example, must sell its earliest purchases first. A hardware store, however, could sell its most recent purchases first. The inventory costing method used to calculate the cost of merchandise sold should not, however, be determined by the order in which items are sold. A business should choose the inventory costing method that provides its managers with the best accounting information.

A comparison of inventory costing methods

The inventory costs for the 16 music stands were calculated using fifo, lifo, and weighted-average methods during a fiscal period of rising prices. To show the effect of falling prices, purchase information for this item is reversed as shown below.

	Units	Unit Price	Total Cost
February 1, beginning inventory...........	4	$48.00	$ 192.00
April 14, purchases......................	10	45.00	450.00
June 22, purchases	8	44.00	352.00
September 6, purchases	16	42.00	672.00
November 28, purchases	12	40.00	480.00
Totals................................	50		$2,146.00

Using the fifo method, the 16 inventory units are priced at the most recent unit prices. The most recent unit prices are $40.00 and $42.00. The inventory cost using the fifo method is calculated as shown below.

Most recent purchase, November 28, 12 units @ $40.00	$480.00
Next most recent purchase, September 6, 4 units @ $42.00	168.00
Total cost of 16 units	$648.00

Using the lifo method, the 16 inventory units are priced at the earliest unit prices. The earliest unit prices are $48.00, $45.00, and $44.00. The inventory cost using the lifo method is calculated as shown below.

Beginning inventory, February 1, 4 units @ $48.00	$192.00
Next earliest purchase, April 14, 10 units @ $45.00	450.00
Next earliest purchase, June 22, 2 units @ $44.00...............	88.00
Total cost of 16 units	$730.00

Using the weighted-average method, the 16 inventory units are priced at the average price of beginning inventory plus the cost of all items purchased during the fiscal period. The inventory cost using the weighted-average method is calculated as shown below.

Total of Beginning Inventory and Purchases	÷	Total Units	=	Weighted-Average Price per Unit
$2,146.00	÷	50	=	$42.92

Units in Ending Inventory	×	Weighted-Average Price per Unit	=	Cost of Ending Inventory
16	×	$42.92	=	$686.72

A comparison of the three inventory methods used in determining the cost of merchandise sold is shown in Illustration 29-4.

	Rising Prices			Falling Prices		
	Fifo	Lifo	Weighted Average	Fifo	Lifo	Weighted Average
Cost of Merchandise Sold:						
Merchandise Inventory, Feb. 1 ...	$ 160.00	$ 160.00	$ 160.00	$ 192.00	$ 192.00	$ 192.00
Net Purchases	2,068.00	2,068.00	2,068.00	1,954.00	1,954.00	1,954.00
Merchandise Available for Sale...	$2,228.00	$2,228.00	$2,228.00	$2,146.00	$2,146.00	$2,146.00
Less Ending Inventory, Jan. 31...	756.00	668.00	712.96	648.00	730.00	686.72
Cost of Merchandise Sold	$1,472.00	$1,560.00	$1,515.04	$1,498.00	$1,416.00	$1,459.28
Relative Cost of Ending Inventory	highest	lowest	intermediate	lowest	highest	intermediate
Relative Cost of Merchandise Sold	lowest	highest	intermediate	highest	lowest	intermediate

Illustration 29-4
Comparison of inventory costing methods

In a year of rising prices, the fifo method gives the highest possible ending inventory cost and the lowest cost of merchandise sold. The lifo method gives the lowest possible ending inventory cost and the highest cost of merchandise sold. The weighted-average method gives ending inventory cost and cost of merchandise sold between fifo and lifo. As the cost of merchandise sold increases, gross profit and net income decrease. Thus, during a year of rising prices, net income is highest under the fifo method, lowest under the lifo method, and intermediate under the weighted-average method.

In a year of falling prices, the fifo method gives the lowest possible ending inventory cost and the highest cost of merchandise sold. The lifo method gives the highest possible ending inventory cost and the lowest cost of merchandise sold. The weighted-average method again gives ending inventory cost and cost of merchandise sold between fifo and lifo. Therefore, during a year of falling prices, net income is the lowest under the fifo method, highest under the lifo method, and intermediate under the weighted-average method.

All three inventory costing methods are acceptable accounting practices. However, a business should select one method and use that same method continuously for each fiscal period. Using the same inventory costing method for all fiscal periods provides financial statements that can be compared with other fiscal period statements. If a business changes inventory costing methods, part of the difference in gross profit and net income may be caused by the change in methods. Therefore, to provide financial statements that can be analyzed and compared with statements of other fiscal periods, the same inventory costing method should be used each fiscal period. (CONCEPT: Consistent Reporting)

ESTIMATING THE COST OF MERCHANDISE INVENTORY

Estimating inventory by using the previous years' percentage of gross profit on operations is called the gross profit method of estimating inventory. The gross profit method of estimating inventory is often used to estimate the cost of the monthly ending inventory. The ending inventory cost is used to prepare monthly financial statements. The gross profit method of estimating inventory provides a business with a method of calculating inventory costs that is less expensive than taking a periodic inventory or maintaining a perpetual inventory system.

MusiCo prepares an income statement at the end of each month. *(CONCEPT: Accounting Period Cycle)* To estimate the ending merchandise inventory on April 30, the following information is obtained.

Beginning inventory, February 1..........................	$ 45,790.00
Net purchases for the period, February 1 to April 30	170,670.00
Net sales for the period, February 1 to April 30	285,790.00
Gross profit on operations (percentage based on records of previous year's operations)........................	40.0%

MusiCo's fiscal year ends on January 31. A periodic inventory was taken on January 31 to provide an accurate cost of ending inventory for annual financial statements. The ending inventory on January 31, $45,790.00, is also the beginning inventory on February 1. Therefore, the February 1 inventory cost, which has been verified by taking a periodic inventory, is used as the basis for estimating monthly ending inventory.

In the prior fiscal period, MusiCo's gross profit was 40.0% of its net sales. MusiCo can use this percentage in the current fiscal period to estimate the cost of merchandise sold and gross profit.

Four steps are followed to estimate the ending merchandise inventory for MusiCo on April 30.

1 Determine the cost of merchandise available for sale.

Beginning inventory, February 1	$ 45,790.00
Plus net purchases, February 1 to April 30	+170,670.00
Equals cost of merchandise available for sale.........	$216,460.00

2 Estimate the gross profit on operations.

Net sales for February 1 to April 30................	$285,790.00
Times previous year's gross profit percentage	× 40.0%
Equals estimated gross profit on operations	$114,316.00

3 Estimate the cost of merchandise sold.

Net sales for February 1 to April 30................	$285,790.00
Less estimated gross profit on operations (from Step 2).................................	−114,316.00
Equals estimated cost of merchandise sold...........	$171,474.00

4 Estimate the cost of ending merchandise inventory.

Cost of merchandise available for sale (from Step 1) ..	$216,460.00
Less estimated cost of merchandise sold (from Step 3)...................................	−171,474.00
Equals estimated ending merchandise inventory	$ 44,986.00

The estimated ending merchandise inventory for MusiCo on April 30, $44,986.00, is used to prepare the April income statement. MusiCo's income statement prepared on April 30 is shown in Illustration 29-5.

MusiCo, Inc. Income Statement For Month Ended April 30, 19--		
		% of Net Sales
Operating Revenue:		
Net Sales............................	$96,720.00	100.0
Cost of Merchandise Sold:		
Estimated Beginning Inventory, April 1 ..	$ 45,178.00	
Net Purchases	57,840.00	
Merchandise Available for Sale	$103,018.00	
Less Estimated Ending Inv., April 30	44,986.00	
Cost of Merchandise Sold	58,032.00	60.0
Gross Profit on Operations	$38,688.00	40.0
Operating Expenses....................	24,858.00	25.7
Net Income...........................	$13,830.00	14.3

Illustration 29-5
Income statement with
estimated inventory

The beginning inventory on April 1, $45,178.00, is the estimated ending inventory from the income statement on March 31. The amount of merchandise inventory purchased in April, $57,840.00, is obtained from the general ledger. By using the $44,986.00 estimate of ending merchandise inventory, MusiCo calculated its estimated cost of merchandise sold to be $58,032.00.

An estimated inventory is not completely accurate. The actual rate of gross profit on operations may not be exactly the percentage used in the estimate. Also, some merchandise may have been stolen or damaged. However, an estimated ending inventory is accurate enough for management to prepare a monthly income statement without taking the time to count the inventory. Businesses using a monthly estimate of the merchandise inventory usually take an annual periodic inventory. This is necessary in order to have accurate information for the end-of-year tax reports.

SUMMARY OF AN INVENTORY SYSTEM

At the end of the fiscal year, a merchandising business will usually determine the actual quantity of each item by taking a periodic inventory. The cost of merchandise inventory can be calculated using the fifo, lifo, or weighted-average inventory costing method, as shown in Illustration 29-6.

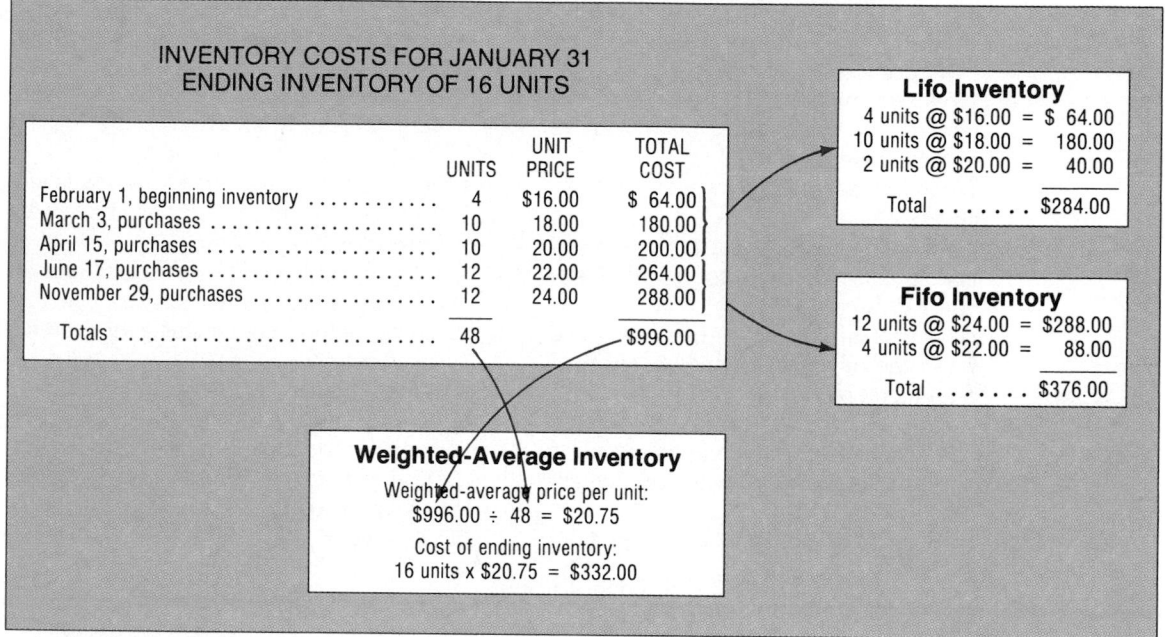

INVENTORY COSTS FOR JANUARY 31
ENDING INVENTORY OF 16 UNITS

	UNITS	UNIT PRICE	TOTAL COST
February 1, beginning inventory	4	$16.00	$ 64.00
March 3, purchases	10	18.00	180.00
April 15, purchases	10	20.00	200.00
June 17, purchases	12	22.00	264.00
November 29, purchases	12	24.00	288.00
Totals	48		$996.00

Lifo Inventory

4 units @ $16.00 =	$ 64.00
10 units @ $18.00 =	180.00
2 units @ $20.00 =	40.00
Total	$284.00

Fifo Inventory

12 units @ $24.00 =	$288.00
4 units @ $22.00 =	88.00
Total	$376.00

Weighted-Average Inventory

Weighted-average price per unit:
$996.00 ÷ 48 = $20.75

Cost of ending inventory:
16 units x $20.75 = $332.00

Illustration 29-6
Summary of fifo, lifo, and weighted-average inventory costing methods

A merchandising business can control its merchandise inventory by maintaining a continuous record of item quantities known as a perpetual inventory. At any time a business can determine the quantity of any inventory item on hand by examining the stock record in the stock ledger.

A merchandising business can also estimate monthly ending merchandise inventory costs by using the gross profit method of estimating inventory. The previous years' percentage of gross profit on operations is used to estimate the cost of merchandise inventory sold during the period. This estimate is subtracted from the merchandise available for sale to calculate the estimated ending merchandise inventory.

■ ACCOUNTING TERMS

What is the meaning of each of the following?

1. periodic inventory
2. perpetual inventory
3. inventory record
4. stock record
5. stock ledger

6. first-in, first-out inventory costing method
7. last-in, first-out inventory costing method
8. weighted-average inventory costing method
9. gross profit method of estimating inventory

◼ QUESTIONS FOR INDIVIDUAL STUDY

1. What item is typically the largest asset of a merchandising business?
2. Why do successful businesses need an effective inventory system?
3. Identify four reasons why a merchandise inventory that is larger than needed may decrease the net income of a business.
4. What two methods can be used to determine the quantity of each item of merchandise on hand?
5. When are periodic inventories normally taken?
6. How do inventory levels affect the period a business selects for its fiscal year? Why?
7. What action should a business take when the minimum balance is reached on a stock record?
8. When a perpetual inventory of merchandise is kept, what entries are made on a stock record and when are the entries made?
9. How is the accuracy of a perpetual inventory checked?
10. When the fifo method is used, how is the price of each kind of merchandise determined?
11. On what idea is the lifo method based?
12. When the weighted-average method is used, how is the price of each kind of merchandise determined?
13. In a year of rising prices, which inventory costing method gives the highest cost of merchandise sold?
14. In a year of falling prices, which inventory costing method gives the lowest cost of ending inventory?
15. Why should a business select one inventory costing method and use that same method continuously for each fiscal period?
16. When neither a perpetual system is maintained nor a periodic inventory is taken, how can an ending merchandise inventory be determined that is accurate enough for a monthly income statement?

◼ CASES FOR MANAGEMENT DECISION

CASE 1 Williams, Inc., recently started a perpetual inventory system. Mr. Fleming, the manager, asks if there is any reason for the company to continue with periodic inventories now that a perpetual inventory system is used. How would you answer Mr. Fleming?

CASE 2 Marshall Company uses the fifo method of costing its merchandise inventory. The manager is considering a change to the lifo method. Prices have increased steadily over the past three years. What effect will the change have on the following items? (1) The amount of net income on the income statement. (2) The amount of income taxes to be paid. (3) The quantity of each item of merchandise that must be kept in stock. Why?

CASE 3 The Craft Shop stocks many kinds of merchandise. The store has always taken a periodic inventory at the end of a fiscal year. The store has not kept a perpetual inventory because of the cost. However, the manager wants a reasonably accurate cost of merchandise inventory at the end of each month. The manager needs the amount to prepare monthly income statements and to help in making decisions about the business. What would you recommend?

◼ DRILL FOR UNDERSTANDING

DRILL 29-D1 Determining quantities of merchandise on hand using a perpetual inventory

Accounting records at Blette Company show the following inventory increases and decreases for one item of merchandise. Beginning inventory on July 1 was 68 units.

Increases		Decreases	
Date	**Quantity**	**Date**	**Quantity**
		July 5	34
		July 7	25
July 8	50		
		July 12	15
July 15	125		
		July 16	108
		July 23	52
July 28	100		

Instructions: 1. Use a stock record similar to the following. Record the increases and decreases.

Increases		Decreases		Balance
Date	**Quantity**	**Date**	**Quantity**	**Quantity**
July 1				68

2. Calculate and record the balance of units on hand for each date a transaction occurred.

■ APPLICATION PROBLEMS

PROBLEM 29-1 **Determining cost of ending inventory using the fifo, lifo, and weighted-average methods**

Accounting records at Wimberly Company show the following purchases and periodic inventory counts.

Model No.	Beginning Inventory January 1	First Purchase	Second Purchase	Third Purchase	Periodic Inventory Count December 31
A48	15 @ $12.00	24 @ $14.00	20 @ $15.00	16 @ $18.00	29
G56	6 @ $40.00	8 @ $42.00	4 @ $44.00	9 @ $45.00	12
Q392	24 @ $ 7.00	18 @ $ 6.00	30 @ $ 6.00	26 @ $ 5.00	42
S49	6 @ $40.00	8 @ $45.00	10 @ $45.00	5 @ $48.00	16
P32	14 @ $12.00	12 @ $10.00	22 @ $ 9.00	10 @ $ 8.00	30
K235	4 @ $30.00	16 @ $35.00	8 @ $35.00	10 @ $38.00	19

Instructions: 1. Figure the total cost of ending inventory on December 31 using the fifo method. Use a form similar to the following. The inventory cost for Model No. A48 is given as an example.

Model No.	No. of Units on Hand	Unit Price	Cost of Ending Inventory
A48	29	16 @ $18.00 13 @ 15.00	$483.00

Use the following procedure to complete the form.

(a) Record the model number and number of units of each model on hand on December 31.
(b) Record the unit price of each model. When more than one unit price is used, list the units and unit prices on separate lines as shown in the example.
(c) Calculate the cost of ending inventory of each model, and write the amount in the Cost of Ending Inventory column.
(d) Add the amounts in the Cost of Ending Inventory column to calculate the total cost of ending inventory.

    2. On another form calculate the total cost of ending inventory using the lifo method. Follow the steps given in Instruction 1.

    3. On another form calculate the total cost of ending inventory using the weighted-average method. Use the following procedure.

(a) Record the model number and number of units of each model on hand on December 31.
(b) Calculate the weighted-average price per unit for each model. Round the amount per unit to the nearest cent. Write the amount in the Unit Price column.
(c) Calculate the cost of ending inventory of each model, and write the amount in the Cost of Ending Inventory column.
(d) Add the amounts in the Cost of Ending Inventory column to calculate the total cost of ending inventory.

    4. Compare the total cost of ending inventory obtained in Instructions 1, 2, and 3. Which method, fifo, lifo, or weighted-average, resulted in the lowest cost of ending inventory?

PROBLEM 29-2   Estimating inventory using the gross profit method of estimating inventory

The following information is from the accounting records of two different companies for July of the current year.

	Companies	
	Daniel	**Pearson**
Beginning inventory, July 1............................	$12,900.00	$32,900.00
Net purchases for July..................................	32,300.00	63,200.00
Net sales for July	76,500.00	98,500.00
Gross profit on operation as a percent of sales...........	60.0%	45.0%
Operating expenses for July	25,400.00	37,600.00

Instructions: 1. For each company estimate the ending inventory for July of the current year using the gross profit method of estimating inventory.
    2. Prepare an income statement for each company similar to the one shown in Illustration 29-5 for the month ended July 31 of the current year.

■ ENRICHMENT PROBLEMS

MASTERY PROBLEM 29-M   Determining cost of ending inventory using the fifo, lifo, and weighted-average methods

Accounting records at SummerSport Company show the following purchases and periodic inventory counts.

Model No.	Beginning Inventory January 1	First Purchase	Second Purchase	Third Purchase	Periodic Inventory Count December 31
23B2	4 @ $4.50	12 @ $4.75	8 @ $4.90	15 @ $5.20	22
13M2	3 @ $3.50	6 @ $3.30	2 @ $3.20	5 @ $3.10	8
45V23	23 @ $1.20	45 @ $1.25	35 @ $1.30	40 @ $1.40	35
90F2	12 @ $7.40	15 @ $7.50	16 @ $7.80	20 @ $7.90	30
10K3	32 @ $5.40	38 @ $5.10	19 @ $4.90	26 @ $4.80	40
34P2	2 @ $2.50	5 @ $2.70	4 @ $2.80	3 @ $3.00	4

Instructions: 1. Figure the total cost of ending inventory on October 31 using the fifo method. Use a form similar to the following. The inventory cost for Model No. 23B2 is given as an example.

Model No.	No. of Units on Hand	Unit Price	Cost of Ending Inventory
23B2	22	15 @ $5.20 7 @ 4.90	$112.30

Use the following procedure to complete the form.

(a) Record the model number and number of units of each model on hand on December 31.
(b) Record the unit price of each model. When more than one unit price is used, list the units and unit prices on separate lines as shown in the example.
(c) Calculate the cost of ending inventory of each model, and write the amount in the Cost of Ending Inventory column.
(d) Add the amounts in the Cost of Ending Inventory column to calculate the total cost of ending inventory.

2. On another form calculate the total cost of ending inventory using the lifo method. Follow the steps given in Instruction 1.

3. On another form calculate the total cost of ending inventory using the weighted-average method. Use the following procedure.

(a) Record the model number and number of units of each model on hand on December 31.
(b) Calculate the weighted-average price per unit for each model. Round the amount per unit to the nearest cent. Write the amount in the Unit Price column.
(c) Calculate the cost of ending inventory of each model, and write the amount in the Cost of Ending Inventory column.
(d) Add the amounts in the Cost of Ending Inventory column to calculate the total cost of ending inventory.

4. Compare the total cost of ending inventory obtained in Instructions 1, 2, and 3. Which method, fifo, lifo, or weighted-average, resulted in the lowest cost of ending inventory?

CHALLENGE PROBLEM 29-C   Determining the cost of merchandise inventory destroyed in a fire

A fire completely destroyed the warehouse of Fleming Lighting Company on the night of October 12. The accounting records of the company and $6,500 of merchandise inventory remained safe in the company's showroom. The company does not maintain a perpetual inventory system. The insurance company, therefore, has requested an estimate of the merchandise inventory destroyed in the fire.

The following income statement is for the previous fiscal year.

Fleming Lighting Company		
Income Statement		
For Year Ended July 31, 19--		
Operating Revenue:		
Net Sales		$746,900.00
Cost of Merchandise Sold:		
Beginning Merchandise Inventory, Aug. 1..........	$ 72,430.00	
Net Purchases	291,300.00	
Merchandise Available for Sale..................	$363,730.00	
Less Ending Inventory, July 31	79,610.00	
Cost of Merchandise Sold		284,120.00
Gross Profit on Operations......................		$462,780.00
Operating Expenses............................		416,900.00
Net Income....................................		$ 45,880.00

The following additional financial information is obtained from the current year's accounting records.

Net purchases, August 1 to October 12.............................	$ 70,190.00
Net sales, August 1 to October 12	162,790.00
Operating expenses, August 1 to October 12........................	87,280.00

Instructions: 1. Calculate the prior year's gross profit on operations as a percentage of net sales. Round the percentage calculation to the nearest whole percent.

2. Use the percentage calculated in Instruction 1 and the current year's financial information to calculate an estimate of the total merchandise inventory as of October 12.

3. To calculate the cost of the inventory destroyed in the fire, subtract the cost of the merchandise inventory from the estimate of the total merchandise inventory as of October 12.

4. Prepare an income statement for the period August 1 to October 12.

Accounting Concepts

The following accounting concepts and their definitions are provided in this appendix for ready reference.

ACCOUNTING CONCEPTS

Accounting personnel are guided in their work by generally accepted accounting concepts. Ten commonly accepted accounting concepts are described in this appendix. Each concept is fully explained in the text the first time an application of the concept is described. Throughout the textbook, each time a concept application occurs, a concept reference is given, such as *(CONCEPT: Business Entity)*.

1. ACCOUNTING PERIOD CYCLE. [Chapter 7]
   Changes in financial information are reported for a specific period of time in the form of financial statements.
2. ADEQUATE DISCLOSURE. [Chapter 8]
   Financial statements contain all information necessary to understand a business' financial condition.
3. BUSINESS ENTITY. [Chapter 1]
   Financial information is recorded and reported separately from the owner's personal financial information.
4. CONSISTENT REPORTING. [Chapter 7]
   The same accounting procedures are followed in the same way in each accounting period.
5. GOING CONCERN. [Chapter 1]
   Financial statements are prepared with the expectation that a business will remain in operation indefinitely.
6. HISTORICAL COST. [Chapter 12]
   The actual amount paid for merchandise or other items bought is recorded.

7. MATCHING EXPENSES WITH REVENUE. [Chapter 7]
   Revenue from business activities and expenses associated with earning that revenue are recorded in the same accounting period.
8. OBJECTIVE EVIDENCE. [Chapter 4]
   A source document is prepared for each transaction.
9. REALIZATION OF REVENUE. [Chapter 13]
   Revenue is recorded at the time goods or services are sold.
10. UNIT OF MEASUREMENT. [Chapter 1]
    Business transactions are stated in numbers that have common values, that is, using a common unit of measurement.

SHARP

APPENDIX
B

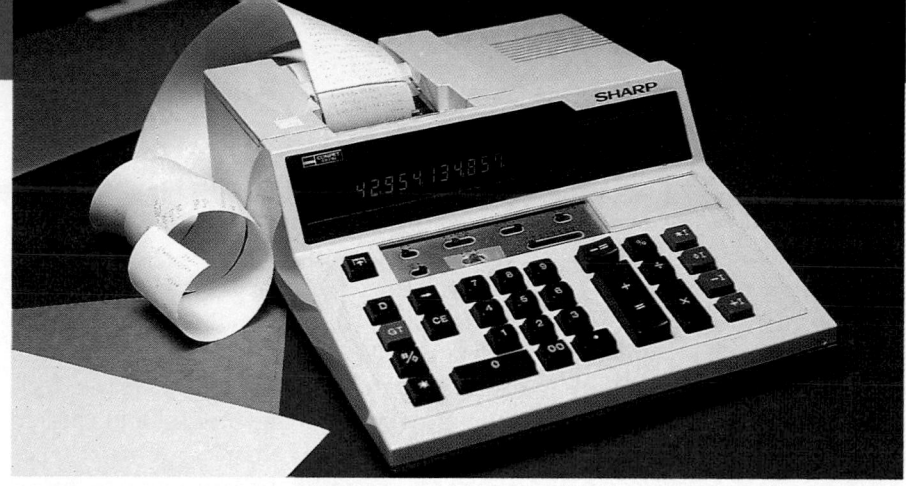

Using a Calculator

KINDS OF CALCULATORS

Many different models of calculators, both desktop and hand held, are available. However, all calculators have their own features and particular placement of operating keys. Therefore, it is necessary to refer to the operator's manual for specific instructions and locations of the operating keys for the calculator being used. A typical keyboard of a desktop calculator is shown in Illustration B-1.

Illustration B-1
Typical desktop calculator keyboard

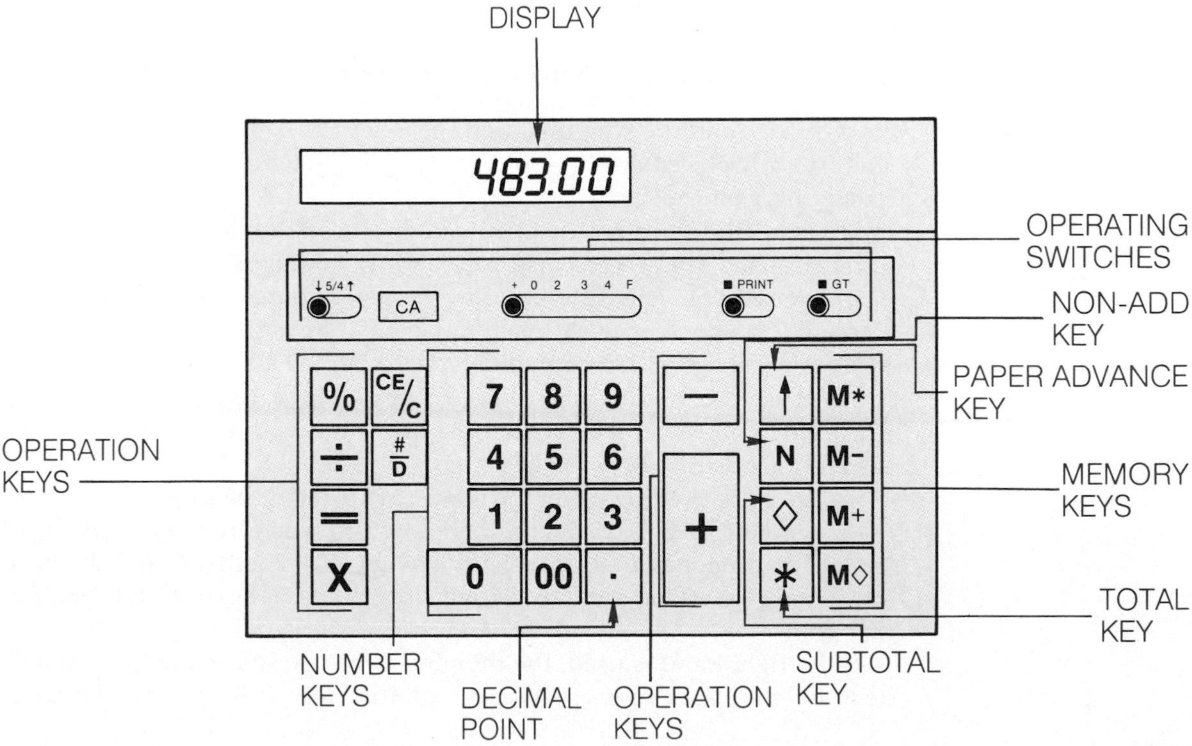
DISPLAY
483.00
OPERATING SWITCHES
NON-ADD KEY
PAPER ADVANCE KEY
MEMORY KEYS
TOTAL KEY
OPERATION KEYS
NUMBER KEYS
DECIMAL POINT
OPERATION KEYS
SUBTOTAL KEY
↓5/4↑
CA
+ 0 2 3 4 F
PRINT
GT
%
CE/C
÷
#/D
=
X
7
8
9
4
5
6
1
2
3
0
00
·
—
+
↑
N
◇
*
M*
M-
M+
M◇

DESKTOP CALCULATOR SETTINGS

Several operating switches on a desktop calculator must be engaged before the calculator will produce the desired results.

The *decimal selector* sets the appropriate decimal places necessary for the numbers that will be entered. For example, if the decimal selector is set at 2, both the numbers entered and the answer will have two decimal places. If the decimal selector is set at F, the calculator automatically sets the decimal places. The F setting allows the answer to be unrounded and carried out to the maximum number of decimal places possible.

The *decimal rounding selector* rounds the answers. The down arrow position will drop any digits beyond the last digit desired. The up arrow position will drop any digits beyond the last digit desired and round the last digit up. In the 5/4 position, the calculator rounds the last desired digit up only when the following digit is 5 or greater. If the following digit is less than 5, the last desired digit remains unchanged.

The *GT* or *grand total switch* in the on position accumulates totals.

TEN-KEY TOUCH SYSTEM

Striking the numbers 0 to 9 on a calculator without looking at the keyboard is called the touch system. Using the touch system develops both speed and accuracy.

The 4, 5, and 6 keys are called the home row. If the right hand is used for the keyboard, the index finger is placed on the 4 key, the middle finger on the 5 key, and the ring finger on the 6 key. If the left hand is used, the ring finger is placed on the 4 key, the middle finger on the 5 key, and the index finger on the 6 key.

Place the fingers on the home row keys. Curve the fingers and keep the wrist straight. These keys may feel slightly concaved or the 5 key may have a raised dot. The differences in the home row allow the operator to recognize the home row by touch rather than by sight.

Maintain the position of the fingers on the home row. The finger used to strike the 4 key will also strike the 7 key and the 1 key. Stretch the finger up to reach the 7; then stretch the finger down to reach the 1 key. Visualize the position of these keys.

Again, place the fingers on the home row. Stretch the finger that strikes the 5 key up to reach the 8 key, then down to reach the 2 key. Likewise, stretch the finger that strikes the 6 key up to strike the 9 and down to strike the 3 key. This same finger will stretch down again to hit the decimal point.

If the right hand is used, the thumb will be used to strike the 0 and 00 keys and the little finger to strike the addition key. If the left hand is used, the little finger will be used to strike the 0 and 00 keys and the thumb to strike the addition key.

The touch system may also be used on a microcomputer numeric keypad. However, the software being used must have a calculator feature in order to use the keypad as a calculator.

PERFORMING MATHEMATICAL OPERATIONS

Mathematical operations can be performed on a calculator both quickly and efficiently. The basic operations of addition, subtraction, multiplication, and division are used frequently on a calculator.

Addition

Each number to be added is called an addend. The answer to an addition problem is called the sum.

Addition is performed by entering an addend and striking the addition key (+). All numbers are entered on a calculator in the exact order they are given. To enter the number 4,455.65, strike the 4, 4, 5, 5, decimal, 6, and 5 keys in that order, and then strike the addition key. Commas are not entered. Continue in this manner until all addends have been entered. To obtain the sum, strike the total key.

Subtraction

The top number or first number of a subtraction problem is called the minuend. The number to be subtracted from the minuend is called the subtrahend. The answer to a subtraction problem is called the difference.

Subtraction is performed by first entering the minuend and striking the addition key (+). The subtrahend is then entered, followed by the minus key (−), followed by the total key.

Multiplication

The number to be multiplied is called the multiplicand. The number of times the multiplicand will be multiplied is called the multiplier. The answer to a multiplication problem is called the product.

Multiplication is performed by entering the multiplicand and striking the multiplication key (×). The multiplier is then entered, followed by the equals key (=). The calculator will automatically multiply and give the product.

Division

The number to be divided is called the dividend. The number the dividend will be divided by is called the divisor. The answer to a division problem is called the quotient.

Division is performed by entering the dividend and striking the division key (÷). The divisor is then entered, followed by the equals key (=). The calculator will automatically divide and give the quotient.

Correcting errors

If an error is made while using a calculator, several methods of correction may be used. If an incorrect number has been entered and the addition key or equals key has not yet been struck, strike the clear entry (CE) key one time. This key will clear only the last number that was entered. However, if the clear entry key is depressed more than one time, the entire problem will be cleared on some calculators. If an incorrect number has been entered and the addition key has been struck, strike the minus key one time only. This will automatically subtract the last number added, thus removing it from the total.

HAND-HELD CALCULATORS

Hand-held calculators are slightly different from desktop calculators, not only in their size and model but also in their operation. Refer to the operator's manual for specific instructions for the calculator being used.

On a hand-held calculator, the numeric keys are usually very close together. In addition, the keys do not respond to touch as easily as on a desktop calculator. Therefore, the touch system is usually not used on a hand-held calculator.

On a hand-held calculator, addition is performed in much the same way as on a desktop calculator. However, after the + key is depressed, the display usually shows the accumulated total. Therefore, it is not necessary to strike the total key.

Subtraction is performed differently on many hand-held calculators. The minuend is usually entered, followed by the minus (−) key. Then the subtrahend is entered. Pressing either the + key or the = key will display the difference.

Multiplication and division are performed the same way on a hand-held calculator as on a desktop calculator.

SAFETY CONCERNS

Whenever electrical equipment such as a calculator is being operated in a classroom or office, several safety rules apply. These rules protect the operator of the equipment, other persons in the environment, and the equipment itself.

1. Do not unplug the calculator by pulling on the electrical cord. Instead, grasp the plug at the outlet and remove it.

2. Do not stretch the electrical cord across an aisle where someone might trip over it.
3. Avoid food and beverages near a calculator where a spill might result in an electrical short.
4. Do not attempt to remove the cover of a calculator for any reason while the power is turned on.
5. Do not attempt to repair a calculator while it is plugged in.
6. Always turn the power off or unplug a calculator when finished using it.

◼ CALCULATOR DRILLS

Instructions: Complete each drill using the touch method. Set the decimal selector at the setting indicated in each drill. Compare the answer on the calculator to the answer in the book. If the two are the same, progress to the next problem. It is not necessary to enter 00 in the cents column if the decimal selector is set at 0-F. However, digits other than zeros in the cents column must be entered preceded by a decimal point.

DRILL D-1   Performing addition using the home row keys
Decimal Selector—2

4.00	44.00	444.00	4,444.00	44,444.00
5.00	55.00	555.00	5,555.00	55,555.00
6.00	66.00	666.00	6,666.00	66,666.00
5.00	45.00	455.00	4,455.00	44,556.00
4.00	46.00	466.00	4,466.00	44,565.00
5.00	54.00	544.00	5,544.00	55,446.00
6.00	56.00	566.00	5,566.00	55,664.00
5.00	65.00	655.00	6,655.00	66,554.00
4.00	64.00	644.00	6,644.00	66,555.00
5.00	66.00	654.00	6,545.00	65,465.00
49.00	561.00	5,649.00	56,540.00	565,470.00

DRILL D-2   Performing addition using the 0, 1, 4, and 7 keys
Decimal Selector—2

4.00	11.00	444.00	4,440.00	44,000.00
7.00	44.00	777.00	7,770.00	77,000.00
4.00	74.00	111.00	1,110.00	11,000.00
1.00	71.00	741.00	4,400.00	41,000.00
4.00	70.00	740.00	1,100.00	71,000.00
7.00	10.00	101.00	4,007.00	10,000.00
4.00	14.00	140.00	7,001.00	10,100.00
1.00	17.00	701.00	1,007.00	40,100.00
4.00	40.00	700.00	1,004.00	70,100.00
7.00	77.00	407.00	7,700.00	74,100.00
43.00	428.00	4,862.00	39,539.00	448,400.00

DRILL D-3 Performing addition using the 2, 5, and 8 keys
Decimal Selector—2

5.00	58.00	588.00	8,888.00	88,855.00
8.00	52.00	522.00	5,555.00	88,822.00
5.00	85.00	888.00	2,222.00	88,852.00
2.00	52.00	222.00	8,525.00	88,222.00
5.00	25.00	258.00	2,585.00	85,258.00
8.00	58.00	852.00	8,258.00	22,255.00
5.00	82.00	225.00	8,585.00	22,288.00
2.00	28.00	885.00	5,258.00	22,258.00
5.00	88.00	882.00	2,852.00	22,888.00
8.00	22.00	228.00	2,288.00	25,852.00
53.00	550.00	5,550.00	55,016.00	555,550.00

DRILL D-4 Performing addition using the 3, 6, 9, and decimal point keys
Decimal Selector—2

6.00	66.66	666.66	6,666.99	66,699.33
9.00	99.99	999.99	9,999.66	99,966.66
6.00	33.33	333.33	3,333.99	33,366.33
3.00	33.66	666.99	3,366.99	36,963.36
6.36	33.99	999.66	6,699.33	69,636.36
3.36	99.66	333.66	9,966.33	33,333.66
9.36	99.33	696.36	9,636.69	66,666.99
9.63	33.36	369.63	3,696.36	99,999.33
6.33	33.69	336.69	6,963.99	96,369.63
9.93	69.63	963.36	6,699.33	36,963.36
68.97	603.30	6,366.33	67,029.66	639,965.01

DRILL D-5 Performing subtraction using all number keys
Decimal Selector—F

456.73	789.01	741.00	852.55	987.98
−123.21	−456.00	−258.10	−369.88	−102.55
333.52	333.01	482.90	482.67	885.43

DRILL D-6 Performing multiplication using all number keys
Decimal Selector—F

654.05	975.01	487.10	123.56	803.75
×12.66	× 27.19	× 30.21	×50.09	× 1.45
8,280.273	26,510.5219	14,715.291	6,189.1204	1,165.4375

DRILL D-7 Performing division using all number keys
Decimal Selector—F

900.56 ÷ 450.28 = 2.
500.25 ÷ 100.05 = 5.
135.66 ÷   6.65 = 20.4
269.155 ÷ 105.55 = 2.550023685*
985.66 ÷ 22.66 = 43.49779346*

Number of decimal places may vary due to machine capacity.

Recycling Problems

RECYCLING PROBLEM 1-R   **Determining how transactions change an accounting equation and preparing a balance sheet**

Kim Suomi is starting Suomi Service Center, a telephone-answering business. Suomi Service Center uses the accounts shown in the following accounting equation. Use a form similar to the following to complete this problem.

Trans. No.	Assets			=	Liabilities	+	Owner's Equity
	Cash +	Supplies +	Prepaid Insurance	=	Olson Office Supply	+	Kim Suomi, Capital
Beg. Bal. 1.	0 +700	0	0		0		0 +700 (investment)
New Bal. 2.	700	0	0		0		700

Transactions
1. Received cash from owner as an investment, $700.00.
2. Bought supplies on account from Olson Office Supply, $100.00.
3. Paid cash for insurance, $150.00.
4. Paid cash for supplies, $50.00.
5. Paid cash on account to Olson Office Supply, $50.00.

Instructions: 1. For each transaction, complete the following. Transaction 1 is given as an example.
a. Analyze the transaction to determine which accounts in the accounting equation are affected.
b. Write the amount in the appropriate columns, using a plus (+) if the account increases or a minus (−) if the account decreases.
c. For transactions that change owner's equity, write in parentheses a description of the transaction to the right of the amount.
d. Calculate the new balance for each account in the accounting equation.
e. Before going on to the next transaction, determine that the accounting equation is still in balance.

2. Using the final balances in the accounting equation, prepare a balance sheet. Use February 7 of the current year as the date of the balance sheet.

RECYCLING PROBLEM 2-R   **Determining how transactions change an accounting equation and preparing a balance sheet**

Steve Bird operates a service business called Office Plants Company. Office Plants Company uses the accounts shown in the following accounting equation. Use a form similar to the following to complete the problem.

Trans. No.	Assets			=	Liabilities	+	Owner's Equity
	Cash +	Supplies +	Prepaid Insurance	=	Stanton Company	+	Steve Bird, Capital
Beg. Bal. 1.	1,600 −90	200	400		500		1,700 −90 (expense)
New Bal. 2.	1,510	200	400		500		1,610

Transactions
1. Paid cash for telephone bill, $90.00.
2. Received cash from sales, $230.00.
3. Paid cash for equipment repair, $25.00.
4. Received cash from owner as an investment, $300.00.
5. Paid cash for rent, $400.00.
6. Received cash from sales, $250.00.
7. Paid cash for advertising, $100.00.
8. Paid cash on account to Stanton Company, $500.00.
9. Paid cash for water bill, $60.00.
10. Paid cash for miscellaneous expense, $10.00.
11. Bought supplies on account from Stanton Company, $300.00.
12. Paid cash for supplies, $200.00.
13. Received cash from sales, $270.00.
14. Paid cash to owner for personal use, $600.00.
15. Paid cash for insurance, $150.00.

Instructions: 1. For each transaction, complete the following. Transaction 1 is given as an example.
a. Analyze the transaction to determine which accounts in the accounting equation are affected.
b. Write the amount in the appropriate columns, using a plus (+) if the account increases or a minus (−) if the account decreases.
c. For transactions that change owner's equity, write in parentheses a description of the transaction to the right of the amount.
d. Calculate the new balance for each account in the accounting equation.
e. Before going on to the next transaction, determine that the accounting equation is still in balance.
2. Using the final balances in the accounting equation, prepare a balance sheet. Use the date November 15 of the current year.

RECYCLING PROBLEM 3-R   Analyzing transactions into debit and credit parts

Alicia Valdez owns a business called QuickWash. QuickWash uses the following accounts.

Cash
Supplies
Prepaid Insurance
Kishler Office Supplies
Travis Office Supplies
Alicia Valdez, Capital
Alicia Valdez, Drawing

Sales
Advertising Expense
Miscellaneous Expense
Rent Expense
Repair Expense
Utilities Expense

Transactions

Mar. 1. Received cash from owner as an investment, $3,000.00.
      2. Paid cash for supplies, $60.00.
      5. Paid cash for rent, $200.00.
      5. Received cash from sales, $350.00.
      6. Bought supplies on account from Travis Office Supplies, $500.00.
      9. Paid cash for repairs, $10.00.
     12. Received cash from sales, $200.00.
     13. Paid cash for insurance, $100.00.
     17. Bought supplies on account from Kishler Office Supplies, $50.00.
     19. Paid cash for miscellaneous expense, $5.00.
     19. Received cash from owner as an investment, $800.00.
     19. Received cash from sales, $300.00.
     20. Paid cash on account to Travis Office Supplies, $50.00.
     24. Paid cash for telephone bill (utilities expense), $25.00.
     25. Paid cash for advertising, $35.00.
     26. Received cash from sales, $320.00.
     30. Paid cash to owner for personal use, $500.00.
     31. Received cash from sales, $100.00.

Instructions: 1. Prepare a T account for each account.
    2. Analyze each transaction into its debit and credit parts. Write the debit and credit amounts in the proper T accounts to show how each transaction changes account balances. Write the date of the transaction in parentheses before each amount.

RECYCLING PROBLEM 4-R   Journalizing transactions

Mary Ching owns a service business called Ching's Accounting. Ching's Accounting uses the following accounts.

Cash
Supplies
Prepaid Insurance
West Supplies
Wilson's Office Supplies
Mary Ching, Capital
Mary Ching, Drawing

Sales
Advertising Expense
Miscellaneous Expense
Rent Expense
Repair Expense
Utilities Expense

Instructions: 1. Journalize the following transactions completed during October of the current year. Use page 1 of a journal similar to the one described in Chapter 4 for Rugcare. Source documents are abbreviated as follows: check, C; memorandum, M; receipt, R; calculator tape, T.

Oct. 1. Received cash from owner as an investment, $14,000.00. R1.
     2. Paid cash for rent, $700.00. C1.
     5. Paid cash for supplies, $500.00. C2.
     6. Paid cash for insurance, $1,500.00. C3.
     7. Bought supplies on account from West Supplies, $2,000.00. M1.
     9. Paid cash for miscellaneous expense, $5.00. C4.
    12. Paid cash on account to West Supplies, $1,000.00. C5.
    12. Received cash from sales, $450.00. T12.
    13. Received cash from sales, $400.00. T13.
    14. Paid cash for telephone bill, $60.00. C6.
    14. Received cash from sales, $480.00. T14.
    15. Paid cash for repairs, $80.00. C7.
    15. Paid cash to owner for personal use, $400.00. C8.
    15. Received cash from sales, $550.00. T15.
    16. Received cash from sales, $480.00. T16.
    19. Received cash from sales, $380.00. T19.
    20. Received cash from sales, $520.00. T20.
    21. Bought supplies on account from Wilson's Office Supplies, $600.00. M2.
    21. Received cash from sales, $400.00. T21.
    22. Paid cash for supplies, $1,200.00. C9.
    22. Received cash from sales, $550.00. T22.
    23. Received cash from sales, $450.00. T23.

2. Prove and rule page 1 of the journal. Carry the column totals forward to page 2 of the journal.
3. Use page 2 of the journal. Journalize the following transactions completed during October of the current year.

Oct. 26. Paid cash for advertising, $100.00. C10.
    26. Bought supplies on account from West Supplies, $60.00. M3.
    26. Received cash from sales, $460.00. T26.
    27. Received cash from sales, $370.00. T27.
    28. Paid cash for electric bill, $40.00. C11.
    28. Received cash from sales, $400.00. T28.
    29. Paid cash on account to West Supplies, $60.00. C12.
    29. Received cash from sales, $330.00. T29.
    30. Paid cash for supplies, $50.00. C13.
    30. Received cash from sales, $550.00. T30.
    31. Paid cash to owner for personal use, $400.00. C14.

4. Prove page 2 of the journal.
5. Prove cash. The beginning cash balance on October 1 is zero. The balance on the next unused check stub is $14,675.00.
6. Rule page 2 of the journal.

RECYCLING PROBLEM 5-R   Journalizing and posting to a general ledger

Al Burns owns a service business called Burns Cleaning. Burns Cleaning uses the same journal used by Rugcare in Chapter 4.

Instructions: 1. Open a general ledger account for each of the following accounts.

Assets		Revenue	
110	Cash	410	Sales
120	Supplies		Expenses
130	Prepaid Insurance	510	Advertising Expense
	Liabilities	520	Miscellaneous Expense
210	Mitchell Office Supplies	530	Rent Expense
	Owner's Equity	540	Utilities Expense
310	Al Burns, Capital		
320	Al Burns, Drawing		

2. Journalize the following transactions completed during November of the current year. Use page 1 of a journal. Source documents are abbreviated as follows: check, C; memorandum, M; receipt, R; calculator tape, T.

Nov. 1. Received cash from owner as an investment, $7,000.00. R1.
    3. Paid cash for insurance, $250.00. C1.
    5. Paid cash for miscellaneous expense, $5.00. C2.
    6. Received cash from sales, $410.00. T6.
    9. Paid cash for rent, $400.00. C3.
    11. Paid cash for supplies, $550.00. C4.
    13. Bought supplies on account from Mitchell Office Supplies, $700.00.   M1.
    13. Received cash from sales, $380.00. T13.
    16. Paid cash for electric bill, $50.00. C5.
    18. Paid cash on account to Mitchell Office Supplies, $350.00. C6.
    20. Paid cash for advertising, $35.00. C7.
    20. Received cash from sales, $1,020.00. T20.
    25. Paid cash for supplies, $100.00. C8.
    27. Paid cash for supplies, $120.00. C9.
    27. Received cash from sales, $1,660.00. T27.
    30. Paid cash to owner for personal use, $500.00. C10.
    30. Received cash from sales, $450.00. T30.

3. Prove the journal.
4. Prove cash. The beginning cash balance on November 1 is zero. The balance on the next unused check stub is $8,560.00.
5. Rule the journal.
6. Post from the journal to the general ledger.

RECYCLING PROBLEM 6-R   Reconciling a bank statement; journalizing a bank service charge, a dishonored check, and petty cash transactions

Sarah Getz owns a business called Quick Service. Quick Service completed the following transactions during August of the current year.

RECYCLING PROBLEM 9-R   Journalizing adjusting and closing entries

The following information is obtained from the partial work sheet of Lawn Services for the month ended September 30 of the current year.

	3	4	5	6	7	8	
ACCOUNT TITLE	ADJUSTMENTS		INCOME STATEMENT		BALANCE SHEET		
	DEBIT	CREDIT	DEBIT	CREDIT	DEBIT	CREDIT	
1 Cash					3 1 5 0 00		1
2 Supplies		(a) 1 7 5 00			6 7 5 00		2
3 Prepaid Insurance		(b) 2 3 0 00			2 5 0 00		3
4 Lodge Supplies						4 5 0 00	4
5 Verner Supplies						1 0 0 00	5
6 Norman Eli, Capital						3 1 3 0 00	6
7 Norman Eli, Drawing					3 1 5 00		7
8 Income Summary							8
9 Sales				1 6 1 5 00			9
10 Insurance Expense	(b) 2 3 0 00		2 3 0 00				10
11 Miscellaneous Expense			7 5 00				11
12 Rent Expense			4 2 5 00				12
13 Supplies Expense	(a) 1 7 5 00		1 7 5 00				13
14	4 0 5 00	4 0 5 00	9 0 5 00	1 6 1 5 00	4 3 9 0 00	3 6 8 0 00	14
15 Net Income			7 1 0 00			7 1 0 00	15
16			1 6 1 5 00	1 6 1 5 00	4 3 9 0 00	4 3 9 0 00	16
17							17
18							18
19							19
20							20
21							21
22							22
23							23
24							24

Instructions: 1. Use page 3 of a journal. Journalize the adjusting entries.
  2. Continue to use page 3 of the journal. Journalize the closing entries.

RECYCLING PROBLEM 10-R   Preparing a general ledger file maintenance input form and journalizing opening balances

Carpet Magic has the following general ledger chart of accounts and post-closing trial balance on August 31 of the current year.

Balance Sheet Accounts		Income Statement Accounts	
(100) ASSETS		**(400) REVENUE**	
110	Cash	410	Cleaning Fees
120	Petty Cash		**(500) EXPENSES**
130	Supplies—Cleaning		
140	Supplies—Office	510	Advertising Expense
150	Prepaid Insurance	520	Insurance Expense
		530	Miscellaneous Expense
	(200) LIABILITIES	540	Rent Expense
210	Decker Cleaning Supplies	550	Supplies Expense—Cleaning
220	McKenna Office Supply	560	Supplies Expense—Office
		570	Utilities Expense
	(300) OWNER'S EQUITY		
310	Charles Dietz, Capital		
320	Charles Dietz, Drawing		
330	Income Summary		

Carpet Magic
Post-Closing Trial Balance
August 31, 19--

ACCOUNT TITLE	DEBIT	CREDIT
Cash	12 9 2 0 00	
Petty Cash	4 0 0 00	
Supplies—Cleaning	2 6 1 0 00	
Supplies—Office	1 2 4 0 00	
Prepaid Insurance	1 2 0 0 00	
Decker Cleaning Supplies		1 3 1 5 00
McKenna Office Supply		6 6 5 00
Charles Dietz, Capital		16 3 9 0 00
Totals	18 3 7 0 00	18 3 7 0 00

Instructions: 1. Prepare a general ledger file maintenance input form (FORM GL-1) for the general ledger chart of accounts. Use September 1 of the current year as the run date.

2. Journalize the opening balances for Carpet Magic on a general ledger input form (FORM GL-2). Use September 1 of the current year as the run date and the date of the opening balances. Batch No. 1; Memorandum No. 1.

3. Total and prove the Debit Amount and Credit Amount columns. Record the batch totals.

RECYCLING PROBLEM 11-R   Preparing input forms for an automated accounting system

Tien's Hairstyling has the following general ledger chart of accounts.

Balance Sheet Accounts		Income Statement Accounts	
(100) ASSETS		**(400) REVENUE**	
110	Cash	410	Sales
120	Petty Cash		
130	Supplies—Beauty	**(500) EXPENSES**	
140	Supplies—Office		
150	Prepaid Insurance	510	Advertising Expense
		520	Insurance Expense
(200) LIABILITIES		530	Miscellaneous Expense
		540	Rent Expense
210	Comair Beauty Supplies	550	Supplies Expense—Beauty
220	Eagle Office Supplies	560	Supplies Expense—Office
230	Monaco Beauty Supplies		
(300) OWNER'S EQUITY			
310	Damien Tien, Capital		
320	Damien Tien, Drawing		
330	Income Summary		

Tien's Hairstyling performed the following file maintenance activities.

Account Deleted	Account Title Change	Accounts Added
Comair Beauty Supplies	Rent Expense	Grandy Beauty Supplies
	TO	Rent Expense—Computer
	Rent Expense—Building	Utilities Expense

Instructions: 1. Assign account numbers to the new accounts using the unused middle number method.

2. Prepare a general ledger file maintenance input form (FORM GL-1). Use July 1 of the current year as the run date.

3. Journalize the following transactions on a general ledger input form (FORM GL-2). Use July 31 of the current year as the run date. Batch No. 6. Source documents are abbreviated as follows: check, C; receipt, R; cash register tape, T.

Transactions

July 27. Paid cash for advertising, $125.00. C185.
    27. Paid cash for beauty supplies, $175.00. C186.
    28. Paid cash for office supplies, $103.00. C187.
    29. Paid cash on account to Eagle Office Supplies, $297.00. C188.
    29. Received cash from owner as an investment, $2,500.00. R10.
    30. Paid cash for miscellaneous expense, $65.00. C189.
    30. Paid cash to replenish the petty cash fund, $201.00: beauty supplies, $82.00; office supplies, $67.00; miscellaneous, $52.00. C190.
    30. Paid cash for electric bill, $126.00. C191.
    31. Paid cash for computer rent, $880.00. C192.
    31. Paid cash to owner for personal use, $800.00. C193.
    31. Received cash from sales, $1,830.00. T31.

4. Total and prove the Debit Amount and Credit Amount columns. Record the batch totals.

5. The following accounts need adjustment at the end of the fiscal period. Journalize the adjusting entries on a general ledger input form (FORM GL-2). Use July 31 of the current year as the run date. Batch No. 7.

Account Title	Account Balance
Supplies—Beauty	$2,130.00
Supplies—Office	1,427.00
Prepaid Insurance	1,575.00

Adjustment Information, July 31

Value of beauty supplies on hand	$1,560.00
Value of office supplies on hand	1,160.00
Value of prepaid insurance	1,400.00

6. Total and prove the Debit Amount and Credit Amount columns. Record the batch totals.

RECYCLING PROBLEM 12-R   Journalizing purchases, cash payments, and other transactions

Eva Akemi and Daniel Marino, partners, own a furniture store.

Instructions: Journalize the following transactions completed during November of the current year. Use page 19 of a journal similar to the one described in Chapter 12. Source documents are abbreviated as follows: check, C; memorandum, M; purchase invoice, P.

Nov. 2. Paid cash for rent, $1,200.00. C251.
  2. Purchased merchandise on account from Baines Furniture Co., $2,335.00. P88.
  3. Paid cash for office supplies, $66.00. C252.
  5. Paid cash on account to Decor-Concepts, $985.00, covering P85. C253.
  7. Purchased merchandise for cash, $130.00. C254.
  9. Purchased merchandise on account from Metaline Co., $950.00. P89.
  9. Bought store supplies on account from Gateway Supply, $140.00. M40.
  10. Purchased merchandise for cash, $83.00. C255.
  12. Paid cash on account to Furniture Industries, $1,400.00, covering P86. C256.
  12. Bought office supplies on account from Scott Supply, $95.00. M41.
  14. Discovered that a transaction for store supplies bought in October was journalized and posted in error as a debit to Purchases instead of Supplies—Store, $74.00. M42.
  16. Eva Akemi, partner, withdrew cash for personal use, $1,000.00. C257.
  17. Daniel Marino, partner, withdrew cash for personal use, $1,000.00. C258.
  17. Paid cash for advertising, $75.00. C259.
  19. Paid cash on account to Classic Furniture, $1,345.00, covering P87. C260.
  19. Purchased merchandise on account from Metaline Co., $1,250.00. P90.
  20. Daniel Marino, partner, withdrew merchandise for personal use, $152.00. M43.
  22. Purchased merchandise for cash, $60.00. C261.
  24. Paid cash on account to Baines Furniture Co., $2,335.00, covering P88. C262.
  25. Eva Akemi, partner, withdrew merchandise for personal use, $225.00. M44.
  27. Paid cash for store supplies, $78.00. C263.
  30. Paid cash to replenish the petty cash fund, $301.00: office supplies, $78.00; store supplies, $52.00; advertising, $125.00; miscellaneous, $46.00. C264.
  30. Paid cash on account to Metaline Co., $950.00, covering P89. C265.

RECYCLING PROBLEM 13-R   **Journalizing sales and cash receipts**

Ana Lamas and Alex Keyser, partners, own an office supply store.

Instructions: 1. Journalize the following transactions completed during September of the current year. Use page 21 of a journal similar to the one described in Chapter 13. A 4% sales tax has been added to each sale. Source documents are abbreviated as follows: receipt, R; sales invoice, S; cash register tape, T.

Sept. 1. Sold merchandise on account to Samuel Quist, $75.00, plus sales tax, $3.00; total, $78.00. S53.
  1. Received cash on account from David Plouff, $85.28, covering S49. R85.
  2. Sold merchandise on account to Carmen Estevez, $125.00, plus sales tax, $5.00; total, $130.00. S54.
  5. Sold merchandise on account to Keith Aldrich, $265.00, plus sales tax, $10.60; total, $275.60. S55.
  5. Recorded cash and credit card sales, $1,940.00, plus sales tax, $77.60; total, $2,017.60. T5.
  7. Received cash on account from Edward Jarmen, $249.60, covering S50. R86.
  9. Sold merchandise on account to Perez Accounting Co., $345.00, plus sales tax, $13.80; total, $358.80. S56.
  10. Sold merchandise on account to Nancy Cain, $85.00, plus sales tax, $3.40; total, $88.40. S57.
  11. Received cash on account from Bonner Secretarial Service, $249.60, covering S51. R87.
  12. Recorded cash and credit card sales, $2,350.00, plus sales tax, $94.00; total, $2,444.00. T12.
  14. Received cash on account from David Doran, $187.20, covering S52. R88.
  15. Sold merchandise on account to Hazel Ervin, $65.00, plus sales tax, $2.60; total, $67.60. S58.
  18. Received cash on account from Samuel Quist, $78.00, covering S53. R89.
  19. Recorded cash and credit card sales, $2,450.00, plus sales tax, $98.00; total, $2,548.00. T19.
  21. Received cash on account from Carmen Estevez, $130.00, covering S54. R90.
  25. Received cash on account from Keith Aldrich, $275.60, covering S55. R91.
  26. Recorded cash and credit card sales, $2,140.00, plus sales tax, $85.60; total, $2,225.60. T26.
  29. Sold merchandise on account to Susan Gates, $145.00, plus sales tax, $5.80; total, $150.80. S59.
  30. Recorded cash and credit card sales, $1,285.00, plus sales tax, $51.40; total, $1,336.40. T30.

  2. Total the journal. Prove the equality of debits and credits.
  3. Rule the journal.

RECYCLING PROBLEM 14-R   **Opening accounts and journalizing and posting business transactions**

Instructions: 1. Open new pages for the following accounts in the general ledger of Catalina Shoes. Record the balances as of September 1 of the current year.

Account No.	Account Title	Account Balance
1110	Cash	$ 13,200.00
1130	Accounts Receivable	441.00
1140	Supplies—Office..................................	1,830.00
1150	Supplies—Store	1,560.00
2110	Accounts Payable................................	3,820.00
2120	Sales Tax Payable................................	937.50
3120	Sophia Kizer, Drawing	9,820.00
3140	Brian Rankin, Drawing............................	9,600.00
4110	Sales	150,000.00
5110	Purchases.......................................	88,000.00
6110	Advertising Expense..............................	2,310.00
6140	Miscellaneous Expense	1,260.00
6160	Rent Expense....................................	7,600.00
6190	Utilities Expense	1,620.00

2. Open new pages for the following vendor accounts in the accounts payable ledger. Record the balances as of September 1 of the current year.

Vendor No.	Vendor Name	Purchase No.	Account Balance
210	A & J Shoes	P66	$1,480.00
220	Colormate Shoes..............................	—	—
230	Sanz Supply	—	—
240	Suave Shoe Co................................	P65	2,340.00

3. Open new pages for the following customer accounts in the accounts receivable ledger. Record the balances as of September 1 of the current year.

Customer No.	Customer Name	Sales No.	Account Balance
110	Joyce Abler	S53	$178.50
120	Helen Gorthy...................................	—	—
130	Joshua Lentz...................................	—	—
140	Earl Ward	S52	262.50

4. Journalize the following transactions completed during September of the current year. Use page 15 of a journal similar to the one described in Chapter 14. A 5% sales tax has been added to each sale. Source documents are abbreviated as follows: check, C; memorandum, M; purchase invoice, P; receipt, R; sales invoice, S; cash register tape, T.

Sept. 1. Paid cash for rent, $950.00. C225.
2. Purchased merchandise on account from Colormate Shoes, $1,650.00. P67.
4. Received cash on account from Earl Ward, $262.50, covering S52. R33.
5. Recorded cash and credit card sales, $3,350.00, plus sales tax, $167.50; total, $3,517.50. T5.
    Posting. Post the items that are to be posted individually.
7. Paid cash for electric bill, $158.10. C226.
9. Bought office supplies on account from Sanz Supply, $135.00. M32.
10. Paid cash on account to Suave Shoe Co., $2,340.00, covering P65. C227.
12. Recorded cash and credit card sales, $4,140.00, plus sales tax, $207.00; total, $4,347.00. T12.
    Posting. Post the items that are to be posted individually.
14. Sold merchandise on account to Helen Gorthy, $260.00, plus sales tax, $13.00; total, $273.00. S54.

Sept. 15. Sold merchandise on account to Joshua Lentz, $125.00, plus sales tax, $6.25; total, $131.25. S55.

15. Sophia Kizer, partner, withdrew cash for personal use, $1,200.00. C228.

15. Brian Rankin, partner, withdrew cash for personal use, $1,200.00. C229.

18. Purchased merchandise on account from A & J Shoes, $940.00. P68.

19. Recorded cash and credit card sales, $4,080.00, plus sales tax, $204.00; total, $4,284.00. T19.

    Posting. Post the items that are to be posted individually.

21. Discovered that office supplies bought for cash was journalized and posted in error as a debit to Supplies—Store instead of Supplies—Office, $118.00. M33.

22. Sophia Kizer, partner, withdrew merchandise for personal use, $125.00. M34.

24. Sold merchandise on account to Earl Ward, $135.00, plus sales tax, $6.75; total, $141.75. S56.

25. Sold merchandise on account to Joyce Abler, $95.00, plus sales tax, $4.75; total, $99.75. S57.

26. Recorded cash and credit card sales, $4,530.00, plus sales tax, $226.50; total, $4,756.50. T26.

    Posting. Post the items that are to be posted individually.

28. Received cash on account from Joyce Abler, $178.50, covering S53. R34.

28. Paid cash on account to A & J Shoes, $1,480.00, covering P66. C230.

30. Paid cash to replenish the petty cash fund, $201.50: office supplies, $42.00; store supplies, $57.50; advertising, $64.00; miscellaneous, $38.00. C231.

30. Purchased merchandise on account from Suave Shoe Co., $860.00. P69.

30. Recorded cash and credit card sales, $1,970.00, plus sales tax, $98.50; total, $2,068.50. T30.

    Posting. Post the items that are to be posted individually.

5. Total the journal. Prove the equality of debits and credits.

6. Prove cash. The balance on the next unused check stub is $25,084.90.

7. Rule the journal.

8. Post the totals of the special columns of the journal.

9. Prepare a schedule of accounts payable and a schedule of accounts receivable. Prove the accuracy of the subsidiary ledgers by comparing the schedule totals with the balances of the controlling accounts in the general ledger. If the totals are not the same, find and correct the errors.

RECYCLING PROBLEM 15-R Preparing a semimonthly payroll

The following information is for the semimonthly pay period June 1-15 of the current year.

Employee		Marital Status	No. of Allow-ances	Earnings		Deductions
No.	Name			Regular	Overtime	Health Insurance
3	Cahill, Bryan	S	2	$598.40	$40.00	$25.00
4	Dykes, Eleanor	M	3	525.60		30.00
7	Holcomb, David	S	1	624.00		
1	Kirby, Sharon	S	1	552.00	9.30	
5	Mendez, Thomas	M	2	545.60		25.00
6	Salassi, Carol	M	3	576.00		30.00
8	Tsang, Elaine	M	2	651.20	44.40	25.00

Instructions: 1. Prepare a payroll register. The date of payment is June 16. Use the income tax withholding tables in Illustration 15-4 to find the income tax withholding for each employee. Calculate FICA tax withholding using an 8% tax rate. None of the employee accumulated earnings has exceeded the FICA tax base.

2. Prepare a check for the total amount of the net pay. Make the check payable to Payroll Account, and sign your name as a partner of Riddley Company. The beginning check stub balance is $7,687.89.

3. Prepare payroll checks for David Holcomb, Check No. 332, and Carol Salassi, Check No. 335. Sign your name as a partner of Riddley Company. Record the two payroll check numbers in the payroll register.

RECYCLING PROBLEM 16-R Journalizing payroll taxes

Johnson Manufacturing completed payroll transactions during the period February 28 to April 30 of the current year. Payroll tax rates are as follows: FICA, 8%; federal unemployment, 0.8%; and state unemployment, 5.4%. No total earnings have exceeded the tax base for calculating unemployment taxes.

Instructions: 1. Journalize the following transactions on page 4 of a journal. Source documents are abbreviated as follows: check, C, and memorandum, M.

Feb. 28. Paid cash for monthly payroll, $3,312.16 (total payroll, $4,298.00, less deductions: employee income tax, $642.00; FICA tax, $343.84). C167.
    28. Recorded employer payroll taxes expense. M34.
Mar. 15. Paid cash for liability for employee income tax, $642.00, and for FICA tax, $687.68; total, $1,329.68. C192.
    31. Paid cash for monthly payroll, $3,328.84 (total payroll, $4,327.00, less deductions: employee income tax, $652.00; FICA tax, $346.16). C235.
    31. Recorded employer payroll taxes expense. M39.
Apr. 15. Paid cash for liability for employee income tax, $652.00, and for FICA tax, $692.32; total, $1,344.32. C251.
    30. Paid cash for federal unemployment tax liability for quarter ended March 31, $103.62. C272.
    30. Paid cash for state unemployment tax liability for quarter ended March 31, $699.41. C273.

2. Prove and rule the journal.

RECYCLING PROBLEM 17-R Completing a work sheet

On December 31 of the current year, Klimer has the following general ledger accounts and balances.

Account Title	Balance
Cash	$ 19,865.00
Petty Cash	500.00
Accounts Receivable	9,260.00
Merchandise Inventory	226,320.00
Supplies—Office	5,085.00
Supplies—Store	5,420.00
Prepaid Insurance	4,300.00
Accounts Payable	9,720.00
Sales Tax Payable	950.00
Dorothy Klimer, Capital	107,365.00
Dorothy Klimer, Drawing	15,880.00
Howard Klimer, Capital	106,190.00
Howard Klimer, Drawing	15,730.00
Income Summary	—
Sales	189,540.00
Purchases	85,250.00
Advertising Expense	4,735.00
Credit Card Fee Expense	1,930.00
Insurance Expense	—
Miscellaneous Expense	2,360.00
Rent Expense	14,400.00
Supplies Expense—Office	—
Supplies Expense—Store	—
Utilities Expense	2,730.00

Instructions: Prepare Klimer's work sheet for the fiscal period ended December 31 of the current year.

Adjustment Information, December 31

Merchandise inventory	$218,770.00
Office supplies inventory	2,195.00
Store supplies inventory	2,205.00
Value of prepaid insurance	1,720.00

RECYCLING PROBLEM 18-R   Preparing financial statements

Discount Footwear prepared the work sheet shown on page C-17 for the year ended December 31 of the current year.

Instructions: 1. Prepare an income statement. Figure and record the following component percentages: (a) cost of merchandise sold, (b) gross profit on sales, (c) total expenses, and (d) net income or loss. Round percentage calculations to the nearest 0.1%.

    2. Prepare a distribution of net income statement. Net income or loss is to be shared equally.

    3. Prepare an owners' equity statement. No additional investments were made.

    4. Prepare a balance sheet in report form.

Discount Footwear

Work Sheet

For Year Ended December 31, 19--

		1	2	3	4	5	6	7	8	
	ACCOUNT TITLE	TRIAL BALANCE		ADJUSTMENTS		INCOME STATEMENT		BALANCE SHEET		
		DEBIT	CREDIT	DEBIT	CREDIT	DEBIT	CREDIT	DEBIT	CREDIT	
1	Cash	19 3 9 5 00						19 3 9 5 00		1
2	Petty Cash	3 0 0 00						3 0 0 00		2
3	Accounts Receivable	8 9 3 0 00						8 9 3 0 00		3
4	Merchandise Inventory	257 2 0 0 00			(a) 9 7 5 0 00			247 4 5 0 00		4
5	Supplies—Office	5 1 2 0 00			(b) 2 9 8 0 00			2 1 4 0 00		5
6	Supplies—Store	4 8 7 5 00			(c) 3 1 4 0 00			1 7 3 5 00		6
7	Prepaid Insurance	4 8 3 0 00			(d) 2 7 6 0 00			2 0 7 0 00		7
8	Accounts Payable		8 3 6 0 00						8 3 6 0 00	8
9	Sales Tax Payable		9 8 0 00						9 8 0 00	9
10	Joseph Kane, Capital		111 6 4 0 00						111 6 4 0 00	10
11	Joseph Kane, Drawing	15 8 4 0 00						15 8 4 0 00		11
12	Gail Miles, Capital		110 3 6 0 00						110 3 6 0 00	12
13	Gail Miles, Drawing	15 9 3 0 00						15 9 3 0 00		13
14	Income Summary			(a) 9 7 5 0 00		9 7 5 0 00				14
15	Sales		235 4 5 0 00				235 4 5 0 00			15
16	Purchases	105 9 5 0 00				105 9 5 0 00				16
17	Advertising Expense	4 9 6 5 00				4 9 6 5 00				17
18	Credit Card Fee Expense	2 1 3 0 00				2 1 3 0 00				18
19	Insurance Expense			(d) 2 7 6 0 00		2 7 6 0 00				19
20	Miscellaneous Expense	2 2 8 5 00				2 2 8 5 00				20
21	Rent Expense	16 8 0 0 00				16 8 0 0 00				21
22	Supplies Expense—Office			(b) 2 9 8 0 00		2 9 8 0 00				22
23	Supplies Expense—Store			(c) 3 1 4 0 00		3 1 4 0 00				23
24	Utilities Expense	2 2 4 0 00				2 2 4 0 00				24
25		466 7 9 0 00	466 7 9 0 00	18 6 3 0 00	18 6 3 0 00	153 0 0 0 00	235 4 5 0 00	313 7 9 0 00	231 3 4 0 00	25
26	Net Income					82 4 5 0 00			82 4 5 0 00	26
27						235 4 5 0 00	235 4 5 0 00	313 7 9 0 00	313 7 9 0 00	27
28										28

RECYCLING PROBLEM 19-R   **Journalizing adjusting and closing entries**

Use the following partial work sheet of Cook & Latzco Paints for the year ended December 31 of the current year.

	3	4	5	6
ACCOUNT TITLE	ADJUSTMENTS		INCOME STATEMENT	
	DEBIT	CREDIT	DEBIT	CREDIT
4 *Merchandise Inventory*		(a) 9 8 4 0 00		
5 *Supplies—Office*		(b) 2 5 1 0 00		
6 *Supplies—Store*		(c) 2 6 3 0 00		
7 *Prepaid Insurance*		(d) 2 5 8 0 00		
21 *Income Summary*	(a) 9 8 4 0 00		9 8 4 0 00	
22 *Sales*				310 9 2 0 00
23 *Purchases*			124 3 5 0 00	
24 *Advertising Expense*			4 7 8 0 00	
25 *Credit Card Fee Expense*			3 9 8 0 00	
26 *Insurance Expense*	(d) 2 5 8 0 00		2 5 8 0 00	
27 *Miscellaneous Expense*			2 1 4 0 00	
28 *Payroll Taxes Expense*			7 0 7 0 00	
29 *Rent Expense*			13 2 0 0 00	
30 *Salary Expense*			58 9 2 0 00	
31 *Supplies Expense—Office*	(b) 2 5 1 0 00		2 5 1 0 00	
32 *Supplies Expense—Store*	(c) 2 6 3 0 00		2 6 3 0 00	
33 *Utilities Expense*			2 7 6 0 00	
34	17 5 6 0 00	17 5 6 0 00	234 7 6 0 00	310 9 2 0 00
35 *Net Income*			76 1 6 0 00	
36			310 9 2 0 00	310 9 2 0 00

Instructions: 1. Use page 25 of a journal. Journalize the adjusting entries using information from the partial work sheet.

2. Continue using page 25 of the journal. Journalize the closing entries using information from the work sheet. The distribution of net income statement shows equal distribution of earnings. The partners' drawing accounts show the following debit balances in the work sheet's Balance Sheet Debit column: Angela Cook, Drawing, $14,780.00; Alan Latzco, Drawing, $15,120.00.

RECYCLING PROBLEM 20-R   Journalizing and posting purchases and cash payment transactions

Instructions: 1. Open the following accounts in the general ledger of Dunhill Corporation. Record the balances as of October 1 of the current year.

PARTIAL GENERAL LEDGER

Account Number	Account Title	Account Balance
1105	Cash	$23,410.00
1110	Petty Cash	250.00
1140	Supplies	957.00
2115	Accounts Payable...	1,382.00
5105	Purchases..	—
5110	Purchases Discount	—
5115	Purchases Returns and Allowances	—
6105	Advertising Expense	—
6130	Miscellaneous Expense.......................................	—
6140	Rent Expense	—
8105	Cash Short and Over..	—

2. Open the following vendor accounts in the accounts payable ledger. Record the balances as of October 1 of the current year.

ACCOUNTS PAYABLE LEDGER

Vendor Number	Vendor Name	Terms	Purchase Number	Account Balance
210	Adkin Supplies	n/15	—	—
220	Blair Company	n/30	—	—
230	Friedmans Company...............	n/30	P92	$625.00
240	Hargrove, Inc.....................	1/10, n/30	P100	757.00
250	Stovall Company	2/10, n/30	—	—
260	Winston Company................	1/10, n/30	—	—

3. Journalize the following transactions affecting purchases and cash payments completed during October of the current year. Use page 10 of a purchases journal, a general journal, and a cash payments journal. Source documents are abbreviated as follows: check, C; debit memorandum, DM; memorandum, M; purchase invoice, P.

Oct. 1. Paid cash for rent, $1,500.00. C163.
   1. Purchased merchandise on account from Blair Company, $1,482.00. P101.
   5. Purchased merchandise on account from Winston Company, $225.00. P102.
   5. Returned merchandise to Friedmans Company, $70.00, from P92. DM61.
      Posting. Post the items that are to be posted individually. Post from the journals in this order: purchases journal, general journal, and cash payments journal.
   8. Paid cash on account to Friedmans Company, $555.00, covering P92 for $625.00, less DM61, $70.00; no discount. C164.
   8. Paid cash on account to Hargrove, Inc., $749.43, covering P100 for $757.00, less 1% discount, $7.57. C165.
   12. Purchased merchandise for cash, $720.00. C166.
   14. Purchased merchandise on account from Winston Company, $1,296.00. P103.
   15. Paid cash on account to Winston Company, $222.75, covering P102 for $225.00, less 1% discount, $2.25. C167.
   15. Paid cash to replenish the petty cash fund, $158.80: supplies, $47.50; advertising, $53.60; miscellaneous, $61.75; cash over, $4.05. C168.
   15. Bought supplies on account from Adkin Supplies, $304.00. M17.
      Posting. Post the items that are to be posted individually.
   18. Paid cash for miscellaneous expense, $218.00. C169.

Oct. 20. Purchased merchandise on account from Friedmans Company, $350.00. P104.
  20. Returned merchandise to Blair Company, $177.00, from P101. DM62.
  21. Paid cash on account to Winston Company, $1,283.04, covering P103 for $1,296.00, less 1% discount, $12.96. C170.
  22. Paid cash for advertising, $345.00. C171.
  25. Purchased merchandise on account from Winston Company, $817.00. P105.
  27. Paid cash on account to Blair Company, $1,305.00, covering P101 for $1,482.00, less DM62, $177.00; no discount. C172.
  28. Returned merchandise to Winston Company, $34.00, from P105. DM63.
  29. Paid cash on account to Adkin Supplies, $304.00, covering M17; no discount. C173.
  29. Purchased merchandise on account from Stovall Company, $925.00. P106.
  29. Paid cash to replenish the petty cash fund, $187.80: supplies, $14.30; advertising, $78.60; miscellaneous, $90.00; cash short, $4.90. C174.
     Posting. Post the items that are to be posted individually.

4. Total and rule the purchases journal. Post the total.
5. Prove and rule the cash payments journal. Post the totals of the special columns.
6. Prepare a schedule of accounts payable. Compare the schedule total with the balance of the accounts payable account in the general ledger. The total and balance should be the same.

RECYCLING PROBLEM 21-R   Journalizing and posting sales and cash receipts transactions

Instructions: 1. Open the following accounts in the general ledger of Thompson Company. Record the balances as of June 1 of the current year.

PARTIAL GENERAL LEDGER

Account No.	Account Title	Account Balance
1105	Cash..	$9,216.00
1125	Accounts Receivable	3,024.01
2135	Sales Tax Payable	—
4105	Sales..	—
4110	Sales Discount	—
4115	Sales Returns and Allowances	—

2. Open the following customer accounts in the accounts receivable ledger. Record the balances as of June 1 of the current year.

ACCOUNTS RECEIVABLE LEDGER

Customer No.	Customer Name	Sale No.	Account Balance
110	Bolero Company	S84	$616.45
120	Franklin, Inc.......................	S88	448.20
130	Mooney and Associates............	S85	398.76
140	Powers Company	S89	702.00
150	David Reed......................	S90	858.60

3. Journalize the following transactions affecting sales and cash receipts completed during June of the current year. Use page 6 of a sales journal, a general journal, and a cash receipts journal. Thompson Company offers its customers terms of 2/10, n/30. The sales tax rate is 8%. Source documents are abbreviated as follows: credit memorandum, CM; receipt, R; sales invoice, S; cash register tape, T.

June 1. Received cash on account from Franklin, Inc., $439.24, covering S88 for $448.20 ($415.00 plus sales tax, $33.20), less 2% discount, $8.30, and less sales tax, $0.66. R21.

4. Granted credit to David Reed for merchandise returned, $126.00, plus sales tax, $10.08, from S90; total, $136.08. CM8.

7. Received cash on account from Powers Company, $687.96, covering S89 for $702.00 ($650.00 plus sales tax, $52.00), less 2% discount, $13.00, and less sales tax, $1.04. R22.

7. Recorded cash and credit card sales, $1,980.00, plus sales tax, $158.40; total, $2,138.40. T7.

   Posting. Post the items that are to be posted individually. Post from the journals in this order: sales journal, general journal, and cash receipts journal.

9. Received cash on account from David Reed, $722.52 (covering S90 less CM8), no discount. R23.

9. Received cash on account from Mooney and Associates, $398.76, covering S85; no discount. R24.

11. Recorded cash and credit card sales, $2,358.00, plus sales tax, $188.64; total, $2,546.64. T11.

   Posting. Post the items that are to be posted individually.

13. Sold merchandise on account to Franklin, Inc., $1,236.00, plus sales tax, $98.88; total, $1,334.88. S91.

15. Granted credit to Franklin, Inc., for merchandise returned, $36.40, plus sales tax, $2.91, from S91; total, $39.31. CM9.

15. Received cash on account from Bolero Company, $616.45, covering S84; no discount. R25.

18. Recorded cash and credit card sales, $2,678.00, plus sales tax, $214.24; total, $2,892.24. T18.

   Posting. Post the items that are to be posted individually.

21. Sold merchandise on account to David Reed, $540.00, plus sales tax, $43.20; total, $583.20. S92.

22. Sold merchandise on account to Bolero Company, $415.00, plus sales tax, $33.20; total, $448.20. S93.

22. Sold merchandise on account to Powers Company, $643.00, plus sales tax, $51.44; total, $694.44. S94.

25. Recorded cash and credit card sales, $1,916.00, plus sales tax, $153.28; total, $2,069.28. T25.

   Posting. Post the items that are to be posted individually.

28. Sold merchandise on account to Bolero Company, $756.00, plus sales tax, $60.48; total, $816.48. S95.

29. Received cash on account from Franklin, Inc., $1,295.57 (covering S91 less CM9), no discount. R26.

29. Received cash on account from David Reed, $571.54, covering S92 for $583.20 ($540.00 plus sales tax, $43.20), less 2% discount, $10.80, and less sales tax, $0.86. R27.

30. Sold merchandise on account to Franklin, Inc., $772.50, plus sales tax, $61.80; total, $834.30. S96.

30. Recorded cash and credit card sales, $1,606.00, plus sales tax, $128.48; total, $1,734.48. T30.

   Posting. Post the items that are to be posted individually.

4. Prove and rule the sales journal. Post the totals of the special columns.

5. Prove the equality of debits and credits for the cash receipts journal.

6. Prove cash. The cash balance on hand on June 1 was $9,216.00. The total of the Cash Credit column of the cash payments journal for Thompson Company is $14,753.00. The balance on the next unused check stub on June 30 is $10,576.08.

7. Rule the cash receipts journal. Post the totals of the special columns.

8. Prepare a schedule of accounts receivable similar to the one described in Chapter 14. Compare the schedule total with the balance of the accounts receivable account in the general ledger. The total and the balance should be the same.

RECYCLING PROBLEM 22-R Recording entries for uncollectible accounts

Colonial Plastics has the following accounts in its accounts receivable ledger.

PARTIAL ACCOUNTS RECEIVABLE LEDGER

Account No. and Title	Date	Post. Ref.	Debit	Debit Balance
125 Dixon Company	May 19	S5	$ 621.00	$ 621.00
135 Fire Star Co.	Mar. 25	S3	1,295.00	1,295.00
140 Haber Corporation	Jan. 26	S1	916.00	916.00
190 Tri-State Corporation	Feb. 1	S2	384.00	384.00

Instructions: 1. Journalize the following transactions completed during October, November, and December of the current year. Use pages 10, 11, and 12 of a general journal and pages 11 and 12 of a cash receipts journal. Source documents are abbreviated as follows: memorandum, M; receipt, R.

Oct. 2. Wrote off Tri-State Corporation's past-due account as uncollectible, $384.00. M332.
     14. Wrote off Haber Corporation's past-due account as uncollectible, $916.00. M336.
         Posting. Post each entry to the customer accounts in the accounts receivable ledger.
Nov. 17. Wrote off Dixon Company's past-due account as uncollectible, $621.00. M342.
     22. Received cash in full payment of Tri-State Corporation's account, previously written off as uncollectible, $384.00. M347 and R409.
         Posting. Post each entry to the customer accounts in the accounts receivable ledger.
Dec. 13. Wrote off Fire Star Co.'s past-due account as uncollectible, $1,295.00. M355.
     21. Received cash in full payment of Dixon Company's account, previously written off as uncollectible, $621.00. M362 and R476.
     26. Received cash in full payment of Haber Corporation's account, previously written off as uncollectible, $916.00. M368 and R482.
         Posting. Post each entry to the customer accounts in the accounts receivable ledger.

2. Journalize the December 31 adjusting entry for estimated uncollectible accounts expense for the year. Use page 13 of the general journal. Uncollectible accounts expense is estimated as 1.0% of total sales on account. Total sales on account for the year were $1,206,470.00.

RECYCLING PROBLEM 23-R Calculating depreciation expense and book value of plant assets; journalizing entries affecting plant assets

Magnolia Company records plant assets in two accounts: Office Equipment and Store Equipment. Magnolia Company owns the following plant assets.

Plant Asset	Asset Account	Date Bought	Original Cost	Estimated Salvage Value	Estimated Useful Life
1	Office Equipment	Apr. 1, 19X1	$ 7,500.00	$ 500.00	7 years
2	Store Equipment	Sept. 1, 19X1	18,900.00	2,400.00	10 years
3	Office Equipment	Oct. 1, 19X1	6,300.00	300.00	5 years
4	Store Equipment	Mar. 1, 19X2	5,200.00	1,240.00	6 years
5	Store Equipment	July 1, 19X2	13,700.00	1,100.00	12 years
6	Store Equipment	June 1, 19X3	9,600.00	2,040.00	9 years
7	Office Equipment	Nov. 1, 19X4	1,250.00	350.00	3 years
8	Office Equipment	July 1, 19X5	2,800.00	800.00	4 years

Instructions: 1. Calculate each plant asset's depreciation expense for the year ended December 31, 19X5. Use the straight-line method of calculating depreciation. Round amounts to the nearest cent.

2. Calculate each plant asset's ending book value as of December 31, 19X5.

3. Journalize the two adjusting entries for depreciation expense for the year ended December 31, 19X5. Use page 13 of a general journal.

4. Journalize the following transaction. Use page 4 of a cash receipts journal. Source documents are abbreviated as follows: memorandum, M; receipt, R.

19X6

Apr. 2. Received cash from sale of plant asset number 2, $12,200.00: original cost, $18,900.00; total accumulated depreciation through December 31, 19X5, $7,150.00; additional depreciation to be recorded through April 2, 19X6, $412.50. M125 and R193.

RECYCLING PROBLEM 24-R Journalizing notes payable and notes receivable transactions

The following transactions were completed by Arrowhead Manufacturing during July of the current year.

Instructions: 1. Journalize the following transactions. Use page 7 of a general journal, page 14 of a cash receipts journal, and page 18 of a cash payments journal. Source documents are abbreviated as follows: check, C; memorandum, M; note payable, NP; note receivable, NR; receipt, R.

July   2. Received cash for the maturity value of NR95: principal, $1,100.00, plus interest, $11.00; total, $1,111.00. R132.

5. Issued a 60-day, 10% note, $3,000.00. NP155.

6. Paid cash for the maturity value of NP149: principal, $7,000.00, plus interest, $140.00; total, $7,140.00. C1043.

8. Discounted at 11% a 30-day non-interest-bearing note, $2,500.00; proceeds, $2,477.08, interest, $22.92. NP156.

11. Received cash for the maturity value of NR92: principal, $600.00, plus interest, $12.00; total, $612.00. R147.

13. Received cash for the maturity value of NR94: principal, $575.00, plus interest, $5.75; total, $580.75. R152.

17. Paid cash for the maturity value of NP151: principal, $4,500.00, plus interest, $90.00; total, $4,590.00. C1212.

18. Issued a 3-month, 12% note to McKinney Company for an extension of time on this account payable, $1,700.00. NP157.

21. Melinda Blair dishonored NR80, a 6-month, 12% note, maturity value due today: principal, $500.00; interest, $30.00; total, $530.00. M113.

July 25. Discounted at 11% a 6-month non-interest-bearing note, $12,500.00; proceeds, $11,812.50, interest, $687.50. NP158.
   27. Received a 30-day, 13% note from Miles Browning for an extension of time on his account, $1,500.00. NR96.
   29. Paid cash for the maturity value of NP131: principal, $3,500.00, plus interest, $192.50; total, $3,692.50. C1235.

2. Prove the cash receipts and cash payments journals.

RECYCLING PROBLEM 25-R Journalizing and posting entries for accrued revenue and expenses

The following accounts are from Willem Corporation's general ledger. The balances are recorded as of December 31 of the current year before adjusting entries.

PARTIAL GENERAL LEDGER

Account No.	Account Title	Account Balance
1115	Notes Receivable....................................	$ 720.00
1120	Interest Receivable	—
2105	Notes Payable	4,000.00
2110	Interest Payable	—
3120	Income Summary	—
7110	Interest Income	132.00
8110	Interest Expense	575.00

Willem Corporation completed the following transactions related to notes receivable and notes payable during the current year and the following year. The first two transactions have already been journalized and posted. Note Receivable No. 7 and Note Payable No. 10 are the only notes on hand at the end of the fiscal period. Source documents are abbreviated as follows: check, C; note payable, NP; note receivable, NR; receipt, R.

19X1
Oct. 1. Received a 4-month, 15% note from Joseph Dowd for an extension of time on his account, $720.00. NR7.
Nov. 1. Issued a 6-month, 14% note, $4,000.00. NP10.

19X2
Feb. 1. Received cash for the maturity value of NR7: principal, $720.00, plus interest, $36.00; total, $756.00. R194.
May 1. Paid cash for the maturity value of NP10: principal, $4,000.00, plus interest, $280.00; total, $4,280.00. C426.

Instructions: 1. Open the seven general ledger accounts and record the balances.
   2. Use page 14 of a general journal. Journalize the adjusting entries for accrued interest income and accrued interest expense on December 31. Post these entries.
   3. Continue to use page 14 of a general journal. Journalize the closing entries for interest income and interest expense. Post these entries.
   4. Use page 15 of a general journal. Journalize the reversing entries for accrued interest income and accrued interest expense. Post these entries.
   5. Use page 21 of a cash receipts journal. Journalize the receipt of cash for the maturity value of NR7. Post this entry.
   6. Use page 22 of a cash payments journal. Journalize the cash payment for the maturity value of NP10. Post this entry.

RECYCLING PROBLEM 26-R **Journalizing dividends and preparing a work sheet for a corporation**

On December 31 of the current year, Specialty Design Corporation has the following general ledger accounts and balances.

Account Title	Account Balance
Cash	$ 67,277.00
Petty Cash	300.00
Notes Receivable	5,937.00
Interest Receivable	—
Accounts Receivable	26,115.00
Allowance for Uncollectible Accounts	36.00
Merchandise Inventory	142,806.00
Supplies	3,450.00
Prepaid Insurance	12,300.00
Office Equipment	8,787.50
Accumulated Depreciation—Office Equipment	1,175.00
Store Equipment	27,125.00
Accumulated Depreciation—Store Equipment	6,251.00
Notes Payable	12,500.00
Interest Payable	—
Accounts Payable	38,945.00
Employee Income Tax Payable	1,732.00
Federal Income Tax Payable	—
FICA Tax Payable	2,000.00
Sales Tax Payable	4,980.00
Unemployment Tax Payable—Federal	35.00
Unemployment Tax Payable—State	236.25
Health Insurance Premiums Payable	1,487.00
Dividends Payable	7,000.00
Capital Stock	100,000.00
Retained Earnings	60,487.25
Dividends	28,000.00
Income Summary	—
Sales	1,340,500.00
Sales Discount	3,361.00
Sales Returns and Allowances	3,415.00
Purchases	982,935.00
Purchases Discount	4,807.00
Purchases Returns and Allowances	3,678.00
Advertising Expense	4,039.00
Credit Card Fee Expense	13,446.00
Depreciation Expense—Office Equipment	—
Depreciation Expense—Store Equipment	—
Insurance Expense	—
Miscellaneous Expense	2,225.00
Payroll Taxes Expense	16,910.00
Rent Expense	42,600.00
Salary Expense	179,890.00
Supplies Expense	—
Uncollectible Accounts Expense	—
Utilities Expense	3,227.00
Gain on Plant Assets	75.00
Interest Income	690.00

Account Title	Account Balance
Cash Short and Over (cash short)	14.00
Interest Expense...	1,460.00
Loss on Plant Assets...	95.00
Federal Income Tax Expense....................................	10,900.00

Instructions: 1. Complete a work sheet for the current year ended December 31. Record the adjustments on the work sheet using the following information.

Adjustment Information, December 31

Accrued interest income...	$ 140.00
Uncollectible accounts expense estimated as 2.0% of sales on account. Sales on account for year, $453,800.00.	
Merchandise inventory	140,700.00
Supplies inventory	450.00
Value of prepaid insurance..	4,100.00
Annual depreciation expense—office equipment	950.00
Annual depreciation expense—store equipment.....................	4,065.00
Accrued interest expense...	290.00
Federal income tax expense for the year	12,146.50

2. Use page 30 of a cash payments journal. Journalize the following transaction completed during the next year. The abbreviation for check is C.

Jan. 20. Paid cash for quarterly dividend declared December 20, $7,000.00. C568.

RECYCLING PROBLEM 27-R Preparing financial statements and end-of-fiscal-period entries for a corporation

Just-In-Time Supplies completed the work sheet on pages C-28 and C-29 for the current year ended December 31.

Instructions: 1. Prepare an income statement. Calculate and record the following component percentages. (a) Cost of merchandise sold. (b) Gross profit on operations. (c) Total operating expenses. (d) Income from operations. (e) Net addition or deduction resulting from other revenue and expenses. (f) Net income before federal income tax. Round percentage calculations to the nearest 0.1%.

2. Analyze Just-In-Time's income statement by determining if component percentages are within acceptable levels. If any component percentage is not within an acceptable level, suggest steps that the company should take. Just-In-Time considers the following component percentages acceptable.

Cost of merchandise sold.............................	Not more than 73.0%
Gross profit on operations	Not less than 27.0%
Total operating expenses	Not more than 20.0%
Income from operations	Not less than 7.0%
Net deduction from other revenue and expenses	Not more than 0.5%
Net income before federal income tax...................	Not less than 6.5%

3. Prepare a statement of stockholders' equity. Use the following additional information.

January 1 balance of capital stock account.........................	$80,000.00
(16,000 shares issued for $5.00 per share)	
January 1 balance of retained earnings account.....................	25,928.60

4. Prepare a balance sheet.

5. Calculate Just-In-Time's (a) working capital and (b) current ratio. Determine if these items are within acceptable levels. Just-In-Time considers the following levels acceptable.

Working capital................................   Not less than $90,000.00
Current ratio...................................   Between 2.0 to 1 and 2.5 to 1

6. Use page 15 of a general journal. Journalize the adjusting entries.

7. Use page 16 of a general journal. Journalize the closing entries.

8. Use page 17 of a general journal. Journalize the reversing entries for the accrued interest income and accrued interest expense.

RECYCLING PROBLEM 28-R   Journalizing transactions in a voucher system

Walston Company uses a voucher system, including a voucher register and a check register, similar to those described in Chapter 28.

Instructions: 1. Use page 7 of a check register. Record the bank balance brought forward on May 1 of the current year, $6,597.66.

2. Journalize the following transactions completed during May of the current year. Use page 8 of a voucher register and page 7 of a check register. When a voucher is paid or canceled, make appropriate notations in the voucher register. Source documents are abbreviated as follows: check, C; debit memorandum, DM; voucher, V.

May 1. Purchased merchandise on account from Moraska Company, $790.00. V30.
    2. Bought supplies on account from Waldoch Supplies, $159.78. V31.
    4. Bought store equipment on account from Murphy Equipment, $1,449.77. V32.
    8. Purchased merchandise on account from Westhaven Company, $1,278.00. V33.
    8. Paid cash to Moraska Company, $774.20, covering V30 for $790.00, less 2% discount, $15.80. C19.
    10. Made a deposit in the checking account, $2,957.50.
    14. Received invoice for delivery service from Davis Delivery, $29.50. V34.
    14. Paid cash to Davis Delivery, $29.50, covering V34. C20.
    14. Issued DM5 to Westhaven Company for return of merchandise purchased, $170.00. Cancel V33. V35.
    15. Paid cash to Westhaven Company, $1,085.84, covering V35 for $1,108.00, less 2% discount, $22.16. C21.
    16. Recorded voucher for semimonthly payroll for period ended May 15, $1,396.47 (total payroll, $1,860.00, less deductions: employee income tax payable — federal, $280.50; employee income tax payable — state, $34.23; FICA tax payable, $148.80). V36.
    16. Paid cash for semimonthly payroll, $1,396.47, covering V36. C22.
    22. Paid cash to Waldoch Supplies, $159.78, covering V31. C23.
    25. Bought office furniture on account from Yurik Company, $1,979.99. V37.
    29. Made a deposit in the checking account, $1,279.51.
    30. Purchased merchandise on account from Moraska Company, $1,875.95. V38.

3. Prove and rule both the voucher register and the check register.

Just-In-Time Supplies
Work Sheet
For Year Ended December 31, 19--

| | TRIAL BALANCE | | ADJUSTMENTS | | INCOME STATEMENT | | BALANCE SHEET | |
ACCOUNT TITLE	DEBIT	CREDIT	DEBIT	CREDIT	DEBIT	CREDIT	DEBIT	CREDIT
1 Cash	30 817 00						30 817 00	
2 Petty Cash	3 0 0 00						3 0 0 00	
3 Notes Receivable	5 4 0 0 00						5 4 0 0 00	
4 Interest Receivable			(a) 1 0 8 00				1 0 8 00	
5 Accounts Receivable	23 5 0 3 00						23 5 0 3 00	
6 Allow. for Uncollectible Accts.		3 2 00		(b) 4 8 4 0 56				4 8 7 2 56
7 Merchandise Inventory	88 5 2 5 40		(c) 7 9 1 4 00				96 4 3 9 40	
8 Supplies	3 1 0 0 00			(d) 2 7 0 0 00			4 0 0 00	
9 Prepaid Insurance	11 0 7 0 00			(e) 7 3 8 0 00			3 6 9 0 00	
10 Office Equipment	7 9 1 0 00						7 9 1 0 00	
11 Accum. Depr.—Office Equipment		1 0 5 7 00		(f) 8 5 5 00				1 9 1 2 00
12 Store Equipment	44 4 1 2 00						44 4 1 2 00	
13 Accum. Depr.—Store Equipment		5 6 2 5 90		(g) 3 6 5 8 50				9 2 8 4 40
14 Notes Payable		11 2 5 0 00						11 2 5 0 00
15 Interest Payable				(h) 2 8 1 25				2 8 1 25
16 Accounts Payable		34 4 4 5 90						34 4 4 5 90
17 Employee Income Tax Payable		1 5 5 8 00						1 5 5 8 00
18 Federal Income Tax Payable				(i) 1 0 0 7 10				1 0 0 7 10
19 FICA Tax Payable		1 8 0 0 00						1 8 0 0 00
20 Sales Tax Payable		4 4 8 2 00						4 4 8 2 00
21 Unemploy. Tax Payable—Federal		3 2 00						3 2 00
22 Unemploy. Tax Payable—State		2 1 6 00						2 1 6 00
23 Health Insur. Premiums Payable		1 3 3 8 30						1 3 3 8 30
24 Dividends Payable		6 0 0 0 00						6 0 0 0 00
25 Capital Stock		80 0 0 0 00						80 0 0 0 00

#	Account Title	Trial Balance Debit	Trial Balance Credit	Adjustments Debit	Adjustments Credit	Income Statement Debit	Income Statement Credit	Balance Sheet Debit	Balance Sheet Credit
26	Retained Earnings		25 928 60						25 928 60
27	Dividends	24 000 00						24 000 00	
28	Income Summary				(c) 7 914 00	7 914 00			
29	Sales		1197 640 00				1197 640 00		
30	Sales Discount	3 024 90				3 024 90			
31	Sales Returns and Allowances	3 073 50				3 073 50			
32	Purchases	884 641 50				884 641 50			
33	Purchases Discount		4 326 30				4 326 30		
34	Purchases Returns and Allowances		3 310 20				3 310 20		
35	Advertising Expense	3 635 00				3 635 00			
36	Credit Card Fee Expense	12 101 40				12 101 40			
37	Depr. Expense—Office Equipment			(f) 8 55 00		8 55 00			
38	Depr. Expense—Store Equipment			(g) 3 658 50		3 658 50			
39	Insurance Expense			(e) 7 380 00		7 380 00			
40	Miscellaneous Expense	2 002 50				2 002 50			
41	Payroll Taxes Expense	15 219 00				15 219 00			
42	Rent Expense	38 400 00				38 400 00			
43	Salary Expense	161 901 00				161 901 00			
44	Supplies Expense			(d) 2 700 00		2 700 00			
45	Uncollectible Accounts Expense			(b) 4 840 56		4 840 56			
46	Utilities Expense	2 904 00				2 904 00			
47	Gain on Plant Assets		7 00 00				7 00 00		
48	Interest Income		6 00 00		(a) 1 08 00		7 08 00		
49	Cash Short and Over	7 50				7 50			
50	Interest Expense	3 829 50		(h) 2 81 25		4 110 75			
51	Loss on Plant Assets	8 5 00				8 5 00			
52	Federal Income Tax Expense	9 850 00		(i) 1 007 10		10 857 10			
53		1379 712 20	1379 712 20	28 744 41	28 744 41	1161 397 21	1213 968 50	184 408 11	236 979 40
54	Net Income after Fed. Inc. Tax					52 571 29			52 571 29
55						1213 968 50	1213 968 50	236 979 40	236 979 40
56									
57									

RECYCLING PROBLEM 29-R **Determining cost of ending inventory using the fifo, lifo, and weighted-average methods**

Accounting records at Northland Company show the following purchases and periodic inventory counts.

Model No.	Beginning Inventory January 1	First Purchase	Second Purchase	Third Purchase	Periodic Inventory Count December 31
C23	10 @ $15.00	8 @ $16.00	12 @ $18.00	16 @ $20.00	20
R79	15 @ $ 9.00	18 @ $10.00	20 @ $12.00	12 @ $14.00	25
C152	8 @ $ 6.25	12 @ $ 6.00	15 @ $ 5.90	10 @ $ 5.75	14
D34	42 @ $23.00	35 @ $22.00	40 @ $20.00	40 @ $18.00	67
R493	8 @ $ 5.20	9 @ $ 5.80	5 @ $ 6.30	7 @ $ 6.50	15
G549	20 @ $10.00	15 @ $11.00	15 @ $12.00	25 @ $12.00	35

Instructions: 1. Figure the total cost of ending inventory on July 31 using the fifo method. Use a form similar to the following. The inventory cost for Model No. C23 is given as an example.

Model No.	No. of Units on Hand	Unit Price	Cost of Ending Inventory
C23	20	16 @ $20.00⎫ 4 @ 18.00⎭	$392.00

Use the following procedure to complete the form.

(a) Record the model number and number of units of each model on hand on December 31.
(b) Record the unit price of each model. When more than one unit price is used, list the units and unit prices on separate lines as shown in the example.
(c) Calculate the cost of ending inventory of each model, and write the amount in the Cost of Ending Inventory column.
(d) Add the amounts in the Cost of Ending Inventory column to calculate the total cost of ending inventory.

2. On another form calculate the total cost of ending inventory using the lifo method. Follow the steps given in Instruction 1.

3. On another form calculate the total cost of ending inventory using the weighted-average method. Use the following procedure.

(a) Record the model number and number of units of each model on hand on December 31.
(b) Calculate the weighted-average price per unit for each model. Round the amount per unit to the nearest cent. Write the amount in the Unit Price column.
(c) Calculate the cost of ending inventory of each model, and write the amount in the Cost of Ending Inventory column.
(d) Add the amounts in the Cost of Ending Inventory column to calculate the total cost of ending inventory.

4. Compare the total cost of ending inventory obtained in Instructions 1, 2, and 3. Which method, fifo, lifo, or weighted-average, resulted in the lowest cost of ending inventory?

Index